V!VA Travel Guides Colombia.

ISBN-13: 978-1-937157-08-1

Voice: (831) 824-4395

Website: www.vivatravelguides.com

Information: info@vivatravelguides.com

Travel is inherently dangerous. While we use a superior process for updating guidebooks and have made every effort to ensure accuracy of facts in this book, V!VA Publishing Network, its owners, members, employees, contributors and the authors cannot be held liable for events outside their control and we make no guarantee as to the accuracy of published information. V!VA encourages travelers to keep abreast of the news in order to know the safety situation of the country. Please travel safely, be alert and let us know how your vacation went!

V!VA Travel Guides takes no position on the internal affairs of Colombia. We do not support one faction or another in the country's on-going civil war. The colors and sizes of maps or other features of this guidebook have no political or moral significance.

◊ Color Insert Photos: "Cartagena" by Paula Newton, 2009; "Pilón del Azúcar, Cabo de Vela" (The Guajíra Peninsula), "Interior courtyard of Ecco Homo monastery, Villa del Leyva" and "Sunset at Alto del Águila, Puerto Nariño" by Lorraine Caputo, 2009 ◊

The following photos are licensed under the Creative Commons license (see http://creativecommons.org/licenses/by/2.0/ and http://creativecommons.org/licenses/by/3.0/ for details):

"Museo del Oro - Reg. 025393, Reg. 025394" by kozumel ©, www.flickr.com/photos/kozumel/, 2009; "Ciudad Perdida (the Lost City)" by Liam and Hels - Big Trip ©, www.flickr.com/photos/liam-hels-big-trip/, 2009; "Coffee beans" (Parque Nacional del Café) by Bill Hails ©, www.flickr.com/photos/billhails/, 2009; "Parque Arqueológico de San Agustín" by Mario Carvajal ©, www.flickr.com/photos/mario_carvajal/, 2008; "Tayrona Park, Santa Marta, Colombia 08" by Ben Bowes ©, www.flickr.com/photos/benbowes/, 2009; "Santa Fé de Antioquia" by progresivo ©, www.flickr.com/photos/progresivo/, 2008; "Catedral Primada en Navidad, Bogota" by EduardoZ ©, www.flickr.com/photos/eduardozarate/, 2009; "Ensenada de Utría - Mangroven.jpg" by Philipp Weigell ©, http://commons.wikimedia.org/wiki/File:Ensenada_de_Utr%C3%ADa_-_Mangroven.jpg#filelinks, 2008; "NIC_3192" by (Hiking in Parque Nacional El Cocuy) by Chris Walker Innerwealth ©, www.flickr.com/photos/innerwealth/; "Street, La Candelaria. Bogotá" by paul bridgewater - www.londonmusicphotographer.com ©, www.flickr.com/photos/paulbridgewater/, 2009; "El ultimo tesoro de america" (Treasure Hunt) by Naty Rive ©, www.flickr.com/photos/96952704@N00/, 2007; "Cabo San Juan Beach - Tayrona National Park" (Caribbean Coast) by Roubicek ©, www.flickr.com/photos/roubicek/, 2009; "love is in the air, love is everywere" (Caribbean Coast) by Flowery 'L'u'z'a' ©, www.flickr.com/photos/luchilu/, 2008; "Black-headed Caique" (Jungle) by petepictures ©, www.flickr.com/photos/petepictures/, 2009; "CIMG1583.JPG" (Hike Colombia) by Threat to Democracy ©, www.flickr.com/photos/16725630@N00/, 2007 ◊

◊ Cover Design: Jason Halberstadt ◊ Cover Photos: "Plaza de Bolivar, Bogota, Colombia" by szeke ©, www.flickr.com/photos/pedrosz/5770632336, 2011; "Café maduro colombiano" by Mario Carvajal ©, www.flickr.com/photos/mario_carvajal/3281060185, 2009; "Bay-headed Tanager (Tangara gyrola)" by Aralcal ©, www.flickr.com/photos/aralcal/4374852862, 2009; Untitled by Luz Adriana Villa A. ©, www.flickr.com/photos/luchilu/258603947, 2008. ◊ Back Cover Photo: "Colombia, the only risk is wanting to stay" by Luz Adriana Villa A. ©, http://www.flickr.com/photos/luchilu/, 2008 ◊

CONTENTS

INTRO & INFO

INTRO & INFO

INTRO & INFO

About VIVA Travel Guides

We began VIVA Travel Guides back in 2007 because we simply wanted a better travel guide to our home country of Ecuador. All the guidebooks at the time were years out of date and weren't nearly as helpful as they should have been to real travelers. We knew we could do better.

We asked the question: "What would the travel guidebook look like if it was invented today from the ground up in the era of Google, Facebook, Wikipedia and nearly ubiquitous Internet connectivity?"

We concluded that the key to creating a superior guide is a knowledgeable community of travelers, on-the-ground professional travel writers, local experts and street-smart editors, all collaborating together on the web and working toward the goal of creating the most helpful, up-to-date guide available anywhere.

Continuously Updated

Traveler reports come in daily via the web and we take advantage of highly efficient 'web to book' technology and modern digital printing to speed the latest travel intelligence to the printed page in record time. We update our books at least once per year—more often than any other major publisher. We even print the date that each piece of information in the book was last updated so that you can make informed decisions about every detail of your trip.

A Better Way to Build a Guidebook

We're convinced we make a better guidebook. It's a more costly, painstaking way to make a guidebook, but we think it's worth it, because you're be able to get more out of your trip to Colombia. There are many ways that you can get involved in making VIVA Travel Guides even better.

Help other travelers by writing a review

Did you love a place? Will you never return? Every destination in this guidebook is listed on our website with space for user ratings and reviews. Share your experiences, help out other travelers and let the world know what you think.

Make corrections and suggestions

Prices rise, good places go bad, and bad places go out of business. If you find something that needs to be updated or improved in this book, please let us know. Report any inaccuracies at www.vivatravelguides.com/corrections and we'll incorporate them into our information within a few days. As a small token of our thanks for correcting an error or submitting a suggestion we'll send you a coupon for 50 percent off any of our E-books or 20 percent off any of our printed books.

Make your reservations at www.vivatravelguides.com

You can support VIVA's mission by reserving your hotels and flights at www.vivatravelguides.com. When you buy from our website, we get a commission, which we reinvest in making our guides a better resource for travelers. Find the best price on flights at www.vivatravelguides.com/flights and efficiently reserve your hotels and hostels at www.vivatravelguides.com/hotels.

We sincerely hope you enjoy this book, and your trip to Colombia even more.

Happy Trails,

Jason Halberstadt
Founder, VIVA Travel Guides

About the Authors

Upon re-declaring her independence at age 29, **Lorraine Caputo** packed her trusty Rocinante (so her knapsack's called) and began journeying throughout the Americas, from Alaska to Tierra del Fuego. Her work has appeared in numerous U.S., Canadian and Latin American publications. As the lead writer, Lorraine spent many months exploring the best of Colombia for the first edition. She returned for her 10th Colombian adventure, to update this edition of V!VA Colombia. Lorraine also extensively helped with the editing of this book.

Richard McColl is a British, Colombia-based freelance journalist who now divides his time between his colonial guesthouse in Mompós and the capital Bogotá. He contributed to the chapters on the Pacific Coast, Magdalena River Valley, Tierra Paisa, Valle de Cauca and Bogotá.

Brenda Yun, a freelance writer based in Honolulu, is an avid world traveler who once believed in seeing everything first and then returning to the select places that were most interesting. She fell in love with Colombia on her assignment for V!VA and vows to return sooner rather than later. She continues to write travel-related articles for print and online magazines and is currently completing a book-length memoir about her tumultuous twenties.

MANY THANKS TO:

Lisa Blackwell-Sayles, **Stephanie Witkin**, **Emily Thiersch**, **Eden De Souza** and **Nathan Perry**, the editorial interns who assisted with the production of this edition. Thanks also to all those who helped build the foundation of this book over the years, including: Michelle Lillie, Karen Nagy, Andrea Davoust, Rachel Anderson, Karen Hartburn, Troy Shaheen, Elizabeth Kerjes, Leslie Brown, Nili Larish, Laura Granfortuna, Tammy Portnoy, Lorena Fernández and Ricardo Segreda. Many thanks to Tom Bacon, Daniel Johnson, Nick Rosen, Mark Samcoe, and Joanne Sykes for their input as well.

Further thanks go out to **Jesua Silva**, V!VA's staff cartographer; **Pedro Vasconez,** our talented in-house graphic designer; and **Daniela Viteri,** who helped with the updating process. Also, thanks to the Techie Team, the programming masterminds who keep our parent website www.vivatravelguides.com running smoothly and always lend a hand to the not-always-computer-savvy staff. A big thank you to the whole Metamorf team for their support.

Mil gracias to German, Richard, Shaun, Cristina & Miguel, Oscar & Ivonne, and other Colombia Hostel members, as well as Filip (Mocoa) and Gilbert (Sapzurró) for their invaluable time, information and encouragement. Also to José, the poet in the hotel, Juan and Juan Gabriel; Jayariyú, Katy, Karmen, Amelia and the other Wayuu women who taught us so much about their culture; Shingo (Japan), Kristin & Erika (U.S.) and Daphnis (Belgium) for sharing their North Coast adventures, as did those doing it on two wheels: Aaron (Ireland), Erin & Alan (U.S.) and Ronald & Esther (Holland). Further thanks to Cheryl (Australia) and Ocean Malandra (U.S.) for feedback on the Guajira & Mompós and Cali respectively, and to Tom (Haifa), Yo & Zora (Japan), and all the dozens of other travelers who took the challenge to know Colombia.

Most of all, to the hundreds of Colombians who shared their history and culture, and who even after three generations of civil war, continue to receive travelers with such gracious hospitality. *Hasta el próximo tintico que nos provoque,* this guide is for you.

About the Editors

INTRO & INFO

Jena Davison is the Managing Editor for this edition of *V!VA Colombia*. Shortly after graduating from University of Wisconsin-Madison with a BA in Journalism and Mass Communication, Jena packed her backpack and headed across the equator to travel solo through South America. Born and raised in New Jersey, Jena's itch for travel has previously brought her to 20 countries, mostly in Europe and Latin America. She currently lives in Quito, Ecuador.

Paula Newton was the Managing Editor for the first three editions of this book and for many other V!VA guidebooks. With an MBA and a background in New Media, Paula was the organizing force behind V!VA's editorial team for several years. With an insatiable thirst for off-the-beaten-track travel, Paula has traveled extensively, especially in Europe, Asia and Latin America, and has explored more than 30 countries. She currently lives in Quito.

Dr. Christopher Minster, PhD is a graduate of Penn State University, The University of Montana and Ohio State. He is V!VA Travel Guides' expert on ruins, history and culture, as well as spooky things like haunted museums. "Crit" worked for the U.S. Peace Corps in Guatemala as a volunteer from 1991 to 1994 and has traveled extensively in Latin America.

Regional Summaries

Bogotá (p.76)

Bogotá, Colombia's largest city and one of South America's most happening metropolitan areas, is a Capital District unto itself, between Colombia's Huila and Cundinamarca Departments. This enormous metropolis has everything—the nation's most comprehensive museums, bohemian and trendy nightlife, artisan shops and mega-malls, international restaurants and ones from the country's many regions, and other attractions. Both art and business are booming in this capital, and, although crime and violence is still a part of life here, so are rapid development and tourism. The locals are the most cosmopolitan in the country, and are some of the friendliest and most helpful. As an essential port of international arrival and departure, the city is a sophisticated, increasingly safe and hospitable place to spend a few days. The city itself is situated on the Sabana de Bogotá, the nation's highest plateau, making for cool year-round climate and wet conditions in the winter. After you've had a proper introduction to the country with a visit to its impressive National Museum, escape from the quick urban pace of Bogotá and a taste of slower-paced small-town life. Head an hour north to Zipaquirá to tour the underground cathedral and salt mine, where the country still gets most of its salt. Or search for the legendary El Dorado at Guatavita, or get in some rock climbing at Suesca.

Valle del Cauca (p.110)

The Valle del Cauca is situated between the Pacific Ocean and the western ridge of the Andes, basking in a climate that is perfect for agriculture. The heart of this region is Santiago de Cali, Colombia's third largest city and often-considered salsa capital of Latin America. Visitors regard Cali as a shocking mixture of a maze-like streets, as a happening home to some of the prettiest girls in the Colombia, and, finally, as the mecca for some of the most coordinated hips in the southern hemisphere. If Colombia were three bears and Cartagena is hot and Bogotá is cold, then Cali is "just right"—both in terms of the climate and the people. There's a general feel-good nature to this part of the country. At night, Cali's Avenida Sexta lights up like the Las Vegas Strip. Yet there are plenty of opportunities to relax and enjoy down-time by the Río Cali, which runs its way straight across the city. If you prefer something more tropical, though, head to the San Cipriano jungle and enjoy a ride on a unique open train car. Or, if you're looking for a place to cool off, then take the tourist train inland towards the hills, stopping off in the small towns of Buga and La Tebaida to snap photos of colonial churches and architecture.

Zona Cafetera (p.134)

Colombia's Zona Cafetera (Coffee Zone) is the newest and fastest growing tourist attraction in the country. Comprised of three lush regions—Risaraldas, Quindío and Caldas—it stretches across mountainous terrain at over 1,000 meters (3,280 ft) above sea level. Raspberries, coffee, potatoes and oranges grow naturally among green bamboo and dense forest. This region's Parque Nacional Natural Los Nevados also offers some of the most postcard-perfect scenes of high altitude fauna and natural life. The strange-looking frailejones only survives in the most arid and cold high-altitude climates. On the other end of the spectrum, the national tree called *palma de cera* (wax palm) gracefully towers over the Valle de Cocora near Salento, where the river microclimate explodes with bird and plant life. The coffee zone's three major cities—Pereira, Armenia, and Manizales—all buzz with urban life, while tranquil nature is just a short bus ride away.

Tierra Paisa (p.158)

Inhabitants of Medellín and Santa Fe de Antioquia are referred to as paisas. They are known throughout Colombia for being a hardworking bunch and are bold in nature. A perfect example is the country's former president, Álvaro Uribe Vélez, who had, within one decade, turned crime-ridden and struggling Colombia into a far safer and prosperous place. Indeed, paisas have proven to be the country's most industrious, business-oriented and wealthy members of the nation. At the same time, paisas know how to have a good time and share a unique lingo. For instance, when asking a fellow paisa how it's going, one would say, "Qué hubo pues?" Medellín is really the heart of Tierra Paisa. In the 1980s this violent city was the murder capital of the world, taking center stage as the home to the infamous Pablo Escobar and, along with him, the shady underpinnings of the drug cartel. Within a mere decade, however, Medellín has almost completely reversed its image, highlighting its artistic and vibrant cultural life. In recent years, paisas have actively promoted their land for tourism, and for good reason: the region is spotted with delightful, white-washed colonial towns and conservative yet accommodating citizens with a desire to maintain their cultural heritage. There are several sites worth visiting in Tierra Paisa, such as the colonial masterpiece of Santa Fe de Antioquia.

Pacific Coast (p.180)

Isolated by the Cordillera Occidental from the rest of the country, Colombia's Pacific coast is difficult to reach and a world unto itself. The region's rich cultural biodiversity rewards those travelers who undertake the rigorous journey to this area. Tumaco, easily reached from Ipiales or Pasto, has one of Africa's purest expressions in the New World, and several mangrove reserves like Parque Nacional Natural Sanquianga, with great birdwatching, and relaxing beaches at Bocagrande. Buenaventura is the jumping-off point for two other national parks: Malpelo and Gorgona. The Chocó, along the northern coast, presents whale watching at Juanchaco and Ladrilleros, surfing, birdwatching and other outdoor adventures. Here the Embera indigenous maintain their culture. Those with guts, time and patience can undertake a coastal journey by local *chalupas* (boats).

Magdalena River Valley, upper (p.204), lower (p.216)

Shaped by the Magdalena River and stretching over 1,500 kilometers (900 mi) across the interior of Colombia from south to north, the Magdalena River Valley runs from the southern extremes of the Andes (at the river's source in Huila), through the arid badlands of the Tatacoa Desert, past the towering snow-capped mountain of Nevado del Tolima in Ibagué and the hot and sticky swamps of Mompós to the Caribbean seaport of Barranquilla. Willing travelers to this area will be pleasantly surprised by the contrasts and the differences in each town. Starting at Honda, known as both the City of Bridges and Cartagena of the Interior (thanks to its narrow colonial streets), travelers can venture on to Ibagué, Colombia's music capital. Here you can explore verdant canyons nearby and try to catch a glimpse of a spectacled bear. Then, follow the main cattle route to the Caribbean coast, passing through humid, hot and flat terrain where cattle farming remains the dominant industry. Enormous ranches extend out from towns along the Magdalena River and any journey will undoubtedly be delayed by a passing cattle train ambling along a major byway. At Puerto Berrío or the petroleum capital of Barrancabermeja, hop a boat down the Magdalena to Mompós. You won't want to miss the smoke stacks, nodding donkeys that dot the horizons, or the Nazarenes on procession in the austere Semana Santa of Mompós, a sleepy UNESCO World Heritage Site.

Caribbean Coast (p.230)

In the great spirit of regionalism that defines Colombia, most people along the Caribbean coastal area are referred to as costeños. These coastal dwellers are full of a zest for life. The low-lying Caribbean is certainly Colombia's tropical heart and soul, and costeños take to the pursuit of leisure with great ease and delight. Whether you visit Tolú, Cartagena, Barranquilla, Santa Marta or Valledupar, the pace of life is slower than the urban centers in Colombia's interior. Yet the area is equally as vibrant as metropolitan areas. This coast is, after all, where colonization started back in 1525 with the first European settlers arriving on the shores of Santa Marta. For three centuries, pirates plagued these Caribbean cities, and slavery was a part of life. Impressive stone walls and fortresses were built to protect important ports. Cartagena remains one of Colombia's best-preserved colonial cities. To immerse yourself in the region's vibrant rhythms, Barranquilla's Carnival and Valledupar's vallenato festival should not be missed. Of course, Parque Tayrona near Santa Marta is a tropical paradise like no other and a place where many choose to spend their entire vacation relaxing in hammocks or private bungalows beside the tranquil sea. A five-day trek to the archeological ruins of Ciudad Perdida (the Lost City) is a rare opportunity to see an ancient city in the middle of a cloud forest and to meet the indigenous Kogis who live in thatched huts and live as they had centuries ago. Finally, get out to San Andrés Islands for a taste of Raizal culture, or way off the beaten track to Sapzurró and other jungle villages near Panamá.

La Guajira (p.344)

The arid plains and indigenous Wayuu culture of the Guajira Peninsula create a remote yet rewarding travel destination. Its capital, Riohacha, is surrounded by the desert and Caribbean Sea, and is the launching point for the rest of the region. The southern section of Guajira reaches the Sierra Nevada de Santa Marta, and has heavy farming, cattle raising and the world's largest coal mine. Manaure, the major town in the Media Guajira (Middle Guajira) glitters with salt flats and beaches fine for birdwatching. The northern region, the Alta Guajira, includes the scenic deserts of Cabo de Vela, Nazareth and Punta Gallinas. The eastern oasis of Macuira is a cloud forest that even the most adventurous travelers have difficulty reaching. To be certain, the heat and lack of good roads in the Guajira make it Colombia's "no-man's land."

Eastern Colombia (p.370)

The central Andean regions of Boyacá, Cundinamarca, Santander and Norte de Santander are at the geographical, cultural and historical epicenter of Colombia itself. The gold-worshipping pre-Columbian Muisca Indians played an important role in forging Colombia's national identity. It was near Tunja, one of the nation's oldest cities, that Bolívar defeated the Spanish army in 1819, clearing the way for independence. Just two hours from Tunja is Villa de Leyva, a well-preserved colonial town that is a weekend hotspot for city dwellers. The town center boasts the largest cobblestone plaza in the country. Just outside of town, there are an important archaeological site and an amazing pre-historic crocodile on display in a museum. Farther east lie San Gil, the nation's adventure capital, and the impressive Chicamocha Canyon. Both places provide adrenaline junkies with whitewater rafting, rappelling, kayaking and paragliding. Then, just 20 minutes by bus from San Gil is charming Barichara, a small colonial town with colonial architecture. On the border with Venezuela lies Cúcuta, where ties were forged between Colombia, Ecuador and Venezuela in 1821. Up deep in the Andes is Parque Nacional Natural El Cocuy, with trekking circuits around 21 snowcapped peaks.

Southern Colombia (p.456)

Lovely, colonial Popayán, Colombia's *joya blanca* (white jewel), serves as the perfect launching point for grand adventures in the must-see archaeological sites, San Agustín and Tierradentro. You will have to endure a rough and bumpy six-hour bus ride to either locale, but the rewards upon arrival are worth the pain in the neck. San Agustín's enigmatic stone monoliths—some twice the size of humans—are scattered throughout the surrounding hills. Tierradentro's fascinating subterranean burial tombs, decorated with symbols of moons, salamanders and human faces, provide yet another intriguing glimpse into pre- Columbian times. Both locales are steeped in myth and legend, and situated among gorgeous mountains. Travelers often spend weeks hiking and horseback riding in the cloudy mists and exploring the rolling hills. Midway between Popayán and the San Agustín is Parque Nacional Natural Puracé, where condors soar over páramo plains and volcanoes. Further south are Pasto with nearby Laguna de la Cocha, whose shores are dotted with eco-farms, and Ipiales, the last town before hopping the border into Ecuador. Southern Colombia has many traditional villages, like Silvia and Cumbal, and nature reserves perfect for hiking and birdwatching.

Llanos and Selva (p.512)

Just over the Cordillera Oriental's brow from Bogotá is Villavicencio, gateway into the Llanos. Here you can savor a different Colombian culture, of *coleos* (rodeos) and BBQs. Capybara, the world's largest rodent, roam the plains where anaconda slither and roseate spoonbills glide. Adventuresome souls can explore three remote national parks: Sierra de la Macarena ,Tuparro and Sumapaz. Just south of the Llanos begins Colombia's Selva. On the western edge is Mocoa, capital of the Putumayo. In the extreme southeast is Leticia and its surrounding Amazon jungle, a stone's throw from Brazil and Peru. Only reachable by plane from Bogotá, Leticia is adjacent by land to the Brazilian town of Tabatinga and by boat to the Peruvian village Santa Rosa. Travelers seeking a unique Amazon experience don't need to venture far to witness the jungle wildlife in action. Catch the monkeys in Parque Nacional Natural Amacayacu and the pink dolphins near Puerto Nariño.

!!!!!

A Country of Contrasts

Colombia is certainly a country of contrasts. You may find yourself paragliding off of an enormous mountain one day and sunbathing on the beach the next. If you're searching for a blend of both, try some of these pairings:

Desierto Tatacoa & Isla Gorgona—Do you prefer dry or wet conditions? You're in luck, because Colombia offers both extremes. Tatacoa offers a glimpse of dry desert with cactus, sand and wildflowers, while Isla Gorgona, the country's largest Pacific island, is covered with lush, tropical rainforest, and you can spot humpback and sperm whale.

Salento & Coveñas—Both of these small towns are perfectly secluded, and offer tourists privacy, but in very different settings. In Salento, visitors delight in the crisp air and gorgeous Valle de Cocora, where the hillside is dotted with palmas de cera, Colombia's tall, skinny national tree. Then, in Coveñas, the warm tropical beach is yours for the taking.

Ciudad Perdida & Parque Tayrona—Three full days of hiking in the northern Sierra Nevada will take you to an abandoned pre-Columbian town in the clouds, Ciudad Perdida (the Lost City). At 1,000 meters above sea level, tourists who have endured the trek will bask in the glory of old times. Then, at sea level, on the way back to Santa Marta, is the equally lovely and relaxing Parque Tayrona, another home to the Tayrona Indians, set in calm bays and palm trees.

San Gil & Barichara—One of the country's centers for eco-adventure is San Gil, where rappelling, whitewater rafting and paragliding over the stunning Chicamocha Canyons shouldn't be missed. Just 20 minutes by bus from San Gil is the sleepy colonial town of Barichara, where the buildings are perfectly white-washed. Walking along the cobblestone streets, listening to the patter of horse hooves, and observing the stone carvers leaves little to the imagination of how life used to be.

Villavicencio & El Cocuy—From lowland plains to skyscraping mountain peaks, Colombia can take you from one extreme to the other. Villavicencio is the gateway into the country's low-lying Llanos, where joropo music and rodeos reign. Parque Nacional El Cocuy, at over 4,000 meters (13,130 ft) altitude, is home to northern South America's largest ice pack. Here, travelers can spend days trekking around and scaling the almost two dozen snowy peaks.

Leticia & Providencia—The most extreme of contrasts is the immense Amazon jungle setting in Leticia with the small, Caribbean island life in Providencia. There's nothing more Colombian about both: in Leticia, you laze around in small villages camped along the Amazon River; in Providencia, you walk or bike your way around, chatting it up with the Raizal. The opportunity to interact with locals abounds, and both cities are great ports to further exploration of Latin America. Leticia borders both Brazil and Peru, and Providencia is a very short plane ride from Costa Rica. Updated Sep 02, 2011.

!!!!!

Basic Facts

Official Name: Republic of Colombia
Capital: Bogotá
Population: 4.8 million (July 2011 estimate)
People: mestizo 58%, white 20%, mulatto 14%, black 4%, mixed black-Amerindian 3%, Amerindian 1%
Literacy Rate: 90.4%
Religion: Roman Catholic (90%)
Language: Spanish (official)
Government: republic; executive branch dominates government structure. President Juan Manuel Santos Calderón (since August 7, 2010); Vice President Angelino Garzón (since August 7, 2010). (The president is both the chief of state and head of government.)
Provinces: Colombia has 32 Departments and one capital district(*): Amazonas, Antioquia, Arauca, Atlántico, Bolívar, Boyacá, Caldas, Caquetá, Casanare, Cauca, Cesar, Chocó, Córdoba, Cundinamarca, Guainía, Guaviare, Huila, La Guajira, Magdalena, Meta, Nariño, Norte de Santander, Putumayo, Quindío, Risaralda, San Andrés y Providencia, Distrito Capital de Santa Fe de Bogotá*, Santander, Sucre, Tolima, Valle del Cauca, Vaupés, Vichada
Economic Facts: As of June 2011, unemployment is 11.6%, and public debt is 44.8% of GDP. In 2010, 44.4% of the population lived below the poverty line.
Agriculture: coffee, cut flowers, bananas, rice, tobacco, corn, sugarcane, cocoa beans, oilseed, vegetables; forest products; shrimp.
Main exports: petroleum, coffee, coal, apparel, bananas, cut flowers
Main industries: textiles, food processing, oil, clothing and footwear, beverages, chemicals, cement; gold, coal, emeralds.
Time: GMT minus 5
Electricity: 110/120 Volts AC, U.S. 2 pin plugs are used.
Updated: Sep 16, 2011.

Introduction

Say "Colombia" and most people will immediately think of something negative: drugs, guerrilla warfare, corruption, kidnappings or crime. This is hardly surprising, since the international press regularly features these facts about Colombia.

In truth, Colombia is one of the most beautiful countries in Latin America, and many places are just as safe to visit as other destinations on the continent. So, if you don't stray too far from the tourist areas and heed current safety advice, there is no reason why you shouldn't include Colombia in your itinerary. You will be well rewarded if you do. Caribbean beaches, Andean highlands and fertile rainforest claim the highest diversity of flora and fauna on the continent after Brazil, making it a perfect spot for nature lovers. Yet even those places deemed safe and developed for tourism have hardly been touched by outside visitors.

It's not, however, just natural wonders that draw travelers to come here; good food, great bars and fantastic coffee are a Colombian trademark, while the locals are reputed to be some of the friendliest and most welcoming in the world, and certainly haven't lost their party spirit. It's no wonder the national tourism board has adopted as its saying, "The only risk is wanting to stay." Updated: Sep 01, 2011.

Geography

Colombia is virtually all coasts to the west, and all valleys and basin to the east. The northernmost tip of the Andes mountains, which extend all along the west coast of South America, can be found in Colombia, where they stretch out in three parallel ranges known as the Cordillera Occidental, Cordillera Central and Cordillera Oriental.

The Cordillera Oriental, the most easterly, varies from short, finite ridges descending into the Amazon basin to summits high enough for snow. The capital city of Bogotá, at an altitude of 2,640 meters (8,661 ft), sits on one of the high basins in this region.

The Cordillera Central offers the highest peak at its northern end—Cristóbal Colón—in Colombia at 5,776 meters (18,945 ft), and many high and active volcanoes, including the Tolima at 5,215 meters (17,105 ft). Some valleys here host small communities, but the region overall is largely unpopulated.

The Cordillera Occidental runs parallel to the Pacific coast, peaks only at 3,050 meters (10,000 ft) while its hills slide into the coasts. The range's rivers deposits create thick sediment beds under the coastal waters.

The Caribbean coast east of the Panama isthmus is a low-level plain born of sediment deposits, interlaced by various rivers, especially the Magdalena River, and intermingled with some hills. This area is home to such major port cities as Cartagena and Barranquilla.

The territory that border Venezuela, Brazil, Peru and eastern Ecuador comprise almost two-thirds of Colombia. Within the Orinoco River basin, the geography is floodplains, great rivers and the spurs of the Guiana Highlands. Only three percent of the nation's population lives here, mostly along the rivers. Updated: Sep 01, 2011.

Climate

Colombia has two seasons—wet and dry—though you can experience each more than once in a calendar year depending on where you are. In Bogotá, for example, there are two rainy seasons (April-June and October-December), while the coastal town of Cartagena typically has one rainy season from May to November. Colombia's temperatures, on the other hand, are generally dictated by altitude, with temperatures in the eastern lowlands among the hottest in South America and temperatures in the Andean range that can fall well below freezing. Temperatures in Cartagena, for example, are what you might expect from a tropical beach town, with highs around30°C (85°F). Temperatures in Bogotá average around 14°C (57°F). Generally, expect to wear a sweater at night along the coast and a jacket in higher elevations. Also be aware that precipitation tends to be heavier on the Pacific coast and in the Andes, with annual rainfall in excess of 2,540 millimeters (100 in).Updated: Sep 01, 2011.

Flora and Fauna

Overall, Colombia is the second most diverse country in the world in terms of its concentration of flora and fauna species, and has the greatest concentration of species indigenous to a particular region. Indeed, 10 percent of the entire world's species live in Colombia, many of which can be found in Parque Nacional

Photo by: Mario Carvajal

Natural Amacayacu. Colombia even has the largest number of land mammals on the planet. This includes such creatures as jaguars, pumas, tapirs, anteaters, sloths, armadillos, monkeys and red deer—456 species total—of which 22 percent are at risk of extinction. Colombia is also home to the spectacled bear, so named because the light fur around its eyes give it the appearance of wearing glasses. It is currently being challenged both by habitat loss through deforestation, and hunters who seek its claws for alleged fertility and vigor.

In addition to mammals, reptiles and amphibians, Colombia is home to an almost uncountable number of birds like toucans, cockatoos, storks, cranes, parrots, vultures and hummingbirds. The largest avifauna is the Andean condor. Colombia's waterways are populated by such notable swimmers as the huge yubarta whale along the Pacific coast and the predator piranha in the Amazonian rivers.

Colombia also has the highest concentration of diverse plants—over 130,000 species—including the highest amount of plant life—55,000 species—that is native only to its host country. Hot and humid regions in the Amazon basin give rise to high trees and dense vegetation, while coastal regions are home to mangroves. Foliage similarly varies according to climate throughout the country. Updated: Sep 01, 2011.

National Parks and Reserves

Colombia has 56 national parks and reserves, from the Caribbean Islands to the Amazon jungle, along both coasts and deep into the Llanos. Over 12 percent of the national land and marine territory, representing a total area of 12,602,321 hectares (31,127,733 ac), is protected.

There are five types of protected areas. The largest group, containing 41 reserves, is the Parque Nacional Natural (PNN). (Note: In Colombia, a Parque Nacional is one that belongs to the nation and therefore is not necessarily a wildlife reserve, whereas a Parque Nacional Natural is a protected area.) The 12 Santuario de Flora y Fauna (SFF) preserve sensitive flora and fauna zones. The two Reserva Nacional Natural (RNN) parks are located deep in the Llano plains. The last protected area is Isla de Salamanca, the only Vía Parque (VP).

Almost half of the parks are designated Parque Ecoturísticos (Ecotouristic Parks), providing lodging, tour guides and other infrastructure. Among these are: Los Nevados in the Zona Cafetera; Utría, Malpelo and Gorgona in the Pacific Coast area; Corales del Rosario y de San Bernardo, Isla de Salamanca (adjoining the Ciénaga Grande de Santa Marta), Sierra Nevada de Santa Marta Tayrona and Old Providence McBean Lagoon in the Caribbean Coast and Islands region; Los Flamencos and Macuira in the Guajira; Iguaque and El Cocuy in Eastern Colombia; Puracé, Galeras and Isla de la Carota in Southern Colombia; and Tuparro in the Llanos and Amacayacu near Leticia in the Selva. See the respective chapters for more information on these reserves.

Some of the parks are recognized by international agencies as being unique environments, thus providing them with more protection. Two of the reserves—PNN Los Katíos near the Panamá border and SFF Malpelo off the Pacific Coast—are UNESCO World Heritage Sites. UNESCO also has recognized some of Colombia's geography as Biosphere Reserves: the Cinturón Andino (which includes PNN Nevado del Huila, Puracé and Cueva de los Guárachos); El Tuparro (PNN El Tuparro); Sierra Nevada de Santa Marta (PNN Sierra Nevada de Santa Marta and SFF Los Flamencos); Ciénaga Grande de Santa Marta (VP Isla de Salamanca y SFF Ciénaga Grande de Santa Marta); and Seaflower (encompassing the entire San Andrés archipelago, including PNN Old Providence a McBean Lagoon). As well, almost

460,000 hectares (1,136,200 ac) are Ramsar Wetlands Sites of International Importance. These are the Río Magdalena estuary in SFF Ciénaga Grande de Santa Marta; Laguna de la Cocha (SFF Isla de la Carota); Río Baudó delta; Otún Lagoon marshlands in PNN Los Nevados; and PNN Chingaza's watershed.

Colombia's National Park Service accepts Colombian and foreign volunteers for one-to six-month-long stints. For more information about volunteering, or about the national parks themselves, visit: www.parquesnacionales.gov.co. Updated Sep 02, 2011.

Environmental Issues

Colombia has one of the richest eco-systems in the world. The country is roughly 51 percent rainforest and 68 percent forest in total, producing a significant amount of the Earth's oxygen. Though only one-tenth the size of neighboring Brazil, it has just as many animal species. In fact, Colombia is home to 10 percent of the world's living creatures. A UNESCO study ranks Colombia at number four in the world with regards to water reserves per area unit.

Unfortunately, Colombia is a developing nation, and despite its vast reserves of petroleum, historical widespread poverty, greed and corruption have taken their toll on this paradise. Deforestation, soil erosion, pesticides, and the contamination wrought by inadequately monitored drilling and mining have imperiled many of its native species—the Colombian grebe and the Caribbean monk seal have already become extinct—while another 114 creatures and 429 plant species are currently at risk. This is partly a consequence of up to 600,000 hectares (1,482,632 ac) of forest that have disappeared each year for the last several decades.

With most farm land owned by a minority of the country's citizens, poor farmers are forced to seek new ground to cultivate, often the very habitats of at-risk species of plants and animals, resulting in an ecological crisis. The "drug war" has also contributed to this as coca, marijuana and poppy growers have escaped into virgin territory to grow their crops.

By the early 1990s, out of 194 countries in the world, Colombia ranked 43rd in industrial carbon emissions, totaling 63.3 million metric tons by 1996, not including vehicle emissions. While drinkable water is available to 99 percent of city residents, only 70 percent of the rural populace enjoys this privilege.

An environmental consciousness has emerged in Colombia, but it has been slow to evolve, and has been hampered by political and economic turbulence. By 1959, the government had passed measures protecting forests and the Pacific coast. In 1969 the Institute for Development of Renewable Natural Resources and the Environment (INDERENA) was established with the intention of training government employees working in conservation, forestry and fishing. The National Resources and Environment Code was established in 1973. In 1982, the Colombia Sanitary Code instituted pollution control standards.

Although the government has set aside nine percent of the country's land as protected national park territory, effective safeguarding of the land has been hindered by the exhaustion of law enforcement in fighting drug trafficking, which in itself has contributed heavily to ecological damage through the chemicals used in the manufacture of cocaine, as well as the retaliatory fumigation of coca crops by the government.

Some of the private environmental groups that have emerged in the last few decades include Ecofondo, Censat Agua Viva and Semillas. These organizations often work with or alongside international environmental organizations such as Greenpeace and the World Wild Fund for Nature, as well as with non-environmental organizations such as the Center for Indigenous Cooperation in advising rural communities, who often engage in illegal logging as a means of survival, in cultivating environmental awareness.

In 2006, the Colombian government adopted a controversial General Forestry Law, whose intent is to provide state support for commercial logging in areas of Colombia that are not officially protected regions. The administration of then-President Álvaro Uribe argued that such a measure was necessary to stimulate job and economic growth. Opponents argued that the bill received was backed by multinational corporations, such as the paper and pulp manufacturer Smurfit Carton, and that the communities (mostly indigenous and Afro-Colombian) who live in the areas most impacted by the law were not consulted.

Surprisingly, however, a joint 2008 Yale/Colombia University study placed Colombia among the world's top ten countries in terms of management of natural resources and pollution control. Updated: Sep 01, 2011.

History

PRE-CONQUEST

The geographical area of present-day Colombia has been inhabited for centuries, since at least 10,000 BC. Various cultures came and went, many of them centered in the Magdalena River valley. At the time of the Spanish conquest, the two most important ethnic groups were the Muisca culture, which was an advanced but small culture near Bogotá, and the Tayrona people on the Caribbean coast. Neither culture was able to hold off the Spanish conquest for long and subsequent revolts by the Tayrona caused the Spanish to almost completely stamp out their culture. Some fled into the Sierra Nevada de Santa Marta, where their descendants yet maintain their traditions. The Muisca, in spite of years of repression, have managed to maintain some of their original culture.

THE CONQUEST

When Spanish forces under the command of Sebastián de Belalcázar and Gonzalo Jiménez de Quesada arrived in the area in the late 1530s, the Muisca were feuding. Rival Zipa and Zaque people were fighting over land and salt mines. Because of this division, the Muisca culture was easily divided and conquered. The gold artifacts found near Guativita fueled the Spaniards' search for El Dorado, and many towns in the south were founded as base camps for their explorations.

THE COLONIAL ERA

By 1549, the strategic location of Colombia had been recognized by Spain, and Santa Fe de Bogotá was named an audiencia, which was a certain form of legal district with a court. It thus became the most important city in the region, which was then referred to as Nueva Granada. Nueva Granada contained Colombia, Venezuela, Panama and part of Ecuador, and was elevated to the status of Viceroyalty in the early 18th century. Even when it was raised to the status of Viceroyalty, Nueva Granada was considered something of a backwater in comparison with wealthier Lima and Mexico City.

INDEPENDENCE

Bogotá was one of the first places in the Americas to declare independence from Spain, in July 1810. The definitive moment for Colombian independence came in August 1819, when a large force of rebel Colombians and Venezuelans, reinforced by the British Legion

INTRO & INFO

INTRO & INFO

The Sack of Cartagena

By the 1580s, Spanish power in the New World had reached its zenith and the rich colonies were making Spain very wealthy. This wealth naturally attracted Spain's many enemies, chief among them the English. Spanish ships and treasure ports had to be constantly on their guard against pirates, privateers and other thieves.

The greatest sea-dog of the Elizabethan Era was Sir Francis Drake. One of the great sea-captains and adventurers of history, Drake had been raiding the Spanish for decades. In 1573, he had captured a Spanish mule train carrying literally tons of silver and managed to make off with most of it. In 1578, he sailed around South America to attack unsuspecting Spanish treasure fleets in the Pacific: Once again, he made off with thousands of pounds of gold, silver and other treasures. The Spanish hated Drake, and his predations on their treasure put great strain on the fragile relations between England and Spain.

In 1584, the English began plotting another large-scale raid of Spanish treasure fleets and ports: Drake was the natural choice to lead it. By late 1585, Drake was ready to set sail. He had a fleet of 21 ships manned by 2,000 soldiers and sailors, one of the most impressive war fleets ever at the time. He first attacked the Spanish port of Vigo before sacking the Canary Islands. Crossing the ocean, he landed his men on Hispaniola and marched on Santo Domingo. Capturing the city, he looted it and then held it for ransom, collecting another 25,000 ducats.

Drake now set his sights on Cartagena. Cartagena was, at the time, one of the richest ports in the world, as much of the vast wealth of South America passed through it on its way to Spain. The Spanish there weren't very worried, however, as the port was well guarded with forts, two large Spanish warships and hundreds of armed Spanish troops. Drake attacked anyway.

On February 9, 1586, Drake landed his soldiers on La Caleta, a spit of land where the forts were located. These were soon captured. Drake then sailed his ships into the harbor and met up with the soldiers for an assault on the town itself. The English charged and the Spanish defenses broke. The men on the warships, in fear of the raiders, jumped ship and ran into the jungle.

Soon the town belonged to Drake. Cartagena was thoroughly looted, netting the attackers some 250,000 pieces-of-eight. Drake ransomed the city for another 100,000. Drake lost only 30 men. His daring had paid off in one of the most successful raids in the history of privateering. Drake and his men attacked and looted St. Augustine (Florida) before heading home. Drake arrived just in time to help defeat the Spanish Armada.

Cartagena recovered, and continued to be an important Spanish treasure port. Many of the defensive forts and walls can still be seen today!

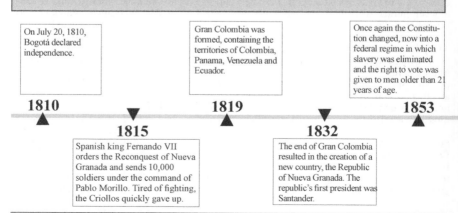

On July 20, 1810, Bogotá declared independence.

Gran Colombia was formed, containing the territories of Colombia, Panama, Venezuela and Ecuador.

Once again the Constitution changed, now into a federal regime in which slavery was eliminated and the right to vote was given to men older than 21 years of age.

1810   **1819**   **1853**

1815   **1832**

Spanish king Fernando VII orders the Reconquest of Nueva Granada and sends 10,000 soldiers under the command of Pablo Morillo. Tired of fighting, the Criollos quickly gave up.

The end of Gran Colombia resulted in the creation of a new country, the Republic of Nueva Granada. The republic's first president was Santander.

of almost 1,000 British and Irish volunteers, clashed with royalist forces at theBattle of Boyacá and defeated them.

GRAN COLOMBIA

In 1819, the historic Congress of Angostura established the nation of Gran Colombia, which included all of present-day Colombia, Venezuela, Ecuador and Panama and parts of Brazil, Costa Rica, Peru and Guyana. Gran Colombia was the brainchild of Simón Bolívar, who saw it as the first step to his dream of a united South America that would compete with the United States and Europe as a world power. Unfortunately for Bolívar, the petty ambitions of local leaders and logistics (the mountains, rivers and dense jungles of northern South America which made communication and government very difficult) doomed Gran Colombia from the start. By 1831 it had dissolved into the smaller nations that we see on the map today.

THE REPUBLICAN ERA

From 1831 to 1863, the new nation was known as the Republic of New Granada. It changed its name in 1863 to the United States of Colombia and in 1886 it changed once again to the Republic of Colombia, a name it retains to this day. In 1843, the new Constitution for the Republic turned it into an Authoritative Regime under President General Pedro Alcántara Herrán, in order to control the nation's first civil war, the War of the Supremes.

During the 19th century, the citizens of Colombia fractured into two competing ideologies: Conservatives and Liberals. The Conservatives believed in a strong central government, limited voting rights for citizens and strong ties to the Catholic Church. The Liberals were just the opposite: They wanted the right to vote for all citizens, an absolute division between church and state, and stronger regional government. The Liberals had strong support from the coffee plantation owners, who favored their looser taxes and controls.

The conflict between Conservatives and Liberals would become a long-running and violent one, erupting into the Thousand Days War (1899-1902), the nation's second civil war. By some estimates, as many as 100,000 people were killed as Liberal and Conservative armies fought each other all over the nation. The result was a nominal victory for the Conservatives, but in reality the war simply devastated the nation.

THE TWENTIETH CENTURY

In 1902, The United States picked up the Panama Canal project abandoned by the French a few years earlier. When Colombia rejected the U.S.' terms for future administration of the canal, the United States encouraged wealthy Panamanian families to separate from Colombia...and backed them up with several warships. At that time, Colombia was still reeling from the Thousand Days War and had little choice. Panama formally became independent from Colombia in November 1903, although Colombia did not officially recognize this until 1921.

EL BOGOTAZO

Tensions between Conservatives and Liberals continued to smolder during the first half of the 20th century. They erupted once more in 1948, after extremely popular Liberal presidential candidate Jorge Eliécer Gaitán was assassinated in Bogotá. Much like other political assassinations, such as that of John F. Kennedy, conspiracy theories abound as to the architects of the murder.

Just as Colombians were beginning to recover from the last civil war, came the most traumatizing event of the century for the nation: the separation of Panama, which was encouraged and coordinated by the United States.

A worker strike broke out on the Caribbean coast and national armies were sent in to control the over 11,000 protesting United Fruit workers. The army opened fire on the crowd, killing a number of people that was never factually determined. As a result of the scandal, President Miguel Abadía Méndez was voted out of office in 1930.

1903   **1928**

1886   **1921**   **1948**

A new constitution finally cancelled out federalism in the now-called Republic of Colombia. A movement of "regeneration" brought another civil war named Thousand Days Civil War (1899-1902).

Colombia recognized Panama's independence and signed the Thompson-Urrutia Treaty with the U.S., in which the U.S. gave Colombia an indemnity of $25 million.

The murder of presidential candidate Jorge Eliécer Gaitán unleashed a series of conflicts that lasted until the mid-1950s. The period, known as La Violencia began that same night with riots in Bogotá that would later on be named El Bogotazo.

Among the common "culprits" are the CIA, the Soviet Union, the Conservatives and even Fidel Castro, who had a meeting scheduled with Gaitán on the day he was killed.

The city, already swollen with impoverished people from the countryside who had come looking for work and saw Gaitán as a savior, went mad. Radio stations urged listeners to take the streets, blaming the Conservative Mariano Ospina Pérez government for the murder. The crowd broke into hardware stores and even police stations looking for weapons. Liberal leaders and the Conservative government tried to work together to stop the violence, which by then had spread to all of Colombia's other large cities. But there was nothing they could do. By dawn Bogotá was in ruins, and many institutions and buildings had been burned to the ground. Almost every store in the city had been looted, and informal markets had sprung up on the outskirts of the city. All in all, over 3,000 people were killed in the uprising, and it launched the period known as La Violencia.

LA VIOLENCIA

Following the murder of Gaitán and the Bogotazo, Colombia descended even further into chaos and its third civil war. The Conservative government clamped down on civil liberties, and every major political entity began forming its own death squads. These squads operated in every city, town and village in Colombia, murdering any and all who disagreed with them. The weapons of choice were clubs, knives and machetes, and became it was common to find hacked-up bodies in the streets. Institutions such as the press were afraid to speak up against the violence for fear of reprisal, and the Catholic Church was openly siding with the Conservatives, telling followers to kill Liberals.

By the time La Violencia came to an end around 1958, between 180,000 and 300,000 Colombians had been killed. This horrific period closed when a military administration was replaced by a moderate compromise government formed by Liberals and Conservatives. In a way, Colombia is still suffering the effects of La Violencia: It was during this time that the revolutionary groups that would become the FARC, which still operates in Colombia, were formed.

COCAINE

With rise of the international popularity of marijuana and cocaine in the 1970s, Colombia grew into a major producer and exporter of the two drugs within the next decade. During the 1980s, Colombia became a battleground between two rival drug cartels: Cali, controlled by the Orejuela brothers, and Medellín, under the command of Pablo Escobar. Up until the early 1990s, Colombia would suffer as the two cartels fought for control of all aspects of the trade, from production to exportation—including of the police forces, politicians and media—through bombings, kidnappings, assassinations and other acts of intimidation. Against this backdrop, the guerrilla armies—the FARC, ELN and M-19—grew in strength and in response, paramilitary armies were formed under the auspices of Antioquian land owners.

THE 1990S

The 1990s brought about a period of relative peace for Colombia. Many of the smaller rebel groups, including the once-feared M-19, laid down their arms in favor of legal change, although other groups (most notably the FARC) remained. With Escobar dead, the cartels lost a lot of their power and mainly fought among themselves. By the

After 5 years of civil war, General Gustavo Rojas led a coup d'état to throw out president Laureano Gómez, and granted amnesty to over 5,000 Liberal guerrilla members who, in return dropped their weapons.

What started as a small Communist guerrilla group in 1949 grew stronger despite the national army's efforts. The group came together as the Southern Bloc and then renamed itself Fuerzas Armadas Revolucionarias de Colombia (FARC).

Newly elected Conservative president Belisario Betancur initiated peace talks with representatives of FARC.

1953   ▼   **1964**   ▼   **1983**   ▼

▲   **1958**   ▲   **1974**   ▲   **1985**

Rojas' dictatorship, filled with police abuse, media censorship and raw violence, came to an end. After 9 years, the National Congress was reinstituted and a power-sharing government composed of Liberals and Conservatives was established. Although La Violencia was over, organized guerrilla groups began to develop.

Liberal presidential candidate Alfonso López Michelsen won the first free election since 1958 by a margin of 3 million votes.

On November 6, M-19 guerrillas seized the Palacio de Justicia (Supreme Court) in Bogotá, taking 350 hostages. The Colombian military attacked. The resultant firefight resulted in 95 deaths.

time the cartels collapsed, the guerilla and paramilitary armies had carved out a chunk of the lucrative drug trade for themselves.

The era was far from utopian; election fraud and government corruption were still extremely high. Since the late 1990s, Colombian leaders have been trying to modernize the economy, crush the drug cartels and improve human rights in Colombia. The U.S. has been a vital partner in their efforts, giving billions of aid to help destroy the drug lords and the FARC. In 1998, in an effort to negotiate with the FARC, President Andrés Pastrana ceded 42,000 square kilometers (16,216 sq mi) of land to the guerrilla movement as its territory, Farclandia, deep in the Llanos. But because of stalled peace negotiations, Pastrana threw in the towel with this novice approach in 2002 and declared an all-out war on the FARC.

THE NEW MILLENIUM

In 2002 Álvaro Uribe was elected president. He adopted a very aggressive, hard line against the drug lords and the FARC. He pushed for a constitutional amendment allowing presidents to serve a second term of office; he was reelected and served until 2010. His policies included military strikes not only within his own country, but also inside of neighboring Ecuador in early 2008 which killed several important FARC leaders but caused an ugly international incident. Since leaving office, he has faced allegations of corruption, human rights abuses and ties with paramilitary organizations.

Despite efforts to allow it, Uribe was ruled ineligible to run for third term in 2010. His former defense minister, Juan Manuel Santos faced Green Party candidate Antanas Mockus in run-off elections.

Santos won. Since then, Uribe has accused Santos of becoming too lenient with the rebel groups. Updated: September 20, 2011.

Politics

Like the U.S. system of government, Colombia's political structure is divided into executive, judicial and legislative branches of government, with the latter, like the U.S. system, divided into a Senate and a House of Representatives. Senators are elected via a national ballot, while representatives are elected by their local constituents. Congress convenes twice annually, and the president can summon a special session when necessary. However, unlike the U.S. system, the Colombian president is chosen directly by the electorate, without the intervention of an electoral college. He then serves as both head of state and head of government, overseeing a multi-party representative democracy. The president serves for four years and may only be elected for two terms.

There are two high courts in Colombia that serve separate functions: the Constitutional court, which as its name indicates, interprets the Constitution and monitors observance of laws, and then there is the Supreme Court, consisting of 23 judges who are appointed by the legislature for eight-year terms. This court is divided into three chambers: a civil-agrarian, a labor and a penal.

The Constitution was reformed in 1991 to allow for greater civil liberties, such as divorce and dual citizenship, and most importantly, the right to request a tribunal if a citizen can provide evidence that his or her constitutional rights are not being honored. In 2004, Article 197 of the Constitution was amended to allow presidents to serve two terms, and not just one. Updated: Sep 16, 2011.

Chief of the Medellín cartel, Pablo Escobar, orders the death of Guillermo Cano, director of the newspaper El Espectador. The event unleashes a war against drug trafficking.

Independent Liberal candidate Álvaro Uribe won the presidential election by promising to put military pressure on the biggest guerrilla organization in the country, the FARC. Within two years, governmental data showed that homicides, kidnappings and terrorist attacks in Colombia decreased by 50 percent. The security policy implemented by Uribe kept the public happy.

Former presidential candidate Ingrid Betancourt was freed after being held hostage for 6 years by the FARC.

1994 ▼ **2002** ▼ **2008** ▼

▲ **1994** ▲ **2006** **2010**

Liberal presidential candidate Ernesto Samper won the election. His opponent showed recordings that implicate Samper's campaign to have been funded by drug cartels. The scandal, later dubbed "Process 8,000," took two years to resolve, and after countless investigations, interrogations and many murders, Samper got off the hook in 1996.

With the Constitution modified to allow a second term, Álvaro Uribe was reelected to serve another term until 2010.

Uribe protégé Juan Manuel Santos is elected president, but soon faces criticism from Uribe about becoming "too soft" with the guerrilla movements.

The Banana Companies

The history of the banana companies in Colombia shadows that of Central America. The same U.S.-based *bananeras* operated in both parts of the Americas, but the major player in Colombia would be United Fruit Company, who opened its plantation doors in Magdalena Department in 1899.

The Caribbean coast was rocked with banana worker strike that lasted several months. They were appealing for nine rights, including eight-hour days, written contracts, the abolition of food coupons—to be spent only in company stores—and no more than six days a week of work. In December 1928, the Colombia government put down the strike in Ciénaga, near Santa Marta. Military forces rolled in and the massacre of United Fruit (now known as Chiquita) employees began—the worst in the banana trade's history. The government was afraid unions would give way to communism. The army barricaded the plaza and then proceeded to machine-gun down hundreds of workers from the rooftops.

The Colombian government claims that the violent incident was necessary to avoid U.S. intervention on behalf of the United Fruit Company's interests. The true number of deaths is unknown as the governmental and company archives have never been made public. Most figures claim it to be between nine (the official report) and 2,000. The history was brushed under the carpet for decades, until the publication of Gabriel García Márquez' "One Hundred Years of Solitude." The novels' version of the Macondo *masacre de las bananeras* seems to have been accepted more as historical, rather than fictional, truth. Márquez's exaggeration of the death toll, which intended to convey the repressive nature of the conservative government and the brutality of United Fruit, has now become *la historia oficial*. The massacre was a pivotal event in Colombian politics, which bolstered support for the left.

The history of United Fruit, which became Chiquita in 1984, doesn't stop there: Chiquita was fined $25 million upon discovery that it had made 100 monthly payments totaling $1.7 million to the United Self-Defense Forces of Colombia (AUC), a Colombian right-wing terrorist group, between 1997 and 2004. While the company claims the payments were made to protect its workers, union organizers were targeted by the very same groups financed by Chiquita.

Oddly enough, the Urabá plantation in Colombia was the most lucrative of all of Chiquita's global properties during the payment period. Additional reports allege that Chiquita boats have couriered cocaine and smuggled in machine guns for the AUC; a civil lawsuit filed on behalf of hundreds of Colombian families asserts that Chiquita's payments financed both torture and murder.

Colombia's Attorney General even demanded that Chiquita executives be extradited and tried in the country for their crimes, but to no avail. The U.S. refused. The disturbing reality of Colombia under the banana companies seems to move closer to Macondo every day, as history repeats itself and one hundred years of silence dawns to a close. Updated: Sep 16, 2011.

CURRENT POLITICAL SITUATION

As with most Latin American countries, Colombia's political history has been one of civil wars, social injustice, corruption and violence. A fraudulent election in 1970 prompted the organization of the guerrilla movement M-19 four years later, and in the latter half of the 20th century high-profile kidnappings, right-wing, leftwing and criminal terrorism—along with repressive countermeasures—have pretty much defined this nation.

The gravest threat to Colombian stability came about through the rise of drug cartels in the 1970s and 1980s. Exploiting the increasingly high demand for cocaine in North America and Europe, their lucrative operations enabled them to bribe and/or coerce police and politicians, as well as ordinary (and usually) poor citizens. They combined their buying-off with barbarity; apart from their own pattern of abductions and violence, they also financed both right-wing paramilitaries and left-wing guerrillas, all to undermine law enforcement.

In 1999, President Andrés Pastrana began "Plan Colombia," an aggressive effort to fight the drug trade, along with minor attempts to address the underlying social issues that sustain it. The military facet of the plan was backed by the United States, with money, arms and advisors. Plan Colombia, however, failed to affect much change. The next president, Álvaro Uribe, enacted an aggressive hard line against guerrilla groups, which reduced crime and violence, and in turn produced notable economic growth, but major social problems—poverty, illiteracy, class and political polarization—remained. Under the present president, Juan Manuel Santos, Plan Colombia continues, with increased U.S. presence; an agreement was signed to allow eight U.S. military bases in Colombia, on which construction has begun.

The civil society also is playing a more active role in the nation's politics. Communities like San José de Apartadó have taken a non-partisan, non-violence stance against the Civil War—and as a result have faced attacks by guerrilla, paramilitary and (according to some reports) Colombian military forces. Former Senator Piedad Córdova continues to mediate with the FARC for release of the kidnap victims they hold. Updated: Sep 09, 2011.

Economy

Colombia's economy has for decades been among the best in Latin America, thanks in large part to steady agricultural production, a healthy textile industry and a wealth of natural resources. Colombia is among the world leaders in the production of coffee, petroleum, textiles and flowers, and is South America's leading provider of gold, nickel and coal.

These and other growing sectors have in recent years helped Colombia's economy grow by an average of 6.8 percent a year, some two percentage points higher than the Latin American average. Former President Álvaro Uribe's efforts to increase security in Colombia have certainly helped, going a long way in rebuilding confianza, or trust, in the country's economy. As killings and abductions have declined, foreign investment from multinational corporations has soared, flooding Colombia's economy with money and industries geared toward future growth.

Other signs of economic strength abound. Declining inflation and unemployment have improved the country's quality of life, tourism to Colombia has nearly tripled in the last five years, and real estate is once again a stable investment. Taken together, it's not surprising to see once-dangerous or impoverished neighborhoods and districts beginning to turn around.

PAST AND PRESENT

In the latter half of the 20th century, with the emergence of cocaine as a major international commodity, probably no other country in the world has suffered the slings and arrows of outrageous economic fortune as much as Colombia. A country rich in natural resources, Colombia nonetheless has had grave economic inequalities among its population from the very beginning. Mestizos and indigenous—who make up the most of the population—have experienced the most marginalization: low wages and few opportunities for upward mobility. This conflict between a mostly poor majority and an affluent minority has always been an ongoing source of political conflict and economic instability, but it took the new cocaine market to bring Colombia to the verge of financial and social chaos.

This new wealth was a boon for the already affluent, who were eager to launder these ill-gotten gains into real estate, construction and other investment ventures. This, in turn, provided well-paying jobs and marginal benefits for the middle-class and to a lesser extent, the poor. But it also wreaked havoc on the overall economy. The influx of U.S. dollars accelerated inflation. Decades- long extreme violence profoundly damaged Colombia's infrastructure. Drug cartels not only had the firepower to wage war on law enforcement and society, they also financed left and right-wing terrorist groups. The unstable climate, which included attacks on petroleum drilling operations, discouraged foreign investment.

Despite this, Colombia's economy was remarkably stable and productive in comparison to that of its Latin American neighbors. This was in part because of its wealth of organic and mineral resources. Another factor encouraging steady growth was Colombia's commitment to a free and open market. During the 1980s, Colombia was the only Latin American country not to default on its international loans.

During the 1970s, in an ambitious attempt to improve the quality of life for Colombia's vast poor while maintaining a strong economy, President Alfonso López (1974-1978) initiated a development plan centered on exports, farming, regional growth and manufacturing.

Julio César Turbay (1978-1982) invested public resources in Colombia's energy and mining sector, and improving communication and transportation services, while decentralizing the economy.

However, by 1982, an economic crisis, in part brought on by the growing social disorder wrought by the drug trade, forced President Belisario Betancur (1982- 1986) to issue decrees revising banking and fiscal guidelines before the Virgilio Barco (1986-1990) administration attempted to reduce unemployment while promoting economic growth.

In 1990, President César Gaviria Trujillo (1990-1994) reduced tariffs, deregulated many private markets, and privatized state-owned industries, including airports, seaports, power plants, banks and highways, as a means of drawing foreign investors. Gaviria forged regional trading blocs like the Latin American Integration Association (LAIA), a free-trade agreement between Chile and the G-3 (Colombia, Mexico and Venezuela). With tariffs lowered and increased trade with the U.S., jobs were lost in certain sectors, but food prices were kept low and the economy grew at a rate of 4.5 percent.

President Ernesto Samper (1994-1998) inaugurated more progressive social policies for the poor, but higher public spending expanded the fiscal deficit. A recession resulted and unemployment rose to 20 percent. By the end of 1999 Colombia's total foreign debt was $34.5 billion; credit rating organizations ranked the country as a poor risk investment.

Andrés Pastrana Arango (1998-2002) devalued the peso and accepted a $2.7 billion International Monetary Fund loan contingent on fiduciary restraint and restructuring. Nonetheless, with the influx of borrowed money, new austerity policies and the competitive price of its petroleum and other exports (due to the peso's devaluation), the economy began to recuperate. In 2000 the U.S. loaned Colombia $1.3 billion in military aid against the drug cartels and leftist rebels, but right-wing, left-wing and criminal violence still prevailed in 40 percent of the country.

It was against this background of fear that Álvaro Uribe (2002-2010) was elected, promising to restore peace and security. In his first term, defense spending nearly tripled. U.S. troops were sent in to guard the country's largest pipeline. With loans from international agencies, social spending was increased, but this necessitated cutting pensions and other social programs in order to moderate the deficit.

By 2003, GDP growth reached as high as four percent, and continued to increase ever. His 2004 plan involved shrinking the public-sector deficit to less than 2.5 percent of the Gross Domestic Product (GDP); he was able to reduce it to 1.5 percent. The economic growth, along with increased security, improved investor and business confidence. In 2007, foreign investment reached a record $5 billion. However, with the onset of the world financial crisis in 2009, the Colombian peso weakened by 6.4 percent and the overall economy declined as foreign exports failed. Colombia was one of the hardest hit Latin American countries. In 2010, the markets began to recover, notably in the oil sector.

President Juan Manuel Santos (2010-) has vowed to continue Uribe's promarket policies, stimulating growth in agriculture, extractive and innovative industries, while investing in infrastructure and housing. He introduced legislation to use some oil revenue to recompense Colombians who lost land due to the Civil War violence. The U.S. continues to be a major trading partner; Colombia is its third larger supplier of oil. A free trade agreement between the two countries continues to be stalled, with strong opposition from labor and human rights groups. Santos is encouraging market expansion to Canada, Europe and Latin America.

Still a vast number of Colombians live in extreme poverty—11 million live on less than a dollar a day. Working conditions, particularly in the mining sector, are dangerous. Reportedly, right-wing paramilitaries have routinely assassinated union organizers. While the powerful Medellín and Cali cartels have experienced significant losses in the last twenty years, the very law of supply-and-demand has kept the lucrative cocaine trade active, which in turn continues to fund any attempted subversion of Colombian security. Updated: Sep 22, 2011.

Population

Although—according to the national census—the vast majority of Colombia's population is mestizo (mixed Amerindian and white, 58 percent) or white (20 percent), the nation wears many faces within those and in other ethnic groups.

Much of the white population traces its origins to Spain. Besides during the Spanish colony era, other waves of immigrations came from the Iberian Peninsula, most notably during and after the Spanish Civil War. In the latter half of the 19th century and into the 20th, other Europeans arrived, especially during World War I and II. Italians settled primarily in the major Caribbean ports, and Germans found a home in Santander and Boyacá Departments. Other significant ethnicities that came were Romani (Gypsies), Russians and French.

During the same period, the largest immigrant group came from the Levantine countries: Lebanon, Syria and Palestine. Most of the first arrivals were Christians, thus assimilating quickly into Colombia's society. Later, Muslims came to the Caribbean coast, where until today their communities have mosques and Islamic schools. Also from this region, as well as from Europe, many Jews arrived, choosing to settle in Barranquilla, Medellín, Bogotá and Cali.

Colombia's African descendants, constituting a total of 21 percent of the population, came through slave trafficking. They have had a tremendous influence on the country's culture and sciences. But even within this population, there are three major sub-groups. The most predominant and most well-known is on the Caribbean coast. In this region, though, are palenquero communities, like San Basilio de Palenque near Cartagena, which preserve African traditions and language. The most traditional African culture is said to be found along the Pacific coast, where the labyrinthine mangroves gave refuge to Maroons, or escaped slaves. It was here where the first uprisings against Spanish rule occurred.

Official government figures state indigenous (Amerindian) peoples make up only one percent of the population, though some organizations say it is as high as 3.4 percent. Of the over 80 nations, the largest is the Wayuu in the Guajira peninsula. Other significant ones are the Nasa in Southern Colombia, Senú on the western Caribbean coast and the Emberá in the Pacific Chocó region. The Sierra Nevada de Santa Marta is home to about 30,000 people of the Arhuaco, Kogi, Kankuamo and Wiwa nations. The departments with the highest concentration of indigenous are La Guajira (40 percent), Guainía (32 percent), Vichada (31 percent), Vaupés (29 percent) and Amazonas (27 percent). Even though the law now recognizes the indigenous' territorial and self-governing rights, these peoples have been hit by the civil war, drug trafficking, and the pressure of multinational corporations wanting to appropriate natural resources from indigenous and sacred lands. In recent years, the U'wa of Eastern Colombia threatened mass suicide at the threat of oil exploration in their territory.

Language

Spanish is the official language of Colombia. Not all Colombians speak the same, however, as the spoken Spanish varies (sometimes dramatically) from region to region. In Bogotá, people speak what is called the Rolo dialect (also referred to as cachaco, meaning educated or refined) while those from northwest Colombia speak with the "hissing S" usually recognized as the Spanish of Spain. Other dialects include Cundiboyacense, which still uses an archaic variant of usted; and the coastal, similar to the Spanish spoken throughout the Caribbean.

Many of the more than 180 indigenous languages of the country's ethnic groups are constitutionally recognized as official languages within their respective territories. Wuyuunaiki (of the Guajira) has the most speakers. On San Andrés, Providencia and Santa Catalina Islands, a creole English is traditionally spoken; only on the last two isles is it preserved, however. Some Afro-Colombian communities on the Caribbean coast speak Palenquero, a Spanish Creole based on Kongo and other African languages. While bilingual education is mandatory in these territories, it is more geared toward Spanish replacement, rather than native language literacy. Therefore, most Colombians speak Spanish as either their first or second language.

If traveling to Colombia, it is recommended that you brush up on your Spanish. English is taught in schools, but not exceptionally well. Most Colombians understand much more English than one might imagine, but relatively few are fluent. Updated: May 11, 2011.

Religion

When it comes to religions in Colombia, Roman Catholicism is far and away the most prevalent. Brought from Spain in the early 1500s, Catholicism is popularly thought to have been spread by fear, intimidation and bribery. The truth is a little more complex. While some missionaries relied on such tactics, others, such as Bartolomé de las Casas, were instrumental in the defense of the Indians and in

INTRO & INFO

promoting a religion of love. Either way, Catholicism became firmly established and for centuries was the official religion of Colombia.

By hosting the Medellín Conference in 1968, Colombia played an important role in the development and dissemination of Liberation Theology, the idea of utilizing the Christian mission to bring justice to the poor. Despite these developments, the Catholic Church in Colombia has seen its influence wane in recent decades. In 1973, Colombia changed Catholicism from the country's official religion to "the religion of the great majority of Colombians." Perhaps more damning, the government revoked some of the church's power. In particular, Catholic missionaries no longer possessed greater jurisdiction than the government over education and health care in the Colombia's mission territories (land with primarily indigenous populations). The church was forced to surrender any right to censor public university texts and enforce the use of the Catholic doctrine in public schools. For good measure, Colombians were also granted the right to contract civil marriages without renouncing their Catholic faith.

Colombia's government expanded religious tolerance in 1991, when it guaranteed its citizens freedom of religion. Christian evangelicals and Mormons have made inroads here in recent years. On San Andrés, Old Providence and Santa Catalina Islands, the Baptist church has always been the predominant religion. Because of the large wave of Middle Eastern immigration the late-19th to early-20th century, Colombia also has quite a significant Muslim population, especially along the Caribbean coast. Maicao's mosque is the second largest in Latin America. Colombia also has small populations of Jews, Baha'is and Buddhists, who all have houses of worship in the country.

Even though other religions have grown in Colombia in recent years, they still pale in comparison to the overwhelming reach of Catholicism. According to most polls on the subject, approximately 90 percent of Colombians identify themselves as Catholic. But signs also point to a decline in Catholic faith. A 2001 poll conducted by one of Colombia's premier newspapers indicated that as many as 60 percent of Colombians did not actively practice their faith, and more recently, Colombia overturned a long-standing law prohibiting some forms of abortion despite opposition from the Catholic Church. Updated: May 11, 2011.

Social Issues

Despite Colombia's wealth of natural resources, geographical position and advantageous climate, historical circumstances have bequeathed this Andean nation a multitude of social problems: high unemployment, a housing shortage, malnutrition and hunger, high rates of infant mortality and abandoned children, widespread poverty, pervasive alcoholism and drug abuse, widespread juvenile delinquency, high rates of crime and violence, human rights abuses, entrenched and violently polarized guerrilla factions, and inadequate health and education services.

The roots of these problems can be traced back to the legacy of Spanish colonialism and imperialism. Even after Colombia's independence from Spain, the new governors did not establish a political and social structure for the benefit of all of its citizens, but rather for only for the very small, mostly Spanish-descendant class. The effect of such institutionalized inequality has proven to be disastrous for the overall quality of life of Colombia's citizens, including, ironically, its wealthiest, who have to live in fear of being kidnapped or murdered.

In the years following World War II, the situation was exacerbated by two major factors: the new market for cocaine, and the Cold War, which resulted in the United States and the Soviet Union subsidizing opposing and often violent ideological factions in Colombia, both of which used the fight against the other as an excuse for committing atrocities on innocent civilians. Extremists on both the right and the left also accepted funding and arms from the highly lucrative cocaine trade, which had a vested interest in undermining any form of social order which interfered with its traffic.

Colombia's rural poor, in particular, have experienced the brunt of suffering, often being the target of extreme violence and having their territory appropriated and/or pillaged by wealthy landowners, and multinational interests—such as the Chiquita Banana, which was exposed recently for subsidizing paramilitaries near their plantations, both for "protection" and to repress any attempts by Chiquita's low-paid workers to form unions. Guerrilla warfare, paramilitaries and the narcotics trade are additional factors resulting in the displacement of millions of refugees, who have fled to the overcrowded cities, or more frequently, left to other countries—Ecuador in particular—in search of safety and better

Refugees of the War on Drugs

Since 1985, over 4.1 million Colombians have been displaced from their homes because of the war. At least 20,000 others have disappeared and over 5,000 have been found in communal graves by authorities. While the rest of the world makes "recreational" use of the white powder, this country is chained to the cultivation, production, commerce and power struggle that come as the result of being the provider of over 80 percent of the world's cocaine.

The war in Colombia, though fueled by narcotics, is not a war on drugs. Nor does it affect the substantial drug trade in the country, which accounts for almost three percent of Colombia's GDP. Confrontation between FARC guerrillas and paramilitary forces—backed by the national army and international forces—have turned Colombia into their battlefield and used civilians as tools of extortion, terror and income.

According to Human Rights Watch, the paramilitaries are causing the biggest hardship on civilians: it reports paramilitary forces are responsible for 78 percent of human rights violations in Colombia. Police authorities say between 1982 and 2005, paramilitaries—who joined in a consolidated organization in 1997 called United Self-Defense Forces of Colombia, or AUC—conducted over 3,500 massacres and robbed over six million hectares of land from farmers in different areas of the country.

From 2003 until 2006, 35,353 members of the AUC were demobilized. However paramilitary groups and delinquent activities have not ceased. Today an estimated 3,000 Colombians take part in emerging groups. The number of threats against labor unionists, human rights workers and communities nearly doubled between 2007 and 2009, and continues to grow.

Another cause of the flood of refugees in Colombia is government's use of glyphosate in coca field eradication. This herbicide kills not only the source for the white powder, but also peasants' food crops and causes health problems. Tens of thousands of Colombians have fled over the borders to escape the fumigations.

Colombia has the highest displaced population in the world, with a significant number of refugees in its neighboring countries, Ecuador and Venezuela. The United Nations High Commission on Refugees operates field offices in key zones within Colombia and in Ecuador. Other international refugee organizations are also present.

In the south, Ecuadorian NGOs have adopted different strategies to handle the large amounts of Colombian families crossing the border. As the numbers of immigrants increased from 1999, Ecuadorian organizations have periodically consulted civilians from both nations in forums and seminars. In 2008, Ecuador reformed its refugee visa policy, thus allowing many Colombians to legalize their status. However, xenophobia is on the increase in this southern neighbor. Since January 2011, Ecuador has received on average 1,500 refugees per month.

Venezuela has also seen a significant number of refugees come in at the border. However, they have not always been received with open arms. In 1999, Human Rights Watch sent a letter to Venezuelan president, Hugo Chávez, expressing concern with the way a number of Colombian refugees were transported back to their homeland forcefully, even though there was still eminent danger from paramilitary forces circulating the area.

On February 4, 2008, thousands of people in cities across the globe put on "Colombia soy yo" (I am Colombia) T-shirts and marched for peace in the country and against the FARC. Parting from that initiative, another walk was organized for March 6 to support and remember all of the victims and refugees of the war on drugs. Updated: Sep 20, 2011.

INTRO & INFO

opportunities. Women comprise 55 percent of internal refugees, and are often at high risk of sexual violence and unwanted pregnancies.

The Colombian government's response to this crisis has been criticized as being deficient. While over 90 percent of Colombians over the age of 15 can read and write, education in the rural provinces is often inadequate, with poorly qualified and underpaid teachers offering only the basics of primary school education, with no vocational or higher education opportunities.

During the 1990s, Colombia led the world in kidnapping rates, and was almost as high in murder rates, particularly in its cities. However, even though violence and crime still exists, over the past 10 years, crime and violence have declined, due in part to the decline in the power of drug cartels and the government's hard-line stance. Furthermore, in the last few years, Colombia's GDP growth has been constant, unemployment has not risen and rates of poverty, including rates of extreme poverty, have dropped several percentage points—all of which has attracted increasing national and international investments. Updated: Sep 16, 2011.

Culture

Culturally, Colombia is one of the richest countries in South America, integrating three continents' worth of tradition through music, dance, painting, sculpture, folk craft and literature.

The first cultures to arise out of this region were from pre-Columbian peoples who inhabited the area over 10,000 years ago. Such pre-Incan civilizations as the Carib, Chibca, Quimbaya, Tolima, as well as the Incans were master metallurgists and craftsman, fashioning basketry, wood carvings, textiles and pottery. Almost all of it served a combination of religious, political and practical ends.

The Spanish conquest brought the florid passions of Catholic religiosity to the region. Tall, large and lavish cathedrals and the iconic image of the martyred, emaciated, bleeding Christ, as well as the Holy Virgin, often adorned with gold-encrusted attire, a crown and an equally elegant baby Jesus on her arm. The veneration of Mary, particularly, was eagerly received by indigenous populations who saw in her the same maternal majesty they attributed to their own matriarch deities,

such as Mama Kilya. In addition, with colonization came the tradition of secular European painting, literature and music.

The Spanish also imported African slaves, whose own culture mingled with the locals, resulting in such percussion-heavy musical genres as cumbia, vallenato, porro and champeta. The cumbia also refers to a courtship dance ritual popular with the common folk. Vallenato began in the northeastern valleys along Colombia's Caribbean coast, by farmers who incorporated West African styles of music. The Carnaval of Barranquilla serves as a large-scale celebration of the many dimensions of Colombian music and dance, and of its multi-racial, multi-ethnic roots.

In 1871 Colombia established the Academy of Spanish Language, the first in South America. Beginning with Simón Bolívar, Colombia has one of the most noteworthy literary traditions on the continent, ranging from historical chroniclers to poets to novelists. As with the rest of South America, Colombia's writers evolved from religious to secular concerns, integrating and reflecting the changes in Western thought overall.

Gabriel García Márquez, who won the 1982 Nobel Prize for literature, is Colombia's most famous writer and an exponent of the modernist Magic Realism genre. Some of Colombia's other recognized writers include the 19th-century Jorge Isaacs, whose romantic chronicle of the lives of Colombia's mestizos, "Maria," actually inspired a minor Japanese migration to the country, while other notable 20th-century scribes include Álvaro Mutis, Laura Restrepo, Germán Espinosa and Fernando Vallejo, who also directs films, though the film adaptation of his most famous novel, "Our Lady of the Assassins" was directed by the Swiss Barbet Schroeder, who spent part of his childhood in Colombia. Colombia's most famous sculptor and painter is Ferdinand Botero, celebrated (as well as criticized) for his "fat" subjects.

Much of modern Colombian culture—movies, TV programs, as well as music—has been strongly influenced by Hollywood, European cinema, and U.S. popular music, from rock to soul to rap. Colombia is one of Latin America's major producers of telenovelas (soap operas). Singer-songwriter Shakira from Barranquilla is an international superstar, while Medellín-native Juanes is one of the biggest rock stars in Latin America. Estefano, from Cali, has become famous both for his own music as part of the duo Donato and Estefano, and as a songwriter for such Latin artists as Gloria Estefan, Ricky Martin, and Jennifer Lopez.

Colombia is also noteworthy for its high number of beauty pageants, a major fashion industry and the highest numberof museums of any Latin American country.

Sociologically, Colombia has tended toward being socially conservative, with family of key importance in the lives of its citizens. However, recently it has become more liberal in the area of divorce and gay rights. Spanish is the predominant language, Roman Catholicism is the dominant religion (though protestant evangelism is growing) and fútbol (soccer) is the most popular sport. Updated: Sep 14, 2011.

ART

The history of art in Colombia divides into four periods: 1) pre-Columbian, 2) colonial, 3) post-independence and 4) modern.

Pottery bearing animal, human and geometric designs and other evidence of pre-Columbian culture date as far back as 7,000 BC. However, the information regarding this people is scarce. Later civilizations such as the Tairona and the Muisca were skilled metallurgists, particularly with gold, and their work—pendants, figurines, necklaces—was rich with political and religious detail.

However, much of this gold work has been lost owing to the officially sanctioned looting on behalf of the Spanish crown, which resulted in many sacred and ceremonial artifacts and sculptures being taken to Spain and melted down.

After the Spanish conquest, Colombian art was almost entirely thematically ecclesiastical and derived from previous medieval, Mannerist, and Renaissance styles imported from Europe. Nonetheless, native Colombians who were trained in these arts retained some of their own cultural legacy in their work. This can be seen particularly in the older churches in Colombia, which evidence elements of indigenous design.

However, at this stage in history, Spanish-born or Spanish-descended artists prevailed on Colombian soil. The dominant style during this time was Baroque: emotional to the point of visual melodrama. The first artist of note is Alonso de Narváez. He is known less for a particular originality than for a legend about a portrait he painted on cloth of the Virgin and child, flanked by two saints. Reportedly the colors quickly faded and the canvas began to rot, yet after it was put away in storage it was found years later to have become completely restored. Baltasar de Figueroa, from Seville, integrated native influences to his European sensibility. His legacy was continued by his sons.

The most important artist of the colonial era was Gregorio Vázquez de Arce y Ceballos. A prolific painter, his original portrait of the Trinity as a three-faced being (inverting Dante's three-faced Satan from the "Divine Comedy") was later condemned as heresy partly due to its resemblance to Hindu idols. The artist responsible for the Sopo Archangels series is unknown, but the paintings are notable for the androgynous nature of their subjects.

The 19th-century post-independence Republican period is considered negligible by most scholars. Some attribute this to Colombia's geography, which kept artists isolated from each other and the world, and thus retarded the evolution of new forms. However, two noteworthy painters in the latter part of the century were Mercedes Delgado Mallarino de Martínez, one of the few women artists of the time, and Ricardo Acevedo Bernal, who was not only a painter, but also composer, photographer and even diplomat.

Colombia's Modern Art movement began in 1920, when artists such as Santiago Martínez Delgado and Pedro Nel Gómez imported the Mexican muralist movement to their native country. Later artists, such as Ricardo Gómez Campuzano and Carlos Correa, revealed the influence of Post-Impressionism and Cubism in their work. Spanish-born Alejandro Obregón introduced his own Expressionist Romanticism, influenced by Picasso that exhibited a heavy environmental, political and sexual focus. Along with Eduardo Ramírez Villamizar, Édgar Negret, Enrique Grau and FernandoBotero, he was considered a member of Colombia's "Big Five" artists. Of the latter, Botero is also the most famous Colombian artist ever, sharing a celebrity status rivaled only by novelist Gabriel García Márquez and singer Shakira. His "fat people" and "fat animal" sculptures and paintings, often humorous, are sold for millions, yet he has not shied away from tackling any number of controversial themes, from criticizing the Church to human rights abuses committed by the U.S. government. Updated: Sep 13, 2011.

MUSEUMS

Colombia has more museums than any other country in Latin America. You will find many opportunities to intellectually and spiritually immerse yourself into the culture and geography of this region.

The more notable museums in Bogotá include the Museo Nacional de Colombia, one of the oldest and biggest museums in all of Latin America. This museum housed in a former prison was established in 1823. The imposing edifice, with arches and domes, and made of stone and brick, offers a 20,000-plus piece collection. What once were prison cells now showcase impressive accomplishments in archaeology, ethnography, history and art. The collection contains items from European, Afro-Colombian and indigenous cultures, from 10,000 BC to the present. Paintings on permanent display include works by such masters as Fernando Botero.

The most famous museum in the capital is the Museo del Oro of Colombia's Banco de la República. Offering the largest and most impressive gold metallurgy collection of the pre-Columbian period—including a golden raft used in ceremonies—along with ancient stoneware, shell, wood and textile artifacts, Bogotá's Gold Museum is one of the most memorable testaments to South America's early civilizations.

Other noteworthy bogatano institutions are the Museo de Arte Colonial, Museo de Arte Moderno, Museo Iglesia de SantaClara, a former and breathtakingly beautiful monastery, and the modern, interactive Maloka Museum of Science.

Outside of Bogotá, noteworthy museums include the Museo de Antioquia in Medellín, the second oldest in the country and one of the most important. It serves as the virtual national house gallery for world-famous painter and sculptor Fernando Botero. Armenia's Museo del Oro Quimbaya and Santa Marta's Museo de Oro Tairona have impressive pre-Columbian gold collections. Cartagena offersMuseo Naval del Caribe, a Museo de Arte Moderno, Museo de la Inquisición and the Museo San Pedro de Claver, annexed to the church and plaza where a 17th-century Spanish priest who advocated for the human rights of the local population had lived. Updated: Sep 13, 2011.

MUSIC

Melodic and multi-rhythmic, Colombia's musical genres evoke and integrate a multitude of traditions: indigenous, Spanish, African and North American. There was music in Colombia, of course, before the arrival of Spanish conquerors, and the haunting pan flute melodies of Andean cultures echoes in the more contemporary bambuco, also known as the "music in the interior." Integrating European waltzes—which set it apart from the more purely indigenous music in Peru, Ecuador and Bolivia—it is notable for its melancholy mood. Long popular, it peaked with the public in the 1920s and 1930s. Pasillo, guabina and torbellino are similar blends of folk and European music.

The Spanish brought not only their tunes, both ecclesiastical and secular, but also stringed instruments such as the guitar, violin, cello and bass. Through slavery, they also brought over an African population whose music added a strong element of rhythm.

Hence, Colombia's music evolved in accordance with geography and demography. Much of Colombia's musical genres originated on the Caribbean coast which was the main disembarkation point for imported African slaves. Cumbia, along with vallenato, is Colombia's signature contribution to world music and is a variation of African Guinea's own cumbe, from which this genre gets its name.

Heavy on percussion, cumbia originally consisted of a vocals and a polyrhythmic combination of drum and wooden stick (known as claves) beats. It is accompaniedby a style of dance purportedly associated with the iron shackles worn by the slaves themselves. Over time wind, keyboard and string instruments along with more Europeanized melodies were incorporated.

However, it was not until the 1940s when cumbia was legitimized by urban and middle-class Colombians. One cumbia song, the "Cumbia Cienaguera," is known as Colombia's unofficial national anthem. Notable cumbiastars include Los Teen Agers, Los Graduados and Los Corraleros de Majagual.

Vallenato also developed in Colombia's Caribbean region, but in the valleys which gave the genre its name. A popular legend attributes its beginnings to a musician by the name of Francisco el Hombre who defeated Satan in a contest of musical skills. More probably, it is a derivation of cumbia which spread through the region by traveling, musically skilled farmers for whom music was both a sole source of entertainment and means of bringing news to other areas. Its key instruments

Shakira

You're in a sweaty nightclub, a dark bar, a packed bus or a local restaurant—and if the music is blasting, you're likely to hear singer-songwriter Shakira, the most successful Colombian musician of all time. Known for her unique vocals, passionate lyrics and sensual belly-dance moves, Shakira is a global phenomenon.

Born in Barranquilla to parents of Colombian and Lebanese descent, Shakira began her professional singing career at age 13. After creating two commercially unsuccessful albums at a young age, Shakira released Pies Descalzos (Bare Feet) in 1996. Pies Descalzos, which sold over three million copies, featured Shakira's now signature style—a blend of Latin, Arabic and rock influences—and marked her arrival to the Latin music scene. Major singles off that album include: "Estoy Aquí"; "Dónde Estás Corazón?"; "Antología"; "Pienso en Ti"; "Un Pocode Amor" and "Se Quiere, Se Mata." During this time, Shakira also founded the Pies Descalzos Foundation to help impoverished children in Colombia (www.fundacionpiesdescalzos.com)

Her 1998 follow-up record, Dónde Están Los Ladrones?(Where Are the Thieves?) was an even bigger global success. Songs such as "Ciega, Sormuda," "Tú" and especially the heavily Arabic-influenced, Grammy-winning "Ojos Asi" led Shakira to the top of the Billboard's Latin album chart, paving the way for her explosion on the American music market.

Upon enlisting Emilio Estefan (Gloria Estefan's husband) as her manager and producer, dying her hair blonde and playing up her sex appeal, Shakira moved to Miami to create her first English-language album, Laundry Service, in 2001. This album was an instant success, entering the U.S. pop charts at number three and selling over 200,000 copies in the first week. Hugely popular singles off this album include the hip-shaking "Whenever, Wherever" and the soulful "Underneath Your Clothes."

After an extensive tour of Laundry Service, the next few years were spent working on two albums simultaneously. The Spanish-language Fijacion Oral, Vol. 1 won her a second Grammy Award for Best Latin Rock/Alternative Album. The English-language Oral Fixation, Vol. 2, featuring her immensely popular collaboration with Wyclef Jean, "Hips Don't Lie," shot to the top of the Billboard Hot 100 chart, and became the most played song in pop-radio history during the summer of 2006. Shakira's sixth studio album She Wolf was released at the end of 2009 and was closely followed by her seventh studio album Sale el Sol released in October 2010. Updated: March 23, 2011.

guacharaca (a gourd rasped with a stick), caja (box) drum and accordion. Guitars, bass and other instruments have been added over time.

Another variation of cumbia is porro, which originated in such towns as Sucre and Córdoba. It blends the "big band" sound of military brass ensembles. Champeta, popular in Cartagena and elsewhere on the Atlantic coast, is noteworthy because it has remained close to its African roots, though it has been influenced by such other Caribbean music as reggae, mento and calypso. Salsa may have begun in Cuba, but starting in Cali, it became Colombian genre in its own right.

Currulao, which originated on Colombia's Pacific coast, is also close to its African origins. This musical genre uses marimbas, bass drums and guasas, which are like maracas, but tubular.

Joropo is style of music popular along the Colombian-Venezuelan border. It is strong on harp and improvisational lyrics. Joropo blends folk, European and African influences. North American rock, pop, funk, soul and rap have all had a tremendous impact during the last few decades. One of the most famous musicians to emerge is "Hips Don't Lie" phenomenon Shakira. Another is Juanes, one of the most popular singer-songwriters in all of Latin America. Both these artists have won numerous Grammy awards. ChoQuibTown, a hip hop group from the Pacific Chocó, won a Latin Grammy in 2010. Updated: May 11, 2011.

DANCE

As long as there has been music, there has also been dance, and as with Colombian music, Colombian dance evolved from Old and New World traditions, culminating in a variety of unique and colorful styles of movement and dress.

Cumbia

The purest representation of African, indigenous and Spanish fusion and Colombia's most significant musical art form, cumbia originated on the Caribbean coast as instrumental music created with drums, bagpipes and maracas. The word cumbia is a derivative of the African word "cumbé," which means party or celebration.

Cumbia is considered by many the queen of Afro-Caribbean rhythms, yet to get to what it is today, this musical genre has transcended races, cultural backgrounds and social classes. During the 1930s, cumbia rose from the working classes to the urban high society of Colombia, validating itself as an authentic art form. As it gained popularity, it added lyrics and instruments like the accordion. Today three types of cumbia prevail: classic cumbia, which is instrumental; modern cumbia, with various drums and animated lyrics; and cumbiamba, differing from cumbia in both musical instruments and dance rituals. With Spanish-inspired clothing—long skirts for women and hats and red handkerchiefs for men—the dancing portion of cumbia is a courtship ritual that follows the beat of African drums with a style of indigenous movements.

The rhythms of cumbia have spread all through Latin America. Argentina, Chile, Mexico, Peru and other countries have developed a taste for creating and dancing the Colombian sound, but with their own national flavors. Updated: Sep 14, 2011.

Indeed, one cannot talk about Colombian dance without its accompanying costumes. For most dances, the women are barefoot, wear a short-sleeved blouse, and most importantly, wear a floor-length, multi-pleated, flowing skirt, the edges of which are gracefully held and swayed by the dancers, both in their pas-de-deux with their male partners, and when they dance as women together in a group.

The bambuco is identified as Colombia's national dance. Its music incorporates Andean and African melodies, as well as European waltzes and polkas, but with a ¾ meter and whose music is sung by two voices. There are six varieties of this particular courtship dance, all of which the groups of pairs move serenely and suggestively, and in which the men discreetly pursue the women, and they coquettishly respond.

The second most famous Colombian dance, as with the most famous genre of Colombian music, is cumbia. African in its origin, cumbia, a word that translates into revelry or festival, was born in Colombia's fields and plantations around Cartagena as a recreational dance for slave workers. Consisting of five key steps, the cumbia features a seductive motif in which the man beseeches his beloved, and which she in turn alternately flirts with and snubs him. The woman traditionally holds a cluster of candles.

The sanjuanero is another courtship dance, from Colombia's valley region. Dancers on occasion extend a scarf between each other as an index of the man's longing to win the object of his affection. Beginning with a series of overtures by the man toward the woman, the dance then proceeds into an ornamental series of turns, with steps backward and sideways, in which the couple come close then pull apart. It is a variation of the bambuco.

Abozao, from Colombia's Pacific Chocó region, is a more spontaneous dance, with less defined choreography in which moves are improvised. A group dance featuring many pairs, it can also be a courtship dance. It has a noticeably sensual element, with the woman teasingly moving her hips, provoking the man to beg for more, which she does not offer.

Mapalé is Colombia's sexiest dance, as well as its most overtly African, with movements that can be traced directly back to Guinea. It is one in which the woman does indeed respond to the implied proposal in the man's physical movements and gestures. Popular along Colombia's Caribbean coast, the dance is named after a fish in the Magdalena River and the dancers perform with a distinctly rippling cadence meant to evoke fish. In this dance, the woman often wears a short grass skirt, while the man is always shirtless. Both thrust their hips to a fast beat made of drums, handclaps and a collective vocal chant of "mapaleeé, mapaleeé!"

Other notable traditional dances include joropo, with roots in flamenco and Andalusian dances; pasillo, adapted from Austrian waltzes, but with faster, more vertiginous gestures and smaller steps, which gave the dance its name; and bunde, a religious and ceremonial dance that is often performed only by women or only by men, and whose music is entirely percussive, made up only of hand slaps, drums and vocal chants.

The most famous modern dance in Colombia is salsa, with Cali being the capital. Here, both the music and dance have a faster rhythm than in Cuba or Puerto Rico. In recent years, Colombians have taken home the grand prize in international salsa dance competitions. Updated: September 14, 2011.

THEATER

Theater existed for pre-colonial peoples of Colombia, as religious ceremony celebrating gods and related to seasons, wars and harvests—and on occasions even incorporating human sacrifices. The arrival of the Spanish introduced western theater to the New World, though apart from opera and other European genres, it too was mostly religious and pedagogical in nature. The 19th century introduced more ambitiously secular and historical themes, especially in the Costumbrismo style brought over from Spain which focused on the daily lives of the common population. Some of

the more notable authors of this period include Luis Vargas Tejada, José María Samper and José María Vergara y Vergara.

However, it was not until the early 20th century that a distinctly Colombian theater came into being through the efforts of Antonio Álvarez Lleras and Luis Enrique Osorio who wrote politically themed, realistic plays. They also trained actors, produced theater journals and sponsored companies, all of which laid the foundation for the new directions Colombian theater was to take in the years that followed.

Following World War II, Colombian artists, influenced by European existentialists and the experimental works of Antonin Artaud and Bertolt Brecht, felt even more emboldened to tackle ideological themes. The cataclysmic events from 1948 to 1955 known as La Violencia ended the popularity of the more genteel Costumbrismo of the previous century.

In Medellín, the Experimental Theater of the Institute of Fine Arts questioned the bourgeois values of Colombian culture, exploring such issues as racism, class inequality and historical oppression. It often did so in an abstract manner, with characters identified as numbers or symbols as an index of their dehumanization. Other theater groups revived elements of pre-Columbian ceremony in theater as a means of honoring the heretofore devalued indigenous culture.

In addition to Brecht and Artaud, the vanguard innovations of Stanislavski and Grototowski influenced Colombian theater. These methods were imported by writers and directors such as Enrique Buenaventura and Santiago García, who had lived in Paris and Prague. This art form was simultaneously more realistic (especially in acting) but more experimental and modernist in its staging.

The success of the Socialist revolution in Cuba was yet another notable historical factor in the evolution of Colombian theater, inspiring a generation of university-based young writers, actors and directors. This movement, called Nuevo Teatro, created newer forms of community-based, cooperatively created theater that addressed the needs and issues of the people, particularly the poor, minorities and the disenfranchised, and became widely popular. These works incorporated elements of folklore and revisionist views of history. One of the most popular plays was "I Took Panama," staged by the Teatro Popular de Bogotá, which discussed Colombia's loss of Panama through the interventionist policies of Theodore Roosevelt.

However, due to the left-leaning bent of this movement, many of the artists involved had to struggle with government censorship and harassment. Buenaventura and García were both dismissed from their university positions. Some theater companies were shut down on charges of "subversion."

The 1980s saw a resurgence of more conventionally scripted drama, particularly as paramilitary and cartel violence resulted in a decline in the popularity of activist theater. Argentine actress Fanny Mikey successfully produced the works of Edward Albee and Neil Simon, and co-founded the Ibero-American Theater Festival, the largest of its kind in all of South America, attracting established repertories from all over the world, such as the Royal Shakespeare Company. In Bogotá, Medellín, Cali and Cartagena, lively theatrical communities still thrive. Updated: Sep 14, 2011.

COMEDY

Considering the level of chaos in Colombia's history, it would have been impossible for Colombians not to have a sense of humor, but it was not until the arrival of TV in the 1950s that a distinctly Colombian comedy came into being. Shows such as "Yo y Tú" and later "Don Chinche," used family life as a starting point for satirical barbs aimed at local culture and politics, often burlesquing regional dialects and attitudes.

One innovative program, "Sábados Felices," ("Happy Saturdays") offered a showcase for comics from all over Colombia, along with sketches poking fun at politicians and celebrities. A show called "No Me Lo Cambie" ("Don't Change the Channel on Me") integrated bits from European and American shows along with "Candid Camera"-style practical jokes.

In the 1990s, Jaime Garzón initiated a more sophisticated style of political comedy, combining an opinionated acuity, often at the expense of the government, with a theatrical flair for parodying people from all walks of Colombian life. Unfortunately, his open partisanship played a hand in his death when he was assassinated on August 13, 1999, reportedly by right-wing paramilitaries. This had the effect since of inhibiting overtly critical comedy in Colombia.

Still, political comedy, as long as it was impartial, continued and in radio. Crisanto Alfonso Vargas and Guillermo Díaz Salamanca became enormously successful with their gibes at the state and citizenry, with Salamanca lauded as the "man of a thousand voices" for his aptitude at imitating public figures in all spheres of prominence. Martín de Francisco and Santiago Moure, who began in TV and later moved on to radio, gained notoriety for pushing the boundaries of decorum in their humor.

In 2004 comic Jose Ordóñez occasioned a moment of national pride when he set the Guinness Book of World Records for the longest duration—65 hours—in telling continuous jokes. However, in the last decade, Colombia's two most notable contributions to world humor have come in the form of another comic, Andrés López and a TV program, "Betty la Fea."

The former popularized the American tradition of stand-up and monologue comedy and achieved international renown for his one-man show "The Ball of Letters," a sardonic and observant take on generational and cultural divisions in Colombia. "Betty la Fea," a comedy-drama about a homely but brainy administrative assistant at a fashion agency who gets her revenge against the more easily appreciated beauties in her midst by virtue of her I.Q. and work ethic, not only became a massive hit across Latin America, but inspired no less than thirteen remakes in as many countries, including Greece, Turkey, Russia, India, Israel and the United States, where it was known as "Ugly Betty."

John Leguizamo is a well-known actor and comedian who was born in Bogotá and immigrated to the United States at the age of four. His monologues and shows have poked fun at both Latino culture in the United States as well as popular stereotypes about Hispanics. Updated: Sep 14, 2011.

CINEMA

Colombians have been trying, in fits and starts, to establish a national film industry virtually since the dawn of the medium itself, but until very recently, their success has been at best limited. Not only have aspiring producers, writers and directors been faced with Hollywood's domination of the market, Colombian filmmakers were also far behind Mexico and Argentina in creating a niche for themselves as a Latin film industry, even within Colombia.

Shortly after movies were introduced to Colombia at the turn of the 20th century, the entrepreneurial Di Domenico brothers produced a historical documentary, "The Drama of October the 15th," regarding the Battle of Boyacá, and a more controversial one about the then-recent assassination of Rafael Uribe Uribe, a key political figure. For the most part, however, cinema was still a novelty for Colombians until the 1920s, and creative ambition did not go much further than the Lumière-like filming of everyday life.

The first full-length feature film, "María," based on a novel by native author Jorge Isaacs, appeared in 1922. In 1924,"Under the Antioquia Sky" and "The Tragedy of Silence" opened to a generally enthusiastic response. These films were followed by "Claws of Gold" in 1926, a critical take on the U.S.' intervention in Colombian politics which resulted in the loss of Panama.

However, these sporadic efforts could not compete with the flood of popular and expensively produced cinema coming from Hollywood and Germany which featured such stars as Charlie Chaplin and Greta Garbo. When sound arrived in 1928, Colombian filmmakers could not afford the costly equipment needed to make their own "talkies," and were thus finished for many years. What was left of the local industry shifted entirely from production to importation.

With the production of Colombia's first sound film in 1941, national cinema saw a new beginning. Shortly thereafter a Bogotá businessman Oswaldo Duperly started a production company which, for a few years, made a minor incursion into the Latin market dominated by Mexico and Argentina.

In 1954, in the manner of Luis Buñuel and Salvador Dalí with "Un Chien Andalou," novelist Gabriel García Márquez and painter Enrique Grau collaborated on a surrealist short film, "The Blue Lobster." Their hopes of manifesting a renaissance in Colombian film art did not happen.

In the 1970s, social problems gave rise to an exploitative genre dubbed "pornomisery." Influenced by the popularity of the lurid Mondo Cane "shockumentaries," pornomisery captured some of the worst scenes of poverty and degradation in Colombia at the time, but without any accompanying insight or explanation.

Around the same time a new box office tax was instituted in order to subsidize the production of short films. Aspiring filmmakers responded eagerly. By the end of the 1970s, the state-sponsored production company, FOCINE, folded due to mismanagement and an economic crisis. During its existence, it was a notable boost to a new generation of ambitious auteurs, and actually resulted in some successes.

This past decade has seen Colombian cinema recover, in part because of new government measures to finance and promote filmmaking, and in part due to the international success of films such as "Our Lady of the Assassins" and "María Full of Grace," which ironically were made by a Frenchman and an American respectively. However, native filmmakers like Sergio Cabrera, Rodrigo Triana and Victor Gaviria have succeeded both at home and abroad, winning prizes and box office earnings for works that have tackled Colombia's many social problems. Ciro Guerra's "Los Viajes del Viento" won a Cannes Film Festival award in 2009. In addition, Colombia's film festivals in Bogotá and Cartagena are among the best regarded in Latin America, and the one is Mompós is quickly gaining fame. Updated: Sep 15, 2011.

LITERATURE

Though for many the notion of Colombian literature immediately brings to mind Gabriel García Márquez and the style of Magic

Colombia Fun Facts

► Colombia borders **Brazil, Venezuela, Panama, Peru, and Ecuador**.
► Total landmass of Colombia is roughly **1,140,000 square kilometers** (440,156 sq mi), which is slightly less than twice the size of Texas or France.
► Highest point: **Pico Cristóbal Colón**, 5,775 meters (18,942 ft).(Note: nearby Pico Simón Bolívar has the same elevation.)
► Lowest point: **Pacific Coast**, 0 meters
► Colombia is the **oldest democracy** in Latin America.
► Colombian women got the right to vote in **1957**.
► The 2011 Global Peace Index of the Institute for Economics & Peace and The Economist magazine ranked 153 countries according to how peaceful they were and how hard they strived for peace. Iceland was first, Iraq was 152nd. **Colombia was ranked 139th**, last in Latin America, behind countries like Uganda and Lebanon. (In case you're curious, the U.S. came in 82nd, between Gabon and Bangladesh; its northern neighbor, Canada, ranked 8th.)
► There are **80 different indigenous nations** in Colombia, speaking **180 languages**.
► Experts believe there are 14,000 species of **butterflies** in the world: about 3,000 of them are found in Colombia.
► Colombia has the world's greatest diversity of **orchid species** (3,500) and birds (1,754 species). It also takes second place for amphibians and third for reptiles.
► Colombia's Pacific coast is home to the **golden dart frog**; one gram of its poison is enough to kill about 15,000 humans.
► According to the International Union for Conservation of Nature and Natural Resources, Colombia is home to **593 endangered species**, which puts them 8th on the international list. Ecuador is first, with 2,151 species.
► Colombian **María Isabel Urrutia** is the only South American to win Olympic gold in weightlifting.
► Colombia has been to the FIFA World Cup playoffs **four times**.
► **Tourism** in Colombia fell 21 percent between 1995 and 1999 and rose 48 percent between 2005 and 2006; in the first six months of 2011, it increased 14.3% over 2010.
► Ninety-five percent of the world's **emeralds** come from Colombia.
► Colombia is the world's third-leading producer of **women's lingerie**.
► Some experts estimate that Colombia can produce 545 metric tons of pure cocaine annually. The country is the world's largest grower of the **coca plant**.
► Brazil produces the most coffee annually in the world; Colombia is second, providing **12 percent of the world's coffee**.
► It is estimated that people drink 400 billion cups of coffee each year, second only to water.
► After petroleum, coffee is the world's second most traded commodity.
Updated: Sep 16, 2011.

Realism, the literary movements and authors this country has seen are as diverse as the culture itself. The common denominator of Latin American literature can be clearly defined in Colombian authors from the colonial era, passing through the Independence authors, and the styles like Costumbrismo, Los Nuevos, Nadaísmo and the Boom Generation.

Colonial literature in Colombia was heavily influenced by religion, since only religious men were educated in the art of writing and it would have been difficult to publish stories of heroes who weren't saints because the church controlled printers. By the time the people of Nueva Granada began fighting for independence, the political discourse became the spark that ignited the fire of patriotic poetry and a general search for a national identity in narration. Antonio Nariño, a republican journalist known as the father of political journalism in Colombia, was a key figure in the literature that lead up to independence. In mid-1810, Nariño founded the political newspaper La Bagadela, an outlet for his centrist discourse which served him to later get elected president of Cundinamarca.

Ringing in the New Year

Like any place in the world, Colombians celebrate New Year's Eve with music, dancing, confetti and lots of noise. And like its Latin American kin, Colombians create Old Men (Año Viejo), firework-stuffed effigies representing the past year's worst politicians, athletes and celebrities. At midnight, these are set ablaze in the middle of town streets, lighting the sky with explosions and sparks. Colombians, though, have some of their own customs (agüeros) to ensure the New Year brings all their desires.

To get rid of negative energy, pray Psalm 91 at precisely midnight, or stand on a chair to allow the past year's bad luck pass below. To have good luck, eat 12 grapes, one at each toll of midnight's bell. Another way to draw good energy, happiness and good times is to wear yellow underwear. It's best to wear them inside out, and then after midnight, turn them right-side out. To fulfill wishes for sexual pleasure, use red underwear.

Champagne plays a part in many other agüeros. A champagne bath at midnight is said to ensure prosperity and good fortune. To guarantee wealth, personal jewels are placed in a goblet of the bubbly. Another ritual entails thrusting hands into a sugar-water fountain, and then washing them with the sparkling wine.

Colombians believe placing coins on a mirror or counting money over and over while midnight tolls secures lots of money in the next year. Throwing coins outside the door and sweeping them back into the house is another way to bring wealth. Putting coins in shoes also attracts money.

A cheaper alternative to draw moolah is to eat lentils or put some in a pocket. Another use of this legume is to take 33 of them (representing the 33 creeds said during Easter Week), tie them in a napkin and safeguard them in a wallet until midnight of the next year. To have both money and travel in the New Year, pack a large suitcase and at 12 sharp, walk around the block.

A divination is performed by breaking two eggs in a glass. The yolks' shapes foretell what the New Year will bring. To find a husband or wife in the next 12 months, sit down and stand up with each stroke of midnight. A final New Year's Eve act is to burn colored candles, to draw energy: blue (peace), yellow (abundance), red (passion), green (health), white (clarity) or orange (intelligence). Updated: Nov 16, 2010.

The second half of the 19th century and the beginning of the 20th century, the style known as Costumbrismo emerged and became the first defined mark of what we know today as Colombian literature. Costumbrismo concentrated on narrating real characters in society as a way of defining the culture and its people. The critical style acquired during the Independence era continued in Costumbrismo; in fact, it has continued to question quotidian rules and government throughout published pages of every literary era. The poet Gregorio Gutiérrez Gonzáles (known as the man of the three Gs) is a particularly good example of Costumbrismo. His descriptions of romantic style gave details of everyday family life, and exposed the melancholy and love of common places.

León de Greiff, Luis Vidales and Tomás Carrasquilla, some of the best writers in the 1920s, belonged to the literary movement referred to as Los Nuevos (The New Ones). This style consisted of a hidden romanticism and a negation of the past. The ugly was emphasized. Narrations were often dark and mysterious. De Greiff was the best-known bohemian in Los Nuevos movement. His work was heavily criticized because of his constant experimentation with form, style and vocabulary. He was awarded the National Prize for Poetry in 1970.

The movement funded by journalist Gonzálo Arango came to be the trend of the 50s. Nadaísmo adhered itself to existentialist and nihilist principles. The movement began before Arango, with Fernando

Gonzáles Ochoa who produced the first writings that would later be cataloged as Nadaísta. Arango was a disciple of Ochoa. Considered one of the greatest Colombian thinkers of all times, Ochoa spent his life developing original philosophies and artistic works. Though he was nominated for a Nobel Prize of Literature in 1995, he did not win the recognition. In 2006, however, Colombian president Álvaro Uribe approved a law in which the nation would remember the life and works of Ochoa and declared his house near Medellín, la Casa Museo Otraparte, a cultural landmark.

With the Boom Generation came the acclaimed Gabriel García Márquez, who moved Colombian and Latin American literature into the realm of magical realism. In this genre, magical elements or illogical scenarios appear in an otherwise realistic setting. Márquez went on to achieve world admiration, receiving the 1982 Nobel Prize of Literature for his novel "Cien Años de Soledad."This movement advanced Colombian literature to the top of the list. However, it was followed by a generation of pessimistic authors for some years before contemporary authors took back the characteristic everyday descriptions and magical realism of today's publications.

Other important late-20th century writers are Laura Restrepo, who has won several literary prizes, and Manuel Zapata Olivella, who is recognized as one of the hemisphere's most important Afro-Latino fiction writers and folklorists. Updated: Sep 15, 2011.

Holidays and Festivals

HOLIDAYS
These are Colombia's national holidays. Those marked with an asterisk (*) are celebrated on the nearest Monday and known as a puente (a three-day holiday weekend). On most holidays, expect processions and other events. These are times when many Colombians take a break; hotel and transportation prices increase substantially and reservations should be made.

January 1—New Year's Day

*January 6—Epiphany (Day of the Three Kings)

*March 19—San José—To honor husbands and fathers.

March/April—Semana Santa (Thursday and Friday before Easter Sunday)—The most renowned observances are in Popayán and Mompós.

May 1—Primero de Mayo (Labor Day)

*May 15—Ascención de Jesús (Ascent of Christ)

*June 10—Sagrado Corazón (Sacred Heart)

*June 29—San Pablo y San Pedro—Celebrated with flair in Neiva (which has a national bambuco dance festival) and in coastal communities

July 20—Declaration of Independence

August 7—Battle of Boyacá—To observe the decisive battle against the Spanish crown, in 1819

*August 15—Asunción de la Virgen María (Feast of the Assumption)

*October 12—Descubrimiento de América (Columbus Day)

*November 1—Día de Todos los Santos (All Saints Day)

*November 11—Independencia de Cartagena (Independence of Cartagena)

*December 8—Inmaculada Concepción (Immaculate Conception)

December 25—Navidad (Christmas)—Be sure to check out Bogotá's special festival in Parque Bolívar.
Updated: May 11, 2011.

FESTIVALS
If secular and non-patriotic celebrations are more your style, Colombia has plenty to offer of festivals where you can experience traditions and culture:

January 5 and 6—Carnaval de Blanco y Negro—A huge powder and grease-tossing parade celebrated in Pasto and other southern Colombia towns.

February/March (moveable feast)—Carnaval—The big party is in Barranquilla, but also check it out in any Caribbean town or in Tumaco, on the Pacific coast.

February/ March—Festival Internacional de Cine de Cartagena de Indias —One of Latin America's most prestigious film festivals.

March/April—Festival Iberoamericano de Teatro—A huge, biennial theater festival in Bogotá, drawing troupes from around the world.

April—Festival de Poesía de Medellín—One of the most important international poetry gatherings in Latin America.

Last week of April—Festival de la Leyenda Vallenata—Vallenato music rocks Valledupar.

May—Festival de la Cultura Wayuu—Wayuu culture is highlighted at this annual festival held in Uribia in the Guajira.

Mid-July—Festival Internacional de la Confraternidad Amazónica—Annual international gathering of Amazonian indigenous nations in Leticia.

Mid-October—Encuentro Mundial de Coleo—rodeo competitions down on the Llanos, in Villavicencio (the women's rodeo is in March).

December—Festival de Cine Mompox—Another film festival to round out the year. Updated: Sep 16, 2011.

)!!!!

Information

BEFORE YOU GO

You have dreamed of going to Colombia, to savor its natural and cultural richness. Now it's time to get prepared. Be sure your passport is valid for at least six-months and check visa requirements. Draw up an itinerary, book your passage, pack your bags and you're ready to go.

Not quite. There are a few odds and ends to take care of yet. Check your medical and travel insurance policies for coverage. Be sure to toss in a first aid kit and any medications you regularly take. Lastly, Colombia can be a tumultuous country, therefore it is recommendable to check news updates on political and guerrilla situations and make sure the areas you are visiting are safe. Updated: Sep 07, 2011.

Visas

Please note that while usual visa requirements have been detailed below, it is essential that you check on the details with your closest consulate, as requirements change frequently and can vary from place to place.

TOURIST VISA

Residents of Latin American countries, the U.S., Canada, Western Europe, and several others in Asia and the Middle East (a total of 69 nations around the world) do not need a tourist visa to enter Colombia. When citizens of the aforementioned nations come to Colombia, an immigration officer will stamp an entry seal in their passport which will say how many days the person is allowed to stay. Although the maximum amount of days for most nationalities to visit Colombia is 90, the officer generally will stamp 30 or 60 days, so be sure to ask for more if you need it. U.S. and some European nations now only receive a maximum of 60 days upon entering Colombia.

Tourists may stay in Colombia for up to a total of 180 days. To apply for an extension, go to any DAS office in the country (located in departmental capitals; URL: www.das. gov.co). *Note: at the time of press, DAS was in the process of being dissolved but is still responsible for immigration matters in the meanwhile. Consult the DAS website for further developments.* You'll need passport, a photocopy of the passport's information pages, two three-centimeter by four-centimeter color photos (blue background) and

a ticket exiting the country. The person also needs to complete the required form and pay 72,350 COP (at the designated bank). A complete set of fingerprints will be taken. The Bogotá DAS office can give up to 60 additional days. Offices in other parts of the country give only 30 days more, and require two each of photocopies and photos. Travelers report DAS is more stringent on requirements in Bogotá, Cartagena and other places with many foreigners. It is easier in towns off the "gringo" trail.

For residents of nations who do need a tourist visa (check with the local Colombia consulate) the most important thing to know is that your visa will take approximately 15 days to process. You will need three passport pictures, a valid passport, a filled application form, a photocopy of passport, bank statement, round-trip ticket and information on the place where you plan to stay. An appointment and a $40 fee will complete the transaction. Updated: Apr 05, 2011.

BUSINESS VISA

To conduct business in Colombia or perform marketing studies, it is necessary to apply for a business visa, which can last for a maximum of three years. The visa does not allow the business person to live in the country, thus every visit should last no longer than six months. In order to apply for this visa, applicants will need three passport pictures, a valid passport, a filled application form, a photocopy of the passport, and a letter from the company the person works for describing the operations its employee will carry out in Colombia or a letter from the applicant if he or she is self-employed explaining the purpose of the visit.

If these last two options don't apply to your situation, then the letter must come from the Colombian entity—private or public—inviting you, as they will be responsible for your stay. Lastly, you must present a certificate of incorporation and legal representation issued no more than three months previously. Note that the letter and the certificate you present must be notarized and certified with an apostille from the secretary of the state where it was issued.

Independent business people must show a non-refundable round-trip ticket and bank statements for the three months previous to the visa application date. Though the applicant must go to a consulate for the request, the visa takes about three working days to come through for U.S. citizens and it can take up to two weeks for other nationalities. The cost of application for a business visa is $150, and it is necessary to make an appointment at the consulate.

WORK VISA

To be eligible for a Colombian work visa, an applicant must meet one of the following criteria: be employed by a Colombian company; work in Colombia under an academic agreement between countries; get transferred by a multinational to a Colombian subsidiary; get hired by a news agency as a correspondent in Colombia; participate in an artistic or cultural group coming for a performance or work as a volunteer or missioner for a religious organization.

For any of these circumstances, the applicant needs three passport pictures, a valid passport, a filled application form, a photocopy of passport, a letter of the company that is employing the applicant, a certificate of incorporation and legal representation issued no more than three months previous, a certificate of proportionality, which must be issued by the Ministry of Work and Social Security of Colombia, proof that the applicant is qualified for the position (diplomas, licenses or certificates) and a police report translated into Spanish. The cost to apply for a work visa is $205; the applicant must make an appointment at the nearest consulate for the request.

STUDENT VISA

The student visa can be requested by someone planning to attend a private or public educational organization recognized by the national government. The applicant must sustain a minimum of 10 hours per week schedule in the institution to be eligible for the visa. It is also possible to ask for a student visa if you are completing an internship as part of an academic program or if you are participating in an exchange program recognized by the government.

A student visa in Colombia lasts for a maximum time of one year, however, you may renew the visa as many times as needed to complete an educational program, after which, if you intend to stay in Colombia, the visa can be exchanged for another of a category. To apply, you need a valid passport, a filled form, three passport photos, an authorization from parents or legal guardians (if applicant is under 18), a medical certificate stating the physical and mental health of the applicant, a certificate of acceptance from the Colombian educational institute the applicant is planning to attend, and certificates of economic solvency from parents or person who will be responsible for the expenses of the applicant.

Embassies in Colombia

Australia
Bogotá: Ca. 69, 7,-51, apt 302. Tel: 694-6320.

Argentina
Bogotá: Av. 40A, 13-09, 16th floor. Tel: 288-0900, Fax: 288-8868, E-mail: embargentina@etb.net.co

Bolivia
Bogotá: Ca. 108A, 21- 42, Chico Navarra. Tel: 619 5509/214 2325, Fax: 619-6050, E-mail: central@embajadaboliviacolombia.org, URL: http://embajadaboliviacolombia.org/

Brazil
Bogotá: Ca. 93, 14-20, 8th floor. Tel: 218-0800, Fax: 218-8393, E-mail: embaixada@brasil.org.co, URL: http://bogota.itamaraty.gov.br/pt-br/

Canada
Bogotá: Cra. 7, 114-33, 14th floor. Tel: 657-9800, Fax: 657-9912, E-mail: bgota@international.gc.ca, URL: www.canadainternational.gc.ca/colombia-colombie/index.aspx?lang=eng

Chile
Bogotá: Calle 100, 11 B-44. Tel: 620-6613/2417/215-6886, Fax: 619-3863, E-mail: echileco@colomsat.net.co

China
Bogotá: Cra. 16, 98-30. Tel: 622-3213/3126/3215, Fax: 622-3114, E-mail: chinaemb_co@mfa.gov.cn, URL: http://co.china-embassy.org

Costa Rica
Bogotá: Cra. 12, 114-37, Barrio Santa Bárbara Central. Tel: 629-5095/5072, E-mail: embacosta@etb.net.co, URL: www.embajadadecostarica.org

Ecuador
Bogotá: Ca. 72, 6-30, Edificio Mazuera, 7th floor. Tel: 212-6512/23/25/41/49/69, Fax: 212-6536, E-mail: eecucolombia@mmrree.gov.ec

France
Bogotá: Cra. 11, 93-12. Tel: 638-1400, Fax: 638-1430, E-mail: presse@ambafrance-co.org, URL: www.ambafrance-co.org

Germany
Bogotá: Cra. 69, 25B-44, 7th floor. Tel: 423-2600, Fax: 429-3145, URL: www.bogota.diplo.de

INTRO & INFO

INTRO & INFO

Guatemala
Bogotá: Ca. 87, 20-27, office 302, Tel: 636-1724, E-mail: embcolombia@minex.gob.gt

Ireland
Bogotá: De Las Americas 56-41. Tel: 446-6114, Fax: 446-6120, E-mail: gomezconsulirlanda@smurfitkappa.com.co

Israel
Bogotá: Ca. 35, 7-25, 14th floor, Edificio Caxdac. Tel: 327-7500 (ext 507), Fax: 327-7555, E-mail: consular@bogota.mfa.gov.il, URL: http://bogota.mfa.gov.il

Italy
Bogotá: Ca. 93B, 9-92. Tel: 218-7206/0252/6608, Fax: 610-5886, E-mail: ambbogo.mail@esteri.it, URL: www.ambbogota.esteri.it/Ambasciata_Bogota

Japan
Bogotá: Cra. 7, 71-21, Torre B, 11th floor. Tel: 317-5001, Fax: 317-4989, URL: www.colombia.emb-japan.go.jp

Mexico
Bogotá: Ca. 113, 7-21, Teleport Business Park, office 204, Barrio Santa Ana. Tel: 629-4992, E-mail: consulmexcol@etb.net.co, URL: www.sre.gob.mx/colombia/

Netherlands
Bogotá: Cra, 13, 93-40, 5th floor. Tel: 638-4200, Fax: 623-3020, E-mail: bog@minbuza.nl, URL: www.mfa.nl/bog

New Zealand
Bogotá: Diagonal 109, 1-39 Este, apt 401, Santa Ana. Tel: 633-1322, Fax: 274-7135, E-mail: pearsona@cable.net.co

Panama
Bogotá: Ca. 92, 7A-40. Tel: 257-5067, Fax: 257-5068, URL: www.empacol.org

Peru
Bogotá: Ca. 80A, 6-50. Tel: 257-0505, Fax: 249-8581, E-mail: embaperu@embajadadelperu.org.co, URL: www.embajadadelperu.org.co

Poland
Bogotá: Cra. 21 Bis, 104A-15. Tel: 214-0400/2931, Fax: 214-0854, E-mail: bogota.amb.sekretariat@msz.gov.pl, www.bogota.polemb.net

Spain
Bogotá: Ca. 94A, 11A-70. Tel: 628-3910 (ext 340), Fax: 628-3938/39, E-mail:cog.bogota@maec.es, URL: www.maec.es/subwebs/Consulados/Bogota/es/home/Paginas/Home_Bogota.aspx

Sweden
Bogotá: Ca. 72 Bis, 5-83, 9th floor, Edificio Avenida Chile. Tel: 325-6180, E-mail: ambassaden.bogota@foreign.ministry.se, URL: www.swedenabroad.com/bogota

Switzerland
Bogotá: Cra. 9, 74-08, 11th floor. Tel: 349-7230, Fax: 349-7195, E-mail: vertretung@bog.rep.admin.ch, URL: www.eda.admin.ch/bogota

United Kingdom
Cra. 9, 76-49, 8th floor. Tel: 326-8300, Fax: 326-8302, URL: http://ukincolombia.fco.gov.uk/en

United States of America
Bogotá: Ca. 24 Bis, 48-50. Tel: 315-0811, Fax: 315-2197, URL: http://bogota.usembassy.gov/

Uruguay
Bogotá: Cra. 9, 80-15, 11th floor. Tel: 235-2968/1462/2748, Fax: 248-3734, E-mail: urucolom@etb.net.co

Venezuela
Bogotá: Cra. 11, 87-51, 5th floor. Tel: 644-5555, Fax: 640-1242, E-mail: correspondencia.colombia@mppre.gob.ve, URL: www.embaven.org.co

Updated: Sep 28, 2011.

Travel Insurance
It's a good idea to purchase travel insurance if you're going to be visiting Colombia. Policies cover everything from trip cancellation, delays, the loss or theft of luggage and valuables, and legal costs. Numerous insurers offering a variety of policies, so do some solid research before choosing the policy that's best for you. Check with your bank or credit card company to find out if you already have coverage. If you have a policy for health, life or homeowner's insurance, you may also have some travel insurance coverage.

MEDICAL INSURANCE
The most essential part of any Colombia travel insurance policy is the medical provision.

Photo by: Ben Bowes

Medical treatment costs for serious injuries can quickly add up. Look into how much your insurance will pay for necessary emergency expenses and if your policy covers helicopter rescue and emergency evacuation, should you need to return home for serious medical attention. Most Colombian hospitals demand you pay for your medical treatment up front, usually in cash. If you have to pay cash at a hospital, obtain receipts for any medical care you receive so you can provide copies when making your insurance claim.

Before you leave, make sure your travel insurance policy covers all the activities you intend on doing, or think you might try. Activities such as zip-lining, mountain biking and climbing are often considered "adventurous" and are therefore not covered under a basic policy.

LOST OR STOLEN ITEMS

Most travel insurance claims relate to lost or stolen goods. If you intend on taking expensive belongings such as laptops, smart phones or cameras to Colombia, there is a chance these items could be damaged, misplaced or stolen. Purchase a policy that offers an adequate level of protection to cover all the items you intend to take to Colombia, or consider leaving any highly expensive items at home.

If you are robbed while in Colombia, report the incident to the police within 24 hours. Make sure to obtain a copy of the police report, as your Colombia travel insurance company may demand this (along with a receipt for the stolen item) when you make your claim.

Basic travel insurance policies may not provide for the loss or theft of valuables and, in general, the more money you are willing to spend on travel insurance, the greater the level of protection you will receive. If you purchase a more comprehensive policy, the deductibles will be smaller, single item limits will be higher, and there may even be coverage for cash and the cost of reissuing a passport. Read the fine print to make sure you are satisfied with the level of coverage your policy provides.

STUDENT TRAVEL INSURANCE

When studying in Colombia, it is important to make sure you are covered by appropriate travel insurance. Many study abroad programs require proof of medical insurance or ask students to purchase special policies before leaving. If you need to purchase coverage yourself, shop around for the best policy that suits your needs.

As a student abroad, you may be able to collect additional benefits not covered under normal policies, including benefits that help refund course fees in the event of cancellation for medical reasons. It may also be easier to insure valuables such as laptops under study abroad insurance policies, and you may even be able to get coverage for part-time employment or participation in sports and other activities while in Colombia.

INSURANCE TIPS

Be sure to have your travel insurance company's 24-hour emergency contact number, your insurance card and preferably a complete copy of your policy. (You can also scan the policy and e-mail it to yourself, so you can access the information wherever you are, even if someone steals your bags.) Insurance companies also recommend taking written records of any medical conditions and proper names of any medication you are taking, plus copies of any prescriptions. Updated: Sep 18, 2011.

Getting To and Away

Entering Colombia is not a difficult transition. A valid passport—for some a visa—and a return ticket to wherever you came from will be enough to get you inside. To ensure your departure is as trouble-free as the entry, keep the customs form you're given when you fly in with your passport; it will entitle you to a refund of sales taxes, if you have spent enough.

BY AIR

Flights to Colombia arrive from neighboring Panama, Venezuela, Brazil, Peru and Ecuador, as well as elsewhere in South America. There are also numerous flights to Colombia from North and Central America, and Europe. The only international Colombian airline is Avianca, which is also the biggest operator for domestic flights. Other airlines, however, like British Airways, Continental Airlines, American Airlines, Mexicana de Aviación and Aerolíneas Argentinas frequently go to Colombia. Main airports include El Dorado in Bogotá, Rafael Núñez in Cartagena, José María Córdova in Medellín, Alfonso Bonilla Aragón in Cali and Ernesto Cortissoz in Barranquilla.

DEPARTURE TAX

If flying out from Bogotá, you must pay a departure tax. For stays of less than 60 days, it is $33 (or 65,400 COP). If you have been in the country for more than 60 days, or are a Colombian or a foreign resident, the fee is $64 (124,400 COP). The tax may be paid in US dollars, Colombian pesos (COP); travelers checks and credit cards are not accepted. If you are flying with a North American or European courier, the tax may already be included in your ticket. Updated: May 11, 2011.

BY BUS

Land border crossings exist between Colombia and Venezuela, Ecuador and Brazil. International bus service only operates along the Caribbean coast, from Cartagena, Barranquilla and other Colombian cities, to Maracaibo, Valencia and Caracas, Venezuela.

BY BOAT

Boat is the only way to enter Colombia in some regions. Arriving from Panama is only possible by air and by chalupas (local boats) or by sailboat. International boats also run between Esmeraldas, Ecuador, and Tumaco on the Pacific coast, and along the Amazon River, between Santa Rosa and Iquitos, Peru, and Manaus, Brazil, to Leticia. It is also possible to navigate rivers from Colombia to Venezuela; even though these are now heavily patrolled by Colombian military, accessing the waterways' ports is difficult as the roads pass through the war zone. If you are sailing on your own to Colombia, the major Caribbean Sea ports—Cartagena, Barranquilla, Santa Marta and San Andrés—all have marinas. You can also drop anchor in such places as Taganga, Riohacha or Cabo de la Vela. Updated: Sep 08, 2011.

Border Crossings

NOTE: For details on any of these border crossings, see the specific cities in this guide.

COLOMBIA-VENEZUELA

The most common border crossings between Colombia and Venezuela are at Cúcuta, through the cordillera, and at Maicao, the coastal route. Other crossings exist in the Llanos region, at Puerto Carreño, Colombia-Puerto Páez, Venezuela and Casuarito, Colombia-Puerto Ayacucho, Venezuela. Nevertheless, these crossings cannot be recommended at this time due to civil war fighting. Additionally, the few travelers that have attempted these routes report that immigration facilities for either or both countries were non-existent. Venezuela is a half-hour ahead of Colombia time.

COLOMBIA-PANAMÁ

No overland route connects the Central American republic Panamá with Colombia; in the debate of building a highway, the jungle—known as the Darien Gap—won. The famous crossing of the Gap on foot is prohibitively dangerous now, due to guerillas, paramilitaries, drug labs and other hazards. Missionary groups and the rangers at Los Katíos National Park have pulled out, thus leaving the potential adventurer without the traditional safety nets.

The most secure border crossings between the two countries are on the Caribbean coast of the isthmus. Other routes exist on the Pacific side, but these are rarely used due to the dangers. Colombia does not require an onward ticket for those arriving by land or sea. Many airlines are hesitant to sell a one-way ticket from Panamá to Colombia since they claim they will be fined if you are called on it. Depending on your luck, you may get a flight between the two countries for $350. Panamá requires a demonstration of sufficient funds ($600) and an onward ticket. However, for travelers from "first-world" countries, the sufficient funds and/or credit card usually suffices. Citizens from many Eastern European countries need a visa to enter Panamá. For specific requirements, check: www.migracion. gob.pa. Panamá has consulates all along the coast, including in Capurganá for those going up the coast, as well as in Bogotá. There are no ATMs between Cartagena and Panama City.

Rumors have always abounded about hitching a ride with a cargo boat out of Cartagena, Barranquilla or another Caribbean coast port to Panamá. Such opportunities are, quite frankly, a pie-in-the-sky dream. Ships must use only licensed crew. Additionally, there are many contraband-running ships that are hesitant to carry passengers. If the boat is caught doing illegal activities, you and the captain will have a whole lot of explaining to do. Better to spend a bit more and get to Panama or Colombia safely and legally.

Along the Caribbean coast are four means of getting north to Panamá. Sailboating from Cartagena through Kuna Yala (San Blas Islands) to Portobello, Panamá, has been the most popular way in recent years. The other three routes begin at Turbo on the Golfo de Urabá and go up the Caribbean coast. For decades, backpackers have been taking the local chalupas (boats) from Turbo to Capurganá, then to Puerto Obaldía, Panamá, from where there are flights to Panama City. A new option is to take the chalupas to Capurganá and Zapzurró, then the Darien Gapster boat through Kuna Yala to Porvenir, Panamá. An alternative to this is island hopping from Zapzurró to Portobello or Porvenir. If going through Kuna Yala, read "In Kuna Yala" in the Caribbean Coast and Islands chapter, to learn more about local laws and customs.

COLOMBIA-ECUADOR

Most travelers cross into Ecuador at the Rumichaca border crossing near Ipiales, in Southern Colombian. For those wanting to get off the beaten track, though, there exist two other possibilities. Along the Pacific Coast is a maritime route, from Tumaco to San Lorenzo and Esmeraldas, Ecuador. The third way is through the Selva, starting at Mocoa in the Putumayo, to the international bridge at San Miguel. This alternative takes you to Lago Agrio, Ecuador.

COLOMBIA-PERU-BRAZIL

At Leticia in the southeast corner of Colombia, is a triple frontier: Colombia, Peru and Brazil. Travelers heading upriver to Iquitos, Peru, will have to boat across the river from Leticia to Santa Rosa, Peru, to officially check into Peru. Those taking a boat to Manaus or other Brazilian towns down the Amazon, will have to walk across the border from Leticia to Tabatinga, Brazil, to take care of Brazilian immigration procedures. Updated: Sep 06, 2011.

Getting Around

BY AIR

If you have only a short holiday, it would be worth flying from destination and destination. At times, domestic Colombian flights can be cheaper (or slightly more expensive) than bus fares. Competition between the carriers is great, causing fare wars. Check their websites for super-saver rates. Taxes on ticket sales are high, accounting for about 30 percent of the price. The major domestic carriers are:

Ada—www.ada-aero.com (specializing in flights within Antioquia):

AeroRepública (now owned by Copa)—www.copaair.com

Aires—www.aires.aero

Avianca—www.avianca.com

Satena—www.satena.com

BY BUS

Colombian buses are some of the best in South America. Often, companies will have several levels of service, from corriente(average) to lujo (luxury). Bus terminals often display the safety record of all carriers, with the monthly and yearly accident, injury and death figures. Many companies issue baggage claim tickets. By law, bus outfits have a maximum fare they can charge during the high season. In the low season there are substantial reductions, particularly with buses to or from Caribbean coast destinations. The trick is to arrive some 10 or 15 minutes before the bus leaves, and when told the price of the fare, ask (ever so sweetly) for a discount. Colombians alsorecommend talking directly with the driver about a cheaper rate.

During holidays, you may have to reserve your ticket at least several days in advance; some companies have online reservations, requiring a credit card. Websites for the major lines are:

Berlinas—www.berlinasdelfonce.com

Bolivariano—www.bolivariano.com.co

Brasilia—www.expresobrasilia.com

Coomotor—www.coomotor.com.co

Copetrán—www.copetran.com.co

As far as traveling at night, in the past Colombians would either advise against it or at least say it's a risk. These days highways are heavily patrolled by the Colombia military and the only persons likely to be stopping your bus in the middle of the night are young regimented soldiers. Colombians now feel more confident traveling after dark. Still, in some parts of the country, buses do not run at night.

BY TRAIN

Most trains in Colombia are now tourist oriented and run only on weekends and holidays. The La Sabana steam train chugs from Bogotá to Zipaquirá. Cali has a variety of tourist trains: the Tren Turístico Azúcar y Café and the Tren Rumbero. The Tren Ecoturístico de las Flores rattles and sways from Barranquilla to Las Bocas de Cenizas at the mouth of the Magdalena River. See the principal cities for more information onschedules and fares. The Ruta de Maconda, from Santa Marta to Aracataca, is still on hold.

The only normal passenger service still in operation is the Barrancabermeja-Puerto Berrío train. Residents of San Cipriano near Cali are running a small operation to maintain contact with the outside world.

BY TAXI

Not all cities enforce the use of taxi meters, so whether you catch a cab with or without it, check fares with your hostel concierge before going out. If the cab has no meter, negotiate a price with the driver before boarding the cab. Although it is more expensive, ask your hotel to phone for a taxi to the station or airport instead of trying to hail one on the street. Use licensed taxis. The license plate number should be painted on the sides of the vehicle, as well as on its roof. Do not enter one if someone else is in it. Keep your baggage with you. To borders, collective taxis (colectivos, or por puesto in cities bordering Venezuela) are the norm. For short jaunts around town, mototaxis (motorcycle taxis) are cheaper.

BY CAR OR MOTORCYCLE

In Colombia gas prices are on average $4.50 per gallon. For both car and motorcycle travelers, an international driver's license and insurance are obligatory, as is vehicle registration. Highways in general are in excellent condition. Invías (www.invias.gov.co) publishes road reports on its website. Motorcycles do not pay tolls. Night driving and riding are not recommended. Check with DIAN (the customs office) for the latest procedures for entering and exiting Colombia with your own vehicle. Cars pay a tax, motorcycles do not. When you leave the country, turn in the permit document. Although DIAN might not ask motorcyclists for proof of insurance, if you are stopped by police you could be asked to show it.

A recommended website for those traveling in their own vehicle is www.drivetheamericas.com, which has information on vehicle shipping between South and Central America. Motorcyclists recommend www.horizonsunlimited.com.

Motorcyclists can get their bikes from Central America to Colombia in several ways:

•Stahlretter is the only sailboat-ferry that presently takes motorcycles and their riders from Cartagena to Portobello, Panama. Check the Caribbean Coast and Islands chapter for details.

•Some bikers join together to share shipping by private sailboat from Portobello, Panama to Cartagena, but there is no insurance or warranty. The sea can be rough with big waves. The cost for both you and your bike is $900.

•Cargo ship is another option, but captains don't like to take passengers along.

•You can ship your motorcycle by cargo air-lines to Bogotá (drain gasoline and disconnect battery; $550) and travel yourself by passenger plane ($350-500). With this option, your bike is insured.

Motorcyclists must purchase a reflective vest with their license plate number emblazoned on it, as well as have the number put on the back of their helmets (cost for both comes to about $10 in any given shop). Helmet use is mandatory by law for both rider and passenger.

If you have to order parts from overseas, it can take 45 days or more. Most foreigners take off-road bikes because parts are easier to find. Bogotá has several small part shops where you can get just about anything you might need. Accommodations that accept motorcycles are common (free parking), especially in small towns. A few, like Casa Kiwi in Medellín, give a discount to motorcyclists.

BY BOAT

More remote areas of Colombia can only be reached by boat. From Turbo, chalupas (launches) depart for Capurganá and other villages along the North Coast. Other launches run along the Pacific coast between Nuquí, Buenaventura and Tumaco, though this is a less-taken route due to the nation's civil war. River travel is the norm in the Amazon, whether heading to other Colombian villages or traveling downstream to Manaus, Brazil, or upstream to Iquitos, Peru.

BY BIKE

Bicycling is quite common in Colombia. Even small villages have repair shops. Most cyclists advise to stay on the main roads, avoid going into jungle areas and do not travel at night. All admit the biggest security issue is not with factions of the country's civil war, but with ordinary theft. Remember Colombia has three mountain ranges with passes of up to 4,000 meters (13,129 feet).

Many cyclists have their own websites detailing their adventures: www.roundtheworldbybike.com, www.ride-forclimate.com, www.mundocaracol.com, www.pedaleandoelglobo.com and www.crazyguyonabike.com. Although it is a bit dated, Iris en Tore op reis (www.irisentoreopreis.nl) has excellent travelogues and maps in English. Panamericana on a Recumbent Bike (www.panamerica.ch) lists reports and altitudes for all points between Alaska and Ushuaia.

Casa de Ciclistas is a network of local bicycle enthusiasts providing home stays and logistics for bikers. They don't have a central website, though. Just search the term and city, and you'll find contacts' information.

BY HITCHHIKING

As always, hitchhiking is an iffy proposition in terms of success and safety. Male-female couples say they encounter few problems in traversing Colombia this way. Solo males report poor luck. Lone females should probably forget this option for travel. Always trust your gut instinct about a prospective ride; another vehicle will eventually come along. Truck drivers are likely to be looking for a passenger (illegally) to help keep them awake with conversation. Updated: Sep 08, 2011.

Tours

With the expansion of the tourist industry in Colombia, the number of organized travel options continues to grow. Various types of tours are available, encompassing many of Colombia's historical and natural delights. Whether it is hiking through the Andes, being guided through one of Colombia's principal cities, visiting ancient landmarks or taking a boat trip down the Amazon, the opportunities available are extensive. Although low demand previously restricted tours to either being short-duration or solely in Spanish, the development of the industry is constantly opening new horizons. Updated: Apr 10, 2008.

PRE-ARRANGED TOURS

The combined expansion of both Colombia's tourist market and Internet-based excursion companies has led to the growth of organized packages throughout parts of the country. The options of packages available vary in duration, from one week inside Colombia, to six months throughout various South America countries. Understandably, considering the higher price of the packages, these tours entail most costs including accommodation and transportation although they are rarely fully inclusive and you should inquire about hidden costs beforehand. Not best for those searching for a relaxing break, these types of tours usually encompass a host of activities and visits to multiple locations. As well as general tours, more specific adventure travel trips and nature-orientated visits can be found. Although without as many guarantees, it is often cheaper and can be more liberating to organize trips once inside Colombia. Updated: May 18, 2009.

INTRO & INFO

AMAZON TOURS

The vast expanse of the Amazon jungle provides an ideal location for various day and multi-day guided tours. Most tours leave from Leticia in the southeastern pinnacle of Colombia and generally include trips along parts of the Amazon River and some of its multiple tributaries. Often an excellent way to see the extensive elements of jungle life, Amazon tours not only enable you to see incredible varieties of flora and fauna but also provide an insight into indigenous lifestyles. English-speaking guides are available at numerous organizations and some tours include visits to the Parque Nacional Amacayacu or stays in jungle lodges. Updated: Sep 08, 2011.

ANDES TOURS

Colombia is intersected by the presence of the overwhelming Andes. Split into three ranges, the Occidental, Central and Oriental, Colombia's Andean mountains are a host of volcanoes, glacial formations and impressive lakes. They provide perfect terrain for mountain biking, trekking and both rock and ice climbing. Parque Nacional Natural El Cocuy encompasses snow-peaked mountains and vast lakes, a perfect landscape for trekking. The mountains also offer less energetic aspirations, like birdwatching. Various tour guides operate in the regions. Whether it be sports and physical challenges or a more relaxed enjoyment of natural delights that appeals to you, it is likely that there will be an Andean tour to fit your interests. Updated: Sep 08, 2011.

SPECIAL RUINS/LANDMARK TOURS

Guided tours to special landmarks are easy to book and usually depart from Bogotá. If, for example, you are planning to visit the Salt Cathedral in Zipaquirá—one of the seven wonders of Colombia—and are also interested in the enchanted lagoon of Guativita nearby, the best way to learn the history and maximize your time is probably to let a tour guide lead and arrange transportation. From Bogotá you can also take a day tour to Villa de Leyva, one of the oldest towns in Colombia, or a multiday excursion for the famous archeological park San Agustín, a large UNESCO site that contains much history and many myths. For a more complex tour, like going around Zona Cafetera, air transportation and extra time is necessary. Updated: Sep 08, 2011.

CITY TOURS

Most of Colombia's principal cities have organized city tours. While some bus tours are available, seeing a city by foot is often the best way to get around and take in the location's atmosphere. It is best to visit the local tourist office to discover what type of tours a city has on offer. In Bogotá for example, walking tours offer enchanting strolls around the delights of La Candelaria and Plaza de Bolívar. In Cartagena, you can opt to explore the city in a horse-drawn carriage. Updated: Sep 08, 2011.

CHIVAS

Although still an important means of transport across some parts of Colombia, the life of the chiva has taken a new meaning in many Colombian cities. Rides on chivas have become a popular means of nightlife entertainment. Often organized by travel agents, nighttime chiva tours can include numerous stops at a city's top party spots, various samples of aguardiente (sugar cane alcohol) and great live music. If the party lifestyle is one you enjoy, a trip on a chiva will provide guaranteed fun.

NATIONAL PARK CONCESSIONAIRES

Most of Colombia's national parks with an eco-touristic focus are operated in coordination with local communities. The hotels, guides and other infrastructure of four of them, though, are managed by the national travel agency Aviatur (www.aviatur.com/www.concesionesparquesnaturales.com). It is the official concessionaire for Tayrona, Gorgona, Amacayacu and Nevados national parks. Aviatur also offers special tours on river houseboats and catamaran in other parts of Colombia. Updated: Sep 8, 2011.

OTHERS

Numerous other organized trips are available throughout Colombia. With some of the world's top sites for scuba diving, many companies are organizing tours to see Colombia's underwater delights, incredible coral reefs and maritime wildlife. Organized excursions to parts of Colombia's coastline can also include whale-watching, eco-lodge stays, surfing and relaxation on beautiful beaches. Tours are also organized through Colombia's famous coffee region and can stretch from two days to one week in duration. Updated: Apr 10, 2008.

Responsible Tourism

Tourism in Colombia is experiencing rapid growth that is hoped will bring considerable benefits to the country. Unfortunately, some aspects of tourism can have negative social, environmental and even economic consequences. Responsible tourism benefits both the traveler and the local community alike. The traveler gets an insight into local

Ecotourism in Colombia

By the end of 2007 the Colombian Ministry of Commerce, Industry and Tourism reported approximately 1,260,000 tourists visited Colombia in that year, a major improvement in the industry. Colombia hopes to attract four million international tourists in 2014.

Colombia is a multifaceted nation that offers visitors a wide range of ecotourism options. Under Colombian law, ecotourism is defined as a specialized way of tourism developed in areas with a unique natural attractions and that fits within parameters of sustainable human development. Ultimately, ecotourism looks to entertain and educate the visitor through observation and study of natural resources and cultural aspects related a place.

The Natural National Parks System has 24 areas with an ecotourism vocation and activities that respect nature and show visitors unique fauna and flora. Many of these places have campgrounds, restaurants, information centers, trails and other facilities. Ecotourism is an important tool to strengthen the park system, because it generates financial resources through concessions, services and fees, allowing redistribution throughout the entire system.

Though controlled ecotourism can represent an improvement in the life of people living in unique areas, it is essential to consider some places are not willing nor meant to be exposed to any kind of tourism. Don't push yourself into people's homes or privacy, and don't trespass limits of trails in parks. Colombia has an organized way of ecotourism and looks to conserve its natural areas and sanctuaries. Taking advantage of the opportunities available will expose you to a variety of valuable sights and activities, in addition to allowing you to help with your contributions to maintain the parks and communities. Updated: Sep 08, 2011.

cultures while the local community gains from low-impact, sustainable income. Responsible actions are crucial to the future of the industry and we all play an essential part.

Problems associated with illicit drugs in Colombia are well documented. Aside from being aware of the direct and indirect dangers associated with the drug industry, it is vital to act responsibly to avoid serious punishment.

DO:
•Research your location prior to traveling and upon arrival visit the local information center or tourist office to discover any potential hidden delights. Try and learn at least the basics of Spanish as this will not only make things easier and more enjoyable but can also leave a positive impression with locals.

•Inquire about the environmental records of tour operators and, when appropriate, give preferential treatment to local guides, restaurants and accommodation over multinational firms that have a poor ecological reputation.

•Buy crafts from family workshops and community cooperatives. This will enhance your experience and often ensures that your money goes directly to local people.

•Respect cultural and religious traditions. Colombia is a Catholic country and always act with consideration when in the vicinity of religious establishments. When visiting indigenous communities, respect their traditions.

•Be courteous and considerate when taking photos of people and always ask for their permission beforehand. Be aware that in many indigenous communities, taking photos of people is prohibited.

•Practice safe sex. The consequences of not doing so can be severe for both parties.

DO NOT:
•Abuse privileges such as water and electricity, especially in smaller communities where resources are scarce. Some more expensive hotels provide the option of having your linen and towels washed daily. This is an unnecessary luxury that uses considerable energy and water.

•Drop litter. Although rubbish dropping may be a more common problem in Colombia than where you are from, it is not OK to join this trend. Provide a good example; pack a plastic bag for trash and recycle when possible.

•Interfere in local ecology. However beautiful a flower may be, do not pick any and avoid interfering in wildlife habitats. Small actions can have devastating, long-term impacts on local environments. Updated: Sep 08, 2011.

Sports and Recreation

Colombia's natural wonders make it an excellent place for adventure travel and sports. Although its sport and recreation industry is still growing, Colombia's Pacific and Caribbean coasts, Andean mountains, vast natural expanses and extensive rivers all cater to those keen on outdoor activities.

The incredible scenery and beautiful lakes at Túquerres and the waterfall at La Chorrera are popular with hikers, while visits to the marvelous tombs of Tierradentro are frequently combined with long day walks. For the more extreme walker Colombia also hosts a variety of inviting challenges. Various trekking routes, such as those in Parque Nacional Natural El Cocuy, can be combined with rock or ice climbing. Suesca's diverse rock formations are a heaven for climbing fans of different levels of skill. Cavers can delve into incredible stalagmite and stalactite-filled caves near San Gil. When caving and going on long treks it is advisable to always go with a guide. In instances of day trips, at the very least speak to someone in the know about the safety of the area.

Mountain biking and paragliding are alternative ways of witnessing Colombia's natural beauty and diverse flora and fauna. Reserva Natural Laguna de Sonso is a great site for birdwatching as over 100 different species can be seen.

Its numerous rivers make Colombia an attractive place for rafting and kayaking, and its lakes are great for different water sports and fishing. Windsurfing and both off-shore and lake sailing are also becoming increasingly popular. Colombia's coastline attracts surfers and scuba divers of all levels. The Pacific coast is considered best for surfing. Many diving enthusiasts are flocking to experience the wonders hidden within the Caribbean Sea.

As well as being a fantastic location to participate in sports, Colombia also is extremely enjoyable for the spectator. Although somewhat tarnished by the happenings of the 1994 World Cup, fútbol (soccer) is exceptionally popular both to play and to watch.

Going to a match of one of Colombia's top teams is guaranteed to provide an electric atmosphere. Baseball, polo, basketball and bull fighting are found in many of Colombia's major cities, also. As increasing numbers of competitions come to Colombia's shores, surfing is riding the wave of national enthusiasm. Try and find somewhere to watch tejo, a national sport that is over 500 years old. Be sure to keep your distance however, as tejo involves throwing a weight towards a target filled with clay and gunpowder. Other traditional sports are chaza, played in the Pasto region, and bolo, common in Eastern Colombia. Updated: May 11, 2011.

HIKING

The notorious reputation of Colombia's mountains and jungles as the province of terrorists, armed revolutionaries, paramilitaries, drug cartels, and even ordinary kidnappers and thieves makes the very idea of venturing beyond Colombia's cities seem brave and/or foolish. While a decades-long civil war has made many of Colombia's rural areas dangerous, a high portion of Colombia's breathtaking mountains are now safely accessible.

The most popular destination for foreign hiking enthusiasts, who make up 80 percent of its visitors, is the Sierra Nevada of Santa Marta's pre-Columbian Ciudad Perdida (Lost City), which was a secret to the western world until 1975. Located halfway up the mountains' northern side at 1,000 meters (3,280 ft), it can only be reached on foot with one of three authorized tour operators, all based in Santa Marta and Taganga. The entire journey takes three days to walk up and two days to return. The agencies provide guide, food and hammocks. The risk of dangerous confrontations is about less than five percent, but there is a greater risk of malaria, so travelers are advised to bring repellent and wear long-sleeved shirts at night. The degree of humidity is also very high, and visitors to the Sierra de Santa Marta during the rainy season—which runs from April to June, and later from October to December—have nicknamed it "the Green Hell."

Also on the north side of the pyramid-like Santa Marta range, hikers can explore the trails at the San Lorenzo station of PNN Sierra Nevada de Santa Marta. In the coastal foothills is Parque Tayrona, notable not only for its beaches, but for some pleasant hiking opportunities through jungle to El Pueblito, another pre-Columbian city. On the southwestern slopes of the sierra lies the town of Valledupar, from which many intrepid trekkers can hike to various isolated indigenous villages. The rest of the Sierra Nevada de Santa Marta is inaccessible, due to security issues and the wishes of the native nations who consider those mountains sacred lands.

Further south, along the border with Venezuela, the Cordillera Oriental has the Sierra Nevada del Cocuy, and its Parque Nacional Natural El Cocuy at 4,000-meter (13,120 ft) altitude. The park offers treks lasting up to 10 days, as well as mountain, ice and rock climbing. This region is well guarded by the Colombian army, with no reported guerrilla activity. Continuing south along the Venezuelan border, the village of Puerto Inírida offers rock climbing and hiking opportunities. Unfortunately, this area still is in the civil war's red zone.

Heading inland, Bogotá is surrounded by mountains that offer many four- to eight-hour-long day hikes, as well as safe one-, two- and three-day treks. Other places to head to for multi-day hiking excursions are Medellín and Manizales, both of which border Parque Nevados. This is also a premier birdwatching area.

At the lower end of Huila Department is San Agustín with a Parque Arqueológico which is a rich repository of pre-Columbian culture. San Agustín is also a starting point for many hikes and treks outside the park area. The entire area is now well-patrolled. Professional guides can not only take you through the park, but through El Macizo Colombiano to the source of the Río Magdalena, a large river which stretches nearly the length of Colombia itself. The latter is a 4-5 day walking trip.

On the southern Pacific coast, Gorgona Island, which for 50 years served as a penal colony, offers the pleasures associated with an island, as well as many hiking paths. Boats going to Gorgona routinely depart from the port city of Buenaventura. Updated: May 11, 2011.

SURFING

Foaming at the top, they rise high and move fast towards the wide Colombian shore, which extends over 3,200 kilometers (1,952 mi) along the Pacific Ocean and the Caribbean Sea. Long ignored by surfers, Colombian waves are increasingly gaining attention from both locals and tourists at every skill level who want to ride the clear water on long boards. The best surfing spots in the country are on the Pacific Coast, particularly the Department of Chocó, however, the Caribbean coast also has some good waves.

El Chocó is the poorest department of Colombia; the rainfall (one of the heaviest in the world) does not allow for much agriculture, and industrial development has lagged behind in the department. The potential for tourism is what gives locals an incentive of income, and as a result surfing tours and lessons have become popular.

Particularly Nuquí has become a major surfing destination because of its deserted beaches and diverse lodging options. Hotels like El Cantil organize surfing tours lasting 2-5 nights in which parties are taken in a motorboat to specific isolated surfingspots. They also have alliances with surfing schools like Olaviento Indoor, where beginners can learn to balance themselves on simulators before going out into the ocean.

Surfing-oriented lodging has also opened up in El Rodadero (near Santa Marta) and other Caribbean coast towns. Not only is long-boarding practiced in this region, but also kite boarding and wind surfing.

Beginners or travelers looking for a lesson usually go to Terquito beach in Nuquí or La V beach in Puerto Colombia, near Barranquilla. Intermediate-level surfers have a wide range of beaches from Mendihuaca and Los Naranjos in the Department of Magdalena to Bahía Solano in the Chocó to El Bolsillo in Puerto Colombia. Finally, experts looking for a challenge go to Pela Pela or Pico de Loro in Nuquí.

Surfing in Colombia has surpassed an amateur point and is now a major competitive sport at a national level, not to mention a popular destination often recommended by international surfing publications. Colombia's surfing culture is blooming with talent as new generations learn the sport at earlier ages than they did 10 years ago. Kids of ages 5 and 6 are picking up boards and stroking up to waves, whereas the previous generations would start surfing at ages 15 and up.

In the last decade over 40 national surfing competitions and three Latin American tournaments have taken place on the beaches of Colombia. Events like the Circuito Nacional de Surf OP PRO 2008 have pulled considerable crowds to places like Cartagena, Parque

Tayrona and Barrranquilla in order to proclaim a national champion.

If you plan to surf on the Caribbean coast, note that the best months to surf on are December-March and July-September. The Pacific, however, is considered a higher quality surf coast. Updated: Sep 15, 2011.

RAFTING
Colombia has some excellent rivers for rafting, and some reliable operators to take you there. The premier rafting center is in and around San Gil, where local operators generally will take you to one of three nearby rivers: Fonce, Chichamocha, or Suárez.

The Fonce River has a good mix of rapids, with long sections of everything from class II to class IV rapids. Short trips can be made to the slower parts, a good option for novices or mixed groups. The Fonce can get a bit rough, too, in other sections: up to class IV, suitable for intermediate and advanced rafters.

The Chichamocha is generally a bit rougher that the Fonce, and rafting trips pass through the scenic Chicamocha canyon. The Suárez is the roughest of all. One reputable operator in the region is Colombia Rafting Expeditions (www.colombiarafting.com), located in San Gil. The Chicamocha can also be rafted further upstream, at Capitanejo.

Another good spot for shooting the rapids is in San Agustín. Here, the Río Magdalena provides class II to IV white waters. Magdalena Rafting (www.magdalenarafting.com) is an experienced agency that offers daily runs, and can arrange multi-day excursions down the river canyon .

If you're in Bogotá, there is some rafting to be had on the Río Negro, not far outside of town. The class III river is good for beginners. For a slightly different rafting experience, Paisa Travel (www.paisatravel.com) offers a trip on a balsa wood raft through Colombia's coffee-growing region on the La Vieja River. The river is not particularly rough and participants are encouraged to swim off the raft as it makes its way along the river. Updated: Sep 15, 2011.

HORSEBACK RIDING
Horseback riding is a popular sport in Colombia, and the country's Andes and Llanos provide an ideal climate for equestrian enthusiasts. However, as can be expected, the degree of safety varies from region to region in Colombia.

In the countryside near Popayán, in the southwest department of Cauca, many adventure outfits rent horses and lead guided tours. The Circuito Ancestral, in particular, has a world-famous reputation for its scenic and historical value. East of Popayán, you can visit the ancient rock sculptures of San Agustín on horseback or undertake the adventure of traveling to Otavalo, Ecuador, on a noble beast.

The eastern Llanos are home to Colombian *coleo* (rodeo), and hosts international competitions for men and women. It is also a well-known destination for horseback riding. Unfortunately, many parts of the region are not the safest.

Many towns have their own equestrian festivals from Christmas to New Year's Eve. Most notable are the festivities in Cali, where in 2007, drunken residents mistreated the horses to the point that cabalgatas, or horse processions, were canceled. There has been less controversy with traveling horse shows sponsored by local restaurants, which feature actual dancing horses.

A final note: It is the custom to have a shot of the potent aguardiente while on a horse. Updated: Sep 15, 2011.

MOUNTAIN BIKING
The most popular mountain biking routes for foreigners who travel to Colombia are located around such places as Bogotá, Villa de Leyva near Tunja and Cartagena. Due to safety reasons, most routes are one-day only, though in some areas multi-day routes exist. For those willing to brave it, and use precautions, Colombia offers some of the most spectacular scenery in the world on sierras as high as 4,000 meters (13,000 feet).

North of Bogotá, mountain biking is very popular in the city of Suesca, where there are specially designed routes and trails. Many shops in that town rent bikes and offer tours. In Cartagena, you can rent a bike and ride to La Boquilla beach, Playa Blanca and other attractions outside the city. There are also relatively safe biking areas in Santa Marta, near Tayrona, as well as in the Zona Cafetera. Two- and three-day expeditions are available in Parque de Los Nevados near Manizales.

The best times to mountain bike are those months with the least amount of rainfall: November-December and July-August. Due to the high risk of theft, only a handful of places in Colombia rent bicycles. The cost is generally $40 per day, and you can hire a guide for an additional $35. However, group tours generally charge only $15 per person.

Colombia sponsors a variety of mountain biking, cross-country, downhill and biking marathons. There are a number of successful biking Colombians, such as María Luisa Calle, Olympic Bronze Medal Velodrome winner in 2004, and Fabio Parra, who came in third at the 1998 Tour de France. Updated: Sep 15, 2011.

Birdwatching

A trip to Colombia should be at the top of every devoted birdwatcher's list. It is one of the most biodiverse countries in the world, especially where birds are concerned. Colombia is home to more than 1,800 species of birds, about 150 of which are considered rare or endangered. Roughly an additional 1,000 species more also come through on their annual migration path. A quarter of the 800 bird species of Colombia's Chocó department are unique to that area.

In recent years Colombian tourist infrastructure has improved significantly, and generally you will face little risk at the reserves (although don't expect any luxury accommodations). Nevertheless, don't think you can just go wandering around by yourself–there have been a few instances of birdwatchers getting kidnapped. Do make sure to inquire about possible risks before entering an area, and stay abreast of safety developments. Many of the national parks require visitors to first obtain a permit from local authorities before entering. Here are a few of Colombia's birding highlights by region:

AROUND CALI
El 18
This forest habitat, with its many varieties of tanager, is a good place to get your feet wet. The Multicolored Tanager is the most sought after, but you are also likely to see Beryl-spangled, Saffron-crowned, Golden, Blue-capped, Golden-naped, Metallic-green, Scrub, Fawn-breasted, Purplish-mantled and Blue-necked Tanagers, as well as several species of woodpecker and hummingbird. There are around 140 different species in total, although in one visit you'll probably only see about half of that. Unfortunately, deforestation is beginning to affect the region. The habitat is 18 kilometers (11 mi) from Cali, heading down the Buenaventura road, to the village of Dapa. It is an unmarked area of forest, so it is better to hire a guide or at least ask a cab driver who knows the area rather than attempting to go it alone.

Bosque Yotoco
Located in the Western Cordillera, this reserve is especially notable for having Cauca Guan, Turquoise Dacnis Tanager and Multicolored Tanager. You must request permission from the Corporación Autónoma Regional del Valle del Cauca (CVC) in Buga Efrén to be able to visit. Tel: 2-227-8347, Fax: 2-228-6172, URL: www.cvc.gov.co.

Reserva Natural Laguna de Sonso, Cali
There are about 160 species of bird inhabit this wet land area.

AROUND MEDELLÍN
Yellow-Eared Parrot Reserve
The Yellow-eared Parrot is a critically endangered species now found only in a few small areas in the Colombian Andes. In addition to being a haven for these rare parrots, the 130-hectare (321-ac) Loro Orejiamarillo reserve is also home to Tawny-breasted Tinamou, Purple-throated Woodstar, Yellow-vented Woodpecker, Spillman's Tapaculo, Chestnut-crested Cotinga, Black-tipped Cotinga, Sharpe's Wren, Indigo Flowerpierce, handsome flycatchers and tanager finches. 2.5 hours from Medellín, near Jardín.

Chestnut-capped Piha Reserve
At Arrierito Antioqueno (Chestnut-capped Piha) Bird Reserve, besides the Piha, you may encounter Stile's Tapaculo, Red-bellied Grackle, Multicolored Tanager, Black-and-gold Tanager, Parker's Antbird, Black Tinamou, Blue-fronted Parrotlet, Colombian Screech Owl, Red-faced Spinetail, Striped Woodhaunter, Purplish-mantled Tanager, Scarlet and White tanager, Sharp-tailed Streamcreeper, Fulvous-breasted Flatbill and Chestnut-breasted Wren. 4-5 hours from Medellín.

PACIFIC COAST
Río Ñambi
This reserve sits between Altaquer and Junín on the Pasto-Tumaco highway at El Barro. It has around 300 documented species of birds, among which are some of the rarest on earth. Species include the Dark-backed Woodquail, Plumbeous Hawk and Forest Falcon, Pale-eyed Thrush, Rufous Brown Solitaire, Toucan Barbet, Beautiful Jay, Torrent Duck and Fasciated Tiger Heron. You can get to the reserve on any bus coming from Ipiales or Pasto to Tumaco. From the entrance it is a four-kilometer (2.5-mi) walk to the reserve center. Lodging can be arranged on the reserve, and it is best to book in advance. URL: www.felca-colombia.org.

Pueblo Nuevo

Of all the places listed, this birding area may be the most difficult to access. Also located along the Pasto-Tumaco highway, the little village of Pueblo Nuevo is a six-hour walk through the woods (although you do not necessarily need to walk all the way to the village to see flapping beauties). The best way to get there is to hire a guide nearby at Altaquer or Río Ñambi. Count on only the most basic lodging. Despite its frustrating obscurity, Pueblo Nuevo is worth the trouble for a determined birder. Species in this area include a variety of tanagers (including, if you're very lucky, the Yellow-green Bush Tanager), woodpeckers, toucans, antbirds, Stripe-billed Araçari, Chestnut-headed Oropendola, Purple Honeycreeper, Purple-crowned Fairy, Spot-crowned Antvireo and a great number of Five-colored Barbet.

La Planada

This indigenous-run, 3,200-hectare (7,904-ac) reserve, also off the Pasto-Tumaco road, is one of the most prominent in the country, and protects several species of rare birds, including the White-face Nunbird. The reserve, which forms part of the Chocó eco-region, is also home to the Dark-backed Wood Quail, Semicollared Hawk, Black-and-chestnut Eagle, Colombian Screech Owl, Cloud-forest Pygmy Owl, Velvet Purple Coronet, Orange-breasted Fruiteater, Plate-billed Mountain Toucan, Violet-tailed Sylph and Crimson-rumped Toucanet, as well as an assortment of tanagers. Cel: 321-738-9385, E-mail: jaimecaicedog@hotmail.com, URL: http://reservalaplanada.blogspot.com).

OTHER RESERVES

Parque Nacional Natural Amacayacu
This national park near Leticia is comprised of both swampland and forest. It is made up of different zones, each with its own distinct list of bird species. From the reserve center itself you can see several species of tanager and parrots, as well as others including the Black-fronted Nunbird, Black-crested Antshrike, Boat-billed Flycatcher, Golden-tailed Sapphire and Southern Beardless Tyrannulet. Another fruitful region of the park for birdwatchers is Isla Mocagua. This is a good location for viewing waterfowl, especially Hoatzin, or Stinkbird. You may also see a few varieties of hawk, heron and vulture. To visit Amacayacu, it is mandatory you go with a guide. To get the most out of the park, it is best to go during the wet season.

Parque Nacional Natural Tayrona

This 16,650-heactare (37,000-ac) park outside Santa Marta is home to more than 200 species of birds.

Santa Marta Mountains (Minca Road)

A good place to become familiar with Colombia's many endemic birds. In a 4x4 vehicle, take the Minca road up to the Parque Nacional Natural Sierra Nevada de Santa Marta ranger station at San Lorenzo, where the is lodging and guides.

Sanctuario de Flora y Fauna Los Flamencos

Made up of two areas—Perico and Camarones—both located near Riohacha in the Guajira. At the reserve reside Rufous-vented Chachalaca as well as a variety of aquatic birds, including the Greater Flamingo.

Ucumarí & Los Nevados

Ucumarí, near Pereira, is located in the Zona Cafetera's Central Cordillera on the edge of Parque Nacional Natural Los Nevados. Both parks have incredible amounts of species.

Volcán Chiles

At this inactive volcano on the Colombia-Ecuador border near Ipiales, it is possible to spot famous Andean Condor. Updated: Sep 07, 2011.

GUIDES

Granted, some of the best birding locations require a little sense of adventure and an affinity for off-the-beaten-path travel. But there are still amazing birdwatching opportunities for those who prefer to stick to more heavily trafficked areas. Whatever you chose, you will most likely need to make some arrangements in advance or hire a guide.

Birding Tropics

Santa Marta
Cel: 311-402-3799
E-mail: mariqui@birdingtropics.com
URL: www.birdingtropics.com

Cansa Trading

Bogotá
Tel: 1-694-9331
E-mail: cansatrading@gmail.com
URL: www.cansatrading.com

Colombia Birding

Medellín
Cel: 314-896-3151
E-mail: diego@colombiabirding.com
URL: www.colombiabirding.com

Dunanzhe Tours
Santa Marta
Cel: 300-428-4443
E-mail: waly@dunanzhe.com
URL: www.dunanzhe.com

Ecotours
Bogotá
Tel: 1-245-5134
E-mail: info@ecoturs.org / angelagomez@gmail.com
URL: www.ecoturs.com.co

Hansa Tours
Bogotá
Tel: 1-601-5311
E-mail: erik@hansatours.net
URL: www.hansatours.com
Meridian 72°
Cel: 314-331-6351
E-mail: asaavedra@meridian72.com
URL: www.meridian72.com

To discover more about reserves, guides, trip reports, bird lists, maps and more birding information, visit Birding Colombia (www.birdingcolombia.com) or Fat Birder (www.fatbirder.com). A national birding NGO is Pro Aves (www.proaves.org), which operates a number of reserves and accepts volunteers. Updated: Sep 07, 2011.

Shopping

Traveling through the Colombia, you will find plenty of souvenirs that represent the rich culture of this country. From a miniature figure of a chiva to a vueltiao sombrero or a pair of emerald earrings,there are endless choices at every price rangeand often with the possibility of bargaining.

WHAT TO BUY

Aside from being the largest producer of emeralds in the world, for which you can get the best bargains in Bogotá and Muzo, Colombia is also well known for making arguably the best-quality coffee. Pick some up at the Zona Cafetera, along with plenty of caramels and other sweets. Crafts like baskets, 3-D paintings, tagua (vegetable ivory) figurines and beaded necklaces vary depending on the region you are visiting, but generally are very similar in every weekly market. Ruanas (short ponchos) and other woolen clothing are made in small Andean villages, like Cumbal and Concepción. Colombia is also a good place for picking up quality and inexpensive leather items.

WHAT NOT TO BUY

It is not possible to export animal and plant products from Colombia and most nations reject the importation of any of these three products. Avoid buying products made out of insects, feathers or endangered species of flora and fauna. It is not advisable to get involved in buying or smuggling cocaine, which is punished with severe penalties and indirectly contributes to the damage caused to communities caught up in the production chain.

WHERE TO BUY

Although some crafts and traditional artifacts can be found throughout the country (and even international boutiques, as Colombians have migrated in considerable numbers, taking their culture with them), Southern and eastern towns in the country hold weekly markets. Cities in the Caribbean coast, Guajira, Llanos or the jungle rely on craft workshops and strip malls. Different towns and regions specialize in typical Colombian goods. Villavicencio offers comfortable chinchorro hammocks and magnificent musical instruments like harps. Traditional gaita flutes are made in Tubará on the Caribbean coast. Ráquira is known for its pottery. For elaborate woodwork and delicious candy, try to get to Málaga. Bogotá's La Candelaria district holds some of the cheapest emerald. The indigenous nations of Sierra Nevada de Santa Marta and La Guajira are known for making resistant woven bags.

HOW TO BUY

Practice your bargaining skills all over Colombia when you are buying souvenirs and other goods. Businesses like grocery stores and malls are not up for the bargaining game. However, if you are in a market, a souvenir shop in a small town or a crafts fair, prepare to offer about half of what the asking price is and start negotiating. Try to keep a good humor as you settle on a price, and consider the effort and time it could have taken to create the piece you have your eyes on.

All major credit cards are accepted in urban areas; however, as you get further away from major cities, it will be more difficult to find both businesses that accept credit cards and places to cash travelers' checks and currency exchange houses.

WHEN TO BUY

Businesses are open Monday- Friday 8 a.m.-noon and 2-6 p.m., yet commercial-stores stay open for a bit longer and a lot of them open on Saturdays. Generally, shopping hours are subject to the climate of each city; colder places like Bogotá are usually open for business Monday-Saturday 11 a.m.-9 p.m., while warmer cities tend to close at lunch hours (11 a.m.–3 p.m.) yet open at around 9 a.m. In small towns, shops close at lunch, and close early in the evening. Take into consideration that Colombians see Sundays, holidays and lunchtimes as personal time, so try to shop around that. Updated: Sep 8, 2011.

Studying Spanish

Out of all the places in Latin America to study Spanish, Colombia is not the ideal place to study. Someone beginning to learn Spanish may find the Colombian accents difficult to understand. In addition, there is not the abundance of Spanish language schools here that are found in other countries. If you choose to study in Colombia, make sure you obtain a student visa prior to your arrival. Overall, when looking for a place to study Spanish, Bogotá, Medellín and Cartagena provide the best options. Schools arrange airport pick-up, housing and offer a variety of excursions and activities in addition to language classes, such as cooking classes or field trips to local museums and historical sites. Many of these extracurricular activities will be offered for an additional, yet low, cost.

International language school agencies allow you to book your classes before you arrive. However, these are often more expensive, and you won't know how the school is until you arrive. **Languages in Action** has general, medical and business Spanish courses in Bogotá and Cartagena (URL: www.languagesinaction. com). With **Cactus Language School**, you can choose to study Spanish and volunteer in Bogotá, Cartagena, Medellín or Leticia (Tel: 1-888-577-8451 (U.S.), URL: www.cactuslanguage.com). **Adventure Travel**, affiliated with the World's Best Language School, has Spanish courses teamed with scuba diving, salsa dance lessons or volunteering in Cartagena (E-mail: info@learnspanishanddive. com, URL: www.learnspanishanddive.com). Canadian-based **Voyage International** arranges courses in Cartagena, with additional options of volunteer work, or courses in scuba, kiteboarding or sailing (Tel: 1-514-844-2831, Fax: 1-514-844-2018, E-mail: info@ langage.com, URL: www.vuvoyage.com).

A better option is to wait until you arrive in Colombia, so you can check out the school and its offerings firsthand. Also, it will work out to be cheaper. **Nueva Lengua** (www.

nuevalengua.com) has locations in Cartagena, Bogotá and Medellín. Aside from intensive languages classes, Nueva Lengua also offers specialty, like medical Spanish, or combination courses, such as Spanish and scuba diving. The course prices vary depending on location.

In Bogotá, **High Technology Learning** or more commonly known as HTL (URL: www. htl-online.com/international_s.php) offers each three, five or ten week courses. The longer courses offer fewer classes per week.

Foreign students coming to learn Spanish at the **Universidad del Norte in Barranquilla** (URL: www.uninorte.edu.co) can choose between month long sessions offered according to the school sessions or private classes. The university partners foreign students with university students and offers foreign students the opportunity to attend all activities provided for all university students.

Lastly, at **EAFIT University** in Medellín (URL: www.eafit.edu.co) the Spanish language classes are guaranteed to have a maximum of 10 students to a class and one-on-one conversational programs are set up for extra practice. Updated: Jun 16, 2011.

Living in Colombia

A great number of people end up coming to Colombia and falling in love with the country and its oft-flaunted attractions. For the most part, tourists arrive on a regular three-month tourist visa and either prefer to leave the country in order to obtain an extension or run through the demands required of them by the DAS office.

For those who are intent on actually living in Colombia there are a number of ways of doing so.

1. **Study:** There are a number of world-class universities in Colombia, all of which accept foreign students. Check their websites. If you are already in the country and thinking of this option, it is worthwhile to visit the university/academic institution to find out enrollment requirements.

2. **Teach English:** The pay is notoriously low, but most English teachers supplement their income by also offering private classes in addition to being affiliated to a language school. It is fundamental to have a TESL or TEFL.

3. **Become an investor:** Check with the Ministry of Foreign Affairs to see what is

required of an investor in Colombia to receive a visa. There is a minimum investment fee that frees up a lot of paperwork.

Any of these listed options should present you with a good opportunity to live, earn and fully enjoy Colombia. We strongly advise against people attempting to slip under the radar and go about their business without the correct paperwork. Colombian bureaucracy is substantial. A failure to comply with the required norms is frowned upon and could result in deportation, a hefty fine or some time in a particularly unpleasant Colombian prison. Updated: Sep 05, 2011.

Volunteering in Colombia

While the opportunities to volunteer in Colombia are increasing, there is still a long way to go for the country to reach the levels now experienced in Ecuador or Costa Rica. Given that many places in Colombia are still very much "out of bounds," charities can be forgiven for not sending people into the zona roja. Things are changing, however, and foreign-run NGOs as well as local outfits are beginning to recognize the value that willing volunteers can bring.

Many language schools now give students the opportunity to roll up their sleeves and help with local projects, like working with poor children. Several environmental organizations accepts volunteers, like **Pro Aves**, an NGO dedicated to birding (URL: www.ecovolunteer.com) and **Colombia's national parks** (URL: www.parquesnacionales.gov. co). Several dive shops in Taganga on the Caribbean Coast are reforesting coral reefs; see Tours under Taganga for more information. Out on Providencia Island, **Trees and Reefs Foundation** (URL: treesreefsfoundation. blogspot.com) is looking for natural and social scientists to work on a variety of projects.

Aside from showing up and lending your services, it is worthwhile doing some research and perhaps organizing your volunteering stint from your home country so as to be sure of what you are getting yourself into. One source for information about the groups and charities that are currently receiving volunteers is the Catholic Church, which maintains an up-to-date list of all outfits; contact your local parish. If you are a in the medical or education professions, your opportunity for long-term stints is greater; many organizations listed in the "Information Resources" section take volunteers.

Obviously most organizations will require a voluntary contribution and a minimum commitment period. In order to work with children it is recommended that you make your enquiries from your home country and provide the chosen organization with a background check to ensure the safety and security of the children with whom you intend to work. These organizations list volunteer opportunities:

Globalteer—www.globalteer.org

Idealist—www.idealist.org

United Planet—www.unitedplanet.org

Updated: Sep 05, 2011.

Working in Colombia

Most people residing and working in Colombia have come here sponsored by an international private school or a multinational firm. For these individuals securing the correct documents is straightforward. For others this is not the case. It is fundamental to have your papers in order. To do this you must have a legitimate reason for being here, be it teaching English, starting a business or being of some obvious benefit to the country. In order to have everything correct you must first contact the Minsterio de Relaciones Exteriores (Ministry of Foreign Affairs; www.cancilleria. gov.co) and have all your forms approved there before then getting your ID card at your local DAS office.

If you have the means and the visa to stay longer, such as by working for an NGO or working as a journalist, then the ideal situation would be to organize a visa in your home country and then to organize the issuance of a Cédula de Extranjería from the DAS office once you have arrived. Updated: Sep 05, 2011.

Lodging

HOTELS AND HOSTELS

As the image of Colombia improves in the eyes of international travelers and tourism takes on a bigger role in the economy of the country, the quality of hotels becomes a priority for those in the tourism industry. The cities receiving the majority of tourists—over 10 cities throughout Colombia—all have lodging options of international standards and several franchises for those more comfortable with the familiar. There are, however, plenty of unique hotels set in historical buildings, ranches, residential areas and even protected natural areas that enhance the experience of visiting Colombia.

As far as hostels go, there are plenty of affordable options in urban areas. Many have dormitories, as well as private rooms. Travelers who are members of Hostelling International (URL: www.hihostels.com), minihostels (URL: www.minihostels.com) or Hola Hostels (URL: www.holahostels.com) receive discounts at hostels belonging to those networks. Colombian Hostels is a nationwide chain (URL: www.colombianhostels.com.co). Updated Sep 06, 2011.

ECO-LODGES

In 2006, then-Colombian President Álvaro Uribe opened the first 20 eco-lodges in the Sierra Nevada for a program called "Fostering Families," which helps the families highly affected by cocaine production. The program has blossomed into the Posadas Turísticas de Colombia (URL: www.posadasturisticasdecolombia.com), with family-run hostels from Providencia to Putumayo, from the Guajira to Nuquí.

Most eco-lodges in Colombia have package (sometimes all-inclusive) deals that can be arranged through travel agents. Look for packages that specialize in relaxation, whale-watching, surfing, scuba diving, birdwatching, fishing or jungle walks.

The Chocó region along the Pacific Ocean provides some of the best choices for environmentally friendly eco-lodges. **Pijiba Lodge** near Nuquí offers transportation in a glass-bottom boat. **El Almejal** in El Valle really focuses on conservation and teaching.

On Colombia's Caribbean side, taste the organic fruits grown in the garden at Playa Koralia, but leave the laptop at home, or it could be confiscated. They're serious about being one with nature. Also, check out El Refugio de Mr. Jerry, Lodge Piedra Piedra, Hotel Kipara, Finca Raval Jardín Ecológico, El Cantil or Estado Natural. Updated: Sep 21, 2011.

SPAS

Colombia offers many variations on the stereotypical relaxing and tranquil spa vacation. If you want to indulge in the local specialty, cacao, try the choco-therapy at the Thermaé Spa at the **Hotel Opera in Bogotá** (Ca. 10, 5-72, Bogotá. Tel: 1-336-2066, 1-336-5285, E-mail: sales@hotelopera.com.co, URL: www.hotelopera.com.co). The New York Times calls **Casa Boutique Veranera in Cartagena** "a jewel box of a hotel with a spa and yoga studio" (Ca. Quero 9-65, San Diego, Cartagena. Tel: 5-644-8908, E-mail: reservation@casaveranera.com, URL: http://casaveranera.com). Don't skimp on the insect repellent during beachside massages or meditation sessions at Playa Koralia, east of Santa Marta (Cel: 310-642-2574, E-mail: koralia@koralia.com, URL: www.koralia.com). As well, many luxury hotels throughout the country, like Radisson Hotels, have massage rooms.

The Hare Krishnas have six ecological reserve finca lodges in Colombia where guests may enjoy vegetarian cuisine, yoga and meditation classes, hiking trails, temazcales (sweathouses) and other natural therapies. Some of the retreat centers are: **Gambhira** near Santa Marta (Tel: 315-375-5591, E-mail: costavaisnava@gmail.com), **Finca Raval Jardín Ecológico**, near Bucaramanga (Tel: 7-680-2045 /680-2075, Cel: 312-351-0209, E-mail: govindap@intercable.net.co) and **Varsana Jardínes Ecológicos**, near Bogotá (Tel: 1-323-2195, Cel: 320-899-5159/313-806-5031, E-mail: info@varsana.com, URL: www.varsana.com). Many of the fincas also take volunteers. For more information about these, visit: www.inboundtours.com.

If you prefer to relax in hot springs, one place to go is **Termales de Santa Rosa de Cabal**, located in Risalda in the Zona Cafetera (Tel: 6-364-5500, E-mail: informacion@termales.com.co, URL: www.termales.com.co). Other thermal resorts are found in Paipa and at **Termales de Rivera** near Neiva. More rustic hot springs are **Agua Hirviendo** and **Aguatibia** near Coconuco in Southern Colombia, and **Güicán** near Parque Nacional Natural El Cocuy.

Lastly, while in Medellín, don't miss out on treating your tootsies—for free—to the foot spas in Parque de los Pies Descalzos. Updated: Sep 07, 2011.

CAMPING

If you are interested in camping in Colombia, contact local tourist authorities for information on camp sites, or suitable areas to put up your tent or park your camper van. Camping, especially if unplanned, can be dangerous as it generally done away from safer urban centers. However, as the security situation improves and Colombia's tourism industry grows, the popularity and number of camping opportunities is expanding.

Although the number of campsites is growing throughout the country, they are rarely signposted from main roads and can often be difficult to find. In no instance should you camp on private land without permission. This is not only illegal but extremely dangerous. You should always ask permission to camp on someone's land but only do so when assured of the area's security.

A few free sites can be found throughout the country and others go from as little as $1 per person per night. Some national parks also offer the opportunity to camp and are generally safer than non-supervised camping. Hostels are increasingly catching on to the popularity of camping for budget travelers and nature lovers and are offering camping opportunities in their grounds.

NOTE: White gas (gasolina blanca) is now virtually impossible to obtain in Colombia. There are only a few places in Bogotá where it can be bought, one place in Bucaramanga. Campers now have to use gasolina roja (i.e. regular gasoline) in their camp stoves. If you are going to use a camp stove in Colombia, it must be a multi-fuel equipped to use regular gasoline. Updated: Sep 07, 2011.

RENTING
Renting an apartment outright is a tricky issue. Should you go through a licensed agent and receive the security and legal sureness offered you will need a proof of income, a Colombian national to countersign your contract and then have the documents notarized. Unfortunately most Colombian apartments to let are unfurnished. The easiest way around this is searching the web and checking out ads in windows for people offering private furnished properties. Updated: Sep 07, 2011.

Food and Drink
Colombian recipes rely heavily on fresh, regionally available ingredients. While Colombian cuisine may not have the boldest or most adventurous flavors, the traveler will have no trouble finding filling and inexpensive traditional dishes, snacks, street food, and tropical produce that hit the spot.

Colombian arepas (fried cornmeal patties) are a street food sold and eaten all over the country, but in western Colombia are often breakfast (along with hot chocolate). Plain arepas are rather bland and are typically eaten with cheese or butter, though several variations are also popular. Stuffed arepas include the arepa de choclo, made with corn and cheese; arepa de huevo, egg arepa; and arepa de queso and arepa boyacense, which are filled with savory and sweet cheeses. Packaged arepas can also be bought in the supermarkets.

Empanadas (fried pastries stuffed with meat or cheese) and buñuelos (fried, cheesy cornflour balls) are two more deep-fried foods that are also quite common, among others.

REGIONAL SPECIALTIES
An ever-popular dish you are likely to encounter, especially in and around Bogotá, is *ajiaco*, a riff on chicken soup that contains corn and potatoes. It is usually served with heavy cream and avocados, making it a hearty lunch on its own.

Though typical of Medellín and the northwest, another nationally favorite dish is the *bandeja paisa*, or paisa platter, which includes rice, beans, ground beef, plantain, sausage, chicharrón, arepa, avocado and a fried egg.

Sancocho, a stew that is typical of Cali and the southwest, is often prepared on special occasions or weekends. Another hearty dish, it usually contains chicken, fish or oxtail, plantains, *yucca* (manioc), potatoes, cilantro and spices.

Both Pacific and Caribbean coastal cuisines are unsurprisingly heavy on spicy fish and lobster, often accompanied by coconut rice. Seafood is generally difficult to find inland.

In the Llanos, or eastern plains, where large ranches and *vaqueros* (cowboys) punctuate the open landscape, barbecued meat or *asado* is the main staple, and the most common dish is *mamona*, or barbecued veal.

Goat meat commonly appears on the menus in several parts of Colombia. In the Guajira, this meat is often served in a stew called *friche*. In San Gil, Capitanejo and other villages in Santander Department, the roasted meat is served with *pipitoria*, rice prepared with goat blood and finely chopped innards. Another treat in this region is roasted fat-bottom ants.

In Nariño Department bordering Ecuador, adventurous meat-lovers also can try fried or roasted *cuy*, or guinea pig. Though cuy is generally consumed in the household, many tourist-oriented restaurants have it on offer.

Colombian Coffee

Colombian Coffee. Those two words just sort of seem to roll together, don't they? Colombian coffee. Mmm. Go say them to the nearest java-head. You know who I'm talking about, there's one in every office. Watch him grin with joy and maybe even twitch a little. Colombian coffee. There's magic in those words, my friend.

Coffee was first introduced to Colombia in the early 19th century by java-heads who were sick of going all the way to Brazil to get their fix. It soon became the country's main export and before long, Colombia was one of the world leaders in coffee production.

Coffee grows well on mountainsides, particularly the Arabica bean, which is the highest quality bean there is. The other type of coffee bean, Robusta, is apparently more like a weed than a real crop, and the beans it produces are best suited for high school students planning all-nighters or grinding into brick mortar. Well, that's what the Colombian Coffee Board says, anyway. Did I mention that all Colombian coffee is Arabica?

Colombian coffee is hand-picked by Juan Valdez look-a-likes, loaded on to donkeys or mules, and brought to special machines, which separate the pulp from the seed. If you've never seen a real live coffee bean, they're a little like a small red cherry, except the part you want is the stone and not the fruit, which has no caffeine in it and is therefore useless, much like a real cherry. So anyway, the seeds are removed and the fruity part is separated out and used for compost, which is a nice way of saying it's left out to rot. The beans are rinsed out a couple of times, which is one of the reasons why Colombian coffee is special.

Once the beans have been washed, they are left to dry in the sun for a few days. They are lovingly covered at night and when it rains, leading some to suspect that Colombians take better care of their coffee beans than their pets.

Once the beans are dried, it's time to roast them. Coffee beans are roasted according to a complicated scale with such levels as "full city roast," "Italian roast," "high-school kid pulling an all-nighter roast" and "roast of the death of a thousand twitches." These different levels refer to how long the bean is roasted, and therefore how dark it gets. The lightest roasts are given a couple of minutes under one of those French fry lights, while the darkest roasts are run through leaky old Soviet nuclear reactors by political prisoners given a suit made of tinfoil for protection. Be sure to try some of the fine local coffee on your trip!

PRODUCE

Particularly pleasing is Colombia's abundance of delicious exotic fruits, many of which do not have names in English. Lulo and guanabana make particularly good juices and *curuba* (banana passion fruit), feijoa, mamey, *guayabamanzana* (hybrid between guava and apple) and níspero, among many others, are all worth a try.

Vegetables are rather hard to come by in Colombia. The most commonly served are roots, like carrots, potatoes, *batata* and yucca. Also expect *plátanos* (plantains), squash and salads made of cabbage, tomato and onion.

BEVERAGES

By far the most famous of all Colombian beverages is, of course, its internationally consumed coffee. Be warned, however, that coffee quality varies and your *tinto* (small black coffee) may be weaker and sweeter than expected. The word tinto can also mean a glass of red wine, but avoid Colombian wines–Chilean and Argentine wines are widely available and of a much higher quality.

Other alcoholic drinks of Colombian origin that are indeed worth trying include *aguardiente*, sugarcane alcohol; *guarapo*, a drink made of fermented fruits and sugar; *canelazo*, a warm, fruity drink made with aguardiente and cinnamon; *refajo*, a mixed drink of rum or beer and cream soda; and *chicha*, a fermented corn drink made by the indigenous in the Andes. Of course national beers are also widely available; top brands are Poker, Águila, Pilsener and Club Colombia.

Culinary Vocabulary

Aborrajados ► Banana dessert.

Almojábana ► Type of bread made with cheese and flour; also called pan de bono.

Arepa ► Corn-flour patty that can come plain or stuffed with other ingredients. Popular as a breakfast food; also found in Venezuela.

Arequipe ► Soft caramel made out of milk and cinnamon.

Arracacha ► Elongated tuber that is brown on the outside and yellow on the inside.

Auyama ► Though in the dictionary it means pumpkin, Colombians call auyama a type of squash with green peel and orange insides.

Batata ► Sweet potato.

Bocadillo ► A sweet made out of the guayaba (guava) fruit. Sometimes people call bocadillo a small snack.

Buñuelo ► A deep-fried dough served as dessert with syrup.

Caldocorto ► Broth made out of legumes and herbs. It is used to cook fish and seafood.

Cañón ► Pork meat.

Caspiroleta ► Drink made out of milk, eggs, brandy, cinnamon and sugar.

Champús ► Traditional beverage prepared with corn meal, corn, cinnamon, panela (raw sugar) and fruits like pineapple and lulo.

Changua ► Soup made out of milk, onion, cilantro and egg.

Chicharrón ► Fried pig skin.

Cuchuco ► Barley and pork meat soup.

Curuba ► Acidic fruit of yellow skin and lots of small seeds.

Guasca ► An edible leaf.

Malta ► Sweet drink made out of barley, not fermented.

Marranitas ► Little balls prepared with pork rind and plantain.

Merengues ► Also known as besitos, or kisses, these baked sweets are made of beaten egg whites and sugar. They are found all over Latin America.

Muchachorelleno ► Literally "stuffed boy," the dish is actually stuffed beef.

Oblea ► Thin, round cookie wafer made of flour and water. It's served with jams and sweet sauces or caramel.

Pasabocas ► Finger foods served in social gatherings. Generally come on a toothpick or over a small cracker.

Patacón ► Found in other adjacent countries, this side dish is made from plantains cut, squashed and fried.

Pocillo Tintero ► A small cup of coffee.

Ponqué ► Basic cake made out of flour, butter, eggs and sugar.

Salpicón ► Drink made out of juice of varying flavor with diced fruit. It can also mean a beef or fish stew.

Tinto ► Strong black coffee.

Zapote ► A fruit of brown peel and fibrous, orange insides with a big, black seed in the middle.

Updated: May 11, 2011.

If alcohol isn't your thing, the many nonalcoholic drink options are worth a try. Colombian hot chocolate is made with a special pitcher and a *molinillo* for stirring, and is often served with cinnamon and cheese. *Aguapanela* is a drink of dissolved sugarcane in water with lime juice and sometimes cheese added in for flavor. Both *champú* and *lulada* are thick drinks that utilize Colombia's wondrous spread of unique fruits, and *salpicón*, which translates into large splash, is a refreshing drink of soda and chopped fruit. Coca-cola and other sodas are available everywhere as well, as are fresh fruit drinks.

DESSERTS

Like entrées, desserts are a regional affair in Colombia. *Mazamorra,* cornmeal boiled in milk, a common sweet in Antioquia. On the Caribbean coast, try the *crema de arroz,* a delicious rice and coconut milk pudding. A cheap dessert is obleas, large circular wafers sandwiching *arequipe* (soft caramel) or fruit sauces. Colombia's many fruits also can satisfy your sweet tooth.

WHERE TO EAT ON THE CHEAP

Like in neighboring countries, many restaurants in Colombia offer inexpensive multi-course set lunches, which usually include soup, meat, rice, French fries, a small salad and grilled plantains. This is the best way for the traveler on a budget to fill up on hearty, hot food. These and other restaurants do not usually have printed menus, so if your Spanish is rusty, it might be useful to have a pocket dictionary handy while the server gives you the run-down on what is available. Colombians tend to take siesta in the afternoon, so most lunch spots serve meals between noon and 2 p.m.

VEGETARIAN FARE

In restaurants, vegetarians may find it difficult to find satisfying options aside from arepas, rice, beans, salad and potatoes. Luckily, most cities have at least one vegetarian-oriented restaurant. The Hare Krishnas operate a chain of eateries called Govindas.

INTERNATIONAL FARE

Should you tire of Colombian food and require something different, the three big cities of Bogotá, Cartagena and Medellín offer quite a few nice restaurants with international fare to choose from. Also, in the Caribbean coast cities, where many Middle Eastern and other foreigners have settled, you can venture into other culinary worlds. Updated: Sep 13, 2011.

Maps

Buying maps in Colombia can be a difficult process and some suppliers provide out of date copies. The best source is the Instituto Geográfico Augustín Codazzi (Bogotá: Monday-Friday 8.00 a.m.–4.30 p.m. Cra. 30, 48-51. Tel: 1-368-3443, E-mail: cig@igac.gov.co, URL: www.igac.gov.co), which has offices in most departmental capitals. Here you can obtain copies of a variety of national, departmental, regional and city maps that range in price from $2-5 per sheet. It also publishes Mapas de Ruta, a spiral-bound collection of maps perfect for motorists and bicyclists ($7).

It is always worth visiting the local tourist information center and asking in your hotel or hostel if they have, or know where best to obtain, local maps. Most Colombian cities are structured around the grid system thus making it relatively easy to find your way around. Calles are generally oriented North to South, and Carreras run East to West.

Outside of Colombia, one of the best sources for maps is International Travel Maps& Books (12300 Bridgeport Road, Richmond, BC V6V 1J5, Canada. Tel: 604-879-3621, Fax: 604-879-4521, URL: www.itmb.ca).Updated: Sep 21, 2011.

Media

Colombia is a tough country for journalism. Human rights organizations like Amnesty International and Human Rights First, as well as professional journalist organizations such as Committee to Protect Journalists and Reporters Without Borders, rank Colombia as one of the four most dangerous countries for journalists. They also report that Colombia suffers one of the highest assassination and exile rates of any country in the world.

Gabriel García Márquez and other Latin American journalists have established the Fundación para un Nuevo Periodismo Iberoamericano to train the new generation of journalists. The Institute has regular seminars, workshops and other programs. (Ca. San Juan de Dios 3-121, Cartagena de Indias. Tel.: 5-664-5890, Fax: 5-664-5904, URL: www.fnpi.org).

The established media in Colombia play a major role in the government's anti-terrorism program. We also list some of the independent media of the country. More listings for Colombia media may be found at Internet Public Library (URL: www.ipl.org) or at World Press (URL: www.worldpress.org).

NEWSPAPERS

El Espectador (Bogotá)—www.elespectador.com

El Heraldo (Barranquilla)—www.elheraldo.com.co

El Mundo (Medellín) www.elmundo.com

El País (Cali)—www.elpais.com.co

El Tiempo (Bogotá)—www.eltiempo.com

El Universal (Cartagena)—www.eluniversal.com.co

MAGAZINES

Cromos (Centrist, news)—www.cromos.com.co

El Malpensante (literary)—www.elmalpensante.com

Número (Leftist, cultural)—www.revistanumero.com

Revista Cambio (Liberal)—www.revista-cambio.com

Semana (Centrist, news)—www.semana.com

TELEVISION AND RADIO
Caracola—www.canalcaracol.com

RCN—www.canalrcn.com/in English: www.ntn24news.com

Telesur—www.telesurtv.net—Colombia is not officially part of the Telesur consortia, but it can be received in some parts of the country

ONLINE
CM & la Noticia—www.cmi.com.co

Colombia Indy Media—colombia.indymedia.org

Colombian Journal (journalist Gary Leech)—www.colombiajournal.org

Colombia Reports—www.colombiareports.com

El yesQuero (lawyer-journalist Rafael Rincón)—elyesquero.blogspot.com

Reuters Alert Net: Colombia Displacement—www.alertnet.org/printable.htm, with excellent articles with figures on War on Drugs, narcotrafficking and refugees

Updated: May 10, 2011.

Money and Costs
In Colombia, prices (particularly for hotels and transportation) as a rule increase 5.5-6 percent at the beginning of each year. Hotel and other rates have increased more in popular destinations, like Bogotá and Cartagena, since tourism has been growing in Colombia. Expect all prices to be higher at holiday times. Since research began for this guide, the dollar has decreased in value about six percent against the Colombia peso (COP).

Budget travelers can easily get by on about $20 per person per day, including the occasional national park visit and meal at a fancy restaurant. With a bit of an eye on expenses, though, you could survive on $15 per day. In much of the country, basic lodging can be had for $8-10 per night. Set meals of the day cost $3 on average. Transportation is the major expense. See the Budget Travelers

section in this chapter for ways to travel for less money in Colombia.

Mid-range travelers should allow $50-60 per day for basic expenses. Hotel rooms in this class cost from $25 per night (less per person for couples), and have private bath (with hot water in cold climates, with only cold water in hotter parts of the country), cable TV and air conditioning. Meals usually cost about $10-12, including a drink.

Luxury travelers will find Colombia to be quite a bargain, especially if you are from Europe. Very nice hotels go for $70 on up. Count on having private bathroom with hot water in all climates, air conditioning, swimming pool, sauna and other amenities. You can enjoy a dinner with wine for $20-30, at the least. Be sure to add to your itinerary an Amazon jungle lodge, a Llanos hotel campestre and national park accommodations at Tayrona, Gorgona or Amacayacu. Updated: May 11, 2011.

MONEY
The official currency of Colombia is the peso (abbreviated COP). There are 50, 100 and 500 peso coins; the 10 and 20 pesos coins are rarely used now. Bills come in denominations of 1,000, 2,000, 5,000, 10,000, 20,000 and 50,000 COP. The symbol used before prices is: $.Even though most people travel only with a bank card, a variety of money options should be employed.

CASH
Carry some U.S. cash in perfect condition for changing at border crossings or for areas where ATMs may not be available. Casas de cambio (exchange houses) in major cities will change euros. Currency of other countries is difficult to change into pesos anywhere.

BANKS
ATMS are common, connected with both Latin American and international networks (redes), including Cirrus and Plus. ATH (A Todo Hora) 24-hour cash machines usually give better rates and have a higher daily withdrawal limit. Davienda is said to have the highest withdrawal limit.

CREDIT CARDS
High-end businesses accept credit cards. Mastercard and Visa are the most common; some also take Diners or American Express. Many bank ATMs take credit cards as well. Visa cash advances can be obtained at Banco de Bogotá and Banco Popular.

TRAVELER'S CHECKS
Bancolombia and some branches of Banco Santander exchange U.S. dollar or euro American Express travelers checks. Go prepared with a photocopy of the front page and entry stamp of your passport. You will also have to fill out a form and give your right index finger print. Few casas de cambio and businesses accept travelers checks. Bancolombia is American Express' representative in Colombia for financial matters.

WIRING MONEY
Some travelers find they need to have folks back home wire money to them through Western Union (URL: www.westernunion.com) or MoneyGram (URL: www.moneygram.com). You receive it in COP, though you can buy U.S. dollars, if they are available. Branches of money wiring services at banks typically handle transactions only for Colombians. Foreigners will have to go to Giros y Finanzas (URL: www.girosyfinanzas.com) for Western Union wires and Cambiamos (URL: www.cambiamos.com) for MoneyGram. Check the websites for office locations. Updated: May 11, 2011.

Keeping in Touch

MAIL AND PACKAGES
The main national postal service is Correos de Colombia, also called 4-72 (www.4-72.com). Most towns have an office. Letters and packages take up to a week for national delivery, 8-12 days for addresses in the Americas and about two weeks for other overseas destinations. All overseas post, even to neighboring countries, is sent air mail. There have been reports of letters arriving opened and taped back shut. Prices for letters and packages is quite high: a letter (up to 20 grams) costs $3.20-3.70 and up to 501-1,000 grams, $28.40-35.50. Certified mail is about $4-7 more, depending on destination. Letters weighing up to two kilograms may be sent by normal (uncertified) mail. Packages up to 30 kilograms may be sent by certified mail. See 4-72's website for complete rates.

Courier companies are common throughout Colombia as well. The major ones are **Servientrega Internacional** (URL: www.servientrega.com), **DHL** (URL: www.dhl.com), **Deprisa** (Avianca Airlines; URL: www.deprisa.com) and **Federal Express** (URL: fedex.com).

You can have mail sent to you by way of the post office's general delivery. Have your post addressed: your full name (as it appears in your passport, last name in capitals), Poste Restante, Lista de Correos, Correo Central, city or town, Colombia. If you hold an American Express credit card, you can also receive your mail at one of its offices (www.americanexpress.com). These days, very few embassies hold mail for their citizens. Updated: Mar 18, 2011.

TELEPHONE
In many smaller towns, Telecom has an office with phone service to local, national and international numbers. To make a local or national phone call, you can also go to a shop with a sign stating Minutos or Llamadas. They charge $0.10-0.20 per minute to cellular calls, more to land lines (fijo).

Local phone numbers have seven digits and begin with a number from 2 to 8; 9 is reserved for pay phones. For mobile-to-mobile calls, the phone number is prefixed by a three-digit access code (see below).

When calling from a landline to a cell phone, dial **03 + access code + phone number**. For calls made from a cell phone to a landline, dial **03 + city/region code + phone number**.

EMERGENCY PHONE NUMBERS
For police, fire and general emergencies, dial: 112 (nation-wide) or 123 (in Bogotá, Medellín and Cúcuta).

DOMESTIC LONG DISTANCE
For domestic long distance, Colombia has three carriers covering specific cities and regions of the country. Only ETB is nation-wide.

Domestic long distance calls are prefixed with "0," followed by the code for the carrier: 5 for Orbitel, 7 for ETB and 9 for Telefónica. The third digit is the city (region) code (see below), which is then followed by the seven-digit number (ex. 091-XXX-XXXX).

Colombia City (Region) Codes:
1—Bogotá (Cundinamarca)

2—Cali (Valle del Cauca), Popayán (Cauca), Pasto (Nariño)

3—Not used

4—Montería (Córdoba), Quibdó (Chocó), Medellín (Antioquia)

5—Riohacha (La Guajira), Barranquilla (Atlántico), Santa Marta (Magdalena), Valledupar (Cesar), Sincelejo (Sucre), Cartagena (Bolívar)

6—Manizales (Caldas), Pereira (Risaralda), Armenia (Quindío)

7—Cúcuta (Norte de Santander), Bucaramanga (Santander), Arauca (Arauca)

8—Tunja (Boyacá), Ibagué (Tolima), Yopal (Casanare), Neiva (Huila), Villavicencio (Meta), Puerto Carreño (Vichada), Florencia (Caquetá), San José de Guaviare (Guaviare), Puerto Inírida (Guainía), Leticia (Amazonas), San Andrés (San Andrés), Mocoa (Putumayo), Mitú (Vaupés)

INTERNATIONAL LONG DISTANCE

You can call home from Colombia with a mobile phone, landline or Skype. Some Internet cafés and cabinas (phone centers) have international phone service, charging $0.15-0.30 per minute to the U.S., and more for other countries. It is cheaper to call home on a landline than a mobile phone. Skype is the most affordable option, though in some parts of the country it is unavailable (especially in the Southern and Eastern regions). It is also possible to make collect calls from Colombia. International calling cards are available in bigger cities.

The prefix for international calls is 00. If using one of the national long distance carriers, the prefix is followed by the carrier code (see above). Then follow the country code + area code + phone number. For example, to call the U.S. or Canada, you would dial: **009 + 1 + area code + phone number.**

Other country codes are:
France: + 33
Germany: +49
Poland: + 48
United Kingdom: + 44

Argentina: + 54
Bolivia: +591
Brazil: + 55
Chile: + 56
Ecuador: + 593
Peru: + 51

Australia: + 61
Japan: + 81
New Zealand: + 64
South Korea: + 82

CALLING COLOMBIA FROM ABROAD

The country code for Colombia is 57. When dialing, this will be prefixed by your country's international calling number, and be followed by the city (regional) code (see above) + the phone number. For example, a person calling from North America would dial: 011 + 57 + city/region code + seven-digit phone number. See your home telephone directory for specifics for your country.

When calling a Colombian cell phone from abroad, substitute the cell phone carrier access code (see Colombia Cell Phone Providers) for the city/region code.

It is cheaper to call a Colombian landline than a cell phone. To make cheap calls to Colombia, you can either use a voice-over-internet system like Skype, or buy a phone card.

CELL PHONES

Cell phone use in Colombia is overtaking traditional landline use. Mobile phones in Colombia have SMS and MMS capabilities; more expensive phones have Internet access. Cell phone coverage in Colombia is reliable, even in the mountains and jungle.

It may be possible to use your cell phone from home while traveling in Colombia. Colombia's cell phone carriers operate on GSM networks; Tigo uses the 850 Hz band, and Comcel and Movistar use both 850 and 1900 Hz bands. Dual-band phones from Europe, Africa, Asia and Oceania will not work, but GSM-enabled phones from North or South America likely will. All quad-band, and most tri-band, phones will work in Colombia. Cell phones from outside the western hemisphere will need a flat blade plug adapter and 110-volt converter in order to charge safely. Colombian mobile phone companies have roaming agreements with many international cell phone companies, so, while extremely expensive, it may be possible to use your existing phone plan in Colombia.

COLOMBIAN CELL PHONE PROVIDERS

There are three service providers in Colombia: Tigo, Comcel and Movistar. All three offer monthly pre-paid-a good idea for longer stays, and pay-as-you-go services. Cell phones can be purchased at retailers throughout the country; shop around, as the three companies are quite competitive. In larger cities, many small shops specialize in the sale of refurbished cell phones.

The codes for each of the three carriers are:
Tigo: 300, 301, 302, 304
Comcel: 310, 311, 312, 313, 314
Movistar: 315, 316, 317
Phone shops will also sell SIM cards that will give you a local phone number and allow you

to place and receive calls. Purchase minutes for your mobile phone at Tigo, Comcel or Movistar stores, or at most convenience stores. Cards to recharge your *saldo* (credit) come in 5,000, 10,000 and 20,000 COP denominations.

INTERNET

Internet cafés are found in towns of any significant size. Connections are usually fast (most have broadband) and $0.80-1.55 per hour. There are still many small villages where the populace does not have access to the Internet. A trend throughout Colombia is to boycott Microsoft programs, instead using Open Office. Only hostels geared to international or higher-budget travelers have on-site Internet. WiFi is still uncommon in much of the country and sometimes is charged for. Before sitting down with your laptop and logging in, make sure you will not be charged for this connection. Updated: Sep 12, 2011.

Photography

FILM

At the Airport

Take all your film with you in your carry-on luggage. The scanning process for checked luggage will damage your fi lm. Passing your film more than five times through the X-ray can also damage it, but in this unlikely situation you can just ask for a hand check.

What Kind of Film to Buy

Use a film that has an ISO (ASA or sensitivity to light) 100 or 200 for outdoor shooting, 400 for indoor, and 800 or 1000 for near-darkness. Fuji Velvia slide film is known for producing rich colors and good sharpness and contrast —great for vacation photos. The downside: it's a little pricey, and if you want the pictures in something other than slide format you'll have to get the slides scanned or scan them yourself.

PURCHASE, REPAIR AND DEVELOPING

Bogotá

ABC Digital Center Servicio Técnico— Camera and video camera repair. Ca. 9, 37-40, L-2015/2016. Tel: 1-247-5589.

Artecámaras Reparaciones—Camera sale and repair. Cra. 9, 18-51, L-101. Tel: 1-282-7195.

Super Foto Digital—Film developing. Ca. 23, 4-22. Tel: 1-281-6112.

Medellín

Colormatic—Film developing. Cra.66B, 34B-14. Tel: 4-351-0081.

Electronippon Asistencia Técnica Integral—Authorized service for: Sony, Samsung, JVC, Toshiba and Sharp; camera and camera accessory sale; camera and video camera repair. Ca. 46, 79-64. Tel: 4-411-1085.

Cali

Universal Fotográfica—Develops all brands and types of film; transfer to CD, slides. Ca. 13, 3-41. Tel: 2-880-5050, E-Mail: info@universalfotografica.com, URL: www.universalfotografica.com. Updated: Sep 21, 2011.

COLOMBIAN PHOTOGRAPHY

If you are interested in looking at photos and not just taking them, Colombia has a lot to offer. The national photography museum in Bogotá, **Fotomuseo** (URL: www.fotomuseo.org), is an innovative non-profit organization that brings photography to all levels of society through its outdoor exhibitions. It holds five annual street exhibitions of national and international photographs in three different areas of the city, with each exhibit lasting 45 days. In doing this, Fotomuseo hopes to share the value of this art form with the public without elitism or pretension.

The museum holds two other events during the year: Fotomaratón, which brings together the works of professional, amateur and student photographers from Colombia and neighboring countries, and Fotográfica Bogotá, which involves street and gallery exhibitions of work from the most important national and international photographers. This occurs twice a year.

Another important institution is **Club Fotográfico Medellín** (Cámara de Comercio del Poblado, Avenida Oriental 52-82. Tel: 4-444-8822, URL: www.clubfotograficomedellin.org), Colombia's oldest photography association. Founded in 1955, the Club organizes exhibitions, conferences, workshops and competitions, including the Salón Colombiano de Fotografía, probably the nation's most prestigious photo competition. The Club's website includes information about ongoing photography events in the country.

Colombia has produced several notable photographers, among them Leo Matiz, Saúl Orduz Vega, Abdú Eljaiek, Sady González Moreno and Gabriel Carvajal Pérez. You can view their work at www.fotografoscolombianos.com.

Health

Many people prior to travel get too preoccupied with the dangers associated with tropical diseases and what they will do if they fall sick. Other than the somewhat inevitable and rarely threatening diarrhea associated with changes in diet, very few travelers suffer serious illness when inside Colombia. A key to avoiding sickness while abroad is preparation. Although less equipped in rural areas, most Colombian cities have good health facilities and numerous pharmacies that will provide medicines in the eventuality that you become ill during your travels.

One obvious precautionary measure is to take out travel insurance that covers medical necessities. Bring along a copy of your insurance card or policy. If you are undertaking travel for an extensive period of time there are a few recommendations to consider before departing. A dental check-up could prove useful. For those who suffer from diabetes, heart trouble/cardio-pulmonary disease, high blood pressure or cholesterol problems, consultation with your doctor is highly advised.

Pack a small first aid kit with any medicine you take on a regular basis, plus some anti-diarrheal pills, aspirin, insect repellent and sunscreen. Most of these items are available in cities all around Colombia, however if you prefer or require a certain type or brand—hypoallergenic, for example—it is best to bring it from home than to risk not finding what you want. Mentacol (mentholated rubbing alcohol), which is available at local pharmacies, provides refreshing relief to insect bites. Insurance companies recommend taking written records of any medical conditions and their proper names of any medication you are taking.

For more information on traveling and diseases, consult the U.S. government's Centers for Disease Control (URL: www.cdc.gov), the U.K.'s National Travel Health Network and Centre (URL: www.nathnac.org) or your embassy's website. Another useful independent site is the British-based Travel Health (URL: www.travelhealth.co.uk).

MINOR HEALTH PROBLEMS

Altitude Sickness

When traveling in the Colombian Andes it is important to rest the first few days and drink lots of bottled water. Should you suffer from a severe headache, drowsiness, confusion, dry cough, and/or breathlessness, drink lots of water and rest. If the symptoms continue, move to a lower altitude. Anyone planning to hike at high altitudes is advised to relax in high altitude locations for a few days before any physical exertion. Note that altitude sickness, locally called soroche, can come on suddenly if you experience a sudden change of altitude. You may suffer from it when traveling to the likes of Parque Nacional Natural El Cocuy. Sickness can also affect locals so be prepared and take care!

Frostbite

Frostbite is simply the freezing of the skin and is more commonly suffered at higher altitudes. This can usually be avoided if you wear proper clothing—double thick socks, gloves and a ski-mask can all help. Wear water-resistant clothing and change out of wet clothes immediately if you can. Smoking and drinking alcohol also raise your risk because they decrease your circulation. The most common places to get frostbite are on the hands and feet, although exposed facial areas like the ears, nose and cheeks are also vulnerable areas. The first signs of frostbite are usually tingling, numbness, and discoloration of the skin to white or yellow. When you begin to warm up you will start feeling pain in the affected area, and it may turn red and swell. The best way to treat frostbite is to soak the skin in warm, but not hot, water until feeling returns. Only begin treatment when you are safely out of the cold.

Fungal Infections

These are most common in hot and humid areas and generally accumulate between the toes or fingers, or around the groin. Spread by infected animals or people, fungi thrive in moist conditions. If you suffer from a fungal infection it is best to ensure the affected area is kept dry and clean and avoid scratching. Wear loose clothing and avoid artificial materials. Treating with anti-fungal cream or powder can also help.

Motion Sickness

Even the hardiest of travelers can be hit by motion sickness on the buses in the Andesor boat trips along the coast or to Malpelo Island. Sit near the front of the bus or stay above deck on the boat and focus on the horizon. If you are prone to motion sickness, eat light, non-greasy food before traveling and avoid drinking too much, particularly alcohol. Over-the-counter medications such as Dramamine can prevent it. Eating ginger candy or drinking ginger tea 20 minutes before a trip also provides relief to many. If you suffer from severe motion sickness, you may want consult a pharmacist to get a prescription for something stronger.

Sunburn/Heat Exhaustion

Even at high altitudes where cool breezes constantly blow and snow can accumulate, the sun is incredibly strong. Apply sunscreen with at least an SPF of 30 every few hours you are outside. The sun on the coast is particularly strong and unprepared visitors can get badly burned. If you get severe sunburn, treat it with a cream and stay out of the sun for a while.

To avoid overheating, wear a hat and sunglasses, and drink lots of water. Overweight people are more susceptible to sun stroke. The symptoms of heat exhaustion are profuse sweating, weakness, exhaustion, muscle cramps, rapid pulse and vomiting. If you experience heat stroke, go to a cool, shaded area until your body temperature normalizes and drink lots of non-caffeinated drinks, like Gatorade, to replenish vital salts. If the symptoms continue, consult a doctor.

Traveler's Diarrhea

This is probably the most common illness that travelers suffer from. There is no vaccine to protect you from traveler's diarrhea; it is avoided by eating sensibly. It is most often transmitted by food, though also by contaminated water. Eat only steaming hot food that has been cooked all the way through in clean establishments. Avoid raw lettuce and fruit that cannot be peeled, like strawberries. Vegetables are usually safer than meat. Some supermarkets stock vegetable wash and this can be a good way to ensure clean fruit and vegetables if you are cooking your own meals. Make sure any milk you drink has been boiled. Avoid ice cream that could have melted and been refrozen, such as anything for sale in the street. Use purified water. You can filter or boil it, or use Aguasafe purifying drops, which are available at pharmacies.

If you do get diarrhea, it is best to let it run its course while staying hydrated with clear soups, lemon tea, a Gatorade-type drink and soda that has gone flat. Bananas are also a good source of potassium and help stop diarrhea. Coconut milk can also prove an effective remedy. You can make a rehydration fluid by mixing a half-teaspoon of salt and four tablespoons of sugar to a liter of boiled or purified water. If you need to travel and can't afford to let the illness run its course, any pharmacy will give

you something that will make you comfortable enough for a bus trip. If the diarrhea persists for more than five days, see a doctor.

MAJOR HEALTH PROBLEMS

AIDS (SIDA)

As in many parts of the world, AIDS infections are increasing. The virus, HIV, is transmitted through injection by unsterilized needles previously used by a HIV sufferer and, increasingly, via unprotected sex. Contrary to popular belief, HIV in Colombia is more commonly transmitted by heterosexuals rather than homosexuals. It is worth avoiding the likes of acupuncture and tattooing unless certain of the location's hygiene standards and safety. You should always practice safe sex. The HIV infection does not always trigger an automatic illness and only can be confirmed by a blood test.

Cholera

Although the risks of cholera in Colombia are small and vaccinations are generally not necessary for international travel, there are some precautionary measures that can be taken to avoid contracting this potentially fatal disease. As cholera is an intestinal disease contracted from contaminated food or water, it is advisable to undertake similar precautions to those relating to diarrhea. Cholera triggers vomiting and a watery, rice-textured diarrhea that can lead to severe dehydration. If you contract it seek immediate medical attention.

Dengue Fever

At times, Colombia experiences outbreaks of dengue fever, especially along the northern coast. Dengue fever is a mosquito-transmitted, viral infection that is most common in densely populated urban areas. The best prevention is avoiding insect bites (see box article, "Don't Get Bitten!").The symptoms, which appear seven to 10 days after exposure, are similar to a severe flu: intense joint and muscle pains, fever, vomiting and headaches. Often a rash follows. There is no immediate cure for dengue fever and, as well as taking plenty of fluids and non-aspirin pain killer (acetaminophen or paracetamol), medical assistance should be sought in the unlikely eventuality that you contract the hemorrhagic form of the disease.

Hepatitis

It is advisable to be vaccinated against hepatitis A and B. A vaccine covering both types is good for 10 years. Hepatitis A is typically passed through food; Hepatitis B, through dirty needles or sexual encounters. Avoid situations where you could be subject to being exposed. Needless to say, it is a good idea to stay away from any sort of questionable injection and to not get a piercing while traveling, especially at the popular outdoor markets.

Malaria

Most doctors around the world will tell you that if you travel anywhere in Colombia, you must take pills to prevent malaria. This is not true, as there are parts of Colombia where malaria is not present. If you are only traveling above 2,500 meters (8,200 ft), where mosquitoes do not thrive, you do not need to take preventative medicine. However, if you plan to spend time along the eastern Llanos, Colombia's coastline, inland river valleys or in Amazonia, it is a good idea to take the proper measures to prevent the disease.

To prevent getting bitten, see the box article, "Don't Get Bitten!" You are advised to consult a physician prior to travel, as various malarial medicines are available. Depending on the type of medication you take, you will begin it a few days or a few weeks before entering a malarial area, and continue taking it two to six weeks after leaving. Pregnant women and children are particularly vulnerable to malaria and should be vigilant with their preventative regime.

Malaria is caused by a parasite. The general initial symptoms of malaria are high fever, shivering, sweats, headaches, body pains and possible diarrhea or vomiting. It can lead to death. If you are or were in a malaria area and start to have these symptoms, get to a medical facility quickly. Time is of the essence for successful treatment.

Pulmonary Edema

Associated with a rapid climb in altitude and a severe deterioration of altitude sickness, some people can suffer from the potentially fatal pulmonary edema. As well as those associated with altitude sickness, symptoms of pulmonary edema can be a persistent cough, bloody phlegm, wheezing, a sensation of drowning and blue or bruised lips. The illness can also trigger a loss of orientation and hallucinations. An assisted descent in altitude is essential to avoid the intensification of these conditions and possible death.

Rabies

There are stray dogs throughout Colombia that are usually harmless. Avoid all dogs that are behaving strangely. Some home-owners train guard dogs to attack trespassers. On long hikes

Don't Get Bitten!

Avoidance of mosquito bites is the key to preventing dengue and malaria. Unfortunately, the mosquitoes that carry these diseases are active at different times of the day: the Aedes aegypti, which transmits dengue, from dusk to dawn, and the Anopheles, which carries malaria, from dusk to dawn. This means mosquito bite prevention is a 24-hour job. Use DEET-based mosquito repellent (avoid contact with plastics) and wear long, loose garments. Avoid dark colors, shiny jewelry and scented soaps or perfumes, as these attract mosquitoes. Look for lodging that is away from standing pools of water, and that provides screens on doors and windows, or a mosquito net on the bed (or tote your own, preferably permethrin-treated). Burn mosquito coils in your room. Additionally, mosquitoes do not, as a rule, like moving air, so sleep with a fan blowing on you. Do not scratch the bite; this can lead to infection in tropical climes. Updated: Sep 21, 2011.

in rural areas, always carry a walking attack. In the Llanos and Amazonia regions ensure you are covered at night, especially on the feet, as some vampire bats can bite. In case you are bitten by a dog or a wild animal, clean the wound thoroughly and seek immediate medical consultation. If required, rabies vaccinations are readily available in most major cities. Try to identify the animal or its owner and inform the relevant authorities. If you are planning to visit particularly isolated areas or will be working in a field that involves contact with animals, it is advisable to consult a doctor about having the rabies vaccination prior to travel.

Typhoid

This is transmitted by infected food or drink. An oral capsule or injection should be taken before travel if you are planning to travel in Colombia or South America for an extended period of time (six months or more). The injection needs booster every three years.

Water Hazards

Before swimming in local waters you should always enquire about their safety. Be extremely careful about swimming in piranha or caribe infested rivers. Do not swim naked as some waters are populated by candirú fish that trace urine currents and can enter bodily orifices. When bathing, wear sandals as some tropical fish eject venom if trodden on.

INTRO & INFO

Yellow Fever

There is a risk of this mosquito-borne disease, especially in the jungle. Talk to your doctor before taking the vaccine, as it is not recommended for people with certain allergies (including to eggs), pregnant women, children under nine months and other special cases. The vaccine lasts for 10 years and has minimal, if any, side effects. When vaccinated, you will be given a Certificate of Yellow Fever Vaccination that should be carried with you. Visits to some places in Colombia and South America may ask for it.

HOSPITALS AND PHARMACIES

Major Colombian cities have adequate general and pediatric hospitals. Rural areas have only basic medical facilities. In Bogotá, many travelers choose to go to the **Fundación Santa Fe de Bogotá** (Ca. 119, 9-33. Tel: 1-603-0303.) Another good option in the capital is the **Clínica Del Country** (Cra. 16, 82-57. Tel: 1-530-0470/530-1270. URL: www. clinicadelcountry.com).

Several well-equipped hospitals are on the Caribbean coast. In Cartagena are **Hospital Bocagrande** (Cra. 6 and Ca. 5, Bocagrande. Tel: 5-665-5270) and **Hospital Naval** (Cra. 2, 14-10, Bocagrande. Tel: 5-655-5759.) In Barranquilla, they are **Clínica del Caribe** (Ca. 80, 49C-65. Tel: 5-356-4861, URL: www.clinicadelcaribe. com), **Clínica La Asunción** (Ca. 70B, 41-93. Tel: 5-368-1148, URL: www.clinicalaasuncion.com) and **Clínica Bautista** (Cra. 38, 71-10. Tel: 5-360-2200, URL: www.clinicabautista.org). **AMI** (Asistencia Medica Inmediata; URL: www. amisap.dioestudio.com), a medical service in Barranquilla and Cartagena, provides ambulance service, 24-hour house calls, pharmacy service and blood work.

Should a life-threatening medical problem arise, you may have to be evacuated to a country with more developed facilities. Check with your health insurance provider to make sure you are covered should this occur.

Pharmacy chains recommended by the U.S. embassy in Bogotá include Cafam, Colsubsidio, Olímpica and Sideral; most of these are connected to major supermarkets and all offer delivery service. Often many pharmacies are near hospitals, as well. In some parts of Colombia, pharmacies follow the de turno system, in which one is assigned to be open for off-hour emergencies.

It is important to note that while "medical tourism" has become increasingly popular in Colombia, (particularly elective, aesthetic surgeries) these operations are inherently dangerous. Should you choose to undergo this kind of procedure in Colombia, be sure to thoroughly investigate the facilities and your surgeon beforehand. Updated: Sep 22, 2011.

Safety

The security situation in the country is generally safe. However, there are areas where it is more "fluid" and others that remain in the red zone of the nation's civil war. These include parts of the Pacific coast, Río Magdalena valley, Norte Santander, the Llanos and the interior (southern and eastern) jungles. We have, as much as possible, pointed these out in the text. At the time our correspondents went to places, it was safe to do so. If you are considering going off the beaten track or into one of the problematic zones, check the news and ask for local advice. Colombia is an earthquake-prone country. Also, its Pacific coast has experienced tsunamis; move to higher ground as fast as possible. In the event of these or other type of natural disaster, follow authorities' instructions.

In more mundane matters, here are a few suggestions for your personal safety:

Do not accept food, drink, cigarettes or other items from strangers, especially on buses. They may be drugged and you'll wake up days later without a memory or belongings. These drugs have no taste or smell, and are fine enough to be blown into your face. Also watch your drink in nightclubs, that it doesn't get drugged.

Do not carry a package for another person, as it might contain drugs. Be polite to any approaching police office. However, beware of police officers searching you and planting drugs. Get a trustworthy witness, especially if they raid your room. Such incidences have been reported on the Caribbean coast, San Andrés and other popular foreigner destinations. Ignore any offers of drugs in the street, as the "dealer" might be setting you up to be arrested.

There are no plainclothes cops in Colombia. Ignore any person coming up to you who claims to be one, and demands to see your passport and sufficient funds. Often the "cop" will ask the same of another "foreigner" (an accomplice). Another common ploy to relieve travelers of their belongings is to distract their attention: spritzing mustard, shampoo, excrement or other goo on the victim and offer to clean it up (while cleaning out pockets), or a soccer ball innocently hitting your leg.

Use locally produced shoulder bags so you blend in more, wearing the strap across the chest. Day and fanny packs attract thieves. In bus terminals and airports, keep a close eye on your baggage, especially at holiday times. Always keep an arm or leg through the strap. Arrive to your destination during daylight.

Make a photocopy of the front (information) page of your passport to carry with you around town and to use when buying bus tickets. This will save headaches in having to spell your "weird" name to the ticket seller, and you won't have to dig out your valuable document in public. Also scan the information pages of your passport and e-mail them to yourself. This can help speed a replacement if your passport gets lost or stolen.

Wear a money belt under your beltline, with the opening against your skin. Preferably use one with two compartments (one for passport, credit cards, etc.; the other for cash, travelers checks) to more evenly distribute the bulk across your midriff. On trips through iffy parts of the country, distribute money around your body (in your shoe; in hidden pocket pinned or sewn into the inside of clothes; elastic bandage pouches used above the elbow or below the knee).

When day tripping, carry only what you need. Leave all valuables at your hotel. When depositing valuables in your accommodation's safe, make an inventory of your possessions. Leave one copy with what you're depositing and keep another copy for yourself. Check the contents when you pick the items back up. Updated: May 03, 2011.

Etiquette and Dress

Colombia is an extremely courteous country. When addressing strangers, a Colombian calls someone *primo(a)* (cousin) or *vecino(a)* (neighbor). In the countryside, a high form of respect you can show to a campesino is to call him Don or her Doña. To address someone with these titles is considered a bit old-fashioned in the cities, where you should stick with Señor and Señora. In eastern Colombia, particularly Boyacá Department, the very formal su merced is used instead of usted. In greeting people, men shake hands with men, and women receive barely a kiss on the right cheek.

Dress in Colombia is conservative, with plain, simple lines. For business encounters, men should wear suits with tie; women can wear a dress, skirt or pants. The key for both genders is well-tailored, well-pressed clothing. Even on the Caribbean coast, fashions are a bit conservative, with the guayabera (short-sleeve shirt) being considered almost formal. Updated: Jul 11, 2008.

Officialdom and Business

Colombia has a very business-oriented society. Arrive to appointments on time, even though the other party may not. When dealing with public officials, be courteous. Usually they are patient—if you are. When going to an office, greet the person from the doorway. It is considered rude to enter uninvited.

Although such occurrences are rarer than in the recent past, when stopped by the military on the highways, remember these recruits are only doing their job. Usually only men are asked to step off the bus. Women stay on board. However, documents of all passengers are checked. Men may be patted down, in the search for weapons. Updated: Sep 9, 2011.

Travel Tips for Specific Groups

WOMEN TRAVELERS

Colombia is a good country for the lone woman traveler. They are hassled less here by the stereotypical Latino whistling and cat-calling. However, if you do experience any such treatment, the best course of action is to ignore it and carry on walking. You may be considered a bit of an oddity, though, as most Colombians of either gender travel in groups. If it makes you feel more comfortable, use the old ploys: say your partner is near-by, carry a photo of your "partner," wear a wedding ring or travel with a companion. Wearing a cross or Star of David (which many Christians wear) does wonders to change people's attitudes, as well, as they seem to believe you are a "good girl." Birth control and tampons (expensive) are difficult to buy outside the major cities, so stock up before you leave.

GLBT TRAVELERS

Colombia has one of the more accepting scenes for gays and lesbians—at least legally. In 2007 the National Legislature passed a law guaranteeing equal rights for same-sex couples in issues of finances, insurance and inheritance. It is estimated that 300,000 same-sex couples live in this country. This having been said, society in general is yet a bit up-tight about the open expressions of love. The large cities, like Bogotá, Cali and Medellín, and

INTRO & INFO

Caribbean port towns have quite large GLBT communities that celebrate annual Gay Pride Day. A source of information about gay-friendly businesses is: www.guiagaycolombia.com.

SENIOR TRAVELERS

As Colombia becomes safer, more retirees are heading to this country to explore the jungle, trek to Ciudad Perdida or just relax on the beach. Senior citizens—those of the tercera edad or "third age," as they say in Colombia—will find Colombia to be quite enjoyable. Discounts on everything from bus fares to museum entries are given to those over 65 years (and in some places, even younger). As in Latin cultures, much respect is shown to older adults.

DISABLED TRAVELERS

Travel for disabled persons is a mixed bag in Colombia. Much understanding is lent to these travelers, as quite a high percentage of the nation's population is disabled, due to land mines and other incidences of the civil war. However, the infrastructure is not quite designed for persons with disabilities. Newer constructions and more upscale businesses are trying to be more conscious of this population's special needs. If you are sojourning in a wheelchair, keep an upbeat attitude. Travel with a companion who can help you get over that doorstep or wherever you might need a hand. Phone hotels and restaurants beforehand to inquire about their accessibility.

TRAVELING WITH CHILDREN

Because families are the center of Colombian society, you will find you receive different—if not better—treatment when traveling with children. When Colombians travel, the whole family goes. It is common that mid-range and above hotels have a kiddies pool, playground or other special amenities for the children. Some of the more upscale inns even have suites with a bedding area just for the young ones. Often the Banco de la República cultural centers have story hour or other programs for kids. On buses, fares for children are cheaper if they ride in a parent's lap. At hotels, ask about the children's rate or bargain for one. It is acceptable to share a meal with a young one. Teach your kids to say simple niceties like gracias and por favor. Updated: Sep 22, 2011.

Tips for Budget Travelers

Colombia is a "swing" country for travelers spending six months to two years traveling in the Americas, northward from Argentina to Mexico or southward. Many will be flying out of an expensive country like the U.S., Mexico,

Chile or Brazil. Here are some tips to help you experience Colombia more economically.

LODGING

Cheaper hostels include hospedajes and residencias, often located near the markets. Skip the extras, like private bath, air conditioning and TV. If staying for more than a few nights, ask about a possible discount. Room prices are generally cheaper per person for couples than for the solo traveler. Camp or sleep in hammocks wherever offered. A new option that many budget travelers of all ages and professions are using is couch surfing (URL: www.couchsurfing.com), home stays that allow you a glimpse into daily life.

FOOD AND DRINK

Breakfast is a poor-value meal; fix it in. Inexpensive meals are the comida corriente, or set meal available at lunch and dinner, and those found in the comedor section of the public market. Buy a portable heating element to warm water for tea or coffee. Look for hostels that have cooking facilities. Purify your own water by filter or drops (some pharmacies sell Aquasafe).

Going out to Colombian nightclubs is almost prohibitively expensive for the shoestring traveler. Consider that often the cover charge alone is about $10, plus your drinks on top of it. Save such activities for a special occasion. Buying beer at the store is relatively cheap; wine is quite pricey.

TRANSPORTATION

Journeying long legs is cheaper than short ones in Colombia. Outside the high season, ask for a discount ("No sería posible un descuentico?"). Couples report success hitchhiking, though remember that this is not without its risks.

ACTIVITIES

Many museums and archaeological sites in Colombia are free. Discounts are frequently given to those with an ISIC card, and often with your university's own ID. Children and seniors get substantial reductions. For free entertainment, check out exhibits, concerts, movies and other events at cultural centers or universities. Some active sports are absolutely free, like swimming, snorkeling and hiking the numerous old stone roads that lace the Colombian countryside.

GENERAL

Avoid prime Colombian destinations during holidays, when prices for lodging and food at least double, and in some places up to quadruple. Limit travel at these times, also. Although it may seem tedious, keep a daily accounting of your expenses. You can then see how you are spending your money, and know where to cut back if you find you are overspending. An additional advantage to this is you will always have handy the figures of hotels and transport to pass along to other travelers. Updated: Sep 13, 2011.

Information Resources

These Information Resources will help you keep a pulse on what is happening in Colombia. For Media and Online resources, see Media in Colombia.

GOVERNMENT PAGES

Colombia—www.gobiernoenlinea.gov.co

Ministerio de Relaciones Exteriores—www.cancilleria.gov.co (addresses of embassies and consulates)

Ejército Nacional, Republica de Colombia—www.ejercito.mil.co

British Embassy—www.ukincolombia.fco.gov.uk

Canadian Embassy—www.canadainternational.gc.ca

U.S. Embassy (Bogotá)—bogota.usembassy.gov

FACTIONS

Autodefensas Unidas de Colombia (AUC)—no longer maintains a website; officially disbanded

Ejército de Liberación Nacional de Colombia (ELN)—www.nodo50.org/patrialibre

Fuerzas Armadas Revolucionarias de Colombia (FARC)—www.resistencia-colombia.org

TOURISM

Colombia.com—www.colombia.com

Fondo de Promoción Turístico Colombia — www. fondodepromocionturistica.com

Instituto Colombiano de Arqueología e Historia—www.icanh.gov.co

Instituto Geográfico Agustín Codazzi—www.igac.gov.co

Instituto Nacional de Vías—www.invias.gov.co (road conditions, maps, etc.)

Parques Nacionales—www.parquesnacionales.gov.co

BLOGS AND OTHER SITES

Colombian Paradise—www.colombian-paradise.com

Couch Surfing—www.couchsurfing.com (homestays)

Gringo (in Hebrew)—www.gringo.co.il/country_page.asp?countryID=9

Hospitality Club—www.hospitalityclub.org (homestays)

Mochileros.org—www.mochileros.org

Paisa Tours Colombia Travel Guides — www.paisatours.com

Plan B Bogotá—www.planb.com.co

Platypus—www.platypusbogota.com

Poor But Happy—www.poorbuthappy.com/colombia

Third World Traveler—www.thirdworldtraveler.com

HUMAN RIGHTS ORGANIZATIONS AND OTHER NGOS

Amnesty International (International)— www.amnesty.org

Amnesty International (U.S.)—www.amnestyusa.org

CODHES (Consultoria para los Derechos Humanos y el Desplazamiento)—www.codhes.org

Fellowship of Reconciliation—www.forcolombia.org

Global Exchange—www.globalexchange.org

Human Rights Watch—www.hrw.org
Peace Brigades International—www.pbi-colombia.org/pbi-colombia.html

Refugees International—www.refugeesinternational.org

United Nations High Commission on Refugees—www.unhcr.org

Witness for Peace—www.witnessforpeace.org

INDIGENOUS RIGHTS

Colombia Indígena—http://colombiaindigena.blogspot.com

Cultural Survival—www.culturalsurvival.org

Indigenous Environmental Network—www.ienearth.org

NotiWayúu—www.notiwayuu.blogspot.com

Organización Nacional Indígena de Colombia—www.onic.org.co

Survival—www.survival-international.org

Updated: Sep 02, 2011.

Colombia Bibliography

If you cannot find these books at your local vendor or for purchase on-line, ask your public library if you can obtain them through interlibrary loan (there may be a small fee for this service). This is just a sample of books about Colombia; please write us with more of your suggestions.

HISTORY AND POLITICS

Betancourt, Ingrid. *Until Death Do Us Part: My Struggle to Reclaim Colombia* (Ecco, 2002)—The former presidential candidate's memoir about fighting against the drug cartels and corruption in her country.

Betancourt, Ingrid. *Even Silence Has an End.* (Penguin Press, 2010)—Betancourt's recounting of six years as a FARC hostage. Others that were released at the same time have penned books of their experiences: Clara Rojas, *Captivity* (Atria, 2010); and Marc Gonsalves and the other U.S. contractors, *Out of Captivity* (Harper, 2010).

Borden, Mark. *Killing Pablo: The Hunt for the World's Greatest Outlaw* (Atlantic Monthly Press, 2001)—The rise and fall of Pablo Escobar.

Braun, Herbert. *The Assassination of Gaitan: Public Life and Urban Violence in Colombia* (University of Wisconsin Press, 1986)—How the assassination of presidential candidate Jorge Eliecer Gaitán affected the course of Colombian history.

Broderick, Walter. *Camilo Torres: A Biography of the Priest Guerrillero* (Doubleday, 1975)—A biography of the priest-turned-guerrilla-fighter Camilo Torres.

Bushnell, David. *The Making of Modern Colombia: A Nation in Spite of Itself* (University of California Press, 1993)—The first book on Colombian history published in English.

Gaitán, Jorge Eliecer. *1928 La masacre en las bananeras* (Editorial Cometa de Papel, 1997)—Gaitán's presentation of eyewitness reports of the 1928 banana worker massacre in Ciénaga.

Lynch, John. *Simón Bolívar: A Life* (Yale University Press, 2006)—The first biography in English of the Great Liberator in over 50 years.

Safford, Frank and Palacios, Marco. *Colombia: Fragmented Land, Divided Society* (Oxford University Press, 2001)—Colombian history and culture from before Columbus to the modern day.

Toledo, Rebecca, et al. *War in Colombia: Made in USA* (International Action Center, 2003)—A collection of essays by US and Latin American analysts, examining the US' role in Colombia's civil war.

Vallejo, Virginia. *Loving Pablo, Hating Escobar* (Random House, 2008)—A book by a TV journalist who also was the coke kingpin's lover.

SOCIAL AND ENVIRONMENTAL ISSUES

MacNeil, Suzanne. "Reflections on Mining in Colombia: When 'Development' Creates Deprivation," Colombia Journal Online, August 13, 2007 (www.colombiajournal.org/colombia262.htm)

Molano, Lafredo. *The Dispossessed: Chronicles of the Desterrados of Colombia* (Haymarket Books, 2005)—Testimonies from internal refugees of Colombia's civil war.

Murillo, Mario. *Colombia and the United States: War, Terrorism and Destabilization* (Seven Stories Press, 2003)—The effects on Colombian civilians of the U.S. War on Drugs.

Reuters Alert Net. *Colombia Displacement*—An excellent series of articles with about the effects of the War on Drugs, narcotrafficking and refugees (www.alertnet.org/printable.htm?URL=/db/crisisprofiles/CO_DIS.htm)

Weisman, Alan. *Gaviotas: A Village to Re-invent the World* (Chelsea Green Publishing, 2008)—About the alternative, sustainable community deep in Colombia's Llanos.

LITERATURE

García Márquez, Gabriel—Nobel-prize winner Gabo is more well-known for his novels and short stories, like *A Hundred Years of Solitude and Love in the Time of Cholera*. But he began his career as a journalist. The only book available in English is *News of a Kidnapping* (*Noticia de un secuestro*). If you read Spanish, other titles include *Cuando era feliz e indocumentado* and *Crónicos y reportajes*.

Isaacs, Jorge. *María.*—A piece of classic Colombian literature.

Olivella, Manuel Zapata. *Chambacu: Black Slum* (Latin American Literary Review Press, 1989), *A Saint is Born In Chima* (University of Texas Press, 1991) and *Changó, the Biggest Badass* (Texas Tech University Press, 2010)—Zapata Olivella was one of the most important Afro-Colombian writers and ethnographers.

Restrepo, Laura. *Delirium* (Vintage, 2008) and *Leopard in the Sun* (Vintage, 2000)—These are just of the many two works by this prolific, post-Boom Generation novelist. Several of her books are published in bilingual editions.

Vallejo, Fernando. *Our Lady of the Assassins* (Serpent's Tail, 2001)—The novel upon which the movie was based.

TRAVELOGUES AND JOURNALISM

Balf, Todd. *The Darkest Jungle: The True Story of the Darién Expedition and America's Ill-fated Race to Connect the Seas* (Crown Publishers, 2003)—About the 1850s US Darien Exploring Expedition that explored the Darien Gap looking for a suitable place to build a canal.

Dudley, Steven S. *Walking Ghosts: Murder and Guerrilla Politics in Colombia* (Routledge, 2004)—Chronicles based on Dudley's five years reporting from Colombia for National Public Radio.

Egan, Andrew Niall. *Crossing the Darien Gap* (Adventura, 2008)—A Canadian's journey through the famed Gap when he was a teen.

Ereira, Alan. *Heart of the World: The Elder Brothers* (Knopf, 1992)—About the Kogui beliefs and way of life deep in the Sierra Nevada de Santa Marta.

Guillermoprieto, Alma. *The Heart that Bleeds: Latin America Now* (Knopf, 1994) and Looking for History: Dispatches from Latin America (Vintage Books, 2002)—A collection of this Mexican journalist's articles for the New Yorker magazine.

Howe, Jason P. *Colombia: Between the Lines* (Cheshire, UK: Conflict Pics, 2008)—A photographic journey in the Red Zone.

Nicholl, Charles. *The Fruit Palace: An Odyssey through Colombia's Cocaine Underground* (Saint Martin's Press, 1986)—A gripping travelogue into the world of cocaine, from cultivation to smuggling.

NATURE GUIDES

Gentry Alwyn H., and Vasquez, Rodolfo. *A Field Guide to the Families and Genera of Woody Plants of Northwest South America* (University Of Chicago Press, 1996).

McMullen, Miles; Donegan, Thomas M.; Quevedo, Alonso. *Field Guide to the Birds of Colombia* (Colombia: ProAves, 2010; www.proaves.org).

Restall, Robin; Rodner, Clemencia; Lentino, Miguel. *Birds of Northern South America* (Yale University Press, 2007)—One of the highest regarded bird guides for Colombia, in two volumes.

FOR CHILDREN

DuBois, Jill. *Colombia* (Marshall Cavendish, 2002)—A primer on Colombia.

Montgomery, Sy. *Encantado: Pink Dolphin of the Amazon* (Houghton Mifflin, 2002)—An invitation to learn about the magic and diversity of Colombia's Amazon.

Rawlins, Carol. *The Orinoco River* (Franklin Watts, 1999)—Getting to know the second greatest river of South America, the Orinoco. Spengler, Kremena. *Colombia: A Question and Answer Book* (Capstone Press, 2006)—An introduction to Colombia's history, geography and culture. Updated: Sep 22, 2011.

)))))

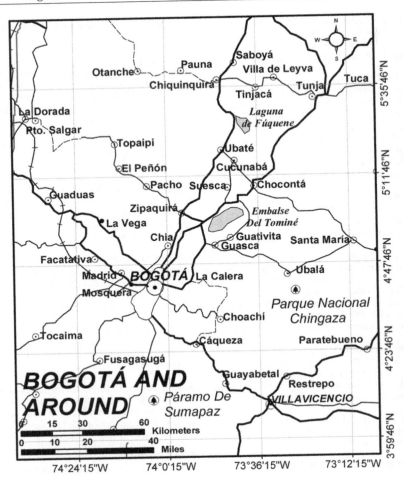

Bogotá

| 🏔 2,600m | 🧍 7,457,000 | 📞 1 |

In many ways Bogotá epitomizes the Latin American city, with its mix of crumbling colonial architecture and modern office blocks, vast divide between the rich and poor, and soaring population. It is both highly cosmopolitan and, in some regards, stuck in the past. With much to attract the artist, the historian, the pleasure-seeker and even perhaps the naturalist, Bogotá has become a big destination for world travelers, though it is so markedly different from other Colombian cities.

Located in the center of Colombia atop an Andean plateau, Bogotá is flanked by the Cordillera Oriente to the east and smaller mountain ranges to the west. With an altitude of 2,600 meters (8,530 ft) above sea level, the capital takes third place for highest major city in the world. Travelers will find that, much like Medellín, Bogotá has recently undergone a serious makeover: with massive investments in reviving public spaces, expanding infrastructure and improving social services, the Colombian capital now thrives as a case study of urban transformation in South America. In due time, its reputation will catch up. However, crime is still prevalent and visitors should be alert around tourist areas and government buildings.

The colonial part of Bogotá is alternately called La Candelaria and Centro Histórico. This area provides travelers with a pleasant sense of history and a great selection of cafés, theatres and museums. Considered by many to be the intellectual and cultural center of Bogotá, La Candelaria is a must-see district. A strong university presence here results in low prices and a prevalent bohemian culture.

In contrast to the historic La Candelaria, in the north of Bogotá (which comprises the neighborhoods of Centro Internacional/La Macarena, Chapinero, Zona Rosa, Parque de la 93, and Usaquén), a far more modern, commercial atmosphere presides. Luxury hotels, glitzy apartments and swanky shopping malls, like the Hacienda Santa Bárbara in Usaquén, are the norm. The Museo de "El Chicó" Mercedes de Pérez (formerly the Hacienda de El Chicó) offers an expansive collection of 18th century art.

Day trips outside of the city are also popular due to Bogotá's central location. Restless travelers can stretch their legs as they explore the surrounding landscape. The cliffs of Suesca offer world-class rock climbing, while short journeys to La guna de Guativa provide great views of the Cundinamarca countryside.

Highlights

Visit the **Jardín Botánico**—Botanical Garden—(p. 86) for a tranquil escape from the hustle and bustle of downtown Bogotá.

Stroll through the exhibitions of the **Gold Museum** and discover the history behind the famous myth of El Dorado (p. 84).

Become part of the lively atmosphere in the cafés of **La Candelaria** (p. 92).

Bike through the streets of Bogotá on the **Ciclovía** (p. 86).

Take a ride to the stunning **Cerro de Monserrate** (p. 94) for a spectacular view of the city.

Explore the life and art of this Colombian literary legend at the **Centro Cultural Gabriel García Márquez** (p. 94).

History

Bogotá, originally Bacatá, was the capital city of one of the region's most advanced pre-Columbian civilizations, the Muisca. Spanish conquistador Gonzalo Jiménez de Quesada reached Bacatá in the 16th century. Struck by its location near several rivers and the allure of rumored gold–the Muisca were master goldsmiths–Quesada attacked, defeating the tribe and re-christening the location Santa Fe de Bogotá.

With the flow of riches moving from present-day Ecuador and Peru up through Colombia, Bogotá grew rapidly as an important administrative center. In 1740 the city was declared the capital of the Viceroyalty of New Granada, an area that includes present-day Colombia, Venezuela, Ecuador and Panama. In the following years, Bogotá first welcomed the arrival of South America's Liberator Simón Bolívar, then reportedly shunned him from the city limits. The city came to be defined by its remarkable and ornate Republican architecture, which can be observed in and around the Plaza de Bolívar.

Despite considerable growth, Bogotá still only had a population of about 100,000 at the turn of the 20th century. It wasn't until the middle of the century that, in a drive to industrialize, the city began to thrive.

In a turn of events that has resulted in the socially fractured Colombia we know today, Liberal leader Jorge Eliécer Gaitán was assassinated on April 9, 1948, in Bogotá. What ensued is known as the Bogotazo, a period of mayhem when the city was under attack from within. A tenuously organized mob took control, sacking and burning churches, public offices and buildings and killing thousands. Since, Bogotá has been regaining its confidence and evolving into a vibrant capital city. Updated: Feb 26, 2008.

When to Go

Often referred to, by its many polite and well-educated citizens, as the "Athens of South America," Bogotá virtually always has culturally stimulating events to enjoy. Check local listings, bill stickers on the walls of La Candelaria or the directories in the newspaper, El Tiempo (URL: www.eltiempo.com), for continuously updated event listings.

Given the city's altitude and location on the *altiplano* (high plain), it should come as no surprise that the average temperature

BOGOTÁ

BOGOTÁ

in Bogotá is roughly 13°C (55°F). It can drop to a low of 6°C (42°F) on chilly evenings, and on some occasions has been known to reach a high of around 19°C (66°F). Be warned that it rains a good deal in Bogotá. Updated: Feb 26, 2008.

Major cultural events are listed below. Those that are "in the park" are in the Parque Central Simón Bolívar, while the rest are celebrated across the city unless otherwise noted. Updated: Mar 07, 2011.

Month	Event
January	Arrival of the Three Kings in the Barrio Egipto
February	Bullfighting season starts
March/ April	Iberoamerican Theater Festival (2008 and every other year)
April	Feria del Libro (Corferías)
August	Summer Festival, Bogotá's Birthday, Salsa in the Park
September	Jazz in the Park
October	Bogotá Film Festival, Rock in the Park
November	Opera in the Park
December	Christmas Lights Festival

Getting To and Away
BY AIR
International and internal flights with **Aeropública** leave from and arrive at the Aeropuerto El Dorado (Av. El Dorado, 93-30. Tel: 425-1000). A newer terminal has been built about a half-mile from El Dorado and is called the Aeropuente; only domestic flights with Avianca leave from here. When traveling by taxi, the driver will ask you to specify which airport, El Dorado or the Aeropuente. The major domestic airlines have offices in Bogotá: **Avianca** (Ca. 19, 4-37. Tel: 401-3434; also Cra. 10, 26-53. Tel: 342-607; airport 425-1000, URL: www.avianca.com), **Aires** (Cra. 15, 100-654. Tel: 294-0300 (reservations)/413-9473 (airport), URL: www.aires.aero), **Satena** (Cra. 10, 26-21, 1st floor. Tel: 423-8500/605-2222 (airport), URL: www.satena.gov.co). For information about getting to and from the airport, see "Getting Around Bogotá: By Taxi".

BY BUS
The Terminal de Transporte (Diagonal 23, 69-60. Tel: 416-3951. URL: www.terminaldetransporte.gov.co) is the main hub for land travel to destinations across the country. The terminal is divided into five color-coded modules, according to destinations: 1/yellow—south; 2/blue—east,west; 3/red— north; 4/green—interdepartmental taxis; 5/purple—arrivals. A tourism office is in Módulo 5. For bus travel to closer destinations such as Zipaquirá, Guatavita, Suesca and Villa de Leyva, take the Transmilenio to the northernmost station (Portal del Norte) and then catch a small interurban bus. Bear in mind that you can negotiate bus fares in Colombia. Do not accept the first rate offered.

BY TRAIN
The Turistren, which runs its course to Zipaquirá and the surrounding area, leaves from the Sabana Station only on Saturdays, Sundays and holidays. This is not a regular transport train but a tourist activity. (Ca. 13, 18-24, Estación de la Sabana. Tel: 375-0558). More information can be found on the website, URL: www.turistren.com.co. Updated: Mar 07, 2011.

Getting Around
At first glance, Bogotá's city layout seems unruly and disorderly, but it is actually pretty easy to negotiate. The most important thing to remember is that streets labeled as "Avenida" and "Carrera" run North and South and those labeled as "Calle" run East and West. Understand also that the mountains in Bogotá are at the extreme eastern edge of the city and that the major thoroughfares are Carrera 7 and Carrera 10.

Note: Eight years ago, beginning on the north side of the city, Bogotá began changing its numbering of Calles and Carreras. However, this has been a slow process. Some parts of the city already have changed names, and others (like La Candelaria) are just now being affected. Where possible, we include both the old address, and the new (in parantheses)." Keep in mind that taxi drivers tend to use the old addresses.

There are three ways to get around the city: taxi, regular city bus, and Transmilenio (a rapid-transit bus system).

BOGOTÁ

BY TAXI

Taxis are inexpensive and abundant throughout the city. Late at night try to catch an official taxi to avoid being cheated. Taxis should have the license number printed on the side and roof of the vehicle, and drivers should also display identification (the photo should match the driver, of course; men without credentials sometimes pay cabbies for use of registered cabs). All taxis run on meters, which should comply with a rate chart visible to the passenger. Fares after 8 p.m., on public holidays and Sundays, and to and from the airport include special surcharges. One recommended taxi company is **Taxis Express** (411-1111).

From the airport, you can either wait in the queue for an airport-sponsored (and therefore more secure) taxi, or you can cross the two small streets in front of the airport to where the "regular" taxis (which will charge a few dollars less) line up.

A cab from the Candelaria neighborhood to the bus terminal costs about $7, and to the airport $11-12. Taxis are scarce at rush hours and when it's raining.

BY BUS

Bogotás Transmilenio rapid transit bus system has made travel in Bogotá less stressful. The ordinary city buses, however, can also be a great asset to travelers. Careening around street corners and racing to make the green light are part of standard operating procedure for drivers of Bogotá's aging bus fleet. The bus' destination is indicated by a sign in its front window, and the fare is normally in the region of $0.60. If you are in doubt about anything ask a fellow traveler. Buses tend to stop frequently, as needed, rather than only at conventional bus stops. To reach Candelaria from the Terminal de Transportes, catch the black "Germania" bus from outside Módulo 5.

Transmilenio

This fast, convenient bus system has been in operation since 2000. However, be prepared for stressful rides during peak hours, with delayed service and overcrowded buses (a boon for pickpockets). Also be warned that the Transmilenio maps are not particularly clear and often the buses are poorly labeled. Construction is underway to extend the service and add a route to the airport. Calle 19, Avenida Jiménez and other major thoroughfares are currently torn up from this project. Single fare is $0.90. Tel: 364-9400. Updated: March 22, 2011.

BY CAR

The following international car rental agencies have offices in Bogotá: **Budget** (Av. 15, 107-08. Tel: 612-5807, E-mail: counter@budgetcolombia.com, URL: www.budgetcolombia.com), **Dollar** (Ca.

BOGOTÁ

Gay Bogotá

Although an amendment ensuring equal rights for gay citizens was passed in 1991, homophobia is still quite prevalent throughout the machista culture of Colombia–with the exception of Bogotá. Although most rural regions of the country maintain strictly traditional notions of gender and sexuality, Bogotá has developed a progressive gay culture that thrives in a variety of clubs, bars and social networks. The Colombian capital has come a long way in terms of tolerance and acceptance. In 1996, just 32 people participated in Colomia's first annual Gay Pride Parade; in 2008, the number was in the thousands. Participants mock Colombian machismo: men in bishop and soldier costumes stand alongside drag queens. Conservative Bogotanos continue to frown upon what they see as an indecent spectacle, but that has not stopped the movement from picking up momentum. Today, Bogotá is one of Latin America's leaders in the acceptance and celebration of LGBT culture.

Bogotá's gay scene is most vibrant in the north. The Chapinero district–affectionately nicknamed "gay ghetto," "gay hills" and "bodygay"–is home to a majority of the city's gay-friendly establishments. Dance clubs like **Theatron** (Ca. 58, 10-34. Tel: 1-249-2092, URL: www.theatrondepelicula.com) and **Lottus** (Ca. 58 10-42, piso 3) provide lively rumbas for the gay traveler within the Chapinero. Both have a cover charge of $7 that usually includes several drinks. Lottus is open to male patrons only. Outside of the Chapinero, **Cats** (Ca. 74, 15-51. Cel: 310-555-4699) and **Club G** (Cra. 17, 14-68 Sur. Tel: 278-3030) are also popular spots. For the high-end traveler looking to venture a bit outside the city, **El Closet Lounge** (Km 5, Via Calera. Tel: 520-7126, URL: www.elclosetbogota.com) is a luxurious club with a great view of Bogotá and a great sound system. These are only a few of Bogotá's many gay bars and clubs.

Bogotá also offers hotels geared toward homosexual guests. **High Park Hotel** (Cra. 4, 58-58. Tel: 753-7724) advertises itself as 100 percent gay and lesbian. Other lodging options include **Residencias Gays** (Cra. 15, 86a-42, Apt. 201. Cel: 315-613-3670) and **Green House** (Av. Caracas, 55-52. Tel: 346-0461).

Gay travelers will also find restaurants, gyms and tour agencies specifically geared toward LGBT patrons. For a complete listing of gay services, communities and entertainment in Bogotá, visit www.guiagaycolombia.com/bogota.

90, 11a-09, Tel: 691-4700, E-mail: dollar_col@hotmail.com, URL: www.dollar.com), **Hertz** (Cra. 11, 75-19, Tel: 210-1907), and **National** (Cra. 15, 93-47. Tel: 612-5635).

To decrease smog, Bogotá has a Pico y Placa system, limiting the days of circulation for private vehicles. Twice weekly license plates ending with designated numbers are not permitted on the road. The system is in effect Monday-Friday 6 a.m.-8 p.m. Updated: Mar 07, 2011.

Safety

Gone are the days when travelers to Bogotá were nervous to walk through La Candelaria even during the day and would hurry back to their accommodation at dusk. However, the Candelaria has seen an increase in assaults in recent years, especially by teenage gang members; as a result, police patrols have increased.

Begging is common, especially in La Candelaria, and tourists would be wise to not stray west of Carrera 10 in this area. Caution should be exercised as in other big cities. Be especially careful with your personal belongings on buses and on the Transmilenio. It is best to call for a cab at night. At the very least, always be sure you are taking only registered taxis with certified drivers. Also, beware of scams, such as "undercover police officers" who ask to see your passport. If you are the victim of any crime, you can report the incident to the Policía de Turismo (Hotel Tequendama, Cra. 13, 26-62. Tel: 337-4413/243-1175). Updated: Feb 26, 2008.

Services

TOURISM

In the southwest corner of the Plaza de Bolívar in the Candelaria there is a helpful Tourist Information office (Monday-Saturday 8

Religion in Bogotá

Although Bogotá traditionally has strong Catholic ties, other religious groups have been encouraged to lay down their roots. There are many Protestant sects represented here: the Baptists, Lutherans, Presbyterians, Methodists, Disciples of Christ and Menonites all have houses of worship.

Colombian Episcopalians and Anglicans have their own website to help orientate visitors (URL: www.iglesiaepiscopal.org.co). There is even an Orthodox church. For addresses of these temples, check the Páginas Amarillas under "Iglesias Bautistas." Bogotá has a Monthly Friends Meeting; for the most recent contact information see: URL: fwccworld.org/find_friends/index.php.

The capital's synagogue is **Bet Chabad** (Ca. 94, 9-52. Tel.: 635-8261/8251). For Islamic travelers there is **Centro Cultural Islámico** (Monday-Friday 9 a.m.-noon and 2-5 p.m. Diagonal 22B 43A-13, Tel: 335-0364, E-mail: centroculturalislamicocolombia@yahoo.com). Also, there are a number of Buddhist temples; for listings consult the wesbite: URL: www.budismo.cl/dir/colombia.html. Updated: March 22, 2011.

a.m.-6 p.m.; Sunday and holidays 10 a.m.-4 p.m. Cra. 8, Ca. 10, Palacio Liévano, 1st floor. Tel: 283-7115, E-mail: pitcentrohistorico@idt.gov.co, URL: www.turismobogota.gov.co). You can also find tourism offices at the Terminal de Transporte (Módulo 5. Tel: 295-4460), in the airport (413-9053), and at Transmilenio stops Las Aguas, Alcalá and Biblioteca Tintal. Additional resources include *Ciudad Viva*, the city's monthly publication of cultural events, and *The City Paper*, a monthly English-language newspaper (URL: www.thecitypaperbogota.com).

For tourism card/visa extensions, go to **DAS** (Monday-Thursday 7:30 a.m.-4 p.m., Friday 7:30 a.m.-3 p.m. Ca. 100, 11b-27, Edificio Platino. Tel: 595-3525).

MONEY

The Carrera 7 running north from the Plaza de Bolívar is the most convenient place to locate the banks and financial institutions that you might need. There are many ATH (A Toda Hora) ATM machines that work with every type of card. The main branches of major banks are: **HSBC** (Cra. 8, 15-46), **Bancolombia** (Cra. 8, 13-17; Cra. 10, 17-54)—exchanges American Express travelers checks, **Citicorp** (Cra. 13, 29-25), BBVA (Cra. 14, 19-71). There are a couple of well-policed ATMs close to the Museo del Oro. Additionally, several exchange houses can be found in the Emerald Trade Center (open Monday-Saturday until 6 p.m. Av Jiménex 5-43); some exchange Thomas Cook and American Express travelers checks. Others can be located on

Avenida Jiménez, between Carreras 5 and 6. Another reliable place is **Titan** (Cra. 7, 18-42, local 116). People often jostle for a position on street corners near the Avenida de Jiménez Transmilenio station offering to exchange money. Do not change money in the street. Go to one of the official offices nearby instead. **American Express** office is at Calle 85, 20-32 (Tel: 313-1146 /800-912-3054). Western Union is represented by **Palma Real** (Ca. 28, 13-22, local 28). **Money Gram** is at Calle 47, 9-53. Updated: May 24, 2011.

KEEPING IN TOUCH

In Bogotá, and in particular in the Candelaria, you have your pick of Internet cafés and telephone cabins. International calls can be made easily and cheaply, while an hour on the Internet should cost no more than $1. To mail a letter, go to the 4-72 post office (Monday-Friday 8 a.m.-5 p.m., Saturday 8 a.m.-noon. Cra. 8, 12A-03). Other Bogotá branches are listed at URL: www.4-72.com.co/seccion/oficinas. Updated: May 24, 2011.

MEDICAL

Pharmacies can be found on almost every block along the Carrera 7 and inside most major supermarket chains (Éxito, Carrulla and Carrefour). Recommended hospitals are **Fundación Santa Fe de Bogotá** (Ca. 116, 9-02, Tel: 629-0766) in Usaquén, **Clínica del Country** (Cra. 16, 82-57. Tel: 530-0470, URL: www.clinicadelcountry.com) in Zona Rosa. Yellow fever vaccinations are available at **Clínica Marly** (Monday-Friday 8 a.m.-6 p.m. Ca. 50, 9-67. Tel: 343-6680) in Chapinero for $30.

LAUNDRY

Most hotels will have a laundry service that you can use. However, for those in the Candelaria that don't, try **Lavaseco La Colonial** (Cra. 3, 13-88).

CAMERA REPAIR

Foto Almacén Buitrago is a second-floor shop (Monday-Friday 9 a.m.-2:30 p.m. Cra. 7, 21-65) that can assist with most camera needs. You can also seek camera repairs at Carrera 7, 22-31, local 231 (Tel: 286-3369). Updated: Mar 07, 2011.

SHOPPING

From the polished marble surfaces in the ultra-modern shopping malls in the north to the street markets in San Andresito, there are many shopping opportunities to take advantage of in Bogotá. Should you need hiking equipment, be lusting after new books in English, require repairs for your iPod or simply wish to pick up some local ground coffee and Colombian keepsakes, all can be found here in Bogotá with relative ease.

Centro Comercial el Andino

An incredibly popular shopping center in the heart of the Zona Rosa, Centro Comercial el Andino offers everything from quality clothing stores to designer sunglasses emporiums. What makes this mall a destination for visitors is its six-screen cinema and enormous food court. Just a few streets over, on Calle 81, is the **Atlantis Plaza**, another mall with more cinemas and similarly styled stores. Open 10 a.m. to 9 p.m. (Cra. 11, 82-71. Tel: 621-3111. URL: www.centroandino.co.com). Updated: Jun 11, 2009

Herencias de Artesanías

There is no doubt that you can find tourist trinkets and ground coffee cheaper in nearby galleries located close to the Museo del Oro, but if you have no time to bargain and need to buy high-quality and nicely packaged gifts, this place will meet your needs. The shop stocks good Colombian coffee and interestingly crafted artesanias. Ca. 16, 4-92. Tel: 243-0195, E-mail: herencias@herenciasdecolombia.com.

San Andresito

More a collection of warehouses than a store, San Andresito is spread over four or five square blocks and sells just about everything, from knock-off shoes and clothes to the latest consumer electronic devices. Cheap alcohol and DVDs abound. Negotiating is a necessity, and be sure to compare prices between stalls before making a final purchase. Be advised to watch your belongings here. Cra. 38, Ca. 6.

MacTools

For travelers toting Mac products, it is comforting to know that there is an Apple certified technician in Bogotá who can tend to any glitches. Of course, they also stock all the new software for Apple products. Ca. 90, 13-53. Tel: 622-3188, E-mail: camilovega@cable.net.co, URL: www.applemactools.com.

Hacienda Santa Bárbara

Yet another enormous shopping center in Bogotá, the Hacienda Santa Barbara is located in Usaquén in the north of the city. Part of the shopping mall is housed in what remains of a sprawling colonial building, which would have been a weekend retreat for a wealthy Bogotano in times past. The number of shops, cafés and eateries is astounding. Any trip to Usaquen should include a brief look through the Hacienda Santa Barbara. Cra. 7, 115-60. Tel: 612-0388.

Usaquén Flea Market

The Sunday flea market is close to the amenities of the Hacienda Santa Barbara and the delightful Usaquén plaza, surrounded by restaurants and charming cafés. Artists, designers and craftsmen display their wares here. T-shirts, shawls, carvings and other items are for sale here, prices negotiable. Ca. 119b.

Mercado de Pulgas San Alejo

This flea market occupies a parking lot near Museo Nacional on Sundays. Flea market enthusiasts can find some real steals here, or just while away a few hours sifting through antiques and trinkets. Cra. 7 and Ca. 24.

Emeralds

If you are keen on buying an emerald, head to legitimate shops located in the **Emerald Trade Center** (Av. Jiménex 5-43), on Carrera 6 between Calles 10 and 12. These dealers are licensed, and will give a certificate of authentication of the gemstone you purchase. Vendors also gather on street corners along Avenida Jimenez and Carrera 7 from Monday to Saturday; if you just show up around here you will likely be approached by a number of salesmen. It's best to not get involved or purchase emeralds here, but it can be interesting to come and take a look.

CAMPING

So, after a long flight, you arrive in Bogotá and discover that in those hurried last-minute packing you've forgotten the tent. Or

Camping Supply Stores

The biggest camping supply store chain is **140chomiles,** (Cra. 15, 96-67. Tel: 218-1125, URL: www.140chomiles.com), the Colombia branch of the South American chain **Tatoo Adventure Gear** (URL: www.tatoo.ws/home). The store is a top source for brand-name sportswear, trekking and camping equipment, biking accessories and more, operatin at three stores in Bogotá, (Cra. 15, 96 - 67; Ca. 122, 18-56; and C.C. Andino, Local 340, Cra. 11, 82-71). The adventure gear distributor also stocks guidebooks and maps, and the knowledgeable staff provides information on mountaineering courses and seminars, and gives tips on everything from the best routes to climb to the perfect hiking boot. Open Monday-Friday 11 a.m.-7:30 p.m., Saturday 10:30 a.m.-7:30 p.m. Closed Sundays. Updated: Mar 09, 2011.

Other camping supply stores include:
Nómada (Ca. 45 and Av. Caracas, 2nd floor). Stocks climbing, hiking and camping equipment, keeps lists of credible mountain guides and offers advice on treks and hikes throughout Colombia.
Manglares (Cra. 5, 55-68. Tel: 346-4132/310-565-5352. URL: www.manglares-jp.com). Offers cycling and kayaking equipment and dry bags.
Clínica de Calzado Ambiental/El Eje Ambiental (Av. Jiménez 3-55. Tel: 301-556-8641). Does quick, quality repairs of knapsacks, leather goods and other items.
Montaña Accesorios (Cra. 13a, 79-52, E-mail: montanaccesorios@hotmail.com, Tel: 530-6103. URL: www.montanaccesorios.net).
Montaña Rescate (Ca. 100, 41-40, local 501 and Ca. 95a, 51-11, La Floresta).
Acampar/Camping Vive (Diagonal 5a, 73c-16, Barrio Mandalay. E-mail: manufacgramas@hotmail.com Tel: 608-7457/452-8731).
Camping Amarelo (Ca. 57, 9-29, office 301. Tel: 217-4480/211-8082. URL: www.campingamarelo.com).
Acampamos Iglu Ltda (Cra. 24, 48-90. Tel: 245-2369, E-mail: internacional@iglu.co.com, URL: www.iglu.com.co)
Aventura Almacenes (Cra. 13, 67-26.)

Some of the larger supermarkets, such as **Éxito** in Chapinero, stock some camping gear. Updated: Mar 07, 2011.

hearing the tales of other travelers, you've learned Colombia is a great place to go camping–and camping is a great way to save cash. Bogotá has a number of stores carrying everything you need to sleep under the stars and to scale the nearby mountains (see box, Camping Supply Stores). Parks near Bogotá with campsites include Tobia, Villeta, Sasaima, Anolaima and Anapoima.

White gas (camp stove fuel) is next to impossible to find in Colombia, as its sales have been restricted. However, one place that still carries it located at Calle 7, 3-65. Updated: Mar 07,2011

BOOKSHOPS

For just about any book you would ever want, whether current bestsellers or those long out-of-print, head to Calle 15 between Carreras 8 and 9. Spend hours (or even days) browsing dozens of shops that sprawl for several square blocks and entire malls jammed with stalls. Among the packed bookshelves, you can find books in English and other foreign languages. In many places you can bargain a bit. For bookworms interested in collector's and antiquarian items, check out **Merlín** (Cra. 8a, 15-70. Tel: 284-4008/4301, E-mail: senec52@yahoo.es). **Authors Books** (Ca. 70, 5-23. Tel: 217-7788, URL: www.authors.com.co) stocks new releases, classics and a variety of English-language magazines, though the books here have been marked up significantly. One reason to try this place is its attractive café, a great place to grab a drink and peruse before you buy. If the prices here are too steep then try your luck in **Tower Records** in Atlantis Plaza and Centro Comercial Andino, where there are some limited English-language offerings. Updated: Feb 28, 2011.

BOGOTÁ

The Myth of El Dorado and Bogotá's Museo del Oro

By Wilson Lievano, V!VA List contributor, 2007

Legend tells that when the Muiscas, the native civilization that first settled the site where present-day Bogotá stands, had to crown a new cacique, or chief, they congregated at the nearby Guatavita lagoon. Their candidate was then covered in gold dust, and he and the tribe's shamans would sail to the center of the lagoon in a raft loaded with offerings of gold, emeralds and other precious objects. As the shamans offered these objects to the god of the lagoon, the would-be cacique would jump into the icy waters. If he emerged unharmed, he became their new leader.

When the Spaniards arrived in the region and heard of this rite, they started to call the Muisca cacique "El Dorado"—"the gilded one." Finding hundreds of pieces of gold along the edge of Lake Guatavita when they tried to dredge it in 1545, the Spaniards began searching for a mountain city where gold treasure abounded, believing that such a place had to exist. Many greedy Spaniards were drawn to Muisca territory to participate in the search, but to no avail.

This quest was the first incarnation of the hunt for "El Dorado," a term that has really come to describe a concept—that of a rumored site in South America where massive amounts of gold treasure could be found—more so than a specific legend. El Dorado was later the Spaniards' name for a rumored Amazonian city of gold; the myth even extended to Patagonia in a slightly different form as the "Ciudad de los Cesares," a city made of gold, silver and diamonds founded by survivors of a Spanish shipwreck.

In 1939, to honor the memory of the Muisca and to preserve Colombian archeological heritage, the Colombian government created its own Dorado: El Museo del Oro (the Gold Museum), a permanent collection of more than 35,000 gold ornaments, tools and art pieces made by the native prehispanic cultures of Colombia.

One of the most famous pieces of the exhibit is a solid-gold statue of a raft with the Muisca cacique and his priests on it. The level of detail and historic significance of this statue have made it the museum's highlight. There are other fascinating pieces, such as the Poporo Quimbaya, a golden urn decorated with perfectly round spheres—an impressive achievement since these cultures didn't know the advanced metallurgical techniques used in Europe at the time.

Things to See and Do

No trip to Bogotá is complete without a few hours spent gaping at the craftsmanship on display at the world-renowned **Museo del Oro.** This can be combined with wandering through the colonial streets of La Candelaria, spending some time in the **Donación Botero,** and heading into the striking and imposing Plaza de Bolívar. If there is any event taking place at the elegant Teatro Colón, you are strongly advised to make space in your itinerary to marvel at the décor found within. For further information, have a look at *Ciudad Viva*, the city's monthly publication of cultural events. Updated: Feb 29, 2008.

Museo del Oro !

The Museo del Oro, located in downtown Bogotá, has three floors. The first floor houses temporary exhibitions. The second floor displays the main collection: a voyage through the history and customs of the prehispanic tribes that lived in present-day Colombia, organized by the types of metallurgical processes they used. The third floor contains a history of gold and its significance to prehispanic cultures, along with an exhibit of pieces made by cultures originally from the Colombian southwest. Visitors will learn of the legends, myths and stories that are associated with these pieces. Other pieces were made during the Spanish conquest and tell the story of the native resistance and of their defeat at the hands of the Spanish invaders. (For more information, see box: The Myth of El Dorado and Bogotá's Museo del Oro). The museum has its own stop on the Transmilenio, Bogotá's mass transportation system. To visit, get off the Avenida Jiménez line at the station Museo del Oro and walk two blocks to the museum. Entrance to the museum is $2 Monday–Saturday, free on Sunday. Cra. 6, 15-88, Parque Santander. Tel: 343-2222.

Casa Museo Jorge Eliécer Gaitán

This musuem preserves the home and office of the man who, without a doubt, was the most important social leader in modern Colombian history. Shortly after graduating from law school, the brilliant attorney became a progressive Congressman of the Partido Liberal (Liberal Party) in the 1920s. Before the legislature, Gaitán presented testimony he compiled from survivors of the 1928 Ciénaga banana massacre. This stunning documentation is still widely available. His entire career was focused on improving the social rights of his country-people, which made him a tremendously popular presidential candidate in 1948. But on April 9 of the same year he was assassinated in downtown Bogotá. His killing sparked the present-day civil war that has now lasted more than 60 years. Casa Museo Jorge Eliecer Gaitán teaches visitors about the life, work and philosophy of this illustrious Colombian. Tuesday-Friday 9 a.m-5 p.m., Saturday-Sunday 10 a.m.-2 p.m. Ca. 42, 15-52. Tel: 604-4747, ext. 29226, E-mail: casagaitan@unal.edu.co, URL: www.colarte.arts.co/Museos/JorgeEliecer-Gaitan/general.htm. Updated: Mar 10, 2011.

Museo de Arte Moderno

The MAMBo was opened in 1976 and has emerged as one of the premier museums of its kind in Latin America. Here you can admire, or critique, avante guard cinematic arts, installation pieces, and classic media such as photography, drawing and painting. The MAMBo also collaborates with the opera to create sets and help put the works together for shows in the Teatro Colón. Taking a taxi is recommended. Tuesday-Saturday 10 a.m.-6 p.m, Sunday noon-5 p.m. Ca. 24, 6-00. Tel: 286-0466, URL: www.mambogota.com. Updated: Mar 01, 2011.

Museo Nacional

Ten blocks north of La Candelaria and in the shadow of the Plaza de Toros stands the Museo Nacional, which resembles a fortress and once served as a prison. With more than 20,000 objects and 17 permanent exhibition galleries, the Museo Nacional is well funded and maintained. Be sure to check out the exhibits on Afro-Colombian history and ethnology and one of the many fabulous temporary exhibitions In previous years, the museum has displayed the Terracotta Army and the jewels of Sipán. Worth

Hosts of Literary Readings

Casa de Poesía Silva—Ca. 14, 3-41. Tel: 286-5710, URL: www.casadepoesiasilva.com.
Academia de la Lengua—Cra. 3, 17-34. Tel: 334-3152, E-mail: jaime_posada2004@yahoo.es.
Centro Cultural Gabriel García Márquez— Ca. 11, 5-60, La Candelaria. URL: www.fce.com.co/index.asp.
Prólogo Café y Libros—Tertulias Thursdays. Ca. 96, 11A-46. Tel: 757-8069, URL: www.prologolibros.com, E-mail: prologolibros@cable.net.co.
Loto Azul—Open mic music and poetry, Friday 6-11 p.m. Carrera 5, 14-00. Tel: 334-2346, E-mail: lotoazulvegetariano@yahoo.com.
Museo Arte y Cultura—Tertulias Fridays. Ca. 36, 5A-19, La Merced. Tel: 245-3780/4492.
Arte Letra Librería Café—Cra. 7, 70-18.
Atrio Café Bar—Cra. 11, 67-34, Chapinero. Tel: 249-5828.
Authors Bookstore and Café—Ca. 70, 5-23. Tel: 217-7788, E-mail: info@authors.com.co, URL: www.authors.com.co.
Biblos Librería—Av. 82, 12A-21. Tel: 218-1831. URL: www.biblioslibreria.com, E-mail: atencionalcliente@biblioslibreria.com.
Café Gaitán—Ca. 23, 7-73. Tel: 480-1325. URL: www.cafegaitan.com.
Casa de las Citas—Cra. 3, 13-35.
Updated: Mar 10, 2011

looking into are the free talks on weeknights that discuss points of historical interest.To get there from the Candelaria, if you are too tired to walk the 10 or so blocks north to the museum, catch any bus going north on Cra. 7; get off when you see the fortress-like museum—you can't miss it. Tuesday-Saturday 10 a.m.-6 p.m., Sunday 10 a.m.-5 p.m. Cra. 7, 28-66. Tel: 381-6470, E-mail: info@museonacional.gov.co, URL: www.museonacional.gov.co. Updated: Mar 10, 2011.

Corferías

Corferias is a huge conference and exhibition center. Whether you are a literature fanatic and need to get your fix at the book fair or you fancy coming to Expoartesanias to see the

---

Loved it? Loathed it? Write a review and help other travelers.

finest crafts that Colombia has to offer, there is likely something going on at Corferias that appeals to you. Check out the website for the dates of events. 8:30 a.m.-5:30 p.m. (Cra. 37, 24-67. Tel: 381-0000, E-mail: info@corferias.com, URL: www.corferias.com).

Corferías Events:
February: Travel Fair
April: Book Fair
August: Health and Beauty
September: Home Show
November: Food Show
December: Expoartesanias
Updated: Feb 28, 2011.

Bogotá's Literary Scene
Colombia's present-day writers tend to swing through the nation's capital, where they find receptive audiences. Hit Bogotá's blossoming literary café scene and hear the latest in literature from the poets and authors themselves (see box for a list of places that host *tertulias,* or public readings). Some venues even open the microphone up to the public, giving the opportunity to share some verses.

Parque Central Simón Bolívar
The lungs of Bogotá, Parque Central Simón Bolívar offers the largest area (more than 400 hectares) of greenery in the city. Open from early morning to early evening, on a sunny day this park is a great place to wander around the lake, participate in water sports, jog, cycle or picnic. The park also hosts concerts and has welcomed international stars like Roger Waters and Iron Maiden onto its verdant grounds. Ca. 63 and 53 between Cra. 48 and 68. Updated: Feb 07, 2008.

Jardín Botánico José Celestino Mutis
For nature lovers and travelers seeking to escape the mayhem of downtown Bogotá, a trip to the Jardín Botánico should be high up on the list of things to do. Wide lawns and snaking pathways lead through plant life from Colombia's diverse regions. Throughout the year various exhibitions are held, the most popular of which is the butterfly house, which attracts hundreds of tourists and schoolchildren every day. Arriving by taxi is recommended; it should cost about $4 from the Candelaria. 9 a.m.-5 p.m Ca. 63, 68-95. Tel: 437-7060, E-mail: bogotanico@jbb.gov.co, URL: www.jbb.gov.co. Updated: Feb 28, 2011.

Ciclovía
Every Sunday, many of Bogotá's major roads are blocked off for cyclists, roller-bladers and pedestrians. People also meet up on the streets to socialize and head to parks for free aerobic workouts. The ciclovía starts early in the morning and continues until 2 p.m., so if you are keen on getting some high-altitude exercise or just taking a stroll, then join in. This event takes place all over Bogotá, including the Carrera 7. If you run into bike problems along the way, there are state-sponsored bike mechanics all along the route. Updated: Mar 31, 2011.

Photo by: nati fg

Fitness Centers
Aside from the Sunday morning Ciclovía, there are a number of options that allow the visitor to keep fit while in the capital, including several decent gyms with day pass entries. In La Candelaria there is a cheap and relatively respectable gym at the corner of the Parque de los Periodistas and the Avenida Jiménez. The cheapest of the lot in La Candelaria is on Avenida 19, but the equipment is severely lacking. Further north and into the area of Chapinero is **Body Care Gym** (Ca. 45, 15-38). This is a far better option than those previously mentioned. If you must have the best, head to any of the branches of **BodyTech** based around the city—the closest to downtown is on Carrera 7 and Calle 62. BodyTech has hot showers, but the others do not. Bring your own towel. Updated: Mar 31, 2011.

El Campin
If you can, try to get to a soccer game between the two city rivals, Santa Fe and Millonarios. Even better, get to an international match at the Nemesio Camacho Stadium (otherwise known as El Campin). See almost 50,000 rabid fans cheering in true Latin American style, complete with whistles, fireworks and toilet paper rolls. Take the Transmilenio bus to the El Campin stop. Best enjoyed with friends while seated in the Colombia section. Av. Norte-Quito-Sur (NQS) with Ca. 57, Teusaquillo. Updated: Mar 01, 2011.

Rumba Bogotana

Bogotá has some of Latin America's greatest nightlife spots. Your options are vast and varied, from clubbing the night away in the Zona Rosa, the Candelaria or Usaquen to a night at the theater. Locals will recommend that you take a nightime chiva tour, where open, wooden-sided buses, decked out with lights, play loud music and serve alcohol. You can find chivas all over the city. Updated: May 15, 2009.

Studying Spanish

To study Spanish in depth, sign up for a course offered at any one of the following universities in Bogotá. All have internationally recognized courses and can offer different levels of instruction:

Universidad Javeriana–
www.puj.edu.co
Universidad Externado–
www.uexternado.edu.co.
Universidad de la Sabana–
www.unisabana.edu.co.
Universidad Nacional de Colombia–
www.unal.edu.co. Updated: May 15, 2009.

Tours

There are dozens of tour outfits in Bogotá offering all kinds of tours. Popular tours include rumba tours in a chiva and tours to Zipaquirá and Villa de Leyva. For a complete list of tour companies go to URL: www.bogotaturismo. gov.co. Updated: May 12, 2009.

Empresa Turística y Cultural La Candelaria (ETC)

Acting as both a chamber of commerce for Candelaria's local businesses and a tour provider, Empresa Turística y Cultural La Candelaria (ETC) offers a diverse range of tours for the eager tourist. Every individual's needs can be met; whether architecture is your thing or you're feeling romantic and want to surprise your other half with a private nighttime tour. You can even travel in style in a Chevrolet 1946 and see many of the sites of interest in Bogotá's colonial Candelaria center. The choices are endless. (Cra. 8, 11-39, office 716 , Plaza de Bolivar, La Candelaria. Tel: 283-2319, E-mail: info@lacandelaria.info, URL: www. lacandelaria.info). Updated: Jun 15, 2011.

Destino Bogotá

DestinoBogota.com is a division of **Via Colombia Travel Services**, which is a leading company that specializes in travel in Bogotá and surrounding areas. They have a qualified and experienced team of professional drivers and multilingual guides who provide customers with a personal service dedicated to meeting specific travelers' needs. Furthermore, the company is accredited by the Ministry of Industry, Commerce and Tourism as a Tourism Operating Agency. Ca. 72 (Av. Chile), 12-65, office 405. Tel: 753-4887, E-mail: info@ destinobogota.com, URL: www.destinobogota.com. Updated: Mar 10, 2011.

Tesoro Tours

Tesoro tours have been operating for a few years and specialize in everything that Bogotá and the surrounding area have to offer. Available tours include a night tour, a shopping tour, a city tour or a trip as far out as Zipaquira. They also provide custom tours. Monday-Friday 8 a.m.-6 p.m., Saturday-Sunday 9 a.m.-2 p.m. Ca. 93, 47a-11, La Castella. Tel: 691-3011, ext. 102, URL: www.tesorotours.com. Updated: Feb 28, 2011.

Colombia Oculta Tourism

Colombia Oculta is an adventure tour operator aiming to show tourists the landscapes that can't be found anywhere but Colombia. The company invites you to discover the mountains, jungles, lakes, rivers and deserts of the country, as well as the endless colors of Colombia's endemic plant and animal life. Tel: 630-3172, ext. 112, Cel: 311-239-7809, E-mail: info@colombiaoculta.org, URL: www.colombiaoculta.org. Updated: Mar 10, 2011.

Colombian Travels

Colombian Travels, a new tour operator with a strong belief in responsible tourism, specializes in small group tours of the Caribbean Coast and Islands, La Guajíra, East Andean Highlands and Zona Cafetera. Based in Bogotá, with another office in Sydney, Australia, Colombian Travels can arrange city tours, rumbas, visits to national parks and indigenous communities or excursions further off the beaten path. Choose from one of Colombian Travels' set itineraries, which last around two weeks, or book a shorter or more individually tailored trip. Accommodations, travel and outings are included in the price, and all tours are led by English-speaking locals. Tel: 481-7695 (Bogotá)/61-4-2563-4502/3523-1818 (Australia), Skype: colombiantravels, E-mail: contact@colombiantravels.com,

URL: www.colombiantravels.com. Updated: Mar 30, 2011.

Caminar Colombia

If you're tired of Bogotá's concrete and smog, then join Caminar Colombia for its Sunday *caminata ecológica* hikes into the nation's wilds. These all-day excursions go to little-visited nature spots through cloud forests, across páramos, along ancient stone roads or to out-of-the-way villages. These outings are relaxed affairs, not strenuous marches. Reservations must be made by phone before noon the Saturday before. Most hikes cost $18 and include transportation and guide; discounts are given for early payment. Ca. 18 Sur, 11b-44. Tel: 366-3059, URL: www.caminarcolombia.com. Updated: Mar 18, 2011.

Bike Tours

On a rain-free day, bicycling is a fun way to see Bogota and get a little exercise at the same time. The guides are bilingual and also knowledgeable about the country's history, social problems and the long-standing armed conflict. The tour visits several parks, including one with a camp of displaced people. If you are renting a bike to ride on your own without a guide, take a good look at the map they lend you and try to take quieter back streets; ask in the office about recommended routes. The office is located in La Candelaria. 9 a.m.-6 p.m. Cra. 3, 12-72. Tel: 281-9924, E-mail: bogotabiketours@gmail.com, URL: www.bogotabiketours.com. Updated: Mar 10, 2011.

Lodging

From chic boutique hotels to homey backpacker hostels, Bogotá caters to every budget, as you would expect from a major capital city. In La Candelaria, you will find a large number of budget hotels and hostels set in charming restored buildings. Options in this neighborhood have tripled in recent years and range from the calm and quiet, where you can sleep peacefully, to the raucous, where you can party until dawn with your new backpacker friends. Family-run establishments and luxury options tend to do business in the historic center and further north. Bogotá also has a number of good-value places to stay, as well as several global luxury chain hotels near the airport. Updated: Jun 25, 2010.

BUDGET AND MID-RANGE

A little goes a long way at budget hotels in Bogotá: most have excellent extra services, such as on-site cafés, bars and restaurants, and rooms have a host of amenities, including WiFi. Bogotá's budget and mid-range hotels lie in La Candelaria and scattered across the city. Private rooms cost between $15 and $50, depending on your level of comfort; dorms can be found for as low as $10. The Chapinero neighborhood has a few inexpensive, basic hotels options, which provide great access to the sights in La Candelaria and the hip nightlife of Zona Rosa. Bogotá B&Bs, while generally more expensive ($50 a night on average), offer relaxed accommodation in quaint residences. B&B rates are lower for longer stays.

HIGH-END

Luxury hotels in Bogotá tend to do business in La Candelaria and the business district. Old homes in the historic center have been reborn as posh boutique hotels ($60-200 per night), and feature extras such as spas and pizzerías; meanwhile, high-end hotels in the Centro Internacional/La Macarena and Rosales neighborhoods charge in the hundreds for a night's stay, and are within walking distance of Zona T and Parque de la 93.

INDEPENDENT LODGING

Colombian families in Bogotá offer homestay options, with meals often included in the price. Nightly rates for a private room are around $40, and the price decreases the longer you stay. If you're planning to stay in Bogotá for several weeks or more, there are many affordable private apartments throughout the city. From studios to multi-room apartments, longer-term accommodations in Bogotá are fully furnished and come with added bonuses like WiFi, swimming pools and fitness center access. Bogotá newspapers are a good place to find information on apartment rentals.

North House Hostel Bogotá

(BEDS: $11.50-14, ROOMS: $31-42) North House Hostel Bogotá is located in the Chico neighborhood in the north of Bogotá, close to the popular nightlife and dining areas, the "Zona Rosa" (between Ca. 79 and Ca. 85 and Cra. 11 and Cra. 15) and Parque 93. It is right across from the Universidad San Martin and less than a five-minute walk from los Heroes transmilenio stop. It is also close to the Carulla supermarket (open 24/7).

North House Hostel is set in an old two-story house. The first floor comprises a T.V. and lounge area, large dining room, kitchen, laundry area, garden for relaxing and restaurant/café with an outdoor seating area. The second floor consists of dormitories and bathrooms. There are five dormitories and one private room with a total of 31 beds. A taxi will get you here from the airport in 25 minutes and will cost $8-10. Cra. 18, 80-66. Tel: 530-1968, E-mail: northhouse@ northhousehostel.com, URL: www.north-househostel.com. Updated: Mar 01, 2011.

Martha's Place

(ROOMS: $18-79) This is a fully furnished three-bedroom vacation rental, which can be rented by room or fully. Each room has a TV and WiFi. Martha's Place is two blocks from the US Embassy and a ten-minute walk to the largest mall in South America. Cheaper and nicer than most hotels, Martha's Place fills a niche for budget travelers who don't want to rough it and is 25 minutes by taxi from the airport. Ca. 22, 48-65, Conjunto Salitre Pijao. URL: www.apartmentinbogota. com. Updated: May 15, 2009.

Hotel Zaragoza

(ROOMS: $25-60) The Hotel Zaragoza has become a favorite haunt among European budget travelers. Set in a four-story, green-and-hot-pink building that blends into the modern architecture of Avenida Jiménez, this inn offers medium-sized rooms with cable TV and private, hot water baths. Some rooms have balconies that look out over the avenue. The beds are good and come with several blankets to keep you warm on those chilly Bogotá nights. This hotel is often full because the word of its quality accommodations is spreading quickly in budget traveler circles. The price for couples matches what you'll find in hostels. Av. Jiménez 4-56. Tel: 284-5411/608-8290. Updated: Feb 28, 2011.

Restaurants

Whether you need to stick to a rigid budget of $5 per day for food or have the money to spend on a gourmet feast, Bogotá has what you want. Small restaurants all over the city run lunch deals starting around $2 that will fill your stomach with hearty fare (typically a soup to start, followed by a cut of meat served with rice, potatoes and beans). If you fancy something more chic, newer establishments in the Candelaria and the Macarena will fit the bill. Trendy places can also be found in the Zona Rosa and Parque la 93. Bogotá offers a wealth of nightlife options. Fashionable clubs line the streets in the north and student hangouts are sprinkled amid the colonial mayhem of the Candelaria. Most clubs close between 2-3 a.m., but those with an appetite for more can go on to well-known after-parties. The locations of these parties are passed on by *voceros* via hostel networks (the *voceros* receive a commission for each person they bring, and parties charge an entry fee). Bogotá's arts scene is a lively one too, with art-house cinemas, theaters and live music venues putting on shows to big crowds. Updated: Jul 10, 2009.

Bogotá Beer Company

The Bogota Beer Company, with 10 locations in Bogotá (including in Zona Rosa, Usaquén, and Parque la 93), models itself on U.S.-style micro-breweries. The artisanal beers and pub setting draw crowds here, not to mention the large-screen TVs permanently tuned to sporting events. Contact information is as follows for locations in Zona Rosa, Usaquén and Parque de la 93, respectively (for other locations and hours, check out the URL listed below): Cra. 12, 83-33 (across from Centro Comercial Andino); Cra. 6, 119-24; Cra. 11a, 93-94. Tel: 802-6737/9762/6784/6765. URL: www.bogo-tabeercompany.com. Updated: Apr 1, 2011.

Photo by: Jack Zalium

Capachos Asadero !

(ENTREES: $7.25-8.25) If your itinerary doesn't include a hop down to Villavicencio and the Colombian plains, you can still try *mamona*, the typical BBQ from the plains, at Capachos. The veal is slow-cooked on stakes to succulent perfection. Capachos also grills pork and mojarra fish. Your cut of meat comes with various sauces for dipping and with the traditional sides of roasted plantain, potatoes and yucca. From Thursday to Sunday, there is live

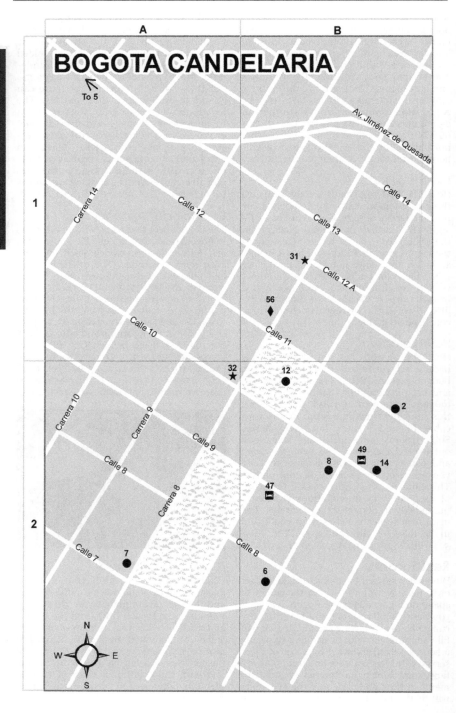

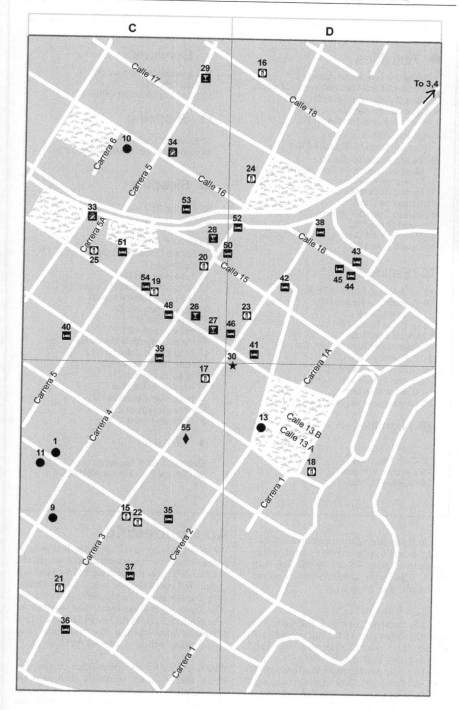

BOGOTÁ

BOGOTÁ

● Activities

1 Biblioteca Luis Angel Arango C2
2 Centro Cultural Garbriel García Márquez B2
3 Casa Quinta del Bolivar D1
4 Cerro de Monserrate
  (Funicular and Teleférico) D1
5 Estación de la Sabana
  (Steam Train to Zipaquirá) A1
6 Museo Arqueológico B2
7 Museo Claustro De San Agustín A2
8 Museo de Arte Colonial B2
9 Museo de Bogotá C2
10 Museo de Oro C1
11 Museo Donación Botero C2
12 Plaza Bolívar B2
13 Plazoleta del Chorro de Quevedo D2
14 Teatro Colón B2

⑩ Eating

15 An Andante Ma Non Troppo C2
16 Capachos Asadero D1
17 Casa de Citas C2
18 El Bolón Verde D2
19 La Vida en Rosa C1
20 Pastelería Organización Gers C1
21 Pimienta y Café C2
22 Quinua y Amaranto C2
23 Restaurante Café Israelí L´Jaim D1
24 Restaurante Donde Tatiana D1
25 Restaurante Vegetariano Loto C1

☒ Nightlife

26 Café del Sol C1
27 Café Para Dos C1
28 Escobar y Rosas C1
29 Quiebra Canto C1

★ Services

30 Lavaseco la Colonial D2
31 Post Office B1
32 Tourist Information Office A2

☒ Shopping

33 Emerald Trade Center C1
34 Herencias de Artesanías y Café C1

▦ Sleeping

35 Abadía Colonial C2
36 Anandamayi C2
37 ApartaEstudios C2
38 Casa Platypus D1
39 Centro Plaza Hotel C1
40 Dorantes C1
41 Fátima Hostal D1
42 Hospedaje Cacique Sugamaxi D1
43 Hostal La Candelaria D1
44 Hostal Platypus D1
45 Hostal Sue D1
46 Hotel Aragón D1
47 Hotel Casa de la Bótica B2
48 Hotel Dann Colonial C1
49 Hotel de la Opera B2
50 Hotel El Dorado C1
51 Hotel Internacional C1
52 Hotel San Sebastian D1
53 Hotel Zaragoza C1
54 Oceanía Hotels C1

◆ Tours

55 Bogotá Bike Tours B1
56 Cultural Tours in Candelaria C2

music from the Colombian countryside. Daily noon-6 p.m., Friday and Saturday until 7 p.m. Ca. 18, 4-68. Tel: 243-4607, URL: www.asaderocapachos.com. Updated: Mar 01, 2011.

El Café Internet Bar

El Café Internet Bar is a popular, gay-friendly hangout with loud music, stiff drinks, fast computers, cute boys (and a few girls) and comfy seats. It's busy most evenings. Sunday-Wednesday 10 a.m.-midnight, Thursday-Sunday 10 a.m.-2 a.m. Ca. 59, 13-32. Tel: 249-6512. Updated: Feb 07, 2008.

La Candelaria

With a colonial flavor, eclectic bookstores, dance academies, museums and restaurants, La Candelaria is the beating heart of old Bogotá. One could spend several days wandering the streets of La Candelaria, exploring the Plaza de Bolívar under the shadows of the opulent Palacio de Justicia and Catedral Primada and visiting the museums and many other points of interest on Calle 10.

With a handful of universities in the district, there is a considerable student presence here that keeps the prices down and the cultural activity, including dining and nightlife, vibrant. Most of Bogotá's affordable accommodations are located in La Candelaria, as are some luxury options. There are a few bars and clubs in Escobar and Rosas (Cra. 5 and 14) and Quiebracanto (Cra. 5, 17-76). Updated: Mar 03, 2008.

Things to See and Do

Museo de Arte Colonial

Originally built in the late 17th century as the seat of the Colegio Máximo de la Compañía de Jesús, this Spanish colonial-style building was converted into a museum in the 1940s and renovated in the late 1990s. The museum houses unforgettable works by Vásquez and Figeroa and portraits of key players in the colonial period. There are scattered antiquities and furniture from the colonial era as well. To get there, go east (uphill) from the Plaza de Bolívar on Calle 10 to Carrera 6, then turn right (the museum will be on the right side of the road). Tuesday-Friday 9 a.m.-5 p.m., Saturday-Sunday 10 a.m.-4 p.m. Free guided tours Tuesday, Friday 3 p.m. Cra. 6a, 9-77. Tel: 341-6017, E-mail: museocolonial@mincultura.gov.co URL: www.museocolonial.gove.co. Updated: Mar 10, 2011.

Claustro San Agustín

Built in 1583 and formerly an Augustinian cloister, this is certainly one of the oldest surviving buildings in Bogotá. The museum, once the home of the Museo de Artes y Tradiciones Populares, now specializes in temporary exhibits by national and international photographers and artists. It also features special archaeological shows. Just one block from the famous Palacio NariNo, the museum is easily located. Monday-Saturday 9 a.m.-5 p.m. Cra. 8, 7-21. Tel: 284-2670. Updated: Mar 10, 2011.

Museo Donación Botero ⚑

This museum should be at the top any art enthusiast's list of things to do in Bogotá. Of the musuem's two sections, the first is dedicated to the famous Colombian artist Fernando Botero, who, in the words of most Colombians, "paints fat people." This wing displays 123 examples of Botero's work. As the museum's name suggests, Botero donated many of his own pieces to the collection. The second section of the museum displays 85 works by internationally renowned artists from the 19th century, such as Renoir, Chagall, Picasso, Bacon and Moore. The museum is located just three blocks up from the Plaza Bolívar. Free

guided tours are offered Monday-Friday 10 a.m. and 4 p.m. Monday-Saturday 9 a.m.-7 p.m. (last entry 6:30 p.m.), Sunday and holidays 10 a.m.-5 p.m. (last entry 4:30 p.m.). Ca. 11, 4-41. Tel: 343-1340, URL: www.lablaa.org/museobotero.htm. Updated: Mar 10, 2011.

Museo Arqueológico

The Museo Arqueológico, or MUSA, houses an impressive permanent collection of pre-Columbian ceramics in a 17th-century mansion. The mansion has a fascinating history. For a period of time, it belonged to the Marquís de San Jorge, a viceroy best known for his cruelty. Opened to the public in 1973, the museum has permanent ceramics and colonial art exhibits as well as seasonal exhibits. Close to the Plaza Bolívar. Monday-Friday 8:30 a.m.-5 p.m., Saturday 9 a.m.-4 p.m. Cra. 6, 7-43. Tel: 243-1048/0465, E-mail: fpcdireccion@etb.net.co, URL: www.museo-arqueologico.com. Updated: Mar 10, 2011.

Plaza de Bolívar

The opulent grandeur that meets you when you enter Bogotá's Plaza de Bolívar is overwhelming. Around the plaza, whose center is marked by a Simón Bolívar statue, rise tall, stately buildings, including the Capitol building, the Palacio Liévano (seat of the mayor of Bogotá), the Catedral Primada and the Palacio de Justicia. This plaza was the very location where Bogotá was declared the seat of Nueva Granada's colonial government. In its earlier days, the Plaza de Bolívar was cut through by trams and traffic. The Palacio de Justicia has been renovated after besieged in 1985 by the M-19 guerrilla group. The Palacio de Nariño (Presidential Palace), which is located just south of the Plaza, was rebuilt in 1949 after the massive Bogotazo riots. Today, the plaza and its environs are a place where peaceful demonstrations head, children chase pigeons and photographers vie for your business. Be wary in this area after dark. If you head south from the plaza, between Calles 9 and 8 you will find a large park, within which is the old Observatorio Nacional (an astronomical observatory); further south between Calles 8 and 7 is the Palacio de Nariño, or the Presidential Palace. The Plaza de Bolívar is between Cra. 7 and 8, and between Ca. 10 and 11. Updated: May 18, 2009.

Casa Quinta de Bolívar

The Quinta, not far from the Universidad de los Andes in the Candelaria, is perhaps best known as the most stable residence Simón Bolívar had in his adult life—he spent 423 days here, though not consecutively. The elegant hillside mansion, with its well-preserved gardens, European architecture and courtyards, was a gift to Bolívar from the Colombian State, and he remained its sole owner for 10 years. The Quinta later changed hands many times and was even owned by a brewery before being bought back by the State for the purpose of creating a museum. Tours (in Spanish) take you through the key rooms, pointing out interesting antiquities such as Bolívar's bed and other objects from the republican era. Tuesday-Friday 9 a.m.-4 p.m., Sautrday-Sunday 10 a.m.-4 p.m. Ca. 20, 2-91. Tel: 336-6419, URL: www.quintadebolivar.gov.co. Updated: Mar 01, 2011.

Teatro Colón

Right in the thick of things on Calle 10 (across the road from the Ministry of Foreign Relations) and one block up the hill from the Plaza de Bolívar is the ornate and decorative Teatro Colón, opened in 1892. Seating up to 900 people, this is really Colombia's centerpiece theater. Plan your visit to coincide with a performance or concert that will allow you to fully appreciate one of the continent's most beautiful theaters. To get there, simply find Calle 10 from Plaza de Bolívar and climb one block. *Note: Teatro Colón is currently under renovation; call the theater directly for additional information on its reopening.* Monday-Saturday 8 a.m.-8 p.m., Sunday 8 a.m.-4 p.m. Ca. 10, 5-32. Tel: 284-7420. Updated: Mar 09, 2011.

Museo de Bogotá

The Museo de Bogotá has a new home in the historic center of the city, in Casa Sámano, the former home of Nueva Granada's last viceroy. The late-18th-century structure has a new, urban-chic annex with manholes encased in glass floors on the back. The building is as much a work of interest as the exhibits that fill the spaces. The displays, which change every three months, show off different facets of Bogotá's history. Topics include the city's oldest radio station, publishing and other themes. The building is wheelchair accessible. Tuesday-Friday 9 a.m.-6 p.m., Saturday-Sunday 10 a.m.-5 p.m. Casa Sámano, Cra. 4, 10-18. Tel: 352-1865, URL: www.patrimoniocultural.gov.co. Updated: Mar 18, 2011.

Plazoleta del Chorro de Quevedo

Deep in the student heartland of the Candelaria is this small plaza, with bars, restaurants and eclectic shops that appeal to an off-beat crowd. Here in the Plazoleta del Chorro de Quevedo is where Gonzalo Jimenez de Quesada—the founder of Bogotá—stopped and drank from a stream in his push south, not that you would know there was ever a stream. On weeknights the place buzzes with students, musicians and storytellers. On weekends, the barrio empties out and feels less safe. Ca. 13 and Cra. 2. Updated: May 15, 2009.

Centro Cultural Gabriel García Márquez

Although Colombian author Gabriel García Márquez set his prize-winning novel *One Hundred Years of Solitude* in his homeland, the book was born in Mexico, where Márquez has resided for many years. As a gesture of appreciation, the Fondo Cultura Económico, a major Mexican publisher, had the Centro Cultural Gabriel García Márquez built. Inaugurated in 2008, the building has a modern design, with curved walls enclosing circular patios. In the cultural center is a bookstore, record shop, auditorium, exhibition hall, restaurant and café. The ground level features a biographical display about García Márquez on large panels. The center frequently hosts literary and other cultural events. Ca. 11 (Ca. de la Enseñanza) 5-60. URL: www.fce.com.co/index.asp. Updated: May 18, 2009.

Biblioteca Luis Ángel Arango

Bogotanos proudly declare that their library, Luis Ángel Arango, is one of the most visited in the world, with more people walking through the entrance here per week than at the New York Public Library. While the accuracy of these claims is dubious, there is no doubt the universities in La Candelaria contribute a steady flow of students. The library is worth visiting for its often-changing exhibits and occasional recitals. Monday-Sunday from 8 a.m. Ca. 11, 4-14. Tel: 343-1212, URL: www.lablaa.org. Updated: Mar 01, 2011.

Cerro de Monserrate

If you would like a truly impressive view of the city, head up to the top of the Cerro de Monserrate, 3,152 meters (10,341 ft) above sea level. The view on a clear day is breathtaking. Opened in 1929, the sanctuary at the top of the mountain, which holds a replica of Barcelona's *Virgen Morena* (Black Virgin) statue, is a pilgrimage site. Some visitors even make the journey to the

top of the mountain on their knees. Since there have been robberies here, especially when the pathway is deserted, it is not recommended that you walk to the top. Further, you should be in decent shape, as it is an hour-long hike at a high altitude. If you do walk the route, it is best to go on the weekend or on a religious holiday, when the number of visitors increases. There are two other forms of reaching the top: by cable car or on the Funicular. Often, if one of these is running and in service, the other is not. The Cerro is open to visitors every day and in the evenings. Taking a taxi to the mountain is recommended. Funicular: Monday-Saturday 7:45 a.m.-11:45 a.m.; Sunday and holidays 6 a.m.-6:30 p.m. Teleférico: Monday-Saturday noon-midnight, Sunday 9 a.m.-5 p.m. Cra. 2, 21-48, Paseo Bolívar. Tel: 284-5700, URL: www.cerromonserrate.com. Updated: Mar 10, 2011.

Lodging

La Candelaria is the most popular neighborhood to stay in Bogota. It has an abundance of cheap lodging options set in lovely colonial buildings. Budget hostels, with beds for as low as $10 are plentiful, but you might want to consider something a bit more pricey with private rooms and more space, such as the U.S. $12 per night **Hostel La Candelaria**. Another popular option is **Platypus**, a hostel run by Bogotá fixture Germán Escobar and a hub for travelers. It offers all the important amenities, including laundry, full kitchen and vast amounts of information and advice. Updated: Jul 05, 2010.

BUDGET

Oceania Hotels

(ROOMS: $3-25) Opened in 2007, the Oceania is clean and well-run and has rooms for up to five people. The restaurant downstairs serves economical lunches. To get there, take any bus running into the Candelaria district en route to the Biblioteca Luis Angel Arango. Get off at the corner of Carrera 4 and Calle 14, and the hotel is just meters away. *Note: this hotel is currently under renovation; call for more information on its status and expected reopening date.* Ca. 14, 4-48. Tel: 342-0650/0561/0562, Fax: 342-1879. Updated: Mar 09, 2011.

Hostal Platypus

(BEDS: $9-26.50) In front of Platypus, a drawing of the hostal's namesake animal greets guests in lieu of its actual name—the first indication that this is a unique place. Enormously popular amongst travelers, the Platypus offers all the comforts the tired traveler would want. Germán Escobar, the owner, is himself a backpacker who has traveled around the world and knows how wonderful it is to have free coffee and tea all day long, a kitchen to use, laundry service, and a great common room with wood-burning fireplace. Other services include a free book exchange and a collection of travel information books. Germán himself is a tremendous source of information about what to see in Colombia, his native land. He speaks Spanish, English, German, French and Italian. If there is no room at the hostel when you arrive, the staff will gladly call around to other hotels for you. Reservations are highly recommended. From the bus terminal, take a black bus that says "Germania" going to the Candelaria district. Tell the driver you want to get off at Calle 16. Then walk along Calle 16 towards the mountains for two blocks. It will be a green building on your right. Ca. 16, 2-43 (Ca. 12F, 2-43). Tel: 341-3104/2874, E-mail: platypushotel@yahoo.com, URL: www.platypusbogota.com. Updated: Mar 11, 2011.

Hotel Internacional

(ROOMS: $10-17) Several stories of rooms, with common or private baths and all with hot water, await the weary journeyer at this hotel, which is often full due to its popularity. Budget traveler conveniences, like a common kitchen and book exchange, are a bonus. You can even sip on some free coffee while making a Skype call. First-floor accommodations are better for those who are less mobile. Ca. 5, 14-45. Tel: 341-3151/8731, Cel: 312-595-1480, E-mail: hotelinternacionalbogota@hotmail.com, URL: www.hotelinternacionalbogota.com. Updated: Mar 01, 2011.

Hostal Sue

(ROOMS: $10-31) Definitely a worthy rival to the mighty neighboring Platypus, Hostal Sue boasts a lively social atmosphere, exhaustive DVD collection, heated terrace and all the know-how about how to have a good time in Bogotá. Dormitories and private rooms are available either in Sue One or just two short blocks away in Sue Two. The hostal is located conveniently close to the Parque de Los Periodistas, and therefore very close to the transport amenities of the Las Aguas Transmilenio stop and the countless buses that reach the Avenida 19. Ca. 16, 2-55. Tel: 334-8894, Cel: 310-877-5381, E-mail: reservations@hostalsue.com, URL: www.hostalsue.com. Updated: Mar 01, 2011.

Hotel El Dorado

(ROOMS: $12-26) Hotel Dorado is undoubtedly the least expensive hostel in the center of Bogotá, between the Candelaria district and downtown. The rooms at El Dorado are basic, if a bit small, and most have windows. The headless showers spew hot water. Rooms on the terrace have beautiful views over the city and of Montserrate, but share a common bath. Pay a few extra dollars for a room with private bath downstairs. Among some journeyers, the Hotel Dorado has earned a poor reputation for security; nonetheless, it is a cheap lodging option. Cra. 4, 15-00. Tel: 334-3988/281-7271, E-mail: doradohotel@hotmail.com. Updated: Mar 01, 2011.

Hospedaje Cacique Sugamuxi

(BEDS: $12-26) Hospedaje Cacique Sugamuxi is one of La Candelaria's newest hostels, having opened in 2008. This hostel is located above a restaurant and fruit shop. Many of the rooms are small, but they are well-furnished for the traveler who needs to relax and catch up on journal writing. Common or shared baths. Smoking is prohibited. The kitchen is well equipped and has a sunny eating area. Hospedaje Cacique Sugamuxi offers its guests the cheapest in-house Internet ($0.50 per hour) and laundry service ($1.05 per kilogram) in the neighborhood. Corner of Cra. 3 and Ca. 15a. Tel: 337-4326/317-331-1071, E-mail: caciquesugamuxi@hotmail.com, URL: www.caciquesugamuxi.com. Updated: May 01, 2011.

Hotel Centro Plaza

(BEDS: $12-40) This hostel is a hit with Israeli travelers, as the Star of David subtly adorning the entrance might suggest. Dorms are furnished with single beds (no bunks here) and large private rooms have 24-hour hot water baths. Hotel Centro Plaza also has special features, like a game room with billiards and ping-pong tables, a fruit shop and a kosher restaurant. Cra. 4, 13-12. Tel: 243-3818/286-1580, E-mail: hotelcentralplaza@hotmail.com. URL: www.hotelcentralplaza.com. Updated: Mar 01, 2011.

Hotel Aragon

(ROOMS: $14-22) For those seeking a cheap and quiet room, the Hotel Aragon is a viable option. But be warned, last we checked it appeared as though the management hadn't invested in hotel upkeep since the 1950s. Still, private rooms are available for bargain basement prices. The hotel is close to the Parque de los Periodistas, an easy stroll from Las Aguas or Museo del Oro Transmilenio stops. The nearest bus will take you to Carrera 4 with Calle 14, one block away. Cra. 3, 14-13. Tel: 342-5239/284-8325. Updated: Mar 10, 2011.

Hostal Fátima

(ROOMS: $16-50) Opened in September 2007, the Hostal Fátima has other hostal owners in La Candelaria reaching for their checkbooks to update their facilities in order to keep up. The ownership has placed special emphasis on comfort. The treats include spanking-new bathrooms with Jacuzzi, complimentary breakfasts, and a sauna and solarium. It is a hit among backpackers looking to socialize. The hostal is about a five minute walk from the Las

Aguas Transmilenio Station across the Parque de Los Periodistas. A bus will drop you at Carrera 4 and Calle 14 so only two blocks away. Ca. 14, 2-24. Tel: 281-6389/283-6411, E-mail: contacto@hostalfatima.com, URL: www.hostalfatima.com. Updated: Mar 01, 2011.

Anandamayi

(ROOMS: $17-68) The Anandamayi Hostel is a stylish, comfortable and cheap place to stay in La Candelaria. Spacious internal patios with hammocks lend themselves to spending idle hours relaxing. Dormitories are large and very clean and a country-style kitchen is available to all. With an open layout and a verdant garden out back, this is one of the more relaxing hostels in Bogota. Dorms are priced at $17, $50-68 for a single. To get there, stroll up Calle 10 from the southwest corner of the Plaza de Bolívar, or catch a bus to Carrera 4 with Calle 10 and walk up the hill for about three blocks. Alternatively, catch a cab from Avenida Circunvalar. Ca. 9, 2-81. Tel: 341-7208, Cel: 315-215-5778, E-mail: anandamayihostel@yahoo.com, URL: www.anandamayihostel.com. Updated: Mar 10, 2011.

MID-RANGE

Hostal La Candelaria

(ROOMS: $19-40) This five-star guesthouse has rooms with a bathroom, rooms with shared bathrooms and duplex apartments in a colonial house with a quiet and safe atmosphere. A taxi from the airport is recommended. Ca. 16, 2-38. Tel: 600-7559, E-mail: info@hostallacandelaria.com, URL: www.hostallacandelaria.com. Updated: Mar 01, 2011.

Hotel Dorantes

(ROOMS: $21-32) In the mid-19th century, Hotel Dorantes was a family mansion. Elegant woodwork and parquet floors remain from when the house was built, and original art adorns the lobby, hallways and staircases. The rooms are airy and come with private pathrooms, hot water and cable TV. Some have balconies. Before starting your day's sightseeing, you can relax in the lobby and read the daily newspapers. The staff speaks some English. Ca. 13, 5-07. Tel: 334-6640, E-mail: administradora@hoteldorantes.com, URL: www.hoteldorantes.com. Updated: Mar 01, 2011.

Casa Platypus

(ROOMS: $22-94) After over three years of careful restoration, this transformed republican-era home has made its debut as the grown-up, high-class sibling of the Hostal Platypus. Located in La Candelaria across from the Parque de los Periodistas, this hotel offers spacious, private rooms that are tastefully decorated and come with cable TV and private bath. Extras include the comfortable sitting room with hearth, a well-equipped kitchen and a rooftop terrace with a stunning view of Montserrate. A large breakfast is included in the price, as are parking, Internet and taxes. Dorms are $22, private rooms $72-$94 for one to three people. Cra. 3, 16-28 (Cra. 3, 12F-28). Tel: 281-1801/1643, E-mail: casaplatypus@yahoo.com, URL: www.casaplatypus.com. Updated: Mar 18, 2011.

Hotel San Sebastián

(ROOMS: $36-47) The San Sebastián is a safe and decent hotel with clean rooms. Cable TV included. Situated between the Transmilenio stops of Las Aguas and the Museo del Oro in La Candelaria, the hotel is a few minutes on foot from each. Any bus heading along Carrera 7 to the Luis Ángel Arango Library will drop you right outside. Av. Jiménez, 3-97. Tel: 337-5031. Updated: Mar 10, 2011.

Hotel Dann Colonial

(ROOMS: $58-66) Resembling a 1970s relic in terms of both its architecture and its style, the hotel Dann Colonial could use a makeover. However, the hotel offers the conveniences of cable TV and minibar, and Monday to Friday there is an economical buffet lunch available. Any bus heading to the Biblioteca Luis Angel Arango along Carrera 4 will drop you right at the corner above the hotel. Otherwise a taxi will negotiate the streets of the Candelaria with relative ease. Ca. 14, 4-21. Tel: 341-1680/1681. E-mail: administradordanncolonial.com, URL: www.danncolonial.com. Updated: Mar 01, 2011.

HIGH-END

Abadia Colonial

(ROOMS: $63-83) Do not be put off by the raucous student bars opposite Abacadia. This boutique hotel's rooms are all at the back of the building, centered around a garden and courtyard, and remain unaffected by the noise. Great care has been put into the details at this hotel, and the dècor is warm and tasteful, making this a charming place in the heart of Bogotá's bohemia. To get to the hotel, which is higher up in the Candelaria district, taking a taxi is recommended. Otherwise, it is an uphill walk with your bags, either from the bus at Carrera 4 or even further from the Transmilenio station at Las Aguas. Ca. 11, 2-32. Tel: 341-1884, E-mail: abadiacolonial@gmail. com, URL: www.abadiacolonial.com. Updated: Mar 01, 2011.

Hotel Casa de la Botica

(ROOMS: $131-200) Outstanding craftsmanship and design are evident in every facet of this hotel. From the courtyard and salon to the fireplaces and balconies in the rooms, beautiful brick and woodwork make this restored republican house feel earthy yet stylish. There are two accommodation options: standard and suite. Guests have access to a pizzeria, a French bakery and a snazzy restaurant. Other bonuses include free WiFi in rooms and public spaces, laundry service, cable TV, and transport to and from the airport. Soon to open are a full-service spa, Turkish bath, Roman pool and sauna; check the website or call to find out more about when exactly these facilities will be available. To get there, catching a cab is easiest, as the hotel is at the far end of the Candelaria. Otherwise, walk south along Carrera 7 along the Plaza de Bolívar, then hang a left. Ca. 9, 6-45. Tel: 281-0811, E-mail: ventas@hotelcasadelabotica.com, URL: www.hotelcasadelabotica.com. Updated: Apr 04, 2011.

Hotel de la Ópera

(ROOMS: $180-220) Set in two beautifully restored houses next door to the Presidential Plaza on one side and the opulent Teatro Colón on the other, Hotel de la Ópera is La Candelaria's most luxurious lodging option. Everything about this hotel is utterly romantic and polished, from the elegant dining rooms to the Italian-styled suites. Amenities include an on-site pool, a spa, restaurants with magnificent views of colonial Bogotá and a business center with free Internet. Ten-percent tax not included in the price. If you decide against a taxi, head to the Plaza de Bolivar at the Southern end of the Carrera 7 and then walk through the plaza to Calle 10. Ca. 10, 5-72. Tel: 336-2066/5285, E-mail: sales@hotelopera.com.co, URL: www.hotelopera.com.co. Updated: Apr 4, 2011.

ApartaEstudios La Candelaria

(APARTMENTS: $230-380/week; $370-775/month) If Bogotá is more than just a brief stopover for you, consider renting a studio apartment by the week or month. ApartaEstudios offers four types of apartments to choose from, the cheapest being about what you would expect from a studio and the most expensive decked out with spiraling staircases, chimneys and stylish kitchens. All apartments are fully furnished and come with WiFi. Any bus to Germania and beyond will get you close. Ca. 10, 2-40. Tel: 281-6923, Cel: 313-442-1805, E-mail: contactenos@apartaestudioslacandelaria. com, URL: www.apartaestudioslacandelaria.com. Updated: Mar 01, 2011

Restaurants

Restaurants in La Candelaria run the gamut from traditional Colombian restaurants serving dishes like *ajiaco* (potato soup), *sancocho* (a traditional soup made with meat, plantains and yucca) and *asados* (BBQs) to Middle Eastern, Italian, French, Japanese, Thai, and Mexican restaurants. Because several universities are in the area, hamburger, arepa and pizza fast-food joints are common. At many Novo-Colombian bistros, live jazz and other relaxing music set the mood. A word of caution, however: many restaurants are closed on Sunday. Candelaria has several neighborhood grocery stores and bakeries. **Olímpica** supermarkets (Av. Jiménez 4-74 and Cra. 4, 18-42) and Ley (Cra. 7, near Plaza Bolívar) offer a greater variety of goods. Updated: Mar 10, 2011

Pastelería Organización Gers

This bakery may have an unusual name, but it cooks up some mighty delicious desserts. Just walking along Carrera 4, your eye will latch on to the pastries gleaming in the glass case. There are the usual goodies, like *milhojas* (cake made with puff pastry) and *alfajores* (soft cookie filled with caramel), as well as some unique ones, like the raspberry-filled, lemon-iced chocolate cake. Pastelería Organización Gers also has overflowing baskets of fine breads, including a tasty rye with raisins and seeds. Monday-Saturday 11 a.m.-10 p.m., Sunday 11 a.m.-6 p.m. Cra. 4, 14-95. Tel: 482-0742. Updated: Mar 10, 2011.

Donde Tatiana

(ENTREES: $2-3) Many Bogotanos go to Donde Tatiana for the lunch or dinner special. Choose from a variety of meats such as beef, *sobrebarriga* (stuffed roasted beef) and fish. The plates come heaped with salad, *patacones* (fried plantains), French fries, rice and beans. The mealtime spread comes with soup and a drink. The restaurant is just blocks from La Candelaria, which makes it a good place to fuel up after a long day of traveling into the capital. Daily 11 a.m.- 5 p.m. Cra. 4, 16-63. Updated: Mar 10, 2011.

An Andante Ma Non Troppo

(ENTREES: $8-13) It would be easy to stride past this restaurant without noticing it—one entrance lies at the back of a gift shop and the other is fairly nondescript. The inside, however, comprises four spacious rooms. Pastries, good coffee and a killer lunchtime promotion of two courses for around $6 are all on offer. Try the grilled chicken in herbs with Mexican soup, patacones and salad, and wash it down with a freshly squeezed fruit juice. Cra. 3, 10-92. Tel: 342-3237. Updated: Mar 10, 2011.

Quinua y Amaranto

(LUNCH: $7-8.50) This is one of two excellent vegetarian restaurants in La Candelaria. Due to its popularity, this charming and atmospheric place gets pretty packed—arrive early to avoid disappointment. Watch the culinary staff at work up front. We recommend the tortilla española. Monday noon-4 p.m, Tuesday-Saturday noon-7:30 p.m. Ca. 11, 2-95. Tel: 565-9982. Updated: Mar 10, 2011.

Café del Sol

(ENTREES: $2 and up) Perfect for couples wanting a romantic meal, Café del Sol is an atmospheric and intimate locale. Its dimly lit rooms span back from the bar on the street, ideal for those who don't want to be seen. Monday-Wednesday 8 a.m.-9 p.m., Thursday-Friday 8 a.m.-10 p.m., Saturday 9 a.m.-7 p.m. Ca. 14, 3-60. E-mail: cafedelsolcolombia@gmail.com Updated: Mar 10, 2011.

Café Para Dos

(ENTREES: $4-12) Behind a window decorated with multicolored bottles lies Café Para Dos: check out the rooms scattered with scattered with Moroccan throws and cushions. Upstairs there is an open fire, making this café an ideal place to sit back, drag on a hookah, enjoy a coffee or cocktail, and relax. Located at Ca. 14, 3-12 on the corner by Hotel Aragon. Monday-Thursday 11 a.m.-10 p.m., Friday, Saturday 11 a.m.-1 a.m. Tel: 600-5702, E-mail: cafeparados2003@yahoo.com.mx. Updated: Jun 14, 2011.

Casa de Citas

(ENTREES: $6.50-13) Formerly a brothel (hence the name), the Casa de Citas has converted itself into a cool hangout for live music and easy bites. Don't let the cover charge put you off. Once inside, knock back a rum or aguardiente, and listen to Cumbia, Bolero or Cuban Son music while checking out the balcony where *women de la vida alegre* (prostitutes) once stood to promote themselves to potential customers. The restaurant specializes in Peruvian cuisine. Daily noon-10 p.m. Cra. 3, 13-35. Tel: 286-6944/282-6368, E-mail: casa_de_citas1992@yahoo.es. Updated: Mar 10, 2011.

Escobar y Rosas

From Wednesday night onwards, there are lines of people left in the cold as this wildly popular bar/club reaches capacity. Inside, loads of fashionably dressed people are crammed into two tiny floors while the DJ plays funky tunes. The name of this establishment has nothing to do with the former head of the Medellín Cartel, but instead refers to a pharmacy that was formerly situated where the club is now. Only cash is accepted here. Cra. 4, 15-01. Tel: 341-7903. Updated: Jan 11, 2008.

La Vida en Rosa

(ENTREES: $4-9) La Vida en Rosa has an extraordinarily large menu and appears to have an enormous turnover, filling all five of its rooms at lunchtime. The set menu looks of particular quality and the lasagnas are enormous. This is a popular joint for brisk lunchtime service. Ca. 14, 4-38. Tel: 284-1609. Updated: Mar 10, 2011.

Pimienta y Café

(LUNCH: $4.50-8, ENTREES: $10-12) For a couple of dollars, you can feast on a set lunch menu that would fill even the emptiest stomach. Pimienta y Café is clean, friendly and spacious, and is often frequented by politicians climbing up the hill from Congress. The service is fast, and the food is substantial and flavorful. Monday-Friday noon-3 p.m., Saturday noon-4 p.m. Cra. 3, 9-27. Tel: 341-6805, Fax: 352-1158, E-mail: mijaro@hotmail.com. Updated: Mar 10, 2011.

Plaza del Chorro de Quevedo

In the heart of La Candelaria, at the steep end of the hill, is the Plaza del Chorro de Quevedo. On any given evening you can find a host of interesting and eclectic bars to frequent here. In front of the small chapel, there is normally a *cuentero* (storyteller) regaling a crowd for his dinner. Recommended bars are **Pequeña Santa Fe**, **El Gato Gris** and **Merlín**. Plaza del Chorro de Quevedo, Ca. 13 and Cra. 2. Updated: Jan 11, 2008.

Quiebra Canto

Quiebra Canto is the brainchild of a group of students from the Universidad Nacional. Twenty-nine years ago, they decided to create a place to play Silvio Rodríguez songs and start the revolution. Very little

of that original theme remains, but none-theless, Quiebra Canto is one of Bogotá's most popular haunts for a Wednesday night. Here, funk is mixed in with salsa and often washed down with a healthy dose of samba. Students dance the night away and loners stand at the bar looking moody. For a bird's eye view of the dance-floor, head to the second level. Cra. 5, 17-76. Tel: 243-1630. Updated: Jan 11, 2008.

Restaurante Vegetariano Loto Azul

(LUNCH: $2.45-4) For more than two de-cades, Loto Azul has been serving Bogo-tanos and foreigners delicious vegetarian food. Besides whipping up breakfasts and lunches accompanied by the salad bar ($2.45 main course only, $3.20 complete with soup), Loto Azul also prepares lasagnas,

sandwiches and buffets. Several times per week, it presents special dishes. In addition, the restaurant offers special programs: cook-ing courses, Bakhti yoga sessions (Tuesday 5 p.m.), videos (Thursday 6:15 p.m.), and open mic poetry and music (Friday 6-11 p.m.). Food is served Monday-Saturday 7 a.m.-4 p.m. Cra. 5a, 14-00. Tel: 334-2346/286-3954. Updated: Mar 10, 2011.

Restaurante Café Israelí L'Jaim

(ENTREES: $3-9) Hummus, matbuja, falafel, shawarma (lamb, veal or chick-en), lafa, zoarim, shakshuka—this place has any Middle Eastern comfort food that your stomach aches for. Made from millennia-old recipes, L'Jaim prepares traditional Israeli food for the discern-ing public. If you can't quite make up

● Activities

1 Casa Quinta de Bolívar B2
2 Cerro de Monserrate B2
3 Museo de Arte Moderno A2
4 Museo Nacional A1
5 Parque Nacional Olaya Herrera B1
6 Plaza de Toros la Santamaría A1

⑪ Eating

7 América Dulce América A1
8 Cha Cha A1
9 Frida A1
10 La Hamburguesería B1
11 La Juguetería A1
12 La Macarena A2
13 Leo Cocina y Cave A1

★ Services

14 Camera Repair Foto
 Almacén Buitriago A2
15 Camera Repair Local 231 A2
16 Policia Turismo A1

⊠ Shopping

17 Mercado de Pulgas San Alejo A2

▣ Sleeping

18 El Cafecito B1
19 Tequendama International A1

BOGOTÁ

your mind, you and a companion can try a combination plate. Vegetarian plates are also on the menu. Most dishes come with French fries. Don't forget to take home some pita, lafa or hummus. Sunday-Friday, and holidays 11 a.m.-5:30 p.m. Cra. 3, 14-79. Tel: 281-8635, Cel: 300-563-3654, E-mail: ljaim.restaurante@hotmail.com, URL: www.restauranteljaim.tripod.com. Updated: Mar 10, 2011.

El Bolón Verde ✦

(ENTREES: $9-15) Creative haute cuisine dished up with sweet jazz awaits you at El Bolón Verde. The eats cannot get more inspired than at this bistro. Choose from seafood like shrimp, squid and octopus, or beef tenderloin and pork served in curry or a ground coffee and whiskey sauce. Other dishes that grace the menu are julienned mango, bread with eggplant butter, and the meat platters accompanied by mashed potatoes, salad and bread. Don't forget to try the home-brewed beers. There's live jazz music Thursday-Saturday nights, with public jams on Friday or Saturday nights. On Wednesday evenings, the house band rehearses. Prices include tax, but not the 10 percent tip. Wednesday noon-11:30 p.m., Thursday noon-1:30 a.m., Friday-Saturday noon-3 a.m., Sunday noon-10 p.m. Cra. 1a (Callejón de las Brujas), 13-20, Plazoleta de El Chorro de Quevedo. Tel: 337-5290, Cel: 316-876-3771, E-mail: bolondeverde@hotmail.com. Updated: Mar 10, 2011.

Centro Internacional/ La Macarena

If you take the **Hotel Tequendama** as a reference point or are visiting the **Museo Nacional**, then you are standing in the small but perfectly located district of Centro Internacional. This neighborhood, which older maps call "Samper," is filled with fancy restaurants that cater to a highly paid clientele on weekdays. La Macarena is up the hill behind the Museo Nacional and beyond the Plaza de Toros. In La Macarena, you can find eclectic, artsy shops and funky restaurants and bars. Residents of La Macarena are probably what one describes as "alternative," and they are battling to keep their area that way. Bohemian and funky alike head here for a chilled glass of wine or cocktail before wandering in and out of local art galleries. Updated: Mar 14, 2011.

Things to See and Do

Plaza de Toros la Santamaría

If you think you can handle it, head to the bull ring in the early morning during the months of January and February to see young *toreros* (bullfighters) training. The Plaza de Toros la Santamaría routinely fills to capacity during these months, as it is a big deal here in Colombia. To get there, follow Carrera 7 north from the Candelaria as if you were going to the Museo Nacional. Just before reaching the museum, head right up the hill. Cra. 6 and Ca. 26, La Macarena. Tel: 334-1482. Updated: Feb 08, 2008.

Lodging

If you're looking for lodging in the Bogotá neighborhood of Centro Internacional/La Macarena, good luck. Hotels and hostels in this area are rare; the one notable option is the **Tequendama Intercontinental Hotel**, which offers a wide range of rooms including presidential suites and small singles. Updated: Jul 05, 2010.

Tequendama Intercontinental

(ROOMS: $168-226) Don't let the 50s-era architecture fool you—Tequendama is all luxury on the inside. Rooms come in various sizes, from standard and business to junior and presidential suites. At the lowest level, rooms come with cable TV, mini-bar, 24-hour room service, a tub or Jacuzzi, and a daily paper; amenities increase as you climb the ladder. On-site restaurants offer Colombian and international cuisine (mostly Italian), and the well-stocked hotel bar is certainly quite chic. Other amenities include a business center with Internet access, a putting green, and an on-site sauna and spa. Another advantage to this hotel is its close proximity to the historical center and to Plaza de Toros. It also has easy travel options to the airport, the fashionable Zona Rosa and Parque 93. All buses heading south on Carrera 7 will pass by the Tequendama. From the airport, a taxi is the quickest and easiest option. Cra. 10, 26-21. Tel: 382-2930, Fax: 282-2860, E-mail: bogharsv@interconti.com, URL: www.intertequendama.com.co. Updated: Mar 02, 2011

Restaurants

América Dulce América

(ENTREES: $5-14) Previously known as La Moderna, América Dulce América is a wonderful restaurant across from the National Museum in one of Bogota's beautiful brick buildings. With a pleasant view of Monserrate, América Dulce América is perfect for lunch, dinner or simply to enjoy a few authentic salsa tunes. The cuisine includes typical Colombian favorites and the chef's own fabulous creations. The service is exceptional and the staff treats you like a guest in their home. América Dulce América is ideal for lunch with a friend, drinks and appetizers after work, or a night of dancing to great music. Monday-Friday noon-3:30 p.m. Closed Saturday and Sunday. Cra. 13 and Ca. 28a, local 301, Edificio Falcasparque Central Bavaria. Tel: 288-7964. E-mails: americadulceamerica@gmail.com. Updated: Mar 10, 2011.

La Hamburguesería

(ENTREES: $7-13) Small and brightly decorated, with a streetside heated patio, La Hamburguesería is a good option if you are craving a succulent burger. Medallions of beef and the *calentao* are recommended. Cra. 4a, 27-27. Tel: 281-1286, URL: www.lahamburgueseria.com. Updated: Mar 02, 2011.

Frida

(ENTREES: $9-13) Although out of reach for most budget travelers, Frida's is quite simply the best Mexican restaurant in town. The flavorsome pork ribs bathed in a *rosa de jamaica* (Jamaican rose) salsa are a must-try. For more traditional meals, try fajitas or the aztec soup. Beautifully decorated and with incredible service, this is the place to come for Mexican food while in Bogotá. Cra. 10, 26-40. Tel: 562-0606, E-mail: elisa-mendoza@hotmail.com. Updated: Mar 02, 2011.

La Juguetería

(ENTREES: $13-17) Where else can you dine on fine steaks while surrounded by toys? Dozens of slightly creepy dolls are suspended from the beams and rafters here; nonethless, it is hard to be distracted from the scrumptious food on offer. Bring along some old toys and receive a discount. Ca. 27, 4a-03. Tel: 341-1188. Updated: Mar 10, 2011.

Leo Cocina y Cava

(ENTREES: $14-35) Leo is quite simply the most exclusive and expensive restaurant in Bogotá, and with good reason. Chef Leonor Espinosa has dedicated this establishment to Colombian coastal food with a gourmet twist. If you can make a reservation and secure a table then be sure to try the tuna cut, encrusted with santanderean ants. Come well dressed—you'll be brushing shoulders with the highest-ranking politicians. Ca. 27b, 6-75. Tel: 286-7091/281-6267, E-mail: reservaciones@leonorespinosa.com, URL: www.leococinaycava.com. Updated: Mar 02, 2011.

Tapas Macarena

(ENTREES: $15-25) A hip Dutch/Colombian couple opened Tapas Macarena back in 2007 to fill the city's lack of a traditional tapas bar and to create an intimate space to share food with friends. All meals in this tiny corner spot begin with tasty homemade bruschetta, and the menu offers international whiskeys and Belgian beers. Stop by on a Saturday for live music. Cra. 4a, 26-01. Tel: 243-9004, E-mail: tapasmacarena@yahoo.com. Updated: Mar 02, 2011.

Chapinero

The Chapinero, traditionally popular with students and young couples because it is close to business centers and universities, is undergoing a construction boom. The old apartment buildings that filled the neighborhood are being replaced with flashy new constructions. Any bus from La Candelaria running north on Carrera Septima will take you through Chapinero. There are some decent choices of restaurants and nightclubs here, but for backpackers, this will remain largely a transit area between La Candelaria and Zona T. Updated: May 13, 2009.

Things to See and Do

Parque Nacional Olaya Herrera

If the Parque Central Simón Bolívar is simply too far away, a far easier option is to head to Parque Nacional Olaya Herrera, located in Chapinero. Not as large or as scenic as Parque Central Simón Bolívar, it is still very popular with Bogotanos. There are fountains, plazoletas, football pitches, tennis courts and play areas for children. On weekends, and Sundays in particular, the park is very well attended. Take any bus heading north on Carrera 7 as far as Calle 36. Between Ca. 36 to 39 and Cra. Séptima to Quinta. Updated: Feb 08, 2008.

Lodging

If you're in Bogotá and looking for a hotel, Chapinero may not be the best place to look; options are somewhat limited, though the neighborhood is undergoing massive amounts of construction that could increase its appeal. The neighborhood is close to the business center of Bogotá, so if you're here on business, this would be a good place to look. One of the best options here is **El Cafecito** (with rooms starting at $12), which is part of a chain of hostels under the same name with locations in Quito and Cuenca, Ecuador. If you're looking for a bit more class, check out the **G Hotel**, with rooms starting in the mid $50s. Updated: Jul 05, 2010.

MID-RANGE

El Cafecito

(ROOMS: $12-50) The El Cafecito chain (with branches in Quito and Cuenca, Ecuador) has earned its place on Bogotá's growing list of fine hostels. One block from the Parque Nacional, 20 minutes from the Candelaria, and perhaps 10 minutes from the Macarena, El Cafecito is setting the pace. The location is a beautifully restored Bogotá townhouse with large rooms, wooden floors, an ample garden, and a downstairs café and bar. Accommodating up to 40 guests, the hostel has a few dormitories as well as one double and one private room. Since the only neighbors are office buildings, there is no problem if your BBQ or party in the garden gets a little raucous. Cra. 6, 34-70. Tel: 285-8308, E-mail: bogota@cafecito.net, URL: www.cafecito.net. Updated: Mar 01, 2011.

La Casona del Patio Amarillo

(ROOMS: $50-85) Positioned almost equidistant between the Candelaria and the Zona Rosa, La Casona has long been a favorite for those with a little more cash and a desire to get out of the traditional gringo ghettos. Attentive staff, a great breakfast, and well-cared for rooms and communal areas make La Casona arguably the best value mid-range option in Bogotá. The hotel is located between two major thoroughfares flowing both North and South - the Carrera 7 and the Carrera 9 respectively, so most buses that trundle these routes will bring you within two blocks. Cra. 8, 69–24. Tel: 212-8805/1991, E-mail: casona@telecom.com.co, URL: www.lacasonadelpatio.net. Updated: Mar 01, 2011.

High Park Suites

(ROOMS: $52-105) This refined boutique hotel, the only 100 percent LGBT hotel in Bogotá, is conveniently located at the heart of the city's gay culture. Rooms at the High Park are spacious and comfortable, have great views, and include WiFi, telephones, cable TVs and bathrooms (some with tubs). Hotel facilities include a terrace, café-bar, and a dining room where a delicious Colombian breakfast (included in the room price) is served. The staff will make you feel at home, and if you're looking for a tour of Bogotá, the hotel has excellent English- and Spanish-speaking guides. Cra. 4, 58-58. Tel: 249-5149/5152, E-mail: reservations@hotelhighpark.com, URL: www.highparksuites.com. Updated: Mar 01, 2011.

G Hotel

(ROOMS: $85-130) Located in this gay-friendly neighborhood, near the best gay nightlife in the city, this hotel is a great gay hotel option in Bogotá. It's a smaller hotel, with only 12 rooms, but the attention is very good, the breakfast is delicious and the rooms are comfortable. Services include WiFi, private bath and cable TV. The hotel can also provide tours of Bogotá. Price includes all taxes and service charges and coffee in the mornings. Ca. 63 and Cra. 20. E-mail: reservas@gayhotelbogota.com, URL: www.gayhotelbogota.com. Updated: Dec 10, 2010.

BOGOTÁ

BOGOTÁ

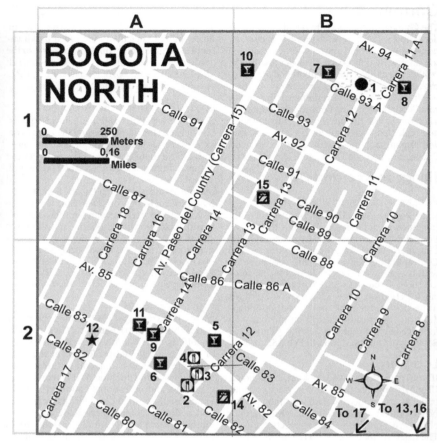

Nightlife

Cha Cha

The winning ticket for Cha Cha is its lofty location on the 41st floor of an otherwise nondespcript Bogotá skyscraper. With views over all of Bogotá, clubbers can enjoy electronica music and chill out on open-air patios. The club is available to rent for private functions during the week and then becomes a proper club from Thursday night onward, with a total capacity nudging 900 liquored-up, dancing bodies. Cra. 7, 32-26, 41st floor. Tel: 350-5074, E-mail: info@elchacha.com, URL: www.elchacha.com. Updated: Mar 10, 2011.

ROSALES

Young professionals in Chapinero dream of upgrading to Rosales. Here the streets are tree-lined, security is high, and the beautiful people drift from cafés to design stores to award-winning restaurants. New bars are springing up, and theaters and fancy shops can be found around every street corner. This is not a backpacker destination, but if you feel like leaving behind the dirt-encrusted cargo pants and fleece and taking a few more pesos out with you, Rosales is a fun place to dress up. Updated: May 13, 2009.

Lodging

The wealthy Rosales neighborhood is home to a few expensive hotels, including **Estelar La Fontana**, which is replete with all the trappings of any American luxury hotel. Your priciest option is the **Hotel Casa Medina**, a popular destination for business travelers due to its location in the heart of the business district and its posh amenities. Hostels and other cheaper options don't really exist because the rent is so high. Updated: Jul 05, 2010.

● **Activities**

1 Parque de la 93B1

⊕ **Eating**

2 Bogotá Beer Company A2
3 Luna A2
4 The Irish Pub B2

▣ **Nightlife**

5 Alma A2
6 Bar 201 A2
7 El Salto del Ángel B2
8 El Sitio B1
9 Gótica A2
10 Kukaranakara B1
11 Penélope A2

★ **Services**

12 Hospital Clínica del Country A2

▨ **Shopping**

13 Authors Bookstore B2
14 Centro Comercial El Andino A2
15 Mac Tools B1

▥ **Sleeping**

16 Hostal Casa de Medina B2
17 La Casona del Patio Amarillo B2

BOGOTÁ

HIGH END

Estelar La Fontana

(ROOMS: $210-411) Estelar La Fontana is located in the north, next to the shops and restaurants of the Unicentro mall. With 193 rooms and high-end amenities, this stately construction is a sight to behold. From standard rooms to the Estelar Suite, spaces are decorated along the lines of upscale U.S. hotel chains. The on-site restaurant features live music and a rotating buffet, and the English-style bar is a great place to start or end your night. Given Estelar's location in the North, it is advised to catch a taxi from the airport. Av. 127, 15a-10. Tel: 615-4400, E-mail: reservas@hotelesestelar.com, URL: www.hotelesestelar.com. Updated: Mar 02, 2011.

Hotel Casa Medina

(ROOMS: $430-609) Located in the heart of Bogotá's business district and within short walking distance of some of Rosales' fashionable bars and restaurants, Casa Medina is an ideal destination for business travelers. Built in 1945 and displaying a blend of Spanish and French influences, its rooms boast a modern-chic ambiance without sacrificing comfort. Casa Medina's restaurant isn't lacking in elegance either, with international cuisine available in a sophisticated dining area. Menu options include Thai chicken supreme, salmon medallions in a citrus fruit sauce, and broiled veal escalope in a cherry sauce. If work is on the menu, the hotel offers a fax, copy center, translation services, a secretary center and audiovisual equipment. Try the on-site gym or massage room when work gets you down. Head into town on Carrera 7 and the hotel is located on the left as you head south towards the center. Cra. 7, 69a-22. Tel: 217-0288/312-0299, Fax: 312-3769, E-mail: red@charlestoncasamedina.com, URL: www.hoteles-charleston.com/casamedina. Updated: Mar 02, 2011.

Zona Rosa

Located between Calles 79 and 85 and Carreras 11 and 15, this lively area on the northern part of the city is a trendy night spot where younger crowds meet and party along the streets lined with fine restaurants and hot nightclubs. Updated: Jun 03, 2008.

Nightlife

Gótica

Gótica is a long-time clubber's favorite in Bogotá for its seemingly endless list of world-class DJs invited to spin their business in one of its three rooms. You will find yourself immersed in either electronica, crossover or buoyed up on hip hop if you decide to make Gótica your club of choice on a Friday or Saturday night. Prices are steep for those who are not affiliates of the club but for one evening, you will enjoy yourself enough to forget about the money you are dropping here. *Note: Gótica is currently closed for renovation; call or check the website for information on its reopening.* Cra. 14, 82-50. Tel: 218-0727, URL: www.myspace.com/clubgotica. Updated: Mar 09, 2011.

Bar 201

(COVER: $5) Designed to look like an apartment, complete with paintings, sofas and table lamps, Bar 201 is a fun place to listen to tunes and have a drink. On occasion, there is live music. There is usually no line to get in. Ca. 82, 13-26. Tel: 530-4051. Updated: Dec 19, 2007.

Penélope

(COVER: $10) While other clubs are succumbing to the fad of minimalist themes and furnishing, Penélope, a classic club in Bogotá, refuses to be bullied and maintains its glam style and purpose. The music here, electronica and crossover, is excellent and can be heard in the two dance rooms. Cra. 14a, 83-49. Tel: 606-3568, E-mail: info@club-penelope.com, URL: www.club-penelope.com. Updated: Dec 19, 2007.

El Sitio

(ENTREES: $17-25) El Sitio, "The Place," is exactly that if you want to get back to good old-fashioned partying, Colombian style. Basic furnishings make this bar/restaurant/club a place to buy a bottle with some friends, kick back to some live music, and then leap up and dance energetically with the rest of the patrons. Considered one of the best places to go for a party, El Sitio rarely disappoints. Arrive early to avoid long lines. Tuesday noon-midnight, Wednesday-Saturday noon-3 a.m. Cra. 11a, 93b-12. Tel: 616-7372, E-mail: info@elsitiogroup.com, URL: www.elsitiogroup.com. Updated: Mar 02, 2011.

Alma

Alma is the most happening club in Bogotá. Entry is tough but not impossible; it is best to find friends in high places who can guarantee your entry. If that's not possible, be sure to arrive early. People call weeks ahead of time to reserve the VIP sofas. Wednesday night is strictly salsa and Thursday is 80s night with a sprinkling of Latin rock. On Fridays and Saturdays, the three rooms are split into funk, soul and acid jazz. Ca. 85, 12-51. Tel: 622-8289. Updated: Dec 19, 2007.

Zona T

So-called for its two pedestrian streets that meet in a "T", the Zona T has some of Bogotá's best shopping and nightlife. Rival restaurants and bars blast music in efforts to drown each other out and lure in patrons. Fine restaurants as well as staple favorites such as **Crepes and Waffles** and the **Irish Bar** are located here. If you're not interested in the bars, restaurants or clubs, there are three enormous shopping malls in the immediate vicinity. **Atlantis** and **Andino** have multiscreen cinemas, and **El Retiro** is considered a luxury mall. Updated: Dec 05, 2007.

Restaurants

The Irish Pub

Popular with young Colombians, the Irish Pub really does not resemble an Irish establishment at all. However, on weekends the forecourt that spills onto the pedestrianized section of the Zona T fills with revelers. For a pint and some traditional pub food you could do a lot worse. Cra. 12a, 83-48. Tel: 691-8711. Updated: Mar 10, 2011.

Luna

(ENTREES: $8-35) In the heart of the Zona T, Luna—along with many of its neighbors in the area—is an upmarket Italian restaurant, specializing in risotto and pastas. The décor sets it apart from the rest and the food will have you purring appreciatively. Ca. 83, 12-20. Tel: 257-2088, E-mail: lunazonak@hotmail.com, URL: www.zonak.com.co. Updated: Mar 02, 2011.

V!VA ONLINE REVIEW

LUNA

Nothing on the menu will disappoint. Pastas are authentic and well done. This place is both affordable and a luxury dining experience!

April 25, 2009

Parque de la 93

Along with Zona T, Parque de la 93 is a key area in Bogotá for merrymaking. With abundant restaurants, bars and clubs, the area has transformed from a residential district into a commercial one. With fewer students, this area appeals to a more mature crowd than the Zona T, which is evident when you compare prices. For an excellent night out, you should head to **Salto del Ángel** on the western edge of the park, where you can enjoy dinner and watch the restaurant morph into a late-night bar and nightclub complete with open fireplaces inside and terraces upon which to gaze down onto the dance floor.

You would be hard pressed to call Parque de la 93 a real park. It is more of an upmarket grassy tree-lined plaza. Parque 93 is somewhere to go when you have had your fill of colonial buildings and the mayhem of La Candelaria. Here you can spy on how the other half lives; this area is full of luxury apartments and expensive restaurants. There are a couple of places that accommodate the traveler's budget, namely the **Bogotá Beer Company** on the corner of Juan Valdéz. If money is not an issue, you can indulge in many places here. Updated: Feb 06, 2008.

Nightlife

El Salto del Ángel Bar

Mainly appealing to young, moneyed professionals, El Salto del Ángel is filled with beautiful people every Friday and Saturday, and often midweek. Tables are moved aside as 80s music, electronica and contemporary latin beats are turned up. Cra. 13, 93a-45. Tel: 635-9307. Updated: Dec 19, 2007.

Kukaramakara Bar

Another effervescent option in northern Bogotá for those who can get their tongues around the twister of a name and want to head out and hear some live music covered by the house band. The band plays latin tunes, with a DJ spinning records during its breaks to keep the dancefloor heaving with the crowded and sweaty bodies. Arrive early to secure a table. Cra. 15, 93-57. Tel: 642-3166, E-mail: bogota@kukaramakara.com, URL: www.kukaramaka-ra.com. Updated: Mar 10, 2011.

Usaquén

Usaquén, at one time a separate village on the outskirts of Bogotá, has been consumed by the capital's unrelenting sprawl. Now Usaquén resembles a village within Bogotá with chic boutiques, quality restaurants and some equally enticing bars. These businesses are all clustered around an attractive plaza in an area inhabited by wealthier residents. A great day to visit is Sunday, when the flea market is in full flow with interesting bric-a-brac. Updated: Mar 10, 2011.

Things to See and Do

Museo de "El Chicó" Mercedes de Pérez

(ADMISSION: $1.50 adults, $1 students/senior Citizens, $0.50 children under 5) Once a typical hacienda of la Sabana of Bogota, the Museo de "El Chico" is home to a vast and valuable collection of artifacts from the 18th century, ranging from religious paintings to copper and bronze tools from the colonial age. In 1992 it was declared a place of cultural interest within the district. Surrounded by beautiful parks, the museum offers a calming and relaxing way to escape the ever-expanding city life. Monday-Friday 10 a.m.-5 p.m. Saturdays 8 a.m.-noon. Closed Sundays and holidays. Cra.7, 93-01. Tel: 623-1066, Fax: 622 2183, Email: info@museodelchico.com, URL: www.museodelchico.com. Updated May 18, 2011.

Restaurants

Zhang China Gourmet

(ENTREES: $10) Good Chinese restaurants in Bogotá are pretty hard to come by, so the discovery of this eatery in Usaquén was quite well received. The setting is ideal, right on the corner of the plaza, and the interior is modern and stylish. Cra. 6, 119-01. Tel: 213-3979. Updated: May 18, 2009.

Restaurante Casa Vieja

(ENTREES: $14-18) Restaurante Casa Vieja (formerly known as Alfredo's Bistro), placed right in the heart of the village-like district of Usaquén, is a perfect place to settle down to a long lunch after a shopping excursion in the Hacienda Santa Barbara. When the weather holds, the place to be is on the patio, otherwise there are plenty of tables indoors. The Thai Chicken Salad is good value for its size at $10; also recommended are the Dill Salmon and the Grilled Chicken in a Blue cheese sauce. Monday-Saturday noon-10 p.m., Sunday noon-6 p.m. Cra. 6a, 117-35. Tel: 213-3246, E-mail: info@casavieja.com.co. Updated: Mar 03, 2011

V!VA ONLINE REVIEW

RESTAURANTE CASA VIEJA

" At this restaurant, they have the best food ever. It has an excellent atmosphere, mostly if you want a calm place to have a good conversation. "

January 10, 2011

BOGOTÁ

80 Sillas

(ENTREES: $14-25) 80 Sillas lists itself as an "informal restaurant." However, at first glance it appears to be anything but that. This seafood restaurant and cevichería is fast becoming a favorite for yuppies working in the Usaquén area. The ceviche is very good, and the staff is insistent that the ingredients arrived fresh that morning from the coast. Ca. 118, 6a-05. Tel: 619-2471. Updated: Mar 10, 2011.

AROUND BOGOTÁ
ZIPAQUIRÁ

 2,600m 62,000 📞 1

Zipaquirá is mostly known for its enormous underground salt cathedral. What visitors don't necessarily know is that this is one of the more attractive colonial towns in the country, and that it is worth spending a day or two here to bask in the sun and surrounding greenery. The main plaza boasts the history of this salt mining town, and the wealth of Zipaquirá is immediately evident in a brief glance at the immense cathedral on the square and the immaculately clean condition of the narrow surrounding streets.

In pre-Columbian times, this town was home to the Muisca people. Zipaquirá, which in Chibcha (the Muiscan language) means "the land of the *zipa* (king)," suggests that this was a prosperous region, likely due to the region's salt supplies. The Muisca people would sell salt or trade it for goods.

The salt, which is still being mined from the mountainside to this day, was formed thousands of years ago when Zipaquirá was once under water. To get to Zipaquirá from Bogotá, take the Transmilenio to Portal del Norte ($0.95), then a bus to Zipaquirá ($2).

Things to See and Do

Salt Cathedral ❗

(ADMISSION: $11) Dark passages beneath the mountain had been traditionally associated in the Christian culture with Hell and the devil, but a group of miners transformed their workplace into a place of worship, which became a symbol of their devotion. For more than 500 years, the salt mountains that surround the town of Zipaquirá have been exploited, first by the Muiscas, the native culture of the region, and then by the Spaniards and their descendants.

After Christianity was introduced into the region, the miners started to hang religious images in the walls of the mine for protection. The fervor of the workers inspired the government to build a shrine in the mines. The project was completed in 1954 and soon began to attract visitors. The salt cathedral is a must-see for Catholics that visit Bogotá, (Zipaquirá is just 15.5 mi from Bogotá and is accessible by car or train), but the architecture and the fine carving of statues and religious symbols appeal to all kinds of visitors.

The current cathedral is not the original one. As time passed, the water that seeped in from outside started to damage the cathedral and posed a threat to visitors. In 1990, the government closed the shrine and started to build a new one 60 meters (197 ft) below the old cathedral. The project was completed in 1995 and now covers 0.8 hectares (2.1 ac) of underground tunnels and chambers.

The cathedral is composed of three sections. First there is the Stations of the Cross, where small shrines carved in salt guide visitors through the scenes of the passion and death of Christ. The tradition says that depending on the gravity of your sins and your willingness to repent, you can take one of three stairs to the next level. The more sins, the longer the stairway. Cold tunnels illuminated by blue and white lights lead to the second section, the dome. A ramp takes the visitors deep into the mountain where they can see in the distance a 16-meter (52-ft) cross carved into the wall of the central chamber of the cathedral. Mass is held there every Sunday and on special occasions.

At the bottom is the central chamber, which is supported by four columns that represent the four evangelists, and a round marble sculpture of the creation of man, inspired by Michelangelo's Sistine chapel fresco painting. The chamber is also decorated with several angel sculptures meant to be a reproduction of the Pietà, as well as a Nativity scene carved in stone. Further down, there is a concert hall and a path that leads to the surface and a small park dominated by a statue honoring the salt miners that worked in the mine over the centuries.

There are no religious requirements for admittance. People with heart conditions, fear of darkness or enclosed spaces are not encouraged to take the tour. Daily 9 a.m.-3 p.m. Updated: Mar 10, 2011.

Steam Train to Zipaquirá

(TICKETS: $21 adults, $17 senior citizens, $12.50 children) An interesting and fun way to get out to the Salt Cathedral at Zipaquirá is to travel on the Sabana Steam train from central Bogotá. The train only runs on Saturdays, Sundays and public holidays, and it is imperative that you head to the Estación de La Sabana a couple of days in advance to secure your seat. There is a buffet carriage on the train, but purchases here are not included in the price of your ticket. Saddle up and settle down, and let the touring papayera band play their tunes as you roll out to Zipaquirá. Daily 8:30 a.m.-5:30 p.m. Estación de la Sabana, Ca. 13, 18-24. Tel: 375-0557, URL: www.turistren.com.co. Updated: Mar 07, 2011

Lodging

Hotel Colonial

(ROOMS: $7-15) A fantastic find in the center of town (just 2 blocks from the main plaza and another 2 blocks from the salt cathedral), Hotel Colonial has everything you are looking for in an economic yet stylish and comfortable hotel. With 50 rooms among two well-manicured courtyards and a cozy, green backyard, you're sure to find the right setting and accommodation. All rooms (except the dorm) have a private bathroom with hot water and cable TV. Facing the mountain from the main plaza, walk one street to the left, then take the first to the right. Hotel Colonial is the yellow hotel on the left side of the street. Ca. 3, 6-57. Tel: 852-2690. Updated: Mar 10, 2011

Restaurants

Sakura Japonés

(LUNCH: $3.50) Although Sakura Japonés doesn't serve the most authentic Japanese cuisine in the country, you can still count on having a complete meal here in a pleasant atmosphere. There is a set lunch menu that includes juice, soup, salad, vegetables, meat or chicken, rice or potatoes, and a pastry dessert for just $3.50. You can always order á la carte from the general menu, where noodle soups and basic sushi items are freshly prepared in the tiny kitchen out back. Catering or take-out service is also available upon request. Ca. 4, 12-37, in front of Parque la Esperanza. Tel: 851-0261, Cel: 313-244-8555/4197. Updated: May 28, 2008.

Restaurante Sabor a Leña

With so many similar restaurants to choose from, it would be easy to skip Sabor a Leña. However, it shouldn't be overlooked, as its great prices, tasty local food and convenient location make it perfect for travelers needing a good, quick meal. The menu, which changes daily, can be found outside the main entrance. Sabor a Leña is across the square from the archaeological museum, at the foot of the hill of the salt cathedral. Ca. 1, 7-12/16. Tel: 852-2213. Updated: Mar 10, 2011.

SUESCA

Suesca is a rock climber's wonderland. Rocks come in all shapes and sizes, catering to experts, beginners and those in between. Not only can you have fun on the rocks, but you can also try your hand at rafting, mountain biking, camping and hiking. Suesca makes for an excellent weekend break from Bogotá, and can be combined with trips to Guatavita and perhaps Villa de Leyva. There is a fair amount of guesthouses and restaurants throughout the area. Take the Transmilenio to the Portal del Norte station (the northern end of the line) and then catch any bus within the station heading to Suesca (40 min-1 hr). Updated: May 16, 2008.

GUATAVITA

Guatavita is a pleasant day trip from Bogotá, a place where travelers can escape the city fumes and explore a little of the Cundinamarca countryside. The original Laguna de Guatavita was a sacred site to the local Muisca people, who were known to have enormous reserves of gold. Here in the lake the leader of the Muisca would bathe while covered in gold. This most likely gave rise to the idea held by Spanish conquistadors—in particular Gonzalo Jiménez de Quesada, who discovered the lake in 1537—that the lake was one of the possible sites of the mythical El Dorado. There is an interesting wedge cut out of the side of the lake where the Spanish attempted to drain it to extract its riches. Over the years, there have been several attempts to recover gold from the lake and all have ended in failure.

The town as it is today was built in a traditional colonial fashion, but it is obviously artificial. It was moved to its present location in 1970 after the waters from the Bogotá River flooded. There are some decent restaurants and plenty of stalls to purchase Colombian gifts. Brave souls can also partake in aquatic sports in the chilly lake waters. The laguna is open Tuesday-Sunday 9 a.m.-4 p.m., and costs $4.50 for nationals and $7 for foreigners From Bogotá, take the Transmilenio to the Portal del Norte station, then catch a bus from within the station. Updated: Mar 09, 2011

!))))

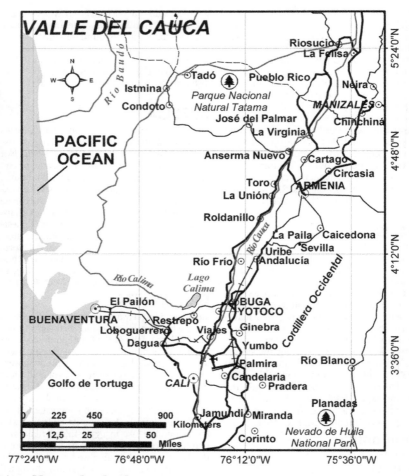

Valle del Cauca

The raucous epicenter of Cali makes the department of Valle del Cauca the powerhouse of southwestern Colombia. Throughout the region, the average altitude is roughly 1,000 meters (3,280 ft) above sea level. In Valle del Cauca's extreme west lies Cali's ugly sister, Buenaventura, a port city flanked by the waters of the Pacific Ocean. The department's other boundaries are defined by the mountain ranges that make up the central and western ridges of the Andes. The Cauca, one of Colombia's most powerful and longest rivers, flows through these mountains.

The department has always been strategically important for overland travel and import/export, so there is no shortage of interesting

sites to visit. From Cartago in the north, bordering the neighboring department of Risaralda, there is a steady line of religious monuments that follow the Cauca River and span south. Notable churches can be found in Cartago, Toro, Roldanillo, Bugalagrande, Guacari, Guadalajara de Buga and Jamundí.

If following the route of the river, take time to check out the traditional vallecaucana estancias, coffee farms, adventure sports and natural sights in Calima, El Cerrito and Palmira. Also, don't miss an opportunity to check out locally woven crafts made from plantain fibers or try the nationally famous vallecaucana *champús* (traditional fruit and herbs drink) , *marranitas* (fried plantain balls) and *aborrajados* (banana dessert) dishes. Updated: Sep 01, 2011.

History

Until the arrival of the Spaniards, the territory now called Valle del Cauca was inhabited by hunter-gatherer tribes, which were prevalent in and around the Calima River. The Spanish empire grew and both Popayán and Cali were founded by the conquistador Sebastián de Belalcázar in 1536, Popayán being first.

During this colonial period, the area fell under the auspices of the governing body in Quito, Ecuador. Later, after independence and the annexation of the Valle del Cauca, the territory was split between Popayán and Buenaventura. In 1857, a state was created that included the departments of Chocó, Caquetá and Pasto. However, in 1908, these territories were divided, creating Valle del Cauca as we know it today.

During the industrialization of the 20th century, a deteriorating economy and violence pushed people toward the major urban areas of Cali, Cartago and Palmira, which influenced the growth of the department. To this day, Cali and other towns suffer from ill distribution of wealth, mass migration due to conflict, and the destruction that accompanies the rise and fall of powerful cocaine cartels. Updated: Sep 01, 2011.

When to Go

During just about every month of the year, there is a festival or feria taking place somewhere in the Valle del Cauca, from the remotest hamlet to downtown Cali. Every December, thousands of people gather for the Feria de Cali, a rowdy music festival complete with bullfighting and a parade—an event not to be missed. Shortly after the Feria de Cali, the Carnaval de Juanchito is held in the municipality of Candelaria at the beginning of every year. Salsa dancing is also on display here, as well as vallecaucan sights, tastes and sounds. In June, the town of Ginebra holds its festival of Andean music. The Feria Nacional de la Caña de Azúcar is yet another important festival held in Florida each March and is worth a peek. The sweet taste of sugarcane is celebrated and locals parade wearing native costumes.

It is difficult to predict weather conditions along the coast. A squall can blow up at any time, but the two defined rainy seasons take place from March to May and then from October to November. During these seasons, Cali is badly affected; escape closer to the mountain ranges for a cooler climate. Average temperatures hover around 24°C (75°F). Updated: Sep 01, 2011.

Safety

Travel in Valle del Cauca is generally safe. You should be aware, however, of the red zone in the southeastern corner of the region, an area disputed between the government and FARC rebels. The FARC has suggested that the government create a demilitarized zone to negotiate prisoner exchanges near the towns of Florida and Pradera. In Cali, standard precautions are advised, as for any major city. Updated: Sep 01, 2011.

Things to See and Do

Should you tire of dancing salsa in Cali (the self-proclaimed salsa capital of the world), head outdoors and partake in one of the many activities at Lake Calima or at the national parks in the area. Given the region's geography, which includes plains, mountains, cloud forest, jungle and coast, there are a great deal of attractions in this southwestern Colombian department. Besides the main destinations, tourists will find rewards in exploring the small towns of Valle de Cauca, where religious relics and pre-Colombian settlements lurk around every corner. Updated: Sep 01, 2011.

Tours

For tours close to Cali, contact the **Centro Cultural de Cali** (Tel: 885-8855, E-mail: oficinadeturismo@cali.gov.co). If you want to organize tours further afield in Valle del Cauca, call the **Fondo Mixto de Promoción del Valle del Cauca** (Tel: 886-1300, ext 500). Updated: May 05, 2007.

Lodging

Tourism is growing in the Valle del Cauca, and this growth is reflected in the prevalence of decent, if not above-average, accommodation options. If you are happy with a cheap and cheerful backpacker haunt, then you will not be disappointed with the offerings available in Cali. One step up and you can find family-run places that make you feel at home. There are also stylishly rustic haciendas—usually kept in the family for eons—that have been thoughtfully restored and converted into tourist attractions and wonderful guesthouses. Of course, if money is no object, you'll also be able to find boutique hotels and luxury chains in most of the major cities. Updated: Jul 09, 2011.

VALLE DEL CAUCA

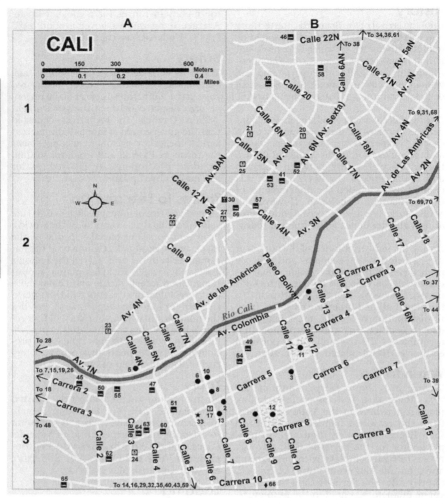

CALI

A 757m **👤** 2,100,000 **📞** 2

Colombia's third largest city is one of many contrasts. Watched over by the statue of the Cristo Rey and the monument of the Tres Cruces, the capital of the Valle del Cauca region is the industrial heart of Colombia's southwest. Cali entices all who visit with promises of balmy nights spent in the company of beguiling caleñas with salsa rhythms and days spent idly wandering through chic areas lined with boutiques or historic districts steeped in art and culture.

In the outlying areas of Cali, there are many recommended sights that include the zoo, Buga, Sonso, Parque Nacional Natural los Farallones and the Ecoparque Río Pance. Cali has much more to offer beyond its renowned nightlife and it is gradually becoming a well-rounded tourist destination. Nonetheless, it is the contagious desire to shake those hips that brings people together in the packed discotecas of the Colombian salsa capital.

Cali is coming to terms with its violent past and unruly present. Unlike other Colombian cities of its size, Cali's geography means that poorer neighborhoods are mixed in with richer ones to a greater extent than in Bogotá or Medellín.

● Activities

1 Capilla de la Inmaculada B3
2 Casa Proartes A3
3 Iglesia San Pedro B3
4 La Ermita B2
5 Los Gatos A3
6 Museo Arqueológico La Merced A3
7 Museo de Arte Moderno A3
8 Museo de Oro Calima A3
9 Museo Nacional de Transporte B1
10 Museo Religioso y Colonial
   San Francisco A3
11 Plaza de Caicedo B3
12 Plaza San Francisco B3
13 Teatro Municipal Enrique Buena A3
14 Universidad Santiago de Cali A3
15 Zoológico de Cali A3

⑩ Eating

16 Al Lado del Camino A3
17 Arte y Cocina A3
18 Café Mulatto A3
19 Cali Viejo A3
20 Cathay B1
21 Granada Faro B1
22 Inca Gaucho A2
23 La Joroba de Carmello A2
24 Macondo A3
25 Palo Alto B1
26 Piccolo Pomadoro A3
27 San Borondón A2
28 Vinos del Río A3

▣ Nightlife

29 El Habanero A3
30 Faro 2004 A2
31 Kukaramakara B1
32 Tin Tin Deo A3

★ Services

33 Centro Cultural de Cali A3
34 Edicameras B1
35 Hospital Universitario
   del Valle A3
36 Post Office B1

▨ Shopping

37 Centro Comercial Único B2
38 Chipichape B1
39 Jardín Plaza B3
40 Loma de la Cruz
   Artisan Park A3

▬ Sleeping

41 Cali Plaza Hotel B2
42 Calidad House B1
43 Casa Aguacanela A3
44 Casa Toscano B2
45 Design Hotel Austral A3
46 Hostal Iguana B1
47 Hostal San Fernando A3
48 Hostal Santa Rita A3
49 Hotel Camino Real B3
50 Hotel Dann A3
51 Hotel Del Puente A3
52 Hotel Don Jaime B1
53 Hotel Granada Real B2
54 Hotel Imperial B3
55 Hotel Intercontinental A3
56 Hotel Nevada B2
57 Hotel Posada Colonial B2
58 Hotel Sartor B1
59 Jardín Azul Casa Hotel A3
60 Jovitas A3
61 Kaffee Erde B1
62 La Casa Café A3
63 Posada de San Antonio A3
64 Sabor I Arte A3
65 Tostaky A3

♦ Tours

66 Chivas Tour B3
67 Christian Dojoseba (See 61)

▦ Transportation

68 Airport B1
69 Bus Terminal B2
70 Train Station B2

VALLE DEL CAUCA

It may not be a city to everybody's liking, but given Cali's geographical location, there is no denying its importance for those travelling to or from Ecuador. There are attractions here and in the surrounding areas that can keep the visitor entertained for a few days or more. Updated: Mar 06, 2008.

History

VALLE DEL CAUCA

Santiago de Cali was founded on July 25, 1536 in a fertile valley of the Lili River by the Spanish conquistador Sebastián de Belalcázar, who was also the founder of Ecuador's capital city, Quito. The original site of the city is in the southern end of the current metropolis. The city was moved roughly 17 kilometers (10.6 mi) away from the original site due to interference from the native Jamundí people.

During this period, Cali played second fiddle to Popayán and long into the 18th century, the city was more or less dominated by the existence of large fincas. In 1810, Cali declared its independence from Popayán, which led to several battles between royalists and the local militia.

Due to its location, easily within reach of the industries of Antioquia, the ports of the Pacific and the eastern edge of the Andes, Cali is very much a city near the frontline of the current Colombian conflict. Throughout the 1980s, the infamous Cali cartel was the major rival of it's better-publicized Medellín brethren (of Pablo Escobar fame) to the north. Updated: Sep 01, 2011.

Highlights

Put some salsa rhythm to your trip at the endless dance clubs of chic neighborhoods like **El Peñón** and **La Granada**.

The colonial neighborhood of **San Antonio** provides a beautiful view of the city and is the cultural center of Cali.

If you intend to ever learn salsa, this is the place! Take advantage of the wide range of schools available in the city.

When to Go

Cali is blessed with favorable weather patterns. The temperature averages 24-30°C (75-85°F) year round. Cali has two rainy seasons, and though you can expect the showers to be short, they are tremendous in volume.

The first wet season runs March-May and the second, which is briefer, happens October-November. Updated: Feb 18, 2008.

HOLIDAYS AND FESTIVALS

Cali's (and one of Colombia's) biggest festival is, without a doubt, Feria de Cali, which takes place every December 25-30. It has been a yearly event since 1957, a time when work ceases and partying persists. This event is the city's version of Carnaval; nights are alive with salsa concerts, horse races and exhibitions. Days are packed with bullfights, beauty and fashion pageants, parades, food festivals, sports events and city-wide street festivities. Music is integral to the event, with national and international acts performing.

In late August, the Petronio Alverez festival takes place, which is the country's largest Afro-Colombian festival. This five-day festival features food and music from the Pacific coast. Ajazzgo, a large jazz festival attracting hosts of international jazz artists, happens in early September. Late September is the time for the Festival Mundial de Salsa, when all the Cali salsa teams compete in several different categories for the crown of the Valle. Free salsa classes and conferences also take place during the day. Another worthwhile event is the Festival Internacional de Cine de Cali. Only a few years old, this international film festival is held in early November.

To close the year on December 31, there is always a huge concert on the hill in Plaza San Antonio, where song and dance is the center of the New Year's party.

Although there are Easter processions in Cali, they are not particularly notable. You are better off heading a couple of hours away to Popayán. Prices generally increase in Cali around and during Semana Santa—when all Colombians travel—and during the famous Feria de Cali. Updated: Sep 01, 2011.

Getting To and Away

BY BUS

The **Centrales de Transportes S.A. de Cali** (Ca. 30N, 2AN-29. Tel: 668-3655, E-Mail: info@terminalcali.com, URL: www.terminalcali.com) is a sprawling, three-story cement building and may appear somewhat daunting at first glance. It is well

policed and fairly easy to navigate, though. All bus companies are on the second floor.

Several bus companies, including **Expreso Palmiro** (Tel: 668-5341), **Expreso Bolivariano** (Tel: 668-7617) and **Velotax** (Tel: 668-7200/5587), offer services from Cali to Bogotá. Buses leave at least hourly between 3:30 a.m. and 11:45 p.m. The trip takes about 10 hours and costs $28-45.

Expreso Palmira runs buses to Popayán (3 hr, $5.60-28) every 15 minutes between 4 a.m. and 7 p.m. Multiple other companies do this same route, with the last bus leaving at 10 p.m.

Bus, taxis and vans serviced by Cooredor Vial del Pacífico leave for Buenaventura every 30 minutes between 4 a.m. and 7:30 p.m., costing $9-12 and taking about 3.5 hours.

A few different companies do the Cali-Medellín route (7-8 hr, $21-39), including Expreso Bolivariano, Expreso Trejos, Expreso Palmira and Flota Magdalena. The first bus leaves at 5 a.m. and the last at 11:40 p.m.

Buses to Buga (1 hr, $3-4) leave every 10 minutes between 6 a.m. and 9:30 p.m., with less frequent departures before and after those times. Updated: Jun 23, 2011.

BY TRAIN

The tourist train, **Tren Turístico Café y Azúcar** (Av. Vásquez Cobo 23N-47. Tel: 666-6899/620-2324, E-mail: trenturistico@ert.com.co, URL: www.trenturisticocafeyazucar.com), runs trips to Cumbre, Buga, La Tebaida, San Cipriano and Zarzal on weekends. Trains leave at various times; call for schedules. This service is not just transport, but includes live music and partying as well.

BY AIR

Alfonso Bonilla Aragón airport, also known as Palmaseca airport (Tel: 418-5000, URL: www.aerocali.com.co) is located about 16 kilometers (9.9 mi) outside of Cali. Both international flights and internal flights land here.

A taxi from the city to the airport, and vice versa, will set you back more than $25. The cheapest way to get here from the center is to go to the bus terminal first and head to Lineas Consul, which has vans leaving every 15 minutes for the 30-minute ride. The cost for one passenger is about $1.75. To get from the airport to the city center is the same—go to the exit point for national flights and from there, you can catch a similar van for the same price. Updated: Feb 13, 2008.

Getting Around

Cali is a confusing city, as street numbers appear to have little rhyme or reason. Use the river and the Intercontinental Hotel as major landmarks, or look up at the hills to see statue of the Cristo Rey and the monument of the Tres Cruces; these will help you gain your bearings.

Avenida Sexta, one of the main thoroughfares, is also known as Avenida 6 Norte, and may be marked as such on maps. Wherever you are going, be sure to have the address written correctly, since Avenida 4 is not the same as Avenida 4 Norte. The best way to avoid such problems is by finding out exactly which neighborhood it is in.

Buses are fairly straightforward and have their destinations plastered over the front window. For the most part, they travel on the main roads, and each journey costs $0.70. An efficient, new bus system called the MIO covers most of the city and runs in designated lanes. The flat fare is about $0.60 per trip.Updated: May 15, 2009.

Safety

Cali, as with any similar large city, is beset with problems. Colombia's unrest has led many displaced people to the city in search of security and access to money.

Panhandlers are common in the downtown area. In Granada and El Peñón, you won't be bothered too much. Pay attention to your belongings and heed local advice. Cali beggars are not persistent; they'll ask for money once and then move on. Updated: Feb 13, 2008.

Services

TOURISM

There is a helpful tourist information office in the bus terminal on the ground floor. For more detailed information, go to the **Centro Cultural de Cali** (Ca. 6 and Cra. 5. Tel: 885-8855, ext. 122, E-mail: oficinadeturismo@cali.gov.co, URL: www.caliturismo.com).

MONEY

Banks and cash machines are prevalent in the city. On Avenida Sexta, as well as in the Plaza de Caizedo and downtown, you can easily find all the major banks.

KEEPING IN TOUCH

While in Cali, you won't ever be more than a few blocks from an Internet café or telephone call center. Avenida Sexta has them by the

dozen, with **Cyberphone Club** (Av. 6N, 4-52, San Fernando. Tel: 514-6563) being a recommended choice. **Correos de Colombia** (Av. 6N, 30-21) will assist with all postal needs.

MEDICAL

In the case of a medical emergency, **Clínica Fundación Valle de Lili** (Cra. 98, 18-49. Tel: 331-7474/9090), **Clínica de Occidente** (Ca. 18N, 5N-34. Tel: 660-3000) and **Hospital Universitario del Valle** (Ca. 6, 36-08. Tel: 558-6355) all provide adequate care.

LAUNDRY

Laundry places are common so there should be at least one near any accommodation. Some hostels also offer on-site laundry services.

CAMERA REPAIR

Should you encounter any camera troubles, **Edicameras** (Av. 6N, 30-11. Tel: 558-3893) or **Tecno Cameras** (Av. 6N, 24-84, opposite the Biblioteca Departamental) should be able to help out. Updated: Mar 06, 2008.

SHOPPING

Cali may just offer everything that a shop-a-holic craves, from chic boutiques in the upscale neighborhoods of Granada and El Peñon to the sleek and ultra-modern shopping centers of Palmetto Plaza, Jardín Plaza, Cosmocentro, Unicentro, Chipichape and Centenario. Updated: June 09, 2008.

Jardín Plaza

This well-stocked shopping center in the southern part of Cali has a wide range of modern clothing and electronics stores. You are sure to find all of the major brand-name accessories here, and there's even a movie theater. It is also one of the few places with WiFi access. Cra. 98, 16-200.

Chipichape

Chipichape, located in the north, is currently *the* mall of choice. By day, shoppers come in hordes searching for the latest bargains or simply to sit and people-watch on one of the many benches scattered throughout. Chipichape's eateries are especially popular at lunchtime. The mall's 12-screen movie theater is another draw and is a common place for caleños to catch a flick. Come nighttime, they head to the cool reggae and pop bar or other hip nightspots here to salsa until late. Daily 6 a.m.-midnight. Ca. 38N, 6-35. Tel: 659-2198/2199, URL: www.chipichape.com. Updated: Jun 23, 2011.

Salsa in Cali

Ride in a public bus, sit in a bar or walk down Avenida Sexta in barrio Granada and you will know that this city is all about salsa. There are dozens of salsa schools in Cali where a novice can learn a few steps to impress friends back home. In addition, there are many clubs where the irresistible urge to get up and strut one's stuff will be too overwhelming to resist.

No one should pass through Cali without attempting to salsa with a local at least once. Salsa is the pulsating heart of this city, and from cab drivers listening to the beats on their vehicle radios to live performances in public spaces and theaters, you can't avoid it. Pick up some of the steps at one of the salsa schools, where even the most lead-footed foreigner will be left eager to give it a go.

If you left your dancing shoes at home, head to the chic barrios of El Peñón or Granada to browse the boutiques for a solid pair. Afterward, stick around and enjoy a sumptuous meal in one of the city's most exclusive restaurants. Updated: Sep 01, 2011.

SALSA SCHOOLS IN CALI

Swing Latino
World salsa champions offer a progressive level group class open to the public. Cra. 31, 7-25, El Cedro. Tel: 380-9202/9168.

El Manicero
Inexpensive and popular salsa school that has large group classes twice a night, every night of the week. Cra. 39, 9-56. Tel: 513-0231.

RU Café
Cuban rueda and casino-style salsa classes on three floors. Cra. 36, 8-49. Tel: 557-8833/682-6705/ 556-5840.

Tango Viva y Salsa Vivo
Tango and salsa clases in group and private settings in a brand new two-story studio. Ca. 5 B5, 36-94. Tel: 557-0618/514 5827/514 5692.

Loma de la Cruz
Little stores line the streets around Loma de la Cruz, making this area your best bet for purchasing artisan goods. There is a strange, locally known legend called "Mano del Negro" (The Black Hand) surrounding this part of town. Long ago, a black slave was unjustly killed here and legend says that if you pass through the area late at night, you can see the slave's hand emerge from the ground.

Centro Comercial Único
If you are looking for quality goods at a discounted price, this is the outlet mall for you. It is the only place in the city where leading brands are sold at 50 percent off the retail price. If you get tired of shopping, you can rest your feet while watching a movie at the 12-screen cinema. Ca. 52, between Cra. 3 and 4. Updated: Apr 27, 2008.

Things to See and Do
Cali can easily keep travelers occupied for a number of days, whether it be sleeping off late nights in salsatecas or wandering the colonial streets of San Antonio. The historic center has a plethora of museums, and the northern neighborhoods of Granada and El Peñón boast upmarket restaurants and boutiques that would not be out of place in Los Angeles or Miami. Updated: Sep 01, 2011.

MUSEUMS & CHURCHES
Should you find yourself downtown in the Centro of Cali, there's a few possible reasons why you're here. You are either lost,

VALLE DEL CAUCA

you are trying to find an information center or you are in need of a culture fix. If the latter is true, read on!

A good place to start is the **Teatro Municipal Enrique Buenaventura** (Ca. 6 and Cra. 6) that stands imposing and yellow in all its Baroque glory.

From here, head to the **Museo Religioso y Colonial San Francisco** (Cra. 4, 6N-117) to see over 350 pieces of priceless religious works of art held within. Your next stop should be the **Museo Arqueológico La Merced** (Cra. 4, 6-59) and then the short stroll over to the **Museo de Oro Calima** (Ca. 7A, 4-69).

Should you tire of the noise and pollution of the Centro, head toward the river and the north to the Museo de Arte Moderno La Tertulia. Updated: May 22, 2009.

Museo Nacional del Transporte

If you have time on the way to or from the airport, it's well worth stopping in for a quick whirl around the national museum of transportation. This museum has an impressive collection of classic cars, historical planes, steam trains, motorcycles, bicycles, combustible engines, model cars, helicopters and other modes of transportation. There is a cafeteria if you need a bite to eat, as well as free parking for visitors. Rápido Aerpuerto buses to and from the terminal and airport, passing the museum every 15 minutes. Monday–Friday 8 a.m.–4 p.m., Saturday–Sunday and holidays 10 a.m.–5 p.m. Next to the Alfonso Bonilla Aragón airport in the Zona Franca de Palmaseca. Tel: 651-1154, E-mail: museodetransporte@yahoo.com. Updated: Apr 27, 2008.

Museo del Oro Calima

A respectable collection of gold and ceramics is housed in the Banco de la República building. This is a fairly recent collection of Calima cultural artifacts (Calima is the name of the original indigenous group in the Valle de Cauca), which dates back nearly 9,000 years. Unlike the Quimbayá collection in Armenia, this museum does not have an English translation along each panel to guide you through. There is, however, a helpful English brochure that outlines the history of the Calima people and their customs. After you are finished browsing the Calima artifacts, head down the hall into the second exhibition room. Here there are several paintings and works of art that describe and illustrate the six stages of development of

Latin American art and are well worth a look. Tuesday-Friday 9 am.-5 p.m., Saturday 10 a.m.-5 p.m. Ca. 7, 4-69. Tel: 883-6945, URL: www.banrepcultural.org/cali. Updated: Jun 22, 2011.

Museo de Arte Moderno La Tertulia

For a little taste of modern art, Museo de Arte Moderno La Tertulia is your best bet. This place is much more than just an art museum, though. There is also an outdoor auditorium where you can catch musical performances, especially at the beginning and end of every month. Next to it is the Cinemateca art house, which plays independent films and frequently hosts passing film festivals. Behind the theater is the XV Salón de Arte BBVA, a bank-sponsored art hall designed for continuing education of the modern arts. Finally, there are temporary and permanent exhibitions on display in two separate buildings. Monday-Saturday 10 a.m.-6 p.m. Av. Colombia 5-105 Oeste. Tel: 893-2941/2939, Fax: 893-2961, E-mail: museolatertulia@telesat.com.co. Updated: Mar 29, 2011.

La Merced/Museo de Arte Colonial

Housed in the La Merced church, the Museo de Arte Colonial contains pottery and pre-colonial relics. Built in 1545, La Merced is the oldest church in Cali. The church is a well-preserved, white colonial-style building, which is a really nice contrast to the uglier city buildings in the neighborhood. Monday-Saturday 9 a.m.-1 p.m. and 2-6 p.m., Sunday and holidays 9 a.m.-noon. Cra. 3, 6-40. Tel: 880-4737, Cel: 313-659-5182. Updated: Mar 31, 2011.

La Ermita !

Its original name was "Ermita de Nuestra Señora de la Soledad del Río," and in the early 1600s, it was a small Baroque chapel. In 1787, it was destroyed. Today La Ermita stands as a very different yet gorgeous gothic structure, built in 1942 and modeled after the cathedral in Cologne, Germany. The attention to detail and its curious pale blue and white color makes La Ermita a city symbol and it is certainly the most photographed church in all of Cali. Cra. 1 and Ca. 13. Tel: 881-8553/1378, E-mail: catedraldesanpedro@hotmailcom. Updated: Mar 31, 2011.

Iglesia San Pedro

First erected for the Priest of Quito in 1539, then later torn down and rebuilt in 1772, again in 1841, and one last time in 1930, this church has undergone several alterations. Inside and out, it is simple and understated, with stark white walls and ceilings, accentuated by seven gorgeous crystal chandeliers above the center aisle and an enormous wooden organ on the second floor. Take some time to admire the nice marble image of Jesus seated next to St. Peter. The side chapel is also a solemn place to pay homage to the Virgin Mary. On the way out, look at the bronze work by artist William Echeverría on the doors. Ca. 11, 5-53. Updated: Mar 29, 2011.

Capilla de la Inmaculada

Built in 1762, the Capilla de la Inmaculada has a modern and modest interior, but is worth a quick peek because it remains the church of choice at midday. This narrow and long chapel is a homage to the Virgin Mary, who solemnly stands at the front altar. The interior is accented with seven arcs and several white columns with a blue and gold trim. Mass is held at 6:30 a.m., 10 a.m., 3 p.m., 6 p.m. and 8:30 p.m. It is located in Plaza San Francisco. Updated: Mar 31, 2011.

PLAZAS & MONUMENTS

Plaza de Caicedo

Plaza de Caicedo has always been the center of public, commercial and political life in Cali. During the colonial period, it was called the Plaza Mayor. Between 1674 and 1897, the park was used for public markets. In 1813, it took the name of Plaza de la Constitución. In 1913, the name was changed to Plaza de Caicedo to honor caleño Joaquín de Caicedo, a martyr of the nation's independence. This plaza is the best place to people-watch during lunchtime. There is a stunning, stark white judicial building on the northern edge of the plaza, as well as a few small fountains around the perimeter and Caicedo's bronze statue in the center. Bounded by Ca. 11 and 12 and Cra. 4 and 5. Updated: Mar 31, 2011.

Plaza San Francisco

San Francisco is an enormous brick plaza and one of the largest in Cali, where pigeons (and humans) gather to catch some rays and chill out. This plaza was actually destroyed in 1960 and rebuilt in 1969. Be sure to check out the black fountain near the entrance to Capilla de la Inmaculada. This modern monument was erected in 1970 to honor the reverend father Damián González. Bounded by Cra. 6 and 8 and Ca. 9 and 10. Updated: Mar 31, 2011.

Monumento de las Tres Cruces

Standing at 1,500 meters (4,921 ft) above sea level, the three crosses that comprise this high-altitude monument were constructed in 1837. Every May 3 (Colombia's Labor Day), caleños climb to the top of this hill to pay homage to Santa Cruz and to celebrate their city's independence from Spain. There's a good view of the city from the top. An interesting fact to keep in mind is that the center cross is 26 meters (85 ft) tall and 22 meters (72 ft) wide. You can safely walk to the monument on a path from barrio Normandía, or simply flag one of the taxi jeeps marked "Las Cruces," which shuttle sightseers to and from Normandía Plaza and the monument. Updated: May 13, 2008.

Los Gatos

In 1996, renowned painter and sculptor Hernando Tejada began what came to be a collection of a dozen cat sculptures along the Cali River, close to El Peñón. Tejada's original cat, "El Gato del Río," is the largest of the collection. The subsequent cats are half its size but some have twice the charisma. These latter felines were painted by other significant Colombian artists and are all decorated to match. Examples include "Magic Cat," "Coquette Cat" and "Seven Lives Cat." This is a great place to stroll along the river and to appreciate some interesting modern Colombian art. Along the Río Cali and Av. 4N Oeste. Updated: Apr 04, 2011.

THEATERS

Cali Teatro

(TICKETS: $11 adults, $5.60 students) One of the few places in the city where you can get fresh air and a fine view of Cali is atop the hill in barrio San Antonio. Here you will find an 18th-century chapel and a park. The Cali Teatro, a block from the park, has seasonal performances that could be worth an evening out if your Spanish is strong enough to understand the dialogue. Visit the Cali Teatro website for upcoming events. Cra. 12, 4-51, San Antonio. Tel: 893-8790/8811, URL: www. caliteatro.com. Updated: Jun 22, 2011.

Casa Proartes

This great little Neoclassic-style building, next door to the Teatro Municipal, is yet another center for the arts in Cali. Built in 1871 and beautifully restored in 1991, several free temporary art exhibits and arts performances are on the center stage inside. There is a small cinema on the ground floor and across the way, there is a pleasant cafeteria open for lunch on the weekdays. Check the front entrance for the latest evening performances and daytime exhibitions, most of which are free. Cra. 5, 7-02. Tel: 885-1179/880-4650/4602, E-mail: proartes@proartescali.com, URL: www. proartescali.com. Updated: Mar 31, 2011.

Teatro Municipal Enrique Buenaventura

On April 9, 1918, construction of this beautiful yellow theater began. Ten years later, it was completed, with remodeling done in the 1950s. Modeled like an Italian opera theater, this Neoclassical theater holds up to 1,200 people in its stylish and elaborate European-like interior. It was declared a national monument in June of 2002. The ticket office is open in the afternoons, but even if it's not, the security guard can give you free tickets to private performances if you ask or let you in to take a look at the stage when there are no rehearsals. Cra. 5a, 6-64 and Ca. 7. Tel: 883-9106/07/684-0570/3578/0593, URL: www.cali.gov.co/teatromunicipal/. Updated: Mar 31, 2011.

PARKS & NATURE

Ecoparque Río Pance

The Río Pance runs to the south of Cali, by the city garden and the university district. A very popular spot that sees hundreds of city folk on the weekends, the Ecoparque Río Pance is a convenient place to relax by the river. The park has open-air gym stations, a lake for recreational fishing, a botanical garden, and food and bathroom facilities. There are wonderful views of the Cali countryside throughout the park. Buses to Ecoparque Río Pance leave the bus terminal every 30 minutes and cost $1.50 each way. Updated: Mar 29, 2011.

Lake Calima

Spanning an area of 70 square kilometers (27 sq mi), Lake Calima is the largest artificial body of water in Colombia. The lake was created in 1964, when the government undertook a massive dam project to provide energy for that region. Just 90 kilometers (56 mi) from Cali, it has become one of the top weekend destinations for residents of Cali and lovers of water sports. Visitors can either rent a cabin or camp if they want to spend the night. Sports available include windsurfing, kitesurfing, sailing, canoing and water skiing, and there are options for parascending and canopy tours nearby. El Darién, Calima. To get there, catch any bus from the bus terminal to Calima. Updated: Mar 30, 2011.

Reserva Natural Laguna de Sonso

Roughly 10 kilometers (6.2 mi) southwest of the municipality of Buga, the Reserva Natural Laguna de Sonso is a wetland reserve that offers delights to the birdwatchers. The eastern margins of the River Cauca pour into this area, also known as the Laguna de Chircal, and create an area of 2045 hectares (5053 ac), 90 percent of which is wetlands.

Studies have revealed that up to 162 species of bird make the wetlands here a migratory resting point or home. Of these 162 species, 55 are aquatic birds and in mating season, up to 15,000 Grayish Piculets descend into the area. Other prevalent species include the Blue-winged Teal and the Apical Flycatcher.

To get there, catch a bus from the Terminal de Transportes to Buga (every 15 min, journey time roughly 45 min). At the terminal in Buga, take a local bus heading southwest. The journey from here should take approximately 30 minutes. Bring clothes that will protect you from the elements, your binoculars, a camera and patience. Updated: Mar 28, 2011.

Zoológico de Cali

(ADMISSION: $5.60 adults, $4 children) What is likely the best place in Colombia to see the widest variety of animal life resides in the western portion of the city, in Barrio Santa Teresita. The Zoológico de Cali is a surprisingly clean and well-organized spread with every imaginable mammal (lions, tigers, pumas, jaguars and spectacled bears— oh my!), native birds (including condors and parrots) and snakes from the Valle de Cauca.

Free transportation to and from the zoo is available in northern and southern city routes. The north route stops at La 14 de Calima, Sameco, Menga, Chipichape, Avenida Vásquez Cobo, Avenida Las Américas, CAM, Avenida Del Río, Portada al Mar and the zoo. The south route stops at Cosmocentro, Calle 5, La Tertulia and the zoo. Buses to the zoo leave at 11 a.m., noon and 1 p.m. and return at 11:30 a.m., 12:30 p.m., 3:30 p.m., 4:30 p.m. and 5:30 p.m. The zoo is open daily 9 a.m.-4:30 p.m. during low season and 9 a.m.-5 p.m. during high season. Cra. 2 Oeste and Ca. 14, Barrio Santa Teresita. Tel: 892-7474/682-6764, URL: www.zoologicodecali.com.co. Updated: Mar 29, 2011.

OTHER ACTIVITIES

Tren Turístico Café y Azúcar

(TRIPS: $14-50) Much like the Sabana train that runs from Bogotá, the Tren Turístico Café y Azúcar runs trips from the station in downtown Cali to points in the Valle del Cauca countryside and beyond. Choose from a variety of journeys that leave in the morning and return in the later afternoon, such as Cali to Buga, Cali to the Recreational Park La Cumbre, or Cali to Finca Villa Karen or Finca Turística la Gran Béligica.

Trips can resemble that of a party atmosphere, complete with a papayera band that plays its way through the carriages and stewardesses who attend to all of your eating and drinking needs. If you buy a package on any of the above trips, lunch and park entries are included as well. An option for the true reveler is the Tren Rumbero—the Party Train. This makes a round trip from Cali to the club Hostal del Pipe and includes entry to the club and a DJ on board. It leaves for Cali at 2 a.m.

This train does not run on a daily basis; check well beforehand to be sure when it is operating. During rainy season, the train is often cancelled since the tracks become covered by small landslides. To get there, catch a bus to the bus terminal; the train station is next door. Estación del Ferrocarril, Av. Vásquez Cobo, 23N-47, 2nd floor. Tel: 620-2326/7/8, Cel: 314-618-6278/619-2608, E-mail: contacto@trenturisticocafeyazucar.com.co, URL: www.trenturisticocafeyazucar.com.co. Updated: Jun 21, 2011.

Fútbol

Catching a fútbol game in any city in Colombia is nothing short of a religious experience. Hordes flock to the stadiums, screaming furious chants at the opposition while voicing praise on their side. Cali has two teams that call the Estadio Pascual Guerrero home. America de Cali (red) and Deportivo Cali (green) have their tribes of supporters—for your safety do not get the two confused! Perhaps the most extreme fútbol experience you can have is to go to a local game between the two bitter city rivals. You are advised to go with someone knowledgeable, since more than 40,000 fans show up to these games. It's best not to take valuables or large amounts of money with you. To get there, take any bus that runs down the Calle 5. Get off when you see the flags in front of the stadium. Updated: Mar 28, 2011.

Studying Spanish

Cali is not as developed as Bogotá, Medellín and Cartagena when it comes to Spanish study. However, the big city universities have established language learning centers and offer courses almost all year round.

Javeriana University

Javeriana University, a Jesuit school located in southern Cali, offers a special "Functional Spanish for Foreigners" language and culture program through its humanities and social science department. This program aims to immerse foreign students in practical, social and cultural interactions in class and through various activities and excursions around the city. Colombian culture is the focus of the course, through which you will attain more fluency with the Spanish language and a better understanding of the country. Ca. 18, 118-250. Tel: 321-8200, E-mail: mtorres@javerianacali.edu.co, URL: www.javerianacali.edu.co. Updated: Mar 29, 2011.

Universidad Santiago de Cali

Specifically designed for foreigners, the Universidad Santiago de Cali offers a Spanish-language course with a good deal of social interaction and cultural activity. It places students in three levels (basic, intermediate and advanced) to focus on improving their verbal communication and written fluency. To complement the Spanish study, Universidad Santiago de Cali organizes cultural trips to the Valle de Cauca, salsa dance outings and lively rumba excursions. The program includes 120 hours of lessons and costs $690. Ca. 5 between Cra. 62 and 63a, Campus Pampalinda. Tel: 518-3000, ext. 421, URL: http://virtual.usc.edu.co/espaextranjeros. Updated: Jun 21, 2011.

International Student Services Organization

For a shorter Spanish language program, you could opt for the one offered at ISSO, which provides online, small group and private lessons. You can start the online program anytime, using its online lesson book and with communication taking place via E-mail. Semi-private lessons begin every two weeks and include materials and 40 hours of lessons for $250. Private lessons can be arranged for $14 per hour, or a 25-hour program costs $350. For an additional fee, ISSO can assist with securing homestays, furnished apartments or hotel accommodations. Av. 5cN, 23dN-86, office 301. Tel: 680-2001/660-1798, E-mail: isso@estudiosexterior.com. Updated: Mar 29, 2011.

Tours

Chivas Tour

Cali is a great place to take a chiva tour, a tour of the city on an open-air party bus. By day, this company will show you around the city and show you the important sights. A Spanish-speaking guide can provide you with historical information and general orientation. Then, at night, get your boogie on and ride around on the party chiva to the numerous salsa hotspots. For $50, you will get a full-day chiva tour with a Spanish-speaking guide and evening transport along Avenida Sexta. The night chiva costs $10, but does not include nightclub cover charge. Ca. 8, 10-70. Tel: 680-3535. Updated: Mar 31, 2011.

Motolombia

Motolombia is Colombia's only motorcycle rental operator when it comes to large enduro bikes and ATV tours. The fleet consists of Kawasaki KLR650s and an Aprilia ETV1000, plus a couple of 450cc ATVs for jungle/mountain tours near Cali. Enduro bikes can be rented for day or week-long tours around Colombia with or without guide. Av. 6N bis, Ca. 26N, 57, Santa Monica. Tel: 396-3849, Fax: 668-9986, E-mail: mike@motolombia. com/booking@casablancahostel.com, URL: www.motolombia.com/www.motolombia. wordpress.com. Updated: Mar 28, 2011.

Christian Dojoseba

Christian, the owner of Kaffee Erde Hostal, is a very accommodating tour operator who is more than happy to take you on a jungle trip to San Cipriano or to closer locales like Ecoparque Río Pance. Having lived in Cali for several years, he takes tourists on informative strolls around the city. He'll often stop to buy fresh fruit on the way and will take you back to his hostel and make you fresh juice, while telling you about the joys of living in Cali. Kaffee Erde, Av. 7N, 42-30, Barrio Centenario. Tel: 301-400-0914. Updated: Mar 29, 2011.

Max Viedmon

Frequently referred by travelers passing through Cali, Max is a great reference should you speak Spanish and want to experience the region like a local. If you would rather he pick you up on the other side of Colombia and show you around, he is happy to accommodate and personalize a countrywide tour. He takes security and safety very seriously and guarantees discounted rates and a wealth of information. His affiliate, Jenny, provides horseback riding tours on fast-trotting Colombian horses (called *caballo de paso Colombiano*). She even accommodates for physical rehabilitation programs and camping trips by horse. These services cost approximately $30-50 per day, plus food, accommodation and transportation. Max and Jenny are both based in Buga but can pick you up anywhere in the city. Cel: 312-843-4902, URL: www. maxviedman.blogspot.com/www.santaelenaelparaiso.org. Updated: Mar 29, 2011.

Neighborhoods of Cali

The three barrios of San Fernando, El Peñón and Granada were originally residential areas and have slowly morphed into high-rent, trendy zones. In San Fernando, you will find the Parque del Perro—with a statue of a dog in the middle—lined with small bars and more than a dozen restaurants. This park appeals to a young crowd and during the weekends it is bursting with people.

El Peñón, on the other hand, is behind the Intercontinental Hotel and close to the Museo de Arte Moderno La Tertulia. Its bars, shops and restaurants appeal to a more mature clientele, who are intent on eating well and being seen in the right place. The circular park in the middle of El Peñón features art fairs on the weekends.

Granada is the largest of the three areas and stretches for 10 city blocks. Dining in this barrio is expensive and exclusive, though budget places also exist. The nightlife corridor of La Sexta is located here, between Calle 15 N and Calle 19 N, and features mostly salsa and crossover clubs. A few blocks up on La Novena, more upscale lounges, electronic music clubs and a wide variety of high-end restaurants are located. A string of rock clubs is located on Calle 17N, between Novena and Sexta, as well.

The next barrio heading north from Granada in the evening shadows of the mountains, Santa Monica Residencial starts at Calle 21, where a couple of decent hostels are located, and stretches up to Chipichape, a very large shopping center with a multi-screen cinema and trendy brand name shops, bars and restaurants. Avenida Sexta, also known as the "Zona Rosa," runs from south to north, and is bustling, busy and vibrant at night with clubs, bars, discos and street BBQs.

San Antonio is Cali's bohemian center, and a large number of expatriates call this area home. This neighborhood is historic and is protected by the city from further development. Across the road and up the hill from the museums, its streets are lined with small and independent theaters, interesting cafés and artists workshops. At night, caleños come to the park beneath the San Antonio Chapel (constructed in 1747). Up here, they enjoy the breeze and occasional live music while watching the sparkling lights of Cali down below—this makes a great evening out. Updated: Sep 01, 2011.

Lodging

Cali's reputation as a tourist destination is growing and every possible type of accommodation can now be found. In San Antonio, Miraflores and near Granada, there are hostels and guesthouses for those on a budget, while the most exclusive new hotels and boutiques are located in El Peñón. If you are looking for something in-between, there are plenty of mid-range options near the center of the city. Updated: Jun 29, 2011.

BUDGET

Hotel Posada Colonial

(ROOMS: $6-20) A hotspot for budget travelers, Hotel Posada Colonial is a curious establishment with 22 rooms, each of different quality and price. One room is like a closet with a tiny twin bed and a tiny bathroom, which costs $6 a night (not recommended). Others are more spacious and have large, private bathrooms. There is little natural light, though, so the place feels a bit more like a prison than a hotel. However, it is conveniently located, since it is half a block from Avenida Sexta. Plus, there is a decent restaurant next door, which is nice to use as your lounge. Ca. 14, 6-42. Tel: 661-2925. Updated: Apr 28, 2008.

Jovita's !

(BEDS: $8.50, ROOMS: $11.50) This recommended hostel in San Antonio offers free salsa and yoga classes to its guests. Housed in a renovated colonial building, with a courtyard filled with hammocks, Jovita's has a lot to offer: a mini-gym, a BBQ, a garden and stocked TV room for socializing, a small bar, and even local food workshops weekly. Rooms are also available for monthly rent, costing around $200 per month. Cra. 5, 4-56, San Antonio. Tel: 893-8342, Cel: 317-640-6813, E-mail: info@jovitashostel.com, URL: www.jovitashostel.com. Updated: Sep 01, 2011.

La Casa Café

(BEDS $8.50, ROOMS: $14-31) La Casa Café is a beautiful, small family-run hostel. Three private rooms, named after popular coffee drinks, hold one to three people. The forth room is a dorm room with four beds and it has access to a small terrace. There is free coffee, tourist information, WiFi, a communal kitchen, TV room, library books and movies. The hostel is commited to cultural and heritage tourism, with the goal of exposing travelers to local customs and typical life. It also has a chilled-out café downstairs, where you can sip on artisanal coffee or have a snack while playing some board games. Cra. 6, 2-13, San Antonio. Tel: 893-7011, Cel: 316-521-7388, E-mail: lacasacafecali@yahoo.com/lacasacafecali@gmail.com, URL: www.lacasacafecali.blogspot.com. Updated: Apr 04, 2011.

Kaffee Erde

(BEDS: $9-18) Kaffee Erde has quickly become a good alternative to the other backpacking hostels in Cali. This converted house in Barrio Centenario makes guests feel right at home, and Christian, the owner of the place, makes you feel like part of his family. Although the house itself is a little lackluster and in need of some updating, there is a very redeeming living room and outdoor lounge area, where guests spend most of their time. Also, dorm rooms have only three beds, which give the place an airy feel. There are separate male and female bathrooms. You are more than welcome to use the kitchen and to drink all the free Colombian coffee you like. Christian's sister provides free salsa lessons in the evenings, and on the weekends, Christian will escort his guests to the best salsa clubs in town or serve as their guide on a jungle trip. Av. 7N, 42-30. Cel: 301-400-0914, E-mail: dojoseva@hotmail.com, URL: www.kaffeeerde.com. Updated: Jun 21, 2011.

Calidad House

(BEDS: $9, ROOMS: $20) The Calidad House has eight simple but comfortable rooms, including three- and four-bed dormitories. Private rooms sleep between one and three people, and vary in quality. All bathrooms throughout the hostel are shared and hot water is hard to come by. However, the location at the heart of the exclusive barrio Granada is unrivaled. Once in the Granada neighborhood, find the Juan Valdez coffee shop, and from there, walk up the hill two blocks and you will be at the hostel. Ca. 17N, 9AN-39, Granada. Tel: 661-2338, E-mail: calidadhouse@yahoo.com, URL: www.calidadhouse.com. Updated: Mar 30, 2011.

Tostaky !

(BEDS: $10, ROOMS: 12.50-17) Owned by French-Colombian couple Vincent and Claudia, Tostaky is one of the most popular hostels in San Antonio, and with good reason. Its location is ideal, across from the neighborhood's park. Recently expanded, Tostaky offers both dorm beds and private rooms, along with free Internet, a kitchen and a book exchange. The laidback, backpacker atmosphere is what keeps travelers coming. Cra. 10, 1-76. Tel:

893-0651, Cel: 300-355-1650, E-mail: cafe-tostaky@gmail.com, URL: http://cafeto-staky.blogspot.com. Updated: Sep 01, 2011.

Iguana
(BEDS: $10, ROOMS: $18-28) Boasting to be the destination of choice for all backpackers passing through Cali, the Iguana is a great place to settle down and spend a few days. Dorm rooms and communal areas are the name of the game here, not forgetting that this place is located in the one of the choicest neighborhoods of Cali, near exclusive restaurants and bars. Make your way to the barrio Granada and wander down Avenida 9 Norte until the end. The Iguana is up on the right, a block and a half past the Argentine restaurant. Av. 9N, 22N-46. Tel: 660-8937, Cel: 313-768-6024, E-mail: iguana_cali@yahoo.com, URL: www.iguana.com.co. Updated: Jun 22, 2011.

The Pelican Larry Hostel
(BEDS: $11-18) A modern backpacker hostel with a social vibe, Pelican Larry is located just five minutes from the Zona Rosa bars. Facilities include hot showers, comfy beds, nice computers, a well-stocked kitchen, a sundeck and a BBQ. The hostel's twice weekly BBQs are a bit hit, and its TV room with a good selection of DVDs is a nice place to relax. Prices include taxes, free linen and towels, all day coffee, travel tips and help with visa extensions. Spanish and salsa classes can also be arranged. From the bus terminal, ask for "La Glorieta" roundabout, and then take Calle 23 Norte; keep walking for 10 minutes and you will arrive at the hostel. A taxi from the bus terminal should be around $2. Ca. 20N, 6AN-44, Granada. Tel: 392-1407, Cel: 315-770-6770, E-mail: gunty@pelicanlarrycali.com, URL: www.pelicanlarry-cali.com. Updated: Jun 22, 2011.

V!VA ONLINE REVIEW

THE PELICAN LARRY HOSTEL

Pelican Larry is a great place to meet other travelers, party and/or chill. The weekly BBQs are stellar.

September 18, 2009

MID-RANGE
Hotel Camino Real 1A
(ROOMS: $17-40) This is another option in the hustle and bustle of downtown, which is cheaper than the Hotel Imperial. There are 50 rooms, so reservations usually aren't an issue. Each room comes with cable TV, private bathroom and fan. Ca. 9, 3-54. Tel: 680-2626/884-2525, Fax: 684-1175, E-mail: camino-real9@hotmail.com, URL: www.ho-telcaminoreal1a.com. Updated: Mar 31, 2011.

Hotel Sartor
(ROOMS: $20-40) Having been on the backpacker trail for some time now, Hotel Sartor offers pretty decent accommodations close to the Avenida Sexta nightlife. This is a good option for travelers seeking a convenient location and good value. All rooms have private baths and surround a little courtyard. There is a computer with Internet available for $2 per hour, and an Italian restaurant attached to the lobby. Av. 8N, 20-50. Tel: 668-7443/6482, Fax: 661-5037, E-mail: hotelsartor@yahoo.com. Updated: Mar 30, 2011.

Hotel Nevada
(ROOMS: $22-46) Hotel Nevada was built to satisfy tourists seeking refuge in the city's busy yet safe and heavily patrolled "Zona Rosa." Just one block from the nightlife on Avenida Sexta and 15 minutes from El Centro, Nevada is like a home away from home with 21 comfortable guest rooms and luxuries such as a sauna, steam room and Jacuzzi. All rooms have private baths with hot water and cable TV, and are classily decorated. Av. 8N, 14N-15. Tel: 667-9693/660-3689, Fax: 660-3689, E-mail: hotelnevadacolombia@yahoo.com, URL: www.hotelnevadacolom-bia.com. Updated: Mar 29, 2011.

Hotel del Puente
(ROOMS: $25-30) Smack dab on the bridge bordering barrio San Antonio and the Centro, this four-story hotel has an unfortunate view of one of the busiest byways in the city. The rooms here are basic, just a bed, window and private bath. The advantage here is the location, just steps away from all of the major sites in Cali. As the hotel is technically in the San Antonio neighboorhood, good cafés and restaurants are also just around the corner. Ca. 5, 4-36. Tel: 893-8484. Updated: Mar 30, 2011.

Hostal San Fernando
(ROOMS: $29-49) Just up the hill and within a block of the Parque del Perro is the Hostal San Fernando. Its 12 rooms are all equipped with air conditioning and private bathrooms, but are a little dark. It is a decent place, but perhaps not ideal for those traveling with a partner—all the room windows open onto the central courtyard, making it easy to hear conversations in other quarters. To get here, tell your taxi to

take the Quinta toward the stadium, then turn up toward the Parque del Perro; from here, you are less than a block away. Ca. 3, 27-87. Tel: 556-2226, Fax: 489-6081, E-mail: calihotel@hotmail.com, URL: www.calihotel.com. Updated: May 20, 2009.

Posada de San Antonio !

(ROOMS: $30-40) Located in a beautifully restored colonial mansion in the antique barrio of San Antonio, this posada's familiar style and relaxed ambiance have made it a favorite with those wishing to stay in an establishment a step up from grungy backpacker digs. With a capacity to hold 45 people, Posada de San Antonio has 14 rooms, and its helpful staff will move or add beds to accommodate groups. Each room has its own bathroom with hot water, TV with cable and fan. Breakfast is included. Catching a taxi into the myriad of streets in this part of town may seem daunting, but make sure the driver knows to take you to Barrio San Antonio; once this is clear, there should be no problems. Cra. 5, 3-37. Tel: 893-7413, Cel: 313-583-6091, Fax: 893-7413, E-mail: info@posadadesanantonio. com, URL: www.posadadesanantonio.com Updated: Feb 09, 2011.

Hotel Imperial

(ROOMS: $36-50) There are plenty of reasons to not stay downtown, but if you must, you may find yourself checking into one of a number of hotels that now seem dated and claustrophobic. The Hotel Imperial may have been stylish in the 1970s, but it has aged badly. If you choose to stay here, you'll be in a 50-room high-rise close to the city's museums. Breakfast is included, as are all taxes. If you come in groups of 20 or more guests, the prices will lower to $14 per night. From the airport, catch a bus to the bus terminal or you will find yourself $25 out of pocket. From here, a cab will get you downtown for $3. The hotel is close to the Buenaventura Theater. Ca. 9, 3-93. Tel: 889-9571/75, E-mail: hotelimperialdecali@ hotmail.com, URL: www.hotelimperialdecali. com. Updated: Mar 31, 2011.

Casa Aguacanela

(ROOMS: $40-45) Run by the delightful Esperanza, the Casa Aguacanela is a true home away from home in the safe residential area of Miraflores. The guesthouse has three rooms; two rooms are dormitories with three beds each and the last room is a private double. Limited sleeping capacity makes this a calm retreat in the mayhem of Cali. There is a communal kitchen and a pleasant balcony with views over the city. Cra. 24a, 2A-55, Miraflores.

Tel: 556-8382, Cel: 311-325-0578, E-mail: casaaguacanela@gmail.com/etrujil@yahoo. com, URL: www.casaaguacanelacali.com. Updated: Mar 20, 2011.

Jardin Azul Casa Hotel

(ROOMS: $50-65) Jardin Azul is a delightful small hotel in a quiet and safe neighborhood. It was renovated in February of 2010 and offers six spacious rooms that combine modern design with classical elements; some of them have balconies overlooking the garden. The beautiful garden, yoga zone and swimming pool provide an ideal opportunity to relax and refresh the body and soul. Jardin Azul is near the departamental library on Calle Quinta, between San Antonio and San Fernando. Cra. 24A, 2A-59, Barrio Miraflores. Tel: 556- 8380, Cell: 321-305-0375. E-mail: reservas@jardinazul.com, URL: www.jardinazul.com. Updated: Mar 30, 2011.

Casa Toscano

(ROOMS: $50-70) Casa Toscano offers apartment-style accommodations for executives and tourists visiting Cali. Located on a quiet side street in the peaceful neighborhood Centenario, guests enjoy the privacy and comfort of ample suites. There are eight tastefully decorated suites with wicker furniture and ceramic pottery that sleep up to six people, making it an ideal place for a family if you have the cash. There are significant discounts if you plan to stay longer than 10 and 20 days. A 24-hour, secure, covered parking garage is available for guest use. Ca. 4N, 1N-41. Tel: 660-3459, Cel: 318-642-4343, E-mail: casa. toscano@hotmail.com, URL: www.casatoscano.com. Updated: Mar 31, 2011.

Hostal Santa Rita

(ROOMS: $53-89) A delightful place for families or for those just passing through, the Santa Rita is located in northern Cali, one block from the river of the same name in a colonial-style house dating back to 1945. The seven rooms are immaculate and have private bathrooms, hot water, air conditioning, Internet and cable TV. Guests are treated to a hearty breakfast. Ask the taxi driver to take you to the barrio Santa Rita near the Carulla supermarket and the Hostal Santa Rita is the yellow colonial building further up the road. To get here by bus, take any one that is heading to the zoo and asked to be dropped off. Av. 3 Oeste, 7-131. Tel: 2-892- 0021, Cel: 316-482-2931, Fax: 2-892-6143, E-mail: info@ hostalsantarita.com, URL: www.hostalsantarita.com. Updated: Mar 31, 2011.

Hotel Granada Real

(ROOMS: $53-111) The Hotel Granada Real sits alone on Avenida 8 Norte, but is near the amenities and nightlife attractions of Avenida 6 and barrio Granada. Definitely a place for patrons in town for a conference, the hotel's 61 rooms are all equipped with air conditioning, cable TV, mini-bar and refrigerator. It also conveniently offers private parking and front-desk safe boxes. Av. 8N, 15AN-31. Tel: 2-661-4920, E-mail: ventas@ hotelgranadareal.com.co, URL: www.hotel-granadareal.com. Updated: Mar 29, 2011.

Sabor I Arte

(ROOMS: $84-101) With four rooms and a suite set apart in a different building, the hostel Sabor I Arte is an artist's concept of how a guesthouse should be run. The rooms are named after fruits, and the owner prepares meals while you sit and relax in the tranquil settings of a colonial house in the barrio San Antonio. There's no sign outside, so use the Posada de San Antonio as your reference point and the Sabor I Arte will be next door. Cra. 5, 3-23, Barrio San Antonio. Tel: 2-893-7064, Fax: 2-893-7064. E-mail: soniaserna7@ yahoo.com, URL: www.saboriarte.com. Updated: Apr 29, 2009.

HIGH-END

Cali Plaza Hotel

(ROOMS: $73-187) Aside from providing accommodations that include one- to three-bedroom apartments, Cali Plaza Hotel is a very popular and centrally located meeting place. The café is one of the only places in town where you can get free WiFi reception, which makes it a perfect place to socialize with locals and foreigners. It is right off Avenida 6, so guests can easily stumble back to their Cali home after visiting the nightclub of their choice. Discounts available if you pay in cash. Ca. 15N, 6N-37. Tel: 2-668-2611, Cel: 312-287-9840, E-mail: claude@ledbetter.com, URL: www.caliplaza.com. Updated: Mar 30, 2011.

V!VA ONLINE REVIEW

CALI PLAZA HOTEL

I felt like I was at home as opposed to staying at a hotel. People were great and I will be coming back soon.

May 07, 2009

Hotel Don Jaime

(ROOMS: $77-85) Hotel Don Jaime seems to appeal to business types and it bears all the hallmarks of an establishment of this kind. The renovated hotel has 29 rooms with air conditioning, WiFi, cable TV, mini-bar, refrigerator and clock radio. There is a restaurant open to the public on the ground floor and a terrace bar on the top floor. Conference rooms are also available. Av. 6N, 15N-25. Tel: 667-2828, Fax: 668-7098, E-mail: reservas@hoteldonjaime.com, URL: www.hoteldonjaime.com. Updated: Mar 29, 2011.

Design Hotel Austral

(ROOMS: $100-155) With 19 rooms, this hotel is clearly aimed at those looking at options in the "boutique" range. The whole place has a sparkling new feel with its simplistic designs and spartan décor. Its rooms, which have a Swiss modern feel, have all the conveniences you would expect, though you won't be spending much time indoors with all the quality restaurants and bars in barrio El Peñón. To get here, the nearest landmark is the Hotel Intercontinental. Ca. 1 Oeste, 2-18. Tel: 892-2828/893-0608, Fax: 893-3697, E-mail: reservas@hotel-austral.com, URL: www.hotel-austral.com. Updated: Mar, 31, 2011.

V!VA ONLINE REVIEW

DESIGN HOTEL AUSTRAL

My experience at the hotel was great. The people and the amenities of the place are excellent.

February 10, 2009

Hotel Dann and Dann Carlton

(ROOMS: $111-655) Two towers stretching across Calle 2 connected by a third-floor footbridge make up the very large and luxurious Hotel Dann and Dann Carlton. The Carlton tower is the newer, noticeably more modern and shiny one, with a gorgeous covered third-floor pool and bar. Together, the brick towers provide nearly 200 guest quarters complete with mini-bar, Internet and flat-screen TV. If that's not enough to tickle your fancy, there is also a fully stocked convention center, a Tony Roma's restaurant and a free guest parking garage. Av. Colombia 1-40. Tel: 886-2000, E-mail: reservas@ hotelesdanncali.com.co, URL: www.hotelesdann.com. Updated: Mar 29, 2011.

Hotel Intercontinental

(ROOMS: $120-896) An enormous luxury hotel conveniently located by the river and close to El Centro, Intercontinental is part of the Hotel Estelar chain spread throughout Colombia. This one features almost 300 spacious guest rooms and suites. Despite its immense size, this hotel offers surprisingly personalized service and impeccable amenities, such as three restaurants, a spa, a travel agency, an attractive courtyard and upscale shops. Av. Colombia 2-72. Tel: 882-3225, E-mail: cali@interconti.com/icali. reservas@ihg.com/servicioalcliente.hinter@hotelesestelar.com. Updated: Mar 29, 2011.

Restaurants

As with every major city, the variety and availability of good places to eat is enormous in Cali. Should you wish for a dining experience that you could get back in your home country, then head to the upper class neighborhoods of El Peñón and Granada. Otherwise, you are advised to do a little bit of hunting around for budget places. They spring up and close down routinely, but usually, within a couple of blocks of the ultra posh and expensive places, you can find restaurants that offer set meals and ridiculously low prices.

There are a string of budget vegetarian restaurants on Avenida 6 in the city center, just a couple blocks over from Calle 5, if coming from San Antonio. Plaza Alameda, where fresh seafood comes into Cali daily from the Pacific coast, is surrounded by cheap seafood restaurants that are only open for lunch, but which offer dishes like *pescado de sancocho* and *cazuela* at bargain prices. Updated: Sep 01, 2011.

CAFÉS

Nutricentro

(LUNCH: $3.50-5) This gourmet café is perfectly situated down the street from Teatro Municipal in El Centro. Here you can grab a healthy and hearty vegetarian buffet for $3.50. If you arrive early enough, before they run out, you can also order its "special" plate for just $5. Meals come with juice or soy milk, fruit, salad, vegetarian side dishes and a small dessert. There are two other branches north and south of the city that offer more specialized health treatments like therapeutic massages, reflexology, shiatsu, relaxation gym, yoga and Arabic dance lessons. Centro: Ca. 5, N7-40. Tel: 895-9777; North: Ca. 23AN, 3-66. Tel: 660-3794; South: Cra. 39, 5A-69. Tel: 556-0875. Updated: Mar 31, 2011.

Café Mulato

A few blocks from the Museo de Arte Moderno La Tertulia is Café Mulato, a place that clearly takes pride in the quality of its bean and the ambience created for its frequent patrons. Light music wafts from speakers accompanying your strong organic roast, making this place a chilled retreat. Wraps, salads and other options are available. Ca. 5 Oeste, 3-05, El Peñón. Tel: 893-2963. Updated: May 21, 2009.

Macondo !

Macondo caters to the bohemian crowd that frequents the barrio of San Antonio. At this café, patrons arrive fresh from theater workshops and art studios to enjoy booze-fortified coffees, sandwiches and cocktails. A veggie sandwich will set you back around $3 and is full of mushrooms, cheese and other goodies. Cra. 6, 3-03. Updated: Nov 13, 2007.

COLOMBIAN/SOUTH AMERICAN

El Canelazo

(LUNCH: $2.25) Just a block or so from the Parque del Perro and its pricey restaurants, this is a cheap, family-run establishment that specializes in home-cooked set meals. The menu changes daily here, but you can expect grilled chicken breast or pork chop proceeded by plantain soup for $2.25. Ca. 4b, 35-91. Updated: Mar 30, 2011.

Romani

(LUNCH: $3.75) Romani is another bargain restaurant alongside the Parque del Perro. This Colombian-Italian fusion place offers home-cooked set meals at lunchtime, and is popular with office workers and students. For your hard-earned $3.75, you get a choice of soup or spaghetti as a starter, one of two types of meat accompanied by rice, salad, potatoes, and fresh juice to wash it all down. Ca. 3A, 34-57. Tel: 556-1341. Updated: Mar 30, 2011.

Arte y Cocina

(LUNCH: $4) Behind the Centro Cultural de Cali, Arte y Cocina is an ideal place to escape the heat of downtown after picking up tourist information. Situated at the back of the courtyard, this restaurant provides much needed tranquility and respite from the heat and traffic of the Centro. You can get a gourmet buffet lunch for $4. On Thursdays, there are tango lessons from 6:30-8:30 p.m. Cra. 5 and Ca. 7, Centro. Tel: 896-1992, E-mail: fundacrearte@hotmail.com, URL: www.fundacrearteorg.com. Updated: Mar 31, 2011.

VALLE DEL CAUCA

Al Lado del Camino

Cheap and cheerful, Al Lado del Camino (On the Side of the Road) is frequented by droves of medical students from the nearby hospital. The restaurant has a menu that changes daily, but always has three choices for starters and three choices for a main course. Vegetable soups and grilled chicken breast are the norm, but the high turnover of patrons and bustle make this an entertaining place for lunch. Ca. 5, 4B-18. Updated: Mar 30, 2011.

Inca Gaucho

How Inca Gaucho (formerly La Antorcha) can ever hope to fill every seat is a mystery. This vast restaurant is another in the zone that specializes in parrillas and Peruvian food, but its live music on Friday and Saturday nights definitely sets it apart from the rest. Av. 9aN, 9-69. Tel: 653-6131. Updated: Mar 31, 2011.

Patio Valluca

This pleasantly decorated café and restaurant is one of the classier places to try authentic caleño cuisine. More of a dinner spot than a lunch one, Patio Valluca has a variety of special regional dishes. A popular dish here is the *arroz atoyado*, a delicious casserole that resembles a risotto with chicken, sausage and potatoes. All of the main plates are filling and reasonably priced. Daily 7:30 a.m.–11 p.m. Ca. 2 Oeste, 1-07. Tel: 893-3322. Updated: May 13, 2008.

Cali Viejo !

The city's premier location for dining out on vallecaucano food is found in a sprawling finca built in 1870 along the river Cali and close to the city's zoo. With a musical trio wandering between tables playing traditional Colombian Andean music and waitstaff dressed as if from the 19th century, you'll be forgiven if you feel that you have stepped back in time. The food is typical of the region and is by no means cheap, but the helpings are enormous, the location is incredible and the whole experience makes for a great meal out. Try the traditional *champus* (Indian beverage prepared with corn meal, corn, pineapple, lulo, cinnamon and panela) and follow it with a hearty grill accompanied by a *marranita* (a little ball prepared with pork rind and plantain). Casona Vieja Bosque Municipal, 200 meters (656 ft) beyond the zoo. Tel: 893-4927/521-5140, E-mail: comercialcaliviejo@telesat.com.co, URL: www.restaurantecaliviejo.com. Updated: Mar 29, 2011.

INTERNATIONAL

Cathay

(ENTREES: $4-12) Just like many other Chinese restaurants you have probably set foot in, the menu at Cathay is not constrained to dishes merely from the Orient, but fried local platters and French fries as well. Nonetheless, if you are in the neighborhood and hankering for some quality dim sum or sweet and sour pork, then this is the place to come. Av. 8N, 16-70. Tel: 660-1654. Updated: Mar 31, 2011.

La Joroba de Camello

This joint above a jazz club is a place only a local would know. The Joroba de Camello (Camel's Hump) is dark and moody with loud music, cold beers and great slices of pizza. You can pile up the toppings on your slice for $2. The cocktails are killer and appeal to a younger crowd. Av. 4a Oeste, 1-65. Updated: Mar 29, 2011.

Palo Alto

Less chic than the surrounding places in Granada yet far from a dump, Palo Alto is where you come if you need a good coffee, a wrap or juice after browsing boutiques in this exclusive area. In addition to the above, Palo Alto serves pita sandwiches and salads, and has a great terrace. Av. 9N, 14N-73. Tel: 653-5390, E-mail: cafepaloalto@gmail.com. Updated: Nov 13, 2007.

Vinos del Río

Across from Los Gatos Park and the river is Vinos del Río, a nice wine store that offers free wine tasting with snacks. The wine is primarily from Argentina, but there are also some selections from Chile and Spain. Tasting is professional and obligation-free, making it a nice place to rest your feet, sip on award-winning wine and have a snack. Monday-Saturday 10 a.m.-8 p.m. Av. 4 Oeste, 3-88. Tel: 892-0343, Cell: 315-570-7733, Fax: 893-1874, E-mail: megatrading@vinosdelrio.com, URL: www.vinosdelrio.com. Updated: Apr 04, 2011.

VALLE DEL CAUCA

Piccolo Pomodoro

A very cozy Italian eatery with pizza and pasta and all the desirable fixings, Piccolo Pomodoro aims to please, and does so effortlessly. All of the food here, including several different types of ravioli (even asparagus!), is homemade and absolutely delicious. There are some yummy appetizers like carpaccio salad to start your meal, and you can cap it off with a big slice of tiramisu. Monday-Saturday noon-3 p.m. and 7 p.m.-1 a.m. Cra. 2a Oeste, 2-34, El Peñón. Tel: 893-0780, E-mail: piccolopomodorocali@gmail.com/claudigo7@yahoo.com. Updated: Apr 04, 2011.

V!VA ONLINE REVIEW

PICCOLO POMODORO

Everything about this small Italian restaurant is really good, you have got to try it during your next visit to Cali!

July 28, 2009

Restaurante Pizca Arte y Sabor

(ENTREES: $10-18) Up the hill of the ever-hip El Peñón is this trendy Mediterranean lunch and dinner spot. The place is rather artsy, with modern paintings, nice décor, stylish furniture and warm-colored walls. The food here isn't bad, though you'll need deep pockets. Appetizers are between $6-8 and mains like seafood and pasta cost between $10-18. Monday-Friday 11:30 a.m.-2 p.m., Tuesday-Saturday 6 p.m. until around 11 p.m. Cra. 3a Oeste, 2-05, El Peñón. Tel: 893-9659. Updated: May 13, 2008.

San Borondón

Claiming to offer the flavor of two worlds, the San Borondón caters to dining caleños who cannot decide between sushi or an Argentine parrilla. The terrace, with its cooling breeze, is the place to settle down to a juicy steak or a platter of sushi. Ca. 10N, 8N-43. Tel: 668-3326, E-mail: restaurante@sanborondonrestaurante.com, URL: www.sanborondonrestaurante.com. Updated: May 18, 2009.

Granada Faró

(ENTREES: $12-30) Customers frequent Granada Faró for its sophisticated ambiance. The restaurant features three distinct dining rooms: a main salon with windows facing the street, a private salon specially designed for private engagements and an airy salon for socializing with friends. The food here is primarily of the Mediterranean variety and is made to order. There is another branch of the same restaurant in Jardín Plaza, in the southern part of the city. Av. 9N, 15AN-02. Tel: 661-1782/667-4625, E-mail: info@granadafaro.com, URL: www.granadafaro.com. Updated: Mar 31, 2011.

Pacífico

(ENTREES: $14-29) Hidden from the street by potted palms, the Pacífico is a decidedly elegant establishment that specializes in seafood. Ideal for a romantic dinner, try the cazuela del Pacífico, which includes shrimp, squid, clams, crab, paingua clam and coconut. Otherwise, go for the guiso de piangua, a local dish from the southwest made with clams harvested from the roots of mangroves. Av. 9N, 12-18. Tel: 653-3753, E-mail: gerencia@pacificorestaurante.com, URL: www.pacificorestaurante.com. Updated: Mar 31, 2011.

Petite France

(ENTREES: $10-17) This warm, cozy restaurant in El Peñón serves what is arguably the best French cuisine in Cali. The dishes at Petite France, which include crab bisque, quiche and fondue, bring a little bit of Paris to this city. Although the food here is not cheap, but it is tasty and authentic. Cra. 3a Oeste, 3-53, behind the Colegio Sagrada Familia. Tel: 893-3079, E-mail: petitefrancecali@hotmail.com. Updated: Apr 04, 2011.

Nightlife

Known for its salsa dancing, Cali becomes alive at night. The major nightlife districts of Cali are just outside of the city limits, mostly due to the fact that they don't have to close at the times stated by municipal laws.

After partying in the city a bit, many people head to either Menga or Juanchito to continue the rumba, both of which feature a long avenue lined with discos. Menga is located in the north, just past barrio Santa Monica and is considered more upscale. The city's largest electronic and pop clubs are located here. Juanchito is where Cali's salsa scene started and is located in the east. There are several large classic salsa clubs here including the legendary Chango.

Ask around for the most fashionable dancing spots, though you are sure to bump into salsa wherever you go. If you crave a more relaxed atmosphere—or need a night off from dancing—trendy lounges are springing up in

VALLE DEL CAUCA

VALLE DEL CAUCA

Photo by: inyucho

Granada and Parque del Perro. Alternatively, check out the eclectic bars in the barrio San Antonio. Updated: Sep 01, 2011.

Tin Tin Deo !

Tin Tin Deo is routinely described as being one of the best places to go for salsa music and dancing in Cali. Come here to watch in awe as beautiful people show off what their limber bodies and seemingly effortless ear for music can do. Prices are discounted on

Thursdays. Ca. 5, 38-71. Tel: 514-1537/557-4534/5111, E-mail: peronellgp@hotmail.com/tintindeo@yahoo.es, URL: www.tintindeo.com. Updated: Mar 21, 2011.

Soneros

Often equipped with a live salsa band, Soneros has a different vibe from other salsa haunts, though it is hard to put your finger exactly on how. Nonetheless, the dancing is still first rate, the ambience is excellent and any night out spent here will be one to remember. The music and the company make the place and the night. Ca. 12AN, 6N-119 and Av. Octava. Tel: 660-4074. Updated: May 21, 2009.

El Habanero

As the name might suggest, spicy, hot and tingling are all sensations likely to be felt after a long night of salsa at El Habanero. Expect a variety of music here, with nothing getting in the way of the crowds who demand to dance. Ca. 7A, 23A-01. Tel: 557-4390. Updated: May 21, 2009.

La Matraca

La Matraca is a salsoteca with a long-standing tradition of playing salsa dura, but also Cuban son and bolero. On Sundays, the place changes somewhat and offers revelers a taste of tango. Cra. 11, 22-80, Barrio Obrero. Tel: 885-7113. Updated: Nov 15, 2007.

Kukaramakara

(COVER: $6) Always a good bet on weekends, Kukaramakara pumps salsa, rock and pop music from open to close. Don't be surprised when locals start to dance on chairs and tables late in the evening at this rowdy place. Occasionally, the house band will play live Latin pop songs. Drinks are by the bottle. Servers are always circulating around, keeping a drink in your hand as you dance the night away. Thursday–Saturday 6 p.m.-2 a.m. Ca. 28N, 2bis-97. Tel: 653-5389/660-2933. Updated: Mar 30, 2011.

Faro 2004

Faro 2004 occupies a prime location on a corner in the trendy Granada barrio. Live music plays in the expansive front courtyard on weekend evenings, making this an ideal place for enjoying a cocktail from its extensive drink list. More a bar than a restaurant, the food is nonetheless sizeable and flavorsome. This is not a place for a quiet meal, but somewhere to begin the evening's festivities. Av. 9N, 12-76. Tel: 409-6518. Updated: May 25, 2009.

AROUND CALI

BUGA

Only 80 kilometers away from Cali, Buga is another world from Cali's busy salsa dancing streets. One of the oldest cities in Colombia, Buga was founded by the Spanish in 1555, then called Guadalajara de Buga. This medium-sized city is famous for the **Basílica del Señor de los Milagros** (Cra. 14, 3-62. Tel: 228-2823, URL: www.milagrosdebuga.com), which is home to the gold-plated El Señor de los Milagros (The Lord of Miracles). This church attracts nearly a million visitors and pilgrims every year, who come to pay their respects and to pray for miracles. Although completed in the 18th century and later destroyed by an earthquake, the Ermita was bestowed with the title of basílica in August of 1937 by Pope Pius XI.

From Cali, through several companies, you can catch a van from the main bus terminal for around $2-3. The ride takes about 40 minutes and the van will drop you at the terminal in Buga. From there, it is a straight 10-minute walk to the town center and the Basílica. Updated: April 21, 2009.

Lodging

Buga Hostel

(BEDS: $9, ROOMS: $19.50) Buga Hostel is a backpacker's dream right in the heart of Buga, near the Basilica. This old house with beautiful tiled floors and comfortable sitting areas offers a spacious 10-bed dormitory with lockers for stowing your knapsack away. The hostel also has a private room for two, with its own balcony overlooking the street and shared bath. Guests may use the common kitchen. After a day of sightseeing, relax on the rooftop terrace in one of the hammocks. The real treat of Buga Hostel is its on-site bakery, pizzeria and microbrewery, the Holy Water Ale Café, creating delights from old-world recipes. Cra 13, 4-83. Tel: 032-236-7752, E-mail: bugahostel@gmail.com, URL: www.bugahostel.com.

YOTOCO

Some 18 kilometers (11 mi) from Buga and 56 kilometers (34.8 mi) from Cali, the natural reserve of Yotoco covers 560 hectares (1,384 ac) and its altitude oscillates between 1,200 and 1,600 meters (3,937-5,249 ft) above sea level.

The town of Yotoco itself was founded in 1622 by Captain Diego Rengifo Salazar who took full advantage of the Yotoco settlement already in place. What you find today is a small town with some colonial buildings of interest, but the range of flora and fauna in the area is more fascinating.

VALLE DEL CAUCA

All the flora that covers the eastern edge of the Andean cordillera is represented here. Birdwatching is also possible. Aside from fishing in the Escondite and Picapiedra rivers, you can also bathe in the natural pools of the Iso Chorros river.

SAN CIPRIANO

San Cipriano is fast becoming a must-do activity for adventure-seeking travelers. At Córdoba, two hours from Cali on the road to Buenaventura, there are train tracks where trains no longer run. Due

to this, the town of San Cipriano has effectively been cut off from civilization. Nonetheless, the locals have devised an ingenious way of attracting visitors: They have created their own carts that travel the train tracks. You can choose to ride either a hand-pumped cart or one attached to a motorcycle. Hop aboard and take in the stunning, lush scenery on the way to San Cipriano.

When you finally arrive to San Cipriano, you'll find a very small town with rope bridges, a few streets and a beautiful river.

The river has some rapids that make it a fun place to hire inner tubes and spend an afternoon drifting down the river.

To get there, catch a bus from Cali going to Buenaventura and ask to be dropped off at Córdoba. From Córdoba, wander down the hill, avoiding the unnecessary touts, and pick out your cart of choice. Fifteen minutes later, you'll be in San Cipriano. Be sure to leave San Cipriano before dusk to be able to catch a day-time bus back to Cali. Updated: Nov 11, 2009.

PARQUE DE LOS FARALLONES

Only 20 minutes from Cali's city limits and with borders that include the slopes to the Pacific coast, the Eastern cordillera of the Andes and the River Cauca, the Parque de los Farallones is a sight to behold. Created in 1968, its ecosystems include that of the Andes and the Choco and everything in between, ranging from 1,600 meters (5,249 ft) above sea level to over 4,000 meters (13,123 ft).

Spanning 150,000 hectares (370,658 ac), the park takes in steep mountain ranges, cloud forest, numerous water sources and rainforest, as well as lowland jungle. Due to the variety of altitudes, precipitation and temperatures found within the park, the environment plays host to around 700 species of birds, 200 species of snakes, peccary, deer, pumas and monkeys.

There are visitor centers and campsites, but permission to enter the park must be sought prior to arrival. **Topacio Visitors Center** is found near to the River Pance, where there are two campsites and bathrooms. **Quebra-da Honda Visitors Center** is at Kilometer 28 on the route to Peñas Blancas and Pichinde and has one campsite. The **Park Authorities** are located in Cali (Av 4, 37AN-37. Tel: 664-9334). Updated: May 19, 2009.

!!!!!

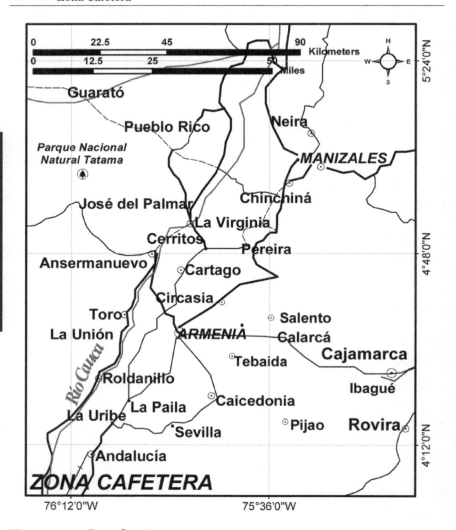

Zona Cafetera

The smell of tangy oranges, the taste of smooth coffee and the sound of bird songs can all be found in the impressive green lands of the Zona Cafetera, a region made up of the provincial departments of Caldas, Risaralda and Quindío. Made up of valleys filled with bamboo, mountain peaks that tickle the sky and rolling landscapes, this coffee-growing region is throbbing with natural life, tranquility and adventure.

Colombia's coffee zone only has two million inhabitants. Its major cities, Manizales, Pereira and Armenia, are all less than 200 years old,

illustrating how this part of the country is richer in rural cultivation and natural beauty than in urban growth and prosperity. Coffee is just one of many reasons why this region has gained popularity. Other draws include its large natural parks, like Parque Nacional Natural Los Nevados and Valle de Cocora, and the thermal springs in Santa Rosa de Cabal.

The inhabitants here undoubtedly value tradition and a slower-paced rural lifestyle. Still, with modern cities close by, the traveler who hungers for peace and quiet but still wants to be near the action can be satisfied.

History

Two thousand years before the Spanish conquest, the Cauca Medio/Zona Cafetera was populated by agricultural workers, gold and salt miners, ceramic artists and farmers. Gold and ceramic art were highly valued in these early societies, and the abundance of gold and clay spurred a great proliferation of art for centuries. Metal works were created with unique methods combining gold and copper, and surviving ceramics depict simple yet beautiful zoomorphic and anthropomorphic figures.

Until 1540, there were so many different indigenous customs, traditions and languages present in this area that European settlers classified the cultures into provinces: Caramanta, Anserma, Arma, Picara, Carrapa, Quimbaya, Quindío and others. Among all of these groups, the most impressive gold and masterful art came from the Quimbaya.

In the late 1500s, the indigenous and native people in metropolitan centers like Manizales and Pereira moved to quieter, more comfortable mountain villages. This is why there are so many lovely colonial *pueblos* (towns) and buildings in this region. Rural farm life continues to be important for the people here, and traditional customs are still practiced in the more remote parts of Risaralda and Quindío.

As the nation's green region, Zona Cafetera has a perfect microclimate for plant life. Coffee, berries, potatoes, and many other fruits and vegetables grow here almost effortlessly. As populations in the area flourished, these industries continued to develop.

UNESCO declared the Zona Cafetera a World Heritage Site in July of 2011, due to its sustainable coffee-producing terrain, which represents traditional coffee-growing techniques and is an example of environmental adaptation. Updated: Jul 07, 2011.

Highlights

Visit one of the coffee fincas surrounding **Armenia** (p. 137) or **Manizales** (p. 152) to see how the caffeinated drink is made from bean to cup.

Don't miss the **Parque Nacional del Café** (p. 140), an educational amusement park with live shows, rides, shops and more.

Indulge your outdoorsy side in the **Valle de Cocora** (p. 146), where hiking, horseback riding and wildlife spotting opportunities abound.

Explore the peaks, valleys, craters and lagoons of **Parque Nacional Natural Los Nevados** (p. 157), where snowy mountains, desert and evergreen forest coexist.

When to Go

The rich, fertile land of the Zona Cafetera is 1,000 meters (3,281 ft) above sea level, so the climate in this region is almost always cool or cold, especially in the mountains. The rainy seasons of March to May and September to November can be downright depressing, sometimes with pounding rain all day. The drier seasons are quite temperate and tend to favor warmer temperatures.

The *feria* (fair) in Manizales is one of the largest festivals in Colombia and always draws a crowd of locals and tourists alike. Salento's population seems to double every weekend, as food tents and artisan stalls pop up on the main square. In January, Salento also has a very popular, raucous celebration in remembrance of the town's founding. Updated: Jul 07, 2011.

Safety

The Zona Cafetera is a very laid-back part of Colombia. Travelers will feel particularly safe and secure in the smaller towns. The larger cities are generally safe, even at night. However, the usual precautions are advised.

Until recently, Pijao, a town near Armenia, was known by locals as a base for the FARC. However, the situation has improved

ZONA CAFETERA

Photo by: Christopher Minster

significantly and you shouldn't experience any problems here.

Always ask tourist information offices about areas to avoid, or ask your hotel about the city's dangerous neighborhoods. These locations change fairly frequently, as both rural and urban areas in this region are experiencing growth. Updated: Jul 11, 2011.

Things to See and Do

The Zona Cafetera is a place to indulge the senses—from hot thermal springs to the cold Valle de Cocora; sweet berries to bitterly rich coffee. Manizales, Pereira and Armenia are the capitals of the departments that make up the Zona Cafetera, and each provides a different take on the many riches Colombia has to offer.

In Manizales, a treacherous trip to the top of La Basílica is a must. Near Pereira, travelers should set aside a full day in the Parque del Café or spend a few hours basking in the hot thermal springs of Santa Rosa. The Museo del Oro Quimbaya in Armenia remains one of Colombia's best-preserved and most organized gold collections. Also of note is Salento, a small town tucked neatly beside a mountain, where

farm-grown trout is deliciously served on a large *patacón* (fried plantain).

Tours

The Zona Cafetera is the ideal place to enjoy the gorgeous Colombian countryside, and to fully do so, you will need a guide. In fact, Parque Nacional Natural Los Nevados requires that visitors be accompanied by a park ranger or guide. This is not only for your safety but also to help you navigate through the high, winding park roads. Valle de Cocora, near Salento, is another place where you might benefit from a guided tour. While trails into the valley are well marked, a good guide can help you get the most out of your experience.

Finally, if you're coming to this region, you should stop by a coffee farm. You are, after all, in Colombia, where the highest grade of coffee is produced and exported throughout the world. You will find there is a great deal to learn about coffee, and it is well worth the extra money to hire a local farmer to show you around and teach you the tricks of the trade.

Many tours and guides can be found upon arrival in your destination of choice. In the case of Parque Nacional Natural Los Nevados, it is wise to arrange a tour in Manizales that includes transportation to and from the park. Horseback riding is also a very popular activity in this region. It costs about $20 for a day tour (4-6 hr) in the countryside.

Lodging

In general, the municipalities in the Zona Cafetera have a wide range of accommodation options for foreigners. Manizales and Salento in particular have good, low-cost backpacking hostels. Only a handful of places offer dorm beds, the cheapest option for budget travelers. You will be surprised, though, how far your cash can go if you break from the backpacker route and search for your own accommodations in town.

It is a little more difficult to find cheap lodging in Armenia and Pereira, as these cities have less developed tourism infrastructures. If you plan on spending a night or two in either of these places, first go to the information booth at the bus terminal. This is the best place to get some good suggestions for accommodation and to pick up some business cards. It will also give you a chance to get your bearings and learn which neighborhoods are safe and which to avoid. As the entire region is temperate and often cool, you will appreciate that all accommodations have 24-hour hot water. Updated: Jul 09, 2011.

ARMENIA

 1,500m   350,000 6

Armenia was founded on October 14, 1889, by Jesús María Ocampo, also known as Tigrero (or the "Tiger Killer") because of his love of hunting jaguars (known locally as tigers). Ocampo came to Armenia, which is located on the Río Quindío, looking for shelter in the mountains of Quindío. He paid 100 pesos in gold coins for land on which to build a trade center, not only for himself but also for other colonists from Antioquia, Manizales and areas surrounding the river. He proceeded to sell land for settlement. Six months after its founding, in August of 1890, Armenia had reached a population of 100 people, allowing it to gain legal recognition by the government. The city became known as Armenia to honor the people murdered in the Hamidian massacres of 1894-96.

Armenia's enviable geographical location at 1,500 meters (4,921 ft) above sea level, next to two rivers, and within five hours from the country's three largest cities (Bogotá, Medellín and Cali), made it a commercial hub during the 1900s, especially when the city welcomed train and car transportation in the late 1920s. In January of 1999, Armenia experienced a devastating earthquake that left 200,000 people homeless. However, international aid quickly brought modern buildings to the city, including a modern bus terminal and a pedestrian mall in the center of town. A collection of gold that is often regarded as the best in the country is located in northern Armenia at the Museo del Oro Quimbaya. Updated: May 14, 2009.

When to Go

The nice, temperate climate in Armenia often allows for pleasant days and cool evenings. Just as in other areas of the Quindío, it is usually wetter in the months of April and October.

A really neat festival worth catching if you are in the region around February is Armenia's Yipao, or Jeep Parade. Jeeps, which have become the beloved symbol of the coffee culture in this part of Colombia, gather together and parade around the city carrying heaps of produce such as plantains and fruits. The cars carrying the most harmonious arrangements of produce win prizes. In 2006, Armenia and nearby Calarcá were inaugurated into the Guinness Book of World Records for having the longest caravan of nearly 400 jeeps. Updated: Jul 21, 2011.

Getting To and Away

The city of Armenia is conveniently situated between some of Colombia's largest cities. Bogotá and Medellín are just six hours away by bus; Cali and Ibagué are three hours away; and Pereira and Manizales are one and two hours away respectively. Getting to and away from Armenia by bus is the easiest and safest option.

The city's secure, modern bus terminal is located on the southern edge of the city, a short five-minute taxi ride ($1.50) from Plaza Bolívar, the city's center. Walking from the terminal to Plaza Bolívar is not advised. You can take any local bus from the terminal to the "Centro" ($0.75), which will pass through the center on its route around the city.

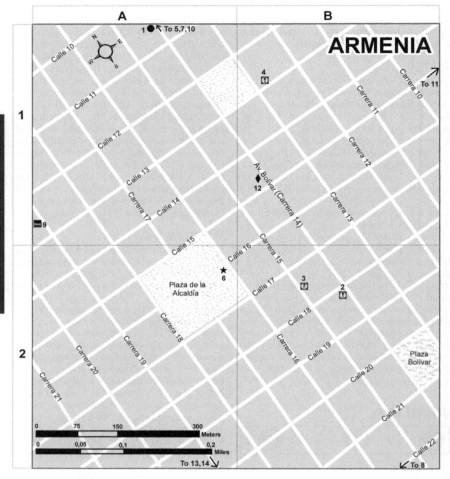

ZONA CAFETERA

There is very little reason to fly here. If you do decide to fly, the Pereira airport services Armenia by airport shuttle every hour. Updated: May 14, 2009.

Getting Around

With the opening of Armenia's pedestrian mall running through the center of the city, getting around by foot is the best option. Yellow taxis buzz around town at all hours, though, if you'd rather not walk (minimum price during the day is $1.50, night $2.50). Red "Tinto" buses run along Armenia's main thoroughfares for $0.75 per ride, and are the best way to get to the Museo del Oro Quimbaya in the north of the city. Updated: May 14, 2009.

Safety

Armenia is a surprisingly clean and safe city. However, the few blocks around Plaza Bolívar can get a bit shady at night. There is little crime to speak of in this town, but the usual precautions should apply when wandering the city alone or after dusk. Updated: May 27, 2011.

Services

The city's tourism office, **Corporación de Cultura y Turismo de Armenia** (Monday-Friday 7:30 a.m.-noon and 2-6:30 p.m. Tel: 741-2991/3144), is located in the **alcaldía** (Cra. 17, 16-00, Centro Administrativo Municipal CAM). Alternatively, you can get tourist information from the booth in the bus terminal, which is at the top of the stairs. The agents

● **Activities**

1 Museo del Oro Quimbaya A1

◫ **Eating**

2 El Toque Pizzeria B2
3 Home B2
4 Rincón Vegetariano B1

★ **Services**

5 Hospital San Juan de Dios A1
6 Tourism Office A2

▦ **Sleeping**

7 Eco Hotel Santa Barbara A1
8 HC Comfortel B2
9 Hotel Alpino de Armenia A1
10 Hotel El Edén Country Inn A1
11 La Floresta Hotel Campestre B1

◆ **Tours**

12 Territorio Aventura B1

▦ **Transportation**

13 Airport A2
14 Bus Terminal A2

there are very attentive and helpful, and can provide you with maps, handouts and any other pertinent information you might need.

Banks, ATMs, postal services, pharmacies and Internet hubs are found around Plaza Bolívar or along the pedestrian mall. Armenia's public hospital is **Hospital San Juan de Dios** (corner of Av. Bolívar and Ca. 17N. Tel: 749-3500). Updated: Aug 04, 2011.

Things to See and Do

Armenia is a gateway to the rich Quindío region, but the city itself offers little to see and do. Other than the educational Museo del Oro Quimbaya at the northern edge of the city and the interesting Parque Nacional del Café closeby, most visitors head to the hills to experience the surrounding nature. There are many hiking, rafting and fishing opportunities outside Armenia as well as other adventurous activities that could be worthwhile should you choose to stay for longer than a day. Updated: Jun 09, 2011.

Pedestrian Mall

There is plenty of shopping along Avenida Bolívar (or Cra. 14), where you can walk a dozen blocks down a pedestrian walkway that extends from Plaza Bolívar (cross street: Ca. 21) to the hospital (on Ca. 9). On weekends, this street is packed with people in need of some retail therapy. Artisan shops, drugstores, clothing

boutiques and bigger malls line both sides of the street, so you'll be sure to find what you're looking for. Pedestrians are the privileged ones here as cars cross the road slowly, giving shoppers the right of way. Updated: Apr 04, 2011.

Museo del Oro Quimbaya ♪

The most impressive permanent gold collection in the Zona Cafetera is found at the northern edge of Armenia on the way to Salento and Pereira. This museum is the primary reason travelers pass through the city. It is housed in a fantastic brick structure, surrounded by green courtyards and complete with a kid's library and lecture hall, cafeteria, temporary exhibition hall, and two rooms holding Quimbaya gold and pottery.

The first room begins with the history of the Quimbaya, the indigenous people who occupied the mid-Cauca region (the departments of Caldas, Risaralda and Quindío) long before the Spanish conquered this area in the early 16th century. The gold on display is a fascinating collection of body ornaments, musical instruments, tools and objects used to check coca leaves. The pottery is mostly comprised of human figures and pumpkin-shaped urns and pots. Animal, female and pumpkin shapes dominate the gold and clay objects because they represent life, reproduction and fertility—three important Quimbaya values. The pinkish glow of the gold

Parque Nacional del Café

By Wilson Lievano, V!VA List Contributor, 2007

If Juan Valdez, the image of Colombian coffee throughout the world, had a farm, it would probably be on the grounds of the Parque Nacional del Café, the theme park for all things coffee related.

Located in the town of Montenegro, Quindío, 257 kilometers (160 mi) west of Bogotá, in the heart of the coffee-growing region of Colombia, the park is a blend of mechanical attractions, ecotourism and family entertainment. All pay homage to the production of the smoothest, tastiest coffee in the world.

The park sits in a small valley. To get there from the entrance, visitors can take a cable car, which gives a broad view of the park and its surroundings, or a path that allows them to see and touch all the varieties of coffee plants that are grown in Colombia, along with several other varieties from around the world. The path forks, one way leading to the auditorium where a dance troupe performs the typical dances of the region twice a day. The other arm goes to several stations where park officials give a step-by-step explanation of how coffee goes from the Colombian highlands to your favorite mug.

Both paths converge on a big colonial-style square filled with statues and stores. During the Christmas season, the square has a large tree and live re-enactments of the Nativity. From the square, visitors can walk to the mechanical attractions area that has everything from carousels for the kids to roller coasters and go-karts for the grown-ups. A little further down the road is the lake of the legends, a place that offers boat rides and several tales of the myths and legends of the original inhabitants of the region.

No visit to Parque Nacional del Café is complete without taking some time to sit in one of the many coffee houses scattered all over the park to enjoy a *tinto* (the name that locals give to a cup of regular coffee). These shops also offer a wide variety of candy made from coffee.

It is easier to get to the park from Armenia than from Pereira. Take any bus from Armenia to Cicasia (15 min, $1; leaves the terminal every 15 min), where you can ask to be dropped off near the park entrance. Additionally, buses from Salento to Armenia (20 min, $1; leaves every half hour) pass through Cicasia. Alternatively, you can rent a car and drive here. Updated: Apr 25, 2008.

Photo by: Christopher Minster

ZONA CAFETERA

comes from a mixture of gold and copper alloy; gold symbolizes males and copper symbolizes females. The second room details the importance of ceremonies and the conservation of tradition after the Spanish conquest.

To date, there have been two significant discoveries of Quimbaya gold. The first, called the "Quimbaya Treasure," was a collection of over 200 golden objects and numerous pieces of pottery. The entire collection was regrettably given to Spain as a gift and is now on display in the Museo de América in Madrid. A second group of objects was uncovered in the Antioquia region and is on display in a traveling exhibition through the Banco de la República. Check its website (URL: www.banrep.gov.co) to find its current location.

Admission is free, and both rooms have English guidebooks that you can carry with you. Take any bus to Circasia and get off at the rotary with the black steam train in the center. Tuesday-Saturday 10 a.m.-5 p.m., closed Mondays and public holidays. Av. Bolívar, 40N-80. Tel: 749-8433, E-mail: museoquimbaya@banrep.org, URL: www.banrepcultural.org/armenia. Updated: Apr 04, 2011.

Jardín Botánico de Quindío/ Mariposario

(ADMISSION: $8) Not far from Armenia is the Quindío Botanical Garden, a jungle-like sanctuary full of plants, trees and animals. The highlight of the garden is the Mariposario, or butterfly building. It's essentially a butterfly-shaped greenhouse where dozens of species of butterflies flourish. Besides the butterflies, there is a canopy tower, a museum dedicated to a roadway tunnel, a kids' maze, a hanging bridge and many trails. Guides are available, even in English. KM3 va Calarcá. URL: www.jardinbotanicoquindio.org.

Recuca

In the Zona Cafetera there are several coffee plantations that welcome visitors with tours, activities and lunch. One such place is Recuca (short for *Recorrido de la Cultura Cafetera*), located about 20 minutes from Armenia near "la Y," a Y-shaped intersection (a bus traveling between Barcelona and Armenia can drop you off on the road leading there, about a 20 minute walk). Recuca is a working coffee plantation and guests learn everything from how to plant coffee to how to prepare the perfect cup of joe. They'll even dress you up in traditional coffee region clothes and teach you how to properly challenge a rival to a machete fight! The coffee tour takes about 2 hours and costs approximately $10-15. A hearty lunch of traditional fare (similar to a *bandeja paisa*) will cost an additional $5 or so and is a good deal. They'll be happy to sell you a fine bag of coffee to take home, too. URL: http://www.recuca.com/en/home.htm Email: luchore-cuca@hotmail.com. Phones: 310 830 3779 or 311 383 9885. Updated: November 5, 2011.

Tours

Territorio Aventura

Just 30 minutes from Armenia, you can visit a natural park, try your hand at fishing, go kayaking or rafting, or see the world from great heights as you rappel or parasail above the Quindío countryside. Territorio Aventura is ready to plan these adventurous activities for you. Longer trips include *finca* (farm) stays in peaceful haciendas outside the city. Cra. 14, 14N-6 Edificio Acuarium, local 1. Tel: 749-5448/3352, Cel: 310-422-0596/504-3555, URL: www.territorioaventura.com.co. Updated: Jul 08, 2011.

Lodging

Some good economical hotels are a few blocks from the city's pedestrian mall, along Avenida Bolívar between Calle 21 and 9. Basic accommodations include a clean, well-lit room with private bath, and usually just a fan. It never gets hot enough in Armenia to justify air conditioning, so don't expect many places to have it. Sticking to the area next to the pedestrian mall is the safest option, since there are always people bustling about. There are some less desirable parts of towns that are best to avoid, like Simón Bolívar (not to be confused with Plaza de Bolívar).

In the green hills around Armenia are a host of converted "fincas:" country homes that are now hotels. Some are simple and some quite elaborate, with swimming pools, activites, horses, and more. These are great places for those vacationing with kids or those looking to relax. Updated: Nov 09, 2010.

Hotel Alpino de Armenia

(ROOMS: $9-11) Hotel Alpino is a good budget option at the northern end of the city. Although this place is a little farther away from the pedestrian mall, Plaza Bolívar and the busy Carrera 19, it can still be rather loud. But with a clean room that includes private

bath, hot water and TV for around $10 a night, it's hard to complain. You can negotiate to have breakfast included. Cra. 19, 12-41. Tel: 745-4040. Updated: Apr 04, 2011.

Casa Quimbaya

(BEDS: $11 and up) Casa Quimbaya is Armenia's first backpacker's hostel. It is a red-tile roofed bungalow on the corner of a residential street, located near restaurants, discos and other services. Casa Quimbaya offers budget travelers three dormitories and two private, double rooms to choose from. The hostel also has 24-hour hot water, a fully equipped kitchen, DVD library, WiFi and other services, as well as Spanish, guitar and singing lessons. Guests can swap travel tales in the common room or out in the hammock-strung patio. Ca 15 Norte, 14-92. Tel: 732-3086, Cel: 320-683-4959, E-mail: info@casaquimbaya.com, URL: www.casaquimbaya.com.

HC Comfortel

(ROOMS: $18-20) Manager Rubiel keeps this 10-room hotel spic-and-span and makes sure his guests are happy during their stay. The rooms here are spacious with private bath and cable TV. For convenience and comfort on a budget, Comfortel's location—a few blocks from Plaza Bolívar—and its prices will hit the spot. Ca. 22, 17-30. Tel: 741-4852, Cel: 311-777-7133, E-mail: confortel-armenia@hotmail.com. Updated: Apr 04, 2011.

Finca Hotel Los Ancestros Sorrento

(ROOMS: $40-50) Los Ancestros is a laid-back, homey hotel located about 15 minutes by car outside of Armenia. It's in the middle of nowhere, and difficult to find (arrange pick-up with hotel staff). Its remoteness is the best part, however: it's quiet, cozy and in the morning you'll hear roosters instead of car alarms. There is an outdoor pool and a small playground. Breakfast and dinner is included. Best for those with driver or private transportation. Cel: 3125967127 3174348325, Updated: Nov 04, 2011.

Eco Hotel Santa Barbara

(ROOMS: $30-75) This eco-friendly hacienda outside of Armenia is a great base for exploring the surrounding coffee-growing area. The hotel has a coffee trail on its property and offers hour-long tours with a guide to learn about the process of coffee production, ending with a cup of organic coffee from its own farm. Eco Hotel Santa Barbara has

49spacious rooms with private bathroom, TV and balcony. With an on-site restaurant serving up regional dishes, a swimming pool, a Jacuzzi, a game room and a nightclub (9:30 p.m.-close), it will be hard to find a reason to ever leave. Vereda La Siria Circasia. Tel: 740-4800, Fax: 740-4868, E-mail: mercadeo@ecohotelsantabarbara.com, URL: www.santabarbaraecohotel/www.ecohotelsantabarbara.com. Updated: Apr 04, 2011.

Hotel El Eden Country Inn

(ROOMS: $52-88) This neat and colorful inn between Armenia and Circasia is the perfect place to experience the major sites in Quindío. Set in brightly colored colonial buildings, this inn has 15 guest rooms: 11 standard rooms, two family suites and two presidential suites. It also has a pool, Jacuzzi, gym and a restaurant (Monday-Saturday noon-9 p.m., Sunday noon-6 p.m.). The living room fits 100 people and is occasionally used for social events and meetings. Take any bus to Circasia, Salento and Pereira and have the driver drop you off at the entrance to the hotel—on your left, up the hill. Km. 4, outside Armenia. Cel: 315-547-5347/316-527-8558/314-635-3228, E-mail: reservasedencountry@hotmail.com, URL: www.hoteledencountryinn.com. Updated: Apr 04, 2011.

Finca Cafetera El Balso

(ROOMS: $54-60 per person) Finca Cafetera El Balso is one of the most attractive destinations to stay in outside of the city. Located five kilometers (3 mi) outside of Armenia, you can enjoy privacy coupled with the beauty of the coffee country. This hacienda offers five comfortable rooms with a total capacity for 14 guests. You'll want to stay for a while to fully enjoy the farm's beautiful gardens, green fields, coffee and fruit crops. Km. 5, Vía Armenia. Tel: 749-4280, Cel: 300-656-5656, E-mail: reservas@fincaelbalso.com, URL: www.fincaelbalso.com. Updated: Jul 11, 2011.

La Floresta Hotel Campestre !

(ROOMS: $71-136) Directly outside Armenia lies La Floresta Hotel Campestre, a charming rural escape on a beautiful old estate. Its three suites and 15 standard rooms all have WiFi, TV, phone with international calling, and doors leading outside to the plants and gardens that surround the hotel. Lots of activities will keep visitors occupied on La Floresta's property, which has a pool, tennis courts, a golf course, a gym, nature trails, an events room and a communal terrace with hammocks. The downstairs restaurant, La Terraza (Daily 6:30 a.m.-9 p.m.) serves up both international and national dishes. Km. 3, Vía El Edén airport, Vereda Santana. Tel: 747-2508, E-mail: reservas@laflorestahotelcampestre.com, URL: www.laflorestahotelcampestre.com. Updated: Jul 12, 2011.

Restaurants

Delectable, fresh treats can be found on nearly every street corner in Armenia. This area of the country is the leading producer of flour, apples, potatoes and berries. The city is also big on fresh meat and fish. There are several decent eateries right in the center of town that serve vegetarian food, traditional Colombian dishes and more. Updated: Dec 19, 2007.

Rincón Vegetariano !

(LUNCH: $3.50-4) Serving what is arguably the best vegetarian food in all of Colombia, Rincón Vegetariano is a fantastic find in the heart of Armenia. The menu is set every day, but includes juice and milk, fruit, soup, four small vegetarian dishes and a dessert. Service is quick and the second-floor balcony seating is ideal. For just $3.50 in house and $4 take-out, you really can't go wrong here. It also delivers. Ca. 13, 13-24. Tel: 744-5055, Cel: 311-634-7767, E-mail: negramona56@hotmail.com. Updated: Apr 14, 2011.

El Toque Pizzeria

(PIZZA: $2.50-6) This clean, blue-themed pizzeria next to Plaza Bolívar prepares hearty pizzas 16 different ways for a good price. There is free delivery service as well as an online menu if you wish to order from home. Small (1 slice), medium (personal pizza) and large (8 slices) orders are all quite generous and, more importantly, delicious. Closed on Sundays. Cra. 14, 18-02, Centro Comercial Yuldana, local 9. Tel: 741-0134. Updated: Apr 14, 2011.

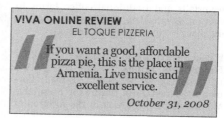

V!VA ONLINE REVIEW
EL TOQUE PIZZERIA

If you want a good, affordable pizza pie, this is the place in Armenia. Live music and excellent service.

October 31, 2008

ZONA CAFETERA

Home

(ENTREES: $7-10) A nice establishment with an enormous flat-screen TV in the front room, a buzzing kitchen and a pleasant back patio, Home does, in fact, offer the comforts of home. The name of the game here is meat—lots and lots of churrasco, chorizo and pork. There's also trout, but in this kind of hearty setting, you'll be more inspired to order a big plate of churrasco and potatoes with a Colombian beer. Prices are a bit expensive. Cra. 15, between Ca. 17 and 18. Updated: Apr 14, 2011.

PIJAO

 1,650m 10,149 6

Although Pijao may have been avoided by travelers just a year ago due to FARC activity in the area, the situation has improved immensely and the city now sees more and more foreigners passing through. Located 31 kilometers (19.3 mi) from Armenia, Pijao—named after the indigenous tribe that populated the area prior to the arrival of the Spanish—is a small agricultural city of 10,149 inhabitants.

Interestingly, Pijao is one of two cities (the other being Marsella) in Colombia at the center of the country's Slow Food movement. Slow Food, an international movement that began in Italy in 1986, rejects agricultural globalization and fast food culture while favoring organic, locally grown food. Furthermore, in June of 2010, Pijao became the first Latin American city to be certified as a Cittaslow, or Slow City, an offshoot of the Slow Food movement. As a Slow City, Pijao residents have committed themselves to slowing down their pace of living, decreasing environmental degradation, preserving their culture, promoting sustainable tourism and educating future generations on ecological topics.

The city itself doesn't offer much to tourists beyond walking around and soaking in the local culture and architecture. However, there are hiking and biking opportunities, waterfalls and traditional coffee farms to visit on its outskirts, making Pijao a relaxing place to stop while in the region.

If you'd like to spend the night in Pijao, try **Hostal Las Nubes** (Rooms: $10-30. Ca. 11, 5-81. Cel: 312-825-5613, E-mail: flormonica@gmail.com), run by the hospitable Mónica Flóres, who was at the forefront of securing Pijao's Slow City certification. The hostel, which can hold 10 people, has a kitchen, a garden, bike rental and free coffee throughout the day. Updated: Jul 12, 2011.

SALENTO

 1,800m 10,000 6

What we now regard as the town of Salento used to be in another location and have a different name. On January 5, 1830, Simón Bolívar passed through the original town (called Barcinales) on his "Camino Nacional," which took him from Cartago to Ibagué. A dozen years later, the town moved to its current location, higher in the mountains at 1,800 meters (5,906 ft), and was renamed Villa de Nuevo Salento. In time, just Salento became the town's name. Salento was officially declared its own municipality much later, in 1908.

Despite it's youth, Salento is still considered the "Father of Quindío," and you will fully understand this term upon visiting this beautifully scenic town. With only 10,000 residents, infinite natural beauty, architectural uniformity and quaintness, as well as a general adherence to and appreciation for tradition and culture, it is no wonder Colombians and foreigners fall in love with this place.

The colorful two-story buildings along Carrera 6 off the main plaza to the stairs of the *mirador* (lookout point) have been excellently preserved. Aside from the occasional car or motorcycle passing through and the fact that nearly every building along this street has been converted into a restaurant or handicraft shop, not much has changed here. The men still wear their country gear, playing cards or billiards at the local bar.

The town is surrounded on all sides by lush, vista-filled countryside. This is a place to explore nature at its finest, whether by horseback along the Quindío River, by foot along dozens of mountain paths or by jeep to the gorgeous Cocora Valley. Don't forget to snap a photo of the national tree, the Palma de Cera, which is a very tall and thin palm tree native to this part of the country. And, of course, your trip to Salento is not complete without trying *trucha con patacón* (trout with a very thin and very large plantain pancake). Updated: Jul 16, 2011.

Photo by: Christopher Minster

ZONA CAFETERA

When to Go
Similar to the other 12 municipalities in the department of Quindío, the weather in Salento is always temperate if not cool. It rains more in the months of March, April, September, and October. Other times of the year, T-shirts and jeans will suit you just fine.

Every January 5-12, Salento celebrates the founding of its city with a major festival called Palma de Cera. Some interesting contests highlighting Salento's lack of technology are held, as well as theater and cultural events. At this time, you will also see one of the biggests fried patacones you'll ever witness. Updated: Jul 16, 2011.

Getting To and Away
Buses converge in the main square. There are three buses that leave to and from Pereira per day. Buses to Armenia come and go hourly. If you're heading to the Valle de Cocora for the day, there are three departures by jeep on the other side of the square. There are several buses back to Salento, with the last bus leaving from the valley at 5 p.m. It takes about one hour to get to each of these destinations. Updated: Apr 23, 2008.

Getting Around
Salento is a very small town, easily manageable by foot. There are no local buses or taxis, but you can hitch a ride from one end to the other if need be. If you'd like to visit the restaurants down by the river, hop on any bus heading out of town. The road to Salento is windy, and cars zoom by at an alarming rate, so it's best to travel out of town by bus even if you're just going down the hill. Updated: Apr 23, 2008.

Safety
The residents of Salento's small urban center are used to seeing both national and international visitors year round. Locals are helpful and accommodating, and you don't have to worry excessively about crime or theft. The tap water here comes from the mountains and is fresh enough to drink, so say goodbye to bottled water and fill up straight from the faucet. Updated: Jul 16, 2011.

Services
The information office at the mirador has useful tips about activities in and around Salento. There is an ATM in the main square on Carrera 7 in the yellow and blue building. There is no sign, so you have to look for it or just ask. Sometimes the machine is out of money, so be

Juan Valdez

Good coffee seems to often come with the face of a mustached man accompanied by a donkey. Though Juan Valdez is a fictional character who borders the stereotypical, his face represents over 500,000 Colombian men who are part of the National Federation of Coffee Growers. Formed in 1927, the federation protects farmers from the threat of international prices falling by saving up any extra income when prices are high and therefore guaranteeing a steady salary throughout the year. In 1981 the logo of Juan Valdez took on the new role of distinguishing 100% Colombian coffee from mixed brands.

Thirteen years later, Juan Valdez made his first TV appearance along with his mule, Conchita, and ever since the trademark has become popular in pop culture. A non-profit organization, the National Federation of Coffee Growers, handles several programs for the economical and educational advancement of Colombian *cafeteros* and their families. Projects like sanitation of living environments, electricity installed, potable water installed, schools for both children and adults, among other things have helped strengthen the communities of coffee growers.

sure to stock up on cash in Pereira or Armenia before going to Salento. Some restaurants and stores accept Visa and MasterCard, but most of the hotels in town do not. There are two decent Internet cafés on Carrera 6 that charge $1 per hour. The hospital is at the corner of Carrera 7 and Calle 7. There is no laundry service in town. Updated: Apr 23, 2008.

Things to See and Do

Coming to Salento requires taking a deep breath of fresh mountain air and enjoying the peace and tranquility of a slow-paced lifestyle. Most activities revolve around the outdoors, whether is be taking a walk, riding a horse or climbing a mountain. There are a handful of beautiful natural sights within arm's reach. Valle de Cocora, with its diverse cloud forest and river running through it, is a must-see, as is the town's Mirador de Salento. Also take a moment to browse the artisan stores on Calle de Real. If you haven't had enough of the outdoors, saddle up and ride out of town on horseback. Updated: Jul 09, 2011.

El Mirador de Salento

The Mirador de Salento is much more than a lookout point. First, you must climb 200 stairs to the big cross at the top. Along the way, you will find signs that tell the story of Jesus. Follow the path to your left to the mirador, which is a covered viewpoint with a grand vista of the Valle de Cocora. The path by the parking lot will lead you down to the river and to other trails in the valley. Updated: Apr 04, 2011.

Valle de Cocora

Cocora Valley is a great launching point for nature hikes and wildlife spotting. There are several trails leading up the mountain, along the river and farther into the valley. A peaceful cloud forest with little manmade pedestrian bridges over the river is about an hour away by foot. Another 30 minutes up the valley will take you to Acaime, a small home with dozens of hummingbirds. You can sleep here for $5 a night, or enjoy a refreshment and snack for $2.

A different trail on the hillside takes you back to Cocora, or you can hoof it up the hill five more kilometers (3 mi) to another lookout. If you don't want to walk the trail, a horse and guide will take you wherever you want for $8 an hour.

Jeeps leave for the Cocora Valley from the main plaza in Salento at 7:30 a.m., 11:30 a.m. and 4 p.m. It costs about $2 per person each way and takes one hour. Head back to Salento from the valley at 8:30 a.m., 12:30 p.m. or 5 p.m. Updated: Apr 04, 2011.

Horseback Riding

Another great way to see the beautiful and vast countryside around Salento is by horse. Paulino Callejas, a local cowboy, has 35 willing horses and a crew of cowboys ready to take you on trails up the mountain or along the Río Cocora. Trips range from 1.5 hours up to six hours, and Paulino charges $10-35, depending on the length and difficulty of the ride. Bigger groups receive discounted rates. Find Paulino at the white house with red trim at the corner of Calle 7 and Carrera 8 in barrio Boquerón. Tel: 313-320-4277. Updated: Apr 04, 2011.

Lodging

Most hostels and hotels in Salento are clustered along Calle 6 and Carrera 6. You will be much happier staying closer to the plaza, and there is always a room available somewhere unless you're coming for festival week in January. All accommodations are about the same price and provide similar amenities: private bath with hot water, plenty of blankets, and hopefully a window with a view of the countryside. If you arrive mid-week or during low season, you can bargain for a better rate. If you're looking for other accommodation options in Salento, camping may be the answer. A popular Salento camping site called **Monteroca** (Cel: 315-413-6862/310-422-3720, URL: www.campingmonterroca.com) is located about four kilometers (2.5 mi) outside of the city, toward the Valle del Río Quindío. The Monte Roca camping site has tents for sale, and even a museum, Museo del Camino Nacional, in a restored colonial house. Updated: Jun 30, 2010.

Hostel Tralala Salento

(ROOMS: $10-17 per person) Perfectly situated close to the town center, Hostel Tralala Salento is ideal for the tired traveler in search of peace and quiet. Recently renovated (2010), this small hostel of four rooms (one of which is a dorm) has a comfortable, relaxing environment complete with a beautiful sun terrace and a patio with hammocks. Along with having a book exchange, cable TV and free WiFi, Tralala Salento's two kitchens are clean and well equipped. For any food supplies, just head to the supermarket around the corner. Hostel Tralala Salento is the white/orange building in front of the local hospital. Cra. 7, 6-45. Cel: 314-850-5543, E-mail: tralalasalento@gmail.com, URL: www.hosteltralalasalento.com. Updated: Jul 6, 2011.

Plantation House

(ROOMS: $10-25 per person) If you are after a taste of Salento's local history, the Plantation House is an ideal place to stay. Originally a coffee plantation house, the hostel has been reconstructed into three separate areas to suit the needs of those staying in the heart of Colombian's coffee country. There are still various coffee plants in the hostel's spacious gardens. Both dormitory-style and private accommodation is available, with access to kitchen facilities, Internet and hot water. Even though Plantation House is a bit far from the town center, located several blocks from the main plaza, it seems to be continuously packed with backpackers. The nearest bus stop is right by the fire station, just at the entrance of Salento. From there, the hostel is 150 meters (492 ft) away. Alto de Coronel, Ca. 7, 1-04. Cel: 315-409-7039, E-mail:theplantationhousesalento@yahoo.co.uk, URL: www.theplantationhousesalento.com. Updated: Jul 06, 2011.

Posada del Angel 🔔

(ROOMS: $15-20) This hostel is the best find in town and just a few paces from the main plaza. Most tourists don't know about this place because it is not in an obvious location. Upon arrival at the plaza, instead of heading back through town from where you came, head down the hill half a block on Calle 6, where you will see this cute white hostel with blue trim on the left. Elsa, the owner, resident and local expert, is a sweet lady who will make you feel right at home. Her house has four bright and airy rooms, each with cable TV and a private bath. The room next to the kitchen has a nice balcony looking out over the countryside. Elsa will cook breakfast for you for $2.50, or you can use the kitchen for free. Ca. 6, 7-47. Tel: 759-3507, Cel: 311-609-0977/317-257-7314. Updated: Apr 23, 2008.

Balcones de Ayer

(ROOMS: $18-25) This attractive colonial home provides basic but modern accommodations half a block from the plaza. All six rooms are the same, with cable TV, a clean private bath (with hot water) and a comfortable queen-size bed. The price includes breakfast in the first-floor restaurant, which also serves traditional lunches and dinners (meat and fish) for $8-10 per plate. Ca. 6a, 5-40. Tel: 759-3273, Cel: 312-226-2921, URL: www.balconesdelayer.com. Updated: Apr 04, 2011.

V!VA ONLINE REVIEW
BALCONES DE AYER

The rooms are small but very clean, and with hot water. Great location on the main square, and friendly owners. Good value.

October 31, 2008

ZONA CAFETERA

Posada El Mirador de Salento

(ROOMS: $18-25) La Posada is an elegant and comfortable house of traditional Colombian architecture. It has comfortable private rooms, complete with showers, hot water, cable TV and breakfast. The spaces are very open and the atmosphere is relaxed. Located near a beautiful viewing point, the hostel is five minutes off Calle Real and the principal square, where you'll find everything you could need. It is a great opportunity to feel the amiability of the Colombians. Cra 3, 1-40, barrio las Colinas. Tel: 759-3500, Cel: 317-624-5553, E-mail: posadaelmiradordesalento@gmail. com, URL: www.posadaelmiradordesalento. blogspot.com. Updated: Apr 04, 2011.

Restaurants

All of Salento's restaurants are located around the plaza and along Carrera 6. There are enough restaurants to last you a week without going back to the same one, though most serve up the same dishes, so it's a good idea to ask the locals which are popular. The specialty here is fresh trout, available eight different ways, and served with a large patacón. Typical paisa dishes are also common. Updated: Apr 04, 2011.

Super Patacón con Trucha

Its name deserves a prize, as does its monstrously delicious trout and patacón. This place is no secret to either locals or tourists. If you ask anyone where to go for the best trout in town, you'll wind up here. Super Patacón is right on the square, and the portions are enormous and tasty. Depending on how you order the trout, it will come in a bubbling soup with garlic and mushrooms, or sit right on top of the big yellow fried plantain. Use the sweet and crispy pieces of patacón to scoop up your fish and enjoy! Updated: Apr 04, 2011.

Las Mariposas !

This artisan store has a lovely restaurant in its back garden, which serves traditional Colombian cuisine, including regular and half portions of trout with patacón. Trout plates can be prepared various ways, all including a fresh salad with tangy dressing. The restaurant has a perfect view of the colorful stairs to the mirador, making it an ideal lunch spot. Updated: Apr 04, 2011.

Las Tapias

This classic Italian and French eatery is a tasty option if you're seeking something other than trout or fried meat. It has a central spot in the middle of Carrera 6, and is brightly decorated with heavy wooden tables and chairs. The crepes, pizza and pasta here are all cheap and delicious. Updated: Apr 04, 2011.

PEREIRA

 1,500m   450,000   6

Before it became Pereira, the capital of the Risaralda region, it was first the town of Cartago, which was moved to the place it is today in 1691. The Cartago-Pereira area was culturally influenced by the fierce Quimbaya tribes. The Quimbaya people are famous for their gold work, which is considered among the best representations of pre-Columbian culture. Settlers from Antioquia occupied the area during expansion efforts that developed much of Colombia. Because of its economically strategic location, fertile soil and good weather, Pereira experienced significant growth during the time of colonization. Settlers grew large quantities of coffee, which is still the most important crop produced in the area.

Unlike Manizales, Pereira had many settlers from Valle del Cauca, Bogotá and other major Colombian cities, and even today, the city has a diverse population. In 1921, with the arrival of the locomotive train, Pereira quickly became known as "The Prodigious City," as it experienced quick economic growth. Fifty years later, the city had doubled in population and now has 450,000 residents. Today, it continues to buzz with agroindustrial manufacturing and financial activity.

Although it's an urban place, it is still a city in need of infrastructure for foreign travelers. The two tourist offices in town are more like bookshelves with flyers and business cards, and the hotels cater to business travelers rather than backpackers. Still, if you set aside a day in Pereira, chances are you will find a suitable place to sleep and something interesting to do. Updated: Jul 14, 2011.

When to Go

Pereira is the warmest city in the Zona Cafetera and sees a fair amount of sunshine. Still, it can be a bit cooler and rainier in April and October. Small food festivals are held in the Plaza Bolívar three times a year to celebrate a variety of local foods, such as *mazamorra* (a dessert made from corn, milk and sugar water). For

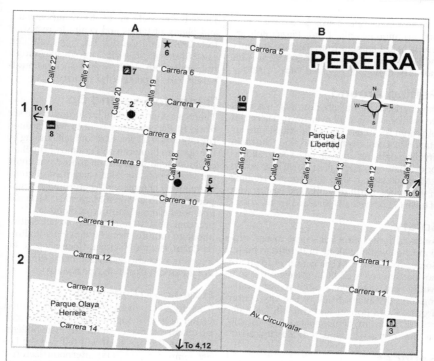

Activities

1 Banco de la República   A1
2 Plaza Bolívar A1

Eating

3 Kilaba   B2
4 La Catorce A2

★ Services

5 Fomento del Turismo A1
6 Clínica Risaralda A1

Shopping

7 Estación Central A1

Sleeping

8 Hotel Abadía Plaza A1
9 Hotel Santa Rosa B1
10 Hotel Suite Center B1

Transportation

11 Aeropuerto Matecaña A1
12 Bus Terminal A2

about five days at the end of August, the city holds its annual Fiestas de la Cosecha, which celebrates the harvest season with food and drink. Updated: Jul 11, 2011.

Getting To and Away

Pereira's international airport, Aeropuerto Matecaña, the largest in the region, is located a short 20 minutes from the city center (about $5 by taxi). A few different airlines offer flights between Pereira and Bogotá (Aires, Avianca and Satena), Medellín (Aires, ADA and Satena), Cali (Aexpa) and Panama City (Copa Airlines Colombia). Check their individual websites for exact schedules.

The city's bus terminal, **Terminal de Transportes de Pereira** (Tel: 315-2323, URL:

www.terminalpereira.com), is an easy and safe 20-minute walk from Plaza Bolívar. Pereira is just an hour from Salento, Armenia and Manizales, and about four hours from Cali and six from Bogotá. Updated: May 14, 2009.

Getting Around

The city is easily walkable on foot, but taxis are readily available all over town. There is a minimum $1.50 day and $2.50 night rate for a taxi ride. Local city buses run along the main city thoroughfares and will take you to all major destinations ($0.75 per ride). There is also a Megabús system with three routes running in the center, north to south, and east to west of town ($1 per ride). Updated: May 14, 2009.

Safety

As in all larger cities, it's best to use caution when walking alone in Pereira at night. Some streets even in the center of town are not particularly well lit in the evening, so it would be wise to take a cab if you are walking long distances. Stick to the city center around Plaza Bolívar and you will feel safe, but still be aware of pickpockets and use basic common sense. Updated: May 29, 2010.

Services

There are two tourism offices in Pereira. The Fomento del Turismo, located in the big mall on Calle 17 and Carrera 9, has brochures and maps to pick and choose from but no office attendant. The other office is located in the city's government building two blocks down the hill. The people at this location can help you make local calls to arrange accommodations or tours.

There is a plethora of pharmacies, banks, ATMs and Internet cafés on the main Plaza Bolívar. **Hospital Universitario San Jorge** (Cra. 4, 24-88. Tel: 335-6333) and **Clínica Risaralda** (Ca 19, 5-13. Tel: 335-5666) are two of Pereira's major medical facilities. Another hospital and some medical clinics are also located just outside of the city's center by the bus terminal. Updated: Jul 11, 2011.

SHOPPING

Estacíon Central

This shopping mall, just a block from Plaza Bolívar, is still filling up with modern stores and food stalls. Retail and electronics stores are on the top three floors, and there's a variety of food options (fast food, bakery goods, and Russian desserts and sweets) downstairs.

There is free WiFi in the downstairs atrium, and plenty of tables and chairs to rest your feet. Cra. 6 and Ca. 20. Tel: 335-5122, Cel: 314-889-5795, E-mail: info@estacioncentralpereira.com, URL: www.estacioncentralpereira.com. Updated: Jul 11, 2011.

Things to See and Do

There is nothing special for foreigners to see or do in Pereira other than to walk around the city center. If you find yourself passing by the obscure Fomento de Turismo or the Banco de la República, pop in to find out about current events or local activities. Pereira is mainly a commercial center and a transportation hub between Manizales, Armenia, and northern and southern Colombia. There are some nice thermal springs worth visiting about 20 minutes from Pereira in Santa Rosa de Cabal. Parque Nacional Ucumarí is 30 kilometers (18.6 mi) southeast, in the direction of La Florida. Updated: Apr 04, 2011.

Banco de la República

The city's very modern library and cultural center is worth stopping by if only to catch up on current events in the city. The bulletin board on the first floor will tell you the latest temporary exhibits, afternoon lectures, educational talks or evening concerts held on-site. The third floor has a good collection of Colombian magazines, newspapers and literature, which, if you're Spanish is good enough, could prove to be an afternoon well spent. The third floor also has a nice reading area with desks, and a pleasant outdoor terrace with tables and chairs that visitors are encouraged to use. Daily 10 a.m.-5 p.m. Ca. 18bis, 9-57. Tel: 324-3400, URL: www.banrep.org. Updated: Apr 11, 2011.

Lodging

Not particularly accommodating to backpacking tourists, hotels in Pereira tend to be expensive and modern. There are no cheap hotels or hostels in the city worth recommending. The best accommodations are within a three-block radius of Plaza Bolívar. Cheaper family homestays and other lodges are located out of town on the way to Manizales. Updated: Jul 09, 2010.

Sweet Home Hostel

(BEDS: $11, ROOMS: $19.50-31) Sweet Home Hostel is travelers' home away from home while in Colombia's coffee region. This local owned hostel offers two four-bed dorms, and a six-bed room, all with lockers. There are also two private rooms, for couples or families, with common bath. This hostel's beds are larger than the norm, guaranteeing travelers a restful night's sleep. Bathrooms have hot water. Other amenities Sweet Home Hostel offers are smokers' patio, hammocks, common kitchen and WiFi. Sweet Home Hostel's bilingual staff provides guests with information about the area's many activities. This hostel is near the bus terminal and many cultural attractions. Cra 11, 44-30, Barrio Maraya. Tel: 345-4453, Cel: 313-422-4605, E-mail: sweethomehostel@gmail.com, URL: www.sweethomehostel.com.

Hotel Suite Center !

(ROOMS: $21-40) Smack dab in the center of Pereira, Hotel Suite Center is likely the most affordable and comfortable option. Rooms range from a bit shabby (with metal bunk beds), to pretty posh (canopy bed, large TV and a bathtub in the bedroom). All rooms have hot water and a fair share of comfort and security. The restaurant on the main floor serves decent Colombian fare. Ca. 16, 7-56. Tel: 333-0989, Cel: 310-388-1520, Fax: 333-9018. Updated: Apr 04, 2011.

Hotel Royal

(ROOMS: $25-45) Located in the center of Pereira, Hotel Royal has simple single, double and triple bedrooms, all with private bathroom, TV, metal-framed beds, hot water and telephone. Ca. 16, 5-78. Tel: 335-2501/2502, Cel: 311-711-4660, Fax: 335-2500, E-mail: hotelroyal@yahoo.com. Updated: Jul 12, 2011.

Hotel Termales Santa Rosa de Cabal

(ROOMS: $130-200) Travel 15 minutes out of town to Santa Rosa de Cabal and you will find this comfortable, luxurious hotel, complete with a naturally heated pool filled with fresh water from thermal springs. Aside from its decadent furnishings, the hotel has two private Jacuzzis, a massage parlor, secure parking, a restaurant and a bar. Its 30 family-friendly rooms are situated in two different buildings. Tents are also available for rent for those interested in camping on the grounds. The hotel can accommodate meetings or special events in its 60-person conference room as well. A 15-minute walk down the surrounding trails lead you to mountain waterfalls or to the town of Santa Rosa. Ca. 14, 15-41. Tel: 364-6500, Cel: 320-680-3604 ,Fax: 364-1490, E-mail: informacion@termales.com.co, URL: www.termales.com.co. Updated: Sep 06, 2011.

Hotel Abadia Plaza

(ROOMS: $100-120) The best of the best in Pereira, Hotel Abadia is a high-end establishment in the heart of the city. The 50 modern, tastefully decorated rooms have first-class amenities, including a flat screen TV. Breakfast in the hotel's restaurant is included in your stay, and guests are also free to use the hotel gym and sauna. Cra. 8, 21-67. Tel: 335-8398, Fax: 334-2471, E-mail: reservas@hotelabadiaplaza.com, URL: www.hotelabadiaplaza.com. Updated: Apr 05, 2011.

Restaurants

The cuisine in Pereira isn't too varied. You'll find typical arepas, empanadas and other Colombian plates on most menus. Like in Manizales, the restaurants in Pereira's nicer hotels tend to have more creative dishes, but are pricier. Shopping mall food courts are cluttered with different stalls that have small menus. Updated: Apr 05, 2011.

La Catorce

La Catorce shopping mall, across from the bus terminal, is a convenient eating spot for those just passing through Pereira. It has a food court with fast food as well as a variety of restaurants. Since there is little to no atmosphere at La Catorce, this place is best for travelers on the go, or those who plan on doing some retail shopping in addition to having a quick bite to eat. Updated: Apr 04, 2011.

Kilaba !

(ENTREES: $8-16) This unique eatery, with an Arabian take on Colombian cuisine, serves up *bandeja paisa* and other traditional dishes with some Middle Eastern flair. In addition to Colombian specialties, you can also order some unique dishes and desserts, such as stuffed grape leaves or baklava. This is one of the few nice establishments that stays open until late in the evening. The restaurant is a few blocks from Plaza Bolívar and comfortably seats 30 guests in its warmly decorated dining hall. Av. Circunvalar Ca. 11, 12B-27. Tel: 334-9207, Cel: 300-275-8570, URL: www.kilaba.com. Updated: Aug 04, 2011.

AROUND PEREIRA
PARQUE NACIONAL UCUMARÍ

Parque Nacional Ucumarí is one of Colombia's best locations to spot birds, animals and plant life. The variations in altitude in this area are what make Ucumarí so biologically diverse. Because the park covers some 16 kilometers (10 mi) in diameter, the best, and practically only way, to experience it is to hire a guide who can take you to the park via chiva bus. With a guide, you can visit waterfalls, hike in the forest, and see unique birds as well as Andean spectacled bears (if you're lucky), which dwell in this region.

Dormitories and camping sites are available in the park, about 30 minutes from the entrance by foot. There are accommodations and tourist services to Ucumarí in nearby Parque Nacional Natural Los Nevados as well. If you are serious about visiting Ucumarí, plan on spending at least a full day in the park with a guide and be sure to account for the time needed to travel to and from Pereira. Updated: Apr 04, 2011.

MANIZALES

 2,150m   386,931   6

Manizales was founded by a group of 20 antioquians on October 12, 1849, in the middle of a civil war. Even though it is the capital city of the department of Caldas and the most important city in the nation's coffee region, Manizales is still physically part of Antioquia, the region where Medellín reigns supreme. This city's culture has a strong Spanish influence, but its initial homogeneity has been tempered by other ethnic groups migrating to the city to attend its outstanding universities. Tango and rumba are the dances of choice here, and jazz is widely enjoyed as well.

Because of the climate, culture and landscape, Manizales resembles San Francisco, California, with its trendy eateries, chilled-out lifestyle and proximity to the outdoors. At 2,150 meters (7,054 ft), this city has a cool factor all its own. While the city's commercial center around Plaza Bolívar is a historical area, the university district and Zona Rosa show how Manizales can keep up with the times. The city's harmonious blending of old and new makes it a pleasant place to spend a few days.

When to Go

Because of its elevation, temperatures are cool year round. Expect more rain from March to May and September to November.The biggest festival is the Feria de Manizales, which takes place in January. There are parades, craft fairs, arts and literature events, and a beauty pageant where the coffee queen is crowned. Bullfighting is also an important aspect of this festival. The Festival Latinoamericano de Teatro takes place in late September, when there are free concerts in Plaza Bolívar and special theater events throughout the city. Updated: Apr 24, 2011.

Getting To and Away

Manizales is the perfect stopover between Bogotá and Medellín, which are both five hours away. Buses to Pereira (1 hr, $4.50) and onward to Armenia (2 hr, $9) and Cali (5 hr, $15) leave every 15 minutes. The road to Manizales is very curvy, so you will be much more comfortable riding in a bigger bus rather than a van or *colectivo* (smaller bus). Updated: Apr 24, 2008.

Getting Around

Manizales' city center is best managed on foot. The Zona Rosa is about 10 minutes from Plaza Bolívar by car. You can hail a cab, which should cost you about $2.50, or flag down any bus with a sign for "Avenida Santander" and either "Estadio" or "Cable" in the window. All municipal buses cost $0.75 per ride. Updated: Apr 24, 2008.

Safety

There have been reports of theft in Manizales, especially in the city center between the bus terminal and Plaza Bolívar. The sidewalks are not particularly well-lit at night, so it is not advisable to walk around the city alone after dark. Updated: Apr 24, 2008.

Services

A small yet informative touriost office is located on Plaza Bolívar, by La Basílica. Here you can pick up a map, get other relevant info about the city, and look into the activities Manziales has to offer. The area around the plaza is also considered the commercial center of the city, so it is the best place to find ATMs, cheap Internet and postal services.

Photo by: Christopher Minster

Hospitals and universities, however, are located outside of the historical center along Avenida Santander on the way to the Zona Rosa. Head in that direction if you are looking for pharmacies, laundry services or grocery stores.

If you want to rent camping or climbing equipment, or mountain bikes, you can do so at **Manizales Hostel** (Ca. 67, 23-A33, barrio Palermo. Tel: 887-0871, Cel: 300-521-6120). Updated: Apr 05, 2011.

SHOPPING

Cable Plaza !

This modern mall has it all: a supermarket, fashionable clothing stores on three floors, a deck with nice views of the greater Manizales countryside, a food court with free WiFi, and a six-screen cinema playing newly released films in English with Spanish subtitles. Movie tickets cost $5 on all days except Tuesdays, when they cost $4.50. Take the bus on Avenida Santander toward El Estadio or El Cable and get off at Calle 65. Updated: Apr 05, 2011.

Things to See and Do

Most of the best sights and activities in the area involve being outdoors in the crisp, cool air. There are several parks spread around this hilly city where you can spend a few hours if the weather is nice. The Parque Nacional Natural Los Nevados should be high on your list of activities; time your visit for a clear, sunny day.

La Basílica

The two bronze doors at the front entrance of La Basílica tell the story of this neo-Gothic church. This religious center was first built in 1854, but was destroyed in an earthquake in 1878. The wooden structure that replaced the original church burned down in 1925. Construction of the current structure began in 1929. It is an impressive building both inside and out. Colorful stained glass is on display on all sides of this church. You can walk up the main tower, which is 106 meters (348 ft) high—the highest in the country—for $3. The stairway to the top is twisty and steep, so it's not for the faint-hearted. The tower is open Tuesday-Sunday 9 a.m.-5 p.m. Purchase your ticket from the western entrance. Cra. 22, between Ca. 22 and 23, Plaza Bolívar. Updated: Apr 05, 2011.

Río Blanco Ecological Reserve

This well-organized eco-park is ready for a high volume of tourists, but few foreigners make the time to visit it. The water of Río Blanco is considered some of the purest in the world, and 35 percent of the water used in Manizales comes from here. Start your visit at the museum by gathering info about the surrounding natural sites. Afterwards, follow a well-mapped route and walk along any of the four distinct trails in the park. Observe the flora and fauna in the cloud forest, then visit the exhibitions and the environmental workshops. There is a pair of spectacled bears here, as well as 256 species of birds and 350 species of butterflies. Bring your raincoat and wear sneakers or boots. It is also best to wear dark-colored clothing to blend in better with the surroundings. Bring binoculars if you have some. Updated: Apr 05, 2011.

Botanical Garden

The Botanical Garden in the university district is yet another great place to spend a sunny day. There are plenty of colorful flowers and fauna to admire, as well as benches to sit on to read or people-watch. The park is smaller than the others in the city, but the free entrance into the garden is a major draw, as is the peace and quiet of the place. Located on the campus of the Universidad de Caldas. Updated: Apr 05, 2011.

Recinto el Pensamiento

This cloud forest with a biotic and hydroid resource has several walkable ecological trails, a butterfly farm, an orchid garden and a gorgeous bamboo pavilion. The café in the park sells *Buendia* (locally farmed) coffee and other local products. Recinto el Pensamiento is just 20 minutes from Plaza Bolívar and the hustle and bustle of city life. Closed on Mondays. Km 11, Vía Magdalena. Tel: 889-7070 Ex. 2990/313, E-mail: Expoferias@cpdcaldas.org Updated: Apr 05, 2011.

Los Yarumos Ecological Park

Los Yarumos Ecological Park is a lush, green forest reserve situated in the city's surrounding cloud forest. Visitors can enjoy trails and lovely views of the countryside, and can even participate in extreme sports like rock climbing or canopy tours. The park is home to nearly 30 species of birds and hundreds of endemic flowers and trees. Outdoor concerts or cinema functions are held on weekends in the park's amphitheater. While you're here, you might as well take a quick peek at the park library and natural history museum. Updated: Apr 05, 2011.

Tierra Viva

Tierra Viva is a private agricultural and ecological park where you can rest, take part in some outdoor activities, and learn about nature and the cultural values associated with this area of the country. The park's thermal springs are natural and clean, and horseback riding as well as park and interactive farm tours are possible. Even if you aren't quite satisfied with all of the activities, you can just lounge around and sip a cup of Colombian coffee as you take in the beautiful green views from the park's comfortable restaurant and café. Daily 9 a.m.-1 p.m. and 3-6 p.m. Ca. Ines Salcedo 1-52 and Federico Proaño (behind the Clínica Santa Ines and the Universidad Estatal de Cuenca). Tel: 927-7966/288-3131, URL: www.migunecuador.com. Updated: Apr 05, 2011.

ZONA CAFETERA

Lodging

Hostels are easy to come by in Manizales, and are refreshingly clean and delightfully cheap. The best hotels are located within two blocks of Plaza Bolívar, with cheaper ones found down the hill a few blocks the away, near the tunnel for the city. The other option is to stay in the part of the city near Zona Rosa, along Avenida Santander, which is 10 minutes away by bus. Accommodations in this part of town are more modern, quiet, and are also closer to Manizales' nightlife, the stadium and the main shopping malls. Updated: Jun 30, 2011.

BUDGET

Mountain House !

(ROOMS: $10-25) This lively hostel in Zona Rosa is run like a well-oiled machine. The owners, both named Christina, have a really good system of service. Mountain House has four dorm rooms that sleep up to eight people, and two private rooms. Relax in a hammock while eating your complimentary breakfast, or mingle with the other guests at the hostel's weekly BBQ. It also has a spotless 24-hour kitchen. The staff members are amiable local experts with a vast knowledge of Manizales. Ca. 66, 23B-137 (Av. Paralela in barrio Guayacanes). Tel: 887-4736, Cel: 300-439-7387/311-745-3761, E-mail: info@mountainhousemanizales.com, URL: www.mountainhousemanizales.com. Updated: Apr 04, 2011.

Manizales Hostel

(ROOMS: $10-25) Another sociable hostel in Zona Rosa, close to the city's vibrant nightlife, Manizales Hostel has dorm rooms for three, four or 10 people, as well as private rooms. The large, fully furnished kitchen and living room area are ideal for meeting other travelers. Conveniently, two supermarkets, a shopping mall and a movie theater are all close by, and the hostel has Internet and laundry service. Breakfast is included in the price, and free coffee is available all day long. The staff is knowledgable regarding tours and treks in the surrounding mountains, so you can spend more time relaxing and less time figuring out your plans. Ca. 67, 23-A33, Palermo. Tel: 887-0871, Cel: 300-521-620, Email: info@manizaleshostel.com, URL: www.manizaleshostel.com. Updated: Jul 08, 2011.

Hotel Los Sauces

(ROOMS: $12-15) A decent, economical option in El Centro, Los Sauces has 22 rooms, all with private bath with hot water, TV and radio. The bathrooms are tiny but functional, and the beds are very soft. Although it is located in the industrial heart of the city, this is a clean and comfortable option for travelers on a budget. It is close to all the major city sites and the bus terminal. From Plaza Bolívar, walk downhill three blocks on Calle 23. The hotel is on your right. Ca. 23, 18-55. Tel: 882-1228/884-9881. Updated: Apr 04, 2011.

PitStop Hostel

(ROOMS: $11-37) Located in Zona Rosa, PitStop hostel is right in the thick of all the action. The owners of this Spanish colonial house have two popular hostels in Medellín (PitStop and Tiger Paw), so they know what they are doing. Guests can choose between dorms and private rooms, which come with either shared or private bathrooms. With a Jacuzzi, a terrace, and an on-site bar with a DJ and music events, the PitStop promises travelers an exciting stay. Ca. 65, 23B-19. Tel: 887-3797, E-mail: pitstopmanizales@hotmail.com, URL: www.pitstophostelmanizales.com. Updated: Jul 08, 2011.

MID-RANGE

Hacienda Venecia

(ROOMS: $17-84 per person) This magnificent plantation in Manizales is home to one of Colombia's many quality coffee producers. Juan Pablo Echeverri, the hacienda owner, offers extensive tours to his visitors, educating them on all there is to know about coffee. Surrounded by beautiful scenery and the friendliest of locals, it's not surprising that many travelers are keen to spend more time here! The hacienda has two areas of lodging available, the main accommodation house being the original plantation house. However, don't be disheartened if money is an issue for you. Both tours and lodging types vary and are by no means out of reach for those on a modest budget. Rates include breakfast. Cra. 24A, 58A-61. Tel: 636-5719, E-mail: gerencia@haciendavenecia.com, URL: www.hacien-davenecia.com. Updated: Jul 07, 2011.

Hacienda Guayabal !

(ROOMS: $45) If you don't mind staying outside of Manizales to get an hacienda experience, this gorgeous coffee farm and homestay in Chinchiná is a fantastic option. Hacienda Guayabal is a totally self-sufficient farm that exports its coffee overseas to places like Japan and Spain. For $8, you can take a three-hour tour and learn everything you'll need to know about the production of coffee. If you work on the farm, you can sleep on-site for free. Or, you can just relax here for $45 per night (all-inclusive). From Manizales, take the bus to Chinchina ($2, 30 min). Catch another bus in front of the main church to Guayabal ($0.50, 10 min). Get off at Guayabal and walk through the town and up the hill to the hacienda (10 min). Cra. 3, 15-72, Chinchiná. Tel: 4-840-1463, Cel: 315-540-7639, E-mail: haciendaguayabal@hotmail.com, URL: www.haciendaguayabal.com. Updated: Apr 05, 2011.

HIGH-END

Hotel Escorial
(ROOMS: $50-92) This conveniently located upscale hotel is a great option for travelers with a bigger budget. Several uniformed concierges, doormen and maids roam about all day making sure guests feel at home. Just one block from Plaza Bolívar, Hotel Escorial has about 60 rooms with all the major amenities as well as a parking lot for guests. Restaurante Los Vitrales on the third floor is set in a pleasant, colorful courtyard. The same menu is served for breakfast, lunch and dinner (appetizers $3, entrees $15), and the food is meticulously prepared. Ca. 21, 21-11. Tel: 884-7646/8271, Fax: 884-7722, E-mail:escorial@hotelesmanizales.com, URL: www.hotelesmanizales.com. Updated: Apr 05, 2011.

Regine's Hotel
(ROOMS: $65-80) Regine's Hotel is a small, European-style accommodation option steps from Zona Rosa. Its 10 rooms are elegantly decorated with classy wooden furnishings and each has a mini-bar. The tidy and comfortable common areas, where you can read and relax, are also a major bonus. Although this hotel is close to nightclubs and bars, it is tucked away on a quiet street, so you can easily spend a peaceful evening here if you so desire. Ca. 65a, 23B-113. Tel: 887-5360, Cel: 311-762-1572, Fax: 887-5686, E-mail: regineshotel@hotmail.com, URL: www.regineshotel.com. Updated: Apr 05, 2011.

Hotel Bolívar Plaza
(ROOMS: $65-95) You can't beat the location, price, atmosphere or view from Hotel Bolívar Plaza. This clean hotel has 18 rooms on three floors of a building that faces La Basílica. All rooms include cable TV, Internet, breakfast and a private bath with hot water. Ask for one of the rooms facing the church; it will be a bit noisier, but the view is worth it. Ca. 22, 22-40. Tel: 884-7777, Cel: 313-684-7246, Fax: 884-7396, E-mail: bolivarplaza@hotelesmanisales.com, URL: www.hotelesmanizales.com. Updated: Apr 05, 2011.

Restaurants
There is not much variety to speak of in Manizales. Most restaurants are fast food joints with typical fare such as arepas, empanadas, and traditional plates with meat or fish. Some of the nicer hotels in the city serve up more exotic dishes, but expect to pay up to three times as much for these special meals. Manizales is still considered paisa country, so *bandeja paisa* (varieties of meat served with avocado, egg, beans and grilled banana) is worth a try if it's on the menu. The *cazuela* (seafood or meat stew) is also very tasty in this part of the country. If you'd rather take advantage of your hostel's kitchen and cook instead, there is a Cafam supermarket at Calle 22, 21-51. Updated: Apr 05, 2011.

Don Juaco
If you're looking for a hearty meal at a reasonable price, Don Juaco will deliver. This is a great little find with warm, comfortable indoor and outdoor seating. Traditional dishes are served in generous portions, complete with a salad, French fries and half of a canned peach. Main plates (like the lasagna and cazuela) come in clay bowls with plenty of melted cheese on top. A local dish to try is the *mazamorra con panela* ($3), which is a corn and milk soup with a caramel cookie on the side. Ca. 65, 23A-44. Tel: 855-0610, Cel: 310-830-2218, E-mail: bervigo@epm.net.co. Updated: Apr 24, 2008.

Plaza 22
This three-in-one restaurant, café and cevichería has every little snack or big meal your belly could desire. Downstairs is a cafeteria serving bread, fruit and refreshments, while the upstairs is a restaurant serving seafood, meat and local plates like bandeja paisa. You can also opt

for the $4 lunch special that changes every day. Cra. 22, 21-47, Plaza Bolívar. Tel: 882-5308. Updated: May 19, 2009.

El Mural

On the third floor of the Estelar Las Colinas Hotel, El Mural is a pricey but high-quality option if you need a break from typical Colombian cuisine. Here, you can order some nicely prepared seafood or pasta dishes. The $10 buffet, available on weekdays, is perfect for those who want to splurge. Estelar Las Colinas Hotel, Cra. 22, 20-20. Tel: 884-2009, Fax: 884-1590, E-mail: reservas@ hotelesestelar.com. Updated: Apr 04, 2011.

AROUND MANIZALES

PARQUE NACIONAL NATURAL LOS NEVADOS !

Nevado del Ruíz, Crater de la Olleta, Nevado de Santa Isabel, Laguna Verde and Valle del Silencio are just a few of the reasons to visit Parque Nacional Natural Los Nevados.

The trip to Los Nevados, which means "Snow-capped Mountains," starts in Manizales and covers almost 59,000 hectares (145, 792 ac) of territory. In the midst of the Colombian central mountain chain, snow and sand live side by side, and small spouts of water surge to supply nearby towns. You can pass through desert landscapes with bright red rocks at Ruiz, photograph wild flowers and evergreens at Santa Isabel, or admire the glittering snow of Laguna Verde.

Lodging is available at El Cisne Visitors Center ($45-90), or you can camp at one of the park's two designated camping areas. Tours of the park require a guide, which will cost about $30 a day. If you plan on walking up Nevado del Ruíz, be sure to drink a lot of water the day before—even so, you still may experience altitude sickness once you reach the top. Choose a clear, sunny day to visit, and bring cold-weather gear as it can get quite chilly at this elevation.

The park is located about 45 minutes from Manizales. Buses to the park lodge and entrance leave from the terminal every hour, but guides are required upon entrance to the park. The altitude increases quickly, so on the way up, keep the windows open.

Reservation information for Parque Nacional Natural Los Nevados can be found at www.concesionesparquesnaturales. com. Updated: Apr 05, 2011.

)))))

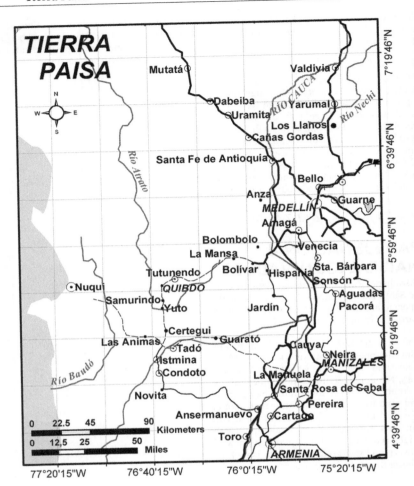

Tierra Paisa

Tierra Paisa is a fertile and verdant swath of land that includes not only the massive department of Antioquia, but also Caldas, Risaralda and Quindío, taking up most of the area known as the Eje Cafetero.

As you would expect, inhabitants of the Tierra Paisa are referred to as *paisas*, and they are considered among the friendliest and hardest working Colombians. In fact, paisas are known throughout Colombia for their proactive business sense, including arguably the most famous of the paisas, former President Álvaro Uribe Vélez.

Keeping with their nature, paisas have successfully established all types of high-yield industries in the region, such as coffee growing, coal mining and commerce, making it an economic powerhouse within Colombia.

In recent years, paisas have actively promoted their land as one for tourism, and with good reason: The area is strewn with beautiful colonial villages with whitewashed walls striving to keep their cultural heritage alive.

Medellín is the region's capital and a major tourist destination, but there are other sites in the region that are worth a visit. These include the Gulf of Urabá on the Caribbean coast, the scenery in and around the coffee town of Salento in Quindío, the colonial masterpiece of Santa Fe de Antioquia, and the towns of Manizales, Pereira and Armenia. Updated: Aug 11, 2011.

Highlights

Explore the urban landscape of the culturally charged and business-centered city of **Medellín** (p. 160), Tierra Paisa's capital city, complete with ample parks and an electric nightlife scene.

Delve into the region's agricultural tourism with a trip to the numerous **coffee plantations** and **estancias**, alternating horseback rides with savory coffee breaks.

For something in between rural stillness and urban chaos, visit the colonia-era towns of **Santa Fe de Antioquia** (p. 177), **Marinilla** (p. 170), and **Jericó**, rich with archeological and historical sites of interest.

History

Tierra Paisa was first discovered in 1541 by the conquistador Jorge Robledo, who was responsible for founding Santa Fe de Antioquia.

The first tribes encountered in the Tierra Paisa were the Nutabes and their allies, the Catíos. Neither tribe took the arrival of the Spanish conquistadores particularly well, evidenced by continuous battles waged against the first colonial capital, Santa Fe de Antioquia.

The region's history has since been characterized by violence and power struggles, including calls for and acts of independence from both the Spanish Crown and from Colombia itself. This can easily be understood given the rising wealth of the region.

Throughout the 18th, 19th and 20th centuries, the economy of Tierra Paisa flourished. It suffered a major setback in the 1970s, however, allowing for the rise of the Medellín cartel, which put the city and the region on the map for all the wrong reasons. With drug lord Pablo Escobar's death in 1993, a relative peace settled on Medellín, and the city has since turned itself around. Updated: Sep 28, 2011.

When to Go

In terms of climate, there is no right or wrong time to go to Tierra Paisa. The region's varied terrain, ranging from the tropical Caribbean coast in the north to the cooler strip of Andes running from north to south, allows for a wide variety of temperatures at any time of year. On the western slopes of the Andes, the mountain terrain transitions into the humid jungle of the Chocó, and on the northeastern frontiers reaching Puerto Berrío, the land is flat, humid and hot. Updated: Sep 20, 2011.

Safety

In the major cities such as Medellín, visitors will be pleasantly surprised at the overriding sense of security. However, you should exercise caution at night, especially in the downtown areas.

Road travel for the most part is safe, though travel is not recommended in the western parts of Risaralda that lead to the Chocó. On occasion, night travel on buses from Medellín east into Santander (through the Magdalena Medio region) can be suspended due to activities by one of the armed groups rife in Colombia. Updated: Sep 20, 2011.

Things to See and Do

The Tierra Paisa could stand as a tourist destination in its own right. It has everything from captivating colonial villages to pre-Columbian historical sites. Head in one direction and you are in the heart of the coffee-producing region near Pereira; travel in another direction and you could reach the Nevado del Ruiz near Manizales, ideal for climbing and trekking. Conveniently, adventure seekers can also temper physical exertion with cultural activities and nights out in Medellín. Updated: Sep 20, 2011.

Tours

Since Medellín is the capital of the region and the seat of business, many tour companies offering routes throughout the region can be found there. **The Corporación Turístico del Suroeste Antioqueño** (Carrera 65, 8B-91, Oficina 248 C.C Terminal del Sur. Tel: 361-2022, E-mail: ctdelsuroeste@yahoo.com) is a good place to start, as it offers rafting trips, coffee tours through Jardín, tours into the Eje Cafetero, trips to Jericó, horseback excursions through the southwest and other options. Updated: Dec 04, 2007.

TIERRA PAISA

Lodging

Given that paisas are expert business people, it should come as no surprise that accommodation options for every budget can be found in the region. Although the quality varies greatly, hostels throughout Tierra Paisa should be decent for the most part. There are also many family-run guesthouses that specialize in home cooking and first-rate service, but they may require some advance notice.

In Medellín, you can find Colombia's finest hotels, the ubiquitous backpacker digs—complete with travelers chilling in hammocks and gearing up for another night out—and everything in between. Often, if you are organizing trips through a company in Medellín or another city, it will have its own choice of accommodation on offer. Updated: Dec 04, 2007.

MEDELLÍN

 1,495m   2,750,000   4

Medellín is one of the most compelling cities in Colombia, and perhaps its greatest turnaround story. The city, once known for drug violence, has become a safe venue to soak up culture and nightlife, and it has a way of luring visitors into staying longer than they had intended. Travelers can enjoy the Botero-sculpture-filled Parque Barrio to the exclusive bars, restaurants and hotels of El Pobaldo. There is also the cable car that takes you high over the less affluent barrios in Medellín, offering a bird's-eye view of the city. If the bar scene isn't your thing–though Medellín and the friendly nature of the locals may convert you–there are frequently free concerts in the Teatro Metropolitano and a lively arts scene to quench any cultural thirst. If you are in the area in July and August, try to catch the Flower Festival, and once you've had your fill, stroll to the Parque de los Pies Descalzos to marvel at modern and inclusive architecture. Updated: Dec 01, 2010.

Highlights

One of the seven Cerros Tutelares, **Cerro Nutibara** (p. 168) is arguably the most interesting for visitors. The oversized mount houses the allegory to the areas of the region, Pueblito Paisa, the 3,800-capacity outdoor theater "Carlos Vieco" and the park of sculptures, a permanent exhibition of the work of 11 renowned artists from Colombia and around the world.

A **walking tour** (p. 166) of the city is the best way to appreciate the art of Medellín. Be sure to stop at the **Museo de Antioquia** (p. 169) for the largest collection of Botero paintings.

Follow in the footsteps of cocaine legend **Pablo Escobar**, starting with a tour of his old estate, Hacienda Nápoles.

Head to **Parque Lleras** in El Poblado to sample Medellín infamous nightlife scene.

History

Lying deep in the Valle de Aburrá, Medellín was founded in 1616 by Spanish explorer and conquistador Francisco Herrera y Campuzano. The city's name was changed from the original San Lorenzo de Aburrá to Villa de Nuestra Señora de la Candelaria de Medellín in 1675 and was subsequently granted city status in 1813.

Populated for the most part by Spanish settlers from the province of Extremadura, known for their work ethic and hardy lifestyles, Medellín became a major hub for commerce and industry over the years, particularly in textiles, making the city one of the fashion centers of South America.

In spite of Medellín's best efforts to alter its image, it has been a city tainted by death. One of the most infamous incidents was the murder of the Colombian soccer player Andrés Escobar in 1994. Escobar was gunned down in front of a nightclub for accidentally kicking in the self-goal that resulted in the national team's elimination from the World Cup.

In a history that remains, unfortunately, too well known throughout the world, Medellín gained a justifiably terrible reputation in the 1980s and 1990s as the world capital of

Pablo Escobar (1949-1993)

Cocaine-legend Pablo Escobar began his criminal career inauspiciously as a grave robber, ripping up tombstones and re-selling them. Through underworld connections, he soon began smuggling cocaine, a job in which success proves lucrative. In a series of calculated moves, he became head honcho of the Medellín Cartel, earning $1 million a day in cocaine money by controlling charter-flight deliveries to the U.S. In the 1980s, Colombia controlled 75-80 percent of the cocaine trade and of that, Escobar's cartel ran the majority of it. Coca soon became the biggest cash crop in Latin America as international cocaine use exploded.

A drug baron worth $3 billion, Escobar's power and fame was widespread. Pablo was fierce and bought up influence by intimidating, threatening or killing anyone in his path, be it man, woman or child. Politicians were offered two alternatives: pay-off or death.

Despite his corrupt character, El Patrón—or "The Godfather" as Pablo is also called—was able to win the hearts and minds of Colombia's disenfranchised by financing charity works á la Robin Hood. He built churches and football fields, quickly winning the support of the Catholic Church and the working class.

He is credited with several political assassinations and the bombing of Avianca flight 203, which killed several Americans on-board, spurring DEA involvement in Colombia. In order to stop a law from being passed that would allow narco-traffickers to be extradited, Pablo's men—the M19—turned a November 6, 1985 Supreme Court meeting into a bloodbath, killing half the senators. The granddaddy of the cocaine industry also created his own political party and was elected to congress, establishing himself as head of a veritable mafia (and earning himself a limited immunity for criminal acts).

Escobar was allowed to build and design his own prison, La Catedral, as part of a deal with the government. In exchange for giving himself up to the authorities, he was granted immunity from extradition to the U.S. So many were his enemies that when Escobar escaped from his plush private jail in 1992, government teams, both Colombian and American, joined hands with the vigilante group Los Pepes (People Persecuted by Pablo Escobar) to track him down. The manhunt, as well as Escobar's life, ended in a shootout between Pablo and a U.S. army contingent on the rooftops of a Medellín neighborhood in 1993.

His legend lives on, especially in Hollywood. Multiple movies over the years have centered around Escobar's life, including *Blow* (2001), starring Johnny Depp. In Medellín, the city that made him famous, visitors are able to see Escobar's grave at the **Cemetery of Jardines de Montesacro**; his former estate, **Hacienda Nápoles**, which is now an amusement park; and some of his personal belongings, including his Harley-Davidson motorcycle and personal gun collection, at the **Museo de Policia Nacional**. Some tour companies, such as **Zorba**, organize Pablo Escobar-themed tours that hit on some or all of these, plus more.

murder, kidnapping and crime. Pablo Escobar's cartel and its rivals were responsible for countless deaths, making the city one of the most dangerous on earth.

In December of 1993, the godfather of the international cocaine trade was hunted down and shot in his hometown of Medellín. In the years since, violence in the city has decreased considerably. Updated: Jan 03, 2008.

When to Go

Known as "the city of eternal spring," Medellín maintains a warm temperature between 27 and 28°C (81-82°F) throughout the year. A constant, refreshing breeze runs through the city, but every once in a while (usually in the second half of the calendar year) a rainy season reduces overall temperatures. The lowest temperature in Medellín oscillates around 16°C (61°F). If you

TIERRA PAISA

TIERRA PAISA

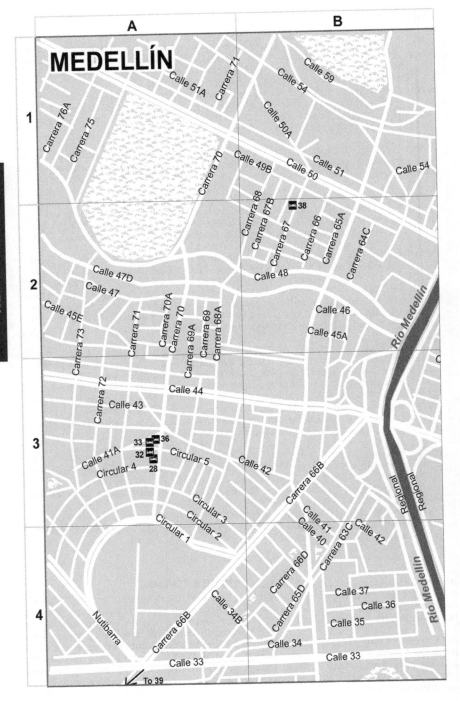

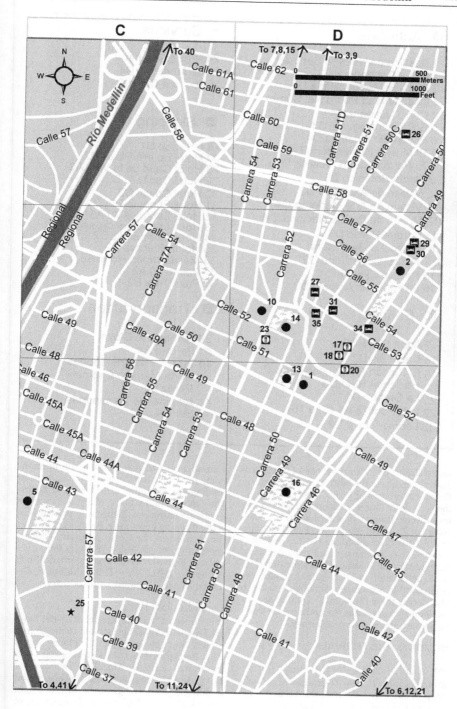

● Activities

1 Basílica de Nuestra Señora de La Candelaría D3
2 Basílica Metropolitana D2
3 Casa Museo Pedro Nel Gómez D1
4 Cerro Nutibara C4
5 Edifício Inteligente C3
6 El Castillo Museum D4
7 El Museo Universitario D1
8 El Parque de los Deseos D1
9 Jardín Botánico D1
10 Museo de Antioquia D2
11 Museo de Arte Moderno C4
12 Museo de Policía Nacional D4
13 Parque Berrío D3
14 Palacio de la Cultura Rafael Uribe Uribe D2
15 Parque Explora D1
16 Parque San Antonio D3

⑪ Eating

17 Agua Clara D2
18 Cazuelas D2
19 El Rincón Antioqueño (See 18)
20 Hacienda Real D3
21 La Grappa D4
22 Latin Coffee A1 (See 18)
23 Leomar No. 2 D2

★ Services

24 Hospital General de Medellín C4
25 Tourism Office C4

■ Sleeping

26 61Prado D1
27 Hotel Botero Plaza D2
28 Hotel Cabo de la Vela A3
29 Hotel Capitolio D2
30 Hotel Cristal D2
31 Hotel Eupacia D2
32 Hotel Laureles 70 A3
33 Hotel Los Almendros A3
34 Hotel Normandia D2
35 Hotel Nutibara D2
36 Mediterraneo Hotel A3
37 Palma 70 A3
38 Palm Tree B2

▣ Transportation

39 Aeropuerto Olaya Herrera A4
40 Terminal de Transportes Norte Mariano Ospina Pérez C1
41 Terminal de Transportes Sur C4

TIERRA PAISA

would like to be in town for one of Medellín's festivals, check out the Festival Internacional de Poesía (International Poetry Festival) in July; the Feria de las Flores, a celebration of the country's diverse flowers, in July/August; the Feria Nacional de las Artesanías, a national arts fair, in July; the ColombiaModa (URL: www.inexmoda.org.co), an international fashion display, in August; or the Medellín Medio Maratón (Medellín half marathon. URL: http://maratonmedellin.com) in September. Although it is fun to visit during these times, be aware that accommodation prices usually rise and advance reservations are almost always necessary.

HOLIDAYS AND FESTIVALS

International Poetry Festival

From its inception in 1991 against a backdrop of extreme violence, the Medellín international poetry festival has grown from a small event to a national phenomenon. Poets from all over the world participate in readings at Medellín's theaters and parks. The festival takes place every July and is worth checking out. Especially worthwhile is the opening ceremony, held every year in the theater on the Cerro Nutibara. Transversal 39a, 72-52. Tel: 541-2944, Fax: 412-8822, E-mail: festivalpoesiamedellin@yahoo.es, URL: www.festivaldepoesiademedellin.org. Updated: Jun 10, 2011.

Feria de las Flores

It is no secret that 80 percent of all cut flowers grown in Colombia are sold to the United States, and the Feria de las Flores shows why. Recognized as the most important and traditional feria in Medellín, this festival brings the city to a halt in a flower-scented and brightly colored gridlock for more than a week at the end of July and beginning of

August. Parades of garlands float through the city streets, but it is the Silleteros Parade (2007 marked the 50th year of this competition) that defines the whole week, when elaborate and complex presentation of flowers are paraded and judged. Also to be enjoyed are the classic car, mule and orchid parades. Alcaldía de Medellín, Ca. 44, 52-165, 7th floor. Tel: 385-5097, E-mail: feriadeflores@ medellin.gov.co, URL: www.feriadelasflores-medellin.gov.co. Updated: May 18, 2009.

Feria Nacional de las Artesanías

Beginning on the first Saturday of July each year, hundreds of artists–from Medellín and other parts of Colombia–display their ceramics, jewelry and works made of glass, wood, stones and other materials. The artwork is part of an exhibition but is also for sale. This multi-day event takes place in the Unidad Deportiva Atanasio Girardot at Calle 48, 73-10. Updated: Jun 10, 2011.

Getting To and Away

BY AIR

Medellín has two airports. Aeropuerto Olaya Herrera (Cra. 65, 13-157. Tel: 285-9999) is located downtown and is the older of the two. This airport is only equipped to receive small aircrafts and thus is limited to internal flights. Flights to Chocó are available from here.

Aeropuerto José Maréa Córdova (Tel: 562-2828), located outside Medellín in the neighboring municipality of Río Negro, is the international hub. Travel time between here and downtown takes at least 30 minutes.

BY BUS

Medellín has two bus terminals: the Terminal de Transportes Norte Mariano Ospina Pérez and the Terminal de Transportes Sur. As you would imagine, the north terminal is located in the north of the city, connected to the Caribe metro station, and the south terminal is close to the Olaya Herrera Airport. Terminal de Transportes Sur is part of a large shopping complex that has many services, including a movie theater and luggage storage.

City bus route 313 goes between the two stations. It takes 30 minutes, and costs about $0.80.

Terminal de Transportes Norte

Buses to and from Bogotá and the North Coast and surrounding towns.

Gómez Hernández and Sotrauraba work on alternate days, running buses every hour to Santa Fe de Antioquia for $4-4.50. Trips last 1.5 hours.

Expreso Brasilia, Rápido Tolima, Flota Magdalena, Expreso Bolivariano and Rápido Ochoa have frequent departures to Bogotá between 5 a.m. and 11:45 p.m. Trips take approximately nine hours and cost $20-28.

Copetran has 10 buses a day to Bucaramanga (8 hr, $28-42), the first one at 6:30 a.m. and the last at 11 p.m.

Buses to Cartagena (13 hr, $28-45) are serviced by **Copetran** (2 daily, 4 a.m. and 10 p.m.), **Rápido Ochoa** (6 daily, 5:30 a.m.-9:30 p.m.), **Expreso Brasilia** (6 daily, 5:15 a.m.-9:30 p.m.) and **Unitransco** (2 daily, 8:30 p.m. and 10 p.m.).

Expreso Brasilia goes to Magangue (12 hr, $40) at 7:40 p.m. every evening, and returns from Magangue at 4:30 p.m. daily.

Other destinations you can reach from this terminal include Valledupar (12 hr), Turbo (8 hr), Tolú (10 hr), Santa Marta (15 hr), Barrancabermeja (12 hr) and Barranquilla (14 hr).

Terminal de Transportes Sur

Expreso Arauca services buses to Manizales (every hr 4:30 a.m.-7:30 p.m.; 4 hr, $16.50), Pereira (every 2 hr 4:30 a.m.-5 p.m.; 5 hr, $14), Armenia (every 2 hr 4:30 a.m.-5 p.m.; 6 hr, $16) and Cali (14 daily, 5:30 a.m.-11 p.m.; 8 hr, $20).

Other companies that do the trip to Cali include **Expreso Bolivariano** (5 daily, 10 a.m.-10:30 p.m.; $22), **Flota Magdalena** (9 daily, 7:30 a.m.-10 p.m.; $17) and **S26** (5 daily, 8:30 a.m.-11 p.m; $17).

There are five buses daily to Popayán (10 hr, $28-33), Pasto (18 hr, $40-43) and Ipiales (20 hr, $40-44), all running between 2:30 p.m. and 11:15 p.m. Expreso Bolivariano and Flota Magdalena service these destinations, with Flota Magdalena being the cheaper option. Updated: Apr 25, 2011.

Getting Around

The city of Medellín may still be paying for the metro system built in 1995, but it is dazzlingly new, easy to use and gets you just about everywhere. For a $0.80 fare, you are able to reach 25 stations on lines

TIERRA PAISA

A and B and the connecting lines to the cable car, which run from Acevedo Station to the Barrio Santo Domingo Savio.

Buses are frequent and have their destinations plastered on the front windscreen. Taxis are an easy alternative, being inexpensive and efficient. Updated: Jun 06, 2011.

Safety

Modern-day Medellín may lull the traveler into a false sense of security, but every big city has its problems. The dark days of Escobarian terror are gone, but drug trafficking is still an issue, and visitors should be wary in the evening, especially downtown. Security is tight in El Poblado, a popular neighborhood for tourists to stay in. Updated: Jun 14, 2011.

Services

TOURISM

There is an extremely helpful, well-informed tourist information booth in the Parque Berrío, near the station. Otherwise, information booths are located in both airports and in both bus terminals.

MONEY

Every bank and ATM can be found all over the city, especially downtown. Supermarkets also have branches, many with extended hours. *Casas del cambio* are common downtown, in El Poblado and in shopping malls.

KEEPING IN TOUCH

Locating telephone exchanges and Internet cafés is not a problem in any sector of Medellín.

MEDICAL

If you need medical care while in Medellín, **Hospital General de Medellín** (Cra. 48, 32-102. Tel: 384-7300) and **Clinica El Rosario** (Cra. 20, 2 Sur-185. Tel: 326-9216) will fulfill your needs. Updated: Nov 25, 2007.

LAUNDRY

Most hotels and hostels have laundry service.

CAMERA

A few camera repair shops can be found in the Centro. Specific camera manufacturers also have repair shops in some shopping malls.

SHOPPING

Medellín, perhaps more than other major Colombian cities, is a treasure-trove for shopaholics. Because it's a hub of the textile and fashion industry, major name brands are available here at bargain prices. Vast shopping malls now take up areas of hillside and have rapidly become major meeting points for people of all ages.

Some major shopping centers include: **Centro Comercial San Diego** (Ca. 34, 43-66. Tel: 232-0624), **Parque Comercial El Tesoro** (Loma del Tesoro with Transversal superior. Tel: 321-1010), **Cuidadela Comercial Unicentro** (Cra. 66B, 34A-76. Tel: 265-1116), **Centro Comercial Oviedo** (Ca. Sur, 43A-127. Tel: 321-6116) and **Centro Comercial Mayorca** (Ca. 51 Sur, 48-57. Tel: 373-0335). Updated: Apr 05, 2011.

Things to See and Do

Medellín spoils visitors with its abundance of compelling features, ranging from the luxurious nightspots of Parque Lleras to culturally rich museums and offbeat activites like riding a cable car over the city's shanty towns. Popular tourist attractions include the Cerro Nutibara, with its Pueblito Paisa, and the Botanical Garden.

More awaits the visitor beyond nightlife and museums, though. Medellín emphasizes the arts, and frequently, there are free concerts in one of the city's theaters or improvised performances in the streets near El Poblado.

A brief stroll through the downtown area will enlighten you to what Medellín has to offer, as you move into the shadows thrown by the startling modernity of the library in the Plaza Cisneros and the town hall before looking over at the striking Edificio Inteligente.

Medellín is also a fantastic destination for those seeking the thrill of adventure sports. On the city's outskirts, there are opportunities for rock climbing, rafting, paragliding, trekking, rafting and kayaking. Updated: April 22, 2009.

Walking Tour

In a day, you can cover most of what the old center of Medellín has to offer on foot—and there is no better way to see this part of town.

Start the day at the **Basílica Metropolitana de Medellín**, located at the far end of the Carrera Junín. Enjoy a tinto coffee in the park while admiring this immense brick structure. From here, you can then walk along the **Carrera Junín**, browsing the shops in the downtown sector. As you reach the end, cross the road and make your way

Fernando Botero (1932-)

The most famous living Latin American artist, Fernando Botero, is best known for his paintings of very fat subjects. His art is abstract, in that the colors, figures and people depicted are not meant to be a representational likeness of the subject. The obesity of the subjects is designed to mock the bourgeois middle class. In one portrait, a corpulent family of four poses by an apple tree and even the pet monkey is grossly overweight.

Born in Medellín, Botero had limited exposure to art at an early age, as most commonly accessible art in Colombia at that time was of religious images such as Madonnas and crucifixes. He originally trained as a matador, and bullfights and rings figure prominently in his early works.

In his teens, he went to Spain and Italy where he studied art and art history. He spent a few years in Mexico, where the muralist works of Diego Rivera and others greatly influenced his work. He moved to the United States in 1960, and has lived in New York and Paris ever since.

In spite of his long absence, his paintings continue to display a distinctive Colombian flavor. Botero is very highly regarded in international art circles, and is becoming well-known outside of Colombia and New York.

In the last few years, his work has become increasingly political. In 2005, he released a series of paintings and sketches concerning the U.S. torture abuse scandal at the Iraqi prison of Abu Ghraib. He has also tackled issues from his native Colombia, such as a rebel gas cylinder attack that killed 120 people in a church in May 2002.

In 2004, Bogotá welcomed Botero's donation of his personal collection of work to the city, and these prize pieces are now housed in the Botero Museum and the Museo Nacional de Colombia. His works were given on two conditions; the first, that the museum would be free to the public, the second being that Botero himself was in charge of the arrangement and color scheme of his paintings.

Visitors to Medellín with an interest in Botero's art should head to the Museo de Antioquia, home to the largest collection of Botero paintings. More Botero sculptures are on public display at the Plaza de las Esculturas and at Parque Berrío, as requested by Botero himself.

TIERRA PAISA

to the **Basílica de Nuestra Señora de La Candelaría.** This colonial-style building stands at odds with its environment of 1970s high-rise office blocks.

Just a few blocks from here, on the other side of the metro station, you can find the attractions of **Parque Berrío** with its museums and Botero sculptures. The **Museo de Antioquia** is the large building toward the back of the square; it holds a permanent collection of 119 pieces donated by Fernando Botero himself. Pose for photos in front of the grotesque, reclining lady before moving south a few more blocks.

The **Parque San Antonio** really isn't a park at all. It more closely resembles an enormous parking lot in front of a shopping mall. However, there are two Botero sculptures here that are of interest to visitors. The original bird of

peace sculpture was placed here by Botero and was subsequently blown up by a suspected FARC bomb, tragically killing a dozen passersby. Instead of replacing or moving the mangled sculpture, in brave defiance, Botero created an identical sculpture to the original and placed it alongside its disfigured predecessor.

Move down from the Parque San Antonio to the **Estación Central**, where all rail travel used to pass into Medellín. Now a visitor center, the Estación is a good place to relax with a cold juice before moving through the large buildings that make up the town hall of Medellín and finally passing by the **Plaza de Cisneros** in front of the city library.

From here, you will be able to see the **Edificio Inteligente**—literally the "Intelligent Building"—which was built with environmental

Photo by: I.D.R.J

concerns in mind. Before reaching this building, pass through the **Parque de los Pies Descalzos (Park of the Bare Feet)**, where kids like to come to play in the cool fountain jets after visiting the nearby children's museum.

The only notable geographic feature in this part of the Aburra Valley, the **Cerro Nutibara**, should now be easily visible. From this 80-meter (263-ft) high hill, you gain a nice view of the downtown area and Pueblito Paisa, constructed here to show what a typical antioquian village should resemble. To get to Cerro Nutibara, first catch the metro to Parque Berrío, then do the rest on foot or by taxi. Don't forget to bring your camera and some cash. Apr 07, 2011.

Jardín Botánico de Medellín

Considered the lungs of Medellín, the Jardín Botánico Joaquín Antonio Uribe is a delightfully leafy and tranquil destination within the confines of the bustling city. The verdant wealth contained within the garden's 14 hectares (2.5 ac) ranges from a spectacular orchid collection (the country's national flower) to flora found throughout Colombia.

The garden's emphasis is on ecology, education and entertainment. Schools frequently bring students here to expose them to the importance of environmental preservation,

and researchers regularly visit the garden's library. Concerts are often performed in the garden as well, so be sure to check listings. Catch the metro to the Universidad station and follow the signs. Daily 9 a.m.-5 p.m. Cra. 52, 73-298. Tel: 444-5500, Fax: 571-8967, E-mail: comunicaciones@jbotanicomedellin.org, URL: www.jbmed.org. Updated: Dec 19, 2007.

Cemetery of Jardines de Montesacro

It may seem a particularly macabre and even inappropriate activity, but people are making pilgrimages of sorts to the Cemetery of Jardines de Montesacro. Fame is a curious thing, and for this reason, travelers make the trip to pay their respects to the former head of the Medellín Cartel, Pablo Escobar, whose notoriety lives on. At the cemetery, you can chat with many well-wishers from the poorer neighborhoods of Medellín, who continue to see Pablo Escobar as the "papa de los pobres," the father to the poor. Talking to these people is in itself a revealing experience.

Take the metro to Itagui and continue walking for 15-20 minutes as if you were heading out of town; the cemetery will appear on the right. If you don't fancy the walk, either take a cab or catch a bus along the road. Remain respectful; Pablo Escobar still means a great deal to many here. Updated: Apr 06, 2011.

The Medellín Cable Car

It is hard to imagine a more delightful and relaxing way to make your daily commute to work than drifting over the rooftops in a cable car. In Medellín, this dream for commuters is a reality. Since building a metro running up the valley wall into the poorer neighborhoods of Medellín was logistically impossible, the city developed this mode of transport instead. The cable car connects these districts with the main metro line at Acevedo station. From Acevedo, the cable car runs through two stations, Andalusia and Popular, before reaching the end of the line at Santo Domingo Savio and then commencing the return journey. The trip over the less affluent barrios of Medellín is a great introduction to the troubles that still haunt the city. Hop on or off, and you will find a willing local ready to chat, share some wisdom and point out the sights of the city from up high. Take a camera and snap some shots of the city from Santo Domingo Savio. Updated: Apr 05, 2011.

El Parque de los Deseos

El Parque de Los Deseos (The Park of Wishes) is described as an open space to observe the universe. Fundación Empresas Públicas de Medellín began this work to encourage visitors to lie back and get lost in the stars. Built close to the planetarium and the Botanic Garden, the idea was to promote interest in the cosmos and make science popular. There are 11 interactive activities with public services and astronomy, and the parking garage serves as a theater that shows movies about astronomy.   Daily 6 a.m.-11:30 p.m. Ca. 71 and 72, and Cra. 52 and 53. Tel: 516-6005/6404. Updated: Apr 06, 2011.

Museo de Arte Moderno

(ADMISSION: $4, free for students with valid ID, seniors over the age of 60 and children under 12 years old) The pride and joy of Medellín artists is the Museo de Arte Moderno (MAMM). And so it should be: By placing an emphasis on homegrown Colombian talent, it effectively displays the high quality of art this nation produces. Exhibiting around 1,400 pieces of art, including works by recognized Colombian artists such as painter Debora Arango and sculptor Hernando Tejada, the MAMM is well worth a peek. Spend a morning or afternoon exploring the museum and the surrounding Suramericana district. To get to the museum, catch the metro to the Suramericana station, and from there, walk along Carrera 65 before turning right on the major road and walking a few blocks down. Tuesday-Friday 9-5:30, Saturday 10 a.m.-5:30 p.m., Sunday 10 a.m.-5 p.m. Closed Mondays. Cra. 44, 19A-100, Av. Las Vegas. Tel: 444-2622, E-mail: museodearte@une.net.co, URL: www.mammedellin.org. Updated: Apr 06, 2011.

Parque Explora

(ADMISSION: $15 general admission, $4 planetarium) Parque Explora is a 22,000-square-meter (236,806 sq ft) interactive science center built to promote knowledge and technology. Committed to protecting the diversity of life, Parque Explora's 15,000 public displays offer visitors the opportunity to explore, learn and enjoy through interactive experiments. With a 3D auditorium, planetarium, a television studio, a kids room and its famous aquarium, this place is worth the somewhat expensive admission ticket. As South America's largest aquarium, the Aquario Explora is home to nearly 4,000 organisms and 400 of Colombia's most common species, a must-see for any sea creature lovers.

Parque Explora is located in the northern area of Medellín between the Parque Norte and the Botanical Gardens. Walking is ideal if you are already in the Zona Norte but if you are not, it can be reached by the Medellín Metro on the A line; get off at the Estación Universidad (University Station). A number of buses also serve this area. Daily 10:30 a.m.-6:30 p.m., box office closes at 5 p.m. Cra. 52, 73-75. Tel: 516-8300, URL: www.parqueexplora.org/parqueexplora. Updated: Jun 21, 2011.

Palacio de la Cultura Rafael Uribe Uribe

Constructed by a Belgian engineer beginning in 1925, the Palacio de la Cultura is a brilliant work of mathematical architecture with Renaissance influence. The building is by far one of Medellín's most widely recognized architectural works. It is home to the Department of Culture's historical archives and the setting for a variety of events, including a permanent art gallery on the first floor. In addition to frequent exhibitions, the Palacio de la Cultura holds several examples of Antioquia culture with department libraries, a sound library, the Center for Musical Documentation, a café and culture shop. Cra. 51N, 52-03. Tel: 512-4669/251-8461. Updated: Jun 21, 2011.

El Museo Antioquia

As the first established in Antioquia and the second in Colombia, this art museum houses works by Medellín natives Fernando Botero and Pedro Nel Gómez. A few of the many

TIERRA PAISA

permanent galleries include: Pre-Hispanic, Murals, Photographs, National Artists, International Artists, Sculptures, Contemporary, and the most visited gallery: Botero. Cra. 52, 52-43. Tel: 251-3636, E-mail: proyectos@museodeantioquia.org. Updated: Jun 21, 2011.

Casa Museo Pedro Nel Gómez

The Casa Museo Maestro Pedro Nel Gómez is a very special cultural site in the city of Medellín. It was established by the engineer, painter, city planner and sculpter Pedro Nel Gómez and his family. He is considered one of the most important muralists of the 20th century and has been called the "painter of Colombian pride." Much of the artist's work, including his drawings and paintings, is preserved in this museum. Cra. 51b, 85-24, Barrio Aranjuez. Tel: 233-2623, E-mail: programacion@museopedronelgomez.org/comunicaciones@museopedronelgomez.org. Updated: Jun 21, 2011.

Museo de Policia de Nacional

If you are in search of local history with a twist, head to the Museo de Policia de Nacional. This museum is devoted to the history of Bogotá's police force, and you will find police uniforms from 100 different countries and an impressive set of weapons confiscated over the years on display. The star of the museum can be found in the basement. Here, a special exhibit is dedicated to Colombian drug lord Pablo Escobar and the Medellín cartel. A model of his bullet-ridden corpse as well as Escobar's vast collection of guns are showcased, telling the story of the "world's greatest oulaw," his life on the run and his eventual surrender. Tours are given in English, French, Spanish and Sign Language. Admission is free. Daily 8 a.m.-5:30 p.m. Located west of the Plaza de Bolívar, Ca. 9, 9-27, La Candelaria. Tel: 233-5911/281-3284, E-mail: museopolicia@correo.policia.gov.co, URL: www.policia.gov.co/portal/page/portal/MUSEO. Updated: Jun 17, 2011.

El Castillo Museum

El Castillo Museum is often used for fairs and cultural festivals due to its lavish beauty. It is an architectural jewel of gothic medieval design in the style of the French Loire castles. It houses a collection of paintings by national and foreign artists that once belonged to the wealthy family who lived there. The museum is south of the center. Take the El Poblado-San Lucas bus from Parque Berrío and get off at Loma de Los Balsos. It's a short walk down the side street to the museum. Monday-Friday

9-11:30 a.m. and 2-5:30 p.m., Saturday 9 a.m.-noon and 2-4 p.m. Ca. 9 Sur, 32-269. Tel: 266-0900, E-mail: proyectoselcastillo@une.net.co, URL: www.museodelcastillo.org. Updated: Apr 06, 2011.

El Museo Universitario

The internally recognized El Museo Universitario was issued to be created in 1970 by the University of Antioquia's Honorary Council for means of fusing the Natural Science and Anthropology Museums into one. The entire museum contains over 5,500 objects, with over 2,700 pieces in the Collection of Visual Arts. The Galileo Room in the Interactive Museum is quite new to the museum and is a brilliant display of some main topics in the field of the natural sciences. Ca. 67, 53-108, Bloque 15. Tel: 219-5180, E-mail: museo@quimbaya.udea.edu.co. Updated: Jun 21, 2011.

Hiking

On the last Sunday of every month, **Inder** (Tel: 260-6611) plans hiking trips to rural areas around Medellín. The small towns of San Cristóbal, Palmitas, San Antonio de Prado, Santa Elena and Altavista are used as points of departure or arrival. Six guides and a coordinator take the hike along ecological paths, which offer terrific views of the city since they follow some of the highest points around the city. The hike is free and lasts five or six hours. To participate, call the Inder office to find out the point of departure. Hikes begin at 8 a.m. Updated: Apr 06, 2011.

Marinilla, El Peñol and Guatapé

Marinilla, El Peñol and Guatapé are small municipalities roughly 50 kilometers (31 mi) from Medellín, easily reachable from the Terminal del Norte.

Marinilla is of great importance in the region of Antioquia as a site of historical and artistic interest. Founded in 1690, it bears all the hallmarks of a religiously motivated town with ornate and austere churches. It is said that despite the introduction of black slaves into the community and the existence of indigenous peoples, the colonial settlers never intermarried, and, to this day, their descendants are still fair-haired.

El Peñol was founded in 1714, and in contemporary times has risen to prominence as a tourist haven. When a dam was built nearby, a massive artificial lake was formed, making this a great place to practice water sports.

Guatapé, which neighbors El Peñol, is also a major destination for people from Medellín looking to enjoy the lake. Visitors can join the fun, participating in ecotourism, exploring the religious sites, boarding or trekking. From the northern bus terminal in Medellín, buses leave every 15 minutes and take 30 minutes to an hour to arrive.

If you want to spend a night in the area, **Hostel El Encuentro** (Vereda Quebrada Arriba. Tel: 861-1374, E-mail: info@hostelelencuentro.com, URL: www.hostelelencuentro.com) is a good choice. This eco-hostel, on a private peninsula overlooking Guatapé, has a camping area and on-site tent rental in addition to shared dorms ($10)and private rooms with private baths ($37). Free use of its yoga/meditation area and its six-person row boats are additional perks. Updated: Apr 08, 2011.

Studying Spanish

Due to its favorable climate, cultural activities and unstoppable nightlife, Medellín is fast becoming a firm favorite for those wishing to study Spanish. Several good language schools have been established here and are making a name for themselves, including **Nueva Lengua Escuela de Español** (E-mail: contactenos@nuevalengua.com, URL: www.nuevalengua.com/spanish/medellin.htm), **Medellín Spanish School** (Connected to the Black Sheep Hostal. E-mail: info@blacksheepmedellin.com, URL: www.spanishinmedellin.com) and **EAFIT University** (E-mail: abotero@eafit.edu.co, URL: www.eafit.edu.co/EafitCn/Idiomas/spanishprogram/Index.htm. Updated: Apr 05, 2011.

Tours

A few years ago, Medellín still had to realize its tourism potential, but now many tour operators are in existence, though not as many as you would imagine, given all that Medellín has to offer. Updated: Apr 22, 2009.

Expediciones Makondo Expeditions

Expediciones Makondo Expeditions (EME) offers a wide variety of tours and activities including eco-tours, horseback riding, city tours, night tours, tours of archaeological ruins, climbing, rafting, hiking, birdwatching, trekking, water sports, whale watching, wildlife tours and coffee landscape tours. Spanish, English, Danish, German, French, Italian and Quechua are spoken. Ca. 9, 39-09, Parque Lleras.

Cel: 310-373-1176, URL: www.expedicionesmakondoexpeditions.wordpress.com Updated: Feb 05, 2010.

Zorba

Offering a variety of private tours, Zorba's local and informative guides aim to show you all Medellín and its surroundings have to offer. Besides its basic city tour ($85), Zorba organizes themed tours such as the Carlos Gardel tour (4 hr, $100), the Pablo Escobar tour (3 hr, $125) and the Fernando Botero tour (4 hr, $93). All tours can be customized to suit individual budgets and interests. If you have more time to spare, you can take one of Zorba's day tours to nearby Guatape and Santa Fe de Antioquia ($160), or multi-day tours to the Zona Cafetera ($1,070). Ca. 8, 42-33, El Poblado. Tel: 268-8921, E-mail: info@zorba.com.co, URL: www.zorba.com.co. Updated: Jun 14, 2011.

Medellín Experience

The Medellín Experience caters to small groups and arranges tailor-made travel plans. It offers horseback riding trips, parascending, rafting, treks, coffee tours, city tours and advice on hotels and other trips in the region. Known for its personal attention and advice, Medellín Experience will gladly give you a free quote on your dream tour. Cel: 312-220-2047, E-mail: andrespuldain@hotmail.com, URL: www.medellinexperience.com. Updated: Nov 25, 2007.

Turibus

Turibus runs city tours all day from 9 a.m. until 5 p.m. They hit the major city sights such as Parque el Poblado, Plaza Botero and the Parque de los Pies Descalzados, making Turibus a good solution for those who do not have a lot of time. The company also offers party buses for night tours, and once booked on the tour, you will gain discounts to various restaurants and bars. URL: www.seditrans.com. Updated: Apr 06, 2011.

Turixmo Receptivo Medellín

Offering a metro tour of the city, a regular city tour, a shopping tour, a chiva party tour, tours to the east of Antioquia and tours to the west of Antioquia, Turixmo is perhaps the most comprehensive tour agency in Medellín. Tel: 266-2846, E-mail: turixmo@geo.net.co. Updated: Nov 25, 2007.

Boomerang Paragliding

For over 10 years, Boomerang Paragliding has been introducing travelers to the sport of paragliding, both with internationally certified

TIERRA PAISA

courses and 25-minute tandem flights offering a fantastic view of the entire Medellín valley and western area close to Santa Fe de Antioquia. Pilots are some of the best and most experienced competition pilots in Colombia. Besides paragliding, Boomerang organizes trekking, mountain biking and canyoning adventures. English is also spoken. Cel: 320-693-3032, E-mail: piloto_x@hotmailc.com, URL: www.boomerangparagliding.com. Updated: Apr 06, 2011.

Lodging

As a tourist and business destination, Medellín has a great variety of accommodation options. There are cheap backpacker digs in desirable areas with a good nightlife scene—fine places to go back to and recover from a night of serious partying. Business options abound in El Poblado and the barrio of Laureles, making the decision of where to stay a difficult one. Mid-range hotels can be found in converted townhouses. The most economical hotels are in the stadium neighborhood, near Medellín's downtown. Updated: Jun 05, 2010.

BUDGET

Hostal Tamarindo

(ROOMS: $8-20) With a maximum capacity of 16 people, the Hostal Tamarindo is one of the smaller accommodation choices in El Poblado. There are two cleanly kept and well-maintained mixed dormitories of six and eight beds respectively, as well as one double room. As with most hostels, the Tamarindo comes with a communal TV room, book exchange and a small terrace. Take the metro to the Pobaldo station and go up Calle 10 until Carrera 36 (Domino's Pizza) and take a right. Walk to the end of the street and make a left. The hostel is the last brick house on the left side, half a block up from Próximo mini market. Ca. 7, 35-36. Tel: 268-9828, Cel: 300-255-8232 E-mail: hostaltamarindo@gmail.com, URL: www.hostaltamarindo.com. Updated: Apr 07, 2011.

The Blacksheep Hostel

(ROOMS: $9-25) This New Zealand-owned party hostel is an excellent choice for travelers looking for a laid back, social atmosphere. Room options include four-, six- and eight-bed dorms as well as private rooms with both ensuite and shared bathrooms. The owner, Kelvin, knows a great deal about all things Colombian and will gladly dish out advice. The hostel's hammocks add to the relaxing vibe, and there is a communal kitchen and TV room with an extensive DVD collection for gathering. Every Sunday, the Blacksheep staff cooks up a delicious BBQ on the outdoor patio. Private Spanish courses ($9 per hour) on the hostel's balcony can be arranged. Transversal 5a, 45-133 Tel: 311-1589, Cel: 311-341-3048, E-mail: kelvin@blacksheepmedellin.com URL: www.blacksheepmedellin.com. Updated: Jun 14, 2011.

Buddha Hostel

(BEDS: $10-12, ROOMS: $28-50) Buddha Hostel is different from any other backpacker lodging. This is a boutique hotel, featuring retro-Asian architecture and gardens. Artworks decorate the interior. The onsite restaurant serves international cuisine. The bilingual staff helps travelers get to know Medellín's attractions and nightclubs. Dormitories and private rooms are cozy, with firm mattresses, 24-hour hot water and other necessities to help travelers rest well. Guests may relax watching a movie from the DVD collection, or in a hammock on the terrace. As if all this weren't enough, Buddha Hostel also offers classes in Spanish, salsa, and world wines and cocktails. Ca 94B Sur, 51-121, La Estrella. Tel: 279-5152, Cel: 312-892-6521, E-mail: urban@buddhahostels.com, URL: www.buddhahostel.com.

Palm Tree

(ROOMS: $10-18) Perhaps the "grand dame" of Medellín hostels, the Palm Tree has maintained a steady record over the years as a popular backpacker haunt. This townhouse, which sits in a residential neighborhood close to cheap restaurants and next door to a massive supermarket, has everything a budget traveler could need. With nice dorms, free Internet, a communal kitchen, hammocks, a BBQ and a bar area, what more could you ask for? Catch a metro to the Suramericana station and head toward the Exito supermarket. The Palm Tree is located behind Exito and is visible due to its orange color and great deal of flags outside. Cra. 67, 48D-63. Tel: 260-2805, E-mail: info@palmtreemedellin.com. URL: www.palmtreemedellin.com. Updated: Apr 06, 2011.

Casa Kiwi !

(ROOMS: $10-30) The Casa Kiwi has become a travelers' institution in Medellín, especially when you only have to walk five blocks downhill to get to the buzzing nightlife area of Parque Lleras. The hostel has dorm rooms, luxury dorm rooms, private rooms and other rooms in a newer wing. In addition to a big screen television, the communal area is equipped with sofas, hammocks and a pool table. The hostel is easy to find—if coming by metro, get off at Poblado, walk up the hill for 10-15 minutes and then hang a right past the pizza place. Cra. 36, 7-10. Tel: 268-2668/ 352-1109, E-mail: casakiwi@gmail.com, URL: www.casakiwihostel.com. Updated: Apr 06, 2011.

Waypoint Hostel

(ROOMS: $12-37) Perhaps Waypoint's biggest perk is its swimming pool, not something most budget travelers expect when dishing out money for their dorm bed. Additional amenities include a BBQ area, hammocks, free coffee, a TV room, free WiFi and a kitchen. If you would prefer more privacy and space, Waypoint also has single, double and triple rooms. It is located in a quieter part of the El Poblado neighborhood called La Aguacatala, but is still close to nightlife. Take the metro to Aguacatala station and the hostel is three blocks away. Cra. 48B, 10 Sur-08. Tel: 312-5294, Cel: 300-671-9912, E-mail: waypointhostel@gmail.com/info@waypointhostel.com, URL: www.waypointhostel.com. Updated: Jun 14, 2011.

Hostal Odeon

(ROOMS: $13-15) This hostel has three floors of decent rooms near Parque Bolívar. There is a private bathroom, mini-fridge, fan, cable TV and stereo in every room. Cheerful staff and free coffee greet you in the lobby, next to the giant fish tank. Ca. 54, 49-38. Tel: 513-1404/511-1360. Updated: Apr 07, 2011.

MID-RANGE

La Bella Villa

(ROOMS: $15-20) In the same mold as the Hotel Eupacla, the Bella Villa has seen more prosperous days. The hotel has been a bit neglected, with travelers now leaning toward the more desirable areas of El Poblado and Laureles. The inside of the hotel can make you feel a bit claustrophobic; the low ceilings and heavy drapery do not help. If every other hotel in Medellín is occupied and the Bella Villa meets your budgetary requirements, then this place is suitable. Ca. 53, 50-28. Tel: 511-4915, Fax: 512-9477, E-mail: bellavilla-hotel@hotmail.com. Updated: Apr 07, 2011.

Hotel Normandia

(ROOMS: $17-25) Hotel Normandia's 47 large, spotless rooms is complemented by a chic, comfortable lobby. Every room comes with cable TV, fan, private bathroom and stereo. Some rooms have balconies overlooking Calle 53. Among the perks are a restaurant downstairs and a late 3 p.m. checkout. Ca. 53, 49-100. Tel: 251-2296. Fax: 293-5981. Updated: Apr 07, 2011.

Hotel Cristal

(ROOMS: $20-55) Located across the street from the Catedral Metropolitana, Hotel Cristal is composed of 24 clean rooms complete with private bathroom, cable TV, ceiling fan and mini-fridge. Cra. 49, 57-12. Tel: 511-5631. Updated: Apr 07, 2011.

61Prado

(ROOMS: $22-42) 61Prado is a Dutch-owned guesthouse with 18 rooms, each with private bathrooms. Amenities include free high-speed WiFi, a fully-equipped kitchen and laundry service. Stays can be reserved on a daily, weekly or monthly basis. It is close to Plaza Botero, a five-minute walk from the nearest metro station. Ca. 61 (Moore), 50A-60. Tel: 254-9743, Cel: 310-848-3031 (English)/314-666-5137 (Spanish), E-mail: 61prado@gmail.com, URL: www.61prado.com. Updated: Jun 14, 2011.

Hotel Eupacla

(ROOMS: $23-65) If you're really keen on being in the Centro rather than Laureles or El Poblado, then this is a reasonable option. The hotel has dated furnishings and an overall worn feel to it, but if you need to be downtown for business or by preference, then so be it. With over 60 rooms, the only time this hotel is likely to be filled to capacity is when there is a massive conference in town. Get off the metro at Parque Berrío and walk beyond and behind the Hotel Nutibara and you will find the Eupacla easily. Cra. 50, 53-16. Tel: 231-1765, Fax: 251-6969, E-mail: hoteleupacla@hotmail.com. Updated: Apr 07, 2011.

Hotel Capitolio

(ROOMS: $25-60) This is an excellent value, next door to the Hotel Cristal. A wide spiral staircase leads up to five floors of clean, spacious rooms, which all have cable TV, private bathroom, ceiling fan and mini-fridge. There is also a small pool on the ground floor next to the bar. Cra. 49, 57-24. Tel: 512-0012. Fax: 511-5631. Updated: Apr 07, 2011.

Hotel Los Almendros

(ROOMS: $30-45) A family-run venture in the executive district of Laureles, Hotel Los Almendros has 25 comfortably furnished rooms for those not wishing to spend a fortune in the area. Breakfast comes included, and the staff

TIERRA PAISA

tries to make your stay as enjoyable as possible. Your best bet is to hail a taxi, as the roads in Laureles can be misleading. Ca. 41A, 70-78. Tel: 412-9002/8266. Updated: Apr 06, 2011.

Hostal Portón de Provenza

(ROOMS: $35-50) Hostal Portón de Provenza has a new feel about it, probably because the owners take great care of their investment. The management's major desire is to take care of their patrons, so the rooms (private and dorms) are spotless, the communal areas are well kept and, in short, the place is spic-and-span. From Poblado metro station, you will need to walk up the hill for 20 minutes past Parque el Poblado and Parque Lleras, then hang a right on Carrera 35. Cra. 35, 7-108. Tel: 311-5452, E-mail: portondeprovenza@une.net.co. Updated: Jun 15, 2011.

Alcazar de Patio Bonito

(ROOMS: $40-65) This family-run B&B of few rooms but plenty of charm is ideally located close to the Poblado metro station, the Exito supermarket, the Oviedo shopping center and the nightlife area of Parque Lleras. The rooms may need a little updating but they are clean, and each has its own private bathroom, cable TV, refrigerator and constant hot water. From the Poblado metro station, ask for directions from the Exito parking lot. You are within three blocks. Cra. 45, 6-68. Tel: 266-2583, E-mail: carmensofic_16@hotmail.com, URL: www.hotelalcazardepatiobonito.com. Updated: Apr 06, 2011.

Hotel Botero Plaza

(ROOMS: $42-80) This hotel is stylish, modern and located right in the city center. The 84 rooms all come with air conditioning, mini-bar, private bathroom and cable TV. A sauna, steam bath and gym are available for guests, plus there is a restaurant downstairs. Request a room on the upper floors for great views of the city. Cra. 50A, 53-45. Tel: 511-2155. URL: www.hotelboteroplaza.com. Updated: Apr 07, 2011.

Hotel Nutibara

(ROOMS: $48-140 per person) Opened in 1945, this behemoth of a hotel in the downtown area was built at a time when the Centro was the height of fashion and security. Things have changed somewhat, but the Nutibara still maintains high standards. With 137 rooms, it is the largest hotel of its type in this part of Medellín. Each conventionally furnished room comes with cable TV, mini-bar, private bathroom and air conditioning. It

is not a bad choice if you've got the cash and need to be in this part of town. Prices include tax. You can get to Nutibara easily by taxi, but another option is to catch the metro to Parque Berrío and walk the two blocks from there. Ca. 52A, 50-46. Tel: 511-5111, Fax: 512-4693, E-mail: info@hotelnutibara.com, URL: www.hotelnutibara.com. Updated: Jun 10, 2011.

Palma 70

(ROOMS: $50-65) The Palma 70 is yet another hotel looking to cash in on the conference center in Medellín, and by all accounts, it appears to be doing a good job at it. Rooms are standard fare with the traditional hotel furnishing, and are kept in good condition and clean. Prices are negotiable if paying in cash. Take a taxi into the Laureles district. Circular 5, 70-37. Tel: 409-1020, Fax: 412-5751, E-mail: hotelpalma70@gmail.com, URL: www.hotelpalma70.com. Updated: Apr 06, 2011.

HIGH-END

Hotel Cabo de la Vela

(ROOMS: $65-75) Another hotel in Laureles aimed at the executive market, Hotel Cabo de la Vela is clean, modern and well located on a tree-lined residential street. In addition to rooms fully equipped with all the conveniences you would expect, the hotel offers a large conference room, a restaurant and a staff knowledgeable about Medellín. To get here on the metro, get off at Estadio Station and walk down Carrera 70 until you meet Circular 4. Otherwise, catch a taxi from the station. Circular 4, 70-72. Tel: 413-8400, Fax: 413-8410, E-mail: mercadeo@hotelacabodelavela.com, URL: hotelcabodelavela.com. Updated: Apr 06, 2011.

Mediterraneo Hotel

(ROOMS: $73-128) Modern and sleek, this hotel is banking on its Swiss modern style to attract clientele. The 32-room novelty offers everything that the executive might need. With WiFi, sauna, gym, breakfast and parking, the owners place a premium on service. Discounts are offered if you stay for more than two days and if you pay in cash. A taxi is the most convenient way to reach this hotel. Cra. 10, Circular 5-23. Tel: 410-2510, Fax: 250-5059, E-mail: info@mediterraneomedellin.com, URL: www.mediterraneomedellin.com. Updated: Apr 06, 2011.

Hotel Laureles 70

(ROOMS: $75-110) In an area flooded with hotels for the "executive," this is another offering that is comfortable, well decorated and equipped with helpful staff. Its 38 rooms range from junior suites to single and double options, making Laureles 70 is a fine option for a short stay. A taxi will get you here no problem. Circular 5, 70-13. Tel: 411-2828, Fax: 411-7268, E-mail: la70@une.net.co, URL: www.hotel-laureles70.com. Updated: Apr 06, 2011.

Hotel Poblado Plaza

(ROOMS: $122-225) Right next door to the Oviedo mall, the Estelar Poblado Plaza is a luxury hotel for those with no limit on their budget. Its 84 rooms range from suites with two private bathrooms to superior rooms with twin beds. In truth, if you were to stay here, you could be forgiven if you forgot which country you were in. In addition to WiFi access in the rooms, there are free computers on every floor for those who failed to bring their laptop with them. Should you book to stay on a weekend when it's quieter, the prices drop. Cra. 43A, 4 Sur 75. Tel: 268-5555, Fax: 268-6949, E-mail: info@hotelpoblado-plaza.com, URL: www.hotelpobladoplaza.com. Updated: Apr 07, 2011.

Restaurants

There are world-class eateries in Medellín, ranging from locales that can offer the finest and freshest seafood—flown in that day from the Pacific—to vast cavernous steakhouses and sushi restaurants. For those on a budget, a short wander into the areas around Parque el Poblado will reveal various locations that can provide set lunchtime meals for around $2. The same goes for restaurants in the Centro.

BUDGET

Donde Paco !

For people staying at the Casa Kiwi or the Hostal Portón de Provenza, Donde Paco will be very familiar. Since it is a reasonably cheap and very cheerful restaurant located close to these hostels, it is always popular. Servings are a good size, the food is tasty, and for those suffering from the effects of the night before, it is only a short walk to get to. Cra. 35N, 8A-80. Tel: 311-9097, E-mail: dondepaco@hotmail.com. Updated: Dec 19, 2007.

> **V!VA ONLINE REVIEW**
> DONDE PACO
>
> "It has a family-oriented, very relaxed atmosphere and very good homemade-style cuisine. We had a very tasty experience."
> *August 11, 2008*

Leomar No. 2

This busy little café is next to the Plazoleta de las Esculturas. It is a great place to fill up on *bandeja paisa* after a few hours in the Museo Antioquia. Also serves up good, cheap lunches and snacks. Cra. 52, 51-54. Tel: 513-8736. Updated: Apr 07, 2011.

MID-RANGE

Amazonia

Amazonia sits in the hot nightlife area of Parque Lleras, the heart of Medellín's Zona Rosa. The restaurant offers exotic foods from lesser known regions of Colombia.

TIERRA PAISA

Bandeja Paisa

Perhaps the most terrifying dish available in Colombia comes from this region. Not terrifying in the nature of the food—it won't be compared to toasted ants, brains or the like. In truth, it's similar to a full English breakfast, but it is eaten in the heat. With every mouthful, you can feel your arteries thickening.

A bandeja paisa consists of beans, ground beef, rice, chorizo, blood sausage, pork scratchings, avocado, arepas and plantains, topped off with an arepa and a fried egg.

If that doesn't make your heart skip a beat in fear then nothing will. And if you can finish this hearty platter, you are doing better than most. With any luck, the sugar and grease rush will make you feel superhuman and not on the verge of suffering a heart attack.

You can find this dish in any restaurant downtown. If you want to give it a try, make sure you don't eat breakfast beforehand; come to the table with an empty stomach. Updated: Apr 05, 2011.

While Amazonia claims to offer bites from the Amazon and beyond, if these are not to your liking, there are many traditional dishes as well, such as *ajiaco* (a typical chicken soup made with potatoes, sour cream and capers) parrilla. Cra. 8A-32, Parque Lleras. Tel: 266-6307. Updated: Dec 19, 2007.

Cazuelas 1, 2, 3

(ENTREES: $3.50 and up) Cazuelas 1, 2, 3 is a decent and reasonably priced restaurant downtown where you can sample a whole load of culinary delights from the Antioquia region. If you are hankering for a paisa stew—beans, pork scratchings, salsa, avocado, rice, arepa and plantain then you can get it here for $3.50. Cra. 49, 52-107. Tel: 293-2180. Updated: Dec 19, 2007.

Latin Coffee

(LUNCH: $4) With set-lunch menus at $4 in a clean and calm area in the Centro, you won't do a great deal better than Latin Coffee if you're in this part of town. All lunches come with soup, then either roast chicken or grilled beef with rice, salad, an arepa and a juice to wash it down. Union Centro Comercial, local 217, Cra. 52-107. Updated: Apr 07, 2011.

El Rincón Antioqueño

(LUNCH: $4) In the same food court as Latin Coffee and Las Cazuelas, El Rincón Antioqueño is another option set back from the bustle of the Carrera Junín, above the mayhem on the second floor. Sink your teeth into standard fare from the region. A set menu with beef goes for $4. Breakfast costs around $2.50. Union Centro Comercial, Balcón de Comidas, local 221, Cra. 49, 52-107. Updated: Apr 07, 2011.

Hacienda Real !

If your curiosity is piqued by talk of the famed dish from Antioquia—the bandeja paisa—this is one place you should check out in the historical district of the Centro. The Hacienda Real is located above the noise and hurried existence of the street vendors on the Carrera Junín. The dish is well prepared and large, enough to keep you full for the rest of the day. Cra. Junín 52-98. Updated: Apr 07, 2011.

Agua Clara

(LUNCH: $4) This is another good eatery located above the Carrera Junín in the Centro. You can get a set menu lunch for $4, and that's never bad. The servings are generous and flavorsome, and the locale is clean and

welcoming. You know what you're getting here: beef or chicken accompanied by rice, beans and potatoes with some garnish. Cra. Junín 52-141. Updated: Apr 07, 2011.

El Acontista Café

This hip café is popular with the student crowd. The walls are decorated with vintage posters and photographs of American jazz musicians. It has daily specials, free WiFi and delicious cheesecake. Ca. 53, 43-81. Tel: 512-4501. Updated: Apr 07, 2011.

V!VA ONLINE REVIEW
EL ACONTISTA CAFE

I love this place. It has a nice environment in the middle of downtown, and the food is great.

October 20, 2009

El Zócalo

This restaurant in El Poblado has excellent fajitas and quesadillas. Live shows every Friday from 9 p.m. to 12 a.m. Cra. 43B, 11-84. Tel: 311-4217. Updated: Apr 07, 2011.

HIGH-END

La Grappa

La Grappa, another chic offering in the continually buzzing Parque Lleras, specializes in Mediterranean cooking, pastas and meats. Perhaps its setting attracts revelers more so than diners: Tall glass windows and a deck on the second floor make this a very stylish place to sip a cocktail before heading out for the evening. Ca. 8A, 37A-01. Tel: 312-7266. Updated: May 18, 2009.

Nightlife

Medellín's nightlife centers around the bright lights of the bars and clubs in El Poblado. The place to go, without a doubt, is Parque Lleras. From there, see where the crowd and your new-found friends will lead you; certainly, it will be an entertaining evening. You can find anything from dance clubs playing electronica to traditional salsa haunts. Choose a place on a whim and you won't be disappointed.

Discoteca Mango's

(COVER: $8) Located on the road out of town, Mango's is immensely popular despite its Wild West theme. The hordes come out to this institution week-in and week-out and dance the night away to the sounds spun by excellent

DJs. Catch a cab out to Mango's with some friends and you probably won't regret it. Cra. 42, 67A-151. Tel: 277-6123, E-mail: invensionesmangos@une.net.co, URL: www.discotecamangos.com. Updated: Apr 06, 2011.

Berlin 1930

Berlin 1930 appears to have been around as long as Medellín itself. No one knows when it opened, but one thing remains a constant: its popularity. A great place for an early evening beer or cocktail and a game of pool, it is located close to the clubs and other nightspots of the Parque Lleras. Ca. 10, 41-65. Updated: Apr 07, 2011.

Blue !

The place to go on a Thursday night, Blue is a Medellín institution, and very popular with backpackers. Paisas and foreigners alike dance along to the electronica music flowing out of its massive speakers. Capacity is often reached here, such is its reputation among the traveling crowd, so you might want to get in early. Cra. 41 and Ca. 10. Updated: Apr 07, 2011.

Oz

(COVER: $8) Becoming increasingly popular with travelers, Oz delivers loud music in a variety of rooms through enormous, booming speakers. Not only popular with visitors to the city, Oz is a firm favorite with many of the beautiful people of Medellín. Cra. 37A, 8A-28. Tel: 311-5781. Updated: Apr 07, 2011.

Sam Pues

If you are itching to dance, Sam Pues may be the place for you. Tables and chairs lay scattered about as people, normally relatively dormant by nature, spring up and start to strut their stuff. Located close to Parque Lleras, Sam Pues has been around for some years and has solidly established itself on Medellín's nightlife map. Ca. 10A, 40-37. Tel: 266-9404. Updated: Dec 19, 2007.

AROUND MEDELLÍN

SANTA FE DE ANTIOQUIA

When the city planners of Medellín came up with the idea of creating a Pueblito Paisa replica—a typical antioquian village—on the Nutibara hill, Santa Fe de Antioquia was what they had in mind.

A bus journey of one-and-a-half to two hours from Medellín's Terminal del Norte bus station takes you out of the Aburra valley and into the heartland of the region. At the station, head to either Gómez Hernández or Sotrauraba companies, which run to Santa Fe about once an hour on alternating days (van $4.50, bus $4).

Also known as "Ciudad Madre," the town is a national monument recognized for its antiquated but well-maintained cobbled streets, whitewashed walls, historical churches and breezy plazas.

The first Spanish settlement in the area was founded in 1541 by Mariscal Jorge Robledo and was an agricultural and mining village.

Aside from wandering the streets, you can visit the Museo de Arte Religioso, Museo Juan del Corral and the Casa del Niño Tomás. Some six kilometers (3.7 mi) away there is the famous Puente de Occidente, or east bridge, measuring 291 meters (955 ft) in length, which was constructed in 1895. E-mail: turismo@antioquia.gov.co, URL: www.antioquia.gov.co. Updated: Dec 19, 2007.

Things to See and Do

Puente de Occidente

The bridge of the West, or Puente de Occidente, is a 291-meter-long (955-ft) bridge over the Río Cauca, linking the municipalities of Olaya and Santa Fe de Antioquia. Designed by José Maria Villa and built between 1887 and 1895, it is a showpiece of late 19th-century engineering. The wooden platform has a capacity for two pedestrian and one vehicular route. Pull yourself up the hill using the rope near the west towers for a great view from above. Stand in the middle as trucks rattle across to feel the whole structure wobble. The bridge is five kilometers (3 mi) east of town. Negotiate a return trip by taxi or hire a motorcycle to zip you there and back. Walking takes about an hour and can be grueling in the afternoon heat. Updated: Oct 09, 2008.

Museums and Churches

The Museo de Arte Religioso Francisco Cristóbal Toro has a collection of paintings, sculptures and goldwork from the 18th century on (admission $1. Saturday-Sunday and holidays 10 a.m.-5 p.m. Ca. 11, 8-12. Tel: 853-2345). You may also want to explore Santa Fe's five churches, including

TIERRA PAISA

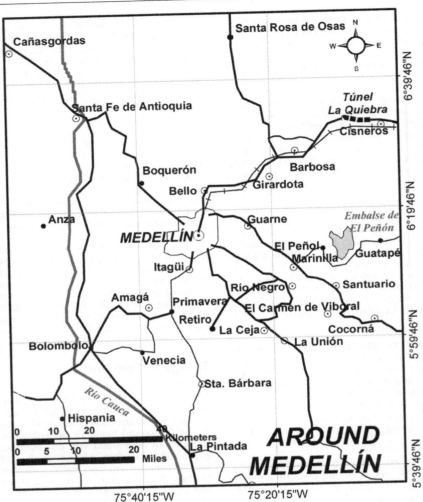

the **Catedral Metropolitana**, constructed between 1797 and 1837 (Plaza Mayor; morning and evening mass, as well as Sunday morning services), and the **Iglesia de Santa Barbara**, built in baroque style in the middle of the 18th century, named "grandmother of the churches" in the province of Antioquia (Daily 5-6:30 p.m. and Sunday mass. Corner of Ca. 11 and Cra. 8). Updated: May 18, 2009.

Lodging

Lodging is limited in the colonial town Santa Fe de Antioquia because it is primarily a day-trip destination from Medellín. However, there are a few hostels and hospedajes around that offer sufficiently clean, modest rooms for about $7 per night. For a bit more, you should stay at one of the few Santa Fe de Antioquia hotels, which offer more in the way of a quaint, cozy experience, starting around $35 for a single room. Updated: Jul 05, 2010.

Hospedaje Franco

(ROOMS: $7.50-10) One of the cheapest in Santa Fe, Hospedaje Franco has an open-air courtyard with a large TV and children scurrying about. Rooms have TV and ceiling fans and some have private bathrooms. Prices nearly double during weekends and festivals. Cra. 10, 8A-14. Tel: 853-1654. Updated: Apr 22, 2009.

El Mesón de la Abuela !

(ROOMS: $8-10) El Mesón de la Abuela is a welcoming little hospedaje with six rooms, including a six-bed dorm. Each room has TV, private bathroom and ceiling fan. There is a well-priced restaurant downstairs and hammocks for lounging. Cra. 11, 9-31. Tel: 853-1053, Cel: 311-394-3325. Updated: Jul 07, 2009.

Restaurants

Restaurante Plaza Mayor

(ENTREES: $3.50-5) Located on the ground floor of the Hostal Plaza Mayor, this restaurant serves up great grilled dishes and typical Colombian fare for great prices. When it's not raining, it pulls tables out into the plaza. Parque Principal, 4-59. Tel: 853-3448, Cel: 310-334-4501. Updated: Apr 22, 2009.

Santa Fe Restaurante

(ENTREES: $4-5) This is a great place to enjoy a cold beer and reasonably priced regional cuisine while people-watching under a giant sun umbrella in Plaza Mayor. It has a rainbowed assortment of cakes and other snacks for dessert. Parque Principal, 9-39. Updated: Apr 22, 2009.

!!!!!

TIERRA PAISA

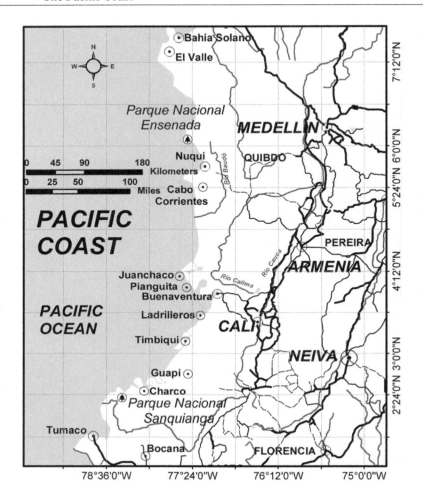

The Pacific Coast

The Colombian Pacific region, made up of four departments (Chocó, Valle del Cauca, Cauca and Nariño), remains a largely unvisited and unknown part of Colombia. That shouldn't dissuade you from visiting, however. This part of Colombia offers travelers a variety of things to do, from adventure and ecotourism to cultural experiences and attractions.

The region itself is dominated by two rivers, the Atrato in the north and the San Juan in the south. It is cordoned off from the rest of the country by the spine of the Andes to the east. In the extreme north, the border with Panama is defined by the famous Darien Gap. While in-roads are being made into the more unknown

areas, many journeys to this part of Colombia (including trips to eco-lodges on the Chocó coast) require taking internal flights and then being transferred by boat. In order to get to the Pacific Coast by bus, visitors must come from either Medellín or Cali in the north or Pasto or Ipiales in the south. Most of the roads here wind their way toward important ports, while the tangle and mesh of rivers serve as highways for *chalupas* (boats)and canoes. Due to the density of the jungle and the extreme climatic conditions present here, it seems highly unlikely for roads to be constructed anytime soon.

Security remains an issue throughout parts of the region, especially on the mass of land extending from the ports of Tumaco and

Buenaventura near the border with Ecuador, to Bahía Solano and the border with Panama in the north. The inhabitants of this region—mostly descendants of African slaves and Embera Indians—increasingly find themselves in the crossfire between the government troops and leftist FARC guerrillas. For this reason, it is advisable to use common sense and to plan ahead. Updated: May 18, 2009.

History

Chocó, given its distance from Bogotá, its hostile environment for travelers and its poor infrastructure, has remained a relatively unexplored region inhabited largely by Embera Indian communities and former African slaves. Until recently, their history

Highlights

Get a taste of Afro-Colombian culture during **Tumaco's colorful Carnaval celebration** (p. 182), complete with traditional music, dance and parades.

Wonder at the site of migrating humpback whales from the resort towns of **Juanchaco and Ladrilleros** (p. 191), or from **Isla Gorgona** (p. 191).

Book a tour to **Parque Nacional Natural Malpelo** (p. 192) for some of the world's best diving sites, and to admire the rocky island's volcanic formations.

Spend a night or more at one of the award-winning eco-lodges around **Nuquí** (p. 195) to explore the area's mangroves, beaches and national parks.

has been one of indifference, but struggles between the government and guerrilla groups have converted this region into the front lines of the battle.

Nariño, Valle del Cauca and Cauca have an altogether different history. First home to hunter-gatherers—relics and artifacts have been found in and around Cali—before being used as a thoroughfare by the Spaniards en route to Quito, these departments have seen much of Colombia's troubles throughout history. Cauca, in particular, suffered in the Colombian Civil War of 1860–62. Nowadays, trouble lingers—major ports such as Buenaventura and Tumaco are

coveted by both the government and the guerrillas, and fighting breaks out here with regularity. Updated: May 18, 2009.

Things to See and Do

Cultural curiosities, natural wonders, colonial opulence and adventure sports are just some of the attractions available in abundance along Colombia's Pacific coast.

Visit Isla Gorgona, Ladrilleros, Juanchaco, Nuquí or Bahía Solano to marvel at humpback whales. From Nuquí, make the short trip south to Cabo Corrientes, where surfers claim to find the best surf conditions along Colombia's Pacific coast. Finally, make your way to Sanquianga National Park to spy enormous sea turtles hauling their massive bodies up the beach to lay their eggs. If you can't make this, arrive to watch the offspring hatch and strike out alone for the ocean. Updated: May 18, 2009.

Tours

If whale watching is on the itinerary, tours are a must. Most places are now aware of the correct behavior around the whales and their young, and most guides maintain a respectful distance. Along the entire coast, tours are easily found for trips to places like Parque Nacional Natural Ensenada de Utría. To get to Isla Gorgona, it may be necessary to organize a tour through Aviatur. Many sightseeing opportunities on this Pacific coast are available through big package tours. Signing up with a company in advance will usually mean having all your meals and accommodations looked after, and is the cheaper option.

Tours to Isla Guacán and Isla Verde cost $15 and last about five hours, departing at 9 a.m. and 2 p.m. You must have a group of at least five or pay for the empty spaces. Tours can be arranged by Enrique Barrera at Carrera 1A, 18-35, a restaurant near the river bank close to Plaza del Moral. Updated: Apr 11, 2011.

Lodging

You are advised to shop around for Pacific coast accommodations. It may not be a question of always looking for the cheapest option, but rather paying a few dollars more for a place where you and your belongings are safe. Because tourists to Chocó are sparse, places like Quibdó are severely short on good hotels (hostels are all but impossible to find). Along coastal destinations in the Chocó, however, one is spoiled by choices with eco-hotels. Natural luxury is provided through

PACIFIC COAST

well-thought-out lodges delivering on every promise made. Most of these places are package deals and can be arranged in Medellín. Updated: Jul 22, 2010.

Restaurants

Thanks to its geography, restaurants outside of the major cities in this part of Colombia are small and tailored toward locals. Don't expect to find much of a variety here, either. Due to its isolation over the years, food is distinctly regional here.

TUMACO

 2m   185,000   📞 2

San Andrés de Tumaco, Colombia's second most important Pacific port, is 304 kilometers (189 mi) from Pasto. It is situated on three islands, all connected by bridge: Tumaco, Viciosa and El Morro. Isla Tumaco is the principal population center. Seen from the air, it seems a coast-to-coast blanket of human civilization. Isla El Morro hosts the city's air and maritime ports, as well as a major military base.

Tumaco is called La Perla del Pacífico—The Pearl of the Pacific. But its luster is a bit dulled in spots. Upon arriving, what strikes you is the chaotic bustle, streets under repair and the smell of polluted sea. The growth it has sustained in the past decade—primarily due to internal refugees from Colombia's civil war—has stretched this city beyond its already limited infrastructure. Street signs on Isla Tumaco are scarce and use the numbered calle-carrera system; locals use different names. Barrio Puentes and others in tsunami-risk areas are soon to be a thing of the past. They are being relocated to safer grounds.

Tumaco has been declared a Special Port, Ecotourism and Biodiversity District, thus allowing infrastructure improvement and tourism promotion. Tumaco's most distinctive feature is its mangroves: Parque Nacional Sanquianga is along the north coast. The clean beaches of Isla El Morro and Bocagrande provide welcomed escapes from the bedlam of Isla Tumaco. Tuma indigenous and Afro-Colombian cultures live along the coast. The marimba music and traditional chants of the Afro-Colombian communities in Tumaco and the southern Pacific coast are recognized by UNESCO as part of Intangible Cultural heritage of Humanity.

Besides its beach resorts, mangrove reserves and unique cultures, Tumaco has yet another attraction: an alternative crossing to Ecuador—by sea. Updated: Feb 15, 2011

History

The Tumaco region was settled over 4,000 years ago by the Tumaco-La Tolita peoples, whose reign stretched along the Pacific coast from northern Ecuador to southern Colombia. Hidden among the coast's tangled mangroves are reminders of this nation, largely unstudied and unexcavated.

In 1526, Francisco Pizarro arrived on the islands. Father Onofre Estéban founded the present-day city in 1610. Several times Tuma indigenous attempted to push these invaders away, but never successfully.

By 1628, Tumaco had become an important port between Panama and Callao, growing haphazardly, a mélange of peoples and cultures. During the 18th century, Tumaco served as a base camp for the defense of Spain's Pacific American ports assaulted by pirates. But in 1681, 1684 and 1687, English and Dutch corsairs attacked the town. Such raids continued until the early 19th century. Legend says Henry Morgan hid his loot in the Isla del Morro caves.

The Comuneros de Tumaco revolted against Spanish rule in 1781. The rebellion was suppressed the following year. Slaves who escaped from this uprising retreated into the swamps. Those Maroons form the base of modern Tumaco's Afro-Colombian culture.

Twentieth-century Tumaco was twice destroyed by tsunamis: in 1906 and 1979; the latter wave left over 400 dead and 1000 missing. Updated: Feb 15, 2011.

When to Go

Tumaco is said to be one of the rainiest places on earth. The wettest months are May to July, and the driest are April and August. Temperatures range from 25-35°C (77-95°F).

Tumaco is popular with vacationing Colombians. Beaches get pretty crowded during holidays, especially around Christmas and New Years, Easter week (Semana Santa) and July to August. Prices go down out of these seasons.

Tumaco is famous for its Carnaval, highlighting regional Afro-Colombian music, dance and cultural traditions. The town

Photo by: tío tigre

PACIFIC COAST

moves to the rhythm of currulao, bambuco and la juga during the week before Ash Wednesday. Parades, *murgas* (drum-dance troupes) and beauty queens are all featured. Every August, marimba music fills the air for the Festival de Currulao, drawing participants from Colombia's and Ecuador's Pacific coast. On November 30, thanks are given to San Andrés for having saved the town from a tsunami. Updated: Feb 21, 2011.

Getting To and Away

BY AIR

Tumaco's airport (Tel: 727-2598) is located on Isla del Morro. Satena flies to Cali (5 weekly, $67 and up) and Bogotá (4 weekly, $87 and up). Avianca has daily flights to Cali ($70 and up). Other carriers are Easy Fly (to Cali, Bogotá; competitive prices) and TCA (to Cali). Updated: Feb 15, 2011.

BY BUS

Tumaco has two city bus routes: Ruta 1 to Playa El Morro (about 30 min) and Ruta 2 to the airport. Fares are $0.35. The last bus from downtown to El Morro leaves at about 7:45 p.m. and from El Morro to town at 8 p.m.

Taxis charge $3 between Isla Tumaco and Isla El Morro. Intercity buses have their offices on Calle 13, including **Transipiales** (Tel: 727-2426), **Cootranar** (Tel: 727-2562) and **SuperTaxis**.

To Cali: 14-18 hr—**Transipiales** (3 p.m., 7 p.m., 8:45 p.m.; $33), **Cootranar** (5

a.m., 2:30 p.m., 8 p.m.; $31), **SuperTaxis** (5:30 a.m., $28) and **Flota Guaitara** (combi, 5 a.m., $44; taxis, leave when full, $50). Buses stop in Popayán ($25-30).

To Pasto: 6-6.5 hr—**Transipiales** (hourly 4 a.m.-7 p.m., $14), **Cootranar** (hourly, 5:30 a.m.-2:30 p.m., $14), **SuperTaxis** (combi, hourly, $12; taxi, leave when full, 5 hr, $18), **Flota Guaitara** (leave when full, 5 a.m.-7 p.m.; $16).

To Ipiales: SuperTaxis (combi, 5 a.m., 6 hr, $11; taxi, 1 p.m., 5.5 hr, $17), **Flota Guaitara** (station wagon, 5 a.m., $14; taxis, leave when full, $18). Updated: Feb 15, 2011.

BY BOAT

For launches to Bocagrande and various small villages in the coastal mangroves, go to Transmart on the *muelle* (dock) at Calle San Carlos and Calle de Comercio (Cel: 315-643-8128). The *puerto marítimo* (seaport) is on Isla El Morro, about one kilometer (0.6 mi) from Playa El Morro. Boats to Esmeraldas, Ecuador, also depart from this port. See "Border Crossing: Tumaco-Esmeraldas" for more information. Updated: Feb 15, 2011.

Border Crossing: Tumaco-Esmeraldas

For a different adventure in making the journey to Ecuador, consider going by sea. Service has much improved in recent years. You don't have to travel in launch through mangroves and into the open sea anymore—now it is done by cargo-passenger boat.

Servimar runs a ship from Tumaco's puerto marítima on Isla El Morro to Esmeraldas every Friday evening, arriving in Ecuador Saturday morning; the trip takes 10-12 hours.

Buy your passage from Servimar's office across from the maritime port, where the two palm trees are (Monday-Friday, 8 a.m.-noon and 2-6 p.m. Cel: 315-491-7821, E-mail: gutierrez_balvino@hotmail.com). Tickets are sold all day Thursday and Friday until 6 p.m., and cost $15 one way.

The DAS office is Tumaco is now authorized to give entry and exit stamps. Its offices are located about 1.5 kilometers (1 mi) from the port, toward Isla Tumaco; it is the green-trimmed, yellow-ochre building opposite and just past the military base. You are responsible for going there before departure to get your exit stamp (or, if arriving to Colombia, for your entry stamp).

Boarding of passengers on the ship begins at 7 p.m. Friday night; departure is at 8 p.m. (or so). You will receive a bed in a nine-bunk room. No food or drink is provided or sold; bring your own.

Upon arrival in Esmeraldas, Ecuadorian immigration and customs will greet you dockside. Expect a very thorough search of your belongings.

From Esmeraldas to Tumaco, the boat leaves on Wednesday night, arriving in Tumaco on Thursday morning. The Esmeraldas agent is **Sarjento Campaña**.

Whether departing or arriving to Colombia with this ship, it is more convenient to stay at Playa El Morro, just one kilometer (0.6 mi) from the maritime port.

Note: This service has been on hold since mid-2010, but is expected to resume in the near future. Contact Servimar in Tumaco or Sarjento Campaña in Esmeraldas for the boat's latest status.

Launches still do run down the coast. Check at Tumaco's dock at Calle San Carlos and Calle de Comercio for boats. The usual route is: land transporation from Tumaco to Invilí, from where a launch is taken to Puerto Palmas. From there, a vehicle goes to Desembocadero and then a launch to San Lorenzo, Ecuador. Immigration procedures are done in Tumaco and San Lorenzo. Updated: Feb 21, 2011.

Safety

Bear in mind that Tumaco is a port town with endemic poverty. Take extra care navigating the crowded daytime and barren nighttime streets. If going out night clubbing, take a taxi home.

The road to Tumaco is still in a zone seeing sporadic activity by armed factions of the civil war and narco-traffickers. However, with the heavy Colombian military presence, the situation has much improved. Check on safety conditions before embarking on your journey. At the time of writing, the road was okay.

The threat of tsunamis is now taken very seriously in Tumaco. If there is an earthquake, follow instructions and get to higher ground. As the area experiences great rainfall, take precautions against malaria and dengue. Many hotels have screened windows; those in Playa El Morro also have *toldillos* (bed mosquito nets).

Take particular care with food and water. Treat all tap water or drink bottled water; the tap water at El Morro is only suitable for bathing, as it has mangrove particulate matter. Updated: Jul 20, 2011.

Services

TOURISM

Tumaco's tourism office is on the third floor of the Alcaldía building (Monday-Friday 8 a.m.-noon and 2-5 p.m. Ca. 11/Caldas and Cra. 9/Ca. Mosquera). If it is not open, try the very helpful **Cámara de Comercio** (Monday-Friday 8 a.m.-noon and 2-5 p.m. Ca. Sucre, half a block from Ca. Mosquera). The Policía Nacional is located in downtown Tumaco (Ca. Mosquera and Av. Ferrera Esquina. Tel: 727-2020), and the city's **DAS office** (Monday-Friday 7:30-noon and 2-5 p.m.) is at Calle 17, 29-70.

MONEY

Calle Sucre is nicknamed Calle de los Bancos (Street of the Banks), because it has branches of all of Colombia's major banks. None, however, change traveler's checks or cash. They do have ATMs, though; Bancolombia's handles any type of bank card. A few agencies exchange U.S. dollars, but only if the manager is in: **Viaje Turismo** (Monday-Friday 8 a.m.-noon and 2-6 p.m. Ca. Sucre, two blocks from Ca. del Comercio) and **Giros and Finanzas/Western Union** (Monday-Friday 8 a.m.-noon and 2-5:30 p.m., Saturday, 8 a.m.-noon. Ca. Mosquera, half a block from the cathedral, in Centro Comercial La Sultana).

PACIFIC COAST

KEEPING IN TOUCH

Internet cafés are scattered throughout Isla Tumaco, but service is basic—don't expect to make a Skype call or to burn photos onto a CD. Internet costs around $1.50 per hour.

You can make local and national calls from any store or street stall announcing llamadas. **Pacific Net** offers international phone calls (Ca. Ovando/Crs. 9B, 11-55, next to Hotel Las Lajas).

Avianca Depris (Ca. Caldas/Ca. 11, near Cra. 9) ships certified packages and letters. It costs a pricey $30 to send a letter to the U.S.

At El Morro beach, it is harder to keep in touch. Local and national calls are available, but not international calls or Internet services.

MEDICAL

Hospital San Andrés (Ca. 7 de Agosto and Cra. 12B. Tel: 727-1099) is a level-two hospital with many emergency care services. However, be advised that it does not have a hyperbolic chamber, making scuba diving a risky activity in these parts. *Droguerías*, or pharmacies, are especially found on Calle 13 and Calle 9B (Calle Ovando). Updated: Feb 15, 2011.

SHOPPING

Asociación de Artesanos José el Artesano

Asociación de Artesanos José el Artesano is a small, non-descript building of white-painted brick stands alone on an "island" lot at the bend of Playa El Morro's beach road. Peering into the windows, you can glimpse drums, baskets and jewelry. Once inside, you walk into the creative world of Tumaco's artisans using natural materials from these islands: earrings from coconut, jewelry made from sea shells, and handmade conuno drums and marimbas accompanied by rampira-wrapped maracas. This same plant is used to craft covered bowls. Tetera is another plant woven into containers.

If the shop is not open, ask doña Clara at the workshop on the corner across the road. José el Artesano also now has a shop in Tumaco town. It features all the same crafts, as well as gold and silver filagree jewelry (Av.Los Estudiantes, 200 m/700 ft past Cancha San Judás, across from Hotel San Andrés). Across from the Hotel Reynolds, Playa El Morro. Updated: Feb 15, 2011.

Things to See and Do

Don't let first impressions of Tumaco put you off from spending a bit of time here. The streets are crazy, but you can seek refuge in the cathedral, then stroll to Parque Colón across the road and search for the iguanas in the trees—or battle the market streets' madness until you reach the home of Virgen de la Merced, Tumaco's patron saint, on Parque Nariño.

The Casa de la Cultura has a small museum and library (Monday-Friday 8 a.m.-noon and 2-6 p.m. Ca. Bolívar and Ca. San Carlos). Then there are beach temptations like Playa El Bajito, on Isla Viciosa, near Puente El Morro. The waters are still too polluted to swim, so while at Playa El Bajito, have a quick bite to eat instead. Across the bridge, at the end of Isla El Morro, is that island's beach, with tranquil waters and black sands. If you can, take the trip through the mangroves to Isla Bocagrande, where the region's best beaches are.

For nature lovers, Parque Nacional Sanquianga, four hours north on the coast, is home to waterfowl, sea turtles and 30 percent of Colombia's Pacific Coast mangrove. On the mainland is Reserva La Planada, a private reserve of 3,200 hectares (7,907 ac) of nature created in 1982 by the FES Foundation La Planada. This patch of dense cloud forest surrounded by flat-top mountains is home to a wide variety of flora and fauna and, it is believed, one of the largest concentrations of bird species native to South America.

If you can't be in Tumaco for one of the festivals, you can still catch performances of the traditional Afro-Colombian dances of the region. Every Wednesday and Thursday night, rehearsals are held at the *cancha* (ball court) on Calle San Judás and Calle de los Estudiantes from 7-9 p.m. Updated: Feb 21, 2011.

Playa El Morro

The Isla Tumaco-Isla El Morro road ends in a loop at a glistening, black-sand beach and warm-watered sea. Just offshore is the haystack-shaped El Morro rock formation.

The main strand is the most popular place to swim and sunbathe. After spending the day in the warm sea, take in the sunset while having a fresh seafood dinner. Afterwards, hit one of the beach-disco-bar kiosks right on the beach, and chill beneath the palm trees to the tune of jazz-foreign oldies-salsa-vallenato. Spending the night at Playa El Morro is much more peaceful than in Tumaco town. The entire loop of the beach road is lined with hotels for every budget.

At the far end of the beach road loop is the famed Arco del Morro; as the tide lowers, its tranquil pool drains in a rushing creek to the sea. Beyond the arch, a several-kilometer-long beach is being exposed. The swimming here is not great, due to mangrove sediment, but the beachcombing and birdwatching are rewarding. This is also the time you can visit the cuevas, where legend says pirate Henry Morgan hid his treasure (admission: $1.60).

Do not wild camp on the beaches, due to the high wash of the incoming tide and possible robbery. (The town itself is patrolled.) Also, avoid swimming at low tide when poisonous rays and *pez de sapo* (frogfish) are exposed.

Frequent busetas run between Isla Tumaco and Playa El Morro (5 a.m.-7:45 p.m. from Tumaco, until 8 p.m. from El Morro; $0.35, 30 min). A taxi costs $2.75 each way. Updated: Apr 14, 2011.

Playa Bocagrande

Bocagrande is a small island, tucked into the mangrove estuaries near Tumaco. A magical place to spend a few days, the crystalline sea washes upon fine silvery sand and soft breezes moderate the warm days (temperature averages 27°C/81°F). Opportunities for scuba diving or snorkeling are nonexistent, as there are no coral reefs. However, waterfowl abound, which is great for birdwatchers, and the fishing is also astounding. Bocagrande is the perfect paradise for those looking to kick back in a hammock and escape civilization for a few days.

Transmart (in Tumaco, along the dock at the end of Ca. la Merced, and Ca. del Comercio. Cel: 315-643-8128) runs launches to Bocagrande, only at high tide. In high season, it goes daily; in the low season, on demand. Updated: Apr 08, 2011.

Parque Nacional Sanquianga !

Located on the Pacific coast in the north-western Nariño Department, Parque Nacional Sanquianga contains 30 percent of Colombia's Pacific mangrove forests. This 80,000-hectare (197,684-ac) park protects a complex estuary delta system formed by the Sanquianga, Patía, La Tola, Aguacatal and Tapaje Rivers. The ecosystem also includes 60 kilometers (36 mi) of sandy beaches, swamps and *guadual* (giant bamboo) forests.

A great diversity of marine species lives within the shelter of the red mangrove: sponges, mollusks, crabs, piangua and more. This sanctuary has the highest concentration of shore and seabirds on the Colombian Pacific coast and is a primary nesting ground for Brown Wood-rail, Gull-billed Tern, Tumaco Seedeater and Neotropical Cormorant, as well as for Caguama sea turtles. Other fauna include sloths, iguanas, babillas and rodents. The labyrinths of Sanquianga additionally harbor small indigenous and Afro-Colombian communities, with a total population of about 11,000.

While canoeing through the mangroves, you can observe the diverse flora and fauna Parque Nacional Sanquianga contains and experience one of the best preserved mangroves. Interpretive trails at El Secadero and El Carboncillo, and to Lagunas de Mulatos and de Amarales, allow you to penetrate the forest. On Playas Guascama, Barrera, Tasquita, Mulatos, Amarales and Vigía, you may swim, and play soccer or beach volleyball. Cultural activities also await you in the villages tucked into the filagree of this coast.

From Tumaco, check the various boating companies located on the pier at the end of Calle de la Merced, near Calle del Comercio for launches to the national park (4 hr, $33-42 one way). Sanquianga is also accessible by boat from Buenaventura (12 hr). Updated: Apr 14, 2011.

Tours

Tour operators are beginning to open in Tumaco. A handful of travel agencies will also help you buy flights or tour packages from here to other Colombian destinations. SENA (Servicio Nacional de Apredizaje) is training people in lower economic brackets as guides. This is just one of the steps being taken to develop the local tourist industry. Updated: Jul 11, 2011.

Viaje Turismo

The women of this two-person office can sell you tickets with major airlines from Tumaco's La Florida airport to any place in the country. They also handle the airlines' tourist packages to Cartegena, Medellín and other attractive resorts, and courier services. When the owner is in, you can change U.S. dollars for pesos—one of the few places in Tumaco you can do so. Monday-Friday 8 a.m.-noon and 2-6 p.m. Ca. Sucre, 1.5 blocks from Ca. del Comercio. Updated: Apr 08, 2011.

Guía T.P. Viajes y Turismo-SENA

SENA has a program to train economically disadvantaged people of the Tumaco region to be tour guides. The students' travel agency, Guía T.P. Viajes y Turismo, can guide you to major attractions in the city itself, at Playa El Morro and Bocagrande, or to small indigenous and Afro-Colombian settlements deep within the mangroves. Some have private vehicles to chauffeur you to the sites. Negotiate the cost of your excursion with your individual student-guide. Ca. El Comercio, 1 block from Parque Colón. Tel: 315-447-1973 (Professor Patricia Coronado). Updated: Feb 15, 2011.

Tours La Sultana

Tours La Sultana has opened its doors to help visitors appreciate Tumaco's natural wonders. An escape to the fine-sand beaches of Bocagrande, a 20-minute boat ride from the city, is one adventure this agency offers ($21, including transportation and lunch). Or, travelers can opt to spend several hours touring the bay and weaving through the mangroves to observe the multitudes of birds around ($17). In July, when the humpbacks breach the blue ocean waves, Tours La Sultana takes folks out to whale watch ($28). All prices are per person. Hotel La Sultana, Ca. Sucre and Ca. del Comercio. Tel: 727-2438, URL: www.hotellasultana.com. Updated: Feb 21, 2011.

Lodging

All classes of hostels exist on Isla Tumaco. Accommodations are diverse, and travelers of all budgets will find a place here. At this time, many of the upper-end hotels are booked long-term by military personnel. If your inn is close to the seafront, you may be bothered by the stench of the water.

Playa El Morro has better options for budget backpackers and couples looking for a romantic getaway. If coming from or going to Ecuador by the weekly ship, it's better to stay here; DAS (Departamento Administrativo de Seguridad) offices and port are nearby. **Panorama Kioss** provides shaded campsites for $2.60-4.20 (back loop of beach road, up from Hotel El Morro. Cel: 318-356-7454/316-570-0463). Beach camping is not recommended, because of tides and robberies. Prices rise during holidays. Updated: Feb 15, 2011.

Hotel El Dorado

(ROOMS: $6-14) El Dorado is one of the oldest lodging options in Tumaco, serving travelers for over 35 years. The second floor is full of rooms sharing clean-enough common baths with cold water only. On the roof, surrounding a garden patio, are very nice cabañas for one to three people, with private, cold-water bathrooms and TV. These are more expensive. The front cabins have a balcony over the street; the back ones have a sea view. As this hostel is right on the waterfront, the smell of the centuries-polluted sea may leave a bad taste in the mouths of some. Ca. El Comercio, between Ca. La Merced and Ca. Parque Colón. Updated: Apr 08, 2011.

Hotel Guaduales del Pacífico

(ROOMS: $14 per person) Hotel Guaduales, built from giant bamboo, is an example of the traditional architecture found in this region. The rooms are simple—a bit rough, but adequate—with a private bath (cold water only) and mosquito nets over the beds. The screened windows make the rooms light and airy. The common upstairs balcony has a tranquil sea view, making it the perfect place to relax or read. The restaurant has seating on the front veranda and serves *comida corriente* (daily special) for $3.50. It also serves beer. Owner Doña Yolanda, a jolly but no-nonsense woman, is always ready to ask you, "¿Le provoca un tinto?" ("Would you like a coffee?") Beachside road, Playa El Morro. Tel: 727-2927. Updated: Feb 15, 2011.

Los Veleros

(ROOMS: $19-33) Los Veleros is clean, safe and has several terraces. There is free WiFi and several computers available for use. The hotel is located one block away from the bus terminal, right next to the police station in the center of downtown. Ca. Mosquera, next to the Polícia Nacional post. Tel: 727-0836. Updated: Apr 08, 2011.

Hotel Barranquilla

(ROOMS: $31-61) The most luxurious hotel at Playa El Morro, Hotel Barranquilla is a sharp high rise with well-equipped rooms. All have air-conditioning, private bath, hot water, fridge and cable TV, while some also sport a balcony and sea view. If you'd like to explore nearby sights, the owners of Hotel Barranquilla can arrange tours. Be sure to check out the top-floor restaurant and the kiosk disco on the beach. Beachside road, Playa El Morro. Tel: 727-1760, E-mail: hotelbarranquilla@hotmail.com. Updated: Feb 15, 2011.

Hotel Los Corales

(ROOMS: $74-150) By far, Hotel Los Corales is the best hotel-resort in the whole area. This beachside hotel has 80 guest rooms, suites and a presidential suite (with Jacuzzi), each with air conditioning, private bathtub, hot water, linens, towels, satellite TV, fridge and balcony. The amenities of this hotel include an adult's pool, kid's pool, Jacuzzi, gym, free

PACIFIC COAST

WiFi, laundry service, meeting rooms, pool bar, terrace karaoke bar, kiosk bar-disco right on the beach and more. Tours can be arranged and dispatched from the 24-hour reception.the restaurant offers breakfast, lunch and dinner with reasonable prices, including an á la carte menu with seafood, traditional Colombian dishes and some international food. Beachside Road, Playa El Morro. Tel: 727-2779. Tel: 305-760-4888, Email: info@ hotelloscorales.com, URL: www.hotelloscorales.com. Updated: Feb 15, 2011.

Restaurants

Food prices in Tumaco tend to be higher than in inland cities. The mercado hustles daily on many of the streets of Tumaco, especially on Calle de Comercio, and Calle de la Merced to Plaza Nariño.

The Calle de Comercio sector has inexpensive eateries serving fish and wild game. Fish and seafood, of course, are the town's specialties. Try the encocados, or dishes prepared in coconut milk, and the ceviche (raw, marinated fish or seafood). A local drink to cool sultry afternoons is champú—a non-alcoholic brew of fermented corn, tropical fruits and panela (raw sugar). Updated: Feb 15, 2011.

Pollos Wilson

(CHICKEN MEAL: $1.60) Pollos Wilson is only one of the dozens of fried chicken joints that crowd Tumaco's chaotic streets. Its proximity to the bus terminals make it a convenient place to grab a plate of chicken, fries and rice before heading down the road. Pollos Wilson isn't just about winged servings on a platter, though. It also serves up arepas, papa rellena (stuffed potato ball) and other fast food. Wash it down with a tinto, hot chocolate or other available drinks. Ca. 13 (Ca. La Merced), in front of the Cootranar bus station. Updated: Apr 08, 2011.

Restaurante La Corvina

(LUNCH: $4) At the bend of the beach road, not too far from the Arco del Morro, is a double row of kiosk restaurants, all serving cheap fish specials. The menu at La Corvina, however, sticks out from the rest. Not only does its proprietor, Doña Nata, prepare à la carte seafood dishes such as crayfish, oysters, squid, shrimp, clams, crabs and lobster, but she also offers other wild game meats. These include familiar animals (rabbit and venison) as well as exotic ones (fox, wild pig and guatín). The set meals at lunch and dinner are an economical alternative

to the à la carte selections ($4-28). Fourth restaurant on right, Kiosk Row, Playa El Morro. Updated: Apr 08, 2011.

Restaurante Alta Mar

(LUNCH: $5.50) The open-sided dining room at Restaurante Alta Mar gives a commanding view of the sea. The fresh morning breeze creates an enjoyable breakfast experience from 7-9 a.m. ($4). The excellently prepared lunch special, served 11 a.m.-2 p.m., includes soup, a main dish of fish or meat, rice, patacones (fried plaintains), salad and a large fresh fruit drink. The lunch costs $5.50. The seafood á la carte menu ($10-14) is served all day until 9 p.m., giving you the opportunity to watch the sunset and appreciate the evening breeze. Hotel Barranquilla, Beachside Road, Playa del Morro. Updated: Apr 08, 2011.

Nightlife

Tumaco has a number of dance spots to entertain locals as well as military personnel. Forget the workday—it's time to rumbear! A cluster of clubs on Calle de los Estudiantes are near the cancha (ball court). But the most happening scenes are at the El Morro bridge. Out at Playa El Morro are other clubs, with kiosk bars, tables beneath palm trees and a lawn-tent dance floor with pulsating lights, all set on the sand. Most clubs close at 1 a.m. No matter where you decide to rumbear the night away, take a taxi home (unless you are partying and staying at El Morro). Updated: Feb 15, 2011.

Punto Baré

When asked, SENA student guides Deysy and Claudia were unanimous in revealing the most happening place for a rumba: Punto Baré. Here, the party begins at 7 p.m. and goes until 3 a.m., grooving to the beat of salsa, with a bit of merengue and reggaeton thrown into the mix. So hit that huge dance floor and sway under the pulsating lights. Sidle up to the long bar for a drink--but if you're looking for something non-alcoholic, you're going to be out of luck. There is no door charge, but there is a steep minimum consumption of $11. Claudia and Deysy warn it's elegant—so, men, no shorts. Subida del Puente del Morro, fifth from the bridge on the left side of the road. Updated: Apr 08, 2011.

Kiosko El Caído del Sol

At a table beneath palm trees at Kiosko El Caído del Sol, friends nurse beers over a quiet conversation. The cool blue light of the dance floor gleams on couples swaying to the sensual rhythm of Cuban Son. There's no hassle here at the Kiosko El Caído del Sol: no door charge (well, this beach bar has no door) and no minimum consumption. Just chill with a cold drink and some salsa, son and jazz. Daily 8 p.m.-1 a.m. Across from Hotel Barranquilla, Playa del Morro. Updated: Apr 08, 2011.

BUENAVENTURA

 7m   324,000   2

Situated 128 kilometers (79.5 mi) from Cali, Buenaventura is a sweltering port on the Colombian Pacific coast. Make no mistake: Buenaventura is a dangerous place with the guerrilla, paramilitaries and government all jostling for control of this pivotally important communication and transportation hub.

The place is architecturally unappealing with its city center built mainly on the island of Cascajal. If you find yourself here, it is likely that you are lost and way off course or you have come to make a connection to the nearby tourist areas and whale-watching retreats of Juanchaco and Ladrilleros.

Despite the unspeakably high murder rate, visitors will be pleasantly surprised with shopping opportunities and the hotels and restaurants on Calle 1.

Should you have to spend a night or more than a few hours here before making the connection to one of the surrounding sights, then be sure to visit the San Andresito area of town for bargain shopping. Then head to the Muelle Turístico to slurp on a freshly squeezed fruit juice and watch the massive tankers power their way out into the open ocean. Updated: May 18, 2009.

History

Founded in the 16th century, Buenaventura was a major world player before the creation of the Panama Canal. Ships going to and from the California Gold Rush would pass through these waters, increasing the city's importance. Currently, Buenaventura is Colombia's leading port on the Pacific coast and is crucial for importing cargo to surrounding areas, particularly Cali. Updated: Jul 15, 2011.

When to Go

Between late July and early October, people descend on the resorts of Juanchaco and Ladrilleros to catch a glimpse of the migrating humpback whales. Updated: Jul 17, 2011.

Getting to and Away

BY AIR

The airport is a 30-minute drive from downtown Buenaventura; a taxi ride costs around $9. Satena has flights here several times a week.

BY BUS

The Terminal de Transportes is downtown. Even though it is close to the hotels on Calle 1, it is recommended to always take a taxi (about $2) to and from there.

Buses from the terminal leave for Cali frequently. Given the areas the journey passes through, it would be wise to go during daylight hours. The road to Cali winds through valleys and tunnels, and has been blocked on occasion after landslides from heavy rains. Numerous companies run buses to Cali from Buenaventura. Two reputable companies are Palmira and Transmar. Buses cost $10-11 per person. Taxis, which leave when full, cost $15-40 per person. The journey takes three to four hours.

Additionally, there are also bus services to Medellín, Bogotá, Manizales, Armenia, Pereira, Buga, Tulua, Cartago and Istmina.

BY BOAT

You can organize your transport north to Juanchaco, Ladrilleros, Guapi and Charco from the Muelle Turístico; trips to all of these places cost around $25-30. Other destinations include Bocana, La Cangreja, Pianguita and Timbiquí (about $45). There are half a dozen boat operators, and most leave for their destinations from 9-11 a.m. However, departure times are always changing and costs often depend on how many passengers are going. Two recommended companies are Pacífico Express and Transmilenio. Updated: Jul 25, 2011.

Safety

Security should be on any visitor's mind when coming to Buenaventura. This is ground zero for turf wars between the paramilitaries and the guerrillas who want to control a lucrative area for the drug trade. The murder rate in the city is startlingly high and tourists are advised not to stray from Calle 1 at night. There is high unemployment and therefore, problems of delinquency. Updated: Apr 22, 2009.

Services

For tourist information, head to the Muelle Turístico. The office there can provide you with maps and trip ideas. Buenaventura's DAS office is located at Calle 1A, 3-16 (Tel:

PACIFIC COAST

242-6637/6638/241-9759). Bancolombia, on Calle 1, has an ATM that accepts Visa, or you can go to the Davivienda branch on Calle 2 and Carrera 3. **Cyber Pacífico** (Ca. 2-11) is best for Internet; it is opposite the Olímpica supermarket. Medical Clínica Buenaventura can be found on Calle 6, 16-24 (Tel: 255-4755).

SHOPPING
For knock-off sports shoes, clothes and alcohol, head to San Andresito to bargain for various items. San Andresito is located on Calle 9 with Carrera 6. Updated: Nov 15, 2007.

Tours
When you arrive at the Muelle Turístico, various individuals will confront you who claim to be official tour guides. Some of them are scam artists posing as tour operators who have taken brochures from reputable companies and pretend they are associated with those companies. Head straight to the tourism office (the yellow building located off to the left) to make sure you get an accredited guide. The office staff can provide you with maps and prices. Whale-watching tours should cost about $12 per person. A tour that covers all of Cascajal Island will cost around $45. Updated: Mar 15, 2011.

Lodging
Buenaventura has limited lodging options since it doesn't have much of a tourist draw beyond its status as a jumping-off point for places along the coast. There are a few nice hotels in the city, but unfortunately budget options are limited; hostels are almost unheard of in Buenaventura. Updated: Jul 21, 2010.

Hotel Tropicana
(ROOMS: $12-15) Don't let Hotel Tropicana's drab green exterior fool you. Its interior is actually quite nice, with a friendly staff eager to help. The hotel's four floors of comfortable rooms come with private bathrooms, cable TV and air conditioning. Hotel Tropicana is located a block off of the Calle 1 drag. From Muelle Turístico, head down Calle 1 and turn left on Carrera 5. Walk up a block and it's the large green building on your right. Cra. 5A, 2-22. Tel: 241-7573. Updated: Apr 08, 2011.

Hotel Los Delfines
(ROOMS: $15-40) This beautiful hotel has nine floors of spotless rooms, with wide verandas on every floor offering panoramic views of the Pacific. Rooms have air conditioning, private bathrooms, telephone and cable TV. It also has laundry service downstairs, and free Internet access in rooms and on the

balconies. Hotel Los Delfines is in an excellent location, just a few blocks away from the Muelle Turístico. Ca. 1, 5A-03. Tel: 241-5450, Fax: 241-5463, E-mail: hotellosdelfines@mibuenaventura.com. Updated: Jul 25, 2011.

Hotel Titanic
(ROOMS: $29-45) The Hotel Titanic does not do a great deal to inspire the visitor with its name. But all the same, it is another respectable establishment along Calle 1 in the safer part of Buenaventura. The hotel has 37 rooms equipped with cable TV, mini-bar, private bathroom, air conditioning and telephone. It also has a restaurant and bar. Ca. 1a, 2A-55, in front of the park. Tel: 241-2046/1566. Updated: Apr 08, 2011.

Gran Hotel
(ROOMS: $36-42) With 28 well-appointed rooms all containing a private bathroom, much-needed air conditioning, cable TV, and mini-bar, the Gran Hotel is a place where you would gladly spend the night. The hotel's reception is helpful and friendly. There is an on-site restaurant and all rooms come with WiFi access. If you are coming from the Muelle Turístico, walk across the road and a block to the right up Calle 1. Ca. 1a, 2A-71. Tel: 243-4527, Fax: 243-4846, E-mail: granhotel1@telecom.com.co/granhotel@mibuenaventura.com. Updated: Jul 25, 2011.

Hotel Capilla del Sol
(ROOMS: $62-115) Nine floors of hotel rooms provide the visitor with plenty of options for ocean views from Cascajal Island. All rooms have air conditioning, private bathroom, mini-bar, WiFi and balcony. The rooms are well attended and comfortable. On the roof terrace, there is a well-regarded restaurant that stays open until 10 pm. Corner of Ca. 1a and Cra. 2a, 2nd floor. Tel: 242-3000/2100, E-mail: hotelcapilladelsol@gmail.com. Updated: Apr 08, 2011.

Hotel Estelar Estación
(ROOMS: $75-155) Designed and constructed in an era when opulence and class meant everything, the Hotel Estelar Estación cuts an awkward gait in today's Buenaventura. Its stucco-fronted balconies set it apart as the only true upscale hotel in the city. If it is luxury you are after, pick any one of its 75 suites, take a dip in its pool or just enjoy one of its restaurants. Ca. 2, 1A-08. Tel: 243-4070, Fax: 243-4118, E-mail: recepcion.hestacion@hotelesestelar.com, URL: www.hotelesestelar.com. Updated: Apr 08, 2011.

PACIFIC COAST

Restaurants

Primos

Although it is not the most inviting establishment in the Zona Rosa, lacking the quality and setting of some of the other places in the neighborhood, Primos is another decent option on Calle 1. Offering the usual fare for the coast, including fried fish, cuts of meat and generous helpings, you could do a lot worse. Prices run up to $22. Ca. 1, 3rd block. Tel: 242-3109. Updated: Apr 08, 2011.

Soles

On the 11th floor of the Capilla del Sol Hotel, Soles makes for a pleasant respite from the noise of cars along the Zona Rosa strip. Standard eats are available, and while the food is better than passable, the main reason to come here is for the view of the city lights overlooking the Pacific. Soles serves breakfast ($3.50) and fixed-price lunches ($5) as well. Corner of Ca. 1a and Cra. 2a, 11th floor. Tel: 242-3000. Updated: Apr 08, 2011.

Rapy Taylor

One of six fast food stalls on the shore side of Calle 1 in the Zona Rosa, Rapy Taylor serves up exactly what you would expect. Pizza, hamburgers, hot dogs and other fast food fare is available for diners in a hurry. Ca. 1, opposite the hotels. Updated: Dec 19, 2007.

Sabrosuras del Pacífico

Delightfully positioned on the second floor of a building facing the sea, Sabrosuras del Pacífico specializes in seafood dishes native to this area. Although this is an ideal place for lunch, it may not be to everyone's liking for dinner, when the neighboring club opens and smothers the restaurant with loud music. Ca. 1, opposite Hotel Los Delfines. Tel: 241-7944. Updated: Apr 08, 2011.

Leños y Mariscos

In the heart of Buenaventura's Zona Rosa on Calle 1, Leños y Mariscos is an upscale eatery that offers fairly standard fish, chicken and beef dishes. However, the helpings are sizeable and accompanied at lunchtime by a salad and small dessert. Ca. 1, 5A-08, in front of Hotel Los Delfines. Tel: 241-7000. Updated: Sep 05, 2011.

Nightlife

Because it is a major port, Buenaventura has a colorful nightlife, to put it mildly. As a tourist, you are recommended to stick to the Zona Rosa on Calle 1, which extends from the Muelle Turístico up the hill to the Mirador Azul bar. Between these two landmarks, you should be less likely to run into problems. Party the night away in one of dozens of places, like Krypton or Chaplins. Updated: Nov 15, 2007.

AROUND BUENAVENTURA

The area around Buenaventura is certainly a bigger draw than the city itself, and with good reason. These surroundings are made up of interesting natural attractions, ranging from the excellent diving sites at Parque Nacional Natural Malpelo to the whale-watching opportunities at Juanchaco, Ladrilleros and Isla Gorgona. Transportation and tours can be arranged from the offices located along the Muelle Turístico in Buenaventura. Transjuanchaco is a reputable company, also with an office in the Muelle Turístico. Updated: Apr 18, 2011.

JUANCHACO AND LADRILLEROS !

Both Juanchaco and Ladrilleros are swamped during the whale-watching season, which runs from late July into the early weeks of October. Every long weekend or public holiday brings with it hordes of vacationers from Cali eager to catch a glimpse of the migrating humpbacks. Whale-watching tours cost $11.50-14.

Juanchaco's beach is littered with driftwood and is not a place one would spread out a towel in order to catch some sun; Ladrilleros is much more suited to this. When the tide is out, the beach widens enormously and vendors set up their stalls providing everything from fortified coconut cocktails to fried fish lunches. There are places to stay here in both areas, many of which are arranged through pre-organized package deals. In both towns, there are smaller residences, which rent rooms.

Take a boat to Ladrilleros from the pier in Buenaventura. The ride takes between four and five hours and costs around $31-34 each way. Once you get to Ladrilleros, it is a 30-minute walk to the beach, or you can wait for 4x4 transport (around $1) to take you there. Updated: Jul 25, 2011.

ISLA GORGONA

Gorgona used to be a prison island before being converted into a national park. It sits some 30 kilometers (19 mi) off the coast, and is home to a great variety of venomous snakes and migrating birds. Its waters are also a favored destination for migrating humpback whales. Diving is very popular here, with opportunities to see marine turtles, sharks and many species of fish.

You can arrange to get to Isla Gorgona from the Muelle Turístico in Buenaventura. There are two options: either take the express boat service, which takes about four hours, or take a cargo boat, which is less expensive but takes three times as long. Cargo boats leave each evening at 6 p.m., arriving at Isla Gorgona at 6 a.m. Alternatively, you can take a boat to the island from Guapi. Boats leave from Guapi's pier every day and the trip takes an hour and a half.

There is a park fee of $10, payable prior to arrival. The national Colombian travel agency Aviatur is the official concessionaire that organizes trips to Gorgona. The Aviatur company sells packages, which include meals and transport. All information (services, prices) for trips to Gorgona Island is posted on its website: www.aviatur.com.

Lodging and food are available on the island. Accommodations include private rooms with private bathrooms as well as 10 houses with four rooms each. There is a pool, Jacuzzi, and basketball and volleyball courts on-site. The restaurant serves typical regional fare, including several different types of fish. Updated: Jul 25, 2011.

PARQUE NACIONAL NATURAL MALPELO!

(ADMISSION: $50 per day) If you love diving, marine wildlife and exploring untouched nature, then it is worth your time to arrange transportation from Buenaventura to the rocky island of Malpelo.

Located 322 kilometers (200 mi) off the coast, the tiny island is only 0.4 kilometers (0.25 mi) by 3.2 kilometers (2 mi), but the surrounding water is recognized as one of the best diving sites in the world (many say that it is similar to Cocos, Costa Rica). The diving sites include the Three Musketeers, La Gringa and the Altar of the Virgin. Divers have the opportunity to see Moray eels, dolphins, manta rays, white-tipped reef sharks, hammerheads, angelfish, starfish, whales, silky sharks and many other sea creatures.

In addition to life under the sea, Malpelo's volcanic formations make it a wonder to behold and it is easy to believe why it's

referred to as one of Colombia's treasures. The island is also home to a quarter of the world's population of Nazca boobies.

Fishing is illegal within a 40-kilometer (25 mi) radius. In 2006, Malpelo was declared a UNESCO World Heritage Site. However, the wildlife, especially the sharks, are still considered in danger.

In order to visit Malpelo, you must book a package tour through either the Fundación Malpelo (Malpelo Foundation) or through La Oficina de Ecoturismo en Parques Nacionales (the Office of Ecotourism in the National Parks office). Three ships go to the island from Colombia: Nemo (a catamaran), Maria Patricia and Sea Wolf; the ride takes 36 hours. Trips are for a minimum of eight days and cost between $2,000-3,500. All nationals and foreigners must get permission to go to the park from the offices of Parques Naturales Nacionales de Colombia in Bogotá. Boats also leave from Panama; see www.inula-diving.com or www.coibadiveexpeditions.com/coiba for more information on this alternative option.

For more information about Malpelo's surrounding waters, check out www.fundacionmalpelo.org. Fundación Malpelo has an office in Bogotá (Cra. 7, 32-33, 27th floor. Tel: 285-0700/0701). Updated: Mar 28, 2011.

The Chocó

Chocó is one of the least visited departments of Colombia, and yet it is one with perhaps the largest helping of natural wonders. The whole area is covered by humid tropical rainforest, which, from the air, appears as if it has been poured onto the land. Its geography, consisting of impenetrable forests, swollen rivers and nearly six meters (19.7 ft) of annual rainfall, make this one of the wettest and most bio-diverse places on the planet.

Former African slaves and Embera Indians now populate the department, recognized for its poverty and lack of infrastructure. Slowly the region is opening thanks to increasing tourism and prospectors keen on exploiting the area's rich natural and mineral resources.

Security in the Chocó can be an issue, mainly due to the coastline's role in the country's illegal drug and arms trade. These issues make it a hotly disputed region between the government and the guerrillas, and common sense is essential for travelers. Updated: May 18, 2009.

History

Given Chocó's geography, it is no wonder that the department feels like its been left behind. The department originally was inhabited only by indigenous tribes, and in the era of Spanish imperialism, the colonizers for the most part left the area alone. In the 16th century, a Spaniard by the name of Alonso de Ojeda, who had accompanied Christopher Columbus on his second journey to the Western Hemisphere, created new settlements in the Gulf of Urabá on the Caribbean side of the Chocó. The settlements did not last long, however, as they continually ran low on food and suffered constant attacks from hostile tribes. Currently, the department suffers from mining and logging issues, and has become a major region for pitched battles between the government and the guerrillas in the interior and along the coast.

When to Go

Visit the Chocó in September for the month-long Fiestas of San Pacho, which celebrate Chocó's patron saint, St. Francis of Assisi. In June and July, annual sports fishing competitions are held. Fishermen from all over the world come out to try and snare marlin in catch and release tournaments. From late July to the end of September, marvel at the migrating humpback whales.

The year-round average temperature is 28°C (82°F). It rains less in the early part of the year, though precipitation is expected daily. Chocó is considered one of the wettest places on earth. It is said to receive up to six meters (19.7 ft) of rainfall every year, and meteorologists have found that it rains at least 20 days out of every month.

Safety

Although the government has made significant progress in recent years in securing the area, safety remains a concern in Chocó. Travel overland from Quibdó to the coast by river is not recommended, and neither is travel from Risaralda in Chocó. The regions of Nuquí, El Valle and Bahía Solano are now safe, though local DAS officers keep a keen eye on goings-on, and all tourists coming into the area—especially into Bahía Solano—are expected to register with them. Do not, under any circumstances, become involved

with drugs here. If you find a discarded packet, leave it alone and report it immediately to the appropriate authorities. Do not take photos of any military installations or personnel.

Things to See and Do

As one of the world's most diverse ecosystems containing a cornucopia of species not found anywhere else on the planet, Chocó offers a wealth of natural pursuits. It is well worth the money to stay in one of the region's excellent eco-lodges, from where you can spot the annual migration of humpback whales. If getting out to interact with the area is more your thing, you can kayak to and explore one of the many mangroves, visit Embera tribes and see their way of life, or dive to the wreck off Bahía Solano. Other options include surfing at Cabo Corrientes, relaxing at Morromico, hiking through the Utría National Park and sports fishing (best in June or July) off the coast. Updated: Apr 11, 2011.

Tours

Should you arrive as part of a package holiday, a great deal of tours will be made available to you, from dipping in thermal hot springs to day trips to Utría and whale-watching excursions. Most hotels can organize everything. For diving, contact Rodrigo at the Hostal del Mar in Bahía Solano. Updated: Apr 11, 2011.

Lodging

The majority of Chocó hotels are some sort of all-inclusive eco-lodge. These can be found on the edges of towns and sometimes are up to a couple of hours away by boat. Within the towns themselves, the range is greater but the quality may not be, and there aren't a lot of luxury hotels. Updated: Apr 11, 2011.

QUIBDÓ

 50m   109,000   4

Quibdó's skyline is dominated by the immense San Francisco de Asís Cathedral, which towers over the banks of the Atrato River. The river is the city's most important means of communication, aside from the frequent flights into the airport, since Quibdó remains poorly connected to the world by two ill-maintained roads.

Overall and aesthetically, Quibdó is an unlovely place. Its architecture and infrastructure have suffered from harsh

PACIFIC COAST

climatic conditions, leaving its streets potholed and buildings stained as if burnt by the humidity. But for the intrepid traveler, these hindrances are only minor hurdles.

Indeed, upon arrival you are sure to be the only tourist, and once this is known, the people here, mainly of Embera Indian and descendants of African slaves, will adopt you as one of their own.

Accommodation is not as developed and established as you would find elsewhere, since Quibdó mainly plays host to soldiers and officials from Doctors Without Borders. Be sure to take a stroll along the riverfront in the early evening and wonder at the bizarre fruits that lack names in English. Updated: Apr 11, 2011.

History

Quibdó's history is largely uncharted except for a few mentions thanks to the work of Fray Matias Abbot in 1648, when the Franciscan order was granted the lands in the area by Embera Indians.

While the city was destroyed by subsequent attacks by hostile tribes, it was rebuilt in 1654 under the watch of the Jesuits Pedro Caceres and Francisco de Orta. Later, Quibdó declared its independence in February of 1813, and in 1825, the city was officially named San Francisco de Quibdó.

When the department of Chocó was created in 1948, Quibdó was named its capital. In 1966, the city was ravaged by fire. Currently, it is better known as being in the heart of the Zona Roja (Red Zone), and for suffering from malaria and poverty.

When to Go

Quibdó is a hot and wet city. There is no effective wet or dry season, since the rain is likely to fall at any time of the year. The rainiest month is August and the driest is February, but really there is little to differentiate between the months.

In April, there is a celebration for typical chocoano dances and foods. If you are in the area in September, stop by for Quibdó's Fiesta of San Francisco de Asís. Updated: Aug 15, 2011.

Getting To and Away

Satena and Aires have regular flights from Quibdó's **Al Carano Airport** (Tel: 671-9048) to Bogotá, Medellín and Pereira,

and vice versa. In addition to those major cities, travelers can buy flights to Nuquí and Bahía Solano from Quibdó.

Traveling here by road from Risaralda or Medellín is strongly discouraged, despite the beautiful scenery. The western regions of Antioquía, Risaralda and Quindío that border the Chocó are dangerous. However, if you decide to waive caution, Rápido Ochoa has buses that leave three times a day from Medellín to Quibdó. River travel is not recommended either. Your best option is to fly. Updated: Nov 15, 2007.

Safety

The people in Quibdó are very polite and helpful, but as in all cities, there are dangers.

Avoid walking off main roads and on unlit streets at night, especially if alone. Remember that Quibdó is a port town and comes with typical port disturbances.

Since Quibdó sometimes seems like a major garrison town and hardly a tourist destination, the police and military will regard visitors with a bit of suspicion. Be sure to keep cameras hidden, and don't even look like you are taking photos that may contain military personnel or buildings. The DAS officers will be curious about who you are, so be sure to have all of your papers in order. Updated: Nov 15, 2007.

Services

The **Government of Chocó** (Tel: 671-1415) can provide you with some tourist information. Quibdó's **DAS office** (Ca. 25, 6-08, Barrio Pan de Yuca. Tel: 671-1402) is open Monday-Friday 7:30 a.m.-noon and 2-6 p.m. There are lots of cash machines that accept Visa in Quibdó. Bancolombia is on the corner of Calle 24 Carrera 2. There is a decent Internet café with telephone booths at Calle 25 and Carrera 5. Seek medical attention at **San Francisco de Asís Hospital** (Cra. 1, 31-25. Tel: 671-1160) or **Hospital Local Ismael Roldan Valencia**, but if your condition is bad and you can travel, get on the earliest flight to Medellín. Updated: May 18, 2009.

Things to See and Do

There are no obvious attractions in Quibdó, but it does make for an interesting couple of days spent off the beaten track. Until the security situation gets better and tourism increases, Quibdó is a place to mix it up with the locals, stroll along the riverfront and spend time at the market.

Check out the Atrato River, a vast river that flows alongside Quilbdó, running 750 kilometers (460 mi) north to the Gulf of Uraba. Watching the boats coming and going from the port and bringing in goods will pass some time. Otherwise, you can marvel at the enormity of the beautiful riverside San Francisco de Asís Cathedral. Nov 15, 2007.

Lodging

Quibdó's tourism infrastructure has remained undeveloped to the point of despair, but given the low number of visitors, this is to be understood. The Hotel Malecón is the only recommended option; other hotels appear to rent rooms by the hour. Updated: May 18, 2009.

Hotel Malecón

(ROOMS: $25-32.50) As the name suggests, this hotel is located right next to the port, which straddles the Atrato River. Its drab stairwell is hard to miss. Don't let the façade put you off, though; Hotel Malecón is a good option. It is safe; its 25 rooms are clean; and Ramón, the concierge, is a great source of information about the area and city. Rooms are equipped with either a fan or air conditioning, and come with a mini-bar and private bathroom. There is no hot water, but this is hardly a necessity in Quibdó. Do not mistake the Hotel Malecón with the Hotel Central, which is reached by the same flight of stairs and rents rooms by the hour. From the airport, any taxi costs roughly $2.50. For a collectivo bus, ask to be dropped off at the convent. The Hotel Malecón is across the road. Tel: 671-4662/2725. Updated: Apr 11, 2011.

Restaurants

There are a number of restaurants to choose from in Quibdó. If you want to have a true Chocó experience and eat some fish, head to the market, pick out what you want and select one of the stalls to prepare it for you. Otherwise, La Terraza is a good option. Along the riverfront, you can get any type of fresh-squeezed, cheap fruit juices.

The Mercado

Although not an official restaurant, the market is a great place for fresh fish. Here, locals fry up the morning's catch and accompany it with the ubiquitous plantain and rice. Cheap and cheerful, if you are looking for a true Quibdó experience, this is it. Atrato Riverfront, past the cathedral. Updated: Apr 11, 2011.

Pizzería Maestro Pierro

Pizzería Maestro Pierro is Quibdó's first pizzeria. It has decent pizza, some varied pasta dishes and the usual Colombian fare. Cra. 3 and Ca. 31. Updated: Apr 11, 2011.

Rapi-Pollo

Not the healthiest option but a definite possibility for a quick bite to eat, this establishment specializes in chicken. Hunks of fried or roast chicken come with side orders of salted potatoes at reasonable prices. Cra. 4, behind the Banco de la República. Updated: Apr 11, 2011.

La Terraza

Situated on the first floor of a nondescript corner building, La Terraza is an oasis of calm and a definite place to gorge yourself. Offering massive servings of obvious dishes such as fried fish with patacones and rice or the wildly popular and artery-clogging Bandeja Paisa, La Terraza is welcoming and popular with the locals. If you don't fancy a large meal, then come in for a sancocho soup and a cheap Poker beer and mix it up with the fine people of Quibdó. Cra. 4, 24-197. Tel: 671-1940. Updated: Apr 11, 2011.

Nightlife

Bold claims among locals declare Quibdó the party capital of the Chocó, if not of Colombia. There is a small Zona Rosa, along Calle 31 on Carreras 2 and 3, that caters to those who want to dance and drink.

NUQUÍ

 5m   6,300   ☎ 4

Nuquí has some services that cater to tourism, but it is better known as the base for excursions into the surrounding area. Its expansive beachfront looks out into the vast Gulf of Tribuga and is strewn with driftwood.

If you have arranged to spend your time at one of the nearby award-winning eco-lodges, then you'll likely be picked up at the airport on the eastern end of town. After you register with the DAS official and pay the tourist tax ($2.80), a motorboat will take you to your chosen destination.

There are no banks in Nuquí, and electricity is scarce. The town's hotels are in the northern sector, a five-minute walk from the airport. Aside from these, Nuquí itself offers little to tourists. It is the

PACIFIC COAST

PACIFIC COAST

surroundings that most people have come here for: to explore the mangroves in Coquí, the hot springs at Termales, the surf at Cabo Corrientes, and the waterfalls and wonder of the Utría National Park. Updated: Jul 21, 2011.

History
Located 120 kilometers (75 mi) from the capital of Chocó, Nuquí was established as a town in 1917 by Juanito Castro. The area was historically used by hunter-gatherers and Embera Indians. Now it is populated by a few paisas from Medellín who are cashing in on the tourist industry, and descendants of African slaves. Updated: Apr 22, 2009.

When to Go
Nuquí is a year-round destination. However, to catch the real flavor of the Chocó and the natural sights, it's best to there for the whale-watching season. It will most likely rain during your time in Nuquí, but it is unlikely you will ever get cold, since the average year-round temperature is 28°C (82°F).

Getting To and Away
Unless you have arranged for a trip on a cargo boat from Buenaventura in the south, the only way of getting here is to fly in from Medellin, Pereira or Quibdó. From Medellín, Aexpa and Satena have flights directly to Nuquí, which leave on Mondays, Wednesdays, Fridays and Sundays. Both airlines also have flights from Bahía Solano and Quibdó. In addition, Aexpa covers the route from Pereira to Nuquí.

Boats come into Nuquí, bringing supplies from Buenaventura. If you are an adventurer, try buying a seat in a fisherman's vessel coming or going from El Valle or Bahía Solano. This journey is not made frequently, though, due to shortages of gasoline. Updated: Jul 21, 2011.

Safety
Nuquí is a safe town and the surrounding areas are unaffected by the conflict. Leave your worries behind; nearly all you need to think about is avoiding suburns and riptides. Updated: Aug 16, 2011.

Services
There are no banks or ATMs in Nuquí. Come prepared with plenty of cash. The main lodges maintain radio contact with Medellín. However, the phone lines and electricity are often down, and there is no Internet. If necessary, you can make calls from rented cell phones in Nuquí.

SHOPPING
Next to the airport, there are some decent shops selling goods created by Embera Indians, including paddles and woven baskets. Be sure to stock up on anything you may need before leaving major cities. Updated: Nov 16, 2007.

Things to See and Do
Activities around Nuquí mostly revolve around the outdoors, whether it be hiking, kayaking, surfing, wildlife watching or relaxing in hot springs.

Guachalito and the beaches to the south of Nuquí are beautiful; take a boat from town and sun-bathe the afternoon away. Check out Coquí's amazing mangroves, which are situated near an indigenous village. Visit the hot springs of Termales town, sure to be a relaxing escape. At Cabo Corrientes, surf in the company of turtles, lobsters and abundant species of fish. Alternatively, hike through Parque Nacional Natural Ensenada de Utría, a stunning natural reserve located to the north of Nuquí. If you are in the area between late July and October, marvel at the annual migration of the humpback whales as they swim south with their young. Updated: Jul 21, 2011.

Water Activities
Nuquí offers many delights to the adventurous traveler with an eye on adrenalin-packed watersports. Each hotel that lines the rugged and dramatic coast near to the town of Nuquí can provide you with a kayak with which to hopefully view whales and explore the rocky promontories between each bay. If kayaking is not your thing, you can rent surf boards and hire guides to tow you out to areas of good surf near to Cabo Corrientes. Should you want to go below the ocean surface, diving and snorkelling excursions can also be arranged, giving visitors the chance of spotting large groups of green turtles. Check all equipment before heading out and make sure you are familiar with the tidal movements in the area. Do not attempt to touch the wildlife. Updated: Apr 11, 2010.

Lodging
The visitor is spoiled with choices in the environs of Nuquí. There are a couple of good options in that town itself that can organize tours and offer half-board packages, but it is beyond the town's limits that you reach paradise. Eco-lodges such as the Morromico, Pijiba and Piedra Piedra are not cheap, but all thoughts of cost are quickly banished when you reach their

lush settings. Private cabañas stocked with everything you might need are complemented by delicious full-board catering. Updated: Jul 21, 2010.

Iraka del Mar Eco-Hotel

(ROOMS: $35-50) The brightly painted Iraka del Mar Eco-Hotel is the best hotel in the town of Nuquí itself (surrounding ecolodes are fancier). The hotel welcomes guests with 12 inviting cabins, all equipped with private bathrooms and decks with hammocks. The staff can arrange tours and transport to other parts of the Chocó, including trips to the thermal springs and to Utría park, and whale-watching tours. Since this hotel relies on package tours from Medellín, the deals include two meals a day. Just before the military football field and in front of the Palmas del Pacífico Hotel. Tel: 683-6016, E-mail: info@nuqui.com. Updated: May 18, 2009.

Piedra Piedra !

(ROOMS: $85-119 per person) Perched atop a rocky bluff that looks out onto the Pacific Ocean, Piedra Piedra has a stunning location. With a capacity for 17 people in its four rooms, the owners at Piedra Piedra are insistent on keeping their operation small to safeguard the natural beauty of the area. Available tours include scuba diving and kayaking. However, if you fancy just lying around, there's also a tanning deck. All meals are included in the price. Prices rise during high season. Camping is also possible ($20 per person). From Nuquí, you should be met by your boat driver and taken 40 minutes south. Otherwise, you'll need to wait for the collectivo boat to leave. Cel: 315-510-8216, E-mail: info@piedrapiedra.com, URL: www.piedrapiedra.com. Updated: Jul 21, 2011.

V!VA ONLINE REVIEW
PIEDRA PIEDRA

This is paradise...

June 30, 2008

Palmas del Pacífico

(ROOMS: $93) The Palmas del Pacífico is a block behind the other accommodation choices in Nuquí. The cabañas are comfortable yet dated, and guests enjoy the sea breeze from the terraces. As with most hotels in the region, the Palmas del Pacífico relies on tourists coming from Medellín on package trips. It includes two meals in the price. Walk toward the beach and turn right on the second-to-last block. Palmas is just before the military football field and one block back from the Iraka del Mar Eco-Hotel. Tel: 683-6010/6127, E-mail: bea_104@hotmail.com. Updated: Sep 05, 2011.

El Cantil

(ROOMS: $275-354) El Cantil is located right next door to the Pijiba Lodge. The lodge's seven cabins each sleep up to six people. Rooms are self-contained, independent units, spread evenly apart on the hillside, ensuring that each has a sea view and a bit of privacy. All deals include three meals and transportation from Nuquí to the lodge. El Cantil has surfboards and kayaks, and offers scuba diving excursions. Two-night minimum. Prices rise during high season. It is 40 minutes down the coast from Nuquí. Tel: 252-0707/352-0729, E-mail: elcantil@elcantil.com, URL: www.elcantil.com. Updated: Apr 11, 2011.

V!VA ONLINE REVIEW
EL CANTIL

This is a great nature lodge. The service and seafood were great!

August 04, 2009

Morromico

(ROOMS: $102 per person) With four rooms that sleep a maximum of 12 people in total, Morromico Hotel is definitely a quiet place to kick back and enjoy what Chocó has to offer. The emphasis is on harmony—with nature, with one another and with the other guests. Ample communal areas for relaxing means you will make friends quickly. All meals are included. Minimum of three-night stay. Tel: 312-735-6321, E-mail: playa@morromico.com, URL: www.morromico.com. Updated: July 11, 2011.

Pijiba Lodge

(ROOMS: $125-166 per person) Pijiba Lodge is hands down the most environmentally friendly lodge on this stretch of coast. In fact, it won an award from Conservation International. The lodge's three cabañas are each split into two rooms, and there is some overflow accommodation. The maximum occupancy in the lodge is 18. Each room has a private bathroom and comes equipped with mosquito nets and candles. All meals are included in the price, as are various excursions. Pre-booked packages (3-night minimum) to the Pijiba Lodge include airport pick-up and boat ride. If you do not have reservations, then catch a colectivo boat south. Tel: 474-5221, E- mail: gonzatrujillo@une.net.co, URL: www.pijibalodge.com. Updated: Jul 21, 2011.

Restaurants

Nuquí has a few basic restaurants specializing in fish dishes. Near the airport, there are places that offer cheap fish empanadas and arepas. Most likely, wherever you stay will provide you with meals.

Nightlife

There are discos in Nuquí, albeit very basic ones, including one that offers a striptease show at an entry cost of $2.50. For something more relaxing, kick back on someone's front porch with a beer. Updated: Nov 15, 2007.

AROUND NUQUÍ

PARQUE NACIONAL NATURAL ENSENADA DE UTRÍA

(ADMISSION: $19.50 foreigners, $7.50 nationals, $4 children) Located in the state of Chocó, Parque Nacional Natural Ensenada de Utría covers an area of almost 545 square kilometers (210 sq mi), with topographical features such as the Utría Fjord and the Baudó Hills that border onto the town of El Valle. The year-round temperature hovers around 28°C (82°F), and due to the mists off the hills and the fact that the area has one of the highest rainfalls in the world, it is humid.

The park consists of vast swaths of rainforest—home to the increasingly rare Chocó Tinamou bird—as well as tangles of mangrove swamps, coral reefs and 17,401 hectares (43,000 ac) of Pacific coastline. Marine fauna in the area is very diverse, including 105 species of crustaceans and several species of whales, among them the famous humpback whales. Utría has two diving sites: Punta Diego and Punta Esperanza, as well as two beaches: Playa Cocalito and Playa Blanca. In addition, there are two Indian reserves in the area. Overall, the entire park displays the diversity of what the Chocó has to offer.

Mano Cambiada (Tel: 316-822-6157/311-872-7887/313-400-5094, URL: www.nuquipacifico.com), a community

organization, handles the park's lodging and food services. You can spend a night in one of its cabañas, which can collectively sleep 31 people, or grab a bite to eat at its restaurant called Yubarta. Mano Cambiada also organizes tours to Utría, which include accommodation, three meals a day, activities, and transport from Nuquí or Bahía Solano to the park, and vice versa.

If you are going to the park without booking a tour, you can reach Utría by boat or through a combination of 4x4 and hiking. Boats leave from Buenaventura (8 hr), Bahía Solano (1.5 hr), Nuquí (1 hr) or El Valle (30 min). Alternatively, you can take a jeep from Bahía Solano to El Valle (40 min) and walk the trail (9.46 km/5.88 mi; 3 hr) to the park.

The other land trail in Utría, called Cocalito, is about 990 meters (3,248 ft) long, and takes approximately 50 minutes to hike. On the way, you can see frogs, insects, snakes, birds and other wildlife, while passing mangroves, beaches and estuaries. Utría also has an underwater path (1.1 km/0.68 mi; 50 min), where you can appreciate coral reefs, turtles, eels and lots of different species of fish.

Bring adequate water with you and stay hydrated in the heat. If in any doubt at all, contract a local guide and be sure that the park authorities know you are in the area. Updated: Jul 25, 2011.

EL VALLE

 5m 1,000   4

Take the only road south from Bahía Solano for about 20 kilometers (12.4 mi) and you'll reach El Valle. Contrary to what its name would suggest, the town is distinctly un-valley like. El Valle is gradually stepping out of the shadow of its larger neighbor to the north, Bahía Solano, and El Almejal Nature Reserve is helping it become a destination in its own right.

For now, the town consists of two roads and a pathway to Playa Almejal. There has been a massive construction push along this beach, which looks like it could have some positive effects in this area.

Electricity cuts and communication problems are the norm. If you desperately need medical attention, or just want to run an errand, you must head north to Bahía Sola-no. When the weather is at its worst, provisions in El Valle become scarce. During one recent October, torrential rain caused several places to run out of beer!

Soak in everything, as little as that might be, that El Valle has to offer. The town's skyline displays the spurs of the Baudo mountainous region and a variety of species of migrating birds. El Valle is also great for whale-watching trips. Hop on a launch from the expansive stretch of beach, which runs south from the town into the Utría National Park, and is populated by lazy dogs and coconut harvesters. Updated: Apr 11, 2011.

History

El Valle's history is one defined by the river and its exit into the Pacific Ocean. El Valle is inhabited by Embera Indians, who survive on small-scale hunting and fishing and are descendants of African slaves brought in during the Spanish rule.

When to Go

Come for whale-watching season to enjoy one of El Valle's biggest draws. Otherwise, the sport fishing tournaments in June and July are a sight to see. The best time for a trip to the turtle conservation project is in September, when the hatchlings emerge. Updated: Jul 22, 2011.

Getting To and Away

Unless you arrive to El Valle by sea, you must first fly into Bahía Solano. It is about an hour flight from Medellín, Pereira or Cali. From the airport, it should be easy enough to hire a jeep or chiva for the hour-long journey. Be warned: during the wetter seasons, parts of the road are impassable. When rivers burst their banks, the mud on the road can be very deep. Authorities have been attempting to pave the route. Updated: Jul 22, 2011.

Safety

El Valle is generally safe, though usual precautions do apply. People are friendly and willing to help, should you require assistance. Updated: Feb 18, 2008.

Things to See and Do

Stroll to the stunning beaches of Cuevita and El Almejal for some sun and fun. Take a canoe trip through the mangroves of the Tundo River or visit the waterfalls by Playa Larga, El Tigre, Chado River and Juna River. There are plenty of ecological tours into the nearby Utría National Park as well. Updated: Feb 12, 2008.

Playa El Almejal

One of Colombia's most spectacular beaches is El Almejal. The beach stretches two kilometers (1.2 mi) and ends dramatically as the ocean's fury makes a meal of the surrounding rocks. Here, you have nature in all its glory, along with the opportunity to surf, swim or just relax in the shallow waters.

El Almejal may also be a good indication of future development. In recent years, diggers and trucks have trundled along the beach collecting rocks and sand for nearby resorts. Sadly, that which is most precious to El Almejal—its tranquility—may be lost in the coming years. Visit now before the hordes discover one of Colombia's best-kept secrets! Walk a few of kilometers north from the town; you can't miss El Almejal. Out of season, the beach is deserted and many of the guesthouses are closed. Updated: Apr 11, 2011.

Lodging

There are few tourist accommodation options in the actual town of El Valle. Sleeping choices are north of town along the fringes of Playa El Almejal. Here, there is a massive drive to increase tourism. Away from the construction work, there are some pleasant eco-lodges. Hostels haven't really been established yet, due to a lack of tourist interest in the area. However, this may change as the town develops a larger tourism infrastructure. Updated: Jul 21, 2010.

The Humpback Turtle !

(BEDS: $5.60-33.50) Budget travelers have a place to stay, now at Playa Almejal. The Humpback Turtle, a community-run eco-lodge, has rustic, thatched cabañas made of guadua (giant bamboo) and wood. Whether swaying in a hammock or sharing a dorm room with other backpackers, you can chill in this corner of Colombia's Chocó. For a bit more money, you can have a private room with a sea view. The hostel's bar grooves with reggae and tasty native cocktails. The restaurant serves delicious fish, seafood and regionally specialties, with ingredients from its own organic garden. The Humpback Turtle offers a sustainable, eco-friendly alternative at very comfortable prices. Cel: 312-756-3439, E-mail: thehumpbackturtle@gmail.com. Updated: Nov 01, 2011.

Hotel Valle

(ROOMS: $24-28 per person) The Hotel Valle offers a roof over the traveler's head, some food and little more. Double rooms are cramped, with sheets that don't fully cover the mattresses. Towels are provided, and rooms are available with private bathrooms. There are two pleasant terraces on the second level. The ají sauce prepared by the owner, Lorena, is only for those with a high chili tolerance! If arriving from the south, cross the long bridge from the agricultural college and follow the road. Otherwise, ask for directions to the main crossroads. Tel: 682-7907, Cel: 314-612-8970, E-mail: hotelvalle@hotmail.com.Updated: Apr 11, 2011.

Kipara Hotel

(ROOMS: $40-50) An attractive swimming pool and a pleasant location near the stunning El Almejal beach make the Kipara Hotel a choice escape for people from Medellín. A restaurant and bar are also on-site, though the family-run Kipara is no luxury resort. Tel: 682-7909, Cel: 311-634-4428/310-849-7585, E-mail: hotel_kipara@hotmail.com, URL: www.hotelkipara.com. Updated: Apr 11, 2011.

El Almejal Lodge

(ROOMS: $100 and up) This lodge is a destination all on its own. It offers all-inclusive per-person packages for a minimum of three nights and a maximum of seven. The sustainable eco-lodge features hammocks surrounded by palm trees, 12 open-air lodges (each with its own bathroom), butterfly gardens and hiking paths. The restaurant uses herbs and vegetables grown on-site in its worm-fed garden. Also, El Almejal runs a sea turtle conservation program (Proyecto Golfina: www.almejal.com.co/proyectogolfina). Fly into Bahía Solano, then take a jeep to El Valle and down the road to the lodge. Tel: 230-6060, Cel: 320-686-7177/674-6023, E-mail: info@almejal.com.co, URL: www.almejal.com.co. Updated: Apr 11, 2011.

Restaurants

Most of the lodges and hotels are package deals that include meals. Most likely, you will end up eating where you stay. Food is basic, but enough to stick to your ribs and keep you satiated. Expect fish preceded by fish soup. There are few options in town. The restaurant at the Hotel Valle serves roast chicken and also doubles as a bakery.

Nightlife

Nightlife in the area is next to non-existent. Your best bet is to settle down for a few beers with the locals. However, the town has been known to run out of beers when the roads are closed and supplies can't get through. Updated: Feb 12, 2008.

BAHÍA SOLANO

 5m   10,000   ☎ 4

Bahía Solano is poised to take advantage of its location to become the Pacific Coast's major tourist destination. The town, protected by a vast bay, is descended upon by hundreds of tourists during the whale-watching and sport-fishing seasons. Beyond these times, however, you can have the city to yourself.

The town itself is similar to others along the Pacific Coast, as tourism is kept separate from the daily life of the locals. All hotels in Bahía Solano are located in the southern end of the town. Use the massive Hotel Balboa Plaza as a reference point and it is highly unlikely that you'll get lost. There are just a few restaurants and places to stay, so a great deal of vacationers head to the next beach along the coast, Huina. The polite and captivating people of Bahía Solano dedicate themselves to various industries: fishing, cattle, agriculture, tourism and the more sinister industry of cocaine. The DAS office and military have a significant presence here. Do not, under any circumstances, attempt to photograph military installations or involve yourself in any way in the drug trade. Updated: Apr 11, 2011.

History

Founded in 1935, the original name of Bahía Solano was Puerto Mutis, but over time, this name fell by the wayside. As with the rest of the Pacific Coast, the original settlers were the Embera Indians whose territory reaches north into Panama. Today, the majority of the population is a mix of descendants of African slaves and people who moved from Medellín about 50 years ago. Those from Medellín came expecting Bahía Solano to explode on the tourist circuit, because at the time, there were plans to build the Pan-American highway through this area. The plans changed and the highway's route has effectively cut Bahía Solano adrift. Both guerillas and Colombia's armed forces covet Bahía Solano for its strategic geographic location. Updated: Feb 08, 2008.

When to Go

Bahía Solano has the typical chocano climate, so expect heat and rain. Of course, Bahía also a big whale-watching destination, so try to plan your trip around whale-watching season if you'd like to participate. Updated: Jul 25, 2011.

The Cocaine Industry in Bahía Solano

Bahía Solano's pivotal location in the transportation of narcotics has made local involvement inevitable. Although there is no obvious consumption of the product in Bahía Solano, the industry, made lucrative by the U.S. and Europe, certainly makes waves here.

In recent years, fishermen no longer fish as much for the traditional catch, but instead for 25-kilogram parcels of cocaine thrown overboard from drug boats on their way north, under threat of capture by the Colombian authorities. A fisherman stands to gain $25,000 by collecting the parcel, hiding it on a secluded beach, informing a buyer and essentially selling it back to its owner. The profit margins are so great that neither party is particularly upset.

One strange side-effect of the cocaine industry is that Bahía Solano—with an oceanfront abundant in fish—is often left without fish to buy. Restaurants are void of fish to prepare. The supply aircrafts from Medellín stop making trips to the area since they make the return route without fish to sell. Then the vicious circle continues...

Getting To and Away

Unless you arrive by cargo boat from Buenaventura or hire a boat from El Valle or Nuquí, the only other way to get to Bahía is by plane. There are frequent flights with Satena and Aexpa to Medellín, and connecting flights can be picked up from there.

The only road in this stretch of the Colombian Pacific connects Bahía Solano to El Valle. Large portions of the road are unpaved, making delays inevitable. Four-by-fours make the 20-kilometer journey in the morning for $5 per person. Updated: Feb 08, 2008.

Safety

The military presence is strong in Bahía Solano. Any suspicious activities are reported and recorded. Since the conflict is an issue to the north of Bahía Solano, the military checks each hotel and hostel every day to receive updates on guests. Hotel owners are expected to attend security update briefings at least once every fortnight. If you plan on spending any time in Bahía Solano, or are traveling in the region, it is recommended you register with the DAS office. Registered travelers will receive updates about security issues in the area. Updated: Mar 10, 2008.

Services

There is one bank in Bahía Solano and it accepts Visa. It is located at the main crossroads, opposite the **DAS office** (on the waterfront. Tel: 682-6984, Cel: 313-745-8611). Only some cell phone companies have coverage here. Many kiosks and individuals will rent cell phones that charge by the minute. There is a Telecom office opposite the Hotel Bahía with Internet access. However, Bahía Solano's frequent energy shortages mean the connection is not always functioning. Get all your vaccinations before going. There is a clinic in Bahía Solano, but for any emergencies, go to Medellín. Updated: Mar 10, 2008.

Things to See and Do

Visit the deserted beaches of Huina to the south and Mecana to the north. These are great places for diving and observing marine life. Take a fishing trip off the coast if you are interested in snaring some bluefin tuna. Hike to the waterfalls, just past the military checkpoints along the coast, which explode with fresh water. Dive to the bottom of the sea to see the wreck of the Sebastián de Belalcázar. During May and September, migrating humpback whales are so abundant that they are easily visible from the shore. Hikes up to the statue of the Virgin offer inspirational views of the city and the bay. For more trip or activity ideas, contact Enrique at the Hotel Rocas de Cabo Marzo. Updated: Feb 11, 2008.

Diving

Almost 34 meters (110 ft) below the sea, the wreck of the former Colombian Navy vessel, the Sebastián de Belalcázar, is a mystical attraction. The site is out of reach to open-water divers, but remains an enticing destination for more advanced divers. The ship, scuttled to provide a haven for marine life, has an incredibly interesting history. Originally a U.S. Navy boat that survived Pearl Harbor, it was decommissioned by the U.S., sold to Colombia and named after a Spanish conquistador. At that time, the vessel and crew were responsible for intercepting the largest shipment of weapons destined for the M19 guerrilla group.

PACIFIC COAST

Today, experienced divers glide over the ship's hull, looking into the control room and spotting massive snappers, groupers and the occasional shark. For very experienced divers, there are possibilities of exploring within if the conditions are appropriate. For more information on diving, contact **Rodrigo Fajardo** at the Posada del Mar (Tel: 682-7415, E-mail: rfajardo@bis.com.co); he runs all diving trips from Bahía Solano. Updated: Apr 11, 2011.

Sport Fishing

Every June and July, fishing enthusiasts descend onto the murky Pacific waters in Bahía Solano, Cupica and Tribuga for catch-and-release tournaments. The reward isn't really the money as much as the bragging rights that come with snagging a marlin. People also haul in tuna, barracuda and sharks. Remember that these types of trips will be costly, given the nature of the sport. Plus, gasoline needs to be stockpiled. Contact expert fisherman **Enrique García Reyes** (Tel: 682-7525, Cel: 313-681-4001/312-895-8682, E-mail: enriquerestrepo@telecom.com.co) for more information. Updated: Apr 11, 2011.

Lodging

There are a variety of accommodations in Bahía Solano. While some are truly opulent, others clearly rent by the hour. During high season, you'll want to book a room in advance, especially on the longer holiday weekends when the town is overrun by Colombian vacationers. Updated: Mar 21, 2011.

Posada del Mar

(ROOMS: $10-15) Previously known as Hostal del Mar, Posada del Mar is run by the town's dive center. This comfortable and friendly budget hostel has four cabañas with rooms that can accommodate one to six people. It caters to the backpacking and diving crowd. The diving school and hostel are owned by Rodrigo, who has over 30 years of diving experience and who has lived in Bahía Solano for many years. Two blocks south of Hotel Balboa Plaza, next to the Satena office. Cel: 313-746-0680, E-mail: posadadelmarbahiasolano@yahoo.es. Updated: Feb 11, 2011.

Hotel Bahía

(ROOMS: $14-28) This 15-room hotel is the better of the two facing buildings on the so-called Calle de Comercio. Rooms are unimpressive, but are clean and come with private bathroom. The hotel has a decent restaurant on the ground floor and a small kiosk for making phone calls. Ask any taxi driver from the airport and he'll have you there within 15 minutes. Otherwise, just look for the towering Hotel Balboa Plaza, head for that and the Hotel Bahía is across the way. Ca. 3, 2-34, Tel: 682-7047/7048. Updated: Apr 11, 2011.

Hotel Balboa Plaza

(ROOMS: $35-153) In the hands of its original owner and creator, Pablo Escobar, this hotel must have been opulent. Now its glory has faded considerably and the external features are desperately in need of some love and affection. Torn and stained awnings flutter in tatters over windows, the garden—while still a good place to have a cold beer—has seen better days, and the mural beside the pool is weathering into nothingness. One can see the grandeur that was once here in the high-gated entrance. Now, people slink in through a side entrance. The restaurant is passable, and several of the rooms have been renovated. Tel: 682-7075, Fax: 682-7401, E-mail: hotelbalboap@telecom.com.co. Updated: Apr 11, 2011.

El Refugio de Mr. Jerry

(ROOMS: $50-80) A 10-minute boat ride around the bay from Bahía Solano to Huina reveals a further beach that has more accommodations available, one of these being Mr. Jerry's. Needing some superficial work, Mr. Jerry's can sleep 50 people comfortably and works on the basis of people buying packages including all three meals and flights beforehand. If you have arranged a package tour, you will be met at the airport and taken to the oceanfront in Bahía Solano and then transferred to Huina. If not, you'll need to contract a fisherman to get you there. Tel: 682-7233, E-mail: mrjerrybahiasolano@telesat.com.co. Updated: Apr 22, 2009.

Posada Turística Hotel Rocas de Cabo Marzo ⏎

(ROOMS: $60 and up) Owners Nancy and Enrique have lived in Bahía Solano for almost two decades and know everything there is to know about the area. With only five rooms, this hotel feels like a family-run guesthouse. Rooms come with double beds, private bathrooms and mosquito nets. Enrique is a committed sports fisherman and diver, and Nancy, a former nurse with first-aid knowledge, is a phenomenal cook. They make the Posada Turística Rocas de Cabo Marzo the best place to stay in Bahía Solano. They also offer a tour called Ruta Biopacífico, that follows the Pacific coast to Parque Nacional Natural Ensenada de Utría, Guachalito and Termales. Tel: 682-7525/7433,

Cel: 313-681-4001/312-895-8682, E-mail: bahiatebada@hotmail.com, URL: www.posadasturisticasdecolombia.com/posada/rocas-de-cabo-marzo-3. Updated: Apr 11, 2011.

Playa de Oro Lodge

(ROOMS: $81 and up) The Playa de Oro Lodge is a massive construction on Huina beach that caters to package tourists from Medellín. The resort is made up of four blocks, each with eight rooms. All have private bathrooms, fans and a hammock on a private terrace. The package deal includes transportation from the airport in Bahía Solano and a transfer to Huina. Cel: 361-7809, Fax: 285-7333, E-mail: info@hotelesdecostaacosta.com, URL: www.hotelesdecostaacosta.com. Updated: Apr 11, 2011.

Restaurants

The restaurants in Bahía Solano offer the standard fare of the region—fried fish, patacones and rice. Remember, sometimes the fishermen are distracted by the prominent drug industry and restaurants could run low on fresh catch. The majority of restaurants also offer set meals as an alternative.

Las Palmas

The expression "cheap and cheerful" could not apply to a nicer, more pleasant place in Bahía Solano. This restaurant is family run and owned. Las Palmas has set menus for lunch and dinner that cost roughly $4. A dish of fried fish, rice and plantains is preceded by soup. It also stocks cuts of beef and chicken. It is next door to the Hotel Bahía. Updated: Apr 11, 2011.

Oh! Solano Mio

Run by Enrique of the Posada Turística Rocas de Cabo Marzo Hotel, this pizzeria offers far more than simple pizza. Nancy is an excellent cook and can conjure up culinary delights, particularly incredible fish dishes. The atmosphere is familiar and relaxed, and Enrique will certainly want to regale you with some stories of sports fishing or advice on unmissable sights in this region. Posada Turística Las Rocas de Cabo Marzo. Tel: 682-7525, Cel: 313-681-4001/312-895-8682. Updated: May 11, 2009.

Hotel Bahía Restaurant

Offering standard set meals at lunch and dinner, the Hotel Bahía's restaurant is a good budget option. Fish, of course, is the most prevalent dish on the menu, but cuts of pork, beef and chicken are also available. Everything is freshly prepared and accompanied by rice, salad and patacones. Ca. 3, 2-34. Tel: 682-7047. Updated: Mar 10, 2008.

Balboa Plaza Restaurant

One peek inside the hotel tells you all you need to know: this restaurant could be anywhere in the world. The food is standard, but since the number of visitors is low, the establishment does not see fit to replenish dwindling provisions. Sometimes tuna can be the only thing on the menu for multiple nights in a row. Inside the Hotel Balboa Plaza. Tel: 682-7075, E-mail: hotelbalboap@telecom.com.co. Updated: Mar 10, 2008.

Puerto Ventura

Puerto Ventura is one of two fast food restaurants in Bahía Solano. This place does a brisk trade in hamburgers, hot dogs and other ubiquitous fast-food items. It also squeezes an excellent, fresh fruit juice. The juice may seem pricey, but rest assured: it is large and refreshing. Located at the crossroads. Updated: Apr 11, 2011.

Jimmy's

The other fast food restaurant in town, Jimmy's is at the end of the main road past the DAS office. Pizza and hamburgers are the house specialties, and the dining experience is enhanced by a lovely sea view. The place does a roaring trade on weekends and is a fine spot to have a beer while watching the sunset. Updated: Apr 11, 2011.

Nightlife

The discos and bars in Bahía Solano are for the locals. Grab a beer, sit down and you'll make friends. At the crossroads beyond the DAS office, there is typically a small crowd enjoying excessively loud music at any hour of the day. Updated: Feb 11, 2008.

¡¡¡¡¡

PACIFIC COAST

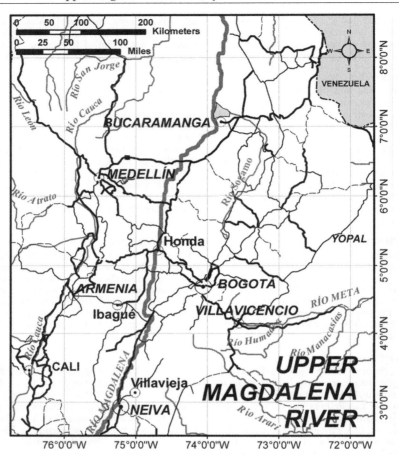

The Upper Magdalena River Valley

If the Magdalena River could speak, it would boast of the countless riches that have been transported on its waters through the years. Shaped by the river, the Upper Magdalena River Valley runs from the lower extremes of the Andes, at the river's source in Huila, to the well-preserved statues of San Agustín. It continues its run through the arid badlands of the Tatacoa Desert and past Nevado del Tolima, a mountain towering 5,200 meters (17,060 ft) over the departmental capital of Ibagué, before encountering the last navigable point from the coast inland, Honda.

Travelers to this area will be pleasantly surprised by the unique offerings in each town. Starting in Honda, known as both "the City of Bridges" and the "Cartagena of the Interior" (thanks to its narrow colonial streets), venture on to Ibagué, Colombia's music capital. Nearby, explore verdant canyons and try to catch a glimpse of a Spectacled Bear. Move south to encounter the archeological wonder of Neiva, which will whet your appetite for the wonders further down the road at San Agustín.

Many of these towns and settlements date back to earlier than 1,000 B.C. So, given their history and the importance of the river as one of Colombia's principal highways, it is no wonder that they have been of major significance in Colombia. Updated: Mar 14, 2008.

Highlights

Visit the magnificent anthropomorphic statues on display in the parks around San Agustín.

Lesser known but well-worth a visit are the badlands of the **Tatacoa Desert** (p. 209), which are perfect for camping.

Lush, sunny valleys and charming towns create a must-experience environment around **Ibagué** (p. 210).

History

The departments of Tolima and Huila, which make up the majority of the Upper Magdalena River Valley, have a fascinating past. This includes advanced pre-Columbian tribes who created the wonders found around San Agustín. The history of the region is full of tales of indigenous royalty martyred by the Spanish. Indigenous tribes flourished until the arrival of the Spanish conquistadors in 1538. Records show how several thriving communities along the Magdalena violently opposed the invaders and made Spanish settlement of this region difficult, to say the least. Eventually Spanish influence grew and local opposition abated. During the Colonial and Republican eras, the Magdalena turned into a major commercial and transit route through Colombia. Honda, in particular, rose to prominence as Colombia's wealth passed through this inland port. Updated: Apr 14, 2008.

When to Go

December to March are the driest months around Upper Magdalena. However, it is in your best interest to keep a rain jacket and umbrella handy throughout the year. Consider timing your trip to coincide with local festivals, such as Honda's Festival de la Subienda in February, or Neiva's Reinado del Bambuco and Ibagué's Folkloric Festival, which both take place in June. Updated: Mar 14, 2008.

Safety

The Upper Magdalena River Valley is generally considered a safe place for traveling. However, Neiva is the gateway to the regions of Caquetá and Putumayo, which are considered the red zone, so there is always a possibility that some violence, normally restricted around Neiva, may spill over. Updated: Mar 14, 2008.

Things to See and Do

Traveling around the Upper Magdalena River Valley is typically an unconventional route, but it is one that will not disappoint. In the same day it is possible to revel in the striking contrasts between the Tatacoa Desert and the rock sculptures in San Agustín. For walkers, hikers, climbers and rafters, the region includes the Combeima Canyon, the Nevado del Tolima and the rapids on the Magdalena. For the non-outdoorsy types, there are plenty of cultural pastimes around, many of which can be found in Ibagué. Those who appreciate good food shouldn't pass up trying a *tamale tolimense* (a regional tamale made with meat, rice, peas and egg wrapped in a banana leaf). Updated: Dec 19, 2007.

Tours

Although tourism is not as popular in the Upper Magdalena River Valley as in other regions of Colombia, some tour operators do exist. Contact the following organizations for more specific details:

Ibagué	Proyectos de Promoción Turística. Tel: 267-8906
Nevado de Tolima	Fundación Yulima. Tel: 261-2902
Tolima (general)	Gobernación de Tolima. Tel: 1-288-2349, E-mail: casatolima@etb. net.co/turismotolima@ gov.co, URL: www. tolima.gov.co
Huila (general)	Secretaría de Cultura y Turismo del Huila. Tel: 874-1198
Tatacoa	Secretaría de Cultura y Turismo Villavieja. Tel: 879-7744 (ext. 110)

Lodging

Accommodation options in the Upper Magdalena River Valley are surprisingly varied and, on the whole, of pretty good quality. Since it has been on the tourist map for a few years, traditional backpacker and traveler haunts are readily available in San Agustín. In Ibagué and Neiva, however, expect cheap hotel options with little character or sense of community. If you decide to visit the Tatacoa Desert, your accommodation options are limited to camping. Updated: Jul 23, 2010.

UPPER MAGDALENA

NEIVA

 442m   331,000 📞 8

Neiva is moving ahead in terms of tourism. A key intermediary city in this part of the country, Neiva has traditionally connected conventional tourist destinations like Popayán and San Agustí n to more off-the-beaten-track places such as Caquetá and Putumayo. But major efforts are being made to make the city itself more aesthetically pleasing, which is drawing tourists.

From the shady Parque Santander in the heart of the city to the Malecón del Río Magdalena at the river's edge, visitors here will find Neiva has increasingly more to offer. And even if the city doesn't capture your fancy, it still makes a perfect base from which to explore the attractions in the surrounding parts of Huila, such as the Tatacoa Desert in the north and Parque Isla on the opposite side of the Magdalena. If you can, be sure to get to Neiva in June for the notoriously riotous festivals that take place here. Updated: May 18, 2009.

History

Prior to the arrival of the Spanish in 1538, a complex and developed indigenous civilization existed around the Huila region. The Augustinian culture reined supreme here between 1,000 B.C. and 1,650 A.D., before fading away—though not without a fight. Famed sites, like those in San Agustín, are what's left of the culture today. Local tribes, like the Pijao, the Andiquie, the Yalcones, the Paeces and the Tamas, all fiercely opposed the conquistadores. They made imperial expansion difficult in this region.

Neiva was first founded in 1539 by Juan de Cabrera, but was subsequently destroyed. The city was founded a second time by Juan Alonso on the present-day site of Villavieja to the north, though this was also destroyed. Finally, in May 1612, Diego de Ospina y Medinilla, chancellor of Nueva Granada, founded "Limpia Concepción del Valle de Neiva," where Neiva has stood ever since. Updated: Feb 27, 2008.

When to Go

Given its relatively low altitude and the fact that it is near the equator, Neiva is always hot, with temperatures continually in the 30s °C (high 80s-90s°F). If you want to partake in Neiva's festival season, May-June is the time to come. Locals celebrate the Birthday of Neiva in May, and both the Festival of Folklore and Señorita Neiva and the Fiesta de San Pedro in June. Updated: Feb 27, 2008.

Getting To and Away

Aeropuerto Benito Sala de Neiva is a five-minute taxi ride from downtown. Buses to Bogotá ($10) with Cootranshuila and Coomotor leave at 1 p.m. and take five hours. Neiva is also a key connection point for buses into the lesser known regions of Caquetá and Putumayo. To get to the Tatacoa desert, take the Coomotor collectivo van at the far end of the terminal to Villavieja ($2.50, 1 hr). Updated: Feb 27, 2008.

Safety

Neiva is generally safe and there really is no feeling of personal danger or aggression toward tourists. However, as recently as January of 2011, three bombs exploded in Neiva, leaving houses damaged and one person injured. The government claims that the FARC was responsible for these attacks. Updated: Jun 30, 2011.

Services

There is a good tourist info booth in the Terminal de Transportes. For further information, contact the **Secretaría de Cultura y Turismo de Huila** (Cra. 5, 21-81. Tel: 875-3042). Around Parque Santander, you will find every bank and ATM you could need. Internet cafés are commonplace throughout the city. **Hospital Universitario Hernando Moncaleano** (Ca. 9, 15-25. Tel: 871-5907) and **Clínica Nueva** (Cra. 4, 9-46. Tel: 871-0998) are reputable medical facilities, should you need medical attention. Updated: Feb 27, 2008.

SHOPPING

Although there are some shopping centers around Neiva, such as **Centro Comercial Metropolitan** (Cra. 5, 6-28) and **Centro Comercial La Decima** (Ca. 4, 5-41), this is not a shopaholic's destination. If you want to pick up some trinkets and souvenirs from the region, head to the Malecón del Río Magdalena, where there are a number of artisan stalls set up. Updated: Apr 13, 2011.

Things to See and Do

From the arid Tatacoa desert in the north to the ecological park, restaurants and nightlife along the Magdalena, Neiva has enough to keep travelers busy. Even if none of these activities   pique your

interest, Neiva is worth coming to in June for the riotous party atmosphere that happens during its festival celebrations. Updated: Jun 29, 2011.

Termales de Rivera

About a half-hour south of Neiva, the Rivera Hot Springs make for a good day trip or overnight excursion, especially for families. The natural hot springs have been made into a water park of sorts, with well-designed warm and cool pools, some of which have slides. There is also a spa, and visitors have the opportunity to go horseback riding and hiking as well. Although it is not frequented by tourists much, this place is very popular with locals. The park is reasonably priced, and there is an on-site hotel and restaurant. Termales de Rivera is open in the afternoons during the week and all day on weekends; it is closed on Mondays. Located just outside the town of Rivera, about 30 kilometers (18.6 mi) south of Neiva. Tel: 838-7147, E-mail: recreacion@comfamiliarhuila.com. Updated: Apr 21, 2008.

Piedra Pintada Aipe

Over six meters (19.7 ft) long and three meters (9.8 ft) high, the Piedra Pintada, in the municipality of Aipe, is a marvel that has survived the ages. Experts believe this was likely a meeting point for commerce and trade, and you can try to make meaning of the marks carved into the rock by both the Paeces and Pijaos tribes. In the immediate vicinity, archeologists have also found burial grounds and ceramic utensils, perhaps proving this to have once been a sizeable community. Updated: Apr 13, 2011.

Lodging

One thing to bear in mind in Neiva is that any establishment listing itself as a "hostel" is actually a place that rents its rooms by the hour and is not a hotel. On the whole, there are decent options in Neiva for those on a budget, such as the Hotel Andino. If money is not a consideration then the Hotel Khalifa is not a bad choice. Rooms will book up fast in June for the festival, so making reservations in advance is recommended. Updated: Jul 21, 2010.

Hotel Andino

(ROOMS: $13-20) Set back from the noisy Calle 9, the Hotel Andino is the budget destination of choice in Neiva. Its 20 rooms all contain a fan, private bathroom, cable TV and telephone. Don't expect luxury here, but you will be in a secure place in the center of town. You can walk to all sites of interest and are very close to all the major banks. Catch a cab in or head to Carrera 5 and find Calle 9 from there. Any resident will be able to point you in the right direction. Ca. 9, 5-82. Tel: 871-7844, Fax: 871-3853. Updated: Apr 13, 2011.

Hotel Geminis

(ROOMS: $20-25) The Hotel Geminis makes the cut, as it is obvious that the proprietors have made significant efforts to clean the place up and present a respectable façade. Don't be mistaken, this hotel caters to the rent-by-the-hour crowd as well as to those who wish to stay several nights. Rooms are accommodating, with all the necessary amenities. The only aspect that will remind you about the hotel's other, less salubrious side is that most rooms have mirrors on the ceiling. The hotel is located in front of the Concha Acustica, near to the Parque Santander. Ca. 7, 8-37. Updated: Apr 13, 2011.

Hotel Casa Pablo

(ROOMS: $24-73) Up the hill out of the hubbub of central Neiva you will find Hotel Casa Pablo. Three stories tall, this hotel has plenty of rooms, ranging from cheaper ones on the ground floor with fans and no air conditioning to more luxurious ones higher up. All rooms have private en-suite bathrooms and cable TV, and the owner is very knowledgeable about things to see and do in and around Neiva. Ca. 5, 12-45. Tel: 872-3100, Fax: 871-2807, E-mail: hotelcasapablo@gmail.com. Updated: Apr 13, 2011.

Hotel Khalifa

(ROOMS: $43-50) A more regal option in Neiva if your budget is up to it, and even more so if you can negotiate the price down by paying in cash, Hotel Khalifa has 48 comfortably equipped rooms. Rooms with fans instead of air conditioning are cheaper. The place is unlikely to be full unless its during a holiday or conference. The prices are higher if you choose to pay with plastic. Cra. 6, 8-76. Tel: 871-2021/2369. Fax: 871-0023. URL: http://hotelkhalifa.byethost9.com. Updated: Apr 13, 2011.

Restaurants

If downing a chilled, freshly blended juice is your vice, then you have come to the right city—Neiva has a vast quantity of fruterías. Along the Magdalena River's main boardwalk, there are a dozen or so options for dining that all more or less offer the same fare, so take your pick. The mayor's office set this area aside to promote tourism and increase nightlife options in Neiva.

Things are pretty low-key during the week, but on weekends, Neiva's nightlife really kicks off along the Magdalena. Open-air bars and clubs all tend to get pretty lively. Otherwise, the Neiva Plaza Hotel on the Parque Santander claims to have the best nightclub in town. It wouldn't be unreasonable to try out a few different options and then decide what you like best. Updated: Feb 27, 2008.

Super Jugos La Ñapa

Super Jugos La Ñapa is nothing to look at but the locals love it. Fruits of all shapes and sizes are blended up here into juices, and you can even enjoy tropical flavors that have no names in the English language for as little as $0.65. Fancy a snack? Sandwiches cost around $1.50. Cra. 5, 12-26. Tel: 871-2251. Updated: Apr 13, 2011.

Brasas del Río

The Brasas del Río is one of the establishments along the Magdalena River. In this pleasant riverside setting, surrounded by abundant greenery and artisan stalls, feast on *huilense parilla* (a local pork specialty) or more familiar fare such as grilled beef, chicken or fish. Prices are reasonable, and the restaurant is a nice place to enjoy a cold beer and people-watch. Malecón del Río Magdalena. Updated: Apr 13, 2011.

Tijuana

Wedged between a Renault dealership on one side and a garage on the other, the proprietors of Tijuana could have chosen a more tranquil spot for their restaurant and bar. Despite this, the adobe-style architecture, Mexican flags and good food make this somewhere to enjoy something different than the usual fare in Neiva. Prices are reasonable and the margaritas are perfect for those who want to cool off from the equatorial heat. Cra. 5, between Ca. 11 and 12. Tel: 871-3526. Updated: Apr 13, 2011.

Frutería y Heladería Alaska

With a juice bar called "Alaska" in the hot region of Neiva, the owners of Frutería y Heladería Alaska are clearly trying to entice customers seeking a cool drink and refuge from the sun. Here the patron is presented with an exhaustive list of fruit juices and some interesting house concoctions. One is "El Boxeador," which has a raw egg mixed in with fruit, and another is "Explosivo," which includes crab! Some may not be to your liking, but the conventional and the exotic—curuba, cebada, chulupa, borojo—are all on offer at low prices. Cra. 6, 8-40. Tel: 871-2475. Updated: Apr 13, 2011.

Huila Café

Located on the second floor of an elegant hall with high ceilings, wooshing fans and ample space, the Huila Café is more than just your average café. Don't be put off by the couples canoodling in private corners; the coffee is excellent and the location is among Neiva's best. If you are hungry, a croissant will set you back $1.50. Ca. 7, 6-59 on the second floor, opposite the post office. Tel: 871-0799. Updated: May 25, 2009.

VILLAVIEJA

 347m 2,000 📞 8

Villavieja is a tiny village close to the Tatacoa Desert. There are no real attractions in the village itself, but it is the jumping-off point to the desert. Near Villavieja is Aipe, which is across the river and on the main highway that runs between Neiva and Bogotá. Be aware that villaviejans don't like residents of Aipe; they believe people from Aipe are thieves. Neither town wants to build a bridge to make transportation easier for each other or visitors to the Tatacoa Desert. Based on the bad blood between these two towns, some say it may be safer to bypass Aipe altogether. That said, it does not feel dangerous. Updated: Feb 06, 2008.

V!VA ONLINE REVIEW
VILLAVIEJA

Villavieja is great if you are looking to slow down and escape from the everyday hassle.

July 9, 2008

Getting To and Away

The easiest way to get to Villavieja is from Neiva (1 hr, $3). Collectivos run hourly from 9 a.m.-6 p.m. The closest town to Villavieja is Aipe, which is located across the river and on the main highway running between Neiva and Bogotá. If you're heading to Villavieja from Ibagué or Bogotá and you prefer not to travel to Neiva and backtrack to Villavieja, you can take any bus to Neiva and get dropped off on the highway in Aipe. Walk through Aipe town and down the hill to the river bank (1.6 km/0.9 mi, 20 min). There is a motored canoe that shuttles people back and forth between Aipe and Villavieja every half hour during the day (15 min, $1). From the drop off point on the other side of the river, it's a short 10-minute walk to Villavieja center. A morning bus to Bogotá (5 hr, $12) leaves Villavieja at 5 a.m. Updated: Aug 13, 2011.

Tours

You can easily contract a guide to the Tatcoa desert as you enter the town of Villavieja. To hire one in advance, contact the Alcaldía at 8-879-7744 (ext 110). Updated: Feb 27, 2008.

Chopo Taxi

Chopo, a most enthusiastic local villaviejan, is more than happy to serve as your local guide and taxi driver during your visit to the Tatacoa Desert and around. He knows the best places to go and best times to visit the different places in the desert. His family also owns a small store in Villavieja. He charges $1 for a ride around town, $5 to the observatory and $20 for a full five-hour excursion in the desert. Cel: 313-865-8710. E-mail: chopotaxi@hotmail.com, URL: www.chopotaxi.com. Updated: Apr 13, 2011.

Lodging
Hospedaje La Casona

(BEDS: $8-12) Pretty much the only official place to stay in Villavieja, La Casona has three enormous dorm rooms, one of which can sleep more than 10 people. Its huge backyard serves as the restaurant. There is even an empty, dry swimming pool that might or might not be functioning someday. Since there are so few visitors to Villavieja, reserving a room in this one hotel in town is not necessary right now, but this might change once word spreads more. Next to the church on the main square. Updated: Apr 13, 2011.

Nightlife
El Tizón

If you're looking for some good, old-fashioned live music, dancing and fun, El Tizón has got just that. This place gets packed in the evenings and stays open until the folk decide to ride their horses (or motorcycles) home, which is often when the sun rises the next morning. The vallenatos and rancheras music—complete with accordion, acoustic guitar, drumming and twangy vocals—booms from this happening nightspot at the edge of town. There is a five-piece live band that plays on the weekends. Updated: May 28, 2008.

AROUND VILLAVIEJA
DESIERTO DE LA TATACOA!

Right up in the northern part of the department of Huila is a little-known and little-visited attraction, the Tatacoa Desert. However, it should really be on every traveler's list of things to do in Colombia and rates highly with all those who do manage to get out to the 330 square kilometers (127 sq mi) of red and gray stained rock. In addition to incredible scenery, with towering cacti and interesting rock formations, the Tatacoa Desert is arguably a huge paleontological cemetery. Another reason to come here is that you can camp out for free under the stars. The desert can be accessed from Villavieja (approx 40 min from Neiva). From Neiva, look for the Coomotor colectivo vans, which leave when full from the far end of the bus terminal. Take plenty of water and sunblock. Updated: Apr 13, 2011.

Things to See and Do

Piscina Orfanda
(ADMISSION: $3 adults, $2 children) Not quite an oasis but certainly a perfect location for a pool, Piscina Orfanda is a private pool about 10 kilometers (6.2 mi) into the desert. It provides visitors with perfect freshwater relaxation amid picturesque gray sand and green cacti. The water comes from a natural spring just up the hill from the pool. It's crystal clear and just the right temperature. The pool is on the small side; you can't swim laps. It is a popular spot for locals on the weekend, so head there early (before 10 a.m.) if you want it all to yourself. Updated: Apr 13, 2011.

Lodging

El Observatorio
(BEDS: $6-10) The observatory at the entrance of the Tatacoa Desert isn't just for watching the sunset, the moon rise and the world turn. Owners Pisco and Alberto also provide a variety of accommodations for sleeping under the stars in the desert. They hang hammocks on the front porch, rent tents and have two cabañas with private bathrooms. The idea here is to really get the desert experience from dusk 'til dawn. There are mosquitoes and other invisible biting bugs at night, so bring repellent or a net. No need to call ahead for reservations. Hire a local taxi (a small tri-wheel tuk tuk) to take you to the desert along the paved road from Villavieja. The observatory will be on the left just before the road becomes unpaved. Updated: Apr 13, 2011.

Estadero Sol de Veran de Soña Lilia
(BEDS: $12) Estadero Sol de Veran de Soña Lilia is located in the Tatotoca Desert, 250 meters (820 ft) from the observatory. The posada has beds and hammocks

on offer, as well as a camping area. Besides having an on-site restaurant, it also sells homemade cactus sweets. Cel: 313-311-8828/317-0896. Updated: Feb 15, 2011.

PARQUE NACIONAL NATURAL NEVADO DEL HUILA

The Parque Nacional Natural Nevado del Huila attracts thousands of trekkers, hikers and climbers each year. If you are coming here to participate, it is recommended to hire a guide and to bring warm hiking clothes. Birdwatchers might find this park especially interesting, since it is home to birds like the Golden Eagle, Andean Condor, tanagers and hummingbirds. Founded in 1977, this 158,000-hectare park (390,426 ac) is located close to the Magdalena River and is divided between the Colombian departments of Huila, Tolima and Cauca.

The park features indigenous ruins, Laguna Paez, and an area of volcanic wasteland that includes Colombia's highest and not-so-dormant volcano. The snow-capped Nevado del Huila stands at 5,364 meters (17,602 ft) and is 241 kilometers (150 mi) southwest of Bogotá. Dormant for more than 400 years, the volcano woke up in 2007 and has erupted numerous times since then. According to the Smithsonian Institution's Global Volcanism Program, the eruptions have caused damaging mudslides and thousands of residents were evacuated from their homes. Check with government agencies and/or the Smithsonian before traveling to this area. Camping is the only sleeping option inside the park. Daily 8 a.m.-4 p.m. Updated: Jun 30, 2011.

Note: The closest hospital to Parque Nacional Natural Nevado del Huila is in Neiva. Therefore, make sure to be bring along your own first aid kit when going hiking, and take necessary precautions against altitude sickness and frostbite.

IBAGUÉ

 1,285m 440,000 8

Ibagué resembles Bucaramanga but is smaller. The city's recent growth reflects its growing importance, as multinational chain stores have sprung up on the city's edge. As if trapped in a breathless valley, temperatures average 24°C (75°F), keeping Ibagué a pleasant year-round destination. As the capital of the Tolima department, it also plays an important role in the cultural development of the country by hosting the Colombian Festival of Folklore. For more than 30 years, the tolimenses have been blending music, dance and gastronomy beneath the towering Nevado del Tolima and welcoming all to participate. Updated: May 27, 2009.

History

Andrés López de Galarza founded Ibagué— originally called Villa de San Bonifacio de Ibagué del Valle de las Lanzas—in 1550 on the current-day site of Cajamarca. A year later, it was moved to escape the spears and continuing attacks of the Pijao Indians. The town grew steadily and was drawn into the spotlight for a brief spell as the capital of Nueva Granada after a coup d'etat in 1854. Updated: Feb 27, 2008.

When to Go

Due to the valley it resides in, the temperature in Ibagué is frequently in the mid 20s°C (high 60s-low 80s°F), making the city a pleasant destination year round. A few festivals take place here, including the National Duets Competition in March, as well as the Colombian Festival of Folklore and the Fiestas de San Pablo in June. Updated: Jun 30, 2011.

Getting To and Away

Ibagué's airport, **Aeropuerto Perales de Ibagué** (Tel: 267-5662/268-5600), is located on the outskirts of town. The airport only receives and sends off domestic flights serviced by Aires or Avianca airlines. The bus station, **Terminal de Transporte de Ibagué** (Cra. 2, 20-86. Tel: 261-8122), has bus connections all over Colombia. Over 25 different bus companies collectively offer services to major cities such as Bogotá, Medellín, Cali and Pasto and to smaller regional destinations like Neiva and Honda. Updated: Feb 27, 2008.

Safety

Exercise caution when walking in the city center around Carrera 1, as there are several abandoned areas. The tourist office in the bus station does not recommend walking from the bus terminal to the town center, since this will lead you through an abandoned park frequented by undesirables. Besides keeping these tips in mind, Ibagué is generally is safe place to visit. Updated: Sep 26, 2008.

Services

There is a helpful tourism information booth in the bus terminal. For further details, contact the **Cámara de Comercio** (Tel: 263-1784). Two of Ibagué's medical facilities are: **Hospital Federico Lleras Acosta** (Ca. 33, 4A-50. Tel: 264-0888) and **Clínica Tolima** (Cra. 1, 12-22. Tel: 261-0367). Updated: Feb 27, 2008.

SHOPPING

The city is well known for its music, and there are several music shops downtown, just off Carrera 3. Since Ibagué is a large city, it also has a few good shopping centers, such as **Centro Comercial Multicentro** (Av. El Jordan, Ca. 64 Centro), **Comercial La Quinta** (Cra. 5, 29-32) and **Centro Comercial Combeim** (Cra. 3, 12-54). Updated: Feb 27, 2008.

Things to See and Do

As Colombia's "Musical City," Ibagué places a strong emphasis on the arts. This can be observed in the bars and restaurants downtown as well as at the events at Teatro Tolima. In addition to the city's art and culture, the valley surrounding Ibagué provides outdoor pursuits, especially in the Combeima Canyon. Experienced hikers may also attempt to conquer the Nevado del Tolima peak. Updated: Mar 04, 2008.

Teatro Tolima

Ibagué's arts scene is most apparent at the Teatro Tolima. Built in 1915 and then later renovated and constructed in an imposing Art Deco style, the theater can house up to 1,000 people. It shows movies, hosts concerts, and presents dance, music and theater performances. Check the website for a list of events. Cra. 3, 11-76. Tel: 261-1608, Fax: 261-0328, E-mail: info@teatrotolima.com, URL: www.teatrotolima.com. Updated: Jun 30, 2011.

Combeima Canyon !

The Combeima Canyon is the gateway to the Nevado del Tolima and a favorite weekend getaway for ibaguenos due to its clean air, beautiful scenery, and interesting flora and fauna. Approximately 30 kilometers (18.6 mi) from the city of Ibagué, visitors can enjoy typical dishes from the region, bathe in waterfalls, take bike rides or do some rock climbing. There are also opportunities to take in the towns of Chapeton, Tres

UPPER MAGDALENA

Esquinas, Llanitos, Pastales, Villerestrepo and Juntas along the way. Should you come here after the grueling ascent of Nevado del Tolima, head to El Rancho, which has medicinal hot springs recognized for their healing properties. To get here, take a bus from the Terminal de Transportes de Ibagué. Updated: Apr 12, 2011.

Climbing the Nevado del Tolima

With its snowy peak, the Nevado del Tolima is a challenge that hikers, climbing enthusiasts and adventure sports junkies should not miss. At 5,200 meters (17,060 ft), the Nevado del Tolima is one of the most difficult (but also one of the most beautiful) peaks in Colombia. The route up is steep and rocky, and it seems you are at the mercy of a downpour at any moment. In order to truly appreciate the ascent and descent of the mountain, plan for a trip of three days. Bring as much of your own equipment as possible to make the trip more economical. Start inquiring about guides and information at least two days before your proposed start. Updated: Apr 12, 2011.

Tours

Ibagué has yet to fully grasp the tourism bull by the horns, but slowly and surely the potential for growth in this field is being recognized. For further information on tours and packages, contact **JM Logística y Eventos** (Cra. 2, 20-86, Terminal de Transportes. Tel: 263-8061, Cel: 315-213-9176/320-281-5384/301-361-3372, E-mail: jmturislocal@hotmail.com, URL: http://jmlogisticayeventos.com/index.html). Updated: Jun 24, 2011.

Lodging

You can find most budget and mid-range hotels downtown, where standards vary from the decidedly seedy to the passable to outright good value. Worthy of note for their low prices, hospitality and helpfulness are Nelson's Inn and the Hotel Center. In general, budget hotels offer comparable amenities and prices. Updated: Jul 21, 2010.

Hotel Lafont

(ROOMS: $17-25) The Hotel Lafont is in a shabby, 1970s-style building right in the heart of Ibagué. Upon entry, you're greeted by a cracked stairwell, poor paintwork and worn decór, which offers an insight into how the establishment is run. However, these are only surface flaws. This really is a decent, cheap option in the center of town. The hotel has 22 rooms, all with private bathrooms and cable TV. In the lobby there is a restaurant, laundry, conference room and a few computers for Internet use. Head to Carrera 3 and you will see Hotel Lafont towering above Calle 14. Ca. 14, 3-19. Tel: 263-1519, Cel: 315-831-9984. Fax: 261-2814, E-mail: hotellafont2008@hotmail.com. Updated: Apr 12, 2011.

Hotel Center !

(ROOMS: $19-25) In a perfect world, every hotel would be a little more like the Hotel Center. Its location—in the center of Ibagué, within close reach of great restaurants—is unrivaled. Beyond that, the hotel has clean, comfortable and affordable rooms with WiFi and cable TV, which come with private bathrooms that have hot water. The staff does everything within its power to make your stay a pleasant one, giving advice on sites of interest and liaising with tour companies. One downside is that the hotel doesn't offer breakfast. Cra. 4, 12-52. Tel: 263-7181, Fax: 263-7186, E-mail: info@hotelcenteribague.com, URL: www.hotelcenteribague.com. Updated: Apr 12, 2011.

Nelson's Inn Hotel

(ROOMS: $36-50) A step up from the Hotel Center, Nelson's Inn has nothing to do with the English Naval hero and is simply named after the owner. Located right on the doorstep of Ibagué's pedestrianized Carrera 3 and close to amenities such as restaurants, bars and shops, Nelson's Inn is a fine place if you are passing through on business. The hotel has 41 rooms, all containing a fan, cable TV, a private bathroom with hot water and some with balconies. Internet is not available in the rooms, but the hotel's foyer has some computers guests can use for free, and WiFi is available here as well. Ca. 13, 2-94. Tel: 261-1867/1819, Fax: 261-1810, E-mail: gerenciahotel@hotmail.com, URL: www.hotelnelsoninn.com. Updated: Apr 12, 2011.

Restaurants

The department of Tolima is recognized throughout Colombia for its tasty pork dishes and flavorful tamales, neither of which are hard to come by anywhere in Ibagué. Ask locals; they'll happily direct you to their favorite eatery in the downtown area. Updated: Apr 22, 2009.

Chuzo Restaurante

From the finely polished red awnings that single out Chuzo as a landmark in downtown Ibagué to the neatly arranged and stylishly decorated interior, Chuzo is an uppercrust eatery. With sophisticated takes on hamburgers and steaks, customers can feast on hearty patties in mushroom sauces or delicately grilled skewers of beef or chicken, all within a WiFi hotspot. Ca. 31, 4a - 10, barrio Cádiz. Tel: 278-9796, E-mail: gerencia@chuzorestaurante.com. Updated: Feb 01, 2011.

El Gran Chalet
For budget eats in the city center, you can't beat El Gran Chalet. The inside wall has been decorated by local artists and the set meals ($1.50) are economical and generous, served by smiling waitresses. Cra. 4a, 12-12. Tel: 263-9153. Updated: Apr 22, 2009.

HONDA

 229m   40,000   8

Honda mainly exists because for a long time, it has been the last stop on the river journey to Bogotá. From Honda, conquistadors and royalty had to rough the rest of their journey overland. The city was declared a national monument based on its historically significant location.

Honda is also known as the "City of Bridges," due to the 29 bridges that cross back and forth over the Magdalena River. Some architecturally interesting buildings remain on the river from the colonial era.

All bus lines that run in from the Caribbean Coast come through Honda and pause briefly to let a few passengers off. Therefore, to most travelers Honda represents little more than a hot and nameless stop on an overnight bus to Bogotá. There is no central terminal, so in the darkness, it just looks like a confusing crossroads on the highway.

Others also know Honda as the "City of Peace," because it avoided the violence in the 1950s that affected so many of Colombia's major cities. As a whole, the city has a worn and used-up feel and has definitely known better days. Updated: Sept 24, 2009.

History
Founded in August 1539 by Conquistador Francisco Nuñez Pedroso, Honda grew into its golden age during the latter half of the 19th century, thanks to the steam boats that traversed the Magdalena. The elegant and imposing structures that still exist from this era hark to a time of expansion and hope. Unfortunately, the same thing that happened to Mompós happened to Honda—the river changed its course and steam travel became a thing of the past. Honda was left to flounder without purpose as a major transshipment route. Updated: Feb 27, 2008.

When to Go
Honda is hot all year round, with temperatures almost always in the 30s°C (high 80s-low 100s°F). If you are around in February, check out the plundering of the river during the Subienda Fishing Festival.

Subienda Fishing Festival
Every February, Honda's population swells to nearly 60,000 for the Subienda Fishing Festival. During the festival, participants fish the waters of the mighty Magdalena River. Fish like nicuro, bagre, kapax, bocachico and tolomba are caught in abundance and offered to all to share. Although the main focus of the festival is the fish, other events take place. One lucky lady wins a beauty pageant and is elected to the Reinado de la Subienda (the festival's royal court). There are also rodeos and parades. The Festival de la Subienda is Honda's main event of the year. It transforms a decaying city into a party location, so don't forget to book a room far enough in advance. Updated: Apr 11, 2011.

Getting To and Away
There is no official bus terminal. The stretch of highway that cuts through Honda is used by all the bus companies. Brasilia, Copetrans, Rápido Ochoa, Omega, Bolivariano and others all have offices here. Bogotá is a mere four hours away and Ibagué, three. Updated: Feb 27, 2008.

Safety
Honda does not feel unsafe, but keep your normal traveler's wits about you. Watch out for bag snatchings or muggings near bus stops. Updated: Feb 27, 2008.

Services
Honda's tourism office is located in the Alcaldía and can be reached at 8-251-4145 or 8-251-3500. In the case of medical need,

UPPER MAGDALENA

head to **Hospital San Juan de Dios** (Ca. 9, 16-38. Tel: 251-3577) or **Clínica Honda** (Ca. 11, 17-66). Updated: Feb 27, 2008.

Things to See and Do

Honda doesn't have many captivating attractions, though history enthusiasts will enjoy the city's colonial-era buildings, which pay tribute to the first attempts at settlement in northern South America. Fisherman may also find themselves entertained here for the famous Subienda Fishing Festival in February. Other travelers passing through can head to one of the few museums or to the Teatro Honda. Updated: Apr 27, 2011.

Museo del Río Magdalena

(ADMISSION: $1) River enthusiasts will want to check out the Museo del Río Magdalena, located along the overgrown riverwalk by the water's edge. It's not something you'll want to make a pilgrimage for, but if you have an hour to waste, the museum provides the history of the Magdelena River, spanning from its first human inhabitants until the present. It also has information about the flora and fauna found in and along its banks. Tuesday-Saturday, 9 a.m.-noon and 2-6 p.m. Ca. 10, 9-01. Tel: 251-4480. Updated: Apr 11, 2011.

Museo Alfonso López Pumarejo

(ADMISSION: $1) Museo Alfonso López Pumarejo is located in the former home of two-time Colombian president Alfonso López Pumarejo. It houses an interesting collection documenting his life and work. Monday 8 a.m.-noon, Wednesday-Friday 8 a.m.-noon and 2-6 p.m., Saturday-Sunday 8 a.m.-6 pm. Closed Tuesdays. Ca. 13, 11-75, Plaza de América. Tel: 251-3484. E-mail: museoalfonsolopez@mincultura. gov.co. Updated: Apr 11, 2011.

Teatro Honda

(ADMISSION: $5 adults, $2.50 children) For relatively recent Hollywood flicks, head over to the historical Teatro Honda. Cra. 11, 14-57. Cel: 313-368-2259. Updated: Apr 11, 2011.

Lodging

Honda accommodations are varied, and increase in quality the further you get out of the city proper. Nicer hotels that cater to Colombian holidaymakers and their families can be found in the suburbs. Otherwise you will be presented with the unwelcome prospect of poorly-maintained establishments near to the city center. Most Honda hotels look as if they have not been updated since the 1960s and are still using the same bedding. During the fishing festival in February, all rooms book up fast. Updated: Jul 21, 2010.

Hotel Villa Real

(ROOMS: $5-11) Located away from the mayhem of the Pan-American Highway crossroads, Hotel Villa Real is decent and safe. All of the dozen rooms have air conditioning, and there is a pool to cool off in. Don't expect luxury here, but you'll have fine place to rest your head. Get off the bus in front of the line of bakeries, cross the road and follow the road up the hill from the cathedral. The Villa Real is opposite a large vacant apartment building. Updated: Feb 06, 2008.

Hotel Los Puentes

(ROOMS: $7-15) This family-friendly hotel has 25 brightly colored rooms with cable TV, private bathrooms and wall fans to provide relief from the sticky Honda heat. There is a secure lot to park your car, as well as a flower-filled veranda on the second floor and friendly staff. Three bedrooms are also available for groups. Just make sure your TV and fan are functioning before agreeing to a room. Cra. 12, 17-12B (Ca. San Miguel). Tel: 251-3070. Updated: Apr 11, 2011.

Asturia Plaza Hotel

(ROOMS: $10-20) Although not stunning, Asturias Plaza is one of the better places to spend a night in Honda. It's located near the river, and has 45 single and double rooms, all with private bathroom, cable TV and ceiling fan. There is a clean pool downstairs to cool off in as well as a restaurant. Free Internet is available downstairs upon request, though the connection is quite slow. Cra. 11, 16-38. Tel: 251-3326. E-Mail: jomafra3@ hotmail.com. Updated: Apr 11, 2011.

Casa Belle Epoque

(ROOMS: $43-77) This 10-room hotel is small but sweet, with comfortable single, double and triple rooms, all with private bathrooms. It has a swimming pool, a Jacuzzi, a rooftop terrace and a lounge area with hammocks, so there are plenty of different atmospheres to relax in. Free WiFi access is available throughout the hotel, and a European- or Colombian-style breakfast is included in the price. Ca. 12, 12A-21, Cuesta de San Francisco, Centro Histórico. Tel: 251-1176, Cel: 310-481-4090/312-478-0173, E-mail: casabelleepoque@yahoo. com.com, URL: www.casabelleepoque.com. Updated: Jun 30, 2011.

Restaurants

There are plenty of bakeries and places to get cheap set meals around the Pan-American crossroads where the buses drop and pick up passengers, including **Restaurante La Cazón** (Cra. 12a, 17-20. Cel: 315-331-8515) and **Restaurante La Mejor Salud** (Cra. 12A, 17-40). None of them are particularly enchanting, and all of them serve basically the same food for around $3. Up the hill, across the Magdalena River, there are some more options with better fare. Updated: Apr 11, 2011.

Restaurante El Agrado

(ENTREES: $3-5) Popular with locals, this little restaurant has been going strong for 35 years. It serves up the regular Colombian á la carte fare as well as daily specials for breakfast, lunch and dinner. Ca. 10, 26-48. Tel: 251-5261. Updated: Apr 11, 2011.

Restaurante Las Delicias del Mar

(ENTREES: $4-6) Located close to one of Honda's numerous bridges, Restaurante Las Delicias del Mar serves up seafood, freshwater fish dishes and has some delicious juices. Av. Ernesto Soto Camero. Tel: 251-3214, Cel: 310-329-8727. Updated: Apr 11, 2011.

Chamaco

(ENTREES: $8 and up) This cozy local favorite has endearing paper hearts dangling about the restaurant and serves up typical Colombian cuisine and great seafood. Private dining booths are available. Ca. 13, 2-60. Tel: 261-2774. Updated: Apr 22, 2009.

Toy Wan

(ENTREES: $10 and up) Clean and classy with a great location in the city center, Ton Wans serves up delicious Chinese cuisine with impeccable service. Popular with local businessmen and rated one of the city's top choices, this establishmnet has great afternoon specials from 3-6 p.m. and a generous list of wines to choose from. Cra. 4, 11-14. Tel: 261-0861. Updated: Apr 11, 2011.

Nightlife

Honda still has a reputation for being overrun by whiskey bars and brothels, perhaps a throwback to the colonial era when sailors would have to dock here. These days, there are a couple of bars and clubs that thump out loud music just up the hill from the bus stop. However, exercise caution when visiting this area. Updated: Feb 27, 2008.

!!!!!

UPPER MAGDALENA

Lower Magdalena River Valley

Strategic and fertile are two words that describe the vast stretches of flood plain comprising the Lower Magdalena River Valley. This area, originally a strategic main route from the coast to the interior of Colombia, now prospers with some of the nation's largest cattle ranches.

Spend any time here and you'll see that cattle farming is the dominant industry. Enormous ranches extend out of the towns along the river, and any journey you make will undoubtedly be delayed by a passing cattle train ambling along a major byway.

As ranching is life to the people here, town festivals often resemble rodeos, with bull riding and drinking that evoke scenes reminiscent of a long disappeared American West. In the spirit of Colombian regionalism, most people in this area are referred to by other Colombians as costeños (from the coast) despite the fact that towns like Mompós, Puerto Berrío and Barrancabermeja are located several hundred kilometers from the nearest shore. However, this relative misnomer is justified when you learn that residents of these towns are defined by the freshwater of the Magdalena River.

From the smokestacks and nodding donkeys in Barrancabermeja to the silversmiths and Nazarenes on procession in the austere Semana Santa of Mompós, the Lower Magdalena River Valley is an area you will not want to miss. The García Márquez-like idiosyncrasies and welcoming inhabitants will leave a lasting impression on any traveler. Updated: Sep 29, 2009.

Highlights

Well kept in its hard-to-reach location, **Mompós** (p. 223) is one of the colonial jewels in Colombia's opulent crown.

The **Oil Museum** (p. 221) of Barrancabermeja is a good resource to understand the importance of the oil industry in Colombia.

Take a **ride on a speed boat** up the Magdalena River for the full experience of this region's activities and beauty.

History

Prior to Spanish occupation, this area was solely inhabited by indigenous tribes. Despite the injustices that have occurred on their land, the current settlements in this part of the Magdalena River Valley are distinctly defined by their hospitality toward visitors.

As the Spanish colonial empire flourished, the main highway from principal towns and ports was the river. Everything, including silver from the mines in Potosí, Bolivia, and contraband from the Caribbean Islands, passed through these waters. During the drive for independence, the towns along the Lower Magdalena were pivotal in Simón Bolívar's push for separation from Spain. Since Mompós and other settlements gained more income through contraband, which the Spanish crown was intent on curtailing, locals quickly sided with the Venezuelan-born liberator in the fight against Spain.

Toward the end of the Republican era in Colombia, the Magdalena River started to change its course. Silt levels rose and many branches of the river became impassable for the old paddle steamboats. The importance of the river as a major highway diminished, and towns formerly at the heart of trade routes became became backwaters and were left in isolation.

In contemporary years, the Lower Magdalena has seen its fair share of violence from both paramilitaries and left-wing guerrillas. Barrancabermeja, in particular, has been at the heart of these struggles. Updated: Jan 21, 2008.

When to Go

When planning your trip to Lower Magdalena, take into consideration the unrelenting heat, which rarely dips below the high 20s°C (high 70s/low 80s°F). Travelers should be aware of when rainy seasons hit, since there is widespread flooding in the Lower Magdalena and journeys can be delayed. Keep an eye out for floods in January and April-May. Updated: Jan 21, 2008.

Safety

Since the government has made special efforts to secure all major highways, most routes in the Lower Magdalena are safe. However, you are advised not to travel on the road from Medellín via Puerto Berrío to other destinations at night, since the paramilitaries have a large presence in these areas. Updated: Jan 21, 2008.

Things to See and Do

No visit to the Lower Magdalena is complete without some time spent on or beside the river itself. The Magdalena River is intrinsic to Colombian identity, and has characterized Colombia's history through thick and thin. With its handsome churches and curious histories, the town of Mompós is the river's main attraction. By letting go of luxuries and going beyond the normal tourist traps and attractions, travelers will be able to experience the real heartland of Colombia. Updated: Jan 21, 2008.

Lodging

Accommodation quality varies considerably from town to town. Small port towns, such as Puerto Berrío and Puerto Boyacá, offer decent and relatively inexpensive hotels. These are much better than the cheaper, brothel-like options. Mompós has a selection of overpriced hotels, but there are some reasonable places as well, such as **La Casa Amarilla**. Barrancabermeja is an industrial capital and its hotels, though plentiful, cater to engineers sent to the city on a work ticket. Nonetheless, decent options are possible to find. Updated: Jul 23, 2010.

PUERTO BERRÍO

 125m   38,000   4

The first thing you notice upon arriving in Puerto Berrío is the staggering heat and humidity. Temperatures average above

LOWER MAGDALENA

30°C (87°F). Once you have become accustomed to the dank humidity that leaves everyone covered in a shimmer of sweat, you note the obvious absence of the typical hills. Puerto Berrío and this region of the Magdalena River are quite flat.

Formerly, Puerto Berrío had greater significance as a transport hub for the rail network, moving coal and other products through Colombia. Now, the railroad service is gone and the town is little more than a vital port on the Magdalena River. All that remains are some forlorn tracks and a historic engine in front of the military base.

In the past, Puerto Berrío was renowned for its bawdy *whiskerías* (brothels) and *chicas de la vida alegre* (prostitutes), fulfilling its role as a transit hub among linking river and rail networks. To some extent, this is still the case around the port area, where some of these establishments can still be found. Updated: Sept 24, 2009.

History

Located on the banks of the Magdalena River and on the border between the departments of Antioquia and Santander, Puerto Berrío occupies a region known to Colombians as the Magdalena Medio. This is because it has little in common with the rest of its department and more in common with other settlements along the Magdalena.

Founded in 1875 by Pedro Javier Cisneros, Puerto Berrío's fate has been inextricably linked to the business its port and railway hub has drawn. In 1925, the town was all but destroyed by a fire. Due to the loss of the railway and the shifting river, Puerto Berrío is no longer the important hub that it once was. Updated: Nov 27, 2007.

Getting To and Away

BY BUS

There is no bus terminal per se, but all buses come to a halt on the main plaza in Puerto Berrío. This leaves you close to all hotels, banks and restaurants. There are three main transportation companies that make the trip to Puerto Berrío: **Cootransmagdalena**, **Rápido Ochoa** (mainly to Medellín) and **Rápido Tolima** (taxi services).

Buses make the trip to Bucaramanga (6 buses daily, $13), Barrancabermeja (7 buses daily, $8) and Medellín (26 buses daily, $9-10.50).

Alternatively, it is possible to take a taxi to Honda (1 taxi daily, $9), Ibagué (6 taxis daily, $12.50) or Puerto Boyacá (2 taxis daily, $5).

BY BOAT

Cootransfluviales Unidos (Tel: 833-3238) has an office right in the port and runs *chalupas* (fast boats) to Barrancabermeja (2.5 hr) at 9 a.m. and 2:30 a.m. for $10.

Trans Fluvial runs boats from Puerto Berrío to La Sierra at 7:30 a.m., 10:30 a.m., 1:30 p.m. and 4 p.m. Updated: Nov 27, 2007.

Safety

Puerto Berrío is a relatively safe town. As long as you stay away from the port after dark, you should encounter little trouble. The most dangerous moments of any visitor's trip is the time spent on public transportation. From time to time, the roads to and from Medellín and Barrancabermeja are closed due to military or guerrilla operations in the area. Updated: Nov 27, 2007.

Services

TOURISM

There is no tourism office in Puerto Berrío, as you would suspect from a place with little tourism industry. Upon asking what there was to see in Puerto Berrío, a traveler received the bewildering reply from a hotel manager: "In reality, there's nothing."

MONEY

In the Plaza Mayor, there is a BBVA with ATMs and an adjacent **Bancolombia** with similar facilities.

KEEPING IN TOUCH

You can make international calls at any of the many call centers in town. There are also three Internet cafés for further communication needs: **Edetel**, in front of the military base; **Enter.Net**, on Calle 54 between Carreras 4 and 5; and **Mundo Digital**, on the corner of Calle 54 and Carrera 5.

MEDICAL

A recommended clinic is located next door to Bancolombia on Plaza Mayor. Pharmacies abound and can be found throughout Puerto Berrío. Updated: May 15, 2009.

Tours

There are plenty of side trips that can be taken from Puerto Berrío. You can go to Puerto Olaya and enjoy a plate of fish served with fried macho plantain and rice. Nearby El Zuam has one of the most beautiful places to swim. Alternatively, take a nice trip in a lancha on the Magdalena River or just relax with a beer at La Malena.

Lodging

Puerto Berrío has hotels of all shapes, sizes and costs. Visitors are advised to stay within a few blocks of Plaza Mayor and to avoid the cheaper options near the port where security is questionable. Many of the cheap port motels rent rooms by the hour. The hotels listed here are credible establishments that do not cater to the rent-by-the-hour crowd. Updated: Jul 22, 2009.

Las Golondrinas

(ROOMS: $15-35) Right on the corner of the main square in Puerto Berrío, this is one of two recommended hotels in town. Rooms come with air conditioning, refrigerator, cable TV and darkened windows to keep out the blazing sunshine. Each room has a private bathroom (without hot water, since it's unecessary here). Ca. 7 and Cra. 4. Tel: 833-4846. Updated: Apr 14, 2011.

Hotel Las Dos Palmas

(ROOMS: $20-25) Hotel Las Dos Palmas is quite simply one of the best hotels in Puerto Berrío. Located a few blocks from a seedy port area and a few blocks from the main square and its conveniences, this hotel has 20 rooms, all equipped with air conditioning (an absolute necessity in this sweltering town). If you're arriving by bus, the hotel is four blocks away. Ca. 53, Cra. 2. Tel: 833-3339/3338. Updated: May 19, 2009.

Restaurants

Those easily satisfied with an enormous and freshly blended fruit juice from a market stall ($0.50) will be more than happy in Puerto Berrío. There are many levels of restaurants to choose from, but keep in mind that the quality does not match that of Medellín. Cheap eats are available and lunchtime deals abound. Updated: Nov 26, 2007.

Chara

(LUNCH: $2) Located beneath the Residencias Bahía, about a block back from the town square, Restaurante Chara is a functional and clean establishment. It won't win any Michelin stars, but it will provide the traveler with a hearty and reasonably priced meal. A breakfast of *calentao* (rice, beans and meat) goes for only $1.25, and you can enjoy a set lunch for roughly $2. Ca. 52 and Cra. 4. Updated: Apr 13, 2011.

Las Dos Palmas

(LUNCH: $2) Situated on the ground floor of the hotel by the same name, this restaurant is a decent option for a quick, decent breakfast. Lunch is a set menu ($2), and drinks are an additional $0.60. The restaurant is clean, the staff is attentive, the fans go some way to cooling you off and the TV blares at all hours. Ca. 53 and Cra. 2. Tel: 833-3339. Updated: May 19, 2009.

El Portón de los Frijoles

(ENTREES: $5-20) Without a doubt the best place to eat in Puerto Berrío, El Portón de los Frijoles' extensive menu and quality of food have few rivals in town. Sit outside in the still, humid air while sipping a cold beer and attacking a steak, or retreat to the dining room with soothing air conditioning. The restaurant specializes in grilled food, with an emphasis on beef and fish dishes. The grilled river fish is particularly appetizing. Ca. 49, behind Bancolombia. Tel: 832-7473, E-mail: alcapris@hotmail.com URL: www.portondelosfrijoles.com. Updated: Apr 14, 2011.

Casa Vieja

On the corner next to Bancolombia, Casa Vieja sets out to be the elegant dining option in Puerto Berrío. It does reasonably well too, with its shaded tables out front and its general keen eye for detail. The dishes are not cheap, but you will find them to your liking if you are into seafood. Almost all speciality dishes include some sort of river fish, bagre in particular. Ca. 50, beside Bancolombia. Updated: Apr 14, 2011.

Fresas y Moras Frutería

Ever tried *níspero, uchuva* or *corozo*? Come to Fresas y Moras Frutería. Here you can get your hands on a fine, fresh-squeezed fruit juice, fruit salad or even a breakfast omelet. The staff at this street-corner restaurant are helpful and accommodating and will advise you on the fruits in season. Cra. 7, 5-18. Tel: 833-2679/5992. Updated: Apr 14, 2011.

BARRANCABERMEJA

 126m 300,000 📞 7

Barrancabermeja is first and foremost an oil town. This detail is not lost on the visitor as a massive refinery looms large over this sweltering settlement on the Magdalena River. Temperatures rarely dip below 30°C (85°F) and more often edge near 40°C (105°F). Barrancabermeja was the

LOWER MAGDALENA

first city in Colombia with an international airport, since its refinery drew in prospectors from all over the world.

Until the early 2000s, Barrancabermeja was plagued by urban violence resulting from the conflict in Colombia. To this day, the citizens talk of three different Barrancabermejas. The first being the refinery, which is pretty much its own city; the second being the leafy and pleasant middle-class neighborhoods like Las Colinas; and the third being the poor barrios on the other side of the tracks, which were held by the guerrillas up until recently.

Barrancabermeja is a great place to mix it up with the locals, as the people are very friendly and accommodating. Don't be surprised if you are invited on day trips to nearby ciénagas, where you can swim in the cooling waters, enjoy various aquatic sports and lunch on freshwater fish. Updated: Feb 08, 2008.

History

Although Barrancabermeja has many remnants of small indigenous settlements that existed in the area dating as far back as the 16th century, the town as it is now known was not created until the Spanish came along. Explorer Gonzalo Jiménez de Quesada named the area on account of the ravines (*barranca* means ravine in Spanish). The city expanded rapidly as an oil boom town in the 1920s when Standard Oil moved in to exploit this wealth.

In addition to its petroleum history, the city has long been in the crossfire of the long-running Colombian conflict with the ELN. This guerilla organization staked their claim to the region in the 1970s and 1980s, and later in the 1990s when the FARC arrived. In 1998, Barrancabermeja suffered a massacre: 32 civilians were killed as paramilitary forces declared their intent to intimidate the region. Updated: Jul 08, 2011.

When to Go

Barrancabermeja is inextricably associated with oppressive heat. Temperatures rarely drop below 30°C (85°F). Even though rains fall in September and October, this hardly alters the heat.

Major events that take place in Barrancabermeja include the Reina Internacional de Petróleo pageant in April and the Fiesta del Petróleo in August. Both revolving around its main industry, the latter is complete with concerts, parades and other cultural displays. Additionally,

Barrancabermeja hosted its first International Theatre Festival for Peace on May 21-29, 2011, with a focus on social transformation and emancipation, remembrance, and peace and reconciliation in both national and international contexts. Updated: May 31, 2011.

Getting To and Away

BY BUS
There is no bus terminal, but most bus companies have offices downtown on or near Carrera 6. Main bus companies include: **Cootransmagdalena**, **Brasilia** and **Copetrans**.

To Bucaramanga: every half hour, prices vary.

To Puerto Berrío: 5:30 a.m. and 6 a.m., prices vary.

To Barranquilla: 7 p.m. and 9:30 p.m., $35-40.

To Bogotá: 6 a.m., 10 a.m., 2:30 p.m., 9:30 p.m., 10 p.m. and 10:30 p.m.; $35.

To Cartagena: 7 a.m., 7 p.m., 8:30 p.m. and 9 p.m.; $40-46.

To Maicao: 7 p.m., $35.

To Cali: 7 a.m., 3 p.m., 7 p.m. and 9 p.m.; $30.

To Medellín: 8 a.m., 2 p.m. and 10 p.m.; $35.

BY TRAIN
A functioning train service runs from Barrancabermeja to Puerto Berrío daily at 5 a.m. and 1 p.m. Carriages are small, and the journey takes three hours and costs $7.50. Tel: 602-7684.

BY BOAT
Barrancabermeja is situated on the Magdalena River, so river transport is vital. Journeys are long and tend to be expensive.

Cootransfluviales has services Puerto Berrío (6:30 a.m., $10), Gamarra (7 a.m.), El Banco (connection from here to Mompox; 5 hr, $24) and San Pablo (9 a.m., 10 a.m., noon, 12:30 p.m.). **Transportes San Pablo** goes to Magangué, with connections to Mompox, at 6 a.m. (9 hr, $40). Updated: Feb 08, 2008.

Safety
Since the conflict has been forced out of the city limits and into other areas, Barrancabermeja has become a pretty safe place. However,

visitors must use common sense. Travelers should be especially vigilant when withdrawing money from ATMs. Especially watch out for motorcycle-riding thieves who follow those who just took out cash and rob them as they exit their taxi. Updated: Mar 11, 2011.

Services

TOURISM

There is no official tourism office in Barrancabermeja. For further information, contact the **Corporación Mixta de Promoción de Santander** (Cra. 19, 35-02. Tel: 630-7589) or the **Instituto Municipal de Cultura** (Ca. 30, 26-117. Tel: 634-1132).

MONEY

Banks are located throughout the city and cash machines are easily accessible.

KEEPING IN TOUCH

There are Internet cafés throughout every district of the city.

MEDICAL

If in need of medical attention, head to **Clínica Primero de Mayo** (Cra. 21A, 47-30. Tel: 622-2468.).

SHOPPING

All things considered, there is very little to shop for in Barrancabermeja. Due to the heat, sunblock, a hat or after-sun cream are necessary and are easily found around downtown. Updated: Feb 08, 2008.

Things to See and Do

If you find youself in Barrancabermeja, there are probably one of three reasons why you are here:

1) You are an engineer or an oil prospector brought in on a business gig.

2) You are making the incredible journey by river from the Colombian coast to the interior or vice versa.

3) You are lost or stranded.

Despite all the negative comments you might have heard about the city—with its oppressive heat and the ever-present silhouette of the refinery—Barrancabermeja has a few attractions to keep tourists occupied.

The surrounding countryside, fed by the waters of the Magdalena River, is surprisingly beautiful. The large lakes nearby are good for day trips, where you can take a dip in the cool waters, water ski, hire a jet ski or dine on fantastic fish dishes. During weekends, you'll find that most barramejos descend upon these areas to escape from the heat. Updated: Feb 08, 2008.

Oil Museum ❗

Walk around the port of Barrancabermeja and the importance of the oil industry becomes clear when you see the dozens of oil rigs that line the coast and the statue of Christ dedicated to oil. The Oil Museum (Museo del Petróleo) gives a concrete idea about the city with the largest oil refinery in the country, the history of oil and the current progress of the oil industry. Look for the museum on the road to the center of Barrancabermeja, about 15 minutes out of town and right near where the crude oil refining process begins. Updated: Apr 13, 2011.

Ciénaga San Silvestre

Likened to a freshwater "ocean," the Ciénaga San Silvestre spans out from Barrancabermeja to as far as Puerto Wilches, making it a vast body of water measuring nine square kilometers (3.5 sq mi).

On the banks of San Silvestre, a 10-minute drive from Barrancabermeja, various water sports resorts have sprung up. At these family-friendly places, you can swim in the delectable waters of the ciénaga, waterski, parascend and fish. Normally, there is a beach volleyball court set up, a live band playing on the weekend and spaces to set up your own BBQ.

Too much action? Take a hammock, string it up in the shade of some trees and have a serious siesta in the breeze coming off the ciénaga. To keep costs down, you can bring your own picnic. Make sure to bring plenty of sun protection and watch out for freshwater stingrays near the shore in dry season. To get there, catch a taxi from downtown Barrancabermeja. Updated: Apr 13, 2011.

Lodging

Accommodation options in Barrancabermeja range from luxurious to seedy. At the high end of the scale, businessmen working for oil companies lounge by swimming pools in the finer establishments. The next rung of hotels cater to the contracted engineers brought in for short-term jobs; these are typically decent and efficient places. Finally, there are cheaper options downtown in the city's Zona Rosa. Many are just fine, but the majority cater to people renting rooms by the hour. Updated: Jul 21, 2011.

LOWER MAGDALENA

The River Train

"Peto, peto," Doña Sorelly calls. She opens her milk can, steam from the corn drink escaping into this slightly cool morning. The toot of the autoferro's horn warns of our imminent passage. We leave Barrancabermeja, entering this new day swaying, occasionally jolting down narrow-gauge tracks. Wheels upon rails sharply clack and rumble as we pass homes with still-sleeping families. Mango trees scrape our sides. The cloud-silhouetted dawn is just beginning to lighten. In the distance, on the banks of the Río Magdalena, refinery stack smoke and derrick flames billow. Lightning streaks the western sky. A thin rain sheens off bronze cacao leaves.

This landscape begins to define itself as waterlilied swamps and stands of bamboo. Cattle rise, the dew and drizzle glistening on their hides. Passengers come, cargo goes. Slowly, these villages and settlements we visit are awakening; stalls are mounted in the light of lamps. Garzas rise from their trees, white blips winging across the gray sky. There's a hollow clatter as we cross over bridges above small rivers flowing to that great Río. Workers board, workers leave; it's just another day of labor. This land, so flat, begins to undulate. The rain ceases, though the day is yet subdued. Thin-limbed, potbellied children stand in their golden-lit doorways, lethargically watching us shudder past.

After Puerto Olaya, the Río Magdalena comes into view. Soldiers patrol the bridge we soon cross. The river glimmers silver and brown beneath us, its sandbars exposed. Swooshing, swaying, clattering past shack homes, we arrive to our destination, Puerto Berrío.

Check the Getting To and Away from Barrancabermeja section for the train's latest schedule, or call the offices. Tel: 602-7684.

San Cristóbal

(ROOMS: $18-30) Although the San Cristóbal is in the city's Zona Rosa, this respectable hotel is definitely separate from the many seedy, rent-by-the-hour options nearby. The price for one of the 40 rooms is cheaper if you choose a fan over air conditioning. The rooms are generally clean, and all come with cable TV, a cooling option and telephone. To get there, catch any bus heading downtown and ask to be dropped off on Calle 50. Ca. 50, 12-36. Tel: 622-4346/602-1982, Fax: 621-1163. Updated: Apr 14, 2011.

Hotel Cacique

(ROOMS: $30-46) Just next door to the Pipatón is the characterless and charmless Hotel Cacique. It really does live in the shadow of its neighbor and is nothing more than a location for businessmen coming through Barrancabermeja. Rooms are standard, with TV, air conditioning and private bathrooms. Ca. 49, 1-14. Tel: 622-3350/621-4714, Fax: 622-6672, E-mail: hotelcaciquebarranca@yahoo.es. Updated: Apr 14, 2011.

San Carlos

(ROOMS: $65-80) Just down the hill and around the corner from Pipatón, the San Carlos is another hotel aimed at the engineering crowd. Each of the 30 rooms and seven apartments have air conditioning, cable TV, minibar, WiFi and a private bathroom. The San Carlos is functional but lacks character and feeling; it does exactly what is says on its card and nothing more. It also loses customers to the Pipatón since that hotel has a pool. Ca. 49, 5-104. Tel: 602-2010, Fax: 622-4372, E-mail: reservas@suhotelsancarlos.com/hsanca@yahoo.es, URL: www.suhotelsancarlos.com. Updated: Apr 13, 2011.

Hotel Bachue

(ROOMS: $75-100) Located in the center of town, the Bachue underwent a complete renovation in August of 2007 of everything down to tiling in the bathrooms and linen on the beds. The entry still has a 1970s feel to it, but the 40 rooms are top class, offering guests WiFi, air conditioning, a private bathroom and a refrigerator. Breakfast is included, and weekend rates are significantly lowered, as hotel occupancy drops considerably. Cra. 17, 49-12. Tel: 622-2599/611-2007, Fax: 622-2474, E-mail: hotelbahue@gmail.com. Updated: Apr 14, 2011.

Pipatón

(ROOMS: $75-125) This colonial-style building stands tall, affording great views over the

Magdalena River. Once you stroll through its welcoming doors, you'll note the swimming pool and the air-conditioned lobby. All rooms have WiFi, air conditioning, private bathroom, TV with cable, refrigerator and breakfast included. If coming in from the airport, call the hotel in advance and it will have a taxi pick you up free of charge. Av. del Rio 47-16. Tel: 602-0250, Fax: 602-0258, E-mail: reservas@hotelpipaton.net, URL: www.hotelpipaton.net. Updated: Apr 13, 2011.

Restaurants
The best food in Barrancabermeja comes fresh from the river. Head to the river banks, not far from the **Cacique Hotel**, to find a number of set-ups preparing delicious bagre and bocachica fish dishes. Go downtown to find anything else to eat.

Avenida del Río
Avenida del Río is a great stroll for anyone with an appetite. A line of unnamed and numbered stalls along the riverfront specialize in local delicacies like sancocho de pescado, bagre and bocachica fish dishes. Don't be put off by the backdrop of the massive refinery; this is the place to come to enjoy fish with the locals. On weekends, all of the stands are full to capacity. Choose a stand that suits you and settle in for a sumptuous feast. Updated: Apr 13, 2011.

Café Bohemia !
Intimate places like Café Bohemia are beginning to spring up, diversifying the options available here. Small tables line the narrow establishment but take nothing away from its ambience. Come for a cocktail or a coffee, or try some of their sandwiches. Café Bohemia may just be a perfect escape from Barrancebermeja within the confines of the city. Ca. 49, 19-30. Tel: 611-2575. E-mail: angelaperez@hotmail.com. Updated: May 25, 2009.

Nightlife
The Zona Rosa, a string of clubs downtown, constantly produces loud Vallenato music and salsa. Barrancabermeja does not have the same level of nightlife as Medellín or Bogotá, but prices are low and the entertainment value is premium. Updated: Feb 08, 2008.

Carrera 10
Often just referred to as "la 10," Barrancabermeja's Zona Rosa positively buzzes on Fridays and Saturdays. La Via Lactea is a pizzeria/bar with an open-air section and unintrusive music; it is the ideal spot for an early evening beer. The following clubs are all found on

Carrera 10 and are close to the Parque de la Vida: **Amnesia**, **Evolution**, **Cucaracho**, **Seven**, **Amatista** and **La Ciudad**. All of these play a variety of music and, for most, entry is free and beer is cheap! Cra. 10. Updated: Apr 13, 2011.

MOMPÓS

 18m 31,000 📞 5

To visitors and locals alike, Mompós represents an older, forgotten colonial Colombia. It is a city of tradition, family ties, and a mix of García-Márquian myth and religious piety. The culture remains largely untouched by the conflict found throughout the rest of the country.

Two hundred kilometers (124 mi) east of Cartagena, this island town is difficult to reach. However, it is well worth the effort. Colonial Mompós has been a UNESCO World Heritage Site since 1995. It is comprised of three long, whitewashed streets, which run parallel to the Magdalena River. Mompós' stifling heat and backwater status do not create the most favorable place for tourists. However, anyone interested in colonial Colombia and the European Diaspora, or in observing one of Latin America's most austere Semana Santa celebrations, should consider a visit. Updated: Feb 18, 2008.

History
Like similar colonial settlements, Mompós came about due to its favorable location along the Magdalena. The absence of unfriendly indigenous tribes also helped foster a successful colony. Mompós grew considerably during the colonial era, when the river was the fastest route to Honda, and subsequently Bogotá. It is said that more money passed through Mompós than through Cartagena, thanks to the bootlegging of precious metals, tobacco and alcohol to and from the Ecuadorian port of Guayaquil.

Simón Bolívar's numerous stays in Mompós create another historical connection to Latin American history. While there, Bolívar raised an army of willing momposino volunteers to aid in his march on Caracas. It is rumored that Gabriel García Márquez built this history into "The General and His Labyrinth," and possibly into his other books as well. Bolívar once proclaimed, "If to Caracas I owe my life, to Mompós I owe my glory."

LOWER MAGDALENA

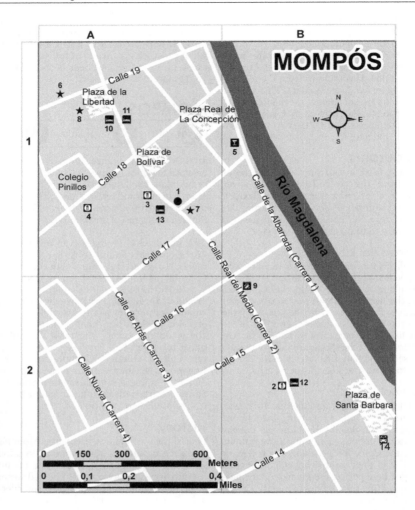

The aforementioned are high points in the history of this colonial wonderland, but all of this came to an end when the river somewhat changed its course and fluvial travel became less important. Updated: Feb 18, 2008.

When to Go

Semana Santa is Mompós' one real high season. During this time, streets are filled with Nazarenes and Colombian tourists. The normally sleepy town also receives an economic boost during December and January from family members who return for the holidays and tourists coming from the coast. Aside from these times, life in Mompós is pretty slow.

The wet season stretches over the months of April and May, and September through October. During these months, downpours can keep normally high temperatures in the upper 20s°C (70s°F). Outside of these months, Mompós is hot and dry, typically hovering above 30°C (86°F).

August 6 marks the Independence of Mompós. On and around this date, revelers enjoy more than a few cold ones while watching the rodeos and listening to the booming street music.

In 2008, Juan Ensuncho Bárcena founded the Mompós Independent Film Festival. Since then, thousands of locals and foreigners

● **Activities**

1 Museo Cultural A1

⑩ **Eating**

2 Asadero Patio Bonito B2
3 Crepes D´ La Villa A1
4 Dely Bross A1

▣ **Nightlife**

5 Luna de Mompox B1

★ **Services**

6 Hospital A1
7 Planet Net A1
8 Tourism Office A1

🛍 **Shopping**

9 Taller y Joyería Jimmy B2

■ **Sleeping**

10 Bioma Boutique Hotel A1
11 Casa Hotel La Casona A1
12 Casa Hotel Villa de Mompox B2
13 Hostal Doña Manuela A1

🚌 **Transportation**

14 Unitransco B2

Semana Santa in Mompós

For one of the most unforgettable Semana Santa experiences in Colombia, head straight to Mompós. Not only are the parades austere in their religious significance and the floats ornate, but the willingness of the people to be involved and pitch in is legendary. Nazarene pilgrims dressed in heavy smocks sweat uncontrollably in the heat as they jostle for favorable positions underneath the weighty religious artifacts. Whole families parade to the old cemetery to light candles and place them on the tombs of their dear departed while a band plays a somber tune.

Later in the week, budding artists decorate the streets in chalk and sawdust etchings of religious figures and events, only to later see them destroyed underfoot by yet another procession. Coming to Mompós at any time of year is special but it is doubly so during this period, when you have the opportunity to see the seven immaculate churches in all their pomp and majesty, and to observe one of Colombia's best-preserved sites at its finest. Updated: May 15, 2009.

have gathered in town each year to appreciate over 150 independent films with democratic, political and social themes. This event is free and typically takes place over four or five days, though the date changes each year. In 2010, the festival was cancelled due to flooding in Mompós. The festival will resume in 2011. For more information, check out the festival's Facebook page (URL: www.facebook.com/festicinemompox). Updated: Feb 22, 2011.

Getting To and Away

Mompós is not easy to reach. However, through a combination of buses, taxis, water transportation and maybe a 4X4, any traveler can make it.

FROM THE CARIBBEAN COAST:
The fastest but most expensive way to get to Mompós is to fly into Cartagena or Barranquilla and organize an inter-city taxi to Magangué. Taxis to Magangué from Cartagena take 3-3.5 hours and cost $15-20; they leave when full. From Magangué, you can catch a motorized canoe across the river to Bodega (25 min, $3), then head on to Mompós via shared taxi (1 hr, $3-6.50). **Unitransco** also provides direct service from Cartagena to Mompós at 7 a.m. from the terminal. The price varies ($30-40), depending on the season.

Direct vans leave from both Santa Marta ($23) and Taganga ($28) for Mompós. Alternatively, you can take an early bus from Santa Marta to Bucaramanga, tranferring in Bosconia, where there are direct buses to Mompós.

Otherwise, Mompós has buses leaving every day to Barranquilla, Cartagena and Sincelejo (connections to Tolu, Coveñas and Medellin).

LOWER MAGDALENA

A reputable bus company in Mompós is **Copetran** (Ca. del Cementerio 3-74. Tel: 685-5768). However, if you are stuck in Mompós and have to leave, the best bet is to get to Magangué and try your luck there since there are more options. Updated: Apr 04, 2011.

COMING FROM COLOMBIA'S INTERIOR AND BOGOTÁ:

Omega and **Copetran** have direct overnight buses from Bogotá to El Banco, which leave every evening at 5 p.m. (13 hr, $40). Buses also leave from Bucaramanga to El Banco at 3:30 a.m., 5 a.m., 5:30 a.m., 8:30 a.m., 11 a.m. and 10 p.m. **Cotaxi** (Tel: 637-2999), **Cootramagdalena** (Tel: 637-3400) and **Coopetran** (Tel: 637-6100) collectively provide these services; all charge $28 for the journey. There are also direct buses from Barrancabermeja to El Banco as well (6 hr), leaving at 5 a.m., 6 a.m. and 8 a.m.

From El Banco, you will need to catch one of the waiting 4x4s that run the arduous two- to three-hour journey over bad roads to Mompós ($11-14).

If you are coming from Medellín, you can either take a direct bus to Magangué (12 hr, $49) or catch a bus to Sincelejo and connect to Magangué from there (8-10 hr, $54). The former only leaves once daily, at 8:45 p.m., and is serviced by **Expreso Brasilia** (Tel: 230-9871); more frequent departures leave for Sincelejo.

Either way, once you get to Magangué, you will need to cross the river via water transport and continue on to Mompós by taxi. Updated: May 04, 2011.

RIVER TRAVEL

From Barrancabermeja and other points on the Magdalena River, there are infrequent departures to Magangué and El Banco. Small boats leave for El Banco from Barrancabermeja every morning at 6 a.m. Be sure to ask around; the river journey will be far more pleasant than one by road. The Colombian government has stated its intent to make the waterways in this region passable, so there should be more available long-distance river travel options in the future. Updated: May 04, 2011.

Safety

Imagine a town where, once the sun has set, entire families pull their rocking chairs out onto their front porches and sit, doors open, chatting with passersby. Mompós is a town that has been largely unaffected by many of Colombia's ills. Simply put, on an island with nowhere to run and fewer places to hide, Mompós has been left alone. In the outer neighborhoods on the other side of the highway, Mompós is growing significantly due to land invasions by people displaced by the conflict in other areas. Mompós itself is incredibly safe, though. Updated: Feb 18, 2008.

Services

TOURISM

The tourism office is located on the second floor of the Palacio Municipal on the western side of Plaza de la Libertad. It is open Monday-Friday 7 a.m.-noon and 2-5 p.m. For additional information about Mompós, ask at the **Museo Cultural** on Calle del Real Medio. Updated: Mar 29, 2011.

MONEY

There are three ATMs in town. All are on the corner of the Parque Bolívar and the Camellón del Colegio. The ATMs provided by the Banco Popular accept all cards, and the cash point provided by BBVA accepts Visa.

NOTE: During Semana Santa, demand for cash is at a premium and ATMs have been known to run out.

KEEPING IN TOUCH

There is an Internet café on the Alberrada, across the corner from the El Éxito supermarket. There is also **Planet Net**, which has telephones and computers available at Calle del Medio, 12-06. Both charge $1 per hour.

MEDICAL

Be aware that if you are ever in dire need of serious medical attention, there is every possibility that it will not be available in Mompós. However, you can try your luck at the pharmacies and clinics in the Plaza del Mercado.

SHOPPING

Taller y Joyería Jimmy (Ca. del Medio, Cra. 2, 15-86. Tel: 685-5383) offers some of the finest metal ornaments in Mompós. **Joyería William Vargas** (Tel: 684-0453) sells a selection of the typical jewelry sold in the area. Updated: Feb 18, 2008.

Things to See and Do

If you are not making your way to this river city for the major Semana Santa festivities, it is good to remember that a visit to Mompós is not all about seeing and doing. The activities are slim pickings; a trip here is more about soaking up the atmosphere.

While there are ornate churches to be seen, Masonic histories to be investigated and walks to be had, Mompós lends itself to rising early to view the howler monkeys in the park. Afterwards, stroll down Calle del Medio, making a detour to the Plaza del Mercado, and observe life here before heading back along the shady riverfront to where the wealthier residents live in the Portales de la Marquesa.

Tours of the Ciénaga are offered at the ludicrously hot hour of 2 p.m., and you can rent bicycles at some establishments to make your own trips. For those interested, cockfights are also held around town on most weekends.

Mompós has a few beautiful churches and two museums. **The Museo Cultural** (Admission $1.50; Monday-Saturday 9 a.m.-noon) houses a collection of religious art and memorabilia related to Simón Bolívar. **The Casa de la Cultura** (Admission $0.50; Monday-Friday 8 a.m.-5 p.m.) is a museum documenting Mompós' history. Updated: Apr 13, 2011.

Tours

Hostal Doña Manuela
In addition to being one of the finest accommodation options in Mompós, Hostal Doña Manuela offers city tours and wildlife tours of the local ciénagas, allowing visitors to marvel at the abundant birdlife. It also runs a finca outside of Mompós with a swimming pool and horses. Tel: 685-5142, E-mail: mabe642@hotmail.com. Updated: Jan 21, 2008.

Mompós Tour
Mompós Tour takes tourists from Cartagena to Mompós on Tuesdays, Thursdays and Fridays in a fully air-conditioned minivan. Prices are steep, but if you only have a few precious days in the area, this is a good choice, as it organizes all transportation. Tel: 685-5142. Updated: Jan 21, 2008.

Lodging
In addition to being hard to reach, Mompós has suffered at the hands of hoteliers who have taken advantage of their distance from other tourist sites and hotel options. Room prices here are steep, even in the off season. That said, service is good and most places offer clean accommodations topped off with air conditioning and efficient services.

Be advised: During Semana Santa, hotel prices tend to increase considerably. Rooms book up fast, though locals have been known to rent out their spare rooms. It is advisable to book your accomodation and if possible your bus tickets in advance. Updated: Jul 21, 2010.

La Casa Amarilla !
(ROOMS: $8-66) Way overdue, there is finally a budget option for travelers in Mompós. La Casa Amarilla is a large, renovated colonial mansion with views over the Magdalena River. The kioscos are in a great place, out where you can enjoy an ice cold beer and watch the howler monkeys. Prices, as you would expect, increase during Semana Santa, but the rest of the year they are reasonable. The mansion consists of two dormitories (three- and four-people rooms), each with private bathroom, and two private rooms with double beds (one with en-suite). For a basic dorm bed, prices average at $8 per bed. If your sights are set a little higher however, La Casa Amarilla has six luxurious suites on offer, prices averaging at $44 per person, including breakfast and WiFi.

La Casa Amarilla is the backpacker choice. The British owner has installed a TV and DVD player in the second entry room, renovated the garden, put in a communal kitchen, and has done his best to make this a place where you want to kick back and chill for a few days. If you come in on the Unitransco bus, this will drop you right outside La Casa Amarilla. Coming in from El Banco, head to the Albarrada (the road by the river) and follow it upstream to La Iglesia Santa Barbara; one block beyond is the hostel. Ca. 13, 1-05, La Albarrada with Santa Barbara. Tel: 685-6326, Cel: 301-362-7065, E-mail: lacasaamarillamompos@gmail.com. URL: www.lacasaamarillamompos.com. Updated: Apr 13, 2011.

Casa Hotel Villa de Mompox
(ROOMS: $10-17.50) Perhaps best described as one step up from backpacker comfort and charm, the Villa de Mompox sits on the edge of everything colonial in Mompós and one block

back from the Magdalena River. Prices are probably a bit steep for what is on offer, but the owners cannot be faulted in creating an "alternative" lodging in the other more expensive options in this town. All rooms come with air conditioning, ceiling fans and private bathrooms. A comfortable communal area for guests to relax is lacking, but all in all, if nowhere cheaper is available and you are on a budget, this is probably your best option. The hotel sleeps up to 43 on its premises, and across the road there are a couple of other rooms for the overflow that inevitably happens during Semana Santa. The bus drops you off next to the Iglesia Santa Barbara and from there, you should head one block away from the river and you will find the hotel. Ca. Real del Medio 14-108. Tel: 685-5208, Cel: 311-848-4324, E-mail: casahotelvilladememompox@yahoo.com. Updated: Apr 13, 2011.

Casa Hotel La Casona

(ROOMS: $14-56) As one of the leading hotels in Mompós, the expectation is that La Casona should be a paradise. It is not. The rooms are dark, the furniture could use some updating and the communal areas need work.

For too long it seems the establishment has been resting on its laurels knowing full well that a steady stream of tourists would continue visiting during Semana Santa. While the staff is helpful and friendly, you can do better for the price. Head to the Real Calle del Medio and follow it, downstream, until you reach La Casona. Cra. 2, 18-58. Tel: 685-5307, E-mail: eucaris@hotelmompos.com, URL: www.hotelmompos.com. Updated: Apr 13, 2011.

Hostal Doña Manuela

(ROOMS: $62-85) This 28-room behemoth of a colonial mansion sits proudly in the center of Mompós' main street, Calle del Medio. Routinely used as a location for wealthy Momposinos to hold events such as weddings, it is quite simply the best and most elegant place to stay in town. Prices are not cheap, but you get what you are paying for: air conditioning, cable TV, elegance, and a swimming pool, which is an excellent addition in the Mompós heat.

The owners also own a farm on the outskirts of Mompós where guests can choose to take horse rides or swim in its other pool. For those not interested in paying the lofty prices to stay at the Hostal Doña Manuela, the establishment offers a day pass for $10 that allows use of the pool and some free drinks for the

whole day, or you can purchase a pool pass for $3. The hotel's rooms vary from doubles to as many as six beds (maximum capacity 90 people). Prices increase during Semana Santa. Head to the Calle del Medio and the hostel is smack bang in the middle. Ca. Real del Medio 17-41. Tel: 685-5142, E-mail: hostaldonamanuela@hotmail.com. Updated: May 13, 2009.

Bioma Boutique Hotel

(ROOMS: $95-240) Opened in April of 2011, Bioma is a brand-new boutique hotel born from the meticulous restoration and expansion of a colonial house. It is strategically located in the heart of Mompós' historical center. This hotel offers its guests a unique escape from their everyday life by immersing them into the magical settings of a beautiful colonial UNESCO World Heritage Site.

This hotel delivers all the modern comfort and amenities expected of today's discerning traveler. Offering rooms equipped with comfortable beds, elegant bathrooms, air conditioner and ceiling fan, high definition TV with local and international channels, WiFi, in-room safe, mini-bar and iPod docking station, Bioma Boutique Hotel has it all. Additionally, Bioma amenities include gardens, restaurant, swimming pool, terrace with 360-degree views of the city, Jacuzzi and lounge. Ca. Real del Medio 18-59. Tel: 685-6733, Cel: 315-308-6365, Fax: 685-6733, E-mail: info@bioma.co, URL: www.bioma.co. Updated Apr 27, 2011.

Restaurants

Restaurants in Mompós offer Creole meals as well as standard regional fare. If you are looking for salads and light foods, you won't have much luck. Most dishes consist of chicken or beef, though one place does offer crepes. If you are looking for more unusual foods, then Mompós might be the ideal destination. Locals here eat just about everything, including sea turtles (Galápagos/icotea), peccary (ponche/chiguiro) and the occasional iguana.

There are some decent bars along the riverfront on the Alberrada that blast out different genres of music alongside one another. The pick of the bunch and the most historic is **Luna de Mompox**. Updated: Feb 18, 2008.

Asadero Patio Bonito

(ENTREES: $3 and up) Asadero Patio Bonito is cheap and cheerful. This restaurant stands out from the crowd thanks to its good-sized portions and inexpensive

nature. The dirt floors are hardly notice-
able, since the place is only open at night
and the lighting is dim. All platters cost
about $3. Don't forget to specify whether
you want beef or chicken. Opposite the
Hotel Villa de Mompox, on Calle Real del
Medio. Updated: Apr 13, 2011.

Dely Bross
Run by an efficient and friendly paisa
(a native of Medellín), the Dely Bross is
an unassuming restaurant near Parque
Bolívar. Locals must truly enjoy the owner's decent-sized platters of grilled chick-
en, beef and river fish, since almost every
lunchtime and evening the crowd is near
capacity. Ca. 18, 2B-59 and El Camellon
del Colegio, opposite the Colegio Pinillos.
Updated: May 19, 2009.

Crepes Helados Pan D' la Villa
Although the service is slow and the staff
isn't very friendly, Crepes Helados Pan D'
la Villa's has a great location right at the
heart of Real Calle del Medio, making it an
ideal spot to break from the stifling heat.
Enjoy a light crepe lunch at the only place
where crepes are available in Mompós.
Wash it all down with a sweet, chilled *jugo
de corozo*. The site can seat up to 40, but
keep in mind that service slows considerably with larger crowds. Ca. Real del Medio
17-51. Updated: Apr 03, 2011.

Nightlife

Luna de Mompox 🍴
As the oldest and most established bar in
Mompós, the Luna de Mompox is a classy
spot. On the corner of the Alberrada de los
Angeles, it has a prime location that over-
looks the Magdalena. This is a great place for
a happy hour drink that could extend into an
impromptu late-night party.

A few other bars rest along the Alberrada,
including **Bar D' Rumba** and **Mango Bi-
che Bar**, which both vie for more clients by
drowning eachother out with loud music.
Updated: Apr 03, 2011.

LOWER MAGDALENA

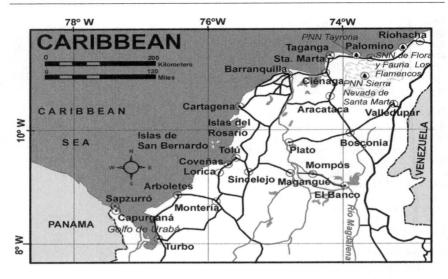

The Caribbean Coast and Islands

Along Colombia's Caribbean coast are gorgeous and deserted beaches, both on the mainland and islands. All are virtually unspoiled, with a couple of notable exceptions.

By far the most popular visitor spot on the coast is Cartagena. The colonial architecture in Cartagena's old town is among the best-preserved in Latin America, and there are also many impressive buildings from the republican era. History buffs will be fascinated by the fortified wall and castle that protected the old city, time and time again, from pirates and other invaders. And with Cartagena's laidback vibe, bustling streets and exciting nightlife, it's easy to see why so many people come here for holidays.

But the beaches in Cartagena's immediate vicinity aren't the best; serious beach lovers, divers and snorkelers head to the Islas de Rosario, with wide, sandy bays, palm trees and off-shore reefs that teem with colorful sea life. There are a couple of places to stay on the islands, but they're so close to Cartagena that most people just go for a day trip. Just up the coast from Cartagena is the fishing village of Boquilla, which livens up on weekends, when little wooden huts open up to serve up the catch of the day alongside rice and plantains.

Further north, Santa Marta is reachable in a day from Cartagena. There's not much to do in the town itself—most people come en route to Parque Nacional Natural Tayrona, which arguably has Colombia's best beaches. Most of the beaches are set in deep bays surrounded by forest, and there's a good chance you'll have one all to yourself. Santa Marta is also a good base from which to organize trips to Ciudad Perdida (The Lost City), an ancient pre-Columbian town that remained hidden deep in the thick rainforest until it was discovered by accident in 1975. There are no roads, and the city can only be reached by foot. It's a five-day hike there and back.

Colombia also lays claim to two Caribbean Islands, San Andrés and Providencia, each of which has a completely different feel. San Andrés is more visitor-oriented, with a resort atmosphere that attracts sun-seekers and watersport enthusiasts, many from South America. The beaches are good and the diving is said to be the best in Colombia. In contrast, Providencia's tourist industry is not nearly as well-developed, which, for some, is the best thing about it. It is far quieter, the beaches are pristine, and there are plenty of good dive spots here, too. Updated: Feb 1, 2011.

Baseball

Take me out to the ballgame, take me out with the crowd
Buy me some perros and cerveza
I don't care if I ever...

It has often been said you can trace U.S. military occupations by baseball. To this rule, though, Colombia is an exception. Here, the sport was introduced by local boys who learned it in other countries and thought it would be cool to play it in their Caribbean hometowns.

Gonzalo and Hibraim Zúñiga Ángel, brothers from the Chocó, went to the U.S. to study. When they got off the ship in Cartagena in 1903, they were toting bats, balls and other strange equipment. They and Fernando Gómez and Guillermo de la Espriella began playing the sport in that city. In the case of Barranquilla, three brothers—Venancio, Abraham and José García—brought the game in 1906 from Cuba; two years later they formed the Barranquilla Cubans team. The first game between these two rival cities was November 11, 1916; Cartagena won 6 to 2.

And it's root, root, root for the home team
If they don't win it's a shame...

The professional season in Colombia depends on the major leagues in the U.S., as many players on State-side teams come down to play in the off-season. Generally, it's from October to February. Only six cities have pro teams: Barranquilla Caimanes, Cartagena Indios, Montería Cardenales, Cali Toros (formerly of Sincelejo), and new-comers Medellín Potros and Bogotá Águilas.

What is big in this country is the minor leagues, or Liga Menor, which runs from March to September or October. Most towns along the Caribbean coast from Sucre Department to the Guajira have several teams, including Montería, Sincelejo, Cartagena, Barranquilla, Ciénaga and Santa Marta. Even Bogotá has a team, and Chiquinquirá will soon have one. Games are on Saturdays and Sundays at 3 p.m. So if you happen to be on the coast during the season, drop by the ballpark and catch the action!

So it's one, two, three strikes, you're out at the ol' ballgame....

History

The indigenous Arawak-Caribe were the original inhabitants of Colombia's Caribbean coast and the San Andrés Islands. Included in this ethnic group were the Tayrona, goldsmith masters and ancestors of the modern-day Kogi, who still inhabit the Sierra Nevada de Santa Marta. These nations had extensive trade networks throughout the hemisphere. (Their products have been found as far north as the Ohio River Valley.)

When Santa Marta was founded in 1525, it was the first Spanish settlement in South America. Soon other ports were settled along the coast. The most important was Cartagena in 1533, which became the main storehouse and port for the riches mined in the Spanish colonies. The cities were targets for pirates for more than a century. Some of the famous sea dogs who hit up this area were Sir Francis Drake and the Cote brothers.

These foundling cities played important roles in the struggle for independence from Spain. Cartagena was one of the first cities of Nueva Granada to declare freedom and under whose patronage Simón Bolívar fought. In 1830, the Great Liberator died in Santa Marta. After the breakup of Gran Colombia, the region along the Río Magdalena suffered from civil wars, including the War of One Thousand Days, which raged in the late 19th century.

CARIBBEAN COAST

Highlights

The quintessential colonial port of **Cartagena** (p. 244) with its brightly colored buildings boasts almost 500 years of history.

A five-day trek deep into the jungles near Santa Marta takes you to the fabled **Ciudad Perdida** (p. 315), the Lost City.

Head out to the ballpark and munch down on *fritos* and beer while enjoying a **baseball** (p. 231) game.

The annual vallenato music festival in **Valledupar** (p. 319) every April is a great opportunity to learn about the extended music culture of Colombia.

From the **San Andrés Islands** (p. 329) to **Parque Nacional Natural Tayrona** (p. 311), divers can explore coral reef as well as old Spanish galleons.

At the end of the 19th century, the US banana companies arrived. United Fruit Company had plantations stretching across the Lower Magdalena River Valley, operating under various names, including Sevilla Fruit Company and Magdalena Fruit Company. In 1928 the workers went on strike, leading to a massacre of the *bananeros* and their families in Ciénaga. The United Fruit Company is still here (now known as Chiquita); its plantations stretch all the way to the Urubá Gulf. Dole and Fyffes also have a presence in the region.

The Magdalena River Valley, Sierra Nevada de Santa Marta and the Chocó have been hot points in the civil war, which still wages to this day. The ELN is the major guerrilla group in the area, but there are some FARC and paramilitary forces, too. Updated: Feb 1, 2011.

When to Go

The Caribbean Coast and islands have a hot climate. Daytime temperatures reach the upper 20s°C to mid-30s°C (80-95°F). Typically there are two rainy seasons, May to June and August to November. Storms can be torrential and sometimes cause local flooding. From the end of the year into March, high winds come blowing out of the north. Small craft advisories may be issued during this period. In the San Andrés Islands, watch out for tropical storm and hurricane advisories from May to September. Historically, hurricanes do not strike as far south as the northern coast of South America. Updated: Mar 13, 2011.

Safety

Petty crimes occur in large tourist cities, like Cartagena, Barranquilla and Santa Marta. In these areas use common sense and leave valuables in your hotel. When out and about, be aware of your surroundings and keep an eye on your camera and backpack.

These major population areas are outside of the red zone of Colombia's civil war. Security has improved greatly in the past few years, but problems still exist in the hinter regions along the Río Magdalena and in the Sierra Nevada de Santa Marta. The mangrove swamps between Coveñas and Turbo are hideouts for narcotraffickers. For the most part, however, it is safe to visit towns in those areas—as long as you don't go wandering off into the back country. Keep informed of current situations and always ask local advice. Updated: Jun 11, 2011.

Things to See and Do

The Caribbean Coast and islands aren't just about white sand beaches and scuba diving. You can delve into colonial and republican history in such cities as Cartagena and Santa Marta, tracing the steps of Spanish explorers and Simón Bolívar. Many astounding national parks and reserves, like Tayrona, Los Flamencos, Ciénaga and Sierra Nevada de Santa Marta, provide opportunities to see sea turtles and spectacular birds. Let your footfalls echo through ancestral ruins of the Tayrona civilization: Ciudad Perdida (Lost City) in Parque Nacional Natural Sierra Nevada and El Pueblito in Parque Nacional Natural Tayrona. Aracataca, author Gabriel García Márquez' hometown, is the inspiration for Macondo (the mythical town in *One Hundred Years of Solitude*, where absurd happenings are the norm). But along this coast, every village is a Macondo, with strange festivals to celebrate with the locals like the caiman fiesta in Ciénaga or the donkey pageant in San Antero. Of course, don't forget to join the bigger parties along the Caribbean, drinking whiskey in Valledupar at the vallenato music festival and dancing traditional cumbia in Barranquilla's Carnaval. And there's much to see in the way of visual arts,

CARIBBEAN COAST

Photo by: Luis Alejandro Bernal Romero

CARIBBEAN COAST

from world-class art museums in the major cities to the film festival in Cartagena. San Andrés, whose culture is English-based, has the best of beaches and scuba diving.

Tours

Many agencies throughout Colombia and overseas offer package excursions to the San Andrés Islands, Cartagena and other tourist destinations. Cruise ships have begun return-ing to the ports here, the most popular call being Cartagena. If you make it to the coast on your own, tour operators can help you with exploring local sights or destinations like Parque Nacional Natural Tayrona and Ciudad Perdida. Some go even further to Cabo de la Vela and the Guajira Peninsula.

Many agencies handle the arrangements for the most popular sport in the Caribbean region—scuba diving. Whether you are an experienced diver or a novice wanting to learn, get ready to discover the world beneath these crystalline waters. You'll swim with colorful fishes and manta, and searching sunken ships. The most popular places to study for PADI certification are Santa Marta and Taganga.

Lodging

The full gamut of lodging types exists on Colombian's Caribbean coast, from *mala muerte* inns that may double as brothels to five-star hotels. In villages, expect only basic accommodations. Backpacker hostels are opening up in more towns, allowing safe and inexpensive options to budget travelers. Most hotels will have only showers with room-temperature water—which in these latitudes is quite warm. Luxury resorts will be the only places to have heated water. Lower-cost hostels will only have fans; mid-range accommodations will give you the choice between a room with a fan or with more expensive air conditioning.

In tourist destinations (Cartagena, Barranquilla and Santa Marta) hotels have one price for the low season and a much higher price in the high. At these times, reservations are advisable. During Carnaval, room rates may quadruple in Barranquilla. Any place along the coast it is worth asking for a discount in the *temporada baja*, especially if you will be staying for more than a few days. Updated: May 15, 2009.

COLOMBIA-PANAMÁ BORDER CROSSINGS

BY SAILBOAT

The most popular way now to journey between Colombia and Panamá is by sailboat, plying the waves between Cartagena and Portobello, Panamá, by way of Kuna Yala (San Blas Islands), home of the Kuna indigenous. The trip takes four to six days: a two-day open sea crossing from Cartagena, then two to three days in the islands. The entire package costs $450-550, and includes transportation, food and water, as well as customs and immigration procedures. Most boats take only five to seven passengers. Bicycles cost an additional $60.

Be warned that the sea can be rough at times and people frequently complain of seasickness. Travelers that have taken this route report Panamá immigration officials are usually more lenient on the entrance requirements, figuring if the tourist can afford the passage on a sailboat, then he has the financial means to visit their country.

The best sources of information are Casa Viena in Cartagena, and in Panama City, **Luna's Castle Hostel** (URL: www.lunascastlehostel.com) or **Mamallena** (URL: www.mamallena.com). Travelers coming down from Panama are now going directly to the Caribbean ports from where the sailboats are departing. Recommended places to gather information are **Hostel Wunderbar in Puerto Lindo** (URL: www.hostelwunderbar.com) and **Captain Jack's Hostel Portobello**, where many captains hang out (URL: www.hostelportobelo.com).

A frequently recommended boat is Fantasy, a 50-foot Vagabond built for the TV show, *Fantasy Island*, that Captain Jack operates (www.captainjackvoyages.com). The only reputable ships taking motorcycles ($500 extra) are Fritz the Cat (www.fritz-the-cat.com) and Stahlretter (www.stahlratte.org).

There are captains out there who are out to make a quick buck. (They can pull down a neat $5,000 in one run.) For tips on how to choose a sailboat, read "Safety on the Seventh Sea."

BY CARIBBEAN COASTAL ROUTE

The traditional route for backpackers traversing the isthmus from Colombia to Panamá has been along the North Coast from Turbo to Puerto Obaldía, Panamá. As long as you stay in the villages along the way and do not wander out, you should be safe. There is a trail that runs between Aguacate to Acandí, Capurganá, Sapzurró and over the brow of the hill to Puerto Obaldía. Ask local advice before heading out on it, as some parts may still have security problems. Panamanian officials will prevent tourists from walking the trail between La Miel and Puerto Obaldía. Be safe, be wise and you will see one of the most beautiful parts of Colombia.

Your journey begins at **Turbo**, the main port on the Golfo de Urabá. It is accessible by bus from Medellín by way of a rough road (8-17 hr, depending on road conditions, $34). Break the long journey midways with a visit to Santa Fé de Antioquia, a beautiful, safe colonial town.

You can also reach Turbo from Cartagena, by way of Montería (Cartagena-Turbo: 5 hr,

Safety On The Seventh Sea

Everyone dreams of being a pirate of the Caribbean, sailing the turquoise sea in search of deserted islands. Perhaps that's why the Colombia-Panama sailboat crossing has become so popular in recent years.

But unlike pirates of ole, you don't have the right to mutiny and make the captain walk the plank! You're a guest on his ship and have to spend up to five days with him—no dry land in sight.

Horror tales abound of bad crossings: drunk (or drugged up) or inexperienced captains, insufficient or poor food, water out of rivers (and resultant diarrhea), engines malfunctioning and being adrift for several days, overcrowding with passengers sleeping on deck—the list goes on.

It's become a lucrative business for some. Consider that at present prices, a captain can pull down a treasure trove of $5,000 on one run, by jamming people aboard. No regulations control these cruises.

To make your cruise as safe as possible, here are a few suggestions. Don't be afraid to ask pointed questions.

•Meet the captain personally and if possible the skipper and crew, to feel out their vibes. (Anybody can put up slick poster advertisements.)
•Check out the boat. It should have life boats and life jackets sufficient for the number of passengers and crew; flares, emergency radio.
•Ask to see the accommodations, to see about their conditions and cleanliness.
•Ask specifics about food (type, how many meals) and where the water comes from (is it treated?)
•Ask to see the boat's registry, license to make such runs and insurance. If the captain refuses to show these, don't go.
•How waste and trash are disposed
•What type of relations the captain has with the Kuna. (See In Kuna Yala for more about local laws and customs).
•The website Sail Panama and Colombia has a checklist with more questions to ask (www.sanblascartagena.com/safety).

Seaworthies recommend that to minimize such incidences and to have a safer voyage that you avoid boats under 37 feet, since they are not as stable. A sailboat that is 37 to 44-foot is better. Best is a 44 to 66 footer. Catamarans are the most stable.

Panamanians consider the eastern Caribbean coast to be a No Man's Land. Real pirates lurk not too far away. If pressed, some captains claim pirates operate along the coast. But in reality, pirates tend to make raids at open sea. Yachters have reported problems near Islas del Rosario, and the Caribbean coast from the Guajira to Trinidad. It's amazing there haven't been pirate attacks on these sailboats shuttling foreigners across the Caribbean (or at least what's being talked about). It would be rich rewards from such sitting ducks. It's also lucky—considering the condition of some boats and overcrowding—that there haven't been shipwrecks. Hopefully there won't be any in the future, either. Updated: Jun 16, 2011.

CARIBBEAN COAST

$20; Montería-Turbo: 7 hr, $20). You will have to break the journey up in two. Montería has security issues; it is best to stay in Arboletes. Check Aires (www.aires.aero) or ADA (www.ada-aero.com) for cheap airfares from Medellín to Apartadó, near Turbo.

Turbo is an ugly port with many safety issues. Get out as soon as you can. If you're stuck there, a recommended hotel is **Hotel Florida** (Parque Principal, near docks. Tel: 827-3531/Cel: 311-327-2569. Single $9-11). It is difficult to change

In Kuna Yala

The allure for many travelers of taking the Colombia-Panama sailboats is passing through the San Blas Islands. It is an exotic locale, with crystalline seas, powder-white beaches and traditional indigenous people. A real foreign land—which is precisely what it is.

Welcome to Kuna Yala, an autonomous region within Panamanian territory, with the right to lay down its own laws. The official website of the Congreso General Kuna (Kuna Yala's governing body) has useful information (in Spanish) about Kuna culture, history and other aspects, and details the norms of tourism and tourist behavior (www.congresogeneralkuna.com). Some of the laws are:

•Photographs and videos of the Kuna or the community may not be taken without the permission of local authorities and individuals.
•Natural resources (including the plentiful coconuts and shells) may not be removed.
•Local authorities may search tourists.
•Tourists must respect sacred sites, cemeteries and religious rituals.
•The use or trafficking of drugs or other illegal substances is prohibited.
•People may not wear bathing suits in public streets.
•Nudity in all forms is prohibited (including skinny-dipping).
•Guides must be Kuna.
•No littering. Only biodegradable materials may be used.
•Fines up to $100,000 may be levied, and the violator may be expelled from the Kuna community.

These laws are intended to preserve Kuna traditions and way of life. Nonetheless, sociologists and anthropologists have noted the impact sailboat tourism is already having on Kuna culture.

Updated: May 12, 2011.

money in Turbo. The *chalupas*, or boats, up the coast will take payment in either Colombian pesos or U.S. dollars.

From Turbo, twin-engine speedboats leave almost daily (usually in the early morning when the sea is calmer) for villages along the coast, including San Francisco and Capurganá. If heading for Panamá, go to Capurganá (leaves 8:30 a.m., $31, 2-3 hours) for your Colombian exit stamp. Buy tickets the night before (in the low season, it may be possible to buy the same morning). Show up about 6 a.m. to get a seat in the back, which will be less bumpy and damp. The journey can be very wet; be sure to cover yourself and your belongings with a plastic tarp (a shower curtain works great) and wear a life jacket. The seas are rough December-March; this run is not recommended then.

Midways between Turbo and Capuraganá is the small hamlet **San Francisco**, accessible by launch (from Turbo: 8:30 a.m., noon; 1.5-2 hr, $17). Travelers willing to get way off the beaten track can pass the days relaxing, fishing, kayaking, hiking or horseback riding. Sea turtle season is May-July. Ralle's Hostel provides lodging with communal kitchen (Cel: 314-703-6151, URL: www. ralles-hostel.com. Dorm: $14, with 2 meals $22; private room with 2 meals $28). Bring insect repellent, sun screen and flashlight.

Capurganá has for many years been a resort town for those moneyed Colombians looking for the ultimate in white-sand beaches and amazingly colored sea. Still, there are affordable inns in this village, e.g. Señora Beatriz' Hostal Capurganá ($9) and Hospedaje Los Delfines (near Ferretería Marta, $7 per person). Restaurante Josefina is said to prepare the best seafood in Colombia.

The DAS (Colombian immigration) office is an 8 to 10-minute walk from the jetty; here you get your passport stamped. It is difficult to change money in Capurganá; the grocery shop reportedly gives poor rates. There is no ATM. From Capurganá chalupas go to **Puerto Obaldía, Panamá** (9 a.m., 30-45 min, $14). Your boat will be met by the Panamanian immigration and customs officials, who can be quite stringent on fulfilling the entry requirements. Be prepared to show sufficient funds ($600), on- or outward ticket (a credit card may suffice in lieu of a ticket), malaria medication and yellow fever vaccination. Have two photocopies of your passport handy. Panama immigration is open only Monday-Friday.

A hotel in Puerto Obaldía is Pensión Cande ($5). The internet café gives good rates of exchange. Air Panamá has flights to Panama City four times weekly (URL: www.flyairpanama.com. $92, including taxes). Upon arriving at the Panama City airport, passengers are held for interrogation about drugs. Passports are stamped in Puerto Obaldía, but tourist cards issued on the plane. Up to 90 days are given.

ALTERNATIVE ROUTE THROUGH SAN BLAS

Foreigners are re-blazing the old, alternative route through the San Blas Islands. **Sapzurró**, a 250-soul village, is accessed from Capurganá by chalupa (several daily, 10 min, $4). Camping Paraíso, also called Chilli's Hostel, has hammock-mosquito net accommodations ($5.50), as well as camping and cabañas (near the bay, Cel: 313-685-9862). Wittenberg Camp, at the base of the hill to La Miel, is quieter. It also lets hammock-mosquito net ($5.50) and a one-person cabaña ($11), and makes meals (Cel: 311-436-6215, E-mail: wittenberg2000@hotmail.com).

Darien Gapster runs a speedboat from Sapzurró to Porvenir, Panamá, passing through Kuna Yala (Tel/Colombia: 314-567-3978, URL: www.thedariengapster.com). The three-day trip includes transport, lodging and meals in San Blas Islands ($279; book ahead; $25 deposit required), but not water. The group of travelers meets in Cartagena, from where they travel together to Turbo by land, and then Capurganá and Sapzurró by chalupa (these costs are not included). Passengers can also join in Sapzurró. The captain handles all immigration procedures. Alternately, you can await a Kuna merchant ship to take you to Miramar ($30-100, depending on your bargaining skills; 4-5 days). The journey is rudimentary, with only wooden benches and small servings of food; bring a hammock and extra food and water; Teresa

(UK) recommends the Tabualá 2.

Daphnis (Belgium) island-hopped his way through the San Blas archipelago. Going South, this was his route:

Miramar-Porvenir: common speedboat 8 a.m. (can be delayed), 2 hr, $25

Porvenir-Narganá: cargo ship, 2 hr, $25

Narganá-Ustupu: passenger speedboat, 2 hr, $25

Ustupu-Calendonia: slow cargo ship, many stops; 6 hr, $5

Calendonia-Puerto Obaldía: hired single engine speedboat, 4 hr, $25

In Puerto Obaldía, luggage was searched and immigration procedures done. Daphnis counsels that patience is needed, as it may be two or three days between boats. Don't rely on local information for the next boat; take it upon yourself to ask every boat coming into port. Also, take plenty of money with you.

There reportedly is a weekly launch from Porvenir to Puerto Obaldía ($40-80, depending on the number of passengers). Updated: May 20, 2011.

COVEÑAS

 0m   11,000   5

The more amiable and interesting area of Coveñas township is Segunda Ensenada of Punta de Piedra. This horseshoe-shaped bay extends over 2 kilometers (1.2 mi) west of the mouth of Ciénaga de Caimanera. Over a dozen hotels and even more restaurants line the white-sand beach. The Golfo de Morrosquillo here is shallow for a long ways out to sea.

Mornings by the sea are calm, but the sea breezes are at full gust by noon. The ocean is the warmest you will find in all of South America. Combined with the hot tropical sun, it will feel more like a Jacuzzi! Several pleasant days can be spent without notice here, as time somehow slips its way through your fingers. Colombians mob the beach on the weekends, while weekdays often see empty sand and sea.

The actual town of Coveñas is six kilometers (3.6 mi) down the road. It has Internet and other basic services, but hey, you're at a wonderful beach get-away! Leave your laptop behind, kick back and relax your very own coastal paradise. Updated: Jun 15, 2011.

When to Go

Like Tolú, Coveñas is tropical year-round. The beach gets crowded on the weekends and during holidays. Hotels fill up on Sundays in particular, and clear out by Tuesday. If you are seeking a private plot of sand, come on a weekday. Occasionally the hotels see so few guests and are so quiet it is spooky. San Antero, a village 7.5 kilometers (4.7 mi) from Coveñas, hosts the Festival del Burro every Semana Santa, featuring a donkey beauty pageant and traditional costeño music and dances. Updated: May 09, 2011.

Getting To and Away

From Tolú, minibuses to Coveñas depart from a half block north of the plaza (Cra 2, between Ca 16 and 17. Every 10 min 5 a.m.-7 p.m., 0.5 hr, $1.70). Tolú to Segunda Ensenada costs $2.25, and Segunda Ensenada to downtown Coveñas $1.25. Beware of overcharging. Brasilia and Rápido Ochoa share a terminal on the highway near downtown Coveñas. They provide service to **Montería**, **Medellín**, **Bogotá** and other destinations. Fares are about the same as from Tolú. For **San Antero** and **Cispatá**, flag down a bus along the highway or go into Coveñas and catch one from the terminal across from the Ochoa-Brasilia station. Any bus going to Lorica passes through San Antero ($1.70). Updated: Jun 15, 2011.

Getting Around

It is very easy to walk around beachside Coveñas. There is also the slower alternative of a two-peddle cart along the boardwalk, costing about $0.50. A mototaxi between downtown and Segunda Ensenada cost $0.80. Official motorcycle drivers for hire wear dark or orange vests. If you prefer a regular cab, Los Taxis has a stand near the Segunda Ensenada bus stop (Tel: 288-0933). Updated: Jun 15, 2011.

Safety

In Coveñas. you will have surprisingly more to worry about during the day here than at night. That is, if you spend your day on the beach. Hawkers selling everything imaginable under the sun beg you to buy something. The biggest danger is probably at sea, with boats doing banana and tube rides, or other tours. These craft sometimes can get too close to swimmers. Coveñas is within a malaria and dengue zone.

Take precautions against being bitten and take malarial medication, especially during the rainy season. *Jejenes* (no-see-ums, sand flies) are quite vicious. Tap water is not potable. Updated: Jun 16, 2011.

Services

Most services are located in downtown Coveñas, including the police station, Bancolombia (ATM), **Centro de Salud** (health post; Cell: 312-669-1324) and pharmacies. Several Internet cafés are near the bus terminals on the highway. The tourism office is in the *alcaldía* (city hall); for more information about Coveñas, visit www.covenas-sucre.gov.co or www.destinomorrosquillo.com. At Segunda Ensenada, there is a Bancolombia ATM at Villa Melissa. Locals set up cell phone stands (local and national services only). Updated: Jun 16, 2011.

Things to See and Do

Coveñas is all about relaxing on the beach or under the shade of a thatched umbrella. You can also get your dose of R&R in at Playa Blanca, a pleasant, less-developed beach, and Volcán de Lodo, a healing mud bath. Both are West of Coveñas, near San Antero. If it's flora and fauna or natural life you are seeking, you don't have to look far. Manglares de Cispatá, to the West, and Ciénaga de Caimanera, on the way to Tolú, both are great half-day excursions.Updated: Jun 21, 2011.

Playa Blanca

Very few foreigners know of Playa Blanca, 30 minutes west of Coveñas. This town has small beaches separated by jetties. It's where Colombians seeking sand and sun come to vacation. During the holidays, weekends, and in July, the beach fills up with people. At other times of the year this place is completely empty and, therefore, a perfect getaway should you find Coveñas not to your liking. Hotel Playa Blanca, the only hotel in town (URL: www.hotelplayablancasanantero.com; $50 per night), offers clean and modern cabañas with hammocks, and has a large pool. Other, less expensive, accommodations are in homes across from the beach that can only be arranged upon arrival. Stock up on snacks before you leave for Playa Blanca, as the handful of restaurants here serve plain meals at high prices. To get to Playa Blanca, take a bus to San Antero ($1.70) and from there a mototaxi ($1-2) to Playa Blanca. Updated: Jun 16, 2011.

Volcán de Lodo
(ADMISSION: $3) Treat yourself to a healing mud bath at Volcán de Lodo, where the mud supposedly has special healing properties. The great thing about this place is the price: For just $3 you can play in the mud while feeling your skin transform and soften. The facilities here are basic. Get yourself dirty, and then rinse yourself off. It's a great way to break up your day on the beach.From Coveñas, take a San Antero- or Lorica-bound bus and ask the driver to let you off at *Volcán de Lodo* ($1.70). Updated: May 09, 2011.

Manglares de Cispatá
Spend an interesting half-day trip at the Manglares de Cispatá in the Sinú River delta. Visit a small animal sanctuary with turtles and caimans. You can touch and hold most of the animals. A guide explains the kind of preservation work currently done in the area. If you come by boat, you also can visit a bird sanctuary with pelicans and tour a sardine farm. To get to Manglares de Cispatá, take a bus to San Antero ($1.70) and from there, transport to Cispatá ($1). Or hire a boat from Playa Blanca to show you around for $50 and make a day of it. At Bahía de Cispatá is Camping Cispatá (URL: www.camping-cispata.com), Resort Cispatá Marina Hotel (Tel: 811-0707, URL: www.cispata.com) and other lodging. Updated: May 09, 2011.

Tours
Deportes Náuticos offers scuba, kite boarding, water skiing and other water sports, as well as catamaran cruises (Cabañas La Candelita, Primera Ensenada. Cell: 314-561-6513). **Nicolás Teherán** is a Sena-trained guide who does boating tours of Ciénaga La Caimanera ($11 per person) and fishing trips. You can also hire him to take you by motorcycle to Volcán del Lodo ($7 round trip, with 1-hr wait) (Boca de Ciénaga, Cell: 311-671-0184, E-mail: nicolascaimanera@hotmail.com). Some hotels offer boating tours to Islas de San Bernardo, Isla Fuerte and other destinations, as well as jet ski and other aquatic sport equipment rentals. Updated: Jun 16, 2011.

Lodging
Downtown Coveñas has few lodging options. The best variety is at Segunda Ensenada of Punta de Piedras, between Tolú and Coveñas. Here are basic hotels, cabañas and vacation apartments. Some places also have campsites. If Coveñas isn't quiet enough, you

can head westward to Playa Blanca at San Antero or Playa del Viento at San Bernardo del Viento. In the Coveñas region, hotel prices rise steeply at holiday times. In the low season, bargain for a cheaper rate if spending several days. Updated: Jun 16, 2011.

Los Corales
(ROOMS: $10-39) Los Corales' Swiss owner keeps a watchful eye over the hotel and can tell you firsthand how much Coveñas has changed since his hotel opened more than a decade ago. Back then, it offered just three rooms and basic accommodations. Now, this place has 27 rooms, public shower and bathroom facilities, and a fully functioning dining hall and beachfront restaurant. For half as much as you would pay at other hotels at Segunda Ensenada, you get a spacious and modern room with air conditioning or a fan. Prices rise in high season. Av. La Playa, Segunda Ensenada. Tel: 288-0336, Fax: 288-0573, URL: www.loscoraleshotel.com. Updated: May 09, 2011.

Hotel Villa Lina
(ROOMS: $13-15) Hotel Villa Lina is a quiet retreat in the heart of Coveñas' Segunda Ensenada. The English-speaking owner, José, makes every effort to welcome his guests. He is knowledgeable about what to see and do in the area. The rooms (some with king-sized beds) are spacious and have private baths. The shaded lawn has camping. Bicyclists and motorcyclists are welcome. The restaurant, which is open daily, serves local cuisine on the beach, where hammocks hang, ready for guests' siesta. Special all-inclusive packages (with lodging and three meals) are available, and prices rise in high season. Segunda Ensenada, Cel: 312-763-6971, E-mail: josebarguil@yahoo.com, URL: www.destino-morrosquillo.com. Updated: May 17, 2011.

Hotel Nitana
(ROOMS: $42-69) Hotel Nitana, a Spanish-owned and -run inn, is an excellent option for anyone considering a few days on this stretch of beach in Coveñas. Rooms are new, clean and comfortably equipped with air conditioning, refrigerator, new mattresses and fine bathrooms. The beach out front is narrow and far from ideal, but a 15-minute stroll will take you to wider, sandier points. The hotel can help guests arrange tours to San Bernardo islands and Ciénaga de Caimanera, and activities like water skiing, fishing and scuba diving. Room rates include breakfast, and go up in high season. If arriving on the bus from Cartagena, ask

to be dropped on the outskirts of Coveñas. Keep an eye out for the signs to the hotel, clearly seen on the right-hand side. Segunda Ensenada, Tel: 288-0363/Cel: 315-755-4774, E-mail: info@nitana.com, URL: www.nitana.com. Updated: May 14, 2009.

La Fragata

(ROOMS: $50-145) La Fragata is a lively, resort-like hotel comprised six distinct buildings: three cabaña-style structures; the main reception hall, which includes second-floor rooms overlooking the ocean; a six-story structure, which has hotel rooms; and, lastly, a pool area and hut for relaxing. Having almost 100 guest rooms and styles to choose from is a bonus, but the rooms themselves are all a bit simple and in need of updating. However, La Fragata does have the best facilities in town, with a solarium deck and bar on a protected beach, shaded huts with hammocks, and a game room and lounge on the second floor of a large thatched hut. This is definitely the best option for families and large groups. La Fragata can help arrange kayak rental, scuba diving or tours. Sister hotel Cabañas la Fragata (Tel: 311-420-8382. URL: www.hotelestropical-inn.com/covenas. html) in the Puerto Viejo sector (between Coveñas and Tolú) rents out six cabañas that house three to 18 people. Cabañas share a barbecue area and kiddie park. Segunda Ensenada, Tel: 249-9361, Cel: 312-665-8975, URL: www.hotel-lafragata.com. Updated: May 09, 2011.

Villa Melissa

(ROOMS: $50-150) Villa Melissa is one of Coveñas' best hotel options. The owners are friendly workaholics who will do everything within their power to make your stay a pleasant one, and their dedication to their investment shows. An impeccably clean pool welcomes people in from the beach. The accommodations are large, well-furnished and comfortable. Villa Melissa has one-, two-, and three-room apartments; each has a balcony, air conditioning, fans and cable TV. The hotel is six kilometers (4 mi) outside of Coveñas. Ask the bus driver to let you off at Villa Melissa (you will see the sign along the road) or catch a taxi from Coveñas. Look at the web site for a map of how to get there. Segunda Ensenada. Tel: 288-0249, Cel: 311-665-9228. E-mail: info@hotelvillamelissa.com, URL: www.hotelvillamelissa.com. Updated: May 09, 2011.

Estado Natural Eco-lodge

(ROOMS: $30-37 per person) Immerse yourself in nature at Estado Natural Eco-lodge, about 46 kilometers (28.6 mi) west of Coveñas, near San Bernardo del Viento. You can lie on a pristine beach, snorkel around the reefs of Isla Fuerte, canoe through mangrove forests or the delta of the Sinú River, hike to a tropical dry-forest private reserve or watch your feathered friends at Ciénaga de Bañó, one of the top birdwatching spots in Colombia.

The one- or two-story cabañas (the two-story ones come with a private kitchen and have a full ocean view from the bedroom) are constructed sustainably with local materials and are modeled on ancient indigenous circular huts. Be warned: here, eco-friendly equals compost (waterless) toilets, although some cabañas have regular toilets.

Your money also goes toward supporting this 10-year-old eco-lodge, which calls itself "a nature retreat that will hopefully teach you something." Estado Natural has been reforesting the local mangrove forests and teaching local children about environmental responsibility. A volunteer program is available with the hotel. Room rates rise in high season. Playa del Viento, San Bernardo del Viento, Cordoba. Cel: 301-442-2438, E-mail: info@estado-natural.com, URL: www.estado-natural.com. Updated: Jun 16, 2011.

Restaurants

The few dining options in Coveñas are all comparable in price and quality. The typical fare at every restaurant is a plate of fish, meat or chicken with a side of salad and plantains. The most you can expect from these eateries is that you leave full and satisfied. Rest assured the seafood is always fresh and of particularly good value. At Segunda Ensenada, many restaurants line the beach. Some are attached to hotels; La Fragata, Villa Melissa and Los Corales each have extensive menus. In the low season, many are closed during the week. About midway down Avenida La Playa is a row of basic *comedor* eateries. A good option for a mid-day snack is to buy ceviche or oyster cocktail from a food vendor roaming the beach and boardwalk. Updated: May 09, 2011.

Punta de Piedra

(ENTREES: $6-10) Restaurante Punta de Piedra is a peaceful place to have dinner. The owner, Saul, is super friendly and fre-

---

quently hosts card games with his friends in one corner of the dining room. The openness of this restaurant and the amiable locals make this a great place to wind down, people-watch, and enjoy a home-cooked meal. The food here is decent and reasonably priced—especially the seafood. Daily 9 a.m.-9 p.m. Segunda Ensenada, at far south end of beach Tel: Cell: 310-705-0561. Updated: May 18, 2009.

Palmar

(ENTREES: $7 and up) When the local youth turn up the music and chill out in the shade, Restaurante Palmar becomes a pretty lively place for lunching. The food here is just average, so come more for the atmosphere than the cuisine. There is a second-floor balcony with hammocks and seating that you are free to use even after you finished your meal. Segunda Ensenada, Punta de Piedra (next to Hotel Los Corales), Cel: 313-576-5075. Daily 7 a.m.-7:30 p.m. Updated: Jun 16, 2011.

TOLÚ

 0m   28,000   5

Santiago de Tolú is a sleepy fishing port founded in 1535—making it one of the oldest Spanish towns in Colombia. There's nothing particularly attractive about it aside from the warm ocean. It has friendly locals and a light-hearted, free-spirited vibe due to the abundance of bars along the boardwalk that blast champeta music all day long. During holidays and weekends, when Colombian tourists flock here, the town doubles in size.

Tolú is the ideal launching point to see natural sights or to lounge on a white sand beach. Some interesting places, like the San Bernardo Islands, Coveñas, Caimanera, Volcán de Lodo and Playa Blanca, are 30 minutes to an hour from Tolú.

There are a far greater number of Colombians here on vacation than foreigners, but backpackers are slowly discovering Tolú, too. Most people spend just a day or two in Tolú, then head further West along the coast. Updated: May 09, 2011.

When to Go

Tolú, like Cartagena, has the benefit of year-round tropical weather—generally hot and clear conditions. During December, January and Semana Santa this place gets so packed that, depending on what kind of beach holiday you are looking for, it may not be worth stopping here. On weekdays, this town is very quiet and peaceful. Updated: Jun 21, 2011.

Getting To and Away

BY BUS

Tolú has two bus terminals. Minibuses to Coveñas depart from a half block north of the plaza (Cra 2, between Ca 16 and 17. Every 10 min 5 a.m.-7 p.m., 0.5 hr, $1.70). Buses to all other destinations leave from the gas stations (bomba) at Calle 16 and the highway, nine blocks east of the plaza. Brasilia has a ticket office on the Carrera 3 side of the plaza. Rápido Ochoa has one at Supermercado Popular (Cra 2, between Ca 16 and 17).

To Cartagena: hourly 7:15 a.m.-8:15 p.m., 3 hr, $17
To Montería: hourly 8 a.m.-6 p.m., 4-5 hr, $10-12
To Medellín: Brasilia (8 a.m., 10:30 p.m.; 3 buses 5:30-7 p.m., 12 hr, $47-49)
To Bogotá: Brasilia (8 a.m., 5:30 p.m., 24 hr, $69)

BY AIR

Montería has an airport, as does Cartagena. Check the website of Avianca and other couriers for special fares. These can save much money and time in traveling to/from Bogotá. Updated: May 09, 2011

Getting Around

Tolú is small and manageable on foot. The major activity happens around Parque Principal and the boardwalk along the beach. If you're hard-pressed to get somewhere quickly, hitch a ride with a bicicletero (a man pedaling a bicycle rickshaw), who will take you anywhere in town for $0.60, or from the long distance bus terminal to downtown for $1.25 (beware overcharging). If you want to get around on your own power, Corpoguitur rents bicycles for $7 the entire day (Telemar Internet Café, Ca 15, 1-31. Tel: 288-5094, Cel: 301-684-4772). Updated: May 09, 2011.

Safety

Tolú is a generally safe town. Its residents are curious about where you come from, and will want to look after you and ensure you have a good time. Still, it is best to stick to the main streets at night and not wander too far out of the city limits. Tolú is within a malaria and dengue zone. Take malarial medications and precautions against being bitten, especially during the rainy season. Tap water is not potable. Updated: Jun 16, 2011.

Services

TOURISM

The tourism office is at the Casa de la Cultura (Monday-Friday 8 a.m.-noon, 2-6 p.m. Ca 20, between Cra 2 and 3. E.-mail: turismo@santiagodetolu-sucre.gov.co, URL: www.santiagodetolu-sucre.gov.co). The police station is on Calle 16, between Carreras 3 and 4.

MONEY

Bancolombia is across from the main plaza (Ca 15, between Cra 2 and 3). Banco Agrario and Banco Popular also have ATMs (Ca 16, between Cra 3 and 4). Estanco 20 de enero, near the plaza, buys US dollars (Ca 16, between Cra 2 and Av La Playa).

KEEPING IN TOUCH

I-Café is the best internet in town (Ca 17, between Cra 2 and 3). Llamadas Telemar has international phone service (Ca 15, between Cra 2 and Av La Playa). Tolú has no post office.

MEDICAL

The local hospital is at Ca 16, 9-43 (Tel: 286-0596). Several pharmacies are around the main plaza.

LAUNDRY

Laundry is available at any home-for-rent or hotel, and all charge about $2 per kilo. Updated: May 09, 2011.

Things to See and Do

Tolú itself has little to offer in terms of historical sights or other activities. If you'd like to spend a few days in town, you can take a boat trip, spend some time on the beach, walk or ride with a bicicletero around town, or make your way to Ciénaga de Caimanera for some time in nature. In the evenings, make your way along the boardwalk and take some time to enjoy the sea breeze, shopping, lively music and warm atmosphere. Updated: May 09, 2011.

Bicicletero

A good way to get out and see Tolú and its malecón (boardwalk) is to hire a bicicletero and ride around town for an hour or two. Many of these "bikers" sit around the main square and by the bus terminals and are very happy to show you the sights and sounds of Tolú for $1.25 per hour. A jaunt around on one of the six-passenger bikes (on which each person has a pedal to push) costs $1.25 per person. Updated: May 09, 2011.

La Ciénaga de Caimanera

Just fifteen minutes out of town, between Tolú and Coveñas, is a pleasant natural half-fresh and half-salt water lagoon, Ciénaga de Caimanera. Here, you can take a boat around the lagoon, pick and eat raw oysters, spot jaibas (small crabs) scurrying around the exposed roots of the mangrove forest, and see shrimp by the dozen. Most excursions go as far as the floating house, where at sunset you can watch the birds returning to their roosts. Take a taxi from Parque Principal to La Boca de Ciénaga ($4 one way) or take a Coveñas-bound bus as far as the Boca de la Ciénaga ($1). Book a tour through your hotel, or go to La Boca de Ciénaga. Excursions should cost $9 per person, but operators may try to charge as much as $22; bargain hard. Updated: Jun 16, 2011.

San Bernardo Islands

In an effort to attract affluent clientele and foreign revenue, the Colombian tourism industry has recently begun actively promoting the tiny 10-island archipelago of San Bernardo, which is part of PNN Corales del Rosario y de San Bernardo, founded in 1977. Tours include visits Isla Palma, with its ecological park and ill-equipped aquarium; El Islote de Santa Cruz, a tiny fisherman's community built on top of the sea and one of the most densely populated islands in the world; Isla Mucura, which is known for its beaches; and Isla Tintipán, known for its mangrove forests. Be warned that locals on Isla Mucura tend to overcharge for beach chair rentals.

A Norwegian couple has a small hostel on Isla Palma ($28 per person). Tours to Islas de San Bernardo can be arranged through any of the clubes náuticos on Avenida La Playa or through your hotel (in the high seasons, book in advance). The excursions supposedly leave at 8 a.m. and return at 4 p.m., but may leave later and return earlier. Rates run $31-35, depending on the company and season, and includes transportation, aquarium entry fee and lunch.

If you plan to stay on Isla Palma, talk with a local fisherman who'll charge $11 one way for the one-hour ride out; arrange for pick-up in advance. Nautical clubs charge $17 for this same service, and $20 round trip for same-day trips.

Did a unique trek? Got way off the beaten path? Tell other travelers at vivatravelguides.com

Tours

Nautical clubs offices abound along Avenida La Playa. All offer tours to Islas San Bernardo. Some also do fishing and scuba excursions. Some agents are **Club Naútico Mundo Marino** (Avenida La Playa, 14 - 40. Tel: 288-4431 / Cell: 321-525-1855, E-mail: mundomarinotol@yahoo.es, URL: www.clubnauticomundomarino.com) and **Club Náutico Mar Adentro** (Av La Playa, between Ca 11 and 12. Tel: 288-5481, Cel: 310-638-7648, E-mail: maradentrotolu@hotmail.com, URL: www.clubnauticomaradentro.com). **Corporguitur**—Cooporación de Guías de Turismo—rents bicycles and offers tours to Ciénaga de la Leche, a lagoon with waterfalls and a variety of avifauna, including toucans. It also rents kayaks ($11 per hour). (Telemar Internet Café, Ca 15, 1-31. Tel: 288-5094/ Cel: 301-684-4772). Updated: May 09, 2011.

Lodging

You will have little trouble finding accommodation upon arrival in Tolú. On every block close to the boardwalk there are at least two or three houses, hostels, hotels and rooms for rent. Accommodations are basic but satisfactory. Places across from the ocean are more expensive. Loud music from bars along this stretch make the hotels on perpendicular streets a more attractive choice. For cheaper (and quieter) accommodations, try on Carrera 2, between Calles 11 and 12. Updated: May 09, 2011.

Hostal Rokalpa

(ROOMS: $9 per person) Hostal Rokalpa is one of several centrally located and clean hostels worth a try. The rooms here all have cable T.V., but are basic and small. The airy courtyard in the middle of this home is a nice place to relax or have breakfast (which you must ask to be included in your stay). Bargain with the owner for a more economical price. Ca. 17, between Cra 1 and Cra. 2. Cel: 313-531-4986. Updated: May 09, 2011.

Hotel Darimar

(ROOMS: $15-25) The clean, trim exterior of Hotel Darimar makes it seem more tcomfortable than it actually is. The rooms are small and stuffed with three short, hard beds. The bathrooms are hardly functional. This place feels more like a hospital than a hotel, but it's quiet and peaceful and conveniently located just off the boardwalk, and near the best Internet in town and the local bus terminal. Ca. 17, 1-60. Tel: 288-5153, Cel: 313-551-4977. E-mail:

hoteldarimar@hotmail.com. URL: www.hoteldarimar.com. Updated: May 09,2011

Villa Babilla

(ROOMS: $15-28) Owners Laffi and Alex opened this hostel hoping to bring foreign tourists to Tolú, and slowly their plan is working. The only problem with Villa Babilla, a well-known hostel on the backpacker route, is that it is a bit out of the way from town activity. This is a peaceful hostel, though, with lots of hammocks, a nice outdoor patio, a clean community kitchen and clean, spacious rooms. Room rates rise in the high seasons. Ca. 20, 3-40. Tel: 288-6124, Cel: 312-677-1325, E-mail: info@villababillahostel.com, URL: www.villababillahostel.com. Updated: May 09, 2011.

Hotel Caribe

(ROOMS: $17-34) Although Hotel Caribe offers basic rooms, its location in the center of the boardwalk across from the beach is ideal. Admittedly, the rooms here need updating, the lighting is dim and the bathrooms are a bit tight. Nonetheless, the rooms are a good value. Prices are higher at vacation times. Av. La Playa 18-8. Tel: 5-288-5115, E-mail: hotelcariberoyal@telecom.co, URL: www.hotelesdelmar.com. Updated: May 09, 2011.

Restaurants

Restaurants in Tolú are consolidated along the beachfront. Unfortunately, there's not a lot of variety in this town. Essentially, you have a choice between meat, chicken, fish, lobster and shrimp. These dishes are served with either plantains or rice, salad, and occasionally a scoop of beans. Try the local *bandeja típica* of fish, *patacones*, coconut rice and salad. Lobster and prawns (*langostinos*) are reasonably priced in Tolú. Prices are relatively the same everywhere you go. *Comida corriente* specials cost a bit more than in other coastal cities. Most restaurants close before 9 p.m. On the boardwalk are many fruit juice and ceviche stands. Fast food stands set up at Carrera 2 and Calle 15 in the evenings. Pick up groceries at the Mercamaceo supermarket near the plaza (Ca 15 and Cra 2). Updated: May 09, 2011.

Varadero Restaurant and Bar

(ENTREES: $4-13) Ideally located just a block from Parque Principal, Varadero serves a fantastic breakfast complete with scrambled eggs (with ham, tomato and onions), *arepa*, cheese, and your choice of hot chocolate or coffee. Prices on the menu are outdated, so be sure to find out the price of your food before you order it.

Daily 7 a.m.-8 p.m. (or later, if enough clientele). Av. La Playa, between Ca. 14 and Ca. 15 . Tel: 5-288-2916. Updated: May 10, 2011.

Restaurant Row

(ENTREES: $3-9) For a decent, cheap lunch, head to Tolú's Restaurant Row, which begins at the boardwalk and extends one block along Calle 20. Twenty great little stalls serve up fresh fish with rice and salad at a super-economical price. Around lunchtime the stalls are packed with locals, especially the most popular one, Fonda La Gordita. Most eateries are open daily 8 a.m. to 7 p.m. (some until 9 p.m.). Ca. 20, between Av. La Playa and Cra. 2. Updated: May 09, 2011.

Terraza Restaurante La 15

(ENTREES: $6-20) Terraza Restaurante La 15 is one of Tolú's better restaurants. The service here is quick and the food is tasty (though the prices are a bit high). You can't complain about the setting either, since Terraza is on a breezy corner of the boardwalk with tables by the beach and a covered patio. Daily 7 a.m.-3 a.m. Av. La Playa and Ca. 15. Tel: .288-6226. Updated: May 09, 2011.

Restaurante Donde Carlos

(LUNCH: $4.50, ENTREES: $8-33) Donde Carlos looks great from the outside: clean with its peach and cream colored decor. But the food here is expensive and not very tasty. Instead of asking for *la carta* (the menu), ask directly about *la comida corriente* (daily special), which will be half the price. Daily 7:30 a.m.-9 p.m. Ca. 17, between Av. La Playa and Cra. 2. Tel: 288-5895. Updated: May 09, 2011.

CARTAGENA DE INDIAS

 0m   895,000   5

Foreboding fortresses, narrow streets, hidden patios and enchanting colonial houses characterize Cartagena, a vibrant city rich in history and Caribbean culture. It is often referred to as one of the most beautiful cities in South America, and was designated a UNESCO World Heritage site in 1984. Frequent trade winds temper the heat.

Cartagena's strategic position on the Caribbean coast near the Magdalena and Sinú river deltas made it an important port for the Spanish Empire and a favorite target of pirates. A series of stone-walled forts—the largest such complex in the Americas—spread throughout the city stand as ominous reminders of Cartagena's colonial past.

Cartagena has plenty of sights and sounds to offer travelers. One of the best ways to enjoy this intriguing city is to amble along its historic streets, exploring its nooks and crannies and savoring its small surprises. The inner sector of the walled city—El Centro and San Diego—have multitudes of plazas, museums and churches.

The rampart walls around Plaza de la Bóvedas provide a space for watching the sea and relaxing. A lighted underground passage and drawbridge lead from here to the fortress of La Tenaza, occupying a formidable spot at the water's edge.

Daytrips abound from Cartagena. Just outside the center are Castillo San Felipe de Barajas and the spectacular viewpoint La Popa hill, where the church and monastery of Santa Cruz and restored ruins of a convent dating back to 1608 are found, along with a well-preserved image of Virgin of La Candelaria, whose festival is celebrated on February 2. Beaches at Marbella and Bocagrande invite a lazy day in the sea and sun. La Boquilla, a small village to the east, offers not only a long strand, but also windsurfing and mangrove boat tours. Other boating excursions are to Playa Blanca on Isla Barú, Islas del Rosario for scuba diving and snorkeling, and Isla de Tierra Bomba's Bocachica fortresses and Punta Arena beach. If beaches aren't your bag then head to the clay baths at Volcán Totumo. San Basilio del Palenque, a village founded by run-away slaves in the 17th century and which still strongly holds on to its African roots, was declared a UNESCO Intangible Cultural Heritage of Humanity in 2008 (47 km/29 mi south of Cartagena). Updated: May 05, 2011.

History

The first humans to live in the area were the Puerto Hormiga settlements (7,000-3,000 BC), which produced some of the oldest pottery in the Americas, followed by the much more developed Monsú culture. By the time the Europeans came, various Carib-Arawak nations lived on the coast and off-shore islands.

On an island separated from the mainland by marshes and lagoons, Pedro de Heredia founded Cartagena de Indias in 1533.

For years, it served as a storage point for items sent from Spain, and for treasure extracted from the Americas. Over the next 200 years, Cartagena experienced several sieges. The most notable attacks were by Sir Francis Drake in 1586, Baron de Pointis and Ducasse in 1697, and Sir Edward Vernon in 1741. This latter assault was repelled by the famous one-eyed, one-armed, and one-legged hero Blas de Lezo, whose statue stands at the entrance of the San Felipe fortress. These severe attacks led to the building of the old city's protective wall and forts, such as San Fernando, San Sebastián del Pastelillo and San Felipe de Barajas.

In 1811, Cartagena declared independence from Spain. The following year, Simón Bolívar used the city as a jumping-off point for his Magdalena campaign. Pablo Morillo and the royalists re-took control in 1815. Cartagena gained full independence in 1821. Updated: May 03, 2011.

When to Go

Temperatures in Cartagena range from warm to hot—and it's usually hot. The only distinguishing factor in the weather is the humidity. Rain falls between August and November, but this doesn't deter tourists. Prices of accommodations are 20 percent higher in December and January and during Semana Santa.

HOLIDAYS AND FESTIVALS

The city's patroness, **Virgen de La Candelaria**, is honored at La Popa on February 2. For nine days before the feast, thousands go up the hill by foot, horse, or car and, on the ninth day, they carry candles. There is a **Caribbean music festival** at the end of the year and for five days in March. Cartagena's **International Film Festival** is held in the spring (usually in March; URL: ficcifestival. com). The **Festival of Sweets** is held during La Semana Santa in Plaza de los Coches. Last, but not least, a great feast is held from November 11-14 to celebrate the **city's independence**, when men and women in masks and fancy dress roam and dance in the street to celebrate the independence of Cartagena. Colombia's **national beauty contest** is held during this festival. For a list of cultural events, check out www.cartagena-caribe.com. Updated: May 05, 2011.

Getting To and Away

BY BUS

Cartagena's **Terminal de Transpor** (Diagonal 57, 54-236, Pozón. Tel: 6 0289) is about 30 minutes from downtown, on the road to Barranquilla. The station has restaurants, shops, ATMS, 24-hour taxi stand, phone and internet stands and other services. See Getting Around Cartagena for information on how to there. Buses depart for many corners of the country. Various companies have service to destinations. For Barranquilla (2 hr, $6-7), see Santa Marta; for Maicao (8.5 hr, $34), see Riohacha. For Turbo, transfer at Montería.

To	Departure	Time	Price
Tolú	Hourly	3 hr	$20
Montería	Hourly	5 hr	$20
Mompós	7 a.m.	5-6 hr	$30
Medellín	Hourly mornings/ evenings	13 hr	$66
Santa Marta	Hourly	4 hr	$13-19
Rioha-cha	Frequent	6.5 hr	$30
Valledu-par	3 buses daily	6 hr	$22
Bucara-manga	Hourly mornings/ evenings	8 hr	$48
Bogotá	Frequent	18-24 hr	$77-80

MarSol (Ca. 70, 6A-120, Crespo. Tel: 656-4172) has direct service to Santa Marta ($22), as well as to Barranquilla and Valledupar. In Getsemaní, tickets may be bought at Luna Nueva Restaurante-Bar (Ca. de la Media Luna 10-36). Also ask at your hostel.

BY AIR

Aeropuerto Rafael Núñez has service to national and international destinations. The airport has a variety of services, including car rental agencies, ATMs and an exchange house

CARIBBEAN COAST

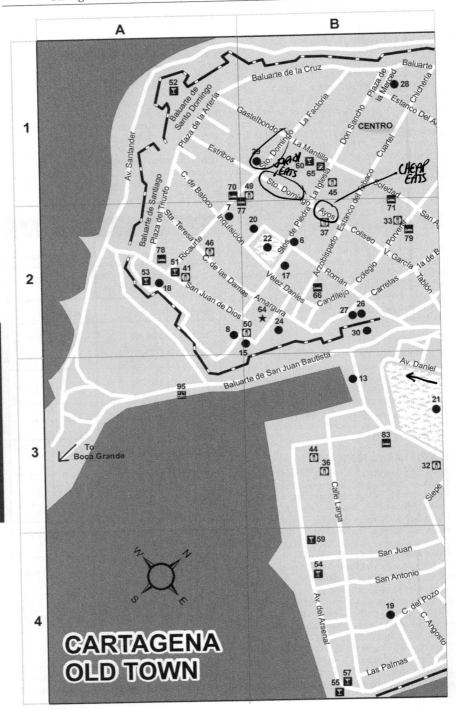

CARTAGENA OLD TOWN

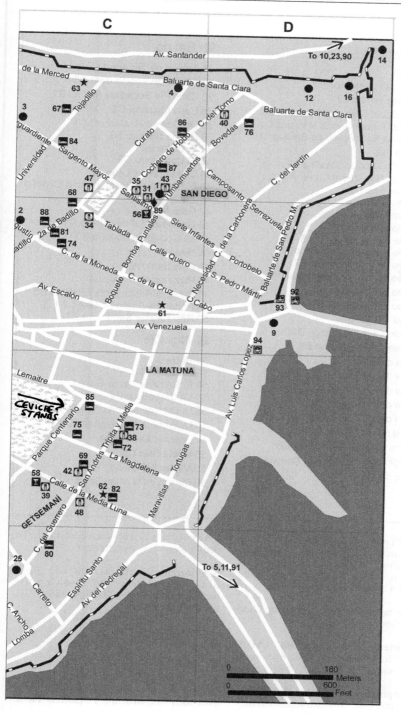

● Activities

1 Babel C1
2 Cartagena International
   Language School C2
3 Casa Cultural Colombo Alemana C1
4 Casa de Gabriel García Márquez C1
5 Castillo de San Felipe de Barajas D4
6 Catedral B2
7 Centro de Idiomas Catalina A2
8 Iglesia de San Pedro Claver A2
9 India Catalina D2
10 La Boquilla D1
11 La Popa D4
12 Las Bóvedas D1
13 Muelle de los Pegasos B3
14 Museo Casa Rafael Núñez D1
15 Museo de Arte Moderno B2
16 Museo de las Fortificaciones D1
17 Museo del Oro Zenú B2
18 Museo Naval del Caribe A2
19 Nueva Lengua B4
20 Palacio de la Inquisición B2
21 Parque del Centenario B3
22 Plaza de Bolívar B2
23 Playa Marbella D1
24 Plaza de la Aduana B2
25 Plaza de la Trinidad C4
26 Plaza de los Coches B2
27 Portal de los Dulces B2
28 Teatro Heredia Adolfo Mejía B1
29 Templo and Plaza Santo Domingo B1
30 Torre del Reloj B1

⑩ Eating

31 Arepas del Santísimo C1
32 Australian Fusion Café C3
33 Cafetería Bocaditos Madrid B2
34 Casa Majagna C2
35 Da Danni's Restaurant C1
36 Donde Socorro B3
37 El Bistro B2
38 El Coroncoro C3
39 El Parche del León C3
40 El Santísimo Restaurante & Café D1
41 Enoteca A2
42 Gato Negro C3
43 Govindas Sol de la India C1
44 La Cocina de Socorro B3
45 Mila B1
46 Palo Santo A2
47 Pizza en el Parque C1
48 Pizzaría Restaurante I Balconi C3
49 Portón de Santo Domingo B1
50 Restaurante San Pedro B2

🍸 Nightlife

51 Babar A2
52 Café del Mar A1
53 El Baluarte Tasca-Bar A2
54 La Carbonera B4
55 La Casa de la Cerveza B4
56 La Esquina Sandiegana C2
57 León de Baviera B4
58 María Félix C3
59 Mister Babilla B4
60 Rincón de la Mantilla B1

(open daily; also exchanges American Express travelers checks). The airport is 1.5 kilometers (1 mi) from downtown, in the Crespo district. For information on getting there, see Getting Around Cartagena. It opens at 4:30 a.m.

The following airlines serve Cartagena. Check their websites for super-saver fares.

—Aerolíneas de Antioquia (ADA) (Aeropuerto Rafael Núñez. Tel: 658-4095, URL: www.ada-aero.com)

—AeroRepública (Cra. 6, 8-116, Bocagrande. Tel: 665-0428. URL: www.aerorepublica.com)

—Aires (Cra. 3, 8-128, local 2, Bocagrande. Tel: 666-8919, URL: www.aires.aero)

—Avianca (Ca. del Arzobispado 34-52, El Centro. Tel: 664-7376. Also Ca 7,7-17, local 7, Bocagrande, Tel: 655-0287. URL: www.avianca.com)

—Lan (Aeropuerto Rafel Núñez. Tel: 01800-956-4509, URL: www.lan.com)

BY BOAT
Boats to Playa Blanca, Islas del Rosario, Isla de Tierra Bomba and Bocachica depart form the **Muelle Turístico La Bo**

★ **Services**

61 Citibank C2
62 Laundry Service C3
63 Lavamejor C1
64 Tourism Office B2

📖 **Shopping**

65 Ábaco B1

🛏 **Sleeping**

66 Alfiz Hotel B2
67 Casa del Tejadillo C1
68 Casa la Fé C2
69 Casa Viena C3
70 El Marqués Hotel
   Boutique A1
71 Hospedaje Cartagena B2
72 Hospedaje Marta C3
73 Hostal La Casona
   Getsemaní C3
74 Hostal Mar Azul C2
75 Hostal Real C3
76 Hostal San Diego D1
77 Hostal Santo Domingo B1
78 Hotel Charleston A2
79 Hotel El Viajero A2

80 Hotel Familiar C4
81 Hotel Los Balcones
   de Badillo C2
82 Hotel Marlin C3
83 Hotel Monterrey B3
84 Hotel Puertas de
   Cartagena C1
85 Hotel San Felipe C3
86 Hotel Santa Clara C1
87 Hotel Tres Banderas C1
88 Portal de San Diego C2

♦ **Tours**

89 Adventure Colombia C2

🚍 **Transportation**

90 Aeropuerto Rafael Núñez D1
91 Bus terminal D4
92 Buses to Bocagrande,
   La Boquilla D2
93 Buses to bus terminal D2
94 Buses to La Popa D2
95 Muelle Turístico
   La Bodeguita A3

CARIBBEAN COAST

deguita (Av. Blas de Lezo). To the west of the docks are ticket windows of 10 agencies that also offer trips to Volcán Totumo, chiva tours and other excursions. Buy tickets to Playa Blanca and Islas del Rosario directly from the window ($20-28); the touts charge more. Tours Playa Blanca has service to Bocachica (every 0.5 hr 8 a.m.-4 p.m., last return 4 p.m.; $8 round trip, $14 with lunch). The local boat is cheaper ($3-4 one way), but you'll have to be insistent to get the regular price. The Muelle charges an additional $3 dock fee. Lanchas (launches) to Punta Arena on Isla de Tierra Bomba depart from next to the Hilton Hotel in Laguito, Bocagrande ($3-6). From **Mercado Bazuarto** (between Av. Pedro de Herredia and Av. del Lago, 3.5 km east of downtown), local cargo-passenger launches leave 7-9 a.m. for Isla Barú and Playa Blanca ($3 one way). These are rudimentary craft, leaving from a non-salubrious locale. Deal only with the captain. The **yacht club** (Club Naútico) is on Avenida Miramar on Isla Manga. For information about boats to Panama, see Colombia-Panama Border Crossings. Updated: May 04, 2011.

Getting Around

Officially all of Cartagena has numbered Carreras and Calles, as in the rest of Colombia, but it is only used in Bocagrande. The old city still uses street names, which change every block. Some businesses, however, do use the numbered system.

It is easy to get around the walled city and to Bocagrande on foot. For longer distances, catch a *buseta* (city bus, $0.80 from India Catalina monument). Buses to Bocagrande, the airport and La Boquilla depart from the northeast corner, and the white and green Metrocar to the bus terminal from the northwest corner (30-60 min, $0.90). For San Felipe fortress or La Popa, catch one from the southwest corner. Busetas from Bocagrande to downtown pass along Carrera 3. TransCaribe, similar to Bogotá's Transmilenio bus service, will run between the bus terminal and Muelle Turístico La Bodeguita; it will (hopefully) be done by the end of 2011.

Taxis are unmetered. Settle on a price before boarding. Taxi stands at the bus terminal and airport post official prices and sell vouchers. To downtown the fare is $6.50 and $9 respectively. A cab caught a block from the terminal complexes charge $4-5 and $5-7.

Most car rental agencies are at the airport or in Bocagrande. Three dealers are in Bocagrande's Edificio Torremolinos (Cra. 2 and Ca. 10): National (Tel: 301-756-0313), Car Renta (Tel: 666-4120) and International Car Rental (Tel: 665-5148). Hertz is at the airport (Ca. 70, 1D-124, local 4, Crespo. Tel: 690-6232). Cartagena has *pica y placa*, which designates vehicular circulation days according to license plate number. Shops leasing bicycles are cropping up all over, especially in Getsemaní; most charge $3 per hour. Ciclo Sport gives discounts for all-day and multi-day rentals (Ca. Larga 8B-74, Centro Comercial Getsemaní, local 1B-174, Getsemaní. Tel: 660-1582, Cel: 314-547-5758, E-mail: ciclosport412@hotmail.com). Updated: May 02, 2011.

Safety

El Centro and San Diego are well-lit after dark and are safe for tourists. Nonetheless, tourists should always use caution when walking around at night. Some areas in La Matuna and Getsemaní are not so well lit. Keep valuables back at your hotel, but carry a photocopy of your passport with you at all times. Keep an eye on your belongings when sitting in plazas or on the ramparts. Don't let distractions (like a "stray" soccer ball hitting your leg) let your guard down. Be especially vigilant at holiday times, above all at the bus station. The street money changers are notorious for ripping off tourists; use only banks or casas de cambio for those transactions. Be wary of iced drinks if you aren't at a nicer establishment (the ice might be made from non-purified water). Updated: May 04, 2011.

Services

TOURISM

The main **tourism office** is at Plaza de la Aduana (Monday-Saturday 9 a.m.-1 p.m., 2-6 p.m.; Sunday 9 a.m.-5 p.m. Yel: 660-1583, E-mail: puntadeinformacionturistica@yahoo.com, URL: www.cartagenadeindias.travel). It also has kiosks at the Torre del Reloj and Plaza San Pedro Claver. The administration office is at the Muelle Turístico La Bodeguita (Av. Blas de Lezo. Tel: 655-0211), but it will refer you to the main office.

In the historic center, **police** posts are at the Muelle Turístico La Bodeguita, Parque El Centenario (Getsemaní) and Centro Comercial La Plazoleta (La Matuna). In Bocagrande, the station is near Parque Flanaga (Av. Malecón and Ca 3).

DAS handles immigration matters (Monday-Friday 7:30-11 a.m., 2-4 p.m. Ca. 20B, 29-18. Tel: 666-0438). **Instituto Geográfico Agustín Codazzi** sells Mapas de Rutas, a handy 12-map, spiral-bound atlas for motorists and bicyclists (Monday-Friday 8 a.m.-4:30 p.m. Ca. 34, 3A-31, Parque de Bolívar, Centro. Tel: 664-4169).

Twenty-six countries have **consulates** in Cartagena. See the back of the telephone directory for a complete list of offices: Venezuela (Cra. 3, 8-129, Edificio Centro Ejecutivo, oficina 802, Bocagrande. Tel: 665-0382; possible to obtain visa in one day), Panama (Cra. 1, 10-10, Bocagrande. Tel: 665-4400), Canada (Cra. 3, 8-129, Edificio Ejecutivo, Bocagrande. Tel: 665-5838), France (Parque Fernández de Madrid 37-34, San Diego. Tel: 664-6714), Great Britain (Cra. 13B, 26-78, Edificio Chambacú, oficina 416, Centro. Tel: 664-7590). Other European countries with diplomatic representatives in Cartagena are Austria, Belgium, Czech Republic, Finland, Germany, Greece, Hungary, Italy, Poland, Portugal, Russia, Spain, Sweden and Switzerland. The nearest US consulate is in Barranquilla.

MONEY

Banking hours are Monday-Friday 8-11:30 a.m. and 2-4 p.m. Most change U.S. dollars; Bancolombia handles American Express travelers checks. Bancolombia, BBVA and Santander are on Plaza de la Aduana. Citibank is in the La Matuna district (Ca. 35, 8B-05). Most institutions have branches

Pirates and the Sacking of Cartagena

Long before throngs of vacationers flocked here for the surf, sand and shopping, Cartagena attracted visitors of a different sort: pirates. As one of the great treasure ports of Spain's colonial conquests, Cartagena saw a fair share of gold, jewelry and gems pass through its waters. Thus, the city was also one of the prime targets for English, Dutch and French buccaneers. The Spanish did everything they could to deter attacks, but they suffered many setbacks before achieving lasting peace.

One of the first pirate attacks of note involved Robert Baal, a pirate of French descent who in 1551 was able to wrest more than 600 pounds of gold from the governor of Cartagena as ransom. The King of Spain reacted swiftly, commissioning engineers from Europe to construct fortifications around the city—a task that would install some of Cartagena's most lasting and iconic symbols. The fortifications took nearly 200 years to complete, and in the first decades of their construction, pirates continued to successfully attack Cartagena.

The pirates' standard operating procedure involved calculated sieges of the city followed by demands for ransom. In return, pirates promised not to completely destroy the city. French pirate Martin Cote exacted a large sum of money this way not long after Baal.

Sir Francis Drake, perhaps the most famous swashbuckler to leave his mark on Cartagena, attacked the port in 1586. Spaniards fled the city in droves, leaving the port largely unprotected. According to lore, Drake burned much of the city to the ground, including a nave of the Cathedral. He received a very large ransom (one report estimated it at more than 100,000 ducats), a large amount of gems and jewels, artillery pieces and other assorted goods.

By the 1600s, Spanish engineers had improved the city's fortifications enough to thwart most attempts on the city. The last successful invasion came in 1697, when Baron de Pointis was able to enter the city, thanks in large part to a slave rebellion that took place inside the city's walls. Spain again strengthened fortifications in response, leading to one of the city's greatest defensive successes in 1741, when Admiral Edward Vernon led the English Navy in an attack against Cartagena. After fierce fighting and some 350 bombs, Cartagena was able to repel the English attack. Cartagena's success proved a defining moment for the city, as it brought a halt to attacks on the city. Another attack would not take place until the 19th century, when the war for Colombian independence was underway.

along Avenida Venezuela and along Calle del Arsenal. In Bocagrande, banks are on Avenida San Martín (Cra. 2), between Calles 9 and 11. HBSC's main branch is in this neighborhood (Av. San Martín 10-21).

Casas de cambio typically exchange U.S. dollars, Euros and bolívares fuertes. Many are on Plaza de los Coches, Calle de las Carretas and Parque de Bolívar. Take your passport. Recommended ones are Oscar (Cra. 7, 32-91, Portal de los Dulces) and Comisiones Las Bóvedas (Ca. del Colegio 34-53). In Bocagrande are several exchange houses, including Cambiamos (Cra. 2, 1-100; a variety of currencies, American Express travelers checks; also MoneyGram agent). Do not change money on the street.

MoneyGram has 20 offices in the city (most at Davivienda banks) and Western Union has 19 branches, including Giros y Finanzas (Av. Venezuela 8A-87, local 3, La Matuna). Check their websites for the nearest agent.

KEEPING IN TOUCH

To send that tropical paradise postcard to the folks back home, go to 4-72 post office (Ca. 32C, 10B-30, Edificio Telecom, La Matuna. Also at Ca. del Arsenal 8B-173, Getsemaní). Both branches are open Monday-Friday 8 a.m.-noon, 2-5:45 p.m.; Saturday 9 a.m.-1 p.m. Internet is common; many places have Skype. Likewise, phone stands are everywhere. In Getsemaní is a small internet place with computers, Skype, and national and international call service (Ca. del Guerrero 29-69).

MEDICAL

The main health facility is **Hospital Bocagrande** (Cra. 6 and Ca. 5, Bocagrande. Tel: 665-5270). The **Hospital Naval** has a recompression chamber (Cra. 2, 14-10, Bocagrande. Tel: 665-4306). Pharmacies (*droguerías*) are found all over the city. Several are on Avenida Venezuela. Drogas La Rebaja has over two dozen stores with delivery; the one in Bocagrande is open 24 hours (Cra. 2, 7-179. Tel: 655-12009, Cel: 320-788-7583).

LAUNDRY

Laundries are present in all neighborhoods. Expect to pay about $2 per kilogram for wash and dry. Most are open Monday-Saturday and have same-day service. Lavamejor, a laundromat and dry cleaner, has shops in El Centro (Edificio del Tejadillo, local 101, Playa Tejadillo and Ca. del Tejadillo. Tel: 664-5620) and Bocagrande (Cra. 4, 5-11. Tel: 665-0546). In Getsemaní is Laundry Service (Ca. de la Media Luna 10-19). Updated: May 02,2011.

SHOPPING

High-fashion, Caribbean women's apparel, handicrafts and Colombia's famous emeralds are easily found within the walls of the old city. The clothing and shoes can be expensive along Calle Santo Domingo in El Centro, but the boutiques are classy and colorful. Mementos and handicrafts make Las Bóvedas a perfect place to practice your bargaining skills. Out at Mercado Bazuarto (between Av Pedro de Herredia and del Lago, 3.5 km east of downtown), cheap hammocks can be bought at the shops in the alley between the Olímpica grocery store and Centro Comercial Globo Centro; try Cacharería Miriam. Updated: May 02, 2011.

Ábaco

At the corner of Calle de la Mantenilla and Calle de la Iglesia in the old city, you will find Ábaco, a trendy café and bookstore. Nicely furnished with dark wooden chairs, tables and bookshelves, this is a great place to find a small selection of literature in English. Some people spend a whole day here, drinking freshly brewed coffee and reading the newspaper or a book pulled straight off a shelf. Monday-Saturday 9:00 a.m.-8:30 p.m., Sunday and Holidays 4:00 p.m.-8:30 p.m. Ca. de la Mantenilla and Ca. de la Iglesia, 3-86, El Centro. Tel: 664-8338, E-mail: info@abacolibros.com, URL: www.abacolibros.com. Updated: Apr 16, 2011.

Emerald Shopping

El Centro houses an overwhelming selection of emerald shops, which are concentrated around Calle del Ladrinal. Many sell gems found in Boyacá Department. Jewelry ranges in quality and size, but prices are consistently high. If you're serious about buying, expect to bargain down to about 50 percent of the price quoted, which might explain why some stores have "50 percent off" slogans permanently painted on their windows. Also, don't be fooled by the elegant interior of a place—some of the cloudiest emeralds can be found at the seemingly fanciest places. Hired men will try to lure you in to their stores for you to take a look. Note that "Museo de la Esmeralda" is a jewelry store like its competitors and not a museum at all. Nonetheless, if you are selective, inquisitive and keen enough, you could still find that gorgeous piece you are seeking. Updated: Apr 16, 2011.

Santo Domingo Boutiques

Ladies will be impressed with the trendy boutique shopping along Calle Santo Domingo, between Plaza Santo Domingo and Baluarte San Francisco Javier. You could spend hours hopping in and out of these stores displaying swimsuits, shoes and clothing. The loose, clean styles, creative designs, and vibrant Caribbean colors characterize Cartagena's hip and lively fashion scene. The prices are rather high (about 100 U.S. dollars for a swimsuit, sandals, or dress), so for better bargains, you will have better success shopping on the blocks around Calles Badillo and Moneda. Calle Santo Domingo is also called Calle Santa Teresa and Calle Ricuarte, El Centro. Updated: Apr 16, 2011.

Things to See and Do

The best way to experience Cartagena is on foot. Cartagena has a long history, complete with pirates, rum, legend and lore; to make the sights you see more meaningful, visit a museum and the forts to get a sense of the fascinating events that have taken place here. Walk through the plazas and along Las Murallas, the city's famed wall, to enjoy the sea breezes. On a particularly lazy day, go to the beach. And for the snap-happy, be prepared to take lots of photographs of the colorful buildings. Updated: Jun 21, 2011.

Muelle de los Pegasos and El Camellón de los Martires

Along the walkways separating El Centro from Getsemaní, you will find some interesting monuments marking Cartagena's independence. Three impressive bronze Pegasus statues look out to the sea beside the city convention center. Between the Centro de Convenciones and Parque del Centenario is the grand Camellón de los Mártires (Walk of the Martyrs), whose centerpiece is a lovely white statue of a woman also looking out to sea. These monuments together come to represent the peace and independence so earnestly fought for and won. They serve as an affirmation of the bloodshed and looting that once plagued the city is long past. Av. Blas de Lezo. Updated: Apr 15, 2011.

Casa Museo Rafael Núñez

(ADMISSION: $0.60 adults, $0.40 students with card, $0.30 children) Casa Museo Rafael Núñez was the home of former Colombian President Rafael Núñez. This native-born cartagenero was the country's only four-time ruler and served his last two terms in this port city. Núñez was much more than a mere governor: He wrote the 1886 Constitution (which was in effect until 1991) and the national anthem's lyrics. The Caribbean-Antillan-styled house, where he and his mistress (later, his second wife) lived, is brilliant proof of breezy pre-air conditioned houses. It has an unusual octagonal dining porch. The museum displays the home's original furnishings and Núñez' personal items. Explanatory signs are in Spanish. Tours (in Spanish) are available; tip the guide. Núñez and his wife are interred in the Hermit de el Cabrero church across the street. Tuesday-Friday 9 a.m.-5:30 p.m., Saturday 10 a.m.-5:30 p.m., Sunday 10 a.m.-4 p.m. Closed Monday. Ca. Real de El Cabrero 41-89, Barrio El Cabrero, one block east of the Museo de las Fortificacions. Tel: 664-9440. Updated: Apr 29, 2011.

India Catalina

This monument was sculpted by Eladio Gil Zambrana and erected in 1974. India Catalina, an indigenous woman and the supposed daughter of a chief from Colombia's Atlantic coast, accompanied Pedro de Heredia to Cartagena's shores in the 16th century and served as his interpreter during the Spanish conquest. She was fluent in Spanish and the native language, adopted the Catholic religion, and later married Pedro de Heredia's nephew. Heredia's conquest went on to completely annihilate the Calamari people who had previously lived in Cartagena. Today, India Catalina symbolizes the fading pre-Colombian inhabitants. At the same time, she serves as a tribute to the Caribe culture and the original inhabitants of this region. Smaller replicas of her statue are used to award winners of the Cartagena Film Festival. Av. Venezuela and Av. Luis Carlos López. Updated: Apr 15, 2011.

Castillo de San Felipe de Barajas

(ADMISSION: $8 adults, $4.50 children) A statue of Blas de Lazo, who famously and successfully defended Cartagena from invasion in 1741, stands in front of Castillo de San Felipe de Barajas, Cartagena's strongest and largest military fortress. This fortress was built on San Lázaro Hill over the course of nearly 150 years and features advanced military engineering that was directed by engineer Antonio de Arévalo. Wander through the underground passageways, which are now lit so that visitors can see the impressive design. This military wonder remains a symbol of Cartagena's history under siege and its people's long journey toward independence. The fortress is a 20-minute walk from the old town, or take a local bus from Parque del Centenario. Daily 8 a.m.-6 p.m. Av. Arévalo, San Lázaro. Tel: 666-4790. Updated: Apr 15, 2011.

La Popa

(ADMISSION: $4 adults; $3 Children) Atop the highest point in the city sits Convento de Nuestra Señora de la Candelaria. Founded in 1607, this church is also known as Convento de la Popa, (Stern of the Galley) because of its location behind the city and because many thought the hill looked like a ship's poop. An image of La Virgen de la Candelaria, the patroness of the city, still hangs inside the chapel and an important festivity in her honor is held on February 2nd. There have been reports of armed robbers on the road leading to La Popa, so it is advisable to visit only by taxi and not on foot. Monday-Saturday 8 a.m.-5 p.m. Tel: 666-2331.Updated: Apr 15, 2011.

Cartagena's Beaches

(ADMISSION: free) After spending hours wandering Cartagena's narrow streets, a perfect way to cool down is to hit the beach. **Marbella** is the closest to the city. This several-kilometer-long beach begins just 300 meters (1,000 ft) east of Las Bóvedas and Museo de las Fortificacions and las Murallas. It is composed of five coves created by breakwaters. Marbella is the most popular playa with the locals. Out on **Bocagrande**, the L-shaped peninsula south of the city, are a variety of beaches to choose from: the west coast (which has less mangrove debris further south), the south coast of Castillogrande (the bottom leg of the "L"), and Laguito (the curly-cue on the L's bottom). The clearest water is at Laguito, just behind the Hilton Hotel. The best beaches are further from Cartagena: **La Boquilla** (6 km/3.6 mi) east and **Playa Blanca** on Isla Barú. Most beaches have lifeguards. Bocagrande's beaches are open 8 a.m.-6 p.m. and the others dawn-dusk. On weekends and holidays, all beaches are crowded.

Cartagena Water Sports

Sea breezes usually dance into Cartagena in the early afternoon, making this a perfect time to play in the water. Surfers can hit the waves off the north coast of Isla Barú. The best spot for windsurfing and sailboarding is La Boquilla. Scuba divers can explore the coral reefs and shipwrecks along Isla Barú's coasts and in PNN Islas del Rosario, both of which also offer excellent snorkeling. The following shops offer gear rentals and/or lessons:

Kiteboarding, Wind Surfing and Surfing: **Aqua Náutica** (Cra 9, 22-802, near Hotel Las Américas, La Boquilla. Tel: 656-8243 / Cell: 311-410-8883, E-mail: jhbwind@yahoo.com, URL: www.kitesurfcolombia.com) also has kayaking. **Mokaná Club** (Las Velas beach, Laguito, Bocagrande. Tel: 644 6444 / Cell: 300-810-7502, E-mail: mokanaclub@yahoo.com, URL: www.mokanaclub.com).

Scuba Diving: **Diving Planet** (Ca. del Estanco del Aguardiente 5-94, Centro. Tel: 664-2171, E-mail: info@divingplanet.org, URL: www.divingplanet.org), **Buzos de Barú** (Cra 1, 2-87, Hotel Cariba, Bocagrande. Tel: 665-7675/Cell: 320-573-2045, E-mail: dive@buzosdebaru.com, URL: www.buzosdebaru.com). Updated: May 02, 2011.

Studying Spanish

Nowhere else in Colombia will you be able to study Spanish in a tropical paradise and participate in water sports later that day, as well as learn about the Caribbean coast's unique Afro-Colombian culture and music. Well aware of Cartagena's multitudinous draws, several Spanish language schools in the city combine work with play, offering afternoon cultural activities like dance and sports in conjunction with morning Spanish lessons. It is the perfect blend of schoolwork and recess that you wished you had as a kid. Updated: Apr 16, 2011.

Babel International Language Institute

Just a block from Plaza San Diego in Cartagena's Old Town is Babel International Language Institute. This school offers Spanish courses for travelers wishing to spend some time in this colonial city. The experienced teachers speak English. Classes are limited to eight students.

It isn't just all Spanish at Babel. With its affiliate, Crazy Salsa, it also has Spanish and salsa combination courses. The dance academy also teaches the steps to merengue, bachata, vallenato, champeta, mapalé and cumbia rhythms (E-mail: info@crazysalsa.net, URL: www.crazysalsa.net). Ca. Tumbamuertos 8-55, San Diego. Tel: 660-1809/Cel: 300-561-9428, E-mail: info@babelschoolcartagena.com, URL: www.babelschoolcartagena.com. Updated: May 02, 2011.

Cartagena International Language School

Cartagena Intentional Language School is the newest kid on the Spanish school block. This small academy has intensive courses (20 hr/week, $225) and private tutoring ($400). A crash course in traveler Spanish is also taught just for backpackers. Students may also opt for a combined Spanish-salsa course (30 hr/week, $325) or only salsa (10 hr/week, $125). Hourly, one-on-one sessions of Spanish ($25) and salsa ($15) are also on the slate. Discounts are given for two weeks or more. Class size is limited to six persons. Teachers are Colombians who speak English. Classroom materials are included. Ca. San Agustín 6-55, Edificio Balcones de San Agustín, Centro. Tel: 670-048, E-mail: roger@cartagenaschool.com / daniel@cartagenaschool.com, URL: www.cartagenaschool.com. Updated: Jun 16, 2011.

Casa Cultural Colombo Alemana

The Casa Cultural Colombo Alemana, in the historic center of Cartagena and close to Teatro Heredia and the city beaches, provides a relaxed and friendly atmosphere for inter-cultural exchange and learning Spanish. Three different types of Spanish are taught at this small school: beginner to advanced Spanish, Spanish for tourism, and Spanish for the workplace. Individual classes or small groups provide students with a flexible schedule. In addition, afternoon cultural activities are available to enhance students' practical learning of the language. Ca. Estanco del Aguardiente (Ca. 38) 5-31, Centro. Tel: 660-2522, E-mail: cartagen@colomboalemana.org, URL: www.colomboalemana.org. Updated: Apr 11, 2011.

Centro de Idiomas Catalina

Centro de Idiomas Catalina is one of Cartagena's newest language schools. Run by two native speakers, this center offers basic and intensive Spanish classes in the morning. Afternoons are set aside for special courses on culture, history, literature, music, dance and other

Free in Cartagena

Upon arriving in Cartagena, budget travelers are slammed with the reality of how expensive the museums and excursions to Playa Blanca and Islas del Rosario are. These journeyers might wonder just what they can do on a shoe string. The answer is: Plenty!

Grab the camera and had out to wander the streets of the Old City. The most picturesque parts are Centro, San Diego and Getsemaní neighborhoods. It costs nary a cent to sit on the fortress walls, meditate on the Caribbean Sea, people-watch or catch up on the old journal. Another pleasurable walk is along Isla Manga's Avenida Miramar, which begins with Fuerte del Pastelillo (now the Fishing Club) and ends with a viewpoint gazebo.

To cool off on a sultry day, pack a picnic and head to the beach. The nearest to town is Marbella, just east of the Bóvedas. Bocagrande peninsula to the west of downtown is draped with playas, including at Castillogrande and Laguito. All of these are super packed on weekends and holidays. If you have a few bucks to spare, hop a combi out to La Boquilla where the best mainland strand is.

Because Cartagena's museums are beyond the reach of most Colombian's wallets, the Cultural Ministry has dictated they must be free one day per month. The last Sunday of each month, these are gratis: Museo Naval, Palacio de la Inquisición, Museo de las Fortificacions and las Murallas, as well as the fortresses San Felipe de Barajas, and San Fernando and Batería San Rafael (both at Bocachica, Isla de Tierra Bomba). The Museo de Arte Moderno is free every Wednesday. The Museo del Oro Zenú and Museo de la Esmeralda are always gratis.

At the end of the day (5-6 p.m.), head down to **Plaza de los Coches** to watch the youth dance and music troupes performing regional Afro-Colombian rhythms: (toss a small tip in the hat). Free cultural events, like movies and art exhibits, are hosted by the various cultural centers: **Casa Cultural Colombo Alemana** (Ca. Estanco del Aguardiente 5-31, Centro. URL: www.colomboalemana.org), **Alliance Française** (Parque Fernández de Madrid 37-34, San Diego. URL: www.afcartagena.org), **Centro de Formación de la Cooperación Española** (Cra 34, 2-74, Plaza Santo Domingo, Centro. URL: www.aecidcf.org.co) and **Centro Cultural Colombo Americano** (Ca. de la Factoría 36-27, Centro. URL: www.colombocartagena.com). The **Banco de la República** (URL: www.banrepcultural.org/cartagena) has two venues that host events: **Biblioteca Bartolomé Calvo** (Ca. de la Inquisición 3-44) and **Casa de Bolívar** (Ca. San Agustín 6-49). These cultural centers also offer concerts and theater (for which a modest fee may be charged). Check the monthly publication, Donde (available at the tourism office), daily newspapers and Guía Cultural Karamairi (URL: karamairi.blogspot.com) for event announcements.

topics. The special three-class tourism Spanish course helps travelers handle restaurants, hotels and shops during their Colombian soirees. Class size is limited to eight students. One-on-one tutoring is also available. Centro Catalina also coordinates a volunteer program working with children from poor neighborhoods. Basic course $139-159/week, Intensive course $179-199/week, Special courses $20-40. Ca. Santo Domingo and Ca. de la Inquisición, Centro. Tel: 41-79-460-7148 (Europe), Cel: 310-761-2157 (Cartagena), E-mail: info@centrocatalina.com, URL: www.centrocatalina.com. Updated: May 02, 2011.

Escuela De Español Nueva Lengua

With its convenient Getsemní location, it's no wonder Nueva Lengua is foreign backpackers' most popular choice for studying Spanish. All the teachers are native Colombians with university degrees in languages, and they speak English. Nueva Lengua offers elementary to advanced (basic reading) level classes, as well as intensive courses. Private tutoring is also available. Nueva Lengua also provides Internet and excursions to the fortresses, Volcán Totumo and other sights. Spanish courses may be combined with dance, windsurfing, kiteboarding or scuba diving lessons. Nueva Lengua has a travel agency and schools in Bogotá and Medellín. Classes $200/week; intensive $220/week; private tutoring (15 hr/week, $500). One week minimum sign-up. Discount for enrollment of five weeks or more. Ca..del Pozón 25-95, Getsemaní. Tel: 660-1736, URL: www.nuevalengua.com. Updated: May 04, 2011.

Tours

If you prefer not to wilt while walking in the city's sometimes unbearable tropical heat, or would like to visit the sites outside of the walled city without hassle, consider booking a tour through an operator in Cartagena. Expert guides will offer up local knowledge, history and lore. Boat tours head to the islands of Tierra Bomba, Barú and Rosario. Transportation time and fees are often discounted when joining a group trip to the islands and Totume.

Tourists visiting Cartagena can see the city in three ways: on foot, in horse-drawn carriage or in chiva. Authorized tour guides, dressed in beige vests, wait at at Plaza de Bolívar. They offer **walking tours** through the inner city's labyrinth of streets. These guides take people to the most important sights, talking about architecture, culture, history and legends of the colonial town. Also at Plaza de Bolívar, as well as Plaza San Diego, tourists can hop on a **horse-drawn carriage**. A 45-minute spin around the inner and outer parts of the walled city costs $25. The third manner to check out Cartagena is in *chiva*—the colorful, old-style, wooden buses that are still used in rural Colombia. The tours take two styles: a seated drive through the city to see the historical sights or a rumba tour, complete with dancing and *aguardiente* shots. Most chivas depart from Carrera 2 (Av San Martín) in Bocagrande and charge $14-17 per person. These city tours may also be booked through travel agencies. Updated: May 04, 2011.

Adventure Ecotours

Adventure Ecoturismo is a great tour operator providing superior city tours or arranging tours in northern Colombia. Trips and excursions can be arranged for groups of two to eight people and range from one hour to a full day in Cartagena de Indias. You can also participate in trips of up to a week with affiliated operators in the country, such as TurCol in Santa Marta for the five-day trek to La Ciudad Perdida. Other destinations include Islas Rosario, Playa Blanca, Mompox, San Andrés and Parque Tayrona. Rates are reasonable (and negotiable). Guides speak Spanish, English or French. Ca. del Santísimo, 8-55, San Diego. Tel: 664-8500, Cel: 300-558-0874, URL: www.adventurecolombia.com. Updated: May 03, 2011.

Arrecifes Tours

Arrecifes Tours specializes in giving local tours and arranging accommodations (including providing transportation to your hotel) in and around Cartagena. The guided city tours are pretty basic. If you are looking for a private vacation away from the crowds, this agency can book a nice cabaña for you at beach locations close to the city. Arrecifes Tours' cabaña on Isla de Tierra Bomba is equipped with air-conditioned rooms, an airy terrace and a spacious kitchen. In the mornings, drink Colombian coffee with a private view of the sea from the front porch. Centro Comercial Getsemaní, local 1 B-115, Getsemaní. Tel: 665-6477, Cel: 310-611-5842/301-576-0504, E-mail: arrecifesoperadora@hotmail.com. Updated: Feb 04, 2011 .

Diving Planet

Diving Planet Centro de Buceo can help you leave dry land behind while you're in Cartagena. This scuba center, one of the longest-established in the city, specializes in dives in PNN Islas del Rosario's crystalline waters. Diving Planet offers excursions every day (beginning at 8:30 a.m.). Packages include two dives, transportation, all gear and a light lunch—but not the national park entry fee ($7.25). These outings to explore the Caribbean depths are for both PADI certified ($139) and novice divers ($147). Ca. Estanco del Aguardiente 5-94, Centro. Tel: 664-2171, Cel: 300-603-7284, URL: www.divingplanet.org. Updated: Apr 29, 2011.

Isla del Encanto

Isla del Encanto can help you arrange an affordable visit to the Rosario Islands or Totumo volcano, plan a tour around the city (including trips to Castillo de San Felipe and La Popa), or organize a ride in a chiva party bus. Whether you'd like to rent a boat for a day, go camping, jet skiing, diving or snorkeling, Isla del Encanto will happily assist you. Visit its office in Bocagrande or at the Muelle Turístico La Bodeguita in downtown. Av. San Martín (Cra 2) 5-94, Michel Center, local 5, Bocagrande. Tel: 5-655-5454, Cel: 300-816-9666, URL: www.isladelencanto.com.co. Updated: May 05, 2011.

Ocean and Land Tours

Ocean and Land Tours offers exactly what its name alludes to: organized tours of land and sea. The guides speak English and Spanish, providing city tours both near and far. Here, you can also book a rumba ride in a chiva—a mobile party. This operator can organize boat trips, arrange for your accommodations, or book your trip to Islas del Rosario, Playa Blanca, Santa Marta, or other places. Ocean and Land Tours also has an office at Muelle Turístico La Bodeguita. Cra. 2, 5-15, Centro Comercial El Pueblito, local 19, Bocagrande. Tel: 5-655-2300, Cel: 317-820-0411. Updated: May 03, 2011.

Lodging

Cartagena's cheapest accommodation can be found in Getsemaní. Around here, you will find backpacker hostels that have basic rooms, with a stiff bed and cold water showers. Nonetheless, in recent years, some B&Bs and boutique hotels have opened their doors. Once you cross over Avenida Venezuela into the Centro and San Diego neighborhoods, both price and quality rise. Hotels in the Centro are right in the thick of daily activity, those in San Diego are quiet and serene. Bocagrande has vacation-resort-styled hostels and apartments for rent. No matter the class of accommodations, rates rise in the high seasons. Updated: Jun 12, 2011.

Cartagena Rental Accommodations (ROOMS: $80-150) Cartagena Rental Accommodations provides a great option if you plan to stay in Cartagena for a week or longer. With studios, one-, and two-bedroom apartments in the old city, Bocagrande and Laguito, you are sure to have the privacy you are seeking. Guests feel "at home" in these convenient, modern condos. This alternative is ideal for traveling professionals or families on vacation. Cartagena Rental Accommodations has English-speaking staff, to help foreigners arrange leases. Cel: 316-685-3499, URL: www.colombiarental.net. Updated: Jun 11, 2011.

Restaurants

Eating in Cartagena is a gastronomical adventure. Take time to savor the many facets of Colombian-Caribbean cuisine. Street food can be found around every corner, like the Caribbean ladies balancing bowls of fruit on their heads. Ceviche stands line the Avenida Daniel Lemaitre side of Parque del Centenario. In the Centro, cheaper restaurants are found on Calle de Ayos. Mid-range restaurants are between Plaza Fernández de Madrid and Plaza San Diego. Pricier, more delectable dishes are on Calle Santo Domingo. The Éxito supermarket is convenient for Walled City lodgers (Avenida Venezuela and Calle del Boquete, La Matuna). In Bocagrande, there's an Olímpica grocery store (Cra 2 and Ca 12). Mercado Bazuarto, just past the Barrio Chino, is the open-air market (between Av Pedro de Herredia and del Lago, 3.5 km east of downtown). Regionally, watermelon is called *paitilla*. Updated: May 02, 2011.

Nightlife

Avenida del Arsenal, which runs from the convention center to Baluarte San Lorenzo del Reducto, lights up and vibrates every night from 10 p.m. until dawn. You can choose from an array of pubs, bars, lounges and clubs. The streets between Plaza Santa Teresa and Plaza Santo Domingo are well-populated with locals and foreigners too. Plaza San Diego and Plaza Fernández de Madrid in the old city also offer several chic hangouts, but these spots are not open quite as late. If you are looking for a more relaxed local nightlife scene, head to Avenida San Martín in Bocagrande.

Neighborhoods

The original part of Cartagena is surrounded by massive fortress walls. It is divided into two sectors: the inner city, with the Centro and San Diego neighborhoods, and the outer, with La Matuna and Getsemaní.

Centro is where the majority of Cartagena's tourist attractions are consolidated. This is where governmental and ecclesiastical bodies had their seats, and high officials and nobility lived. Today, some of Cartagena's most exclusive hotels, restaurants and shops are here. Plaza Santo Domingo is lined with delightful sidewalk cafés. **San Diego** was home to colonial Cartagena's middle class. This neighborhood, dotted with small, shady plazas, has a quieter pace by day and a sophisticated buzz by night.

The outer walled city was where the artisan classes lived. **La Matuna**, a triangular wedge between Venezuela and Lemaitre Avenues, was always the business sector. With the urban modernization ideals of the 1970s, La Matuna lost its colonial architecture and fortress walls. Today its streets are crowded with vendors.

Getsemaní, south of Avenida Lemaitre, retains much of its original centuries-old architecture. Many cartagenera families still reside here, sitting on their stoops, sharing the day's news. An important community gathering spot in the evenings is Plaza de la Trinidad. Getsemaní has many budget hostels (though every year, more upscale B&Bs are opening) and a lively night scene.

Most tourists prefer to stay in the old city, whereas vacationing Colombians tend to head to **Bocagrande**, located on an L-shaped peninsula south of the ramparts. The bottom bar of the "L" is called Castillogrande. The curlycue on the bottom of the peninsula is Laguito.

Other neighborhoods of import are **Isla Manga**, an island south of Getsemaní and where travelers arriving from Panama by sailboat or cruise ship will dock, and **Crespo**, northeast of downtown and home to the airport. Updated: May 06, 2011.

El Centro

All of Cartagena's major museums, plazas, and churches are consolidated in El Centro. This part of the city starts at the Torre del Reloj and extends outwards, covering roughly 50 blocks filled with colorful colonial buildings draped with bougainvillea. If you have just one day in Cartagena, spend it in this neighborhood, as there is much to see and do here. The shopping, hotels and restaurants in El Centro are the most expensive in the city. Still, it is worth the extra cash just to meander the quaintest and most breathtaking city center in all of Colombia. Updated: Apr 15, 2011.

Things to See and Do

El Torre del Reloj

The yellow clock tower at Plaza de los Coches, above the main entrance gate into the walled city, is one of the primary emblems of Cartagena. Built in the early 18th century, the four-faced clock was originally called "Bridge Gate" because it joined Getsemaní with El Centro. In 1888, the republican-style tower was added to hold the clock. The Torre del Reloj, as it is known now, continues to be a landmark meeting place for residents in the city. Av. Venezuela and Av. Carlos Escallón. Updated: Apr 15, 2011.

Plaza de los Coches

Walking under the Torre del Reloj into El Centro, you come to Plaza de los Coches. Today, this space bustles with shops and vendors. But try to imagine it 300 years ago, when Plaza de los Coches was the center for transportation, and where slaves were bartered and sold. A statue of Pedro de Heredia, the city's founder, has been erected where the slave market used to be. The large buildings with colonial arches and balconies that surround this plaza are some of the oldest in the city. Along the north side is the Portal de los Dulces. Ca. de las Carretas and Ca. Portocarrero. Updated: Apr 15, 2011.

Portal de los Dulces

Strange Caribbean sweets can be found throughout the day and evening along the Portal de los Dulces arcade. Here, stalls display glass jars stuffed with chocolates, flavored rock candy, coconut delights, dried fruits and other treats like *muñecas de leche* ("milk dolls") or *bolas de panela* (brown sugar balls) that will make your sweet tooth ache. Some may not look appetizing, but if you're in Cartagena, you should give at least one treat a try. The Festival de los Dulces falls in March in the Plaza and features an even stickier assortment of sweets. Ca. de las Carretas, Plaza de los Coches. Updated: Apr 15, 2011.

Plaza de la Aduana

This is Cartagena's oldest and largest plaza. It serves as the commercial heart of the city and the parade grounds for festival days. People mingle here throughout the day and into the evening. It is the ideal meeting place for day-trippers taking the ferry to Isla Barú or for travelers visiting the tourist office. A few local banks and ATMs are also on the square. A statue of Christopher Columbus stands in the center of the plaza. Ca. Amargura and Ca. del Río. Updated: Apr 15, 2011.

Museo de Arte Moderno

(ADMISSION: $3 adults, $2 children) Housed in two buildings—the first built in the 17th century, the second added during the end of the 19th century—the Museo de Arte Moderno houses a permanent collection and temporary displays of post-1950s Colombian, Caribbean and Latin American art. Exhibits are frequently changed. The museum also has a library and gift shop. Monday-Friday 9 a.m.-noon, 3-7 p.m.; Saturday 10 a.m.- 1 p.m. Calle 30, 4-08, Plaza San Pedro Claver. Tel: 664-5815, E-mail: mamcartagena@gmail.com. Updated: Apr 15, 2011.

Iglesia de San Pedro Claver

(ADMISSION: $4 adults, $3 children). First constructed in the 17th century by the Jesuits, this church's convent served as the residence for Saint Pedro Claver (1580-1654), a priest whose missionary work focused on helping slaves from Africa. He was often regarded as the "Slave of Slaves" or the "Apostle of the Blacks." He lived here until his death and was canonized in 1888. The high altar is made from marble imported from Italy. Under the altar are his relics (physical remains), which are visible through a glass coffin. Inside the cloister is a museum displaying articles from his mission. On the second floor is a small Afro-Caribbean museum. Beyond the cloister, a convent for the Society of Jesus was built, which served as a charity hospital for the poor. Later it was headquarters to republican troops. Guided tour: in Spanish $8, in other language (English, French, German, Italian) $10. Now, the former convent is the site of the Naval Museum. Daily 8 a.m.-6 p.m. Cra. 4, 30-01. Tel: 664-4991. Updated: Apr 15, 2011.

Museo Naval del Caribe

(ADMISSION: $4.50 adults, students and children $2) This extensive museum recounts Cartagena's remarkable naval history. The building comprises two wings, separated by gardens. The west, or colonial, wing was constructed in the early 17th century as a Jesuit school, in association with the Iglesia de San Pedro Claver next door, and later became a hospital. In the early 20th century, the east, or republican, wing was built to quarter the first batallion of the Colombian Marines. Upstairs, you can find naval weapons and ship parts. Artifacts such as anchors, cannons and other sea instruments are also on display. This museum is a great way to learn about the city's maritime legends and history. Tuesday-Sunday 10 a.m.-5:30 p.m. Ca. San Juan de Dios 3-62. Tel: 664-9672. Updated: Apr 15, 2011.

Plaza de Bolívar

Plaza Bolívar is the ideal place for relaxation in the center of the old city. At lunchtime, locals take advantage of the shade offered around the center statue of Simon Bolívar on his horse, and the tourists sit down to rest their feet and people-watch. Women dressed in bright, typical Caribbean dresses balance bowls of fruit atop their heads, ready to whip up a delightful tropical salad. Cheap food stalls are around the Plaza, as well as some of the city's best known sites, such as the Catedral, the Museo de Oro Zenú and the Palacio de la Inquisición. Ca. de la Inquisición and Ca. del Ladrinal. Updated: Apr 15, 2011.

Museo del Oro Zenú

(ADMISSION: free) This informative and surprisingly educational gold museum is nicely curated and features pre-Colombian gold from the Zenú nation that lived on the Golfo de Morrosquillo and Sinú River valley (200 BC-1600 AD). Displays explain that the gold was used for burial and other ceremonies. In the Zenú tradition, gold was placed in urns, then the urns were buried under trees to symbolize fertility and new life. One wing on

the second floor explains the agriculture and resources used during pre-colonial times. A six-minute video in English, French or Spanish, describes how canals were built for agricultural purposes. Tuesday-Friday 10 a.m.-1 p.m., 3-7 p.m.; Saturday 10 a.m.-1 p.m., 2-5 p.m.; Sundays and Holidays 11 a.m.-4 p.m. Cra. 4, 33-36, Plaza Bolívar. Tel: 660-0778. Updated: Apr 15, 2011.

La Catedral

(ADMISSION: $6.70 adults, $4.40 children and third-agers) Construction of Cartagena's first cathedral began in 1575, using the modest materials of wood and cane. Plans were revamped by Simón González, who performed the greater part of its construction from 1577 until 1612. Francis Drake famously destroyed it in the midst of construction in 1586. It took nearly 100 years to complete this grand cathedral, and it underwent further renovation in 2007. The final product is a perfect blend of colonial and modern styles. It has a gaping doorway opening up to its imple interior, and contains a gilded 18th century alter and marble pulpit. The nave is flanked by thick white columns and impressive, tall arches. Tourist visits are allowed only when there is not a mass being celebrated. The audio tour (included in admission; in Spanish, English, French, German and Italian) explains the church's history and other items found inside. Monday-Saturday 10:30 a.m.-7 p.m., Sunday 9 a.m.-6 p.m. Ca. de los Santos de Piedra, diagional to Parque Bolívar. Tel: 664-5511. Updated: Apr 15, 2011.

Palacio de la Inquisición

(ADMISSION: $7 adults, $5.50 children) With its large, baroque-style stone entrance, external balconies facing the Plaza de Bolívar and Spanish coat of arms, the Palacio de la Inquisición is one of the city's best examples of late colonial architecture. Beginning in 1610, this palace was the site of the Punishment Tribunal of the Holy Office, but construction wasn't completed until 150 years later. It is now the Museo Histórico de Cartagena de Indias, displaying instruments of torture, pottery, paintings, furniture and other artifacts from both the colonial and independent eras. Visitors can wander through this old palace and step back in time to chronicle the history and legend of the city, and of the 17th century Spanish Inquisition. Guided tours for 1-5 persons: in Spanish $17, in other languages $20. Free admission the last Sunday of each month. Monday-Saturday 9 a.m.-6 p.m.;

Sunday, holidays 10 a.m.-4 p.m. Ca. 34, 3-11, Plaza de Bolívar. Tel: 664-4570, URL: www.museodecartagenadeindias.gov.co. Updated: Apr 15, 2011.

Teatro Heredia Adolfo Mejía

(ADMISSION: $6) If you are a fan of interpretive arts, the Teatro Heredia Adolfo Mejía is not to be missed. Located in Plaza de la Merced in the old city, this theater was built in the 19th century atop the ruins of a convent. Its original neo-classical style imitated the famous European theaters of the time. The remodeled theater remains the epicenter for theater, ballet, folkloric dance and performances in the city. Admission includes a guided tour. Monday-Friday 8-11:30 a.m., 2-5:30 p.m. Cra. 4, 38-10, Plaza de la Merced. Tel: 664-9631. Updated: Apr 15, 2011.

Plaza Santo Domingo

The always-happening Plaza Santo Domingo is filled with classy cafés ideal for people-watching. The brick plaza and the shops that dot the plaza's periphery seem unchanged by time, so it is easy to imagine colonial life while you enjoy a *limonada de coco* (coconut lemonade) under the shade of a table umbrella. The square is set among elegant colonial houses, and Botero's famous fat lady statue is situated in front of the church. Touching her supposedly brings you good luck. Ca. de Santo Domingo and Ca. de los Estribos. Updated: Apr 15, 2011.

Templo de Santo Domingo

(ADMISSION: $6.70 adults, $4.40 children and third-agers) Templo de Santo Domingo was originally located in Plaza de los Coches, but after a terrible fire that consumed the city, it was destroyed and relocated to where it stands today. The church's construction began in the late 16th century, making it Cartagena's oldest temple. Santo Domingo has a Spanish renaissance architectural style and looks as if it were carved out of a very large rock. There is one unfinished tower and the other one is twisted—by the devil, according to local legend. Inside, foreboding tombstones pave the floor at the baroque-style, marble altar. A 16th century image of Christ carved from wood as well as an image of the Virgin with her gold and emerald crown draw worshippers. Admission includes an audio tour (in Spanish, English, French, German and Italian). Tourist visits are allowed only when there is not a mass being celebrated. Daily 8 a.m.-6 p.m. Ca. Santo Domingo and Ca. de los Estribos, Plaza Santo Domingo. Tel: 655-1916, URL: www.tierramagna.com. Updated: Apr 15, 2011.

Lodging

BUDGET

Hospedaje Cartagena

(ROOMS: $19-28) If you're not daunted this conveniently located hostel's hourly rate, you will get a pretty good bang for your buck here. Up the hotel's steep stairs, you'll come face-to-face with a lady behind a glass booth. Take a nap or stay for a night, but don't expect any fancy treatment. All rooms have private bath, and fan or air conditioning. Two pluses are its convenient location and second-floor balcony overlooking the street. Ca. de la Soledad .5-52. Cel: 301-545-7582. Updated: Apr 16, 2011.

MID-RANGE

Hotel El Viajero

(ROOMS: $21-38) Talk about great location for a decent price, Hotel El Viajero is one of the few hotels in El Centro that you will find under $50 per night. This is an 18-room hotel with basic rooms—some with air conditioning, all with cold showers. El Viajero has been around long enough to know how to keep guests satisfied and happy. It has a sizable front lounge overlooking cute Calle Porvenir and a clean kitchen for guest use. This really is the cleanest and best option for visitors looking for a place with a little style. Ca. de Porvenir 35-68, 2nd floor. Tel: 664-3289, E-mail: hotelelviajero@gmail.com, URL: www.hotelelviajero.com. Updated: Apr 16, 2011.

Hostal Mar Azul !

(ROOMS: $30-40) By far the best value in El Centro, Hostal Mar Azul is a colorful little gem on the second floor of a colonial building on Calle de la Moneda. The walls are painted with bright Caribbean colors and the place exudes a happy vibe. Some of the 10 rooms have air conditioning and all have private baths. A computer with internet is available for guest use. The only downside to this cute hostel is that the hallways are narrow and the rooms are a bit small. Ca. de la Moneda 7-51, 2nd floor. Cel: 312-605-6023, E-mail: Chepr1@hotmail.com. Updated: Apr 16, 2011.

Hostal Santo Domingo !

(ROOMS: $36-65) Right in the center of Calle Santo Domingo, this small 9-room hostel is steps from nearly every major site in the old city. Set back from the street in a two-story colonial building, the place is clean and quaint with a courtyard and two-person tables in front of each room. Smaller rooms just have fans and cold showers, but the location is unbeatable. Discounts available for retirees and groups. Ca. Santo Domingo 33-46. Cel: 300-347-3625, E-mail: hsantodomingopiret@yahoo.es, URL: www.cartagenainfo.com. Updated: Apr 16, 2011.

Hotel los Balcones de Badillo

(ROOMS: $62-188) If you're seeking a great alternative to often-booked Hotel Tres Banderas in San Diego, look no further than Balcones de Badillo. With a dozen white balconies overseeing the activity of the streets below, this is a great place to relax and people-watch. This hotel might look a bit shabby and maze-like from the stairwell, but the rooms here are all nicely furnished and, for the most part, worth the price. Room 303 is the best suite of the 11 rooms, with two queen-size beds and an enormous wrap-around balcony. The price includes a hearty breakfast on a very pleasant rooftop that overlooks the city. Rates increase in high season. Ca. Segunda de Badillo 36-12. Tel: 660-1703, Cel: 300-805-0916, E-mail: losbalconesdebadillo@hotmail.co, URL: www.hotellosbalconesdebadillo.com. Updated: Apr 16, 2011.

HIGH-END

Portal de San Diego

(ROOMS: $83-110) A lovely white hotel in a central location between El Centro and San Diego, Portal de San Diego has 11 quaint rooms around a pleasant courtyard. The modern design of the place—from the clean, white stairwell up to the lobby on the second floor to the stylish paintings and decorations in the common areas—give the hotel a sophisticated air. The pleasant hotel staff let you feel as if Cartagena is your home away from home. Ca. Segunda de Badillo 36-17. Tel: 660-1083, E-mail: portaldesandiego@gmail.com, URL: www.portaldesandiego.com. Updated: Apr 16, 2011.

Hotel Alfiz

(ROOM: $185-250) Located in Cartagena's historic Old Town, the award-winning Hotel Alfiz is a short distance from some of the city's key tourist attractions. This boutique hotel is drenched in local history and culture, and the staff is always eager to share stories with guests. This small, beautiful, 17th-century residence was restored in 2007. Each of this boutique hotel's eight rooms are decorated in motifs reflecting Cartagena's different epochs. Alfiz' guests may relax on the terraces and at the pool.

The hotel is run by a hospitable Colombian family, who provides a warm welcome. Ca. Cochera del Gobernador 33-28. Tel: 660-0006, E-mail: sales@alfizhotel.com, URL: www.alfizhotel.com. Updated: Jun 11, 2011.

El Marqués Hotel Boutique

(ROOMS: $320-450) El Marqués provides quality accommodations in a 17th-century colonial house. The central courtyard has comfortable patio seating and fountain beneath palm trees. Spend a few nights in one of the eight modern, spacious, beige- and wood-themed suites. Guests are treated like royalty and can enjoy the small pool, sushi bar and terrace at their leisure. This place is a dream: contemporary comfort at its best. Ca. Nuestra Señora del Carmen (Calle Santo Domingo) 33-41. Tel: 664-4438, Cel: 314-581-0743, E-mail: reservas@elmarqueshotelboutique.com / reservas.elmarques@gmail.com, URL: www.elmarqueshotelboutique.com. Updated: Apr 16, 2011.

Hotel Charleston

(ROOMS: $481-700) Housed in a magnificently restored 17th-century convent in the old walled city, Hotel Charleston in Plaza Santa Teresa is designed with impeccable taste and attention to detail. Its burnt orange exterior blends perfectly with its classy interior, balancing both the colonial and republican styles evident in the city's architecture. The hotel features 90 guest rooms and suites, as well as an enormous presidential suite, all of which are decorated with fine ornaments representative of Cartagena's traditional style. The rooftop pool has one of the best views of the old city; you can sit up there for tea or a reasonably priced light lunch. Cra. 3, 31-23, Plaza de Santa Teresa. Tel: 664-9494, E-mail: info@hoteles-charleston.com, URL: www.hoteles-charleston.com. Updated: Apr 16, 2011.

Restaurants

Mila

At Mila, pastry chef and cook Camila Andrea Vargas bakes up some delightful breads and French pastries. The brownies are sinful and the cheesecakes heavenly. Local treats like *churros* are also available. The atmosphere feels like a French café. Bakery items on display in a shiny glass case, and above the fresh bread along the wall hangs an enormous chalkboard with soup, salad, sandwich, wrap and drink descriptions. This great place for a light lunch or mid-day snack. Mila also has a shop in Bocagrande (Ca. 6, 3-52, Tel: 655-1780). Ca. de la Iglesia 35-76. Tel: 664-4607, E-mail: admin@pasteleriamilavargas.com, URL: www.pasteleriamilavargas.com. Updated: Apr 16, 2011.

Cafetería Bocaditos Madrid

(LUNCH: $3.50) Locals crowd into this café that serves traditional Colombian lunch for an unbeatable price. Pull up to a stool at the the bar and ask for the lunch. It comes with a cup of *agua de panela* (sweet water), a bowl of soup, and a lunch plate with lentils, salad, plantains and your choice of meat. If you're in the mood for lighter fare, take your pick between various *arepas* and empanadas on display in the glass case on the counter. Open Monday-Saturday 8 a.m.-6 p.m. Ca. del Porvenir 35-10. Tel: 664-6021. Updated: Apr 16, 2011.

El Bistro !

(ENTREES: $6-10) Particularly popular among foreigners, this bakery serves up some of the tastiest breads, desserts, pastas, salads and sandwiches in the area. Customers sit beneath whirling fans to sip coffee and read something from El Bistro's small multi-language bookshelf. If you can't bear the heat, order take-out or have the food delivered. Breakfast, lunch and dinner specials are posted outside on a chalkboard. Daily 6:30 a.m.-10:00 p.m. Ca. de Ayos 4-46. Tel: 660-2065. Updated: Mar 03, 2011.

Palo Santo

(ENTREES: $12-27) Cooking up some of the most delicious Arabic and international cuisine in El Centro, Palo Santo is a great dinner spot right off of Calle Santo Domingo. The kibbeh—two different meatballs served with pita and hummus—is a tasty appetizer. Try the dinner special, which includes a soup or salad, your choice of three entrées, a dessert and a glass of house wine. Take your meal in the quaint courtyard or inside the brightly decorated restaurant. Live music entertains diners Thursday-Saturday evenings. Prices do not include tax or tip. Monday-Saturday noon-3 p.m., 7-11 p.m. Ca. de las Damas 3-13. Tel: 664-4783, E-mail: palosanto_1@hotmail.com, URL: www.restaurantepalosanto.com. Updated: Apr 16, 2011.

Portón de Santo Domingo

(ENTREES: $14-47) Portón de Santo Domingo is a high-class establishment that has been cooking up creative culinary masterpieces for over 100 years. It continues to draw wealthy clientele in search of excellently prepared plates, like stuffed lobster, and decadent desserts. Choose from four different environments: the lobby bar for mingling, the patio with fountains for tropical inspiration, the wine cave for an elegant setting or the salon for a romantic evening. Live tropical and Cuban music plays in the courtyard Monday-Saturdays, starting at 8:00 p.m. Daily noon-midnight. Ca. Santo Domingo 33-66. Tel: 664-8897, URL: www.portondesantodomingo.com. Updated: Apr 16, 2011.

Restaurante San Pedro

(ENTREES: $15-20) This enormous restaurant and café has fantastic food and outdoor seating directly facing the Iglesia San Pedro Claver. The restaurant produces divine Asian-fusion food like sushi, nasi goreng and pad thai noodles, and the café-bar serves an extensive list of wine, cocktails, fresh juices and beer. All the food is prepared with lovely garnishes and colorful Caribbean touches. The servers are friendly, well mannered and accommodating. Depending on the evening, you may have to wait for a seat outside on the plaza, so it would be wise to call ahead if you plan on having dinner. Open noon-3 p.m., 7-11:30 p.m. Plaza San Pedro Claver 30-11. Tel: 664-5121, Cel: 315-664-9675. E-mail: cafesanpedro@decameron.com. Updated: Mar 03, 2011.

Enoteca

(ENTREES: $18-44) Near the Museo Naval and Plaza Santa Teresa is this high-class Italian restaurant. The large interior courtyard creates a comfortable ambiance for the fine dining you will experience. All dishes are made with imported Italian ingredients. Most pastas are made in-house, and come with a choice of a dozen sauces. You may also choose from the 20 varieties of pizza or a succulent seafood entrée. The extensive wine list features *vinos* from all regions of Italy. Daily 11:30 a.m.-11:30 p.m. Ca. San Juan de Dios 3-39. Tel: 664-3806, E-mail: nuovaenoteca@telecom.com.co, URL: www.nuovaenoteca.com. Updated: May 04, 2011.

Nightlife

Babar

(COVER: $6) Babar is one of Cartagena's most successful nightclubs in El Centro. Across the street from the Naval Museum, you will find this very hip and colorful spot on the second floor, with three balconies overlooking the night's activities in Plaza Santa Teresa. The cocktail menu is extensive (many have Caribbean rum in them). Babar is packed with flirtatious foreigners socializing and dancing until the morning hours. Open Thursday-Saturday 9 p.m.-3 a.m. (daily in high seasons). Ca. San Juan de Dios 3-37. Tel: 664-4083. Updated: Apr 16, 2011.

El Baluarte Tasca-Bar

An ideal location for an afternoon to late night cocktail, El Baluarte is located precisely on Baluarte San Francisco Javier ramparts, in front of Plaza Santa Teresa. This is a perfect place to watch the sun set over the Caribbean or to bask in Cartagena's evening hum. Savor delicious grilled foods or have a romantic nightcap by moon- and starlight. On Friday and Saturday nights, El Baluarte hosts live music. Open daily after 6 p.m. Ca. San Juan de Dios and Ca. Ricaurte Baluarte San Francisco Javier. 664-2425, E-mail: baluartesanfrancisco@yahoo.com, URL: baluartejaviersanfrancisocjavier.com. Updated: Apr 16, 2011.

Café del Mar

Café del Mar, on Baluarte de Santo Domingo, is one of the few long-standing night spots that continues to be a popular place to enjoy the sunset, meet new people and party on the weekends. People aren't drawn by the food (Entrées: $9-21) or pricey drinks; they come for the great outdoor atmosphere, infectious house music, lovely evening scenery and happy-go-lucky crowd. Sometimes, especially on the weekends, this place gets so packed that guests spill out into the street. On quieter nights Café del Mar is a great place to unwind. Baluarte de Santo Domingo. Open 5 p.m.-2 a.m. Baluarte de Santo Domingo. Tel: 664-6513, URL: www.cafedelmarcolombia.com. Updated: Apr 16, 2011.

Rincón de la Mantilla

This large, woody restaurant and bar is a huge draw for locals and foreigners seeking a good spot to drink a local beer and people-watch. What likely attracts people to this lively place is the wall of refrigerators stocked with bottles of Águila and Club Colombia beer. Help yourself to a seat outside, inside, or at the bar with your friends and get the party started. Rincón de la Mantilla also serves a lunch special ($5.50) and á la carte dishes ($11-16). Monday-Saturday 8 a.m.-midnight. Ca. de la Mantilla 3-32. Tel: 660-1430, E-mail: gonzalezsegreraehijos@hotmail.com. Updated: May 03, 2011.

San Diego

San Diego is the classiest and most sophisticated part of Cartagena. Like in El Centro, there are plenty of picturesque buildings and narrow streets here—but also a higher concentration of fancy restaurants and luxury hotels. The pace of life in San Diego is slower and privacy is easier to find. This is also the area of the city that inspired bits of Gabriel García Márquez' Love in the Time of Cholera. (In fact, the famed writer's house is here.) In the plaza, you are likely to brush elbows with the city's elite. Updated: Apr 21, 2011.

Things to See and Do

Casa de Gabriel García Márquez

Gabriel García Márquez's house in San Diego has not been turned into a museum or tourist attraction. If it were, it would be one of the most popular sites in Cartagena. The inspirational house still stands today near Baluarte de Santa Clara. From the 5th floor terrace of Hotel Santa Clara you can get a peek of his old courtyard. Tierra Magna (URL: www.tierramagna.com) has a recorded walking tour ($36, in five languages) of Cartagena sites related to Gabriel García Márquez and his work. For more information, ask at Tierra Magna's kiosk at Templo Santo Domingo. Ca. del Curato and Baluarte de Santa Clara. Updated: May 02, 2011.

Las Bóvedas

The same engineer that designed Castillo San Felipe de Barajas built Las Bóvedas to serve as military quarters for the city in the late 18th century. Within this yellow building comprised of 46 arches, are 23 vaults that were used to lodge military personnel and to store ammunition, provisions and tools. During the republican era, these vaults were used as jail cells. The structure has been renovated and now houses artisan shops selling Colombian and Caribbean handicrafts and souvenirs. Las Bóvedas is located at the northern perimeter of San Diego, next to Museo de las Fortificaciones. Its shops are open everyday from 10:00 a.m.-5:00 p.m. Updated: May 02, 2011

Museo de las Fortificaciones and Las Murallas

(ADMISSION: $4 adults, $2.25 children) Construction of Las Murallas, the walls protecting Cartagena de Indias, began in 1586 when Bautista Antonelli, an Italian engineer, was hired by the Spanish

Crown. They were later fortified by Cristóbal de Roda in 1608, who focused on the section separating the city from the open sea. From 1631 to 1633, Francisco de Murga worked to further protect the city on the other side, in Getsemaní. Repairs after several sieges were made in the late 17th century and early 18th century. Many of the wall's old canons are still in place, and visitors can walk around the walls themselves to get a taste of Cartagena's military past. The museum is located next to Las Bóvedas. Be careful, especially if walking at night, not to step in any holes; some are quite large. Daily 8 a.m.-6 p.m. Ca. del Jardín and Ca. Recula del Oveja, Baluarte de Santa Catalina. Tel: 664-4790. Updated: Apr 15, 2011.

Lodging

Hostal San Diego

(ROOMS: $35-49) Hostal San Diego may seem a bit overpriced for what you get (a small air-conditioned room with a cold shower), but it earns points for its location and charms. Its convenient Internet café next door, inviting white exterior and quaint interior courtyard make this hostel appealing. It is also the closest accommodation to the shopping at Las Bóvedas and to Baluarte de Santa Catalina bastion, where you can watch the sunset. This place is the cheapest option in the heart of San Diego., though like other places, rates rise in the high seasons. Ca. de las Bóvedas 39-120. Tel: 5-660-1433, E-mail: hostalsandiego@telecom.com.co, URL: www.hostalsandiego.com. Updated: Apr 15, 2011.

Hotel Tres Banderas

(ROOMS: $103-155) Hotel Tres Banderas' convenient location, relaxing atmosphere and reasonable rates make it a popular accommodation for both locals and foreigners. This hotel's 22 rooms come in three styles—standard, superior with balcony and the Canadá suite—guaranteeing to satisfy all travelers. Rooms are done in earth tones and tasteful décor, and have private bath, air conditioning and cable TV. At the end of a day of sightseeing, relax in one of the two waterfall-bedecked patios, or on a rooftop terrace. WiFi and a typical Colombian breakfast are complimentary. You can also enjoy a free ferry transport to its sister hotel on Isla Tierrabomba, for a beachside respite from Cartagena's bustle. Ca. Cochera de Hobo 38-66. Tel: 660-2112, E-mail: info@hotel3banderas.com, URL: www.hotel3banderas.com. Updated: Apr 25, 2011.

Casa La Fe

(ROOMS: $135-209) If you stay at this great little B&B in the sophisticated Plaza Fernández de Madrid, you will be pampered until the day you tear yourself away from Cartagena. Fifteen neatly decorated and comfortable rooms, all with private bathrooms and air conditioning, surround the house's lush garden courtyard, where guests are served breakfast. Don't miss an opportunity to relax in the lounge on the roof, which offers shade and WiFi. A solid alternative to Hotel Tres Banderas around the corner, La Fe is a bit pricier, but packs a punch. Ca. Segundo de Badillo 36-125. Tel: 5-664-0306, Fax: 5-660-0164, E-mail: admin@casalafe.com, URL: www.casalafe.com. Updated: Apr 15, 2011.

Casa del Tejadillo

(ROOMS: $150-194) This gorgeous republican house, built in the 19th century, provides the same luxury and comfort as El Marqués Boutique Hotel. Perfectly situated on quiet Calle del Tejadillo, this immaculate historical home has been meticulously restored and refurbished to provide superior accommodations. This house has eight clean and spacious rooms. It can be rented out as a whole for large groups. Ca. del Tejadillo 38-53. Cel: 311-221-8167, E-mail: casadeltejadillo@gmail.com / casadeltejadillo@hotmail.com, URL: www.casadeltejadillo.com. Updated: Mar 04, 2011.

Sofitel Santa Clara Hotel

(ROOMS: $364-2,889) This architectural gem, built as a monastery in 1621, is a delight to wander around, with its exquisitely decorated eating and lounging areas, lush gardens and pool. Choose from two fine dining options providing French-fusion cuisine, or sip a drink from the chic bar and café. Sofitel Santa Clara Hotel has 120 luxury guest rooms (including 17 suites) that are distributed in two different environments—colonial and republican. The interior design is impeccable and makes for an atmosphere of quiet order and beauty. Rooms have views of the old city, the ocean, and/or the hotel's well-manicured gardens and pool. Ca. del Torno 39-29, Tel: 650-4700, E-mail: reservas@hotelsantaclara.com, URL: www.sofitel.com/gb/hotel-1871-sofitel-cartagena-santa-clara/index.shtml. Updated: Mar 04, 2011.

Restaurants

Arepas del Santísimo

(ENTREES: $1.70-4.20) This small but affordable café is difficult to spot from the street. But once you do find it, it is worth the search. Enjoy arepas with several different fillings, like cheese, ham, chicken, beef and *chorizo*. They are made to order on one small grill. The café is minimally decorated inside a small, pleasant courtyard and has just five tables. The food here is tasty. Daily 3-10 p.m.Ca. del Santísimo 8-55. Cel.: 310-305-1142. Updated: Apr 15, 2011.

Pizza en el Parque

(ENTREES: $3 and up) Local late-night partygoers end up at this unassuming pizza joint in Plaza Fernandéz de Madrid. Choose from 10 types of pizzas with the usual toppings, then take your pizza outside, sit in the park, and enjoy your meal under the stars. Daily 5 p.m.-1 a.m. Calle Segundo de Badillo 36-167. Updated: Apr 15, 2011.

Govindas Sol De La India

(LUNCH: $4.50-6.50, ENTREES: $6-18) Sol de la India is not just another Hare Krishna Govinda restaurant. This bistro serves gourmet vegetarian cuisine. At the noon hour, it offers an excellently seasones, three-course luncheon special (which can also be ordered as a buffet). À la carte dishes include curries and other Indian delicacies, served with mango chutney and chapati. Hindu music plays softly through the patio and interior dining hall, decorated with posters of Krishna, Lakshmi and Bollywood starlets. Sol de la India also offers yoga, cooking, meditation and other classes, and hosts cultural events. Monday-Saturday 11:30 a.m.-3 p.m, 7-10 p.m. Ca. Tumbamuertos 38-43. Tel: 660-9476, Cel: 318-360-7190. Updated: May 04, 2011.

Casa Majagna

(LUNCH: $6 and up, ENTREES: $9-22) Casa Majagna's interesting mix of Italian and local Cartagenan meals, extensive beer and wine menu, and classy, lounge-like setting draw a healthy bunch of local loyals. The tables outside make for a perfect place to meet with friends for dinner and drinks. Casa Majagna serves tasty, hearty dishes. Let your stomach and your mood decide for you which entrée would be best for you tonight. Open Monday-Friday noon-4 p.m., 6-10 p.m.; weekends noon-4 p.m., 6 p.m.-midnight. Ca. de la Tablada 7-12. Tel: 664-7958. Updated: Apr 15, 2011.

Da Danni's Restaurant

(ENTREES: $10-20) Da Danni's, a Cartagena restaurant serving quality Italian pasta, is a really good option for travelers needing a break from typical Caribbean-Colombian cuisine. Stepping into the restaurant feels as if you've walked into a restaurant in Bologna. The food here is superb and the helpings are large, so you get plenty of food for the price. The bread is baked fresh. Service is excellent. Tuesday-Sunday noon-11 pm. Da Danni's also has a bistro in Bocagrande (Cra. 3, 8-69, Centro Comercial La Mansión. Tel: 665-8979). Ca. de Santísimo 8-01. Tel: 660-0030, Cel: 312-617-3529, E-mail: albertosotosierra@hotmail.com, URL: www.restaurante-dadannis.com. Updated: Apr 15, 2011.

Restaurante El Santísimo

(ENTREES: $18-25) This popular, fancy establishment offers quintessential Caribbean cuisine prepared by a cordon bleu chef. Ask about the day's special menu, or enjoy one of the exquisite seafood creations, and pair it with a fine wine from the extensive list. Dine indoors, or outdoors in a romantic, grotto-like courtyard. Interesting, Catholic-themed artwork adorns the walls. Noon-3 p.m., 7 p.m.-midnight. Ca. del Torno 39-76. Tel: 660-1531, E-mail: restauranteelsantisimo@gmail.com, URL: restauranteelsantisimo.com. Updated: Apr 15, 2011.

Nightlife

La Esquina Sandiegana

One of the only authentic salsa bars in Cartagena, La Esquina Sandiegana has friendly local people. The music and dancing gets going once the sun goes down and usually keeps going until the sun comes up. Tourists here are few—this club has loyal local clientele who come to drink, dance and have a good time. Ca. de los Puntales 8-70 and Ca. de la Santísima. Updated: Apr 15, 2011.

Getsemaní

Getsemaní is the traditional budget-travelers' haunt. In recent years, this neighborhood

CARIBBEAN COAST

within the old walled city has been shedding its grungy and lackluster past. New hostels, boutique hotels and B&Bs are opening, as are a plethora of restaurants. The city's best nightlife continues to groove down on Avenida del Arsenal. Yet, Getsemaní keeps its working-class, family air. Another advantage to staying in Getsemaní is its closeness to Cartagena's major sites. Updated: Jun 11, 2011.

Lodging

BUDGET

Hostal Casa Viena

(ROOMS: $9-25) Hands down the most well-known hostel in Cartagena de Indias, Casa Viena continues to be the first choice for backpackers. It has a helpful tourist desk where patrons and walk-ins alike can plan chiva tours and sailing trips to Panama. With only nine rooms in total, however, this place fills up fast. The only way to secure a room is to call ahead, and even that doesn't guarantee it will have a bed for you. The dorm is the only room with air conditioning and sleeps eight ($9 per person). The other eight rooms range in size (from $14). Ca. San Andres 30-53. Tel: 664-6242, E-mail: hotel@casaviena.com, URL: www.casaviena.com. Updated: May 05, 2011.

Hospedaje Marta

(ROOMS: $10-15) If you are in a pinch, this small, 10-room hotel works, though it's not as nice as its neighbors. The rooms are basic—each with a grainy TV and dimly-lit private bathroom. The fans look decades old and about to disintegrate. The room in front is a quad, and the rest are doubles with one or two beds. Ca. Tripita y Media (Cra. 10) 31-16. Tel: 664-7653, Cel: 311-672-5802. Updated: May 04, 2011.

Hotel Marlin

(ROOMS: $12-35) Hotel Marlin offers comfortable accommodations for Colombian and foreign backpackers, business people and tourists. Set in a colonial house, Marlin has 24 rooms, each with a private bathroom and your choice of a ceiling fan or air conditioning. Internet service, cable TV, laundry service, safety boxes and a common kitchen are available for guest use. The building has a comfortable common room and garden. The hotel also provides helpful tourist information for further destinations like Volcán Totume, Playa Blanca or the Islas del Rosario. Ca. de la Media Luna (Ca. 30) 10-35. Tel: 5-664-3507, E-mail: hotelmarlincartagena@hotmail.com, URL: www.hotelmarlin-cartagena.com. Updated: May 05, 2011.

Hotel Familiar ❗

(ROOMS: $15-20) This large, airy hotel has basic rooms that come with a fan, and with or without a private, cold-water bath. The rooms with private bath get booked first because the shared bathrooms are a bit out of the way and rudimentary, though spacious. The hotel's ambiance however, is redeeming enough to justify staying here. With plenty of lounging options and lovely interior balconies, the place maintains a respectable reputation and tourists usually leave satisfied with the price. Hotel Familiar is especially popular with bicyclists and motorcyclists. Ca. del Guerrero 29-66. Tel: 664-2464. Updated: May 05, 2011.

Hostal Real

(ROOMS: $15-25) Hostal Real, located just a half-block from Parque del Centenario, has 20 rooms that will suit your needs. A few rooms have air conditioning and all have private baths with cold water. Though a bit dank and the bathrooms are tight, it is reasonably comfortable. Hostal Real has an altogether airy feel with two connected courtyards extending all the way to the back. The hostel has a nice, big dorm room upstairs that can hold larger groups without a problem. Ca. Primera de la Magdalena 9-33. Tel: 664-7866, Cel: 313-516 -1542, E-mail: hostalreal@yahoo.com, URL: www. hostal-cartagena.com. Updated: May 05, 2011.

MID-RANGE

Hotel Villa Colonial

(BEDS: $18-38) Hotel Villa Colonial is a comfortable, upscale hostel in Cartagena's bohemian Getsemaní neighborhood. The tastefully decorated rooms in this beautifully restored colonial house surround an interior courtyard with balconies. All accommodations come with private bath, cable TV and a choice of air conditioning or fan. The bilingual staff can make reservations for any outing you'd like to do in the area. Hotel Villa Colonial has a sister inn in the Getsemaní neighborhood: the Casa Villa Colonial), which offers deluxe suites (Calle Media Luna 10-89, Tel: 664-5421, URL: www.casavillacolonial.com). Credit cards are accepted. Ca Maravillas 30-60, Getsemaní. Tel: 664-4996, Cel: 311-665-9369, E-mail: hotelvillacolonial@hotmail.com, URL: www.hotelvillacolonial.com. Updated: Nov 01, 2011.

Hostal La Casona Getsemaní

(ROOMS: $27-44) Even though it has 28 rooms around a peaceful courtyard, La Casona is still a slightly overpriced hostel. The rooms are very simple, with nothing more than the basic amenities, like a small TV, fan or air conditioning, and private bath. You will get a better value on of the larger, air conditioned rooms. Prices are higher at vacation times. Ca. Tripita y Media (Cra 10) 31-32. Tel: 664-1301, Cel: 320-567-8720, E-mail: hostal-lacasona@hotmail.com, URL: www.hostallacasona.com.co. Updated: May 05, 2011.

Hotel San Felipe

(ROOMS: $45-53) This centrally located hotel appeals to Colombians on holiday or business, though it is also a good choice for foreign tourists. As part of the Dorado Plaza hotel group (which has hotels in Bocagrande, Isla de Tierra Bomba, and Bogotá), Hotel San Felipe is an industrial hotel with basic amenities. All of its 55 rooms, spread over five floors, have a television with basic cable and a clean bathroom with a cold shower. The 25 rooms facing the street have fans and nice balconies, although this can make them a bit noisier during the day. The 30 interior rooms have air conditioning and are generally quieter. There is 24-hour security in the lobby, a restaurant and bar. The staff is very friendly and helpful. In all, it is a good and spacious alternative to the tight quarters of the hostels around the corner. Cra. 9A (Av. del Centenario) 31-72. Tel: 664-5439, E-mail: mercadeo@doradoplaza.com, URL: www.doradoplaza.com. Updated: May 05, 2011.

HIGH-END

Hotel Monterrey

(ROOMS: $136-149) Next door to the Teatro Cartagena and across the street from the convention center, the Hotel Monterrey displays a quiet colonial elegance with its stark white exterior. The hotel's design is a perfect blend of European style and 19th century Caribbean flair. Its simple décor, understated luxury, peaceful atmosphere and quality of service are easy to take for granted. Guests can enjoy the Jacuzzi and relax in the comfortable lounge. The hotel also offers private parking. Hotel Monterrey's 30 spacious rooms and suites are mostly singles or doubles. Rates include U.S.-style breakfast and taxes. Cra. 8B, 25-103. Tel: 650-3030, E-mail: info@hotel-monterry.com.co, URL: www.hotelmonterrey.com.co. Updated: May 03, 2011.

Restaurants

Plaza De La Trinidad Stalls

(SNACKS: $1-4) For cheap eats, backpackers should head straight down Calle del Guerrero to the 16th century Iglesia de la Santísima Trinidad's plaza. From early morning to late night, stalls offering a variety of Colombian fast food set up around this square. The first to arrive is the woman who whips up fresh fruit juices from whatever the day's harvest brings. As the day wears on, hotdog and hamburger stands fire up their grills. Come evening, other vendors join the crowd. Now stuffed arepas, shish kabobs and quesadillas join the menu. So, grab a beer from the corner store, place your order and join your new neighbors hanging out down at the plaza. Ca. del Guerrero and Ca. del Carretero. Updated: May 04, 2011.

Gato Negro !

(ENTREES: $2-4) The very unassuming sign of a black cat outside a cerulean blue building on Calle San Andrés (two doors down from Hostal Casa Viena) is the only thing that marks this small café's location. This inexpensive restaurant is popular with foreigners. It specializes in vegetarian, breakfast and lunch, preparing crepes, salads, eggs and other light snacks. Gato Negro's décor is plain and sparse. You can call ahead to take your meal out. Monday-Saturday 7 a.m.-2 p.m., Sunday 8 a.m.-2 p.m. Ca. San Andrés 30-39. Tel: 664-0958, URL: gatonegrocartagena.com. Updated: May 05, 2011.

V!VA ONLINE REVIEW
GATO NEGRO

" Lovely place ... The best breakfast in whole Cartagena!!!! "
May 13, 2009

El Coroncoro

(ENTREES: $3-7) Don't be shy to ask to share a table at El Coroncoro, because that's the only way you'll be able to enjoy its cheap, hearty fare. The menu is full of classic Colombian fare, like *bistek a caballo* (steak and eggs). Set meals come with a choice of 13 entrées. El Coroncoro's décor is an eclectic collection of bric-a-brac from the region and the sea, and wind chimes hung from the ceiling. Daily 7:30 a.m.-10 p.m. Ca. Tripita y Media 31-28. Tel: 664-2648. Updated: May 04, 2011.

CARIBBEAN COAST

Australian Fusion Café

(ENTREES: $5-9) English-heritage travelers have a place to go for their comfort foods: Australian Fusion Café. Chef Ian prepares vintage Australian and Commonwealth food with fascinating monikers. The two- and three-course combo meals are a real bargain. Australian Fusion Café may seem a bit pricey for backpackers, but the heaps of food are enough for two to share (and Ian says it's okay if you do). On weekends and holidays breakfast—featuring vegemite on toast—is served. Open Monday-Friday from 11:30 a.m.; weekends and holidays from 9:30 a.m. Ca. 30 (Ca. de la Media Luna) 8B-108. Tel: 664-9870, E-mail: australianfusioncafe@yahoo.com. Updated: May 04, 2011.

Pizzaría Restaurante I Balconi

(ENTREES: $5-14) What could be more romantic, more intimate than having dinner on a private balcony in the heart of bohemian Getsemaní? That is precisely the ambience Pizzaría-Restaurant I Balconi presents to its Colombian and international clientele. The menu is full of Italian appetizers like ham-wrapped melon, bruschetta and carpaccio. Pastas come with 10 choices of sauce. Sixteen varieties of pizza come piping hot out of the oven. I Balconi also presents meat dishes like tadiata and scaloppini. The restaurant also has interior dining. Daily noon-midnight. Ca. del Guerrero 29-146, and Ca. de la Media Luna. Tel: 660-9880, Cel: 311-392-0936, URL: www.ibalconi.com. Updated: May 04, 2011.

El Parche Del León

(ENTREES: $6-10) El Parché del León is a small bistro founded by four Argentines who prepare typical Italo-Argentine fare, like pizzas, pastas and raviolis have fascinating fillings. Other entrées come from around the globe: veal fajitas, sweet-and-sour ribs, smoked pork curry and stir fries. Vegetarians also have much to choose from. Coconut flan and other desserts round out a meal. El Parche del León also offers a smorgasbord of cocktails, wines, beers and juices. Tuesday-Sunday 5:30 p.m.-2 a.m.; food service 7:30 p.m.-midnight. Ca. de la Media Luna 9-44. Cel: 311-680-8037, E-mail: elparchedelleon@hotmail.com. Updated: May 04, 2011.

Donde Socorro

(ENTREES: $9-21) Popular with the locals and offering eccentric cultural foods such as turtle, rabbit, deer and hen, Donde Socorro (formerly called La Casa de Socorro) is a pure Caribbean delight. Its extensive menu, specializing in Cartagenan-Caribbean cuisine, is orientated around hearty dishes with fish, meat and seafood, are hearty and filling. La Casa can seat nearly 100 people, and customers can choose to sit inside the homely, wooded interior or outside on the covered patio. The walls are decorated with stylish Caribbean art painted on wood planks. This place is not for vegetarians. Daily 11 a.m.-10 p.m. Ca. Larga 8B-112. Tel: 664-4658, E-mail: restaurantelacasadesocorro@yahoo.com, URL: www.restaurantelacasadesocorro.com. Updated: May 05, 2011.

La Cocina de Socorro

(ENTREES: $18-45) Not to be mistaken for the other Socorro restaurant in Getsemaní, La Cocina de Socorro is a fancier establishment serving original and traditional Caribbean food. Watching her grandmother cook began María Nelly del Socorro's love affair with food at an early age. She now blends her abuela's cooking secrets with magical Caribbean flavors. Seafood specialties include jumble fish au gratin and the "Festival de Maricos" (a fisherman's platter in creole sauce). This is Caribbean fine dining as you've never seen it before. Monday-Friday noon-4 p.m., 7:30-11 p.m.; Saturday, Sunday, holidays noon-11 p.m. Cra. 8B, 24-38. Tel: 660-2044, E-mail: lacocinadesocorro13@yahoo.es, URL: www.lacocinadesocorro.com. Updated: May 05, 2011.

Nightlife

María Félix Cinema-Café-Bar

(DRINKS: $2 and up, ENTREES: $3-7) María Félix is much more than a bar. It is a cultural space. The small café is decorated with posters of old movie greats, like Brando, Bacall, Bogart and, of course, Mexican Silver Screen legend María Félix. Every night at 7 p.m., folks get comfy in the overstuffed chairs, waiting for the night's movie. Recent U.S., European and Latin American cinema (all subtitled) grace the big-screen TV. This is also Happy Hour (7-9 p.m.), with two-for-one cocktails. Non-imbibers have a cornucopia of fresh juices to sip. Munch on finger foods, pastas and other delights. Live music and literary readings are also on the calendar. Daily from 7 p.m. Ca. de la Media Luna 9-36. Cel: 318-699-7122. Updated: May 04, 2011.

León de Baviera

(DRINKS: $4-8, ENTREES: $6-20) This hot spot is much more than just a restaurant and bar. It is your very own Bavaria in the heart of Cartagena, and a place to meet fellow travelers as well as locals. Playing rock music and serving German beer and food, León de Baviera has a lively atmo-

---

Did a unique trek? Got way off the beaten path? Tell other travelers at vivatravelguides.com

sphere without being too "Oktoberfest" over-the-top. The bar offers live rock music on Thursdays as well as a collection of live music from different groups on Sundays. Tuesday to Sunday after 4:00 p.m. Ca. del Arsenal 10B-65. Tel: 664-4412, E-mail: leondebaviera@yahoo.es. Updated: May 05, 2011.

La Casa de la Cerveza 🍺

(DRINKS: $4 and up, ENTREES: $12 and up) Perfectly perched atop the old wall of the city at the crook of Getsemaní, this hip outdoor restaurant and bar provides lovely views of the inland lagoons and Castillo de San Felipe de Barajas. The patio has comfortable couches and pillowed sofas. Caribbean salsa plays all night. Order from a small assortment of food and wide array of beers in a wide variety of sizes. Try its popular mojito and party the night away. Daily 4 p.m.-4 a.m. Ca. Arsenal, Baluarte San Lorenzo del Reducto. Tel: 664 9261, E-mail: eventoscartagena@casadelacerveza.com.co, URL: www.casadelacerveza.com.co. Updated: May 05, 2011.

La Carbonera

(COVER CHARGE: $9) La Carbonera is reputedly the top night club and lounge in town, with the best house, dance and techno music. Locals consider this hip spot the place to see and to be seen. People pour in late in the evening, so it's best to end the night here. There is a dress code, so dress to impress or it might be difficult to get in. Daily 9 p.m.–4 a.m. Calle del Arsenal (Calle 24) 9A-47. Tel: 664-6237. Updated: May 19, 2009.

Mister Babilla 🍺

The colorful, Caribbean-themed bar in the front of Mister Babilla provides the perfect alluring taste of what awaits inside. As you walk down the hallway, scantily-clad waitresses ask for your order. In the back room, you will understand when they say, *"rumba en la playa"* ("dance on the beach"). This huge, wooden mess hall fills up late in the evening with singing and dancing maniacs. Things here can get a bit crazy, so be prepared. Mister Babilla also serves breakfast, lunch and snacks ($6-21). Ca. del Arsenal (Calle 24) 8B-137. Tel: 664-8616, E-mail: mrbabilla@gmail.com. Updated: May 05, 2011.

Bocagrande

If you are in Cartagena for a few days, hit up Avenida San Martín in the Bocagrande section of town. Located a block from the beach, this street has loads of hostels, restaurants and businesses. Bocagrande's beach is world-renowned. Although it is crowded and the vendors are persistent, the area is still suitable for catching some rays. The clearest water is at the peninsula's far west end, in the Laguito neighborhood. Bocagrande, which literally means "big mouth," is an alternative launching point for boat trips to Isla del Encanto and historical Isla de Tierra Bomba. As for nightlife, it's mellow. Although Bocagrande's bars are more low-key than those of Getsemaní, you can still dance the night away. Updated: May 05, 2011.

Things to See and Do

El Museo De La Esmeralda

(ADMISSION: free) At Joyería Caribe's Museo de la Esmeralda, a guide leads visitors through the large, second-floor museum displaying everything about emeralds. An underground mine replica shows workers excavating the gems. Other galleries explain where emeralds are found and their place in history. Cases feature these amazing stones, including Petra, an 80-centimeter (31-in) long, 140-kilogram (230-lb) rock studded with 60 raw emeralds. Tourists can get a glimpse of jewelers cutting gems and see the finished products in the store below. Tours are offered in Spanish, English and German. Monday-Saturday 8:30 a.m.-6 p.m., Sunday 9:30 a.m.-6 p.m. Ca. 5, 2-51. Tel: 665-4625, URL: www.joyeriacaribe.com. Updated: May 02, 2011.

Río Casino

Río Casino is a great place to spend an evening winning—or losing—money. This casino, which is part of a larger Colombian chain, features Brazilian Carnaval-esque shows (hence the name "Río" for Rio de Janeiro). All of the slots, roulette and blackjack tables have much smaller minimum bets than in the U.S. Monday-Saturday 11 a.m.-5:30 a.m., Sunday 1 p.m.-3:30 a.m. Updated: May 05, 2011.Av. San Martín 5-145. Tel: 655-1197, E-mail: cvillegas@winnergroup.com, URL: www.winnergroup.com. Updated: May 05, 2011.

Lodging

Hostal Leonela

(ROOMS: $36-58) You really can't go wrong staying a few nights at Hostal Leonela, which has over 35 years of service and helpful staff. The hostel's 35 rooms are situated around a calming blue courtyard,

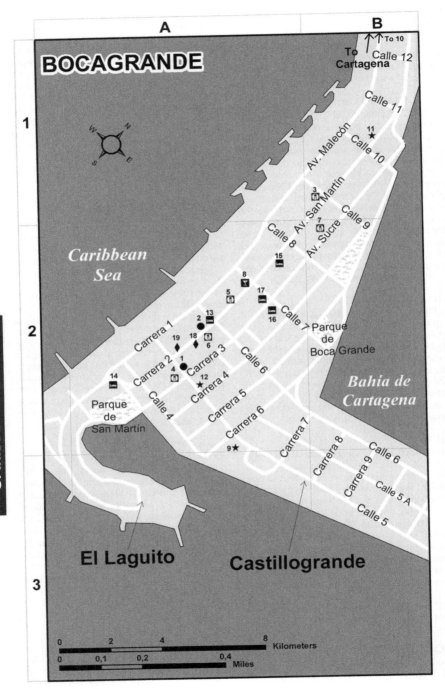

CARIBBEAN COAST

● Activities

1 Joyería Caribe Museo A2
2 Río Casino A2

⑪ Eating

3 Crepes and Waffles B1
4 Da Pietro Restaurant A2
5 La Dulcería A2
6 La Olla Cartagenera A2
7 Restaurante Arabe e Internacional B2

▮ Nightlife

8 REZAK Bar Club A2

★ Services

9 Hospital Bocagrande A2
10 Hospital Naval B1
11 HSBC bank B1

12 Lavamejor A2

▬ Sleeping

13 El Almirante Estelar A2
14 Hotel Caribe A2
15 Hotel Charlotte A2
16 Hotel Leonela A2
17 Hotel Tequendama Inn A2

◆ Tours

18 Isla del Encanto A2
19 Ocean & Land Tours A2

CARIBBEAN COAST

where guests are served their morning breakfast. Some rooms have fans, others air conditioning. All have private bathrooms (cold water only) and a grainy TV with cable. The rooms are spacious and clean. This is a great find with a pleasant atmosphere in a convenient location. Cra. 3, 7-142. Tel: 665-8595, E-mail: hostaleonela@yahoo.com, URL: www.hostaleonela.com. Updated: Updated: May 03, 2011.

Hotel Tequendama Inn

(ROOMS: $112-191) Formerly known as Hotel Parque Real, Hotel Tequendama Inn appears classy from the outside but is a bit more basic than you might think. There's a calm peacefulness here, though, that reminds guests that vacation is all about relaxing. This 30-room hotel draws an older local crowd, but also welcomes foreigners. The rooms here are clean and simple.Cra. 3, 7-171. Tel: 665-5531, E-mail: recepciontequendamainnctg@hotmail.com, URL: www. shc.com.co. Updated: May 03, 2011.

Hotel Charlotte

(ROOMS: $127-150) Smack-dab in the middle of Bocagrande's always-happening Avenida San Martín, Hotel Charlotte is a peaceful getaway. Just one block from the sea, the hotel is a red brick building that is as charming inside as out, decorated with delicate touches and dark wood against a mostly white background. The 34 guest suites are spacious, clean and modern. Relax by the pool or have a drink or meal at the cozy restaurant-bar downstairs. Hotel Charlotte is romantic yet family-friendly. Private parking is available for guests. Av. San Martín 7-126. Tel: 665-9201, E-mail: cartagena@hotelescharlotte.com, URL: www.hotelescharlotte.com. Updated: May 05, 2011

Hotel Caribe

(ROOMS: $159-264) The grand dame of Bocagrande, Hotel Caribe, is a luxurious resort. This historic hotel (designated a national monument), with 363 rooms (17 are suites), is set amid a sprawling estate that includes gardens, outdoor restaurants and, of course, beaches. Eat at one of the hotel's several fine-dining options, meander the grounds at your leisure, exercise in the gym or tan by the enormous pool. Cra. 1, 2-87. Tel: 650-1160, E-mail: hotelcaribe@hotelcaribe.com, URL: www.hotelcaribe.com. Updated: May 03, 2011.

Hotel Almirante Cartagena Estelar

(ROOMS: $237-371) Hotel Almirante Cartagena Estelar is in the center of Bocagrande's scene. Its glass towers house 250 rooms in four styles, including spacious suites decorated in clean, modern lines. Elevators whisk tourists up to these accommodations that have private bath, air conditioning, TV and WiFi connection. Some have sea views. Guests can relax in spa, gym, outdoor pool, billiard salon or casino, and dine in one of the four restaurants or have drinks in the American bar. The hotel also has facilities for meetings and special events, on-site ATM and exchange house. Although Hotel Almirante is rated five-stars, travelers' reviews are mixed. Av. San Martín and Ca. 6. Tel: 655-4700/018000-978000 (toll-free Colombia)/1-866-599-8703 (toll-free U.S., Canada), E-Mail: reservas@hotelesestelar.com, URL: www.hotelesestelar.com. Updated: Jul 10, 2011.

Restaurants

La Dulcería

The sweet smell of baklava lingers in this bright little café. On display in glass cases are various Middle Eastern desserts, but La Dulcería (The Sweet Shop) doesn't just bake its own sweets. One look at its 10-page menu will assure you that you will not go unsatisfied here. Reasonably priced appetizers, soups, empanadas and salads can be made to order. Monday-Saturday noon-10 p.m., Sunday and holidays 1-10 p.m. Cra. 2, 6-53. Tel: 655-0281. Updated: May 05, 2011.

Crepes and Waffles

(ENTREES: $5-18) It's utterly appropriate that a town called Bocagrande, which literally means "large mouth," has this popular food chain on busy San Martín Avenue. With an extensive menu featuring a huge variety of crepes, waffles, pitas, salads and soups, you are certain to leave this place a few pounds heavier. The crepes come either sweet or salty, as do the bread bowls. Make your own salads at the salad bar or order delicious ones off the menu. Av. San Martin (Cra. 2) 8-205. Tel: 665-7258. Updated: May 05, 2011.

Da Pietro Restaurant

(ENTREES: $10 and up) The homemade pasta and pizza at this hotel's restaurant is surprisingly good and probably the best you will find in Bocagrande, if not in Cartagena as a whole. The Italian food is right on par with Da Danni's in San Diego and cheaper, too. The homey decorations make for a romantic evening setting. If you're not in the mood for pizza, ravioli or lasagna, you can always opt for Colombian cuisine prepared with a bit of Italian flair, like seafood casserole and fish fillets. Daily 8 a.m.-midnight. Da Pietro is also a hotel, with rooms ranging $80-91. Cra. 3, 4-401. Tel: 655-2369 , E-mail: hotel@pietro.com, URL: www.pietro.com. Updated: May 05, 2011.

Restaurante Arabe e Internacional

(ENTREES: $12-57) This is one of the few restaurants in Bocagrande that offers half portions of nearly everything on the menu. Specializing in Arabic dishes like quibbe and baba ganoush, this place cooks up mighty fine food in the quaint quarters of a courtyard and relaxing fountain. Local meat and seafood dishes are available here too. Arabic dancers perform for restaurant guests on Fridays and Saturdays. Monday, Wednesday-Friday noon-3 p.m., 7-10 p.m.; Saturday, Sunday noon-10 p.m.; closed Tuesday. Cra. 3, 8-83. Tel: 665-4365, E-mail: arabeinternacional@telecom.com.co. Updated: Jun 16, 2011.

La Olla Cartagenera

(ENTREES: $17-30) Specializing in seafood and Middle Eastern cuisine, La Olla Cartagenera is a fine place to kick back and have a decent meal. There is seating outside on Avenida San Martín, or you can take your meal in the large dining area in the back, where shells and fishing nets decorate the walls. Both food and prices here are good. Av. San Martín (Cra 2) 5-100. Tel: 5-665-3861. Updated: May 05, 2011.

Nightlife

REZAK Bar Club

Bocagrande is not too well-known for its nightlife, so REZAK is an anomaly in this altogether quiet part of Cartagena. Usually hopping on the weekends, this hip night spot can fill up with locals and keep the party going just like its counterparts on Avenida Arsenal in Getsemaní. Av. San Martín 6-155. Tel: 665-4000. Updated: May 05, 2011.

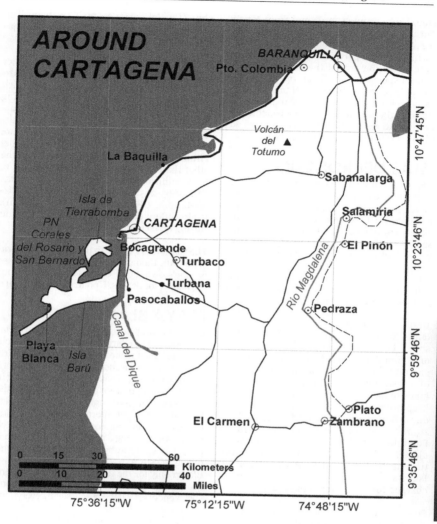

AROUND
CARTAGENA

Pto. Colombia ⊙

BARANQUILLA

10°47'45"N

Volcán
del ▲
Totumo

La Baquilla •

⊙Sabanalarga

Isla de
Tierrabomba

PN
Corales
del Rosario y
San Bernardo

CARTAGENA

Bocagrande

Salamiria
⊙

El Pinón

10°23'46"N

Río Magdalena

Turbaco

Turbana

Pasocaballos

⊙Pedraza

Playa
Blanca   Isla
Barú

Canal del Dique

9°59'46"N

El Carmen

⊙Plato
Zambrano

9°35'46"N

| 0 | 15 | 30 | 60 |
| 0 | 10 | 20 | 40 |

Kilometers

Miles

75°36'15"W   75°12'15"W   74°48'15"W

AROUND CARTAGENA
ISLA DE TIERRA BOMBA

Isla de Tierra Bomba, a rather large island off the coast of Cartagena, remains steeped in history. It was through the strait, Bocachica, that the first pioneers entered Cartagena. The narrow passageway was protected by two fortresses, which may be visited (daily 8 a.m.-6 p.m.): Fuerte San Fernando on Tierra Bomba itself, and Batería del Ángel San Rafael, on a small islet across the channel. The sites share an entry ticket (adults $4.50, children $2.25) and are free the last Sunday of each month. Most day trippers, though, only visit Punta Arena, one of Cartagena's best beaches, and Punta Luna. They spend the day on the playa, eating fresh island fruit and fish, and drinking Águila beer, boating back to Cartagena before sunset.

Hotel Tres Banderas in Cartagena also has luxury lodging at Punta Arena, for those who want to spend the night relaxing under the stars (www.hotel3banderas. com; $105-155, including boat transport).

Lanchas (launches) to Punta Arena depart from next to the Hilton Hotel in Laguito, Bocagrande ($3-6) and from Muelle Turístico La Bodeguita in Cartagena. From the Mueulla Turístico, local boats to Bocachica also depart (every 30-45 min; 15 min, $3-4). Beware of the hard sale of the more expensive tour boat operators ($9 round trip, $15 with lunch). If taking a boat from La Bodeguita, you'll have to pay an additional $3 port fee. Only at Bocachica do non-island residents have to pay a $1.70 additional tax. Updated: May 06, 2011.

ISLAS DEL ROSARIO

About 45 kilometers (27 mi) southwest of Cartagena, Islas del Rosario is a coral islands archipelago with arguably the best beaches and diving in Colombia. The islands were declared a protected area, PNN Corales del Rosario y de San Bernardo, in 1977. The park, which includes 43 islands, covers 120,000 hectares (296,527 ac) of coral reefs, mangroves and associated ecosystems. It extends from the westward from Isla Barú's coast, and includes Playa Blanca.

Underwater delights can be found at the islands' 30 designated diving and snorkeling spots. The diversity of sea life—35 species of echinoderms (such as sea cucumbers and urchins), 45 kinds of sponges, 52 types of coral, 170 different crustaceans, 180 kinds of mollusks, and 215 species of fish—keep even experienced divers occupied for days. Boat tours from Cartagena make a stop the aquarium on at Isla San Martin de Pajarales (adults $12, children 5-12 years old $8; not included in tour price), before turning back around to Playa Blanca on Isla Barú. An additional $7 per person is charged for the national park fee.

Some of the islands have lodging, for those who would like to enjoy the tranquil seas and white beaches at a less-rushed pace. Most hotels are quite plush and provide boat transfer service. Some offer scuba diving excursions. Isla Grande, the archipelago's largest island, has an interpretive hiking path. Several hotels are here, including **Coco Liso Resort** (Cra. 1, 4-12, Hotel El Dorado, local 1, Bocagrande. Tel: 5-665-9339, E-mail: info@cocolisoresort. com, URL: www.cocolisoresort.com) and locally owned **Ecohotel La Cocotera** (Ca. 4, 3-204, Bocagrande. Tel: 5-665-5655, E-mail: reservas@ecohotellacocotera.com, URL: www.ecohotellacocotera. com). **Hotel Majagua** has its own PADI

shop (Ca. del Torno 39-29, San Diego. Tel: 5-664-6070, E-mail: reservas@hotelmajagua.com, URL: www.hotelmajagua.com).

Isla del Encanto, west of Barú, is another one of the larger islands. **Isla del Encanto** tour agency has its own hotel there, which also presents day trips for tourists wishing to enjoy a more tranquil tour (Av San Martín 5-94, Michel Center, local 5, Bocagrande. Tel: 5-655-5454, URL: www.isladelencanto. com.co). One of the smallest isles is Isla del Pirata. Half the island is a reserve, and the other the **Hotel Isla Pirata Resort** (Ca. 6, 2-26, Edificio Granada, local 2, Bocagrnade. Tel: 5-665-2952, E-mail: reservas@hotelislapirata.com, URL: www.hotelislapirata.com). It also offers day tours. For information on staying on Isla Barú, see Playa Blanca.

The easiest way to get to the Islas del Rosario is on tour, though there are ways to get there on one's own. See Getting to and away from Cartagena for details. Updated: May 09, 2011.

PLAYA BLANCA

One of the must-do tours from Cartagena is Playa Blanca, on Isla Barú. This is the dream beach: A palm-shaded white strand of fine sand skirting a crystalline turquoise sea. Many dream of a paradise like this, of passing the days swaying in the hammock, going for a swim—swaying in the hammock some more until lunch with an über-fresh fish, then an afternoon siesta (swaying in the hammock) before kicking back to watch the sunset, drinking a coco loco. Such a place is perfect for easing away weeks of hard travel and hiking. Most Cartagena visitors come to Playa Blanca only for the day. For several hours, the beach is strewn with folks playing in the sun and surf. Vendors stroll the beach, selling everything from snacks and drinks, to kitsch souvenirs and shell necklaces, to massages. When the last boat leaves before sunset, then quiet begins to reign.

But staying on to watch the moonlight snake across the quiet waves is possible. Several luxury resorts have set up on Isla Barú, like **Mona Prieta**, which has two deluxe cabañas to let (URL: www.monaprieta.com) and the national hotel chain **Decameron** (URL: www.decameron.com). **Playa Scondida** also has bungalows (Ca. Larga 8B-55, Getsemaní. Tel: 5-664-2923, URL: www.playascondida. com). Unfortunately, the days of cheap options on Isla Barú are coming to an end. One of the few options left is **Hugo's Place**, which has camping, hammocks and rooms, and a water sports school. Expect a party atmosphere. Some women have reported feeling uncomfortable, though (Tel: 310-716-1021, E-mail: playablanca-2010@hotmail.com).

Travelers coming on day trips to Playa Blanca usually hop on a tour from Cartagena ($20-28). For cheaper alternatives, see Getting to and away from Cartagena. An overland route does exist. From near the India Catalina monument, take a *buseta* to Pasocaballos ($1) and from there a ferry across the Dique del Canal ($0.50). Once on the island, take a mototaxi to Playa Blanca ($6-8). To get back to Cartagena, negotiate for a seat on a returning tour boat ($6-12). Updated: May 05, 2011.

LA BOQUILLA

During the week, the men of La Boquilla still doff their fishermen's caps and head out to sea. But when weekends and holidays come, they are often helping their womenfolk take care of hungry tourists. This little village comes alive with day trippers arriving to enjoy surf, sun and fresh fish. La Boquilla is perhaps the best mainland beach near Cartagena, with over five kilometers (3 mi) of pale-taupe sand washed by clean, tranquil waters. The north end curves into a cove, before turning west to forested hills. La Boquilla is one of the premier windsurfing spots in the region. Another adventure is a boat journey through the mangroves to Punta Ícaros' fine beach. Some beachside eateries, like **Donde Elías** and **Magalí**, offer these trips (1.5 hr, $14-17 per person). **Ocean and Land Tours** in Cartagena also makes this excursion. Palm-thatched *enramadas* preparing fish and seafood platter line the beach for several kilometers (many are closed during the week). These dishes are pricier than in the city, but infinitely fresher. La Boquila has a variety of lodging options, including camping.

La Boquilla is six kilometers (3.6 mi) east-northeast of Cartagena. To get there from the city, catch a *buseta* from near the India Catalina monument (frequent, 20 min, $0.80). The last one back to Cartagena leaves from the beach area at 6 p.m. and from the village's paved main road at 10 p.m. Updated: May 05, 2011.

VOLCÁN DEL TOTUMO

Volcán del Totumo, a volcán de lodo (mud volcano), is 40 minutes northeast of Cartagena. The volcano is not what you would expect—it is more of a hill than a mountain. Climb to the top to take in the volcanic mud's healing properties. Afterwards, wash off in nearby Ciénaga del Totumo, an intense-green marsh aside the sea that is a sanctuary for birds. Entry fee into the volcano is $3; a massage costs $1.70, as does the assisted wash-off at the ciénaga. The spa is open daily 6 a.m.-6 p.m.

Most tourists visit Volcán Totumo in one day. It is best to easier to book a tour from Cartagena ($22, including transport, entry and fish lunch in La Boquilla or Playa de Manzanillo). To get there on your own, from Cartagena's terminal, catch a Galerazumba-bound bus and get off at Lomita Arena (Loma de Arena; 2 hr, $4). Then walk two kilometers down the road to a signed turn-off on the right, from where it is another 1.5 kilometers (45 min total). Or from Lomita Arena, take a mototaxi ($2). Don't start out from Cartagena after 10 a.m., to ensure getting the last bus from Lomita Arena at 3 p.m. Updated: May 02, 2011.

SAN BASILIO DE PALENQUE

San Basilio de Palenque, two hours south of Cartagena, is an African palenque founded by run-away slaves in the late-16th century. It was an important center of resistance against Spanish rule and slavery. Palenque's language is a unique blend of Congo River languages fused with Spanish. The village has preserved its medicinal and other cultural traditions well. For these reasons, UNESCO declared it an Intangible Cultural Heritage of Humanity. Every October, is the Festival de Tambores, when San Basilio's music and other cultural expressions may be savored. The patron saint feast day is June 14. Nonetheless, palanqueros are weary about losing their language and traditions. To learn more about San Balisio, visit: palenquedesanbasilio.masterimpresores.com. Update: Jul 07, 2011.

BARRANQUILLA

 5m   1,112,000 5

Barranquilla, Colombia's principal Caribbean port and capital of Atlántico Department, is midway between Cartagena and Santa Marta on the Troncal del Caribe highway. This city is on the west bank of the Río Magdalena, 22 kilometers (13 mi) from the river's mouth.

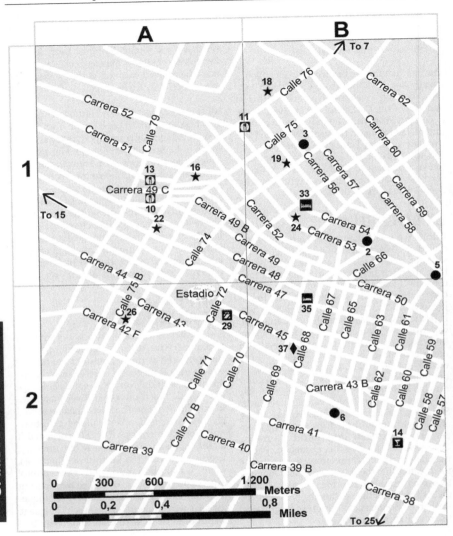

CARIBBEAN COAST

It was a backwater town for several centuries, but in the 19th century it began to rise to international commercial importance. Immigrants arrived from around the world, strongly flavoring the city's ambiance. Barranquilla has a sizable Middle Eastern community, which makes itself evident in commerce, two mosques and the Arabic channels on cable TV. This segment of the population also has its famous sons and daughters, including (most notably) Shakira. Other populations of note are the Afro-Caribbean, which has shaped a number of cultures along the coast, and European immigrants.

Barranquilla, known as El Puerto de Oro de Colombia (Colombia's Gold Port) or La Arenosa (The Sandy One), is most famous for its pre-Lent Carnival, as well as for its music and dance scenes. But there is much more to the city than parties. From museums and stunning architecture to premier beaches and baseball, there is a vast range of ways to pass the sultry barranquillero days. Updated: May 06, 2011.

History

According to historian Alonso de la Espriella, Barranquilla is a city that was

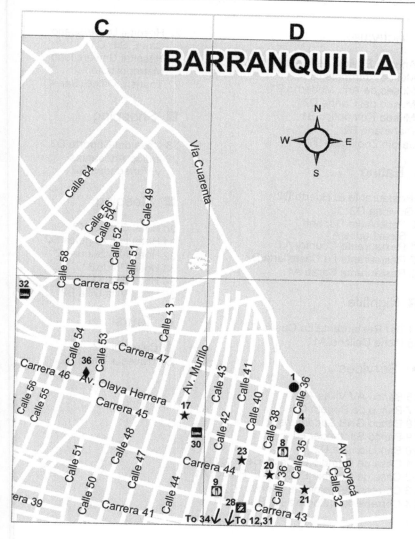

BARRANQUILLA

not founded; rather, it was simply populated. Spanish explorer Rodrigo de Bastidas had discovered the mouth of the Río Magdalena in 1503 but merely sailed on. In the 1620s, Galapa indigenous and cattle farmers who had been displaced by a drought settled the community of Sabanitas de Camacho on the low bluffs. In 1774 the name was changed to Barrancas de San Nicolás. Its official "founding" is recognized as April 7, 1813, when it was called Villas de Barlobento. None of the names really stuck. The city just became Barranquillas, the diminutive of *barrancas* (bluffs).

Simón Bolívar, the Great Liberator, sought rest in the nearby towns of Soledad and San Nicolás (Barlobento). The places where he stayed in Soledad is now the Museo Bolivariano-Casa de Bolivar (Cra. 26,18-10. Tel: 5-342-0207).

The 1940s saw an explosion in Colombian literature in this city: the Grupo de Barranquilla, formed by Gabriel García Márquez, Enrique Grau, Cecilia Porras and Cepeda Samudio, among others. The Cueva, a neighbourhood diner and bar, was their

● Activities

1 Antiguo Edificio de la Armada D2
2 Museo Antropológico B1
3 Museo de Arte Moderno B1
4 Museo del Caribe D2
5 Museo Romántico B1
6 Planetario B2
7 Jardín Zoológico B1

▥ Eating

8 Restaurante El Huerto D2
9 Govinda D2
10 Pepe Anka Bar and
   Steakhouse A1
11 Restaurante Country A1
12 Restaurante La Castellana D2
13 Restaurante Sarab A1

▣ Nightlife

14 Bar Restaurante La Cueva B2
15 Piche Caliche A1

★ Services

16 Banco AV Villas A1
17 Banco de Bogotá C2
18 Banco GNB Sudameris B1
19 Banco Santander B1
20 Bancolombia D2
21 Casa de Cambio El Cairo(Centro) D2
22 Casa de Cambio El Cairo(El Prado) A1
23 Correos de Colombia (Centro) D2
24 Correos de Colombia (El Prado) B1

25 Hospital Universitario
   Cari E.S.E C1
26 Hospital Universitario
   Metropolitano A2
27 Tourism Office (See 4)

▨ Shopping

28 Casa del Deporte D2
29 Indios Artesanías
   y Variedades B2

▬ Sleeping

30 Hotel Girasol C2
31 Hotel Los Ángeles D2
32 Hotel Mezzaluna C2
33 Hotel Prado B1
34 Hotel Skal D2
35 Hotel Villa Dilia B2

◆ Tours

36 Cajacopi C2
37 Travesia Tours B2

CARIBBEAN COAST

meeting point. Their influence continues to be felt to this day. Updated: May 06, 2011.

When to Go

Barranquilla has a hot climate with daytime temperatures averaging between 23ºC and 33ºC (74-92ºF). The rainy seasons are May-June and August-November. During rainy seasons, *arroyos* (creeks) run through the streets. The high curbs, which make walking around the city such an exercise, a necessity, become a necessity. From the end of October to the beginning of January, *aliseos* (high winds out of the North) whip through the city.

Everyone who can comes for Carnaval and pre-Carnaval, which begins two weeks before the main event. Hotel rooms are booked months in advance and prices are up to quadruple the normal amount. Updated: May 06, 2011.

HOLIDAYS AND FESTIVALS

Barranquilla is best known for **Carnaval**, a moveable feast celebrated (i.e. partied) before Lent begins. In February or March. However, barranquilleros invite their guests for other festivals, too:

At th beginning of February is **Carnaval de las Artes**, a four-day, behind-the-scenes look at the art of Carnaval. On February 14 is the **Festival del Bollo**, an Afro-Colombian salute to the *bollo* (a roll made of corn, yucca or plaintain that's cooked in maize or banana leaves) a contribution from Africa to Barranquilla's cuisine.

During the last two weeks of March is the **Festival del Dulce**, another acknowledgment of Afro-Colombian culinary traditions, this time of sweets. The city celebrates its **founding** on April 7, with military and folkloric parades, conferences and concerts.

Poetas del Mundo, an off-shoot of Medellín's Poetry Festival, features local, national and international poets in June. International storytellers unite in August for **El Caribe Cuenta**. September has a double-header: **BarranquiJazz**, an international jazz fest, in addition to the **International Contemporary Dance Festival** (www.barranquijazz.com). Updated: May 06, 2011.

Getting To and Away

BY BUS

Barranquilla's bus terminal is in Soledad, five kilometers (3 mi) from the city. It is divided into four sections. Facilities include restaurants, shops, bakeries, bathrooms, phones, a beauty salon, a casino, Internet and ATMs. To catch a bus to downtown (45 min) or El Prado (1 hr), walk out of the station and cross the road on the left to the corner where buses pass.

To	Departure	Time	Price
Medellín	Every 2 hr 5:45 a.m.-11 p.m.	13 hr	$50-73
Cali	Noon, 8:30 p.m.	24 hr	$90
Santa Marta	Every 10 min 5 a.m.-6:30 p.m.	2 hr	$6-7
Riohacha /Maicao	Every 45 min 3 a.m.-3 p.m., half-hourly 9 -11:45 p.m.	5-6 hr	$18-22
Maracaibo	Daily 11 a.m.	8 hr	$60
Caracas	Daily 11 a.m.	18 hr	$110
Valledupar	Hourly 5 a.m.-4 p.m.	4-5 hr	$12-13
Bucaramanga	Hourly 4 a.m.-11 p.m.	10-12 hr	$48

BY AIR

Aeropuerto Ernesto Cortissoz, 10 kilometers (6 mi) from the city, is one of the five airports in Colombia with international flights, connecting Barranquilla with South, Central and North America. There are *casas de cambio* at the airport. Most airlines have offices in the El Prado district, as well as at the airport: **Aero-República/Copa** (Ca. 72, 57-79. Tel.: 369-0048), **Aires** (Cra.54, 72-27, local 13. Tel.: 360-6629), **American** (Cra. 54, 72-96, local 14. Tel.: 01-800-052-2555),

Avianca (Ca. 72, 57-79), **Delta** (Cra. 54, 68-196, local 107. Tel.: 5-369-2679), **Taca/Lacsa** (Cra. 54, 68-196, oficina 209. Tel.: 5-368-2954). Updated: May 06, 2011

Getting Around

Barranquilla has an extensive public transportation network ($0.60-0.80, slightly higher on Sunday and holidays). To go from the Centro to El Prado, catch a "Uninorte Carrera 54" buseta. From the Centro to the bus terminal, go to Calle 45 (Calle

To	Departure	Time	Price
Cartagena	Every 30 min 4 a.m.-11 p.m.	2 hr	$6-7
Montería	Hourly 3 a.m.-3 p.m., 9 p.m., 9:30 p.m.	6 hr	$22-29
Mompós	Daily 7:30 a.m.	5-6 hr	$36

Museum	Description	Hours	Contact	Price
Museo Romántico	Full of Barranquilla's history and culture.	Monday-Friday 9 a.m.–noon, 3:30–5:30 p.m.	Cra. 54, 59-199, El Prado. Tel: 344-4591.	$2.65 adults, $1.60 children and students
Museo de Arte Moderno	Temporary and permanent exhibits of nationally renowned contemporary artists.	Tuesday-Saturday 9 a.m.–1 p.m., 3–7 p.m.	Carrera 56, 74-22, El Prado. Tel: 360-9952.	Depends on the exhibit.
Planetario	Learn more about the universe at Barranquilla's planetarium.	Wednesday, Friday 6:30–8:30 p.m.	Carrerra 43, 63B -77. Tel: 351-7700/368-2928.	Free.
Museo del Caribe	The nature, people and culture of Colombia's Caribbean region, from the Chocó to the Guajira.	Monday-Friday 8 a.m.–5 p.m.; Saturday, Sunday and holidays 9 a.m.-6 p.m.	Calle 36, 46-66, Centro . Tel: 372-0581, URL: www.culturacaribe.org.	$5 adults; $3 seniors, students and children, $1 extra per person for guide
Antigüo Edificio de la Aduana	The former customs house and railway station are now home to historical and musical archives, and train museum.	Monday-Friday 8 a.m.–6 p.m.	Vía 40, N36-135. Tel: 379-2949	$2.00

Updated: Mar 25, 2011.

Murrillo) for a "Simón Bolívar" or "Tranalianco" transport to Trupillo/Terminal de Transporte. The Transmetro, similar to the Transmilenio, connects downtown with the El Prado district (www.transmetro.gov.co). The system is presently being extended to the bus terminal in Soledad.

The minimum taxi fare is $2.50. It costs $8.50 to the airport or bus terminal. If you are arriving with your own vehicle be aware that many streets in Barranquilla are one way and there are non-circulation days based on license plate numbers. One auto rental company in Barranquilla is Hertz, with offices in El Prado (Cra. 52, 74-39. Tel: 369-0431) and at the airport (Muelle Nacional. Tel: 334-8003).

Often curbs at the corners are up to knee-high, which makes walking through the city quite a workout.

Safety

Not only is Barranquilla a large city, it is also a port city—thus, it is not surprising that there are relatively high crime rates here. Many businesses in the center close before nightfall. The area around the Antiguo Edificio de la Aduana and Parque Cultural del Caribe (Calle 37 to the river, below Carrera 46) is still unsafe even during the day, despite the efforts of the city to reclaim this area in order to make it the downtown district once again. It is best to take a taxi directly that area. Jun 12, 2011.

Services

TOURISM

The Barranquilla tourism office is in the **Parque Cultural del Caribe** (Ca. 36, 46-66. Tel.: 372-0581/372-0582, E-mail: comunicaciones@culturacaribe.org, Web: www.culturacaribe.org). The **Comité Mixto de Promoción del Atlántico**, in the Antiguo Edificio de la Aduana, has excellent free maps and brochures of Barranquilla and Atlántico Department (Monday–Friday 8 a.m.–noon, 2–5 p.m. Vía 40, 36-135. Tel: 330-3862, URL: www.comixto.com). Both these centers are located in a rather shady neighborhood; it is best to arrive by taxi. A further website to visit for tourist information is www.barranquilla.gov.co.

Other useful addresses are: **DAS** (immigration) (Monday–Friday 8–11:30 a.m., 2–5:30 p.m. Ca. 54, 41-133. Tel: 371-7500) and **Instituto Geográfico Agustín Codazzi** (Ca. 36, 45-101. Tel: 341-1683).

Two dozen countries have consuls in Barranquilla. These are just a few: **Brazil** (Monday–Friday 8:30–11:30 a.m., 2:30–5 p.m. Cra. 58, 85-215. Tel: 357-0356), **Panamá** (Monday–Friday 9:30 a.m.–noon, 2–4 p.m. Cra. 57, 72-25, oficina 207-208. Tel: 360-1870), **Venezuela** (Monday–Friday 7:30 a.m.–2 p.m. Cra. 52, 69-96. Tel: 358-0048), **U.K.** (Cra. 44, 45-57, piso 2. Tel: 340-6936), **U.S.** (Monday–Thursday 8:30 a.m.–noon. Ca. 77b, 57-141, office 511. Tel: 353-2182). Check the end of the telephone directory's white pages for others.

MONEY

All banks have their main offices in Barrio El Prado, with branches and ATMs throughout the city. In El Prado, there are many banks found along Calle 70, between Carreras 52 and 54; in the downtown area (centro), there is a dense concentration on Paseo Bolívar (Calle 34). Some of the major banks are: **Banco Citibank Colombia** (Ca. 74, 53-13), **Banco de Bogotá** (Cra. 46, 44-89), **Banco GNB Sudameris** (pay DAS visa extension fee here. Ca. 76, 56-71), **Banco Santander** (Ca. 74, 55-67). **Bancolombia** changes American Express travelers' checks (Cra. 44, 37-19).

Along Calle 76, between Carreras 47 and 49, are a number of exchange houses. The El Prado branch of **El Cairo** (Open 24 hours. Centro: Paseo Bolívar/Ca. 34, 43-117. Tel: 379-9441; El Prado: Ca. 76, 48-30. Tel: 368-1707) changes a number of currencies and cashes traveler's checks. **Western Union/Giros y Finanzas** has eight branches in Barranquilla; check the telephone directory's yellow pages under Giros for the nearest one. **MoneyGram/Cambiamos** has four branches; consult the white pages under Cambiamos.

KEEPING IN TOUCH

The mass of phone stands and shops in Barranquilla has all but done away with the major phone carriers' service offices. Some on Carrera 41, between Calles 39 and 40, have international calls at the bargain prices. You can find internets anywhere in the city. Skype is common. Post office branches are downtown (Monday-Friday 8 a.m.-noon, 2-6 p.m., Saturday 8 a.m.- noon. Calle 40, 44-93, unsigned) and in El Prado (Monday-Friday 8 a.m.-noon, 2-5:30 p.m., Saturday 8 a.m.-noon. Carrera 53, 70-180).

MEDICAL

The major hospitals serving Barranquilla are: **Hospital Universidad del Norte** (Calle 30, Autopista al Aeropuerto, next to Parque Muvdi, Ciudad Rotario. Tel: 371-5555), **Hospital Universitario Cari E.S.E.** (Calle 57, 23-100. Tel: 330-9000) and **Hospital Universitario Metropolitano** (Carrera 42F, 75B-18. Tel: 356-5109). Pharmacies are widespread throughout the metropolis.

CAMERA

Several camera supply stores are located along Paseo Bolívar (Calle 34), between Carreras 39 and 44. For repairs, try **Foto Hora** (Cra. 53 72-39. Tel: 5-358-7390), **Lukkan Reparaciones** (Cra. 53 68-119. Tel: 5-368-3201) or **Serge Gámez Walberto** (Cra. 61, 68-76. Tel: 344-4737).

RELIGION

Non-Catholic Christian churches have a significant presence in Barranquilla. For mass times and faith listings, see the end of the white pages and the yellow pages under "Iglesias" in the phone book. Non-Christian faiths also have practicing communities in this city: **Sinagoga Bet-El** (Ca. 87, 42H-46, Los Nogales. Tel: 359-1949), **Comunidad Budista** (Cra. 50, 80-273. Tel: 5-356-1982) and **Asamblea Espiritual de los Bahais** (Ca. 50C, 3-91. Tel: 363-7927). There are two mosques: one Sunni, the other Shi'ite. Updated: May 06, 2011.

SHOPPING

Casa del Deporte

Casa del Deporte has everything you may need for water and land sports along the Caribbean Coast. It stocks swimming gear, snorkeling equipment and fishing tackle. If a Tayrona beach campsite has your name on it, you might want to pick up gear here, as sporting goods stores are scarce in Santa Marta. At Casa del Deporte, you can purchase two-to-four person tents, sleeping bags and knapsacks. You can get just about anything here for any sport: baseball, rollerblading, tennis, soccer, shooting, darts, ping-pong, and even badminton. Monday-Friday 8 a.m.-noon, 2-6 p.m.; Saturday 8 a.m.-4 p.m. Cra. 43, 39-01, Centro, or Cra. 53, 74-86, local 4, Barrio Norte. Tel: (Centro) 370-5781, (Barrio Norte) 360-7597. Updated: May 06, 2011.

CARIBBEAN COAST

Indio's Artesanías

Indio's Artesanías has crafts from all over the Caribbean coast. There are spoons and other items made from *totumo* (a South American gourd) and bowls made from coconuts. For those looking to prepare for Carnival, there are masks and wineskins (leather bags used to carry wine) for sale. You could even buy all the traditional instruments you would need to equip your own traditional cumbia band, including drums, flutes and maracas, or pick up a cloth hammock for when you head to the beach. Monday-Saturday 8 a.m.-7 p.m. Cra. 45, 70-205. Tel: 356-9423. Updated: Mar 11, 2011.

Things to See and Do

Barranquilla offers many more attractions than its Carnival, such as a zoo, a planetarium, and many historical and art museums. In addition, the city has impressive architecture, which can be seen in such buildings as the Teatro Amira de la Rosa, Iglesia de San Nicolás and the Moorish-inspired El Prado neighborhood. For a breath of fresh air, take the Tren Ecoturístico de las Flores to the mouth of the Río Magdalena. And don't forget the nearby beaches, like those at Puerto Colombia or the village of Tubará. Updated: May 06, 2011.

Jardín Zoológico

(ADMISSION: $4.75 adults, children; $3.35 senior citizens, disabled) Barranquilla's zoo is said to be one of the best on the continent. The majority of the animals (there are more than 140 species) come from Colombia's Caribbean region, but others come from different parts of the country and world. Among the zoo's denizens are spectacled bears, manatees, flamingos, condors, lions, chimpanzees and white-faced monkeys. And for the kiddies, there's a petting zoo. In addition, there is a botanical garden, which preserves plant life from Colombia's Atlántico Department. Tuesdays are discount-entry days. To get there from either downtown or El Prado, catch a "Boston-Boston" or Caldas-Recreo" bus. Daily 9 a.m.-5 p.m. Ca. 76 and Cra. 68. Tel: 360-0314, E-mail: info@zoobaq.org URL: www.zoobaq.org. Updated: May 06, 2011.

Tren Ecoturístiso de las Flores to Las Bocas de Cenizas

(ADMISSION: $41-70 per person, including lunch) The long, covered wooden cars of the Tren Ecoturístico de las Flores move slowly but steadily toward Boca de Cenizas, the mouth of the Río Magdalena River, where powerful currents meet, whirlpooling the silty waters of the river with the azure Carib bean Sea. Not many take this ride, and those who do are in for a relaxing time of listening to folk music as the scenery glides by. The trip is 45 minutes one-way. Cajacopi, a tour company based in Barranquilla is the official operator of the train. In the high season, Cajacopi runs the train twice daily. The tracks are periodically repaired, so sometimes the train does not operate in off-season. For a more rustic ride, go out to Flores, just west of Barranquilla, from where independent operators run out to Las Bocas de Cenizas. Updated: May 06, 2011.

Museo Romántico

(ADMISSION: $2.65 adults, $1.60 children and students) The Museo Romántico is in a republican-era mansion, once home to the U.S. consul in Barranquilla. The museum houses items from the city's history, including letters by Simón Bolívar and the typewriter Gabriel García Márquez used to write the novella La Hojarasca (Leafstorm). Exhibits feature Barranquilla's literary groups, journalistic traditions and Jewish community. The second floor displays the gowns of the Carnival queens, from the very first worn in 1918 to the present-day, and other traditional Carnival costumes. Monday – Friday 9 a.m.–noon, 3:30-5:30 p.m., Cra. 54, 59-199, El Prado. Tel: 344-4591. Updated: Jun 16, 2011.

Tours

Barranquilla has few tour operators. Most specialize in large group trips to local attractions. SENA (Servicio Nacional de Aprendizaje) has an excellent program, training students to become professional guides; for those on a slight budget and interested in supporting education of poor youth, this may be just your ticket (Cra. 43, 42-40. Tel: 351-0799/340-7104, national toll-free: 01-8000-910270). Updated: May 06, 2011.

Cajacopi

Cajacopi specializes in family tour packages to beach resorts and attractions in the Barranquilla area. The company offers packages to Centro Recreacional El Descanso and Castillo de Salgar. In conjunction with the Ministerio de Transporte, it is also the official operator of the Tren Ecoturístico de las Flores. Purchase tickets in advance at Cajacopi's main office. Cra. 46, 53-41, first floor. Tel: 371-4583, URL: www.cajacopi.com. Updated: Mar 11, 2011.

Travesías Tours

Join about 50 merrymakers on one of Travesías Tours' *chiva* (party bus) tours of the city, which take you to four of the hottest dance spots for $20-25 per person (including cover charges, a half bottle of *aguardiente* and fried snacks). During the daytime, this tour company also offers a *chiva panorámica* (sightseeing bus). You'll take in the major sights of the city on a classic, old-style, wooden bus. Travesía Tours also goes further out of the city to other attractions, like Sabanalarga and Santa Verónica. Ca. 45, 68-53. Tel: 369-0371, E-mail: travesiastour@gmail.com. Updated: May 06, 2011.

Lodging

Lodging is much more expensive in Barranquilla than in its coastal cousin cities, Santa Marta and Cartagena. The prices hit the solo traveler's wallet especially hard because it's cheaper to book rooms in pairs. Budget hotels are mainly found in the downtown area, while the most expensive ones are in El Prado. If you are staying for more than a few days in the off-season, it is worth asking about a discount. During pre-Carnaval and Carnaval, hostel prices double to quadruple, and rooms go quick, so make reservations several months in advance. If you're looking to stay here for Carnaval, having a connection to a homestay organization may come in handy. Updated: May 06, 2011.

Hotel Skal

(BEDS: $10-24) Hotel Skal is the most popular hostel among backpackers in Barranquilla. It is the least expensive, decent option in the city. Set in a stunning early 20th-century family home, it has large, clean rooms with private bathrooms, cable TV and a choice of a fan or air conditioning. Only three rooms have one bed and the rest come with two. An extra surprise is the swimming pool out back, the perfect place to cool off in this sultry city. Ca. 41, 41-35, Centro. Tel: 351-2069/351-0074. Updated: Jun 16, 2011.

Hotel Los Angeles

(ROOMS: $15-27) Hotel Los Angeles is a mid-range option in the center of Barranquilla. This four-story hotel has clean rooms that are decent-sized (especially the multi-person rooms), with cable TV and private bathrooms. Many of the rooms surround a central patio on the second floor. The view of the city from the top floor is excellent and the free coffee is a nice plus. Ca. 40, 41-64, Centro. Tel: 351-6666/351-3680 (reservations), E-mail: info@hotellosangelesbq.com, URL: www.hotellosangelesbq.com. Updated: Jun 16, 2011.

Hotel Girasol

(BEDS: $16-27) The Hotel Girasol is in an older building with a circular front drive. All rooms are large, with a fan or air conditioning, private bath, cable TV and a minibar. The environment is family-oriented and quiet. Amenities include free local calls, Internet and private parking. A 10 percent surcharge is added to credit card payments. Guests who stayed at the Hotel Saboy in Santa Marta receive a discount. Ca. 44, 44-103, Centro. Tel: 5-379-3191/1891. Updated: Jun 16, 2011.

Hotel Mezzaluna

(ROOMS: $27-32) The Hotel Mezzaluna is an executive hotel with a friendly administration. The rooms come equipped with good beds, air conditioning, cable TV, telephone, mini-bar (extra charge) and private bathroom. The restaurant next door serves only typical local lunches. Relax in the bar after a day of meeting business clients or sightseeing. Despite its higher-end classification, Hotel Mezzaluna doesn't accept credit cards. Cra. 53, 59-28, El Prado. Tel: 368-4092/4093. Updated: Jun 16, 2011.

Hotel Villa Dilia

(ROOMS: $35-80) Hotel Villa Dilia has excellent service and pleasant rooms. This hotel is worth the few extra bucks. The rooms are simple, with the standard equipment—private bath with room-temperature water, mini-bar (extra charge) and air conditioning. Solid, thick wooden doors guarantee the room's security. Near the El Prado district, it is convenient for both business and leisure activities. Cra. 47, 68-40. Tel: 358-3353 / 5368, E-mail: hotelvilladilia@hotmail.com. Updated: Jun 16, 2011.

CARIBBEAN COAST

Hotel El Prado

(ROOMS: $103-625) Greta Garbo stayed here, as well as Grace Kelly and Carlos Gardel. Their spirits still seem to roam the arcaded balcony halls and gardens of this sophisticated, five-star hotel. Hotel El Prado rolls out the red carpet for guests, whether stars or regular-joe travelers. The 1920s hotel has a large lobby furnished in bamboo that recalls a tropical elegance of times past. The rooms are large and include a sitting area and private baths. All rooms surround a palm-shaded patio garden and swimming pool. Every detail of this hotel conjures up one word—luxury. Who knows, maybe you'll bump into Shakira or Carlos Vives in the lobby. The hotel has special package deals at slower times, which cost about half the normal price and include taxes, insurance and breakfast. Cra. 54, 70-10, El Prado. Tel: 369-7777/01-800-051-1101 (toll free), E-mail: reservas@hotelelpradosa.com, URL: www.hotelelpradosa.com. Updated: Jun 16, 2011.

Restaurants

Barranquilla, Colombia's largest Caribbean port, has a smorgasbord of international foods, including a lot of Middle Eastern restaurants, due to generations of Arab immigrants. (Some are quite chic and have live belly dancing performances.) Vegetarians have so many options that they can try a different restaurant each day of the week. Like everything else in Barranquilla, a set lunch is a little more expensive. Or, check out food options at the market that buzzes across many blocks, between Carreras 34-40 and Calles 40-42.

Restaurante Country

(LUNCH: $2.50-4) Even in the ritzy El Prado neighborhood, daily set-plate specials are available at a reasonable price. At lunch time, blue- and white-collar workers crowd these picnic tables on the large front patio beneath a yellow awning. Don't be shy to ask to share a table. The food here is great, down-home Colombian cooking. The daily special includes soup and drink. À la carte is offered mornings and evenings. Daily 7 a.m. -7 p.m. Ca. 76, between Cra. 53 and 54, El Prado. Tel: 360-8568. Updated: Jun 16, 2011.

Govinda

(LUNCH: $3) Climb the steps to the second floor and push open the door on the right. As you step into the leaf-green room, Krishna greets you from a stained-glass window. New Age music plays low and air conditioning cools the heat of the Barranquilla afternoon. This Govinda, like others in Colombia, serves excellent vegetarian fare, but here it is on porcelain plates. The lunch (soup, main course, salad, drink and dessert) is served 11:30 a.m.–2 p.m. You can also special-order breakfast or dinner to take out. Govinda offers Hatha yoga and cooking classes, as well. Or pick up some baked goodies on your way out. Cra. 43, 41-10. Cel: 301-408-0898. Updated: Jun 16, 2011.

Restaurante La Castellana

(LUNCH: $3-4) Look for Restaurante La Castellana tucked way back from the street and down a long hall. Locals, visitors and the guests of the neighboring Hotel Los Angeles eat here. For a good reason, too. The food is delicious and the service attentive. The set meal (for lunch or dinner) includes a choice of meats, plenty of sides and free refills on drinks, as well as the customary starter soup. Ca. 40, 41-66, Centro. Updated: Jun 16, 2011.

Restaurante Sarab

(ENTREES: $3-9) The menu of Restaurante Sarab is full of typical Middle Eastern dishes. Order labne, fatuch, tahini, taboule, falafel, kabobs, shwarma and other delicacies in full or half portions, and mixed plates, including vegetarian. Top it off with a Middle Eastern dessert. Enjoy your meal inside air-conditioned comfort or out on the shady front patio. Monday 11:30 a.m.–4 p.m., Tuesday–Sunday 11:30 a.m.-9:30 p.m. Cra. 49c, 76-139. Tel: 368-7407. Updated: May 06, 2011.

V!VA ONLINE REVIEW
RESTAURANTE SARAB

The food is superb and the attention is warm and friendly.

November 7, 2010

Restaurante El Huerto

(LUNCH: $3.50-4) Since 1986, Restaurante El Huerto has been preparing meals and baked goods especially for vegetarians and dieters. Its luncheon special is varied, so check the monthly menu calendar (12–3 p.m., $3). Wednesdays feature international cuisine from Mexico, China, Cuba or the Middle East, just to name a few. Tuesdays and Thursdays are free dessert days. Restaurante El Huerto's branch in El Prado has a garden dining terrace, (Cra. 52,

CARIBBEAN COAST

70-139. Tel: 5-368-4573). At both bistros, the staff speaks English. The downtown restaurant is open Monday-Saturday 8 a.m.-7:45 p.m. Cra. 45 and Ca. 36, Centro. Tel: 368-4573/Cel: 310-636-1742. Updated: Jun 16, 2011.

V!VA ONLINE REVIEW
RESTAURANTE EL HUERTO

Love the natural, veggie food! Everything was delicious...

July 24, 2009

Pepe Anca Steakhouse and Bar

(ENTREES: $16-26) Pepe Anca, Barranquilla's finest steakhouse, has everything done right, from the menu to the interior design. The inside of this restaurant has light burnt orange and ochre walls and the tables are clothed in dark blue and peach. The menu features certified Argentine Angus beef and national beef, which you can have plain or in a blue cheese, mustard or balsamic vinegar and red wine sauce. Or, choose from the seafood and fish plates. All dishes come with two sides. Don't forget to select a bottle from the extensive wine list. Monday–Saturday noon–3 p.m., 6–11 p.m., Sunday noon–4 p.m. Cra. 49c, 76-164. Tel: 356-4637/6289, E-mail: pepeancasteakhouse@yahoo.com.mx. Updated: May 06, 2011.

V!VA ONLINE REVIEW
PEPE ANCA STEAKHOUSE AND BAR

I think this is the best kept secret in Barranquilla. I enjoyed the best steak of my life, the service is excellent and the area is very safe.

January 25, 2009

Nightlife

Most of the nightclubs in town are either in the El Prado or El Norte neighborhoods. The downtown area has mainly taverns that appear to serve much more than mere liquor. So if you are staying in this part of town, be prepared to travel quite a distance to wear out your dancing shoes. Something interesting to note is that despite having a renowned annual jazz festival, throughout the rest of the year jazz is strangely absent from the city, except at La Cueva. Updated: May 06, 2011.

Bar Restaurante La Cueva

(DRINKS $3-6, ENTREES $12-18) La Cueva of today is definitely not the laid-back, eating and watering hole it was back when the native writer, Gabriel García Márquez, and his literary friends, the Grupo de Barranquilla, would stay into the wee hours. Today it offers a select menu of exotic dishes with a Caribbean, Italian or Oriental flair at not-so-working-class prices. Even the full bar has some out-of-the-ordinary drinks, like the mango margarita. Sometimes La Cueva hosts literary events, and on Friday and Saturday nights there's live Cuban music or jazz (no minimum consumption or door charge). Monday–Thursday noon–3 p.m., 6–10:30 p.m., Friday and Saturday noon–3 p.m., 6 p.m.–1 a.m. Cra. 43, 59-03. Tel: 340-9813, E-mail: fundacionlacuevayahoo.com, URL: www.fundacionlacueva.org. Updated: May 06, 2011.

Piche Caliche Café Bar

(COVER: $8 women, $10.50 men) Piche Caliche is a serious party bar and claims to have the best rumba in the city. It has an open bar with all-you-can-drink rum or beer for one set price. The clientele are mostly university students. Thursday's Happy Hour (8–10 p.m.) is free to women. Friday is the *rumba universitaria*—there are beer drinking contests and the bar opens at 2 p.m., to start the weekend early. Ca. 96, 46-32, second floor. Cel: 311-407-6834/300-478-1920. Updated: May 06, 2011.

AROUND BARRANQUILLA

TUBARÁ

200m   8,900   5

Tubará is a sleepy, Caribbean village where pastel-colored houses with palm-thatched roofs and the local white-washed church bake in the sun. Twenty-three kilometers (14 mi) from Barranquilla, on the Carretera del Algodón, Tubará is one of the few places where traditional gaita flutes are made from cactus stems, with a thin feather quill for the mouthpiece. While visiting this pre-Hispanic town, check out the Piedra Pintada (also called Petroglífo Mocaná), the Museo Arqueológico (Monday-Friday 8 a.m.-5 p.m. Ca. 1, 10-26. Tel: 331-4333) and Parque El Mirador. Updated Jun 11, 2011.

PUERTO COLOMBIA

 5m 20,000 📞 5

For many generations, Puerto Colombia has been the favorite beach getaway for barranquilleros. The broad, clean, dusky-beige sand beaches and warm sea, which is a bit muddy, are an easy 13-kilometer (8 mi) trip from the city. Many restaurants serving fresh seafood line the beachfront.

In the late 19th century, Puerto Colombia was an important port; its 1893 pier and other buildings of the period are now tourist attractions. Other places to visit include the Spanish fortress Castillo de Salgar, now a national monument with cultural center, exhibit spaces and restaurant, and the beaches at Prado Mar and Sabanilla. Between Barranquilla and Puerto Colombia is Lago del Cisne, a destination for fishing and other water sports. Updated Jun 21, 2011.

SANTA MARTA

 3m 415,200 📞 5

Parrots screech across the rooftops at dawn and dusk. Banana ships enter the harbor while local fishermen prepare to go to out to sea. People stroll along the seafront park, and swim in the warm Caribbean Sea changes that colors all day, from sapphire blue to jade-green, to opal when the sun finally sets. All of this tranquility belongs to Colombia's second most important Atlantic coast port. Santa Marta hides her treasures well to the casual visitor who has come for the larger gems of her region: Ciudad Perdida and Tayrona National Park.

Santa Marta was the first Spanish city founded in South America, at the foot of the Sierra Nevada Mountains where they cascade to the sea. On a clear day, their snowy peaks edge the horizon. This is a port that was repeatedly sacked by pirates and the place where Simón Bolívar died. He lived his last days at Quinta de San Pedro Alejandrino, now a museum to the Liberatador.

With the 21st century's second decade, Santa Marta is experiencing a renaissance. Sailboats and yachts dock into the new international marina at the south end of the camellón (sea front boulevard). Cruise ships call into the main port at the north end. More statues honoring the Tayrona bedeck the seaside park and a monument to local soccer legend El Pibe is at Avenida Libertador and Carrera 19.

Santa Marta's dozen cultural centers and museums frequently host of music, theater and other festivals. Near the city are the beaches of Rodadero, offering all services for the higher budget tourist and excursions to an off-shore aquarium, and Tanganga, popular with backpackers and scuba divers.

To the southwest are two interesting villages: Aracataca, hometown of Gabriel García Márquez and a real-life Macondo, and Ciénaga, set on the east side of a bird-rich lagoon and amid banana plantations, and site of the 1928 massacre. Heading into the mountains are Minca, a cool get-away from the tropical port, and San Lorenzo, gateway into Parque Nacional Sierra Nevada de Santa Marta.

Santa Marta's greatest draws are Parque Nacional Tayrona with white sand beaches, emerald jungles and crystalline waters, and Ciudad Perdida (the Lost City), located five-days trekking deep in the heart of the Sierra Nevada. Updated: Jul 05, 2011.

History

Santa Marta was the first Spanish city established in South America. Officially founded in 1525 by Rodrigo de Bastidas, it quickly developed into an important port. Despite the protection of the bay by two fortresses, 26 known pirates and countless other anonymous ones assailed Santa Marta between 1543 and 1702. These pirates included Sir Francis Drake and Martin Cote. On December 3, 1655, British Vice-Admiral William Goodson attacked and burned the city.

Santa Marta is where Simón Bolívar's journey home to Caracas, Venezuela, came to an abrupt end. He was forced to stop due to intense tuberculosis and was given refuge at Quinta de San Pedro Alejandrino. He died there on December 17, 1830 and was buried in the cathedral. Thirteen years later, Bolívar would finally reach his hometown—his body now rests in Caracas' Panteón.

During the first half of the 20th century, until 1966, the United Fruit Company had its headquarters in Santa Marta. Today, remnants of its Barrio Gringo still exist. Updated: May 27, 2008.

When to Go

It is always hot in Santa Marta. From December to the beginning of March, temperatures are moderated by the winds that come in off the ocean. In January, the winds whipping through the streets from dusk to dawn are called La Loca (The Crazy One). From September to the beginning of December is the rainy season. At times, storms can be very strong, turning the streets into rivers.

Santa Marta is a popular destination for vacationing Colombians, especially during Christmas-New Year's and July-August holidays, and Semana Santa. Updated: Jul 05, 2011.

HOLIDAYS AND FESTIVALS

Like at any place along the coast, locals celebrate Carnival in Santa Marta with *comparsas* (dance troupes) and a flurry of corn starch, spray foam and water. Be ready to dance, dodge and party. Santa Marta and neighboring villages observe the feast days of the Virgen del Carmen, which culminate on July 16 with a boat flotilla from Taganga to Santa Marta and El Rodadero. The city's patron saint, Saint Martha, is commemorated with processions on July 29. Every year Santa Marta hosts a Fiesta del Mar, which may occur in June, July or September. Updated: Jul 05, 2011.

Getting To and Away

BY BUS

Santa Marta's bus terminal is about midway between the city and El Rodadero. It has showers, bathrooms, ATM, luggage storage (7 a.m.-7 p.m.), snack stands, shops, phones and Internet.

To	Departure	Time	Price
Barranquilla	Frequent buses 4 a.m.–7:30 p.m.	2 hr	$6-8
Cartagena	Frequent buses 4:30 a.m.–3:30 p.m.	4 hr	$11-13
Montería	6 buses 8 a.m.-9 p.m.	9 hr	$39
Riohacha	Every half-hour	2.5 hr	$10

To	Departure	Time	Price
Maicao	Every half hour	4.5 hr	$12
Caracas, Venezuela*	Noon and 1 p.m. daily	20 hours	$103
Valledupar	Hourly 4 a.m.-5 p.m.	44 hr	$11-13
Bucaramanga	8:30 a.m.; 5 buses 6:30-10 p.m.	9 hr	$28-33
Bogotá	10 buses 2-8:30 p.m.	17 hr	$39-44
Medellín	10 buses 8 a.m.-8:30 p.m.	17-18 hr	$50-60

Passport needed to book ticket

MarSol (Ca. 23A, 6-54. Tel: 421-2121/ Cel: 300-808-3151) has door-to-door service to Cartagena ($22), as well as to Barranquilla and Valledupar.

BY AIR

Santa Marta's **Aeropuerto Simón Bolívar** is 16 kilometers (9.5 mi) south of the city. Four airlines offer domestic flights, with international connections. Fares to Bogotá cost up to $275 one way (1-1.25 hr), but check their websites for special rates (which can be as low as $100).

Copa (Cra. 3, 17-27. Tel.: 421-0120, URL: www.copaair.com)—To Bogotá: twice daily, with national and international connections.

Aires (Cra. 3, 17-27, local 4. Tel.: 431-1203, URL: www.aires.aero)—To Bogotá: three flights per day.

Avianca (Cra. 2A, 14-17. Tel: 421-4958, URL: www.avianca.com)—To Medellín: daily, $167-444 one way; to Bogotá: four times daily.

Easy Fly (airport, Tel: 431-3370, URL:

www.easyfly.com.co)—To Bucaramanga: daily, from $35 one way.

BY TRAIN

The tourist train Ruta de Macondo, from Santa Marta to Aracataca, is presently on

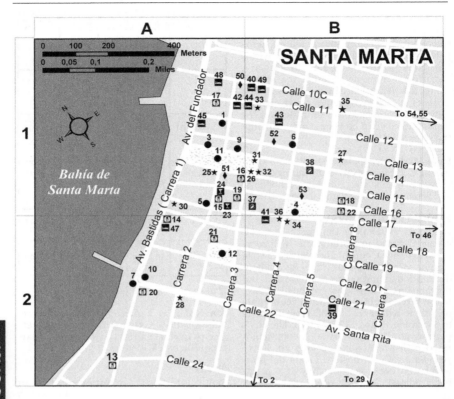

hold until the company offering the services submits the proper studies.

BY BOAT

Travelers cruising the Caribbean in their own sailboat or yacht can dock at Santa Marta's new international marina (Marina Internacional) located at the south end of the *camellón* (Cra. 1, 22-93. Tel: 421-5037, E-mail: info@marinasantamarta.com.co, URL: www.marinasantamarta.com.co). Santa Marta has become a favorite port call for international cruise ships (*cruceros*), which come on Sundays and Tuesdays (and sometimes Thursdays). Updated: Mar 29, 2011.

Getting Around

Santa Marta has a good city bus network. Small *combis* (mini-buses) take people around the town and to El Rodadero and Taganga ($0.70 any destination). To get to the bus terminal, take a bus marked Transporte from along Avenida Bastidas (30 minutes).

Taxis are unmetered. Typical fares from the bus terminal are: to downtown (*el*

centro) $2.80, to the airport $10, to El Rodadero $5.60, to Taganga $6.70. From downtown, rates are: to airport $10, to El Rodadero $4.60, to Taganga $5.60. The following international car leasing agencies have offices in Santa Marta: Hertz (airport, Cel: 313-296-0710) and Avis (Cra. 4, 7-27, Edificio Plaza, local 5. Tel: 422-7807). Updated: Mar 26, 2011.

Safety

Remember, Santa Marta is a port town and a major tourist destination, so keep a close watch on your camera, daypack and other belongings, especially on the beach. Wandering down toward the port gate and old railroad station at anytime of the day or night is never a safe idea. Be careful at night if returning from the bars in the wee hours. There is an active drug scene in the city, and travelers should be warned that foreigners are often set up by police, who then

charge on-the-spot fines. If you want to avoid this, well, keep your distance from the whole scene. Updated: Mar 26, 2011.

● **Activities**

1 Alianza Francesa A1
2 Bananatown A2
3 Biblioteca Banco de la
  República A1
4 Catedral de Santa Marta B1
5 Centro Cultural San Juan
  Nepomuceno A1
6 Iglesia San Francisco B1
7 Monumento a los Tairona A2
8 Museo de Arte (See 5)
9 Museo de Oro Tairona A1
10 Museo Etnográfico de la
   Universidad A2
11 Parque Bolívar A1
12 Parque de los Novios A2

▥ **Eating**

13 Baguettina A2
14 Ben & Josep A2
15 Crêpes Expresso A1
16 Deli Krem A1
17 El Escorial A1
18 Govinda B1
19 La Muzzaría A1
20 Ostras El Juancho A2
21 Restaurante Don
   Chucho A2
22 Restaurant Lucky
   Hong Kong B1

▣ **Nightlife**

23 Bar La Puerta A1
24 Bar Laùtrec A1

★ **Services**

25 Banco Occidental A1
26 Banco Popular B1

27 City Cambios B1
28 Correos de Colombia A2
29 DAS B2
30 Dirección de Cultura y Turismo A1
31 Edificio de Bancos B1
32 Instituto Geográfico Agustín Codazzi B1
33 Lavandería B1
34 National Park Office B2
35 Tayrona Net B1
36 Tourism Information A2

▨ **Shopping**

37 Biosierra B1
38 Vestigios B1

▦ **Sleeping**

39 Aluna B2
40 Hotel Casa Familiar B1
41 Hotel Imperial Caribe B2
42 Hotel Las Vegas Del Caribe A1
43 Hotel Nueva Granada B1
44 Hotel Saboy B1
45 Hotel Yuldama A1
46 Kayros Vivienda Turística B2
47 Park Hotel A2
48 Residencia El Titanic A1
49 Residencia San Jorge B1

◆ **Tours**

50 Atlantic Divers A1
51 Aviatur A1
52 Turcol B1
53 Sierra Tours B1

▣ **Transportation**

54 Transportation to Minca B1
55 Transportation to Parque Nacional
   Tayrona B1

Services

TOURISM

The Santa Marta tourism office, on the second floor of the historic **Casa de Madame Agustine** (Monday-Friday 8 a.m.-noon, 2-6 p.m. Ca. 17 and Cra. 4. Tel: 438-2587, E-mail: turismo@santamarts-magdalena.gov.co, URL: www.santamar-ta-magdalena.gov.co), gives free maps of the city, El Rodadero and Taganga. Information about what to see and do in Magdalena Department is available from the **Dirección de Cultura y Turismo** in the Gobernación building (Monday-Friday 8 a.m.-noon, Cra. 1, Ca. 16 and Ca. 17. URL: www.gobmagdalena.gov.co). For maps of the region, go to the **In-**

stituto Geográfico Agustín Codazzi (Ca. 15 3-25, Edificio BCH, 4th floor. Tel: 421-0157). Dirección Territorial Caribe de la Unidad de **Parques Nacionales Naturales** (Monday-Friday 8 a.m.-noon, 2-6 p.m. Ca. 17 4-06, Tel: 423-0704) coordinates the national parks in Magdalena, including Tayrona, Ciénaga and Sierra Nevada de Santa Marta. **DAS**, or immigration, is at Carrera 8, 26A-15; the phone number for *extranjería* or visa extensions is 5-423-2704. Panama, Spain, Finland, France and Italy all have consulates in Santa Marta; check the telephone directory for contact information.

MONEY
Many banks in Santa Marta are found in the Edificio de Bancos, between Calles 14 and 15 and Carreras 2a and 3, with tellers on the second floor; others are in the same neighborhood, or on Calle 15 along the Parque Bolívar. All have ATH (24-hour) ATMs that accept Visa, Plus, MasterCard and Cirrus cards. Some institutions are: **Bancolombia** (Monday–Thursday 8 – 11:30 a.m., 2–4 p.m., Friday 8–11:30 a.m., 2–4:30 p.m. Cra. 3, Edificio de los Bancos), which exchanges American Express traveler's checks, **Banco de Occidente** (Cra. 2, 15-28), **Banco AV Villas** (Ca. 15, 3-79) and **Banco Popular** (Cra. 3, Edificio de los Bancos). Other banks and ATMs cluster around Plaza San Francisco (Calle 14 and Carrera 4).

To cash U.S. dollars, Euros or bolívares, go to **City Cambios** (Ca. 13 5-22) or **Cambios Tayrona** (Ca. 14, 4-45, local 25, Centro Comercial Royal Plaza).

For receiving *giros* (wired money transfers) in Santa Marta: Western Union/Giros y Finanzas (Ca. 23, between Cra. 7 and Cra. 8, Almacén SAO); and MoneyGram/Cambiamos (Cra. 5 and Ca. 23, Almacén Vivero. Tel: 423-5439).

KEEPING IN TOUCH
Local shops offer local and national call services. Internet is quite common in Santa Marta, as is Skype. A one-stop option for all telecommunications needs is **T@yrona.Net**; ask at the desk for the headset to make Skype calls (daily 9 a.m.-10 p.m. Ca. 11, 5-05). The Correo 4-72 **post office**, of course, is where to mail that "Wish you were here" postcard (Monday-Friday 8 a.m.-noon, 2-5:45 p.m.; Saturday 9 a.m.-1:15 p.m. Ca. 22, 2-08).

MEDICAL
The most recommended medical facility is **Clínica Capri**, near the market in Santa Marta (Ca. 11, 8-21. Tel.: 421-0142). Several drugstores are on Parque Bolívar, and a number more on Carrera 5.

LAUNDRY
Santa Marta does not wont for Laundromats. Two are located side-by-side on Calle 11. **Lavandería Santa Marta** is the cheaper, charging $1.30 per kilo for wash and dry; has same-day service (Monday–Saturday 7:30 a.m.–7:30 p.m., Sunday 7 a.m.–2 p.m., 4–7 p.m. Ca. 11, 2-60. Tel: 423-5906).

CAMERA REPAIR
To purchase film, digital cards, batteries or any other camera accessories, hie over to Carrera 5 where a number of shops can fill your needs. Digital cameras can be repaired at **Servisony** (Ca. 11, between Cra. 5 and Cra. 6).

RELIGION
Santa Marta's telephone directory lists Catholic mass hours and non-Catholic churches at the end of the yellow pages. Protestant faiths in Colombia are called "Iglesias Cristianas Evangélicas"; of the mainstream religions, several Baptist and Presbyterian are listed. Updated: Mar 29, 2011.

SHOPPING

Vestigios
The voices of the ancients speak through the T-shirts Vestigios creates. The company uses designs from petroglyphs, pottery and other artifacts to honor Mother Earth or tell the story of ancient cultures from Colombia and around the world. The 100-percent cotton T-shirts keep you cool in the tropical Caribbean heat and the price is for one is just $6. Moreover, Vestigios has bags made by the present-day indigenous of Sierra Nevada de Santa Marta. Monday-Saturday 7 a.m.-7:30 p.m., Sunday 7 a.m.-2 p.m. Ca. 14, 4-08. Cel: 316-587-1805. Updated: Apr 15, 2011.

Biosierra
Biosierra is Pro-Sierra Nevada de Santa Marta's store, located off the back patio. This foundation works with the mountain's communities on environmental conservation and recuperation. Biosierra brings to the market bags by the Arhuaco, Kankuama, Kogui, Wayuu and Wiwa nations. From the *campesino* settlements are baskets, gourds and woodwork,

Museum	Description	Hours	Contact	Price
Museo de Oro Tayrona	Collections of Tayrona artifacts and information about their society.	Monday–Friday 8:30 a.m.–6 p.m., Saturday 9 a.m.–1 p.m.	Ca. 14, 2-07. Temporary location: Banco de la República, Ca. 14, 1C-37.	Free
Museo de Arte	Three galleries of regional and national artists, with special exhibits.	Monday–Saturday 9:30 a.m.–noon, 3–7 p.m., Sunday and holidays 3–7 p.m.	Cra. 2, 16-44. Tel. 438-2048.	$1.15-2.75
Museo Etnográfico (MEUM)	A people's history of Santa Marta and the Sierra Nevada.	Monday–Saturday 8 a.m.–7 p.m.	Cra. 1 and Ca. 22. Tel: 5-431-7513.	$1.50-2.75
Quinta de San Pedro Alejandrino	The death place of the Great Liberator, Simón Bolívar.	Daily 9:30 a.m.–4:30 p.m.	5 km (3 mi) southeast of the city.	$4.50-6
Museo Bolivariano de Arte Contemporáneo	Special exhibits of modern Colombian and Latin American art.	Daily 9:30 a.m.–4:30 p.m.	Quinta de San Pedro Alejandrino. Tel: 423-7021.	Included in the price of the Quinta

Updated: Mar 26, 2011.

jewelry, T-shirts, puzzles and other products like organic coffee and honey. Biosierra also sells publications on this unique piece of Mother Earth. The book La Sierra de Santa Marta is available in Spanish, English, German, French or Japanese. Monday-Friday 8 a.m.-noon, 2-6 p.m. Ca. 17, 3-83. Tel: 5-431-0551, E-mail: ygutierrez@prosierra.org, URL: www.prosierra.org.Updated: Mar 26, 2011.

Things to See and Do

Many travelers consider Santa Marta just a passing-through point on their way to Taganga, Parque Nacional Natural Tayrona or Ciudad Perdida. However, beneath the surface of this port city, there is much to do. Journeyers interested in history should head for Quinta San Pedro Alejandrina and the Bananatown; ruin rats, to the Museo de Oro, Tayrona's El Pueblito and Bahía Neguanje's archaeological site. Art connoisseurs, take in the several museums and the cultural centers, which often present free events. Nature lovers could take in El Rodadero's aquariums, Santuario de Flora y Fauna Ciénaga Grande or Parque Nacional Natural Sierra Nevada de Santa Marta. Sports enthusiasts, you have a number of sports, from fishing to scuba diving, as well as minor league baseball. Don't forget villages like Minca, Ciénaga or Aracataca—and, of course, Santa Marta's many beaches. Jul 05, 2011.

Catedral de Santa Marta

(ADMISSION: free) The white-washed Catedral of Santa Marta was built within a decade of the city's founding. The front façade is accented by an onion-domed bell tower. The floor plan is a Roman cross. The nave has barrel vaulting and the side aisles quadpartite vaulting. Side chapel screens are made of marble. The front left chapel exhibits a statue of the Virgin that accompanied the Spanish founders. Within this bright, solemn space is the last resting places of founder Rodrigo de Bastidas (to the left of the door) and Bishop Celendón (to the right). For a while, the Great Liberator, Simón Bolívar, reposed here before his remains being taken to Caracas' Pantheon in 1839 (except his heart and intestines, which remain here). His first grave was to the right of the altar and in front of the altar, his second. Cra. 4, between Ca. 16 and Ca. 17. Updated Jul 05, 2011.

Cultural Centers

Just because you are traveling on a tight budget doesn't mean you can't get a fair dose of the arts while you are in Santa Marta. The city's cultural centers often present free events. **Banco de la República** (Ca. 14, 1C-37, Parque Simón Bolívar) is a large cultural center with a library (Monday-Friday 8:30 a.m.-6 p.m., Saturday 9 a.m.-1 p.m.), and occasionally hosts literary readings, concerts, art exhibits and children's programs. The **Alianza Francesa** (Monday-Friday 9 a.m.-noon, 3-7 p.m., Saturday 9 a.m.-noon. Ca. 12, 1C-82. Tel: 423-5971, E-mail: santamarta@alianzacolombofrancesa.org.co, URL: www.santamarta.alianzafrancesa.org.co) has a French-language library and reading room, and art gallery, and screens free movies most Fridays, 7 p.m. **Centro Cultural San Juan Nepomuceno** (Cra. 2, 16-44. Tel: 438-2048, E-mail: centro.cultural@unimagdalena.edu.co, Web: www.unimagdalena.edu.co), the Universidad del Magdalena's cultural center, has an art museum, bookstore, literary readings, lectures and concerts. Updated Jul 05, 2011.

Museo de Oro Tayrona !

(ADMISSION: free) In the building that was once Santa Marta's customs house is the Museo de Oro Tairona, a must-see for those planning to visit El Pueblito in Parque Nacional Natural Tayrona or Ciudad Perdida in Parque Nacional Natural Sierra Nevada de Santa Marta. The museum gives clear, detailed explanations of the society, culture and technology of the Tayrona peoples. A scale model of Teyuna (Ciudad Perdida) will give you a framework within which to take in the ruins when you visit. Also, an impressive collection of Tayrona gold artifacts is displayed alongside an explanation of the processing and forging techniques.   Guided tours in Spanish or English are free. Note: The Aduana building is presently being restored. The Museo de Oro's temporary location is in the Banco de La República (Ca. 14, 1C-37). Monday-Friday 8:30 a.m.-6 p.m., Saturday 9 a.m.-1 p.m. Updated: Mar 25, 2011.

Bananatown

United Fruit Company once had a company town carved in this city that housed its corporate offices and executive housing.

From Calle 25 to the Río Manzanes, between Carreras 4 and 5, was where the executives lived in a walled neighborhood. People had to pass through one of two guarded gates and it had its own railway station where the company's families boarded. Vestiges of the enclave still exist. Part of the 6-meter-high fortification remains near Carrera 5 and Calle 29. The streets are lined with one-story Florida Keys-styled bungalows with expansive grassy lawns. The Centro Colombo-American is in one of these. The Clínica El Prado had been the company hospital and the Atlantis Building at Carrera 5, between Calles 23 and 24, was the headquarters.

The installations of UFC had extended to Carrera 2. In this zone were lower-level workers' housing and other installations, like the *estación del lámbrico*, which can still be seen in the middle of an abandoned lot.

The company facilities in Santa Marta, though, paled in comparison to the town United Fruit Company had out in its plantations at Sevilla; those were complete with casino. To get there, walk southward down Carrera 4 to Calle 24, and begin roaming the streets through this part of town. The neighborhood will soon be obvious by the architecture.

Jimmy Porto, director of the Centro Colombo-Americano (Monday-Friday 8 a.m.-noon and 2-6 p.m. Ca. 26, 4-100), grew up in the Bananatown and is delighted to talk about what life was like in the neighborhood. Updated: May 19, 2009.

Quinta de San Pedro Alejandrino

(ADMISSION: $6 adults, $5 students and seniors, $4.50 children 6-12 years, free children under 6 years). Quinta de San Pedro Alejandrino, founded in 1608 to cultivate sugar cane, is the estate where Simón Bolívar died in 1830. The main house is restored to its original condition, and Bolívar's death bed and the carriage that brought him from Santa Marta to the farm have been preserved. The sprawling green grounds contain other attractions: the **Altar de la Patria**, a massive central monument in remembrance of Bolívar; the impressive **Museo Bolivariano de Arte Contemporáneo**, which showcases Latin American art from the early 20th century to the present day;

and the 22-hectare **Jardín Botánico**. All are included in the price of admission. Guides that speak Spanish and English are at hand (extra charge). Daily 9:30 a.m.-4:30 p.m. The Quinta is five kilometers (3 mi) southeast of the city. From Carrera 1 (Avenida Bastidas) in Santa Marta, take a southbound minibus heading toward Mamatoca. Tell the driver you want to get off at the Quinta de San Pedro Alejandrino ($0.50). Tel: 433-1021, URL: www.museobolivariano.org.co. Updated: Mar 15, 2011.

Santa Marta Beaches

Nothing surpasses the pale sand and warm waters of the Caribbean coast. Santa Marta is no exception. Within the city, there's a beach along the camellón (seafront), which is a bit dirty but very popular with locals and foreigners. The super-bright spotlight rivals the full moon during those evening dips. The premier beaches are El Rodadero and Playa Blanca, where lifeguards are on duty, and beach chairs and water sports gear are available for rent.

Launches to Playa Blanca leave from El Rodadero, from both the main beach and from the other side of the estuary at the right end of the beach (1-4 persons $25, 5 or more persons $5 each). Updated: Jul 05, 2011.

Studying Spanish

Spanish Lessons

If you want to study Spanish in Santa Marta, contact Elsa Valencia. She offers one-on-one classes for all levels of students ($8 per hour). Course materials (textbook, grammar and an audiocourse) are included in the fee. Ms. Valencia also can arrange accommodation, field trips to Cartagena, Tayrona and other destinations for an extra charge. Casa Scania, Ca. 21 3-88. Tel: 431-6714, E-mail: elsaligia@hotmail.com, URL: www.neotropical.se.Updated: Mar 26, 2011.

Tours

Atlantic Divers

Atlantic Divers is one of the oldest scuba shops in Santa Marta. It has more than 25 years experience taking explorers through the underwater wilderness of the Caribbean. Fun dives out to the El Morro shipwrecks or the coral reefs edging the coast cost $67 (two dives) and a two-day, four-dive safari with an overnight stay at Playa Granati is $180 (includes transport, lunch and drinks). If you are a novice, the mini-course is $90 and the three-day course leading to PADI certification is $320. Instruc-

tors speak English. Ca. 10c, 2-14. Tel: 421-4883, Cel: 301-697-2577, E-mail: divers_den_cariba@hotmail.com. Updated: Mar 26, 2011.

Aviatur

Aviatur is the official handler of the National Park Administration's installations inside Parque Nacional Natural Tayrona. The agency manages the operations of the first-class Ecohab cabañas at Cañaveral, as well as lodging and a campsite at Arrecifes. Aviatur provides horseback riding, hikes, guides and other ecotourism activities. This tour operator also offers excursions to other parts of the country, as well as hotel and air reservations. Ca. 15, 3-20. Tel: 421-3848, URL: www.aviatur.travel. Updated: Mar 26, 2011.

Turcol

Turcol is best known for its Ciudad Perdida hike service, a five-day, four-night all-inclusive package for $280. However, Turcol has much more on its agenda, like day trips to El Pueblito in Parque Tayrona with a hike from Calabozo to Cañaveral ($155), and Quebrada Valencia and Buritaca ($45). This operator also does a two-day, one-night excursion to Cabo de la Vela ($150). For day trips, make reservations the day before; for Ciudad Perdida, as soon as possible. Turcol also has an office in Taganga (Casa María, Ca. 19, 5-40, near Casa de Felipe). Ca. 13,3-13, Centro Comercial San Francisco Plaza, local 115. Tel: 421-2256, Cel: 310-640-1875, E-mail: turcol_24@hotmail.com, URL: www.buritaca2000.com. Updated: Mar 26, 2011.

Lodging

Santa Marta has the full spectrum of lodging options, from inexpensive inns to luxury hotels facing the bay. At some of the dirt-cheap hostels it is possible that you will encounter open drug use. For a few dollars more, you can find safer and quieter quarters elsewhere. An unusual feature of Santa Marta is that budget hotels can be found almost anyplace in the city, though most are concentrated on Calles 10c and 11. Most places, even in the luxury price range, have only room-temperature water (which, in this climate, can be quite warm). Many hotels raise prices in the high seasons, when reservations are recommended. Updated: May 15, 2009.

BUDGET

Residencias San Jorge

(ROOMS: $7-10) An understated inn tucked among the partying-budget traveler and shadier hotels on Calle 10C, Residencias

San Jorge promises a family atmosphere. For more than 30 years Javier and Rosealba have offered the weary journeyer comfortable, safe rooms. The 14 simply furnished rooms, which are set around a courtyard, are quite decent-sized and clean. Rooms come with cable TV and a fan, and all save one come with a private bath. The hotel provides a laundry service or you can wash your own clothes. Ca. 10c, 2-68. Tel: 431-1293. Updated: Mar 14, 2011.

The Dreamer Hostel ♪

(BEDS: $9.50-14, ROOMS: $28-47) One of the hottest places on the backpacker circuit is The Dream Hostel. It has many features no other hostel has, like a billard table and swimming pool. If you're not wanting to fix dinner some night in the kitchen, then try the hostel's homemade Italian food. The Dreamer Hostel offers a variety of accommodation choices, from six coed dorms (four- to 10-bed) to private rooms. All accommodations come with either fan or air conditioning, and shared or private bath. The hostel is on the outskirts of Santa Marta, but near a mall and movie theater. Cra. 51, 26D-161 (Diag.32), Los Trupillos de Mamatoco. Tel: 433-3264, Cel: 300-251-6534, E-mail: thedreamerhostel@hotmail.com, URL: www.thedreamerhostel.com. Updated: Updated: Feb 01, 2011.

Hotel Las Vegas del Caribe

(ROOMS: $10-15) Clean, friendly, quiet and safe—this is an apt description of the Hotel Las Vegas del Caribe. Its three-story green structure has mid-sized rooms with private bath, cable TV (with remote control) and your choice of fan or air conditioning. The windows of the rooms in front face the street and during the night the street light shines in. The second and third floors have a common balcony where you can lounge and watch the Calle 11 goings-on. Hotel Las Vegas del Caribe is a good, budget lodging option. Ca. 11, 2-08, Tel: 421-5094, Cel: 311-666-7265, E-mail: hotellasvegas@hotmail.com. Updated: Mar 26, 2011.

Aluna

(BEDS: $11, ROOMS: $22-43) Aluna is one of Santa Marta's newer hostels located in the historic center of Santa Marta. This three-story guesthouse is in a 1920s, Spanish-styled villa with a shady courtyard. The rooftop terrace gives great views of the Sierra Nevada. Aluna has 11 private rooms and four dorms, available with fan or air condi-

tioning. Guests can chill in the hostel's café next door, or prepare meals in the common kitchen. Other extras are Internet, WiFi and free coffee. Ca. 21, 5-72. Tel: 432-4916, E-mail: info@alunahotel.com, URL: www.alunahotel.com. Updated: Mar 17, 2011.

Kayros Vivienda Turística

(BEDS: $11, ROOMS: $26-34) Kayros Vievienda Turística is a Colombian-owned hostel in Santa Marta's historical center, just four blocks from the Catedral.This small, clean hostel offers a seven-bed dormitory with air conditioning and fan, as well as private rooms with TV, air conditioning and private or shared bathrooms. Backpackers can enjoy the common kitchen, BBQ, bar, hammocks, laundry services, and free Internet and WiFi. Kayros' friendly staff provides tourist information to its local and international guests. Check the hostel's website for special offers. Ca. 17, 9-44. Tel: 431-4406, E-mail: viviendaturisticab@hotmail.com, URL: viviendaturistica.es.tl. Updated: Mar 23, 2011.

Hotel Saboy

(ROOMS: $11-22) Hotel Saboy is one of the many sub-mid-range options for the budget traveler, especially anyone not traveling alone. Service is good, and particular attention is paid to ensuring guests receive company safely. Rooms are ample and comfortable, with private bathrooms that have room-temperature water and cable TV. The hotel is quiet and provides a comfortable ambiance. Ca. 11, 2-22. Tel: 421-3799, E-mail: saboysantamarta@hotmail.com. Updated: Mar 26, 2011

Hospedería Casa Familiar

(ROOMS: $11-25) Hospedería Casa Familiar has long been a standby for shoestring travelers who don't want the party atmosphere of the other Calle 10c budget hostels. It's a bit pricier, but that the security and tranquility is worth the extra few dollars. To help save while spending, there's a common kitchen available for guest use. Other amenities include a book exchange, tourist information, Internet and laundry service. Ca. 10c, 2-14. Tel: 421-1697, E-mail: hospedariacasafamiliar@hotmail.com. Updated: Mar 09, 2011.

Hotel Imperial Caribe ♪

(ROOMS: $14-42) Hotel Imperial Caribe is a travel agent's favorite place to put up the tourists. Frequently you'll see the buses pulling up and those travelers stumbling out, looking in awe at their new

Photo by: Ben Bowes

surroundings. This 1920s inn still has a lot of class that's created by the ceramic-tile floors, high ceilings and a feel of those roaring '20s. Rooms are large with private baths (*agua al clima*) and either ceiling fans (just like in the day) or air conditioning. The space is bright from the tropical sun streaming through the long windows. This old hotel has held up nicely over the decades and continues to serve the journeyer well. Ca. 17, 3-96. Tel: 5-421-1556, E-mail: hotelimperialcaribe@gmail.com. Updated: Mar 26, 2011.

V!VA ONLINE REVIEW
HOTEL IMPERIAL CARIBE

The rooms with the high ceiling are spacious and have ambiance.

February 25, 2009

MID-RANGE

Hotel Nueva Granada

(ROOMS: $33-60) The Hotel Nueva Granada's beautifully decorated rooms surround the garden courtyard. Comfortable and quiet, each comes with a spotless private bath and a safe. Sit in the garden and read a book from the in-house library. Or, relax in the Jacuzzi after trekking to the Lost City. The price includes American breakfast and a half-hour of free Internet per day. Hotel Nueva Granada also rents bicycles to guests. Ca. 12, 3-17. Tel: 421-0685/431-2568, E-mail: hotelnuevagranada@hotmail.com, URL: www.hotelnuevagranada.com. Updated: Mar 09, 2011.

Park Hotel

(ROOMS: $35-70) Since its inception in 1927, the same family has lovingly run the Park Hotel, a favorite inn of Colombian TV personalities and international journalists. The outside may have had a facelift a few decades back, but the inside of this inn has the same elegance from its conception. High-relief carvings of dancing figures and tropical vegetation cover the pilasters and stairways. The public areas are accented by paintings and stone sculptures. The tastefully decorated rooms have high ceilings, ceramic-tile floors and private baths. (Here's a secret: the *turista* rooms have a sea view!) On steamy afternoons you can cool off in the swimming pool and come sunset you can relax in the bamboo furniture on the broad, common balcony overlooking the bay. Park Hotel pays attention to the children, too, providing a reading room and pool just for them. Thursday is movie night. Paseo Bastidas (Cra. 1) 18-67. Tel: 421-1215, E-mail: reservas@parkhotel-santamarta.com, URL: www.parkhotel-santamarta.com. Updated: Mar 09, 2011.

Hotel Yuldama

(ROOMS: $50-61) The Hotel Yuldama is a relic of late 1950s architecture. The disappointingly worn rooms have the typical amenities. There's air conditioning, cable TV, minibar (extra charge), telephone, closet and private bathroom. The quarters facing Avenida Bastidas are a bit noisy, though they offer a wonderful view of the bay, especially at sunset. Guests of this hotel can also use the pool and sauna at the Hotel Yuldama Inn in El Rodadero. Cra. 1, 12-19. Tel: 421-0063, E-mail: hotelyuldama@dialnet.net.co, URL: www.hotelyuldama.com. Updated: Mar 26, 2011.

HIGH-END

Playa Koralia

(ROOMS: $105-155, CAMPING: $50-55) Playa Koralia, a secluded eco-lodge on the Caribbean Sea, is a place to get away from it all. Chill outside in simple hammocks while gazing at the beach, but once inside your cabin, you'll wish sleeping at the beach always felt like being an Arab Sheik. The interior decoration is based on inspiration from pre-Columbian symbology, popular Mexican art, Indian Rajastan and the Mediterranean. Koralia offers various activities, like observing local artisans creating, canoe trips, jungle hikes to waterfalls, mountain hikes, snorkeling, massages and flower baths. In addition to a restaurant with a menu inspired by Caribbean, Mediterranean and Asian cuisine, there is a beach-sidebar that has live music and bonfires. Camping is also available if you have your own tent. Playa Koralia offers a pick-up and drop-off transportation from Santa Marta and Barranquilla airports for a fee. Prices include taxes and all meals, and are per person. 48 km/29 mi east of Santa Marta. Cel: 310-642-2574, E-mail: koralia@koralia.com, URL: www.koralia.com. Updated: Mar 26, 2011.

Restaurants

Around this port town, seafood and fish make frequent appearances on menus, no matter the type of establishment. Santa Marta has a broad array of restaurants, including fine dining (less expensive than in El Rodadero) and joints with daily plate specials. International sidewalk cafés line the Carrera 3 pedestrian mall, between Parque Bolívar and Parque de los Novios. All day the stands at Calle 16 and Carrera 5 churn out fresh juices. Come sunset, vendors spring up along Avenida Bastidas and the camellón selling cheese arepas, shish kabobs and other delights. Many restaurants along this stretch are wonderful options for watching the sunset over the bay. For dessert, buy a *crema de arroz* (rice with milk and coconut) from a peddler.

Santa Marta's market sprawls between Avenidas del Libertador and del Ferrocarril, Calles 8 and 12. Centrally located supermarkets include Éxito (Carrera 5 and Calle 19) and Olímpica (Calle 11 8-54). Aguasafe water purifying drops can be bought at Droguería Andina (Carrera 5 18-34) and other pharmacies along Carrera 5. Updated: Mar 27, 2011.

Deli Krem

(ICE CREAM: $1.50-9.50) Sometimes the only thing that will really take away the sting of a blistering day is ice cream. Most locals come to Deli Krem, right on the Parque de Bolívar, to grab a hand-dipped cone in one of 15 flavors. Deli Krem also whips up malts. Grab a container of the creamy delight to take home or down to the seawall. Monday-Saturday 10 a.m.-7 p.m., closed Sundays. Ca. 15, 2-70. Updated: Mar 26, 2011.

Lucky Hong Kong

(LUNCH: $2.25, ENTREES: $3-14) For a different kind of typical set lunch, drop by Restaurante Lucky Hong Kong for Chinese food. Of course, Lucky Hong Kong also has à la carte selections—in fact 135 dishes—and 26 choices of Ray Coling (a *bandeja mixta* of fried rice and stir fry). Vegetarians, you have much to choose from here. Don't forget to ask the quick staff for a pair of chopsticks. Daily 11 a.m.–9 p.m. Ca. 16, 5-56. Tel: 421-6291. Updated: Mar 26, 2011.

Ostras El Juancho !

(ENTREES: $2.75-8.50) For more than 35 years this has been the most trusted place to get a seafood cocktail off the street. Choose shrimp, octopus, conch, oysters and manta ray—or a mixture of seafood—in any size you wish. If the four benches along the wall are full (as they usually are), just take your cup over to the sea wall to watch the sunset. Serves daily 9 a.m.–9 p.m. (except on New Year's Day). Cra. 1, between Ca. 22 and 23, just past the Monumento a los Taironas (also called Los Indios). Updated: Mar 26, 2011.

El Escorial

(LUNCH: $3-6, ENTREES: $5-10) Locals often fill this pleasant, inexpensive restaurant, chowing down on its abundant daily special offered for lunch or dinner (soup;

main course of meat, beans, potatoes, rice and salad; plus drink). À la carte entrées include surf and turf options like simple pastas, arroz con mariscos (seafood rice), bandeja paisa, and a variety of fish and seafood plates. El Escorial serves not only lunch and dinner, but also breakfast. Daily 6:30 a.m.-8:30 p.m. Ca. 11, 1C-60. Tel: 421-3654. Updated: Apr 28, 2011.

Govinda

(LUNCH: $3.50) Like its sister location in Barranquilla, the Hare Krishna's Govinda restaurant location here in Santa Marta is a small, upstairs affair with inside and balcony seating. Music plays low while a set lunch is served, which includes soup, a main course (beans, brown rice, soy or gluten, a vegetable side and salad), dessert and drink. Although the *almuerzo* is officially served from noon until 2 p.m., it often runs out before then. Just like its other locations, besides a restaurant and bakery, Govinda has a few more things on its plate. Stop by the office downstairs to find out about yoga classes or staying at the Gambhira yoga monastery ($28 per day, room and board). Monday-Saturday noon-3 p.m. Ca. 16, 5-67. Cel: 301-239-4332, E-mail: inyasiswami@hotmail.com, URL: www.inboundtours.com. Updated: Mar 26, 2011.

Crêpes Expresso Café Bar

(ENTREES: $3.50-10) The crêpes at Crêpes Expresso Café Bar are named after writers and other figures from French culture. Eric and his crew mount some delicious, freshly prepared additions to Santa Marta's international menu. The Pierre de Ronsard (beef, Roquefort cheese sauce and mushrooms) and the Jules Supervielle (curried shrimp) are savory choices. Dessert crêpes abound, including the simple Anna de Noailles (butter and sugar) and the heavenly Madame de Sévigné (chocolate, almonds, whipped cream, ice cream and strawberries). Vegetarians have several options of delicious entrées, like the Charles Baudelaire (spinach, mushrooms and cream). There is a full bar of alcoholic and non-alcoholic drinks. Monday–Saturday 4–10:30 p.m. Cra. 2, 16-33. E-mail: crepes_expresso@hotmail.com, URL: www.crepesexpresso.com. Updated: Mar 26, 2011.

La Muzzería

(ENTREES: $3.50-$14) La Muzzería is one of a half-dozen sidewalk cafés now adorning the Callejón del Correo (Cra. 3)

pedestrian mall. This pizzeria offers 16 varieties of thin-crust pies for vegetarians and omnivores. A delicious option is its not-so-simple version of the Napolitana, with sweet red pepper, fresh basil, eggplant and tomato smothered with mozzarella cheese. Also on the menu are sandwiches, crepes, tortillas (omelets) and a gourmet *choripapa* (sausage and potato snack). Daily noon-10:30 p.m. Cra. 3, 16-30. Tel: 421-4774, Cel: 301-210-7826, E-mail: pedidas@lamuzaria.com, URL: www.lamuzzaria.com. Updated: Apr 28, 2011.

Baguettina Café

(ENTREES: $4.50-11) Fulfill the yearning for pastrami, prosciutto, salami, tocineta or imported cheeses at Baguettina deli. All sorts of thick sandwiches on fresh-baked baguettes, pita, round French bread or as wraps await you here, whether a meat-eater or vegetarian. Begin your meal with a salad, end it with an incredible pastry and accompany it with a fresh fruit juice, beer or wine. Cocktails are also on the menu, including the intriguing-sounding tamarind daiquiri. Cra. 1c, 23-30. Tel: 421-6378, E-mail: baguettina@gtelecom.com.co, URL: www.baguettina.com. Updated: Mar 10, 2011.

Ben and Josep ⚐

(ENTREES: $11-20) Ben and Josep serves other dishes, but let's talk about what has made this place famous: the steaks. Not just any steak, but the filet mignon. These are tender, even when cooked *medio crudo* (half-raw or very rare). Why are Ben and Josep's steaks so special? Because they directly purchase the animal from the farmer and butcher it themselves. You can have your chunk of meat natural or with a black pepper, BBQ or blue cheese sauce. With a sidewalk table, this is a perfect way to watch the sun set. Open Monday–Saturday 4 p.m.–1 a.m. Food service 6–10:45 p.m. Cra. 1, 18-53. Cel: 317-280-5039. Updated: Mar 26, 2011.

V!VA ONLINE REVIEW
BEN AND JOSEP

*"*Nice wine selection and very good prices. Thursday, Friday and Saturday it's packed with the local rich and famous.*"*

April 19, 2009

Photo by: Jorge Andrade

Mañe Cayón Restaurante

(ENTREES: $12-25) Some say that the best seafood stew in Colombia is right here at Mañe Cayón Restaurante. This sand-floored, lattice-wood-sided eatery has seafood and more seafood to satisfy your taste buds, with some items you don't see on other menus: prawn, lobster, shrimp, octopus and squid. Everything comes with salad and patacones. Fish are offered too—sierra, snapper or a nice fillet. You can have your seafood solo, in one of Mañe Cayón's famous stews, a salad, rice concoction or cocktail. Daily 10 a.m.–8 p.m. Cra. 1, 26-37 (the restaurant is one block further on than you would think by the street numbering scheme, past Calle 27.) Tel: 423-0812. Updated: Mar 10, 2011.

Donde Chucho

(ENTREES: $12-38) Tucked in a quiet corner across from the Parque de los Novios is Donde Chucho, one of Santa Marta's premier gourmet restaurants. It takes pride in specializing in delicacies of old Italy. Pasta plays a major role on this menu. There are six types of noodles and eight sauces, as well as cannelloni, ravioli and four versions of lasagna, plus risottos and antipastos. Seafood is also a principal actor, whether in an antipasto, pasta, risotto or rice. It can also play a solo role (as can chicken or beef), with scant potato sides.

Santa Marta location: Ca. 19, 2-17. Tel: 421-0861, E-mail: restaurantechucho3@hotmail.com . El Rodadero location: Cra. 2, 16-39. Tel: 423-7521. Updated: Mar 26, 2011.

Nightlife

Santa Marta's nightlife is driven by its port town atmosphere. Cafés with live Cuban son music, standard discos and hole-in-the-wall dance-and-brothel clubs vibrate until dawn. There is also a visible gay bar scene, with probably more tolerance than you'll find in hinterland Colombia. A number of casual, international café-bars have opened around Parque de los Novios. Updated: Mar 27, 2011.

La Puerta !

Founded by the same French couple that established Santa Marta's Alliance Française, La Puerta has become the spot to go—even for Taganga backpackers. This café has long been a meeting place for artists and writers, international and local crowds, to drink and share ideas or dance. La Puerta is intimate, with several rooms hung with paintings and a back patio. The *musique* (rock of all eras and all styles, and latin rhythms) is not too loud. On weekends, the rumba really grooves. The bar has domestic and imported beers, French wines and delicious cocktails. Tuesday-Wednesday 6 p.m.-1 a.m.,

Thursday 6 p.m.-2 a.m., Friday-Saturday 6 p.m.-3 a.m. Open Sundays on holiday weekends and daily in high seasons. Ca. 17, 2-29. E-mail: ohlalalapuerta@hotmail.com, URL: www.ohla-lalapuerta.com. Updated: Mar 26, 2011.

Laùtrec Café-Bar

Laùtrec Café Bar is a bar for everyone, it is said, from straight to gay. Bodies sweating in this tropical heat boogie to cross-over music (vallenato, salsa, reggaeton) on the two large dance floors. At times Laùtrec has live bands and fashion shows. Both alcoholic and non-alcoholic drinks are served. So, if you're ready to bop the night away until just before dawn begins painting the sky, head just a half-block from Parque de Bolívar. Tuesday–Sunday 7 p.m.–4 a.m. Cra. 2, 16-08. Tel: 431-9485, Cel: 316-878-4125. Updated: Mar 26, 2011.

El Rodadero

The road from Santa Marta undulates southward through dry hills forested with small-leafed trees and cardoon cactus. From the crest you see the high-rise condos and hotels of the port's richer half-sister, El Rodadero. This is where Colombian families come to spend the holidays, enjoying the warm sea and clean beaches. Along the coast, Colombian musicians and actors have their vacation homes. On the island at the mouth of the bay is Pelican Island, the privately owned retreat of the family of an ex-governor of Magdalena Department (no visits allowed).

Everything in this resort town is geared to tourism. Travelers on excursions with more exclusive tour groups will stay in this part of town. However, that doesn't mean there are not places for journeyers with more modest budgets. Updated: Mar 25, 2011.

History

El Rodadero was just a sparsely populated beach until the 1950s when the first eatery opened. Hotel Tamacá was the first hotel built, in 1959. Since then El Rodadero has grown into the large, moneyed resort it is today. Updated: Mar 27, 2011.

When to Go

The weather is even more sultry in El Rodadero than in Santa Marta. Winds are normal from the end of December to the beginning of March and rain falls regularly from September to the beginning of December. Like Santa Marta, El Rodadero is a trendy vacation destination during Semana Santa, late summer and around the Christmas holidays.

HOLIDAYS AND FESTIVALS

Like Santa Marta, El Rodadero participates in the celebration of the Virgen del Carmen's feast days during the second week of July and the boat flotilla that goes from Taganga to Santa Marta and El Rodadero on July 16.

Getting To and Away

El Rodadero is part of Santa Marta's city bus network. Its *combis* (vans) carry people back and forth from here to the main town; many pass by the bus terminal ($0.70). The typical taxi fare is $5.60 from the bus terminal to El Rodadero and to downtown Santa Marta $4.60.

Many long-distance buses pass through or near El Rodadero. Several companies have offices in El Rodadero where you can advance purchase tickets. Updated: Mar 27, 2011.

Safety

Because it is mainly a wealthier vacationer's resort town, El Rodadero has better security than other towns in this area. On the beach there are posted suggestions to the tourist about steps to take for personal safety, both in Spanish and English. The beaches here have lifeguards. Updated: Jun 05, 2008.

Services

TOURISM

The **Fondo de Promoción Turística de Santa Marta** (Monday–Friday 8 a.m.-noon and 2-6 p.m., Saturday 8 a.m.-noon. Ca. 10, 3-10. Tel: 422-7548, E-mail: fondoturisticasantamarta@gmail.com, URL: www.santamartaturistica.com) dispenses excellent brochures and other information.

MONEY

Most of the banks are located on Calle 9, between Carreras 1 and 3. All have ATMs: **AV Villas** (Ca. 9, 1-47), and **Bancolombia** (Cra. 1a and Ca. 6) and **Colmena** (Cra. 2, between Ca. 6 and 7, next to the Hotel Arhuaco). **Servibanco** (Cra. 3 and Ca. 9) has an ATM that accepts only Visa and Plus cards.

KEEPING IN TOUCH

Phone shops are all over this town; Internet is bit more difficult to find. **Correos de Colombia** is on the corner of Calle 7 and Carrera 2. Updated: Mar 27, 2011.

CARIBBEAN COAST

Things to See and Do

In El Rodadero, you can relax in a lounge chair on the beach, ride a banana boat across the bay, drop a line for marlin or scuba dive and see the world below the waves. If you prefer to see sea creatures from the comfort of dry land, visit one of the two aquariums here. For those who consider shopping a sport, there are plenty of stores to explore here, too.

Acuario y Museo del Mar del Rodadero

(ADMISSION: $14 adults and children from 6 years old) On the shore of Ensenada Inca Inca (Inca Inca Cove), just a few minutes' boat ride along the shoreline from the Rodadero beach, is Latin America's first aquarium, founded in 1966. Its 15 tanks and six sea pools house angel fish, barracudas, sharks, starfish, corals and other species native to this corner of the Caribbean. The sea lions and bottle-nose dolphins put on a show, and you can even swim with the dolphins. (As fascinating as dolphin shows may seem, animal rights groups say they are inhumane. To learn more, visit World Society for the Protection of Animals: www. wspa-usa.org). The adjacent Museo del Mar gives information about the history and maritime ecology of the Caribbean. Buy your combined ticket (boat ride and entry) from the Acuario's office in El Rodadero. Daily 8:30 a.m.-3 p.m. Cra. 1 and Ca. 8, Edificio Fuentemar. Tel: 422-7222, E-mail: acuariorodadero@gmail.com.

Mundo Marino

(ADMISSION: $6 adults, $5 children and senior citizens) This aquarium's marine tunnel and 25 panoramic tanks display more than 700 species local to the region. Mundo Marino also has fish, sea turtle and shark feedings. Children's price is for 2- to 12-year-olds. Daily 8 a.m.-6 p.m. Cra. 2, 11-68. Tel: 422-9334, E-mail: info@mundomarinoacuario.com.co., URL: www.mundomarinoacuario.com.co. Updated: Mar 27, 2011.

Aquatic Sports in El Rodadero

Where there is a sea resort town, there will be water sports. Scuba diving is popular in these parts, and many dive shops are eager to help plan an excursion. There's more to do than diving, though. Rent a kayak or jetski, or take a jostling ride on a *gusano* (water banana). Be sure to wear a life jacket if zipping across the bay. To purchase your own snorkel or scuba gear, stop by the main office of the **Drift Dive Center** (Carrera 2, 11-68. URL: www.divedrift.com).

If you're a bit afraid of the ocean, splash around instead at **Parque Acuático El Rodadero** (admission: $6.75. Tel: 422-7706), a water park with corkscrew slides and pools. The park is located at the left end of the beach and is open Saturday and Sunday 9 a.m.-5 p.m. during low season and daily during high season. Updated: Mar 27, 2011.

Lodging

Most of the lodging options in El Rodadero are resort hotels. Cheap accommodations, however, can be found, especially in the off season when you can negotiate a lower rate. Renting an apartment or condo is another option for those looking to save money. Ask around with locals or check the newspapers for possibilities. El Rodadero also has several campsites, including **Camping Cantamar**, which charges $8 per person and also rents tents $3-6) (Ca. 21, 1-16. Cel: 316-273-3081, E-mail: campingcantamar@hotmail.com, URL: www.campingcantamar.com). Updated: Mar 27, 2011.

Hotel Arrecifes Caribeño

(ROOMS: $11-25) This four-story hostel has rooms for four to eight people, and in the low season a special package (which includes meals) for people traveling in groups. Solo travelers and couples can stay in rooms with private (but cold-water) baths. The entire inside of Hotel Arrecifes Caribeño is covered with murals by a Colombian artist. Prices double in the high season. The inn is about seven blocks from the beach, on the other side of the main highway through El Rodadero. Ca. 19, 6-54. Tel: 422-3265. Updated: Mar 10, 2011.

Camping Bahía Surf Club

(CAMPING: $11 per person, ROOMS: $44-233) Camping Bahía Surf Club in El Rodadero is an all-inclusive resort open all year round that is perfect for adventure seekers. Its five cabins have a kitchen and wireless internet access. The camping ground has showers and electrical outlets. Tents can be rented also. Activities include canoeing and horseback riding, or take a kite surfing course at the Surf Club with professional and international instructors. Equipment rental is available. Bilingual tours include visits to La Guajira and Cabo de la Vela beaches, ideal for kite surfing, and the Sierra Nevada de Santa Marta. Ca. 20, 2A-20. Tel: 436-2590, E-mail: gerencia@bahiacamping.com, URL: www.bahiacamping.com. Updated Jul 8, 2011.

Tima Uraka Hospedaje

(ROOMS: $12-40) Tima Uraka Hospedaje—the "House of the Moon"—is a backpackers'

CARIBBEAN COAST

hostel. Pull up a hammock in the beautiful courtyard garden. All the rooms are nicely decorated and have TV and private bath. You can use the laundry facilities to wash your clothes, or if the hammock won't let you go, give them to the laundry service. A well-equipped kitchen awaits your culinary talents, too. Discount in the low season with Hostelling International card. Ca. 18, 2-59. Tel: 422-8433, Cel: 300-801-6833, E-mail: casalunahostal@hotmail.com, URL: www.timauraka.com. Updated: Mar 10, 2011.

Hotel El Rodadero

(ROOMS: $52-83) The modern Hotel El Rodadero's reception area greets its guests with sea-themed stained glass and sand-filled pillars. Rooms come with cable TV, phone, air conditioning, a tepid-water bath and a minibar (extra charge). The rooms, even those facing the beach, are quiet. The hotel also has a pool with a kids' section and a playground. The inn is partially wheelchair accessible—there are ramps throughout the hotel but the bathrooms have no handrails. Prices include breakfast and dinner. Ca. 11, 1-29. Tel: 422-8323, E-mail: hopertour2007@hotmail.com, URL: www.hopertour.com . Updated: Mar 10, 2011.

Hotel Arhuaco

(ROOMS: $118-263) Every detail in the Hotel Arhuaco is perfect, down to the floral arrangements in the lobby. The rooms are spotless and have air conditioning, satellite TV, personal safe deposit box, mini-bar and private bath. The baths have hot water, a rare find in this climate. A spa and swimming pool make this a perfect getaway for couples and families. The hotel also caters to business travelers, as it has two fully equipped conference rooms. Prices include tax, insurance and U.S.-style breakfast. Cra. 2, 6-49. Tel: 422-7166, E-mail: reservas.sarh@solarhoteles.com, URL: www.solarhoteles.com. Updated: Mar 10, 2011.

Restaurants

Some of Santa Marta's finest restaurants are located in El Rodadero. Here you will find everything from Argentine *parrillas* (BBQs) to Italian bistros. Of course, prices reflect the wealthier tourists who frequent El Rodadero, but that doesn't mean there isn't a fair selection of *comida corriente* (daily special) restaurants here. For these cheap eats, try along Carrera 4 (the main highway through this town). A massive Olímpico supermarket is on Carrera 4, between Calles 12 and 13.

Restaurante El Pibe

(ENTREES: $4-11) El Pibe has arrived from Argentina and unpacked his recipes in El Rodadero. At this sidewalk restaurant you can get Argentine empanadas and other dishes from the Southern Cone. These specialties include *churrasco* (steak), ravioli and *lomito a la parrilla* (grilled tenderloin). To sate a big appetite, you can also get a good, pampas-style barbecue, which includes churrasco, chicken, *ubre* (udder), *chinchulín* (cow intestine), *morcilla* (blood sausage) and *chorizo* (sausage), with potatoes and sauces on the side. Daily 11:30 a.m.-10 p.m. Ca. 6, 1-30. Tel: 422-7973 . Updated: Mar 27, 2011.

Restaurante Punto Marino

(LUNCH: $5.50, ENTREES: $4-20) Beachside Restaurante Punto Marino offers a wide assortment of fish and seafood meals. Under the broad awning, families and tour groups grab a white wicker chair at a table and ponder the extensive menu. Punto Marino has a variety of Menu Tropical set meals that come with soup and main dish (salad, rice, patacones and cassava, plus fish, chicken or beef). À la carte items include *sancocho de pescado* (fish soup), accompanied by coconut rice and patacones), swordfish, shrimp and lobster. To go along with a meal, choose a fresh-fruit juice. Daily 8 a.m.-9 p.m. Cra. 1 and Ca. 11. Updated: Apr 28, 2011.

Ristorante-Viñería El Sabor de Italia

(ENTREES: $11-18) Only true Italian ingredients are used at this *ristorante* to guarantee authentic Italian flavors. Antipastos start the meal off with a traditional touch. Next choose spaghetti or fusseli with one of 14 freshly-made sauces. Lucas, the owner, may be from the north of Italy, but his creations come from all Italian regions. The only non-Italian items on the menu are the Chilean and Argentine wines. Prices include tax, but not tip. Open Wednesday–Monday, noon–2 p.m., 7–10 p.m.; closed Tuesdays. Ca. 17, 1A-77, Edificio Tamacá Country II. Tel: 422-7259, E-mail: mcorrea21@yahoo.com. Updated: Mar 27, 2011.

V!VA ONLINE REVIEW
RISTORANTE VIÑERIA EL SABOR DE ITALIA

Splendid service and delectible sauces. Molto Bene!

May 05, 2011

Nightlife

The nightlife scene in El Rodadero is tailored to this resort town's well-heeled clientele. Get out your finest dancing clothes if you are hitting the clubs, as most have dress codes. Of course, the ebb and flow of crowds in these discos matches that of tourists in Rodadero, with the low season bringing smaller waves of partiers on weekends. Updated: Mar 27, 2011.

TAGANGA

 0m   5,000   5

Located just 5 kilometers (3 mi) from Santa Marta, this one-time small fishing village has become a backpacker's haven. Desert hills steeply slope down to a palm tree-fringed horseshoe bay. On one side of the bay, the fishing boats bob in the sunset; on the other, bathers enjoy the cool waters. Taganga has become a premier center for scuba diving in the region, including as a base for excursions to reefs off neighboring Parque Nacional Natural Tayrona. Days of tranquility end with nights of laid-back partying here, making for an easy pace that many travelers—foreign and Colombian alike—find appealing. Taganga is an escape from the bustling ports and tourist towns of the Caribbean coast, a place where increasing numbers of ex-pats find a home.

But Taganga isn't just for the backpacker. There are inns and restaurants catering to vacationers of all budgets. The town is rapidly growing, with foreigners now owning almost half of the businesses. Increasingly it is able to provide its visitors with the services they want. By the same token, it is starting to become less peaceful, especially on holidays when all accommodations fill up, and losing its appeal to some travelers. The scarcity of water in the area may help to deter unrestrained growth. Updated: Jul 05, 2011.

History

Until the mid-1990s, Taganga was just a small, typical fishing village. Then shoestring travelers looking for a cheap place off the beaten track discovered Taganga's charms. Quickly, the buzz hit the backpacker grapevine, and every year more and more people arrive. The town has experienced a seemingly unstoppable boom, especially since the turn of the millennium.

When to Go

Taganga's climate is hot like Santa Marta's, but a bit drier. The La Loca wind drops in from December to January, helping to moderate temperatures. It rains from September to early December.

Taganga is popular among Colombians as well as foreigners, so expect large crowds during holidays. It is best to make reservations in advance for Easter Week, July-August, Christmas-New Year season and three-day holiday weekends. Updated: Jul 05, 2011.

HOLIDAYS AND FESTIVALS

Taganga celebrates Carnaval with costume parades, music and dancing at dusk. Get your disguise prepared and join in the fun—just don't forget the *maicena* (corn starch) to throw.

Along with Santa Marta and El Rodadero, Taganga honors the Virgen del Carmen, the patroness of fishermen and sailors. This village is the starting point of the boat flotilla on July 16. Updated: Mar 25, 2011.

Getting To and Away

Minibuses to Taganga pass by Carrera 5 in Santa Marta every 10-15 minutes from 6 a.m.-9 p.m. (15 min; last Santa Marta-Taganga van 7 p.m.; last Taganga-Santa Marta 8:30-9 p.m.) and direct from the bus terminal (50 min); either costs $0.70. Taxis charge $5.60 from Taganga to Santa Marta and $6.70 from Taganga to the bus terminal. Moto-taxis are a way to get around Taganga ($0.75); they can also take you all the way to Santa Marta, if you like ($2). Buses to other destinations in Colombia must be caught from Santa Marta's bus terminal.

If you want to reach Taganga on your own bike or vehicle, follow Carerra 11 across the railroad tracks and out of town, up the hill and then down the other side to the beach town. Updated: Mar 29, 2011.

Safety

All told, Taganga is a pretty safe place to hang out. Nevertheless, locals warn to be careful walking to Playa Grande and other beaches, and of leaving your things alone on the sands, due to the possibility of robberies. Such petty crimes increase during high seasons. On the in-town beach, beware of glass and the steep drop just off-shore. Police are vigilant about drugs, and several travelers reported having drugs planted on them.

CARIBBEAN COAST

Photo by: Felipe Mebarak

Since 2006 a number of travelers have reported contracting dengue in this area; it remains unclear whether the contagion zone is Taganga or Parque Nacional Natural Tayrona. Take proper precautions in both areas. Tap water is not safe to drink without treatment.

When La Loca comes calling, seas become rough and small-craft advisories are issued. Keep this in mind when planning boating expeditions. Updated: Mar 26, 2011.

Services

INFORMATION OFFICES

On the beach road (Cra. 1), near Calle 18, is a **tourism information**-tourist police kiosk. The main **police post** is on the main road into Taganga (Cra. 2 and Ca. 18).

MONEY

Bancolombia has an ATM next to Hostal Pelikan, near the police post on Carrera 2. More options, as well as exchange houses, exist in Santa Marta.

KEEPING IN TOUCH

Internet cafés are more common than in the past, though on some days the connection leaves much to be desired. **Mojito Net Internet Cocktail Bar** (Ca. 14 and Cra. 1B-61) seems to be the best of the lot.

MEDICAL

Taganga has a basic health center, **Centro de Salud Taganga** (Ca. 7 and Cra. 3, Tel: 421-9067).

LAUNDRY

Several women offer laundry services so tourists can pass the day at the beach. One is near Casa Felipe, on Ca.19, near Cra. 6).

OUTDOOR GEAR RENTAL AND PURCHASE

Several dive shops, including **Calipso Dive Center** (Ca. 12, 1-40. Tel: 57-5-421-9146, Cel: 315-684-3075, URL: www.calipsodive-center.com.co), sell snorkeling equipment. On the beachfront avenue is **Taganga Xtreme**, which not only sells snorkeling gear, but also rents surfboards and kayaks (Cra. 1, 14. Tel: 421-9350, E-mail: tagangaxtreme@gmail.com). Updated: Mar 29, 2011.

SHOPPING

Literar-té

Head to Literar-té to find just the right book for those lazy hours. With books in 16 different languages, you're bound to find just the right thing. Swiss-native Diana even has guidebooks to help you plan your journey. Literar-té offers more than just books—it has salsa classes, bikes to rent, a cabaña and campsites, and can arrange fishing excursions. Diana keeps no set hours, though she usually opens the shop Monday–Friday mornings. If the shop isn't open, just drop by and call from the gate. Literar-té is uphill and to the right from the soccer field; follow the signs to the sea-shell-covered house on the right. Cel: 317-273-2862. Updated: Apr 29, 2008.

Things to See and Do

Taganga is a great place to kick back, work on your suntan, go swimming, swing in the hammock, eat fresh fish, take a siesta, watch the sunset or head out to Parque Nacional Natural Tayrona to do some more major re-laxation. Hike or boat out to other beaches. Study Spanish or scuba diving. Go on a fish-ing safari. Make an excursion into Santa Marta or El Rodadero to take in a museum, or head up to Ciudad Perdida for the ulti-mate jungle trip. Updated: May 20, 2008.

Playa Grande and Playa Cristal

If the beach in town gets too familiar, try one of the other stretches of sand nearby. The knoll on the right-hand side of Tagan-ga Bay shelters Playa Grande. Restaurants on this pale-golden strand are quite pricey, so pack a picnic. To get to Playa Grande, walk up Taganga Beach to Hotel Bahía Ta-ganga and take the trail that begins behind it (20 min). Alternatively, take a launch to the beach (10 minutes, $2.80 round trip).

Another cruise you can take from the vil-lage is to Parque Nacional Natural Tayrona's closest beach, Playa Cristal, formerly named Playa de Muerte. These launches are now regulated by the national park service; Ex-potur in Taganga is one authorized agency.

During the week both beaches are tranquil, but on weekends and during vacation times Colom-bians come flocking. Updated: Mar 29, 2011.

Scuba Diving

The ocean off Taganga's shores hides many underwater wonders, from coral reefs to old Spanish galleons. Taganga has thus become a hotspot for scuba diving. A dozen dive shops currently operate out of this small village, and many offer courses from basic to divemaster levels. You can choose daytime diving excursions or night dives at more than 30 different sites. One outfitter even does scuba safaris to more distant locales, including Cabo de la Vela in the Guajira. Always check your scuba gear to make sure it is in good condition

and that the scuba agency is PADI-certi-fied. Ask other travelers about their expe-riences with different dive shops. There is no hyperbaric chamber on this stretch of the coast. Updated Jul 05, 2011.

Fishing

Every morning and afternoon local men head out to go fishing, the traditional trade of Taganga. To try your hand at catching some red snapper, albacore, barracuda or shark, see if you can find a local fisherman to take you out. Or, contact Caracol at Liter-ar-té (see Taganga Shopping; Cel: 317-273-2862) about arranging a fishing trip in his boat, followed by a beach BBQ to grill your catch. Either way, you'll be doing it as the locals do, with just a fishing line on a roll, and you'll get to learn about the Caribbean fishing culture. The fishing port is on the right-hand side of the bay. Be warned that from December to January high winds (La Loca) blow in, causing small craft advisories to be issued. Updated: Mar 11, 2011.

Studying Spanish

Academia Latina

If you can't seem to pull yourself away from bucolic Taganga, spend a few hours a day boning up on Spanish. Academia Latina Spanish school allows foreign visitors to study the language while taking in the sand and sea. The teachers at Academia Latina are all Colombians and certified Spanish teachers. A percentage of the tuition goes to local projects, such as programs for poor children. The school can help stu-dents arrange volunteer opportunities. Ca. 14, 1B-75. Tel: 316-600-6410, E-mail: info@academia-latina.com, URL: www.ac-ademia-latina.com. Updated: Mar 14, 2011.

Tours

Most of the tour operators in Taganga are scuba dive centers. Ask around to other journeyers about their experience with these shops before selecting one. Inquire with local *pescadores* about going on a fishing expedi-tion. Recently, the national park service has tightened up boat tours to Playa Cristal and other destinations in Parque Nacional Natu-ral Tayrona, to protect the environment and tourists' well-being. Beware that Taganga is overrun with fly-by-night salesmen and guide organizations, and scams are all too common! A few legitimate tour agencies have offices in this village. They can help you plan your trip to Ciudad Perdida, Tayrona or further afield without having to go all the way in to Santa Marta. Jul 05, 2011.

Expotur

Expotur is a new comer to the Ciudad Perdida trek market. It offers the standard five-day hike to the mythical lost city of Teyuna ($278, including transport, guide, lodging, food and ruins entry fee). Vegetarian meals can be prepared. Expotur is a member of Asoteyuna (Asociación de Turismo Sostenible Comunitario), a network of indigenous and rural communities involved in sustainable tourism. Expotur also does day trips to PNN Tayrona, Minca and other destinations near Santa Marta. It is also authorized to provide boat transport to points within PNN Tayrona. Ca. 18, 2A-07. Tel: 421-9577, Cel: 311-418-2706, URL: www.expotur-eco.com / www.turismoruralcaribe.com. Updated: Apr 25, 2011.

Magic Tours

Magic Tour is a reputable operator that runs well organized hiking trips to the Lost City (Ciudad Perdida). The tours run for five days, and the cost includes guide, entrance to the ruins and all food and accommodation. The food provided by Magic Tour on these treks is of a high quality. The staff provides reliable good service and is friendly. This company can also organize day or overnight trips to the Tayrona national park, Guajira tours and flights. Magic Tour also has an office in Santa Marta, near the Cathedral (Calle 16, 4-41. Tel: 421-5820). Ca. 14, 1B -50 (opposite Casa Holanda). Tel: 421-9429, Cel: 317-679-2441, URL: www.magictourstaganga.com. Updated: Mar 29, 2011.

DIVE CENTERS

Aquantis

Aquantis, part of PADI, offers various courses every day of the year from a bilingual staff. The personalized courses range from the two to four day beginner and recreation courses to the six to eight week PADI Dive Master Course. Other courses include the Emergency First Response Course and the Oxygen Provider Course. Its special night dive is a favorite attraction. Additionally, Aquantis has diving gear available to buy and organizes trips around the area in an effort to educate visitors of the unique ecology in the water and on land. Ca. 18, 1-39. Tel: 421-9344, E-mail: info@aquantisdivecenter.com, URL: www.aquantisdivecenter.com. Updated Jul 10, 2011.

Calipso Dive Center

Travelers whose appetite for underwater exploration has been whetted by dives in Taganga flock to Calipso Dive Center for unique scuba diving safaris.

For beginner divers and divers-to-be, the three-day/two-night trip to Guayaca is ideal. Advanced and fun divers do six day dives and a night dive. Open water and advanced courses in Guayaca cost $378, or $305 for fun divers.

At Cabo de la Vela, experienced divers can explore above and below the waves: there are amazing, rarely-seen dives, and before and after dives there's traditional food, dancing and games from the matriarchal Wayuu indigenous culture. Safarigoers stay in a Wayuu family's beachfront home. This four-day/three-night package costs $611 and includes four dives; these require a minimum of four participants with PADI certification.

Calipso also offers fun dives out of Taganga ($56 per day, 2 dives), and has free dorms for divers. Calipso is working with the national park service in "reforesting" the coral reefs at Gayraca. This project takes volunteers (for more information, contact infocalipsovolunteers@gmail.co). Ca. 12, 1-40. Tel: 421-9146, Cel: 315-684-3075, URL: www.calipsodivecenter.com.co. Updated: Mar 29, 2011.

Océano Scuba

Since 1988, Océano Scuba has offered sport, technical, and professional courses. You will be required to provide your own basic equipment (snorkel, mask, fins, and goggles), have a prior medical exam to prove good health and be at least 12 years of age. The courses are three weeks and you will go to 10 beautiful diving sites along the coast. Rates are competitive but adjust to any budget. Group rates are also available. Océano Scuba does also offer a course for the kids so they will not be waiting on the beach. Océano also has service in Barranquilla (Cra. 43, 80-219, Barranquilla. Tel: 378-5486). Cra. 1, 17-07. Tel: 421-9004, E-mail: oceano@oceanoscuba.com.co, URL: www.oceanoscuba.com.co. Updated: Jul 10, 2011.

Poseidón Dive Center

Poseidon Dive Center is Taganga's oldest and most frequently recommended scuba shop. It offers mini-courses for those who don't have much time but want a little taste of the undersea world ($106). It provides full courses in open water (4-day, $372, 4immersions, leading to PADI certification), as well as advanced, rescue, divemaster and assistant instructor levels. The PADI-certified teachers speak Spanish, English, French and German. Tour options include fun dives ($83 per day, 2 dives), night dives, underwater photography, deep dives and wreck dives. All Poseidón's packages include scuba equipment (bring your own for a discount), boat transport and snacks. Ca. 18, 1-69. Tel: 421-9224, Cel: 314-889-2687, E-mail: info@poseidondivecenter.com, URL: www.poseidondivecenter.com. Updated: Mar 29, 2011.

Vida Marina

Though instructor Santiago is a relative newcomer to the Taganga dive scene, he knows how to make his students comfortable instantly, by taking the most insecure by the hand and joking with the more confident ones underwater. From his center, located a stone's throw from the beach, he teaches basic and professional PADI courses, from open water to advanced, rescue and dive master levels. Two-immersion dives in small groups for certified divers are organized to sites around nearby Parque Tayrona, with all equipment rental, boat ride and a light snack included ($70). Do not hesitate to ask for a discount if you do several dives. Cra. 1 and Ca. 14. Tel: 421 9511, E-mail: escuela@buceovidamarina.com, URL: www.buceovidamarina.com. Updated: Mar 26, 2011.

Lodging

In the past few years, Taganga has seen a boom in the construction of hotels and hostels. Taganga hotels mostly cater to backpackers, though more mid-range options are coming onto the scene. Camping is possible at Diana's house (see Shopping) or at Mónica la Argentina's house, 150 meters (500 ft) past the shop El Esquinazo. Hostel and hotel prices are considerably raised during the high season, and even more so on holidays. At these times of the year, Taganga also becomes crowded and reservations are essential, even for hostels. Tanganga sometimes allows overflow accommodation in hammocks. Water is scarce in Taganga; sometimes accommodations will be without water for a while. Do your part to help conserve. Updated: Jul 26, 2010.

Hotel Oso Perezoso

(HAMMOCKS: $8, ROOMS: $12-27) Hotel Oso Perezoso has three stories with a very relaxed and hospitable feel. There are seven private rooms including singles, doubles and a triple: each has private bathroom. Breakfast is included. The Hotel is equipped with WiFi, free coffee all day and a travelers store. The beach is only a short walk away. The third floor hosts the Tsumami Café and is where Lolita the dog, Simone the cat and Roberto the parrot call home. The co-owner is from the United States and Oso Perezoso is the sister hotel to Miramar Hotel in Santa Marta. Ca. 17, 2-36. Tel: 421-8041, E-mail: HotelOsoPerezoso@yahoo.com, URL: www.hotelosoperezoso.com.

Casa de Felipe !

(BEDS: $9-11, ROOMS: $22-56) Literally built by hand, Casa de Felipe is a product of many years of love. Felipe has created a spectacularly comfortable space for the budget traveler with all the important amenities, including kitchen and laundry facilities. The rooms are spacious and beautifully decorated. The shady garden terraces, hung with hammocks and scattered with tables, have fantastic views of the bay and sunsets. Studios for four or six, complete with private kitchen, BBQ and terrace, are available as well. Casa de Felipe is a quiet hostel away from the beach's weekend and nighttime insanity. The staff speaks Spanish, French and English. Some of the buses from Santa Marta turn up the road toward Casa de Felipe and let you off a block away; otherwise hop off at the road before the police post and walk up the road on the right. Casa de Felipe is 10 minutes uphill from the beach. Cra. 5, 19-13. Tel: 421-9101 , Cel: 316-318-9158, E-mail: info@lacasadefelipe.com, URL: www.lacasadefelipe.com. Updated: Mar 11, 2011.

Casa El Amparo

(COTTAGES: $10-12) A locally owned, small, homey retreat, El Amparo accommodates two to six people. It has a master bedroom that has a double bed and a bathroom. The living room has a fold out sofa-bed and two convertible chair beds while the kitchen has anything you will need. Linen and daily cleaning service is included in the rates. However, it is recommended to hire a washer. Also, at request, El Amparo can help you plan day trips to sites in the area. Casa El Amparo has a decorative iron railing and will be the first house on your right. Ca. 15, 1B-49. Cel: 301-432-1421, E-mail: vargas_amparo@yahoo.com, Updated: Jul 10, 2011.

Hostel Tropical Maison Taganga

(ROOMS: $14-21) For those looking for a cheap option in Taganga, Hostel Tropical Maison might be a good choice. This is not so much a hostel, but rather a few rooms for rent in the home of friendly French owner Jean. Rooms are basic, but clean. The shared bathroom is spotless. Internet is available on Jean's PC. This is not a place for backpackers wanting to meet lots of others to travel, but isn't a bad option for the price. The Maison is across from the Puesto de Salud. Calle 14, 3-06. Tel: 421-9379, Cel: 301-456-5343, E-mail: jeanemilo@hotmail.com. Updated: Mar 26, 2011.

Hotel Pelikan

(ROOMS: $20-28) Hard-to-miss Hotel Pelikan is located on the road into Taganga. It is a brightly-decorated hostel with very friendly and helpful owners. Private rooms are of a decent size and are clean, with private bathrooms. Seemingly always under development, the hostel is regularly adding new rooms. The hotel has a nice shady patio out front for chilling with a book and a beer. Cra. 2, 17-04. Tel: 421-9057, E-mail: hostel-peli.ktrail.com. Updated: Mar 11, 2011.

Casa Holanda

(ROOMS: $28-45) Smack bang in the center of things, Casa Holanda is quickly gaining a reputation as a great place to hang your hat. The twelve private rooms are spacious and spotless with private bathrooms. Owner Edwin and his friendly staff will make you feel at ease. While a little pricier for this town, one of the best things about the Casa Holanda is the included breakfast, with five options to choose from. The on-site restaurant serves delicious sandwiches, snacks and entrées. Ask for a room further away from the entrance—the bars surrounding this place can make it noisy at night sometimes.   Ca. 14, 1B–75, Tel: 421-9390, E-mail: info@micasaholanda.com / casa.holanda@yahoo.com, URL: www.micasaholanda.com. Updated: Mar 26, 2011.

Restaurants

Dining in Taganga is a bit more expensive than in Santa Marta. A number of restaurants serve good international options. Alternatively, for a *comida corriente* (set meal) with fish, check out the beach eateries or the cheaper restaurants on Calle 16, a half-block from the *playa*. To save money, look for accommodation with kitchen facilities for its guests' use. Supertienda Taganga is the closest thing Taganga has to a supermarket; it is conveniently located on the beach road, across from the Parque de los Niños. Updated: Jul 05, 2011.

Los Baguettes de María !

(ENTREES: $4-6) Where do people go to get a nice hot sandwich, its sauce just beginning to seep into the soft interior of a crispy crust baguette? Las Baguettes de María, of course! Its 10 different choices, all named for regional attractions, have made this shop one of the best places to chow in Taganga. Everything is prepared with a cornucopia of toppings—and a lot of Doña María's love. While María prepares your baguette, play a board game at one of the picnic tables or sway in a hammock. The menu is in six languages. Las Baguettes de María is also a hostel that holds up to 22 people (from $13). Open Sunday–Thursday 10 a.m.–10 p.m., Friday 10 a.m.–6 p.m., Saturday only delivery after 6 p.m. Ca. 18, 3-47, in front of the soccer field. Tel: 421-9328, Cel: 316-386-2720 (Spanish)/680-6470 (English), E-mail: losbaguettesdemaria@hotmail.com URL: www.losbaguettesdemaria.com. Updated: Jul 05, 2011.

Restaurante Las Velas

(ENTREES: $6.50-60.50) One of Taganga's finest restaurants is right on the beach. Las Velas offers a full menu, including starters of soup, fruit or salads and light entrees such as seafood cocktail and ceviche. Full meals fresh from the sea come with rice, salad and plantains. If dining in a group, try one of the samplers with an assortment of surf and turf goodies or a paella for six. Daily 8 a.m.-11 p.m.; groups can make special arrangements for later service. Cra. 1, 18-95. Tel: 421-9072/420-6321. URL: www.lasvegastaganga.com. Updated: Mar 14, 2011.

Restaurante Bitácora

(ENTREES: $7-12) Word is spreading fast about Restaurante Bitácora. With well-prepared foods and a seaview porch shaded by potted plants and match-stick bamboo blinds, there is plenty to recommend about this small dining place. Main dishes feature chicken breast, beef or fish with salad and French fries. Restaurante Bitácora also serves vegetarians—try the vegetarian lasagna or the Ensalada Bitácora, with roasted peppers, mushrooms, roasted eggplant, mozzarella cheese, sesame seeds and olive oil. Open daily 8 a.m.–midnight (kitchen closes at 10:30 p.m.) Cra. 1, 17-13. Tel: 421-9234. Updated: Jul 05, 2011.

Mojito Restaurant Bar

(ENTREES: $8 and up) Mojito Restaurant Bar is fairly heavily patronized, in part due to their drinks special, which allows an hour

CARIBBEAN COAST

use of Internet in their adjoining Internet café. This deal is popular with the backpacker crowd. The restaurant itself is open and breezy, serving mainly Italian food. The food's good, though not particularly cheap. The delicious fruit, granola and yogurt breakfast is particularly tasty, with six kinds of fruit and berries. You can sit outside on tall bar stools, or inside in the restaurant proper. Service is also decent. Sometimes Mojito hosts live performances. Daily 10 a.m.-1 a.m. (food service until 11 p.m.). Ca. 14, 1B-61. Tel: 421-9149. Updated: Mar 14,2011.

A La Vista

A La Vista offers reasonably priced snacks, pizzas, crepes and more. Food comes in generous portions, considering the low-ish prices. For a tasty meal that is particularly good value for money, try one of the large selection of crepes. While the place is not much to look at from the outside, it has a view of the sea, is clean and has good service. A La Vista is open only in the evening. Ca. 14 and Cra. 1. Updated: Updated: Mar 14, 2011.

La Casita Del Mar Pizzeria Italiana

This attractive little place on the beach is a solid pizza/pasta restaurant, serving up tasty and familiar Italian favorites. Portion sizes are generous. With a view to the ocean, the friendly owners and staff aim to please and service is good. This place just has a few tables, so the atmosphere is intimate. On the beach. Updated: Mar 14, 2011.

Pachamama !

Pachamama has a reputation as one of the most popular places to dine in Taganga, and with good reason. The two French owners prepare exquisite, well presented food. The service is excellent. Delicious menu items include steak that melts in the mouth, a fiery chicken curry and fish cooked in a variety of styles. In addition, the eager-to-please staff serves good cocktails. While a little pricier than some of the other mid-range options, this place is worth the splurge. Ca. 16 and Cra. 2. Cel: 318-705-6821. Updated: Mar 14, 2011.

Tiki Bar

Right on the seafront, the swanky-for-Taganga Tiki Bar is also home to the surfing-beach gear store, Taganga Xtreme. Menu items include pizzas, sandwiches and snacks. Service at the alfresco café-restaurant is slow, mainly because the staff is busy with the shop in addition to serving food. Also, sometimes menu items can be unavailable. The food itself is decent enough. What Tiki Bar does best is coffee. Cra. 1, 14-50. Updated: Mar 14, 2011.

Nightlife

Taganga now has more places to kick back and have a drink at the end of a hard day of scuba diving or relaxing. Some hostels have rooftops bars. Many restaurants have Happy Hours, serving delicious tropical cocktails. If you're looking for a nightclub scene, though, there's not much. For that type of action, most travelers head into Santa Marta. (Though remember that if you return late, your only option will be by taxi; be sure to not drink up your fare back!) Updated: Jul 08, 2011.

Matasuegra

At first glance this word seems to mean "Mother-In-Law Killer" in Spanish, but this bar actually takes its name from a type of firework. This is the townspeople's bar, with locals sitting out front drinking beer. The foreigners are welcomed in, with full-volume English-language music at times and a rasta décor. There are several small rooms inside to kick back. Open almost every day from 3 p.m. on. Ca. 14, between Cra. 1 and 2. Updated: Mar 14, 2011.

El Garage Bar

El Garage Bar is the oldest nightclub in Taganga. Whereas Matasuegra is more of a local hangout, Garage's clientele is almost exclusively foreigners and caters to foreign music tastes. With inside and patio seating, the backpacking crowd whiles away the nights drinking and dancing. The rumba happens on Wednesday nights, from 8 p.m. to 1 a.m. and from Thursday to Saturday from 8 p.m. to 3 a.m. Ca. 8, 2-127. Tel: 421-9003, E-mail: angelagarage@hotmail.com. Updated: Mar 14, 2011.

AROUND SANTA MARTA

CIÉNAGA

 3m   100,000   5

Amid banana and African palm plantations lies Ciénaga. Bustle and commotion rule the streets as buses en route to destinations along the coast or in the *zona bananera* stop here for passengers. At Calle 17 and Carrera 15 is the former railroad station and plaza, where on December 6, 1928, a massacre of striking banana workers occurred. In the middle of the market, the statue of Juan el Machete commemorates

74°12'15"W   74°6'15"W   74°0'15"W   73°54'15"W

Caribbean Sea

Bahía Neguange

Ensenada de Gayraca
Ensenada de Cinto
Ensenada de Guachiquita
Ensenada de Chengue

Bahía Concha
Isla de la Aguja
Playa Grande
Bahía de Taganga

Cabo San Juan de la Guia
Pueblito
PN Tayrona
Arrecifes
Gayroca
Villa Concha   Calabazo
Cañaveral

Taganga   Palangana
El Zaino

SANTA MARTA
Mamatoco
Río Piedras
Río Mendiguaca
El Mamey

PNN Sierra Nevada de Santa Marta
Machete Pelao

Minca
Río Guachaca

Aeropuerto Simón Bolívar   San Lorenzo
Mutahanzi

Punta de la Gloria
La Tagua
Alto de Mira

Río Toribio
Ciudad Perdida   **AROUND SANTA MARTA**

Río Córdoba
Ye de Ciénega
Ciénega

11°2345"N   11°1745"N   11°11'45"N   11°5'45"N

the victims. Ciénaga has a variety of lodging options, most of them basic hotels. If you can, make it for the town's famed Festival del Caimán in February, when the mythical man-beast comes to party down.

On the way to Ciénaga, 20 kilometers (12 miles) from Santa Marta, are the Aguas Termales de Ciénaga, or Cordobita, whose waters and mud are said to be curative (Open daily 9 a.m.–4 p.m., not safe after dark. Admission: $2.65). Between Ciénaga and Barranquilla is Santuario de Flora y Fauna Ciénaga Grande de Santa Marta, a complex of over 100 swamps in the Magdalena River delta. Updated: Mar 27, 2011.

Getting To and Away

Frequent buses leave from Santa Marta (every five minutes, 4:30 a.m.–6:30 p.m., 30 min, $1.70) and Barranquilla. If coming south from Valledupar or Aracataca, take a Barranquilla-bound bus and get off at Ciénaga.

To get to Aguas Termales de Ciénaga from Santa Marta, hop off at the Cordobita bridge. The entrance to the hot springs is near the gas station. Updated: Mar 29, 2011.

Things to See and Do

Santuario de Flora y Fauna Ciénaga Grande de Santa Marta

Santuario de Flora y Fauna Ciénaga Grande de Santa Marta is a 23,000-hectare (56,834-ac) mangrove ecosystem within the deltas of the Río Magdalena and rivers streaming from the Sierra Nevada de Santa Marta. Created in 1977, it was declared a Ramsar site in 1998 and a UNESCO Human and Biosphere Reserve in 2000. Its swamps are refuge for

CARIBBEAN COAST

mangrove foxes, chigüiros, manatees, caimans, boas, rattlesnakes, slider turtles and several types of monkeys, as well as flamingos and many other birds. The mangrove ecosystem was almost totally destroyed by the Troncal del Caribe highway's construction, which cut off its connection with the sea. However, thanks to conservation efforts, it is once again becoming a haven for many at-risk species.

A hiking path heads into the Ciénaga at Los Cocos (Km 12 via Barranquilla-Ciénaga). The national park service is working with the community at Villa Parque Isla de Salamanca to provide lodging and other tourism services. At El Jobo and La Conda are upper-scale cabins. Due to the swampy nature of the ground, camping is impossible anywhere else. The abundance of mosquitoes makes sleeping in hammock difficult.

To get there from Santa Marta or Barranquilla, travel as far as the Puente de la Barra, where you can hire a privately operated boat to take you south through the Ciénaga Grande de Santa Marta to the mouth of the Río Fundación and the El Jobo canal.

For more information about the Santuario de Flora y Fauna Ciénaga Grande de Santa Marta, stop by the national park office in Santa Marta (Ca. 17, 4-06. Tel: 423-0752). Updated: Mar 27, 2011.

ARACATACA

 40m　 34,000　☎ 5

All along the coast, locals will sometimes say when recounting some strange occurrence, "Well, it's a Macondo." Macondo has long represented the the commonplace nature of small-town absurdities. The inspiration for the fictional town of Macondo is a town deep in the heart of plantations, Aracataca, where Gabriel García Márquez was born and raised on the tales of his grandmother. A few short blocks away from the Arabesque church where García Marquez was baptized is the author's childhood home, the Casa Museo. If you're familiar with Garcia Márquez's work, a tour of this town will take you right back into his magical tales. The Casa del Telegrafista (featured in some of Gabo's works) is at Calle 9 5-30. Next to the railway station, Remedios lies upon an open book, yellow butterflies dancing around her. If you want to

stay in Aracataca for a while and check out why it is Macondo, there are several basic hotels. Catequeros are friendly—and great storytellers. Updated: Mar 27, 2011.

Getting To and Away

From Santa Marta, take any Fundación-bound bus as far as Aracataca (every half-hour 4:30 a.m.-6 p.m., 2 hr, $5). You'll be let off at the roadside. To get to the center of town, take a mototaxi ($0.75) or walk the kilometer (0.6 mi). A motocycle taxi will take visitors to all the main sights for about $12. Updated: Mar 29, 2011.

Things to See and Do

Casa Museo Gabriel García Márquez

(ADMISSION: free) In the rooms of Casa Museo Gabriel García Márquez, the future Nobel Prize winning author was raised by his grandparents. After several years of careful reconstruction based on the testimonies of neighbors and writings of the García Márquez clan, the house has been restored to its early-20th century essence. The 14 rooms exhibit grandfather's silver workshop and office, the kitchen where Gabo sat listening to his grandmother's tales of this land, which later would be known as Macondo, and the bedroom of the famed writer. Monday-Friday 8 a.m.-noon, 2-6 p.m.; Saturday, holidays 8 a.m.-1 p.m. Cra. 5, 6-21. Tel: 425-6588, E-mail: casamuseogabo@gmail.com. Updated: Mar 27, 2011.

Lodging

Don't expect luxury accommodations in Aracataca. Most hotels in this typical Caribbean village are basic *residencias*, or inns with common bathrooms and fans. There are a few acceptable budget options, as well as a backpacker's hostel. Updated: Mar 27, 2011.

Residencia Ocaña

(ROOMS: $5) Located in the back courtyard of a grocery store, this hotel is not exactly pleasing to the eye, but it's acceptable for a night. The ten rooms have private bathrooms, ceiling fans and TV. Doubles are also available. Ca. 8, 2-64. Cel: 313-506-5972/301-684-3975. Updated: Jul 01, 2009.

Residencia Bucaramanga

(ROOMS: $9-13) Another option along Calle 8, the Residencia Bucaramanga is a little more tidy than Residencia Ocaña, but still nothing to get excited about. The

CARIBBEAN COAST

twelve rooms come with private bathroom, ceiling fan and TV. A dormitory is available for larger groups. Ca. 8, 1-69. Cel: 313-542-8182. Updated: Mar 31, 2011.

The Gypsy Residence

(BEDS: $11, ROOMS: $28) The Gypsy Residence welcomes backpackers to Moconda. This small hostel, with only two double rooms and a six-bed dormitory, is intimate and inviting. Relax in the common room, hang out on the front patio, or swayin a hammock in the shady backyard. Backpackers will find everything they need here, including a kitchen. The owner, Tim, a Dutch Gypsy lost in the imagination of magic realism, invites guests to deepen their magical experience by joining his bicycle tour of Aracataca, visiting places associated with Gabriel García Márquez and his works. Ca. 9, 1-74. Cel. 321-251-7420/301-593-3691, E-mail: info@thegypsyresidence.com, URL: www.thegypsyresidence.com. Updated Jul 08, 2011.

PARQUE NACIONAL NATURAL TAYRONA!

Tayrona National Park is said to be one of the most beautiful spots in Colombia. The park consists of 37,000 acres of pristine beaches, coral reefs, mangrove forests, Tayrona Indian ruins, and a vast diversity of plant and animal species. There are more than 770 species of plants in the National Park. The true draw, though, is peace and quiet in a slice of Paradise. If you're looking for a truly secluded trip, head farther into the park, as the beaches closer to town tend to fill up with locals during weekends and holidays.

Various accommodation options are available inside the park. Book through Aviatur (see Tours under Santa Marta), the only agency with permission from the government to make bookings at the cabañas and lodges. Or, if you prefer a rustic, tropical experience, string your hammock up between two trees—just don't forget a mosquito net, and watch for falling coconuts. As a bonus, you might be able to reach a ripe mango from the comfort of your bed. Bring your own water, as it gets pricey. Also, be prepared for bugs and cool nights. Don't forget insect repellent, a flashlight and long sleeves, pants and socks.

The entry fee to Parque Nacional Natural Tayrona is $14 for foreigners, $7.25 for Colombians, and $4 for children 5-12 years old and students with ID; visitors under five and over 65 get in free. Pay at El Zaíno (access point for Cañaveral and Arrecifes), Calabazo and Palagana (access point for Bahía Neguanje and Playa Brava). The park service issues plastic bracelets, which allow reentry into the park.

Travelers should be aware that it is not unusual for people entering the park to be searched for drugs, as the park was once a hotbed for narcotic activities. Updated: Mar 27, 2011.

When to Go

The rainy season is from May-June and September-November. The eastern end of the park, where the Cañaveral and Arrecifes beaches are, receives up to 2,000 millimeters (78 in) of precipitation per year.

Parque Nacional Tayrona has become a popular destination for foreigners and Colombians alike, and during holidays the park gets crowded. During Christmas-New Years and other holidays, overnight visitors are limited to 3,000 in the Cañaveral-Arrecifes-Cabo San Juan del Guía sectors. The number of day trippers are not limited. For a more tranquil visit and for the sake of the wildlife, consider avoiding these peak times. Updated: Mar 27, 2011.

Getting To and Away

Parque Nacional Natural Tayrona is located along the main Caribbean highway, just east of Santa Marta.

From Santa Marta, take a Granero Super Estrella bus from the corner of Calle 11 and Carrera 11 to the park entry at El Zaíno (1 hr, $2.80). A jeep will take you the four kilometers (2.4 mi) to the parking lot (10 min, $1.10 per person). From there it is a five-minute walk to the crossroads for Cañaveral and Arrecifes. Cañaveral is a five-minute walk to the right; Arrecifes is a 45-minute walk to the left. If you prefer to go by horse, the charge is $12. Bikes are also available to rent.

From Santa Marta, transport for Palaganga (access point for Bahía Neguanje and Playa Brava) departs from the mercado area from 6 a.m. to 4 p.m., with the last return to Santa Marta at 4 p.m. ($3 one way). For Bahía Concha, vehicles leave from Barrio Fundadores ($2 one way).

La Piscina is a 15-minute walk beyond Arrecifes, and Cabo San Juan del Guía is another 20 minutes. Updated: Mar 27, 2011.

CARIBBEAN COAST

Safety

The more remote areas of the park are reportedly much safer than they were 10 years ago. However, if hiking more isolated trails (e.g., from Calabozo to Cabo San Juan del Guía), it is advisable to do so in a group or with a guide. Take no valuables.

If visiting beaches or entering the park by boat, be aware of small-craft advisories issued during December and January due to high winds. Swimming is not safe at Cañaveral and Arrecifes, due to strong surf and currents.

Take proper protection against mosquitoes. At times yellow fever is reported in the area, and the park is closed entirely or entrance is restricted to those with proof of vaccination. Since 2006, a number of cases of dengue fever have been reported by travelers; it's unclear if the culprit zone is the park or nearby villages. Also, beware of ticks and other bloodsuckers when walking along overgrown paths. Watch out for bigger pests, too: errant, omnivorous donkeys, especially at Arrecifes, may munch on your belongings if you don't hang them out of reach. Updated: May 13, 2008.

Things to See and Do

The main reason people come to Parque Nacional Natural Tayrona is to relax, swaying in a hammock in the jungle by the sea. To stretch your legs, hike the Nueve Piedras trail and visit the archaeological Museo Chairama at Cañaveral. Or, climb up to the incredible ruins of El Pueblito. A longer trek is from Calabozo to Cañaveral.

Snorkeling can be quite rewarding at La Piscina, a large natural sea pool. A nudist beach lies beyond Cabo San Juan del Guía. Other less-visited beaches are Bahía Concha and Bahía Neguanje, both easily accessible from Santa Marta. Certain zones of the park allow scuba diving and fishing, and tour operators in Santa Marta and Taganga can help you plan excursions. Updated: Mar 29, 2011.

Museo Chairama and Sendero Nueve Piedras

At Cañaveral, visitors to PNN Tayrona can learn a bit more about Tayrona culture. Museo Chairama has a 7,000-piece collection of items from that pre-Hispanic culture, displayed in two galleries. The artifacts are from El Pueblito and other sites within the park. Beginning at the museum is Sendero Nueve Piedras (1 km, 0.5 hr). The interpretive trail, which cuts through the jungle to nine rocks that the Tayrona nation used for rituals, explains Tayrona cosmology. The hike ends at El Mirador, with great views of the coast. The museum and trail are at the Cañaveral sector. From Arrecifes, it is about a 45-minute walk. (Monday-Friday 8 a.m.-noon, 2-5 p.m. Cañaveral sector. Tel: 420-4504, E-mail: caribe@telesantamarta.net.co). Updated Jul 10, 2011.

La Piscina !

La Piscina is a natural sea pool surrounded by rock and reef. Large and tranquil with warm waters, La Piscina is home to many species of colorful fish, which dart among the coral. Manta rays silently wing through the liquid blue, the white sand billowing beneath their forms. Snorkelers can follow a *sendero subacuático*, or underwater trail, through the coral forests and marine grass meadows. Gear can be bought or rented in El Rodadero or Tangaga. La Piscina is a 15-minute walk beyond Arrecifes. Do not touch or step on the coral, as this may kill it. Pack all your trash out. Updated: Mar 27, 2011.

El Pueblito (Chairama) !

The Tayrona nation built their cities in the cool, lush forests of the mountains. Within this park are the wonderfully preserved ruins of Chairama (popularly known as El Pueblito), a once-great fortified town. Footfalls echo along the paved path from Cabo San Juan del Guía, which would have alerted El Pueblito's residents of approaching visitors. Throughout the ruins, you can observe drainage canals and other engineering feats. If you can't make it all the way to Ciudad Perdida, this site will give you a good sense of the Tayrona's impressive civilization. Guides are available on-site. From Cañaveral or Arrecifes, walk along the beach to Cabo San Juan del Guía; from there follow the sign up the mountainside. It takes 1.5 hours to climb the well-paved path through the forest. Updated: Mar 15, 2011.

Hike: Calabozo to Cañaveral

Parque Nacional Natural Tayrona's humid tropical forest blankets you with its very alive, vibrating sort of quiet, as cicadas hum and the wind rustles through leaves. In the mosaic of forest you can catch glimpses of howler monkeys swinging overhead or of iguanas, skinkers and other lizards darting through the brush. It is not hard to appreciate the reverence the Tayrona felt for these places.

Tayrona Culture

About 1,800 years ago, the Tayrona culture began on the Caribbean coast and up the Sierra Nevada de Santa Marta's lower slopes. Excavations at Bahía Chengue and Pueblito, both within PNN Tayrona, and at Teyuna (Ciudad Perdida) show that these sites were inhabited as early as 650 AD. In the 11th-12th centuries AD, the Tayrona began extending their territory deeper into the Sierra Nevada. In the 12th-15th centuries, Tayrona settlements had extensive road networks, as well as irrigation systems, agricultural terraces and drainage canals.

The Tayrona shared a Chibcha dialect and architectural styles. Their villages, however, were independent one from another. A few leaders held political influence over expanses of territory, but none controlled the entire Tayrona population or territory. This nation grew to be great traders, with routes extending to Central America and the Greater Antilles. They also worked in pottery, stone and gold, for which they are most famous.

In 1498, when Spaniard Gonzalo Fernández de Oviedo anchored in Santa Marta Bay, more than 250 Tayrona settlements stretched across 5,000 square kilometers (1,930 sq mi) from the coast to 2,700 meters (8,858 ft) altitude. The Tayrona fought the Spanish invasion, and networked with French and English pirates to burn Santa Marta several times in the late-16th century. In 1599 Santa Marta's governor, Juan Guiral Velón, conducted an intense military campaign that captured and killed 67 Tayrona leaders.

This extermination campaign and the introduction of new diseases decimated the Tayrona population. Surviving Tayrona retreated deep into the folds of the Sierra Nevada de Santa Marta. Some historians believe the Kogi are the Tayrona's modern-day descendants.

To learn more about the Tayrona, check out: Álvaro Soto-Holguin, *The Lost City of the Tayrona* (Bogotá: I/M Editores, 2006); Carl Henrik Langebaek, *The Pre-Hispanic Population of the Santa Marta Bays* (Pittsburgh: University of Pittsburgh, Dept. of Anthropology, 2005); Gerardo Reichel-Dolmatoff, *The Sacred Mountain of Colombia's Kogi Indians* (New York: E.J. Brill, 1990); Gerardo Reichel-Dolmatoff and Alicia Reichel-Dolmatoff, *Sierra Nevada de Santa Marta* (Medellín, Colombia: Editorial Colina, 1999); and Toby Muse, *"Lost City,"* Archaeology (Volume 57, Number 5, September/October 2004). Updated: Jul 26, 2011.

Perhaps the best way to see the forest is to walk the trail from Calabozo to Cañaveral. The path takes you from the park entrance at Calabozo to El Pueblito (2 hr). From here, follow the path laid by the Tayrona, your steps echoing along the stones, to Cabo San Juan del Guía (1.5 hr). Then take the jungle trail to La Piscina (20 min) and on to Arrecifes (15 min), finally arriving at Cañaveral and the main park entry at El Zaíno.

This hike is best done in a group or with a guide. Take no valuables. It is possible to do the trip in the opposite direction, from Cañaveral to Calabozo, although it is a more demanding trek, as much of it is uphill. If you opt to start a day-trip hike at Cañaveral, plan to begin early in the day; you must leave Santa Marta by 7 a.m.

You can eat at Cabo San Juan del Guía, Arrecifes or Cañaveral, although it is expensive.

To get here, take a bus to the Calabozo entry to the park. The route is is well-marked by signs and you can always ask for directions. Updated: Mar 25, 2011.

Beaches

Most visitors to Parque Nacional Natural Tayrona go to the beaches near Cañaveral and Arrecifes in the humid forest zone of the park. On the western end of Tayrona are other less-frequented beaches with quite different vegetation. Bahía Concha, the nearest beach to Santa Marta, has a dry, scrub forest habitat with mangrove trees at the mouth of the Quebrada Concha. The coral reefs make for excellent scuba diving. Playa Brava at the wide Bahía Neguanje also has dry scrub, mangrove forest and coral reefs, as well as an archaeological site, parking and restaurant. Camping is possible at both locations. To get to any of these beaches,

CARIBBEAN COAST

see Getting To and Away. At present, the park entry fee is only charged for Neguanje, and not for Bahía Concha; this will probably change in the future. Updated: Mar 27, 2011.

Tours

There are no tour operators within Parque Nacional Natural Tayrona. Individuals at the El Zaíno-Cañaveral car park have horses for hire (pay extra for a guide). Day excursions to Tayrona, including hiking from Calabozo to Cañaveral, can be arranged with tour operators in Santa Marta and Taganga. The tourist agency Aviatur in Santa Marta handles the park's cabañas at Cañaveral and Arrecifes. All scuba shops in Santa Marta and Taganga offer dives at the many bays lacing the park's coastline. Taganguero fishermen can take you on fishing expeditions to Granale in the extreme west of the park. Updated: Mar 27, 2011.

Lodging

Lodging in Parque Nacional Natural Tayrona goes from one extreme to the other. At Cañaveral you have a full-luxury spa, privately operated by Aviatur; this agency also has not-too-bad cabañas at Arrecifes, as well as campsites. On the other end of the scale are hammocks spaces, campsites and simple cabins run by families at Arrecifes. All in all, accommodations are comparatively expensive at Tayrona, but the nature and peacefulness are priceless. Camping is also possible at Cabo San Juan del Guía.

A number of campsites and lodges have opened up just outside the park boundaries, yet claim to be "in" Tayrona Park. Check the business' location on a map before making a reservation, if you are determined to stay within the park proper. Updated: Mar 25, 2011.

Independent Lodging

(HAMMOCKS: $8.50-13, CAMPING: $11-15) For many years, families have owned and operated lodging options within the park, specifically at Arrecifes. That is where most backpackers head, to sway in a hammock slung in an *enrramada* (open-sided, palm-thatch shelter). This is the ultimate Eden, with the surf's wash just meters away. One of the options at Arrecifes is Camping Don Pedro, which has hammocks, camping and cabañas (Tel: 315-320-8001/317-253-3020, E-mail: fincadonpedro@latinmail. com / fincadedonpedro@hotmail.com). Prices are uniform between these places. A family at Cabo San Juan del Guía also rents hammocks and camp sites (hammock $13, camping $15). Updated: Apr 12, 2011.

Concesión Tayrona

(ROOMS: $195-292, CAMPING: $6.50-11) These eco-huts at Cañaveral are styled on traditional Tayrona houses, but come with all the modern comforts. The spa offers every luxury treatment imaginable, including even a caviar massage. The cabins at Arrecifes are less opulent. Aviatur also provides campsites and hammock spaces (hammock and mosquito net not available to rent) for travelers with simpler tastes and slimmer budgets. Ca. 15, 3-20, Santa Marta. Tel: 423-5655, E-mail: carlosrheebilcock@aviatur.com.co / reservasparques@aviatur.com.co, URL: www.aviatur.com. Updated: Mar 15, 2011.

Restaurants

All restaurants in Tayrona are associated with lodging establishments and can be pricey for budget travelers. A basic vegetable and rice plate costs $6, and a fish meal costs $8-12; a beer is $2 and water is $2.50. Many backpackers and shoe-string travelers prefer to buy supplies in Santa Marta. If you choose to do this, please pack all your trash (especially bottles, cans and bags) back out to civilization. Fresh water, which can be purified, is available. Updated: Mar 27, 2011.

MINCA

Are you getting a bit tired of the heat, the sun, the salty sea? Then get away to where samarios (Santa Marta residents) go: Minca, a small village on the slopes of the Sierra Nevada de Santa Marta. Here, the climate is temperate, clouds swirl around the forested mountains and the air is scented with coffee blossoms on the fincas. Crystalline pools of cool, sweet water await you. Several farms and country houses lodge guests thirsting to enjoy this magical landscape for a longer while.

Getting To and Away

Pick-up trucks and other transport leave from Calle 11 and Carrera 12 in Santa Marta (every 1.5 hr 9 a.m.–4 p.m., last return to Santa Marta 5 p.m., 1 hr, $2.75). A direct taxi from Santa Marta costs about $27 one way. Updated: Apr 05, 2011.

Lodging

Casa Loma Minca

(CAMPING: $5.75, HAMMOCKS: $7, ROOMS: $11-17) Casa Loma Minca, a hand-crafted wooden house set atop a hill, is the perfect place for travelers to get away from Santa Marta's sweltering heat and bustling streets. This hostel's bilingual British owners create a wonderfully peaceful retreat. Casa Loma offers camping, dorms and private rooms. From the tree-house-style porch, enjoy watching the sun set over the Caribbean and Santa Marta's nighttime lights glittering on the horizon. Spend the day relaxing in the many hammocks or strolling down the tropical garden's stone paths, or have a massage. The hostel's restaurant serves international-styled dishes for meat-lovers and vegetarians alike. Upon arriving in Minca, walk to the church and follow the signs from there. Walk up the staircase between the church and the pizza parlor, then continue past the school and sports court. The Hostel's gate is at the back of the sporting field. Cel: 313-808-6134, E-mail: casalomaminca@gmail.com, URL: www.casalomaminca.blogspot.com.

PARQUE NACIONAL NATURAL SIERRA NEVADA DE SANTA MARTA

On a clear day, the snow-streaked peaks of the Sierra Nevada de Santa Marta can be seen from the city of Santa Marta. This cordillera is the highest coastal range on the planet, only 45 kilometers (27 mi) from the sea. Its three crown jewels are Pico Cristóbal Colón (5,775 m/18,942 ft), Pico Bolívar (5,775 m/18,942 ft) and Pico Codazzi (5,375 m/17,630 ft). Much of the area—383,000 hectares (XX acr) of it—is protected lands. The Parque Nacional Natural Sierra Nevada de Santa Marta spreads out across parts of Magdalena, Guajira and Cesar Departments. It is the birthplace of 30 rivers. Animals like jaguars, mountain tapirs, condors, páramo deers, paujils and mountain parrots inhabit the forests. The Arhuaco, Kogui, Kankuama and Wuiwa indigenous nations also call this home.

Most of the Sierra Nevada is closed to outsiders. Still some deep recesses of the mountain range is a "hot zone" with coca cultivation and cocaine processing labs (especially on the Santa Marta side of the range), plus the perseverance of a few guerrilla and paramilitary forces. Likewise, the indigenous are fiercely protective of these mountains, which they consider sacred land, and resent outsiders intruding into their depths.

There are, however, several places we can visit, including Ciudad Perdida of Teyuna and the research station at San Lorenzo, which is the only access point into the national park itself (Admission: $10.50 Foreigners; Colombians: $4.50 adults,$2.25 children; persons under 5 years old or over 65 years, free). A yellow fever shot is necessary. The San Lorenzo station has hiking trails allowing visitors to observe wildlife, visit archaeological sites and get to know the region's indigenous people. San Lorenzo also has two 18-person cabin-dormitories (low season $13 per person per night; high season $18). Bring insect repellant, mosquito net, food and water (or water purification drops or filter). If you plan to cook in the cabin-dormitory kitchen, bring along propane gas or your own camp stove (all other utensils are provided).

Contact the national park office in Santa Marta for more information about the station's services, and a list certified guides and independent drivers to San Lorenzo (Calle 17, 4-06. Tel: 5-421-3805, E-mail: sierranevada@parquesnacionales.gov.co). Updated: Mar 27, 2011.

Getting To and Away

Public transportation for various villages on the northern slopes of the range leaves from Santa Marta's market area on Calle 11. For information on independent drivers to the San Lorenzo research station, visit the National Park office in Santa Marta. Some tour operators in Santa Marta and Taganga offer excursions into this part of the Parque Nacional Natural Sierra Nevada de Santa Marta. Also, it may be possible to find a guide in Palomino to take you there.

The Southern sector of the park is accessible from Valledupar, where several indigenous villages are easily reached. Updated: Mar 27, 2011.

CIUDAD PERDIDA (LOST CITY) !

Deep in the recesses of the Sierra Nevada de Santa Marta, in the upper Río Buritaca valley, lies one of the ancient Tayrona nation's most impressive cities, Teyuna, or Ciudad Perdida (Lost City). The archaeological site earns its name well. Until tomb robbers began raiding the city in July 1975, Teyuna was unknown to the white world.

In March 1976, the Colombian authorities were alerted of this new site and began to protect it from further sacking. For 10 years, the Instituto Colombiano de

5-Day Trek to Ciudad Perdida

The only authorized route is up the Río Buritaca valley. Tour operators' itineraries are essentially the same:

Day 1–At 8-9 a.m., tours leave Taganga and Santa Marta for El Mamey/Machete de Pelado (2-3 hr). After lunch, the trek to Ciudad Perdida begins. The uphill path has some stretches that are in good condition, and others that are muddy. Some sections have little shade. There is one river crossing. After about 3 hours, trekkers arrive at the first camp, which has hammocks with mosquito nets strung in a roofed shelter and showers. Dinner is served.

Day 2–After a 7 a.m. breakfast, trekkers strike out for a relatively easy, 2.5-4 hour hike uphill to the next camp. Along the way is a waterfall. After lunch and a swim in a river near camp, hikers visit the traditional Kogi village, Mutanyi.

Day 3–This day begins with the wake-up call at 5-6 a.m. for breakfast. Afterwards, the trek begins, with several river crossings (the first in a cable car) and lots of uphill stretches. After 4-6 hours, hikers arrive at the campsite, where dinner is served. This night's lodging is in tents.

Day 4–After an early breakfast, trekkers set off for Ciudad Perdida. The one-hour hike cuts through jungle, then fords a river and continues up the 1200 steps to the site. After spending 3-4 hours exploring Teyuna with a guide (and lots of heavily armed Colombian soldiers), hikers head back to camp for lunch. Then it's downhill to Day 2's camp (3-4 hours), where they dine and sleep.

Day 5–Breakfasting before dawn, hikers begin the long-day hike (5-8 hr) downhill to El Mamey, taking a swim break along the way. After lunch at El Mamey, it's back to Santa Marta and Taganga, arriving at 5:30 or 6 p.m.

Rains can delay departure times. Most agencies provide snacks along the way. The depth and strength of rivers depend on recent rains.

Updated Jul 28, 2011.

Antropología e Historia (ICANH) carried out in-depth research and restoration projects. Because of the dense vegetative coverage, about 85 percent of the ruins were still well-preserved. After clearing away the jungle, Teyuna opened to the public in 1981. Since then, Ciudad Perdida has become one of the must-do treks in Colombia.

Tayrona architecture is distinguished in the manner of construction. First, the sides of steep mountains were terraced with containment walls and drainage ditches. Then atop the terraces, round buildings were constructed. Settlements were connected with an extensive network of stone roads. Because of the steep terrain (as much as 60 percent incline), defensive walls were not necessary.

Within Teyuna, which covers 30 hectares (74 ac) at an altitude of 900-1,200 meters

(2,953-3,937 ft), are the ruins of over 200 structures, including living quarters, stone roads and staircases, terraces, canals, plazas, ceremonial buildings and storehouses. The North sector has the oldest buildings, dating to the Neguanje Period (650 AD). These were used until 1100-1200 AD, and built over 1200-1600 AD.

In the upper Río Buritaca valley, 26 other sites have been discovered. Because of its size and monumental character, it is believed Teyuna was the political seat for the region. Some archaeologists estimate Teyuna itself had a population of 1,500-2,000 and with the surrounding settlements, the region's inhabitants numbered over 10,000. Ciudad Perdida was abandoned between 1580 and 1650 AD, but continued to be and remains sacred ground to the Kogi and other indigenous peoples of the Sierra Nevada.

PACKING LIST
Ciudad Perdida Trek

When you go on the Lost City hike you need to be prepared for jungle heat and humidity. Don't forget your sunscreen. Mosquitoes are prevalent and you'll want plenty of repellent, and to keep yourself covered up, so that you minimize the number of bites. Be sure you are up-to-date on your tetanus and yellow fever vaccinations. Finally, one of the biggest challenges on the hike is to keep your stuff dry, so be sure to bring a few plastic bags with you for this purpose. **Do not use army clothing or gear.** You will need:

• Day pack
• Plastic bags (including one to pack out trash and another to keep wet clothes in)
• Photocopies of passport or ID
• Some cash
• Large water bottle
• Flashlight or Headlamp
• Pocket knife

• 2 lightweight hiking pants and/or shorts
• 2 or 3 lightweight hiking tops
• Extra set of clothes (packed in plastic bag)
• Warm top layer or two
• Warm pants/long underwear
• Rain wear (jacket and pants)
• Swimwear
• Socks
• Underwear
• Baseball Cap
• Hiking boots (but not leather; once wet these won't dry)
• Sandals or tennis shoes (for river crossings)

• Basic first aid kit with moleskin, bandages, a small tube of anti-itch cream, antihistamine tablets (Benedryl, difenhidramina)
• Sunscreen
• Sun Glasses
• Insect Repellent
• Insect repellent soap
• Lightweight camping towel
• Personal toiletries – including biodegradable soap and shampoo
• Toilet paper (kept in plastic bag)

Optional:
• Hiking poles
• Binoculars
• Camera
• Extra batteries
• Playing cards
• Lightweight sleeping bag – or alternatively use the blankets provided
• Peanuts, granola bars, raisins and chocolate (for energy while trekking)

Updated: Jul 27, 2011.

CARIBBEAN COAST

Ciudad Perdida lies deep in undisturbed jungle. Among the 628 bird species of the Sierra are several endemic species of toucanets, toucans, chachalacas, hummingbirds, woodpeckers and parakeets. Resident mammals include paca, agouti, coati, brocket deer, peccary and wild cats like the jaguar and ocelot. Howler monkeys visit the ruins. It is common to encounter serpents in the park; most are non-venomous with the exceptions of the fer-de-lance and the coral, both of which are deadly.

ICANH (URL: www.icanh.gov.co) has a guide to Teyuna in Spanish and English that can be downloaded for free. At present, the only authorized route to Teyuna is up the Río Buritaca valley. ICANH, the national park office and indigenous authorities require treks be done with a guide. Helicopter fly-overs are forbidden. Also, at the request of the indigenous, overnight stays in Teyuna are now prohibited. The number of visitors admitted to the archaeological site is limited to 50 per day. In 2003 a group of foreigners were kidnapped by an armed group; there were no such incidents known before or that have occurred since that event. The area is heavily patrolled by Colombian military. Updated Jul 27, 2011.

La Ciudad Perdida (Lost City) Hike

Treks to Teyuna (or Ciudad Perdida) combine the opportunity to see some of Colombia's natural beauty with a fascinating insight into the ancient indigenous Tayrona culture. Usually a five-day trek, the moderately difficult, 40-kilometer (25-mi) hike passes though the Sierra Nevada de Santa Marta's incredible rainforest, taking you across various streams and rivers, through Kogi Indian communities, alongside a beautiful waterfall and finally up a set of 1,200 or so steps to this immense ancient site.

To get to Cuidad Perdida, use a tour operator from Santa Marta or Taganga. Agencies authorized to run the trek have agreed upon a standard price of $280 for an all-inclusive five-day/four-night hike. This fee includes transportation, guide (usually Spanish-speaking, though English translators are available), lodging (usually hammocks with mosquito nets), food, water, entry fee and insurance. Travelers carry their own packs; mules haul the food. Solo travelers or small groups need not worry about finding companions for the trek; tour operators compile a list of people who want to go to Ciudad Perdida and send out groups of

four to 12 almost every day. Sometimes, when demand is low, operators group together with others. During the tourist high seasons, the end-of-year and Semana Santa (Easter) holidays, advance reservations are necessary. Facilities along the way are basic.

Entry to the park is limited to 50 people per day, and tickets are distributed among the authorized operators; thus, making the trip with an independent guide is not advised. Local authorization is essential as your guide will be required to provide legitimate documentation and a visiting permit during the tour. Always check beforehand what equipment is necessary as different operators require you to bring different things, though you can check out **VIVA's Lost City Hike Packing List**. Be sure you are up-to-date on your tetanus and yellow fever vaccinations.

While on many days you'll only be hiking a few hours a day, this trek cannot be considered "easy." The jungle climate makes the hike challenging. Daytime temperatures average 26°C (79°F) with high humidity and frequent rains. At night, it gets down to 18-22°C (64-72°F). This part of the Sierra Nevada experiences two dry seasons (*verano*, January-March, and *veranillo*, July-August) and two rainy seasons or *invierno* (April-June and heavier rains September-December). The depth and strength of rivers depend on recent rains. The park may close temporarily, depending on natural, access, maintenance and other conditions.

A few of ICANH's recommendations about trekking to Ciudad Perdida are:

. Pack only the essential; limit weight to 10 kilograms (22 lb).

. Do not damage the ruins or natural environment.

. Do not bother the wildlife.

. Respect the privacy of locals: Do not enter their homes, or take photos of them or their belongings without permission.

. There is no cell phone reception or other communication means in the park.

To enhance your overall experience and learn about Tayrona culture, check out Santa Marta's Museo de Oro Tayrona before the trek. Updated: Jul 28, 2011.

CARIBBEAN COAST

VALLEDUPAR

 169m   348,000   5

From Bucaramanga, the north highway continues to Bosconia (405 km/243 mi). There the road turns eastward, skirting the Sierra Nevada de Santa Marta mountain range. From a night bus the sunrise reflected off the snow peaks is spectacular. After another 89 kilometers (53 mi) the road arrives at Valledupar, the purported birthplace of Vallenato music. It is the capital of Colombia's newest department, César, which was carved out of the old Magdalena political district in 1967. This is the beginning of the Caribbean region of Colombia. The nearby Sierra Nevada de Santa Marta is home to four indigenous nations. The Valledupar region is the furthest south of Wayuu territory. This city's main square, Plaza Alfonso López, is a mango tree-lined island in a sea of wonderful colonial buildings with plaques proclaiming which figures of Valduparense, or Vallenato, history lived within. Updated: Mar 27, 2011.

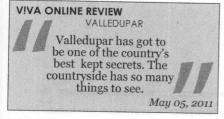

V!VA ONLINE REVIEW
VALLEDUPAR

Valledupar has got to be one of the country's best kept secrets. The countryside has so many things to see.
May 05, 2011

History

When Spaniard Hernando de Santana and his legions arrived here in 1550, Tupe and Chimila indigenous occupied this valley of the Río Guatapurí, or Cold Water River. The invaders called their new city Ciudad de los Santos Reyes del Valle del Cacique Upar—or, to make it short, Valle de Upar. This shortened to today's Valledupar. According to legend, the Tupe set Valledupar on fire and poisoned the water supplies in revenge for the Spaniards' ill treatment, but the Virgen del Rosario miraculously rescued the Europeans. The settlement was refounded and the Spaniards promptly hung 15 Tupe chiefs on La Popa hill in retaliation. In 1813, María Concepción Loperena Fernández de Castro declared Valledupar's independence from Spain and sent 300 horses to Simón Bolívar. During the 1,000-Day War (1899-1902), Valledupar was witness to some of the battles.

In the late 20th century this region became a hotspot in the country's civil war, with clashes first between the ELN and government forces followed by a cleansing by paramilitaries. In 2008, the departmental government faced charges of connections with *paracos*, or paramilitaries. Updated: Mar 18, 2011.

When to Go

The rainy season lasts from February to April. The rest of the year the weather is deliciously hot in this valley, with daytime temperatures reaching 32-36°C (90-97°F), and sometimes peaking above 40°C (104°F). Evening temperatures drop to a balmy 22-24°C (72-75°F). Updated: Apr 23, 2008.

HOLIDAYS AND FESTIVALS

Valledupar is most famous for its Vallenato Music Festival, but there are other fiestas where you can catch well-known groups live.

January 6—Día de los Santos Reyes is also the founding of the Spanish city; celebrated with civic ceremonies, a marathon and free Vallenato concerts at the Parque de la Leyenda Vallenata.

Easter Week (Semana Santa)—Santo Ecce Homo, the city's patron saint, is feted here and in nearby Valencia on Holy Monday; on Maudy Thursday, the penitents and Veronicas have a procession.

April—The Festival de la Leyenda Vallenata (Vallenato Music Festival) begins the last weekend of this month. Updated: Mar 18, 2011.

Getting To and Away

BY BUS

The main bus terminal is about 3.5 kilometers (2 mi) from the center, at Carrera 18D (Av Simón Bolívar) and Calle 45, where the Cacique Upar monument is.

To Maicao: Cootracegua (hourly 4:45 a.m.-2:45 p.m., 4 hr, $12). Taxis from in front of the bus terminal, leave when full ($11.55, beware of overcharging). Other buses from Calle 44, near terminal.

To Riohacha: Frequent 5 a.m.-3 p.m., 4.5 hours, $14—Cootaxiexpress, Cooprovincia. Other buses from Calle 44, near terminal. Or take a Maicao-bound bus to Cuatro Vías crossroads and flag down another to Riohacha.

To El Banco: Cootracegua (7 departures 3 a.m.-12:30 p.m., 5 hr, $15).

CARIBBEAN COAST

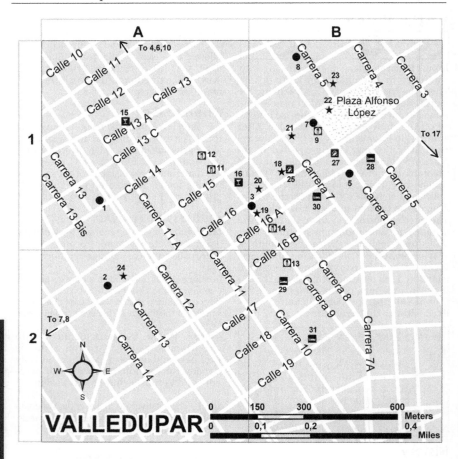

VALLEDUPAR

To Mompós: Lalo (pick-up truck; 4:30 a.m., 4 hr, $28), Cootracegua (bus; 5 a.m., 6:30 a.m., 9:30 a.m., 5 hr, $17)

To Medellín: 3 buses 3-7 p.m., 12 hours, $61—Copetran, Brasilia

To Santa Marta: hourly 4 a.m.-2 p.m., 4hr, $12-14—Costa Line, Cootracegua, Cootracosta. Or take a Barranquilla-bound bus as far as Aracataca, and transfer there for Santa Marta.

To Barranquilla: hourly 5 a.m.-4 p.m., 4 hours, $12-13—Costaline, Cootracosta, Cootracegua, Brasilia.

To Cartagena: Brasilia (3:45 a.m., 10 a.m., 11:45 a.m., 6 hr, $22)

To Bucaramanga: 7 buses 4-9:45 p.m., 8 hours, $39—Copetran, Brasilia

To Bogotá: 8 buses 1-8:30 p.m., 15 hours, $69—Copetran, Brasilia

Pick-up tracks and other transport to villages in the Sierra depart from near the Galería Popular.

To Pueblo Bello: Cootransnevada (Cra 7A, 18B-37. Tel: 574-4115) (leave when full 5 a.m.-3 p.m., 1 hr, $5.50). Transport from Pueblo Bello to **Nabisimake** departs once daily, 8-9:30 a.m. (3 hr, $8).

To La Mina/Atánquez: public pick-up from Galería Popular (Cra 7) (frequent, 8 a.m.-2 p.m., 0.75/1.25 hr, $3.50 to either destination). Continues to Guatapurí (2 hr, $8).

BY AIR
Valledupar's Aeropuerto Alfonso López is located on the road to Codazzi, south of

● Activities

1 Alianza Colombo Francesa A1
2 Biblioteca Pública
  Departamental A2
3 Banco de la República B1
4 Balneario Hurtado A1
5 Casa de la Cultura B1
6 Centro Comercial
  Guatapurí Plaza A1
7 Fundación Pentagrama B1
8 Sayco B1

⬠ Eating

9 Café Plaza Mayor B1
10 Jerusalem Express A1
11 Panaderia Árabe A1
12 Restaurante Muralla China A1
13 Restaurante Nandoburguer B2
14 Restaurante Vegetariano B1

⬚ Nightlife

15 Bartolomé A1
16 Café de la Madres A1

★ Services

17 Academia Andrés "Turco" Gil B1
18 Banco de Bogotá A1
19 Bancolombia B1
20 Banco Popular B1
21 Escuela Talento Vallenato Rafael
   Escalona B1
22 Municipal Tourism Office B1
23 Post Office B1
24 Provincial Turismo B2

⬚ Shopping

25 Artesanías Ebratt B1
26 Asociacion de Artesanos
   De Valledupar (See 25)
27 Tienda Compai Chipuco B1

⬚ Sleeping

28 Hostal Provincia Valledupar B1
29 Hotel Los Cardones B2
30 Hotel Vajamar B1
31 Residencia Kennedy B2

the city. A taxi there costs $3. **Avianca** and **Aires** have direct flights to **Bogotá** ($130-200). Check for specials; sometimes it costs just a bit more to fly than to take a bus. Updated: Mar 29, 2011.

Getting Around

Three modes of transportation are used for getting around Valledupar: taxis (destinations within the city $2.25), motorcycles (you ride on back; $0.50-0.85 per ride) and *busetas*, or city buses (scarce on Sunday; $0.50). Updated: Mar 18, 2011.

Safety

The nighttime streets are well-patroled by police. Still, you should take common-sense measures at late hours. Locals warn about going to Parque de la Leyenda Vallenata, the University and Balneario Hurtado at odd hours—go when there are plenty of people, such as late afternoons.

The Sierra Nevada de Santa Marta mountains are closed to any independent trekking, due in part to the wishes of the four indigenous nations. Some deep recesses of the mountain range are still considered a "hot zone" with coca cultivation and co-caine processing labs, plus the perseverance of a few guerrilla and paramilitary forces. On this side of the Sierra you can visit Pueblo Bello, Nabusimake, Guatepurí and other indigenous villages. Dengue fever has occasionally been reported in Valledupar. Updated: Mar 18, 2011.

Services

TOURISM

You can pick up information about Valledupar at the **city's tourism office** in the base of the bandstand on Plaza Alfonso López (Monday-Friday 8 a.m.-1 p.m. and 3-6 p.m. Ca. 15, between Cra. 5 and Cra. 6. Tel: 584-6981, E-mail: liluzamo@hotmail.com). The **provincial tourism office**, on the fourth floor of the Gobernación del Cesar, has information about the region (Monday-Friday 9 a.m.-noon and 3-5 p.m. Ca. 16 and Cra. 13. Tel: 574-8230, URL: www.gobcesar.gov.co). For tourist card or visa extensions, the Extranjería office of **DAS** is where you have to go (Monday-Friday 7:30 a.m.-noon and 2-6 p.m. Cra. 11A 15-42, Tel: 5-574-2833).

CARIBBEAN COAST

MONEY

Many of Valledupar's banks have branches throughout the city. All have 24-hour ATMs. The principal locations of a few banks are: **Banco Popular** (Ca. 16, 8-20) and **Banco de Bogotá** (Ca. 16, 7-46). **Bancolombia** (Cra. 9, near Ca. 16) changes American Express travelers checks and has a branch at Centro Comercial Guatapurí with extended hours (Monday-Friday 9 a.m.-7 p.m., Saturday 10 a.m.-7 p.m.; Sunday, holidays 10 a.m.-2 p.m. Ca. 19E, between Cra. 9A and Cra. 9C).

Most exchange houses deal only in bank check cashing, but not travelers checks. One exception is **Cambios y Negocios** (Monday–Saturday 8 a.m.-noon and 2-6 p.m. Ca. 16, 17-67), which exchanges cash dollars and Venezulan currency. Giros y Finanzas (Diagonal 16, 17-67, inside Supertiendas Olímpicas) is the Western Union agent.

KEEPING IN TOUCH

Edetel is your telecommunications stop; it has local, national and international call services, as well as internet (Monday-Friday 8 a.m.-noon, 2-6 p.m. Saturday 9 a.m.-noon. Ca. 15, 10-17). Shops and phone stands also offer local or national calls. On Calle 16B, between Carreras 9 and 10, are a bevy of inexpensive internet cafés. It appears no-one has Skype. The **post office** is a half-block from the main plaza (Monday-Friday 8 a.m.-5:45 p.m., Saturday 9 a.m.-1 p.m. Cra. 5, 14-81.)

MEDICAL

Valledupar's public health facility is Hospital Eduardo Arredondo Daza (Cra. 20, 43-63, Tel: 582-6784). There are other medical facilities and pharmacies on Calle 16, between Carreras 15 and 18. More pharmacies are on Carrera 7, between Calles 16 and 17.

CAMERA

On Calles 16 and 16A, between Carreras 7 and 8, are several camera shops that carry digital cameras and accessories, batteries and film. None can repair cameras, though.

RELIGION

As well as Catholic and Christian churches, Valledupar has a small Muslim community that meets to worship, but no mosque. Updated: Mar 18, 2011.

SHOPPING

Asociación de Artesanos de Valledupar

More than two dozen local artisan stalls line the one-story, mall-like Asociación de Artesanos de Valledupar. Handmade wares include molded white hats of the Arhuaco indigenous community of the Sierra Nevada de Santa Marta, densely woven bags of the Wayuu of the Guajira, black and white *sombreros de paja* (straw hats), and vallenato kitsch. You could even form your own vallenato band here if you want, with small accordions, *caja* drums and *guacharaca* (scraper). Monday-Saturday 8 a.m.-7 p.m., Sunday 8 a.m.-1 p.m. Ca. 16, 7-32. Updated: Mar 14, 2011.

Artesanías Ebratt

The Ebratt family has been creating arts and crafts for at least three generations as a member of the Asociación de Artesanos de Valledupar. One son, Ciro, crafts Vallenato and other knickknacks. Another son paints brilliant canvasses depicting the town's culture and life. Doña Esperanza, the mother, gives new life to old treadle sewing machines and other discarded items by turning them into works of art. The father is a cabinetmaker. The family also carries Arhuaco hats and bags, *chinchorros* (hammocks) and other crafts. Monday-Saturday 8 a.m.-7 p.m., Sunday 8 a.m.-1 p.m. Ca. 16, 7-32, local 13. Cel: 310-640-9536. Updated: Mar 19, 2011.

Things to See and Do

Visitors arriving in the cradle of vallenato music in other times than when the festival takes place have the chance to experience Valledupar for what it truly is—a small town with deep artistic roots. You can visit, or even study at, a music school or drop by one of the city's several cultural centers. Wander the streets and take in the colonial architecture of the center and the dozen monuments. To cool off on hot days, dip into the cold waters of Balneario Hurtado or of La Mina. The Sierra Nevada de Santa Marta on the western horizon is home to the Arhuaco villages of Pueblo Bello and Nabusimake, and the Kankuama ones of Atánquez and Guatapurí. Fauna fans can head out the road to Guacoche to find howler monkeys and macaws, or to Los Besotes nature sanctuary. Updated: Mar 19, 2011.

Balneario Hurtado

When Valledupar's heat gets to be a bit much, do as the locals do—head for Balneario Hurtado, a swimming hole where the Río Guatapurí's cool waters flow smooth and cold, pooling along the banks. Young men body surf the few mild rapids rushing by the boulders. Families come to swim, sit at a table or sling a hammock between the trees. There's more than a kilometer of shore, though there's no

Vallenato Music

Valledupar is one birthplace of vallenato, a musical genre reflecting the region's three cultures. A trio of instruments set the tone: accordion (from Europe), *caja* drum (from Africa) and the *guacharaca* (wooden scraper, from the indigenous nations). In recent years, keyboards, guitar, bass and other voices have been added. The three ethnicities are also reflected in the rhythms: Spanish *décima* lyrics, African syncopation and indigenous melancholy. The four styles of vallenato are merengue, paseo, puya and son.

In olden days, accordionists wandered Colombia's Caribbean region, spreading the news—much like medieval troubadours. The most legendary accordionist was Francisco el Hombre, famous for beating the Devil in a squeezebox competition. The songs also are lauds. At *parrandas* (street parties), friends gather to honor someone, singing and drinking whiskey for several days on end. At these events, dancing is not done: the purpose is to listen and share.

Vallenato does have a traditional dance called El Pilón. Women, dressed in long, full-skirted dresses and men in white outfits, sway through Valledupar's streets on the opening day of the **Festival de la Leyenda**, a five-day musical feast beginning the last Wednesday of April (URL: www.festivalvallenato.com). Competitions decide the new kings of professional, amateur, youth, children and unrecorded song categories. Another contest is of Piquería, or improvised vallenato song. The festival was founded in 1968. Thousands of musicians, celebrities and common folk descend on the city to sing, dance and drink.

During the rest of the year, visitors to Valledupar can enjoy vallenato rhythms at holiday concerts. **Café Plaza Mayor** features the music on Friday and Saturday nights, and **Centro Comercial Guatapurí** brings the best musicians to its grounds on Wednesdays. The next generation of talent may be heard at the **music schools** Escuela Talento Vallenato Rafael Escalona and Academia Andrés "Turco" Gil. **Sayco**, headquarters of the region's vallenato composers, has a small museum. On display is a Chinese *sheng*, the accordion's ancestor (Monday-Friday 7:30 a.m.-noon and 2-5:30 p.m. Cra. 5, 13C-40. Tel: 574-3448). **Tienda Compai Chipuco** also has a museum, dedicated to festival co-founder Consuelo Araújo Noguera. The shop sells books, music CDs and local crafts. On the back patio is a cheap restaurant (Ca. 16, 6-05, Plaza Alfonso López. Cel: 316-454-2235). Many of Valledupar's monuments represent symbols associated with vallenato music, or illustrate famous songs. **Patillal** village, birthplace of many composers, has a monument-studded plaza dedicated to its native sons (30 km/18 mi northwest of Valledupar). Updated: Apr 26, 2011.

guarantee you'll be able to avoid the crowds. There are no bathrooms or changing facilities. The party goes on well into the night any day of the week, though locals warn the area can be unsafe after dark. Watch for bottle caps and glass along the banks. The beach is at the north edge of the city at the Río Guatapurí. Take any van that says it is heading for the "Universidad," which is next door to the Balneario ($0.50). The last bus back to town is at 6 p.m. After the last bus, hail a taxi ($2.25). Updated: Mar 19, 2011.

The Cultural Centers of Valledupar

Culture in Valledupar isn't just limited to Vallenato music. **Alianza Colombo Francesa** (Cra. 13A, 13C-66. Tel: 570-3344) has monthly art exhibits, movies (Thursday 6:30 p.m.), concerts and other free events. **Fundación Pentagrama** (Cra. 6, 15-12) presents piano concerts Thursday 7 p.m. The **Casa de la Cultura** (Ca. 16A and Cra. 6) has a small museum; music and dance rehearsals occur on its front patio. **Banco de la República** (Cra. 9 16-13) offers art exhibits and lectures. **Biblioteca Pública Departamental Rafael Carrillo Lúquez** (Ca. 15 and Cra. 14) also has occasional events. **Centro Comercial Guatapurí**, on the road to Balneario Hurtado, has free vallenato concerts (Wednesday 5-6 p.m.). If you are in the mood for a movie, there is a Cinemark theater in the same mall. Updated: Mar 19, 2011.

CARIBBEAN COAST

The Road To Guacoche

The road to Guacoche, a small village where pottery is made, is a wildlife watchers paradise. Rice paddies on either side of a tree-lined lane attract a variety of fauna. Hopping through the canopy are red howler monkeys. Their cries fill the early morning and late afternoon air. The elusive brown capuchin monkeys also cling to the leafy boughs. Upon those branches, hawks and eagles stoically perch, scanning the landscape for their next meal. Dozens of species of birds wing across the sky, including macaws. The best times to spot wildlife are dawn and dusk. Like humans, birds seek cool places in the high heat of the day. Do not make any noises or otherwise bother the fauna. The turn off for the road to Guacoche is 3.6 kilometers (2 mi) north of Valledupar, past Balneario Hurtado. The first seven kilometers (4.2 mi) of the Guacoche road is where fauna can be sighted; Guacoche is another five kilometers (3 mi) down the road. Take a pick-up truck to the turn-off and walk or bicycle from there. A motorcycle taxi will costs about $5. Updated: Apr 26, 2011.

Vallenato Music Schools

Vallenato music isn't confined to festival time in April. You'll hear vallenato strains coming from stereos and from the locals themselves at any time of the year. To catch the next generation learning the trade, stop by some morning or evening to one of the local music schools, such as **Escuela Talento Vallenato Rafael Escalona** (Cra. 7 and Ca. 15) or the famous **Academia Andrés "Turco" Gil** (Ca. 31, 4-265, Tel: 582-4120). You can also sign up for classes if you would like to study the intricacies of this genre. Check a school's policies on visits before going; the schools listed above allow visitors. Updated: Mar 19, 2011.

Lodging

Hotels in Valledupar tend to be a bit expensive. Mid-range options are fairly basic and have an impersonal feel. Upper-priced choices generally are excellent. Hotels and apartment-hotels along Calle 19 and near the bus terminal on Carrera 18D (Av. Bolívar) guarantee a family atmosphere. Make reservations as early as December or January if you plan to visit during the April Vallenato Music Festival. Updated: Mar 19, 2011.

Residencias Kennedy

(ROOMS: $7-9) Residencias Kennedy is a no-frills inn—no plants surround the brick-tile courtyard and there are no TVs in the rooms. The 17 rooms only have double beds, night table and a ceiling fan to keep you cool. All rooms have windows. The elderly owner, Doña Raquel, and her assistant, Jairo, keep it relatively clean. Doña Raquel is a bit hard-of-hearing so she may take a while to answer the door. You can ask to use the laundry basin. Ca. 19, 9-102. Updated: Mar 19, 2011.

Provincia Hostel Valledupar !

(BEDS: $10-16, ROOMS: $26-31) Provincia Hostel Valledupar, located a block from the main plaza, is the perfect place for relaxing. The hostel has both dormitories and private rooms with fan or air conditioning, and many bathrooms to avoid showering bottlenecks. The hostel features many common areas, with game tables, hammocks and big screen TV. The clean kitchen is well equipped. Cristina and Miguel, the Colombian owners, are knowledgeable about what to see and do in the area. They have bikes for guests to use in their explorations of Valledupar. The nice, quiet atmosphere and friendly staff truly make you feel at home. Ca. 16A, 5-25. Tel: 580-0558, E-mail: info@provinciavalledupar.com, URL: www.provinciavalledupar.com. Updated: Mar 14, 2011.

Hotel Los Cardones

(ROOMS: $10.50-19) Hotel Los Cardones' quarters surround a back courtyard. The hotel has a restaurant and sitting room at the front of the building. Some rooms have air conditioning, others have more economical fans. All rooms have cold-water baths and cable TV. The rooms are a bit cramped with two to four beds each. If you want a room with only one bed, call ahead and the family will arrange it. Ca. 17, 9-74. Tel: 574-3023. Updated: Mar 14, 2011.

Hotel Vajamar

(ROOMS: $54-86) One of Valledupar's finest hotels, this establishment has 20 years experience in providing comfortable, tastefully decorated rooms to the discerning traveler. Some of the suites have views over the stunning Sierra Nevada de Santa Marta, and a few have balconies where you can enjoy a meal under the moon. The bathrooms are immaculate and have hot water. The pool out back is free to guests, but non-guests must pay. A Sunday BBQ with free use of the pool is open to all. Room prices include tax and insurance, plus an American breakfast buffet. Cra. 7, 16A-30. Tel: 574-3939, URL: www.hotelvajamar. Com. Updated: Mar 15, 2011.

Restaurants

A small Arab community is quite culinarily ac-

---

tive in Valledupar and sells Arabic food in both restaurants and shops. Chinese food is also available in the city. Otherwise, look forward to more fine Colombian cooking and rotisserie chicken. Some very expensive gourmet and fusion-cuisine restaurants are on Carrera 9, especially between Calles 9 and 11.

The city's central market, Galería Popular, bustles from 6 a.m. to 4 p.m. (between Cra. 7 and Cra. 7A, Ca. 18A and Ca. 18B). The public market is at Carrera 12 and Calle 21. Olímpica (Cra. 9 and Ca. 14) and El Éxito (Cra. 7, 16A-79) supermarkets are conveniently in the heart of the city. For hard-to-find delicacies, try the Carrefour in Centro Comercial Guatapurí. Updated: Mar 14, 2011.

Jerusalem Express ♪
(ENTREES: $3-8) At Jerusalem Express, Lebanese-born Ibraham and his Colombian wife have introduced valduparenses to healthy Middle Eastern cuisine. They prepare quibbes, fatayer (meat or chicken turnovers), malfuf (stuffed cabbage leaves), parra (stuffed grape leaves), stuffed eggplant, cucumber or sweet pepper, and beef or chicken shwarma. There's plenty on the menu for vegetarians as well, such as spinach fatayer, garbanzo or eggplant tahini, and falafel shwarma. If you can't make up your mind, just order the combo plate. The final touch is a small bite of an Arabian dessert. Daily 4:30–11 p.m. Cra. 9, 7C-29. Tel: 573-7217 (bakery)/373-7217 (restaurant). Updated: Mar 19, 2011.

Café Plaza Mayor
(ENTREES: $3.50-15) At this favorite gathering place, Valledupar residents sit at tables on the tree-lined sidewalk, drinking beer and sharing news in the evenings. Inside, small rooms exhibit local artists' works. Another ambiance awaits patrons on the large back patio. There, groups of white sofas create intimate sitting areas. On the stage here, Café Plaza Mayor features live vallenato music Friday and Saturday nights. The restaurant serves sandwiches, steaks and other meals. Daily 9 a.m.-10 p.m. (or later). Cra. 6, 15-70. Tel: 571-2526, Cel: 310-641-2214. Updated: Apr 25, 2011.

Restaurante Vegetariano Vital
(LUNCH: $4) Around the corner from the Vital health store on Carrera 9 is the shop's vegetarian restaurant. A short staircase leads up to a four-table and counter affair where delicious meals are served. The daily lunch special comes with soup, main course and drink. During other times of the day, this vegan eatery offers healthy fast foods for breakfast and dinner. Vital also sells vegetarian "meats," whole-grain breads and fruit juices. Monday-Friday 7:30 a.m.-6:30 p.m. Ca. 16A, 8-65, 2nd floor. Tel: 580-6687, Cel: 315-519-5483. Updated: Apr 27, 2011.

Restaurante Nandoburguer
(ENTREES: $4-6) Despite the name, Restaurante Nandoburguer is better known for its hearty home-cooked meals than for its burgers. With two rooms of indoor seating and a few tables on the front patio, the waiters are kept busy attending to the crowd. At very busy times, like Sunday afternoons, be prepared to display the patience of a saint. The *comida corriente* comes with over a half-dozen choices for the main course. Daily 9 a.m.–9 p.m. Cra. 9, 16B-48. Updated: Mar 19, 2011.

Restaurante Muralla China
(ENTREES: $5-18) Valledupar's resident Chinese restaurant, Muralla China, has more than 80 Chinese dishes and a few international ones. Start off your meal with egg rolls or a seafood cocktail before moving on to a classic Chinese plate, in either half or full order. Mains include chow fan (fried rice), chop suey, chow mein or lo mein prepared with chicken, beef or seafood. Vegetarian options are available as well. Daily 11 a.m.–10 p.m. Cra. 9, 14-30. Tel: 580-0909. Updated: Mar 19, 2011.

Panadería Árabe
Entering Panadería Árabe is like walking into a neighborhood Mediterranean shop. It may call itself a bakery, and sure, there's pita bread and baklava, but that's only the beginning. The shelves are full of everything a native Mediterranean might miss from home, including green olives, artichoke hearts, stuffed eggplant, couscous, pickled vegetables, halvah and olive oil. Turkish candies, dried dates and apricots, and natural pistachios round out the selection. It's the perfect place to pick up a picnic. Daily 8 a.m.-9:30 p.m. Cra. 9, 14-94. Tel: 5-570-8465. Updated: Mar 14, 2011.

Nightlife
Despite being the home of vallenato music, very few nightclubs feature live vallenato bands—or live music at all, for that matter. Most establishments play prerecorded music, and vallenato is the most common, of course. As in many towns

in Colombia, clubs are only open on weekends. The most common beverages are beer, *aguardiente* and whiskey, the liquor associated with vallenato music. Updated: Mar 19, 2011.

Bartolomé

You don't have to come to Valledupar in April to catch live vallenato music. During the off season Bartolomé is one of the few places in town where you can catch bands playing those down-to-earth melodies. Join the crowd by downing some *traguitos* (shots) and singing along about life and love under the roof of this open-sided nightclub. Bathed by the nocturnal breeze and the community vibes, you'll quickly discover why this music is so beloved. Friday and Saturday nights. Cra. 11 and Ca. 13A. Updated: Mar 14, 2011.

Café de las Madres

(DRINKS: $3-15) When the setting sun paints the sky, Valduparenses head to Café de las Madres, tucked behind Parque de las Madres. The wrought-iron garden tables fill quickly with colleagues and couples meeting to have an Atardecer Vallenato (cappuccino and whiskey) or one of the creative coffee shakes, with or without a kick. Other end-of-day beverages include liquored coffees, cocktails, wine, beer, whiskey and vodka. Don't wait for evening to come—escape the day's heat with an iced coffee or a cool glass of white wine. Café de las Madres serves only organically grown Sierra Nevada coffee. Monday–Saturday 8 a.m.–11 p.m. Cra. 9 and Ca. 15, Parque de las Madres. Cel: 301-779-1259, E-mail: cliffordbonilla@hotmail.com. Updated: Mar 19, 2011.

AROUND VALLEDUPAR

PUEBLO BELLO & NABUSIMAKE

The village of Pueblo Bello is in the Sierra Nevada de Santa Marta, on the edge of Arhuaco territory. From here an arduous road winds up to Nabusimake (San Sebastián), a ceremonial center of this native nation. You must get permission to enter Nabusimake upon arrival in Pueblo Bello. The indigenous community will outline where you may hike in the Sierra Nevada and assign you a guide. These mountains are stunning and undisturbed, with waterfalls and good birdwatching. The Arhuaco will also arrange housing in a communal center or may give you permission to camp. Ask permission before taking any photos; in general, it is prohibited. Updated: Jul 10, 2011.

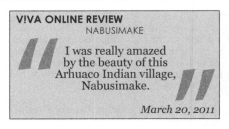

THE ROAD TO GUATAPURÍ

Up until 2008, most roads winding into the Sierra Nevada were off-limits. Now travelers may explore the incredible wonders along them, including the road to Guatapurí. The paved road heads north from Valledupar. Just past the Guacoches turn-off is **Eco-Parque Los Besotes**, a 1,000-hectare (2,470-ac) nature reserve in the foothills. The park, located 10 kilometers (6 mi) off the left side of the highway, protects 250 species of birds, seven of which are endemic, and more than 60 types of mammals. Los Besotes has 14 kilometers (8.5 mi) of hiking trails and campsites (Tel: 573-6761, Cel: 314-540-3733, E-mail: ecobesotes@hotmail.com).

Soon you enter the *resguardo* (reserve) of the Kankuamo indigenous nation at Kilometer 23 as the road to Guatapurí branches off to the left. It crosses **La Vega**, a popular swimming hole on the Badillo River. The next stop is **Patillal**, a village that has produced many Vallenato composers (30 km/18 mi from Valledupar). In the plaza next to the white-washed church are giant medallions to each of the masters. The town's patron saint, Virgen de las Mercedes, is feted September 24. A Vallenato festival is held December 25-27.

Nine kilometers (5.5 mi) further is **La Mina**. The women of this village often gather at Maye's house to weave together. (To see and purchase their works, drop by her place.) Nearby is the Río Badillo which tumbles through massive granite boulders worn smooth by the river. This is a perfect place to cool off on a hot day. From here on, the road is unpaved. The next Kankuamo town is **Atánquez** (17 km/10.5 mi), known for its *panela* (raw sugar), sweets and woolen shoulder bags.

About six kilometers (3.5 mi) deeper into the Sierra, you come to a crossroads for two traditional Kankuamo villages tucked into a spectacular landscape. To the left is **Chemesquemena** (walking: 2 hr, uphill). A short distance to the right is **Guatapurí**. From here, a dirt path rises through forests and countryside, past a sacred well and over a hand-woven bridge, to the Kogi settlement of **Maruamake**.

The indigenous villages, especially Guatapurí, Chemesquemena and Maruamake, are very traditional. Respect their cultural ways, and don't take photos without permission. Remember, these lands are sacred! If going to Maruamake, you will have to overnight it to Guatapurí; contact Provincia Hostel in Valledupar for information on where to stay. Sand flies can be vicious at La Mina; avoid standing pools of water.
Pick-up trucks to La Mina and Atánquez depart from Valledupar's Galería Popular (Cra. 7. frequent, 11 a.m.-2 p.m., 0.75/1.25 hr, $3.50 to either destination). These continue to Guatapurí (2 hr, $8). Hitchhiking back to Valledupar is easy. The public pick-up leaves from Guatapurí at varying times in the morning. Updated: Apr 26, 2011.

San Andrés, Providencia and Santa Catalina

The Archipelago of San Andrés, Providencia and Santa Catalina is located 800 kilometers (497 mi) from Cartagena and a mere 100 nautical miles (185 kilometers) from Nicaragua, in the southwestern Caribbean. Colombia's largest department covers 250,000 square kilometers (96,526 sq mi), or one-tenth of the Caribbean basin.

The archipelago itself spans a total land area of 57 square kilometers (36 sq mi). It consists of the three major islands (San Andrés, Providencia and Santa Catalina), several atolls, including Southwest Cays (Cayos de Albuquerque) and Courtown Cays (Cayos de Este Sudeste), and six outlying shoals and coral banks. Because of the increased mainland Colombian population, many places now have Spanish, as well as English names.

San Andrés, Providencia and Santa Catalina are a world apart from Colombia. The traditional culture is Afro-Caribbean. The native Raizals speak Creole English and are Protestants. The civil strife that affects mainland Colombia is absent here.

In 2000, UNESCO declared the island group the Seaflower Biosphere Reserve. It is the largest marine protected area in the Caribbean, protecting 65,000 square kilometers (25,097 sq mi) of ocean, coral reefs, mangroves and land. Planned oil exploration threatens the reserve.

The islands offer pristine beaches, great scuba diving, aquatic sports, gnarled volcanic hills, and remnants of pirate and Puritan culture, as well as boutiques and dance clubs for when sun and travel become too much. Updated: Aug 1, 2011.

History

The first inhabitants of these Caribbean islands were Miskito Indians from the coast of Nicaragua. In 1620, British Puritans arrived from Europe looking to found a religious society, but instead of building another New England, they soon established the islands as a major base for slave-run plantations and privateering. The Spanish captured the islands in 1641, claiming rightful ownership of them by virtue of their proximity to the Spanish-controlled mainland; the English resisted, even re-capturing the islands for a brief period until they finally recognized Spain's claim in 1793.

The legendary privateer Sir Henry Morgan used these islands as a base in the mid-17th century, launching the sacking of Panama from Providencia. On San Andrés you can visit Morgan's Cave, a natural grotto where Morgan allegedly stashed treasures. As with most places once frequented by pirates, the islanders tell tales of lost loot but no one ever seems to find any.

The islands have variably been under British, Spanish and Dutch control, which has resulted in a blend of languages and cultures. Spanish is most commonly spoken, followed by English. Most of the native islanders, the Raizal, speak a Creole incomprehensible to outsiders, but they can speak standard English and Spanish, too. Different groups of immigrants have come to the islands over the years, including U.S. missionaries, Chinese, Arabs and mainland Colombians.

Colombia claimed the islands in 1822 when it gained independence. Nicaragua has disputed the claim (though it has never challenged it with force) and as recently as 2001 filed a claim with the International Court of Justice to resolve the matter. Colombia responded by establishing military bases on the islands. On December 13, 2007, the International Court ruled the islands were

CARIBBEAN COAST

Colombian territory, but left undecided the maritime border issue. There is also a small movement of native islanders seeking independence from Colombia.

In the 1950s the Colombian Government launched an intensive program to promote the islands' growth and declared them a free-trade zone. As a result, San Andrés has become the package holiday and weekend destination of choice for Colombians from all walks of life. Providencia and Santa Catalina, declared national parks, are protected Caribbean marvels.

Traditional island homes are sturdy, airy, wooden structures with broad porches and old-fashioned wooden shutters. Relatively few remain nowadays, as most residents live in North End or in squat, cement homes built in the last 50 years. One of the best places to see traditional island architecture is at the Casa Museo Isleña (Island House Museum). Updated Aug 2, 2011.

When to Go

All year, the islands are blessed with fine Caribbean weather—except during hurricane season, which can inflict heavy rains, winds and overcast skies from late September through until early December. San Andrés suffers more than Providencia from hurricanes, as favorable currents protect the smaller island. The archipelago has an average temperature of 29°C (84°F) and relative humidity of 89 percent. Annual precipitation is about 1,900 millimeters (75 in). Slight climatic differences exist between the islands.

Casual clothing of light cotton and shirts with short sleeves, and comfortable shoes or sandals are the best for the islands' climate, though have a light wrap on hand for cooler times.

Accommodation rates fluctuate through the year depending on holidays and weather. Flights and all accommodations increase in cost significantly.

High season: late December to late January, Easter Week.

Mid-season: mid-June to mid-August.

Low season: end of January to mid-June, except Easter Week, and mid-August to mid-December.

There are *vedas* (seasonal bans) on certain foods: iguana (January 1-May 31),

Raizals

The natives of the San Andrés archipelago are the Raizals. They are as different to mainland Colombians as the sun is to the moon. Their ethnic roots lie with African slaves, Arawak-Caribe indigenous, and British and other European settlers. The Raizals' native languages are Creole and English, and they are Protestant. Culturally and historically, they are more similar to Caribbean coast Central Americans than they are to Colombians. They are traditionally seafarers, fishermen and farmers.

Since the "Colombinaztion" of the archipelago in the 1950s, the Raizals have faced tremendous repression of their culture and ways. They argue that they suffer from racial, linguistic, racial, socio-economic and political discrimination. Raizals now number less than a third of the archipelago's population. They are a minority on San Andrés Island. On Providencia, Raizal culture still has a stronghold. Their unemployment figures is around 70%. The human rights group Minority Rights recognizes Raizals as an endangered culture.

In response to what they refer to as the "neo-colonial repression"of the Colombia government, in June 2007 the Raizals declared their homeland an independent state: Saint Andrews, Old Providence and St. Kethleena. Updated: Aug 9, 2011.

black crab (April 1-July 31), spiny lobster (April 1-June 30) and conch (June 1-October 31). Bans are in place year-round for coral and turtle. Updated: Aug 2, 2011.

Safety

San Andrés, Providencia and Santa Catalina are remarkably safe. Mainland Colombia's violence and civil war are absent here. Of course, common sense should be used about flashing money and jewels, and leaving things unattended on the beach. Keep valuables in your hotel's safe.

The sun can be strong, so cover up or use sun block. Also keep hydrated. Because San Andrés and Providencia are major tourist destinations, there are programs of control and eradication programs against malaria dengue and leptospirosis. Thus, these diseases rarely occur. A yellow fever vaccination is recommended. Tap water in the islands is not potable.

CARIBBEAN COAST

When in the sea, footwear while snorkeling or swimming is advised, as coral can be sharp. Shuffle feet to avoid unpleasant encounters with sting rays. Also keep an eye out for jellyfish. Watch for high waves and strong currents.

Hurricanes occasionally swipe the islands, and so drills are periodically performed. In the event of a storm, follow public authorities' instructions. Updated Aug 2, 2011.

Things to See and Do

The San Andrés, Providencia and Santa Catalina archipelago is rich in natural and cultural wonders. The islands are home to one national-al park, Old Providence McBean Lagoon, and several nature reserves, including Old Point Regional Mangrove Park and Johnny Cay, which is a popular day trip from San Andrés.

The entire marine area is the Sunflower Biosphere Reserve, protecting this warm, clear water that teems with coral reefs and life. Without a doubt, scuba diving is the most popular activity on the islands. For anyone not certified, PADI certification is not expensive. Or you can stick with snorkeling, an easy alternative. Travelers not into water sports have fine beaches to sun on or trails to take into the hills.

Museums open the doors onto the Islands' past, from the Casa Museo Isleña to the kitschy Morgan's Cave and Pirate Museum. The best is to just kick back with the locals and learn about the unique Raizal culture. Updated Aug 3, 2011.

Tours

Should you arrive on a package tour to San Andrés or Providencia then most of the tours will be included in that deal. Independent travelers, though, can still take in the sights on tours. Agencies on both islands offer excursions to explore the archipelago's surf and turf, as well as its historical curiosities. Updated: Aug 3, 2011.

Lodging

In general most accommodation options on the islands can be arranged from the mainland, since many hotels on San Andrés Island are part of international chains. They range from the ultra-exclusive, five-star resorts to relics of another era of money laundering and narco-influenced extravagance.

On Providencia, the opposite is the norm. The islanders there are intent on protecting their heritage and cultural identity. Most hotels are small, family-run enterprises consisting of few rooms.

The international hotel chain, Decameron, has six exclusive resort hotels on the islands (five on San Andrés and one on Providencia). Updated: Aug 4, 2011.

SAN ANDRÉS ISLAND

 85m   66,000   8

San Andrés (Saint Andrew), the archipelago's largest island, has an interesting history that includes pirates and legends of lost treasures. It is 12 kilometers (7.5 mi) long and three kilometers (1.8 mi) wide, and only about 26 square kilometers (10 sq mi) in size. The northeast tip, North End (San Andrés Town) is where the isle's main city and airport are. The southern tip is home to the Blowing Hole (Hoyo Soplador). Major spots along the west coast are Morgan's Cave and Cove Bay, and along the east coast are Playas de Sound Bay, Rocky Cay and San Luis. In the center of the island is a lagoon called Big Pond (La Laguna). Johnny Cay lies 1.5 kilometers (1.5 mi) off the north coast. Haine's Cay and Aquarium Island are just off the east coast.

The shopping on San Andrés is particularly good, as the town itself is a duty-free zone. There are excellent beaches and scuba diving, too. On an island tour you'll see traditional architecture, a restored traditional home, and some cheesy pirate mannequins à la Disney World at Morgan's Cave. The tour includes snorkeling at West View and a stop at the Blowing Hole, a natural phenomenon which draws many visitors.

San Andrés is a growing resort spot, popular primarily with South American and Canadian tourists. Most visitors stay at large resorts, which are scattered around the island. North End town has lower-budget accommodations. Updated: Aug 1, 2011.

History

San Andrés was "discovered" by the Spanish sometime before 1527 (yet unconfirmed is that Columbus made landfall here), occupied by the Dutch at the end of the 16th century and a British Puritan colony after 1628. Within a decade, the English began bringing African slaves from Jamaica to here to work in the dye-wood, cotton and tobacco plantations. Colonists arrived to San Andrés island first, but later moved to Providencia where freshwater sources existed. The settlers successfully

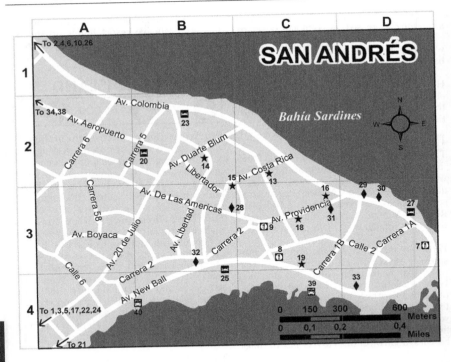

repelled a Spanish invasion. Pirate Henry Morgan used San Andrés as one of his bases of operation in raiding Spanish treasure ports.

Since the early 19th century, Colombia has claimed San Andrés as its territory. In 1902 and 1903 (this second time with the presence of gunboats), the island refused an offer from the U.S. Government to become part of Panama. In the mid-20th century, Colombia began a concerted effort to "Colombianize" San Andrés, first by sending in Catholic missionaries and later by declaring San Andrés a duty-free zone in 1953. Since then, the cultural makeup

of San Andrés has radically changed, with about two-thirds of its population now being from the mainland. Updated Aug 2, 2011.

When to Go

San Andrés is blessed with a year-round Caribbean climate, with temperatures 26 -29°C (79 -84°F). The island has two seasons: wet and dry. The dry season (January-April/ May) eventually segues into the hurricane season (late September to the beginning of December), when rains usually last only 10-20 minutes before the sun shows itself again.

HOLIDAYS AND FIESTAS

July 20–Fiesta Patria. Parades span the island and celebrate the culture of the Archipiélago.

August 7–Fiesta Patria. Parades and expositions of local color and gastrony in the San Luis district.

August 11-14–Feria de las Flores. An annual flower fair.

October 12–Día de La Raza. Cultural activities displaying riches of the island.

November 30–Fiestas Patronales de San Andrés. Celebrations in honor of the island's patron saint. Updated Aug 2, 2011.

Getting To and Away
BY AIR
Flying is the most common way to reach San Andrés. **Aeropuerto Internacional Gustavo Rojas Pinilla** is located within the urban area (Av Aeropuerto, Sector Swamp Ground. Tel: 512-6112). Services include ATMs, exchange house, phone booths, Internet, shops, restaurants and tourism information kiosk.

● **Activities**

1 Blowing Hole A4
2 Casa Museo Isleña A1
3 La Loma A4
4 Morgan's Cave A1
5 Old Point Regional
   Mangrove Park A4
6 West View A1

⊞ **Eating**

7 Margherita e Carbonara D3
8 Miss Celia Restaurant C3
9 Mister Panino C3
10 West View Restaurant A1

▣ **Nightlife**

11 Blue Deep Discotheque (See 25)
12 Melon Kiss Disco (See 25)

★ **Services**

13 Banco de Bogotá C2
14 Banco Davivienda B2
15 Bancolombia B3
16 Cambios y Capitales C3
17 Hospital Departamental
   Amor de Patria A4
18 Macrofinanciera C3
19 Secretaría de Turismo C3

▦ **Sleeping**

20 Cli's Place B2
21 Blue Diamond Hostel A4
22 Hotel Cocoplum A4
23 Portobelo Hotel B2
24 Posada Nativa Licy A4
25 Sunrise Beach Hotel B3
26 Sunset Hotel A1
27 Tres Casitas Apartahotels D3

♦ **Tours**

28 Aviatur B3
29 Banda Dive Shop D3
30 Buzos del Caribe D3
31 Galeón Morgan C3
32 Islatur B3
33 Karibik Diver D4
34 Over Receptour A2
35 Power Boat (See 25)
36 Semi-submarino Manatí (See 27)
37 Viajes Portofino (See 23)

▦ **Transportation**

38 Aeropuerto Internacional
   Gustavo Rojas Pinilla A2
39 Club Náutico C4
40 Nene's Marina A4

During the low season, there are 10 flights per day from Colombia and two international flights; there are more in the high seasons. Domestic flights come from Bogotá, Cartagena, Santa Marta, Medellín, Cali and Barranquilla. They cost anywhere between $250 and $450. Copa has daily service from Panama, with connections to North America and Europe.

Most airline companies have their offices at the airport, as well as in town: **Avianca** (Av Colón, Edificio Onaissi, local 107. Tel: 512-3212; airport: 512-3216), **Aires** (air port. Tel: 512-0774) and **AeroRepública/ Copa** (Centro Comercial San Andrés, local 108-109. Tel: 01-8000-11-2600).

A tourist card for the island is required and can be purchased upon check-in on mainland Colombia or upon arrival in San Andrés. Currently this costs $25 (44,000 pesos) and must be presented at your departure from the island.

Satena (URL: www.satena.com.co) flies twice daily to Providencia ($165-195). **Saerca**, Decameron's carrier, also flies two times per day to the sister island.

BY BOAT
Travelers arriving in their own yacht or sailboat can dock at **Nene's Marina** (Av New-ball. Tel: 512-6139, URL: www.nenesmarina. com) or **Club Náutico** (Av Colombia 8. Tel: 512-3022, URL: www.clubnauticosai.org).

Catamarans and cargo ships go to Providencia. See that town for more information. Updated: Aug 3, 2011.

Getting Around

Public buses ($0.80) are the cheapest way to get around the island. The "El Cove" bus passes through La Loma to El Cove; alight at the Baptist church for Morgan's Cave and La Piscinita. The "San Luis" bus goes down the east coast, through San Luis to the Blowing Hole.

Two main taxi companies operate on the island: **Mega Taxi** (Tel: 512-2222) and **Mío Taxi** (Tel: 512-4888). Rates are around $5 and are doubled midnight-6 a.m. A trip around the island is about $35.

Another way to see the island is by renting wheels. Choose to go by bicycle ($8 half-day, $14 full day), scooter ($28 per day) or golf cart ($56 full day). Almost a dozen local agencies rent cars, including **Portofino Rent-a-Car** (Av Nicaragua 1-115. Tel: 512-6954) and **Millenium Renta Car** (Av. Colombia 1A-51. Tel: 512-3114). Updated: Aug 3, 2011.

Safety

Crime is incredibly low on San Andres and rightly so. The occasional bag snatching is inevitable but hardly the norm in downtown San Andres. Beyond that you should feel very at ease. You are advised not to take valuables to the beach and make full use of the safe in your hotel room. Updated: Aug 2, 2011.

Services

TOURISM

San Andrés' **Secretaría de Turismo** provides tourism information (Av Colombia, Diagonal to Club Náutico. Tel: 512-5058, E-mail: islasvivas@hotmail.com, URL: www.sanadres.gov.co).

Other important offices are **police** (Av. Newball 1-34. Tel: 512-3850/emergency: 123), **Instituto Geográfico Agustín Codazzi** (Monday-Friday 7 a.m.-noon and 2-6 p.m. Av. 20 de Julio, Edificio de la Gobernación. Tel: 512-3096) and **DAS** (Monday-Friday 7:30-11 a.m. and 2-5 p.m. Cra. 7, 2-70, Sector Swamp Ground).

The closest U.S. Consulate in Colombia is in Barranquilla, and of the U.K., in Cartagena.

Costa Rica, Guatemala, Austria and Panama have consulates on the island; check the phone directory for addresses.

MONEY

Banks are open Monday-Thursday 8-11:30 a.m and 2-4 p.m., and Friday until 4:30 p.m. The bilingual ATMs accept Cirrus, MasterCard, American Express, Diners Club and Visa. Several banks and casas de cambio are on Avenida las Américas and Avenida Providencia. Some major ones are: **Banco de Bogotá** (Av. Colón 2-156), **Banco Davivienda** (Av. Duarte Blum 1-110; also Av. Costa Rica 3-19), and **Bancolombia** (Av. Atlántico 1A-35), which also exchanges American Express travelers checks. Money exchange houses include **Cambios y Capitales**, which changes various currencies and travelers checks (Av. Providencia 1-35, local 106) and **Macrofinanciera** (Av. Providencia 1A-48, local 112). To receive wired money, see **Giros & Finanzas**, the Western Union agent (Centro Comercial San Andrés, local 12. Tel: 01-8000-111-999) or the MoneyGram agent, **Cambiamos** (Av. Costa Rica 3-19. Tel: 512-3757).

KEEPING IN TOUCH

Phone booths and Internet cafés are present in downtown and around the island. Cell phone providers are Comcel, Movistar and Tigo. The **post office** is on Avenida Newball (Edif Cámara de Comercio, local 101).

MEDICAL

Hospital Departamental Amor de Patria is the island's main hospital (Vía San Luis. Tel: 5512-3808). San Andrés pharmacies follow the de turno (on-shift) system. **Droguería La Salud Isleña** has free delivery and accepts credit cards (Av. Colón 3-28. Tel: 512-5798).

RELIGION

Baptist, Catholic, Adventist, Spanish Baptist, Christian Missionary and Jehovah's Witness services can all be found. Also, a mosque is located near the Catholic Church of Cristo Salvador. Most services are held in the Islanders' native Creole English. Updated Aug 3, 2011.

SHOPPING

In an attempt at "Colombianization," the Colombian government declared San Andrés a tax-free zone. Now, besides being a beach-goer's paradise, the island is a shopping Eden as well.

CARIBBEAN COAST

The best shopping in the town of San Andrés can be found in the commercial district, known to locals as the North End. Many come here for the bargain American clothes, perfumes, and accessories, real and imitation. Alcohol selections are also cheap and include local liqueurs, such as rum and coffee liqueur. (Be mindful of how much you can actually bring back to your home country; salespeople may be able to advise.) The new pedestrianized area a block from the beach in San Andrés is crammed with exclusive boutiques stocking all of these products in deliciously air-conditioned shops.

With some searching you can bargain for knock-off mp3 players and digital cameras. Large-screen TVs are available in abundance. Respectful bargaining is expected, as very few items actually have a price tag. Other items include scuba and snorkeling gear, flip-flops, water shoes and luggage. Colombians come here to buy everything from kitchen appliances to bed linens. Do not be surprised to see people wandering in and out of these stores dressed in beachwear—they may just be browsing to get out of the heat for a while. Most shops are open from 9 a.m. to 7:30 p.m. with a lunch break. Updated: Aug 3, 2011.

Things to See and Do

Most visitors to San Andrés come to relax on white-sand beaches and to drink piña coladas beside a hotel pool, after hours of duty-free shopping. That's all well and good, but there is much more to do on this tiny island. Once you're done tanning, you might want to check out some of the following activities.

Snorkelers will have many spots to choose from, including nearby Aquarium Island, a favorite among locals and tourists alike. Scuba divers won't want to miss the chance to jump into the warm Caribbean and hit some local hotspots. One of the easiest and best dive sites is the sunken freighter The Blue Diamond, resting in about 12 meters (40 ft) of water off the island's eastern shore.

An island tour is a good investment because it will take you to a number of the best spots. Popular stops on these tours are the Casa Museo Isleña, a restored traditional home, and the Blowing Hole, a somewhat bizarre tourist attraction which features a natural hole in the ground, out of which, occasionally, a strong puff of air bursts. Updated: Aug 3, 2011.

La Loma

(ADMISSION: free) Many San Andrés Island tours will take you to La Loma (120 m/394 ft), the central hill of the island. A hotel there has the best views—you can see the beautiful Caribbean, known for its seven shades of blue and green, some mangrove swamps, and the city of San Andrés at the north end. Nearby are several older homes of the traditional island architecture: simply framed and airy, wooden houses with shutters. Also atop the hill is the Emanuel Baptist Church, which dates back roughly 160 years. It was founded in 1844 by evangelical missionaries from the southern United States. La Loma is home to most of the oldest island families. Updated: Aug 4, 2011.

The Blowing Hole

(ADMISSION: free) Only on a small Caribbean island in the middle of the ocean could a hole in the ground which occasionally blows a strong puff of air be a major tourist attraction. On the southern end of the island, about 10 meters from the ocean, there is a small hole in the rocky ground with a diameter a little larger than a basketball. Every few minutes a wave hits the shore just right, pushing a strong draft of warm air through the tunnel and out of the hole, where there is usually a family of tourists waiting for it. The puff can actually be quite impressive—it can hit you with the force of about 50 hair dryers for a brief moment. Very rarely tides, waves and other conditions are just right, and a geyser of water will erupt from the hole.

The Blowing Hole is a popular stop on the island tour, and there are plenty of vendors on-site willing to sell you a beer, a T-shirt, a necklace, a pretty conch shell or anything else a tourist could want. The vendors aren't aggressive and are even happy to tell you just where to stand or to snap your photo when the blast of air hits your face. Updated: Aug 4, 2011

West View

(ADMISSION: $1) West View, also called La Piscinita, is one of San Andrés' best snorkeling spots. A short pier juts into the ocean. Water-shy tourists toss bread (included in the entrance fee) into the sea, while others snorkel to see the fish feeding. This is also a prime place to swim with manta rays. There is even an underwater apparatus—a large glass helmet connected to an air hose—that you can use to walk around on the sea floor (similar to scuba, but easier). The water is shallow and warm,

CARIBBEAN COAST

and the staff is friendly. West View is included in most island tours, or you can take a local bus there yourself. Updated: Aug 4, 2011.

Casa Museo Isleña

Casa Museo Isleña (Island House Museum) is a restored home, an example of traditional functional island architecture. It is decorated as it would have been decades ago, with family portraits on the walls. The museum is a popular tour stop, and the place is usually either deserted or packed. Occasionally, young girls will start off the tour with a traditional dance. The museum boasts an ocean view and makes for a pleasant, informative visit. Daily 9 a.m.-6 p.m. Av. Circunvalar, Km 5. Tel: 512-3419, E-mail: ecoturismocaribeazul@gmail.com, URL: www.buceocaribeazul.com. Updated: Aug 4, 2011.

Morgan's Cave/Pirate Museum

(ADMISSION: $3) This unassuming freshwater cave, believed to once have been a hiding place for pirate loot, has been transformed into one of San Andrés' main tourist attractions.

A visit starts with a trip to the small Pirate Museum where a Halloween pirate displays a vast collection of fake skulls, fake guns, old treasure-chest-looking trunks, nylon pirate flags and plastic swords. Get your picture taken with the mannequin dressed in stereotypical pirate garb. In the back of the pirate museum you'll find the "Coconut Museum," easy to miss if you're not looking for it. Next it's on to the little art gallery, a squat building notable for the number of old rum bottles built into the walls. The paintings feature mostly seascapes; no parrots or cannons or skulls, unfortunately.

Once you've hit the museum and the art gallery, you get to see the 120-meter (394-ft) long cave itself. According to local legend, infamous privateer Sir Henry Morgan used the cave as a place to stash stolen loot. The place will be a bit of a disappointment if you are expecting to see skeletons or cannons scattered around, but it is a lovely natural cave full of fresh water. You can only descend a few feet into the cave before the water blocks your passage, and according to the pirate-guide it's quite deep. There is an old cannon mounted on concrete nearby.

There are a couple of shops near Morgan's Cave where you can buy a snack or a drink (yes, you can get rum). The usual necklace vendors are there as well. One of the shops is decorated with hanging sea-turtle shells, old lanterns and even a battered microscope.

The whole complex is silly fun, and just a wink away from tongue-in-cheek. You won't learn any more about real pirate lore than you would from a comic-book version of *Treasure Island*, but that's the fun in it. Daily 9 a.m.-5 p.m. Av. Circunvalar, Km 8, Tel: 512-2316. Updated: Aug 4, 2011.

Aquarium Island

Aquarium Island, a small key just 10-20 minutes by boat off the western coast of San Andrés, actually comprises two islands: one small and sandy, the other larger and covered in palm trees. Both islands feature rudimentary tourist facilities, and they are connected by a sand bar just few feet underwater.

The smaller island is popular with snorkelers because the water is warm and clear, and the many fish are easy to see. Snorkeling gear is available on the island, but prices are high. There are small lockers for rent in one of the huts. Glass-bottom boats leave from Aquarium to see shoals of fish, and you can sometimes rent jet-skis.

To get to Aquarium Island, go to the small port on the eastern side of San Andrés and ask to get on the next boat over. You can also book passage through one of the tour operators on San Andrés Island. If you go through a tour agency, expect to pay about $5 per person to get there and back. It's usually cheaper to make your own arrangements at the port.

On weekends, Aquarium Island fills up with locals from San Andrés and tourists. The fish are frightened off, lockers may fill up, locals are sometimes rude to tourists, and every square inch of shade is taken. Weekends are bad, but holiday weekends are unbearable and should be avoided at all costs.

Also note that there are sea urchins in the vicinity. If you're planning on swimming or snorkeling, you'll want good water shoes for protection. Aquarium Island is often packaged together with a trip to larger Johnny Key. Updated: Aug 4, 2011.

The Blue Diamond Wreck Dive

According to local lore, the Blue Diamond was impounded in the 1990s by the Colombian government for running drugs before being scuttled to create a dive attraction. Whatever its history, this medium-sized freighter is an enjoyable wreck, full of little nooks and crannies that divers simply love to explore.

Did a unique trek? Got way off the beaten path? Tell other travelers at vivatravelguides.com

The dive is easy and fun. The wreck rests near the eastern shore of the island in about 10 meters (35 ft) of very warm water—even those most likely to get chilly underwater will not need a wetsuit. The stern, which rests about 12 meters (40 ft) down, is the deepest part of the dive. The boat cracked and split as it sank, and there are several areas through which an adventurous diver can swim without running much risk of getting stuck or caught. Forms of sea life such as fans, corals and small sponges have begun to grow on the wreck, and small, colorful reef fish make it their home.

Highlights include the massive propeller half-buried in the sandy bottom and the bow. You can swim through an open hatch in the bow and come out a hole in the side—just let the divemaster go first. Look for barracuda and other fish darting in and out of the wreckage.

The Blue Diamond is located in a sandy spot, but there are coral gardens and small reefs not far away. If you still have air after completing an exploration of the wreck, you may be able to look around before resurfacing. Updated: Aug 4, 2011.

Johnny Cay Regional Park

One of the most popular tours in San Andrés is boating to Johnny Cay, a four-hectare (11-ac) island two kilometers (1.6 mi) off San Andres' north coast. Since 2002, the islet has been a regional park, which is a natural habitat for green iguana and a nesting ground for a variety of migratory birds. In the translucent sea surrounding the isle live 16 classes of coral and 30 species of fish. On the white-sand beach, visitors will see red crab, and the lizards Isla San Andres Anole and South American whiptail. Flora include bay cedar, lavinda and coconut palm. An entry fee is charged to the cay. Daily 9 a.m.- 4 p.m. Updated: Aug 4, 2011.

Old Point Regional Mangrove Park

Old Point Regional Mangrove Park embraces two bays on San Andrés Island's east coast: Hooker and Haines. The reserve protects the largest and best-preserved expanses of red, black, white and button mangrove forest. In addition, the park preserves coral reefs and pastures of sea grass. Old Point is a good place for observing fauna associated with mangrove eco-systems, snorkeling, swimming and kayaking. There are also hiking trails. Updated: May 9, 2011.

Tours

There are over a dozen tour agencies on San Andrés, many of which work in conjunction with big hotels. They all offer the same tours to more or less the same places—Johnny Cay, Morgan's Cave, The Coconut Museum, La Piscinita and the Blowing Hole. Prices appear to be regulated between them. Many also have boating excursions to the archipelago's other cays. A few selected agencies are: **Aviatur** (Av. Las Américas 1C-93. Tel: 512-7312, E-mail: aviatur@sol.net.co, URL: www.aviatur. com), **Islatur** (Av Newball 4B-12, Edificio Bahía Fragata. Tel: 512-3358, E-mail: islatur@sol.net.co, URL: www.islatur.com), **Viajes Portofino** (Av. La Playa and Av 20 de Julio. Tel: 512-4212/2773, E-mail: receptivos. portofino@hotmail.com/portofino@telecom. com.co, URL: www.portofinocaribe.com) and **Over Receptour** (Cra. 9A, 10-56, Airport, Sector Swamp Ground. Tel: 512-8855, E-mail: sanandres@receptourdelcaribe.com, URL: receptourdelcaribe.com).

Likewise, almost a dozen scuba diving shops operate on San Andrés Island, including: **Banda Dive Shop** (Hotel Lord Pierre, Local 104. Tel: 513-1080, Cel: 315-303-5428, E-mail: dive@bandadiveshop.com, URL: www. bandadiveshop.com), **Buzos del Caribe** (Av Colombia 1-212. Tel: 512-8929, Cel: 312-593-9146, E-mail: engarita2@yahoo.com), **Karibik Diver** (Av Newball 1-248, Edificio Galeón. Tel: 512-0101, E-mail: werneisai@gmx.net, URL: www.karibikdiver.com) and **San Andrés Divers** (Cel: 310-373-0209/317-660-8850, URL: www.sanandresdivers.com).

To experience the sea without diving into its briny depths, **Semi-submarino Manatí** (Av La Playa. Tel: 512 3349, E-mail: info@ semisubmarinomanati.com, URL: www. semisubmarinomanati.com) offers excursions in a glass-sided boat. To recreate those bawdy pirate days of yore, embark on **Galeón Morgan** (Centro Comercial New Point 234. Tel: 512-8787, Fax: 512-1358, E-mail: munmarino@hotmail.com). **Power Boat** (Sunrise Beach Hotel 119. Tel: 512-5208/8296) also does boat tours. Updated Aug 3, 2011.

Lodging

A high percentage of visitors to San Andrés will be staying in one of Decameron's five massive hotels. These hotels sell all-inclusive packages which allow you to dine and see shows at any of the five hotels, as long as you sleep at your own. It's a good way to get to savor several restaurants and shows.

CARIBBEAN COAST

Photo by: Anthony Leimon

CARIBBEAN COAST

There are non-Decameron hotels available on the island, too. Travelers with any size wallet should be able to find a hotel, including budget backpackers. An inexpensive alternative is the small, family-run *posadas nativas* inns, like **Cli's Place** (Av. 20 de Julio 3-47. Tel: 512-6957/0591, E-mail: luciamhj@hotmail.com) and **Posada Native Licy** (La Loma Flowers Hill 39-19. Tel: 513-3972, Cel: 314-488-9890, E-mail: posada.licy@live.com). For a complete list of the over dozen hostels, see: www.posadasturisticasdecolombia.com/posada.

The fanciest hotels are on the coast and have private beaches. The cheapest lodging options are in the town of San Andrés and do not have beaches. Updated: Aug 4, 2011.

Blue Almond Hostel

(ROOMS: $15 and up) This clean, small hotel (3 rooms only) is 20 minutes walking from the sea. It offers amenities budget travelers need, like BBQ pit, kitchen, an outdoor terrace to hang out, book exchange, and sitting room with TV and an extensive DVD collection. Rooms are simply furnished and clean and share common bathrooms. English is spoken. Barrio Almendros, Manzana 4, Casa 3. Tel: 512-2463, URL: www.bluealmondhostel.com. Updated: May 05, 2011.

Sunset Hotel

(ROOMS: $49-91) Situated on the island's west coast, 20 minutes from downtown San Andrés, the Sunset Hotel offers a respite from the hustle and bustle of downtown. The 16 rooms are immaculately laid out with bathroom, air conditioning, TV and fridge, making the Sunset an ideal place to relax. The hotel mainly caters to the scuba diving crowd since Sharky's Dive Shop is attached. A taxi will get you here from downtown in 20 minutes and a bus will take a little longer. Just ask the driver to let you off at kilometer 13 on the coastal road. Carretera Circunvalar, Km 13. Tel: 513-0433, E-mail: reservations@thesunsethotel.net, URL: www.thesunsethotel.net. Updated: Oct 05, 2011.

Tres Casitas Apartahotel

(ROOMS: $60-75) Tres Casitas has ten fully furnished and equipped apartments close to San Andrés' nightlife district. While the furnishings are somewhat dated, the location is unrivaled. The swimming pool and the balconies in every apartment are a nice touch and the communal areas are well-maintained. Right downtown, the Tres Casitas is a five-minute drive from the airport. Av. Colombia 1-60. Tel: 512-6944, E-mail: tres_casitas@hotmail.com, URL: www.apartahoteltrescasitas.com. Updated: Aug 5, 2011.

Portobelo Hotel

(ROOMS: $67-188) Portobelo Hotel has a prime location in San Andrés town: on a pedestrian street along the beachfront and just two blocks from the commercial district. If you are in San Andrés to party or to shop, you can't be in a better location. This hotel could use some upgrades. The rooms' most redeeming feature is the sea views. They also have air conditioning, mini-bar and cable TV. Portobelo also has more expensive condos that feature a kitchenette and other amenities. Av. Colombia 5A-69. Tel: 512-7008, E-mail: reservas@portobelohotel.com, URL: www.portobelohotel.com. Updated: Aug 05, 2011.

Hotel Cocoplum

(ROOMS: $82-228) Cocoplum's most striking feature is its bright, multicolored buildings overlooking palm-shaded walkways. The hotel is set on a clean, private stretch of beach, and there are roomy hammocks to relax in. There are 24 double rooms and 14 family suites, making this a large venture, although the buildings feel a bit cramped. It should be noted that rooms with beach views cost more than front-facing rooms. The on-site restaurant and bar make this a fine family or romantic hotel choice. Spa, childcare, and laundry services are available, as are satellite TV and WiFi. Bilingual staff. Water sports and other activities, such as scuba diving (with a local dive company), snorkeling, and jetskiing, are based from the Cocoplum beach. Vía a San Luis 43-39. Tel: 513-2121, E-mail: informes@cocoplumhotel.com, URL: www.cocoplumhotel.com. Updated: Aug 05, 2011.

Sunrise Beach Hotel

(ROOMS: $210-315) This massive, 300-room hotel looks out-of-place on the coast. It caters to the package tourist crowd, with meals and activities included. Ask for a room with a view of the water, as rooms without a sea view stare over humidity-stained blocks. The pool, however, is wonderful. It is a five-minute taxi ride from the airport. Av. Fancisco Newball 4-169. Tel: 512-3977, E-mail: info@sunrisehotel.com, URL: www.ghlhoteles.com / www.sunrisehotel.com. Updated: Aug 05, 2011.

Restaurants

As the majority of visitors to San Andres arrive here on all inclusive deals, all of their dining arrangements are taken care of within the hotel. While this may be very convenient, it has resulted in a lack of quality restaurants available for the independent traveler. Most restaurants are open Monday-Saturday noon-11 p.m.

It should surprise no one that seafood is the big item on San Andres menus. Crab soup, fish, lobster, shrimp and conch make appearances. One typical dish is rundown (*rondon*), a whatever-is-on-hand stew of fish, conch, yucca, plantain, yam and breadfruit simmered in coconut milk. Other island specialties are lemon pie and beans with smoked pigs tail. Major ingredients also include basil, coconut and breadfruit. Updated: Aug 5, 2011.

West View Restaurant

(ENTREES: $7-13) After a dip in La Piscinita to check out the fish and mantas, stop into West View Restaurant for a plate of fresh seafood. This unassuming eatery offers up fried fish and ceviche, as well as lobster and crab entrées. Typical island cuisine is also served, including the staple rundown stew made of fish, breadfruit, yams and other goodies in a coconut milk broth. To wash it all down, have a *coco loco* (fresh coconut spiked with rum), piña colada or ice-cold beer. For a much more relaxed scene, come after the tourist lunch crowd has left. Carretera Circunvalar Km 11. Tel: 513-0341. Updated Aug 5, 2011.

Margherita e Carbonara

(ENTREES: $10 and up) Travelers (yes, even Italians) frequently rave about Margherita e Carbonara. Pull up a table out on the patio or inside to savor the dishes at this trattoria owned by Vanni from Emilia-Romagna. Risotto, lasagna and a whole gamut of pastas, including tortellini and gnocchi, are prepared to perfection. The pizzas are exceptionally good. As well, the menu has some meat, like scaloppine and cotoletta, and fish dishes. Margherita e Carbonara also has salami and other foods imported from Italy. Service is quick. Av. Colombia 1-93. Tel: 512-1050. Updated Aug 5, 2011.

Miss Celia Restaurant

(ENTREES: $11 and up) For a taste of real Island food, drop by Miss Celia Restaurant. This well-known diner offers fish, conch, lobster and other fruits of the sea. Be sure to try the classic crab soup or the rundown. The menu also includes Colombian favorites like *mondongo* (tripe soup), *chicharrón* (pork fatback) and *bandeja paisa*. There is also a wine cellar. Miss Celia Restaurant is in a colorfully painted, typical San Andrés house with a tropical garden and patio. The ambiance is warm and tranquil. This is the perfect place for a romantic meal. Av. Colombia, across from the Club Náutico. Tel: 513-1062, Cel: 316-690-0074. Updated Aug 5, 2011.

CARIBBEAN COAST

Mister Panino

Mister Panino is an intimate Italian restaurant owned by a native of Naples. The menu is an eclectic affair, using the day's freshest ingredients to create gourmet Italo-Caribbean dishes. One day seafood tortellini may come hot to the table, on another eggplant ravioli. The risotto with asparagus and shrimp is tempting, and the octopus carpaccio is divine. It isn't all about pastas and other Italian fare here, though. Mister Panino also serves T-bone steaks, lamb cutlets and other meats. At the shop you can pick up imported Italian delicacies. Av Colón, Edificio Bread Fruit, local 106-107. Tel: 512-0549, URL: misterpaninosanandres.com. Updated Aug 5, 2011.

Nightlife

Most Colombians are here to party, so naturally, there are some good clubs. Most are located within the big hotels, often on the top floor, so ask around for the current hot spot. Some bars are open until 3 a.m. Updated: Aug 5, 2011

Melon Kiss Disco

(COVER: $7.50) Guests of the Sunrise Beach Hotel and other tourists crowd into Melon Kiss Disco, to dance the night away to electronic beats while washing away any worries with the aid of fancy cocktails. Live sporting events are sometimes screened on large TVs. Daily 9 p.m.-4 a.m.; in low season, only Friday-Sunday. Inside the Hotel Sunrise, Av Newball, 4-169. Tel: 512-3977, E-mail: lorena.morales@ghdtl-hoteles.com. Updated: Aug 5, 2011.

Blue Deep Discotheque

The Blue Deep has been ranked as one of the best nightclubs in all of Latin America. It consists of three distinct bars, two dance floors, a light and laser show, and perfect sound amplification. With a capacity for 800 revelers, be prepared for non-stop dancing. Inside the Hotel Sunrise, Av Newball, 4-169. Tel: 512-3977. Updated: Aug 5, 2011.

PROVIDENCIA AND SANTA CATALINA

 360m   6,000   8

Providencia (Old Providence), the archipelago's second-largest island, is much different than San Andrés. Life here is laid-back and the Raizal culture still reigns.

The main settlement on Providencia is Town (Santa Isabel) on the northern tip, where most businesses are. An 18-kilometer (11-mi) road skirts the outside edge of the island, and so most inhabitants live along the shore. The airport, Rocky Point (Punta Rocosa), Smooth Water Bay (Aguamansa) and Manchineel Bay (Playa Manzanilla) are along the east coast. The west side of the island is where Old Town (Pueblo Viejo), Lazy Hill (San Felipe), Freshwater Bay (Agua Dulce) and South West Bay (Bahía Sudoeste) are. Several *lomas* (hills) rise in the center of the island. Santa Catalina, an isle just to the north, is accessible from Providencia by the "Lover's Bridge." Ten kilometers (6 mi) further north is Low Cay.

Little remains from the early Puritan, slave and pirate settlements, except names and the odd cannon here and there. Santa Isabel has a few ramshackle streets where you can find cafés, a supermarket, banks and a cash machine. Unless you need to withdraw some funds, there should be no urgent need to visit there.

Instead, stick to the island's main attractions—unspoiled beaches, charming islanders conversing in their Creole English, tours of the mangroves and hikes into the interior volcanic hills. Updated: Aug 1, 2011.

History

Providencia has seen its fair share of masters. It was originally a Miskito Indian fishing territory. Columbus may have stepped foot on its shores during his fourth voyage. In 1629, it became a Puritan colony, and later on a pirate lair.

After the Puritan project failed in the mid-17th century, the island fell into Spanish hands but remained ignored by the protectorate in Cartagena. Unbothered by the Spanish, the descendants of African slaves settled on Providencia, and their culture remains intact. Updated Aug 2, 2011.

When to Go

Temperatures on the islands average 25-28° C (77-82°F). October and November are the rainiest months and hurricane season can span from late September into December in a bad year. The dry season is January-April.

HOLIDAYS AND FIESTAS

Saturdays—Gather on South West beach just after 1 p.m. to see one of the most interesting equestrian events in the world—the beach horse races of Providencia.

CARIBBEAN COAST

May-June—Migration of the black crab, a protected and emblematic species.

June 23-26—Festival Folklórico, Cultural y Deportivo de la Vieja Providencia. This is the island's most important festival. It includes sports competitions, gastronomy and a beauty pageant. Updated Aug 2, 2011.

Getting To and Away

BY AIR
Providence's **Aeropuerto El Embrujo** is on the northeast side of the island (Tel: 514-8829). **Satena** (URL: www.satena.com.co) has two daily flights to and from Providencia (20 minutes, $165-195). Book through a travel agency or buy at the Gustavo Rojas Pinilla airport in San Andrés. Purchasing by credit card is difficult. **Saerca** is Decameron's carrier; it also flies two times per day.

BY SEA
Sensation runs a small, catamaran ferry four days per week between San Andrés and Old Providence, departing from San Andrés at 7:30 a.m. and returning 4 p.m. (3 hr; adults $64, children $50). Passengers are allowed to carry up two bags weighing 20 kilograms (44 lb) each (Av. Francisco Newball, Edificio Baypoint, local 9, San Andrés. Tel: 512-5124). Small cargo ships are cheaper but take eight hours. If traveling by boat, prepare for seasickness. Updated: Aug 3, 2011.

Getting Around
Taxis colectivos (shared taxis with set fares and routes) are the most common forms of transport. A taxi from the airport to your hotel should cost about $10. The ride to South West Bay (where most hotels are) takes 20 minutes from the airport. Motorcycles, though, are a popular and cheap way to get around (low season: $30 per day). You can rent them from **Bush Renta Moto** (Cabellete. Tel: 514-8522). **Renta Moto Juanchi** (Fresh Water Bay. Tel: 514-8112) and **Renta Motos Old Providence** (Santa Isabel. Tel: 514-8369) rent both mopeds and cars. **Paradise Tour Contact** rents bicycles and kayaks (Agua Dulce, Tel: 514-8283). Updated: Aug 3, 2011.

Safety
Issues that affect other parts of Colombia are noticeably absent. The main risks here are absent-minded drivers and motorcyclists. If hiking in the highlands, protect yourself against ticks. Updated: Aug 2, 2011.

Services
TOURISM
The **tourism office** is just past the baggage claim in El Embrujo airport (Tel: 514-8003). There is also an office at the Hotel Aury near the harbor (Santa Isabel. Tel: 312-315-6492, info@oldprovidence.com.co, URL: www.oldprovidence.com.co). Other useful websites are: www.providenciaespasion.com and www.sanandres.me.uk.

MONEY
Banco Agrario and **Banco de Bogotá**, both in Santa Isabel, have ATMs. No travelers checks are accepted and U.S. dollars can be changed in some supermarkets or hotels. Most restaurants do not accept credit cards.

KEEPING IN TOUCH
The larger hotels have telephones and fax services. Although harder to come by, an internet café is in Santa Isabel and another in the offices of **Body Contact** travel agent in Sweet Water Bay (Agua Dulce). Expect to pay at least $1.50 per hour to connect with the outside world.

MEDICAL
The **hospital** is in Santa Isabel (Tel: 514-8024/emergency: 11). Ambulances can also be reached at the same number. Severe problems will most likely take you to San Andrés or the mainland. A pharmacy is in the supermarket in Santa Isabel.

RELIGION
Baptist, Adventist, Catholic and other Protestant churches are available. Most services held in English. Updated: Aug 3, 2011.

Things to See and Do
Providencia is a nature lover's paradise, thanks to its idyllic geographical isolation and the fact that it remains largely undeveloped. More than just an ideal place to lie back and relax, Providencia's status as a protected area means that a short stroll will take you from the center of town into a tropical wonderland that seems made for divers and hikers. Highlights are Parque Nacional McBean Lagoon, El Pico hill, Playa Manzanillo and Santa Catalina.
One Saturday, head to South West Bay to see the horse races. Two horses are pitted against each other in a competition that

extends the length of the beach. Millions of pesos change hands in bets and the atmosphere is electric. Updated: Aug 3, 2011.

Parque Nacional
Old Providence McBean Lagoon

(ADMISSION: $2 adults, $1 children) Parque Nacional Natural Old Providence McBean Lagoon, in the extreme northeast of Providencia Island, is the archipelago's only national park. It protects McBean Lagoon, Three Brothers Cays and Crab Cay, as well as reefs and 37 hectares (92 acres) of well-preserved mangroves. Land features include McBean Lagoon and Iron Wood Hill (150 meters / 500 ft), a steep rise with a full 360-degree view of the isle and the seven-color ocean rippling over the exposed reef. In the marine portion is the barrier reef that protects Providence Island's shore and is the second largest in the Caribbean.

McBean Lagoon is nesting ground for a variety of resident and migratory birds. Here, the Seven Colours hiking trail wends through mangrove. Another hike is up through the dry tropical forest of Iron Wood Hill. Crab Cay's fauna includes black crab, and three varieties of lizard: pennie, screeching and blue. The reefs, composed of hard and soft corals, are home to parrotfish, comber, trumpetfish, grunt and other reef fish. Scuba diving and snokeling is good at this cay, as is kayaking. Crab Cay and Three Brothers Cays can only be reached by boat. To get to the mangrove area, take the road that runs along Maracaibo Hill. Extra fees are charged for diving permits. Updated: Aug 8, 2011.

Hike to El Pico, Providencia

Check the skies, consult the weather forecast, speak to some islanders and then choose the ideal day to hike up to El Pico (360 m/1,181 ft). The highest point on the rugged island of Providencia, El Pico offers breathtaking views over the whole island: its azure bays, white sandy beaches, mangroves, quaint settlements and McBean Lagoon. Be sure to bring sunblock and tick repellent. Updated: Aug 8, 2011.

Santa Catalina

The tiny island of Santa Catalina was connected to Providencia at one time, but it is believed that pirates—possibly Henry Morgan or the Dutchman Edward Manswelt—may have cut a 100-meter (328-ft) wide channel to make for an easily defendable, one-square-kilometer base on Santa

Catalina. Today the island is connected to Providencia by a causeway named "Puente de los Enamorados" ("Lover's Bridge"). Across the bridge from Providencia is a path along the waterfront, which is interrupted with placards detailing historical curiosities and identifying where six forts have been placed over the years. What remains today of these bastions, symbols of European imperial designs, are hardened rubble and a few scattered cannons. Be sure to bring along your camera and snap some photos of the views and of the delightfully painted traditional Caribbean architecture. Updated: Aug 8, 2011

Beaches

Providencia has some of the Caribbean's premier beaches with calm waters. The most secluded is Manchaneel (Playa Manzanillo), which is accessible only by taxi or private transport. Get here early to enjoy a full day in the true paradisaical cliché.

Another fine stretch of strand is South West Bay, a 20-minute walk from Freshwater Bay. Here are the archipelago's clearest waters, perfect for snorkeling. Fort Bay on Santa Catalina also has great snorkeling. The path passes by a pirate-era fortress and continues to Morgan's Head.

Freshwater Bay, where most hotels are located, also has a good beach. As well, Providencia and Santa Catalina's coasts are dotted with coves and beaches, like Almond Bay and Pasha Beach, as well as others that are accessible only by boat. Updated: Aug 8, 2011.

Boat Tours

Group boat tours leave every day for a morning at sea to explore Crab Cay, Lovers Bridge, Morgan's Head, Machineel Beach and other sites. Unfortunately, all the tours seem to show up at the same places at the same times.

You can also charter a boat to take in the above sites—and to places others don't go, like the best snorkeling spots. The advantage is that you can arrive when the group tours aren't there. Share the cost with other travelers, and it turns out to be the better option.

Group tours cost about $17 per person and include lunch. To charter a boat for an all-day, private tour costs about $200. Hotels can arrange a ticket on a group tour, or contact Body Contact Tours. To privately charter a boat, ask at your hotel or for a recommended local fisherman. Hippy in Aguadulce and Pirate Morgan Hotel also arrange charters for tour, snorkeling and fishing excursions. Updated: Aug 8, 2011.

Diving in Providencia

Arguably having clearer water that its larger and more frequently visited neighbor, San Andrés, Providencia is a scuba diver's dream. The island has calm, crystalline waters and an abundance of marine life (many of which are endemic species). Both beginners and seasoned professionals will enjoy diving here. Don't be put off by the islanders' laid-back attitudes in their day-to-day business—the diving equipment is well cared-for and the instruction is up to international standards. Updated: Aug 8, 2011.

Volunteering

Trees and Reefs Foundation

Have you ever dreamed of helping a community with vital environmental and cultural issues—on a tropical isle? You have such a chance on Old Providence, where the NGO Trees and Reefs Foundation works together with Coraline, the archipelago's environmental protection agency, on conservation issues and sustainability on the island. Expert natural and social scientists help Islanders with iguana, reef and conch repopulation, sustainable agriculture, a museum, oral history and other projects. You must be a university graduate, understand Spanish and be able to commit at least three months. Volunteers pay for their own food and lodging, staying with local families. Come See Sector, Santa Isabel Town. Cel: 316-424-3192/321-215-4846, E-mail: trees. reefsfoundation@gmail.com / chris@paisatours.com, URL: http://treesreefsfoundation. blogspot.com / www.paisatours.com/volunteer-providencia.htm. Updated: Aug 9, 2011.

Tours

Providencia is a small island where everybody knows everybody, so it is not always necessary to sign up with a tour operator. However, it is advisable to do so for safety reasons. The most comprehensive operator on the island is **Body Contact**, located at Freshwater Bay (Tel: 514-8118, Fax: 514-8283, E-mail: bodycontact2002@ yahoo.com). Another agency is **Rodolfo** (South West Bay, Tel: 514-8626).

Several scuba diving centers operate on Providencia: **Felipe's Diving** (Cabañas El Recreo, Freshwater Bay. Tel: 514-8775, Cel: 312-521-7503, E-mail: info@felipediving.com, URL: www.felipediving.com), **Providencia Marina and Yacht Club** (South West Bay. Cel: 313-747-6238, E-mail: info@providencereefdiving.com, URL: www.providencereefdiving.com), **Scuba Town** (Old Town. Tel: 514-8481, E-mail: jerodive@yahoo.com), **Sirius Dive Center** (South West Bay. Tel: 514-8213, E-mail: info@siriusdivecenter.com) and **Sonny Diving Shop** (Freshwater Bay. Tel: 514-8231, Cel: 313-430-2911, E-mail: gerencia@ sonnydiveshop.com, URL: www.sonnydiveshop.com). Updated: Aug 3, 2011.

Lodging

Lodging on Providencia is a simple affair. Most places do have air conditioning, but not hot water. All told, there are about two dozen hotels and guesthouses strung along the island's coasts. The main tourism spot is Freshwater Bay. Over all, it is more expensive to stay on Providencia than on San Andrés.

As well as one hotel of its own, Decameron has five affiliated hotels on the isle. The majority of hotels, though, on Providencia are independently owned, family-run guesthouses. Renting a house or *cabaña* is an economical choice for families or groups.

Posadas nativas have also begun opening here. **Posada Betito's Place** (Cel: 314-471-5574, E-mail: betitobritton@hotmail.com) is a shipwreck treasure-decorated inn with a view of Crab Cay. **Posada Nativa Sunshine Paradise** is on Santa Catalina Island (Tel: 514-9031, Cel: 311-227-0333, E-mail: franciscarobinson@yahoo.com, URL: www. posadasunshine.com). For a complete list of options, visit Posadas Turísticas de Colombia (URL: www.posadasturisticasdecolombia.com). Updated: Aug 4, 2011.

Posada Vicky

(ROOMS: $10-35) A short walk up the hill from the beach, Posada Vicky is a family home with two converted rooms for tourists. These rooms have air conditioning but lack a good view and sea breeze. Located on the road running down to South West beach, Posada Vicky is an option should other destinations with better locations be full. Posada Vicky is one of the island's *posadas nativas*. Tel: 514-9127. Updated: Aug 8, 2011.

Hotel Sirius Center

(ROOMS: $25-125) The Hotel Sirius Center is at the far end of South West Beach.

This expansive 12-room (30-bed) development is also the site of the Sirius dive center. All rooms have air conditioning, ocean views, TV and a mini-bar. Aside from the convenience of a dive shop on your doorstep, the hotel has a conference room and a restaurant. Prices vary greatly between low and high seasons. The hotel is located at the bottom of the road to South West Bay on the left, opposite from Miss Mary. Tel: 514-8213, E-mail: info@siriushotel.net. Updated: Aug 8, 2011.

Miss Mary

(ROOMS: $40-50) Imagine being able to stroll out of your room and onto a white sandy beach with cool turquoise Caribbean waters lapping the shore. That, in a nutshell, is Cabañas Miss Mary. Located in the tranquil South West Bay, Miss Mary has seven rooms with a total of 14 beds. Four rooms look out onto the ocean while the other three are around the back in a less atmospheric setting. The rooms are comfortable and clean, and it's hard to beat the sense of serenity as you sit on your porch in a hammock watching the sun drip over the horizon. Miss Mary is one of Decameron's affiliates on the island. South West Bay. Tel: 514-8206. Updated: Aug 8, 2011.

Hotel El Pirata Morgan

(ROOMS: $45-75) Hotel El Pirata Morgan is a 30-room hotel (60 beds) on the beach at Freshwater Bay. It's named after the famed pirate who used the island as his base on many occasions. The hotel isn't built in the traditional Caribbean style, but don't let this put you off. Each room has an ocean view and is fully equipped with bathroom, air conditioning, mini-bar and Direct TV. Freshwater Bay. Tel: 514-8067/8528, E-mail: morganhotel@hotmail.com, URL: www.elpiratamorganhotel.org. Updated: Aug 11, 2011.

Hotel Miss Elma

(ROOMS: $65-215) Hotel Miss Elma is found in the "tourist zone" of Freshwater Bay (Bahía de Agua Dulce). All four suites in the hotel have ocean views, air conditioning, mini-bar and cable TV. Well-kept and brightly painted, Hotel Miss Elma is everything a Caribbean hotel should be: effortlessly charming and laid-back. This is a Decameron-affiliated hotel. Freshwater Bay. Tel: 514-8229. Updated: Aug 8, 2011.

Deep Blue

(ROOMS: $172-507) This small luxury hotel has a beautiful and peaceful location with spectacular views of McBean Lagoon National Park. In front of the hotel is Crab Cay, to where it is possible to kayak (kayaks are provided by the hotel). The rooftop has an infinity-edge plunge pool. The seafront restaurant has a lovely wooden deck over the sea and makes a relaxing place. Bahía Maracaibo. Cel: 321-458-2099, E-mail: info@hoteldeepblue.com, URL: www.hoteldeepblue.com. Updated: Aug 8, 2011.

Cabañas El Recreo

Cabañas El Recreo offers beach-side cabins with 15 guestrooms. The accommodations are fully equipped with air conditioning, refrigerator and cable TV. The Happy Sailor Restaurant is located on the grounds. The friendly hotel staff will book trips or organize transport for you. El Recreo is next to Felipe's Diving Shop. This is another one of Decameron's affiliates on Providencia; reservations must be made through Decameron (www.decameron.com). Freshwater Bay. Tel: 514-8010, Cel: 311-333-0519, E-mail: capbryan@hotmail.com. Updated: Aug 8, 2011.

Restaurants

Providencia is a seafood lover's paradise. Black crab is the local delicacy. If ordering lobster, avoid the small-sized ones for ecology sake. Other than that, there's only chicken and tough beef. Vegetarians have few choices. The best restaurants are ones not at hotels. There are several cheap eateries in Santa Isabel. Many restaurants are closed on Sunday, except at South West Bay and at hotels. On Sunday, street vendors open shop and locals put on BBQs. Updated: Aug 8, 2011.

Seaflower Bakery and Coffee Shop

Should you fnd yourself in Town (Santa Isabel) and in need of a sightseeing break, then look no further than Seaflower. This small bakery has pastries, sandwiches, coffees and a bookstore. It's cheap, friendly and very much a local's place. Opposite the Alcaldía, Santa Isabel. Tel: 514-8584. Updated: Aug 8, 2011.

Roland's

Roland Bryan Eden and his son Jason have the best spot on the best beach in Providencia, with its shaded and sheltered homemade tables and chairs clustered in a palm grove. With views of incredible Machineel Beach, Roland's is a place to come for lunch and stay until dinner. Service may be slow, but if you are here you won't want to leave. Try the house spe-

CARIBBEAN COAST

cialty: snapper with vegetables cooked in aluminum foil over an open fire—simply delicious. Reggae beats play at a pleasant volume and on occasion a live band plays in the evening around the burning embers of the central fire. While no credit cards are accepted here, prices are reasonable. Machineel Beach (Playa Manzanillo). Tel: 514-8417, E-mail: rolandsbeach@hotmail. com. Updated: Aug 8, 2011

El Divino Niño

(ENTREES: $5-16) Open only for lunch, El Divino Niño is the quintessential Caribbean beachfront eatery. Wooden tables are placed haphazardly on the sand and the menu is painted primitively on the back wall. Don't let the informality of the place put you off—the prices are reasonable for Providencia and the food is sumptuous. Seafood is, of course, the specialty, but chicken is on the menu as well. An order of fried fish is enough for two people. South West Bay. Updated: Aug 8, 2011.

Richard's Place

Richard's Place is ideal for a sunset on South West Bay. It's a rustic Rasta joint, with hammocks and hand-painted tables. Enjoy a potent piña colada or coco loco, or nurse an ice-cold beer while relaxing in the tranquil setting. Updated: Aug 8, 2011.

Donde Martín

Donde Martín is in the Hotel Cabañas Agua Dulce, at the north end of Freshwater Bay. The menu is extensive and more adventurous than at other restaurants on the island, and spices are used liberally. Particularly recommended are the seafood specials and the chicken and crab entree. Donde Martín has an imaginative marine-themed décor. Tel: 514-8160, Cel: 311-287-7238. Updated: Aug 8, 2011.

Nightlife

The best bars on Providence are Roland's at Manzanillo Beach and Richard's Place at South West Bay. Locals hang out drinking at Lovers Bridge on the weekends. Ask around for discos, but be forewarned these are locals-only places and you'll probably be the only tourist in the joint. Updated: Aug 8, 2011.

CARIBBEAN COAST

!!!!!

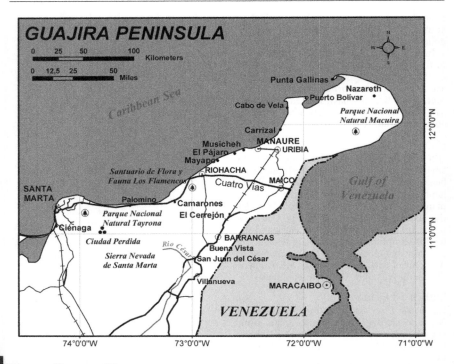

La Guajira Peninsula

The Guajira (Wajirra in the language of the Wayuu) was once considered nothing more than a no-man's land replete with smugglers and outlaws. Due to its isolation, this barren corner of the earth was said to be populated by hostile Indians—a place too dangerous to travel to alone. But after embarking on a journey to this far northeastern region of Colombia, you will soon discover a different face. Welcome to the Land of Dreams and Death, as the Wayuu call their homeland.

The Guajira is divided into three parts, each distinguished by vegetation. Baja Guajira is the southernmost, with lands reaching toward the Sierra Nevada de Santa Marta and with an economy based on agriculture and cattle raising. The world's largest coal mine, El Cerrejón, is also here. Media Guajira, which includes Riohacha Maicao and Manaure, is a hot region, but with moderate temperatures and low-desert flora. Alta Guajira—Uribia, northward to Cabo de Vela and Nazareth—is what we most often think of as Wajirra: desolate deserts. In the eastern

midst of this is the oasis of the Macuira mountain range. Much of this area is difficult to reach with public transport. A sliver of the peninsula belongs to Venezuela, though for the Wayuu, this border does not exist.

The Wayuu (Guajiro) community is a very traditional matrilineal society. Many are willing—after the ice is broken—to teach you about their culture. It is said you make a Wayuu friend for life; even if you return 10 years later, you will be welcomed into the home. Also in the Guajira are significant communities of Afro-Colombians, descendents of Maroons.

Fresh water is scarce in the Media and Alta Guajira, thus affecting the price of every commodity. Hotels may have limited supplies, *comidas corrientes* (specials of the day) often don't include a drink, and transport is more expensive. Have your budget prepared and practice conservation measures.

Access to Guajira is accessible from the Troncal del Caribe highway, as well as from Valledupar in the south. When making travel plans, be aware the southern highway is closed and heavily patrolled from dusk to dawn. The United States have talked

---

Highlights

Take out your binoculars and observe flamingos and other migratory birds at **Santuario Natural Nacional Los Flamencos** (p. 355).

Visit **Cabo de la Vela** (p. 362) for its natural wonders like the Ojo de Agua, the Pilón de Azúcar and Hoyos Sopladores, not to mention the magnificent sunsets.

Celebrate the artistry, gastronomy, music and poetry at the **Festival de Cultura Wayuu** (p. 360), the meeting of the Wayuu nation held at the end of May in Uribia.

The glittering **salt flats of Manaure** (p. 356) are a perfect example of the differences between industrial and traditional extraction of this mineral.

Explore a cloud forest amid the desert: **Parque Nacional Natural Macuira** (p. 368).

about establishing a controversial military base in the peninsula, but it has yet to be done. Updated: Mar 29, 2011.

History

Since time immemorial, the Wayuu have lived in Wajirra. The first Spaniard to sail around the coast was Alonso de Ojeda and the first to step foot on this barren earth was Juan de la Cosa. In the 16th century, the governments of Santa Marta and Venezuela disputed the governance of this peninsula. Each wanted to control the wealth of this land.

The first city in the Guajira Peninsula, Cabo de la Vela, was founded by Martín Fernández de Enciso in 1526. This served as the territory's capital until 1544, when the seat was moved to Riohacha. In 1772, Antonio de Arévalo was sent to pacify the peninsula and establish *caseríos* (small villages) where the indigenous were relocated. These included San José de Bahía Honda (1772), Pedraza (1774), San Bartolomé de Sinamaica (1774) and Santa Ana de Savana del Valle (1776). Until 1871, the Guajira was part of the Magdalena department; only then was it made a territory.

In 1964, it was decreed a new department. During all these centuries of foreign domination, the Wayuu were peons in their own

Responsible Travel in La Guajira

Wayuu suggest the following etiquette practices for visitors to Guajira:

▶ Water is very important. Use only what is necessary for showering.

▶ Always ask permission to take photos.

▶ Cemeteries are sacred grounds. You may enter, but show respect and don't touch anything.

▶ If you give a gift to a family you are visiting, give it to the head of the household.

▶ Drinking alcohol is taboo.

▶ Giving money to beggars is OK, if you feel so inclined. However, don't give candy or money to children.

▶ When eating with Wayuu, do not begin until everyone is present and seated.

▶ After a meal, especially lunch, it is customary to take a nap.

▶ Men may wear shorts. Sleeveless shirts are fine at home. In public, wear a shirt with sleeves. Going shirtless is frowned upon.

▶ Women may wear any type of shirt, with sleeves or without, or even showing the midriff. However, as for men, going shirtless is not accepted. Pants and shorts are OK.

▶ Both genders can swim in whatever attire they like, but no skinny dipping. Updated: Mar 18, 2011.

homeland, forced to labor in the salt and coal mines, in pearling and fishing, on cattle ranches and in contraband running. In the latter part of the 20th century and even now into the 21st, the Wayuu, Afro-Colombians and other inhabitants of the region have seen their communities adversely affected by the massive coal mining and port operations. Remote settlements have been victims of paramilitary attacks, which have caused a tremendous internal refugee problem. Updated: Mar 29, 2011.

LA GUAJIRA

Wayuu Culture

Some describe the Wayuu of the Guajira (Wajirra) as a society where the men do nothing and the women do all the work. From the viewpoint of someone raised in a patriarchal culture, it may seem valid. In truth, these traditionally nomadic people are matrilineal, meaning name, place in society and property pass through the mother. The desert shapes their beliefs, just as the wind shapes the sands: The Wajirra is the land of dreams and death. Wayuu society is divided into 12 clans, each with its own name, symbol and animal. Not only is this identification passed through the mother, but also the definition of who is Wayuu. In the case of marriages with *alijuna* (non-Wayuu), the child is only Wayuu if the mother is.

Community duties follow gender lines. Women are responsible for the household and child-rearing; the men for fishing and goat-rearing. Women fetch precious water; the men, firewood. Women weave *süi* (hammocks) and *susu* (bags); the men, *womu* (hats) and *waireñas* (sandals). Healers may be of either sex. Some specialize in dreams, upon which Wayuu place special significance.

The youngest daughter inherits property, as she is the nearest to life. The eldest daughter, being the closest to death, is responsible for funerary rituals. The Wayuu have two burials: The first is immediately after death and a second occurs five to 10 years later. For this, the daughter undergoes a year-long purification before disinterring and cleaning the bones for the second entombment.

At puberty, only females have a rite of passage. This entails over a year of isolation from the community, during which time she learns the customs of being a woman, songs and dances, and weaving. Because of modern-day demands of school attendance, this ritual now is done in two or three months. Only in isolated *rancherías* (shanty towns) is the longer term still used.

The most important male figure to a child is the eldest maternal uncle. It is he who disciplines. When a potential fiancé asks for a Wayuu woman's hand in marriage, he must go to the uncle, who sets the bride-price. If the husband seeks a divorce, the woman keeps the dowry; if the wife, then she must return half the bequest.

The Wayuu way of dispute resolution, applied by Pütchipü'üi (orators), was recognized in 2010 by UNESCO as an Intangible Cultural Heritage of Humanity. Dance, or *yonna*, is performed only for rituals. Recreational dancing, as at discotheques, is not a part of Wayuu culture. To learn more about Wayuu culture and society (in Spanish), visit: URL: hospitalnazareth.com/cultura_wayuu/estructura_social/estructura_social.html. Updated: May 15, 2009.

When to Go

The Guajira is extremely hot, especially the Media and Alta; temperatures can reach over 40°C (over 100°F). Depending on the region, the most scorching and wettest months vary. In the Media Guajira—Riohacha and Manaure—May-July are the hottest months, with rains coming in April and again between September and November. As you move into the Alta Guajira, patterns change. Inland, around Uribia, showers arrive May-July. Cabo de la Vela, on the coast, has its rains June-August and heat between September-November and January-February. The entire region experiences high winds in January and February.

The beaches of the Guajira, like Palomino and Cabo de la Vela, have become very popular vacation destinations for Colombians. At Christmas and New Years, Semana Santa (especially) and three-day holiday weekends, they are very crowded and prices rise accordingly. Updated: Mar 29, 2011.

Safety

Travel with public transportation is safe in the Guajira, even alone. If traveling by private vehicle, stick to main roads and carry extra gas and water. Hitchhiking in pairs is said to be OK; police and locals can assist. Residents warn not to walk across the desert, whether by trail or road, for danger of

Photo by: Tanenhaus

robbery. Do not drive at night. Much contraband (especially drugs) and paramilitary activities still occur in remote areas.

The Wajirra sun is extremely strong; even Wayuu women wear an earthen mask, a natural sunscreen (Face painting of designs serves another purpose: to express what is going on in her life). During the rainy season, dengue is present. In more humid regions—the coast west of Riohacha and toward the Sierra—malaria and yellow fever exist. Mountain range denizens include the Chagas disease-carrying pito or assassin bug; those of the desert, scorpions and, in secluded areas, snakes. Updated: Mar 18, 2011.

Things to See and Do

Wajirra is a land of contrasts: sea and desert, colonial Riohacha and modern Uribia, untouched landscapes and exploited resources. Sunsets and moon rises are breathtaking, especially at Cabo de la Vela, which also has stunning natural formations to explore. Beaches like Poportín and Palomino are virtually empty during the low season.

Guajira is a birdwatcher's paradise, with flamingos taking haven in lagoons like Laguna de Utta, Carrizal and Musichi. Within the region are several important national parks, among them Macuira, Sierra Nevada de Santa Marta and Santuario de Flora y Fauna Los Flamencos. The region also boasts the world's largest open-pit coal mine, El Cerrejón; one of the biggest wind-turbine electricity projects, Parque Eólico Jepirachi; and the greatest salt extraction at Manaure. You can visit all of them.

The female-centered Wayuu culture remains well-preserved. You can buy *susu* (bags), *chinchorros* (hammocks) or other weavings, spend an evening at a *ranchería* (settlement) eating typical food and drink, or attend the annual Festival de Cultura Wayuu.

Tours

Tour companies across the Caribbean coast offer packages to the Guajira; multi-night trips will find you sleeping in hammocks. These excursions tend to be quite pricey, costing $75-191. One-day trips from Riohacha are also available from $27 per person (minimum of four). Some scuba shops in Santa Marta and Taganga arrange diving safaris at Cabo de la Vela and other points off the Guajira coast. Tour operators also offer a Tarde de Ranchería, a visit to a Wayuu community. During such tours, you learn about the culture and traditions of this nation, see a dance performance, and partake in a typical Wayuu meal including *friche* (goat meat) and *chirrinchi*, the traditional alcoholic drink.

Before deciding on an agency, ensure its vehicles are in good shape and plenty of water is taken along; remember you will be traveling across desert. Also, check the relationship the operator has with the native communities; it should work in partnership with them and not in exploiting them. Updated: Mar 18, 2011.

Lodging

Lodging costs quite a bit more in the Guajira, due in large part to the high cost of water. Shoestring travelers should budget for this. Options to camp or to sling your hammock are also possible in some areas—or may be your only choice. Large chain hotels have yet to arrive on the scene, and Wayuu communities are resisting their entrance into the market. Wayuu prefer to welcome guests in traditional style, thus promoting employment and economic opportunities. In villages and rancherías, do not expect the installed shower to work. You will have to *echar el agua*: a large covered container is provided from which you dip water to throw over you. Keep the water within clean (it can also be treated for drinking) and covered (to minimize mosquito breeding habitats). Updated: Mar 18, 2011.

PALOMINO

Here's a little Colombian secret, one that few foreigners have heard about. It's called Palomino, and it is midway between Riohacha and Santa Marta, flanked by the San Salvador and Palomino Rivers. The town straddles the coastal highway and buses pass through regularly. Head to the beach where the Caribbean lies wide open, waves crashing ashore.

In the dawn light, fishermen push their boats to sea. Comb these amber sands for shells or observe birds in the rivers' mangroves. On clear mornings, the snowy peaks of Sierra Nevada de Santa Marta backdrop the palm trees. Sea turtles nest here in season. Updated: Mar 18, 2011.

When to Go

Palomino, like the rest of coastal Guajira, is hot, especially during May-July. January winds are brisk. September-November is the rainy season, as is April. Palomino is a popular vacation destination for Colombians. If you want the beach to yourself, avoid Christmas, New Years, Semana Santa and three-day holiday weekends, when it can get very crowded. Updated: Mar 18, 2011.

Getting To and Away

Take any Riohacha-Santa Marta bus and ask the driver to let you off at Palomino (from Riohacha, bus $6.35; to Santa Marta buseta $3.70; 1.5 hr either direction). The beach, where most lodging is located, is one kilometer (0.6 mi) away. As the way is confusing and access is difficult, it is best to phone the hostel you'll be staying at for directions. Updated: Jun 11, 2008.

Safety

Many of the available hotels are in fenced grounds where the administrator-family also lives, thus providing some security. Beach camping is not recommended, except possibly during holiday times when many other travelers are pitching their tents, bringing safety in numbers.

The Caribbean here is open sea, meaning strong currents along the shore and at the mouth of the rivers. Most locals, even the kids, go swimming upstream of the rivers, where the water is more placid. During the rainy season, take precautions against mosquitoes, which carry dengue, malaria and yellow fever (for which you should be vaccinated). Updated: Mar 18, 2011.

Lodging

A half-dozen or more inns rest on the beach, but most close during the off-season. They range from camping and hammock places to romantic cabaña getaways. Expect your shower to be unreliable; many shift in temperature and water pressure frequently. Electricity is a bit scarce along here, so be sure you have a flashlight and extra candles with you. Since the nearest restaurants are up by the highway, one kilometer (0.6 mi) away, some hostels have cooking facilities. Call the hotel where you will be staying beforehand so it may arrange for your visit accordingly.

La Casa de Rosa

(BEDS: $3-5) Rosa left a few years back, leaving Eugenio and his young family to run this wonderful backpacker retreat on a wooded ground just 50 meters (164 ft) from the beach. Lodging is either camping ($3.20 per person), a hammock in the enramada (open sided palm-thatch shelter) or front porch of the guesthouse, or a room with bed in the hostel. A rustic shower hut is where you will take a bath; porcelain latrines service your other needs. Prepare your meals in the outdoor kitchen. There is no electricity, though candles are provided. Eugenio also has more luxurious digs, with electricity and other amenities. Call for directions. Cel: 315-752-6287/311-680-6821. Updated: Jun 10, 2008.

La Sirena Eco Hostel and Retreat Center !

(HAMMOCKS: $10 per person, BEDS: $24 per person, CABAÑAS: $37 per person) La Sirena Eco-Hostel and Retreat Center is a peaceful getaway located on the Caribbean Sea. Just 30 minutes from Tayrona Park, the hostel's property—which is part of a coconut plantation—has its own beach and fruit trees, and there are also a few rivers within walking distance. Accommodations include hammocks, bedrooms for two to four people, and private cabañas. Many of the rooms afford views of the sea, and the La Sierra Nevada de Santa Marta, the tallest coastal mountain on earth, can be seen from the grounds. La Sirena hosts yoga, spiritual healing, personal wellness and healing arts retreats at its facility, so check its website for scheduled events. Yoga classes (1.5 hr) take place every Wednesday morning. There is also an on-site restaurant, which serves traditional Colombian meals and snacks. Prices include breakfast. To get there, take a bus from Santa Marta's downtown market or from the Mamatoco bus stop to Palomino (72 km/45 mi, aprox. 1.5 hr). From there, you can walk (about 20 min) to the beach through Don Aires entrance (ask in town); or, take a Moto taxi (no later that 5 p.m.) to La Sirena. Once there, walk on the beach (about 5 min) toward the right until you see a bright multi-colored house close to the water, which is La Sirena. Cel: 313-823-7930/301-640-0484, Email: ecosirena@gmail.com, URL: www.ecosirena.com. Updated: Mar 29, 2011.

Photo by: Tanenhaus

geographical center of the city, is a roundabout with a statue of the town's most famous figure: the legendary Vallenato accordionist Francisco el Hombre, immortalized in song for his duel with the Devil and in Gabriel García Márquez' *Hundred Years of Solitude*. Only one hour from the Venezuelan border, Riohacha makes a convenient resting point before heading to or coming from that sister nation. Updated: Mar 18, 2011.

RIOHACHA

 3m   125,000   5

If you rely on historical Colombian literature to paint the picture of Riohacha (Wayuu: Süchiimma), you would believe it is a Wild West type of town, with lots of contraband running and other shady activities going on. Once arriving, though, you soon discover it's a surprisingly pleasant place with a beautiful malecón and great beach. This is the capital of the Guajira, and the Wayuu, the native residents of this department, are present all over. Welcome to one of the most mysterious corners of Colombia!

The Troncal del Caribe highway passes directly through Riohacha, at Calle 15, cutting the city into two zones. In the center of this roadway, marking more or less the

History

This stretch of the coast had long been a meeting ground of indigenous peoples, the Kogui descending from the Sierra Nevada to trade with the Wayuu and others. In 1535, German explorer Nikolaus Federmann established Riohacha on the west bank of the Río Ranchería. For many years, the most prized pearls came from here, which made it a favorite target of pirates. Sir Francis Drake sacked the port in 1596. With the collapse of the pearl industry in the 18th century, Riohacha became just a tropical backwater, earning the reputation of being an anything-goes town. It was with the creation of the Guajira department in 1965 that Riohacha was declared the official capital. Updated: Jun 10, 2008.

When to Go

Expect rains in Riohacha and the surrounding region September-November. April is also a showery month. January brings fresh

LA GUAJIRA

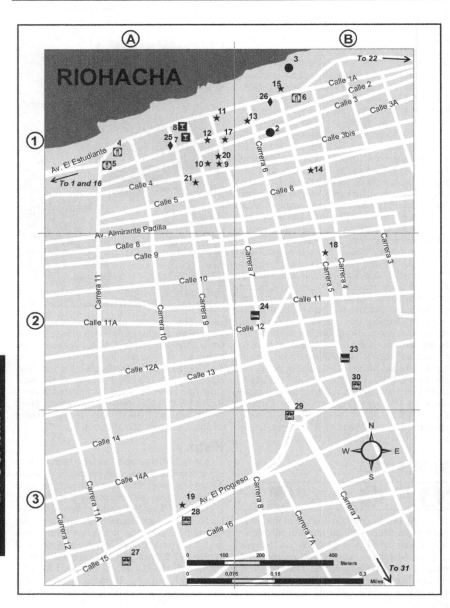

LA GUAJIRA

breezes that roughen the sea; small craft advisories may be issued and scuba diving is nearly impossible. May, June and July are the hottest months, with temperatures reaching 39°C (102°F). Updated: Mar 18, 2011.

HOLIDAYS AND FESTIVALS

Like every town along the Caribbean coast, Riohacha observes the pre-Lent feast of Carnaval beginning the Saturday before Ash Wednesday. It is claimed the one here is the oldest in Colombia. At about 3 a.m. on Sunday morning, men cover themselves with mud, then enter town dancing the *cumbia de pilón*. The Queen of Carnaval and plain folks join in on the procession to the sea, where the

Activities ●

1 Casa de la Cultura A1
2 Centro Cultural Municipal Enrique
   Lallemand B1
3 The Malecón and Beach B1

Eating 🍴

4 Asados Don Pepe A1
5 Marino's Junior A1
6 Restaurante Bar La Tinaja B1

Nightlife ☑

7 Casa Vieja Galería Bar A1
8 Mariano's Bar A1

Services ★

9 Banco AV Villas A1
10 Bancolombia A1
11 Banco Popular A1
12 BBVA A1
13 Correos de Colombia B1
14 DAS B1
15 Dirección de Turismo de la Guajira B1

16 Hospital Nuestra Señora de los
   Remedios A1
17 National Park Office A1
18 Spumas Lavandería y Servicios B2
19 Telecom A3
20 Venezuelan Consulate A1
21 Yejogi Internet A1

Sleeping 🛏

22 Hotel Gimaura B1
23 Hotel Panorama B2
24 Hotel Yalconia del Mar B2

Tours ◆

25 Cabo de la Vela Operadora Turística A1
26 Luna Guajira B1

Transportation 🚌

27 Bus Terminal A3
28 Collective taxis for Valledupar A3
29 Collective taxis to Camarones B3
30 Collective taxis to Maicao, Uribia
   and Manaure B2
31 Pickup trucks to Manaure and Uribia B3

men then wash themselves off. Look forward to lots of *maicena* (corn starch) and water being tossed. Other celebrations to catch are the feast days of the Virgen de los Remedios, Riohacha's patron saint, commemorating May 14, 1663, when she saved the city from a surging tide; and the Festival del Dividivi (Caesalpinia Coriaria), a salute to the arbor symbol of the Guajira department, June 29-July 1. Updated: Mar 18, 2011.

Getting To and Away

There are a variety of ways to get to Riohacha: busetas or small buses ($0.35), taxis ($1.30-1.60) and mototaxis ($0.50). The bus terminal, at Calle 15 and Carrera 11a, has restaurants, a phone, shops and bathrooms.

From Riohacha

To:	Departure	Time	Price
Maicao	5 a.m.-10 p.m.	1 hr	$2.65
Maracaibo	3:30 p.m.	2-3 hr	$24
Caracas	3:30 p.m.	18 hr	$76
Santa Marta	every half hour	2-3 hr	$8-13

To:	Departure	Time	Price
Barranquilla	every half hour	4-5 hr	$11-17
Cartagena	every half hour	6-7 hr	$19-24
Valledupar	4 p.m.	4 hr	$8
Bucaramanga	4 p.m.	12 hr	$49
Bogotá	3 p.m., 3:15 p.m.	20-24 hr	$69

Alternately, you can flag down a bus to your destination as it passes through town on Calle 15. To go to Palomino, take a Santa Marta bus. Shared taxis to Maicao leave from Calle 15 and Carrera 5 (5:30 a.m-5 p.m.), and the last taxi from Maicao to Riohacha leaves at 6 p.m. ($3). To get to Manaure and Uribia, taxis take off from the same neighborhood. Collective taxis for Valledupar depart from Calle 15 and Carrera 10, across from the phone company. To reach Camarones, catch a ride from Calle 15 and Carrera 7.

LA GUAJIRA

Camionetas (pick-up trucks) to Manaure and Uribia leave from the large municipal market on Carrera 7, about five long blocks south of Calle 15.

Aeropuerto Almirante Padilla provides service to Bogotá (end of Cra. 11, south of Ca. 15. Tel: 727-3854). Updated: Jun 10, 2008.

Safety

The central part of Riohacha is said to be safe at night, but not the areas on the far side of Calle 15. During evenings, you will see families sitting in front of their homes, taking advantage of the nocturnal breeze. Care should be taken, also, on more secluded parts of the beach during dark hours. During the rainy season, take precautions against disease-carrying mosquitoes. The tap water is not safe to drink without treatment. Updated: Jun 10, 2008.

Services

TOURISM

The tourism office, Dirección de Turismo de la Guajira, is on the malecón. It dispenses basic, curt information on what to do and see in all the Guajira (daily 8 a.m.-noon and 2-6 p.m., but may close earlier on weekends. Calle 1 and Carrera 5. Tel: 727-1015, E-mail: lourdesmarevalo@yahoo.es).

Other offices of importance are:

• DAS—Monday-Friday 7-11:30 a.m. and 2-3:30 p.m. Ca. 5, 4-48. Tel: 727-2407.

• Instituto Geográfico Agustín Codazzi— Ca. 12, 5-25. Tel: 727-3930.

• National Park office—Cra. 7, 2-15. Tel: 728-2636.

• Venezuelan Consulate—Cra. 7, 3-08, P-7B, Edificio Ejecutivo (next to Banco AV Villas). Tel: 727-4076.

MONEY

As money facilities—banks, ATMs, casas de cambio—are non-existent in the rest of the peninsula, it is best to stock up on pesos here before heading into the hinterlands.

• BBVA ATM—MasterCard, Visa, Plus. Ca. 2 and Cra. 8, across from the church.

• Banco Popular ATH—Visa, MasterCard, Cirrus, Plus. Ca. 1 and Cra. 7; ATM on Cra. 7.

• Banco AV Villas ATM—ATH, Plus, Cirrus, MasterCard, Visa. Cra. 7, 3-16.

• Bancolombia—Exchanges: American Express traveler's checks; ATM—MasterCard, Visa, Cirrus, American Express. Monday-Thursday 8 a.m.-4 p.m., Friday 8 a.m.-4:30 p.m. Cra. 8, 3-09.

KEEPING IN TOUCH

Telecom (Monday–Friday, 8 a.m.-noon and 2-6 p.m., Saturday 8 a.m.-noon. Ca. 15, 10-00) has local, national and international phone services. Shops and street stands also offer local or national call services.

Correos de Colombia has an outpost on Ca. 2, 6-46. It is open Monday-Friday 7:30 a.m.-noon and 2-6 p.m., Saturday 8 a.m.-noon.

Internet is a bit difficult to find. **Yejogi Internet** (Monday-Saturday 9 a.m.-9 p.m., closed Sunday. Ca. 4, 8-29) has a special price of $0.50 per hour from noon to 2 p.m. .

MEDICAL

Hospital Nuestra Señora de los Remedios (Ca. 12, Av. de los Estudiantes. Tel: 727-1374/3077) serves Riohacha's medical needs. Pharmacies are found throughout the city; several are on Calle 7, near Carrera 7.

LAUNDRY

Spumas Lavandería y Servicios is the place to go for laundry. It is more expensive than other parts of Colombia, costing $2.35 per kilogram, owing to the scarcity of water (Monday-Saturday 8 a.m.-7 p.m., closed Sunday and holidays. Cra. 5, 9-27, Tel.: 727-4514/315-749-1064).

CAMERA

A trio of camera shops offering processing, print films (Kodak, Fuji and Konica), cameras (both analog and digital) and accessories, as well as other photographic services, are located on Ca. 3, between Cra. 6 and 7.

SHOPPING

Tienda de Carnaval

Happen to be in Riohacha just in time for Carnaval? Stop by Tienda de Carnaval to get what you need to join riohacheros in this yearly event: rainbow-colored wigs and masks, glittery T-shirts and silly hats—and of course, cans of spritz foam. During the off-season, Tienda de Carnaval sells all sorts of items to help you get ready for any festivity you

A Few Words in Wayuunaiki

Wayuunaiki, or the Wayuu language, is of the Arawak language group. Pronunciation is similar to Spanish, except that the "r" and "rr" have a sound between that of an "r" and an "l"; and "sh" is pronounced as in English. The language reflects the matrilineal aspect of Wayuu society. Many familial relationships are distinguished between that by way of the mother and that by father, for example ashi (paternal uncle) and alaüla (maternal uncle). Another fascinating feature of the language is it has 21 terms for the position of the sun.

Kasashi punuria ▶ What's your name?
Tanoria ▶ My name is
Jamaa pia? ▶ How are you?
Watta'a mal ▶ Good morning
Anas aipa'a ▶ Good night
Ounshi way'a ▶ See you later
Miyaasüütaya ▶ I'm thirsty
Oushutaya jamü ▶ I'm hungry
Wüin ▶ fresh water
aa ▶ yes
nnojo ▶ no
ei ▶ mother
ashi ▶ father
jierü ▶ woman
toolo ▶ man
alijuna ▶ a non-indigenous person
kusina ▶ from other indigenous nation
Updated: Jun 10, 2008.

might celebrate during your stay here. Daily 8 a.m.-noon and 2-6 p.m. Cra. 8, 7-16. Tel: 727-2884. Updated: Mar 15, 2011.

Wayuu Artesanas

Every day Wayuu women come from their rancherías with their communities' craftwork. They pass the day on the south side of Avenida la Marina, in the shade of the buildings, chatting with other *jierü* (women) while crocheting bags. In the evening, when the burning sun begins to set beyond the Caribbean Sea, they all pack up and move to the other side of the road, setting up on the arcades of the malecón. Their bags, hammocks and other goods hang from palm trees and spread on cloths upon the ground. Buying from these women means you are purchasing direct from the producers, cutting out the middleman.Daily 8 a.m.-9 p.m. Updated: Mar 18, 2011.

Things to See and Do

Strolling down the malecón is a pleasurable way to spend a few hours exploring the many facets of Riohachero life. Take a breather from the burning sun by hiding in one of the cultural centers or beneath the shady trees of Parque de Almirante Padilla, the main plaza. Just to the west of the city is Camarones village and Santuario de Flora y Fauna Los Flamencos, a wonderful spot for birdwatching.

The Malecón and Beach

Riohacha's Malecón hugs the shell-strewn, pale beige sand. Depending on the season, the sea is café con leche-colored or turquoise. Along its length are plazuelas where you can rest from the burning sun and buy Wayuu artesanía. From the long wharf at the foot of Carrera 6, try your hand at fishing. Between Carreras 7 and 9 is a grove of palm trees; string up your hammock for a siesta. Just past Carrera 11 are juice and seafood cocktail stands, a delicious snack for refueling. Also here, down on the beach, fishermen sell their catch in the late afternoon. The Malecón ends at the Casa de la Cultura. Begin your walk from the tourism office, at Calle 1 and Carrera 5. Ca. 1 (Av. la Marina). Updated: Mar 15, 2011.

Cultural Centers of Riohacha

The afternoon heat and sun are quite strong in Riohacha. For a respite from the scorch, check out the latest art exhibits at one of the cultural centers. Some also have evening events.

• Centro Cultural Municipal Enrique Lallemand—Art exhibits, movies, dance performances, classes. Monday-Friday 8 a.m.-noon and 2-8 p.m. Ca. 3, 5-49.

• Banco de la República—Art exhibits, library. Monday-Friday 8-11:30 p.m. and 2-6 p.m., Saturday, 9 a.m.-1 p.m. Cra. 7, between Ca. 1 and 2.

• Casa de la Cultura—Art exhibits, concerts, dance, theater, book readings, library and Internet. Ca. 1 and Cra. 15. Updated: Mar 15, 2011.

Tours

Many tour operators are eager to take you into the deep regions of the Guajira. Trips usually include the Salinas de Manaure, Uribia, Parque Eólico Jepirachi and sights around Cabo de la Vela. Three-day outings take you to Nazareth and Parque Nacional Natural Macuira, or to the world's end at Punta Gallina (the most northern point of South America, where desert meets sea). In the past, some agencies also offered boating excursions upriver to virgin mangrove jungles. However, these stopped due to insecurity from the civil war. It's possible that companies may resume trips as stability returns.

Luna Guajira

Luna Guajira presents a variety of packages to get to know Wayuu culture and the beauty of the Guajira Peninsula. One-day packages take in the Santuario Los Flamencos, Cabo de la Vela or the El Cerrejón coal mine ($30 including transportation, guide and entries). Longer excursions, from two days/ one night to seven days/six nights, visit a combination of attractions ($75-400). This agency also goes to Punta Gallinas and Parque Nacional Natural Macuira (five days/four nights, $400. All trips require a four-person minimum. Luna Guajira also has a gift shop with Wayuu artisanía (Monday-Friday 8 a.m.-7 p.m.). Ca. 1, 5-01. Tel: 728-9814/9809, Cel: 300-809-5191/315-738-1161, URL: www.viajesturismolunaguajira.com. Updated: Mar 16, 2011.

Cabo de la Vela Operadora Turística

Cabo de la Vela Tours can not only take you to Cabo de la Vela, but also to other area attractions like the salt mines of Manaure and to Uribia (one- to three-day/two-night packages $47.50-111, minimum four people). A Tarde de Ranchería, a visit to a Wayuu community to learn about the culture, with typical meal, costs $26.50. Cabo de la Vela also offers one-day tours to Santuario Los Flamencos and the El Cerrejón mine. A five-day/four-night excursion goes into the Guajira Alta, including Punta Gallina and Macuira ($343 per person, minimum four people, all inclusive). Monday-Friday 7:30 a.m.-9 p.m. Ca. 1, 9-95, Local 1, Edifico Las Delicias. Tel: 728-3684, Cel: 300-343-0169, Fax: 728-3684, E-mail: turismoyelisgomez2010@hotmail.com. Updated: Mar 18, 2011.

Lodging

Accommodation in Riohacha is more expensive than in other areas, primarily due to competition and the short supply of water. Solo travelers will definitely feel the bite here. If you can, journey with a partner to cut costs, or budget for it. Even the cheaper inns, however, are of fairly good quality. In an effort to conserve water, supplies are cut off during the day at the beginning of each week (Monday and/or Tuesday). Updated: Jul 21, 2010.

Hotel Panorama

(ROOMS: $15-23) The rooms at the two-story Hotel Panorama are spacious enough, with built-in concrete platform beds that sport comfortable mattresses. Other amenities in these quarters are private baths with cold water, cable TV, and your choice of fan or air conditioning. A common balcony on the second floor overlooks Carrera 5, a nice place to watch the sun set over the city. Hotel Panorama offers parking in a locked lot next door and is convenient for the collective taxis to Maicao, Manaure and Uribia. Cra. 5, 13-35. Tel: 727-6580. Updated: Mar 15, 2011.

Hotel Yalconia del Mar

(ROOMS: $18-28) Hotel Yalconia del Mar has upgraded over the years from a basic hotel to one now providing the weary traveler with comfortable, elegant rooms at a mid-range price. The rooms are large, with private bath (cold-water shower), cable TV, and air conditioning or fan. Doña Amanda knows the Guajira region well and has been providing lodging with a homey atmosphere for many years. This inn is on the other side of Calle 12, the broad boulevard that divides the center of Riohacha, thus closer to restaurants and nightclubs. Cra. 7, 11-26. Tel: 727-3487/728-0044, E-mail: hotelyalconia@hotmail.com. Updated: Mar 15, 2011.

Hotel Gimaura

(ROOMS: $58-64) Undoubtedly, Hotel Gimaura is a great lodging choice in Riohacha. Located at the eastern end of Avenida la Marina, this two-story lodge has generous rooms set around a garden or overlooking a field where the heliport used to be. All accommodations have air conditioning to keep you comfortable in the blistering climate, cable TV and private bathroom (cold water only). The swimming pool is another place to cool down and relax. This hotel is also family friendly; children can amuse themselves on the hotel's private playground. Ca. 1, Av. la Marina. Tel: 727-0009/0019/4546, E-mail: hotelgimaura@hotmail.com. Updated: Mar 15, 2011.

Restaurants

Riohacha has a surprising variety of restaurants. Many offer fresh fish and seafood dishes, but also some surprising alternatives. Prices tend to be a bit higher here, due to the shortage of water. *Comida corrientes* (specials of the day) are difficult to find and come without drinks. Carreras 8 and 9, from Calles 13 to 14, buzz with the mercado. A larger municipal

LA GUAJIRA

market is about five blocks south of Calle 15 on Carrera 7. Supermarket Cumaná Express is conveniently downtown (Ca. 2, 7-46). On the beach, at the foot of Carrera 11, fishermen sell their catch in the late afternoon.Updated: Mar 18, 2011.

Asados Don Pepe

(ENTREES: $1.30-3.20) At about 4 p.m., Don Pepe begins firing up the grill under a tarp along Avenida la Marina. By 6 p.m., the line of people throng in. This asadero, though basic, serves up some of the best BBQ you'll find along this coast—and at a very good price. Choose between chorizo sausage ($1.30), chicken ($2.10), goat ($2.65), or beef or pork cutlet ($3.20). All plates come heaping with salad, *bollitos* (boiled corn-dough rolls), yucca or potatoes, and huge slabs of meat. For many it is difficult to finish it all. Daily only 6-10 p.m. Ca. 1 and Cra. 10. Updated: Mar 15, 2011.

Marino's Junior

How many ways can you fix a hotdog? Marino's Junior has over 50 of them. "No," the owner working the grill says, "these are not just ordinary dogs." They are only pure-bred sausages—no mongrel wiener here. The best of the charcoal-grilled sausages is the Suizo, 10 inches of pure beef. Also on the parrilla are six other types of dogs with a variety of fixings: Italian (with mozzarella cheese), Scottish, ranchero, Mexican and Hawaiian. All come with fries. Daily from 4 p.m. until they run out of steam, often until dawn. Ca. 1, 10-97. Cel: 310-705-0117. Updated: Mar 15, 2011.

Restaurante-Bar La Tinaja

Restaurante-Bar La Tinaja's menu includes typical Colombian and Guajiran dishes. However, its specialty is seafood—specifically the *cazuela de mariscos*, a stew made with select fish and shellfish ($10.50). The staff will eagerly explain the recipe to you. It comes served with tasty coconut rice or white rice and patacones. The restaurant has a sea view and the service is stellar. Daily 7 a.m.-9 p.m. Ca. 1, 4-59. Tel: 727-3929, Fax: 727-2731. Updated: Mar 15, 2011.

Nightlife

Along Avenida la Marina, several bars open until late at night, where you can sit at a sidewalk table nursing a beer, watching the riohachero night and singing along with the gang to Vallenatos. Discos are almost exclusively a Thursday to Friday night affair.

Marianos Bar

At the corner of Avenida la Marina and the pedestrian street Carrera 8, there are several yellow tables full of drinkers. An intense strobe light show plays across the ceiling of the second floor, where other imbibers lean against the balcony, watching the night scene below. There is no real dance floor here. Come to relax, enjoy the evening breeze coming off the sea, talk with friends and sing along with Vallenato and tropical music favorites. A full bar is served, as well as several national beers ($1.60-2.65). Daily 1 p.m.-1:30 a.m. Ca. 1 and Cra. 8. Cel: 317-410-2936. Updated: Mar 15, 2011.

Casa Vieja Galería Bar

(DRINKS: $1.30-4.20) Inside, a small dance floor invites you to groove to the music playing—at just the right volume for this place. Nooks and crannies conceal couples chatting over a beer or cocktail. Original paintings by local artists decorate the walls. A few tables and a bar out on the pedestrian street is where you can have your brew, taking in the sea's breeze and Riohacha's nightlife. A beer here costs $1.30-1.60. Cocktails run $2.65-4.20. Daily 4-11 p.m. Cra. 8, between Ca. 1 and 2. Updated: Mar 15, 2011.

AROUND RIOHACHA

SANTUARIO DE FLORA Y FAUNA LOS FLAMENCOS !

With the collapse of the fishing industry on this coast, Santuario de Flora y Fauna Los Flamencos was established in 1977 to recover the ecosystem and provide an alternative income to locals. The park encompasses 7,000 hectares (17,297 ac), protecting four coastal lagoons. It is home to 237 bird species, including the flamingo, Roseate Spoonbill, Black Ibis and Cari Cari. Four species are endemic, 78 resident and 39 migratory.

The best months for sighting flamingos and other migratory fowl are October and November. Other common animals in the area are fox, anteater, rabbits, ñeque and deer, as well as many amphibians and reptiles, including three species of sea turtle. Besides sail-canoe tours through the lagoons and mangroves, several paths wind through the desert forests to lookout towers where you can observe wildlife.

Once you arrive to the other side of the estuary, report to Ilder Gómez at the ranger station, where you will be given an educational tour, which includes the sea turtle hatchery.

LA GUAJIRA

Cost of boat and native guide through the lagoons in sail canoes is $5.50-10 per person, usually requiring a minimum of four people. Ask for José Rodríguez, one of the first locals to provide such a service.

Grupo Asociativo El Santuario, formed by the community within the Santuario, has basic lodging at the reserve, near the ranger hut (per person: camping $2.65, your own hammock in wattle and daub cabaña $3.70, hammock rental in cabaña $6.35). Meals are available (breakfast $2.65, lunch or dinner $5.30-8). The bathrooms are nice, but with toss-water showers; there is no electricity. (Cel: 310-369-7763, E-mail: ecoturismosantuario@yahoo.es/redcimarron21@hotmail.com). Hammock lodging is also available in Camarones (ask around; $5.50 per person).

Santuario de Flora y Fauna Los Flamencos is 20 kilometers (12 mi) west of Riohacha and 165 kilometers (99 mi) east of Santa Marta. From Riohacha, collective taxis for Camarones leave from Calle 15 and Carerra 7 (last back from Camarones at 6 p.m.; $1.05 to Camarones village, $1.60 to the mouth of Río Camarones if enough passengers, 15 minutes). Cel: 310-369-7763, E-mail: ecoturismosantuario@yahoo.es, redcimarron21@hotmail.com. Updated: Mar 24, 2011.

MANAURE

| ▲ | 3m | 👤 | 33,578 | 📞 | 5 |

Amid a flat landscape, where small-leafed trees and cacti meet the blue-green sea, is the small village of Manaure. Northeast of Riohacha, it is called La Novia Blanca (White Bride) of Colombia, for the important salt flats that have been exploited here since long before the Spaniards arrived to these shores. The main plaza has a sculpture commemorating the salt worker. Manaure's Catholic church has an impressive mosaic of Wayuu cosmology on its façade. Updated: Mar 24, 2011.

History

For centuries, this coastal spot was a key sea salt cultivation spot for Wayuu. The present town, San Agustín de Manaure, was founded in 1723 by Capuchin missionary friars. The namesake, Manaure, was a revered Wayuu warrior of the region. Like its neighbor Riohacha, Manaure was visited by pirates in search of salt and riches. Legend says Henry Morgan hid part of his booty here. Updated: Jun 10, 2008.

When to Go

As in the rest of Guajira, it is hot here and even more so due to the salt flats. The most searing time of the year is May-July. Temperatures range 28-38°C (82-101°F). Short, torrential downpours descend on the city during May-June and again from October to November. Refreshing winds are common.

During vacation times, Manaure experiences some increased tourism by Colombians seeking to experience a beautiful and exotic part of their country. It is the Wayuu village closest to major population areas and is the easiest to get to.

HOLIDAYS AND FESTIVALS

The big festival in Manuare occurs in June, saluting all the things most important to its economy: Festival de la Sal, Gas y Flamencos. In addition to being Colombia's greatest producer of marine salt, Manuare also has great reserves of natural gas. The third honoree, flamencos, of course refers to the pink flamingos that reside at Musichi.

Getting To and Away

Manaure is a fairly small town, so it is easy to get around on foot. However, during the hottest part of the day, you might want to consider taking a covered bicycle taxi ($0.50). All transportation in Manaure leaves from the various company offices in the street market district, on Carrera 4 between Calles 6 and 9. Mostly, they are shared taxis that depart when full.

From Manure

To:	Departure Time		Price
Riohacha	5 a.m. -4 p.m.	2 hrs	$6.35
Uribia*	6 a.m. -5 p.m.	20 mins	$2.10
Maicao	5 a.m. -5 p.m.	1 hr	$3.70

*Note: For safety and time reasons it is better to transport to Uribia from sunrise to sunset. Updated: Jun 10, 2008.

From Riohacha, transportation leaves for both Manaure and Uribia from Calle 15 and Carrera 5 (5:30 a.m.-5 p.m.). A less expensive manner to come from Riohacha is to take a bus as far as Cuatro Vías ($2.10), and from there take a pick-up truck or collective taxi ($2.65).

Safety

When asked about how safe Manaure is, especially when staying overnight in the beach kiosks, the response from locals is, "It's too safe." Of course, that does not mean abandoning all safety precautions. Always be aware and careful, and keep valuables and belongings well-protected and within eyesight.Updated: Jun 10, 2008.

Services

TOURISM

The village does not have a tourism office, but it does have a website where you can learn more about Manaure at: manaure-laguajira.gov.co.

MONEY

Manaure has a Banco Agrario, though no ATMs or services for non-residents. Some shops handle transactions for major banks, but again, nothing for the traveler.

Cachaco Carto, in the two-story green building down in the market area, will reportedly change U.S.dollars.Cra.4,betweenCa.8and9.

KEEPING IN TOUCH

The Telecom office in Manaure closed a while back, and the village has no post office. Shops and stands charge $0.10-0.15 per minute for local and national calls. Several Internet cafés are around the plaza, but most close for lunch. Internet is expensive here, costing $1.60-2.10 per hour.

MEDICAL

The public hospital is **E.S.E. Hospital Armando Pabón López** (Ca. 1, 6-35. Tel: 717-8020). There are three pharmacies on Carrera 4, between Calles 4 and 7.

SHOPPING

Artesanías Wayuu Jalianaya

Jalianaya is an *asociación de trabajo* (labor association) comprised of Wayuu women. Walking into its shop, you'll see them seated around the edge of the front showroom, crocheting, talking and buying bundles of yarn.

An assortment of bags (beginning from $19) hang on the walls. Most of these, made of strong acrylic string, are of traditional design, though some are more modern. Hammocks,

woven in synthetic or cotton fiber on an upright loom ($210 and up), hang in the back room. Monday-Friday 8 a.m.-noon and 2-6 p.m. Closed Saturday and Sunday. Ca. 2, 2-07. Tel: 717-8516 (Sales: Manaure) 311-442-1017, (Bogotá) 314-470-7034. E-mail: contactos@jalianaya.com/gerencia@jalianaya.com, URL: www.jalianaya.com. Updated: Mar 30, 2011.

Artesanía Wayuu Mutsia

The wall to one side of Artesanía Wayuu Mutsia's front patio is like a picture dictionary, giving you an introduction to the Wayuu language. Inside, typical items await you, like *wayuusheein* (natural fiber robes) *wayuusupatsu* (sandals with pompoms) and *waireñas* (regular cloth sandals). There are also *susu* (bags), *süi* (hammocks) and ceramics. All items are made by Wayuu.

Original paintings by Chicho Ruiz Ortiz are also available. During the high season, Artesanía Wayuu Mutsia is also open Saturdays. Monday-Friday 8 a.m.-noon and 2-5:30 p.m. Ca. 3, on the Plaza Principal. Tel: 728-1553, Cel: 310-745-3092/3331. Updated: Jun 10, 2008.

Things to See and Do

Manaure has few activities, but all of them are worth doing. Musichi, Carrizal, Poportín and other nearby coastal lagoons are fruitful grounds for birdwatchers. The salt works are the largest of the country, permitting you to see the contrast between the age-old methods of the indigenous Wayuu and the modern-day massive extraction by big industry.

Several women's cooperatives sell everyday articles made by hand and invite you to know about the Wayuu way of life. The beaches are clean and the sea is beautiful, perfect for taking a break from the heat. Updated: Jun 10, 2008.

The Salt Works

The road along the beach connects the two salt works in town. To the east is the industrial one, with high, white mountains glistening in the sun. It is the largest salt extraction in Colombia, covering 4,200 hectares (10,378 ac) and garnering up to 700,000 tons of salt per year. Guides are available for hire to take you through the site.

At the opposite end of the beach road, just past the *barrio popular,* are the salt flats of the local Wayuu community. Rectangular

LA GUAJIRA

plots are carved into the sand. As the water within them evaporates, they turn a brilliant fuchsia, rimmed with crystallizing salt.

It is easy to walk to both of these salt works, or you can hire a bike or motor taxi to take you. Tours to the Guajira make an obligatory stop at the *salinas* (salt flats). Do not underestimate the power of the sun here. Cover up well, drink plenty of fluids and rest in the shade. Updated: Mar 15, 2011.

Musichi !

A spectacular sight is watching a flock of flamingos wading through shallow waters, bending their serpentine necks to sieve food through their bills. A perfect place to observe these majestic, rose-colored birds is at Musichi, 14 kilometers (8.7 mi) from Manaure. Here the sea forms a lagoon, which is a rendezvous point for them, even outside the rainy season. There is also a beach where you can soak up the sun and dip into the fine water. The best time to see the flamingos is 5 -7 a.m. and 3-5 p.m. There is a lookout tower from which to observe them. As they are easily spooked, do not use a motor launch in their vicinity. You can arrive at Musichi by mototaxi ($16) or by 10-person launch ($42 for two-hour trip, takes a half-hour to arrive). Updated: Mar 15, 2011.

Beaches Near Manaure

In and near Manaure are a number of lagoons where you can observe flamingos and other waterfowl. Many also have beaches where you can cool down. In Manaure itself, the beach is a shadeless, pale gray expanse and the sea is a deep teal. **Playas Pájaro** and **Mayapo** have kiosks providing shade and food. Northeast of Manaure is Poportín with white-sand beaches and shallow, clear waters. Here—as well as in Cordón and Carrizal, farther up the coast—birdwatching is excellent. To get to these beaches without your own transportation is a bit difficult. However, you can make arrangements with tour operators in Manaure and Uribia, or hire a taxi. Updated: May 15, 2009.

Tours

Manaure has only one official tour operator, run by a group of Wayuu women. Most agencies in Riohacha and elsewhere include the salt flats in their itinerary of the Guajira, but not Musichi. Your hotel may be able to help you locate a launch or mototaxi to take you out there. One recommended ride is **Antonio de la Rosa** (Cel: 312-606-1987, or through **Hotel Palaima**), who can take you

to both the salinas and Musichi for $16 with a two-hour wait at the latter.

Coopmur

Coopmur—Cooperativa Multiactiva de Trabajo Asociado de Mujeres Rurales—is a cooperative of 12 local Wayuu women with the vision of sharing their world with outsiders. Through guided tours to the salinas, Musichi, local beaches, fishing cooperatives and Ruinas de Santa Rosa, you can get to know corners of the Manaure countryside few other tour agencies go to. These women are eager to share their culture and legends with visitors in an effort to dispel misunderstandings of their unique society. Coopmur also supports the creation of traditional Wayuu crafts, such as bags and hammocks. Ca. 1A, 7-54. Cel: 311-276-8484, E-mail: coopmur@hotmail.com/coopmur@yahoo.com.es, URL: www.visitamanaurelagu-ajira.blogspot.com. Updated: Mar 15, 2011.

Lodging

Surprisingly, Manaure has more places to stay than Uribia does. For the most part, they are basic, well-kept places. Problems with the water supply exist here. Showers are provided with a large container of water from which you take a toss-water bath. On the west end of the beach are a dozen open-sided public kiosks where you can stay overnight, camping or sleeping in a hammock. No facilities are provided at these, and the only security provided is the large spotlight in the center of the grouping. Updated: Jul 22, 2010.

Hotel Unuuipa

(BEDS: $12 and up) Hotel Unuuipa wears the colors of these desert lands: salmon, ochre and melon. Inside are two courtyards around which somewhat cramped rooms are arranged. All have private baths, though for your shower, you have to scoop water out of the provided barrel and toss it over yourself. With a variety of lodging options, you can choose the level of comforts you want and money you want to spend. The staff can help you with any travel needs to nearby sites. Cra. 7, 4-12. Tel: 717-8072. Updated: Mar 16, 2011.

Cabañas Manaure Beach

(BEDS: $10.50) Cabañas Manaure Beach has a basic, four-room hostel: two quarters have three beds each and the other two, four beds each. The windows have shutters, but no glass or nets. Even though the private baths have showers set up, they may not work; a large barrel of water is provided from which to do a toss bath. Don Orlando also rents hammocks if you want to stay in the free public cabañas ($5.30) and can arrange a visit to Musichi by boat. Cel: 310-372-2160/455-5287. Updated: Jun 10, 2008.

Hotel Palaaima !

(ROOMS: $15-32) For many years, Doña Iris has been welcoming visitors to Manaure. Her Hotel Palaaima is the best lodging option in the village. The beautiful white building has 14 airy rooms, simply decorated, with a private bath, TV, and fan or air conditioning. She is knowledgeable about the Guajira and can help you arrange outings. In the courtyard of this inn is a tile-floored, thatched shelter restaurant that serves breakfast, lunch and dinner ($2.10-2.65). Cra. 6, 7-34, Tel: 717-8455/8195, E-mail: irisfaep@hotmail.com. Updated: Jun 10, 2008.

Restaurants

Manaure doesn't have very many restaurants, and they close relatively early. If you like to have a late dinner, you will have to change your schedule to accommodate that of these villagers. Past the west end of the beach are some basic shacks that serve blue-plate specials and fish. Along Carrera 4, between Calles 6 and 9, there is a street market and grocery stores.

The formal municipal market is on Calle 9, between Carreras 2 and 3. In addition to food, check here for Wayuu robes, bags and hammocks. Market day is Saturday. There is not much in the way of nightlife in Manaure. Wayuu society frowns upon drinking establishments, and its culture does not include any dancing other than for ceremonies.

Heladería y Refresquería Marce

To seek refuge from the ardent Manaure sun, pull up a seat at one of the tables on the front walk of Heladería y Refresquería Marce to enjoy a cup of ice cream. No, Doña Marce doesn't mess with cones. It's all served in *tazas*, from two scoops on up. Mix or match any of the eight flavors. She also sells other ice cream treats, milk shakes, sodas, sandwiches and snacks. Monday-Saturday 8 a.m. until whenever, Sunday 2 p.m. until, well, whenever. Ca. 3, next to Banco Agrario on the main plaza Updated: Mar 15, 2011.

Restaurante La Negra

Restaurante La Negra is one of the very few real restaurants in Manaure. At lunchtime, the tables inside and out on the sidewalk are crowded with people chowing down on the comida corriente, which includes soup, choice of meat, beans or lentils, salad and yuca (beef $2.65, fish $3.20-3.70). An unusual feature in these parts is the accompanying drink. At dinner hour, only the *bandeja*, or main course is served. Daily, 6:30 a.m.-6:30 p.m. Cra. 7-67. Updated: Mar 15, 2011.

Restaurante Manaure Beach

(ENTREES: $6 and up) Restaurante Manaure Beach is, as you can expect, right on the shore. The main restaurant is a large, open-sided kiosk with a deck extending out over the sand. The menu is almost exclusively seafood. A meal with fish comes with coconut rice, fried plantains and salad ($6.35 and up). Also on the menu is *cazuela de mariscos*, prepared with shrimp, conch, squid and octopus, with rice and fried plantains on the side ($13.10). Refresh your thirst with a soda or beer. Open daily, 8 a.m.-6 p.m.; if you are staying at the cabañas, you can order for later. Tel: 728-3678, Cel: 301-372-2160/455-5287. Updated: Jun 10, 2008.

URIBIA

 10m   70,850   5

The road heads north from Cuatro Vías to the Uribia-Manaure turn-offs (one tollbooth). To the left is Manaure. Turning right, after four kilometers (2.4 mi) you come to the indigenous capital of Colombia, Uribia. Here is the heart of Guajira, the land of the Wayuu. All roads lead to Uribia. It is the hub of transportation for the Guajira Alta. You must come here first to go to Cabo de la Vela and Nazareth, gateway to Parque Nacional Natural Macuira. The Plaza Parque Colombia, or Plaza Principal, is the center of village life. Here there is an obelisk, gazebo, playground, basketball court and bandstand. Around the perimeter are the important buildings, such as the mayor's office and church, as well as restaurants and other businesses. From the plaza, all streets radiate out. All of the streets have at least three names, making it a bit difficult to give directions. Updated: Mar 16, 2011.

History

Uribia is a 20th-century city, founded on March 1, 1935, by Capitán Eduardo Londoño Villegas. It is named in memory of General Rafael Uribe, one of the leaders during the Guerra de 1000 Días, the civil war that destroyed Colombia at the end of the 19th century. For a while, Uribia was the capital of Guajira Territory, until the department was established in 1954 and the capital moved to Riohacha. This city then became the center for indigenous affairs. Updated: Mar 16, 2011.

LA GUAJIRA

When to Go

Uribia is hot all year long. During the daytime, temperatures climb to 30-35°C (86-95°F). Nights are a cooler 28°C (82°F). In January and February, winds help to moderate the heat. Rains can be expected May-July.

HOLIDAYS AND FESTIVALS

The biggest event in Uribia is the annual Festival de la Cultura Wayuu, held the last week of May. The festival highlights all aspects of this indigenous nation's traditions and the election of their Majayut de Oro, or Miss Gold. For this time, advance reservations should be made at the established hotels.

Pre-Carnaval is celebrated for two weeks before Carnaval, on Friday and Saturday nights. At dusk, the townspeople, dressed in costumes, dance through the streets to the rhythm of bands. Then comes the pre-Lenten party through these streets. Updated: Mar 16, 2011.

Festival de Cultura Wayuu!

The three-day Festival de la Cultura Wayuu draws participants from both Colombia and Venezuela. In Uribia's plaza, three-sided huts exhibit weavings and townsfolk serve gastronomic delights. In the evenings are various programs, like the *yonna*, a dance performed for socially or spiritually important occasions; its different movements are named for the region's fauna.

In other events, contestants out-vie each other in *jayeishi*, a sung poem relating personal experiences and Wayuu culture, and in the playing of such traditional instruments as *kasha* (a drum made of goat or cow hide), *totoroy* (flute) and *wahawai* (a wind instrument that imitates birdsong). The festival's culmination is the election of the *Majayut*, or queen, who must demonstrate a profound knowledge of Wayuu traditions.

For an explanation (in Spanish) of the yonna and other dances and the music of the festival (in Spanish), visit URL: www.colombia.com/turismo/ferias_fiestas/2003/mayo/cultura.asp. Updated: Jun 10, 2008.

Getting To and Away

Bicycle rickshaws ply the streets of Uribia; fares depend on the distance. Transportation leaves from Avenida Fundador, the street on which the market is, or you can ask the company to pick you up at your lodging.

A cheaper way to arrive to Uribia is to take a bus as far as the Cuatro Vías crossroads ($2.10), and from there a collective taxi or pick-up truck ($2.65). Updated: Jun 10, 2008.

To:	Departure	Time	Price
Maicao	Camioneta, 6-8:30 a.m.	1 hr	$2.65
Riohacha	Collective taxi, 6 a.m.-4 p.m.	2 hr	$6.35
Manaure	Collective taxi, 6 a.m.-5 p.m.	20 min	$1.60
Cabo de la Vela	Camioneta, 9-11 a.m., 4 p.m.	1-2 hr	$5-8
Nazareth	Truck, Sunday 8 a.m. or earlier	8-10 hr	$16-19

Safety

Residents of Uribia say the city is very safe. They counsel that if you are going out into the desert, go with someone who knows the area, and, if going on a tour, make sure the company has a back-up plan in case the vehicle breaks down. Take plenty of water with you if going into the Alta Guajira.

Services

TOURISM

There is no tourism office at present, but once the new Palacio Municipal on the corner of the plaza and Avenida Fundador is finished, the city plans to open an Oficina de Cultura y Turismo. URL: www.uribia-laguajira.gov.co. Updated: May 24, 2011.

MONEY

On the plaza, between Avenida La Marina and Avenida Hospital is a **Bancolombia** ATM (MasterCard, Visa, Cirrus, American Express, ATH). The ATM doesn't work all the time. It is best to play it safe and stock up on pesos in Riohacha or Maicao. Apparently, a store down in the market area changes U.S. dollars and bolívares fuertes.

KEEPING IN TOUCH

Thanks to the predominance of cell

phones, Uribia's Telecom has closed. Uribia has no post office either. Plenty of shops offer local and national calls for $0.15 per minute. It is difficult to make international calls. Luckily, **Compartel**, the only trustworthy Internet provider in town, has Skype. Sit down at a computer for $1 per hour. Monday-Friday, 8:30 a.m.-12:30 p.m. and 3-9 p.m., Saturday 9 a.m.-12:30 p.m. and 3-9 p.m. Compartel is located next to Ludoteca on the plaza, near the corner of the street to Hotel Juyasirian.

MEDICAL

Avenida Hospital leads straight to **Hospital de Nuestra Señora del Perpetuo Socorro** (Transversal 8, 6-45. Tel: 717-7033). There is only a handful of pharmacies in Uribia: **Droguería El David** (Diagonal 7, 5-77) and **Droguería Keyris** (Diagonal 8b, 8-32).

CAMERA

Foto Wayuu stocks only batteries and Fuji ASA 100 color film. Monday-Friday, 7 a.m.-9 p.m., irregular hours Saturday and Sunday. The store is located on Av. Fundador, half block from the plaza, on the right-hand side.

SHOPPING

Cecilia Bonivento

At her home in Barrio Abuchairre, Doña Cecilia of the Jusayú clan sits in an open-sided hut. A colleague shows her a new technique for weaving drawstrings for *susu*, or bags. From a line, in the shade of another hut, hangs an assortment of the susu in earthen and brighter colors, mostly in traditional designs. Also strung from pole to pole is a double-faced hammock, thick yet cool and comfortable, woven by her and other women out at the ranchería. Her work is certified by Artesanías de Colombia in Bogotá and carries the Icontec seal of quality. Barrio Abuchairre and Ochoa. Tel: 312-607-8644, Email: eifego019@hotmail.com. Updated: Mar 28, 2011.

Things to See and Do

Uribia is not a destination in and of itself, except as the Capital Indígena de Colombia and during its annual Festival de la Cultural Wayuu. From here, roads weave like threads across the desert into the Alta Guajira: to Cabo de la Vela, Nazareth and the cloud forest reserve Parque Nacional Natural Macuira, or to mythical places like the Rock of Destiny, the lost city of Puerto López and the end of the world at Punta Gallina.

Tours

There are two tour operators in Uribia ready to take you on adventures into the Alta Guajira. Both have connections with the indigenous Wayuu communities, thus providing excursions as seen through the eyes of the people of this land. **SENA** (Tel: 421-1833/672-4115, Cel: 311-264-6903) has a program here in Uribia to train local youths to be guides.

Kaishi

Owned and operated by Andrés Delgado and Ericka Brujes—who is Wayuu and the former tourism officer for Uribia—Kaishi specializes in eco- and ethnotourism. It offers one-day tours to Cabo de la Vela, Manaure, Maicao Minas de El Cerrejón and Tardes de Ranchería en Cabo de la Vela or Riohacha. On longer excursions, it will take you to Cabo de la Vela, or to some of the harder-to-reach destinations of the Alta Guajira, like Piedra del Destino, Nazareth, Parque Nacional Natural Macuira and Punta Gallinas. Birdwatching expeditions can be arranged. Kaishi has bilingual guides. Plaza Principal, between Av. la Marina and the avenue without a name, next to Asados Mana. Tel: 717-7306, Cel: 311-429-6315/316-314-1815, E-mail: kaishiturismo@yahoo.co.uk/info@kaishitravel.com/adelgadorozco@yahoo.com/kekalida@yahoo.com, URL: www.kaishitravel.com. Updated: Mar 28, 2011.

Kai Ecotravel

Kai Ecotravel is a network of Wayuu communities welcoming visitors into the Alta Guajira, providing guides, translators (Spanish and Wayuunaiki), vehicle rental with drivers, lodging and meals. Kai offers an eight-day package to Wosopo, Castilletes, Puerto López, Punta Espada (Piedra del Destino), Nazareth and Macuira, Punta Gallinas, Parque Eólico and Cabo de la Vela. The cost depends on group size and includes driver, guides, lodging and meals. Alternately, hire a vehicle and guide for a two-day/one-night excursion to Punta Gallinas (one to five people, $160; lodging and meals extra) or a one-day outing to El Cardón, Carrizal, Cabo de la Vela and Parque Eólico (one to five people, $80). Daily 8 a.m.-5 p.m. Av. Bogotá (Diagonal 1b) 8-68. Tel: 717-7173, Cel: 311-436-2830, E-mail: info@kaiecotravel.com, URL: www.kaiecotravel.com. Updated: Mar 15, 2011.

Lodging

Uribia doesn't have much in the way of lodging options. For many years, it was a one-hotel town; now it has two decent inns. In the market district is a run-down residencia; when asked about it, locals seemed to

LA GUAJIRA

indicate it really isn't the type of place you'd want to stay, that it handles other activities than putting up travelers. During the Festival de Cultural Wayuu, any place to stay will be difficult to find. Updated: Jun 13, 2008.

Hospedaje Villa María

(ROOMS: $8-21) Hospedaje Villa María is owned and operated by Kaishi tour agency. Along one side of the bare interior patio (which also serves as secure parking for its guests) is a corridor for hammock sleeping (yours or theirs, $8); these guests share the common bath. This is the least expensive inn backpackers will find in Uribia. Off this area are rooms decorated in tropical simplicity, and with air conditioning and private bath ($21 per person). From Plaza Parque Colombia, follow Av. la Marina up one block. Take a left and the inn is about four houses down on your left. Tel: 717-7306/316-314-1815, Cel: 311-429-6315, E-mail: kaishiturismo@yahoo.co.uk/adelgadorozco@yahoo.com, URL: www.kaishitravel.com. Updated: Mar 28, 2011.

Hotel Juyasirian

(ROOMS: $20-25) Walking into Hotel Juyasirian, you can tell it was built specifically for high-ranking government officials and others of that class. The architecture has those refinements that whisper of this former existence. But now anyone can stay in its spacious rooms, most with central air conditioning and private bath. The staff is friendly and attentive. Anytime of the day is a pleasure to sit out on the front veranda or the gazebo, sipping on a free cup of *tinto* (coffee) and chatting with whoever happens to walk by. Hotel Juyasirian is a favorite with tour groups. From the Plaza Parque Colombia, behind the stage, follow the unnamed street that is between the library and the *ludoteca* (toy library) for one block. The hotel is at the next intersection.Ca. 14A, 9-06. Tel: 717-7284, Cel: 312-667-7153, E-mail: juyasirain2009@hotmail.com Updated: Mar 28, 2011.

Restaurants

Uribia has very few restaurants, with a few hole-in-the-wall ones down in the market district on Avenida Fundador, where the majority of general stores are as well. Buy plenty of water here if going into the Alta Guajira, as it is much more expensive elsewhere ($1.60 for a five-liter jug). Uribia's water is brackish and not suitable for purification. Goat forms a principle part of Wayuu cuisine and appears in such dishes as *friche* (stewed goat). Another meal to try is *sahpulana*, a soup made of beans,

corn and squash. The traditional drink is *chinchirri*, a strong alcoholic beverage made from panela (raw sugar) and water.

Because of the presence of military personnel and other non-Wayuu, a few dance clubs and drinking establishments do operate in Uribia, despite such customs not being part of the Wayuu way of life. They are mostly the evening operations of restaurants. Updated: Jun 13, 2008.

Asados Mana

(ENTREES: $2.10) Just before dusk, a few tables are put out on the sidewalk and the ever-present BBQ grill is fired up. Soon the chickens are put on the rotisserie. By nightfall, the smell of *pollo asado* (grilled chicken) is drifting across the park, and plates of poultry and potatoes are being served to eager diners ($2.10 for a quarter of a chicken). Another name for Asados Mana is Mana Restaurante y Disco Licores, because there is a bar in the back room that serves cocktails as well as national and international liquors. On the plaza, three doors to the right of Av. La Marina. Updated: Mar 28, 2011.

Restaurante Juyasirian

(LUNCH: $3.70) In the cool shade on the back patio of Hotel Juyasirian is Restaurante Juyasirian. Parrots and macaws roam freely and lounge on the rafters overhead. In a cage, a mico monkey sways in a hammock, taking interest in female diners. Although it is a bit expensive (breakfast $2.65, lunch with a drink $3.70, à la carte dishes from $5.30), Doña Eugenia and her staff provide excellent food as well as good service. Daily 6:30 a.m.-7:30 p.m.Ca. 14A, 9-06. Tel: 717-7284, Cel: 310-734-0654. Updated: Mar 28, 2011.

CABO DE LA VELA!

 3m   1,500   📞 5

North of the Manaure-Uribia crossroads, the highway continues to parallel the coal railway northward to the turn-off for Cabo de la Vela, eventually passing the Parque Eólico and ending at Puerto Bolívar. The way is rough; low-clearance vehicles will have a difficult time. From the turn-off for Cabo de la Vela, a well-worn track cuts 17 kilometers (10.6 mi) across the desert to the coastal hamlet. Several *arroyos*, or creeks, have to be crossed.

Photo by: d_alzate

Cabo de la Vela is on a bay. Along the south shore, a road edges the waterfront. On the right side are mostly cane-slat buildings serving as restaurants, shops and hostels. On the seaside of the strip are enramadas that are rented out for hanging a hammock or pitching a tent. Behind here are other streets where locals live.

The beach road continues to the desert, then curves westward giving access to inns along the north coast of the bay and ending at El Faro. Updated: Mar 16, 2011.

History

Even though Alonso de Ojeda was the first Spaniard to sail around this cape in about 1498, the first to set foot on this land was Juan de la Cosa. In 1526, Martín Fernández de Enciso founded Nuestra Señora Santa María de los Remedios del Cabo de la Vela as the capital of the Guajira Territory. Later the administrative seat would be moved further south. Updated: Mar 16, 2011.

When to Go

The hottest months in Cabo de la Vela are September-November, with cooling winds in also-toasty January and February. The wet season is June-August.

Cabo de la Vela is a popular vacation destination. Colombians warn that if you want the tranquility Cabo de la Vela has to offer, do not come during population vacation times, especially December-January holidays and during Semana Santa. At these times, the beach is full of campers with loud music until after dawn; everyone then sleeps until mid-morning and then the party resumes. Updated: Mar 16, 2011.

HOLIDAYS AND FESTIVALS

Most of the holidays in Cabo de la Vela are the same as in the rest of Colombia, the most important being December 8, the Velorio de la Virgen; December 24, Christmas Eve; and December 31, New Years Eve, with the burning of effigies representing Old Man Year. A special date is July 16, the feast day of the Virgen del Carmen, when all the hamlet's newborns are baptized. Updated: Mar 16, 2011.

Getting To and Away

If traveling with public transportation to any place outside of Cabo de la Vela, you must first go to Uribia. Three pick-ups leave daily between 4-4:30 a.m., and another possibly at 7 a.m. ($5.30); two of these continue to Maicao ($8). It is best to advise the driver the afternoon or evening before that you will want to travel the next day, so he stops to pick you up.

LA GUAJIRA

From Maicao, a pick-up leaves at about noon, arriving in Uribia at about 4 p.m., then making its way to Cabo de la Vela at about dusk. Updated: Jun 13, 2008.

Safety

Personal safety within Cabo de la Vela and to the nearest sites is OK. Be mindful of personal belongings, especially fresh water, if staying in a beach enramada; these businesses usually have a place where you can stow your pack. Walking away from the village to the highway is considered by locals to be totally unsafe with great chance of attack and robbery.

Be mindful you are in a desert with strong sun: Drink plenty of fluids, use sunscreen and keep under shade in the fiercest part of the day. On the north side of the bay are jellyfish—agua malas—and coral reefs. Strong currents exist at Pilón de Azúcar Updated: Mar 18, 2011.

Services

MONEY

There are no banking or exchange services in Cabo de la Vela, so plan your trip, and your money, in advance. The nearest reliable ATM or place to cash traveler's checks is in Riohacha.

KEEPING IN TOUCH

The village's Telecom is in **Hotel Jarrinapi** (daily 8 a.m.-noon and 2-8 p.m.). It charges $0.25 per minute for local or national cellular calls and $0.30 per minute to land lines; international calls begin at $0.60 per minute ($0.80 to U.S.). Local shops charge $0.30-50 per minute for local and national calls. Cabo de la Vela has no Internet café or post office.

MEDICAL

The **Centro de Salud** is near the entrance to town. The only pharmacy is next door.

CAMERA

Tienda El Jhor, the bright blue concrete block building before Hotel Jarrinapi, sells Kodak color print film. Otherwise, there is nothing else. Updated: Jun 17, 2008.

SHOPPING

Donde Rosita Sánchez

Next to Restaurant y Hospedaje Miramar 2, Donde Rosita Sánchez is a community shop specializing in artesanía. The small front entry patio is hung with a wide assortment of the bags for which the Wayuu are famous. On the racks inside is a selection of *wayuusheein*, or the typical manta dresses of the women, some with traditional designs and others hand-painted. Shelves hold baskets of time-honored medicinal herbs. For a mere $2.65, you can have your photo taken dressed in a wayuusheein and your face painted with Wayuu designs. Daily 6 a.m.-9 p.m. Updated: Mar 18, 2011.

Artesanía Wayuu

The sunlight dapples through the cane slats of the small stand and onto the miscellaneous crafts exhibited. A small selection of bags and hand-painted mantas sway in the wind. The necklaces and earrings, the shell key chains and the sculptures inscribed with Recuerdo de Cabo de la Vela are created by the younger artisans of this village. Also for sale are home remedies like *aceite de tiburón*, shark oil (for coughs and all that ails you), and powdered mother of pearl (for sunburn, which you are highly likely to suffer here). Daily 6 a.m.-8 p.m. Two lots past the Hotel Jarrinapi. Updated: Mar 16, 2011.

Things to See and Do

The biggest activity in Cabo de la Vela is simply getting relief from the sun, whether swinging in a hammock or swimming in the teal-blue sea. Walks to natural features along the coast are best done at dawn or late afternoon to avoid the times of scorching sun. The main road follows the curve of the bay. At the point is the *faro*, or lighthouse. Along the way to the right horizon is El Pilón de Azúcar, Hoyos Sopladores (blow holes), Ojo de Agua (a natural pool) and caves to explore. Ask around for a guide to take you to the more hidden treasures. Between town and El Pilón de Azúcar is Laguna de Utta, a waterfowl refuge. Updated: Mar 16, 2011.

El Pilón de Azúcar

Out on the northeastern horizon, you see an odd triangular-shaped rock rising out of the flat landscape. This is Kamainshi (Kamaici), the Lord of the Things of the Sea—or for alijuna, El Pilón de Azúcar. It has always been a sacred site, believed to be Jepira, where the spirits of the dead arrive. Now a Virgin of Fatima shrine perches atop the white and pale green stone. From that vantage point, you can see the windmills of Parque Eólico Jepirachi twirling in the far distance. At the western foot of Kamainshi is a small, golden-sand beach where you can cool off before continuing your hike. Swimming is fine near the beach, but further offshore, there is a strong current.

LA GUAJIRA

Photo by: Mario Carvajal

To get there, follow the road northward out of town; when you get to the T crossroads, turn right. This will take you directly to El Pilón de Azúcar. From the main part of the village on the south shore, it takes about an hour one way. A loose-gravel path zig-zags to the top. It can be quite windy on the summit, so light-weights will have a go at it; if with young children, hold onto them tight. It is a steep drop down to the sea. The apex is only 2.5-3 meters (7-10 ft) wide. Families sell soft drinks and water in the parking lot at El Pilón de Azúcar. Updated: Mar 16, 2011.

Laguna de Utta

A virtually unexplored birder's paradise awaits you: Laguna de Utta, which stretches across the desert just east of Cabo de la Vela, between the village and El Pilón de Azúcar. Not many visit this lagoon, which is a seasonal haven for waterfowl, such as flamingos and herons, as well as for shorebirds like sandpipers. Despite the immense size of this lagoon, its mangrove ecosystem has been little studied. Laguna de Utta has not yet been designated a protected area either.

Follow the road northward out of town; when you get to the T crossroads, turn right. You will begin seeing the lagoon's shore about 100 meters (328 ft) to the right of the road. From the main part of the village on the south shore, it takes approximately 30-45 minutes. Be careful walking around the shore, as it is marshy. Also beware of snakes. Ask around in the village to see if someone has a launch to hire for boating around the lagoon. Updated: Mar 16, 2011.

El Faro

The lighthouse is located on the very tip of the cape, warning those at sea of the imminent danger of these rocky shores. These days, it is a modern device keeping watch for sailors. The walk through this desert landscape or along the shore strewn with washed-up fragments of large shells and sea urchins is the main appeal to this spot, as is the view of the sea stretching to an indistinct horizon and the glorious sunsets.

If staying to watch the sunset, don't begin the trip back too late. Follow the road northward out of town. When you get to the T crossroads, turn left. This will take you directly to El Faro. From the main part of the village on the south shore, it takes 45 minutes to one hour, one way. Updated: Mar 16, 2011.

Snorkeling

The north side of the bay is rocky with coral reefs. Combined with the clear waters, this is a good place to practice a bit of snorkeling. Beneath the surface are a variety of colorful tropical fish and other marine life to discover among the *arrecife* (coral reef) and plant life.

The water is a bit warmer on this side, with slightly more wave action and the occasion jellyfish. To get there, just walk along the shore, or follow the road out toward El Faro. The sea nears the road just before you arrive to the lighthouse. Updated: Jun 13, 2008.

Aquatic Sports

During Semana Santa (Easter Week) and the December-January holidays, locals open sites renting equipment for different aquatic sports. How about skipping across these crystalline waters on a *velero* (sailboat) or windsurfing? *Gusanos*, or giant rubber water worms, are another way to enjoy a trip across the bay.

People also rent out snorkeling gear and offer *paseos en lancha*, or boat tours around the cape. But to enjoy most of these activities, you'll have to come when everyone else does. Updated: Mar 16, 2011.

Parque Eólico Jepirachi

Like giant stoic soldiers lined up across the flat barren lands, awaiting the charge of a Quijote, hundreds of windmills reel their three arms against the clear azure sky. This is one of the largest electrical projects in the world, generating a good portion of Colombia's energy needs. Here, there is a visitor center, various paths, a botanical garden, the Parque de Leyendas (explaining Wayuu mythology) and an artisan association called Saanain Woumain.

Most tours from Riohacha or Uribia include Parque Eólico Jepirachi on their itineraries. In Cabo de la Vela, you can hire someone to drive you there and back, with a 30-minute wait ($28). Along the main north-south road, midway between the Manaure-Uribia crossroads and Puerto Bolívar, not too far from the turn-off for Cabo de la Vela. Cel: 312-831-8955, E-mail: parqueolico@yahoo.es. Updated: Mar 16, 2011.

Tours

Most tours that come pulling into Cabo de la Vela in big buses originate in Riohacha or Santa Marta. There are no operators in this hamlet, but you can ask around to see if anyone is interested in chauffeuring you out to Pilón de Azúcar or Parque Eólico Jepirachi, or in taking you for a boat ride along the coast or on Laguna de Utta. You will have to negotiate the price for these services. Updated: Jun 13, 2008.

Andrés Gómez

Señor Gómez is the only person in this small village who formally hires out his car and launch for trips to nearby attractions. The land vehicle fits up to six people and the sea one (with life jackets) fits up to seven. If there is fewer than the minimum number, the cost is split among all the passengers. It costs $2.65 (minimum of four) to Pilón de Azúcar or El Faro; he will pick you up at the time you specify for the return journey. Trips to Parque Eólico, with a 30-minute wait, is $26.50 round trip (minimum six people). By sea to Pilón is $37 for the whole boat. To both El Faro and Pilón de Azúcar, a three-hour trip is $10.50 per person (up to seven) or $75 for all. Gómez is located left of the *ferretería* (hardware store), before coming to the curve of the cove. Updated: Mar 16, 2011.

Lodging

All of the lodging options in Cabo de la Vela are local family-run establishments. For the most part, it is sleeping in hammocks in an enramada right on the beach. There are a few more standard hotels, some quite expensive. The village has no electricity; some establishments have generators they fire up only for a few hours at night. Bring a good, strong flashlight and candles.

Due to the scarcity of water, most inns charge extra for a toss-water "shower," and some even for using the restroom facilities (which you flush with water scooped out of the provided reservoir). Updated: Mar 16, 2011.

Restaurant Rosita

(BEDS: $2-8) Doña Rosita is just one of the dozens of restaurants along the south side of the bay as you enter Cabo de la Vela that also rents hammock space. On the beach across from her establishment are three enramadas where you can pass the night in the cooler air, or pitch a tent. Behind the restaurant, in the family's living compound, is a cabaña, if you prefer to hammock sleep in an enclosed space. The restaurant is four lots down, to the left of the church. Cel: 313-595-6111. Updated: Mar 16, 2011.

Kayuusipaa

(BEDS: $7-13.50) Many moons ago, Doña Conchita opened up one of the very first inns in Cabo de la Vela—and it is still known as it has been all this time: Donde Conchita. She is a bit of a legend, known to spend evenings teaching the legends and ways of her people. In rustic cabañas, her guests sleep in hammocks or chinchorros. The clean common baths are out back. The lodge is more isolated and closer to the many natural wonders of this land, making it a perfect choice for those who wish to spend time meditating and hiking. Service is only when Doña Conchita is here, so call or write beforehand. Tell the driver of the pick-up truck from Uribia that you are going to "Donde Conchita;" he will take you to the head of the drive at the roadside. From there, it is about a 100-meter (350-ft) walk down to the compound. On the north shore of the bay, almost at the very end. Cel: 311-442-0427/1-347-9294 (Bogotá) Updated: Mar 16, 2011.

Hotel Jarrinapi

(BEDS: $15-80) The popular Hotel Jarrinapi provides cabañas with hammock or—for those preferring a more conventional sleep—bed, private bath with 24-hour water and fan. Common sitting areas provide refuge during the heat of day and places to relax after a day of hiking. It has its own generator, providing its guests with electricity 5 p.m.-6 a.m. As well as having a restaurant, this hostel also operates a store and the village's Telecom office. Cel: 311-683-4281. Updated: Mar 16, 2011.

Restaurants

As you can expect, the most common item on the menus of Cabo de la Vela's restaurants is seafood. The next most-frequent appearance is made by goat. Exotic dishes like chicken and beef cost a bit more. Few places have a set menu, which does not include soup due to the shortage of water. Beverages are a separate charge and, yes, it is true: beer is cheaper than water here. A few small shops sell canned goods and water, all of which is more expensive than elsewhere. Purchase several jugs of water with you before leaving Uribia. The water in Cabo de la Vela is salty, thus unsuitable for purification. Updated: Jun 13, 2008.

Restaurant Isa

(ENTREES: $3.70-8) A cane-slat picket fence zig-zags around a sand-floored restaurant, located two doors to the left of the church. There are only two tables within this small space. Like the old saying, "great things come in small packages," so it is at Restaurant Isa. Here the señora lends personalized service and dishes up generous portions at the most excellent prices. It's a simple menu: friche ($3.70), arroz con camarones (rice with shrimp) ($3.70), fish ($5.30), langostinos (prawns) ($6.35) and lobster ($8). All come with a tomato-onion salad, rice and fried plantains. A soft drink or beer can accompany your meal. Daily 6 a.m-8 p.m. Updated: Mar 28, 2011.

Restaurante El Wuashi

(LUNCH: $4.20) Restaurante El Wuashi may be part of one of the most expensive, modern hotels in Cabo de la Vela, but its restaurant does have set menus at a rather reasonable price. The breakfast (with eggs) is $3.20; lunch including fish, chicken or beef is $4.20. The menu at El Wuashi also includes à la carte fish and seafood dishes ($5.30-26.50). Open for breakfast 7-9 a.m., lunch 11 a.m.-1 p.m. and dinner 6-10 p.m. El Wuashi is near the entrance to town, before the church. Cel: 311-400-7515/686-0195. Updated: Mar 28, 2011.

Restaurante Donde Mamiche

(ENTREES: $6.35) This is one of the more popular eateries among tour groups and vacationing families, and can be found just three doors down from **Restaurant Rosita**. The blue and white restaurant has a large open-sided patio and an even larger enclosed room where service is rendered. It has a wonderful, unobstructed view of the sea. Of course, the menu is primarily fish and seafood, with dishes beginning at $6.35, accompanied with a simple salad, rice and fried plantains. The wait staff is young, so the service is not always the best. Daily 6 a.m.-8 p.m. Updated: Mar 28, 2011.

THE ALTA GUAJIRA

The Alta Guajira has many impressive sites. On the road to Nazareth is Puerto López, which was once an important port but is now a ghost town abandoned to the desert. Petroglyphs decorate Piedra de Alas at Siapana, a holy spring. There is also Punta Espada, or Piedra del Destino, is a mythical rock that reveals the future of the visitor.

Along the north coast are other places of interest, such as Puerto Bolívar, the port where the El Cerrón mine railway arrives; Bahía Portete, another important port with beaches, mangroves and the only sea crocodiles in the world; Bahía Honda, with fortress ruins; and Punta Gallina, the northernmost point of South America, where golden dunes tumble to a deep-blue sea. Be prepared to spend time and money if traveling on your own, due to infrequent

LA GUAJIRA

transportation. The most important thing to take is plenty of water. Also pack emergency food supplies, sun block, a hat or other items to protect you from the sun, and a tent or hammock. Along the way, you should be able to find shelter and food. In Punta Gallinas, one of the only inns where you can spend the night and eat is **Hospedaje and Comidas Luzmila** (Tel: 521-5005/312-647-9881/626-8121). Another option in Punta Gallinas is **Hospedaje Alexandra** (Tel/Cel: 316-644-4050/315-538-2718. Updated: Jun 17, 2008.

Getting To and Away

Places in the Upper Guajira are difficult to reach, except by private car or on a tour. If you are willing to wait for next week's truck, you could possibly make it to the places along the road to Nazareth. You can also ask around in Nazareth and other villages to see if anyone is heading for the north coast. Updated: Jun 17, 2008.

NAZARETH AND PARQUE NACIONAL NATURAL MACUIRA!

  65m   7,100   5

The village of Nazareth is in an oasis in Alta Guajira's desert. According to Wayuu mythology, this is one of the three sons of the god Maleywa, who had successfully followed his father's orders and was so blessed with this climate and vegetation.

Nazareth serves as the gateway into Parque Nacional Natural Macuira, a unique biological island; it is a cloud forest within the desert. Its 25,000 hectares (2.5 million ac) encompass the Serranía de Macuira, an ancient mountain range that reaches 865 meters (2,837 ft). Among the 249 flora species are mosses and orchids. Fauna includes monkeys, tigrillo, deer, guacharaca and 22 endemic species of birds. Entrance to the national park is free. Updated: Mar 16, 2011.

Getting To and Away

Early Sunday mornings, an unsheltered truck leaves from Maicao, swinging through Uribia, for Nazareth ($18.65-21). In the high season, there may also be one on Wednesdays. It is best to arrive in Uribia at least one day in advance to verify if the truck will be going, as transportation is only once weekly (twice in

high season). The truck returns to Uribia and Maicao on Thursday or Friday.

Another way to reach Nazareth and Parque Nacional Natural Macuira is with one of the tour agencies in Uribia and Riohacha that offer this excursion. Guides in Nazareth charge $5.30-32 per group for trips into the park, depending on the hike. The national park office is in Nazareth. Updated: Jun 10, 2008.

Safety

Be prepared for whatever length of time you will be staying in Nazareth, especially in terms of money. Families in Nazareth rent hammocks at their ranchos. Bring along water, an emergency stash of food, hammock or tent, sun block, insect repellent and hat. There are many snakes in the park, so be aware. Yellow fever is endemic in this area; make sure to get a vaccination at least 10 days before arriving. Updated: Jun 13, 2008.

MAICAO

 20m   123,757   5

Mention you'll be crossing the border at Maicao, and the first response of Colombians and Venezuelans is silence. Then they'll advise you, "Get in and out as fast as possible." Many Maicao natives take offense to this negative characterization. They'll be quick to point out attractions like the beautiful mosque, which is the second most important in Latin America.

Maicao's negative reputation is based on years of contraband running, drug smuggling and robbery. The paramilitary presence since the 1990s has caused a great migration from the city, especially of the Muslim community. Even though its citizens claim it has become a more tranquil place, you are still counseled to be inside before nightfall. Despite all its problems, Maicao continues to be an important land port between Colombia and Venezuela for both legitimate and "other" commerce. La Guajira Peninsula. Updated: Mar 16, 2011.

Border Crossing: Via Maicao

Despite the safety issues Maicao has, in some aspects, this is a preferable Colombia-Venezuela border crossing than the one at Cúcuta. Here, the immigration posts for both countries are next to each other, just like the customs offices (for those

LA GUAJIRA

traveling with their own vehicle), and there is direct international bus service. Venezuela has consulates in Colombia's principal Caribbean coast cities, including Riohacha. At the terminal in Maicao, you can exchange your pesos into Venezuelan bolívares fuertes. *Por puestos* (collective taxis) leave when full for Maracaibo ($3).

Note: be sure the driver understands that you must go through immigration and that he waits for you.

Berlinas has an international service connecting Cartagena, Barranquilla, Santa Marta, Riohacha and Maicao, Colombia, with Maracaibo, Valencia and Caracas, Venezuela. When the bus arrives at the border, it drops passengers off at the immigration post of the country of departure. While travelers go through procedures, the vehicle passes through customs and waits at the bus office on the other side. You then continue on to your destination.

This border crossing is properly called Parguachón in Colombia and Guarero in Venezuela. The border is supposedly open 24 hours a day. If leaving Venezuela, you'll have to pay an exit tax of $16 (at official rate, less at black market rates). Updated: Jun 17, 2011.

!!!!!

LA GUAJIRA

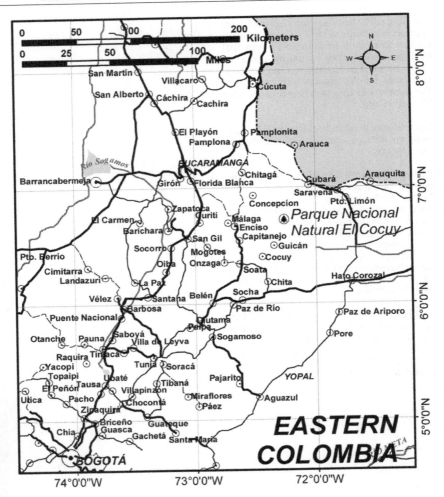

Eastern Colombia

Eastern Colombia consists of those lands northeast of the nation's capital that are defined by the broad lowlands of the Lower Magdalena River valley to the West and the towering heights of the Cordillera Oriental to the East. Within this area are the Departments of Boyacá, Santander and Norte de Santander. A major highway connects Bogotá and Santa Marta, passing through Tunja and Bucaramanga. From Bucaramanga, another thoroughfare heads east to Pamplona, Cúcuta and the Venezuelan border. An older, toll-free road twists through the mountains from Tunja to Capitanejo, Málaga and down to Pamplona, connecting with the Bucaramanga-Cúcuta highway. This is the preferred route for buses and trucks, and the fastest way to get to Parque Nacional Natural El Cocuy and its associated pueblos, El Cocuy and Güican.

The physical beauty and cultural richness of this area of Colombia manage to consistently astound visitors. Colonial villages are plentiful as are reminders of former inhabitants, from prehistoric sea creatures to the pre-Conquest Muisca and Guane nations. The modern-day U'wa indigenous culture clings to its way of life in the Cocuy region, struggling to prevent the violation of their

The Battle of Boyacá

1819: The Spanish and patriot forces at war in present-day Venezuela are locked in a stalemate. There are several armies scattered throughout the land; some rebel, some royalist. None of them are strong enough to wipe out the others and firmly take control of the war-torn land. General Simón Bolivar, himself pinned up against the mountains of western Venezuela, decides on a bold move.

Bolívar ordered his rag-tag army to march west, through reeking swamps, across raging rivers and finally over the frigid Andes themselves. In the process of this brutal march, Bolívar would lose fully a third of his men. But in July of 1819, his men descended into New Granada: present-day Colombia. Once again, Bolívar had done the unexpected: no one thought he would be crazy enough to cross the mountains.

Bolívar regrouped and marched on Bogota, seat of the Spanish Viceroy. Spanish General José María Barreiro was desperately sent out with what men were available to stop the Liberator. On August 7, Barreiro was hurriedly moving his army, hoping to find a place to fight the rebels and keep them out of Bogota.

Bolívar was a lot closer than Barreiro suspected. The liberator struck the extended Spanish army with lightning speed as they marched along the Boyacá River. While General Santander kept the elite Numancia Batallion and the Dragoons at the front of the column pinned down, Bolívar viciously attacked the center, encircling the Spanish army. Barreiro wisely surrendered. The final tally: 200 dead and some 1,600 captured for the Spanish. Bolívar only lost about 13 killed and 50 wounded: the Liberator's victory was one of the most one-sided in history. The Battle of Boyacá would be a turning point in the struggle for liberation of northern South America.

With Barreiro's army out of the way, the route was clear into Bogotá. Bolívar entered the city on August 10 to the cheers of the populace. The Viceroy had left in such a hurry that he even left money behind in the treasury! The struggle for independence in Colombia and Venezuela was basically over, and Bolívar would turn his attention to Ecuador and Peru.

Mother Earth by oil companies. The Cordillera Oriental, with three peaks surpassing 5,300 meters (17,000 ft), includes the largest snow field in northern South America.

Colombians of this region have the reputation of being ultra-courteous, especially in Boyacá. Do not be surprised if locals address you with the medieval *su merced* ("your mercy"). They often call visitors *vecino* (neighbor), and will often ask, "¿Le provoca un tintico?" (Would you like a coffee?). Updated: Apr 4, 2011.

History

Long before humans left their footprints in this region, a sea covered the landscape and left behind multitude of fossils. Eons later, great indigenous nations flourished, the most important being the Muisca and the Guanes. During the Spanish occupation, gold mines flourished for a while near Bucaramanga. The region also had important ports of trade.

Eastern Colombia was a hotbed of rebel activity during New Granada's struggle for independence from Spain. Some of the sparks of this movement ignited in villages around San Gil. In 1819, independence forces, led by Simón Bolívar and Francisco de Paula Santander, won an important victory at Puente de Boyacá near Tunja. Villa del Rosario was the seat for the Congreso Constituyente in 1821 which formed Gran Colombia (Venezuela, Colombia and Ecuador). The first convention of this nascent nation was held in Villa de Leyva.

At the end of the 19th century, Colombia experienced the 1,000-Day War. One of the main areas of fighting was in the Santander Department. The last—and bloodiest—battle of this civil war was fought at Palonegro, near Bucaramanga.

In the 1980s, both the FARC (Fuerzas Armadas Revolucionarias de Colombia) and ELN (Ejército para la Liberación Nacional) gue

Photo by: Amanderson 2

rilla movements began occupying great parts of Eastern Colombia, specifically between the principal North-South highway and the Río Magdalena around the Sierra Nevada El Cocuy (including the national park) and near the less-populated areas along the Venezuela border, particularly in the Norte de Santander Department. The mid-1990s brought paramilitary forces into the region. Some villages, like Málaga and Capitanejo, suffered many killings during what the locals call "a reign of terror." Many fled. Populations in main towns like Bucaramanga and Cúcuta swelled with people fleeing the violence. During the third millennium and under a new president, military forces commenced driving the guerrillas out of populated areas and even now soldiers continue to occupy villages. Remote zones still see armed confrontations between the government, guerrilla and paramilitary armies.

Pamplona is another town with an interesting history, as is Cúcuta and neighboring Villa del Rosario. Updated: Apr 4, 2011.

When to Go

Eastern Colombia generally has two rainy seasons per year, from March to May and from September to November. The drier months are June, July, December, January and February. Due to its diverse topography, some areas, like San Gil and Barichara, receive very little rain year-round while others areas, like Cúcuta and Capitanejo, are downright scorching in the dry periods, with temperatures reaching into the upper 30s°C (upper 90s-lower 100s°F). The best time to visit Parque Nacional Natural El Cocuy and its neighboring villages is during the December-February dry season; however, this is also when temperatures are coldest, occasionally below freezing in the park itself.

Malagá and Pamplona are both college towns. When the universities are in session—January to June and August to the beginning of December—the towns have an energetic atmosphere. Once the students leave on break, these cities revert to quiet highland villages once again.

Villa de Leyva, Barichara, San Gil and Pamplona are extremely popular among vacationing Colombians during major holidays and three-day weekends. Hotel prices rise substantially and reservations are necessary. Parque Nacional Natural El Cocuy is becoming a trendy spot for the December to January vacationers with a little more time. Updated: Sep 28, 2011.

Safety

Eastern Colombia is much safer than it was before 2003. Under President Uribe's program to demobilize paramilitary forces and neutralize the guerrilla armies, roads are now heavily patrolled by the Colombian military. Expect frequent checkpoints, especially when traveling toward the Río Magdalena, the less-frequented areas bordering Venezuela and into the Sierra Nevada de El Cocuy. If journeying to Barrancabermeja, El Banco and other towns on the Magdalena River, stay on the main roads and in the villages; the surrounding countryside may not yet be secure. Trips along the Venezuelan border are not recommended since it is still a "hot zone." Cúcuta, which is the major crossing between Colombia and Venezuela, is the exception. Updated: Mar 14, 2011.

Things to See and Do

The breadth of things to see and do in Eastern Colombia includes nearly everything imaginable, including (but not limited to) cultural activities and high-octane sports. Tunja has many beautiful churches, most notably the Iglesia de Santa Bárbara, which displays embroidery done by Juana la Loca (the "mad" mother of Emperor Carlos V). Villa de Leyva and Barichara are both colonial towns on the national register of historic villages. The countryside surrounding Villa de Leyva bears the fossilized marks of sea monsters from more than 160 million years ago. San Gil is the adventure sports capital of the nation with whitewater rafting, spelunking (cave exploring) and other less extreme options.

Between San Gil and bustling Bucaramanga are the Cañón de Chicamocha and Mesa de Ruitoque, the nation's best places for paragliding. In the deep folds of the Cordillera Oriental are small villages with diverse climates and customs, such as Málaga, Concepción (the wool capital of Colombia) and Capitanejo (the goat, tobacco and melon capital). At the apex of these mountains is the Parque Nacional Natural El Cocuy, which has superb mountain climbing, rock climbing and trekking. Updated: Mar 14, 2011.

Tours

Most of the cities in Eastern Colombia have resident tour operators. The agencies in San Gil specialize in taking visitors on high-adrenaline adventures like whitewater rafting, paragliding, rappelling, spelunking, horseback riding and other such sports. Guides to Parque Nacional Natural El Cocuy are mostly from the local community and have been specially trained in tourism. They specialize in trekking and mountain climbing and some rent out pack mules. Another place to look for inexpensive guides is the local SENA program, which is training low-income residents in tourism. Even villages as small as Capitanejo have SENA training programs. Also, many tour agencies in Bogotá can arrange outings to Eastern Colombia, especially to Villa de Leyva and Parque Nacional Natural El Cocuy. Updated: Sep 28, 2011.

Lodging

Those who travel to Eastern Colombia will find a broad assortment of types and quality of hotels. Smaller villages have homier, simple hostels. In the rural areas, such as those near Málaga and Villa de Leyva, there are working farms where you can stay for a different kind of experience. Near Bucaramanga is a Hare Krishna retreat center. In the warmer zones, hot water is available only in luxury-class accommodations. Most inns' showers have only room temperature water though the sun usually heats the water to a comfortable degree.

In popular vacation destinations, like San Gil, Villa de Leyva and Barichara, hotels charge low season and high season prices and the two prices can vary dramatically. If you insist on going during high season, make reservations well in advance. In the low season you should be able to negotiate a good price for a room, particularly if you are staying for more than a few days. Camping is also an option in this part of Colombia. Updated: Sep 28, 2011.

TUNJA

 2,746m   152,000   8

Tunja is on the main highway heading north from Bogotá, about 135 kilometers (81 mi) away from Santa Marta. There are three toll booths en route from Bogotá to Tunja. Tunja, the capital of the department of Boyacá, is on a high-altitude plateau and is surrounded by mountains. The city's name derives from the Muisca language (of the Chibcha linguistic group) and means "Land of Blankets" or "Royal Mantle."

Some Colombians may tell you there's nothing to see in Tunja, but you should decide for yourself. The city has managed to

EASTERN COLOMBIA

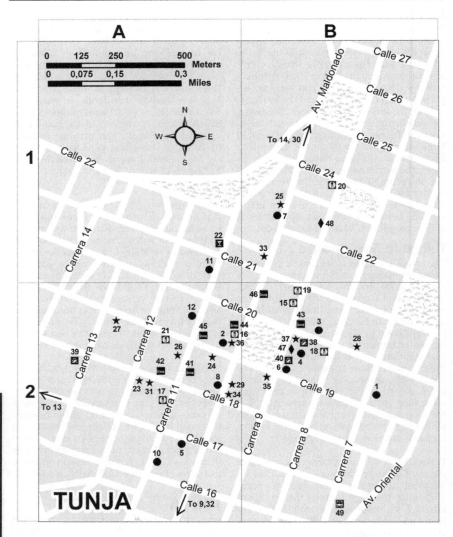

preserve much of its colonial past, including what is said to be the only remaining house in Latin America of the Conquistador Gonzalo Suárez Rendón. Many of the Catholic temples share a gold-leaf-on-red motif, which is most stunningly displayed in the Iglesia de Santo Domingo. A few fragments of the indigenous Muisca culture also remain. Tunja was important during the Wars of Independence. The monumental Batalla de Boyacá was fought 15 kilometers (8 mi) south of Tunja. This battle showed the viceroy of Nueva Granada that the end of the Spanish reign was at hand. Updated: Sep 28, 2011.

Holidays and Festivals

May/April: Semana Santa
June: Fiestas de la Virgen del Milagro
August: Fiestas de San Bartolomé
August 6: Founding of Tunja/Semana de la Cultura Tunjana
August 7: Anniversary of the Battle of Boyacá
September: Fiestas del Señor de la Columna, Festival Internacional de la Cultura and Fiestas de San Lázaro I
October: Festival del Frío
November: Feria Artesanal
December 16-22: Fiestas de San Lázaro II Aguinaldo Boyacense

● **Activities**

1 Capilla y Convento de Santa Clara La Real B2
2 Casa de la Familia Niño y Capitán Martín Rojas A2
3 Casa del Escribano del Rey Don Juan de Vargas B2
4 Casa del Fundador B2
5 Casa del Presidente General Gustavo Rojas Pinilla A2
6 Catedral Santiago de Tunja B2
7 Iglesia San FranciscoB1
8 Iglesia San Ignacio A2
9 Iglesia San Laureano A2
10 Iglesia Santa Bárbara A2
11 Iglesia Santa Clara A1
12 Iglesia Santo Domingo A2
13 Iglesia y Monasterio de El Topo A2
14 Pozo de Hunzahúa B1

⊞ **Eating**

15 Parrilla y Son B2
16 Pussini Café-Bar A2
17 Restaurante China A2
18 Restaurante Pila del Mono B2
19 Restaurante Vegetariano Roma B2
20 Ristorante-Caffe La Buona Vita B1
21 Trigos A2

▣ **Nightlife**

22 Macondo A1

★ **Services**

23 Adpostal A2
24 AV Villas A2

25 Bancolombia B1
26 BBVA (bank) A2
27 Benicnet A2
28 DAS B2
29 Foto Veracruz A2
30 Hospital San Rafael B1
31 Instituto Geográfico Agustín Codazzi A2
32 Lavandería Nuevo Milenio A2
33 Meg@.net B1
34 Santander A2
35 Telecom B2
36 Tourism Office (Boyacá) A2
37 Tourism Office (Tunja) B2

▣ **Shopping**

38 Artesanías de Mi Tierra B2
39 Taller Galería Artesanal Ambar A2
40 Tunja Artesanal B2

▤ **Sleeping**

41 Hotel American A2
42 Hotel Boyacá Plaza A2
43 Hotel Conquistador de América B2
44 Hotel Don Camilo A2
45 Hotel Dux A2
46 Hotel El Cid B2

◆ **Tours**

47 Piri Company Tours B2
48 Viajes Naturaleza y Vida B1

▣ **Transportation**

49 Bus Terminal B2

History

For centuries the Muisca lived in the Boyacá region. At that time, Tunja was known as Hunza, which was the main city of the 800,000 to one million Muisca in the region. This was the most advanced civilization of that time in the region. The Muisca fought hard to keep the Spanish out, but in 1539, the Spaniards succeeded in their conquest. Gonzalo Suárez Rendón established Tunja on the site of Hunza. The city declared its liberty from Spanish rule centuries later in 1811. During the struggle for independence, one of the most decisive battles was fought at Puente de Boyacá. Updated: Sep 28, 2011.

When to Go

Like other areas of the Colombian Andes, Tunja experiences a three-month cycle of wet and dry seasons: wetter months are March-May and September-November. Tunja has a number of civic, cultural and religious celebrations. No matter what time of year you visit, you will almost certainly be here for one. For exact dates visit the tourism office websites.

Getting To and Away

Tunja has a fine network of city buses. The fare is $0.40 ($0.45 Sunday and holidays). The bus terminal is at Carrera 7 and Calle 17. There are two levels: buses on the lower level go to distant cities and buses on the upper level go to Villa de Leyva and surrounding villages.

To Villa de Leyva: half-hourly 6 a.m.-6 p.m.; 45 min, $3.

EASTERN COLOMBIA

To Puente de Bocayá: half-hourly 6 a.m.-6 p.m; 20 min, $1.50.

To Paipa: every 10 min; 30 min, $3.

To Bogotá: every 10 min; 3 hr, $6-7.

To Málaga: 5 buses daily; 8 hr, $14.

To Güicán: 10 a.m. and 10 p.m.; 10 hr, $18.

To San Gil: 11 buses daily.; 6 hr, $14.

To Cúcuta: 9 a.m., 4 p.m., 6 p.m., 8 p.m., 10 p.m., 11:30 p.m.; 12 hr, $32.

Buses also leave to Santa Marta (12:30 p.m.; 19 hr, $58-64), Cartagena (12:30 p.m.; 23 hr, $65-71) and Riohacha (1 p.m., 3 p.m., 11 p.m.; 21 hr, $69). Updated: Jul 04, 2011.

Safety

The areas around the bus terminal and the Iglesia del Carmen neighborhood are dangerous, especially at night. Locals also describe the Los Cojines de Zaque archaeological site as *feo y peligroso* (ugly and dangerous). The Centro Histórico is patrolled by the tourism police and is considered very safe. As in most places around the country, the tap water is not safe to drink. Updated: Sep 28, 2011.

Services

TOURISM

The **tourism office** (Dirección de Cultura y Turismo de Tunja) has excellent maps of the city and hotel information (Monday-Friday 8 a.m.-noon and 2-6 p.m. Closed Saturday and Sunday. Cra. 9, 19-70, Casa del Fundador, Plaza Bolívar. Tel: 742-3272, URL: www.tunja.gov.co) On the other side of the plaza is the **Secretería de Cultura y Turismo of Boyacá Department**, which has information on

VIVA ONLINE REVIEW
TUNJA
"Tunja is a very pretty town. The history and culture are compelling and the architecture is beautiful and well preserved."
February 17, 2009

festivals and other cultural events and attractions all over Boyacá (Cra. 10, 19-17. Tel: 742-6547/3179, URL: www.boyaca.gov.co). You can find maps at the **Instituto Geográfico Agustín Codazzi** (Monday-Friday 8-11:30

a.m. and 2-4 p.m. Ca. 18, 11-31, Banco Agrario building, 5th, 6th and 7th floor. Tel: 742-2268) Immigration, or **DAS**, has an office in Tunja where you can get visa extensions (Monday-Friday 7:30 a.m.-noon and 2-6 p.m. Ca. 20, 7-38. Tel: 742-4017) Updated: Sep 29, 2011.

MONEY

Major banks have branches in Tunja, including: **Bancolombia** (Monday-Friday 8 a.m.-7 p.m. Cra. 10, 22-35, near Iglesia San Francisco), **Santander** (Monday-Friday 8-11:30 a.m. and 2-4:30 p.m. Cra. 10, 18-16), **AV Villas** (Monday-Friday 8 a.m.-3 p.m., Saturday 9 a.m.-3 p.m. Ca. 19, 10-83) and **BBVA** (Monday-Friday 8-11:30 a.m. and 2-4:30 p.m. Cra. 11, 18-41). Many have 24-hour ATMs and both Bancolombia and Santander accept American Express traveler's checks.

The Western Union agent in Tunja is at **Giros and Finanzas** (Monday-Friday 8:30 a.m.-5 p.m., Saturday 8:30 a.m.-1 p.m. Cra. 10, 16-81. Tel: 740-9877) inside Almacén Comfaboy. The **MoneyGram** agent is in the Davivienda bank (Monday-Friday 8 a.m.-4:30 p.m., Saturday 9 a.m.-3 p.m. Cra. 10 and Ca. 14. Tel: 742-4898). Updated: Sep 29, 2011.

KEEPING IN TOUCH

Many shops have local and national phone service for a reasonable rate. **Telecom**, which has international service, is located at the Calle 19, 9 -15 (closed Sundays). A cheaper option for international calls is **Meg@.net**, located at Carrera 10, 21-42, Centro Comercial Pinal. Internet cafés abound in Tunja. **Benicnet** is one of the only cheap places open on Sundays and holidays (Monday-Saturday 8 a.m.-8 p.m., Sunday and holidays 9 a.m.-5 p.m. Ca. 19, 12-69). The **post office** is at Calle 18, 11-77 (Tel: 742-2821, closed Sunday). Updated: Sep 29, 2011.

MEDICAL

The public health facility, **Hospital San Rafael**, is a full-service center (Cra. 11, 27-27. Tel: 740-5050 ext 2114, URL: www.hospitalsanrafaeltunja.gov.co). There are also a number of private clinics. The main *droguerías*, or pharmacies, are on Calle 19. Updated: Sep 29, 2011.

LAUNDRY

Several laundry places are scattered around on the outskirts of the downtown area. One worth trying is **Lavandería Nuevo Milenio**, across from Parque Bosque de la República (Closed on Sunday. Cra. 10, 13-20). Updated: Oct 05, 2011.

CAMERAS

Like all other services in Tunja, camera shops are scattered throughout the town and, apparently, none of the shops repair cameras. The best one-stop option seems to be **Foto Veracruz**, which has all sorts of digital cameras, batteries, chargers and memory cards for sale. It also develops film, print photos, etc. (Monday-Friday 8 a.m.-7:30 p.m., Saturday 9 a.m.-7:30 p.m.; Sunday and holidays 9 a.m.-1 p.m. Cra. 10, 18-24. Tel: 742-3982). Updated: Dec 17, 2007.

SHOPPING

Taller-Galería Artesanal Ambar

Craftsman Rafael Piñeros Bonilla creates simple to sublime jewelry. From seeds, shells and stones to sterling silver, there's a ring, necklace or pair of earrings waiting for you. A unique item is his "Botero" rings: thick and round, some with emeralds and some with other semi-precious gems. You can check out his work at Tunja Artesanal in the Casa del Fundador. Ca. 18, 13-03. Cel: 312-483-3813. Updated: May 18, 2009.

Artesanías de Mi Tierra

Crafts hang from the ceilings, crowd the shelves and are piled in mounds on the floor in this two-story shop. Not only is there pottery from Ráquir, but there are also ceramic miniatures of houses, basketry, woolen *ruanas* (short ponchos) and scarves, net bags, hammocks and cane furniture from other villages in the Boyacá Department. Artesanías de Mi tierra even has honey and scrumptious honey caramel. Everything comes from family workshops. If you can't make it to the villages, Artesanías de Mi Tierra brings it all to you in one shop just a half-block from the main plaza. Daily 8 a.m.-7 p.m. Ca. 20, 8-79 (also Cra. 19-92). Cel: 310-201-8519/320-249-6099/316-472-6003. Updated: Oct 05, 2011.

Tunja Artesanal

This shop presently offers artesanía from family worshops in Tunja. If you are looking for a warm wool sweater, ruana (short poncho) or scarf, a piece of jewelry or a net bag to carry your new purchases, Tunja Artesanal offers a tasteful selection at budget prices. To send greetings home, choose a hand-made paper card. The store also carries crafts from neighboring villages, such as baskets from Tenza. The shop is in the back patio of Casa del Fundador. Cra. 9, 19-56. Cel: 312-586-8328/301-287-8005, E-mail: artesanospachamama@gmail.comUpdated: Sep 24, 2011.

Things to See and Do

Despite having been the capital of its domain, little remains of the Muisca culture in Tunja. The Cojines del Zaque and the Pozo de Hunzahúa are some of the last vestiges of this culture. The colonial era is still evident, however. The city preserves one of the last original conquistador homes in Latin America, the Casa del Fundador Gonzalo Suárez Rendón. Other colonial sites include Casa de la Familia Niño y Capitán Martín de Rojas (now the Boyacá tourism office) and the Paredón de los Mártires in Parque de la República, where you can still see the bullet holes where independence patriots were executed. As with most colonial cities, old churches and convents abound, if that's your sort of thing (see next section for details).

South of the city is the massive monument complex commemorating the Battle of Boyacá. For movie buffs, Tunja has three cinemas. If you are in the mood to shoot 18 holes, there are several golf courses in the area. Sports fans can also check out bullfighting and soccer matches, depending on the season. Updated: Jun 15, 2011.

The Churches of Tunja

Tunja's old churches have architectural features seldom seen elsewhere. A common theme in many of the churches is the gold-leaf-on-red décor. There are open mass hours, except where noted. No photos are allowed inside any of the churches. If you only see one church in Tunja, head to Santa Bárbara.

Catedral Santiago de Tunja—(Basílica Metropolitana de Santiago el Mayor de España) Contains the tomb of Gonzalo Suárez Rendón, the founder of Tunja. It is possible to make an appointment to visit at the office of Cultura and Turismo. Cra. 9, 19-28, Plaza Bolívar.

San Laureano—Cra. 10, between Ca. 13 and 14.

Santa Clara—Cra. 11, between Ca. 20 and 21.

San Ignacio—This church has a stunningly simple interior with bare adobe and whitewashed walls. There is also a fully gilded chapel as well as altar screens. Open Thursday evenings for concerts. Cra. 10, between Ca. 18 and 19.

Santa Bárbara—Cra. 11, between Ca. 16 and 17.

San Francisco—Cra. 10, between Ca. 22 and 23.

Santo Domingo—Impressive red interior with gold-leaf and nacre (mother-of-pearl) accents. The Capilla de la Virgen del Rosario is considered Latin America's "Sistine Chapel." Daily 8 a.m.-noon and 2-7 p.m. Cra. 11, between Ca. 19 and 20.

Capilla y Convento de Santa Clara La Real—Also houses the Museo de Arte Religioso. Daily 8 a.m.-noon and 2-5 p.m. Cra. 7, 19-58.

Iglesia y Monasterio de El Topo—Visits can be arranged through the tourism office. Cra. 17, 17-99. Updated: Sep 30, 2011.

Iglesia de Santa Bárbara

Iglesia Santa Bárbara is perhaps the most unusual of Tunja's churches. To the right of the atrium is a room full of niche tombs. Steps lead from the atrium down into the nave. The color scheme of the sanctuary is impressive: the walls are dark blue-and gray accented with giltwood orchid flowers. Along the transept chapel arches, the designs are simpler. This part of the church was restored after a 1927 earthquake. The ceiling is intertwined with flowering-vine murals. The apse arch is done in bright gold leaf. The apse itself is red and gold. In the left transept chapel is the treasure of this temple: red silk vestments embroidered in gold and silver thread by Juana la Loca, mother of Emperor Charles V. More original murals are located in the chapel on the right. Cra. 11, between Ca. 16 and 17. Updated: Mar 17, 2011.

The Museums of Tunja

All of Tunja's museums are in colonial or Republican-era former homes. Several showcase the buildings themselves, whereas others focus on the art. While on the circuit, don't miss Santa Clara La Real's Religious Art Museum (see churches).

Casa del Escríbano del Rey don Juan de Vargas (ADMISSION: $1.05 adults, $0.50 children)—Built at the end of the 16th century, this colonial mansion displays Mozarab, Andalusian and Tuscan influences. The gift shop sells artesanías, CDs and books by local artists. Tuesday-Friday 9 a.m.-noon and 2-5 p.m., Saturday-Sunday 10 a.m.-4 p.m. Ca. 20, 8-52.

Casa del Presidente General Gustavo Rojas Pinilla (ADMISSION: free)— Once the home of a former president, it's now the Casa de la Cultura, with galleries that feature poetry, music and displays about Rojas Pinilla and other Colombian presidents. Monday-Friday 8 a.m.-noon and 2-6 p.m. Ca. 17, 10-73.

Casa de la Familia Niño y Capitán Martín de Rojas (ADMISSION: free)— Home of the Instituto de Cultura y Turismo de Boyacá (ICTBA) and the Museo de Arte Contemporáneo.Monday-Friday 8 a.m.-noon and 2-6 p.m. Cra. 10, 19-17. Updated: Sep 30, 2011.

Casa del Fundador Gonzalo Suárez Rendón !

(ADMISSION: $0.80) Casa del Fundador was the home of Gonzalo Suárez Rendón, founder of the colonial city of Tunja. It is claimed to be the only original home of a founder still in existence in Latin America. Built in the mid-16th century by Spanish and indigenous laborers, the mansion has Mudéjar and Andalusian features. The upstairs quarters give you an insight into Spanish life of that period, from the austere furnishings to the imaginative ceiling murals depicting a nobleman's favorite pastime, hunting. Guided tours are available in Spanish or English. Updated: Mar 11, 2011.

Puente de Boyacá

On the seventh day of August in 1819, a small liberation force under the command of Generals Francisco de Paula Santander and Simón Bolívar defeated a large column of Spanish troops, effectively ending Spanish control in New Granada. The hallmark of this site is an 18-meter (59-ft) high monument dedicated to Bolívar designed by Ferdinand von Müller. Other structures include a triumphal arch, an obelisk to the Liberator, and the Boyacá Bridge (Puente de Boyacá). Every Saturday a different Boyancense village leads the commemorative ceremonies, complete with honor guards (8 a.m.-5 p.m.).

Puente de Boyacá is 15 minutes south, vía Bogotá. Buses leave from the upper level of Tunja's bus terminal every half-hour ($1.30 each way). It is open daily from 8:30 a.m.-8:30 p.m. Updated: Mar 30, 2011.

Pozo de Hunzahúa

According to legend, Hunzahúa, the Muisca leader who founded Hunza (Tunja), fell in love with his beautiful sister Noncetá, who was much beloved by her people. During a journey, they consummated their love and became husband and wife. When their mother,

---

Faravita, discovered the act, she beat Noncetá with the chicha-making paddle. The chicha urn broke, spilling its endless contents and forming this little lake, now known as Pozo de Hunzahúa. For the Muisca, it was a holy place; gold was offered to its depths. Their leader, Quemuenchatocha, ordered all gold and emeralds to be thrown in to save them from the greedy Spanish conquerors. An early colonizer, Jerónimo Donato, had the pool drained to retrieve the treasure--but found nothing. Stellae located throughout the park illustrate the Muisca culture.

The park is located on Avenida Norte, just past Universidad Pedagógica y Tecnológica de Colombia (UPTC). To get there, take a Muiscas bus. Get off the bus at the pedestrian overpass at Iglesia Santa Inés, just past the railroad station. The Pozo is on the other side of the road, next to the Universidad Pedagógica y Tecnológica de Colomb. The park is open from dawn to dusk. Updated: Mar 17, 2011.

Jardín Botánico José Joaquín Camacho Lago !

The José Joaquín Camacho Lago botanical garden, located on the southeast side of the city, is a center for the study and preservation of endangered Andean flora. Stroll through these 33 hectares (81 ac) that have been set aside and learn about the eco-systems of the Colombian Andes. This is a good introduction before trekking through Parque Nacional Natural El Cocuy or other parts of the region. Vía Soracá, Jardín Botánico José Joaquín Camacho Lago is just past the *Circunvalar* (city bypass). No city buses pass that way. A taxi costs around $1.30-1.60 per vehicle one way. Updated: Sep 30, 2011.

Tours

Tunja has more tour operators than other small cities. Besides the tours to Villa de Leyva and Paipa, a number of tours to villages and natural sites are available. You can arrange a trip to Parque Nacional Natural El Cocuy from Tunja. Most guides only speak Spanish: it is possible (though expensive) to hire a translator. Updated: Mar 17, 2011.

Viajes Naturaleza y Vida

Viajes Naturaleza y Vida offers all-inclusive, multi-day tour packages to some of the region's most popular attractions. Trips are planned at set times of the year, which is great for solo travelers. Check the website for the next excursion to your dream destination. Guides are Spanish-speaking, but Naturaleza y Vida can provide translators (at an extra charge). Naturaleza y Vida can also take you to other parts of Colombia, like the Zona Cafetera, the Caribbean coast and the Llanos. It has an office in Bogotá and another in Villavicencio. Cra. 9, 22-47. Cel: 314-304-7858, URL: http://agenciadeviajestunja.blogspot.com. Updated: Sep 28, 2011.

Piri Company

Piri Company is one of several businesses that can show you around Boyacá. The one-day trips follow the Anillo de Hinojosa, visiting the *páramo* (high moors), waterfalls, mountians and villages of the area. Of course, there are several options in Villa de Leyva. One option is to focus on visiting museums; another option is to explore the pottery village of Ráquira and go to the Candelaria moniastery and a third option is to hike through the Parque National Sanctuary. If the group is smaller than 10 participants, transportation is extra. Translators available but not included. Cra. 9, 19-56, Casa del Fundador, back patio. Tel: 743-1286, Cel: 310-209-3894, E-mail: turism@ piricompany.com. Updated: Mar 31, 2011.

Lodging

Good, inexpensive lodging is difficult to find in Tunja. The cheapest hostels are near the bus terminal—an area which is said to be unsafe and to have a lot of prostitution and drugs. Better hotels are found in the center of the city, but expect to pay more. Several of the more expensive inns have been recently renovated. Updated: Sep 27, 2011.

BUDGET

Hotel Don Camilo

(ROOMS: $5-19) Hotel Don Camilo, one of the least expensive inns in Tunja, is right on the main plaza (look for the small sign). The hostel offers rooms that are a bit worn but clean enough. All rooms have windows and a desk as well as the standard bed. No matter if you choose common or private bathrooms, you'll be guaranteed hot water. Cra. 10, 19-57, Plaza de Bolívar. Tel: 740-9309, Cel: 310-569-0654. Updated: Jul 21, 2010.

Hotel American

(ROOMS: $6.50-20) Another upstairs hostel, Hotel American offers respectable rooms at a comfortable price. Some rooms have private hot water baths and televisions. More basic rooms don't have a TV and the common cold-water bathrooms are shared (one for women, a second for men). The on-site restaurant is located in the covered front patio. In the back courtyard there is a seating area with couches and over-stuffed chairs. Ca. 11, 18-70. Tel: 742-2471, Cel: 311-849-5467. Updated: Mar 17, 2011.

Hotel Dux ♪

(ROOMS: $12.50-20) The creaky old Hotel Dux is a classic place to stay. For several generations, this friendly, family-run hotel has welcomed visitors to Tunja. Rooms are large with at least two beds. All rooms, save one, have private bath and all rooms have TV as well. You can ask permission to wash your clothes in the *pila* out back. At the front entrance is a café run by Marta, who will serve you one dynamite cup of coffee. Marta and her sisters Luzalba and Edilma, who run the hotel, are always ready to chat. Ca. 19, 10-78. Tel: 742-5736, Cel: 320-847-2872, E-mail: claudiagagomez@yahoo.es. Updated: Oct 05, 2011.

MID-RANGE

Hotel Conquistador de América

(ROOMS: $12.50-25) Right on the corner of the Plaza de Bolívar in the heart of Tunja, the two-story Hotel Conquistador de América is a solid mid-range lodging option. Some of the upstairs rooms have balconies over the street. All rooms have private bathrooms with gas-heated hot water as well as TV, phone and shabby carpeting. The first-floor courtyard is quite large, with plants and room to sit and read a book. Ca. 20 8-92 (corner, Plaza de Bolívar). Tel: 742-353, Cel: 310-321-1506. Fax: 742-3534. Updated: Mar 17, 2011.

Hotel El Cid

(ROOMS: $13-32) The Hotel El Cid is located on the second floor above a shopping mall. All of the conservatively decorated rooms have private bath with hot water, cable TV, mini-bar (charges separately) and telephone. Larger rooms (six beds) have balconies over the street. The restaurant only prepares breakfast ($2.65), which is served in a fancy dining room. Cra. 10, 20-78. Tel: 742-3458/744-4179, Fax: 744-4417, E-mail: hotelgidplaza@hotmail.com. Updated: Mar 17, 2011.

HIGH-END

Hotel Boyacá Plaza ♪

(ROOMS: $65-90) One of Tunja's finest lodges, Hotel Boyacá Plaza is in a quieter part of the city. An elevator will whisk you to your carpeted room with a window view of the city. All rooms have a private bath with hot water, plus mini-bar. Smoking and non-smoking rooms are available. Boyacá Plaza has all the amenities you expect from a hotel in its class: security, room service, internet/WiFi, etc. Ca. 18, 11-22. Tel: 740-1116/1117, Fax: 742-7635, E-mail: hotelboyacaplaza@hotmail.com. Updated: Mar 17, 2011.

Restaurants

Tunja doesn't offer much in the way of formal dining establishments, although no visitor will starve in this city. There are plenty of places to purchase your own food: Tunja has two markets, one on either side of the city. The market on the southern end of the city is open on Thursday and Friday and the market on the northern end is open on Saturday and Sunday. Several supermarkets are on Carrera 10, between Calles 18 and 19. One of them is Ley (Monday-Saturday 9 a.m.-9 p.m., Sunday and holidays 9:30 a.m.-7 p.m.). Also, be sure to check out one of Tunja's several pastry shops that bake all sorts of delights, which include *pan integral* (multi-grain) bread and three-seed breads as well. If you want to sit and be served, the average price for a daily *almuerzo* (lunch) or a *comida corriente* (staple food) is about $2 at most local restaurants. Updated: Apr 6, 2011.

Trigos

Grab a basket and the tongs—it's time to hit the bakery. Trigos has an incredible selection of fresh-baked breads—raisin, cheeses, whole-wheat, white, three-seed and a satisfying six-grain with nuts. There are also desserts and smooth ice creams to tempt you. The ice cream comes in twenty-four flavors, made according to an Italian recipe with milk and fresh fruit, and served in a large waffle cone with a dollop of whipped cream. You can choose to kick back and enjoy your treat at one of the tables downstairs or you can sit upstairs in the spacious dining area. So go ahead, sin a bit. Monday-Saturday 7 a.m.-9 p.m., Sunday and holidays 7 a.m.-7 p.m. Ca. 19, 11-35. Tel: 742-3870, E-mail: trigosmch@hotmail.com.co. Updated: Sep 28, 2011.

Restaurante Vegetariano Roma

(ENTREES: $2-3.70) Restaurante Vegetariano Roma appears small, with only a few tables, but up the staircase on the second floor two spacious rooms await you. Formally set tables, with linen cloths and napkins, and attentive service adds to the ambiance. The luncheon menu offers two choices for a main dish, either gluten or soy, with brown rice. Two choices of drink are offered as well, either fresh fruit drink or soy milk ($2-3.70). À la carte pasta dishes, with bread and dessert, ($2.35-3.70) and breakfast ($1.35-1.85) are also available. Daily 9 a.m.-4 p.m. Cra. 9, 20-69. Updated: Jun 02, 2008.

Restaurante China

(ENTREES: $3.70-8.50) The delivery men are hustling, picking up orders and running out to their awaiting motorbikes. Restaurante China is a popular lunch spot. This medium-sized, dimly lit restaurant decorated with typical Chinese bric-a-brac is completely à la carte. The usual oriental fare, made with fish, pork, chicken, beef or seafood, is served here. Combination plates are on the menu for those who can't quite make up their minds. Vegetarians have few choices--either chop suey or chow mein. Sodas, lemonade, pony malta and beer are the beverage options. Daily 11 a.m.-10 p.m. Cra. 11, 17-83. Tel: 740-1878/9423. Updated: Mar 18, 2011.

Ristorante-Caffe La Buona Vita ♪

(ENTREES: $3.95-14.20) A Tuscany-country feel pervades each of the rooms and the patio of this well-appointed restaurant. Many of Tunja's wealthier citizens and visitors are drawn to Ristorante-Caffe La Buona Vita for its distinguished service and for it's homemade pastas, created by a chef who learned his trade in Italy. Begin your meal in traditional fashion with an antipasto ($9-11.50). Then move on to the pasta ($10-15) or a wood-fire-oven-baked pizza ($5.95-20, depending on size) or one of the numerous meat or seafood entrées ($10-16). Unfortunately, there are few dishes suitable for vegetarians. A variety of non-alcoholic and alcoholic drinks are available to accompany your meal; wine is only sold by the bottle. Monday-Saturday noon-9:30 p.m., Sunday and holidays noon-4 p.m. Cra. 9, 23-45. Tel: 742-2198, E-mail: labuonavitarestaurant@yahoo.com.mx. Updated: Mar 18, 2011.

Parrilla y Son Restaurante-Bar

(ENTREES: $4.75-7.95) The second floor of one of Tunja's historic colonial buildings has been converted into a popular restaurant. The main breakfast and lunch area is out on a sky-lit patio and the large front room is the principal nighttime gathering place. Perhaps it is the savory lunches ($2.10) that draw the clientele. Check out the unusual menu items such as lamb hamburgers. There is a variety of chicken and beef dishes, shish kabobs and meats hot from the grill. Some foods are grilled with unusual preparations, like the tropical au

gratin. During the evenings, the full bar is a nice addition. Daily 7 a.m.-10 p.m. Cra. 9, 20-27, 2nd floor. Updated: Feb 22, 2008.

Restaurante Pila del Mono

(ENTREES: $6.35-15.25) On a corner plaza guarded by the Monkey in his fountain is one of Tunja's finest dining establishments, Restaurante Pila del Mono. Take a seat at one of the tables with linen napkins tucked into the water goblets. The menu offers a variety of Boyancense dishes, including meat dishes (beef, pork or chicken), fish or seafood, and there is also a seafood grill. All main courses come with rice and/or potatoes and a salad. For something a bit less expensive, there are pastas, which come accompanied with garlic bread and a salad. Monday-Saturday 10 a.m.-10 p.m., Sunday and holidays 11:30 a.m.-4 p.m. Ca. 20, 8-19, Centro Histórico. Tel: 744-7750, Cel: 300-264-3808/310-550-5983. Updated: Mar 31, 2011.

Nightlife

When in Tunja, do as the tunjanos do! Start the weekend festivities at a café located around the plaza for a small bite and a bit of liquor. The locals turn into dance machines after a long week at work, so make sure you drink plenty of water if you want to keep up with them. After 10 at night, everyone heads to a nightclub. The most happening discos are in the zona rosa and around the university on the north side of the city. Updated: Sep 28, 2011.

Pussini Café-Bar

Come to Pussini Café-Bar to find a friendly dancer to teach you the rumba. The lights are soft and the music is low. In the bar area and up on the balcony people sip on cocktails or have a cold brew. For the non-alcohol drinkers, there are plenty of special coffee choices or tea. A good place to chill out and get ready before heading to a discoteca. Monday-Saturday 8 a.m.-midnight, Sunday and holidays 10 a.m.-10 p.m. Cra. 10, 19-53, Plaza de Bolívar. Tel: 743-2047. Updated: Feb 22, 2008.

Macondo

The discoteca Los Cien Años de Macondo is more commonly known around Tunja as just Macondo. Since the club features pre-1980 bohemian music, it might seem like it is more for the older crowd, but the youngsters come out too. The music also includes salsa and tropical, boleros and ballads. Everyone that comes to Macondo will enjoy a trip back in time via music. Friday and Saturday only 7 p.m.-1 a.m. Cra. 11, 21-47. Tel: 742-4036, E-mail: viejotecamacondo@hotmail.com. Updated: Sep 28, 2011.

EASTERN COLOMBIA

PAIPA

 2,250m 30,000 8

In a valley surrounded by high mountains and softly rolling hills, Paipa is 45 kilometers (28 mi) from Tunja and 184 kilometers (114 mi) from Bogotá. Throughout Colombia this town, which was founded in 1568, is renowned for its thermal springs. The public *piscinas* have large and small pools, as well as 10 individual pools ($5.30). Near Paipa is Lago Sochagota, a man-made lake where you can fish, waterski or enjoy other aquatic sports. There are also several haciendas: El Salitre, three kilometers (1.8 mi) away and Bonza, 10 kilometers (6 mi) down the road. If you feel like spending a night or two in Paipa, many of the main hotels have their own pools. Updated: Mar 18, 2011.

SOGAMOSA

 2,569m 115,134 8

Just an hour east of Tunja, is the Muisca Land of the Sun: Xua Mox or Sogamoso. This mountainous land surrounding Colombia's largest lake, Lago de Tota, was considered to be a sacred place. The recently excavated Templo del Sol concentrated the sun's energy. The temple, which had been burnt to the ground by the Spaniards, is today in archaeological and ethnobotanical garden, Museo Arqueológico de Sogamoso.

Much awaits the casual traveler arriving to this seldom-visited corner of the country. A climb up the hill to Catedral Santa Bárbara gives tremendous views over the rolling countryside. Days may be spent to hiking to other villages, wineries or to Laguna de Siscunsí on the páramo. The city has a daily market, which is liveliest on Tuesday and Friday.

Sogamoso celebrates its birthday September 6. In August is the Fiesta del Huan, a recreation of the indigenous sun ceremony. Sogamoso enjoys a spring-like climate with cool evenings. Updated: Oct 04, 2011.

Lodging

Finca San Pedro ❗
(BEDS: $14, ROOMS: $19.50 per person) Finca San Pedro is a family-run hostel on a two-hectare (4.9 ac) farm on the outskirts of Sogamoso. It offers camping, dormitory, private rooms and a cottage, all set within beautiful gardens. Guests wake up to a delicious and healthy breakfast. The family provides complete information on all Sogamoso has to offer. After a day of sightseeing, relax in one of the spacious living rooms or play with the resident dogs. The finca has many amenities, like laundry, TV, Internet and WiFi, security boxes, sauna and massages. The family also offers classes in yoga, meditation lessons, salsa, tango and joropo dance. Km. 2 vía al Lago de Tota. Tel: 770-4222, Cel: 310-556-2207/312-5677102, Fax: 772-0868, E-mail: info@fincasanpedro.com, URL: www.fincasanpedro.com. Updated: Nov 01, 2011.

VILLA DE LEYVA

 2,149m 12,000 8

The road to Villa de Leyva winds downhill 39 kilometers (23.5 mi) from Tunja through sparse green rocky hills. The twisted strata tilt to almost vertical, revealing a fascinating geological history. The road is well made, with some parts subject to flooding and rockslides. Along the way you will pass Cucaita, a village with a 450-year tradition of art and culture.

Villa de Leyva is big on the destination list for Colombian and foreign vacationers alike. The town, itself a national historic monument, beautifully preserves colonial buildings built with the *tapia pisada* (rammed earth) technique. White-washed buildings hugging cobblestone lanes, the various shops and cultural attractions aren't the only draws here. The entire region is steeped in history, from fossils of Mesozoic sea monsters to the museum homes of important independence leaders. Villa de Leyva has excellent services and fine restaurants for the holidaymaker, although some visitors might find it a bit too touristy. Attractions outside the village are definitely worth several days of exploration. There is something for every type of explorer, including ruins (indigenous and colonial), vineyards and horseracing. The desert and páramo landscapes are also worth investigating. Updated: Sep 28, 2011.

History

During the Mesozoic Era (160-180 million years ago), the valley was part of the great inland Sea of Tetis. Today, marine fossils (including some impressive sea monsters) pepper the Villa de Leyva Desert. Eons later, the Musica, a Chibcha nation, called this valley home. An important ceremonial center, El Infiernito, is a testimony to their presence. The

Spaniards founded Villa de Nuestra Señora de Santa Marís de Leyva on June 12, 1572. The official founder, Andrés Díaz Venero de Leyva, was also the first president of the Nuevo Reino de Granada. Villa de Leyva played an important role during the struggle for Independence from Spain. It was the home of revolutionary heroes Antonio Nariño and Antonio Ricuarte. The village also hosted the First Convention of the United Provinces of Nueva Granada. In 1954, the town was declared a national monument in an effort to preserve its colonial architecture. Updated: Sep 28, 2011.

When to Go

Villa de Leyva enjoys a dry climate, with temperatures averaging 18°C (65°F). The days can get quite warm. The evenings are chilly. January and February are the driest months of the year; October is the wettest.

Thanks to its close proximity to Bogotá, Villa de Leyva is a popular destination for Colombians on weekends and holidays. During the high seasons, expect significantly higher prices and a lot more people. Updated: June 17, 2009.

HOLIDAYS AND FESTIVALS

Everyone flocks to Villa de Leyva for the national holidays. It might seem a bit surprising that this village has the energy to host some of its own festivals, but it does. In addition to the typical Semana Santa celebrations (March/April), Villa de Leyva has its more interesting Astronomy Festival in January, Kite Festival in August and National Tree Festival in October. July is reserved for Fiestas de la Virgen del Carmen (Villa de Leyva's patron saint), complete with gastronomic fairs, and December marks the Festival de las Luces y Concurso de Pesbres, celebrated with riotous bursts of fireworks and a créche, or manger scene, contest. Updated: Jun 27, 2011.

Getting To and Away

Villa de Leyva is a relatively big tourist destination but it isn't really a transportation hub. Many more buses arrive to and leave from nearby Tunja, so it is often easier to hop on a bus there to figure out onward travel. Buses to Tunja leave every 15 minutes between 6 a.m. and 7 p.m. (45 min, $2.50).

Daily buses depart from Villa de Leyva for Bogotá at 5 a.m. and 1 p.m.; on Sundays and holidays, an additional buse leaves at 3 p.m. (3.5 hr, $9.35-10). Other destinations include:

To Santa Sofía: 8 a.m., 9 a.m., 10:15 a.m., 1:15 p.m., 4:15 p.m., 5:45 p.m.; 30 min, $1.75. Buses return to Villa de Leyva at 6:30 a.m., 9 am., 10 a.m., 11:30 a.m., 3:15 p.m. and 5:15 p.m.

To Ráquira: 7:30 a.m., 8:30 a.m., 12:30 p.m., 4:30 p.m.; 30 min, $2.30. From Ráquira: 6 a.m., 8:30 a.m., 1:45 p.m. and 5:30 p.m., or transfer at the crossroads near Tinjacá (on Chiquinquirá-Sutamarchán-Villa de Leyva road).

To Ganchantivá: six departures between 6:45 a.m. and 5:30 p.m.; 1 hr, $2.35.

To Arcabuco: 6:40 a.m., 9:30 a.m., 2 p.m., 5 p.m., 5:30 p.m.; 1 hr, $2.10. Buses return to Villa de Leyva at 5 a.m., 6 a.m., 8:30 a.m., 11:30 a.m. and 4 p.m.

To Chiquinquirá: 7 a.m., 9 a.m., 10 a.m, noon, 2 p.m., 4 p.m.; 1 hr, $3.50. Six buses make the return trip between 8:30 a.m. and 5:30 p.m.

To Sutamarchán: five departures between 7 a.m. and 4 p.m.; 20 min, $1.15.

You can also hire a taxi at the bus station to take you to sites throughout the area. Depending on the route, a four-hour excursion will cost $40-50 per vehicle. Updated: Sep 30, 2011.

Getting Around

Keep in mind, if you are bringing your own car, street parking is prohibited and the speed limit is five kilometers (3.1 mi) per hour in the center of the village. Villa de Leyva is small enough to get around on foot, although the streets are paved with uneven stone, making walking difficult. You can hire a taxi at the bus station to take you to sites throughout the area. Depending on the route, a four-hour excursion will cost $37-45 per vehicle.Updated: Jun 16, 2011.

Safety

As Villa de Leyva is a major tourist destination for Colombians, especially the wealthy ones, the security here has always been tight. You won't hear about the guerrillas or other forces ever harassing the town and the streets are patrolled by soldiers, especially between dusk and dawn.

The region has a species of scorpion that you may encounter. Its sting is said to be like a bee sting and can cause muscle cramping at the site of injection. If camping, staying in a rural area or if you are living in rustic conditions,

EASTERN COLOMBIA

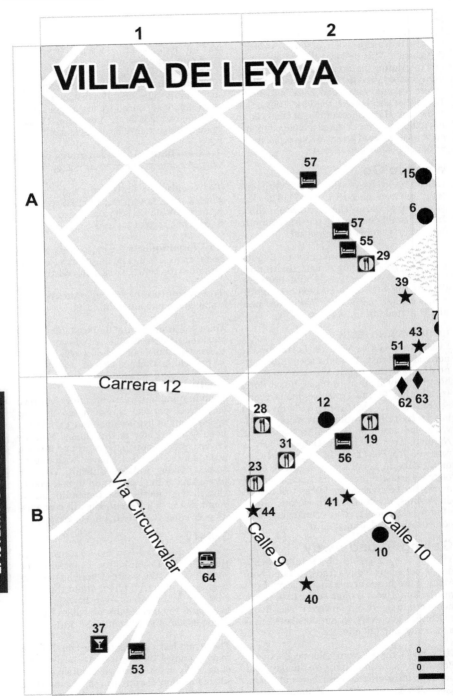

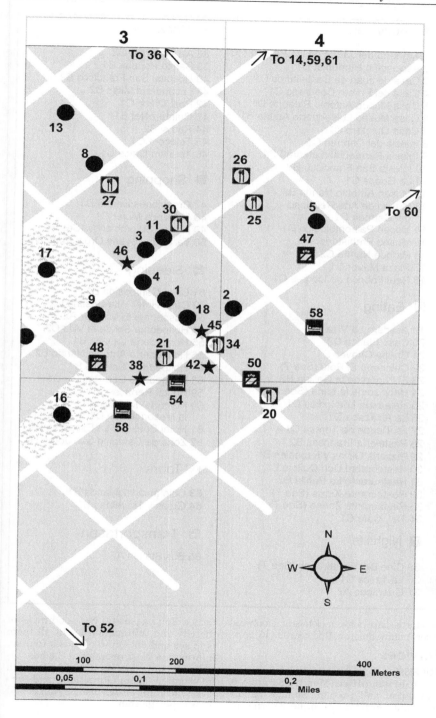

● **Activities**

1 Arquería del Jardín de los Próceres C1
2 Asociación Humboldt D1
3 Casa de Juan de Castellanos C1
4 Casa del Primer Congreso C1
5 Casa Museo Antonio Ricaurte D1
6 Casa Museo Luis Alberto Acuña B1
7 Casa Quintero C1
8 Iglesia del Carmen C1
9 Iglesia Parroquial (catedral) C1
10 Iglesia San Francisco B2
11 La Guaca C1
12 Museo Antonio Nariño B2
13 Museo de Arte Religioso
   del Carmen C1
14 Museo Paleontológico D1
15 Museo Prehistórico B1
16 Parque Nariño C2
17 Plaza Mayor C1
18 Real Fábrica de Licores C1

🍴 **Eating**

19 Asadero La Villa B2
20 Casa Blanca D2
21 Chepa Chavez C1
22 Chichería El Pote (See 7)
23 El Fogón de la Gallina B2
24 Hechizo de la Luna (See 7)
25 Heladería Los Indios D1
26 La Alcazaba D1
27 La Tienda de Teresa C1
28 Pastelería Francesa B2
29 Pizzeria Olivas y Especies B1
30 Restaurante Don Quijote C1
31 Restaurante La Parilla B2
32 Restaurante Xirrus (See 7)
33 Restaurante Zarina (See 7)
34 Té y Café C1

🍸 **Nightlife**

35 Cine Bar El Patriarca (See 7)
36 La Tasca C1
37 Guarapos A2

★ **Services**

38 Azul Internet C2
39 Banco Popular B1
40 Hospital San Francisco B2
41 Lavandería Milán B2
42 Post Office C1
43 QuinteroNet B1
44 Red si B2
45 Telecom C1
46 Tourism Office C1

🛍 **Shopping**

47 Creaciones Bertha D1
48 M Manos Mujer C1
49 Manos Colombianos (See 3)
50 Taller de Joyeria Oro y Plata D1

🛏 **Sleeping**

51 Casa Campesina B1
52 Casa Hotel Villa Cristina C2
53 Hospedaje El Mirador A2
54 Hospedaje Sol de la Villa C2
55 Hospedaría La Villa B1
56 Hospedería Antonio Nariño B2
57 Hospedaría Colonial B1
58 Hospedaría Don Paulino D1
59 Hostal Renacer D1
60 Hostería del Molino
   la Mesopotamia D1
61 Hotel Boutique La Española B1
62 Zona de Camping San Jorge D1

♦ **Tours**

63 Colombia Highlands B1
64 Guías y Travesías B1

🚌 **Transportation**

65 Bus Station A2

---

be sure to shake out your clothes and footwear before putting them on! Updated: Jun 16, 2011.

Services

TOURISM

The **tourism office** (Monday-Saturday 8 a.m.-1 p.m. and 3-6 p.m., Sunday 9 a.m.1 p.m. and 3-6 p.m. Cra. 9, near corner of Ca. 13. Tel: 732-0232) has good maps of the city and information about all there is to see and do. On weekends a tourism information kiosk operates at the bus station. The town has several websites with information about attractions and services, including www.villadeleyva.net and www.expovilla.com.

MONEY

Villa de Leyva has two banks, both on Calle 12, on the Plaza Mayor. Neither cashes traveler's checks. **Banco Popular** does cash advances on international Visa credit cards and its ATM handles Visa, Plus, Cirrus and MasterCard (Monday-Thursday, 8 a.m.-1:30 p.m., Friday, 8 a.m.-2 p.m. Ca. 12, 9-49). The **Comcel**, which is a few doors down from the church, sometimes changes U.S. dollars.

KEEPING IN TOUCH

Telecom has two offices in Villa de Leyva. The main office (daily 8 a.m.-10 p.m. Ca. 13 and Cra. 8) has international phone service beginning at around $0.45 per minute, as well as local and national calls. Its branch office is on the main plaza, down from the cathedral (daily 7 a.m.-10 p.m., Tuesday and Wednesday closed 12:30-1:30 p.m. Cra. 9, 12-36). Many shops have phone service as well; look for the Minutos sign ($0.10-0.20 per minute). Villa de Leyva's **post office** is in Papelería Librería Comercial Fabio (Monday-Friday 8 a.m.-noon and 2-8 p.m. Ca. 13, 7-87). There are a few Internet cafés in this town, including **QuinteroNet** (daily 10 a.m.-1 p.m. and 3-9 p.m., closed Wednesday mornings. Cra. 9, 11-77, around $1 per hour) and **Redsi** (daily 8 a.m.-8 p.m. Cra. 9, 9-99, $1.05 per hour). Both have Skype.

MEDICAL

Hospital San Francisco is at Calle 9 and Carrera 8, next to Iglesia San Francisco (Tel: 732-0516/0244). Pharmacies are distributed throughout the town.

LAUNDRY

Lavandería Milán (Ca. 10, 8-27. Tel: 732-1374) does mainly dry cleaning, though it also does wet wash. A pound of shirts, underclothing and such is $1.30. Pants and jackets are charged per piece.

CAMERA

The two camera shops on Carrera 9 between the Plaza Mayor and the bus station carry basic supplies. They also sell cameras, including disposable ones. Updated: Sep 30, 2011.

SHOPPING

Villa de Leyva is a great place for shopaholics. On the portal side of the Plaza Principal, there are three stores dispensing tons of souvenirs. For unique crafts, stroll down the pedestrian malls of Carrera 9 and Calle 13.

On Carrera 9, between the plaza (Ca. 13) and Puente El Real are many boutiques selling weavings. There is also an antique shop. On the left side of this lane is Casa don Juan de Castellanos with eight artisan shops, including Manos Colombianas and several jewelers. A few doors down is La Guaca, featuring gourmet bistros, shops selling woven goods and an antique store.

Many of the artisans on Calle 13 between Carrera 7 and 8 also specialize in weaving, though there are other shops of interest. Maestro Reinaldo López, one of the village's most noted painters, has a gallery (Ca. 13, 7-97). For leathers, visit **Ricardo Luna** (Ca. 13, 7-54). For fine home details, check out Decorando (Calle 13, 7-35). **Taller de Joyería Oro y Plata** (Ca. 13, 7-52) has exquisite silver and gold jewelry.

Creaciones Bertha 🗡

Creaciones Bertha is an association of families who produce fine hand-made textiles. The entire process is done using by hand, from the carding of the wool, to the dyeing, to the weaving on upright looms. Using mostly virgin sheep yarn, but also cotton and alpaca, they fashion hats, vests and hooded ponchos, all exclusively designed. Other creations include avant-garde wall hangings and rugs. If you don't find what you're looking for, Creaciones Bertha does special orders. Monday-Friday 9 a.m.-6 p.m., Saturday-Sunday 9 a.m.-8 p.m. Cra. 8, 14-81. Tel: 732-0527, Cel: 312-442-2365, E-mail: creacionesbertha1@hotmail.com. Updated: Oct 05, 2011.

M. Manos Mujer

Walking into M. Manos Mujeres (*manos mujeres* means women's hands), you are blasted with color and novelty. Within this space, a collective of 20 women from eight families bring together their handiwork. Through the sales of cards, hand-made paper, jewelry, batiks and weavings, they are supporting their families with their imaginations and skills. Some even delve into arts that for women are non-traditional, like woodworking and sculpture. Original watercolors are for sale at very reasonable prices. Ca. 12, between Cra. 8 and 9, Parque Nariño. Cel: 315-318-0968. Updated: Jun 17, 2009.

Manos Colombianas

If you can't make it to the far corners of Colombia, drop by Manos Colombianas. Here you'll find crafts from near and far made by Colombia's diverse indigenous cultures. On display and for sale are colorful, hand-stitched molas by the Kuna of the Chocó as well as the famous bags made by the Wayuu of the Guajira and the Arhuaco of the Sierra Nevada de Santa Marta. Artisan work comes all the way from the Cordillera Oriental and from the deep Amazon and Llanos regions. Fine Boyacense weavings and Ráquira pottery round out the selection. Casa San Juan de Castellanos, 2nd floor. Cra. 9 and Ca. 13. Updated: Jun 18, 2009.

Taller de Joyería Oro y Plata

Now that you've picked up a new woolen shawl from one of the local weavers, it's time to stop by Taller de Joyería Oro y Plata for the perfect accessory. For over 20 years, the master jeweler of this workshop, Luis Eugenio Guerrero, has been fashioning beautiful rings, pendants, intricate bracelets and necklaces from .950 sterling silver and gold. Some of the pieces feature stones, such as agates, quartzes, zircon and others. Señor Guerrero also does repairs. Tuesday-Sunday 8 a.m.-noon and 2-7 p.m. Ca. 13, 7-52. Cel: 310-556-5522, E-mail: leuguer@ hotmail.com. Updated: Oct 05, 2011.

Things to See and Do

The town itself is a masterpiece of colonial architecture, but if that isn't enough for you, the countryside has fossils, petroglyphs, ancient ruins, vineyards, a dinosaur park and more. Its intense natural beauty spreads across deserts, tropical forests and páramo, embracing 112 waterfalls and the Santuario de Flora y Fauna Iguaque. If you like betting on the ponies, be sure to catch the thoroughbred racing at the Hipódromo. Updated: Jun 16, 2011.

Museo Paleontológico !

Museo Paleontológico, in conjunction with the Science Department of the Universidad Nacional de Colombia, presents impressive exhibitions on the geology and paleontology of what we today call the Desert of Villa de Leyva. The extensive collection, housed in the old Molina de Losada, includes plants as well as fossils of creatures that once lived in the sea, like bivalves, gastropods, ammonites, fishes and sea-going dinosaurs. You can even adopt a fossil as part of a project to establish museum foci around the region and to keep archaeological finds in their original places. Kilometer 1, Vía Arcabuco. Tel: 732-0466, URL: www.unal.edu.co/ museopale. Updated: Mar 21, 2011.

The Churches of Villa de Leyva

The Catedral, on the Plaza Mayor, dates from 1604-1665, and was reconstructed after an earthquake in 1845. A few blocks away, Car-

rera 10 and Calle 14, is Iglesia del Carmen (1836-1845), with a stunning side chapel. Another colonial-era *iglesia* is that of the Carmelitas, built in 1642.

A few of Villa de Leyva's religious temples have taken on new life. The claustro of San Agustín is now the Asociación Humboldt, an environmental studies research center (Cra. 8, between Ca. 13 and 14, Tel: 732-0174). Peek through the door cracks to see ruins of Iglesia de San Francisco (1613) (Ca. 9 and Cra. 8); plans are to restore it. Updated: Mar 18, 2011.

The Museums of Villa de Leyva

The museums in Villa de Leyva are diverse and include homes of Independence war leaders and of a contemporary artist, religious art and fossils. Something for everyone!

Casa Museo Antonio Nariño (ADMISSION: adults $2, students $1.50, children under 12 years $1)—This former home of a major Independence leader was constructed in 1600. Thursday-Tuesday 8 a.m.-noon and 2-6 p.m. Cra. 9, 10-21. Tel: 732-0342.

Museo Prehistórico (ADMISSION: adults $1.50, children $1)—A small private collection of fossils and related paintings, with a Jurassic park in the garden. Daily 9 a.m.-6 p.m. Ca. 13 and Cra. 10.

Museo del Arte Religioso del Carmen (ADMISSION: adults $1, children $0.50)—Considered one of Colombia's finest collections of religious art. Saturday-Sunday and holidays 10 a.m.-1 p.m. and 2-5 p.m.). Ca.14, 10-73. Tel: 732-0214.

Casa Museo Ricaurte (ADMISSION: adults $1, children $0.50)—Home of a local Independence War hero who fought with Bolívar. Wednesday-Friday 9 a.m.-noon and 2-5 p.m. Saturday-Sunday and holidays 9 a.m.-1 p.m. and 2-6 p.m.). Ca. 15, 8-19. Tel: 732-0876.

Museo Paleontológico (ADMISSION: adults $1.50, children $0.50)—An impressive collection of the area's fossils. Tuesday - Saturday 9 a.m.-noon and 2-5 p.m., Sunday and holidays 9 a.m.-3 p.m., closed Tuesday after Puente). Km 1, Vía Arcabuco/Carrera 9. Tel: 732-0466. Updated: Mar 18, 2011.

Casas Coloniales of Villa de Leyva

In addition to the colonial houses in town that were turned into museums, there are a few others you can visit:

Casa del Primer Congreso—This building held the first convention of the United Provinces of Nueva Granada. Tuesday-Thursday, Saturday 8 a.m.-1 p.m. and 2-5 p.m. Cra. 9 and Ca. 13.

Arquería del Jardín de los Próceres—Ca. 13, between Cra. 8 and 9.

Real Fábrica de Licores (1736)—This was the Spanish Crown's first official liquor maker in Nueva Granada. To see the excavated building, ask at the Telecom office next door. Ca. 13, between Cra. 8 and 9.

Casa don Juan de Castellanos—Built 1585-1607, this building has an art gallery with a permanent exhibit on the second floor. Friday-Sunday and holidays 10 a.m.-9 p.m. Cra. 9 and Ca. 13.

Molina Mesopotamia (1568)—existed even before the village was founded. It is currently an upscale hotel. Ask at the reception for permission to see the mill (now a restaurant) and the pond in the back, where you can also go swimming (about $3 for non-guests). Cra. 8, near Vía Arcabuco.

Molina de Losada was another one of the first mills in town and is now home of the Museo Paleontológico (1 km/half mile from town, Vía Arcabuco). **Casa Quintero** has gourmet restaurants (Wednesday-Monday 10 a.m.-11 p.m., closed the Wednesday after a three day holiday. Cra. 9 and Ca. 12). **La Guaca** has handicraft shops and gourmet restaurants (daily 10 a.m.-9 p.m. Cra. 13-57). Updated: Mar 18, 2011.

Casa Museo Luis Alberto Acuña !

Luis Alberto Acuña (1904-1993) is considered one of Colombia's most important 20th-century artists. In 1979 he established this museum to exhibit his own artwork as well as the artwork of others. There are also plenty of antiquities and decorations on display. The Sala de Antigüedades presents antiques from all periods, especially that of the colonial era. The Tapestry Room also focuses on the Master's work. In the patio area are Acuña's murals depicting indigenous legends, in addition to sculptures and masks. Cra. 10, 12-83. Tel: 732-0422, URL: www.gratisweb.com/museoacuna. Updated: Mar 31, 2011.

Viñedo Guananí

Viñedo Guananí wines are in high demand by Colombian connoisseurs. Carbernet Sauvignon, Isabela and Chardonnay grapes are organically grown before heading to the fermentation and ageing vats. At the end of the visit you are offered a free glass of wine! Tours are given only Saturday, Sunday and holidays at 10 a.m. and 2 p.m., with a minimum of six people ($2.10, includes the glass of wine). Aside from the winery, Viñedo Guananí also has an inn with pool, sauna and a restaurant.

The winery has a restaurant that is open daily (make reservations) 8 a.m.-7 p.m. Take Calle 10 to Carrera 11, turn left to Calle 9, after three blocks, cross the Avenida Circunvalar. The winery is 500 meters (1,640 ft) down the dirt road on the right. Vía Casa Fundador. Tel: 732-0398, Fax: 732-1788, E-mail: guanani30@hotmail.com. Updated: Mar 21, 2011.

Tours

In Villa de Leyva, quite a few tour agencies are ready to take you on city tours, out to the local sights or on a chiva ride around town. This village is fortunate to have some experts ready to teach you about the ecology of the region or take you on wild adventure excursions, rappelling into canyons, caves and waterfalls. If you are the independent type, you'll find people renting horses along Avenida Circunvalar, before the cemetery. Updated: May 18, 2009.

Guianzas Pierre LaCour

Pierre LaCour is a professional rafter from France. Here in the Villa de Leyva area, he can take you on many adventure trips, from hiking to horseback riding. However, rappelling is his specialty. Imagine shimmying on a rope down a waterfall or into one of the region's canyons! Depending on the excursion, it costs $10.50-42 per person per day. Pierre also has package tours for groups interested in learning about biodynamic and organic agriculture. Take the road to Santa Sofía. At Carcamo, take a right and follow the signs for eight kilometeters (4.8 mi) to El Arca Verde. It is past Posada San Javier. Cel: 310-773-1556/313-843-5847 E-mail: elarcaverde@hotmail.com, elarcaverde@gmail.com, URL: elarcaverde.com/www.myspace.com/elarcaverde Updated: Mar 18, 2011 .

Colombia Highlands

Colombia Highlands has a variety of half- and full-day outings to the standard Villa de Leyva sights. Adventure tours are another item on the agenda, with rappelling and caving opportunities. Owner Oscar Gilede has something special to offer visitors to this region: scientific tourism. This biologist and eco-instructor can specially tailor your outing for birdwatching, entomology (including spiders), geology, botany or amphibians. He has nighttime stargazing excursions on foot or horseback rides into the desert. Cra. 9, 11-02. Tel: 732-1379, Cel: 311-308-3739, E-mail: info@colombianhighlands.com, URL: www.colombianhighlands.com/www.expovilla.com/colombianhighlands. Updated: Mar 21, 2011.

Guías y Travesías

Focusing on guided walking tours for all ages, Guías y Trvesías will take you on short and long hikes to 70 attractions in and around Villa de Leyva. Trace the Footsteps of the Past to El Fósil, Monasterio de Santo Ecce Homo and El Infiernito, or gather the Jewels of the Desert in Ráquira and Monsterio de la Candelaria (either tour: adults $21, children $17.50, 4 hr). Head out to Santa Sofía for the Caves, Rivers and Roads of Adventure (adults $21, children $17.50; 6 hr), or hike to sacred Laguna de Iguaque (adults $24, children $20; 9 hr). All excursions include guide, transport and entry fees. Guías y Travesías also rents bicycles ($3.20/hour, $10.50/half-day, $18.50/24 hours). Cra. 9, 11-02. Tel: 732-0742, Cel: 311-461-1298, E-mail: guiadevilladeleyva@yahoo.com Updated: Mar 18, 2011.

Lodging

Despite the many inns in Villa de Leyva, budget travelers may have a tough time finding an adequate place, as it is difficult to find a room for under $8 per night. Avoid the high season, when prices double (at least). Camping is a viable alternative. Most hotels are in the mid-range, charging up to $40 per night. Villa de Leyva has a few spectacular luxury hotels (complete with packages for couples who want the ultimate in weddings).

The high season is all national holidays, three-day weekends, July-August, Semana Santa and December 20-January 15. During these times, reservations are necessary. Hotels are not allowed to charge high season prices outside of those dates set by the tourism office. If they do, report the establishment. Updated: Jul 21, 2010.

BUDGET

Hostal Renacer !

(ROOMS: $3-37) Hostal Renacer is a place to be reborn after a day of strenuous sightseeing. Located just outside Villa de Leyva, it's just the place for backpackers to relax and rest. Whether you decide to stay in a dorm, a private room, or set up camp, with super-clean common bath or private bath, there is something to fit every budget. The upstairs suite is perfect for a romantic get-away. The laundry area, kitchen and brick oven, as well as a common room with fireplace are great extra touches. So lay in a hammock on the portico and watch hummingbirds dart around the patio garden flowers and the fountain spray water into the warm day. You've come home. Follow Carrera 9/Vía Arcabuco East out of town. After the bridge, follow Vía Colorado on your right for 600 meters (2,000 ft) to the road that leads to the front gate of Hostal Renacer (60 m/200 ft to the right). Tel: 732-1379/1201, Cell: 311-308-3739, E-mail: info@colombianhighlands.com, URL: www.colombianhighlands.com/www.algo-diferente.net/www.expovilla.com. Updated: Jun 16, 2011.

Zona de Camping San Jorge

(CAMPING: $5.25-5.75) A common complaint about campgrounds in Villa de Leyva is that they merely warehouse people, but experienced outdoors persons say Camping San Jorge, with proper facilities, is the best in Villa de Leyva. The grounds have good-sized sites, bathhouses with hot showers, fire pits and a place to wash your dishes after your meal. Private security and parking are other pluses. Besides camping, San Jorge offers a two-bedroom apartment for six persons with private bath, cable TV, dining nook and kitchenette. Vereda Roble Km 1, vía Arcabuco, in front of the Bomberos (fire station), 300 meters (984 ft) from town. Tel: 732-0328, Cel: 311-213-1125/312-597-9277/300-835-4608, Reservations (Bogotá): 1-612-3130/619-0518, Fax: 732-0328, E-mail: campingsanjorge@gmail.com, URL: www.villaleyvanos.com/pardo. Updated: Sep 28, 2011

Casa Campesina/El Solar Camping !

(BEDS: $5-11) Casa Campesina is a very homey place near the corner of the main plaza. Owner Martha de León has become the surrogate mother of younger travelers, sitting down over a free tea, coffee or juice for breakfast and listening to their travel tales. The rooms have comfy beds and share the common, hot-water baths. Out on the covered back patio is a seating area with BBQ, fireplace and hammocks.

For those on a budget, you can camp in the large garden. Besides Doña Martha, other residents include a dog and a morrocoy turtle. Cra. 9, 11-44. Cell: 311-832-7919, E-mail: campingfamiliar@hotmail.com. Updated: Feb 11, 2011.

Hospedería Don Paulino

(BEDS: $8-10.50) Don Paulino and Doña Olga have established a wonderful inn for visitors to Villa de Leyva. Located on a tranquil street just a few blocks from the Plaza Principal, this hotel has a second-story balcony affording a great view of the sunset over the valley's hills. The rooms are nicely decorated, with clean bathrooms and remote-controlled TV. Mornings, Doña Olga will greet you with fresh orange juice and coffee and will open the kitchen for you to make breakfast. Low room price: $12.50; high room price: $15. Prices depend on the floor you choose to stay on. Ca. 14, 7-46. Tel: 732-1227, Cel: 315-235-9447/313-323-2975, URL: www.villaleyvanos.com. Updated: May 18, 2011.

Hospedería Colonial

(ROOMS: $8-21) Just a half-block from the main plaza is Hospedería Colonial. The family lives in the main part of the house; off their living room are simple rooms for one or two persons that share the family's bathroom. In the back of the dwelling is a terraced yard. The portico porch here has bamboo chairs to relax in after a day of sightseeing. Around the first level of the patio are attractively decorated rooms with private, hot-water baths. Some even come with Jacuzzi. All lodgings come with cable TV. Ca. 12, 10-81. Tel: 732-1364. Updated: Jun 9, 2010.

El Arca Verde

(ROOMS: $10-22.50) El Arca Verde, The Green Ark, is the name of an organic, biodynamic farm outside of Villa de Leyva. Guests lodge in the *maloka*, a traditional, round indigenous hut made of earth, stone and reused materials. The restaurant serves dishes prepared from the farm's produce. The common room serves as a dorm, with beds around the perimeter. Upstairs are two private rooms. A fireplace keeps the house warm on cool evenings. The shower is solar heated. It is possible to trade working on the farm for lodging. Valle Escondido, Vereda Las Vegas 15 km (9 m) from Villa de Leyva. Take the road to Santa Sofía. At Carcamo, take a right and follow the signs for eight kilometers (4.8 mi) to El Arca Verde. It is past Posada San Javier. A taxi costs $15. Cel: 310-773-1556/313-843-5847, E-mail: elarcaverde@gmail.com/elarcaverde@hotmail.com, URL: www.myspace.com/elarcaverde. Updated: Mar 18, 2011.

Hospedería La Villa

(BEDS: $10-74) Hospedería La Villa is one of the few options for budget travelers visiting Villa de Leyva. Located just a half block from the Plaza Principal, this colonial-era styled house has a rambling maze of rooms to let, all with windows facing onto the courtyard. Many of the quarters are quite basic and a bit cramped. Some come with TV and private bath with hot water. Separate from the main building is a penthouse for six people with seating area ($47.50 low season, $95 high season). Ca. 12, 10-11. Tel: 732-0848, Cel: 311-852-4038. Updated: Mar 18, 2011.

Hospedaje El Mirador

(BEDS: $15-20) Located not too far from the bus station on a quiet side street is Hospedaje El Mirador. This hostel is more for those travelers journeying in a group, as all of the well-dressed rooms come with at least two beds. With private bath and cable TV, Hospedaje El Mirador offers the classic creature comforts you find in Colombian inns. One distinction is the riotous courtyard garden filled with plants and pottery fauna (from near-by Ráquira, of course). Ca. 8a, 6-94, between the main streets. Tel: 732-0941. Updated: Mar 21, 2011.

MID-RANGE

Hospedaje Sol de la Villa

(ROOMS: $25-100) Just off Parque Nariño, a few blocks from the bus station, is Hospedaje Sol de la Villa. A modest B&B, it provides tastefully decorated, clean rooms with private, hot-water baths. A continental breakfast (included in price) is served every morning. This is the perfect place for non-smokers, as smoking is not allowed. Reservations are highly recommended. Hospedaje Sol de la Villa accepts credit cards, but with a surcharge. Cra. 8, 12-28. Tel: 732-0224, Fax: 732-0932. Updated: Sep 30, 2011.

Hospedería Antonio Nariño

(ROOMS: $27-63) Hospedería Antonio Nariño is actually a modern construction in the heart of Villa de Leyva, but built with the architecture and techniques of old. Its large, cobblestone courtyards are misted by fountains and surrounded by second-floor balconies. Off these are the spacious, white rooms with modern comforts including double beds, private hot water baths and cable TV. A special feature is the deluxe suite, which comes with Jacuzzi, mini-bar and fireplace ($132 low season, $158 high season). Despite the elegance of this inn, it offers no other side services, such as laundry, breakfast or restaurant. Cra. 9, 10-34. Tel: 732-0211, Cel: 311-440-3901/826-8597, E-mail: hospenarino@hotmail.com, URL: www.hotelantonionarno.com/www.villadeleyva.net/www.villadeleyva.com.co. Updated: Mar 21, 2011.

Casa Hotel Villa Cristina

(ROOMS: $32.50-75) On a quiet dirt street near the center of town is Casa Hotel Villa Christina. This rambling, multi-story house is white with red tile roofs, cobblestoned interior courtyards and terrace and hammocks. Casa Hotel Villa Christina is an intimate B&B offering 10 snug rooms with private bath (hot water) and cable TV with the feel of being at home in a country villa. The tourism information desk provides express tours with guides to local sites and horseback riding. Room prices includes continental breakfast. Ca. 10 3-78. Tel: 732-0594, Cel: 300-568-6828, Email: chvillachristina@yahoo.es, URL: www.villadeleyva.com.co/contenido/hoteles/Otros_alojamientos/Casa_Hotel_villac.htm. Updated: Mar 21, 2011.

Hotel Boutique La Española !

(BEDS: $63-144) Hotel Boutique La Española is a very special hotel on the crowded Villa de Leyva hotel scene. The Soler family's ancient home has been transformed into an intimate inn whose white-washed walls are accented with beautiful tile work throughout. Water flows through the courtyard. Every inch of this space is designed and decorated using Feng Shui principles. The 15

rooms are simply furnished, with TV and spectacular private, hot-water bathrooms. A suite comes with Jacuzzi. The comfortable common room has TV and a fireplace. Prices vary depending on whether it is low or high season. Ca. 12, 11-06. Tel: 732-0464, Cel: 315-842-5393, E-mail: hotel.laespanola@hotmail.com, URL: www.laespanola.villadeleyva.com.co. Updated: Mar 21, 2011.

HIGH-END

Hostería del Molina La Mesopotamia

(ROOMS: $90-225) Built in 1568 as a wheat mill, Hostería del Molina La Mesopotamia is now one of Villa de Leyva's finest inns. You'll feel like you're slipping back in time here, especially because the rooms are furnished with period pieces. Heavy embroidered curtains keep the quarters warm at night while you snuggle in the four-poster beds. Each room has the modern convenience of a private, hot water bath. The millhouse itself is now the restaurant. The millionaire Vanderbilt family and actor Ernest Borgnine, among other famous people, have stayed here. If you aren't a lodger, ask reception for permission to stroll through the immaculate grounds. Non-guests can even enjoy a swim in the warm pond fed by a medicinal spring (about $3). Cra 8, 15a-265 vía Hipodromo, Tel: 313-3491, E-mail: hosteriamesopotamia@hotmail.com, URL: www.hotelmesopotamia.com. Updated: Sep 30, 2011.

Hotel La Posada de San Antonio !

(ROOMS: $100-140) This mid-19th century mansion on Parque Nariño is now the very fine Hotel La Posada de San Antonio. It has the feel of a country mansion, with a pool table in the library, chapel, many antiques and conservative décor. Don Quixote makes frequent appearances throughout the inn. Off the cobbled courtyard is the posada's restaurant. All rooms are super-spacious with king-sized beds and private bath (hot water, of course). At its country annex are conference facilities, swimming pool, horseback riding and other special services. The rooms here are bright and airy, for one to three persons. Hotel La Posada de San Antonio offers wedding and honeymoon packages. Cra. 8 11-61. Tel: 732-0538/0390, Cel: 310-280-7326, E-mail: padelgo@hotmail.com. Updated: Mar 21, 2011.

Hotel Casa de los Fundadores

(ROOMS: $125-150) Casa de los Fundadores (as it is commonly called) is an inn with a bit of a difference: it is a project of the Dominican nuns. Many years ago, their community was on these lands. Now the sisters have built an exclusive hotel with all the luxuries you can imagine, from to sauna and chocolate therapy massages to guided horseback riding tours to (well, yes) their very own chapel. Other special touches are the fire pit, bicycle rental, game room and playground. The guest rooms are immaculately decorated, with private baths. Special vacation packages are offered, as well as all-inclusive wedding plans. Kilometer 1, Vía Viñedo de Guananí. Tel: 732-0880/0878, Fax: 732-0839, Email: admin@casadelos-fundadores.com, URL: www.casadelosfundadores.com Updated: Mar 21, 2011.

Restaurants

Dining in Villa de Leyva tends to be on the high side—both in style of cuisine and in price. Many finer restaurants are closed on Tuesdays, Wednesday and after a three-day holiday weekend, including all those in the Centro Comercial Quintero. You can find good, generous *comida corrientes* for around $2-3. If you are on a budget, some of the budget hostels have common kitchens and there are many shops to buy supplies. Market plaza is a flurry of sights and smells on Saturdays with farmers and other producers coming in from all over the countryside (Ca. 12 and 13, Cra. 5 and 6). Updated: Jun 16, 2011.

Té y Café Saloom

(SNACKS: $0.50-3.70) A quick breakfast or snack or a close-out-the-evening tea and treat can be partaken at Té y Café Saloom. (Despite it being called a saloom, er saloon, no alcohol is served.) All the offerings at this small café are home made, from the cookies to dip in your coffee ($0.50-0.80) to the rich cakes and brownies ($1.30-2.40). Salado or savory goodies are also on the slate, like arepas ($1.85-3.70). The beef or chicken with mushrooms and cheese arepa is worth a taste. Monday-Thursday 8 a.m.-9 p.m., Friday-Sunday 8 a.m.-10 p.m. Cra. 8, 13-00. Tel: 732-0177, Cel: 312-480-5486. Updated: Mar 21, 2011.

Pastelería Francesa

(SNACKS: $0.60 and up) For an escape from Colombia—albeit for a moment—walk into Pastelería Francesa. Here you'll find French pastries created by master baker Patrice Rio. Try a croissant (the croissant de almendras, filled with almond crème filling is divine), a feijao tart (made from a local fruit) or a mini-quiche. Oui, monsieur, there are baguettes as well, white or whole wheat. Thursday-Monday 8 a.m.-6:30 p.m. (until 7 p.m. for carry out). Closed on Tuesday and Wednesday. Ca. 10, 9-41. Updated: Sep 28, 2011.

Heladería Los Indios

(ICE CREAM: $2) Heladería Los Indios is said to have the best ice cream in Villa de Leyva—and it is mighty good. Even the wooden Indians out front are licking cones of one of the dozen flavors available. One scoop is a cool $0.85. Or if you prefer something a bit more decadent, have a sundae ($2), coke float ($1.85) or milk shake ($1.85). Other treats are for the nibbling, too. Sunday-Friday 11:30 a.m.-8 p.m., Saturday 10:30 a.m.-10 p.m. Cra. 9, 14-54. Updated: Jun 16, 2011.

Restaurante La Parrilla

(LUNCH: $2.10) Restaurante La Parrilla is a popular choice among locals and Colombian families having to watch their pennies a bit. The five tables are often full of diners sitting down for the set-plate meals (breakfast $2.10; complete lunch or dinner $2.10 , $1.85 main course and drink only). The midday and evening portions are generous, served with meat, rice, beans, several vegetable sides and salad—so much food, in fact, you might find yourself taking a doggie bag home. You can order the repast with eggs for a lower price. Daily 6:30 a.m.-9 p.m. Cra. 9, 9-17. Updated: Jun 23, 2008.

El Fogón de la Gallina

El Fogón de la Gallina is much the same as its neighbor, Restaurante La Parrilla. El Fogón serves good Colombian classics for its comida corriente, though the portions aren't as generous, and the price is a wee bit higher. Another difference is that the interior of El Fogón de la Gallina is a bit snazzier. Nonetheless, it's one more of the cheaper diners in town where budget travelers—or anyone—can eat well at a comfortable price. Cra. 9, 9-23. Updated: Jun 16, 2011.

Asadero La Villa

(LUNCH: $2.35) At the entrance of Asadero La Villa is an enclosed fire pit where meats roast on an upright spit over the flames. Inside the restaurant is a large, open space with many long, heavy wooden tables, able to accommodate many diners at once. This eatery provides delicious *comida corrientes* for lunch and dinner which include your choice of meat and soda ($2.35, *bandeja* only $1.60). Beer is also available to go with your BBQ ($0.60). Prices include tax. Thursday-Sunday and holidays 7 a.m.-7 p.m. Cra. 9, 10-58. Cel: 314-488-2380/325-8128. Updated: Mar 21, 2011.

EASTERN COLOMBIA

La Tienda de Teresa

(BREAKFAST: $3.50) Tienda de Teresa is a good place to fuel up on a hearty Boyacense breakfast ($3.50) or cazuela boyacense ($3.30) before heading out for a day's hike. But Teresa's is also a good place to drop by anytime of the day to try one of the stuffed arepas with anything and everything, including vegetarian versions ($3.80). In the evening, warm up with canelazo, chocolate or another hot drink while you write a sonnet on the walls that is dedicated to your hostess. Teresa also bakes up some of the region's typical desserts ($1.80). Monday-Friday and Sunday 8 a.m.-8 p.m., Saturday 8 a.m.-11 p.m. Cra. 10, 13-72, Plazoleta del Carmen. Cel: 316-542-0387/311-873-5837. Updated: Sep 28, 2011.

Restaurante Savia

(ENTREES: $6.50-15) Previously known as Restaurant Xirrus, Savia specializes in vegetarian, vegan and organic cuisine with novo-Colombian flair. À la carte dishes include wraps with a torta de plátano and house salad, salads, pastas and soups including miso. Chicken and seafood have their place here, like the shrimp salad prepared with avocado and mango. A full bar of hot, alcoholic and non-alcoholic drinks makes the grade. A plaque outside commemorates the last concert former Elvis Presley drummer Bill Lynn gave before dying in Villa de Leyva. Friday 4-10 p.m., Saturday, and Sunday-Monday holidays 10 a.m.-10 p.m. Centro Comercial Casa Quintero, local 20. Tel: 732-1778, Cel: 312-435-4602, E-mail: olgalucia.cortes@gmail.com. Updated: Sep 28, 2011.

Restaurante Casa Blanca

(LUNCH: $3.20) Many hostels in Villa de Leyva recommend Restaurante Casa Blanca to their guests as an inexpensive dining choice. The diner has earned its reputation from many years of serving classic Colombian dishes and (it is said) to have the best cazuela boyacense around ($2.40). As well as serving set meals for breakfast ($2.60), lunch and dinner ($3.20), Casa Blanca prepares bandejas especiales as well. These special entrées include beef, chicken, fish (including trout) or longaniza sausage, accompanied by yuca, potatoes and salad. For a quick snack, there are arepas and sandwiches. Daily 8 a.m.-9 p.m. Ca. 13, 7-02. Tel: 732-0821, E-mail: restaurantecasablanca@hotmail.com. Updated: Mar 21, 2011.

Hechizo de la Luna

(PIZZA: $4.20-13.50) Hechizo de la Luna (Moonstruck) is one of Villa de Leyva's best pizzerias. The moon theme threads through the dining experience, from the stained glass hurricane lamp lighting your table, to the wine glass with the Man in the Moon amidst a dusting of stars, to the bill on the crescent moon platter. Unique combinations of thin-crust pizzas are delectable. The Pizza de la Luna (smoked ham, prosciutto, salami, mushrooms, roasted peppers, olives, eggplant) and the Sweet Temptation (mozzarella, cherries, apple, smoked bacon, Vienna sausage) are both out of this world. Choose between a small ($4.20-7.40) or medium ($8.50-13.15). Thursday-Monday 11 a.m.-9 p.m. Centro Comercial Casa de Quintero, local 13. Tel: 732-1774. Updated: Jun 16, 2011.

Pizzería Olivas y Especias

(PIZZA: 7-15) On the corner of the main plaza is one of the most recommended pizzerias in Villa de Leyva. This rather large bistro with green and white tables also serves other Italian dishes and crêpes. The pizzas come with a smorgasbord of toppings, in three sizes ($7-14.75). Pasta and lasagna dishes come only with bread ($5.50-7). Vegetarians have several dishes they can try at Pizzaría Olivas y Especias. The restaurant has alcoholic drinks, including canelazo, and fresh juices to go along with your meal. Daily 4-10 p.m. Cra. 10, 11-99. Tel: 732-1261, Cel: 310-262-0664, URL: www.restaurantesvilladeleyva.com.co. Updated: Mar 11, 2011.

Restaurante Don Quijote

(ENTREES: $8-19) The 400-year old kitchen in this colonial style house has lots to offer in the way of culinary delights. Beef, chicken, trout, squid or shrimp accompanied by pasta al pesto and salad ($8-9) might be to your liking this evening, or perhaps the Thai pasta or rice ($9). Stir-fried vegetables with noodles or the tortilla española might fit the bill for a hungry vegetarian. For duo diners, there is the roasted lamb plate ($18.65). On weekdays, Restaurante Don Quijote serves comida corriente ($4.20). On weekends it's only à la carte. Daily noon-9 p.m. Centro Comercial Guaca, Cra. 9 and Ca. 13. Cel: 313-225-2406, URL: www.lacasonacomercial.com. Updated: Mar 21, 2011.

Restaurante Zarina

(ENTREES: $12-15) Restaurante Zarina is an intimate bistro of only four tables, a perfect place for a romantic candlelight dinner. Its Colombian-Lebanese proprietors create the best in Arab, Mediterranean and vegetarian cooking. Some of the menu's highlights are the antipastos, like the a la Charly with Serrano ham, Paipa cheese, olives, dried tomatoes, peppers and eggplant in olive oil, served with whole-wheat bread ($12). Another specialty is the mixed Arab and vegetarian plates ($10-11). Beef, trout and chicken dishes also appear (around $15). Thursday-Monday 11 a.m.-11 p.m. Centro Comercial Casa de Quintero. Tel: 732-0735. Updated: Sep 28, 2011.

Chepa Chaves

(ENTREES: $8.20-10.30) Chepa Chaves, the legend goes, was a charming young women who arrived one day in turn-of-the-20th-century Villa de Leyva. Many fell in love with her—and her cooking. The tradition of fine Colombian cuisine continues at this restaurant named for her, with a small selection of distinctive dishes. The chef creates special house sauces to accompany grilled trout or chicken and braises rounds of beef or pork in red wine. Red snapper and goulash are other offerings on the menu, all coming with salad, rice or vegetable torta and French fries ($8.20-10.30). Chepa Chaves also has an almuerzo ejecutivo during the week ($4.25). Tuesday-Sunday and holidays noon-9 p.m. Cra. 8, between Ca. 12 and 13. Updated: May 25, 2009.

Restaurante Guananí

Restaurante Guananí provides a break from the standard Colombian and haute cuisine eateries in town. This bistro specializes in German cooking, with authentic sausages. Cold platters of ham, cheese or sausage and bread ($5.85-7.50) are on the menu. Among the main dishes are German hamburger, veal or pork scaloppini, chicken goulash and trout. These come with German potato salad or fried potatoes. Be sure to have a glass or a bottle of the house wine (from Guananí's vineyard) with your meal. Monday-Friday by reservation; Saturday-Sunday and holidays 8 a.m.-7 p.m. Viñedo Guananí, 1 km from Plaza Principal vía Hotel Casa de los Fundadores. Tel: 732-0398, Cel: 310-871-1743/ 310-871-1749, E-mail: guanani30@hotmail.com. Updated: Sep 28, 2011.

Nightlife

The rumba in Villa de Leyva only really exists when the tourists come on weekends and holidays. During the week some of the cafés and restaurants around the plaza have guitar music. Your chances of catching live concerts, though, are better during the high season and the holidays. Updated: Sep 28, 2011.

Chichería El Pote

(DRINKS: $1.60-3.70) Chichería El Pote emits the scent of eucalyptus. Pull up a rough-hewn wooden table and settle down to your favorite drink. National and international drinks are on hand ($1.60-3.70) as well as a variety of hard liquors, wines and cocktails. Of course, the traditional drinks are served—canelazo ($3.70) and, yes, *chicha* ($2.10). Before you leave, do not forget to leave your mark on the walls, as guests have been doing for years. Thursday-Tuesday noon-midnight or 1 a.m., depending on the number of people hanging out. Centro Comercial Casa Quintero, 1st floor. Updated: Jun 16, 2011.

La Tasca

(COVER: $2.70) Locals and tourists all shake it at La Tasca. Massive green wooden gates lead to the front courtyard of this large hall. The club is a ways out of town, about 300 meters (984 ft) beyond the cemetery, but that doesn't seem to hurt its popularity much. Check the posters around town for information on what's shaking at La Tasca. During high seasons, La Tasca has live music. This is also a popular place for organizations to host fundraising balls. Open only on Friday and Saturday nights. Ca. 15 (Av. Circunvalar), 12A-25, past the cemetery. Updated: Mar 21, 2011.

La Alcazaba ♪

(ENTREES: $3-8) La Alcazaba is the center of the bohemian scene in Villa de Leyva, the café-bar where intellectuals, writers and artists meet. The antique-filled space has spiral staircases leading to seating areas with fireplaces and balconies. Classic Spanish tapas, fondues and empanadas can accompany your coffee or liquored drink. During the week the house music is boleros, cha cha and other classic suave Latin music. Saturdays and Sundays feature live guitar music or Cuban songs (minimum consumption $8 per person). Sometimes there are literary events as well. Daily 10 a.m.–midnight. Cra. 9, 14-57. Tel: 732-0190, Cel: 311-217-7442, E-mail: info@laalcazabacolombia.com. Updated: Jun 23, 2008.

Cine Bar El Patriarca

(TICKETS: $3.75) It's show time in Villa de Leyva! Instead of just hanging out at a bar, sink down into one of the comfy,

EASTERN COLOMBIA

overstuffed chairs with your *cerveza* or shot (or soda or juice). Munchies include hot dogs, *gringas* and, of course, pop corn. El Patriarca shows mostly international and Colombian films, with the occasional Hollywood sleeper. Movies are shown when at least six viewers are present. Advance tickets may be bought downstairs at QuinteroNet. Centro Comercial Casa Quintero, 2nd floor. Tel: 732-0496. Updated: Sep 28, 2011.

Guarapos

(COVER: $27) Guarapos is another dance club in Villa de Leyva where you can dance to rumba music until dawn. It prides itself on having the best sound system and light show of any nightspot in town. It is also proud of the fact that they bring in the best groups and events. Guarapos offers live music during vacation season and during special holidays (as it should, given the pricey cover charge). Advance purchase tickets can be bought in several neighboring towns, as well as in Villa de Leyva itself. Cra. 9, 7-25. Cel: 310-882-3266. Updated: Jun 16, 2011.

AROUND VILLA DE LEYVA

Road to Santa Sofía

Many attractions await the eager visitor along the 18-kilometer (10.8-mi) stretch of road from Villa de Leyva to Santa Sofía. **Pozos Azules**, three kilometers (1.8 mi) outside of the city, are sapphire pools that sparkle in the desert. One kilometer (0.6 mi) further is the **Amonita**, a large ammonite monument. The left-hand turn-off for **Criadero de Avestruces**, an ostrich farm, is two kilometers (1.2 mi) away from the city (admission: $2.65. daily 9 a.m.-5 p.m.). Just past the Amonita, on the right side of the road, is **Fibas Jardín Botánico del Desierto** (admission: $1.05. Wednesday-Sunday 8:30 a.m-5:30 p.m.).

One kilometer (0.6 mi) on the right is the road to **Museo El Fósil**, which has a massive Kronosaurus fossil (admission: adults $1.30, children $0.80. daily 9 a.m.-5 p.m.). Continuing on the main road, you will pass the **Ruinas de Monquirá**, vestiges of a church built by Fray Bartolomé de Ojeda in 1533 (6 km/3.6 mi from Villa de Leyva). Not too far beyond these church ruins is the track leading to the enigmatic statues of **Parque Arqueológico de Monquirá El Infiernito** (1.5 km/1 mi. admission: adults $1.70, students and children $1.05. Tuesday-Sunday 9 a.m.-noon and 2-5 p.m., closed Tuesday after puente). Another 3.1 kilometers (2 mi) along the Santa Sofía road is the turnoff for **Viñedo Aim Karin**, from where it is 600 meters/1,968 feet to the winery (admission: $2.65). The last major attraction on this route is the 17th-century **Monasterio Santo Ecce Homo** (admission: $1.30. daily 8 a.m.-5 p.m.), 11.7 kilometers (7 mi) from Villa de Leyva and one kilometer (0.6 mi) from the road.

Tour agencies in Villa de Leyva offer half- and full-day trips to these sites (entry fees not included); or, you can hire a taxi at the bus station to take you on this route ($37 for 4 hr). If you are a walker, take a Santa Sofía bus as far as Monaste. Beware, as signs to the different sites often only face in the Villa de Leyva-Santa Sofía directions. Updated: Mar 18, 2011.

Fibas Jardín del Desierto

Fibas Jardín del Desierto is more than just a botanical garden. In the Muisca language, *fibas* means wind. This garden is a project to recover a piece of land that was eroded by the winds. Through this process, Fibas hopes to teach others about xero-culture, or cultivating in desert climates. Two labyrinths of indigenous geometric designs lead you through the maze, representing our relationship with the universe and instructing us on how we should care for the environment.

Take a *buseta* toward Santa Sofía, telling the driver you want to get off at Fibas Jardín del Desierto. The entrance is near the roadside. Some tours include this on their itinerary. Kilometer 4, Vía Santa Sofía, just past Monumento Amonite. Cel: 311-222-2399, E-mail: jaimerodriguez@fibas.org/jrrpu@yahoo.com, URL: www.fibas.org. Updated: Mar 18, 2011.

El Fósil

In 1977 at a hamlet outside Villa de Leyva, some farmers found the skeletal remains of a former inhabitant of this valley: a Kronosaurus who had perished some 110-115 million years earlier. This discovery was tremendous, as it is one of the few nearly complete fossils of this dinosaur in the world. (The others are in Australia.) The 12-meter (39-ft) long creature is joined by other former denizens of this land, such as Ictiosaurus, Elasmosaurus, and other sea and land creatures. Price includes guide

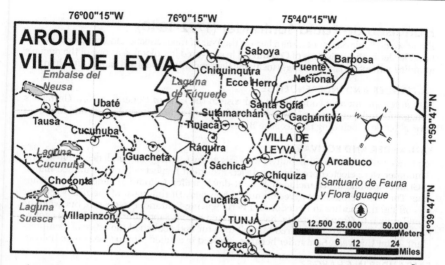

AROUND VILLA DE LEYVA

services (Spanish only), 8 a.m.-noon and 2-5 p.m. No flash photos are allowed.

Take a buseta toward Santa Sofía, telling the driver you want to get off at El Fósil. From the roadside it's about a 10-minute walk to the museum. Many tours include this on their itinerary. Five kilometers (3 mi) from Villa de Leyva, Vía Santa Sofía. Updated: Mar 18, 2011.

El Infiernito !

The official name is Parque Arqueológico de Monquirá, but everyone calls it El Infiernito. This Muisca site was an astronomical center; and, according to archaeologists, a bit more. So it goes, the Muisca (1000-1550 A.D.) believed that when the sun did not cast a shadow of the observatory's twin lines of 36 stones each, then it was busy fertilizing the earth. Planting would begin. To coincide with planting, the women would perform rituals among the forest of phallic statues, hugging and caressing them to ensure fertility and pregnancy. Due east of this is Laguna de Iguaque, the birthplace of humans, according to Muisca mythology. Recent excavations have revealed a tomb and a 4,000-year-old proto-Muisca altar. Take a buseta toward Santa Sofía, telling the driver you want to get off at El Infiernito. From the roadside it's about one kilometer (0.6 mi) to the front gate. Many tours include this on their itinerary. It is seven kilometers (4.2 mi) from Villa de Leyva, Vía Santa Sofía. Updated: Jun 16, 2011.

Monasterio Santo Ecce Homo !

On a green spread of boulder-strewn land, four Dominican monks established a monastery in 1620. Inside this fossil-studded stone edifice, you can tour the original chapel (note the moon and sun in the apse arch) and a dozen galleries exhibiting religious art and the monks' daily life. The choir loft displays parchment musical manuscripts. The cloister patio arcade has 33 columns, representing the years Jesus lived and a Passage of the Dead. Under these bricks, abbots and members of the donor's family are buried. Peeking from beneath the whitewashed walls are murals which were ordered covered in the 18th century.

If the door isn't open during the set hours, ring the bell. Halfway between the main road and the monastery is a signed camino colonial, a stone path going to Santa Sofía. You can begin your day's outing at the Monsterio, then walk back to Villa de Leyva, visiting other sites along the way. It is possible to do retreats at the monastery, living within the community. Public mass is celebrated in the chapel Sundays at 5 p.m. Almost 12 kilometers (7.2 mi) from Villa de Leyva, Vía Santa Sofía. Updated: Mar 18, 2011.

V!VA ONLINE REVIEW
MONASTERIO SANTO ECCE HOMO

A beautiful, energetic and spiritual place.

February 08, 2009

EASTERN COLOMBIA

Francisco de Paula Santander (1792-1840)

Francisco de Paula Santander was a hero of the War of Independence and an important political leader in the early days of Colombia. He is revered in Colombia as one of the nation's founding fathers and many things (including Santander Province) are named after him.

SANTANDER AND INDEPENDENCE

Santander was an able commander and rose to the rank of General in New Granada's struggle for independence. He was a close friend and ally of Simón Bolívar and fought in several battles, including the decisive Battle of Boyaca.

SANTANDER AND BOLIVAR

Santander's friendship with Bolívar was not to last. After independence, Bolívar and Santander were elected president and vice-President respectively of the unified nation of Gran Colombia, which included present-day Ecuador, Colombia, Venezuela and Panama. The two men did not agreè on much, however. During most of the 1820s, Bolivar was off fighting battles in Ecuador and Peru, leaving Santander to govern, but when he would return to Gran Colombia, he would often repeal Santander's laws. Things got so bad that in 1828 Bolivar declared himself dictator and abolished the office of vice-president. Later that year, Santander became involved in a failed plot to assassinate Bolivar.

SANTANDER IN CHARGE

Gran Colombia fell apart in 1830 after the death of Bolívar. Santander returned from exile and became president of Colombia in 1832. He was an able leader and skilled politician who kept both the liberals and conservatives in line. He was a big believer in laws for his people: he famously said, "Arms have given us independence, but laws will give us freedom."

SANTANDER'S LEGACY

In death, Bolívar has become something of a martyr: people remember him for his dream of a united South America and wonder what the present would be like had he succeeded in keeping Gran Colombia together. Santander's legacy has therefore suffered somewhat, as many remember him today only for his public disagreements with the Liberator. This is unfair, as he was a good general, a skilled leader and a man of laws who did much for his people. In Colombia is he still revered as a great hero and visionary leader.

Beyond Santa Sofía

If the road to Santa Sofía is imprinted with the past and present denizens of the Desierto de Villa de Leyva, the road beyond this small village is sculpted by nature herself. Waterfalls, like Cascada Guatoque (80 m/262.5 ft) and Cascadas de Sorocota (3 cascades, the tallest being 30 m/98.5 ft) drape the bluffs. Carved within the auburn earth are caverns and caves, among them Cueva del Indio and Cueva de la Chapa. At Hayal, these elements come togther, with Cascada Hayal (70 m/229.5 ft), Cueva del Hayal and Gruta del Hayal. Paso del Ángel is a narrow ridge between two deep canyons. It is difficult to reach most of these sights without a private car, but tour agencies in Villa de Leyva offer half and full day trips. Updated: Mar 18, 2011.

To Gachantivá

The road to Gachantivá is a pleasant mixture of civilization and nature. Delve into one of the many caves that pockmark the land, like Cueva del Indio and Cueva la Furatena. Practice *torrentismo* (rapelling) in Cascadas la Periquera, camp on the banks of Quebrada la Honda, or hike to Laguna las Coloradas. To wash the sweat off after a long day of adventuring, dip into the Pozo de la Vieja on the banks of Río de la Cebada. To top the day off, visit the ruins of old viceregal Gachantivá Viejo, with its graveyard (segregated by class and race), the old church and other buildings. It is difficult to reach most of these without a private car. Tour agencies in Villa de Leyva offer half- and full-day trips to these sites. Updated: Mar 18, 2011.

Santuario de Flora y Fauna de Iguaque

According to Muisca legend, the goddess Bachue rose from the crystalline waters of Laguna de Iguaque amid the chilly mists swirling across the páramo, and thus mankind was born. It is believed a pilgrimage

Photo by: momentcaptured1

to this sacred place cleanses the soul and purifies the spirit. The Laguna lies in the midst of the 6,800-hectare (16,803 -ac) Santuario de Flora y Fauna de Iguaque. The park includes wetland forests and chilly moors between 2,440 and 3,660 meters (8,000 and 12,000 ft) high as well as eight lagoons. A hiking path to Laguna de Iguaque has signs that describe the special environment of this sanctuary.

Tour agents in Villa de Leyva and Tunja make day trips to the Santuario de Flora y Fauna Iguaque. If on your own, take a bus heading toward Arcabuco and get off at the park entrance. The road at the entrance is rough, and the walk to Laguna de Iguaque takes three and a half hours roundtrip.

Accommodation within the park is available. The *Furachiougua* cabin (Muisca for "good woman") sleeps six to eight people ($14 per person, per night). Camping is only allowed in the designated site near the administrative center. Bring all equipment with you (low season: one-time charge of $2.15 for site, plus $2.15 per night per person/high season: $3.70 for site plus $3.70 per person per night).

There is also a restaurant within the park. Vía Arcabuco. E-mail: norandin@col1. telecom.com.co, URL: www.parquesnacionales.gov.co/areas/lasareas/iguaque/iguaintro.htm. Updated: Jun 16, 2011.

RÁQUIRA

 2,200m 12,300 📞 8

Ráquira in Chibcha means "The City of Pots." To this day, the workshops of this village give credence to the name by making the animal-shaped ceramics for which they are famous. Most visitors come for the Sunday market, but any time is pleasant. The narrow streets are lined with colorful houses and gardens. Ráquira's main temple dates back to around 1600. Six kilometers (3.5 mi) away in the Desierto de la Candelaria is **Convento Monasterio Nuestra Señora de la Candelaria**, an Agustinian monastery founded in 1597. Its museum of religious art and antiques is open to the public ($2.65). The monastery additionally has a restaurant and hostel (Tel: 257-7837, Cel: 310-261-3135. In Bogotá: Ca. 73a, 69A-69, Tel: 1-251-6886/252-9954, Fax: 1-430-1075). Updated: Mar 21, 2011.

EASTERN COLOMBIA

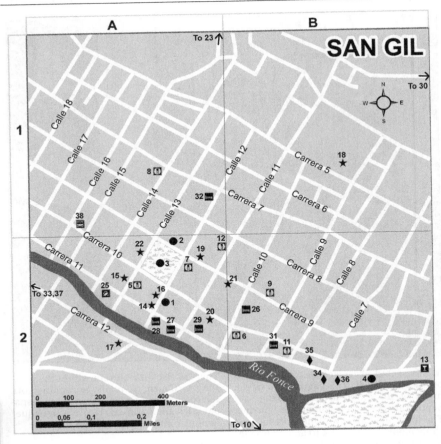

SAN GIL

SAN GIL

⛰ 1,114m	👤 49,500	📞 7

San Gil is great for both extreme sports or just plain relaxing. San Gil has long been popular with Colombians as a weekend and holiday escape. More frequently, travelers come to know of this colonial town in Santander, only six hours from Bogotá.

There are several private nature preserves, the most famous being Parque Gallineral with guided nature tours and swimming pools on the banks of the Río Fonce.

Numerous travel agencies offer extreme sports tours, including paragliding, rappelling, kayaking, caving, biking, horseback riding and day walks. There is whitewater rafting down several local rivers or through the Chicamocha Canyon. Prices for these tours are regulated.

Nearby are several historical towns. Baricha-ra has the Parque de las Aguas and virtually untouched colonial architecture. In Guane there is a paleontology museum, and good opportunities for rock and fossil hunting. Updated: Sep 28, 2011.

● **Activities**

1 Casa de la Cultura A2
2 Catedral A2
3 Parque La Independencia A2
4 Parque Natural El Gallineral B2

🍴 **Eating**

5 Bar Restaurante Carnes y Carnes A2
6 De Santander Tienda Café B2
7 La Polita A2
8 Pizzeria La Ricota A1
9 Restaurant La Casona Criolla B2
10 Restaurante KowLoon Dragones A2
11 Restaurante Rogelia B2
12 Restaurante Saludable Delicia A2

🍸 **Nightlife**

13 Masai Mara B2

★ **Services**

14 Banco Colmena (Western Union) A2
15 Banco Popular A2
16 Bancolombia A2
17 Clinica Santa Cruz de la Loma A2
18 Hospital Regional San Juan de Dios B1
19 MegaRed (Banco de Bogotá) A2
20 Post Office A2
21 Puerto PC B2
22 Telecom A2

🛍 **Shopping**

23 Arte y Naturaleza A2
24 Feria Artesanal (See 1)
25 Mercado A2

🛏 **Sleeping**

26 Centro Real B2
27 Hotel El Viajero A2
28 Hotel San Carlos A2
29 Hotel Victoria A2
30 Hotel Wassiki Campestre B1
31 La Posada Familiar B2
32 Macondo Guesthouse A1
33 Mesón del Cuchicute B1

◆ **Tours**

34 Aventura Total B2
35 Colombia Rafting Expeditions B2
36 Planeta Azul B2

🚌 **Transportation**

37 Bus Terminal A1
38 Buses to Barichara, Curití and other villages A1

History

In pre-Spanish conquest times, the Guanes lived in the San Gil area. They were related to the Muisca, of the Chibcha linguistic family. The Guanes were still here when the Spaniards arrived but were quickly exterminated by the conquering forces. Only 351 survived and were relocated to the village of Guanes.

San Gil as we know it today was founded in 1689 by Don Gil Cabrera y Dávalos, by decree of the Spanish king. The town was originally named for Don Gil and later for the saint of the same moniker.

The sparks of independence ignited in the villages near this colonial town. In 1781 mestizo José Antonio Golán led the comunero revolt in Charalá; similar uprisings occurred in Mogotes, Onzaga and Socorro. A number of important battles occurred in this region. The Batalla de Pienta of 1819 resulted in heavy losses to the viceregal troops, which helped the rebels later win the Battle of Boyacá.

HOLIDAYS AND FESTIVALS

The Fiesta de San Gil on 17 March is celebrated with civic acts and parades. Other civil holidays include 20 July, Fiesta de la Patria, and 7 August, the Batalla de Boyacá. Semana Santa, Easter Week, has religious processions on Maundy Thursday, Good Friday and Holy Saturday. This same week is the Festival de Música Colombiana Andina y Religiosa. The feast of the Immaculate Conception is marked with candlelight

EASTERN COLOMBIA

Photo by momentcaptured1

ceremonies, especially in homes. On any national holiday or three-day weekend expect San Gil to be jammed with Colombians hanging out. Updated: Jun 20, 2011.

Safety

San Gil is a safe place to explore. When participating in any extreme sport, be sure that the company provides you with proper safety equipment and well-trained guides. Do not swim in the Fonce River, which flows through Parque Gallineral and through town, as it has very strong currents; people have drowned in it. The tap water is chlorinated and said to be OK to drink. As in other parts of lowland Colombia, dengue is present in San Gil. Updated: Mar 18, 2011.

Services

TOURISM

Unfortunately, San Gil does not have a tourism office at present. Many hotels do have information on-hand for their guests. Macondo Guesthouse is a great source for information. You can also read more on what San Gil has to offer at www.sangil.com. Updated: Mar 15, 2011.

MONEY

Several banks in San Gil have ATMs. **Bancolombia** has the highest withdrawal limit of $400. It accepts MasterCard, Visa, American Express and Cirrus (Ca. 12, 10-44). **ATH**, or multi-network ATMs, also take Plus cards. You can find these at **Mega Banco/Banco de Bogotá** (Cra. 9, 11-56) and **Banco Popular** (Ca. 13, 10-34). There is no official place to exchange traveler's checks or cash dollars. The local **Western Union** branch in Banco Colmena (Monday-Friday 8-11:30 a.m. and 2-4 p.m. Corner of Cra. 10 and Ca. 12, Parque la Libertad) performs transactions only for Colombians. Updated: Mar 18, 2011.

KEEPING IN TOUCH

Colombia's national phone carrier, **Telecom**, charges $0.10 per minute for local andSan Gil and surrounding towns were flashpoints of the 20th-century civil wars, especially the Guerra de Mil Días at the beginning of the millennium, and the disruptions that arose after Liberal presidential candidate Jorge Eliécer Gaitan's assassination in 1948. Updated: Sep 28, 2011.

When to Go

The weather in San Gil is pretty much the same all year long. There is no real rainy season as in other parts of the country. Temperatures average 25°C (77°F). It is very popular with vacationing Colombians, especially during December-January holidays, Semana Santa (Easter week), July-August holidays and three-day weekends. Hotel prices are higher at these times and reservations are necessary. Updated: Sep 28, 2011.

EASTERN COLOMBIA

Getting To and Away

Getting to San Gil is possible via Bogotá or Tunja. If you're coming from Villa de Leyva, you have to return to Tunja, or else take the back roads, which is cheaper. Go by way of Arcabuco, which is on the main Bogotá-Bucaramanga road. If arriving from the coast, first go to Bucaramanga, then transfer.

San Gil has a good public transportation system (daily 5 a.m.-9 p.m., $0.40). For the long-distance bus terminal, catch a bus that says "Terminal" from Calle 10 and Carrera 11. Taxis cost $1.40.

The long-distance bus terminal, handling traffic to Bogotá, Cucuta and the coast, is located on Carrera 12 and Calle 31, about two kilometers (1.2 mi) from town. Most routes to Santa Marta and other coastal points and to Cucuta transfer in Bucaramanga. It is better to go to Bucaramanga where transport is cheaper and more frequent. Minivans to villages near San Gil leave from the depot at Carrera 11 and Calle 15. For Guanes, first go to Barichara and transfer there.

Direct services are listed below. Primary bus companies include Berlinas, Brasilia, Copetran and Cotrasangil. Schedules and prices vary among companies, so be sure to check them out for yourself, and bear in mind that usually the last bus making the return trip to San Gil will leave earlier than the last bus departing from San Gil to the same destination. national calls, and from $0.30 per minute for international calls (daily 6 a.m.-10 p.m. Ca. 13, 9-70, Parque La Libertad). A national or local call shops costs on average $0.15 per minute. Throughout San Gil you can find Internet cafés; most charge $0.80 per hour. **Puerto PC** charges only $0.60 per hour, and also has special discounts, Skype and inexpensive international calls at $0.25 per minute (Monday-Saturday 8 a.m.-12:30 p.m. and 2-8:30 p.m., Sunday and holidays 8:30 a.m.-1 p.m. Cra, 9, 10-65, local 107, Edifico Venecia). The **post office** (Monday-Friday 8 a.m.-noon and 2-6 p.m., Saturday 8 a.m.-noon) is in the Cajasan mall on Carrera 10, between Calles 10 and 11. Updated: Mar 18, 2011.

MEDICAL

The main public hospital in San Gil is **Hospital Regional San Juan de Dios** (Cra. 5, 9-102. Tel: 243-359). The private **Clínica Santa Cruz de la Loma** is recommended; an English-speaking doctor is available for

To:	Departure	Time	Cost
Bogotá	Every hour	6 hr	$16-24
Cartagena	5 p.m., 7:30 p.m.	14–15 hr	$37-48
Mogotes	7 buses per day	2 hr	$3.20
Barichara	6:10 a.m.- 6:30 p.m.	30 min	$1.60
Cabrera	Mon.-Fri. 5:45 a.m.- 11:30 a.m.; Sat. – Sun. 9 a.m., 11:30 a.m., 5:45 p.m.	1 hr	$2.10
Charalá	Every half hour 6 a.m.- 6:30 p.m.	45 min	$2.10
Curití	Every 15 min. 6 a.m.- 7p.m.	20 min	$0.80
Bucaramanga	Every half hour 4:30-8 p.m.	2.5 hr	$7.40
Páramo	6 a.m.- 7:15 p.m.	30 min	$1.50
Villanueva	Every 20 min. 6 a.m. – 6:50 p.m.	30 min.	$1.30

EASTERN COLOMBIA

emergency cases (Ca. 12, 12-20. Tel: 724-5866/5845/2100). Pharmacies can be found everywhere in the midtown area, about one every block. Carrera 11 has several between Calles 10 and 13. Updated: Sep 27, 2011.

CAMERA

There are only a handful of camera shops in San Gil. Besides providing one-hour film processing, **Fotos Peñaloza** (Monday-Friday 8 a.m.-noon and 2-7 p.m., Saturday 8 a.m.-1 p.m. and 3-7 p.m., Sunday and holidays 8:30 a.m.-12:30 p.m. Cra. 10, 10-101, Tel: 724-2879) has all types of batteries; digital camera cards; old-school film and disposable, underwater and other cameras for sale. It can also connect you to a camera repair person. Updated: Jan 07, 2008.

SHOPPING

Feria Artesanal

It began as a holiday crafts fair, but now is a permanent affair. In the large front hall of San Gil's Casa de la Cultura, 17 Santandereano artesanos—mostly women—bedeck their stalls and tables with their work. To shade yourself during an outing, take along a hat made of palm or *plátano* (plaintain) leaf. Treat your feet to some *fique* sandals or buy napkin holders, placemats or other items to decorate the dining room table. Of course, there's also jewelry. If your sweet tooth starts to ache, take home a bag of honey caramels. Casa de la Cultura, Ca. 12, between Cra. 10 and 11, a half-block from the main plaza. Updated: Mar 30, 2011.

Arte y Naturaleza

Showing off its Santandereano pride, Arte y Naturaleza crochets fashion accessories and other items from natural-colored cotton. You'll need a hat that's guaranteed to keep you cool in these warm lands, especially if you are heading for the Caribbean coast. To make your ensemble complete, don't forget a belt with a metal or wooden buckle and a shoulder bag. You can choose from the many designs crafted. Besides having its home workshop, Arte y Naturaleza also has a stall at the Feria Artesanal in the Casa de la Cultura. Ca. 15, 2-60. Tel: 724-4086, Fax: 724-6315, E-mail: arteynaturalezasangil@yahoo.es URL: www.arteynaturaleza.com. Updated: Mar 30, 2011.

De Santander Tienda Café

De Santander Tienda has gathered the best in Santander's artistry and showcases it all in this small corner shop. Everything in the store is for sale, from the paintings on the wall to the hammock chairs hanging from the ceiling. Shawls, ponchos and bags crafted from fique and linen fill the shelves. As its names implies, De Santander isn't just a shop, but also a café that serves regional coffee, tamales and sweets, which you can purchase to take on the road with you. On Saturdays the café hosts lectures, poetry readings, concerts and other events. Monday-Saturday 8 a.m.-8 p.m. Cra. 10, 10-103 (corner). Tel: 724-3655, E-mail: desantandertiendacafe-com@gmail.com. Updated: Oct 05, 2011.

Things to See and Do

San Gil has much to offer those looking for an adrenaline rush. Water lovers can raft or kayak on rivers with class II-V rapids. If you'd like something really different, there's hydrospeed, or body boarding down the Río Fonce. You can also rappel through waterfalls, or soar like a condor by paragliding from the Parque Nacional Chicamocha, or crawl through some remarkable caves. Stroll and picnic in the botanical gardens of Parque Natural El Gallineral. For those who are more culturally minded, there are nearby villages worth checking out, like Barichara for its colonial architecture and a resident artist community, or Curití, where fique artisans practice their trade. Updated: Sep 28, 2011.

Parque Natural El Gallineral !

Long tendrils of moss hang from ancient trees and sway in the slight breeze. Sunlight sparkles on the torrent of the Río Fonce. This is Parque Natural El Gallineral, four hectares of botanical gardens where the *Quebrada* (creek) Curití meets the robust Río Fonce. Within this park, nine *plazoletas* (squares) are connected by a network of paths through foliage so dense you will not meet another soul. After an enchanting afternoon of wandering through these thickets, bathe in the refreshing spring waters of the *piscina* (pool). Do not swim in the Río Fonce, as it has dangerous currents. The swimming pool is closed for cleaning every two weeks, usually on a Tuesday. There are lockers and showers in an adjoining bathhouse. The restaurant and cafeteria are expensive. Updated: Mar 30, 2011.

The Camino Real from San Gil to the Río Magdalena

I heard a bit of buzz from a friend in San Gil: Go trekking on the old camino real (highway), or Camino de los Guanes, to the Río Magdalena. I checked it out a bit. It appears you can follow the footsteps of the Guane ancestors who had laid down this path (it was later used

EASTERN COLOMBIA

by the Spaniards). The stone road originally extended from Girón, near Bucaramanga, to Barrancabermeja on the River. In this modern era, the trek begins at Cabrera: from there it is a two-hour walk to Barichara. Barichara to Guane is the most-trodden part of the camino (way) (1.5-2 hr). The trail then continues to Villanueva (3 hr). The toughest part of the trek is through the Chicamocha River Canyon, which has a 1,000-meter (3,280-foot) descent and ascent, in over 35°C (95°F) heat. From Villanueva, the road plunges to the ghost town of Jordán at the base of the canyon (3 hr). After a four-hour climb, you arrive at Mesa de los Santos on the other side of the abyss.

The camino originally winded further to the Río Magdalena. According to all sources, it is impossible to continue on from Mesa de los Santos. Some say it is because of safety issues, especially with civil war fighting, but others say it is because bridges no longer exist past that point. Buses leave from San Gil to all the pueblos on the route, except for Jordán. Because of the ongoing civil war in the region, be sure to ask about safety in each village before beginning the next leg. A guide is not necessary, though you will have to ask directions frequently. The entire trek will take two to three days. Accommodations and food are available in all the villages. Updated: Mar 30, 2011.

Waterfalls and Torrentismo

Waterfalls drape the river canyons slicing the countryside around San Gil. At some of the cascades, not only can you gaze upon these natural wonders, but you can also practice a sport offered by the good folk of this area, such as rappelling in waterfalls. Get ready to zip down a slick rock face, misted by tumbling waters. This is just one of the extreme adventures that San Gil has to offer. The easiest fall to get to on your own is 150-meter (500-ft) high Juan Curí, out near Charalá, which has a delightfully cool pool at its base where you can swim.

Contact local tour operators as they offer excursions to several different waterfalls. Alternatively, to get to Juan Curí on your own, catch a Bucaramanga-bound bus or a bus headed to Charalá ($1.60). Tell the driver you're going to Juan Curí.

If rappelling, check the quality of equipment. At Juan Curí, there are two entry points through private property; the first is cheaper ($1.05), though the second includes a tour of the cacao farm ($2.65). To rappel is extra. Updated: Mar 30, 2011.

Whitewater Rafting

San Gil has become renowned for its whitewater rafting. Three main rivers, all with different characteristics, offer adventures for novices and experts alike. The Río Fonce has class II+ rapids. This 1.5-hour trip is popular with beginners and families ($13.25 per person). Río Suárez is considered the best whitewater rafting river, with class IV rapids, depending on the time of year. The six-hour trip includes three hours on the river ($63 per person). Through Cañón Chicamocha is the river of the same name, which has class II to class IV rapids. You can arrange special five-day expeditions down this river. Be sure the rafting company has adequate equipment and practices appropriate safety measures. Updated: Mar 30, 2011.

Other Water Sports

Besides whitewater rafting, there are other aquatic sports to partake in here in San Gil. Check with tour operators in the town for these excursion opportunities.

Kayaking: There are eight rivers to run, though commercial trips are offered only on three of the rivers. Multi-day expeditions may be arranged.

Rappelling: Rappelling in waterfalls is a specialty in the San Gil area.

Hydrospeeding: This is an intense adventure of surfing down 10 kilometers (6 mi) of the Río Fonce's rapids. You receive instruction and are outfitted with board, flippers, life jacket and a helmet. A kayak accompanies you for security. The standard price is $19 per person.

The water temperature of the rivers is 14-18°C (57-64°F). Be sure to check the quality and safety of the equipment used. Updated: Mar 30, 2011.

Caving

Delving into the bowels of the earth (a.k.a caving) is another adventure you can undertake while in San Gil. You can only visit a few of the many caves that gouge the landscape.

Cueva del Indio: This cave out in Páramo is the easiest to spelunk, suitable for the whole family. A special feature is ziplining or jumping 5 meters (16.4 ft) into a pool, then swimming out along a rope.

Cueva la Antigua: This cave is more demanding and hands-on, calling for a lot of crawling through mud. Not for the claustrophobic.

Ojo de Pájaros: This 100-meter (328-ft) deep and 20-meter (65.5-ft) wide cave near Mogotes earns its name from the thousands of oil birds that reside in it.

Other caverns of interest include Cueva del Yeso and Cueva de la Vaca. All caves are on private property and each has only one tour company authorized to lead expeditions. It is illegal to go on your own. Contact the tour operators in town to go caving. Be sure to check the quality of the safety equipment used. Updated: Mar 30, 2011.

Tours

Most "agencies" that exist in San Gil are actually booking agents, arranging your excursion with one of the four tour operators in the town. All offer rafting on the smaller rivers, paragliding, caving, rappelling, and guided tours to Barichara and the waterfalls. San Gil is an OK place to paraglide if you have some experience; however, if you want to take courses, keep in mind that teachers speak only Spanish. There is an English-speaking paragliding guide and instructor in Bucaramanga. All tour operators charge the same for any excursion, as prices are regulated by the city government. Updated: Sep 28, 2011.

Colombia Rafting Expeditions

Whether your interest is simple rafting or any of the other adventure sports on offer in San Gil, like caving or hydrospeeding, Colombia Rafting Expeditions can make it happen. Considered by some to be the better rafting operator in San Gil, Colombia Rafting Expeditions' guides have international experience and many also speak English. This company offers expeditions on all three principal rivers, in raft or kayak, as well as kayaking courses ($50-185). Personnel in another raft or kayak accompany you for your security. The only cavern that Colombia Rafting visits is Cueva Antigua. Hours from 8 a.m.-6 p.m. Cra. 10, 7-83. Cel: 311-283-8647/291-2870, Fax: 724-5800, Email: info@colombiarafting.com/colombiakayak5@hotmail.com, URL: www.colombiarafting.com. Updated: Mar 16, 2011.

Planeta Azul

Planeta Azul has rafting excursions on the various rivers in the region. The company also offers tours into Cuevas del Yeso, de la Vaca, Antigua and del Indio and rappelling and canyoning to Pescaderito, Pinchote and Páramo. You can also choose to go paragliding at Cañón del Chicamocha and Curití or horseback riding to Villa Nueva, Curití or Valle de San José. The horeback riding trip to any of these locations includes a traditional lunch. As if all of the above weren't enough, Planeta Azul will also zip you around on a chiva tour, or suit you up for a good old-fashioned paintball battle. Planeta Azul's guide, who specializes in hikes to Casacada de Juan Curí and the Camino Real from Barichara to Guane, also speaks English. Hours are from 7:30 a.m.-6 p.m. However, you can call cell phone numbers at any hour. Entrance of Parque Natural el Gallineral. Tel: 724-0000, Cel: 310-771-7586/315-823-4796, Fax: 724-7679, E-mail: info@planetaazulcolombia.com planetaazulsg@hotmail.com planetaazulcolombia@hotrmail.com, URL: www.planetaazulcolombia.com. Updated: Mar 16, 2011.

Aventura Total

Aventura Total lives up to its name. The company offers all types of adventures in the San Gil region, from white water rafting on all three main rivers (Fonce, Suárez and Chicamocha) to rappelling at Pinchote and torrentismo at Cascada Juan Curí, to caving at Cuevas Antigua, de la Vaca and del Yeso, as well as horseback riding trips (cabalgatas) to Hacienda Santa Bárbara or Curití ($37.50 per person, all inclusive). Aventura Total's fame rests in its notoriety as San Gil's better operator for paragliding. However, some do not recommend the company for rafting. Office hours are from from 8am-6pm. Hours for the sports and activities are from 8am-4pm. Malecón, in front of Parque Natural el Gallineral Tel: 723-8888, Cel: 316-6939-300/310-551-5254, URL: www.aventuratotal.com.co. Updated: Mar 16, 2011.

Lodging

Accommodation in San Gil is surprisingly inexpensive, and provides good-quality service. The cheaper San Gil hostels are generally found on Carrera 11 between Calles 10 and 13; these generally run from $5-8 per person. By law, hotels must display their prices and may not charge more than the highest shown. Bargains are available in the low season. Most inns double or triple rates in the high season and you will want to make reservations at these times. There are several camping options outside of San Gil. A recommended, free site is Pescadarito, near Curití. Updated: Jul 21, 2010.

BUDGET

Mesón del Cuchicute !

(ROOMS: $5.40-35 per person) As one of San Gil's finest hotels, Mesón del Cuchicute is still remarkably affordable. A country-club-styled inn with park-like grounds, the Mesón has all the comforts that make up a luxury vacation: swimming pool, playground, Jacuzzi, sauna, gymnasium and game room. The brick-floored rooms are amazing with fan, cable TV, mini-bar (separate charge) and private balcony. The hand basins in the hot-water baths are made of rough marble, copper and brass. Rooms for singles or couples are on the third floor. Mesón del Cuchicute also is ecologically conscious: it recycles and has a composting refuse. This has to be one of the best bargains in Colombia. Mesón del Cuchicute is located one kilometer (0.62 mi) from town, past the long-distance bus terminal. Some of the city buses go right to the front gate of the complex, e.g. the one marked "Mesón" ($0.40). A taxi from the center costs $1.40. Km. 1 Vía San Gil-Socorro. Tel: 724-2041/8104/8069, Cel: 312-480-2509, Fax: 724-3171, E-mail: mesondelcuchicute@comfenalcosantander.com.co, URL: www.comfenalcosantander.com.co. Updated: Mar 17, 2011.

Hotel El Viajero

(ROOMS: $7.50-22.50) Conveniently located on Carrera 11, just a few blocks from Parque Gallineral and the market, the Hotel El Viajero provides comfortable accommodations. All rooms have windows, private bath (room-temperature water) and cable TV, as well as a table and chair for catching up on your journal writing. The first floor has a bright, plant-filled courtyard and a balcony overlooking the Río Fonce. The inn guarantees a comfortable atmosphere, suitable for families as well the solo backpacker. Cra. 11, 11-07. Tel: 724-4817, E-mail: hotelelviajero2@hotmail.com. Updated: Mar 17, 2011.

Macondo Guesthouse

(BEDS: $8, ROOMS: $20) Macondo Guesthouse has become *the* place to stay in San Gil. Australian-born Shaun opens the doors of this colonial house, just a few blocks from Parque La Libertad, to backpackers and other travelers. He offers both dorms and private rooms, all sharing baths. Amenities include kitchen, laundry facilities (or use the convenient laundry service), hammocks in the front courtyard, free WiFi, book exchange and much more. Shaun is the best source of information in

town, and can help you organize any adventure activity. Ca. 12, 7-26. Tel: 724-4463, Cel: 311-828-2905, E-mail: macondohostal@hotmail.com/info@macondohostel.com, URL: www.macondohostel.com. Updated: Mar 17, 2011.

Hotel San Carlos

(ROOMS: $10-15) The Hotel San Carlos is one of the budget options in San Gil. It is close to the Parque Central, the central market and Parque Natural Gallineral. A variety of rooms are provided, for one to three persons or families, some with private bath and television. The reception area has cable television. There is a laundry area to wash one's own clothes, and an area for motorcycle parking. This hotel is a good option for travelers watching their wallets. Cra. 11, 11-25. Tel: 724-2542, E-mail: hotelsancarlos2009@hotmail.com. Updated: Mar 17, 2011.

Centro Real

(ROOMS: $10-20) When you walk into Centro Real, you'll likely be welcomed with a smile. This friendly hotel is airy and clean, and there's always someone on call to help you out. It is close to the park and anything else you might want to do in this amazing little town. Rooms are cleaned each day, and you'll be given fresh towls. Ca. 10, 10-41. Tel: 724-0387. Updated: Mar 17, 2011.

MID-RANGE

La Posada Familiar !

(ROOMS: $16-37.50) A small, family-run inn, La Posada Familiar has six rooms with extra touches. The quarters are simply decorated, but come with a ceiling fan, stocked mini-fridge (extra charge for what you consume), and cable TV with a remote control. The private baths are gleaming white, with room-temperature water. All the rooms are outfitted for more than one person, though in the low season the lone traveler can check in too. La Posada Familiar has a small interior patio with a fountain and it also has a garden, an outside balcony, and many other areas to sit and relax after an adrenaline-pumping day of rafting or caving. Cra. 10, 8-55, Tel: 724-8136. Updated: Mar 16, 2011.

Hotel Victoria

(ROOMS: $22-35 per person) Hotel Victoria is a quaint, family-owned hotel near the major attractions of San Gil. The beautiful courtyard has a few different sitting areas, all protected from the rain. Several different types of rooms are available, for one to five people. There are basic ones with a private bath, a fan, a reading lamp and a TV; some with air conditioning, a stereo, a refrigerator and a large-screen TV; and suites with a bathtub. After a pleasant night's sleep on firm mattresses, the family serves morning coffee to their guests. Prices vary according to the room, the amount of days, if its low or high season, and the amount of people staying. Prices raise during the high season. Cra. 11, 10-40, Tel: 723-7960, Fax: 724-5955, E-mail: piedramochuelo@hotmail.com. Updated: Mar 16, 2011.

HIGH-END

Hotel Wassiki Campestre

(ROOMS: $121.50-179) Hotel Wassiki Campestre is the most exclusive place to stay in the area, located five minutes outside of San Gil. Twelve luxurious bedrooms, swimming pool, Jacuzzi, sauna and gym make up this secluded hotel, which also includes a campsite. Prices vary depending on the day, for example the lowest price for a room is from Monday-Thursday is $54 a night, on weekends, $72.50, and on holidays, $125. On the other hand, the highest price for a room from Monday-Thursday is $83 per night, on weekends, $105, and on holidays, $185. Km 3 Vía San Gil-Bogotá (Pinchote entrance). Cel: 320-323-1322/315-371-5000 (reservations), Fax: 724-8386, E-mail: wassiki@hotmail.com, URL: www.hotelwassiki-campestre.com.Updated: Mar 17, 2011.

Restaurants

Comida corriente in San Gil cost $2.10-3.70. Cheaper restaurants are found on Carrera 11, between Calles 9 and 10. The municipal market is a good place to grab breakfast or lunch (daily 6 a.m.-2 p.m., Cra. 11 between Ca. 13 and 14). The market is busiest on Wednesdays and weekends.

Some of the typical dishes you may want to check out are *cabro* (goat), *pipitoria* (rice prepared with finely chopped goat innards and goat's blood), *ubre* (cow udder), *carne oleada* (beef marinated in beer, sun-dried, then grilled) and *hormigas culonas tostadas* (roasted flying ants). Updated: Jun 21, 2011.

Galería y Cafetería La Polita

Considered by some to have the best coffee in San Gil, La Polita is much more than just a good stiff cup of joe. At any time of the day you can come in to have a bit of the hair of the dog that nipped you, a stiff shot of any kind of liquor. It seems everyone comes to La Polita, so at times it can be tough to find a table. Check out the paintings strewn across the walls, which showcase the region's best talents. Ca. 12, 9-35. Tel: 724-4259, E-mail: linasare@latinmail.com. Updated: Sep 28, 2011.

Pizzaría La Ricotta

(PIZZA SLICE: $1.30-1.70, ENTREES: $2.70-3.70) Located up the hill, near several schools and the university, Pizzaría La Ricotta serves up oven-hot pizza at student prices. Whether ordering by the slice or an extra-large pie ($12-14), you can take care of that evening hunger here. A local specialty is the Sangileña, topped with cheese, sausage, corn, cilantro and tomatoes. La Ricotta also has several vegetarian pizzas, like the tropical with an assortment of fruits and cheese and, of course, a plain old-fashioned vegetarian one. If pizza doesn't quite fit the bill, try the lasagna or a panzerotti. Monday-Saturday 3-10 p.m., Sunday 5-10 p.m. Cra. 7, 14-05, Tel: 724-7283. Updated: May 22, 2009.

Restaurante Vegetariano Saludable Delicia

(LUNCH: $2.35) Saludable Delicia lives up to its name, providing delicious, healthful meals to traveling vegetarians. During the morning hours, the shop sells baked goods, teas, supplements, tahini and peanut butter. The set-meal lunch is served from 11 a.m. to 2 p.m. and costs $5. Thereafter until close, only à la carte dishes are available. All meals are served with brown rice. The dining areas are tranquil and airy; the staff, soft-spoken. If adventure sporting has left you a bit twisted, come and have a massage (Sunday-Friday 8-10:30 a.m., 3-7 p.m. $5-15). Sunday-Friday 7 a.m.-8 p.m. Closed Saturdays. Ca. 11, 9-40. Tel: 724-3539, Cel: 320-272-6038/441-1326. Updated: Mar 17, 2011.

Restaurante Rogelia

(LUNCH: $3.50, ENTREES: $8 and up) Restaurante Rogelia presents typical dishes of the Santander region, including *cabro con pipatoria* ($7) and *carne orneada* (beef that has been marinated, then dried and grilled, $8). The *bistec de res a caballo* is not horse meat, but rather a beef steak topped with an egg ($11).

To sample a bit of everything, ask for a *picada* platter ($6-25). The *comida corriente* costs $3.50; only the *bandeja* (main dish) is $8. After 4 p.m. you can order a pizza hot out of the oven. Restaurante Rogelia also serves breakfast ($2.50-$5). Daily 7 a.m.-8 p.m. Cra. 10, 8-09. Tel: 724-0823. Updated: Mar 17, 2011.

Restaurante Kowloon Dragones

You can find Chinese restaurants in every corner of Colombia, even in San Gil. Restaurante Kowloon Dragones presents the visitor with a full menu of Chinese classics prepared with a variety of meats and sauces. Also on the menu are a few choices for the vegetarian, as well as some international dishes. If a group of you are dining together, split one of the *menus familiares*, which include everything from wine to appetizers and soup, plus several types of Chinese fare ($20 for two up to $60 for six). Open daily 10 a.m.-10 p.m. Daily 10 a.m.-10 p.m. Ca. 12, 5-82, La Playa (on the other side of the Río Fonce from the main part of town). Tel: 724-2034/8444 Updated: Mar 17, 2011.

Bar-Restaurante Carnes y Carnes

(ENTREES: $7-15) Beyond the boring gate is one of San Gil's classier eateries. This large restaurant is set in a roofed garden with a brick grill in the center. At the grill, the chef prepares your entrée: chicken, perhaps with an intriguing sauce, pork, beef, fish or seafood. Only rice and potatoes accompany the dishes—but then again, the name of this bistro is "Meat and Meat." While waiting for your repast, read the menu full of tales of the origins and legends of the region's foods. This is the most expensive restaurant in town and has a reputation as being one of the finest. Daily 10 a.m.-10 p.m. Ca. 12, 8-09. Tel: 724-6246. Updated: Sep 28, 2011.

Nightlife

Any night of the week, you can join sangileños and Colombians who sit in front of shops for a beer (or something stronger). The most popular places are along Parque la Libertad. Nightclubs and karaoke joints within the city are required, by law, to close at 1 a.m. No such restrictions hold for those outside the city limits. These businesses are open on weekends until daybreak or when the rumba fizzles—whichever comes first. If heading for the out-of-town hotspots, be sure to save some cash for the cab fare home. Updated: Jun 21, 2011.

Masai Mara Safari Discoteca-Bar

Ask locals what the most happening dance spot is in San Gil, many will tell you Masai Mara. Yeah, everyone seems to try to get there (if they can find a sitter for the kids). Join the crowd at this large club and chill with a beer ($1.60) or something stronger while grooving to the throbbing beats of meringue, salsa, vallenato and reggaetón. Open only on Fridays and Saturdays, beginning at 8 p.m., but the scene doesn't start to get hot until after 11 p.m. and can go on until dawn's first light. Vía a Bella Isla. Tel: 724-0296. Updated: Mar 15, 2011.

BARICHARA

 1,336m   10,000   7

Barichara is the getaway of choice for better-heeled Colombian vacationers seeking to escape metropolitan hassles. This village perches on a plateau overlooking the Río Suárez, 20 kilometers (14 mi) from San Gil, 118 kilometers (80 mi) from Bucaramanga and 307 kilometers (200 mi) from Bogotá. Its well-preserved colonial architecture, made of rammed earth, earns Barichara a place on the national register of historical sites.

Traditionally, this is a village of stone carvers, but in recent years artists of other media have come, inspired by its tranquility and beauty. Whereas neighboring San Gil is for the adventure sports enthusiast, Barichara is for the cultural tourist. Due to the immemorial buildings, the Parque para las Artes, the stone workshops and work of Colombia's premier painters, you can pass days here soaking in Barichara's bohemian atmosphere. Its inhabitants are called *patiamarillas*, for the golden-rust colored soil of their land. Updated: Sep 28, 2011.

History

Bahia-chala (meaning "at the heights of a resting stop") was inhabited by the indigenous Guane people. The Spanish city, Barichara, was founded by Capitán Francisco Pradilla y Ayerbe in 1714. An image of the Immaculate Conception was seen on a rock in 1702. A chapel built to protect it became the nucleus of the new town. In the 18th century, the Guane were rounded up from the region and relocated to Guane village, near Barichara. A dependent of San Gil until 1800, Patiamarillos petitioned for independence; nonetheless, this was not granted until 1821. In 1975, Barichara was

EASTERN COLOMBIA

proclaimed the most beautiful village in Colombia and in 1978, declared a national monument. Updated: Sep 28, 2011.

Getting To and Away

Although a poor road winds from Socorro to Barichara, the better route is from San Gil. This road is paved the entire way. For good views, sit on the driver's side. Buses travel between San Gil and Barichara every half hour daily, from 5:15 a.m. to 6:30 p.m. (40 min, $1.75). Direct busetas leave from Bucaramanga during the week. Updated: Sep 30, 2011.

When to Go

Barichara enjoys a delightfully warm, dry climate year round with average temperatures of 22°C (72°F). It is a trendy getaway destination for Colombians and you'll encounter more crowds at holiday times. On an ordinary week, you'll find Baricahara to be almost sleepy. Many artisan shops and studios are closed, as are local branches of tour operators, and clubs and cafés. Updated: Sep 28, 2011.

HOLIDAYS AND FESTIVALS

A hamlet as ancient as Barichara naturally has a number of festivals. Some are religious and many celebrate the arts for which this town is renowned. The Festival de la Talla en Piedra, or the Stone Carvers Festival, takes place on odd-numbered years.

Semana Santa (Easter Week) is celebrated in Barichara with religious processions. The only summer festival, San Lorenzo Mártir (in honor of the patron saint of Barichara), takes place on August 10. On the last Sunday in January is the Patrimonio Cultural Patiamarillo, which has a focus on stonecarvers, and February 11 marks Virgen de la Piedra, a tribute to the patron saint of carvers. In October, the town comes alive with cultural festivals of solidarity and return for the Fiestas Culturales de la Solidaridad y el Retorno.

At the end of November/beginning of December, Olimpiados Campesinos (the country folks' Olympic Games) occur. December is jam-packed with events:

December 8—Inmaculada Concepción, the other patron saint of the village

December 16-24—Aguinaldo Patiamarillo, the Christmas novena celebrated in Patiamarillo style, with music, theater, poetry and art

December 28—Día de los Angelitos Pichones, akin to April Fool's Day

December 31—Quemado del Viejo, the burning of effigies representing the Old Year. Updated: Sep 30, 2011.

Safety

Barichara has no untoward problems with personal safety, or so swear the locals. No paramilitary or guerrilla presence is reported. It is still important to practice safe travel habits while in Barichara. Updated: Jun 21, 2011.

Services

TOURISM

Barichara's tourism office, **Oficina de Cultura, Turismo y Deportes**, is located on the second floor of the alcaldía building on the main square (Monday-Friday 7 a.m.-noon and 2-6 p.m. Ca. 5, 6-39. Tel: 726-7052/7122/7566, URL: www.barichara-santander.gov.co). It is very helpful and provides excellent bilingual maps of that town and of Guane. On weekends, a tourism information booth is set up across the street at the base of the flagpoles.

MONEY

On the church side of the plaza is an **ATH/Megared ATM**, accepting all cards (except American Express). If you are relying on traveler's checks, your nearest provider for this service is in Bucaramanga or Tunja. There are no official exchange houses.

KEEPING IN TOUCH

The main **Telecom** office, providing local, national and international calls, is a half-block from the Templo de la Inmaculada Concepción (Monday-Saturday 7 a.m.-10 p.m., Sunday and holidays 7 a.m.-9 p.m. Cra. 7, 4-73). **Telecom's Internet service** is three blocks away, near the Casa del Mercado (Monday-Saturday 9 a.m.-9 p.m., Sunday 9 a.m.-2 p.m. Ca. 7, between Cra. 6 and 7). It charges about $1.05 per hour. The **post office** is also a half-block from the main plaza, at Carrera 6, 4-90 (Monday-Friday 8 a.m.-noon and 2-6 p.m.).

MEDICAL

Barichara's **Hospital Integrado San Juan de Dios** is at Carrera 2, 3-90, between Calles 3 and 4 (Tel: 726-7133/7400). Several pharmacies are found on or near the main square. Updated: Sep 30, 2011.

SHOPPING

El Almacencito de Margoth

Right on the plaza, in the Casa de la Cultura, Margarita (Margoth) Bermúdez has a shop. This space features not only her creations, but also those of other artisans of the village. Here you can purchase stone and wood carvings, boxes, fique fashion accessories, paintings and candies, for which this pueblo is renowned (the alfajores are simply divine). A special item Doña Margoth carries is ceramics by the only living Guane indigenous that follows traditional designs and techniques. Ca. 5, 6-29. Cel: 315-379-0217. Updated: May 22, 2009.

Añil, Tienda de Artes Plásticas !

Artists Carlos Santamaría and Yasmith Beltrán have joined up with their colleagues to showcase their pieces. Some are Barichara natives and others have come here to live and create. The 20 of them—about half of them women—decorate Añil's airy space with colorful canvasses and modern sculptures in both stone and wood. If you fall in love with their inspirations, but just can't carry something as bulky or as heavy as that, check the racks of hand-painted T-shirts: Each one is an original work of art and costs $19. Tuesday-Sunday 9 a.m-2:30 and 3-9 p.m. Ca. 6, 10-46. Cel: 311-470-1175/316-886-7394, E-mail: anilartesplasticas@gmail.com. Updated: Oct 05, 2011.

Los Tiestesitos !

Tiestesitos comes from *tiesto*, meaning plant or flowerpot. Indeed, the front patio porch and large interior anteroom of Los Tiestesitos is full of bittersweet orange-colored pottery. Shaped from the golden earth by Doña Alicia and her clan, these vessels come in all sizes and shapes, from the mundane to the exotic. And they're not just for potting, either: they have many purposes. To fill that planter you just bought, check out Los Tiestesitos' *vivero*, or greenhouse, for just the right flora. Cra. 5, 7-62, Tel: 726-7224. Updated: Jun 21, 2011.

Things to See and Do

The main attraction of Barichara is the ageless village itself. Most stone-carver workshops are on Carrera 5, near the entrance to the town. Rock isn't the only material worked here and made into extravagant pieces. There are also fique artisans, painters and cigar makers. To pick up a hand-rolled cigar, stop by Gordelia Tabacos for a free tour (weekends and holidays 9 a.m.-noon and 2-4 p.m. Cra. 5, 0-84, Tel: 726-7684, Cel: 311-531-4771, E-mail: gerencia@gordelia.com, URL: www.gordelia.com).

The Parque para las Artes is another must-do for the culturally minded visitor. To stretch your legs, hike up to the *mirador* overlooking the Río Suárez canyon, or hike to Salto de Mico, 30 minutes along the Barichara bluffs, before hitting the Camino Real to Guane. The Camino Real to Guane has an impressive palaeontological and archaeological museum. Updated: Jun 21, 2011.

Walking Tour of Colonial Barichara !

The real treasure of Barichara is its pristine colonial architecture. Many come to this town just to wander its flagstone lanes, snapping photos of the white-washed, red-tile roofed buildings. Start your exploration at the Templo de la Inmaculada Concepción y San Lorenzo on the main square. It is built of local stone, carved by the village's artisans. Walking west on Carrera 7 to the corner of Calle 3, you come to the Capilla de San Juan de Dios with a noteworthy cemetery. South three blocks on Calle 3 to Carrera 4, then left two blocks to Calle 5 brings you to Capilla de San Antonio, with a small shaded plaza. Another two blocks South, on Carrera 2, between Calles 5 and 6, is Casa Aquileo Parra. Once a home of a former Colombian president (1876-78), it's presently a museum. Returning northward along Calle 6, you will pass the plaza once more and arrive at Capilla Santa Bárbara, now used for cultural events. Updated: Jun 22, 2011.

Parque Para Las Artes

Uphill from the Capilla de Santa Bárbara is Parque para las Artes, a small park dedicated to the main art form Barichara is known for: stone sculpture. Founded after the second Festival Internacional de la Talla en Piedra, it features 27 statues carved by artists from 11 countries. Some are based on European or indigenous American mythology, others are abstract. Small brooks pass through the landscape around these modern sentinels which provide a staggering view over the Río Suárez canyon. Walk up Calle 6 to Capilla de Santa Bárbara, then turn left. About 300 meters (180 feet) on the right-hand side is the entry to the park. The parque is open daily from dawn to dusk. Also, just next door is a public swimming pool. Updated: Mar 22, 2011.

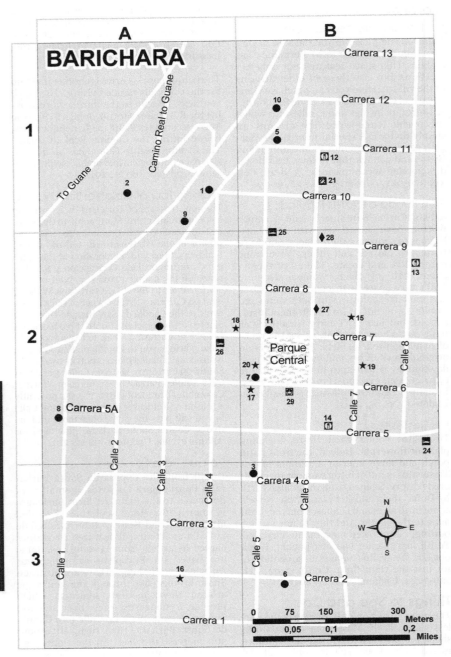

● Activities

1 Camino Real to Guane A1
2 Cañón del Río Suarez A1
3 Capilla de San Antonio B2
4 Capilla San Juan de Dios A2
5 Capilla Santa Barbará B2
6 Casa Aquileo Parra B3
7 Casa de la Cultura B2
8 Gordelia Tobacos A2
9 Mirador A1
10 Parque para las Artes A1
11 Templo Inmaculada B2

🕮 Eating

12 Restaurante Algarabiá B1
13 Restaurante Color de Hormiga B2
14 Restaurante Patiamarilla B2

★ Services

15 ATH/ Mega Red B2
16 Hospital Integrado San
   Juan de Dios A3
17 Post Office B2
18 Telecom A2
19 Telecom Internet B2
20 Tourism Office A2

⊞ Shopping

21 Añil Tienda de Artes Plásticas B1
22 El Almacenito de Margoth(See 7)
23 Los Tiestesitos (See 24)

⊟ Sleeping

24 Hospedaje Los Tiestesitos A2
25 Hostal Misión Santa Barbara B2
26 Hotel Corata A2

◆ Tours

27 Barichara Cultura y Aventura B2
28 Guanecito (Colombian
   Rafting Expeditions) B2

⊞ Transportation

29 Buses to San Gil and Guane B2

Camino Real to Guane

The Camino Real to Guane is part of the old Camino de Herradura that traversed the countryside from Girón, near Bucaramanga, to Barrancabermeja on the banks of the Río Magdalena. It was originally built by the Guane indigenous, and later used by the Spaniards. From Barichara to Guane pueblo is the most trodden stretch these days, having been rebuilt in 1864 by the German George von Lenguerke. The stone-paved trail gently slopes downhill nine kilometers (six miles), passing through a convulsing landscape, where the thick stone strata reveals the geologic history of this region, once part of a great sea some 60 million years ago. From the Parque para las Artes, walk down the path along the rim of the canyon. A sign on the right marks the beginning of the trail. It takes 1.5-2 hours to hike to Guane. The last bus back to Barichara is at 5:30 p.m. ($0.65, 15 minutes). Be sure to pace yourself, unless you want to spend the night in Guane at its simple inn. Updated: Mar 22, 2011.

Tours

Two tour operators exist in Barichara: **Guanecito (Colombia Rafting Expeditions)** (Cra. 9, 6-02. Cel: 311-202-4391/313-365-7755, URL: www.baricharaguanecito.com) and **Barichara Cultura y Aventura** (Ca. 6, 7-72 Cel: 310-809-9784). Both are branch offices of San Gil-based outfits. These offices are closed during the off-season. It may be better to book any activity through the main office. See the San Gil listings for contact information there. Updated: Oct 05, 2011.

Lodging

Most visitors to Barichara come only for the day. If you're looking for some true peace, then spend a night or two, and learn why so many Colombians escape to this pueblo caught in time. Although Barichara has a reputation for being expensive, it does offer a full range of lodging options, from simple hospedajes to luxury inns. Prices rise during the high season, but many families open their homes to the traveler for about $10 per night per person or so;

EASTERN COLOMBIA

for a list of providers, stop by the tourism office. Updated: Jul 21, 2010.

Hospedaje Los Tiestesitos

(ROOMS: $6-8) On the outside, Hospedaje Los Tiestesitos is a pottery workshop. But back behind a small courtyard, Doña Alicia has three rooms to let, all with the private, cold-water bath. Some have one bed, and others have two beds. The simply furnished rooms are snug and kept warm by the thick walls. These quarters have the earthen aroma of the *tapia pisada* (rammed-earth) construction of this house. This much-recommended hostel is probably the cheapest in Barichara. Cra. 5, 7-62. Updated: Jun 22, 2011.

Hotel Coratá

(ROOMS: $20-35) Just a block from Barichara's main plaza is an old casona that has found new life as a hotel. On its first floor, around a corridor porch, are nine spacious rooms for its guests to rest, all adequately furnished. These habitaciones come with TV and private, cold-water bathroom. Stairs lead from the porch to the casona's sunken interior patio, where you can also relax. In the morning, you can order typical Santandereano breakfast ($3.20) before heading out to check out more of what Barichara has to offer. Cra. 7, 4-08 Tel: 726-7110, Cel: 311-481-3195, Fax: 7-726-7071. Updated: Mar 22, 2011.

Hostal Misión Santa Bárbara

(ROOMS: $53-78) This former family mansion is now one of Barichara's most prestigious inns, without being pretentious. The older part of this large house is one story, with a grape-harbor-covered patio. The newer section is two-story, with a five-stroke swimming pool in which to cool down after hiking. Throughout the gardens, hammocks are strung beneath the foliage. The rooms are large, many with an alcove, a child's favorite sleeping space. The bathrooms are spotless and have hot water. To while away the evenings are a game room (complete with a ping pong table). The kids even have their own part of the grounds. Ca. 5, 9-08. In Bogotá: Calle 40A, 13-59. Tel: 726-7163/7373. In Bogotá: 1-288-4949/232-2846. In Bucaramanga: 635-1432, Fax: 726-7060, E-mail: reservas@hostalmisionsantabarbara.info, URL: www.hostalmisionsantabarbara.info. Updated: Mar 22, 2011.

Restaurants

Barichara has an impressive array of food, from classic Colombian cooking to down-home Spanish. Even nouveau cuisine based on *hormigas culonas*, a regional delicacy, makes the platter. During the week in the temporada baja, many restaurants have limited hours. At the corner of Carrera 6 and Calle 7 is the Casa del Mercado where you can pick up on fixings. Panadería Barichara bakes superb breads and desserts (Ca. 5, 5-33). Updated: Jun 22, 2011.

Restaurante Patiamarillo

(LUNCH: $2.50) Restaurante Patiamarillo is a clean, well-lit space, with clothed tables and wooden chairs awaiting its dining clientele. The white-washed walls are hung with a motley collection of *cuadros* (look for the portrait of a very young Clint Eastwood). A simple eating establishment, Patiamarillo serves down-home Colombian and Santandereano dishes, guaranteed to give you enough fuel for a day's worth of Barichara sightseeing and exploring. The comida corriente is a bargain in this town, costing only $2.50. Breakfasts are also prepared and available daily. Daily 7 a.m.-8 p.m. Cra. 5, 6-25. Cel: 314-283-4809/310-581-4722. Updated: Oct 05, 2011.

Restaurante Algarabia

(ENTREES: $4-15) With recipes learned from Yaya, the chef's grandmother, Restaurante Algarabia imparts traditional Spanish cooking to the Barichara tourist. From *tortilla española* ($4) to *paella* ($15), and every Iberian classic in between appears on the menu, including *jamón serrano, queso machego, pavo de castilla and calamares romana*. Additionally, there's wine and sangria to complement your repast, and desserts to put the final touch on the evening. Travelers rave about Algarabia's food; unfortunately, their reports on service are mixed. Open Thursday to Sunday noon-9 p.m.. Thursday-Sunday noon-9 p.m. Ca. 6, 10-96. Tel: 726-7414, Cel: 313-364-8726/388-3268, E-mail: franconmira@gmail.com. Updated: Mar 22, 2011.

Restaurante Color de Hormiga ♪

Color de Hormiga prides itself in serving *comida atípica*—that is precisely what you'll find here. Much of its menu is prepared with a regional delicacy: *hormigas culonas* (fat-bottomed ants). Try the beef tenderloin in ant sauce or, if you're not the adventurous sort, in a blue cheese sauce ($8.50). Color de Hormiga also presents beef shish kabob and a few chicken platters. To accompany your meal, choose a fresh fruit juice, beer or wine. Pull up a table on the covered patio after taking a dip in the pool, then dive into one of these unforgettable dishes. Restaurante Color de Hormiga allows you to be adventurous in a different way. Daily noon-4 p.m., longer hours at holiday times. Ca. 8, 8-44. Tel: 726-7156. Updated: Jun 22, 2011.

Nightlife

If you come to Barichara during the off-season, you may find it a bit boring in the evenings. The village has few nightclubs, most of which are cafés featuring live music, which are fun to relax in after a long day of seeing the sights. They are open only on weekends and holidays. Updated: Jun 22, 2011.

GUANE

 1,573m   170   7

Atop a narrow mesa above the Río Suárez, the Guane people in habited this area long before the Spaniards' arrival. It was here, Guane pueblo, where all the surviving Guane were relocated in the 17th century. This entire hamlet, from its fossils to its *tapia pisada* architecture, is a museum. On the main square is a statue of the last Guane *cacique*, Guananta. On the south side is an attractive stone church; on the east side of the plaza is the **Museo de Paleontología y Arqueología** (admission: $1.05 adults, $0.50 children), containing over 10,000 fossils of fish, ammonites, shells and petrified wood, as well as an indigenous mummy, ceramics and religious art (some from the Quito School). Be sure to pace yourself, unless you want to spend the night in Guane. There is basic lodging. The village produces many products from goat's milk. Try the sabajón, a delicious, slightly alcoholic drink in various flavors.

Guane's feast days are Virgen de la Candelaria (Feb 2), San Isidro Labrador (Sep) and Santa Lucia (Dec 13).

In the Guane region there are a number of petroglyphs and cave paintings: Piedra de Lubigara and Cueva del Pino (near Guane); Hato Viejo (Villanueva); La Custodia, Los Pozos and Cueva de Cartagena (Mesa de los Santos); Cueva Rica (Mogotes), and others, all along the Río Chicamocha. Updated: May 15, 2009.

Getting To and Away

Buses leave from Barichara's main square at 6 a.m., 11:30 a.m., 5 p.m. Likewide, buses leave Guane for Barichara at 6:30 a.m., 11:45 a.m. and 5:30 p.m. ($0.65, 15 min). Also, you can walk the Camino Real. Updated: Mar 22, 2011.

CURITÍ

 1,491m   3,417 7

Curití is a typical Santandereano village of narrow streets lined with white-washed homes. Its residents are famous for their artesanía in fique, or agave sisal. This hamlet offers more to the casual visitor than just shopping. Here you can scrabble underground in Cueva de la Vaca and Cueva del Yeso, or go horseback riding. Near Curití are the crystalline swimming holes Balneario Pescaditos, where you can camp for free (said to be safe) and rappel the cliffs. Updated: May 20, 2008.

Getting To and Away

Curití is seven kilometers (4.2 mi) north of San Gil, off the main highway to Bucaramanga. Take a bus from the terminal at Carrera 11 and 15 ($0.80). Updated: May 06, 2008.

PARQUE NACIONAL DEL CHICAMOCHA (PANACHI)

(ADMISSION: $6 adults, $3 children) Founded in 2006, Parque Nacional del Chicamocha protects part of the rim of the Río Chicamocha's canyon. Located about 50 km (31 mi) outside of Bucaramanga, this national park has much to offer its visitors. The culture connoisseur can enjoy the Museo Guane, Plaza de los Costumbres and the Salón de Exposiciones. The adrenaline junkie can paraglide or zip down the *cable-vuelo* (zipline). For the whole family, there are walking trails, lookouts over the gorge, buggy cars and an ostrich farm. The park is served by a 6.3 km (4 mi) length cable car system ($5 each way). It is one of the longest systems of its type in the world. The system goes across the canyon from the station "Mesa de los Santos" to Panachi. It has three stations. The first station is located inside the park, the middle station is next to the river and the last station is in the "Vereda el Tabacal". The buggies, cable-vuelo and ostrich farm are extra. Updated: Feb 22, 2011.

BUCARAMANGA

 960m   550,000   7

Continuing north on the main highway to the coast is Bucaramanga, 273 kilometers (164 mi) from Tunja. The paved road is in good condition, with four toll booths and several military checkpoints. It is a major transportation hub between the nation's capital and the coast or the Colombo-Venezuelan border at Cúcuta. Built in a much-eroded landscape, Bucaramanga's hills are like crushed paper bags. This capital of Santander department is one of Colombia's largest cities, and is home to 10 universities.

Bucaramanga's appellation is *La Ciudad de Parques*, or "City of Parks." Unfortunately, the ones in the center are in poor repair. Only upon entering the residential areas do you find the better-kept green spaces. Parque García Rovira was the heart of colonial Bucaramanga, whereas Parque Santander is the modern-day center. Several former villages have become bedroom communities of Bucaramanga. Floridablanca, Girón and Piedecuesta are home to museums, botanical gardens and zoological parks that make for great escapes from the city. Bucaramanga is an alternative base for rafting and paragliding adventures on the Río Chicamocha or to visit the Parque Nacional Chicamocha. Logistically, San Gil is still a better spot from which to do these activities. Updated June 22, 2011.

History

Real Minas de Bucaramanga (royal mines of Bucaramanga), was founded on June 3, 1539, by Martín Galeano, some 83 years before the village of the same name was founded by Capitán Andrés Páez de Sotomayor and Father Miguel Trujillo. Ultimately these mines along the Río de Oro ceased. Spanish descendents and mestizos replaced the largely indigenous population and the residents turned to agriculture. In 1857 Bucaramanga became the capital of Santander department; four years later it lost this position to Socorro but regained it in 1896. The 1000-Day War at the end of the 19th century caused economic duress for Bucaramanga, from which it did not recuperate until a century later. The decisive battle of this civil war was fought at Palonegro near the city. Updated: Apr 09, 2008.

When to Go

Ask bucaramanguenses (or búcaros, after their soccer team) when it is best to visit their city and the responses are mixed. Some say the rains come between March and May, while others say September. No one seems to have a definitive answer, but they all agree that almost any month is a fine time to visit. Updated: Apr 09, 2008.

HOLIDAY AND FESTIVALS

Besides celebrating national holidays, Bucaramanga plays host to festivities of its own. These festivals are worth it you find yourself in Bucaramanga when they are occurring:

Día de la Santandereanidad (a celebration of the Santander identity) in April, **Festival Internacional de Piano** (the International Piano Festival) the last week of August, **Feria Bonita** (a celebration and display of cattle, artisan crafts and other commercial wares) in October, **Festival Iberoamericano de Cuenteros** (Ibero-American Storytellers Festival) in October-November and **the Festival de Música Andina Colombiana** (Andean Colombian Music Festival) in the second half of November.

NEIGHBORING TOWNS' FIESTAS:

June: Feria Ganadera—Cattle Fair in Piedecuesta in the first half of the month.

August: Reinado Departamental del Turismo—In Girón the second half of the month.

October: Fiestas del Señor de los Milagros—Processions and celebrations in Girón during the first half of the month.

November: Festival de Cultura, Aire y Dulce-Cultural festival in Floridablanca the second week of November. Updated: Jun 11, 2011.

Getting To and Away

The modern bus terminal is southwest of downtown, on the Girón road. The station is divided into four modules and has several ATMs (outside Module 3), restaurants, phones, elevator, information booth (outside Module 3) and even billiards to pass the time.

Bus companies include: Cotramagdalena, Cotrasangil, Extrarápidos Los Motilones, Copetrán, Omega, Cotaxi, Cotranal, Cooptimotilon, Bolivariano, Cootrasaravita, Transander, Concorde, Costa, Cotrans, Crasilia and Berlinas. Cotrans, Cootrasaravita and Cotranal have offices conveniently located near the center of the city.

The bus system in Bucaramanga is pretty easy to manage and navigate. There are bus routes to many different areas in and around Bucaramanga.

From Bucaramanga

To:	Departures	Time	Price
Barran-cabermeja	Every half hour	2 hr	$8
El Banco		6 hr	$24.20
Pamplo-na/Cúcuta	Every half hour	4/6 hr	$12.10 /18.10
Málaga/ Capitanejo	4:30 a.m., noon	7/8 hr	$17/ $18
San Gil	Every half hour	2 hr	$8
Bogotá	6:30 a.m., 8:30 a.m.-11:30 p.m. every half hour	9 hr	$34
Medellín	8 a.m., 9 a.m., five after-noon/ night buses	9 hr	$37
Cali/Ipi-ales		15 hr/26 hr	$51 /$64
Valledupar	6 a.m., 9 a.m., 11 a.m., six afternoon /night buses	10 hr	$37
Santa Marta	Evening buses	9 hr	$40
Barran-quilla/ Cartagena	9:30 p.m.-12:30 p.m.	9 hr/12 hr	$43/ $49

Bucaramanga's **Aeropuerto Palonegro**, west of Girón, has direct flights to Cúcuta, Me-dellín and Bogotá. Parque Santander Taxi Aero-puerto leaves from a kiosk on Calle 35 (daily 4 a.m.-6 p.m. Tel: 642-5250, Cel: 310-273-2552). Reserve at least two hours before; shared $3.20, solo $5.30). Public busetas ($0.85) toward the airport leave you quite a distance away, but re-portedly taxis shuttle the last leg. Avianca, Sat-ena and Copa have offices on Calle 36, between Carreras 13 and 19. Updated: Jun 22, 2011.

Getting Around

Bucaramanga has good public transporta-tion that runs not only throughout the city, but also connects to the neighboring towns of Floridablanca, Girón and Piedecuesta. In the center, most buses pass Parque de Santos (Cra. 2 and Ca. 31). In-city taxis are metered. Be aware that taxis outside of the city are not metered and be sure to negotiate the rate be-fore agreeing to a ride. Metrolínea, is a mass transit system like Bogotá's Transmilenio. If traveling with your own vehicle, be aware of no-drive days that correspond to your plate's last digit. Updated: Jun 22, 2011.

Safety

Bucaramanga is one of Colombia's five most dangerous cities. Always be street-savvy and be sure to take a taxi after dark. The area just north of Parque Santander, between Calles 33 and 30, Carreras 15 and 21, is one where you should take particular care especially at night. Immediately outside of this area are some of the city's best hotels. Calle 35 is both a market street and where most of the banks are. Take care. Most central city parks have 24-hour Poli-cia Nacional kiosks. Updated: Jun 22, 2011.

Services

TOURISM

Bucaramanga's tourism office, **Instituto Municipal de Cultura y Turismo de Bu-caramanga**, is in Parque de los Niños (Ca. 30, 26-117. Tel: 634-1132/2070, URL: www.imct.gov.co). The Parque Santander Policia Nacional kiosk gives only general informa-tion on sites. The **Cámara de Comercio** has free, hard-to-read maps (Monday-Friday 8 a.m.-noon and 1-5 p.m. Cra. 19. 36-20). This website also can orientate you on Bucara-manga and Santander Department: http://santandertierradeaventura.weebly.com.

Other useful addresses include:
DAS (Monday-Friday, 8 a.m.-noon, 1-4:30 p.m. Cra. 11, 41-13. Tel: 630-2050), **Na-tional Park Office** (Av. Quebrada Seca 30-44, 1st floor. Tel: 645-4868/634-5251),

The Thousand Days' War

Between 1899 and 1902, Colombia was wracked by a long and brutal civil war. Known as the 1000 Days War (a more or less accurate reflection of its length), it left 100,000 Colombians dead and had ramifications for decades.

LIBERALS VS. CONSERVATIVES

At the heart of the conflict were the differences between Colombia's liberals and conservatives. The conservatives favored limited voting rights, close ties between the church and state, and a strong central government. The liberals, on the other hand, favored universal suffrage, weak central government (or strong provincial governments), and no link between the church and the state. These may seem like minor issues, but in 1899, Colombians were willing to die for them.

WAR BREAKS OUT

In 1898, conservative Manuel Antonio Sanclemente became president of Colombia. The liberals were infuriated because they believed that major election fraud had gotten him elected. Liberal generals revolted in Santander Province in late 1899 and shortly scored a major victory at the battle of Peralonso.

CONSERVATIVE VICTORY

The liberals' victory was short-lived. They were vastly outnumbered by the conservative forces, even when they received aid from neighboring Venezuela. In May of 1900, they lost the pivotal battle of Palonegro and before long were on the run across the country. Switching to guerrilla tactics bought the liberals some time, but the end was near. The liberals surrendered in late 1902.

NO WINNERS

The war did nothing to diminish the tension between the two ideologically opposed sides, and the violence would flare up again in the 1940s. Thousands were left dead, the country was destroyed, and to add insult to injury, the United States used the chaos as a cover to make off with the department of Panama.

Instituto Geográfico Agustín Codazzi (Ca. 36, 22-16, 2nd floor. Tel: 763-4257, URL: www.igac.gov.co) and **Venezue**

Ian Consulate (Ca. 37, 52-75. Tel: 643-6621/8942, Fax: 643-6389). France, Italy, Belgium and Spain all have honorary consulates here. Check the end of the telephone directory's white pages for contact information. Updated: Sep 29, 2011.

MONEY

Downtown the major banks are along the pedestrian street Calle 35. Most have usual banking hours, Monday-Friday, 8-11:30 a.m. and 2-4:30 p.m. For traveler's check exchanges, go to Bancolombia or Santander. All have 24-hour ATMs that accept Visa, Plus, MasterCard and Cirrus; Bancolombia also takes American Express: **Bancolombia** (Cra. 18, 35-02), Santander (Ca. 35, 17-87), **Banco de Bogotá** (Ca. 35 and Cra. 17) and **AV Villas** (Ca. 35, 17-45).

In the Centro Comercial Rosedal (Monday-Friday 8 a.m.-noon and 2-6 p.m., Saturday 8 a.m.-

noon. Ca. 35, 18-65, local 121. Tel: 630-3614), there are several casas de cambio. **Cambios Internacionales Euro-Dolar** changes cash U.S. dollars, Pound Sterling, Euros and Bolívares. Money wires may be received through: **Western Union/Giros y Finanzas** (Centro Comercial Cañaveral, local 01, Cra. 25, 29-57, Floridablanca) or **Money-Gram/Cambiamos** (Centro Comercial Cabacera, Etapa 4, local 104, Cra. 35a, 49-07. Tel: 643-8826). Updated: Sep 29, 2011.

KEEPING IN TOUCH

The main **Telecom** branch has local, national and international call service, and private-booth Internet (Ca. 36, 17-75). Shops offer local and national services. Several **Comcel** agents around Parque de Santos (Ca. 33 and Cra. 22) have inexpensive international calls. Most Internet cafés cost $0.80 per hour, including **Barichar@On-Line**, which also has Skype (Cra. 20, 33-34, Tel: 652-0982). To send letters and packages go to the **post office** (Monday-Friday 7:30 a.m.-

noon and 2-6 p.m., Saturday 8 a.m.-noon. Cra. 16, 37-106). Updated: Sep 29, 2011.

MEDICAL

As to be expected in a city the size of Bucaramanga, there are a number of public and private medical facilities. The main one is **Hospital Universitario de Santander**, a.k.a. Hospital Ramón González Valencia (Cra. 33, 28-126. Tel: 634-6110). Pharmacies are common throughout the metropolitan area. Updated: Sep 29, 2011.

CAMERA

A number of camera shops are found on Calle 36, between Parque Santander and Parque García Rovira. All offer film processing; various types of print film and digital camera cards and camera accessories. **Fotografía Colombia** (Ca. 36, 17-31) can put you in touch with someone who does repairs. Updated: Sep 29, 2011.

RELIGION

Bucaramanga is a religiously diverse city. The Hare Krishnas have a strong presence here, with a restaurant and a retreat center. Bahai'is have a home here also (Ca. 35, 21-47. Tel: 645-3203). Purportedly there is a mosque serving Bucaramanga's significant Muslim community. Updated: Sep 29, 2011.

SHOPPING

María

While out in Girón on a daytrip, you may want to take back a reminder of your visit. If you do, you should look up María Pinto. With hands scarred from the resilient material she works with, she'll show you the hats, belts, bags, shoes and sandals she crafts from fique, a palm fiber. All of the items are her own original, innovative designs. Call first before arriving at her workshop, in case you don't find her stall set up on Girón's main square. Ca. 19, 25-95, Portal Campestre, I Etapa, Girón. Tel: 659-3082, Cel: 311-895-2116, E-mail: artesantandermaria@hotmail.com. Updated: Jun 22, 2011.

Acampemos

Before heading up to Parque Nacional El Cocuy, you might want to stop by Acampemos to pick up camping gear and supplies. Not only does it have packs, tents, sleeping bags and pads and rain-proof clothing at wholesale prices, it manufactures it. If you don't see what you need, Acampemos can make it for you. Also on-hand are climbing ropes and clamps. It is also one of the few

places left in Colombia where you can purchase white gas. Ca. 48, 24-57. Tel: 647-4194, Cel: 300-556-5645. Updated: Apr 14, 2008.

Shopping Malls

Need a dose of U.S. culture (or a reminder of why you might have left in the first place)? Hop on a bus towards the burbs. Straddling either side of the highway are *centros comerciales* (shopping malls), all conveniently connected by pedestrian overpass bridges. Spend hours in these air conditioned, glittering palaces of consumerism, window shopping and munching down on food from the food courts. You'll see some familiar "faces" in these places. There are even movie theaters showing the latest Hollywood blockbusters (or duds); Cañaveral has a Muiltplex cinema and La Florida has a Cinemark theater. If you need more pocket money, Cañaveral has banks branches and ATMs. To get there, catch a buseta that says Cañaveral or Autopista ($0.55) from Parque de Santos (Calle 22). Autopista a Floridablanca. Updated: Mar 22, 2011.

Plaza Central

Now that you have had your taste of U.S. culture, it's time to have a real Colombian shopping experience. Head to Plaza Central, Bucaramanga's municipal market, said to be the largest in Colombia. Enter at Calle 34 and grab a shopping cart to begin exploring this crazy world of Colombia's answer to the mall. These four floors are the best of Colombia's products and produce. The first story is where to pick up vegetables and get your watch repaired. Up the ramp to the second level are fruits, juice bars, bakeries, spices and eggs. Third floor is the cheese and meat department. Lastly, the fourth level is where you'll find hats, drinking gourds, hammocks, basketry and other artesanía for your trip or for gifts. Also, you can find colored candles, incenses, soaps or essential oils for your spiritual needs. Refuel at the food court (including a vegetarian restaurant), complete with a great view over the crags surrounding the city. Cra. 16, between Ca. 33 and 34. Updated: Jun 16, 2011.

Things to See and Do

Bucaramanga presents visitors various escapes from the eroded metropolis. Of course, the city has many parks—city, recreational, botanical and zoological—as well as a surprising colonial nugget. The museums cover a range of topics, from the historical Casa de Bolívar and the archaeological Pierda del Sol, to the Museo de Arte Moderno and the Universidad Industrial de Santander's Natural

EASTERN COLOMBIA

History. Neighboring Floridablanca, Piedecuesta and Girón are charming villages and host to some of Bucaramanga's attractions. Updated: May 22, 2009.

The Churches of Bucaramanga

Only a few of Bucaramanga's churches are open outside of mass hours, which are listed in the telephone directory. Some of the city's more interesting Catholic churches are:

Catedral de la Sagrada Familia—Ca. 36, 19-56, Parque Santander.

Capilla de los Dolores—The oldest sanctuary in Bucaramanga. Ca. 35 and Cra. 10, corner of Parque García Rovira.

Iglesia de San Laureano—Cra. 12, 36-08, Parque García Rovira.

Iglesia de San Pío X- Cra. 22, 17-49. Templo Gótico de San Francisco: Cra. 22, 17-49.

Iglesia del Sagrado Corazón de Jesús-Ca. 45, 27A-55. Updated: Mar 23, 2011.

Museo de Arte Moderno de Bucaramanga

The Museo de Arte Moderno de Bucaramanga, or MAMB, is in a Republican-styled house built in the 1940s. Three rooms, one devoted to sculpture by contemporary creators, await your perusal. The museum specializes in itinerant exhibits of mostly national artists, changed every two months. It currently has no permanent collection, but future plans are to extend the building in order to display its growing compilation of impressive works. Stop by and see what is showing this month at the Museum of Modern Art. Be sure to always check out the schedule of exhibits, but remember that at times the museum may be closed in preparation for the next exhibit. Monday-Saturday 8 a.m.-2 p.m. Closed Sundays. Ca. 37, 26-16. Tel: 645-0483, Fax: 645-0483, E-mail: mambucaramanga@yahoo.es, URL: museodeartemodernodebucaramanga.blogspot.com.Updated: Mar 23, 2011.

Cultural Centers of Bucaramanga

Besides attractions like its churches, parks, la Casa de Bolívar and Museo de Arte Moderno, this city has several other foci of culture:

Casa de la Cultura (Ca. 37, 12-46. Tel: 630-2046) has special exhibits and events.

Casa Mexicana's mission is bringing Mexican art, literature and cinema to Colombia (Tuesday-Saturday 10 a.m.-noon and 4-7 p.m. Cra. 28, 49-40. Tel: 647-4869, URL: www.casamexicana.blogspot.com).

Casa Luis Perú de la Croix is home of the 19th-century writer, and will soon become a library (Ca. 37, 11-18).

Banco de la República has free exhibits and concerts (Cra. 19, 34-93. Tel: 630-3174/630-3133, ext. 221, E-mail: sbucaramanga@banrep.gov.co, URL: www.lablaa.org). Updated: Mar 10, 2011.

Casa de Bolívar

This wasn't quite exactly the Liberator's home, but Simón Bolívar did stay here for some 70 days in 1828. In the principal sala are exhibited the belongings he left behind as well as the *mantilla* and comb of a woman who had danced with him. Casa de Bolívar is mainly the home of the History Academy of Santander, displaying other interesting things of the Department's history. Among them is an excellent collection of indigenous Guane textiles. On the back patio are explanations and artifacts of the Battle of Palonegro, the last and bloodiest battle of the 1000-Day War. Monday-Saturday noon-6 p.m. Closed Sundays. Ca. 37, 12-15. Updated: Mar 23, 2011.

The Parks of Bucaramanga

Bucaramanguenses are proud to live in the "Ciudad de Parques," a well-deserved nickname for this city of almost two dozen parks. Parque Santander is the modern downtown parque. Down the bustling streets you'll find Plaza Cívica Luis Carlos Galán, around which are governmental buildings, and Parque García Rovira, the hub of the colonial town; here stands the oldest church of this metropolis. Heading towards Floridablanca is Parque Los Lagos, a popular recreational area. Floridablanca has the Jardín Botánico Eloy Valenzuela. Piedecuesta is home to the zoo. On the northeast edge of Bucaramanga, on the road to Cúcuta, is Parque Morrorico, which has pleasant views. Updated: Sep 29, 2011.

Paragliding !

Well, you can't quite get fitted with a permanent set of wings in Bucaramanga, but nearby Mesa de Ruitoque offers you the next best thing. These heights are considered to be the best place to practice paragliding. Soaring over river valleys and ancient stone roads, you will see Colombia from a vantage point few will ever witness. You needn't worry about being experienced, as agencies offer tandem flights. You will take wing with the pilot riding piggyback. So strap the sail on and take off to see the countryside unfold and flow beneath you. Updated: Mar 23, 2011.

Note: Make sure the tour operator has proper equipment and certification. The great majority of them speak only Spanish. In recent years some accidents have occurred that have led to permanent injury or death.

Tours

Tour operators in Bucaramanga are few and far between; most businesses catering to journeyers are either travel agencies or airline offices. For most adventure sports, such as rafting, go to San Gil. A few specializing in paragliding are located at Mesa de Ruitoque, the premier place in Colombia to do paragliding. Few speak English or a language other than Spanish. One certified parapente instructor is Richi Mantilla Gómez of **Colombia Paragliding** (Cel: 312-432-6266, E-mail: richifly@colombianparagliding.com, URL: www.colombiaparagliding.com). Updated: Mar 18, 2011.

Lodging

Bucaramanga has the full price range of lodging options, from extremely cheap (yet decent) hotels to fine business class hotels. The cheapest options are located right downtown, mainly around Calle 31 and Carrera 20. Be forewarned, however, that some Bucaramanga hostels double as brothels. To be able to recognize those hotels not full of hookers, look for signs that say *ambiente familiar*, or family atmosphere (meaning the place is decent enough for the whole family to stay there). More up-scale hotels are between the Zona Rosa and Cabecera areas of the city. Updated: Jul 22, 2010.

BUDGET

Residencias Las Tres Margaritas
(ROOMS: $7.50-12.50) A family-atmosphere hotel in the city's center that promises three important basics: safety, cleanliness and cheap prices. Las Tres Margaritas is a fairly new, four-story building with amply sized rooms that are clean with private, cold-water baths and cable television. Some of the rooms have balconies overlooking the main street. All is kept clean. The family ensures its guests will have a peaceful stay without incidents while at their inn. With such service, Las Tres Mar-

garitas is often full. Ca. 31, 20-40. Tel: 630-0029, Cel: 316-868-8498, Fax: 630-0029.. Updated: Mar 23, 2011.

Hotel Amparo
(ROOMS: $8-15) A friendly, family-run inn, Hotel Amparo provides its guests with no-frills rooms with or without TV. All have private, cold-water baths and fan to keep you cool in the hot Bucaramanga climate. The beds are okay. The rooms are cleaned daily. In the main lobby of this two-story hotel is a television, and on the front patio there is a restaurant offering inexpensive breakfasts and comida corrientes. If you arrive by motorbike, there's parking inside. This is definitely one of the cheapest hostels with the *ambiente familiar*, guaranteeing you a safe, uneventful stay. Ca. 31, 20-29. Tel: 630-4098, E-mail: hotelamparo@hotamal.com. Updated: Mar 23, 2011.

Kasa Guane Bucaramanga !
(BEDS: $11, ROOMS: $20-28) Kasa Guane Bucaramanga (KGB), a three-story hostel, is the perfect place to meet other travelers. Richi, an enthusiastic traveler himself, offers two private rooms and three dorms. KGB has an equipped kitchen, book exchange, free WiFi, lockers and two spacious terraces with hammocks. The helpful staff arranges tours and activities, from coffee farm tours to waterfall hikes, and on-site Spanish classes and dance lessons. Richi is also a qualified paragliding instructor and has his own paragliding school just 15 minutes from the city. Ca. 49, 28-21. Tel: 657-6960, Cel: 312-432-6266, E-mail: info@kasaguane.com, URL: www.kasaguane.com. Updated: Jul 08, 2011.

MID-RANGE

Finca Raval Jardín Ecológico !
(ROOMS: $15-20) Pamper your physical and spiritual selves at Finca Raval Jardín Ecológico, a Hare Krishna-run spa located 25 kilometers (15 mi) from Bucaramanga. Besides providing simple lodging and vegetarian food, it has a natural swimming pool, volleyball court and hammocks. The price also includes classes on meditation, spirituality, nutrition and yoga. For an extra charge, go for the Finnish-styled sauna or a massage. You may also come for the day to enjoy the facilities. A room with three meals is $20 per person; it is $16 for children six-10 years old, and kids under six stay for free. You can also camp for $17.60 per person, or $14.70 per person if you bring your own tent. Camping also includes three meals. Special packages are available. A sauna with herbs is $16, a relaxation massage is $8 and a total massage is $16. The

EASTERN COLOMBIA

finca is in Raval, about nine kilometers (5.4 mi) from Piedecuesta. From Bucaramanga, board a Trans-Piedecuesta buseta. From that village's market, catch a "Ruta a Curos" bus and alight at Restaurante Caracolí. Ask directions, then, for the Hare Krishna finca. Tel: 680-2045/2075, Cell: 312-351-0209, E-mail: govindap@intercable.net.co. Updated: May 20, 2008.

Hotel Balmoral

(ROOMS: $15-22.50) Conveniently located in the center of the city, Hotel Balmoral is a midrange option for your visit to Bucaramanga. The hostel is a bit worn, but clean. It offers four floors of accommodation, all with windows and some with balconies. The large rooms come equipped with firm beds, air conditioning, cable TV, closet, mini-bar (extra charge) and private bath with hot showers. Hotel Balmoral is the inn of choice for Colombian families and budget businesspersons. Cra. 21, 34-75. Tel: 630-4136/3723, Fax: 630-4663, E-mail: hotelbalmoral@hotmail.com. Updated: Mar 23, 2011.

Hospedaje D'Kpri

(ROOMS: $17.50-25) Hospedaje D'Kpri is essentially a boarding house for university students. However, some rooms are rented out to travelers. The small quarters have all furniture built-in, from the platform bed to the night table. The attached bath is clean and has hot water. If you are planning to stay a while in the city, ask about the special monthly rates. The D'Kpri is located between the Zona Rosa and Cabecera districts of Bucaramanga, not too far from the night clubs. Monthly rates are $150. Ca. 34, 30-47. Tel: 645-2550, Cel: 320-682-9870. Updated: Mar 23, 2011.

HIGH-END

Hotel Chicamocha

(ROOM: $82-125) One of Bucaramanga's finest hostels is Hotel Chicamocha. Providing the best in services to up-scale and corporate business travelers, Hotel Chicamocha provides luxuries few other inns do. Courtesy of the house are a welcoming cocktail, breakfast buffet, a pillow menu (yes, you read correctly), medical assistance, swimming pool, sauna, Turkish bath and gym. Also on-site are event rooms, Internet café, a beauty salon, masseuses, restaurant, bars and a travel agent. Oh, of course the spacious, well-appointed rooms have air conditioning and private bath with hot water. Ca. 34, 31-24. Tel: 634-3000/01-8000-511-723 (national toll-free), Fax: 635-1808, E-mail: reservas.mcch@solarhoteles.com, URL: www.hotelchicamocha.com. Updated: Jan 27, 2010.

Restaurants

Bucaramanga has some mighty fine eats at good prices. A comida corriente, the set-menu, costs $1.60-2.65 at most establishments. Even a premium meal won't cost you an arm and a leg; a repast with wine will set you back about $10. The variety of foods reflects the internationally diverse population of this city. For those staying downtown and eating meals in, an Éxito Vecino is at the corner of Calle 36 and Carrera 16. Also be sure to embark on the adventure through Plaza Central—Bucaramanga's market is reputed to be the largest in Colombia. Updated: Mar 11, 2011.

Govindas

Govindas is an Indian vegetarian delight, courtesy of the Hare Krishnas. For a healthy, flavorful lunch, pull up a table in one of the three rooms and relax to ragas softly playing. Soon your three-course almuerzo will be served: soup and multi-grain bread, the main course with drink, then an herbal tea and dessert ($2.50). During non-midday hours, there's veggie fast food. Adjoining shops sell incense, literature and other items. The bakery has soy cheese, meat, milk and yogurt, as well as natural grain breads, granola and flours. You're sure to leave with your stomach chanting the names of the Lord. Monday-Saturday 7:30 a.m.-6:30 p.m. Cra. 20 34-65. Tel: 680-2045/630-4154, Cel: 312-351-0209, E-mail: academia.bmg@gmail.com/bucaramangagovindas@hotmail.com. Updated: Mar 23, 2011.

La Cocina de la Abuela!

If you're craving some of grandma's cooking hot off the stove, even if it's the middle of the night, then head over to her kitchen. La Cocina de la Abuela prepares Colombian culinary classics, like *carne oreada* (dried beef cooked in beer) and *cabro con pipitoria* (goat with a side of rice prepared with finely chopped goat viscera and blood). Lunchtime is busy—and for good reason. Grandma serves up huge portions in this four-course affair (appetizer, soup, entrée and dessert all for $2.65). Grandpa gets into the action too, firing up his grill a few doors down at La Parrilla del Abuelo. Open daily around the clock. Ca. 34, 32-23.Tel: 645-6083/6691, E-mail: lacocinadela.abuela@hotmail.com. Updated: May 15, 2009.

Repostería Berna

Swiss-owned Repostería Berna is a time-honored place to have a morning treat or afternoon tea. Select a table on one of the three stories (or on the second-floor balcony facing the pedestrian street), and try to decide which of the tasty sweets you'll try this day. Will it be petits-fours, cakes or cookies ($0.45-$1.45)? Perhaps ice cream - whether solo or as a sundae, or a banana split ($1-2.25). To complement your treat, choose coffee, tea, juice or soda ($0.30-$1.35). For something a bit more substantial, there are tamales, sandwiches, empanadas and other goodies. Stop off at the bakery to take home some bread or goat-milk cheese or yogurt. Monday-Friday 8 a.m.-noon and 2-6:30 p.m., Saturday 8 a.m.-6:30 p.m., closed Sunday and holidays. Ca. 35, 18-22. Tel: 630-3371/642-3895.. Updated: Mar 23, 2011.

Restaurante Toy San

(LUNCH: $1.85, ENTREES: $ 5-8) Along pedestrian Calle 35 you'll see the street vendors munching down on some OK-looking Chinese food. Ask where they get it at, and one might have a card from Restaurante Toy San. There you'll find all the tables full of folks enjoying the lunch special. Well, fight your way to the counter for carry out and eat your meal on a park bench instead. Yes, Toy San is THAT popular. À la carte meat or vegetarian chow mein, chop suey and other Chinese dishes are available. Lighter appetites can ask for a half order. Daily 11 a.m.-9 p.m. Cra. 18, 37-44. Tel: 642-4625/0549. Updated: May 15, 2009.

Pizzaría Asturias

(PIZZA: $2.50-14) On this Friday evening a cooling breeze sways the palms lining this veranda in time to the music drifting from the inner sanctuary of Pizzaría Asturias. My finger lazily rounds the curvatures of a wine glass, thinking about a pizza baked in a wood-fired oven that soon will be arriving at this table. It was hard to decide which of the 14 pies to order ($2.50-14), almost half of which are vegetarian, including one of bocadillo (guava paste) and cheese, and the Tutifruti, adorned with apple, peach, plum, pineapple and cheese. Ah, the marinera - chipi-chipi and róbalo fish, squid, shrimp and clams - sounds delightful. Pizzaría Asturias isn't just about pizzas though - it also prepares breakfasts ($2.40-4.50), almuerzos ejecutivos ($4.25) and à la carte dishes ($7-12). Daily 8 a.m.-10 p.m. Cra. 22, 35-01. Hotel Asturias. Tel: 645-7565/1914. Updated: Mar 22, 2011.

Nightlife

Bucaramanga has quite a lively nightlife on weekends. Bars near the universities, though, are open every night. The once-fashionable Zona Rosa (between downtown and Carrera 30) is now lined with strip joints. The happening scene has now shifted to the neighboring Cabecera district. Most clubs are along Carrera 33. Updated: May 06, 2008.

Calle de los Mariachis

When I heard Bucaramanga has a Calle de los Mariachis, visions of Mexico City's Plaza Garibaldi began crooning in my mind. Well, this ciudad's equivalent isn't, well, quite equivalent. Calle 33 is one of the busiest avenues and there are no street-side cafés to sit and nurse a cerveza while listening to the strolling ensembles. At about 5 p.m., in the open windows of upstairs greenrooms, men dress in charro outfits. A trumpet's music waltzes down to the avenida, heard above the rush hour traffic. Those who are ready drink a *tinto* (coffee), waiting for the night's first customer to hire their services. Twenty *conjuntos* will be here until 2 a.m., in case you want to serenade a sweet Colombian. Several clubs—Garibaldi, El Venado del Oro and El Sombrero—have mariachi shows beginning at 10 p.m. every night. Cra. 33, between Ca. 37 and 39. Updated: Mar 22, 2011.

FLORIDABLANCA

 925m   252,267 7

Floridablanca, one of Bucaramanga's bedroom communities eight kilometers (5 mi) away, is a popular place to seek refuge from the city, especially on Sundays. A wondrous fountain in its plaza spritzes the *raspado* (flavored shaved ice) and *oblea* (wafer and caramel sandwich) vendors. A few blocks away is the Piedra del Sol, a massive boulder with spirals and circles carved by Guane ancestors a millenium or more ago. A modern cultural center with an archaeological museum surrounds it. About a kilometer (.62 mi) away is the Jardín Botánico Eloy Valenzuela, once owned by El Paragüitas tobacco company. Updated: May 22, 2009.

Things to See and Do

Jardín Botánico Eloy Valenzuela

On the banks of the Río Frío is the Jardín Botánico Eloy Valenzuela. Paths wind through its nine, lake-dotted hectares ablaze with mini-gardens of orchids, bamboos, palms, aquatic plants, medicinal herbs and other flora. There is even a Japanese meditation garden—a

EASTERN COLOMBIA

perfect place to do a session of aikido or tai chi. Keep an eye out for the red and black squirrels, birds (including ducks and woodpeckers) and turtles that make this parcel their abode. The serenity of the Jardín Botánico Eloy Valenzuela is refreshing. From Bucaramanga, take any buseta that says "Floridablanca" ($0.60, 45 minutes); in the center they pass by Parque de Santos on Calle 22. Oddly, photographs of the flora are forbidden. From Floridablanca's main plaza, walk one kilometer along Carrera 9 to Calle 3. Daily 8 a.m.-5 p.m.Updated: Mar 22, 2011.

Casa de la Cultura Piedra del Sol and Archaeological Museum

The Casa de la Cultura Piedra del Sol takes its name from a mysterious piece sheltered within its courtyard: a boulder carved with spirals and circles. The creators of this work were the Guane, a Chibcha-speaking nation that occupied the Santander region from the seventh century B.C. to the 16th century A.D. Inside, the Museo Arqueológico Regional Piedra del Sol, also known as Museo Arqueológico de los Guanes, presents an impressive collection of textiles, pottery, jewelry and others objects in well-displayed exhibits with excellent explanations on their use and significance. Unfortunately, the Spanish-only descriptions lack information. To get here from Bucaramanga, take any bus that says "Floridablanca" ($0.60, 45 min); in the center they pass by Parque de Santos on Calle 22. From Floridablanca's main plaza, walk up Calle 5 to Carrera 7 and turn right. Cra. 7, 4-35. Updated: Mar 22, 2011.

GIRÓN

 712m 108,466 7

On the banks of the Río de Oro, amid tobacco country, is San Juan de Girón, nine kilometers (5.4 mi) southwest of Bucaramanga. This 17th-century village of white-washed buildings and narrow cobblestone streets is another beloved get-away. The palm-shaded main plaza has artisan booths and a plaque noting how many times Bolívar passed through. Visit the over-400-year-old Mansión del Fraile, a museum of various knickknacks and a room where the Libertador had stayed, and the Museo de Arte Religioso Benedicto XVI. Down by the river, you can try your hand at knitting and munch down on local cuisine. Updated: Sep 29, 2011.

Restaurants

Fritanga

Beneath a centuries-old almond tree, you'll find a market-like place. In today's zephyr, the signs wave, whispering Donde Lola, Donde Maragrita, La Favorita, La Tía Gloria. If you follow a vegetarian, kosher, halal or low-cholesterol diet, ignore the calls. What these women serve up is a traditional must-try for visitors to Girón: the *fritanga*, a heaping plate of sausages, *rellena* (stuffed pork loin) and other pork delicacies, all deep-fried and served hot. You only need a soda or beer to wash it all down and a cardiologist to check you out afterwards. Riverfront malecón (Ca. 27) and Cra. 28. Updated: Apr 14, 2008.

PAMPLONA

 2,287m 77,000 📞 7

At a relatively high altitude, Pamplona enjoys a pleasant spring-like climate year round, thus making it a popular get-away for Colombians and Venezuelans alike. It is a cultural hub, hosting a number of music, dance and cinematographic festivals, and is home to some excellent museums.

This small town has produced poets (Jorge Gaitán Durán, Augusto Ramírez Villamizar, Francisco Valencia) and artists (Eduardo Ramírez Villamizar), as well as military leaders and a president (Rafael Faría Bermúdez).

Pamplona's Semana Santa, or Easter Week, is rated as one of the top three in Colombia, along with Popayán and Mompós. University education has become the basis of Pamplona's economy. Other Colombian cities can't match Pamplona for the number of nicknames it has garnered over its 450 years of existence such as: Founder City of Cities, Patriotic City, The Mitered City, First Capital of the Sovereign State of Santander, The City Spoiled by the Mists and Student Capital of Eastern Colombia. Updated: Sep 28, 2011.

History

Pamplona was established in 1549 by Pedro de Urgúa and Ortún Velasco, who promptly enslaved the indigenous Chitarero nation. A few years later, this new town developed into a gold and silver mining center, one of the richest in the Spanish colonies. Pamplona also became the base for the founding of many cities in both Colombia and Venezuela (Mérida,

San Cristóbal and La Grita), thus earning it the moniker Ciudad Fundadora de Ciudades (founding city of cities). With the rise of the comunero movement against Spanish rule in the late 18th century, Pamplona turned into an important center of rebellion. In 1810 it declared its independence. Between 1817 and 1819, a reign of terror gripped it, meriting another alias, this from Simón Bolívar: Ciudad Patriótica. Once the Colombian Republic was formed, Pamplona was designated the first capital of Santander Department, in 1857. Updated: Sep 28, 2011.

When to Go

The wettest months are usually March to April and October; the driest is December. The town is especially crowded with tourists during Semana Santa and the 4th of July festivities. The city's beat pulses with its university. When there are classes (January to June and August to the beginning of December) Pamplona hops with many cultural events and a vibrant nightclub scene. But, as with all college towns, when students go on break, the city becomes sleepier, with fewer services. Updated: Sep 28, 2011.

HOLIDAYS AND FESTIVALS

Many of Pamplona's holidays have one-week, free cultural festivals associated with them:

On the last Sunday of January, Pamplona celebrates Fiesta del Niño Huertanito. March/April revolves around Semana Santa and the Festival Internacional de Música Sacra Coral (International Sacred Choral Music Festival). July 4 is Grito de la Independencia de Pamplona and the Festival Nacional de Danza Folclórica (Cry of Pamplona's Independence and the National Folk Dance Festival); July 16 is reserved for the Fiesta de la Virgen de Cármen. The Fiesta del Señor del Humilladero takes place on September 14 and the November marks the Founding of Pamplona and the city's Film Festival. Updated: Sep 29, 2011.

Getting To and Away

A good highway leaves eastward from Bucaramanga, climbs to the settlement of Berlín on the páramo, and then descends to Pamplona (120 km/72 mi). Pamplona can also be reached from Málaga to the south.

The Pamplona bus terminal is at the end of Calle 4, one block past the bridge, across from the Policia Nacional base. On the main level of the station are bathrooms, snack shops and phones; on the upper level are restaurants.

To Silos: Extra Rápidos Los Motilones (7 a.m., 11 a.m., 4 p.m., 1.5-2 hr, $4; last return 1 p.m.).

To Cácota: Extra Rápidos Los Motilones (hourly 7 a.m.-4 p.m., 40 min, $3; last return 4 p.m.).

To Chitagá: Extra Rápidos Los Motilones (hourly 7 a.m.-4 p.m., $4; last return 4 p.m.).

To Málaga: 5 hr, $13-15—Cotrans (4 buses, 8 a.m.-5 p.m.), Concorde (2 evening buses).

To Capitanejo: buses leave 2-8 p.m., 6-7 hours, $14-16—Cotrans (2 buses), Concorde (2 buses).

To Cúcuta: Several companies, every half-hour, 2.5 hr, $4-6.

To Bucaramanga: 5 hr, $11—Bolivariano (hourly 11 a.m.-6 p.m.), Copetran (frequent 10 a.m.-midnight).

To El Banco: 12 hr—Omega (8 p.m., $40), Brasilia ($45).

To Bogotá (some go by way of Málaga): most buses leave afternoon and evening, 12-13 hr, $47-49—Copetrán, Omega, Berlinas (also in morning; hourly 4-11 p.m.), Cotrans ($36).

To Cali: Bolivariano (3 buses noon.-8 p.m.), 20 hr, $67).

To Medellín: 12-14 hr—Bolivariano (1 p.m. $56), Copetrán (3 buses 2:30-9:30 p.m., $39).

To Santa Marta: Copetrán (11 p.m., 14 hours, $56), Brasilia ($61).

To Barranquilla/Cartagena: 17/19 hr, $43-61/$47-72—Brasilia (3 p.m., 7:30 p.m.), Copetran (3 buses 5-8:30 p.m.), Berlinas

To Sincelejo/Montería: 16-18/18-19 hr, $47-$72—Copetrán (7:30 p.m.), Brasilia (2:30 p.m., 5:30 p.m.). Updated: Sep 30, 2011.

Safety

Pamplona is a relatively safe town. However, locals say to stay on the busier streets, like Carrera 6 (which goes down to the main night club district) after dark. Also, like when traveling in other foreign places, always practice caution and care and be a smart traveler. Updated: Jun 23, 2011.

Services

TOURISM

The **Instituto de Cultura y Turismo de Pamplona**, or Pamplona's Culture and Tourism Institute, has its office in the Museo Casa Colonial (Monday-Friday 8 a.m.-noon, and 2-6 p.m. Ca. 6, 2-56. Tel: 568-2043). The **Centro Cultural Municipal Ramón González Valencia** (Monday-Friday 8 a.m.-noon and 2-6 p.m. Cra. 7, 5-52) also supplies informative maps of the city. A few useful websites are: http://pamplona-cultural.blogspot.com, www.pamplona.eovirtual.com, www.encuentraloenpamplona.com and www.arcupam.com. Updated: Sep 29, 2011.

MONEY

None of the banks in Pamplona cash traveler's checks. The following have ATMs that takes MasterCard, Cirrus, Visa and Plus cards; Bancolombia's also accepts American Express:

Bancolombia (Ca. 7, 5-76), **Banco de Bogotá** (Cra. 6, 5-47) and **BBVA** (Cra. 6, 5-71, main plaza). There are no casas de cambio, and neither Western Union nor MoneyGram have agents here. Updated: Sep 29, 2011.

KEEPING IN TOUCH

Telecom/Telefónica offers local, national and international calls, as well as Internet (Monday-Saturday 8 a.m.-noon and 2-8 p.m. Ca. 7 and Cra. 5A). A national or local call is cheaper from shops. Some Internet cafés charge less during special hours; shop around. Don't bother looking for Skype; no one seems to know what it is, let alone offer it. Old-school letter or postcard writers should head to the **post office** (Monday-Friday 7:30 a.m.-noon. Ca. 6, 6-17). Updated: Sep 29, 2011.

MEDICAL

Hospital San Juan de Dios is at the end of Calle 5, just over the river (Tel: 568-2482). Most pharmacies are on Carrera 6, between Parque Águeda Gallardo (the main plaza) and at Plazuela Almeida (where the obelisk is). Updated: Sep 29, 2011.

LAUNDRY

Laundry places are few and far between in Colombia; however, Pamplona happens to have two Laundromats. **Lava Express** can wash your clothes for $0.50 per kilo, or wash and dry them for $1.05 per kilo. If you get your dirty clothes in during the morning, they can be done by close the same day (Ca. 9, 7-89. Cel: 312-491-5438). Updated: Sep 29, 2011.

Things to See and Do

Pamplona preserves the beauty of its colonial buildings, unlike many Colombian cities. Several colonial homes have become museums, like the Museo de Arte and the Casa Colonial. Other edifices of the era should not be missed on your stroll around Pamplona are: Casa de Doña Agueda Gallardo (Ca. 5 and Cra. 6), Casa de las Cajas Reales (Cra. 5, between Ca. 4 and 5), and the Casa del Mercado, formerly a Jesuit School (Ca. 6 and Cra. 5). The city is renowned for its religious traditions and Semana Santa celebrations and has a fine selection of churches. Most are only open during mass. Around Pamplona are a number of villages offering crafts, museums, hot springs and natural beauty worthy of day trips. Among these are Silos, Cácota, Chitagá, Mutiscua and Pamplonita. As you can see, there are plenty of activities available in Pamplona. Updated: Jun 24, 2011.

The Museums of Pamplona

One of the city's nicknames is "La Ciudad de Museos." Although few in number, Pamplona's museums cover the spectrum of themes.

Museo de Arte Ramírez Villamizar (ADMISSION: $0.50 children, $0.80 adults)—An impressive collection of art by native son Eduardo Ramírez Villamizar and other modern Colombian and Venezuelan artists. Originally the home of Juan de Maldonado, founder of San Cristóbal de Táchira, this was also once a convent and a brothel—hence its nickname, La Casa de las Marías. Tuesday-Sunday 9 a.m.-noon and 2-6 p.m. Ca. 5, 5-45, Parque Águeda Gallardo. Tel: 568-2999.

Museo Arquidiocesano de Arte Religiosa (ADMISSION: $0.50)—Contains the treasures of Pamplona's churches, including paintings by some of the most important colonial artists. Monday-Saturday 10 a.m.-noon and 3-5 p.m., Sunday and holidays 10 a.m.-noon, closed Tuesdays. Cra. 5, 4-53, Tel: 568-0960.

Museo Casa Azoátegui (ADMISSION: $0.50)—The once-home of Venezuela-born independence general José Antonio Anzoátegui, it is now a museum and archives. Monday-Saturday 9 a.m.-noon and 2-5:30 p.m. Cra. 6, 7-48, Tel: 568-0960, E-mail: museoanzoategui@gmail.com/museoanzoategui@yahoo.com, URL: www.museoanzoategui.blogspot.com).

Museo Casa Colonial (ADMISSION: $0.50)—Also known as the Museo de Pamplona, this museum exhibits small collections of archaeological, paleontological, religious and historical artifacts. Monday-Friday 8 a.m.-noon and 2-6 p.m. Ca. 6, 2-56. Tel: 568-2043. Updated Mar 22, 2011.

The Churches of Pamplona !

Pamplona, renowned for not only its colonial architecture, but also for its Semana Santa and other religious traditions, has a fine selection of churches. Most are open only during mass.

Catedral Santa Clara—Ca. 6, between Cra. 5 and 6, Parque Águeda Gallardo—Formerly the chapel of Santa Clara convent, the now-cathedral was built in 1587 by the daughter of one of Pamplona's co-founders. Check out the angels carved on the apse columns.

Nuestra Señora de las Nieves—Cra. 7 and Ca. 5—Parts of this temple are from the original Convento de Santo Domingo, built in 1563 and destroyed by earthquake in 1875.

San José—Cra. 7, between Ca. 4 and 5—A more modern edifice constructed on the site of the former Santo Domingo monastery.

Ermita del Señor del Humilladero—Ca. 2, between Cra. 7 and 8—This shrine of Pamplona's most holy relic was built shortly after the city's founding, and expanded in 1605.

Convento de Santa Clara—Ca. 6, between Cra. 3 and 4—Of an austere, triple-belled exterior, this convent chapel is home to another important Christ representation, El Huerfanito, which had survived a 17th century earthquake.

Capilla de San Juan de Dios—Cra. 4, between Ca. 6 and 7—A simple, white-washed parish church erected in 1665.

Ermita de las Nieves—Ca. 5 and Cra. 3—Pamplona's first church, dating from 1550.

Nuestra Señora del Carmen—Cra. 3, between Ca. 5 and 6—A younger edifice neighboring the Ermite de las Nieves. Updated: Mar 22, 2011.

El Huerfanito

In the 17th century, an earthquake devastated Pamplona. Only three buildings were left standing. Upon remembering that the statue of the infant Christ was up in the choir loft of the chapel, the nuns of Santa Clara convent cried out, *"Se quedó Huerfanito El Niño!"* The child has been left

an orphan! Removing the debris, her colleagues found the Christ child unharmed and with one arm raised, as if giving a last benediction. Since then, he has resided in the rebuilt temple. Updated: Mar 22, 2011.

Corporación de Turismo de Pamplona

On weekends you can join the Corporación de Turismo de Pamplona's tours to explore the richness of nearby villages. Spend a day in Silos, visiting indigenous tombs, dipping into thermal pools and shopping for a new poncho. Or, travel to Cácota to pick up some ceramics and to canoe across the Laguna de Cácota. You can also drop a fishing line into Laguna del Salado, or spend a while in the Casa de Bolívar and snack on cheese, cakes and peaches in Chitagá. The Corporación de Turismo de Pamplona also has outings to Mutiscua and Pamplonita. All trips include transportation and lunch, and most include a guide, at very reasonable prices ($8-18.65 per person, depending on excursion destination). Tel: 756-0960, Cel: 310-278-6994. Updated: Jun 24, 2011.

Roadtrip to Silos

Between Pamplona and Bucaramanga is a spur road at La Laguna that goes south to the small village of Silos. Surrounded by the foothills of the Cordillera Oriental, Silos is rich in minerals, including marble, coal and limestone. Its inhabitants also weave woolen blankets and *ruanas* (short ponchos). The countryside is dotted with lagoons, some of which offer the fisher a try at trout. Other attractions include pre-Columbian tombs, the Museo Cacique Magará and hot springs. Horseback riding is another possibility.

To get there, Extra Rápidos de Motilones has daily buses at 7 a.m., 11 a.m. and 4 p.m. ($4, 1.5-2 hr). The last departure from Silos to Pamplona is at 1 p.m. You can also go on a tour, but only on weekends. Updated: Sep 29, 2011.

Lodging

Pamplona hotels range from basic boarding to classy resorts. Cheaper *residencias* and *hospedajes* are on the east side of the river, between Calles 7 and 9. Weekends rooms may be a bit more difficult to find due to families making a quick escape to this favored destination. Reservations are highly recommended for the *temporada alta*, or high season, especially Semana Santa (Easter Week) and the July 4th. Updated: Jul 10, 2011.

EASTERN COLOMBIA

Hotel El Llano

(ROOMS: $4.20-10.50) Located a half-block from the obelisk in Plazuela Almeida, the Hotel El Llano is one of Pamplona's cheapest inns promising an *ambiente familiar*, or family atmosphere. Most of the small brick-block rooms have windows facing onto the central patio. The better rooms and common bath are on the second story. All share the common, hot-water baths, except for one that has a private *baño*. The smell of cleanliness permeates the air. However, there is something uncommon about El Llano: no rooms have a TV, thus allowing it to charge such an economical price. Guests can use the laundry area to wash clothes. Ca. 9, 7-30. Tel:-568-3441. Updated: May 19, 2009.

Hotel Ursua ❗

(ROOMS: $8-16) The Hotel Ursua is like your country grandmother's house: big, overstuffed beds and mismatched furniture in the rooms as well as generations of now-antique sewing machines, irons, phonographs and other items scattered throughout. Be sure to check out the LP record collection—you'll be impressed by her wide selection, with LP's such as Seals and Croft and a very young Joan Serrat. Now run by a third generation of this family's women, they greet the weary traveler in this eclectic but comfortable lodge that is part of the over-400-year-old house of Juan de Maldonado. All rooms have private, hot-water baths. Opt for TV or not. The restaurant serves good food. Ca. 5, 5-67, Parque Águeda Gallardo. Tel: 568-2470. Updated: May 12, 2009.

Carionga Hotel

(ROOMS: $26.50-74) A time-worn resort built in the contemporary 1960s architecture of glass and metal, Hotel Carionga still provides the best service to the journeyer to Pamplona. It caters primarily to businesspeople, excursion groups and families. The era-theme continues into the large rooms, in classic 1960s simplicity. Hotel Carionga has many of the usual amenities, plus a few more: audio-visually equipped rooms for conferences, a barbecue patio, and a playground for the children. The parking lot is fenced and guarded. Cra. 5 and Ca. 9, Plazuela Almeida. Tel: 568-1515, E-mail: hotelcarionga2006@yahoo.es. Updated: May 25, 2009.

Restaurants

Like other tourist-oriented services in Pamplona, restaurants are affected when the university is not in session. They tend to close earlier and have a more limited menu. Mostly you will find *criollo* (typical nortesantandereano dishes). The municipal market occupies the entire block between Calles 6 and 7, Carreras 4 and 5. The entrance to the *comedores* (eateries) is on Calle 7. Here you'll find cheap breakfasts and lunches (open 6:30 a.m.-2 p.m.). For inexpensive evening meals, drop by one of the small restaurants down Calle 6, between Carreras 6 and 8.

Restaurante Govinda

(LUNCH: $1.60) In the courtyard of the Hare Krishna-run Hostal Santa Clara in the fourth chakra of Pamplona is Restaurante Govinda, providing this town with well-prepared, nutritious vegetarian food—as is the Hare Krishna tradition. Good soups, mains and fresh fruit juice—a colorful ensemble for your physical and spiritual selves—are all available. Sometimes the "meat" is soy, others times it is gluten. The price of the comida corriente is just right for the poor student or budget traveler: $1.60. When the university students are in town, open 7 a.m.-10 p.m.; out of term, open only for lunch, noon-2 p.m. Cra, 6, 7-21. Tel: 568-4105. Updated: Feb 20, 2008.

Restaurante Desayunadero El Arreiro

(LUNCH: $1.60) An airy restaurant constructed of plaited bamboo slat walls, Restaurante Desayunadero El Arreiro prepares simple criolla dishes. Sit down at one of the tables to a basic, two-course comida corriente (with drink, $1.60) or one of the many à la carte entrées on the menu ($3.20). The señora is friendly and the service is quick. After your repast, just kick back and chat with her and her friends while the soap operas flash on the TV. Daily 9 a.m.-8 p.m. Ca. 6, 7-14. Updated: May 22, 2009.

Restaurante El Solar ❗

(ENTREES: $7-14) This classy, yet rustic dining hall of worn brick and wood exudes a pleasant atmosphere in which to sit down and enjoy an excellent meal. With a menu aimed at the carnivorous crowd, Restaurante El Solar brings sizzling steaks to your table, including what it promises to be an authentic T-bone Americano. There's also several chicken breast and fish platters for those who want a lighter meat. In season, the sounds of live vallenato music drift through the large space, adding to the ambience. Ca. 5. Tel: 568-2966, Cel: 312-522-9225/527-2395. Updated: May 22, 2009.

Nightlife

Pamplona has quite a happening night club scene, with bohemian cafés with live trova music, bars to sit at while talking theories with friends over a few drinks, and discoteques galore. Many are concentrated around Plazuela Almeida, where the obelisk is located. This is the service sector that is most affected when the university is not in session; many are closed. The few that remain open during this downtime do so with limited hours and/or are only open on weekends. Updated: Sep 29, 2011.

Discoteca, Hotel Carionga

On Friday and Saturday nights, pamploneses head here for some elegant dancing. Many make this part of the circuit of hitting the night clubs down near the Plazuela Almeida. As there's no cover charge and no minimum consumption, it's a good, cheap spot to start the night. Merengue, salsa, vallenato and reggaeton (yes, even reggaeton) throb this dance hall until the morning's wee hours. Only rum and *aguardiente* are on hand,. Although if what you want isn't offered, the staff can scare up something different. Friday and Saturday 8:30 p.m.-2 a.m. Cra. 5 and Ca. 9, Plazuela Almeida. Tel: 568-2645. Updated: May 22, 2009.

Siux Coffee Bar

Siux is a comfortable, dimly lit establishment that serves mostly liquor and a little coffee. Despite the canned music that at times can be a bit too loud, it's still one of the most popular places to hang out, chew the fat, expound on a professor's lecture, and have a few drinks. If you're a more solitary soul—or want to be a fly on the wall and watch the unfolding scene—just take a corner table. However, these tables are also sought out by those there with their special someone. During the academic calendar, live music is slated at times. Off-season Friday and Saturday only, 8 p.m.-2 a.m. Ca. 9, 7-16. Updated: May 22, 2009.

CÚCUTA

 320m   920,000   7

Two hours (72 km/43 mi) from Pamplona is San José de Cúcuta, capital of Norte de Santander department. The twisting, paved road has one tollbooth and a military checkpoint. You may at times feel like you are already in Venezuela--with the slang of cucuteños, the fashions and all the cars with Venezuelan plates—but you are still some 20 kilometers (12 mi) from the official border.

Cúcuta is also an important commercial center between the two countries, whether of legitimate wares or contraband (especially gasoline). Since Cúcuta is a popular shopping destination for Venezuelans, everything is geared toward them: numerous ATMs and casas de cambio, shops specializing in clothing and shoes, and fast-food restaurants to fuel frenzied shoppers. Traffic is insane. Two lanes become three or more. Motorcycles disregard what few stoplights there are and use the sidewalk to bypass the traffic. Commerce spills from the stores onto the littered streets.

Those traveling in their own vehicles may find the bustle a bit beyond their experience and prefer to spend the night in Pamplona. Cúcuta is little more than a gateway to Venezuela and a commercial capital. It is also a city steeped in independence history. Nearby, Villa del Rosario preserves important symbols for the bolivariano nations. Updated: Sep 29, 2011.

History

Cúcuta is a relatively modern city, in Colombian terms, having been founded in 1734. The city played significant roles during the Wars of Independence from Spain. It was captured by Simón Bolívar during his Magdalena campaign of 1813. The first congress of Gran Colombia (1821), to unite Venezuela, Colombia and Ecuador, was held in neighboring Villa del Rosario.

In 1875 this town was destroyed by an earthquake and subsequently rebuilt. In recent years, Cúcuta has seen much settlement by *desplazados*, or internal refugees from the war-torn areas in the immediate region. Updated: Sep 29, 2011.

When to Go

It's always hot and sunny in Cúcuta. June and July can see temperatures reaching up to 40°C (104°F). August and September are windy. The rainy season comes in November and December with brief daily showers. The city is even more crowded with vacationers and shoppers in July, August and December. Updated: Sep 29, 2011.

HOLIDAYS AND FESTIVALS

Apart from the national holidays, Cúcuta has its own observances. February 28 is

EASTERN COLOMBIA

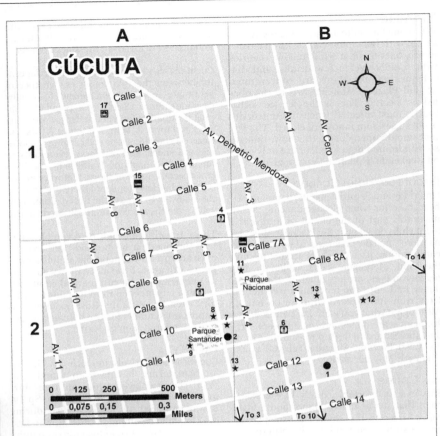

● **Activities**

1 Biblioteca Julio Pérez Ferrero B2
2 Catedral San José A2
3 Monumento Cristo Rey B2

🍽 **Eating**

4 El astillo de Job A1
5 Pastelería La Araña de Oro A2
6 Restaurante Vegetariano Jiarit B2

★ **Services**

7 AV Villas A2
8 Bancolombia A2
9 Banco de Bogotá A2
10 DAS B2
11 Post Office B2
12 Telecom B2
13 Tourism Office B2

🛏 **Sleeping**

14 Hotel Bolívar B2
15 Hotel Casa Real Cúcuta A1
16 Hotel Las Pirámides B2

🚌 **Transportation**

17 Bus Terminal A1

the commemoration of the Battle of Cúcuta; parades wend up to Loma de Bolívar (Bolívar Hill). Cucuteños celebrate San José, the patron saint, on March 19 with processions and fireworks. The city's anniversary, June 17, is another occasion for *pólvora* (fireworks), as well as civic events.

One holiday that is observed on a different day than the rest of the country is Mother's Day, normally the second Sunday of May. The reason, of course, is commerce. In the early 20th century, goods arrived through Maracaibo Lake ports. One year the special goodies for Día de la Madre were delayed. So that the merchants wouldn't be stuck with the merchandise, the date for this holiday was changed to the last Sunday of May, and has remained so ever since. Updated: Feb 07, 2008.

Getting To and Away

Taxis are unmetered, so negotiate a price before boarding. Minimum fare is $2 and transport to the airport costs $4. Note that in Cúcuta carreras are called avenidas. Cúcuta has an extensive public bus system. To go to the Venzuelan consulate or DIAN, catch the "Consulado" buseta from Calle 10 and Avenida 1 ($0.60).

BY BUS

Cúcuta's bus terminal is a madhouse located on Avenida 7 between Calles 2 and 0. Its reputation is notorious (see "Safety"). Plans are underway to build a new facility. If you are heading to the border, Pamplona or other near-by destination, it is better to head straight out to the bus lot and talk directly with the driver.

Bus companies running trips to other major cities include Cotrans, Concorde, Copetrán, Omega, Brasilia, Cootransmagdalena and Bolivariana. Prices and trip times vary. Buses to **Pamplona** (2 hr, $4-6) and **Bucaramanga** (6 hr, $13-18) leave every half hour.

Other popular destinations from Cúcuta include:

Capitanejo (via Málaga) (6 a.m., noon, 3 p.m., 8 p.m.; 8 hr, $25-30), **Bogotá** (5 a.m., 1 p.m., 6 p.m., 3:30-9:30 p.m.; 15 hr, $50-60), **Mompós** (1 p.m. and 8 p.m.; 13 hr, $37), **Barranquilla** (9 a.m.-5:30 p.m.; 16 hr, $58-69), **Cartagena** (9 a.m.-5:30 p.m.; 18 hr, $64-75), **Cali** (11:30 a.m., 9 a.m.-6 p.m.; 20-22 hr, $70-77) and **Medellín** (1:30 p.m., 2:30 p.m., 6:30 p.m., 7:30 p.m.; 13-15 hr, $40-56).

There are frequent buses to the border, $1.20. See "Border Crossing: Via Cúcuta" for more information.

BY AIR

Avianca (Tel: 571-2848, URL: www.avianca.com) and **Aires** (Tel: 583-2941, URL: www.aires.aero) fly out of Cúcuta's Aeropuerto Camilo Daza (Carretera Panamericana, via Sevilla, 5 km/3 mi from downtown. Tel: 587-4886/6324), with departures to Bogotá ($160-200, plus taxes) and to Medellín ($200-250, plus taxes). Aires also flies to Cartagena, Quibdó and other Colombia destinations. Both have offices at the airport. Updated: Sep 29, 2011.

Border Crossing: Via Cúcuta

From Cúcuta, the highway winds 16 kilometers (9.6 mi) to Villa del Rosario, and another four kilometers (2.5 mi) to the Puente Internacional. This is the most common border crossing between Colombia and Venezuela. Local transportation is more geared toward Colombian and Venezuelan citizens who don't need to stop at immigration to deal with bureaucracy. This makes it a bit difficult for foreigners, since buses and collective taxis will not wait for you. For those travelers needing passport procedures, this border is only open 8 a.m.-6 p.m. on either side.

Take a bus as far as the border and debark at the Colombian side of the international bridge ($1.20). A taxi that will wait for you to go through the rigmarole will cost about $25-30. On the left side of the road is DAS in the white house. Then cross back over the road and flag down a bus heading to San Antonio del Táchira, Venezuela, at the other end of the bridge. Tell the driver you are going to the DIEX (a.k.a ONIDEX, or immigration) office. If you are feeling energetic, you could also cross the bridge on foot; however, be very aware of your surroundings, since robbery is a possibility.

Six blocks from the San Antonio side of the bridge is the Venezuelan immigration office. In all, there is about one kilometer (0.6 mi) between the two migración posts. On the Venezuelan side, there is a tourism information booth immediately on the left side of the road. At San Antonio del Táchira, there is frequent transportation to San Cristóbal del Táchira. From there, you can travel to Mérida, Maracaibo, Caracas and other points in Venezuela.

For journeyers traveling with their own vehicle, check with the Venezuelan consulate

EASTERN COLOMBIA

in Cúcuta or the Colombian Consulate in San Antonio for the complete procedures. In general, from Colombia to Venezuela the process will be: DIAN (customs) and then DAS (immigration). The DIAN office is a distance from the border, near the airport. See Cúcuta's "Services" section for addresses for the consulate and Colombian customs and other offices. If leaving Venezuela, the exit tax is approximately $20 (at official rate, less at black market rates). Updated: Jun 17, 2011.

Safety

Like any other border city, Cúcuta has serious problems with security. The streets bustle with commerce and the constant movement all make it easy for a thief to do his/her deed and easily disappear. The entire city is considered to be unsafe after 9 p.m. until daybreak. If needing to move at these hours, take a registered taxi. Otherwise, restrict your activities to daylight hours.

The bus terminal has a long history of people working the traveler trying to create havoc and mischief. Some of the tricks in the past were to have you turn over your valuables for "safe keeping" in the bus office, and the selling of fake tickets. Do not fall for any of this. It is better to go to the bus office window or the bus driver and buy your tickets directly from the personnel. Whenever tensions between Venezuela and Colombia that could affect trade in Cúcuta have flared, the border crossing has seen demonstrations and has even been shut down at times. Keep an eye on the news for any such activities. Updated: Mar 11, 2011

Services

TOURISM

The tourism office in Cúcuta, the **Corporación Mixta de Promoción de Norte de Santander** (Monday-Friday 8-11:45 a.m. and 2-6 p.m.; Saturday 8 a.m.-noon. Ca. 10, 0-30, Edificio Rosetal. Tel: 571-3395, E-mail: info@cucutaturistica.com, URL: www.cucutaturistica.com) has information on sites throughout the department and sells maps of the city ($2). A useful website is: www.cucutanuestra.com.

DIAN, the customs headquarters, is on Avenida Aeropuerto, just past the Venezuelan consulate; those travelers entering or leaving Colombia in their own vehicles will have to pay a visit here. **DAS** (immigration) has two offices in Cúcuta: one for extensions and other such business (Av. 1, 28-53. Tel: 583-6964) and the other for receiving your

entry or exit stamp for Colombia (at the Puente Internacional). If you need a visa for Venezuela or are traveling with your own vehicle, drop by the Venezuelan consulate (Av. Aeropuerto 17N 73, Zona Industrial. Tel: 579-1954). Updated: Sep 29, 2011.

MONEY

Most financial institutions in Cúcuta are around the main plaza, Parque Santander: **AV Villas** (Av. 5, next to the Catedral) and **Banco de Bogotá** (Av. 6, 10-82) both have a multi-network 24-hour ATMs, and **Bancolombia** (Av. 5, 9-80) changes American Express traveler's checks and has an ATM that accepts most major debit cards. Additionally, you can find ATMs in just about any nook of the city.

Avenida 6 also is home to a number of casas de cambio. But as this service is needed by the masses of Venezuelan shoppers, you can actually find exchange houses all over, as well as at the bus terminal and airport.

Both major international money wiring services have main branches in the downtown area: **Western Union/Giros y Finanzas** (Ca. 10 3-42, Edificio Suramericana) and **MoneyGram/Cambiamos** (Cra. 12, 4-47, Centro Comercial Internacional). Updated: Sep 29, 2011.

KEEPING IN TOUCH

Telecom (Monday-Saturday 8 a.m.-8 p.m. Ca. 10 and Av. 0) has local, national and international call service, and Internet. Local/national calls from shops and street stalls cost about the same; they also offer calls to Venezuela. Internet is surprisingly hard to find in Cúcuta. The most centrally located one is in the Centro Comercial Llanomar, to the left of the Catedral. **Correo de Colombia** is on the Parque Nacional (Monday-Friday 8 a.m.-noon and 2-6 p.m., Saturday 8 a.m.-noon. Ca. 8 and Av. 3, Edificio Santander). Updated Sep 29, 2011.

MEDICAL

Cúcuta's two main hospitals neighbor each other on the east side of the city: **Hospital Erasmo Moez** (Av. 11E, 5AN-71. Tel: 574-6888) and **S.E.S. Francisco de Paula Santander** (Av. 11E, 5AN-1511. Tel: 574-1722). Pharmacies are plentiful. A number of them are concentrated on Calle 9, as well as on Avenida 5.

Pharmacies are plentiful. A number of them are concentrated on Calle 9, as well as on Avenida 5. Updated: Sep 29, 2011.

CAMERA

Your camera needs can be met at any of the several shops along Calle 10, between Avenidas 3 and 6. Updated: Sep 29, 2011.

Things to See and Do

Cúcuta does have some historic buildings of note. The **Biblioteca Pública Julio Pérez Ferrero** (Av. 1 and Ca. 12) was built in 1786 and served as the city's first hospital; in 2000 it took on its present duty as the public library, providing many children's and cultural activities. A block away on the other side of Parque is the **Torre del Reloj**, with the distinction of being the only clock in Colombia that tolls the national anthem each hour. It is now home to the department's **Cultural Secretariat**, with exhibits cultural events. **Quinta Teresa**, designed at the end of the 19th century by Domingo Díaz, served as an educational institution. It is presently under restoration.

The city's **cathedral** on Parque Santander is one of almost a dozen Catholic churches you can visit. The **Monumento Cristo Rey**, executed by Marco León Mariño, affords good views. It is 35 meters (174 ft) high with 82 steps to the top (Av. 4 and Ca. 19).

Along the Río Pamplona are the city's most luxurious hotels and several shopping malls. On the road towards the border is **Villa del Rosario**, where the Congreso Constituyente met in 1821 to form Gran Colombia (Venezuela, Colombia and Ecuador). Sites of interest here include the **Templo Histórico**, meeting place of the Congress, and the **Casa-Museo General Santander**, home of one the Independence leaders and the first vice president of Gran Colombia. Updated: Feb 07, 2008.

Lodging

Cúcuta has the whole gamut of lodging choices, from dubious residencies to full-luxury hotels. However, due to the safety issues of the city, it might be more advisable to pass the night in Pamplona, two hours away. For those traveling with their own transportation, it is better to stay away from the city center and its nightmare traffic. Many cheap options are on Avenida 7, near the bus terminal; some are questionable, but those proclaiming "ambiente familiar" are usually decent enough for the whole family to stay in. Only upper-class Cúcuta hotels will have hot water. Updated: Sep 29, 2011.

Hotel Casa Real Cúcuta

(ROOMS: $7-16) Just a few blocks from the bus terminal, Hotel Casa Real Cúcuta is one of the few places along Avenida 7 that has that ambiente familiar, or family atmosphere. It doesn't quite have the shine as in days past, and honestly some of the rooms have become quite shabby (ask to see several before deciding). But it is clean enough for a night's stay. With the children, it can be a bit noisy in the evenings, but thankfully Colombian kids have an early bedtime. All rooms have private, cold-water bathrooms. Depending on your pocketbook, you can choose between having a TV or not, or having a fan or air conditioning. Av. 7, 4-45. Tel: 583-1249 , Cel: 315-853-9738. Updated: May 15, 2009.

Hotel Las Pirámides

(ROOMS: $10-26.50) Located between the bus terminal and downtown, Hotel Las Pirámides is a good mid-range choice for the journeyer needing to spend a night in Cúcuta. The modern building proffers well-appointed rooms with private bath (cold water only), double beds, television and fan or air conditioning. There is one room without television that costs the same for one or two persons, a good choice for budget travelers. The Pérez family is attentive to its guests, thus providing an assuring stay in this hectic city. Cash only is accepted. Ca. 7, 3-73. Tel: 571-9831. Updated: Mar 22, 2011.

Hotel Bolívar

(ROOMS: $88 and up) A member of the Spanish Celuisma hotel chain, Hotel Bolívar is probably the classiest place you can stay in Cúcuta. It was built with a Mediterranean architecture and it has three swimming pools set within a tropical garden. All 128 tile-floored rooms are very spacious and have air conditioning, satellite TV, a mini-bar, sitting area and Internet. Prices include a buffet breakfast. It is located in one of the city's most important commercial zones and is only 15 minutes from the airport. With its easy access to the road, to the border and security, this makes it a good choice for those traveling in their own vehicle. Av. Demetrio Mendoza, Vía San Luis, next to Centro Comercial Bolívar. Tel: 576-0764, Fax: 576-3349, E-mail: reservas@hotel-bolivar.com, URL: www.hotel-bolivar.com. Updated: Jul 06, 2011.

Restaurants

Although the restaurant scene may not be as diverse when school's not in session and students overrun the city, there are still quality options available. Luckily, some of the restaurants in this college town have college prices. The comida corriente is tasty and cheap, and ready to be washed down with a glass of beer or liquor. Unlike the ample supply of restaurants with lunch specials, cafés with real coffee are more elusive. Searching for a cup of brewed coffee may feel like a scavenger hunt at first, but there are some key spots to refuel. Head downtown to feed your caffeine and pastry needs. If you're into a whole-grain, fresh-fruit breakfast instead of a cup of leaded coffee, several cafés offer delicious, healthy dishes. Many have vegetarian options at good prices, too. Updated: Jul 14, 2008.

Pastelería La Araña de Oro

(BREAKFAST: $1.75-3) Mission Impossible: Finding a brewed coffee in downtown Cúcuta, and not having to settle for the sugared, watery java that the street vendors, who are pushing a luggage rack full of thermoses, sell. But a cup of real joe. Most places only have glorified instant coffee machines. But there is hope! Your caffeine-deprived nerves can be soothed at La Araña de Oro. In addition to great coffee, you'll find a luscious assortment of cakes and cookies. Also, for breakfast, you can partake of something savory: a chicken or meat empanada ($0.60), or perhaps, a flaky turnover. Monday-Saturday 8 a.m.-7 p.m., Sunday 8 a.m.-noon. Ca. 9, 5-20. Tel: 571-2651. Updated: Mar 22, 2011.

Restaurante Vegetariano y Tienda Naturalista Jiarit

(BREAKFAST/LUNCH: $2-3) Does Cúcuta ever have a surprise for you, vegetarians—over a half-dozen restaurants to feed your needs. Jiarit is one of the choices, serving breakfast and lunch. The fruit salad is massive, with a generous sprinkling of granola ($1.85). Also on the menu are soy and oat yogurt, and natural fruit juices. A shop provides baked goods. Have a massage or steam bath here as well. A sister restaurant, Salud y Vida, is at Avenida 4, 6-40. Monday-Friday 7 a.m.-6:30 p.m., Sunday 7 a.m.-4 p.m. Ca. 11, 2-81. Tel: 571-8629, Cel: 312-853-8620. Updated: Jun 24, 2011.

El Castillo de Job !

(ENTREES: $2-3.65) In the front courtyard of an old castle, beneath the shade of a large tree, Doña Claudia grills up fish, chicken and steak for the à la carte entrées ($2-3.65). In the small kitchen, the comida corrientes—rice, beans, salad, yucca or potatoes and meat—are dished up ($1.50). All are served with a pint of agua de panela. Expect to share one of the nine tables, as this is an extremely popular lunch place. The al fresco dining experience, with that subtle Cucuteña breeze, is a refreshing alternative to the hot, stuffy restaurants. Daily 7 a.m.-2 p.m.; lunch 10:30 p.m.-whenever the food runs out. Prices include tax. Corner of Ca. 6 and Av. 4. Updated: Mar 22, 2011.

MÁLAGA

 1,400m   15,182   7

The carretera central, the favored route of truck drivers to Cúcuta, continues north 35 kilometers (21 mi) from Capitanejo to Málaga. The road is paved but has potholes and is subject to landslides. The east side affords views of the *cordillera*.

Málaga is home to several small universities and to a growing adventure and agro-tourism industry. You can opt to stay in one of the very reasonably priced hotels or at a farmhouse. Embraced by mountains and páramo carved by waterfalls and caves, the traveler looking for some excitement in practicing spelunking or canyoning will not be amiss in spending a few days here. There are also enjoyable hikes to lagoons and small villages. At the end of the outing, take a refreshing dip in a *balneario's* pool. The surrounding mountains are also home to many elves—or so legends say.

Departing from Málaga, you have two choices for your north-bound journey: the narrow carretera central, which sharply curves down to Pamplona and then joins the main highway to Cúcuta; or, another partially paved road that proceeds through San Andrés and Guacas before joining the major north-south highway to Bucaramanga. Both highways are prone to landslides and have several military checkpoints. Updated: Sep 29, 2011.

History

Hernán Pérez de Quesada and a small group of Spaniards in search of the *Casa del Sol* (house of the sun), rumored to be made of gold, came across the Valle de los Cercados. They called the valley this because the indigenous Chitareros encircled their *bohíos* (huts) with cane poles. Upon hearing of this discovery, Gonzalo Suárez Rendón, Governor of Tunja and originally from Málaga, Spain, ordered Jerónimo de Aguayo to establish a settlement there. On March 10, 1542, Málaga was founded and named in honor of Suárez Rendón's hometown. In 1549, with the creation of Pamplona, Málaga fell under its jurisdiction. In the present era, paramilitary forces entered Málaga around 2000, causing an exodus of the population. Colombian military entered approximately three years later, securing the town. The people have since returned, once more making it a vibrant city to visit. Updated: Sep 29, 2011.

When to Go

The rainy season in the Málaga area is from April to May and September to November, with the wettest months being May, October and November. Typically, January, June and December are drier and warmer. The city hosts several universities, which are in session January to June and August to the beginning of December. Updated: Sep 29, 2011.

HOLIDAYS AND FESTIVALS

Málaga commemorates its patron saint, San Jerónimo, the first week of January. Besides the usual masses and processions, there is a *carrazo* (car float) competition pitting different sectors of population against each other, as well as elections of kings, dog and cattle shows and bull fights.

During the *aguinaldos* (the novena leading up to Christmas), December 16-24, do not be startled by the sight of masked, Cousin-It-looking creatures prowling the streets, swinging a brightly painted, inflated cow's bladder at anyone who dares to challenge them. Nowadays it's young boys (and even a few girls) carrying on the tradition—but it has changed a lot. In the past, grown men dressed like this, with much competition among them for the best costume. Money would be collected from would-be wallop victims; those funds were then used to finance the carrazos at the beginning of January.

To finish off the year is the Festival de Carrancios, or the burning of Old Man Year, on December 31. Updated: Jan 15, 2008.

Getting To and Away

BY BUS

There is no central bus terminal in Málaga. However, there is regular bus service from Bogotá, Bucaramanga and Duitama several times a day, mostly modern big buses.

To Capitanejo: Copetrán—1 p.m., $2.65, 1 hr. For more departure times, see under Bogotá. Also, shared taxis leave, when full, from the corner of Carrera 8 and Calle 12, on Parque García Rovira.

To Capitanejo/Bogotá: Cotrans—3 a.m., 5 a.m., 8 a.m., 6:30 p.m., 8 p.m., 9 p.m., 11 p.m.; $2.65/$23.65, 1 hr/9 hr.

To Pamplona/Cúcuta: Cotrans—4 a.m., 6 a.m., 10 a.m., hourly 9-11 p.m.; $12.60/$17.60, 5 hr/7 hr. Concorde—11 p.m.; $13.25/17.60, 5 hr/7 hr.

To Bucaramanga: Copetrán—4 a.m., 6 a.m., 10 a.m., 1:30 p.m., 3:30 p.m., $18.65; 6-7 hr. Cotrans—2 a.m., 4:30 a.m., 8 a.m., noon, 2 p.m., 5 p.m., $18.65, 7 hr.

To Cúcuta: 4 a.m.-11 p.m.; $18, 7 hr.

BY AIR

Málaga's airport, Aeropuerto Jerónimo de Aguayo, is one kilometer (0.62 mi) from town. Región Air is the only carrier with flights once or twice a week to Bucaramanga ($80, 25 min). You can take small planes from Bucaramanga to Málaga for $56. There are two flights a day. Updated Jun 24, 2011.

Getting Around

There are always taxis waiting in front of the main Cotrans bus terminal. They are cheap and will take you around town and up into the mountains. The shared taxis to Concepción leave from near the main square. They take four to five passengers. Near the exit of town, in the direction of Miranda, is where the shared taxis depart for Miranda and Enciso. Updated: Sep 29, 2011.

Safety

Málaga, everyone says, is a very safe place to stay and there's no problem at all at night. With that being said, it is still important to practice basic safety tips while traveling like keeping your valuables out of plain sight and not venturing anywhere alone. It is always imprtant to be a safety conscious traveler. Updated: Jun 24, 2011.

Services

TOURISM

The **Oficina de Información Turística de los Andes**, Málaga's tourism office, is in the Casa de la Cultura Simón González Reyes (Monday-Friday 8 a.m.-noon and 2-6 p.m. Ca. 13 and Cra. 10). Saturdays and vacation times you can find the staff, composed largely of SENA tourism students, at a booth on the main square, dispensing information about not only Málaga, but also Capitanejo and neighboring villages. Updated: Oct 03, 2011.

MONEY

The two major banks in town, **Bancolombia** and **Banco Popular**, are located across from each other on Calle 12, between Carreras 7 and 8. Their ATMs handle MasterCard, Visa, Cirrus and Plus. An ATH, multi-network ATM is at Carrera 8, 13-38. There is no place to cash traveler's checks, nor any casas de cambio, nor any branches of Western Union or MoneyGram. Updated: Oct 03, 2011.

KEEPING IN TOUCH

Telecom (Monday-Saturday 8 a.m.-noon and 2-7 p.m. Ca. 12, between Cra. 6 and 7) provides local, national and international phone calls. The **post office** (Monday-Friday 7 a.m-noon and 2-6 p.m., Saturday 7 a.m.-noon) is located in the same building. Internet cafés are a bit scarce in Málaga. None have Skype. The largest one, and with the most reliable service, is in **Cafetería y Frutería El Virrey** (Cra. 8, 12-30, Parque García Rovira). Updated: Oct 03, 2011.

MEDICAL

Málaga's main medical facility is **Hospital Santo Domingo** (Ca. 16 and Cra. 7. Tel: 660-7475/7494). Around Parque García Rovira are several major-brand pharmacies; others can be found on Carrera 8. Updated: Oct 03, 2011.

CAMERA

There are scant camera stores found in Málaga. None repairs cameras, and film is limited. Most shops are devoted to taking cédula (ID card) photos or processing. **Foto Art** (Cra. 9, between Ca. 13 and 12) has some camera accessories and 100 ASA color and black-and white rollitos (film). Some drugstores also carry film. Updated: Oct 03, 2011

SHOPPING

Panuchas

You see them for sale all over Colombia, these *malagueño* sweets. Now you can get them direct from Panucha's main store: candied lemon or mandarin rind, or a *breva* (fig) wrapped around a ball of pure *arequipe*; *cocadas* (coconut nuggets), *alfajores* (a delicate cookie sandwich filled with arequipe and edged with coconut), or sugar-coated gummies in a variety of

fruit and other flavors (even celery!) A panucha is an arequipe whipped with coconut. There are even jars of homemade *arequipe* (soft caramel) and jams. If you can't quite make up your mind, choose a sample of goodies. Cra. 9, 13-64. Tel: 660-7080, Updated: Jul 4, 2011.

Mundo Artesanal Titis

Mundo Artesanal Titis is a ma-pa-son operation crafting a variety of useful goods right in their own home. Doña Mariela (ma) will show you around the shop. She makes the small ceramic cups and saucers, candlesticks and candles. Her menfolk create the small wooden boxes. The family also mixes essential oils and incenses. The necklaces and earrings are made by a young man in this same village, and the fique-cotton sandals are made by a woman in a nearby settlement. Cra. 9, 13-35. Cel: 312-359-9497. Updated: Feb 15, 2008.

Artesanía Colombia

Artesanía Colombia is another family workshop, this one concentrating on making wooden household items: boxes, napkin holders, toilet paper dispensers and what-not. It also carries artesanía from other parts of the country, like those fiber sandals and hats from Soatá, a village near Capitanejo. There's even pottery from Ráquira and ceramic chiva buses from the Tunja area. If the doors are closed, just give a knock—the family lives behind the shop. Cra. 9, 13-56. Tel: 661-7600. Updated: Feb 06, 2008.

Things To See and Do

Málaga and its region have plenty for all to do and see. There are numerous lagoons, páramo, waterfalls and caves. Adventure sports people can delve into the depths of Cueva de Culichal, practice torrentismo at Cascadas de Miranda, or rock climb Peñas del Cabío and Colorada, near Enciso. Several of the interesting small villages have balnearios, or swimming spas. Concepción is well-known for woollen textiles; Cerritos for its wind-swept páramo. Tequia ruins and Miranda make an enjoyable day hike, with indigenous cemeteries between the two. While in Málaga, go bowling, whether U.S. ten-pin in town or three-pin *bolo criollo* on the outskirts of town. Updated: Sep 29, 2011.

Cueva de Calichal

Spelunkers, get ready for a bit of exploration. Cueva de Calichal—Calichal Cave—is awaiting you. The first chamber is easily accessed, just slip through that fissure in the rocks. But if you really want to see the bowels of this piece of earth, festooned with stalagmites and stalactites, get your ropes and clamps out. It

A Quick Bolo Primer

Everywhere in Colombia, along country roads and in the hearts of cities, you'll see signs announcing *bolo*, or bowling. There are two types of this very popular sport. Bolo criollo is what you will see most of the time at the outskirts of towns. At the end of an open-air, 18-meter (59-ft)-long court is a backboard, in front of which are three pins in a vertical line. A 300 to 500 gram (11-to 18-oz.) aluminum ball is tossed to a backboard, to knock down the pins. This game has indigenous origins and is strictly for men. *Bolo americano*, or boliche, is good old 10-pin bowling as you find in the U.S. and elsewhere. Colombian woman are said to be quite good *bolicheras*, or bowlers.

takes a bit more expertise and devotion to get into these depths. While you're out this way at Vereda Calichal, enjoy the waterfall and the pool at its base, called the Cascada y Pozo Borbollón. The cave is four kilometers (2.5 mi) from Málaga. Follow the Cúcuta road to La Palma, from where a stone road leads to the road going to the electrical plant. Take a left and soon you'll see the cave. Alternatively, for a more scenic route, before the bridge outside town, follow the *camino herradura* (stone road) that goes behind the monastery. Updated: Sep 29, 2011.

Bolo Americano

Ever wonder what ever happened to all those bowling alleys once the sport lost favor in the United States? Well, it appears everything was shipped to Colombia, lanes, shoes, balls and all (the pinsetters, though, are human beings, so watch for them to get on the rafters before you fire your ball down). Bring back your childhood days; bowling in this country is affordable: $0.95 per *línea* (that is, per game, per person). You don't have to worry about anything—the balls are there (though few over 12 lbs) and shoes are rented (large sizes available; $0.25). Open up a brewski and join the friendly gang at Club Málaga Real for a round on its six lanes. Women are welcome. There are billiards in the front room and upstairs, as well, but this sport is frowned upon for women. Club Málaga Real, Cra. 8, 10-33. Tel: 660-5787. Updated: Feb 06, 2008.

Saturday Market

Saturday is market day in Málaga. The main market area has a roof. The upper part is an ecological market. There are stands for fish and chicken. The lower part is a building for the meat stands, and on the road above the main area is the farmers market, where farmers from nearby sell their products. They set out small tables or just put their wares on the floor. The products sold at the market are the best and freshest very early in the morning. Saturday market sells just about everything and there are lots of people around. Food stalls sell *empanadas* and soups. The market area is down from the main square near the cemetery. Just follow the crowd of people: everyone goes to market on Saturday. If you like markets, don't miss this one. Daily. Updated: Mar 22, 2011.

Tours

Adexpegar

Adexpegar—Asociación para la Promoción y Práctica de los Deportes Extremos y de Aventura del Nororiente Colombiano—is a relatively new company formed by SENA students. The only tour operator in Málaga, Adexpegar specializes in adventure sports: rapelling, torrentismo (rappelling in waterfalls; $30, all equipment provided), canotaje (rafting) on the Río Chicamocha (from Málaga $20; from Capitanejo, on the river, $30 or a 4-hr trip 47.50). They also provide other adventures, but only for those aged 14 to 50. Excursions are guaranteed on weekends; during the week, only when groups of 10 or more are interested. Hours (either location): Monday-Friday 8 a.m.-noon and 2-6 p.m. Cra. 8, 12-05. Magallanes, 2nd floor ; also Ca. 13, 6A-66, Centro Comercial Santander, local 4. Tel: 311-442-7028, Email: adexpegar@yahoo.es/adexpegar_@hotmail.com, URL: http://geocities.com/adexpegar. Updated: Mar 22, 2011.

Lodging

Málaga has a very pleasant surprise awaiting its visitors; a variety of hotels with good rates. Even the town's best inns, in the Zona Rosa, have affordable rates. Eco- and agro-tourism are beginning to get a foot-hold in the surrounding countryside, offering visitors alternatives to the standard hostel. Málaga hostels are also competitively priced, but there aren't too many to choose from. Updated: Sep 29, 2011.

Hotel-Restaurante El Viajero

(BEDS: $3) The Hotel-Restaurante El Viajero is one of the two very inexpensive, very basic hotels right on Málaga's main square, Parque García Rovira. It is only $2.65 per person. All rooms are dark, with no windows, with thin walls separating them, and share the common, cold-water baths. But the rooms are spacious and clean. Ca. 13, 8-56. Tel: 660-7416. Updated: Feb 15, 2008.

Hotel Santander

(ROOMS: $8-25) Hotel Santander is a *ganga*, a bargain, just a half-block from Parque García Rovira, in Málaga's Zona Rosa. The modern rooms are clean and good-sized. All have cable TV and private baths with gas-heated hot showers. To top it off, the friendly family serves you free coffee and orange juice in the morning. If there's anything you need, just pick up the phone in your room and the familia will attend you. Cra. 8, 13-42. Tel: 660-7121, Cel: 311-217-2210, Fax: 661-7586. Updated: Mar 21, 2011.

Granja Agroecoturística Los Guaduales ❗

(ROOMS: $10-15) Get out into the country to a self-sustaining farm. Located 11 kilometers (7 mi) from Málaga on the road to Capitanejo, Granja Agroecoturística Los Guaduales offers its visitors lodging in a hotel-like house or camping, and food straight from the fields. To relax, there's a swimming pool, fishing, video bar and hiking trails. You can even roll up your sleeves and get your hands dirty helping out. If you want to get a bit more of a rush, the folks at the granja can take you rafting on the Chicamocha River or rappelling at four near-by waterfalls (a sport called *torrentismo*). $10-15 per person in the house, plus $10 for meal plan (3 meals per day). Vereda El Espinal, San José de Miranda. Cel: 311-210-0540, E-mail: granjalosguaduales@mnicsena.edu.co, URL: www.senaturistico.blogspot.com. Updated: Mar 21, 2011.

Casa Salzburg

(ROOMS: $25-40) Casa Salzburg is a very friendly family place to stay while in Málaga. The house is beautiful and clean, with a great garden. There is lots to do around where Casa Salzburg is located. Also, the area surrounding this accommodation is fairly safe. Follow CRA 9 down from the main square and turn right at the bakery Pancomer. Casa Salzburg is just opposite. You have to call so someone will open the door, or knock around the corner at CRA 9 No. 10-73. Prices depend on the amount of persons per room and the room you choose. Always call or email before going. Ca. 11, 9-19 or Cra. 9, 10-73. cel: 313-323-6950, Email: casasalzburg@gmail.com, URL: www.casasalzburg.wg.am. Updated: Mar 22, 2011.

Restaurants

Restaurants in Málaga fall into two general categories: fast food and *comida criolla* (home-cooking). The only international cuisine choices are attempts at pizza. Come evenings, it is difficult to get a comida corriente; most dining establishments serve it only for lunch ($1.85-3.20). Vegetarians, you'll find eating a bit trying here, but you can pick up fixings at local supermarkets (Venus is right on the plaza), the innumerable bakeries, and at any of the shops featuring local dairy products. The daily mercado municipal swells on market days, Wednesday and Saturday. Ca. 14 and Cra. 7. Updated: Sep 29, 2011.

La Esperanza Restaurante Típico ❗

(ENTREES: $5-18) La Esperanza brings a hungry traveler's stomach the best in typical Santandereano food. Try the freshest meats from local farms: trout, other fishes and other seafood, chicken and meats, including goat. There are even sampler platters, if you don't quite know what to order ($8-9.25). Main dishes come with salad, yuca, potatoes and dessert. La Esperanza also serves breakfast ($2.10-3.20) and luncheon specials ($3.20-4.75). On the drink list are not only the usual alcoholic and non-alcoholic drinks, but also Colombian wine. Monday-Saturday 7 a.m.-9 p.m., Sunday 9 a.m.-3 p.m., holidays 7 a.m.-3 p.m. Cra. 8, 13-56. Tel: 660-8457, E-mail: restaurantelaesperanza@hotmail.com. Updated: Feb 15, 2008.

Restaurante y Cafetería Las Delicias

Down an alley alongside the market is Restaurante y Cafetería Las Delicias. At noon this place is packed with workers and families sitting down to a typical, home-cooked *comida corriente* of soup, main dish with meat, beans, rice and drink ($1.85). Don't be shy about sharing a table with a perfect stranger—in fact, it'll be the only choice you have. Las Delicias also serves breakfast. Daily 7 a.m.-2 p.m. Cra. 6a between Ca. 12 and 13. Updated: Feb 15, 2008.

Pizza y Lasagna

(PIZZA: $10.60, LASAGNA: $3.70) This restaurant announces on its banner that it also has Mexican food like burritos and tacos. But most days your only choice will be pizza (Hawaiian or chicken and mushroom, $1.50 per slice) or lasagna. The only vegetarian option is specially-ordered pizza, but you'll have to pay for the whole pie. Pizza y Lasagna does its own spin on the classic fast food: cheesy, flaky-crust pizza. No beer or juices are on the drink menu—just sodas. Despite the limited menu, this small, four-table establishment is popular with all Malagueños, whether teens or families, out for a quick bite in the evening. Wednesday-Monday from 5 p.m. on. Cra. 9, 11-53. Updated: May 22, 2009.

Nightlife

Málaga has a quaint Zona Rosa located just off the main plaza, along Carrera 8. Here you will find bars and discos—and yes, even karaoke. However, most are open only on the weekends. Oh, by the way, all those cafeterias and *fuentes de soda* you see around town aren't quite exactly coffee and soft drink joints. They are where most locals go to nurse a beer (or something stronger) while catching up on the news. Updated: Sep 29, 2011.

Bar Karaoke Fuego Verde

Attention, attention: tonight's off-key singing to music videos is being pre-empted by the Nacional-La Equidad soccer game on the big-screen TV. Indeed, sometimes some things are much more important than karaoke and Fuego Verde recognizes that. And at some special times of the year, like Mothers Day, it'll even bring in a mariachi band to play. But most nights you can join the gang here for a few drinks and get crazy pretending you're Shakira, Ricky Martin or Vicente Fernández. Just look for the Tigo sign on the street; as soon as you step into the doorway, you'll see the bar's placard at the foot of the staircase. There's no cover or minimum consumption. Daily 7:30 p.m.-3 a.m. Cra. 8, 13-14. Updated: May 22, 2009.

Jirafas Bar

When I asked where a woman could go alone and have a drink, several people recommended Jirafas Bar. No, you won't be bothered there, they assured me, it's laidback. Music? Oh, you know, salsa, vallenato and the like—and it has a dance floor. Unfortunately, this is like most clubs in Málaga, open only on weekends. It's up on the second floor of a building in the heart of the city's Zona Rosa. Friday and Saturday, 7 p.m.-3 a.m. Cra. 8, 13-29. Updated: May 22, 2009.

SAN JOSÉ DE MIRANDA AND TEQUIA

 1,980m 5,450 7

Tequia was founded in 1539, but due to lack of water and being only two kilometers (1.2 mi) from Málaga, Padre Isidro Miranda moved the town four kilometers (2.5 mi) further on to the Valle de Cutaligua. A few yet

live in Tequia, caretaking the ruins of the old parish church and the balneario, fresh-water swimming pools (even one for children) (admission: $0.80 adults, $0.50 children).

Hiking up a side road into the mountains, you can visit two ancient indigenous cemeteries, one at Vereda de Yerbabuena (preserved in situ at Señor Luis Jesús Gómez' house) and the other at Vereda de Lucusguta. A rough dirt road to the left of the church ruins will take you past farms and brick kilns down to the main "highway" again and into San José de Miranda.

A faux-High-Gothic church sits on San José de Miranda's main plaza like a pastel-iced cake. Follow Carrera 4 out of town. To the right after about 500 meters (300 ft) is Balneario Rosales (admission: $1.05), another spring-fed pool with eucalyptus-fired sauna ($2.65 1 hr, $5.50 2 hr). About seven kilometers (4 mi) down the left of Carrera 4, heading toward Bogotá, is Termales de Salado Bravo at Las Cuevas (admission: free), undeveloped natural hot spring pools. Miranda celebrates its patron saint, Nuestra Señora de los Remedios, in February and the Fiesta de la Gallina (Hen Feast) in June.

There are basic restaurants and an inn in Miranda. The balnearios are guaranteed open Friday-Sunday and Monay holidays, though they are often open during the week, also. A taxi to Tequia costs $3.50 one way; a colectivo taxi to Miranda is $1.50. Or walk to Tequia: the road begins from Calle 1 and Carrera 6C in Málaga.Updated: Mar 21, 2011.

CONCEPCIÓN

 2,005m 7,000 7

Concepción is a weaving center not too far from Málaga. Here, small workshops create blankets, jackets, ponchos and other items from virgin wool—a perfect place to pick up some warm clothing before heading to Parque Nacional Natural El Cocuy. This village is considered the heart of Colombian textiles, hosting the National Wool Fair every December. The home of Salón Wilches, a late-19th-century Liberal politician, is preserved. If you want to take a soak, choose between the fresh-water pools at Balneario Natural de la Quebrada Manaria or the warmer ones of Balneario Natural de Aguas Calientes. You can also visit the indigenous community, Samoré. Collective taxis, when full, leave from the corner of Carrera 8 and Calle 13; $5.30. Mar 21, 2011.

CAPITANEJO

 1,172m   7,800   7

A paved highway wends about 170 kilometers (102 miles) from Tunja up the Eastern Cordillara to Capitanejo. This is the Bogotá-Cúcuta route preferred by trucks and many bus companies, as opposed to the trajectory by way of Bucaramanga: it is shorter and has no peajes, toll booths. On the southern limit of Capitanerjo is the turn-off for the Sierra Nevada de El Cocuy and its hamlets.

Capitanejo is on the Río Chicamocha and serves as an alternative point to raft through that river gorge. The village enjoys a hot, dry climate, perfect for warming up after trekking in Parque Nacional Natural El Cocuy.

The highway forms the main street, Carrera 4. One block west is Plazoleta Municipal Pedro Antonio Ruiz Prada, the main square whose name is as big as the plaza itself, in which most of Capitanejo's population could probably fit. Around this are the church, palacio municipal, bank, two nightclubs and a hotel. In the center is a large ceibo tree which—according to legend whose origin is lost in the mists of time—is over a hidden lagoon. At a 1997 proposal to chop it down, the people rose to protect it. Decorating the plazoleta is a mosaic depicting the products for which Capitanejo is known: tobacco and goat. Indeed, this is the goat, tobacco and melon capital of Colombia. Goats make their appearance on the comida corriente menu and are all-dolled-up for the patron saint processions in August. Updated: Sep 29, 2011.

History

The indigenous peoples who lived in the Capitanejo region were the Lacha. The Spaniards called them Chitareros, as their hair was cut to the mould of the gourd used for preparing chicha (alcohol made from fermented grains, corn or fruit). In 1541, Gerónimo de Aguayos, who had founded Málaga, and 70 other whites arrived in this area. Two years later, Don Juan Rodríguez Parra received these lands along the Río Chicamocha and enslaved the Lacha. It wouldn't be until the following century, in 1630, that Capitán Cristóbal Verde de Aguilar would give Capitanejo its present name. At the turn of the 21st century, paramilitary forces occupied the village; inhabitants recount the massacres and massive exodus that occurred.

The Colombian military moved into Capitanejo in 2003, thus securing it. Capitanejanos have since been returning. Updated: Sep 29, 2011. .

When to Go

The driest months in Capitanejo are December, January, June and July. The rainiest are April and May. The hottest months, with temperatures in the upper 30°s C(upper 90s-lower 100°s F), are January and February. January is also the best month for canotaje, or whitewater rafting. Updated: Sep 29, 2011.

HOLIDAYS AND FESTIVALS

The New Year starts off with the Festival del Río, a time to hit the beaches along the Chicamocha River and to raft down its canyon. In July is the Fiesta de la Virgen del Carmen, patron of all taxi, bus and truck drivers. Goats dressed in earrings and skirts parade through the town as part of the commemorations to San Bartolomé, Capitanejo's patron saint. Honor is further paid to goat friends with the Festival del Cabrito, the third week of December. The year closes with the Fiestas del Retorno y Matachines, which include the aguinaldo novena leading up to Christmas. During this festival, young boys, dressed in costumes, whack challengers with inflated cows' bladders. The burning of Old Man Year rounds out the festival year. Updated: Jan 16, 2008.

Getting To and Away

Capitanejo has no central bus terminal. Most of the transport company offices are located on Carrera 4. All departures times are approximate, as the buses are passing through from various destinations. Many companies only offer trips every other day, so be sure to check schedules carefully. Various bus companies service Capitanejo, including: Coflonorte/Libertadores (Cra. 4, 5-32), Concorde (Cra. 4, 4-19), Copetrán (Ca. 5, 4-84), Cotrans (Cra. 4, 4-12) and Expreso Paz del Río/Gacela (Cra. 4, 4-39).

To El Cocuy: 2 a.m., 3 a.m., 2 p.m., 3:30 p.m.; 4 hr, $5.

To Bogotá (via Tunja): departures 3 a.m.-10 p.m.; 8-9 hr, $16-20.

To Bucaramanga: 3 a.m., 4:30 a.m., 10 a.m.; 7 hr, $20.

To Topal (Casanare): 1 a.m.; 7 hr, $17.

To Cúcuta (via Pamplona): 3 a.m.-10:30 p.m.; 7 hr, $25-30.

To Güicán: 2 a.m., 3 a.m., 2 p.m., 3:30 p.m.; 4 hr, $6. Updated: Oct 03, 2011.

Safety

Everyone assures the visitor that the town and surrounding countryside are perfectly safe now from the presence of guerrilla and paramilitary forces. There is a fortified Policia Nacional station in the village, and motorcycle patrols secure the highway. Cases of dengue have been reported in Capitanejo. Updated: Sep 29, 2011.

Services

TOURISM

The **tourism office** is in the Palacio Municipal (Monday-Friday 8 a.m.-noon. Ca. 5, between Cra. 5 and 6, Plazoleta Municipal. Tel: 660-0092, Cel: 313-495-6465). Updated: Oct 04, 2011.

MONEY

Banco Agrario has a branch in Capitanejo (Ca. 4, between Cra. 5 and 6, Plazoleta Municipal); however, it has no ATM or other services to assist the traveler. Capitanejo has no casa de cambio, so come with plenty of pesos. Updated: Oct 04, 2011.

KEEPING IN TOUCH

Telecom is not only the sole international call center, it is also one of two Internet "cafés" in Capitanejo (Cra. 3, 4-18). The other place to hop on the web is at the public library, **Biblioteca Pública Juan de J. Wilches** (Ca. 3, between Cra. 3 and 2). Several shops along the main street, Carrera 4, offer local and national calls. Skype is nonexistent here. For mailing letters or receiving general delivery, the **post office** (Monday-Friday 8 a.m.-noon and 1-5 p.m., except when the señora pops out to run an errand. Ca. 5, 5-28) is in an unsigned building next to the Palacio Municipal. Updated: Oct 04, 2011.

MEDICAL

Capitanejo's public health facility is **Hospital San Bartolomé** (Cra. 4, vía Bogotá, at the entrance to town. Tel: 660-0015). Several pharmacies are on the same street. Updated: Oct 04, 2011.

CAMERA

Estudio Godoy is the only photo store in town. However, its sole raison d'être is taking photographs. It carries no camera supplies. Updated: Oct 04, 2011.

Things To See and Do

Capitanejo may seem just a scorching town straddling a highway, but it does hide a few cool spots beneath that dust. For the traveler interested in religious attractions, there is the village church, San Bartolomé, the Centro de Peregrinación El Carmen and the Santuario del Sagrado Corazón, with great views over the river valley. Down near the Puente La Palmera spanning the Río Chicamocha are beaches where you can take a free dip. For a more structured swim, go to one of the *balnearios*. Hike out to La Chorrera waterfall, raft down the Chicamocha, drop your line in at the Hacienda La Alejandría for some trout, or rock climb El Tablón and Las Juntas. There's a bit of everything in Capitanejo. Updated: Sep 29, 2011.

Balnearios

To beat the heat in Capitanejo, head for one of the *balnearios*, or swimming holes. There's one for every budget.

Brisas del Chicamocha (ADMISSION: $1.05 adults, $0.80 children under 8) has a large pool with a slide for adults, a shallow pool for children, dressing rooms, shaded seating around the pools and a restaurant. This is the balneario closest to town. Daily 9 a.m.-6 p.m. Cra. 4, via Málaga, just past Restaurante La Pola. Tel: 660-0175.

Avilmar (ADMISSION: $1.60 adults, $1.05 children 12 and under) is near the banks of the Río Chicamocha, one kilometer (0.62 mi) from the village (motorcycle taxi from Calle 4 and Carrera 4, $0.50). Considered a more upscale facility, it not only has a separate pool for the kiddies, but it also has a playground. Its facilities further include sauna and restaurant. Daily 9 a.m.-6 p.m. Cra. 4, via Bogotá. Tel: Tel: 660-0000.

Playas de Chicamocha (ADMISSION: free) is on one of the banks of the river itself. Conditions for swimming here depend on the river's strength; seek local counsel before taking a dip here. Up in the mountains, near La Chorrera waterfall, is yet another option, at Hacienda Loma Linda. Updated: May 15, 2009.

Whitewater Rafting

Rushing down from the Sierra Nevada del Cocuy, the Servitá and Chicamocha Rivers merge at Capitanejo, where their waters, swirling and foaming, leap through a canyon on their way to join the Río Magdalena. Capitanejo is becoming more and more popular as a launching point for doing this river. However, all depends on conditions—the snow melt from the Sierra Nevada might make the river too low or ragingly strong. January is the most certain month. Check with tour operators in Capitanejo or Málaga about taking you on such an expedition. Updated: May 15, 2009.

La Chorrera

Toppling 60 meters (197 ft) down a rock face is La Chorrera waterfall. A motorcycle taxi can take you as far as the Chorrera school ($7) if you don't want to walk the approximately 10 kilometers (6 mi) from town. Still, it's a one-hour hike further into the mountains to see these waters cascading down towards the Río Nevado, its waters eventually mixing with those of the Río Chiamocha. To cool off after this trek, plunge into the pool at Balneario Hacienda Loma Linda. Updated Oct 04, 2011.

Tours

Acolture

Acolture—Asociación Coldinista de Turismo y Recreación—is a project of the local SENA program. Primarily this tour operation is focused on taking groups of 20 or more rafting on the Chicamocha or to visit local attractions like the La Chorrera waterfall. However, Professor Miriam Deysi can help line up a guide if you are only one or two travelers, price to be negotiated. The office can also provide information on hotels, restaurants and other tourist services in the village. Monday-Friday 8 a.m.-noon and 2-6 p.m., Saturday 8 a.m.-noon. Cra. 3, between Ca. 3 and 4. Tel: 660-0098, Cel: 311-513-9450, E-mail: deysymcapi18@hotmail.com. Updated: Jan 16, 2008.

Lodging

Capitanejo hotels are all pretty basic, with only fans to cool your room and cold water showers (though with the heat in Capitanejo, this is barely a hardship). All have the typical, tropical Latin American construction; ventilation is provided through latticed concrete blocks which are unscreened, as are the windows. This, needless to say, allows mosquitoes to come in search of the exotic visitor. Reservations are highly recommended for holiday times. Updated: Jul 22, 2010.

Hotel Cordobés !

(ROOMS: $4-6) Hotel Cordobés is a long-time favorite among budget travelers deciding to experience Capitanejo hospitality for a day or two. Luis and Irene run this basic hostel which has clean rooms that are simply furnished—beds, large table, and nightstand—but suitable for your Capitanejo stay. All the rooms are around the back patio, just off the kitchen. Don Luis and doña Irene are always ready to invite you to sit down and chat over a tinto (coffee) in the morning, or to watch an evening telenovela with them. Ca. 4, 3-58. Tel: 660-0403, Cel: 311-842-6220/313-205-2035. Updated: May 21, 2011.

Hotel Oasis

(ROOMS: $5-16) Three generations of women have been housing visitors here since 1953. It is one of the few inns in Capitanejo that has a dual price list: one for the temporada baja, low season, and another for the temporada alta, high season. All the large, simply dressed rooms have windows and private bath with water al tiempo, or room temperature; as the tank is on the roof, the day's climate will influence the temperature. The rooms upstairs have a TV and fan. Ca. 5 and Cra. 5. Plazoleta Municipal, Tel: 660-0336. Updated: May 22, 2009.

Hotel Colonial

(ROOMS: $7-10) Located a half-block from the Plazoleta Municipal on a quiet street, Hotel Colonial provides its guests with comfortable, clean rooms. Beds are super-fresh, not being made up until you arrive. All upstairs rooms have windows, mostly over the street, private cold-water bath, television and fan. Meals are available in the restaurant upon request. Cra. 5, 3-20. Tel: 7-660-0230. Updated: Mar 21, 2011.

Restaurants

The menu is quite limited in Capitanejo: the comida corriente is primarily cabro (goat) and sometimes gallina criolla (range-raised hen), and is significantly more expensive than in other parts of Colombia. Having said that, the cabro con pipitoria (rice made with goat's blood and finely chopped innards) is less than a third the price here than in restaurants elsewhere featuring it as a plato típico. So, if you want to try this traditional Santandereano dish, wait until you come here. However, take care! Not all of the eating establishments prepare their drinks with boiled or otherwise treated water. The weekly market is on Sunday. Updated Jun 24, 2011.

Asadero Rokoko

If you get tired of the cabro lunches and can't quite afford a meal of range-raised hen, then pop across the street to Asadero Rokoko. Here, a quarter of a roasted chicken costs $1.85. Dip the accompanying yuca and potatoes in the delicious, fresh, homemade chili sauce. The cooler has just about every kind of soft drink on the market in Colombia. Plastic disposable mitts are provided to keep your picking fingers clean (which means, unfortunately, you can't lick 'em clean—and this is finger-lickin' good chicken!) Daily 9 a.m.-10 p.m. Cra. 4, 4-53, Tel: 660-0019, Cel: 311-215-9105. Updated: Mar 11, 2011.

Restaurante La Piragua

(ENTREES: $3-7) Restaurante La Piragua offers excellent, home-cooked meals. The Santandereano classic dish, cabro, is served up traditional-style: *pipitoria* (rice with goat innards and blood), yuca and potatoes. Gallina criolla, or range-fed chicken, is also on the menu, as is occasionally trout. This eatery is tremendously popular with locals and folks passing through town, so go early to catch a lunch table. Restaurant La Piragua also fixes eggs and *caldo de papa* (potato soup) for breakfast. Daily 6 a.m.-6 p.m. Cra. 4, 4-36. Tel: 7-660-0040. Updated: Mar 11, 2011.

Restaurante Chef

(ENTREES: $4-7) Another *comedor* that gets crowded at lunch time, Restaurante Chef serves Capitanejo's typical comida corrientes, or blue-plate specials: cabro and gallina criolla. Yes, the menu is limited, but this is your chance to try goat at a very reasonable price. Daily 11:15 a.m.-5 p.m. Cra. 4, between Ca. 4 and 5. Tel: 660-0042. Updated: Mar 21, 2011.

Nightlife

During the week, if you want to have a beer, hang out at one of the two pool halls in town (men only—Colombian culture frowns upon women in such establishments) or a cafetería. Some of the *estaderos* (adult drinking clubs) may be open. The only disco and only real bar operate only on weekends (Friday, Saturday and Sunday—to close out the market day). Updated: Sep 29, 2011.

La Rumba

Outside the front door, doña Agustina sits on a stool welcoming tonight's imbibers and dancers. She charges no entry nor requires a minimum consumption in her corner discothèque of several dimly lit rooms. Her staff will put on anything the customers request, whether it be salsa, meringue, ranchero, vallenato or Americano. It's a clean place. Take a table and no-one else will bother, even if you're a woman alone. Tables can be reserved. Fri-day-Sunday and Monday holidays 7 p.m.-1 a.m. Ca. 5, 5-70 (corner of Cra. 5), Plazoleta Municipal. Updated: Mar 22, 2011.

Pubs Blue Bar

Soft light bathes the dark blue walls of Pubs Blue Bar. No, this drinking hole doesn't specialize in blues music. You're more likely to hear vallenato, salsa, merengue and the like at a volume too loud for this small space. Early in the evening there are only a few couples in dark corners holding hands, their beers beading in the day's waning heat. Later this pub will be full of sweating bodies throbbing to that music—after all, locals say this is the better dance hall. No admission is charged, nor is there a *consumo mínimo*, except that you must have at least one drink. Friday-Sunday 7 p.m.-3 a.m. Ca. 4, between Cra. 5 and 6, next to Banco Agrario, Plazoleta Municipal. Updated: Feb 22, 2008.

PARQUE NACIONAL NATURAL EL COCUY !

(ADMISSION: $18.25 foreigners, $6.75 nationals, $3.75 students) This national park is officially called Parque Nacional Natural de Sierra Nevada del Cocuy, Chita y Güicán, but most people just call it Parque Nacional Natural El Cocuy. Its 306,000 hectares (756,142 ac) are located in Boyacá, Arauca and Casanare departments.

On this western side of the range, the park boundary is etched at the 4,000-meter (13,120-ft) line. The Sierra Nevada has 21 peaks, several over 5,000 meters (16,400 ft). Ritacu'wa (Ritacuba) Blanco is the highest, at 5,330 meters (17,483 ft). This region has delicate páramo and has been heavily impacted by farming populations. The park service is working with these communities to restore the ecosystem and to develop sustainable alternatives, like ecotourism.

This area abounds with opportunities for trekking and climbing enthusiasts, and for those who just want a feel of the snow. The snowline is, at closest, only a three-hour hike away. This part of the park is divided into three general access points: Las Lagunillas or Alto de la Cueva; La Capilla or La Esperanza; and Rutaku'was (Ritacubas).

At the east side of PNN El Cocuy plunges to its lowest point, 600 meters (1,968 ft) in the Colombian llanos. Climbing the sheer rock here is only for experts. Because of the remoteness of the region and its dense vegetation, it has been less impacted by the human hand. The northern sector of PNN El Cocuy is part of indigenous U'wa territory. This area is the best preserved, in large part due to the U'wa's respect for nature. However, their culture and lands are endangered by the presence of possible oil fields.

Fauna species found in PNN El Cocuy include the spectacled bear, puma, chinchilla, mountain tapir, white-tailed deer and dozens of bird species, among them the condor and the *águila real* (golden eagle). Flora is equally diverse, owing to the many ecosystems of the park: you can see *frailejón*, cardoon cactus, and sietecueros trees, numerous varieties of mosses and lichens and cojines.

The park contains the largest expanse of glacier fields in northern South America but they are quickly receding due to global warming. Scientists estimate that at the present rate of melting, the snow pack will disappear in 15 to 20 years. The Sierra Nevada del Cocuy is the birthplace of rivers flowing both to the Río Magdalena and the Orinoco.

For more information on PNN El Cocuy, visit www.parquesnacionales.gov.co. Updated: Nov 01, 2011.

V!VA ONLINE REVIEW
PARQUE NACIONAL NATURAL EL COCUY
This is an excellent place to go if you love nature and extreme sports.
February 22, 2009

PERMITS
Before entering PNN El Cocuy you must obtain your permit from the park office in El Cocuy village or Güicán. You will be asked on which day you plan to enter and on which day you plan to leave. You can be flexible on the first, but not on the second. If you do not return by that date and report to a park office, search and rescue operations will begin. You can, theoretically, extend the date before expiration, but communications are difficult (including cell phone calls). You will also be asked to which areas you will be traveling.

To go into the northern sectors of the park, you need to apply to the U'wa nation (office in Bogotá), as this is part of its territory. Granting of this permission is not guaranteed.

Entry to PNN El Cocuy is prohibited for those under 12 years or over 60 years, pregnant women, and persons with cardiovascular or pulmonary problems.

The permit is $2.10 for national students (including university, with ID), $4.20 for Colombians and $12.10 for foreigners. Updated: Jul 02, 2008.

History
The history of PNN El Cocuy begins in the Cretaceous period, when this was a vast inland sea. Then, some 15 to 20 million years ago, the land began to rend, mountains uplifted, slowly growing into the Pliocene and Quaternary epochs. An ice field formed throughout this new eastern Cordillera and extended from Laguna de Tota, across the Santander páramo to Norte de Santander Department. In recent centuries, those glaciers have been receding, more rapidly now with global warming. Parque Nacional Natural El Cocuy, Colombia's fifth largest national park, was established in 1977. During the mid-1980s, the entire region (including the park and villages) was occupied by FARC and ELN guerrillas. In 2003 the Colombian military closed in and began clearing out the insurgents from the area. By 2005, the entire western side of the Sierra Nevada del Cocuy was secure. Updated: Sep 29, 2011.

When to Go
Weatherwise, the best months to go into PNN El Cocuy are December to February when it is drier. June and July are also not too bad. The worst months are April, May, August and September when it rains.

Needless to say, these clearer nights are also the coldest, with temperatures dipping below freezing (it's even more frigid deeper within the park). As well, this is a popular destination for vacationing bogotanos, especially in early January. Updated: Sep 29, 2011.

Getting To and Away
From Bogotá and Tunja two routes are possible: one through Duitama, Soatá, La Uvita, Guacamayas and Panqueaba; the other through Capitanejo and on to Cordoncillo. The road at Cordoncillo divides, going right to El Cocuy village and left to Güicán. Both of these towns serve as entries into PNN El Cocuy and have national park offices where you obtain your permit.

From the north you can arrive from Bucaramanga, Pamplona or Cúcuta, by way of Málaga and Capitanejo, to El Espino and the Cordoncillo crossroads. A web of rough roads run in the area immediately adjacent to the national park, leading to haciendas and guide lodges. You can transit this on your own or in a hired vehicle or the *lechero* (milk truck). Express services arranged with the lodges cost around $26.50-45 per vehicle. The daily lechero leaves El Cocuy at 5:30 a.m. ($1.60, regardless of distance). A school bus also leaves from Güicán at 6 a.m. The distance from El Cocuy village to Guaicany is 25 kilometers (15 mi); Guaicany to La Capilla (health post, phone, store), 6 kilometers (3.6 mi); La Capilla to Kanwara turn-off, 7.1 kilometers (4.25 mi); Kanwara turn-off to Güicán, 13.6 kilometers (8.2 mi). From Kanwara is a dirt track leading down into the llanos. Updated: Nov 01, 2011.

Safety

Since the military takeover of the region in 2003, Parque Nacional Natural El Cocuy and surrounding villages are now considered safe. Trekkers report seeing army units patrolling the park interior. However, the llano side of the park, going down into Arauca and Casanare Departments, is still within the *zona caliente* (hot zone) of the country's civil war.

Additionally, much of this area is dense virgin forest and unmapped wilderness, where people have disappeared. It is highly recommended that trekkers ask around locally before planning an itinerary. Military patrols may ask for your identification. A park official in El Cocuy said a notarized photocopy of one's passport would be acceptable in lieu of the original document.

Consider the altitude you are at. The lodges of the park are just below 4,000 meters (13,120 ft) and the park itself is at 4,000 meters or more. If traveling from Bogotá, you will gain significant altitude in a very short time. Do not push yourself to begin any hiking or trekking immediately after arriving. Properly acclimatize. High mountain sickness and pulmonary edema are serious threats, the latter resulting in at least one death per year.

Also take precautions for hypothermia, snow blindness, dehydration and sunburn. Use 30+ factor sun screen and UV-protector sun glasses. Temperatures can drop dramatically, and snow or sleet storms can start with a moment's notice. Have thermal clothing and rain gear at all times. Use sturdy boots. If you bring a cellular phone, Comcel is recommended and you should turn it off and on

every four hours to avoid signal problems. It can be difficult to receive a cell phone signal in the park itself or the neighboring lodges.

As always, be sure to seek local advice about conditions, of both the environment and political climates. Updated: Mar 11, 2011.

MEDICAL AND RESCUE

At La Capilla, about midway on the park road, is a basic *puesto de salud*, or health post. Hospitals exist in the two main villages, with the better being in Güicán. The nearest airport for emergency medical evacuation is in Málaga. If a person does not return by the end of his/her permit time, the national park service contacts the Cruz Roja to begin search and rescue operations. The Red Cross then coordinates its team (some of whom have had high-mountain rescue training), local farmers and military to look for the missing visitor. Don't expect any helicopter rescue if you run into problems. Updated: Jul 02, 2008.

Things to See and Do

If mountaineering and appreciating rare, natural beauty is your cup of tea, then you better start planning now to go to Sierra Nevada del Cocuy. In the May 2007 issue of Condé Nast magazine, Pico Iyer listed the mountain range with 18 snow covered peaks as one of the "20 Places to See Before They Die." But Cocuy's beauty may not live that long: a study published in 2005 said that some of the glaciers will disappear in the next 25 years. This is an especially precarious dilemma, as Iyer says that many of the locals in the area depend on the glaciers for a fresh supply of water. Mountaineering, hiking and trekking in this mountain range are considered some of Colombia's top activities. Treks are best done in the sunny season, December to March. The national park also presents opportunities for fishing and paragliding. Updated: Oct 18, 2011.

Trekking

Another prime activity in PNN El Cocuy is trekking across its plains. A series of old trails traverse the wind-swept landscaped rimed with snow-covered mountains. The solitude makes it a wondrous experience. A highlight is the Valle de Cojines, an area of huge pillows of Plantago rigido carpeting the earth. One–day treks include those to Las Lagunillas, Cueva de Cuchumba and the snow line of Ritaku'wa Blanco. The longest excursion is the Vuelta a las Sierras, or the Sierra Circuit, which can be combined with mountain climbing. A half-circuit can be done around the north sierra,

EASTERN COLOMBIA

returning through Ratoncito Valley (3 days). Treks can also be done to Laguna Verde, Laguna de las Lajas, Laguna Grande de Pachacual or Laguna Grande de la Sierra.

Because all the trekking is at over 4,000 meters (13,120 ft) altitude, it is important to acclimatize first upon arriving to the park. Passes are at 4,200-4,900 meters (13,776 -16,072 ft). The weather can change quite suddenly, with sleet and snow storms. Read the Safety section for more information. You can obtain topographical maps with passes and campsites marked from the national park office in El Cocuy or from the Instituto Geográfico Agustín Codazzi in Bogotá.

If you are properly equipped and have substantial experience at high altitude and alpine/polar trekking, you can do the circuits on your own. A guide, though, is recommended. Pack horses can be hired at many of the lodges. Mar 18, 2011.

Vuelta a las Sierras/The Sierra Circuit

The most challenging of the treks in PNN El Cocuy is around the base of the Sierra Nevada del Cocuy, which is 22 kilometers (13.2 mi) long. The excursion takes five to 10 days. A medical doctor with over 10 years experience trekking in Cocuy suggests this demanding five- to six-day circuit:

Day 1—Through Las Lagunillas district, over Cusirí (4400 m/14,432 ft) and Patio Bolos passes to Laguna La Plaza campsite.

Day 2—To Laguna del Pañuela, over Paso Balcones (4400 m/14,432 ft).

Day 3—To Laguna del Rincón, over Paso de El Castillo (4,600 m/15,088 ft). If you are up to making it a very long day, you can continue to Valle de los Cojines and Laguna El Avellanal, crossing the 4,600-meter (15,088-ft) Paso de la Sierra.

Day 4—Over the mountain passes De los Frailes (4,200 m/13,776 ft) and de Cardenillo (4,100 m/13,448 ft) to Laguna de los Verdes.

Day 5—To Kabañas Kanwara. Each day you will be hiking eight to nine hours. Updated: Mar 18, 2011.

Cueva de Cuchumba !

Not too far from Hacienda La Esperanza, along the Quebrada El Cóncavo, is Cueva de Cuchumba. This cave, with a water-

fall within, was once an important ceremonial center for the U'wa. It was here they kept the image of a woman on cloth that a tall white man with a long white beard, dressed in white, had given them many generations earlier. They kept a fire of wax and "failejón" illuminating it. In 1736, Padre Miguel Blasco was catechizing to the U'wa and gifted them with a small painting of Our Lady of the Rosary. The U'wa responded, "We already have one, much more beautiful and splendorous". The priest had the U'wa textile moved to the church in Güicán, where you can see it today. The magical cave with its cascade bathing the stone walls is still there, though, near the Quebrada El Concavo.

From Hacienda La Esperanza, the walk takes about 10 minutes; from Cabañas Guaicany, one hour. A path from Güicán also goes to the Cueva. Updated: Mar 18, 2011.

Las Lagunillas

It is an easy one-day hike to Las Laguillas. The "camino" is well defined along the Río Lagunilla. A small stream flows across the plain, sculpting the ancient, rock-strewn earth into mounds and forming small crystalline lagoons across the valley. After about 45 minutes you'll arrive to the first of the magical lagoons strung together, Laguna La Pintada, backdropped by Campanilla Negra. The trail climbs through a small pass, and then on to three more lagoons: La Cuadrada, La Atravesada and La Parada.

The road begins at Alto de la Cueva, one kilometer (0.62 mi) from Cabañas Guaicany. One way, the trek is nine kilometers (5.4 mi). Update: Mar 18, 2011.

Rock Climbing

For those who get their adrenaline rush hugging the faces of cliffs, feeling for the next hand hold, PNN El Cocuy has some special treats for you. Perhaps the most popular is El Púlpito del Diablo, a 5l100-meter (16,728-ft), two-pitch challenge of not only rock, but also ice. Other places to climb include Portales (5,100-m/16,728 ft, three pitches) and Morrenas rising amidst glaciers. The most death-defying escarpments lie on the west face of the Sierra Nevada del Cocuy, going down into the *llanos* (eastern plains). On this side of the range are vertical climbs of over 700 meters (2,300 ft), only for the most experienced rock climbers. The views over the llanos is said to be breathtaking.

A guide is necessary. Contact an operator in El Cocuy, Güicán or elsewhere. Basic experience is needed; skill levels are from easy to highly difficult. Unfortunately, the prime area for rock climbing lies in the red zone of the country's civil war, an area in which activities cannot be recommended at this time. Updated: Mar 18, 2011.

Mountain Climbing

One of the biggest draws to PNN El Cocuy is the mountain climbing. The Sierra Nevada del Cocuy is considered to be one of the most beautiful ranges in the country and the lack of tourists makes for an un-crowded, quiet adventure. These peaks were first summited by a Swiss team in 1928. Colombians preparing for Himalayan and Southern Andes expeditions train here. The almost sheer, vertical rises provide challenges for even the most experienced mountaineer. The Sierra Nevada has 21-plus peaks over 4900 meters (16,072 ft). Some of the mountains to conquer are Ritaku'wa Blanco (5,330 m/17,482 ft), Ritaku'wa Negro (5,300 m/17,384 ft), San Pablín Norte (5,200 m/17,056 ft), El Concavo (5,200 m/17,056 ft), and El Castillo (5,030 m/16,500 ft). El Puntiaguado (5,200 m/17,056 ft) is a curious formation of a stone cube crowned by a stone spire.

A guide is essential. Contact an operator in El Cocuy, Güicán or elsewhere. Plan on four to five days for your expedition. The Mountains have many crevasses. Rope, ice axe and crampons are essential equipment (these will most likely be supplied by your guide). Guides in El Cocuy have excursions for those with no experience, as well as a mountain climbing school. Updated: Mar 18, 2011.

Fishing

Don't forget to pack your rod and reel when coming to Parque Nacional Natural El Cocuy. You can whip loose your fly and take a shot at the trout swimming in the icy depths of Laguna Grande de Pachacual, Laguna de la Parada, or in the rivers slicing the páramo. To fish in the lagoons, you must have a permit (obtainable from the national park office in El Cocuy village). To cast a line into the rivers, no special permission is needed. Also, some of the lodges at the edge of the park have stocked ponds. Ah, what better way to end a day of trekking and climbing than with a succulent pan-fried trout! Updated: Mar 18, 2011.

Tours

Guides and horses are available at all of the lodges at the edge of the national park. The park office in El Cocuy village maintains a list of the current prices for each. Depending on the destination, horse rental costs $10.50-26.50 per day and guide services $8-32 per day. Cabañas Guaicany is the most expensive. Prices are set among the guide lodges. Park rules establish that a guide is needed for each group of six persons and that they may only work seven hours per day. El Cocuy and Güicán have tour operators that can make all arrangements for you. If you want to plan your trek in advance, check out Sierra Nevada del Cocuy at www.sierranevadadelcocuy.com or Climbing, Skiing and Trekking Holidays in the Andes at www.andes.org.uk. Updated: Mar 18, 2011.

Lodging

Cabaña-style hotels are concentrated in three areas of the park: Alto de la Cueva (Las Lagunillas), where Cabañas Guaicany and the inns of the Herrera (Miguel and Alejandro) brothers are; La Esperanza (La Capilla); and Ritaku'was, featuring Kabañas Kanwara, Cabañas Peñas Blancas and Posada Sierra Nevada. The majority do not have heat or chimneys. Many have campsites. Make reservations December-January and June-July.

Camping is also possible within the park at several official campsites: El Hotelito, Laguna de la Plaza, Laguna Grande de la Sierra, Laguna de Panuelo, Laguna de los Verdes and other places. A tent with a good rain-fly and a -10ºC (12ºF) sleeping bag with insulation sleep pad are essential. Updated: Jun 24, 2011.

Cabaña Gaicany

(CAMPING: $2.50, BEDS: $7.50-15) In a three-story, A-frame chalet, Juan Carlos Carreño and his family provide simple rooms with bunk beds for up to 35 guests. On the third floor are two rooms, each with a double bed. Up there is also a sitting area for everyone's pleasure with a view onto the snowy peaks. No rooms are heated. There are no private bathrooms, only common. The one shower has an electric heater that barely takes the icy edge off the water. A new dining room and living room with fireplace are presently under construction. The Carreño family rents camping and climbing equipment. They hire guides and horses to all the major attractions in the southern and central range. Alto de la Cueva (Las Lagunillas) sector. Tel: 1-563-5405 (Bogotá), Cel: 310-566-7554, E-mail: cab_guaicany@yahoo.es/guaicany@hotmail.com. Updated: Mar 18, 2011.

Kabañas Kanwara

(BEDS: $3.50-27.50) Kabañas Kanwara is probably the most luxurious inn in the park district. The three cabañas have five rooms each (one to three beds each, plus table) and hot-water shower. Their balconies have a fine view of the Ritaku'was and the cordillera (mountains). Two of the lodges have kitchenettes, but no stove (use your camper). You can even warm up your feet in front of the fireplace before crawling into your blanket-laden bed. The restaurant serves excellent food ($5-6 per meal). Horses and guides are available for treks to Ritacu'wa Blanco and Laguna de los Verdes ($20 and $22.50 per day respectively), as well as to Laguna San Pablín, Púlpito del Diablo and Laguna Grande de la Sierra. Mountain climbing expeditions can also be arranged. Kabañas Kanwara's shop sells weavings by the U'wa and Hormiguitas de la Sierra weaving cooperative in Güicán. From the Kanwara turn-off to Kabañas Kanwara is 4.8 kilometers (3 mi). The rough road is steep, climbing 340 meters (550 ft). You can phone the lodge to meet you at the crossroads where the milk truck will drop you off ($2.60 charge). Tel: 311-231-6004/237-2260, E-mail: infokanwara@gmail.com Updated: Mar 18, 2011.

Hacienda La Esperanza

(BEDS: $10) After being abandoned for a spell, Hacienda La Esperanza has undergone a renovation at the loving hand of Marco Artura Valderrama, once more giving shelter to weary explorers. Its highly polished floors gleam. The thick earthen walls of this 200-year-old farmhouse keep the three multi-bed guest rooms toasty warm. The beds come with several wool blankets. The bathrooms spout hot water showers. Off the central courtyard is a kitchen where you can order meals and a sitting room with a fireplace. Hacienda La Esperanza provides guides and horses to Laguna Grande de la Sierra and other points (horse $20 per day, guide $27.50 per day). The lechero will drop you off at La Capilla, from where it is two kilometers (1.2 mi) to Hacienda La Esperanza. 23 kms from the Cocuy Valley up on the mountain. Cel: 310-209-9812 (Guillermo), E-mail: haciendalaesperanza@gmail.com. Updated: May 18, 2011.

Restaurants

All lodges within PNN El Cocuy serve meals, usually of the high-starch variety. Campers pitching their tents at such establishments may be able to use the kitchen, depending on the inn's policies. Otherwise bring a camp stove.

If backcountry camping, purchase all necessary food and fuel supplies in the nearest villages before coming out to El Cocuy National Park. You may be able to buy some items from locals, but don't bank on it—and very few people live on the eastern side of the range. White gas is scarce in all of Colombia. You can stock up on it in Bogotá or Bucaramanga. Or, else bring a stove that uses multi-fuel or canisters. *Gasolina roja* (car fuel) is available at the gas stations in El Cocuy village and Güicán. Jun 24, 2011.

EL COCUY

 2,750m   7,610   8

The road from Cordoncillo to El Cocuy is unpaved. This colonial town with white and sea-green buildings is the most touristy of the two entries into the Parque Nacional Natural El Cocuy, with better hotel, shopping and nightclub infrastructure. In the main plaza is a diorama of the entire Sierra Nevada del Cocuy mountain range. Otherwise, there isn't much to see or do in El Cocuy village itself. The daily milk truck into the park begins its route here. Updated: Sep 29, 2011.

History

El Cocuy was the fourth Spanish town founded in Nuevo Reino de Granada in 1541 by Captain Gonzalo García Zorro. Before the conquistadors arrived, indigenous Cacique Cocuy ruled the region. Once the Spaniards arrived, they used El Cocuy as a base for explorations for El Dorado in the llanos region. The indigenous were relocated to the warmer, lower regions to work as slaves on farms. El Cocuy was officially declared a residence for Spanish and mestizos in 1720.

In recent decades, El Cocuy and the surrounding region has been affected by Colombia's civil war. Native sons of El Cocuy include José Santos Gutiérrez, president from 1868-1870, engineer Olimpo Gallo Espinel, who discovered the iron mines at Paz del Río, and painter Roberto Arango. Updated: Sep 29, 2011

When to Go

December and January are the best months to come to El Cocuy; nights are colder but the weather is dryer. The wettest months are April, May, August and September. Christmas season and New Year's Eve draw the most tourists to El Cocuy, so make reservations during these times. Updated: Sep 29, 2011

HOLIDAYS AND FESTIVALS

El Cocuy is a typical village with its share of dates important to its people. A few festivals are worth checking out.

Semana Santa is celebrated in March-April with vigorous religious processions (expect to see extreme fasting and flagellation). In June, cocuyanos decorate their Parque Principal with arcades of the region's fruits and a mini zoo to celebrate Corpus Cristi. The Feast of Virgin del Carmen takes place on July 16. From December 7 to 12 is Nuestro Señor de las Misericordias, when El Cocuy pays tribute to its patron saint with an animal fair, artisan exhibits, bullfight and much more.

Getting To and Away

All transportation to the village of El Cocuy arrives and departs from Carrera 5 along the Parque Principal. All the bus companies have their offices on this block. Buses only leave for Güicán and other small nearby villages and for Bogotá.

To go north to Málaga, Bucaramanga, Pamplona or Cúcuta, go first to Capitanejo with a Bogotá-bound bus. Main bus companies include Gacela/Libertadores and Concorde. Buses leave from El Cocuy to Capitanjejo (4-5 a.m. and 6-7 p.m., $6) and Bogotá (via Soatá) (4:30 a.m., 3 buses 4:30-6:30 p.m.; 5:30 p.m., 4 a.m., 5 a.m.; $20-25). Updated: Oct 03, 2011.

Safety

There are armed government forces in El Cocuy village to maintain safety. Assassin bugs (which carry Chagas disease) and non-lethal scorpions are found in this area. Updated: Sep 29, 2011.

Services

TOURISM

The **national park office** is the first place to visit upon arriving in El Cocuy (Monday-Saturday 8 a.m.-noon and 2-5 p.m., Sunday 8 a.m.-noon. Corner of Cra. 5 and Ca. 8. Tel.: 789-0359, E-mail: pnncocuphp@yahoo.com/ pnncocuy@hotmail.com, URL: parquesnacionales.gov.co. The village's official website is www.elcocuyboyaca.com). Not only can the friendly staff help to orientate you to the park's attractions, but they can also supply you with information on transportation, hotels and restaurants in El Cocuy and Güicán villages, and the current prices of lodging, meals, horse rental and guide services of inns located at the edge of the park.

MONEY

Banco Agrario (Ca. 8, between Cra. 3 and 4) is the only money institution in El Cocuy. It has no ATM or other exchange services. Obtain plenty of pesos before coming to the region. Tunja and Málaga are the nearest cities with facilities.

KEEPING IN TOUCH

The **Telecom** office (Monday-Saturday afternoons. Ca. 7, 3-60) in El Cocuy village is closed indefinitely. Local shops charge $0.15 per minute for local and national calls. The lone Internet café in El Cocuy has a slow connection costing $1.05 per hour.

If the Internet fails you, send your loved ones a postcard from the **post office** at Carrera 3, 7-55 (Monday-Friday 8 a.m.-noon and 2-5 p.m., Saturday 8 a.m.-noon)

MEDICAL

Hospital San José (Tel.: 789-0011) and the **Cruz Roja** (Tel: 789-0042) are at the entrance to El Cocuy village on Calle 11 and Carrera 6. The hamlet has few pharmacies. There is one at Calle 7, between Carreras 5 and 6 on the plaza.

CAMERA

Galería Cocuyana (daily 8 a.m.-7 p.m. Ca. 5, 4-20. Tel: 789-0167, Cel: 311-513-9214), the only camera shop in the PNN El Cocuy area, is in El Cocuy village and is owned by photographer Pío Avedaño. He keeps black and white, slide and 100ASA color film in stock, and has cameras for sale. You can also purchase calendars, posters and key chains with his graphic work. Sometimes the gallery may be closed, when Señor Avedaño is out in the field. Updated: Jun 27, 2011.

SHOPPING

Artesanías de Mi Colombia ♪

Artesanías de Mi Colombia specializes in crafts lovingly made in workshops all over Boyacá Department. Pick up a ruana woven in Güicán or El Espino, other woolens from El Cocuy village, or some colorful baskets from Guacamayas. The shop also has a fine selection of fique bags made by the U'wa, cornhusk dolls from Tunja and pottery from Ráquira. Artesanías de Mi Colombia also sells postcards and posters of the national park. Tuesday-Sunday 10 a.m.-1 p.m. and 3 p.m.-7 p.m. Closed Mondays. Cra. 3, between Ca. 7 and 8. Tel: 789-0377, Cel: 310-494-5076/312-352-9121. Updated: Mar 18, 2011.

EASTERN COLOMBIA

Tejidos Katly

Tejidos Katly sells a good selection of *ruanas*, the short wool ponchos that just about everyone wears in El Cocuy, including men, women, boys and girls of every age. To pick one up before venturing into the cold hinterlands of PNN El Cocuy, head to this shop. All Tejidos Katly's ruanas are made of natural-colored virgin wool and prices start at $25. Tejidos Katly sells plenty more to keep warm, including jackets, ski masks, gloves and socks. Margarita Correño will be happy to take a break from her knitting to help you suit up. If the shop isn't open, ring up Doña Margarita. Cra. 5,6-29. Cel: 311-474-0270, E-mail: margaritaga40@hotmail.com. Updated: Mar 18, 2011.

Chirros y Gorras

Chirros y Gorras is your one-stop shopping for hats from every area of Colombia, including native and non-native styles, such as ball caps and pith hats. There's a wide variety of materials to choose from, including felt, leather and paja straw, which is used to make the classic, two-tone sombrero typical of Colombia. The prices aren't too bad, from $7 up. After dropping by Chirros y Gorras you'll find yourself fitting right in with the townsfolk, since hats are a favorite accessory. Cra. 5, 5-78. Updated: Jun 27, 2011.

Things to See and Do

The village of El Cocuy doesn't have many attractions of its own. It has no museums, no hot springs and no cultural centers. It seems to be willing to play a supporting role to the national park by providing good services to the tourist preparing for trekking and mountain climbing. One activity, though, is paragliding from Maohama, a high bluff outside of this hamlet. Updated: Jun 27, 2011.

Paragliding in El Cocuy

To the west of El Cocuy village a dark cliff looms out of the greened landscape. This peak is called Maohama. It is the spot easiest to access in PNN El Cocuy for practicing parapentismo, or paragliding. Any time of the year is good for leaping off its heights and soaring like an Andean condor over the crumpled earth in this corner of Colombia. The best month, though, is in July when El Cocuy pueblo hosts a parapentismo festival. Contact the national park office or Coopserguías in El Cocuy village to arrange an excursion with a guide. Take note that a guide is mandatory for this type of excursion. Updated: Mar 21, 2011.

Tours

Coopserguías

Coopserguías is a cooperative of campesinos residing within Parque Nacional Natural El Cocuy. The down-to-earth souls of Coopserguías know the region like the back of their grizzled hands, and now are pooling together their resources and decades of knowledge to provide services to Cocuy explorers. They offer lodging, horses, equipment for rent and guides for treks and mountain climbing. Coopserguias works in cooperation with the national park service. The sign over the door says Oficina Ecoturismo—AENCO (Asociación Ecoturístico Nevado El Cocuy). The office has irregular hours, so it is best to call or E-mail. Ca. 7 and Cra. 6, Parque Principal. Cel: 313-293-8313/311-880-0875, URL: http://elcocuycoopserguias.com/. Updated: Nov. 17, 2010.

Rodrigo Arias

For many years Rodrigo Arias has been exploring the Sierra Nevada del Cocuy, as well as mountain ranges from California to Patagonia. Hostels in many parts of Colombia often recommend his services to those wanting to experience the grandeur of Cocuy National Park. Arias offers all-inclusive packages for one person or small groups for day hikes, the eight-day circuit trek around the base of the sierra, scaling Ritaku'wa or the other mountains, and climbing El Pulpito. He also teaches courses in mountaineering, rock climbing and rescue, and can arrange special excursions. Rodrigo Arias is now working in conjunction with Coopserguias, a cooperative in Parque Nacional Natural El Cocuy. Cel: 320-339-3839, E-mail: arias_rodrigo@hotmail.com, URL: www.colombiatrek.com. Updated: Mar 18, 2011.

Lodging

El Cocuy village has a growing number of hotels and all are good values. Now even the budget inns have hot water! These are often in the hamlet's oldest structures, in various states of repair, with only common bathrooms located off the back patio (not within the main building). Newer hostels, aimed at travelers with more refined tastes, are still surprisingly affordable. Make reservations for the high seasons, especially the months of December, January, June and July. Updated: Sep 29, 2011.

Hotel Restaurante Casa Vieja

(ROOMS: $4) Hotel Restaurante Casa Vieja is a bit of a misnomer, since it no longer has a restaurant. However, internationally renowned local artist Roberto Arango still opens the doors of his worn colonial home to the weary traveler, offering large rooms, in various states of repair, around the main courtyard. The courtyard makes up for what the sparsely furnished rooms lack. The garden is full of more varieties of geraniums than you thought existed and the portico is a gallery of Arango's Cocuy landscape paintings. The renovated hot water baths are at the back of the house. Cra. 6, between Ca. 7 and 8, Parque Principal. Updated: Jul 01, 2008.

Hotel Villa Real !

(ROOMS: $7-10) A quaint, family run inn, Hotel Villa Real is a comfortable place to stay in El Cocuy—both in price and in ambience. The rooms—all on the upper stories—are finely decorated and come in a variety of sizes (one to six beds) depending on your traveling group. The rooms share the clean common baths with hot showers. One room has its own bathroom. After your park excursion, your rest is assured while lying back on these good mattresses while zoning out to the telly. Downstairs you can conveniently have your meals or grab a drink at the family's store. Ca. 7, 4-50. Cel: 311-475-6495/810-2808, E-mail: hotelvillareal@hotmail.com. Updated: Mar 18, 2011.

Hotel Casa Muñoz

(ROOMS: $10-35) Casa Muñoz has sharp rooms in an annex of a colonial-era house. Each room, named after one of the mountains in the national park, has cable TV and baths with gas-heated hot water. Upstairs rooms have lofts with more mattresses, which are sure to be a hit with the kids. This inn has only one room with a single bed; the others are multi-bed. A restaurant will soon be a part of Casa Muñoz' services. Prices depend on the season and the amount of people in the room. Cra. 5, 7-28, Parque Principal. Tel: 789-0328/0328, Cel: 313 829 1073/332-1980, E-mail: hotelcasamunoz@yahoo.com/hotelcasamunoz@hotmail.com. Updated: Mar 18, 2011.

Restaurants

Eating options in the village of El Cocuy are fairly slim. Some of the hotels have or plan to open restaurants. In the evenings, stands set up around the central park sell cheese arepas and other comidas rápidas. The Mercado, at Carrera 5 and Calle 5, and the *comedor* (dining) section are active weekend mornings, with the principal market day being Friday. The village has several *almacenes*, or general stores, where you can purchase canned goods before heading into the national park.

A traditional dish served only at Christmas and New Years is tamales. These are much different than the Tolimense ones served in most of Colombia. Here, cornmeal mush is filled with pork, beef, chicken and pork skin (all marinated in herbs, spices and beer), garbanzos, onion and carrot. The tamale is steamed in a *hoja de raíz*, also called *bijao* (*Calathea lutea*). Updated: Sep 29, 2011.

Cafetería y Comidas Rápidas Donde Lilia

(SNACKS: $0.50 and up) Cafetería y Comidas Rápidas Donde Lilia is the place to go for a late breakfast or a quick mid-morning snack. This small, no-frills snack stand serves a basic menu of empanadas and *rellenos*, a black sausage filled with potato and rice ($0.50-1). To wash it down, there are coffee and soft drinks. Monday-Saturday 9 a.m.-noon, closed Sunday. Ca. 7, between Cra. 4 and 5. Updated: Mar 11, 2011.

Asadero Nortibrasas

(CHICKEN: $1.60-6.40) Asadero Nortibrasas is a good choice for a break from the hotel-restaurant scene and their typical Colombian fare. In the front room, a large rotisserie rotates chickens over coals. Ask for your plate of roasted chicken and potatoes: a quarter-chicken costs $1.60, half is $3.20 and the whole bird is $6.40. If you want more of a traditional meal, order the grilled chicken breast or fish with rice, potatoes, plantains and salad ($3.70). Daily 10 a.m.-8 p.m. Cra. 5, between Ca. 8 and 9. Updated: Jul 01, 2008.

Restaurant Hotel Villa Real

(LUNCH: $2.10) Steam rising from the pots bathes Doña Marta's face as she dishes up another bowl of soup. Her family is out in the five-table dining rooms, bustling from one customer to another. The main dish comes next with meat, rice and veggies. With a drink made from bottled water, this lunch (or dinner) costs $2.10. Mornings, doña Marta also serves *caldo de papa* (potato soup) or eggs to order with hot chocolate for $1.30. This is one of El Cocuy's most popular restaurants. Daily 7 a.m.-8 p.m., though you may ask for earlier or later service. Ca. 7, 4-50. Tel: 789-0038, Cell 311-475-6495/810-2808, E-mail: hotelvillareal@hotmail.com. Updated: Jul 01, 2008.

Nightlife

The village of El Cocuy has few places for letting off steam and partying down. The only real disco is just open on Fridays, after the weekly market closes. However, there are other places where you can kick back and have a drink. Better still, save up the energy you would otherwise blow on dancing for the treks and climbing you'll be doing in PNN El Cocuy. Updated: May 14, 2009.

Disco T-K

Join the locals in closing out a Friday market day at Disco T-K Fogata, the town's only discoteca. Everyone keeps warm during the chilly nights dancing to the salsa, merengue, reggaeton, electrónica, vallenato or whatever else the crowd requests. There's no cover charge or minimum consumption. Open Friday only, 7 p.m.-2 a.m. Cra. 5, between Ca. 7 and 8, Parque Principal. Updated: May 14, 2009.

Café-Bar Escocés

Café-Bar Escocés is an intimate meeting place on the corner of the plaza in El Cocuy. Low rainbow lights illustrate the paintings of hometown legend Roberto Arango. The drink menu has cocuyano favorites such as canelazo, aguardiente and beer, plus wine for the international customers. Coffee, teas and sodas are also available. If the music inside gets too loud, just pull up one of the benches out front and join in on a jawing session with the locals. Daily 4 p.m.-midnight. Cra. 6 and Ca. 8, next to Hotel Restaurante Casa Vieja. Updated: Jun 27, 2011.

GÜICÁN

 2,928m   9,644   8

From Cordoncillo, a paved road goes to Güicán, which has a more wild-west feel to it than its neighbor El Cocuy. Perhaps Güicán's distinctive atmosphere is because it is the younger of the two main villages, not only in founding date, but also because it was rebuilt after an 1860 fire. Perhaps the difference lies in a closer relationship with the U'wa.

The modern-day U'wa territory is not too far from Güicán, and at times you can see the U'wa in town. Shops around the plaza sell bags and other artesanía created by them. Even though it is the larger village, Güicán has a much more limited selection of hotels and restaurants. Oddly enough, however, it is richer in attractions. Updated: Jun 27, 2011.

History

This sliver of mountain valley was inhabited by U'wa (Güicanes). When their cacique Güaicaní heard the dreaded Spanish were approaching, he lead his people in jumping from El Peñol de los Muertos to escape a life of slavery and disease at the hands of the invaders. The Jesuits subsequently established Güicán on February 26, 1756. Some of the natives fled into the mountains and formed a resistance movement against the Spanish rule. A fire destroyed the village in 1860. After independence, Güicán became a hub of agricultural trade between the highlands and the eastern plains. At the vespers of the 21st century, Güicán found itself in the heated center of the country's civil war and was occupied by the various forces. In 2003, the Colombian military began a clean-up operation of the entire region, and by 2005 the village was once more securely in the government's hands. Updated: Sep 29, 2011.

When to Go

As in other parts of the region, the best time to go to Güicán is when the weather is clear and dry, from December to February. This is also when nights are coldest and the number of national tourists grows. June and July are other good months to visit. The worst months are during the rainy season: April, May, August and September. Updated: Sep 29, 2011.

HOLIDAYS AND FESTIVALS

Güicán's patron saint is the Virgen Morenita whose feast day is February 2 (Candelaria), during which faithful villagers make a romería, or pilgrimage to the Virgin. On this night the traditional Danza de la Clizneja, similar to the maypole dance, is performed. For the next half-week, from February 3 to 6, the town celebrates its Fiestas Reales with processions, horse races, a gastronomic fair and other activities. Updated: Sep 29, 2011.

Getting To and Away

Buses leave only for El Cocuy and other small nearby villages, and direct for Bogotá. To journey north to Málaga, Bucaramanga, Pamplona or Cúcuta, go first to Capitanejo with a Bogotá-bound bus. In Güicán all bus offices are around the town's square. Coflonorte/Libertadores and Gacela/Paz del Río are both on Calle 3, and Concorde at Calle 4 and Carrera 4. The Bogotá bus charges the same fare from Güicán as from El Cocuy. They arrive in this village one hour later from the capital and depart one hour earlier. See El Cocuy for full information.

El Correo, the mail run, is operated by Cootradatil. It leaves three times per day from Güicán to El Cocuy at 7 a.m., 11 a.m., and 2 p.m. ($1.30).

To travel along the park access road, you can either arrange an Expreso service with a lodge ($26.50-42 per vehicle), or catch the daily lechero, leaving Güicán at 5:30 a.m. ($1.60 regardless of distance). Updated: Jun 30, 2008.

Safety

The village and surrounding countryside is generally safe due to the national police and military patrols, though few people go out after 10 p.m. It is still imprtant to practice common sense safety precautions while traveling. Scorpions (non-lethal) and assassin bugs are present in Güicán. Updated: Jun 27, 2011.

Services

TOURISM

A second national park office has been set up in Güicán, on Carrera 4, facing the plaza (Tel: 789-7072, Cel: 310-230-3302), which can provide travelers entering PNN El Cocuy from this village with all the information they should need to know. However, additional information on the park and permits can be obtained from the Policia Nacional kiosk on the corner of the plaza (Cra. 5 and Ca. 4). Updated: Oct 04, 2011.

MONEY

Banco Agrario has a branch office in Güicán. However, it has no ATM or other services for the foreign traveler. There are no casas de cambio in the village, wither. Come with plenty of pesos. Updated: Oct 04, 2011.

KEEPING IN TOUCH

Telecom provides local and national phone service, as well as the cheapest international call rates (Cra. 5, between Ca. 4 and Ca. 5). You can also make local and national calls at shops. Güicán has only one, slow Internet café at Carrera 5, 1-04; it is usually open in the afternoon, though try in the morning, too. The post office is near the plaza (Monday-Friday 8 a.m.-noon and 2-5 p.m. Cra. 5 and Ca. 3). Updated: Oct 04, 2011.

MEDICAL

Güicán's Hospital Andrés Girardot is considered the better equipped facility in the national park area (Ca. 6 and Cra. 6. Tel.: 789-7228). Two droguerías are on Carrera 4, between Calles 4 and 6. Updated: Oct 04, 2011

SHOPPING

Artículos Religiosos La Morenita

Artículos Religiosos La Morenita sells much more than just rosaries, prayer books and other religious articles, most of which are made by Güicán artisans. This shop just around the corner from the church also has what must be Güicán's largest stock of woolen goods—ruana ponchos, hats, gloves and what-not—produced by a collective in this town. You can also pick up a pamphlet explaining the legend of La Morenita and Cuchumba cave (from the Catholic point of view, of course). Cra. 5, between Ca. 4 and 5. Updated: Jun 30, 2008.

Things to See and Do

Even though Güicán has considerably less tourist infrastructure than El Cocuy village, it does have several attractions nearby: Peñol de los Muertos, where U'wa jumped to their deaths upon the arrival of the Spaniards; an incredible monument honoring that indigenous nation; petroglyphs, or rock paintings; and several hot spring pools. An alternative path to Cueva de Cuchumba, near Hacienda La Esperanza within the national park, can be hiked from Güicán. It begins at the end of Carrera 4, at Calle 1. Ask for directions to La Capilla, as the road is not signposted. Updated: Jun 27, 2011.

Peñol de los Muertos

*And it occurred that men with faces of greed
Overthrew and erased our villages
Imposing their way of life by force.
Liberty is a gift that is born with life,
It justifies its existence.
Without it, Mother Earth reclaims us.
And to her breast we return conscious
We have fought for life, the race, for our presence.*
—U'wa history

In the mid-18th century, dust raised by horse hoof began whirling through this valley. The infamous Spaniards were approaching. Cacique Güaicaní knew what this meant for the U'wa people. They had to make a choice. Either live physically enslaved by these white invaders, dying of hunger and their plagues; or, live spiritually in freedom, returning to Mother Earth. An untold multitude chose to leap from El Peñol de los Muertos. Others fled deep into the mountains and to the plains on the other side, thus preserving U'wa culture to this day. Their struggle, however, continues against those men with faces of greed, now lusting after black gold, petroleum. In 1996 and 2003, U'wa threatened to once more leap from El Peñol as Occidental Petroleum exploited resources in U'wa territory.

The path from Güicán begins at the end of Carrera 4, past Calle 1. It is a steep 30-40 minutes uphill, then flat and a last steep rise to the top. Total hike there takes approximately two hours. Or you can walk out of town on Carrera 5, in the direction of the road about 1.5 kilometers (1 mi) away. Updated: Mar 21, 2011.

Monumento a la Dignidad de la Raza U'wa

On the road out of Güicán is a monument facing north towards the indigenous nation it honors. This is Monumento a la Dignidad de la Raza U'wa (Monument to the Dignity of the U'wa Race), created in 2007 by Delfín Ibáñez Carrero. It captures one of the most important events in U'wa history: the mass suicide at El Peñol de los Muertos. From the towering arms of Mother Earth tattooed with petrographs leap bodies of men, women and children. A condor takes flight, indigenous faces peering through its feathers. Engraved on its base is a U'wa proverb for us to remember: "God sleeps in the rocks, breathes in the plants, dreams in the animals, whispers in the waters and awakens in man." Walk down Carrera 5 to the edge of town. The monument is on a roundabout island. The Camino Deshecho and the rock paintings, the Aguas Termales and El Chorrerón, and Peñol de los Muertos are all near Güicán, Parque Nacional Natural El Cocuy. Carrera 5 direction Cordoncillo. Updated: Mar 21, 2011.

The Camino Deshecho and Petrographs

An alternative route down to the hot springs is what the locals call the Camino Deshecho, or the Unmade Road. And that is precisely what this trail is: an old stone road, dating from who knows when, beaten by centuries of foot and hoof trod. It is a pleasant walk downhill through the forest, past the very occasional *casita* tucked behind giant boulders. Keep an eye out for you shall see reminders of the indigenous ancestors along the way. *Pinturas repestres* (rock paintings) decorate the stone outcroppings. Updated: Mar 21, 2011.

Aguas Termales

After all the trekking in Parque Nacional Natural El Cocuy, your muscles may need a bit of relaxation. Near Güicán are Aguas Termales which is perfect as it will help warm you up after hiking, climbing, or strolling through the frigid temperatures in the park. In an old hacienda are two pools: the smaller, shallower one is warmer. If the Aguas Termales happen to be closed, you're not out of luck. About five meters

(20 ft) before the hacienda, on the right side of the dirt road, is El Chorrerón, a small cascade of hot water falling into a natural rock pool. Four kilometers (2.4 mi) from Güicán, walk along the highway towards Cordoncillo or take the camino deshecho. Also, transport from Güicán heading to El Cocuy pueblo or Soatá passes by the turn-off for the hot springs ($0.50). Updated: Mar 21, 2011.

Tours

Güicanes

Victor Correa heads up Güicanes, a collective of professional Sierra Nevada guides ready to lead you in a discovery of their homeland. Correa and his colleagues offer a five-day mountaineering excursion of Ritaku'wa Blanco. Also on their agenda are a four-day trek to Laguna de la Sierra and a five-day jaunt to Laguna de la Plaza. Güicanes also can take you to Suesca for some climbing. Ca. 4, 3-91, Tel: 1-240-5869 (Bogotá)/8-789-7155 (Güicán), Cel: 316-228-7041, E-mail: guicanes@gmail.com/guaicani@gmail.com, URL: www.guaicani.com. Updated: Jun 30, 2008.

Lodging

Your choice of accommodation in Güicán is mighty slim. You don't even have to use one hand to count the number of hotels here. Even though few in number, they do cover the whole range of quality, including high-luxury spas. Prices are budget to low-mid-range. Reservations are necessary at Christmas/New Year and during the summer holidays (June-July). Updated: Jun 30, 2008.

Hotel El Frailejón

(BEDS: $4) Hotel El Frailejón isn't anything special, but it does have two advantages: it's centrally located near the bus offices and it's Güicán's cheapest inn. Perhaps that is why it is frequently full. The rooms are up a narrow staircase, above the restaurant-shop. The quarters are large with little furnishings, including a worn bed or two. Some have a window overlooking the plaza, a few come with no window and view. The old common baths are sufficiently clean. Cra. 4, 3-34. Tel: 789-7037. Updated: Jul 01, 2008.

Hotel Brisas del Nevado

(ROOMS: $6-8) Hotel Brisas del Nevado is a pleasant inn located just a half-block from the main plaza and bus stops. Its clean, simply furnished rooms in the main building are bright with natural light and have one to four beds. Most share the sparkling common baths. Out in the garden is a duplex cabaña with a front patio and private baths. The setting and privacy of these accommodations are a delight—but unfortunately, they are only for larger groups. Cra. 5, 4-57. Tel: 789-7028/1-671-6642 (Bogotá), Cel: 300-273-3190. Updated: Jun 30, 2008.

Hotel La Sierra !

(BEDS: $6.30) No sign marks the presence of Hotel La Sierra. However, this house, a few blocks downhill from the plaza, is a hostel where for years the knowledgeable Profe has offered rooms to trekkers and others heading into the national park. Inside are several floors of rooms with private hot-water baths and televisions. The rooms on the upper floors are airier. If the Profe is around he can fill you in on the park and give knowledgeable advice. Ca. 5, 6-20. Tel: 789-7109/7074, Cel: 311-846-4807. Updated: Mar 21, 2011.

Restaurants

If the eating options are slim in El Cocuy village, they are even more sparse in Güicán. Almost all of the diners are attached to the few hotels. The municipal market is at Carrera 4 and Calle 2. Güicán is famous for its cheeses. The factory here has no store, instead the product is distributed to shops in the town. At times (especially in the high season) the cheese quickly sells out.

Comidas Rápidas Selecta

(SNACKS: $0.50-2.65) Comidas Rápidas Selecta fills with Güicán residents looking for a quick bite to eat in the evening. This snack stand offers the finest selection of hot dogs, hamburgers, sandwiches, empanadas and fruit salads. You can keep your inner kid happy with a cup of gelatin topped with cream for dessert. Daily 6:30-8:30 p.m. Cra. 5, near Ca. 5. Updated: Jul 01, 2008.

Restaurant, Hotel La Sierra

(BREAKFAST: $1.30-1.85, SET MEAL: $1.85-2.10) Hotel La Sierra looks like an old garage, but at mealtimes its five cloth-covered tables are crammed with people. Breakfast is potato soup, or eggs with bread, cheese and coffee or hot chocolate. Comida corriente is served for lunch or dinner. This set plate comes with rice, beans or potatoes, meat and salad. At noon it's accompanied by a fruit drink, in the evening by a hot *agua de panela* ($1.85 main dish only, $2.10

with soup). Daily 6-9:30 a.m., noon-2:30 p.m. and 5-8:30 p.m. Ca. 5, 6-20. Tel: 789-7109/7074. Updated: Jul 01, 2008.

Restaurant, Hotel Brisas del Nevado !

(ENTREES: $2.65) Hotel Brisas del Nevado's restaurant is a surprising member of Güicán's meager dining scene. Its two rooms are smartly decorated in a country style, and the doorways onto the streets are screened with glass and wood inserts accented with a wrought-iron vine motif. In the evening, candlelight illuminates these intimate spaces, creating a romantic place to have a last repast before leaving the Cocuy region behind. Open 7-8 a.m. for breakfast, noon-1:30 p.m. for lunch and 6-8 p.m. for dinner. Cra. 5, 4-57. Tel: 789 7028. Updated: Jun 27, 2011.

Nightlife

Güicán has very few night clubs or drinking establishments and all are rough-and-tumble types of places that even Colombian tourists won't frequent. Updated: Jun 30, 2008

!!!!!

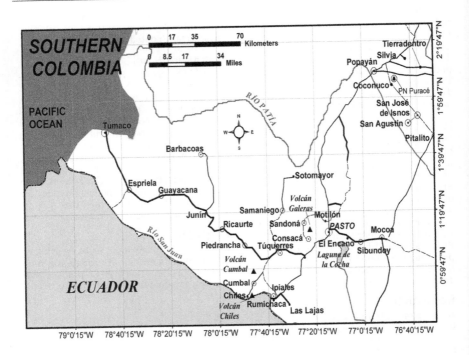

Southern Colombia

Stretching from the southern edge of the Valle de Cauca to the border with Ecuador, the Southern Colombian region contains everything your imagination can conjure: high-altitude páramo plains and snowy volcanoes, flanked by mangrove-filigreed coastline to the west and sultry jungle to the east.

Popayán is a beautiful colonial city, renowned for its Semana Santa processions. Stroll through the narrow streets, stopping in the numerous churches and museums. Popayán serves as the gateway to some of Colombia's premier archaeological sites, both of unknown cultures: Tierradentro, brilliantly painted, human-carved burial caves; and San Agustín, containing several sites of incredible statuary. The countryside surrounding both sites provides great hiking opportunities.

Between the two lies Parque Nacional Puracé. After trekking around the Cadena Volcánica de Coconuco or scaling Volcán Puracé, you can soak your strained muscles in several local hot springs.

Further south on the Pan-American Highway, you arrive at Pasto. This city, overlooked by smoldering Galeras volcano, also has pleasant colonial-era architecture and plazas, as well as a Gold Museum (Museo de Oro).

Accessible from Pasto, you can visit the country's second-largest lake, Laguna La Cocha. On its shores there are many eco-farms that welcome guests. Santuario de Flora y Fauna Isla La Carota is on a small island in the lagoon.

Just north of the Rumichaca border with Ecuador is Ipiales. Eight kilometers (5 mi) away is the Santuario de Nuestra Señora de las Lajas, a neo-Gothic church spanning a river gorge. Also near Ipiales is the indigenous village Cumbal, shadowed by two icy volcanoes.

The entire region has experienced guerrilla and paramilitary activity in recent years. Please read the Southern Colombia Safety section. Updated: Aug 26, 2011.

History

Before the European conquest of the Americas, the mysterious culture we now call San Agustín-Tierradentro, the ancestors of today's Nasa (Páez), lived in the

SOUTHERN COLOMBIA

Highlights

Parque Nacional Puracé (p. 471), at over 3,000 m (9,840 ft) altitude, will literally take your breath away with wild páramo, nearly a dozen volcanoes and thermal springs.

The forests of statues in **San Agustín** (p. 482) are silent witnesses to the country's history. They guard the verdant valleys laced with waterfalls and caverns.

At **Tierradentro** (p. 477), spectacularly painted subterranean burial chambers are scatter across the hilltops of this remote region of southern Colombia. The trip may be a bit arduous and the services basic, but well worth it.

La Ciudad Blanca or the White City of **Popayán** (p. 459) is a wonderful example of Andalusia-Mozarab colonial architecture. Heavily damaged by a 1983 earthquake, the city has since been restored to its original splendor.

Nuestra Señora de las Lajas (p. 509) is a spectacular neo-Gothic church spanning the Guáitra River gorge just outside Ipiales. Updated: Aug 11, 2011.

central cordillera region. They left behind statues and burial tombs. The inter-valley area between the two mountain ranges was home to the many Pasto nations whose traditions yet live in small villages like Cumbal, Saldoná and Túquerres.

The Spanish began making inroads into Southern Colombia in the 1530s. Under orders of Sebastián de Belalcázar, Ipiales, Pasto and Popayán were founded as base camps for the exploration for El Dorado. These population centers fell under the Real Audencia de Quito, thus giving them culturally and politically a closer nexus to Ecuador than to Bogotá and the rest of modern Colombia.

As the colonies' wars against mother Spain intensified in the early 19th century, southern Colombia witnessed the movements of both sides' troops. Pasto remained a royal supporter and suffered quite severely at the hands of Simón Bolívar's forces. When the nascent Gran Colombia split into the

countries we know today, Nariño Department wished to leave with Ecuador but was prevented from doing so.

In the modern era, Popayán has produced 11 Colombian presidents. During the present civil war which has lasted over 50 years, the Fuerzas Armadas Revolucionarias de Colombia (FARC) has been active. However, under former President Uribe's clean-up program and Plan Colombia, they have been pushed toward the nether regions of the Colombia-Ecuador border. This has caused a tremendous growth in the number of *desplazados*, or refugees. Updated: Aug 26, 2011.

When to Go

In Colombia's Southern region—Nariño, Cauca and Huila Departments—altitude affects the climate.

Pasto, Popayán and other population centers in the valley between the Eastern and Central mountain ranges have four seasons of two distinct types of weather. From January to March, it is sunny and warm, and again from June to August, when it is also windy. Invierno, or the rainy season, occurs in April and May, and again from September to December. Most of this area enjoys spring-like climate year round, though Popayán at a lower altitude is a bit hotter in the verano.

November, December and January are the best months to visit the central mountain range region, which includes such attractions as Parque Nacional Natural Puracé, Tierradentro and San Agustín. The clear weather brings the warmest days, but likewise cold nights. The windiest months are July and August, which are also cold. Rain is common the rest of the year; the wettest months are September to October, and February to March. Temperatures depend on altitude. Updated: Aug 26, 2011.

Safety

The Southern Colombia region has seen much guerrilla and paramilitary activity for more than a decade, especially away from the Pan-American Highway. The jungles to the east and west of the highway are also affected by the fumigations of Plan Colombia. Many of the roads are now heavily patrolled by the Colombian military. Checkpoints are common. These include the roads west out to Tumaco and east to San Agustín. Roads radiating into the countryside west of Popayán

SOUTHERN COLOMBIA

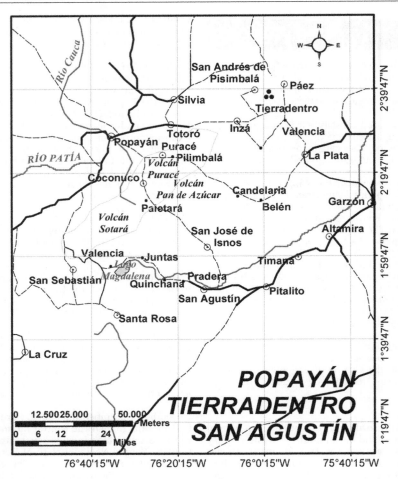

SOUTHERN COLOMBIA

still present problems. Many locals now say nighttime travel between Ipiales, Popayán and Cali is okay. Buses do travel at night upon the Pan-American Highway. In some areas, buses do not travel during dark hours.

The weeks leading up to elections can provide adventures beyond the norm; traditionally this has been when activity by and between the armed factions have increased. Consider twice before going off the well-worn Panamericana path at these times. Review the safety sections of towns we cover for more information. But always seek local advice before heading to your destination. Updated: Aug 26, 2011.

Things to See and Do
Southern Colombia has something to offer, no matter if your interests are adrenaline or culture. Several national park and reserve crown jewels rest in the folds of the south: Volcán Galeras; Puracé National Park, with páramo, volcanoes and thermal springs; and Isla La Corota, covered by low mountain humid forest inhabited by orchids, ferns and 32 bird species.

Other hiking and climbing options include volcanoes Cumbal, Chili and Azufral, and historic routes like Circuito Ancestral and El Macizo Colombiano. You can spend days walking the countryside, exploring the enigmatic tombs and statues of San Agustín and Tierradentro, two premier archaeological sites.

The towns of Cumbal, Sandoná and Silvia have indigenous markets where shoppers can pick up a poncho or other artesanía.

The colorfully-painted *barniz* ceramics of Pasto may be the perfect gift to take home.

Southern Colombia has beautiful colonial architecture, especially in Popayán, and numerous churches and museums. Stunning modern edifices also invite you, like Santuario Nuestra Señora de las Lajas.

Sports aficionados aren't left out of the scene here, either. There's *chaza* in Pasto, *tejo* (with a curious twist) in San Agustín, and some mighty fine trout fishing at Coconuco and Paletará. Updated: Aug 26, 2011.

Tours

In much of Southern Columbia, the tourist infrastructure is still lacking as far as tour operators are concerned. In the cities, most agencies deal in selling airline tour packages to prime destinations like Cartagena. They also book flights, if spending up to a full day on land transportation is not quite appealing to you.

SENA—Servicio Nacional de Aprendizaje—is training guides in such places as Popayán in anticipation of growing tourism. Parque Nacional Natural Puracé is working with the *resguardos indígenas* (indigenous communities) within the park boundaries to provide guiding services there. This provides jobs for the local community, so it does not have to rely on illegal hunting and logging to make a living.

As San Agustín has long been a tourist destination, it has dozens of independent guides (few of whom are certified) and now several tourist operator offices. Updated: Aug 26, 2011.

Lodging

Southern Colombian hotels are surprisingly hard to come by, especially in the luxury class. Popayán has some of the finest, located in colonial buildings. In cities like Ipiales and Pasto, the trend is moving to provide for this group of clientele. Even San Agustín, a long-popular, foreign tourist destination, is seeing a new concept of deluxe vacation homes rising on its landscape. Many smaller towns—like San Agustín, Tierradentro and Puracé—are a budget traveler's paradise. In some of these villages, only the most basic hotels are available. Campgrounds are becoming more common in the region. You'll be able to break out your tent if heading for Parque Nacional Natural Puracé, San Agustín and Tierradentro. Updated: Aug 26, 2011.

POPAYÁN

1,737m   258,653   2

The Pan-American Highway twists and turns for 248 kilometers (149 mi) north from Pasto, arriving at Popayán in the Valle de Pubenza. To the south, east and north of this city are verdant plains studded with mountains. To the southeast is Volcan Puracé and the national park named for it.

Popayán is nicknamed Ciudad Blanca, or the White City. Its narrow streets are lined with two-story buildings constructed in rococo Andalusian-style architecture. Their whitewash is almost blinding on a sunny day. The cathedral is styled in clean, classic Roman lines. The central plaza, Parque Caldas, is a pleasant place to seek shade beneath palms and flowering trees. Here, musicians and comedians frequently entertain the crowds.

Traveling north toward Cali (142 km/85 mi away), you will enter the humid Valle del Cauca, surrounded by mountain ranges on either side. During this journey you can occasionally see Nevado del Huila. Updated: Aug 11, 2011.

History

Popayán was another of the Colombian cities founded by orders of Sebastián de Belalcázar in 1536. It was initially governed by the Audencia Real de Quito, but then transferred under the administration of the Audencia Real de Bogotá. In the modern era, the city serves as the capital for Cauca Department. Eleven of the nation's presidents were patojos, or natives of Popayán. One, Francisco José de Caldas (1771-1815), was also a scientist and director of the observatory in Bogotá. He discovered how to calculate altitude by the temperature at which water boils.

Popayán has suffered from numerous earthquakes over the centuries. One, in 1736, destroyed most of the city. In March 1983, the city was once more leveled by a strong tremor. The colonial sector of Ciudad Blanca has been carefully restored to its previous splendor. Some reconstruction work is still going on. Updated: Aug 11, 2011.

When to Go

Popayán has four seasons of two distinct types of weather. In January-March, expect sunny days, and again June-August, when it is also

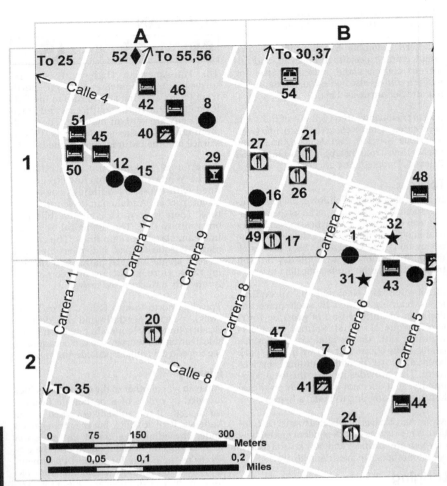

windy, especially in the last month. Those August winds bring two festivals to the Popayán area: the Festival de las Cometas, when kites dance across the azure skies, and paragliding events in Balboa, west of the city. The rainy season comes heavy April-May, and once more with afternoon showers September-December. The average temperature in the Ciudad Blanca is 18ºC (64ºF). Evenings are cool.

HOLIDAYS AND FIESTAS

Like Pasto and other southern Andean towns in Colombia, Popayán celebrates Carnaval de los Blancos y Negros, on January 5 and 6. The city's observance of Semana Santa, Easter Week, is renowned throughout the country. At this time, lodg-

ing prices rise sharply and reservations are necessary far in advance. Mid-April to May is Fiesta de Ecce Homo; on the first day of the festival, a procession of women carry the statue of the Ecce Homo Christ down from the Belén church and on May 1 men return the Christ back to its temple.

Another August festival is the Fiesta del Verano, marked in the villages around the Ciudad Blanca. September is the Festival Gastronómico, or the Gastronomic Festival. Día de los Ánimas, Day of the Dead (November 1-3) is when payusos commemorate their dearly departed with special masses and cemetery events. The first part of December, until Christmas Eve,

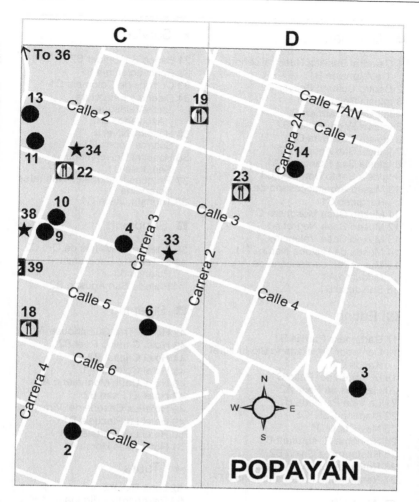

POPAYÁN

chirimías (music groups) pass through Popayán's streets day and night playing drum and flute music. Updated: Aug 11, 2011.

Getting To and Away

Minibuses ply the narrow streets of Popayán ($0.75); catch Transpubenza Ruta 5 from Calle 8 and Carrera 6 for the bus terminal or airport (one block away). Taxis cost about $5.

BY BUS

Traveling the hairpinning Ipiales-Popayán highway in a mini-van or other small vehicle can provoke motion sickness, even in those not prone to such. The bus terminal is a 15-minute walk from downtown. It has a luggage keep, restaurants, internet, phones, bathrooms and ATM (Visa, Plus, Mastercard, Cirrus).

To Silvia: Sotrancauca (Sunday, Tuesday 9 a.m., daily noon; 1.25 hr, $4)

To Puracé: 1 hour, $5-6—Cootranshuila (noon), Sotrancauca (3 daily)

To Tierradentro: Sotrancauca (10:30 a.m., 5 hr, $10). You can also catch a bus going to La Plata and get off at Cruce de Pisimbalá, a.k.a. Cruce de San Andrés.

To Coconuco: Sotrancauca (hourly 6:30 a.m.-5:30 p.m., 1.5 hr, $4-5)

SOUTHERN COLOMBIA

SOUTHERN COLOMBIA

● Activities

1 Catedral Basílica Nuestra Señora De Asunción B1
2 Centro Cultural Bolívar C2
3 Iglesia Belén D2
4 Iglesia El Carmen C1
5 Iglesia Encarnación B2
6 Iglesia La Ermita C2
7 Iglesia San Agustín B2
8 Iglesia San Francisco A1
9 Iglesia Santo Domingo C1
10 Museo Arquidiocesano de Arte Religioso C1
11 Museo Casa Mosquera C1
12 Museo Casa Negret A1
13 Museo Casa Valencia C1
14 Museo de Historia Natural D1
15 Museo Iberoamericano de Arte Moderno A1
16 San José B1

⑪ Eating

17 Carbonera Parrilla B1
18 Comedor Vegetariano Bio-Integral Kanda C2
19 El Portón del Patio C1
20 Helados de Paila A2
21 La Viña Parillada B1
22 Madeira Café C1
23 Mey Chow D1
24 No-name Restaurant B2
25 Restaurante China B2
26 Restaurante La Oficina B1
27 Restaurante Pizzería Italiana B1

☷ Nightlife

28 Bar La Casona Del Virrey (See 48)
29 Imperio A1
30 Viejoteca Rancho Grande B1

★ Services

31 Banco Santander B2
32 Bancocolombia B1
33 Correos de Colombia C1
34 Diseño y Estructura Jorge Velásquez y Asociados C1
35 Hospital Nivel II Susana López D1
36 Hospital Universitario San José C1
37 Parques Nacionales Naturales Surandina B1
38 Tourism Office C1

☒ Shopping

39 Artesanías Manas de Oro C2
40 El Taller to Esperanza Polanco A1
41 Platería San Agustín B2

▬ Sleeping

42 Hostel Trail Guesthouse A1
43 Hotel Camino Real B2
44 Hotel Capital B2
45 Hotel Colonial A1
46 Hotel Dann Monasterio A1
47 Hotel El Paso B2
48 Hotel La Casona del Virrey B1
49 Hotel La Plazuela B1
50 Hotel Los Portales A1
51 Hotel Pass Home A1

♦ Tours

52 Luna Paz A2
53 Resguardo Indígena Guídes (See 37)
54 Sena Student Guides (See 38)

▣ Transportation

55 Terminal Transporte Intermunicipal B1
56 Aeropuerto Guileval A1

To San Agustín: Cootranshuila (4 daily, 6 hr, $17)

To Tumaco: most leave mid-afternoon and evening, 11 hours, $25-30—Transipiales (3 buses), Cootranar (3 buses). Also collective taxis ($44-50).

To Cali: hourly departures, 2-2.5 hours, $8-10—Cootranar, Transipiales, Magdalena, Sotrancauca

To Medellín: 10 hours, $28-32—Bolivariano (2 afternoon, 1 night bus), Magdalena (2 afternoon buses)

To Bogotá: buses leave 4-10 p.m., 12 hours, $35-42—Bolivariano (4 buses), Magdalena (2 buses) and other companies.

To Pasto and Ipiales: Frequent buses with several companies; for details, see those cities.

From Popayán, you can also travel overland to Pitalito, Mocoa, Neiva and other points.

BY AIR

The airport is behind the bus terminal, about a 20-minute walk from the center. **Avianca** has direct flights to Bogotá twice daily ($190-205), with connections to anyplace else in Colombia or the world (Monday-Friday 8 a.m.-noon and 2-6 p.m., Saturday 9 a.m.-1 p.m. Cra. 5 3-85. Tel: 824-3379/315-463-3343, URL: www. avianca.com). Updated: Aug 11, 2011.

Safety

The Valle del Cauca witnessed intense guerrilla activity for several decades. Travel is safer now, thanks to road patrols; even Colombians feel it is now safe to travel on the Ipiales-Cali stretch of the Pan-American Highway at night. Within the city of Popayán, take extra care in the market and bridge areas. A visit to Barrio Alfonso López is not recommended. The El Tambo area west of Popayán has recently experienced civil war activity. Updated: Aug 11, 2011.

Services

TOURISM

The **Oficina de Turismo Popayán** is located on a side street, two blocks from Parque Caldas, across from Santo Domingo church (Monday-Friday 8:30 a.m.-12:30 p.m. and 2:30-6:30 p.m., Saturday 9 a.m.-noon and 2-5 p.m., Sunday 9 a.m.-1 p.m. Cra. 5, 4-68. Tel: 824-2251/311-307-2299, E-mail: oficinaturismopopayan@hotmail. com, URL: www.turismopopayan.com).

For any maps you might need, you can go to the **Instituto Geográfico Agustín Codazzi** (Monday-Friday 8-11:15 a.m. and 1:30-4 p.m. Ca. 3, 7-08). Permits for Parque Nacional Puracé and other national parks in Southern Colombia may be obtained from **Parques Nacionales Naturales de Colombia Surandina** (Monday-Friday 8-11:30 a.m. and 2-4 p.m. Cra. 9, 25N-06. Tel: 823-1279, URL: www.parquesnacionales.gov.co).

MONEY

Most banks are open Monday-Friday 8-11:30 a.m. and 2-4 p.m. Many ATMs take Visa, Mastercard, Plus and Cirrus cards. **Bancolombia** changes only American Express travelers cheques with a small commission; come with a photocopy of your passport's front pages and entry stamp. Its ATM also handles AmEx cards (Cra. 6, 4-49, on Parque Caldas.) **Santander** can also do travelers cheques (Cra. 6, 5-52). Other banks near Parque Caldas include **AV Villas** and **BBVA.**

Western Union/Giros y Finanzas is in the Centro Comercial Colonial (Ca. 3 and Cra. 7, Suite 208). MoneyGram/Cambiamos can be found in the Centro Comercial Rodrival (Monday-Saturday 8 a.m.-6 p.m. Cra. 7 and Ca. 6, Local 9).

KEEPING IN TOUCH

Many phone and internet places are closed on Sunday. For international as well as local and national calls, go to **Telecom** (Cra. 4 and Ca. 3) or **STE Telecolom** (Ca. 5, 7-11), which is cheaper. For inexpensive Internet, head over to Carrera 5: **Diseño y Estructura Jorge Velásquez y Asociados** (Cra. 5, 3-21) and **Intercopias** (Cra. 5, 3-31), which also has Skype. You can send that postcard to Aunt Jane from **Correos de Colombia** at Calle 4, 2-56 (Monday-Friday 8-11 a.m. and 2-5 p.m.).

MEDICAL

Popayán has two public hospitals: **Hospital Nivel II Susana López de Valencia** (Ca. 15, 17A-196. Tel: 821-1721) and **Hospital Universitario San José** (Cra. 6, N-142. Tel: 823-4508). The tourism office says there are English-speaking doctors at the **Clínica La Estancia**, which has emergency services and specialists (Ca. 15N, 2-256. Tel: 823-3950, E-mail: info@clinestancia.com, URL: www. clinestancia.com). Pharmacies, or *droguerías*, are very common, about one every block.

CAMERA

For your camera and needs, most shops are located on Carrera 7 or Calle 5 in the center of town. Compact flash cards can be difficult to find; try **Foto Morillo**, which has five outlets, including on Parque Caldas (Cra. 7, 4-80. Tel: 824-0355). Updated Aug 11, 2011.

SHOPPING

Artesanías Manos de Oro

This shop brings together the works of Cauca's best artisans under one roof. Browse through the two pleasant showrooms, jour-

SOUTHERN COLOMBIA

neying from village to village, and admire the crafts each is renowned for. Woolen ponchos, silk and cotton shawls, items of hand-made paper, and ceramic miniatures of homes and churches can be purchased here. If you haven't time to get to the *pueblos*, you still can take home a bit of artistry made by golden hands. Monday-Friday 9 a.m.-12:30 p.m. and 2-6:30 p.m. Ca. 5, 4-51. Tel: 822-0040, E-mail: cdamanosdeoro@ gmail.com, URL: www.punaprosemanasantapopayan.com. Updated: Aug 11, 2011.

Platería San Agustín

Since 1991, Albeiro Pérez has been crafting fine jewelry. Using sterling silver (.925) from Colombia, Italy, Thailand and Mexico, he creates all sorts of personal ornaments, some with semi-precious stones or glass beads. His filigree work is very delicate. There is bound to be a necklace, bracelet, ring or pair of earrings that strikes your fancy. Don Albeiro also does special orders, if you have a design in mind. Additionally, he repairs jewelry. Monday-Saturday 8 a.m.-noon and 2-7 p.m. Cra. 6, 7-54. Tel: 824-0528. Updated: Aug 11, 2011.

El Taller de Esperanza Polanco F.

Esperanza Polanco forms clay by hand into wonderful candlesticks and lamps, chess sets and nativity crèches, mysterious masks, figurines and miniature scenes. She does tiles also, of original patterns—whether from her own imagination or yours. This small, crowded shop also has works by other patojo artisans and from neighboring Patia villages. There are woven ponchos and bags, wrought-iron work, basketry and other domestic wares from vegetable fibers. If you can't come to Popayán for Easter Week, you can take home a miniature Semana Santa procession. Whatever item you purchase is guaranteed to be an exclusive design of high quality. Monday-Saturday 8:30 a.m.-noon and 1:30-6:30 p.m. Ca. 4, 10-21. Tel: 824-4588, Cel: 300-613-3562, E-mail: esperanzapol@hotmail.com. Updated: Aug 11, 2011.

Things to See and Do

Strolling through the streets of Popayán from park to park and over its historic bridges, Puente de Humilladero and Puente Chiquito, is a great way to enjoy the sunshine. Spend rainy afternoons in the Ciudad Blanca's fine collection of churches and museums. Homes of some of Popayán's illustrious citizens have been turned into museums. Especially noteworthy are the Casa Negret and its

Museo Iberoamericano de Arte Moderno, as well as the Museo de Arte Religioso and the excellent Museo de Historia Natural.

Popayán's Semana Santa commemorations are famous. Every night until Viernes Santo (Good Friday), candlelit processions wend through the narrow streets. The following week are the children's processions. In this season, the Religious Art Museum exhibits the most precious artworks of the city's churches. Due to its universities, Popayán also has a thriving theater and art-movie scene. The beginning of October is the annual Festival de Teatro and Encuentro de Cuenteros, and international meeting of theater and storytelling. During the rest of the year, you can catch theatrical productions and films at the Centro Cultural Bolívar.

Near Popayán are a number of interesting villages, like Silvia and its weekly indigenous market. Several *circuitos*, or tour routes, allow you to visit these *pueblos* on horseback or hiking. To the east is Parque Nacional Puracé with good trekking and climbing. Coconuco, on the south edge of the park, has two hot springs—which can be made as a day trip from Popayán. Along the same road is Paletará which has a trout fishing tournament every October. And don't forget the kite-flying and paragliding festivals in the windy month of August! Updated: Aug 11, 2011.

Museums of Popayán

A good place to get out of Popayán's rains are the museums. Many are the historical homes of past illustrious citizens. A few premier art museums also are on the scene, as well as a distinguished natural history museum.

Museo Casa Mosquera (Admission: $1.05. Monday-Friday 8 a.m.-noon and 2-6 p.m., Saturday, Sunday and holidays 8 a.m.-noon amd 2-5 p.m. Ca. 3, 5-14. Tel: 824-0683)— The 18th-century home of José María Mosquera y Figueroa, whose four sons came to be Presidents of the new republic and diplomats.

Museo Casa Valencia (Admission: $1.05 adults, $0.50 students, $0.25 children 6-12 years old. Tuesday-Sunday and holidays 10 a.m.-noon and 2-5 p.m. Cra. 6, 2-69. Tel: 820-6160)—Home of poet-writer-politician-orator Guillermo Valencia.

Museo Casa Negret (Admission: $1.50. Tuesday-Sunday 8 a.m.-noon, 2-6 p.m. Ca. 5, 10-23. Tel: 824-4546, E-mail: casa.museo.negret@gmail.com , URL: http://museonegret.

Semana Santa

Easily the most important holiday in Popayán, and one that has been celebrated annually for more than 450 years, Semana Santa transforms Popayán into a colorful procession of Catholic tradition, bringing in hundreds of visitors every year.

Following the model of Seville, Spain, the processions in Popayán are all nocturnal, except for the one on Palm Sunday, in which the triumphant entrance of Jesus Christ to Jerusalem is represented with the images of Saint Ecce Homo and El Señor Caído, taken from the chapel of Belén to the Basílica.

On Holy Tuesday white flowers adorn the procession that carries four images from the church of San Agustín to downtown. The procession on Wednesday uses pink flowers in representation of the joy of humanity for his immediate redemption. Holy Thursday is celebrated with a procession of red flowers at the 18th-century church of San Francisco.

Holy Friday begins at the church of Santo Domingo. A symbolic representation of the drama of The Passion is given with purple flowers and a group of men carrying hammers and other tools. Men wear white handkerchiefs with a small purple crown on their shoulders.

The religious significance of this holiday has blended deeply in Popayán with its culture, which makes Semana Santa a major attraction in the city. It has been acknowledged by UNESCO as an Intangible Cultural Heritage of Humanity. For information about the holiday's festivities, see www.semanasantapopayan.com. Updated: Aug 11, 2011.

wordpress.com/casa-museo-negret)—This house built in 1781 was the childhood home of artist Edward Negret. Now it is a museum displaying his early works and family momentos. Adjoining it is the **Museo Iberoamericano de Arte Moderno** (Ca. 5, 10-31. Tel: 824-0468) which exhibits a collection of national and international contemporary art.

Museo Martínez (Cra. 3 Sur Oriente, on road to Calicanto. Tel: 820-6081)—Collection of art by painter Efraín Martínez. Updated: Aug 11, 2011.

Museo Arquidiocesano de Arte Religioso
(ADMISSION: $1.60 adults, $0.80 children 6-12 years old) This museum was founded in 1972 by the city's Archdiocese to protect and conserve the most valuable artworks of Popayán's churches. Over 110 pieces are on exhibit in its 6 halls. During Semana Santa the vault guarding the jewel-encrusted *custodios* is opened for public viewing. You may not photograph any of the works in the collection. Exhibit explanations are in Spanish only; Spanish-language guides are available. Monday-Friday 9 a.m.-12:30 p.m. and 2-6 p.m., Saturday 9 a.m.-2 p.m. Ca. 4, 4-56. Tel: 824-2759. Updated: Aug 11, 2011.

Museo de Historia Natural

(ADMISSION: $1.60 adults, $1.05 children) Under the auspices of the Universidad de Cauca, the Museo de Historia Natural is a nice break from the usual art and miscellanea-housing historical museums. With splendid collections explaining the geology, paleontology, zoology and botany of the region, this is an excellent introduction to what you will see in Parque Nacional Natural Puracé. On the second floor is a botanical garden. Daily 8 a.m.-noon, 2-5:30 p.m. Cra. 2a, 1A-25. Tel: 820-9861, ext. 2602. Updated: Aug 11, 2011.

Centro Cultural Bolívar

(ADMISSION: $3-4) The Central Cultural Bolívar screens art films from Colombia and around the world Thursday to Saturday at 7 p.m. and Sundays at 6 p.m. in this small theater just a few blocks from Parque Caldas. Other days of the week, you can catch documentaries or theater productions; check the websites for scheduled events. The center also hosts the annual Festival de Teatro and Encuentro de Cuenteros every October. A small snack stand sells teas, juices and regional munchies. Ca. 7, 3-17. Tel: 824-0016, E-mail: teatrobolivar@popayancultural.com, URL: www.popayancultural.com. Updated: Aug 11, 2011.

SOUTHERN COLOMBIA

The Churches of Popayán

Take refuge from Popayán's afternoon showers in the sanctuary of one of her churches. The schedule of masses and church hours is in the telephone book.

La Encarnación (Ca. 5 and Cra. 5)— This once-cloister temple was designed by Jesuit Simon Schenherr, who designed many South American churches.

San José (Ca. 5 and Cra. 8)—Another Simon Schenherr creation.

La Ermita (Ca. 5, between Cra. 2 and 3)

Belén (up hill at the end of Calle 4)—The home of the Ecce Homo Christ statue affords great views over the city.

El Carmen (Ca. 4, between Cra. 3 and 4)

Santo Domingo (Ca. 4 and Cra. 5)-The exterior is a good example of rococo Andalusian architecture.

San Francisco (Ca. 4 and Cra. 9)

San Agustín (Ca. 7 and Cra. 6)—In a side chapel is an impressive statue of Christ kneeling upon a silver globe. The altar screen is is repousséed silver, and its Virgen Dolorosa is adorned in silver. Updated: Aug 11, 2011.

Catedral Basílica
Nuestra Señora de Asunción

(ADMISSION: free) Popayán's cathedral is a testament to the clean lines of Roman architecture. The whitewashed exterior is accented only by towering columns with Ionic capitals. The interior of this sanctuary is painted ivory, pale blue and light grey with gold details. The barrel vaulting bands are intertwining vines; a gilded rosette adorns their apices. The aisles are treated with high-relief fleur-de-lis in high relief on the walls, low relief within the span of the arches. Fine silver work is evidenced in the sacristy, and the accoutrements of the Virgin of the Apocalypse. A modern screen with a textured gold background, depicting the Immaculate Conception, adorns the altar. Ca. 5, between Cra. 6 and 7, Parque Caldas. Updated: Aug 11, 2011.

Tours

Despite the number of attractions in Popayán, few tour operators have offices here. The tourism office keeps a list of independent, licensed guides who can show you around the city or take you to places of interest in the area. Many speak English as well as Italian, French, German or another language. Travel agents on or near Parque Caldas can help you make reservations for flights or purchase an airline excursion package to popular destinations in other parts of Colombia. Updated: Aug 15, 2011.

Luna Paz

Ask in Popayán for a tour guide, and many will mention Jairo Paz, owner of Luna Paz. Mr. Paz conducts eco-tours to some of the region's most delectable destinations, including the burial tombs at Tierradentro, hot springs in Parque Nacional Natural Los Nevados, the colonial city of Boyacá and the *fincas* of the Zona Cafetera. He also can take you to Cartagena, Capurganá or Sapzurró on the Caribbean coast or Juanchaco on the Pacific coast, where you can watch whales. Cra. 11, 4-85. Cel: 315-513-9593, E-mail: lunapaztour@hotmail.com, URL: www.agencialunapaztour.com. Updated: Mar 24, 2011.

Resguardo Indígena Guides

What better way to see Parque Nacional Natural Puracé than with a local from the Resguardo Indígena of the Coconuco-Nasa (Páez) people? They know the idiosyncrasies of this land's weather and terrain like no one else. In fact, Surandina prefers you use their services, instead of those of an outsider, for your own safety on the treacherous *páramo* highlands. Furthermore, you will be helping to create employment for those inhabitants of the park who otherwise might have to turn to illegal hunting, logging or other activities to earn money. The national park office in Popayán can help you arrange a guide. You negotiate the price with the guide yourself. The usual rate is $9-11 per day. Cra. 9, 25N-06. Tel: 823-1279 / 1398, E-mail: dtao.sedepopayan@parquesnacionales.gov.co , URL: www.parquesnacionales.gov.co. Updated: Mar 24, 2011.

SENA Student Guides

Servicio Naciónal de Aprendizaje, SENA, and the Oficina de Turismo Popayán are training guides to fill the growing tourism demand of the region. The students, of economically disadvantaged backgrounds, are also receiving language training; many speak English as well as another language. Rates for their services are arranged between the client and the student-guide. For more information, contact SENA (Tel: 822-012) or Carmen Leonor Acosta,

SENA instructor and director of the Oficina de Turismo Popayán. Cra. 5, 4-68. Tel: 824-2251, E-mail: oficinaturismopopayán@hotmail.com, URL: www.turismopopayan.com. Updated: Mar 24, 2011.

Lodging

In Popayán there's a place in the Centro Histórico for any budget, from bottom-dollar dives to luxury hotels in colonial buildings. Most absolute budget places are concentrated between Carreras 3 and 5, and Calles 6 to 8. For those able to spend a dollar or two more per night, or who are traveling as a couple, there are more options. Room prices triple during Semana Santa and hotels fill up—book well in advance. Updated: Jul 2, 2010.

BUDGET

Hotel Boston

(BEDS: $4.20-5.30) For journeyers on a tight budget, the Hotel Boston is one of several good options in the inexpensive sector of the city. As price is charged by bed, not per person, it is especially appealing: the rooms with shared bathroom cost only $4.20 whether you are a solo traveler or a couple. There is only one room with private bath, at $5.30 per bed. Be advised that apparently this hostel accepts hourly guests. Updated: Nov 12, 2007.

Hospedaje Barú

(BEDS: $4.20-5.30) Another possible budget traveler choice, the Hospedaje Barú has three patios, as is typical with old architectural style. The first two have seating areas filled with plants and tables; in the back, the former service courtyard, you can do your laundry. All three are surrounded by rooms, some with rustic private baths. Others share the clean-enough common bathrooms, with cold only showers. This hostel has many long-term guests, including teachers, students and families. Monthly rates are available: $68.50, common bath; $79, private bath. Ca. 7, 3-39. Tel: 824-1220. Updated: May 16, 2008.

Hotel Panamá

(BED: $5.30 – 8) It's cheap, it's clean and the beds aren't bad. The rooms are small, though—not even big enough to swing a cat in—and the ground-floor rooms are dark. There's only common bath with cold-water showers and a laundry basin. You're guaranteed a Latin American lodging experience if your room faces the front patio, thanks to the loud TV that's on from early morning until late night. Still, the Hotel Panamá is probably the better choice among the budget hotels in Popayán. Cra. 5, 7-33. Updated: May 16, 2008.

Hotel Capital

(BEDS: $6-9) If you can afford to spend a dollar more, Hotel Capital is a comfortable choice for budget travelers. All rooms have common baths, but here there is deliciously hot water. The back courtyard garden is a wonderful place to swing from the hammock or sit around with doña María del Carmen and the other women, chatting a rainy afternoon away. You can ask to use the kitchen. While you're there, teach Rebeca, the resident parrot, a few new words. Cra. 5, 7-11. Tel: 838-8363. Updated: Mar 24, 2011.

HostelTrail Guesthouse

(BEDS: $9, ROOMS: $16-33) This backpacker house features all the facilities a traveler could want. It has hot water, WiFi, 24-hour reception, lockers, self-catering kitchen and DVD collection. Hostel Trail presents an eight-bed dorm, as well as private rooms with shared or private bath. It also offers its guests bike rental and laundry service. The hostel is conveniently located in the center of town. From the bus station, turn right onto the main road and turn left onto Carrera 11, then a 10 minutes walk down this road. Cra. 11, 4-16. Cel: 314-696-0805, E-mail: popayan@hosteltrail.com, URL: www.hosteltrailpopayan.com. Updated: Aug 15, 2011.

Hotel Pass Home

(ROOMS: $9-22.50) Located four blocks from the bus terminal and five from the historic center, Hotel Pass Home is a convenient place to stay in Popayán. It's a bare-bones inn, with white walls and small, cot-like beds. All rooms have television and spic-and-span bathrooms with hot-water showers. There is a laundry area where you can wash your own clothes. The English-speaking owner will check you in no matter the hour you get there, no need to make a reservation. Ca. 5, 10-114. Cel: 320-735-5088 / 316-448-9513, E-mail: hotelpasshome@gmail.com. Updated Mar 24, 2011.

MID-RANGE

Hotel El Paso

(ROOMS: $20-38) On the second floor of a colonial-era building is the Hotel El Paso, a good mid-range hostel choice in Popayán. Furnished with solid, carved wood furniture (including a dressing table), all rooms have private bath with hot water and toilets dressed in frilly covers. The wooden doors are thick, guaranteeing to block out any noise from the many sitting areas. A large common balcony overlooks the street corner. This inn is quite popular with Colombian businesspersons. Cra. 7, 7-14. Tel: 824-0227, E-mail: hotelelpasopopayan@hotmail.com. Updated: Mar 24, 2011.

Hotel Colonial

(ROOMS: $23-28) As its name implies, the small Hotel Colonial is in a building from the early centuries of this city. The lobby is tastefully adorned with original artwork and flower-filled vases. The rooms are set off two narrow courtyards. Decorated in wood furniture with wrought-iron accents, all come with private bathrooms with hot-water showers. The beds are firm. This lodge is a pleasant choice for those who are on a mid-range budget. Ca. 5, 10-97. Tel: 831-7848, E-mail: hotelcolonial@hotmail.es. Updated: Mar 24, 2011.

La Casona del Virrey

(ROOMS: $23-38) Hotel La Casona del Virrey, a stylish inn set in a colonial-era building, is a surprisingly affordable alternative right in the heart of Popayán. This is the perfect place to watch the Semana Santa processions from the balconies; however, expect to pay for this privileged view. A broad spiral staircase leads up to the second floor with large, finely furnished guest rooms that have private bathrooms and cable TV. (Here's a secret: there is one three-bed room with an exterior bath that costs significantly less.) Ca. 4, 5-78. Tel: 824-0836, E-mail: hotellacasonadelvirrey@hotmail.com. Updated: Mar 24, 2011.

V!VA ONLINE REVIEW
HOTEL LA CASONA DEL VIRREY

This place if full of great architectural history together with a warm, modern bar atmosphere.

August 13, 2008

Hotel Los Portales

(ROOMS: $30-50) Take a seat in one of the rocking chairs around the front courtyard of Hotel Los Portales and listen to the water spilling from the fountain. Your room will look out upon this patio or one of the other three patios that are part of the colonial building housing the hotel. All the rooms have private bathrooms with a shower with hot water. Ca. 5, 10-125. Tel: 821-0139/5484, E-mail: losportaleshotel@yahoo.com. Updated: Mar 24, 2011.

Hotel La Plazuela

(ROOMS: $60-253) A first-class hotel just across from Iglesia San José, Hotel La Plazuela is in a 1742 building rescued after the 1983 earthquake. Beautiful period pieces furnish the common sitting areas, original watercolors adorn the walls. You can choose a room off the patio or with a street-side balcony. All have carved wood furniture, excellent beds, small refrigerator, cable TV and private bath with gas-heated hot water. This is a perfect romantic get-away for you and your mate, or just to pamper yourself. Ca. 5, 8-13. Tel: 824-1084/1071, E-mail: hotellaplazuela@hotmail.com, URL: www.hotellaplazuela.com.co. Updated: Mar 24, 2011.

V!VA ONLINE REVIEW
HOTEL LA PLAZUELA

Quiet and comfortable, this is a nice place to relax.

June 08, 2009

Hotel Camino Real

(ROOM: $67-106) Food connoisseurs will want to stay at Hotel Camino Real. The hotel's restaurant has been recognized with multiple gastronomy awards and the menu covers a variety of plates. History buffs will also appreciate that the building, completed in 1591, was first used as a center to teach high society women electing to become nuns to read and write. It became a hotel in 1982, and the décor reflects styles from both the Victorian age and the 1980s. Prices include tax and breakfast. Ca. 5, 5-59. Tel: 824-3595/4514, E-mail: hotelcaminorealpopayan@caucanet.net.co, URL: www.hotelcaminoreal.com.co. Updated: Mar 24, 2011.

HIGH-END

Hotel Dann Monasterio

(ROOMS: $136-193) Hotel Dann Monasterio is the cream of the Popayán hotel crop. This Franciscan Monastery turned hotel in 1920 is the only accommodation around with a swimming pool. The 47 rooms still have that feeling of self-repentance, but with an added comfort and sophistication for the guests who prefer not to be in touch with their inner monk. The gourmet restaurant serves local and international food. Wander through the open-air corridors and indulge in a lot of luxury while lounging in the well-kept garden. The hotel includes a bar, in-room satellite TV and breakfast. Ca. 4, 10-14. Tel: 824-2191, E-mail: hotelmonasterio@hotelesdann.com / centralreservas@hotelesdann.co, URL: www.hotelesdann.com. Updated: Mar 24, 2011.

Restaurants

Popayán has offers visitors not only great Colombian food and *parrillas* (BBQ), but also an impressive selection of international food. Many eating establishments are closed on Sunday, and even more so on Sunday evening. The cheapest *almuerzos* and *comidas corrientes* can be found on Calle 8, between Carreras 5 and 6. September is *chonta duro* season, a palm fruit that is served with salt and honey. Pick up one from the many street vendors. If you are self-catering, you can pick up on supplies at the daily market (Ca. 8N and Cra. 6), or at the Ley supermarket (Cra. 5, 6-33). Updated: Aug 15, 2011.

Helados de Paila

(SNACKS: $0.50 and up) On those blindingly hot payanés days, drop by Helados de Paila for homemade ice cream made in a large copper bowl snuggled in a bed of ice. Blackberry, papaya and a variety of other natural fruit flavors await your taste buds. A fresh fruit salad also fits the cool-down bill well. You can come by on a rainy day, too, and warm up with a chicken or beef empanada and a hot drink. On Friday, Saturdays and Sundays the house specialty, pork ribs, is served. Monday-Saturday 8 a.m.-7 p.m. Cra. 9, 7-60. Tel: 824-3436. Updated: Mar 24, 2011.

Madeira Cafe

(SNACKS: $0.75 and up) You can join locals for a quick cup of coffee or tea in this small corner café. Perhaps you'd like to have that accompanied by a brownie or other sweet, or a sandwich. On a hot payanés day, a juice or malt (in chocolate, coffee, amaretto or fruit flavor) can be the thing to cool you down. On chill evenings, a *canelazo* or special coffee with liquor can warm your bones. The earth-tone interior is furnished with wood and wrought-iron tables and chairs. Not only is there ground-floor seating, but also a small balcony for more intimate dining. Madeira has a shop next door selling local *artesanía*, chocolates and coffee. Some evenings there is live music. Monday–Friday 9 a.m-8:30 p.m., Saturday 2-8:30 p.m. Ca. 3, 4-91. Cel: 300-788-6508, E-mail: licetik@hotmail.com. Updated: Aug 16, 2011.

El Portón del Patio

(ENTREES: $1.60-2.10) After spending a few hours in the Museo de Historia Natural, stop by El Portón del Patio for a quick bite to eat. The menu includes not only the usual daily meal for meat-eaters or vegetarians, but also crepes, Mexican tacos and arepas with a variety of fillings. Try the *marranita*, a green plantain filled with meat. Or just sit in the quiet, high-walled courtyard and have a cup of coffee beneath the old trees. If an afternoon shower hits, the porch is also a fine place for your rest. Monday-Saturday 8 a.m.-8 p.m. Cra. 3, 1-83. Tel: 838-0044, Cel: 316-727-7004. Updated: May 21, 2009.

Comedor Vegetariano Bio-Integrales Kanda ♪

(LUNCH: $2) Ah, vegetarians, does Popayán have a surprise for you! A real, honest-to-goodness vegetarian restaurant with flavorful, nutritionally balanced meals. You can be guaranteed your complete proteins at Comedor Vegetariano Bio-Integrales Kanda, as the main dish is brown rice with beans and/or soy meat. The *comida corriente* comes with lots of veggie sides and a salad bar. You can choose between a fruit drink or soy milk to accompany your food. The ambiance is equally delicious, with several small rooms in which to dine and soothing flute music. Unfortunately, Kanda is only open for lunch (11 a.m.-3 p.m.). Ca. 6, 4-52. Tel: 824-0794, Cel: 311-372-6093, E-mail: garpawil@yahoo.es. Updated: Mar 24, 2011.

No-Name Restaurant

(LUNCH: $2) On Calle 8, you can find several cheap restaurants. But this no-name, family-run eatery stands out from its neighbors in the quality of food it prepares (even boiling their water.) Even at the crowded lunch hour, service is quick and friendly here. The standard *comida corriente* is what's on the menu: soup, the main dish of a choice of meats, rice, beans and salad, plus refreshment made of fresh fruit. The only disadvantage is that it is closed on Sundays. Ca. 8, 5-25. Updated: Aug 16, 2011.

Carbonera Parrilla

(ENTREES: $2.50–7.50) Sorry vegetarians: Carbonera Parrilla is for meat eaters only. A generous portion of chicken, pork, fish or succulent beef is served hot off the grill on a wooden plank to your picnic table. If you can't make up your mind, you can order a combination platter. Alongside come potatoes with a bechamel sauce, rice, salad and—to dip your meat into—homemade chimichurri and barbecue sauce. To drink, there's juices and sodas. But, hey, what's a BBQ without a beer? Monday-Saturday noon-9:30 p.m., Sunday noon-4 p.m. Cra. 8, 5-15. Tel: 831-8581. Updated: May 21, 2009.

La Oficina

(LUNCH: $3, ENTREES: $5-7) The interior of Restaurante La Oficina is a bit incongruous with its name: the decorations are rustic, a bit humble, with pink cloths draping the tables—not quite like an office. But nonetheless this is another favorite lunch spot for payaneses escaping from the doldrums of their offices. The evening menu offers classics of Colombia cuisine, such as *bandeja paisa, sancocho de gallina* and *frijoles antioqueños*. Ca. 4, 8-01. Tel: 824-0380. Updated: May 21, 2009.

La Viña Parrillada

(LUNCH: $3.50, ENTREES: $3.50-10.50) Mornings people drop in to catch up on the events or to gossip over a cup of coffee and *pan de oro* from La Viña's in-house bakery. Come afternoon, the place hops with business people and office workers setting down to the scrumptious *comida corriente*. Evenings you can dine until late, choosing from the wide array of à la carte dishes; junior portions are available. You can order wine by the glass or beer on tap. *La viña* means the vineyard, and this motif is carried throughout the restaurant, down to the grape-vine-printed tablecloths. For a more secluded space, retire to the balcony where there are only a few tables. Daily 8 a.m.–midnight. Ca. 4, 7-79. Tel: 824-0602, E-mail: lacosechaparrillada@hotmail.com. Updated: Mar 24, 2011.

Restaurante Pizzería Italiana

(LUNCH: $4, ENTREES: $5-11) Step into this Italian café with its wood-trimmed, mustard colored walls hung with Montreaux Jazz Festival posters. Pull up a wood-and-leather seat at one of the tables. A pizza or pasta, you will ponder, or perhaps an à la carte meat dish? The pastas come with a small salad and delectable garlic-parsley-onion dressing on the side and bread. The cannelloni comes with such generous portions of filling and sauce that the pasta is difficult to find. Wine is an expensive accompaniment to your meal. Restaurante Pizzería Italiano also offers a set-lunch plate. Daily noon–10 p.m. Ca. 4, 8-83. Tel: 824-0607. Updated: May 21, 2009.

Mey Chow

(ENTREES: $8-10) Upon entering Mey Chow through the plain wooden doors, you are not immediately exposed to the grace of this establishment. Step out of the vestibule, past the sandstone reception, and its elegant simplicity is now apparent. The central room is a skylighted courtyard with booths (for up to a dozen or so persons) and tables. Two side rooms provide more secluded dining. All is decorated in green, red and gold. The menu is limited, but has some offerings not seen elsewhere, including Moo Goo Gai Pan and Szechuan Chicken. Any dish can be made vegetarian. Monday-Saturday 6-11 p.m., Sunday noon-3 p.m. and 6-9 p.m. Cra. 2, 2-23. Tel: 824-2761, E-mail: meychow54@yahoo.com. Updated: Mar 25, 2011.

Restaurant China

(ENTREES: $8-12) As you can guess by its name, Restaurant China dishes up Chinese food prepared with chicken, pork, beef or seafood and served with steamed white rice. Vegetarian options are limited to chop suey or chow mein. Multi-course family menus are offered, which are fairly economical if you have a dining partner. The interior is spacious and bright. Despite the bright-red table cloths, clean-lined wood furniture and Chinese silk artwork, this restaurant has an undistinguished feel to it. Daily, 10 a.m.-6 p.m. Ca. 4, 13-31. Tel: 821-9639 . Updated: Mar 24, 2011.

Nightlife

Whether your taste is for dancing to the latest salsa and reggaeton vibes, or to Latin golden oldies, or just chilling over a glass of wine and listening to cool jazz and bossa nova, you will find a place to sit and relax after a day catching the sights of Popayán. Many nightclubs, discos and bars are located right in the historic center, so you will not have to worry about catching a cab home. Updated: Aug 15, 2011.

Bar La Casona del Virrey

(COVER: $5) For a more sophisticated evening out, have a drink at the lounge of the Hotel La Casona del Virrey. The low lights and suave music make for a pleasant retreat from the throbbing discos. On Friday evenings, a live trio performs boleros or tangos. Saturdays feature vallenatos or other types of laid-back music. No cover is charged for guests of the hotel; all others pay. Thursday-Saturday 9 p.m.-late. Ca. 4, 5-78. Tel: 824-0836. Updated: Mar 24, 2011.

Imperio

(COVER:$4.50) This is the place to go for the young and young-at-heart. Imperio is a typical Latin discoteca with the latest reggaeton, electronic, salsa, merengue and vallenato hits, everyone dancing the night away until almost dawn. Open Thursday, Friday and Saturday 9 p.m. -3 a.m. Ladies, if you come before 10 p.m., you get in free. Cra. 9, between Ca. 4 and 5. Updated: May 16, 2008.

Viejoteca, Rancho Grande

Viejoteca: A discoteca where the DJ spins the Latin golden oldies. Sure it draws a more mature crowd, reminiscing to the cumbia, salsa and merengue hits of their youth, the songs perhaps they fell in love to. But even if you are young, you can join in the shaking and swaying. Everyone is given a paper heart to pin on, the color designating civil status (single, engaged, married). The dance party happens only on Thursdays out at Rancho Grande, beginning at 9 p.m. The curfew for all you young'uns is 3 a.m. Buses transit out that way only until 11 p.m. ($1). To return home after that time, take a taxi ($3). Autopista Norte, 32N-50. Tel: 820-5219, Updated: Mar 24, 2011.

AROUND POPAYÁN

SILVIA

At Silvia's Tuesday morning market, you can see the Guambiano indigenous in traditional dress. Afterward, join the Ruta Etno-Ecoturística, featuring nature trails, typical foods (especially trout), *artesanías* and indigenous villages. The route traverses the countryside from Piédamo to Silvia to Las Delicias to El Pueblito, before ending in La Campana. If you want to spend a few days exploring this area northeast of Popayán, Silvia has basic lodging. To rent horses, contact Freddy, a guide that rents them for $2.50 per hour (Cel: 312-758-6963).

It is possible to travel from Silvia to Tierradentro. On market day, transport runs frequently until early afternoon for Totoró. There, hop on a bus going to Inzá. Several times a day pick-up trucks go to Tierradentro and San Andrés de Pisimbalá. Sotrancauca has buses from Popayán to Silvia on Sunday and Tuesday at 9 a.m., and daily at noon ($2.35; 1.25 hours). Updated: Mar 25, 2011.

CIRCUITO ANCESTRAL

The Circuito Ancestral is a tour of small villages east of Popayán. On horseback or on foot, your can enjoy the ecological paths, the headwaters of the Río Molino and the indigenous reservation in Poblazón. Your journey begins in La Unión, also known as La Cabrera, where you can rent horses. It is just a 15-minute bus ride from Popayán. The historic trail then cuts three kilometers (2 mi) crosscountry to Santa Helena. From there, continue to Poblazón (5 km/3 mi) and Santa Barbara (3 km/2 mi). From Santa Helena, you can take a two-kilometer (1.5-mi) detour to the birthplace of the Molino River. The complete 15-kilometer circuit takes about four hours. Try the goodies made from locally grown blackberries. The Popayán tourism office can give you more details on the Circuito Ancestral. Updated: Mar 24, 2011.

CIRCUITO DEL MAÍZ

Traveling west of Popayán, you enter the Circuito del Maíz, or the Corn Circuit, a gastronomic tour of the region. Sample homemade arepas, tamales, sweets, chicha and other typical foods made from *Zea* in the villages of El Charco, Santa Ana and Cajete. You then end your journey at the La Lajita Spa to take a dip in the refreshing La Lajita creek. For more information, visit the tourism office in Popayán. Updated: Mar 24, 2011.

PARQUE NACIONAL PURACÉ

A road heads east from Popayán towards Parque Nacional Natural Puracé. After 18 kilometers (11 mi) it forks: one branch goes to La Plata and Garzón, the other to Pitalito.

The largely unpaved La Plata road skirts the northern edge of the national park. Puracé village (alt: 2,381 m/7,810 ft, pop: 5,264) is at Kilometer 12. Almost 11 kilometers (7 mi) beyond is the Cruce de Mina, the turn-off to a sulfur mine and the main ranger station at Pilimbalá (altitude: 3,350 m/10,988 ft). Continuing along, you encounter other attractions of this sector of Parque Nacional Puracé: a condor observation point (Km 25), Laguna de San Rafael (Km 31), Cascada Bedón (Km 35), Termales San Juan (Km 37) and Cascada San Nicolás (Km 41). This finally arrives at La Plata, 147 kilometers (88 mi) from Popayán.

The southern branch is paved until Coconuco (alt: 2,481 m/8,138 ft, pop: 6,600), where there are two hot springs: Agua Herviendo and Aguas Tibias. Twenty-four kilometers (14 mi) further along is Paletará. Both villages have good trout fishing and are also access points for Parque Nacional Puracé; from Paletará you can reach Laguna del Buey in the park. The next 62 kilometers (37 mi) of road is very rough until Isnos, near some of the archaeological and natural beauties of the San Agustín region. Twenty-seven kilometers (16 mi) beyond is the Cruce de San Agustín, the crossroads to that village.

After another 27 kilometers (16 mi), the main road ends at Pitalito.

Puracé National Park has Andean forests, high Andean forests and páramo. Within its territory are the headwaters of Colombia's mightiest rivers: Cauca, Magdalena, Caquetá and Patía. It is home to over 160 species of birds, spectacled bears, mountain tapirs (*danta de montaña*) and pumas, among other mammals. In the 1990s, the San Diego Zoo in California helped to reintroduce the Andean condor to the region. A study is underway to document the number of orchid species here. Most of the park is *resguardo indígena*, or indigenous reserve lands, of the Coconuco, part of the Nasa (Páez) nation.

Reservations must be made with the national park office, Parques Nacionales Naturales de Colombia Surandina, in Popayán. The entry fee (nationals $3.50, foreigners $8.50) is paid at Pilimbalá and Termales San Juan. Updated: Aug 17, 2011.

History

Parque Nacional Natural Puracé was founded in 1961, the first national park in Cauca Department. During the 1990s the FARC used the park as a base camp. In response, the Colombia military established bases on Volcán Puracé and other areas to combat the FARC. Since 2002, with then-President Uribe's campaign to eradicate the guerrilla movements, Puracé National Park has been cleaned of the forces—according to reports. After years of virtually no tourism, Surandina is repairing service infrastructure to handle the increase of visitors to the park. Updated Aug 16, 2011.

When to Go

November, December and January are the best months to visit Parque Nacional Natural Puracé and the surrounding region. The clear weather brings the highest daytime temperatures (14-16°C/57-61°F) but likewise, the coldest nighttime temperatures, sometimes dropping below freezing.

The windiest, coldest months are July and August. The rest of the year, be prepared for rain that can last all day and all night. The wettest months are September-October, and February-March.

HOLIDAYS AND FESTIVALS

The hamlets neighboring the national park all have their festivals. Puracé village's patron saint is San Miguel Arcangel, celebrated from September 24-30. Sporting, cultural and culinary events, processions, pyrotechnic *vacas locas* and castles, and cock fights all take place during these days.

Coconuco celebrates San Pedro and San Pablo in June. Paletará's annual rainbow trout fishing tournament is the second weekend of October.Coconuco and Puracé celebrate Semana Santa with indigenous processions. In homes, foods such as corn, potatoes and rice, along with a wallet, are placed before a small light, a petition that food and money never be scarce for the family. Updated: Oct 31, 2007.

Getting To and Away

Parque Nacional Natural Puracé and its villages are most easily accessible from Popayán, though you can reach them from Tierradentro (by way of La Plata) or San Agustín.

THE NORTH ROAD (PURACÉ AND PILIMBALÁ)

From Popayán: Several companies run frequent buses to La Plata (Huila). The fare is $2.65 to the town of Puracé (1 hr); it is another $0.50 (30–45 min) to Cruce de Mina (beware of overcharging) and $1.05 (1.5 hr) to Termales San Juan. From the Cruce, walk one kilometer uphill to the turn-off for Pilimbalá (signed), then another 800 meters to the ranger station. The last bus passing by Cruce de Mina for Puracé village is at 5 p.m. From Puracé to Pilimbalá, you can also take the mining company bus at 7 a.m., leaving you about one kilometer from the ranger station.

From Tierradentro: Take the direct Popayán bus or go to Cruce de San Andres de Pisimbalá and await a bus to that city; get off at Cruce de Mina (for Pilimbalá) or at Puracé village. To travel between Puracé and Coconuco, catch a bus or jeep at the fork of the two roads (Puracé-crossroads $1.05, crossroads-Coconuco $0.80).

THE SOUTH ROAD (COCONUCO AND PALETARÁ)

From Popayán: Sotrancauca (hourly to Coconuco 6:30 a.m.-5:30 p.m., 1.5 hr, $1.60).For Paletará, take a San Agustín or Pitalito bus and get off at the village.

From San Agustín: Catch a Popayán-bound bus, which passes through Paletará and Coconuco. Updated: Nov 09, 2007.

Safety

Parque Nacional Puracé is now safe. The military claims all landmines have been removed on Volcán Puracé; nonetheless, it is advised you stay on the trails any place in the park boundaries. The weather on the páramo can change rapidly. Temperatures reach freezing in some months, so bring plenty of warm clothing. Take precautions against hypothermia. Also have gear to protect against rain. Rubber boots are recommended. Folks in the neighboring villages say all is quiet and safe. The military presence is quite notable in all the towns. Updated: Oct 31, 2007.

Services

TOURISM

Before arriving to Parque Nacional Natural Puracé, you must contact **Parques Nacionales Naturales de Colombia Surandina**, in Popayán (Monday-Friday 8-11:30 a.m. and 2-4 p.m. Cra. 9, 25N-06. Tel: 823-1279/1212, URL: www.parquesnacionales. gov.co). The office will fill you in on present safety and weather conditions. It can also help you arrange for a guide. The rangers at the Pilimbalá station can also tell you about the park. In Puracé village, stop by the restaurant Micho for any information you may need about hiking in the area or about the national park.

MONEY

In none of the villages bordering the national park are there banks, ATMs or any place to change cash dollars. Bring plenty of pesos with you.

KEEPING IN TOUCH

The Pilimbalá ranger station has a telephone and radio to communicate with the outside world. In Puracé, the **Telecom** office is on Carrera 7, a half-block from the church; at the time of writing, it had no service. In Coconuco the company's office is on Carrera 2, the main street. In all the *pueblos* people rent their cellular phones for local or national calls. The entire area is devoid of post offices. In some villages the only internet is at the *colegio* (high school), with connection for a few hours Monday to Friday; priority is given to students. There is a privately run internet café in Coconuco (Cra. 3, 2-99).

MEDICAL

When hiking or trekking in Parque Nacional Natural Puracé, carry along a first aid kit with basic medications. The park itself has no medical facilities. The **Centro de Salud** in Puracé village has 24-hour emergency and ambulance services (Cra. 6, 3-50). There is a pharmacy behind the hospital, as well as at the house with the *fotocopias* sign across the street at (Ca 4, 5-18). Coconuco's Centro de Salud also has emergency attention (Cra. 2, 5-59). There is a pharmacy one block away (Cra. 2, 4-15). Updated: May 21, 2009.

Things to See and Do

If you are bored of museums and churches and are ready to get out of the cities, dig out the hiking boots and head to Parque Nacional Natural Puracé. You can climb Volcán Puracé (4,640 m/15,219 ft) or do the two-day trek around Pan de Azúcar (4,670 m/15,318 ft) and the Cadena Volcánica de Coconuco. The pre-Hispanic Camino Nacional is also an off-the-beaten track adventure. The attractions along the north road make a great day excursion. For bird watchers, there are Andean condors and over 160 other species of birds. After days of hiking or trekking, you can soak in the hot springs in Coconuco. For those who like fishing, cast your line in Coconuco or Paletará for some of their famous rainbow trout. Updated: Nov 01, 2007.

Volcán Puracé

The star of this 803,600-hectare national park is Volcán Puracé. A near-perfect cone peak, it rises 4,760 meters (15,613 ft). A well-defined trail leads from the Pilimbalá ranger station through high mountain and páramo ecosystems to its summit. Near the top, loose cinders make the going a bit tough. Even though the volcano last erupted in 1949, its fumaroles still emit sulfur fumes. The trail begins at 3,350 meters (10,988 ft) altitude and no special climbing equipment is needed. However, you are climbing at high altitude and through a landscape that is unrelenting. Clouds and rain can move in at any moment.

The ranger station here has lodging available, which is a convenient place to stay if climbing the volcano. A simple restaurant serves breakfast, lunch and dinner. Even though the military reports all land mines have been removed from the volcano, the park service still recommends you stay on the path. The rangers further recommend you go accompanied, in a group and/or with a guide, as the climate and terrain provide special challenges, and that you begin the climb before 10 a.m. and the descent no later than 4 p.m. Pay attention to the signs warning of fumaroles. Do not enter the crater.

Volcán Puracé is most easily accessed from the north side of the park. A signed trail begins behind the Pilimbalá ranger station. To get to Pilimbalá, see the Puracé: Getting To and Away section. Updated: Dec 19, 2007.

Cascada de Río Bedón

More or less parallel to the Popayán-La Plata road, which passes along the north edge of Parque Nacional Natural Puracé, is the Bedón River. Just past Kilometer 35 the río plunges from 3,060 meters (10,037 ft) altitude to less than 3,000 meters (9,840 ft) before continuing its course eastward through large-leafed foliage. The waters of Cascada de Río Bedón foam white not from the 60-meter (197-ft)-plus fall, but from the sulfur swirling within its depths. You witness its force from the overlook built just 10 meters (33 ft) from the road. Popayán-La Plata road, Km 35, Parque Nacional Natural Puracé. Take a bus from passing along the road to Km 35, or walk from one of the other attractions along the north road. Updated: May 15, 2009.

Termales San Juan

Sulfur-laden waters bubble from out of the earth, rushing to a brook winding across the páramo at 3,200 meter (10,496 ft) altitude. Deep emerald mosses and red lichens carpet the banks. The rocks in the stream are lacquered pale yellow from the minerals. Tall, thin grasses sway in the gentle wind. In the distance rise cragged mountain peaks. You have arrived at Termales San Juan. Sit in the thatched hut for a while and listen to the breeze, the birds, the frogs. Wander the trail that weaves among these waters. As inviting as these pools are, visitors cannot dip into them. Many animals come here and our smell in the waters and earth can scare them.

An uneven stone path next to the ranger station goes one kilometer (0.6 mi) to the thermal pools. Along the way, signs point out special features of the journey, including orchids, a mountain tapir crossing and a view of Pan de Azúcar Volcáno.

On the opposite side of the road is a mirador over the Río Bedón and the Museo Cultural y el Centro de Interpretación Huancayo (Monday-Friday 8 a.m.-5 p.m., $0.75). Meals and drinks can be had at a small shack on the south side of the road, next to the ranger station. Popayán-La Plata road, Km 37, Parque Nacional Natural Puracé. Updated: Aug 17, 2011.

Cadena Volcánica de Coconuco

Like a necklace of rough, uncut jet stones draping the páramo is the Cadena Volcánica de Coconuco. Beginning at Pan de Azúcar, a volcano towering 4,670 meters (15,318 ft), nine more volcanic craters form a chain across the lunar-like landscape within the hinterlands of Parque Nacional Natural Puracé. A two-and-a-half-day trek can be made around their imposing presence, camping on the wild, wind-swept plains. You may be lucky and encounter some of the park's more elusive residents, the mountain tapir, puma and spectacled bear.

To get there, two routes are possible: beginning at and returning to Pilimbalá or Termales San Juan, or starting at Paletará and ending at Pilimbalá or Termales San Juan.

A guide is highly recommended. Contact Parques Nacionales Naturales de Colombia Surandina, in Popayán, to make a reservation and find out about present conditions. It can also help you to arrange the services of a local guide from the indigenous community. The park entry fee is paid at either Pilimbalá or Termales San Juan. Updated: May 18, 2009.

Camino Natural

One of the three park roads, the Camino Natural cuts across the park, from San Sebastián in Cauca to San Agustín in Huila. This pre-Hispanic road takes the average hiker two days to complete, staying the night in San Antonio. Before you start asking if you are there yet, take into consideration it's only an eight-hour walk, but you'll want to stop and talk to the local residents along the way. Camino Natural is stone-paved and a secure route, no longer used by guerrillas. You'll need a guide and a park permit, both of which you can get from the Surandina office in Popayán. Don't miss the chance to take this ancient road through pristine landscapes, visiting indigenous villages along the way and finishing the walk at the site of the mysterious Agustine peoples' stoic statues. Updated: Dec 19, 2007.

Hot Springs

(ADMISSION: Agua Hirviendo $1.75, Aguatibia $3) After days of exploring the natural wonders of Puracé National Park, trekking across the cold, windy páramo, what better way to relax strained muscles and to warm up than to soak in hot springs? Head down to Coconuco, on the south boundary of the park, where not one but two thermal waters await you. Agua Hirviendo is the hotter, bubbling out of the earth at 90°C (194°F)—enough to boil an egg in five minutes, it's said—and mixed with fresh spring water to a perfect temperature. This spa, owned and operated by the Coconuco-Nasa indigenous community, has three large pools and five "personal"-sized ones (the two closest to the source are very hot). The other hot springs is the privately owned Aguatibia. It is more park-like, with thermal lagoons and pools, water slide and thermal "Jacuzzis" with mineral mud.

Agua Hirviendo has changing rooms, but no lockers. Next to the pools are several seating kiosks where you can place your belongings while soaking; keep an eye on them. The hot springs are very crowded during holidays; if you want a more peaceful experience, avoid these times. Both *aguas termales* have restaurants and lodging. At Agua Hirviendo (Tel: 2-822-3649, Cel: 314-618-4178), a cabaña for up to six persons with private bath is $50 and a small one for up to four persons with shared bath is $28; camping costs $6 per tent per night. All options include free, 24-hour access to the pools. Aguatibia (Tel: 2-824-1161, Cel: 315-578-6111, E-mail: termaguatibia@yahoo.es) also has cabañas; camping is $8 per site.

Coconuco is 30 kilometers (18 mi) from Popayán by paved road, thus making this a nice day trip from the city. Agua Hirviendo is one kilometer from the village by paved road (walk, or catch a collective pick-up truck from the main street $0.50 per person, $3.20 whole vehicle). Alternately, take the grassy cow trail that begins just past the Hotel Comfandi through pastures to Agua Hirviendo, though beware of patties and bulls (30 min). Aguatibia is four kilometers (2.4 mi) down the Coconuco-Paletará road. Updated: Aug 17, 2011.

Trout Fishing

Your fly lands softly in the crystalline water of Río Aguasilencio—Silent Water River—or one of its tributaries flowing near Coconuco and Paletará. A subtle breeze passes through the trees and grasses as sunlight dapples the landscape. Tonight you will be frying up the tender rainbow trout you catch here. But for now, it is the meditation of casting and waiting for the gentle tug on the line. If you are in Paletará some last week of October, you can challenge Colombians at the annual rainbow trout fishing tournament.

Coconuco is 30 kilometers (18 mi) from Popayán by paved road, and Paletará 24 kilometers (14.5 mi) further on. You can also reach Coconuco and Paletará from San Agustín. See the Getting To and Away section for Puracé. Updated: Aug 17, 2011.

Tours

Parque Nacional Natural Puracé is beginning to come back onto the radar screen of travelers. A few tour companies and guides in Popayán, San Agustín and Puracé village offer expeditions into the park. Better yet, there are local guides from the indigenous communities within the park who intimately know its terrain; the national park office in Popayán can help arrange their services for you. For more details, see Resguardo Indígena Guides under Popayán. Updated: Aug 17, 2011.

Marino Garces

Prefer to stay in Puracé hamlet? You can still climb Puracé Volcáno in one day. Señor Marino Garces can load you and your friends up in his four-wheel-drive Nissan and guide you to the top and back. He can also take you to visit Termales San Juan. For either excursion he charges a flat rate of $37 for up to eight persons. Bring along your own food and drink (if going to San Juan, you can eat there). For the volcano trek, remember to also have warm clothing, hat, gloves, good shoes or boots and raingear. Ca. 2, 7-28, Puracé village. Tel: 2-847-7032. Updated: May 21, 2009.

Lodging

Accommodations in the area of Parque Nacional Natural Puracé are basic. There are only two options in the town of Puracé, which serves as a base for visiting the attractions along the north road. Within the park itself are cabañas and a campsite, which are more convenient for scaling Volcán Puracé. Of the villages on the south perimeter of the park, Coconuco has more choices, as it is a destination in its own right thanks to the hot springs, where lodging and camping are also available. At vacation times, reservations are necessary, especially for Coconuco. December and January are busy months in the park. Updated: Aug 17, 2011.

Estanco Oficial Residencias

(BEDS: $5.30) The cheapest place to stay in Coconuco is Estanco Oficial Residencias: Official Liquor Store Inn. In the front is where the locals and tourists hang to have a drink (especially popular on weekends and holidays). Beyond another door, along one side of the back courtyard, are the rooms to let. During the week, you can get a restful sleep here. The rooms are spacious and clean, the beds comfy. The four rooms share one clean, cold-water bathroom. Cra. 3, 4-23, Coconuco. Updated: May 15, 2009.

Residencias Cubita

(BEDS: $7) This small, four-room hotel is simple and plain, but the rooms are large, each with two beds. A few potted plants brighten up the patio. The common baths are clean—but brace yourself for the cold-water shower. Extra blankets are available for those nights when it gets frigid. The owners, Marlí and Marino, are hospitable. There is also secure parking for cars or motorcycles, and a laundry area. Ca. 2, 7-28, Puracé village. Updated: Aug 17, 2011.

No-Name Hospedaje

(ROOMS: $8-21) Simple, simple, simple describes this Coconuco hotel. A non-descript green building with a second-floor balcony and carved doors, it is a popular choice for vacationing Colombians—despite the fact that all the basic rooms share the common baths, which have only cold-water showers. But with two hot springs in Coconuco, you can always warm up there. Cra. 2, 6-21, half-block from the church, Coconuco. Updated: Dec 19, 2007.

Parque Nacional Cabañas

(CAMPING: $3.50, CABINS: $11-14.50) Escape to the tranquility of Parque Nacional Natural Puracé. At Pilimbalá ranger station there are three A-frame *cabañas* for rent. After spending all day scaling Volcán Puracé or hiking in the park, cuddle up in front of the sitting room fireplace. The first floor bedroom has bunk beds for six, and on the top floor there are double mattresses for up to four more companions. A private bath is also at your disposal (cold-water shower). Sheets and blankets are provided. For travelers on a tighter budget, the park also has campsites and hammock huts. Cabin reservations must be made with Parques Nacionales Naturales de Colombia Surandina in Popayán (see Popayán Services). Updated: Aug 17, 2011.

Restaurants

Your eating options in the Parque Nacional Natural Puracé region are fairly simple and limited. The menus are restricted almost exclusively to the *comida corriente*, or blue plate specials. Local trout also makes its appearance. At both Pilimbalá and Termales San Juan in the park are small restaurants operated by the indigenous community. Basic supplies can be picked up at general stores or the weekly markets in the villages. Updated: Aug 17, 2011.

Comedor

(SET MEAL: $2.50) Doña Blanca and her neighbors cook up meals in a large hut on the other side of the thermal pools. (Don't get your hopes up too much; due to a 1995 earthquake, the heat and flow of these springs greatly diminished.) From dawn until 8 p.m., these women are serving up standard comidas corrientes for breakfast, lunch and dinner. While waiting for your plate, you can stroll down the Sendero de Orquídeas right behind the restaurant and admire the orchids in bloom. The central fireplace is a wonderful place to warm up on those cold, rainy afternoons. Pilimbalá ranger station. Updated: Aug 17, 2011.

Micho

Open afternoons into the evenings, Micho is the place to hang out for chicken wings, empanadas or other Colombian snacks while playing parcheesi, dominoes or chess. In one back room is a ping-pong table. At any hour you can view a movie from the 100-plus DVD collection on hand. The "theater" is a bare, white-washed lean-to with four plastic lawn chairs. The walls full of popular sayings and riddles are also an interesting way to pass the odd hour in this hamlet ("Does Colombia law prohibit you from marrying your widow's sister?"). Ca. 2, 5-50, Puracé village. Updated: Dec 19, 2007.

No-Name Restaurant

(SET MEAL: $1.50-2) With whatever might be available in this small village, doña Elma whips up simple meals. Breakfast might be eggs, rice, potatoes and coffee. Your lunch or dinner will, of course, have soup—and the main dish, meat or local trout, rice, yucca, tomatoes and a drink. This eatery is very popular with the young soldiers stationed in Puracé. Ca. 2, 6-15, Puracé village. Updated: Dec 19, 2007.

Hato Viejo

(SET MEAL: $2) Behind the green and orange bamboo "picket" fence is the front patio of the Hato Viejo restaurant. Take a table here, or inside in the light and airy dining room. The breeze passing through the large, open windows make the many wind chimes sing. Soon you will have your daily special in front of you. Or perhaps today you're in the mood for some fresh rainbow trout. This eatery is popular with the village's doctors. Cra. 3 and Ca. 5, Coconuco. Cel: 313-867-7172. Updated: Aug 17, 2011.

SOUTHERN COLOMBIA

TIERRADENTRO

 2,464m   6,006   2

Deep within the heart of the hilly countryside around Tierradentro lies one of Colombia's great archaeological gems: mysterious subterranean tombs painted in white-black-red-ochre geometrical patterns which were declared an UNESCO World Heritage Site in 1995. It is a difficult journey to arrive there, especially in the rainy season. You will be rewarded, though, with incredible walking opportunities to explore the ruins and villages of this "Land Within."

A road runs from Popayán to La Plata, passing through Tótoro. The turn-off for Tierradentro is Cruce de Pisimbalá, also called Cruce de San Andrés, near the town of Guadalejo. The Popayán-La Plata road is paved only from El Pital, east of Guadalejo, to La Plata. (Note: this is a different road than that along the north edge of Parque Nacional Natural Puracé.)

From the crossroads, the road heads north towards the "Land Within," Tierradentro. The principal town is San Andrés de Pisimbalá. Two and a half kilometers before that village is Parque Arqueológico, the entrance and museums of this famed archaeological site. The settlement has the major concentration of lodging and restaurants in the area. The road continues uphill to San Andrés, where there are other hotels and eateries. Parque Arqueológico de Tierradentro is part of the Resguardo Indígena de Andrés, an indigenous reservation of the Nasa (Páez) nation. Inzá, a town just west of Guadalejo, has its market day on Saturday, when you can see many Nasa in traditional dress. Updated: Nov 08, 2007.

History

The Chibcha-speaking people arrived in these mountains about 7th–9th century AD. An agricultural society, they crafted weavings, stone carvings and ceramics. Worship focused on death and ancestors. Due to the lack of violent depictions, archaeologists believe the Nasa ancestors were a peaceful nation. Tierradentro and San Agustín were contemporary societies; their sculpture and housing are similar, and their settlements were connected by roads.

When the Spaniards arrived here in the mid-15th century, they called this land of rugged terrain, isolated villages and difficult travel Tierradentro, or "Land Within."

In 1994, Nevado de Huila erupted, causing an avalanche that swept through the valley of the Páez River, killing over 1,000 people. Today, Tierradentro encompasses 21 indigenous reserves. Updated: Nov 06, 2007.

When to Go

As in other parts of this region, November, December and January are the best months to visit Tierradentro. The clear weather brings warm days, but cold nights. The windiest months are July and August, which are also cold. Rain is common the rest of the year; the wettest months are September, October, February and March (when rains are heaviest).

Tierradentro is a popular destination for vacationing Colombians at major holiday times, especially in December. Lodging will be full; likewise, more services, such as restaurants, will be open.

San Andrés has its patron saint ceremonies in mid-November. In the village of Calderas, one hour from San Andrés, you can catch traditional Nasa (Páez) indigenous music and dance during the Tumbichucue celebration held each year on December 31st. The weekly indigenous markets in Inzá and Belalcazar are both on Saturday, beginning at dawn; Guadalejo's market is on Sunday. Updated: Aug 22, 2011.

Getting To and Away

Arriving at Tierradentro is a trip that can be beset by muddy roads and landslides in the rainy season. Vehicles are often overcrowded, with people riding atop and hanging off the back. It is most directly reached from Popayán. However, many visit it in the same breath as San Agustín, which is a full day's journey away; for more details, see below.

If you miss a direct departure for your destination, then take a local pick-up or jeep to Cruce de Pisimbalá, a.k.a. Cruce de San Andrés, and catch other transport there. Both Popayán and La Plata serve as hubs for transportation. When arriving in Tierradentro, tell the driver you want to alight at the Parque Archaeológico, if that is where you will be staying, as San Andrés village is another 2.5 kilometers farther uphill.

To Popayán: Sotranscauca (5:30 a.m., 5 hr, $9.50); from Popayán 10:30 a.m. Or go to the Cruce and catch a La Plata-Popayán bus.

SOUTHERN COLOMBIA

To La Plata: Pick-up trucks (daily 6 a.m., 8 a.m., noon, 4 p.m.), *chiva* (Sunday, Wednesday 7 a.m., Friday 5 a.m.). Both take 1.5-2 hours and cost $7.

The route between Tierradentro and San Agustín will—with a bit of luck—only take about six hours. But if you don't hit the connections right, you will probably have to spend the night in one of the transit points. The route is Tierradentro-La Plata-Pitalito-San Agustín. If you miss a direct La Plata-Pitalito bus, then go to Garzón, from where there is frequent minibuses for both towns. The La Plata bus terminal are quite a distance from town; city buses connect the two ($0.50).

From La Plata to Tierradentro (San Andrés de Pisimbalá): Cootransplateña (every 3-4 hours 6:30 a.m.-4 p.m., 2 hr, $7). Chivas leave from downtown (Sunday, Wednesday, Friday).

To Bogotá: 8 hours, $19-21—Cootranshuila (9:30 p.m.), Coomotor (8:30 a.m., 11 a.m., 9 p.m.).

Pitalito to La Plata: 7 a.m., 10 a.m., 2 p.m., 4 p.m., 3 hours, $9. Or go to Garzón (bus $7, collective taxi $8), then to Pitalito (*buseta* $7, collective taxi $8).

From Pitalito there is also service to Neiva, Bogotá, Isnos and Popayán. Updated: Aug 22, 2011.

Safety

The area is safe for hiking, even alone; however, locals will advise you not to walk at night. Stay on the trails, especially in the back country, as landmines are present. Further afield, deep into the mountains, the FARC is present, but never reportedly in the Tierradentro region itself. Transportation can be dangerously overcrowded. To guarantee a seat, go into San Andrés to catch transport out of Tierradentro; from La Plata to Tierradentro, buy your ticket in advance. Updated: Aug 22, 2011.

Services

TOURISM

Comité Etno Turístico de Tierradentro staffs an information kiosk near the archaeological park (Cel: 312-495-5516/314-734-1453/312-871-9413, E-mail: info@tierradentro-ecoturismo.com, URL: www.tierradentro-ecoturismo.com). In the same sector, a shop offers regional tourist information (daily, 8 a.m.–8 p.m. Green house with the orange door, across from Hospedaje Ricabet. Cel: 313-637-9638/311-337-0573, E-mail: faluza@gmail.com). This store sells locally produced bags, necklaces and other items, and has a restaurant. **The Instituto Colombiano de Arqueología e Historia** has a booklet about the archaeological sites (available in English and Spanish) that can be downloaded for free (URL: www.incanh.gov.co); maps can be printed off from **Tierradentro.Info** (URL: www.tierradentro.info).

MONEY

Neither Tierradentro nor San Andrés de Pisimbalá have banks, places to change cash or travelers checks, nor money wiring services.

KEEPING IN TOUCH

As in many villages in this "Land Within," the high school has internet for several hours per day, Monday to Friday, with priority given to students. Many shops in both the Parque Arqueológico and San Andrés village have phone service; look for the *Minutos* sign. Neither section of Tierradentro has a post office.

MEDICAL

The local medical clinic, **Puesto de Salud San Andrés**, is at the entry of San Andrés village (Monday-Friday 8 a.m.-noon and 2-6 p.m., Saturday 8 a.m.-noon. Cel: 314-662-4446/311-644-9071). Updated: Aug 22, 2011.

Things to See and Do

The main attraction of Tierradentro is its painted, pre-Columbian tombs. A trail connects four sites: Segovia, El Duende, El Tablón (which has statues stylistically similar to San Agustín) and Los Altos de San Andrés. Another burial, Aguacate, lies high in the mountains. The Parque Arqueológico also has two museums on either side of the road: one displays archaeological finds and the other explores the ethnography of the Nasa (Páez) peoples of the region. The village of San Andrés de Pisimbalá has a thatched-roof church. To the west and north of Tierradentro are several stone roads connecting hamlets such as Guanacas, Inzá, Silvia, Chinas and Lame. As security stabilizes, these will make for great off-the-beaten-track hiking. The region also hides multitudinous caverns, waterfalls and other natural wonders. Updated: Nov 16, 2007.

The Museums of Tierradentro

When the rain comes, pass the time in the two fine museums Tierradentro Archaeological Park offers. On the river side of the road is the Museo Etnográfico, describing the history and culture of the Nasa (Páez) peoples of the region. On the other side of the road is the Museo Arqueológico, displaying artifacts from the tombs. One section explains the cultural connection with the area's other great archaeological site, San Agustín. The guard will accompany you on your exploration and answer your questions (Spanish only; exhibition signs in Spanish only).

The museums are located at the entrance of the Parque Arqueológico hamlet, on either side of the road, three kilometers (1.8 mi) before San Andrés de Pisimbalá. They are open 8 a.m.-4 p.m. Entry is included in the archaeological site ticket. Updated: Aug 22, 2011.

The Tombs of Tierradentro

(ADMISSION: $5.60, children under 15 years old free) Four major archaeological sites, all dating from 600 to 900 A.D., make up Tierradentro: three burial and one of statues. The tombs were carved by hand from volcanic rock. Some are up to 3 meters (10 ft) deep. Most are painted within, with geometric and figurative designs in red, black, orange, grey, purple and yellow on white. A few also contain burial urns. Segovia, the first site from the museum, is the crown jewel of the complex. Thirty tombs are open; only 16 are lit. Numbers 8 to 12 are the most impressive. Alto del Duende, the next site, consists of four crypts. The third grouping, El Tablón, holds statues stylistically similar to those of San Agustín. Beyond San Andrés Pisimbalá is Alto de San Andrés with more tombs. Flash photos of the tombs are not allowed. Only a few tombs are lit, and only those at Segovia. Bring a flashlight.

The time it takes to go between sites is as follows: Museo Etnográfico to Segovia, 20 minutes; Segovia to El Duende, 15 minutes; El Duende to El Tablón, 40 minutes; El Tablón to Alto de San Andrés, 30 minutes. The turn-off for the path to Alto de San Andrés is midway between Parque Arqueológico and the village; this can be done as a separate hike. If you do the trek reversed, going from San Andrés de Pisimbalá to El Tablón, Alto del Duende and Segovia, then the walk will be mostly downhill. Check at Parque Arqueológico for availability of horses. Daily 8 a.m.-4 p.m. Tickets are valid for two days. Updated: Aug 22, 2011.

Hiking to the Aguacate Tombs

Historians and Indiana Jones lovers will enjoy hiking to the ruined tombs of Aguacate, near San Andrés Pisimbalá.

Starting just to the left of La Portada bar/restaurant, the four-hour trek climbs hillsides, traverses ridges, and climbs and dips until, astride a mountain, the path reaches the tombs themselves. It's easy to see why people with power once chose to be buried there: If you weren't going anywhere for a few million years, you'd want a view that good, too.

The tombs comprise more than a dozen dramatic and massive holes in the ground, most of which lead to caves of various sizes. Some are painted, others have large columns, and a few are only filled with spiders and dirt. Many have been grave-robbed. The site is less archaeologically important than Segovia. Nonetheless, they are remarkable , especially when you first see the tombs laid out before you, wrapped in an incredible vista.

The trail continues on, mostly downhill, and comes out right by the museums at Parque Arqueológico.

The path is marked at most important forks, and wrong turns down unmarked splits never take long to terminate at farms or fields. Still, to save a bit of time stick to the larger choice when the trail splits. After rains, the trail to Aguacate is especially bad, with mud calf-deep. Rubber boots are recommended. Updated: Aug 22, 2011.

Ritual de Refrescamiento y Limpieza

After months of being on the road, you may need to have a Ritual de Refrescamiento y Limpieza done. The Refresh and Cleansing Ritual is an ancient custom of the indigenous peoples here that is still being preserved. Agriano Piñacue and Victoriano Quinto, two traditional *curanderos* (medicine persons) of the Nasa nation, do these ceremonies. Appointments must be made at least two to three days in advance, as the ritual is timed to the moon phases. To make arrangements for a ritual, contact Dr. Carmen Leonor Acosta, director of the office of tourism in Popayán. She speaks English. (see Popayán Services). There is no charge for the ritual; however, it is suggested that you give a tip of $8-10, or a gift. Updated: Mar 25, 2011.

Tours

Local guides offer guiding services. Many charge only $5 or less, plus transportation. Two who have been recommended are **Pedro and José**, who linger around Hospedaje Ricabet or the hotel next door. **Luza and Fabián**, who have the café-artisan-tourist information shop across from Hospedaje Ricabet, also do tours (Cel: 313-637-9638/311-337-0573, E-mail: faluza@gmail.com). For other guides, contact **Comité Etno Turístico de Tierradentro** for other guides (see Services).

The various tomb sites can also be reached on horseback. Check at Parque Arqueológico for availability of horses or ask at your hotel. Be sure they are in good condition. The typical charge is $2.50 per hour. Updated Aug 22, 2011.

Lodging

Most lodging options are found in the Parque Arqueológico section of Tierradentro. Besides a few formal inns, many families also rent rooms in their homes to tourists. In San Andrés de Pisimbalá there are several other hotels. Comité Etno Turístico de Tierradentro has a half-dozen hostel members.

Most hostels are basic. The only up-scale hotel is **Albergue El Refugio**, featuring a swimming pool, 19 rooms with hot-water, private baths, and campsites (Km 2 vía Inzá, Sector Parque Arqueológico. Cel: 321-811-2395, E-mail: hotelalbergueelrefugio@gmail.com). San Andrés has a heavy military presence, which other travelers have found uncomfortable. They have found the Parque a more relaxing place to stay. Updated: Aug 22, 2011.

Casa de Señora Marta

(BEDS: $4) Perfect for travelers looking for an authentic experience while meeting interesting fellow travelers, Residenciales El Viajero, or Señora Marta's place, could belong to any "interesting" grandmother who wanted to have three rooms and eight beds to spare. House plants abound on ledges across from a cabinet of knick-knacks in the main communal room (which only has three walls) through which an eclectic but steady stream of international travelers has passed through over almost three decades. Señora Marta herself is friendly, neat, welcoming and unobtrusive, and she will cook up cheap and delicious food, including vegetarian dishes, given notice. There's no sign above her door, but anyone in town will tell you where she is. As a fellow traveler said, "staying with her mixes the best of staying in a hostel with the best of a homestay." Ask for la casa de señora Marta. San Andrés de Pisimbalá. Cel: 317-746-5991. Updated: May 15, 2009.

Hospedaje Mi Casita

(ROOMS: $4-5) This sweet little *hospedaje* run by a young family rents out three rooms in what would otherwise just be their private home. Rooms here are spacious enough and the beds are comfortable. The shared bath has a clean toilet and hot water shower. Recuerdo, the resident black labrador retriever, lazes around all day to "keep guard" or just provide entertainment for the kids in the house. The owner's sister runs the shop and juice store next door and will even provide a home-cooked meal, if you ask nicely. Look for the light blue house between the two juice stores in town; also across the street from Hospedaje Lucerne. Sector Parque Arqueológico. Cel: 312-764-1333. Updated: May 28, 2008.

Hospedaje Lucerna

(BEDS: $4.20) Austere on the outside, with only small lettering announcing its presence, Hospedaje Lucerna is big on service. Inside, the rooms are grouped around the flower-filled garden. All share the common bath with hot water (give 20 minutes notice) and have shuttered windows. Mornings, sit down with the lovely elderly couple who open their home to travelers. Don Secundario will tell you about Tierradentro's history while you sip on a free cup of organic coffee from his neighboring farm. Doña Carmelita can also squeeze you up a glass of fresh orange juice—yes, organic, from their own orchard. You can even wash your clothes here. They also offer camping space with full use of the facilities. On the river side of the main road, next to the Museo Etnográfico, Sector Parque Arqueológico. Cel: 312-727-5407. Updated: Dec 19, 2007.

Hospedaje Los Lagos

(BEDS: $4.20-5.25) For those preferring to stay in San Andrés Pisimbalá itself, Hospedaje y Restaurante Los Lagos is one of several options. Located at the end of the village's main road to the right, this Colombian family-run lodging is a very basic inn. The guest rooms come only with beds—no other furnishings appear. One has a private bath and double bed. All bathrooms have cold-water showers. The restaurant is reputed to be good, but advance notice must be given if you wish to dine here. Carrera 2A, 3-17. E-mail: dmonchiviris@hotmail.com. Updated: May 25, 2009.

Hospedaje Pisimbalá

(BEDS: $5-8) Hospedaje Pisimbalá is another old standby for journeyers to Tierradentro. Also a small, family-run inn, this place offers three rooms with shared bathroom and three rooms with private bath. Only one room has a solitary bed; the others are crowded with three beds each, making space to place your packs awfully tight. Hot-water showers are available. Camping is additionally offered, whether in your own tent or camper-van. The front garden is quite nice, with a bamboo gazebo. On the main road, about 200 meters from the Museo Arqueológico, Sector Parque Arqueológico. Cel: 311-605-4835. Updated: Aug 26, 2011.

Hospedaje Ricabet

(ROOMS: $6-11) Located at the upper edge of town, just before the curve heading up the hill to San Andrés center, is Hospedaje Ricabet, which is a mid-range option for travelers looking for a little more than a basic room. Six rooms are situated around a small courtyard—some of which have a private bath with hot water. The rate here is a bit more expensive and a grade more comfortable than the other options in town. Located up the hill from the Tierradentro park entrance, on the right hand side just before heading farther up to San Andrés town, Sector Parque Arqueológico. Cel: 312-795-4636. Updated: Aug 26, 2011.

La Portada

(ROOMS: $7-10) La Portada is a hostel with 11 spacious rooms that have two beds with thick mattresses and fantastic views of the mountains. There are five rooms with private baths and six with a shared bath down the hall. The owners, Leonardo and María Eva, are great and will happily answer any questions you may have about the area. Inquire at their restaurant across the street if there's no one around. The hostel is only 150 meters (500 ft) from a 400-year-old church with a thatched roof. San Andrés de Pisimbalá. Cel: 311-601-7884/311-712-7874. Updated: Mar 28, 2011.

Restaurants

It is very difficult to find a place to eat in Tierradentro. Many places advertising themselves as restaurants in the Parque Arqueológico area don't open or have food in the off-season. It is best to make meal plans in advance with an establishment. More dining choices are had in the village, 2.5 kilometers (1.5 mi) away. In San Andrés de Pisimbalá there's a bakery and a few small stores in the Parque Arqueológico area. Friday is market day in San Andrés. Updated: Nov 06, 2007.

Jugos Ricos

(DRINKS: $1) Its name doesn't lie: Jugos Ricos serves some of the tastiest juices in South America, and not much else. Lots of flavors are available with chilled water or milk bases. You get a glass and a half, roughly—make sure you get the extra bit from the jug! Jugos Ricos Tienda is perfect for an afternoon cool-off or a betweenmuseum, people-watching break. Sector Parque Arqueológico. Cel: 311-721-2771. Updated: Mar 28, 2011.

Restaurante Pisimbalá

(SET MEALS: $2) Restaurante Pisimbalá, located in the the inn of the same name, is virtually your only dining choice in the Parque Arqueológico sector of Tierradentro. The señora makes up a good meal of whatever happens to be at hand, usually consisting of the day's soup, and a main dish or rice, beans, meat, salad and yucca or plátano. You can dine inside or, if the weather is nice, in the gazebo in the front garden. Be sure to give advance notice and set a time if you plan on dining here. In Hospedaje Pisimbalá, on the main road, about 200 meters from the Museo Arqueológico, Sector Parque Arqueológico. Updated: Aug 22, 2011.

La Portada Restaurante-Bar

(SET MEAL: $4-5) La Portada Restaurante-Bar is one of the few dining choices in San Andrés village that is open out of season. This restaurant is light and airy, with a large, covered verandah constructed of *guardanal* (giant bamboo) and brick, with brick-tiled floors. La Portada serves up breakfast, and set-plate meals for lunch and dinner (for a cheaper option, ask for only the *bandeja*, or main dish). La Portada also whips up good vegetarian options. Across the street is the restaurant's new hostel. If you are staying in the Parque Arqueológico sector, remember it is 2.5 kilometers (1.5 mi) away, a dark walk home after dusk. Monday-Saturday 6 a.m.-8 p.m., Sunday 5-8 p.m. San Andrés de Pisimbalá. Cel: 311-601-7884/311-712-7874. Updated: Aug 26, 2011.

V!VA ONLINE REVIEW
LA PORTADA RESTAURANTE-BAR

Built from bamboo, this place has a nice ambiance. The owner is friendly, too.

September 15, 2009

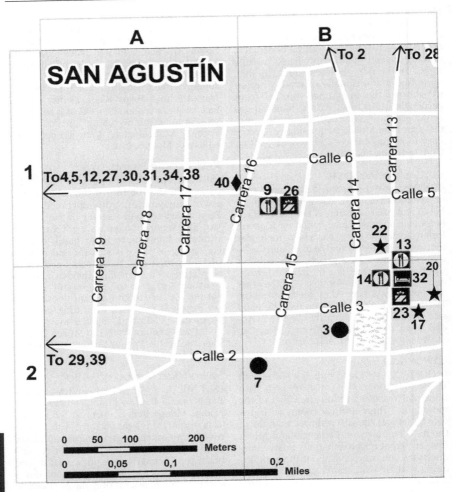

SAN AGUSTÍN

SAN AGUSTÍN

🏔 1,640m	👤 30,000	📞 2

Like silent sentinels guarding the green mountains of southern Colombia, the pre-Columbian statues of San Agustín have long beckoned travelers to wander off the beaten track. The journey can be difficult, but the reward for these sojourners is days of walking through the countryside, exploring the numerous archaeological sites that bestow the name "Archaeological Capital of Colombia" to San Agustín.

Aside from the archaeological park, designated a World Heritage Site by UNESCO,

the landscape also holds attractions: the nascent Río Magdalena, canyons, waterfalls and caves. The road from Popayán skirts the south boundary of Parque Nacional Natural Puracé; it is paved as far as Coconuco, after which it is poor to El Cruce, 27 kilometers (16 mi) from Pitalito. The road from Bogotá, by way of Neiva, Garzón and Pitalito, is completely paved.

Life is laid-back in the village of San Agustín, so much so that many foreigners have decided to stay here to live. Be prepared to spend a bit of time here learning about the enigmatic culture that a millennium ago carved monoliths (every one has a theory), hiking and just relaxing. Updated: Aug 17, 2011.

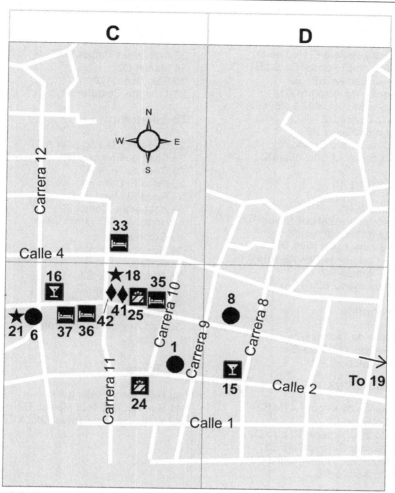

History

The people who carved the monoliths that populate the rolling lands of San Agustín remain a mystery. Today we call their civilization Agustinian, but its real name has been lost in the mists that swirl around these mountains. They are assumed to be the ancestors of the present-day Nasa (Páez) nation of the region. According to radiocarbon dating, the Upper Magdalena area had been inhabited since at least 4,000 years before Christ. The Agustinian culture is usually divided into two periods: the Formative (1000 BC-1 AD) and the Regional Classical (1-900 AD). This latter era was when most of the funerary sites were elaborated. Archaeologists believe the peoples of the pre-Columbian San Agustín and Tierradentro areas were of the same culture; remnants of roads lie beneath the jungle growth.

The Spanish settlement San Agustín was founded by Lucas de Herazo Mendigaña in 1790. It was always a sleepy town, until the latter part of the 20th century, when the civil war took root in the surrounding areas. Travelers' tales of encounters with the *guerrilleros* abounded. However, those days appear to be over with increased Colombian military presence, and once more San Agustín slips back into its quiescence. Updated: Jan 10, 2008.

When to Go

November, December and January are the best months to visit San Agustín, as there is

● Activities

1 Cancha de Tejo El Recreo C1
2 El Tablón-El Purutal Circuit B1
3 Iglesia San Agustín B2
4 Parque Arqueológico A1
5 Piscina Municipal Las Moyas A1
6 Plaza Cívica C2
7 Plaza de Ferias B2
8 Shamanic and Ecological
  Association of Colombia D2

⑪ Eating

9 Brahama B1
10 Cafetería Hotel Los Ídolos (See 37)
11 Hotel Colonial Asadero
   y Restaurante (See 36)
12 La Casona de San Agustín A1
13 La Terraza B2
14 Pizza Manía B2

▼ Nightlife

15 Casa de Tarzan D2
16 Restaurante-Café-Bar
   El Rancho C2

★ Services

17 Banco de Bogotá ATM B2
18 Enter.net C2
19 Hospital Arsenio Repizo D2
20 Internet Galería Café B2
21 Municipal tourism office C2
22 Post office B2

✿ Shopping

23 Artesanías Bambú B2
24 Market C2
25 Solo Cuero C2
26 Taller de Cestería B1

▬ Sleeping

27 Camping San Agustín A1
28 Casa de François B1
29 Casa de Nelly A2
30 Finca El Cielo A1
31 Finca El Maco A1
32 Hospedaje Cambi B2
33 Hospedaje El Jardín Casa
   Colonial C1
34 Hostal Alto de los
   Andaquies A1
35 Hotel Central C2
36 Hotel Colonial C2
37 Hotel Los Ídolos C2
38 Hotel Yalconia A1
39 San Agustín Internacional
   Hotel A2

◆ Tours

40 Magdalena Rafting A1
41 San Agustín Tour Masizo C2
42 World Heritage Travel Office C2

less rain. July and August experience winds and cool temperatures. Rain is common the rest of the year, the wettest months being September, October, February and March.

San Agustín is once more gaining popularity among Colombians as a vacation destination. Keep this in mind if traveling here during July-August, December-January, or Semana Santa holidays and three-day holiday weekends.

San Agustín's principal patron saint is Saint Augustine, whose feast day is August 28. The village also commemorates San Pedro in June. Three noteworthy festivals take place here: In October is the Encuentro Nacional de Cultura (National Cultural Encounter), and in November the Feria Equine (Horse Fair) and the Feria Artesanal y Comercial, highlighting the artisan and other production of the region. Updated: Jan 10, 2008.

Getting To and Away

Buses for the Parque Arqueológico leave from the central park every half-hour (6 a.m.-6 p.m., 20 min, $0.60). Taxis run only until about 9 p.m. and charge $2-4, depending on the distance and time of day.

Chivas for neighboring villages depart from near the market or from Calle 5. Most long-distance transportation leaves from Calle 3, between Carreras 10 and 12.

To Pitalito: Pick-ups leave frequently from Ca. 3 (5 a.m.-6 p.m., 45 min, $2.75)

Pitalito to La Plata: 7 a.m., 10 a.m., 2 p.m., 4 p.m., 3 hr, $9. Or go to Garzón (bus $5, collective taxi $6), then to Pitalito (*buseta* $5, collective taxi $6). From La Plata you can go to Tierradentro. See that section for more details. From Pitalito service is more frequent to Neiva, Bogotá, Isnos and Popayán.

To Neiva: Taxis Verdes (4 services 4 a.m.-1 p.m., 4 hr, $17), Coomotor (2 buses, 5.5 hr, $13-14)

To Bogotá: Taxis Verdes (7 a.m., 7 p.m., 9 hr, $21), Coomotor (5 a.m., 6:30 p.m., 7:30 p.m., 10 hr, $22-27)

To Popayán: $15—Cootranslobayana (1 bus, 6 hr), Cootranshuila, by way of Coconuco (7 a.m., 10 a.m., 4 p.m., 7 hr). Coming from Popayán, the bus may leave you at El Cruce, the crossroads for San Agustín. Catch a pick-up truck coming from Pitalito for San Agustín. Updated: Aug 17, 2011.

Safety

The days of the great adventure to San Agustín appear to be over. In years past, many travelers reported their nighttime bus being stopped by FARC guerrillas and the passengers receiving a political lecture. Since early this present millennium the Colombian military has occupied the town, surrounding countryside and roads. In terms of personal safety, it is safe to do at least the closer walks alone; some locals also say the longer hikes (e.g., to Alto de los Ídolos) are also OK. Updated: May 15, 2009.

Services

TOURISM

The **municipal tourist office** gives out good maps, and has a list of official tour prices (Monday-Friday 8 a.m.-noon and 2-6 p.m. Ca. 3 and Cra. 12, in the Alcaldía building. Tel: 837-3062, E-mail: webmaster@sanagustin.com.co, alcaldia@sanagustin-huila.gov.co, URL: www.sanagustin-huila.gov.co). If the official tourism office is closed, stop by one of the tour operator offices. World Heritage Travel has many years experience orientating visitors to San Agustín.

The **Instituto Colombiano de Antropología e Historia** has a guide to the archaeological sites, available in Spanish and English, that is free to download (URL: www.incanh.gov.co).

MONEY

Banco de Bogotá has a Mega Red ATM (accepts all cards) open 24 hours per day on the main drag at Calle 3, 12-73. There are two other ATMs in town. To change U.S. cash dollars, go to **Almacén De Todos** (Ca. 3, 12-28) or **Tienda Don Lazo** (Ca. 3, 11-62); both give well-below market rates. If you are journeying with travelers checks, you are out of luck in San Agustín; stock up on pesos before coming. Neither Moneygram nor Western Union have offices in San Agustín; the nearest are in Neiva and Popayán.

KEEPING IN TOUCH

San Agustín does have Internet—four cafés, in fact. **Internet Galería Café** (Ca. 3, 12-24) is the cheapest and has a digital camera card reader. While pounding away on the keyboard, you can enjoy a coffee, beer or smoke, or let your eyes rest on the artwork decorating the walls. **Enter.net** (Cra. 11, 3-10) charges more, but has Skype; this non-smoking establishment sells no refreshments. Other communications services in San Agustín seem to hide out in stores. Make local, national and international calls from Telecom in the t-shirt silk-screening shop near the Alcaldía (closed Sunday. Ca. 3). The post office is in the Maxitodo de la 13 store (Monday-Friday 8 a.m.-noon and 2-6 p.m. Cra. 13, 4-09).

MEDICAL

Hospital Arsenio Repizo is the public hospital for San Agustín (Ca. 3 and Cra. 3. Tel: 837-3606). There are many pharmacies on Calle 3, especially between Carreras 9 and 13.

CAMERA

It appears there's only one camera shop in San Agustín: **Foto Color**. Besides developing your film in one hour, it also carries 100, 200 and 400 ASA Kodak and Fuji 110 film; digital camera cards; and disposable, analog and digital cameras. However, it does not repair cameras. Updated: Aug 17, 2011.

SHOPPING

Artesanías Bambú

Walking down the street near Parque Bolívar, you may hear the strands of charango music coming from a shop. Welcome to Artesanías Bambú, where director Manual Una will lay aside his instrument as you enter. The walls are strewn with jewelry, bags and multitudes of items that he and area artisans create from bamboo, clay, wood, guadua and other natural fibers. Or perhaps one of the stone carv

Dulce de Pata

On Calle 3, near Hotel Los Ídolos, Doña María Córdoba passes the day seated on a stool. With two wooden paddles, she works a taffy-like substance into the perfect texture. Occasionally someone stops to buy a wooden stick or small cupful of this tasty sweet called dulce de pata, which literally translates into hooves' sweet. Doña María boils cows' hooves to remove the gelatin, then adds panela (raw sugar) and cooks it until it is thick and molasses-colored. She brings a kettle of this with her everyday and sits right here, working the liquid until it becomes off-white taffy. Go on, don't be squeamish—try a bit. Updated: Apr 11, 2008.

ings—replicas of this valley's statuary—strikes your fancy. Want a charango like don Manual plays? Hand-crafted instruments of all sorts are also for sale. For a special celebration, hire don Manual to perform. Daily 8 a.m.-9 p.m. Cra. 13, 3-06. Cel: 310-759-3408, URL: www. howlingearth.com. Updated: Mar 24, 2011.

Sólo Cuero

A large sign hanging above the door of this small workshop displays naively drawn saddlebag, machete sheaths and boots. In bold print, it announces Only Leather—Manufacture of: coverings, bags, belts, sandals, boots and other horse tackle. Indeed, whether you are preparing for the long journey to Ecuador on a steed or just want to pick up some of Colombia's renowned leatherwork at reasonable prices, Solo Cuero is the place to come. Wooden boards in the doorway display an assortment of sporty sandals. If nothing quite strikes your fancy or meets your needs, Don Isidro can fill your special order. Daily 8 a.m.-7 p.m. Ca. 3, 10-59. Tel: 837-3518. Updated: Apr 14, 2008.

Taller de Cestería

Through the open doors, sunlight dapples the white-washed adobe walls of a small workshop. Within, strands of vejuco alín, a plant fiber, wave through the air as Don Segundo weaves them into baskets and vases. Many times he carefully threads a bead onto the filament, adding colorful touches to his original creations. He passes his days, waiting for you to arrive to purchase one of these cestas to take home. Also leaning against these ancient walls are hand-carved bamboo walking sticks, the

perfect item to steady your pace as you hike to San Agustín's many wonders. Ca. 5, 15-07. Cel: 311-242-9374. Updated: Apr 14, 2008.

Things to See and Do

Be prepared to spend at least a couple of days in San Agustín. The area is perfect for hiking or horseback riding, with the reward of statues, tombs and petroglyphs. Some well-known sites include La Chaquira, Obando, Alto de los Ídolos and Alto de las Piedras. Take the challenge, though, to get to some of the less-visited ones, like Lavaderos or Alto de la Guacas. The Parque Arqueológico encompasses four sites and provides a good introduction. If visiting the Parque Arqueológico, Alto de los Ídolos and Alto de las Piedras, consider buying the specially priced combined ticket ($14).

The scenery is equally stunning with dozens of waterfalls like Salto del Mortiños and de Bordones tumbling through the jungle to join the nascent Río Magdalena, to whose headwaters you can trek or horsback ride. Other adventures include walking the Macizo Colombiano or riding all the way to Ecuador on horse. Sports are not to be forgotten. There's white-water rafting, a huge city swimming pool, and a Colombian favorite, tejo—with an interesting twist. Updated: Aug 18, 2011.

Parque Arqueológico

(ADMISSION: $8.50) The main attraction in San Agustín is the Parque Arqueológico, which encompasses four artificially leveled hills containing tombs and sculptures that are hallmarks of the Agustinian culture. Between these hills are Fuente de Lavapatas, hand-carved pools used for ceremonial purposes, and Alto de Lavapatas, home of more tombs and sculptures. A path near the museum leads into the Bosque de Estatuas (Forest of Statues), which displays over 30 carvings. The museum houses pottery, jewelry and other finds from this site, dating from 1000 BC-900 AD, and explains the society and culture of these mysterious people. It takes at least four hours to visit all the sites in the Parque Arqueólogico.

Guides for hire, some of whom speak several languages, wait near the ticket office ($23 for group of 1-10). Some of the explanatory signs are in English and Spanish. Located three kilometers (1.8 mi) from San Agustín. Busetas leave from Parque Bolívar (every 20 min, 6 a.m.-6 p.m., $0.60). A taxi costs about $2.80 one way. Mesetas and Fuente de Lavapatas are open 8 a.m.–5 p.m., Alto de Lavapatas 8 a.m.–4 p.m., Museum 9 a.m.–5 p.m.; ticket sales 8 a.m.–4 p.m. Updated: Aug 18, 2011.

El Tablón-El Purutal Circuit

Between San Agustín and the Parque Arqueológico are several quite interesting sites. El Tablón, only 1.5 kilometers (1 mi) from the village, is said to be dedicated to the Moon Deity, with five statues and an ethnographic museum. A dirt path wends almost two kilometers (1.2 mi) through the countryside and across a creek to the Río Magdalena. In a spectacular setting mid-way down a canyon are the massive rock carvings of La Chaquira. Continuing the circuit, you arrive next at La Pelota with statuary (including a warrior, and an eagle with a serpent). On the next rise several hundred meters away is El Purutal, a possible ceremonial site, whose statues still retain the colorful paints of their creators.

The entire 15-kilometer (9-mi) hike takes six to seven hours. To begin at El Tablón, walk up Carrera 14 over the hill to the sign. The paths can be quite muddy. You can break the hike up into two days, visiting El Purutal and La Pelota one day, and El Tablón and La Chiquira (2 hr round trip) the other. To save time, you can take a *buseta* ($0.60) to either the turn-off for El Tablón or El Purutal, or hire horses. Refreshments are available only near El Tablón. The El Tablón museum costs $1.20. Updated: Aug 19, 2011.

Piscina Municipal Las Moyas

(ADMISSION: $2) Once the sun begins to shine in San Agustín, it gets downright hot. The perfect way to cool down after visiting the Parque Arqueológico or doing the El Tablón-El Purutal circuit is to swing by the Piscina Municipal Las Moyas. A more-than-Olympic-sized swimming pool full of cool, fresh spring water awaits your laps. There's even a slide to sweep you off your tired feet. After drying off, shoot a few games of billiards in the *ranchito*. Daily 6 a.m.-7 p.m. Off-road to Parque Arqueológico. Head out of town on Calle 5; the marked turn-off for the pool is 400 meters (1,300 ft) along the road to the Parque Arqueológico; the pool is a further 100 meters (320 ft) up the side road. You can also take a buseta from Parque Bolívar ($0.60). Updated: Mar 25, 2011.

Shamanic and Ecological Association of Colombia

Gain fascinating insight into rural community life, alternative agricultural systems, and medicinal and tropical plants on this farm, home to the Shamanic and Ecological Association of Colombia. Participate in a shamanic ceremony ($25), or go on an excursion to enjoy the area's natural beauty (the surrounding woods are home to a vast selection of orchids). The organization, an NGO, also arranges visits to the jungle. People who are planning to participate in the shamanic ceremonies are given proper education and guidance, particularly in diet matters. Basic accommodation in rooms includes food are well-reviewed by guests ($15 a day). The farm is a 30-minute drive from San Agustín. Trips by 4x4 are made to the farm three times a day. Contact the organization through its shop in San Agustín, **El Centro Eco-chamánico** (Ca. 3, 8-44. Tel: 837-9522). Updated: Aug 18, 2011.

Tejo

(ADMISSION: $2) After going through the stands of the market on a lazy Sunday, you might find yourself staring at a sign that reads "Cancha de Tejo El Recreo." Through the courtyard of the rough, tin-roofed *cancha*, you'll find men in various stages of drunkenness throwing a 1.125-kilo (2.5-lb) lead weight at an upright, clay-bedded board 18 meters (59 ft) down court.

Tejo is a popular sport in Southern and Eastern Colombia, often played for a set price that includes a beer. Men and women play in different courts (women's courts are smaller), where you sip on your beer waiting for your turn to throw the weight as hard as you can. In other places, though, the target is called a *bocín*, which has small packets of gun powder attached to it; the object is to explode these. It seems the resourceful citizens of San Agustín have found a new use for the landmines that were laid in the backcountry during the Civil War. (No fear, though—the shrapnel has been taken out.) Ca. 2, 9-40. Updated: Mar 25, 2011.

Hiking Around San Agustín

You can spend weeks hiking through San Agustín's verdant countryside. Trails lead to many of the archaeological sites, making for good day trips. Several-day treks, like the Macizo Colombiano, take you to crystalline lagoons sparkling on the páramo and the headwaters of the Magdalena River. A popular ramble is the El Purutal-El Tablón circuit. Another all-day excursion, now said to be quite safe, is the wending *sendero* to Alto de los Ídolos. Less-visited sites, such as Alto de las Guacas and the caves at Lavaderos, are also worth looking into. Break out the boots and take a hike—scores of adventures await you in these mountains. Updated: Mar 24, 2011.

Horseback Riding

Imagine mounting a beautiful mare to traverse these emerald hills, exploring the silent sentinels that still guard the San Agustín region, or the many lagoons and waterfalls hidden within the folds of this landscape. Prices per hour ($5.20) and per excursion are set by the municipality. The five-hour trip to El Tablón, La Chaquira, La Pelota and El Purutal is about $15, plus another $15 for your guide's horse. Another adventure several travelers have undertaken is to ride with a guide all the way to Otavalo, Ecuador; this takes a major investment of time and money, however. One guide frequently lauded is Pacho Muñoz (Cel: 311-827-7972, E-mail: pachitocampesinito@yahoo.es). Maps provided by the tourism office and travel agencies show the network of trails in the region. Ask for specifics and about safety before heading out. Check your horse to be sure it is in healthy condition. If you take a guide, you will have to pay for his horse as well as his services. Updated: Mar 25, 2011.

Rafting on the Magdalena

As Colombia's greatest river, the Magdalena winds 1,540 kilometers (924 mi) and boils through many canyons before eventually ending in the Caribbean Sea. You can begin this sojourn with the *río* riding on class-II to IV white waters. The most popular course is an 11-kilometer (6.6-mi) run through class II and III rapids, suitable for the whole family. Another route features 30 torrents within 28 kilometers (17 mi). The roughest adventure, for experienced sojourners only, is a 20-kilometer (12-mi) sprint through a canyon, with class III and IV rapids. Two- and three-day excursions can also be arranged. Aptly, the indigenous name for the Magdalena is Guacaayo, meaning River of Tombs.

Contact one of the local tour operators to set up your rafting adventure. Most operators require a minimum age of 12 years and an ability to swim. Make sure the tour operator provides you with proper safety equipment that is in good condition. A wetsuit is necessary, as the water of the Magdalena is quite cold. Updated: Mar 25, 2011.

Tours

Dozens of guides work in San Agustín; however, few of them are officially licensed or speak anything other than Spanish. With the area now under the control of the Colombian military, more tour operators have opened their doors in anticipation of increased numbers of national and foreign tourists. At the Parque Arqueológico there are official guides for hire, many of whom speak English. They charge $23 for groups of one to 10 people. Luis Alfredo Salazar guides in seven languages, including Japanese. Updated: Aug 18, 2011.

Magdalena Rafting

Magdalena Rafting is very highly recommended by travelers seeking the adventure of hitting the rapids of the Upper Río Magdalena. With over 20 years experience on different rivers around the world, owner Amid provides his clients with all the safety equipment—neoprene suits to protect against the frigid waters, helmets and life jackets—to make the run down Colombia's mightiest waterway three times daily, whether in raft or kayak. He also offers other trips, including the 20-kilometer (12-mi) one through the Magdalena River canyon and two- to three-day excursions. Don't yet know how to paddle? No sweat, Magdalena Rafting can pull the strokes for you, or teach you how to stroke in special courses. Ca. 5, 16-04. Cel: 311-271-5333, E-mail: info@magdalenarafting.com, URL: www.magdalenarafting.com. Updated: Mar 25, 2011.

San Agustin Tour Masizo

Juan Arbey, a SENA-certified guide, operates San Agustín Tour Masizo. He offers a one-day package that takes in a wide-range of experiences in exploring the San Agustín region: in the morning, horseback ride the El Tablón-La Chaquira-La Pelota-El Purutal circuit ($50, depending on number of persons), and in the afternoon run in jeep the Obando-Altos de los Ídolos-Alto de las Piedras circuit, taking in a waterfall and the Parque Arqueológico to boot. San Agustín Tour Masizo also provides multi-day ecological tours to Parque Nacional Natural Puracé on horse ($300 for one person, $200 per person for three or four participants). Ca. 3, 10-62. Cel: 312-423-9995/311-234-9448, E-mail: juanarbey@yahoo.com. Updated: Aug 18, 2011.

World Heritage Travel Office/Viajes Patrimonio Mundial

World Heritage Travel Office is San Agustín's oldest tour operator, partly owned and operated by the town's former tourism officer. It is a good alternative for receiving information about the attractions in the region. World Heritage offers everything from hikes or horseback riding to the nearby sites, to rafting the Río Magdalena. The all-day jeep trip is popular, taking in the Narrows of the Magdalena River, Obando, Alto de los Ídolos, Alto de las Piedras and several waterfalls for $13, including driver and transportation, but not lunch, entry fees or guide. Multi-lingual guides are available. Ca. 3, 10-84. Tel: 837-3940, Cell: 311-292-4241, E-mail: viajespatrimoniomundial@yahoo.es. Updated: Apr 14, 2008.

Lodging

San Agustín is a budget traveler's haven. You can choose to lodge in town or out in the countryside on a *finca* (farm). Quite a few places are foreign-owned. Campgrounds are mostly on the road on the way to the Parque Arqueológico, along which higher-price-ranged hotels are also located. Mid-range inns are almost non-existent. Most hotels raise prices in the high seasons. If staying outside the village, consider you will be walking home in the dark after a late dinner or drink, as taxis cease to run after 9 p.m. Updated: Aug 18, 2011.

Hospedaje Cambi

(BEDS: $5-12) Just a half-block from Parque Bolívar, Magola Pérez welcomes San Agustín visitors to these inexpensive, simple, clean rooms in an old colonial building. Nearly all the rooms have TV and private bath; however, three singles with common bath await the solo budget traveler—one of the cheapest options in town. Cambi also has a dormitory. Most importantly, in the cool nights of this village, the quarters are warm and the common baths have hot water. Sitting areas in the flower-filled back patio invite relaxing on sunny days. Prices are higher at holiday times. Cra. 13, 3-36. Tel: 837-3357, Cel: 310-782-4958, E-mail: magolita2@hotmail.com, URL: hotelcambi.redbalsa.com. Updated: Aug 18, 2011.

Hotel Colonial

(BEDS: $5.30-8) On the main street of San Agustín, right where the collective taxis and pick-ups arrive, you can find Hotel Colonial. Set in another classic, aged building, this inn tenders ample, tidy rooms with private or common hot-water bath. Service is attentive and the staff knowledgeable about what to do and see in the region. For those discovering Colombia on motorbike, there's parking for your wheels. On the ground floor is a good restaurant serving up inexpensive set meals. Ca. 3, 11-25. Tel: 837-3159, Cel: 311-459-3314. Updated: Apr 16, 2008.

Hotel Los Ídolos

(ROOMS: $5.30-10.60) Hotel Los Ídolos is definitely the cheapest place to stay in San Agustín if you have a traveling partner. Be warned, however, that the rooms are claustophically small and stuffy, with only a small window set high. These wood-paneled spaces are hot during the day and cold at night. The only furniture is the beds, but even so the rooms are cramped. Nonetheless, if you are only using them as sleeping quarters, they are tolerable. Price doubles for a private bathroom. Ca. 3, 11-47. Tel: 837-3079, Cel: 312-582-3888. Updated: May 25, 2009.

Hotel Central

(BEDS: $6.35-8) This colonial-era hotel is tranquil, despite being on San Agustín's main street. With a family atmosphere, Hotel Central is the preferred choice of some travelers, thanks to its convenient location next to restaurants and bus companies. The wood passageways have lots of seating, tables and plants to while away rainy days. All the rooms are large and adequately furnished, with windows either onto the patio or the street. Those quarters in front have classic wood balconies to watch the village's comings and goings. Unfortunately, only cold water flows from the bathroom taps. Ca. 3, 10-32. Tel: 837-3027. Updated: Apr 16, 2008.

Camping San Agustín

(CAMPING: $8-19) Camping San Agustín is a broad grassy expanse that allows not only tent, but also vehicle camping. If you don't have your own tent, you can rent one, complete with pad, air mattress, sheets and pillow. Under the trees is a cooking area, but you have to supply your own wood. In the main house of Camping San Agustín there are also rooms to rent, either sharing the cold-water showers with the campers or with their own bath. Out back is a three-bedroom cabaña for eight persons with a private, hot-water bath. The camping site fee is $6.35, plus $1.60 per person. Tent rentals go for $5.30, or you can get a room with a shared bath for the same price, or one with a private bath for $8. Cabins are $18.65 per person. 200 m (650 ft) down the road behind the Hotel Yalconia, across from the Piscina Municipal Las Moyas. Follow Calle 5 out of town towards the Parque Arqueológico. Turn right on the first road after Hotel Yalconia. Tel: 8-837-3804. Updated: Apr 16, 2008.

La Casa de François

(BEDS: $8-20) Friendly owner, Frenchman François, makes a stay on his Gaudi-inspired estate one well worth remembering. In fact, many guests of La Casa come for a few days and end up there for weeks, basking in the gorgeous San Agustín town and the country views. François has owned the farm for 15 years and decorated the three cute bamboo and cob cottages with a colorful and classy theme. The dorm room is impeccably designed, with wine bottles in the walls, and holds up to eight people. For a bit more luxury and space, the bamboo hut has three double beds, there are also two private rooms. All rooms share clean bamboo bathrooms with hot water. Prepare meals in François's creative, communal kitchen made from glass mosaics. The hotel can accommodate up to 18 guests. Head up the hill on Carrera 13. Take the second right turn on the steep, dirt road, following the signs for "Hotel." A bit further up the hill, you will find La Casa de François on the left. Tel: 837-3847, Cel: 314-358-2930, URL: www.lacasadefrancois.com. Updated: Mar 25, 2011.

V!VA ONLINE REVIEW
LA CASA DE FRANÇOIS
I loved the owners. They're amazingly nice people and very helpful.
September 8, 2008

Hospedaje El Jardín Casa Colonial !

(BEDS: $8.50-11.50) The Muñoz family opens the doors of its home in this well-preserved colonial house on a quiet side street in San Agustín village. The first thing that strikes you is the restaurant patio, full of hammocks, potted plants, stone replicas of Augustinian statues, a fireplace and aviary. The rooms are just as impressive, all with spectacular views of the surrounding mountains. Some of the rooms even have a balcony. The bathrooms, both common and private, have hot water. Cra. 11, 4-10. Tel: 837-3455/9581, Cel: 312-295-0398, URL: www.hosteltrail.com/eljardin. Updated: Aug 18, 2011.

Finca El Maco

(BEDS: $8.50-17) René has created the wonderful ecological Finca El Maco for those budget travelers who want to stay in fresh country air, eat excellent pizza and relax while checking out all San Agustín has to offer. Creative lodging choices like spending a night in a teepee with a fire pit adds to the adventure in this mysterious world. There are also a malo-

ka, châlet, cabaña and casitas. For a little splurge, have a massage to ease your muscles after a day of hiking or horseback riding. Try the organic dairy products made right on the farm. Spanish, English, German and Italian are spoken. Price depends on type of lodging, and is 50 percent more in high seasons. 1 km (0.6 mi) from the village. Tel: 837-3437, Cel: 311-271-4802, E-mail: info@elmaco.ch, URL: www.elmaco.ch. Updated: Aug 18, 2011.

V!VA ONLINE REVIEW
FINCA EL MACO
This is really the nicest hotel I have stayed at on my trip through Colombia—the most relaxing place on earth!
July 28, 2008

Hostal Alto de los Andaquíes

(BEDS: $10-30) Midway between the village and the archaeological park is Hostal Alto de los Andaquíes. This family farm has been turned into a comfortable hotel surrounded by gardens with spectacular views over the mountains. Guests may choose to stay in one of the three rustic country houses, or have a room in the main cabin. All have private baths. There is also camping. Andaquíes has much to offer its guests: tours to the archaeological sites, waterfalls and the Macizo; horseback riding, mountain biking and rafting. Every night there is music around the campfire. Vereda Nueva Zelanda, 1 km (0.6 mi) from San Agustín. Cel: 312-444-7368, E-mail: aleto@andaquies.com, URL: www.andaquies.com. Updated: Aug 19, 2011.

Hotel Casa de Nelly

(BEDS: $11) Since the mid-1980s, French-owned Casa de Nelly has provided fine cabañas in a beautiful forest. Cats and dogs stroll through the terraced gardens and aviary. Nice touches abound in the sharply decorated, rattan-furnished rooms whose walls are painted with murals. Cabañas have a sitting area for curling up after a long day of visiting ruins. Even the dorm room is quite spacious, fitting only four guests. The Tudor-styled main house serves as lodge and restaurant. If you are on a budget, a common kitchen is also available. 2km (1.2 mi) from the village, off the Vereda La Estrella. Cel: 310-215-9067/311-535-0412, E-mail: hotelcasadenelly@hotmail.com, URL: www.elmaco.ch/Casa%20De%20Nelly/html/menu-eng.htm. Updated: Aug 19, 2011.

Finca El Cielo

(CAMPING: $11, BEDS: $28) Finca El Cielo is a beautiful B&B located in the countryside, near San Agustín's archaeological sites. The rooms are constructed of bamboo and have large beds and modern bathrooms with hot water. The hotel also has a campground. You can relax and enjoy the view of the Cordillera of the Andes, or take a tour organized by the hotel. Afterwards you can dip into the hotel's on-site natural swimming pond. A special feature of Finca El Cielo hotel is its language, dance and horseback riding classes. Via Estrecho, 3 km (1.8 mi) from San Agustín, Cel: 313-493-7446, E-mail: info@fincaelcielo.com, URL: www.fincaelcielo.com. Updated: Aug 19, 2011.

San Agustín Internacional Hotel

(ROOMS: $33-250) These dream houses, perfect for families, are set in estate-like grounds with stone-lined lagoons and emerald lawns. Have you ever fantasized about staying in a typical Mediterranean house, or a Scandinavian? Or how about a TV-perfect U.S. home, or a Colombian hacienda just like on the *telenovelas* (soap operas)? Soon your family can also choose an Arabian one straight out of 1001 Nights, or a pagoda. There is also a traditional indigenous maloka that has individual rooms for let. Vía Vereda La Estrella (end of Ca. 2, at Cra. 19). Tel: 837-3013, Cel: 312-433-2510/311-445-2615, E-mail: inturcol@gmail.com, URL: www.inturcol.com. Updated: Aug 19, 2011.

Hotel Yalconia

(ROOMS: $36-58) Hotel Yalconia is San Agustín's oldest luxury-class hotel. Of modern architecture, this two-story building provides all of the comforts one would want while enjoying the wonders of this region. The sitting areas are bright and airy, as are the guest rooms. The tiled bathrooms are immaculate. All are decorated with furnishings of the Bauhaus era, yet nothing shows its age. The pool out back is perfect for Agustinian sunny days. Yalconia also has rooms for three-five people. The hotel offers packages, which include a floor show of Andean music. Prices do not include taxes and rise in high seasons. Vía al Parque Arqueológico, 400 meters (0.25 mi) from town. Tel: 837-3013, Cel: 316-304-8353, E-mail: hyalconia@gmail.com, URL: www.inturcol.com. Updated: Aug 19, 2011.

Restaurants

The eating scene in San Agustín is pretty boring—just good old Colombian food and little else. A *comida corriente* is inexpensive here. The public market at Carrera 11 and Calle 2 is a great place to grab a cheap meal. The weekly markets, when folks come in from neighboring villages, are Sunday and Monday. While in San Agustín, be sure to try *dulce de pata*, a taffy-like sweet. Updated: Aug 19, 2011.

Cafetería Hotel Los Ídolos

(SET MEAL: $1.60) In the courtyard of the Hotel Los Ídolos is another cheap San Agustín eatery. The friendly women here serve up down-home Colombian meals. The full-helping set lunch is a comfortable price, but the bargain half meal still has quite ample portions for those travelers watching their pennies. This Restaurante-Cafetería is also a good place to stop off for a juice (made with purified water) to recharge your batteries from all the sightseeing. Ca. 3, 11-47. Tel: 831-3079. Updated: Apr 17, 2008.

La Terraza

(SET MEAL: $2, ENTREES: $5-9) Upstairs, above the Banco Agrario, a large orange and white space greets you, made even brighter by the great windows around two sides. Many folks, both local and foreign, chow down on Restaurante La Terraza's specials, which come with a choice of meats at any time of day. A few opt for regular menu items or broasted chicken. The service is quick here, though unfortunately the big-screen TV can be very loud at times. Ca. 4, on the corner of Cra. 13, 2nd floor, Banco Agrario. Cel: 314-229-3796. Updated: Mar 25, 2011.

Hotel Colonial Asadero y Restaurante

(SET MEAL: $2, ENTREES: $6.50-8) The Asadero y Restaurante of the Hotel Colonial fixes up one of the best *comida corrientes*—whether breakfast, lunch or dinner—in San Agustín, and at one of the better prices to boot. For those who prefer something a bit lighter (and cheaper), skip the soup. The Asadero also has specialty dishes: chicken breast, catfish, *mojarra* fish, trout, pork and beef steak hot off the grill. Ca. 3, 11-25. Tel: 837-3159, Cell: 311-459-3314. Updated: Apr 17, 2008.

SOUTHERN COLOMBIA

Brahama !

(SET MEAL: $2.25) As you're heading out one early morning to the Parque Arqueológico, stop by Restaurante Brahama for pancakes, with chocolate or your choice of fruit. On the backswing, its home-cooked vegetarian *comida corriente* lunch hits the spot. If your dining companions are avowed carnivores, they won't feel too out of place. This *restaurante vegetariano* also serves the blue-plate special with meat for the same price. At anytime of day are à la carte plates and fruit salads. These three, two-tone green rooms are a bit worn; off the large one in back is a gate inviting you to the garden. Daily 7 a.m.–7 p.m. Ca. 5, 15-11. Cel: 301-417-1077. Updated: Aug 19, 2011.

La Casona de San Agustín

(ENTREES: $6-9) One of San Agustín's finest restaurants has sophistication from the furnishing to the menu. Cuisine covers the gamut of poultry to red meats to local fish, all prepared fresh and served with house salad and French fries or rice. Take a seat on the front patio, or in the back room with a balcony overlooking the Quebarada Las Moyas. While waiting for your order (the menu advises it'll take 20-30 minutes) challenge your dining partner to a game of chess at the giant board on the back balcony. La Casona also serves breakfast. Ca. 5, 21-125, vía Parque Arqueológico (on right side of road, just past Hotel Yalconia). Tel: 837-9416. Updated: Apr 17, 2008.

Pizza Mania

(ENTREES: $7-15) Just a half-block from the main square, under the soft, hot-pink light, is one of San Agustín's few forays into international cuisine: Pizza Mania, a small, three-table affair. Grab a slice of pizza, whether Hawaiian, meat, chicken with mushrooms, margarita or vegetarian. If a day of hiking has your stomach growling, ask for a whole pie. Order it half one type and half another to share. Saturdays and Sundays the French-German owner whips up a special lasagna. To wash it all down, she can serve you beer, soda or juice. Daily 6–10 p.m. Cra. 13, 3-47, Cel: 311-271-4788. Updated: Mar 25, 2011.

Nightlife

Few choices for nightlife are to be found in San Agustín. Several of the bars and discos are said to be rough-and-tumble types of places. Nonetheless, there are a few more chilled-out places where you can kick back and relax after a long day of hiking. Almost all are located in the village; remember that if you are staying out in the country, taxis stop running at 9 p.m. and you'll have a long, dark walk home. Updated: Jan 10, 2008.

Casa de Tarzan

With rough-paneled walls and tree trunks towering inside this bar, you might be tempted to go swinging from one of the rope-vines hanging from the branches after downing a beer here. But better to just sit back and swap tales with other travelers, or catch the movie or soccer game on the big-screen TV. Monday-Saturday 8 p.m. until whenever, Sundays and holidays from 2 p.m. Ca. 2, 8-04, across from the Bomberos fire station. Tel: 837-3457, Cel: 310-781-8797/312-200-5124. Updated: Apr 17, 2008.

V!VA ONLINE REVIEW
CASA DE TARZAN

Great place Great place to hang out, to party, to drink, to dance, too great! ha, ha, awesome.

December 14, 2010

Restaurante-Café-Bar El Rancho

To get to the restaurant or café, then head down the stairs. To savor a Colombian beer or drink, climb the staircase where a large open space greets you. Pull up one of the leather-covered chairs at a wooden table (the ones on the balcony with a view of Calle 3 are fine for watching the evening Augustinian happenings) and check out the paintings, animal skins and Andean musical instruments bedecking the brick walls. Soon the bartender will be with you not only to ask for your drink order, but also your request for music. Daily 4 p.m.–2 a.m. Ca. 3, 11-60. Updated: Apr 17, 2008.

AROUND SAN AGUSTÍN

SAN JOSÉ DE ISNOS

2,075m   23,756   2

San José de Isnos (Quechua for Sacred Rock) is a small village 26 kilometers (15.5 mi) north of San Agustín. Five kilometers (3 mi) west is one of the most important Agustinian sites, Alto de los Ídolos, consisting of 37 funerary monuments dating 1st century BC– 6th century AD. Some of the sculptures at this crescent-shaped site still retain their paint.

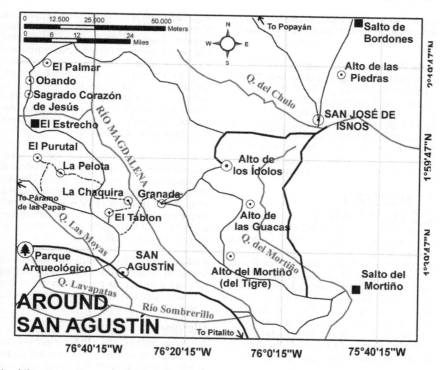

Five kilometers (3 mi) east of Isnos is Alto de las Piedras, a 9th century BC site that is home to the famed Doble-Yo (Double- or Dual-I) figure. This orchid-adorned place contains nine burial mounds with statuary. Another nine kilometers (5.5 mi) along the same road, just before Bordones village, Salto de Bordones, a 300-meter (984-ft) high, chocolate-colored waterfall, plummets through the jungle. A broken stone trail leads to its base (one hour down).

You can also choose to stay in San José and use it as a base for visiting these sites and others. It has several hotels and restaurants. Major celebrations are the Carnaval Blanco y Negro the first week of January and Holy Week; the patron saint day, in honor of San José, is March 19. Market day is Saturday.

All-day jeep tours include Alto de los Ídolos, Alto de las Piedras and Salto de Bordones. Alternately, you can try to visit these sites on your own. First go to the crossroads below San Agustín, then to San José de Isnos (about $3.50 total). Signs at both archaeological sites are only in Spanish. You can hire a guide at Alto de los Ídolos (extra charge).

Jeep tours do not include the entry fees, the lunch in San José de Isnos, or a visit to the Museo Etnográfico at Bordones. Admission to Alto de los Ídolos is $8.50; Salto de Bordones, $1. Updated: Aug 19, 2011.

OBANDO

1,700m   1,000   2

Traveling towards the small village of Obando, you'll cross the Magdalena River at the Estrecho, or Straits, the narrowest point— only 2.2 meters (7 ft) wide. Up a few hundred meters, on the other side of the dirt road, is a signed path to some not-often visited petroglyphs. After a further 2.5-3 kilometers (1.5-1.8 miles) the main path arrives at Obando village, where excavations on burials dating 11th–2nd century BC began in 1992. The painted tombs are now part of the Parque Arqueológico de Obando, which also includes a museum. El Estrecho del Magdalena and nearby petroglyphs are open from dawn to dusk; Parque Arqueológico de Obando (admission: $1.20) is open daily 8 a.m.-noon and 1-5 p.m.

All-day jeep tours include Estrecho del Magdalena and Parque Arqueológico de Obando (minus entry fee) on their route.

At the Parque Arqueológico de Obando, explanatory signs are in English and Spanish. There is a gift shop with locally produced artesanía. You can also visit these sites on your own, although public transportation is a bit more problematic. From Calle 5 and Carrera 14 in San Agustín leave infrequent buses for Obando (about $2). You can get off at the Estrecho, walk to the Petroglyphs and to Obando, then catch a bus back to San Agustín. Updated: Aug 19, 2011.

EL MACIZO COLOMBIANO

If you are yearning to get off the beaten track and experience rural Southern Colombian charm, then go take a hike—from San Agustín to Quinchana and on to Valencia. The five-day trek on a Camino Real (stone and dirt trail) takes you across the Páramo de las Papas (3,685 m/11,976 ft above sea level), passing by farm fields and through small villages. On the way is Laguna de la Magdalena, the birthplace of the Río Magdalena, located 81 kilometers (48.6 mi) from San Agustín. Flora and fauna along the way include orchids, birds and spectacled bear.

It is also possible to do the trip on horseback, which will take three days. The area is now heavily patrolled by the military, along with indigenous guards armed with clubs.

You can do the trek in the opposite direction, from Valencia (reachable from Popayán, 8 hr, $15) to San Agustín. Guides and lodging (Posada Nativa, $4.20 per person) are available in Valencia. For more information on doing it from this village, ask at the Popayán tourism office.

On the road to the Parque Arqueológico is a turn-off heading towards Quichana and Páramo de las Papas. However, because of the environmental conditions, a guide is highly advisable. Updated: Mar 25, 2011.

PASTO

2,527m   400,000   2

Located atop a plateau surrounded by verdant hills to the east and Volcán Galeras to the west, Pasto is 88 kilometers (54 mi) from the Ecuador border, on the Pan-American Highway. This capital of Nariño Department is a pleasant place to spend a few days. With impressive churches, architecture, museums and nearby villages to explore and natural reserves only several hours away, there is something for everyone's taste. Strolling through the streets, you can soon see why Pasto is nicknamed "La Ciudad de los Balcones"—The City of Balconies. Fine woodworking in many styles decorates these personal vantage points over the narrow colonial streets.

If you can, come in time for the city's renowned Black and White Carnival, celebrated in January— but wear your oldest clothes, like the locals do. It's said to be quite a messy party. This Carnival is a time when people celebrate ethnic and social diversity, which has given it UNESCO recognition as an Intangible Cultural Heritage of Humanity.

Pasto identifies itself culturally more with northern Ecuador than Colombia; during colonial times, trade routes connected this city with population centers further south. Updated: Jul 05, 2011.

History

Like other Spanish cities in Southern Colombia, San Juan de Pasto was founded under orders of Sebastián de Belalcázar and was part of the Audencia Real de Quito. First established in 1539 by Capitán Lorenzo de Aldana at Guacanquer, Pedro de Puelles moved it the following year to its present location. During the Independence Wars, Pasto remained a staunch Royalist supporter. Local historians say the city suffered tremendously at the hands of Simón Bolívar's troops. In 1830, Gran Colombia prevented Pasto and Nariño Department from joining the nascent country Ecuador. In recent years, the national government has chosen the city to serve as a resettlement center for demobilized paramilitary forces. Updated: May 14, 2009.

When to Go

Pasto's altitude gives the city a spring-like climate year round. Anytime is fine to visit, but expect rain showers in any month. June, July and August are windy.

HOLIDAYS AND FESTIVALS

The city has a number of festivals worth attending. The most famous is the Festival de Blancos y Negros, or Carnaval. Spanish colonists gave slaves a vacation every January 5, which is why Carnaval is celebrated on that date. But the modern celebration lasts much longer. Beginning on December 28, Day of the Innocents, a ceremony purifies the spirits. New Year's Eve is the Años Viejos, when effigies representing the past year are burnt in the streets. January 2 is Pericles Carnival and January 3 is the Indigenous Carnival—the streets throng with drum troupes, music, dance and horse parades. Then the two great days of celebration: Black Day and White Day, January 5 and 6 respectively, marked with parades, musicians, drum troupes, and grease and talcum powder fights.

As if to get everyone cleaned up from the Carnaval, Pasto has a Fiesta de Aguas—a huge, city-wide water fight—on February 5.

Pasto commemorates its saint, San Pedro, with firework castles, religious processions and *guaguas de pan* (bread babies) the last Sunday of June and the first Sunday of July. Updated: Aug 28, 2011.

Getting To and Away

Pasto has a good city bus network. Busetas ($0.60) begin running at 6 a.m.; most routes operate only until 7:30-8 p.m., with a few until 10 p.m. Rutas C4, C7, C11 and C16 (formerly 4, 6, 7, 9 and 10) connect the bus station with downtown, passing by Calle 17 and Carrera 21. Taxi fares are set by law. For routes within the city the cost is $1.60 per person; for the airport it is $3.60 per person.

BY BUS

Pasto's central bus terminal is located about three kilometers (1.8 mi) from the center, at Carrera 6 and Calle 16. The handicap-accessible building has an information booth, restaurants, shops, phones, an ATM (Visa, Cirrus, Plus), and even casinos and a pool hall to while away the time. Minivans and taxis depart from Módulo 1. Ticket windows for bus companies are in Módulo 2.

To Sandoná: TranSandoná (daily 6:30 a.m., 11 a.m., 4:30 p.m., 5:45 p.m.; 2 hr, $4.50. Buses for Sandoná depart more frequently from the terminal near the university. Take buseta C5, C12 or C13 (Universidad de Nariño) to the station.

To Túquerres: Valle de Atriz (daily, 5:30 a.m., 7:30 a.m.; 2 hr, $2.80).

To Popayán: hourly 5:30 a.m.-11:30 p.m., 5-6 hr—Bolivariano ($16), Transipiales ($14), Cootranar ($13.50), Flota Magdalena ($13)

To Cali: hourly 5:30 a.m.-11:30 p.m., 8 hours, $19.50—Transipiales, Cootranar, Flota Magdalena. Also Bolivariano ($23).

To Bogotá: 18 hr—Bolivariano (hourly 9:30 a.m.-10 p.m., $55), Flota Magdalena (noon, 3:30 p.m., 9 p.m., $47).

To Mocoa: Seven departures daily, 5-6 hours—vans (Cootransmayo, $18) and buses (Transipiales, $12). The companies alternate days.

To Ipiales: half-hourly, 1.5 hr, $5.50—Transipiales, Cootranar, Bolivariano and others; also minvans.

Cheaper trucks and *chivas* leave from a lot terminal at Carrera 9, 16-10.

BY AIR

Aeropuerto Antonio Nariño de Pasto provides direct and connecting services to all of Colombia. It is located 30 kilometers (18 mi) from the city, at **Cano** (Tel: 732-8013). Avianca flies six times daily to Bogotá and four to Cali. Satena has five daily flights to the capital and three daily to Cali. Many travel agencies in downtown Pasto sell tickets for both airlines. Updated: Feb 21, 2011.

Safety

Pastusos proudly claim their city is safe; however, one community historian asserts that relocated, demilitarized paramilitary forces are rearming and thus the face of this town has changed. One area that's a bit dodgy and where you should take particular care is from Carrera 21 to the bus terminal after dark. Many locals now say it is safe Ipiales-Pasto- Popayán-Cali route at night. Updated: Aug 28, 2011.

Services

TOURISM

The extremely helpful **tourism office** has information on things to do and see in the city and surrounding region, as well as several excellent booklets on the artisans, painters and culinary traditions (including recipes) of Nariño (daily 8 a.m.–noon and 2-6 p.m. Ca. 18, 25-25. Tel: 723-4962). It also has a kiosk at the bus terminal. For any maps you might need, go to the Instituto **Geográfico Agustín Codazzi** (Monday-Friday 8-11:15 a.m. and 1:30-4 p.m. Cra. 21b, 18-40). The main **Policía Nacional** post is at Calle 20 and Carrera 27 (Tel: 723-5852).

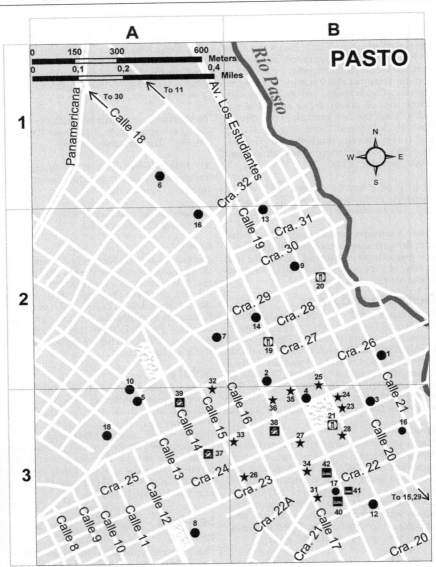

MONEY

Bancolombia (Ca. 19, facing Parque de Nariño) changes Amex traveler's checks only on weekdays (Monday-Friday 8 a.m.-4:30 p.m.); its branch at Calle 19, 25–57 changes them on Saturday mornings. Both branches have ATMs. Santander, also on Calle 19 on the Parque, changes dollar or Euro Amex traveler's checks, but only in the morning (Monday-Thursday 8-11:30 a.m. and 2-4 p.m., Friday 8-11:30 a.m. and 2-4:30 p.m.) Pasto has both a Western Union agent, **Giros and Finanzas** (Paseo del Liceo, corner of Ca. 17 and Cra. 26, local 128) and a MoneyGram agent, **Cambiamos** (Pasaje del Liceo, local 228).

KEEPING IN TOUCH

Internet is common throughout Pasto. **Internel** (Centro Comercial Colombia, Ca. 17, 21A-54, local 103) is one of the few places that has Skype. Make international calls from **Tele**

● **Activities**

1 Casa Museo Taller Relieves B2
2 Catedral B2
3 Iglesia de Cristo Rey B3
4 Iglesia de San Juan B3
5 Iglesia Lourdes A3
6 Iglesia Mariadaz A1
7 Iglesia San Andrés A2
8 Iglesia Santiago Apóstol A3
9 Museo Alfonso Zambrano B2
10 Museo Casona Taminango
de Arte A3
11 Museo de Carnaval A1
12 Museo del Oro B3
13 Museo Fotográfico Luis
Bernardo Esparza B2
14 Museo Juan Lorenzo Lucero B2
15 Museo Luciano Rosero B3
16 Museo Madre Caridad Brader A2
17 Templo de la Merced B3
18 Templo de San Felipe A3

🕮 **Eating**

19 Integrales Pan y Salud B2
20 Mestizo Peña Bar B2
21 Tienda del Café del Parque B3
22 Restaurant Manhattan (See 41)

★ **Services**

23 Banco de Santander B3
24 Bancolombia B3
25 Bancolombia B3
26 Correos de Colombia B3
27 Foto Almacén Tricolor B3
28 Foto Canon Digital B3
29 Hospital DepartamentalB3
30 Hospital San Pedro A1
31 Internel B3
32 Lava Mejor A3
33 Lavandería Perlmatic B3
34 Telecom B3
35 Tourism Office B3
36 Western Union and
Moneygram B3

🗹 **Shopping**

37 Casa del Barniz Obando A3
38 Ecotema B3
39 Vicens A3

▦ **Sleeping**

40 Hotel Casa López B3
41 Hotel Manhattan B3
42 Koala Inn B3

com (Ca. 17 and Cra. 23). Local and national calls can be made from any shop with a sign announcing minutos or llamadas. Mail letters and postcards from **Correos de Colombia** (Monday-Friday 8 a.m.-noon and 2-6 p.m., Saturday 8 a.m.–noon. Ca. 15, 23-60).

MEDICAL
Pasto has two Level-III public hospitals: **Hospital Departamental** (Ca, 22, 7-93. Parque Bolívar. Tel: 721-4625) and **Hospital San Pedro** (Ca. 16, 42-00. Tel: 723-4349). It also has a children's facility, **Hospital Infantil** (Av. los Estudiantes and Cra. 32. Tel: 723-5929). Pharmacies, both national chains and locally-owned stores, are quite common; many can be found on Calle 18, if you are in need of emergency medications.

LAUNDRY
It is hard to find a wet-wash laundry in Pasto, but there are plenty of dry cleaners. One that offers to do a regular wash is **Lavandería Perlmatic** (Cra. 25, 15-40. Tel: 723-3025), but only by piece—an expensive option at $1-2 per garment. **Lava Mejor** (Cra. 27, 15-08, Tel: 722-8088) has one-day service Monday-Saturday, and charges by kilogram: $0.80 for wash and dry, $2.50 with ironing.

CAMERA
Many of your photographic needs can be met right in the heart of Pasto, on Parque Nariño. **Foto Almacén Tricolor** (Cra. 24, 17-82. Tel: 722-3214), a half-block from the plaza, carries digital cameras and photo cards, and 100, 200 and 400 ASA Kodak fi lm. **Foto Canon Digital** (Ca. 19, 23-61. Tel: 723-3818) offers the same items, but has an extra service: Here you can download and print your digital photos or burn them to CD. Updated: Feb 21, 2011.

SHOPPING
Artesanías en Barniz Obandos
Barniz de Pasto is an ancient technique practiced in this region since before the Eu-

SOUTHERN COLOMBIA

ropeans arrived on these shores. The seed of the mapo mapo tree is boiled in water to extract a rubber-like resin that is kneaded until it is flexible, then it is colored with natural dyes, and, lastly, it is applied by hand to carved wood. The famous Casa del Barniz de Pasto may have closed, but the Obando family continues the tradition. Artesanías en Barniz Obandos showcases various generations of work, using traditional, contemporary and unique designs. The items are surprisingly affordable. So, while visiting Pasto, pick up a memento of your visit or a gift for a loved one. Monday-Saturday 8:30 a.m.-12:30 p.m. and 2:30-6:30 p.m. Cra. 25, 13-04. Tel: 722-4045. Updated: Mar 17, 2011.

Ecotema

For over three decades, Ecotema has been clothing Pasto's populace with beautiful, natural-color shawls, ruanas (ponchos), sweaters and shoulder bags. This cooperative of local weavers uses merino sheep wool in their crafts, though sweaters of synthetic fibers are available. Hand embroidery and appliqués trim some pieces. Doña Susana can also show you towels, hot pads and other items to decorate your kitchen. Monday-Saturday 12:30 p.m.-7 p.m. Shop: Ca. 17, 24-77; Factory: Ca. 30, 19-120, Barrio Corazón de Jesús. Shop Tel: 729-2494; Factory Tel: 721-8386. URL: www. coopecotema.es.vg. Updated: Mar 17, 2011.

Vicens

Colombia is renowned for its leather work, and Vicens proudly proclaims it creates "natural designs in leather." If you really want to get dressed up for a night at the discos and desire something special, then drop in at this shop. In its on-site workshop, the craftspersons of Vicens make everything from pants to jackets, vests to micro-mini skirts of fine, glove leather. Want gear a bit more traditional? Try on the hats or belts. For something smaller, there are also wallets, purses and hair barrettes. Monday-Saturday 9 a.m.-7 p.m., Sunday 10 a.m.-2 p.m. Cra. 27, 14-04. Tel: 729-8856, Cel: 315-501-0030, E-mail: vicenscuero@yahoo.com. Updated: Mar 17, 2011.

Things to See and Do

From colonial churches displaying an impressive variety of architectural styles to museums exhibiting arts and history, Pasto has enough to fill any cultural devotee's hours for many days.

For those aching to get out of the city, visit the small villages around the base of Volcán

Galeras, including Sandoná with its weekly market. Túquerres is another village with an interesting weekly mercado; hike to its Volcán Azufral and Laguna Verde.

Several nature reserves are a few hours away, on the road to Tumaco: Reserva Natural Biotopo Selva Húmeda (Pasto office: Cra. 22, 25-35. Tel: 723-3756, E-mail: biotopo@telesat.com.co) and Reserva Natural La Planada (presently closed; Pasto Office: Cra. 30, 19-33. Tel: 731-1323).

Going toward the Putumayo are Laguna La Cocha and the Santuario de Fauna y Flora Isla de la Carota. In this region are a number of Reserva Natural Privadas, community-based reserves you can visit or stay at.

Sports addicts can check out La Chaza, a pre-Columbian ball game played in city parks on the weekends. Updated: Feb 21, 2011.

The Museums of Pasto

Pasto has many museums devoted to just as many topics. Whether your interest is in colonial, graphic, photographic or traditional arts, or natural history, archaeology or ethnography—or even Carnaval—you have some place to spend a few hours. A couple of the museums are by appointment only: **Casa-Museo Taller Relieves EBC** (Admission: free. Ca. 21, 25-40.Tel: 723-3275) and **Museo Fotográfico Luis Bernardo Esparza** (Admission: free. Cra. 31C, 19-72. Tel: 731-0102).

Museo Juan Lorenzo Lucero (Admission: $1.10. Monday-Friday 8-10 a.m. and 2-3:30 p.m. Ca. 18, 28-27. Tel: 731-4414)—A 17th-century priest's collection of daily life objects, musical instruments and art.

Museo Luciano Rosero (Admission: $1.10. Daily 8 a.m.-6:30 p.m. Ca. 23, 17-52. Cel: 310-396-3289)—A once-private collection of religious and secular art, archaeology, coins and natural history.

Museo Alfonso Zambrano (Admission: Free. Monday-Saturday, 8 a.m.-noon and 2-4 p.m. Ca. 20, 29-79. Tel: 731-2837)—Collection of indigenous, colonial and Quiteño-school art.

Museo Madre Caridad Brader (Admission: $0.60. Monday-Friday 8-11:30 a.m. and 3-5 p.m. Ca. 18, 32A-01. Tel: 731-2092)—Religious art, natural history, anthropology and indigenous ethnography.

Museo del Carnaval (Admission: free. Daily 8 a.m.-6:30 p.m. Ca. 19 and Cra. 42, Centro Cultural Pandiaco, Oficina Municipal de Cultura. Tel: 731-4598)—If you can't join pastusos for the Carnaval in January, you can revel in the color here. Updated: Feb 21, 2011.

Museo de Oro

(ADMISSION: free) This small collection of pre-Columbian stone, textile, ceramics, and requisite gold pieces, including some very fine, 2,500-year-old filigree pieces, provides excellent explanations about pre-Conquest, indigenous trade routes in the Americas, and the cultural beliefs and practices of the Pro-to-Pasto (Piartal and Capulí) peoples (Spanish only). At lunch hours, live classical music accompanies your explorations of these galleries on the third floor, and those of modern art located one story below. In the same building is the Banco de la Nación library. Tuesday-Saturday 10 a.m.-5 p.m. Ca. 19, 21-27, Centro Cultural Leopoldo López Álvarez. Tel: 721-9108. Updated: Feb 21, 2011.

Museo Casona Taminango de Artes y Tradiciones Populares de Nariño

(ADMISSION: $1.40 adults, $0.85 children) The casona in which the Taminango museum is housed, built in 1623, is not only the oldest house in Pasto, but also one of the oldest ones in the nation. The guide (Spanish only) will lead you through each room, explaining each of the crafts executed in Nariño Department: woodworking and carving, weaving, blacksmithing, copper and other metalwork, wool and paja weaving. If any craft catches your fancy, you can pick up a work in the small, on-site shop. Monday-Friday, 8 a.m.-noon and 2-4 p.m., Saturday, 9 a.m.-1 p.m. Ca. 13, 27-67. Tel: 723-5539. Updated: Feb 21, 2011.

The Churches of Pasto

Besides the outstanding San Juan Bautista and Cristo Rey churches, other stunning temples have been bestowed upon Pasto during its nearly 500 years of existence. Some other noteworthy ones are:

Catedral (Ca. 17 and Cra. 26)—A red-brick building of simple, classic Roman basilicadesign. Two Art Deco angels hold the baptismal font.

La Merced (Ca. 18 and Cra. 22)—Has a spiral staircase without a central axis pole.

Lourdes (Ca. 13 and Cra. 28)—A typical Latin American parish church.

Also check out these churches:

San Andrés (Ca. 16 and Cra. 28)

San Felipe (Cra. 27, 11-31)

Santiago Apóstol (Ca. 12, 22F-16)

Mariadaz (Ca. 18, 32A-01, across from Universidad Mariana). Updated: Feb 21, 2011.

Iglesia de San Juan

Walking into Iglesia de San Juan's interior is like entering a mosque. Built within a century of the Spanish conquest of the Americas, this temple, Pasto's original cathedral, exhibits a pure Mozarabic style of Islamic-era Spain. Note the almost complete absence of human figures within, the walls instead receiving an interlaced vine-design treatment. The arches are peak-arched with scalloped edges, as in Arab architecture. The ceiling of the apse is mudjedar: a giant wood jigsaw puzzle held together with no glue, nails or pegs. The windows in that part of the church, as well as in the left-hand chapel are covered with wooden, carved screens. Ca. 18 and Cra. 25. Updated: Feb 21, 2011.

Iglesia del Cristo Rey

Whereas the Iglesia de San Juan displays one style of medieval architecture, that of Arab-influenced Spain, a few blocks away the Iglesia the Cristo Rey shows us the architecture of northern Europe of the same period. This church, built in the 1930s, is a stunning example of neo-Early Gothic architecture. Light through the clerestory and apse windows floods the large, open interior. Quadpartite vaulting crowns the ceiling; but that of the transept is octpartite with a rose design. The golden altar is like a giant reliquary coffer. All the interior sculpture and stained glass are by Colombian and Ecuadorian Jesuit artists. Ca. 20 and Cra. 24. Updated: Feb 21, 2011.

Tours

For the number of things to do in and around Pasto, there are surprisingly few tour operators. As in other parts of Southern Colombia, most agencies are devoted only to the booking of air flights. A few officially registered guides can take you to visit Sandoná and other small villages around the base of Volcán Galeras, or to hike and bird watch in Reserva Natural

La Chaza

Sundays, men of all ages partake in Chaza de Bombo, a ball game where four-to eight-man teams hit a tennis ball with a bombo, an 80-centimeter (32-in) -long, wooden racket with a 22-centimeter (9-in) -wide head stretched with hide. When the ball hits the rackets, it sounds like the beating of drums. The game follows the rules of tennis, but with no net. In Chaza de Tabla, the racket head is wooden, studded with rubber. Then there is Chaza de Mano, in which the ball is hit with the bare hand. In these two forms of the game, the 800-gram (28-oz) ball is made of solid rubber. This game of pre-Columbian origin is played only by men. From Calle 17, between Carrera 21 and 22, catch buseta Ruta C3, E1 or E3 "Barrio Florida" to Parque Bolívar; the Estadio de Chaza is across from Ferretería Argentina. To watch a game of chaza de tabla or chaza de mano, catch Ruta C5 or E3 as it passes along Ca. 17. Updated: Feb 21, 2011.

Biotopo Selva Húmeda, Laguna La Cocha and Isla de la Carota, and Volcán Azufral and Laguna Verde. Updated: Aug 28, 2011.

Camino del Viento

Registered guide Orfa Marina Ascuntar specializes in ecological tourism. She can take you on a one-day hiking tour to Túquerres' Volcán Azufral and Laguna Verde, summiting Cumbal's volcanoes, visiting the villages on the skirts of Galeras volcano or soaking in Tajumbía's hot springs. If you want to spend a few more days afield, Ms. Ascuntar will show you the pleasures of the beaches at Tumaco and Bocagrande on the Pacific Coast or the diversity of birds and wildlife at the Reserva Natural Biotopo. She can also design tours specifically to your interests. Tel: 730-4287, Cel: 315-511-7464, E-mail: caminodelvientoTE@hotmail.com, URL: www.caminodelvientoturismo.com. Updated: Feb 17, 2011.

Turismo Aventura

If you are looking to join the condors in soaring over the mountains of Southern Colombia, you can give Carlos Yepes a ring. This professional pilot runs a paragliding outfit out of Pasto. He offers three- and four-day packages, all inclusive, of paragliding over the valleys of Nariño Department and around its impressively active Galeras volcano. He also teaches courses in flying, unfortunately only in Spanish. For more information on activities offered or fees, check out his website. Tel: 731-2951, Cel: 300-617-7304, E-mail: carlosyepes@turismoaventura.com, URL: www.turismoextremo.com.co. Updated: Feb 21, 2011.

Lodging

Most of Pasto's lodging options are concentrated in two areas: near the bus terminal and in the Centro Histórico. A wider variety is found in the historic center—there are some very low-key, beautiful B&Bs, popular budget hotels and a few high-rise, luxury hotels shadowing the Parque de Nariño. Pasto hostels don´t really exist, but cheap hotels offer comparable accommodations. Updated: Jul 05, 2010.

Hotel Manhattan

(BEDS: $5.50-11) With over 30 years of experience, Hotel Manhattan provides travelers with a restful spot to stay in the colonial heart of Pasto. The eclectically furnished rooms surrounding the sitting-area patio of this second-floor inn are spacious and warm; all come with cable TV and balconies. The wood floors throughout are polished and the common bathroom is kept clean. The ground-floor back patio has a laundry area. This is definitely a bargain. Ca. 18, 21B-14. Tel: 721-5675. Updated: Feb 21, 2011.

Koala Inn

(ROOMS: $9-20) On the outside, the Koala Inn looks nondescript. But once mounting the steps up to the inn, you find yourself embraced by classic solar architecture. The rooms, like the exterior, are also a bit plain and showing the wear of more than a decade of travelers from around the world. The hotel offers restaurant and laundry service (no self-laundry washing allowed). Ca. 18, 22-37. Tel: 722-1101. Updated: Feb 21, 2011.

Hotel Casa López

(ROOMS: $45-101) A very understated sign, a solitary H, marks the Casa López. The López have lovingly converted this home that has been in their family for over 70 years into a delightful inn. The natural woodwork and floors of the Republican-era building are polished to a warm sheen. The interior has been designed by a fine hand, with nice touches like glass vases full of Calais lilies. All six rooms come with private, hot water bath,

SOUTHERN COLOMBIA

cable TV, phone and alarm clock radio. Breakfast is served in a separate, second-floor dining room. The López family prides itself on providing European-style service totheir guests. Ca. 18, 21B-11. Tel: 720-8172/733-0223, E-mail: hcasalopez@yahoo.com, URL: www.hotel-casalopez.com. Updated: Feb 21, 2011.

Restaurants

Pasto offers a smorgasbord of dining options. The best restaurants are quite a distance from the downtown district, on the Panamericana and on Avenida de los Estudiantes.

For those on a budget, the cheapest eateries are along Carrera 22 between Calles 16 and 18, and along Calle 17. The city market is located out near the bus terminal. An Éxito Vecino supermarket right in the heart of the city can also fill your self-catering needs (corner of Ca. 18 and Cra. 26). Updated Feb 21, 2011.

Manhattan

(SET MEAL: $1.60-2) You don't have to be a guest to enjoy one of the good meals the women whip up at the Hotel Manhattan. The restaurant is located in the large, skylighted patio. With a smile, they'll serve you a breakfast of eggs, bread or arepa, rice and hot chocolate. The lunch and dinner set meals are the cheapest you can find in this city. So pull up a stool at the counter and chat with the cook while you dine, or grab one of the lace-clothed tables in the alcove to enjoy a more intimate meal. You definitely will not be disappointed. Ca. 18, 21B-14. Tel: 721-5675. Updated: Feb 21, 2011.

Integrales Pan y Salud

(SET MEAL $2.25) This is the only option for vegetarians in downtown Pasto—and unfortunately, only at lunchtime. The midday meal comes with soup, the main plate (with gluten or beans, salad and rice) and drink or soy milk. In other hours, Pan y Salud's bakery has whole-grain breads, sweets and flours. Choose between quinoa, soy, oat and multi-grain goodies. Be sure to taste the unusual radish bread. Monday-Saturday 8 a.m.-7 p.m. Cra. 29, 20-34. Cel: 320-695-1223. Updated: Feb 21, 2011.

Tienda del Café del Parque

Tienda del Café del Parque is a salute to Nariñense coffee and culture. The only coffee it serves is organically grown from Nariño Department, in a two-story shop that itself is a work of art, from the canvases on the walls, right down to the chairs painted with landscapes, abstracts and portraits. Downstairs is a bookshop selling literature by regional writers. Besides coffee, Tienda del Café also has hot cocoa, teas and non-caffeinated drinks, as well as pastries and sandwiches. The second-floor has a full-service bar, and balcony seating overlooking Nariño Park. The ground story has a street-side patio from where you can also watch the daily life of pastusos. Friday nights features live music: jazz, classical or salsa. You can even enjoy this rich coffee back home, thousands of miles away, just grab a sack of coffee on your way out. Monday-Friday 9 a.m.-9 p.m., Friday 9 a.m.-1 a.m., holidays 9 a.m.-noon; closed Sunday. Cra. 24, 18-62, Parque Nariño (next to the Plaza Casino). Cel: 300-657-7115. Updated: Feb 21, 2011.

> **V!VA ONLINE REVIEW**
> TIENDA DEL CAFÉ DEL PARQUE
>
> I liked the drinks and the atmosphere, the music and the different rock bands in the live show.
>
> *May 12, 2009*

Nightlife

The rumba in Pasto only happens on Thursday, Friday and Saturday nights. Most of thedance clubs are on Avenida de las Américas and in the Zona Rosa (Ca. 20, between Cra. 27 and 28). The other nights of the week, you'll have to settle for having a drink at a bar—but not on Mondays, when many are closed. Some of the more down-home joints have canchas de sapo, if you want to try your hand at a Colombian version of darts: tossing coins into a metal frog's mouth. If you are going out for the night, check the bus schedule beforehand, or take a taxi home. Updated: Feb 21, 2011.

Embrujo Andino Peña Bar

Embrujo Andino Peña Bar offers an alternative to local bars and discotheques. At this Carnival-themed club, you may enjoy a variety of Andean musical genres (saya, tinku, tufa, sanjuanito, bambuco and cumbia) and the region's most popular dances (salsa and meringue). The peña also shows videos on a giant screen and features live performances on weekends by folk groups, orchestras, soloists and rock bands. Monday and Tuesday evenings, Embrujo hosts dance therapy sessions, and on Wednesday nights, dance lessons. Don't leave without trying guayuza, a warm alcoholic drink made from herbs. Cra. 23, 19-58. Cel: 313-604-4935, URL: http://embrujoandinobar.bravehost.com. Updated: Feb 21, 2011.

SOUTHERN COLOMBIA

Mestizo Peña-Bar

(COVER: $1.10, LUNCH: $2.25-3) OK, folks—it's time to join an Andean hoedown! If you've gotten bored with the same ol' salsa-cumbia-reggeton down at the other clubs, a seemingly endless repetition of the same throbbing lights, the same too-loud music, the same ol'-same-ol', then you have an alternative right here in Pasto. Every Thursday, Friday and Saturday night Mestizo Peña-Bar presents the best of Andino music live—and occasionally shakes up the mix with a llanera or Afro-Colombian band. The locals hit the large dance floor to shake the workweek doldrums away. Other nights, you can enjoy a drink in this bamboo-paneled space adorned with indigenous artwork. Mestizo also serves breakfast and lunch (8 a.m.-3 p.m.). Monday-Saturday 6 p.m.-1 a.m., closed Sunday. Ca. 18, 27-67. Tel: 723-7754, E-mail: mestizopb@hotmail.com. Updated: Feb 21, 2011.

AROUND PASTO
VOLCÁN GALERAS

Early Pastuso mornings you can catch a glimpse of Galeras, when the clouds lift enough to see it sending up smoke signals. Located only seven kilometers (4.2 mi) from Pasto, the volcano has high Andean páramo and sub-páramo ecosystems woven by over 120 rivers and four lagoons. Butterfl ies, deer, foxes, squirrels, *cusumbo* (kinkajou), *raposa* (fox) and 95 species of birds make their home on these flanks. Two hiking trails begin from the ranger station: Sendero Achichay (4,060 m/13,195 ft) and Sendero Frailajón (3,360-3,960 m/10,920-12,870 ft). Since reawakening from a deep slumber in 1989, Galeras has been closed to hiking and climbing. You can, however, visit towns at its base in the Circumvalar de Galeras. Updated: Feb 21, 2011.

THE CIRCUMVALAR DE GALERAS

The Circumvalar de Galeras (or Ruta Dulce de Nariño) around the base of Volcán Galeras samples historical, colonial villages with long artisan traditions: Nariño, La Florida, Sandoná, Consacá, Yacuanquer and Tangua. The most famous of these is Sandoná, 48 kilometers (29 mi) northwest of Pasto, on the other side of the volcano. It is an indigenous town with a Saturday market. The Panama hats drying in the streets are made by this pueblo's women from paja toquilla (Carludovica palmate) fiber. Several guides offer the Circumvalar tour, or ask the Pasto tourism office for specifics on how to do the circuit yourself. See Pasto's "Getting To and Away" section for details on how to arrive to Sandoná. Updated: Feb 21, 2011.

TÚQUERRES

On the road to Tumaco, 72 kilometers (45 mi) from Pasto, is Túquerres. Founded in 1541 by Miguel de Muñoz at an altitude of 3,051 meters (10,010 ft), this village enjoys a cool climate. On Thursday mornings, Túquerres bustles with its weekly market. If you're looking for a *ruana* (poncho), this is the place to be. Traditionally, paila bowls and other copperware were forged here; but due to the high cost, this craft has all but disappeared.

Overshadowing the village is Volcán Azufral (3,400 m/11,155 ft). Within its crater are three lagoons: La Negra, La Barrosa and the moon-shaped La Verde. Ten fauna species and 476 floral species are found in the area. Guides can be hired in Pasto, Popayán or Túquerres to take you up the two-hour trail that begins from San Roque neighborhood. Túquerres has basic hotels and restaurants, if you want to spend the night here.

Túquerres can be reached from either Pasto or Ipiales; just take any bus heading to Tumaco and alight at this town. Some companies also have several runs per day specifically to Túquerres (2 hr, $2.80). Updated: Feb 21, 2011.

LAGUNA DE LA COCHA

 2,760   5,500   2

On the Eastern slopes of the Nudo de los Pastos, where the Andes branch into the Cordillera Occidental and the Oriental, the road begins to descend towards Macoa, capital of Putumayo Department. On the cloud-misted highlands is Laguna de la Cocha, a place of mystery and legend, a holy place for the ancient indigenous Quillacinga, or People of the Moon. In the icy depths is said to be a lost city. Ley lines of positive energy converge on its central island, Isla de Corota.

Located 25 kilometers (15 mi) southeast of Pasto, Laguna de la Cocha is nuzzled in the world's lowest páramo ecosystem, at only 2,760 meters (9,053 ft) altitude, thanks to the lagoon's unusual geographic characteristics. (Typically páramo zones begin at 3,000 m/9,840 ft.) It is Colombia's second-largest lake and one of the best preserved in the Andes. From this cradle flows Río Guamuéz, its waters rushing to Río Putumayo and the Amazon.

The isle is home to the Santuario de Flora y Fauna Isla La Carota. On the shores of this marsh lake are 32 private reserves run by local communities where you can learn about the area's wildlife, conservation efforts, ecological farming techniques and natural medicine. The entire area affords premier bird watching. Boats connect settlements and the islands around the lake. Updated: Feb 21, 2011.

History

In ancient times, the Laguna and its Isla La Corota were sacred sites for the Quillacinga and other indigenous cultures. Centuries later, the Jesuits arrived on these shores and constructed a chapel to Our Lady of Lourdes on the Isla. Eventually, the Universidad de Nariño, recognizing the unique and fragile ecosystem of the isle, took it over and established a research center. In 1977, Isla La Corota was declared a Santuario de Flora y Fauna, and in 2000, 40,000 hectares (98,800 ac) of the lagoon's region fell under a Ramsar Convention, giving it protection as a páramo ecosystem of international importance. Updated: Aug 28, 2011.

When to Go

The climate of Laguna de la Cocha is cold and humid, with an average temperature of 12°C (54°F), and can drop to 3°C (38°F). Rain is a frequent occurrence here; normally December and January are dryer. In August there are high winds; according to local lore, this is a being that emerges from the lake's waters to overturn unsuspecting boats and drown its passengers.

The second Sunday of February, pilgrims come to visit the Capilla de la Virgen de Lourdes on the Isla de Corota. Updated: May 19, 2008.

Getting To and Away

From the El Encano crossroads on the Pasto-Mocoa road, a dirt road goes to Vereda El Puerto on the north shore of Laguna de la Cocha. From there, the road splits. The west fork leads to Vereda Romerillo; the east fork traverses as far as Vereda Santa Teresita. Departing from Pasto's *cuartel*, white collective taxis to Vereda El Puerto cost $8-10; busetas leave from Calle 20 and Carrera 20. You can also take a Sibundoy or Macoa-bound bus as far as El Encano and walk the last five kilometers (3 mi).

Vereda El Puerto is the port for boat transport to Isla La Corota and hamlets surrounding the lagoon. The five-minute ride out to the island costs about $7 per person (depending on the number of passengers). Updated: Aug 28, 2011.

Safety

Even though the civil war wages not too far away, in the Putumayo, locals assert that El Encano and other settlements around Laguna de la Cocha are safe and tranquil. Because of the constant cold, wet climate of the region, warm clothing and raingear are essential. Eat high-energy foods. Updated: May 19, 2008.

Things to See and Do

The peace of these high mountain humid forests might be enough to draw some people, just looking for a rest from the road. While you are here, though, enjoy a hike in the Santuario de Flora y Fauna Isla La Corota or visit a natural reserve run by the indigenous and *campesino* residents of the lake. Bird watchers, bring along your binoculars because many of those inhabitants await your checklists. Or, to pass a real lazy afternoon, drop a line into these pristine waters and hook a rainbow trout—an introduced species. Updated: May 19, 2008.

Reservas Naturales de la Cocha

Since being declared a Ramsar protected area, local indigenous and campesino communities around Laguna de la Cocha have been taking an active role in conservation and the development of eco-tourism. All told, 32 hamlets are now reservas naturales, practicing sustainable agriculture and teaching environmental education. **La Sombra de un Árbol** and **El Arrayán** specialize in traditional and herbal medicine. **Raíces Andinas** preserves genetic resources, including the seeds of more than 30 varieties of potato. **El Vicundo** has an interpretation trail for birdwatching; **La Casa del Buho** has a museum. Most reservas make home-cooked meals for their visitors; some have basic lodging. Updated: May 19, 2008.

Santuario de Flora y Fauna Isla La Corota

A woman, bewitched by jealousy, was made into an island that to this day floats in the middle of Laguna de la Cocha. The fruit of her womb is the water that bathes her shores...or so legend tells us. This island was a sacred place for the Quillacinta and other indigenous nations. Today it embraces two sanctuaries: a nature one, Santuario de Flora y Fauna Isla La Corota, and a shrine to Our Lady of Lourdes.

The smallest of Colombia's national parks, Santuario de Flora y Fauna Isla La Corota comprises only eight hectares. A half-kilometer path leads up to the island's highest point, at 2,839 meters (9,312 feet). Its ecosystem is low mountain humid forest, exhibiting a great diversity of birds, amphibians and vegetation. At least 32 species of fowl roost here, including pullets, turtledoves, hummingbirds, ducks, wood pigeons, wrens, finches, tanagers, blackbirds and sparrows. Over 500 species of plants carpet the small island, among them *fraillejón*, myrtle, alder, orchids, mosses and ferns.

The environment is quite sensitive. Do not stray off the path. Do not pick any flowers or plants. Take out all your trash. A curious custom is 50 meters (165 ft) before the summit of the island, visitors will take off their shoes, watches and metal items and go hug the Wish Tree. Some claim to be healed of illnesses. To get to the island, take a boat from Vereda El Puerto (5 min, approximately $7). Updated: May 19, 2008.

Lodging

Although Laguna de la Cocha is an easy day trip from Pasto, you may want to spend more time to soak in the tranquility and positive vibes of this corner of the Andes. Around the shores of the lake are several places where you can pass the night. The most formal and luxurious of these is Hotel Sindamanoy, of Swiss-chalet-styled architecture, and the Hotel Guámez. To enjoy Nariñense hospitality, you can also stay in one of the reservas naturales that offer lodging, like Raíces Andinas, Refugio Cristalino or Encanto Andino; El Vicundo has a camping area. Updated: Jul 05, 2010.

Restaurants

Scores of restaurants dot the roadsides at El Encano and El Puerto. The most common item on the menu is rainbow trout fresh out of the lake's icy waters. The family and community-run natural reserves also provide meals with farm-fresh products—including *cuy* (guinea pig.) Most of them can feed large groups. Updated: May 19, 2008.

IPIALES

 2,898m   72,000   2

A Sunday morning stroll around Ipiales belies the reality of this city. These now-quiet streets will soon bustle with travelers and merchants crossing the border, and Ecuadorian and Colombian pilgrims on their way to the Santuario de Nuestra Señora de Las Lajas.

Located on the Pan-American Highway just three kilometers (1.8 mi) north of the Rumichaca border crossing into Ecuador, Ipiales is only a transit point for many. However, it is worth passing a few days here. Services are improving in this southern Colombian city; unfortunately, however, it still lacks a tourism office to orientate visitors, which is a shame, as there are interesting places to get to know. The city has several pleasant parks where you can people watch, and churches to visit. The incredible neo-Gothic Santuario de Nuestra Señora de Las Lajas that spans the Río Guáitra is only eight kilometers (4.8 mi) from Ipiales. Not too far from that pilgrimage site are some petroglyphs of the ancient Pasto indigenous culture. The village of Cumbral presents you with not only incredible vistas of two snow-capped volcanoes, but also walking and climbing opportunities.

So, don't be so hasty in flying through Ipiales to your other destinations in Colombia. Take a break to visit some of the surprises this region hides from fleeting eyes. Updated: Feb 14, 2011.

History

Several indigenous nations, principally of the Pasto who held off the Inca northward, called this region home before the Spanish conquest. Ipiales means People of White Smoke, deriving from Ipial, a Pasto cacique, plus the -es suffix, which means "people." The Villaviciosa de la Concepción de Ipiales was founded in 1537 by Pedro de Puelles, one of several captains sent by Belalcázar to found cities as base camps for the search for El Dorado. In the 1570s, the original city was totally destroyed by fire; at a new site several kilometers away it was rebuilt, with the name Villaje de Ipiales. It was administered by the Audencia Real de Quito. Ipiales joined the fight for independence from Spanish rule in 1809. The Libertador, Simón Bolívar, passed through the city on a number of occasions. Updated: Oct 14, 2007.

When to Go

Ipiales and Nariño Department have an agreeable spring-like climate, due to the high altitude of this southern Colombian region. From June to September it is cold and rainy. The other months see intermittent clear skies and sunshine. No matter the season, the nights are surprisingly crisp.

HOLIDAYS AND FESTIVALS

Ipiales has several festivals. El Festival de

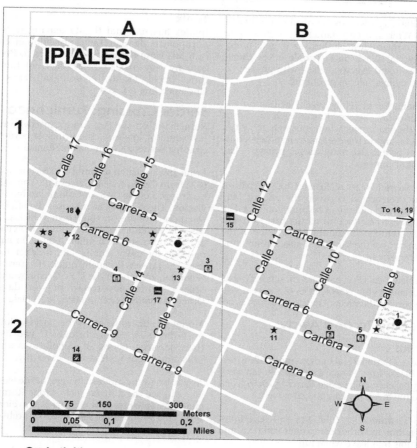

IPIALES

● **Activities**

1 Parque de la Independencia B2
2 Parque La Pola A2

🍴 **Eating**

3 Pan Pan A2
4 Restaurante-Bar Rancho Grande A2
5 Restaurante Mi Casita B2
6 Restaurante Vegetariano Govinda B2

★ **Services**

7 Bancolombia A2
8 Bicicletería JJ A2
9 Ciclo Cadena A2
10 Correo B2
11 Mundo Net B2
12 Sai Telecom A1
13 Western Union A2

🛍 **Shopping**

14 Mercado A2

🛏 **Sleeping**

15 Hotel Belmonte B1
16 Hotel Imperio Real B1
17 Hotel Internacional El Nogal A2

♦ **Tours**

18 Valencia Torres A1

🚌 **Transportation**

19 Bus Terminal B1

SOUTHERN COLOMBIA

los Blancos y Negros (Festival of the Blacks and Whites) occurs January 3-6. Be sure to wear your oldest clothes, as it gets pretty nasty: on Black days, people cover themselves— and everyone else—with grease; on Blanco days, talcum powder flies.

Semana Santa (Holy Week) begins on the Wednesday before Easter. Every morning the via crucis winds through the city's streets, and in the evenings are processions. Many people also make the pilgrimage to Las Lajas at this time.

The Sacred Heart of Jesus is Ipiales' patron saint, celebrated between the end of May and the end of June (a floating holiday). The city is extremely crowded the first fortnight of September during the observance of the feast days of the Virgin of Lajas, culminating September 15.

On New Year's Eve, effigies representing events and noteworthy personalities of the past year are burnt in the streets. Updated: May 18, 2009.

Getting To and Away

BY BUS
The bus terminal is at Carrera 3 and Calle 6, seven blocks from Parque La Pola. You can catch any buseta passing along Carrera 5 ($0.65) or a taxi (up to five persons, $1.40) or walk.

To Tumaco: 5.5-6 hr, $14-16—Supertaxis, Guaitara and other companies run taxis and combis that leave when full.

To Pasto: hourly, 1.5 hr, $5.50—Transipiales, Cootranar, Bolivariano and others.

To Popayán: half-hourly, 8 hr. $16—Transipiales, Cootranar, Bolivariano and others.

To Cali: frequent, 10 hr., $22-25—Transipiales, Cootranar, Bolivariano.

To Medellín: Bolivariano (10 a.m., 3 p.m., 7 p.m., 20 hr, $43).

To Bogotá: Bolivariano (hourly 8 a.m.- 8 p.m., 22 hr, $54-57).

The blue city bus to the Rumichaca border passes along Carrera 7 and drop you off about 100 meters (328 ft) from the border ($0.60). Minivans also leave from the bus terminal ($0.80). Taxis depart from Calle 14 and from Parque La Pola ($3).

BY AIR
Ipiales has national flights leaving from Aeropuerto de San Luís, six kilometres (3.6 mi) from the city. Satena flies to Bogotá by way of Cali (7-hr layover) four times weekly ($130, including all taxes). Updated: Aug 29, 2011.

Border Crossing: Rumichaca
Rumichaca, on the Pan-American Highway just south of Ipiales, is the principle border crossing between Colombia and Ecuador.

From Ipiales, catch a combi ($0.85) or taxi ($3) from Calle 14, near Carrera 10. You will be dropped off at DAS, or Colombian immigration. The complex also houses the offices for those crossing in their own vehicles, a casa de cambio, bathrooms and an Ecuadorian consulate. Colombian migración has one line for entry stamps and another for exit. The process is usually quick. If entering Colombia, citizens of the U.S., Germany and other countries now receive only 60 days. Other nationalities get 90 days, with luck.

Money changers work in the parking lots on either side of the bridge. If you use their services, check all calculations and bills, and count your money carefully.

As you cross the modern bridge, to the west you will see the natural rock bridge Rumichaca is named for. For centuries, travelers used that stone to cross the Río Carchi—even Simón Bolívar and his minions.

On the other side of the river is Ecuador's migración. Usually only 60 days are given upon entering, but go ahead and ask for 90.

Mini-buses ($0.75) and taxis (collective, $1; private, $4-5) leave from the parking lot across the road. The mini-buses and collective taxis will drop you off at Parque Ayora in Tulcán (Ca. Venezuela and Av. Coral); to arrive at Tulcán's bus terminal, take a city bus ($0.80) or walk the 10 blocks. A private taxi from the border will take you directly to the station.

Immigration for both countries is open 6 a.m. to 10 p.m. Transportation fares on either side can be paid in dollars or pesos. Updated: Feb 11, 2011.

Safety
Ipiales, in general, is a safe town. However, like any city near a border, theft can be more

likely than in other towns due to the constant movement of people, making it easy for a would-be thief to disappear. Use common sense: Keep an eye on your belongings at all times. Don't display large amounts of bills; keep only what you immediately need at hand—especially when changing money.

On some routes, many locals travel only during the day, as guerrilla activity and robberies continue to be a problem (though less so than in the past due to the military's presence on the roads and checkpoints). A number of bus companies do offer overnight service to Pasto, Popayán and Cali. Updated: Aug 30, 2011.

Services

TOURISM

There is a **tourism infomation office** at the Rumichaca border crossing. In Ipiales, the **Policía Nacional** post is on Calle 11, between Carrera 5 and 6 (Tel: 773-2577). The Ecuadorian Consulate is one block from Parque La Pola (Monday-Friday 8:30 a.m.-12:30 p.m. Cra. 7, 14-10, 2nd floor. Tel: 772-2272).

MONEY

If coming from Ecuador, exchange only a little money at the border; you'll get a better exchange rate in Ipiales. **Bancolombia** (Monday-Friday 8 a.m.-4 p.m. Ca. 14, on Parque La Pola) is the only bank in Ipiales that changes traveler's checks—and only American Express. Its ATM handles all banking networks, with a daily withdrawal limit of $600. Other banks and casas de cambio will change U.S. cash dollars to pesos. You will find many around Parque La Pola, and on Calle 14 and Carreras 5 and 6. Most are open 8 a.m.-6 p.m., some until 7 p.m. Restaurants and shops at the bus terminal may be able to change money also. For wiring money, the local Western Union office is at **Giros and Finanzas** (Cra. 6, 13-23).

KEEPING IN TOUCH

A fair share of Internet cafés are scattered throughout Ipiales. **Mundo Net** has Skype and can burn your digital photos to CD (Cra. 7, 10-67). To make a local or national phone call, just keep an eye out for the frequent *llamadas* (call) signs. For international calls, try **Sai Telecom** (Ca. 16, 6-47). Old-fashioned snail mail can be posted at the **Correo** in the Alcaldía building complex on the Plaza de la Independencia (Monday-Friday 8 a.m.-noon and 2-6 p.m., Saturday, 8 a.m.-noon).

MEDICAL

The main health facility is **Hospital Civil de Ipiales** (Av. Panameriacana Norte. Tel: 773-3949, Emergencies: 773-3454). The city has a number of *droguerías*, or pharmacies, to cure your ills.

CAMERA

You can find a number of photo shops on Carrera 6, between the two plazas. They sell everything from print film to digital cameras. Foto Almacén Rollei has 100 and 200 ASA film in stock, digital chips, camera batteries and a wide array of conventional and digital cameras. They can process your color-print film in one hour or burn your digital photos onto CD. **Foto Almacén Rollei** also repairs both analog and digital cameras (Cra. 6, 12-133. Tel: 773-3811). Updated: Feb 21, 2011.

SHOPPING

Befitting a border town, the shops in Ipiales offer almost anything you might need. Just stroll through the streets and stop in. For the market scene, head for the daily mercado on Carrera 10, between Calles 14 and 15. Here you can pick up not only fruits and veggies, but also the latest fashions. Ipiales is host to two weekly markets, both carrying out business the full length of Carrera 7. On Fridays is an indigenous market, featuring the produce and products from both Colombian and Ecuadorian pueblos. A run-of-the mill weekly market is on Saturdays.

If you are bicycling your way through the Americas, you can find parts for almost any type of bike, as well as repairs, at **Bicicletería JJ** (Monday-Saturday 8 a.m.-12:30 p.m. and 2-6:30 p.m. Cra. 7, 16-84. Tel: 725-1087; accepts Visa and MasterCard) and **Ciclo Cadena** (Monday-Saturday 8 a.m.-noon and 2-6 p.m. Cra. 7, 16-73. Tel: 725-2149).

Things to See and Do

Ipiales is more than the last Colombian city on the way to the principle border crossing to Ecuador. It is also an important pilgrimage center for both Colombian and Ecuadorian Catholics. Eight kilometers away (4.8 mi) is the Santuario de Nuestra Señora de las Lajas, an impressive church built over a river gorge. From the sanctuary, three kilometers (1.8 mi) along the Río Guáitra, are the rock paintings of Piedra de los Monos, reminding us the area was also sacred to the Pasto ancestors of this region. Numerous indigenous villages speckle the countryside around Ipiales. Visit the weekly market in Cumbal and dine on fresh trout at Laguna de Cumbal. If you're feeling an urge to

SOUTHERN COLOMBIA

do some climbing, Volcán Cumbal and Chilis are awaiting your steps. Updated: Feb 14, 2011.

Churches and Plazas of Ipiales

Ipiales has two pleasant public squares: Parque de la Independencia (also known as Parque 20 de Julio), between Carreras 5 and 6, and Calles 8 and 9, and Parque La Pola, between Carreras 5 and 6, and Calles 13 and 14.

Around Parque de la Independencia are the municipal buildings (the alcaldía) and the city's cathedral. In the center of the park is a tall column atop which is Lady Liberty standing on the back of a soaring condor. The Catedral Bodas de Plata, dedicated to Saint Peter, was constructed in 1823. The church's red-brick exterior of classical lines rises into twin bell towers. Within, the clean style continues. Massive Ionic columns divide the nave from the side aisles, which are lined with chapel screens touched with gold gilt. The left aisle ends in a chapel. Large clerestory windows flood the nave with sunlight. The flat ceilings are of inlaid wood.

Parque La Pola is more the center of Ipiales. Here is where you will find banks and casas de cambio. Combis from the border can drop you off at this park. The center of Parque La Pola is marked with the statue of another woman: independence heroine Policarpa Salavarrieta. She is breaking free from the chains that bind her to a pillar. The blue and white Iglesia de San Felipe Neri, of the same period as the Catedral, has an unusual touch: its two campaniles are topped with onion domes. Inside, the temple's nave is flanked by narrow aisles lined with chapel screens dedicated to various versions of the Virgin. The nave terminates in a square apse. Thick Corinthian columns support the painted, textured-tin ceiling. Small clerestory windows truncate the thick walls, making this church not as bright as the Cathedral. Updated: Feb 14, 2011.

The Cultural Centers of Ipiales

If you find yourself stuck in Ipiales for a few days, don't sweat. There are places where you can while away a few hours.

The **Banco de la República** (Monday-Friday 8:30 a.m.-6 p.m., Saturday 9:30 a.m.-1 p.m. Open evenings for special events. Ca. 17, 7-82) has a cultural center that hosts art exhibits, seminars, concerts, movies and other free cultural events. The building also houses a library, which presents storytelling for children.

The city has its own **Casa de la Cultura**

(Ca. 12, between Cra. 5 and Cra. 4), which also has art galleries and a small library. On Thursday evening and Saturday afternoons, free movies are shown. Nearby fantastic murals adorn the streets.

Tours

As Ipiales is more tuned to commerce than it is to tourism, there are no operators offering tours to the region's attractions. You are pretty much on your own here. Fortunately, you can easily reach them on your own. If you want to save time on traveling to your next Colombia destination, several travel agencies await your business. These are located near the intersection of Carrera 7 and Calle 16. Updated: May 18, 2009.

Valencia Torres

If the prospects of traveling Colombia in a bus for hours—up to a day, a night or even more—make you wince, then consider flying. Valencia Torres can help you book tickets for anywhere you want to go. The small, no-frills office has a helpful staff. Even though it is Ipiales' Avianca agency, Valencia Torres also books with Satena, Aires and other national airlines—and even Tame, in case you want to fly to Quito. This travel agency can also sell you airline tour packages to prime Colombian vacation spots. Need a package sent nationally or internationally? Valencia Torres also handles courier services. Monday-Friday 8 a.m.-noon and 2-6 p.m., Saturday 8 a.m.-noon. Ca. 16, 6-48. Tel: 773-4523, E-mail: valenciatorres@etb.net.co. Updated: Feb 21, 2011.

Lodging

Ipiales has a wide offering of lodging choices for all budgets. Many low-end hostels are located on Calle 13, near the Iglesia San Felipe Neri, and on Carrera 6, between the two plazas. In the past few years, more luxury hotels catering to business travelers have appeared on the ipialeño scene; these are mainly concentrated on Carrera 7. Updated: Feb 14, 2011.

Hotel Belmonte

(BEDS: $6.50-10) Doña Olga proudly states, "This is not a luxurious place. It's basic, secure, clean and cheap"—and that's precisely what the Hotel Belmonte is. The rooms are simply appointed with classic, heavily carved furniture; some rooms come with cable TV. All accommodations share a clean, common bathroom that has 24-hour hot water. Some of the rooms can be a bit noisy. This hostel is popular with backpackers and pilgrims alike. Doña Olga is helpful with tourist information. Cra. 4, 12-111. Tel: 773-2771. Updated: Feb 14, 2011.

Imperio Real

(ROOMS: $13-15) After your long journey, just walk across the street to Hotel Imperio Real, no matter what the hour. Its dim, stone-inlaid hallways quietly lead you to your room. Open the door and walk into a bright room complete with your own private bath (with gas-heated hot water 24-hours a day) and cable TV. If you don't feel like dining downstairs, you can call room service and enjoy your meal in your suite. This hostel also offers laundry service. Cra. 3, 6-26. Tel: 773-4887. Updated: Feb 14, 2011.

Hotel Internacional El Nogal

(ROOMS: $22-108) Hotel Internacional El Nogal is one of the newer luxury inns on the Ipiales scene. The tastefully decorated rooms have telephone, cable TV and private, hot water baths. Unfortunately, some of the rooms do not have windows. But, never mind, if you feel like you really need to unwind, head down to the free sauna and Turkish baths. Also included in the price of this lodge is a buffet American breakfast served in the second-floor restaurant. Other services are free parking in an attached, underground garage, Internet, laundry, room service, transport to/from the airport and money exchange. Cra. 7, 13-77. Tel: 725-3983/3984, E-mail: hotelnogal_ipiales@yahoo.com. Updated: Feb 14, 2011.

Restaurants

For an inexpensive place to eat, check out the *panaderías* on Carrera 6 between Parque La Pola and the Plaza de la Independencia. Many serve *comida corriente* set lunches and dinners. Also, on Parque La Pola are some cheap restaurants. Alkosto supermarket is on Carrera 5, across from Parque de la Independencia. Ipiales also has upscale restaurants specializing in traditional Colombian food; most are around Plaza de la Independencia and on Carrera 7. A specialty of the southern Colombian Andes region is *cuy* (guinea pig) roasted over a wood fire. Updated: Feb 14, 2011.

Restaurant Vegetariano Govinda's

(LUNCH: $1.65) A different breed of revolutionaries has descended upon Ipiales. No, they are not garbed in olive drab, but rather they wear saffron and other colored robes. The only weapons they wave are spoons. Indeed, the Hare Krishnas have arrived and are introducing vegetarian cooking to this border town. Four-course lunches with drink are certain to please the palate (served noon-2 p.m.). Gov-

inda's on-site bakery creates whole-grain goodies. The shop also sells music, videos, books and other delights to feed one's soul. Open until 7 p.m. Cra. 7, 9-56. Tel: 773-8576, URL: larevoluciondelacuchara.org. Updated: Feb 21, 2011.

Pan Pan

(SET MEAL: $1.65-2.25) Pan Pan is just one of the many bakeries that whip up much more than just breads and cakes. It also makes blue-plate specials with hearty soups,followed by a main dish of meat, rice, beans, salad and patacones, washed down with a fresh fruit drink (slightly more expensive on Sundays). Be sure to pick up a cookie right out of the oven on your way out. Pan Pan also serves breakfasts. Monday-Saturday 7 a.m.-9 p.m., Sunday 8 a.m.-7 p.m. Cra. 6, 12-76. Tel: 773-3861. Updated: Feb 14, 2011.

Rancho Grande

(SET MEAL: $3-3.25, ENTREES: $5-10) Styled to look like a humble bohío hut, Restaurante-Bar Rancho Grande sports green-painted bamboo outside and in. But the prices are anything but ignoble in this restaurant. Sit down at one of the green-clothed tables and have an aperitif from the full bar while you study the menu. À la carte dishes include meat, poultry and seafood. All entrées come accompanied with rice, potatoes and salad. Rancho Grande also prepares a daily blue-plate special for lunch, as well as for breakfast ($2-2.50). Daily 7 a.m.–7 p.m. Cra. 7, 14-51. Tel: 773-2662. Updated: Feb 14, 2011.

Restaurante Mi Casita

(SET MEALS: $3.50, ENTREES $5-8) An ipialeño tradition, Restaurante Mi Casita dishes up home-cooked, Colombian favorites. If hunger gnaws you early on, you can breakfast here. Later in the day, choose a plate of meat, chicken or fish prepared with a variety of recipes and accompanied with rice, potatoes and salad. Or try the traditional bandeja paisa. If your wallet is feeling a bit slimmer than that, opt for the comida corriente, offered at lunch and dinner. The only alcohol served by Mi Casita is beer. Daily 8 a.m.–8 p.m. Ca. 9, 6-18. Tel: 773-2754. Updated: Feb 14, 2011.

AROUND IPIALES
SANTUARIO NUESTRA SEÑORA DE LAS LAJAS

One day in 1750 (more or less), María Mueses de Quiñónez was walking from Potosí to Ipiales. Upon her back she carried her young,

SOUTHERN COLOMBIA

deaf-mute daughter Rosa. They decided to rest at Pastarán cave on the banks of the Río Guáitra. When doña María awoke from a nap, she discovered her daughter had wandered off. Upon finding her, Rosa said, "Mamacita, the Mestiza called to me!" She pointed to an image of a woman holding a child and of two men.

Thus begins the story of Santuario Nuestra Señora de las Lajas. A small adobe chapel was built to protect the image of the Virgin in the shallow cave, forming the "altar screen" of the temple. Over the centuries it expanded to the impressive neo-Gothic structure that now spans the Guáitra River. Many Colombians and Ecuadorians make the pilgrimage to this site, beseeching the Virgin Mary for her intercession. The cliff walls are covered with thousands of plaques thanking her for miracles (the Vatican only recognizes one).

Pack a picnic lunch and come spend the day strolling the network of paths that interlace over the grounds. Take a bath in the healing pools at the foot of the waterfall. There's even a playground. The on-site museum ($1.75) has exhibits on the Sanctuary's history and on the Pasto indigenous. On the way back, stop off in El Charco for roasted cuy, a regional specialty.

To get there, colectivo taxis leave Ipiales from Carrera 6 and Calle 6 ($2.25) and from the bus terminal ($1.25). Up the hill, in Las Lajas village, are several hotels, from basic to grand ($3–10 per person, per night), or you can stay at the Casa Pastoral ($4 per night; Tel: 775-4463). The Santuario is crowded at Easter (Semana Santa) and for the Virgen de las Lajas feast days during the first two weeks of September. Las Lajas village, eight kilometers (5 mi) from Ipiales. Tel: 775-4462, E-mail: laslajas08@yahoo.es. Updated: Aug 30, 2011.

PIEDRA DE LOS MONOS

While at Santuario Nuestra Señora de las Lajas, take a hike down to what was certainly a holy site for the previous inhabitants of this region: Piedra de los Monos. Following a well-signed path from the Catholic sanctuary, along the Río Guáitra, you will arrive at these petroglyphs, or rock paintings. In crimson, white and shades of purple, the Pasto people decorated this rock overhang with zoo- and anthropomorphic figures, and their signature sun symbol. The entire "canvas" measures six meters (20 ft) by four meters (13 ft). The age of these creations is not known. Above, on the rim of this gorge, we can witness the

ceremonies of the valley's modern inhabitants. But here, we can only speculate what types of rites the Pasto performed in some past. Located three kilometers (1.8 mi) from Santuario Nuestra Señora de las Lajas. Take public transport to Lajas village (see Santuario Nuestra Señora de las Lajas). Updated: Aug 30, 2011.

CUMBAL

In this small indigenous village on the altiplano, the Sunday market trading is still going strong. Stalls display fruits from highlands and low, or ponchos from local workshops.

Doña Yolanda stops stirring the helado de paila for a moment to serve clients a portion. The copper bowl bedded in ice from Volcán Cumbal appears dull beneath today's clouded sun. On one corner of the Plaza del Mercado, some folks are already loading up on a chiva to return to their pueblos.

Cumbal is the place to be on a Sunday. Other days it's just a quiet village. But it's worth a stay in one of the basic hotels, to set your plans for visiting those two snow-capped volcanoes that you see towering over the hamlet early most mornings. To climb Volcán Cumbal (4,780 m/15,863 ft), ask the locals to accompany them on their daily harvests of ice and sulfur. From the top you'll see the snowy peaks of Ecuador to the south, and to the west, a vast emerald jungle expanse to the Pacific Ocean glittering on that distant horizon.

To summit Volcán Chiles (4,600 m/15, 092 ft), go to the village of the same name on the volcano's slopes. There you may be able to find someone to guide you. It should take about six hours to reach the apex, which lies on the Colombia-Ecuador border. Inquire, also, about the nearby hot springs. Aguas Hediondas, on the southern slopes within Ecuador, are literally boiling sulfurous waters set on a barren páramo plain where condors soar.

Cumbal is 59 kilometers (39 mi) southwest of Ipiales. Collective taxis leave daily for Cumbal, when full, from the Ipiales bus terminal, 5 a.m.-5 p.m. The last vehicle leaves for Ipiales at 4:30 p.m. from the mercado plaza. (1 hr, $2.70 one way). Transport to Chiles leaves from Cumbal. Updated: Feb 21, 2011.

!!!!!

SOUTHERN COLOMBIA

Llanos and Selva

The Llanos (eastern plains) and Selva (jungle) constitute over half of Colombia's territory. Steeped in the history of the Spaniards' lust-driven quest for El Dorado, the region's wilderness succeeded in keeping most of them out, except for the most hardy.

The Llanos, also known as the Región Orinoquia, encompasses the Colombian departments of Meta (capital, Villavicencio), Casanare (Yopal), Arauca (Arauca), Vichada (Puerto Carreño) and Guainía (Puerto Inírida). This area makes up part of the Orinoco River basin and borders Venezuela. The Selva, or the Región Amazonía, is also made up of five departments: Putumayo (capital, Mocoa), Caquetá (Florencia), Guaviare (San José de Guaviare), Vaupés (Mitú) and Amazonas (Leticia). The most famous of these is Amazonas, where Leticia is the crossroads of the Colombian Amazon River basin, with connections to Peru and Brazil.

Roads weave through the Llanos, connecting it with Bogotá and other cities on the western side of the Cordillera Oriental. River travel also exists, and one ageless dream of travelers is to journey down the Río Orinoco into Venezuela. In the Selva, where one goes is dictated by transportation. In most of the region, there are no roads, except for those radiating out from Leticia and one connecting Puerto Asís and other Putumayo towns with population centers in Southern Colombia. Otherwise, travel is exclusively by boat on the many rivers lacing through the jungle.

The mystique of the Llanos and Selva remains today. It is yet an unfathomable region—not only because of the lush vegetation that blankets it, but also because it is the very center of Colombia's civil war. It was here where "Farclandia" existed, a demilitarized zone under guerrilla FARC control at the turn of the millennium. It is also where the heaviest fighting continues to occur as the Colombian military recovers the territory bit by bit. Some places, though, are fine to visit now, such as Villavicencio and Puerto López in the Llanos, Leticia with its neighboring villages, and the Putumayo towns of Sibundoy and Mocoa. Other areas are once more coming within scope of the travelers' route. Keep informed and your ear to the ground to find out where we might next be able to explore this region. Updated: Mar 17, 2011.

Highlights

Visit the **Sibundoy** (p. 529) in the Putumayo, an indigenous community famed for its mask carvings.

Stop by **Leticia** (p. 530), where any Amazon journey begins—whether into the jungle, to Parque Nacional Amacayacu, or floating on the great river's muddy water to Peru or Brazil.

Watch the pink dolphins leap in from the silver waters of **Lago Tarapoto** (p. 543) near Puerto Nariño.

Admire the sunrises and sunsets over the **Llanos**, while observing a myriad of birds and fauna like anaconda, caiman, babilla and chigüiros.

Go whitewater rafting on the **Río Ariari**, **Río Guatiquía** and other rivers slicing through the eastern plains.

Dip into the Caño Cristales in **Parque Nacional Natural La Macarena** (p. 522).

History

After Francisco de Orellana blazed a trail to the Amazon River in 1542, many mid-16th- century conquistadores, like Diego de Orduz, passed through the jungles and plains on their quests for El Dorado. This opened the way for the Catholic missionary orders—the Franciscans, Capuchins, Jesuits and Augustinians—to establish settlements throughout the region. At the time of the Spaniards' arrival, the Llanos were inhabited by independent indigenous villages of the Arawak language group, such as the Guahibos and Sálivas. Their inhabitants were displaced by the Spaniards and forced to live in those Catholic missions. The same happened to the Selva indigenous nations along the Napo, Caquetá, Putumayo and Amazon Rivers.

A great disaster for the indigenous of the jungle came with the rubber boom of the late 19th century. Large swaths of the rainforest were destroyed and slavery was legalized. The Huitoto population, once the Amazon's largest nation, decreased by over 60 percent. La Casa Arana, a major rubber company, is believed to have killed some 50,000 indigenous workers through horrid working conditions, whippings and killings.

Threats to the environment and indigenous peoples continued into the 20th century. With the advent of motorized transportation in the 1930s, roads were built from highland cities like Pasto and Bogotá into the Llanos and Selva. The resulting migration pushed roads further and further into the jungle, not only for new settlers, but also for the extraction of valuable hardwoods and gold reserves. In the 1980s, deep reaches of the jungle became home to vast plantations of marijuana and coca, and to mega-cocaine labs. Tranquilandia—one of the largest with 14 labs, electricity, roads and airfield—processed 3,500 kilograms (7,700 lb) of pure cocaine every month.

Problems continued for the region into the next decade, with the players of Colombia's civil war moving into the relative haven of the Llanos and Selva jungles. A 42,000-square-kilometer (162,163 sq mi) demilitarized zone was established by peace accords between Colombian President Andrés Pastrana and the FARC guerrillas in 1999. Farclandia, as it was nicknamed, covered much of Caquetá and Putumayo Departments, with San Vicente del Caguán as the capital. Pastrana rescinded the deal in 2002, due to the FARC's continued kidnappings and other practices.

Glossary of Rodeo Terms

While in the Llanos region, take the opportunity to go to the rodeo—or, in local parlance, to *el coleo*. To help you with the *llanero* (from the Llanos) terminology for the familiar rodeo phrases, here are some of the major events:

Carrera a Caballo—Horse Racing: one-on-one and competitions of riders on the fastest horse.

Enlazada del Becerro—Calf Roping: Each two-person team has to pursue a calf once it is let loose out of the chute, ride it down, lasso it and tie its feet together in the shortest time possible.

Herrada del Becerro—Calf Branding: Each team, on foot, chases down the calf, lassos it and ties its feet together, then brands the calf in the shortest time possible.

Monta del Potro Cerrero—Bareback Bronco Riding: The participant has to ride an unbroken (untamed) horse without saddle or bridle for the longest period of time.

Ordeño de la Vaca Mañosa—Milking the Ornery Cow: This test, done on foot, consists of wrangling a rascally cow and milking her in the shortest time possible.

Monta del Potro Matrero—Bull Riding: Considered the most dangerous of rodeo events; the winner must ride a bull bareback for at least eight seconds.

Coleo Criollo—Calf Scramble: Practiced the traditional way, barefoot contestants have to pull the tail of a yearling and knock it down.

Llanerazo—Big Llano Event: The hexathlon, so to speak, of the rodeo world. The winner must demonstrate proficiency in the six events listed above (save cow milking), as well as in traditional llanero dancing and musical performance.

With a new president, Álvaro Uribe, coming into power in 2002, FARC strongholds in the Llanos and Selva were systematically attacked. Current President Juan Manuel Santos, who was elected in 2010, continues to prioritize resolving issues with the FARC in this area. Updated: Feb 18, 2011.

Safety

The security situation in the Llanos and Selva can be summed up in two words: War Zone. This is where the FARC and other factions of the Colombian civil war have their strongholds, and where the heaviest fighting between them and the Colombian military is presently taking place.

In the Llanos, the major cities are OK. Avoid traveling off the main roadways. Always ask local advice about the safety of any place further down the road you may want to travel to. Expect many military checkpoints; have your documents at hand. River travel is said to be secure now because of heavy military patrols on the principal waterways. However, the roads to the river ports may not be yet secure.

Likewise, the Selva rivers are reported to be heavily patrolled. The Leticia area is safe, as are the roads to Sibundoy and Mocoa. Around Puerto Asís is considered problematic at this time. Residents on both sides of the Colombia-Ecuador border continue to report fighting. Puerto Leguízamo and Parque Nacional Natural La Paya, located further downstream, are both still off-limits.

In terms of more mundane hazards, malaria and yellow fever are common in both the Selva and the Llanos. Take proper measures against mosquito bites and take malaria medication. A yellow fever vaccination is essential. Both regions are home to spiders, snakes and scorpions. Shake your clothing and shoes before putting them on. Be aware of where you put your hand in the wild, and don't lift logs or rocks. Don't swim in rivers and lakes in early morning or late afternoon, or if you have wounds or are bleeding. This is when piranha and other fish are feeding. Take care near waterways at night, for caimans can be a dangerous threat. Updated: Jul 27, 2011.

Things to See and Do

The biggest draw of the Llanos and Selva is the opportunity to observe wildlife. Caimans, capybaras (the largest rodent in the world), tití leoncitos (the planet's smallest primate), anacondas, boas and pink dolphins are just a few of the intriguing creatures inhabiting these forests and rivers. Birdwatchers are in paradise, with macaws, Harpy Eagles, ibis, hummingbirds, caracaras, Golden Eagles, and almost a thousand other species of avifauna.

Indigenous villages can be visited to learn about their culture and to purchase artisan work. In Leticia and Puerto Nariño, there are annual festivals celebrating the native culture. The Llanos have a mestizo culture distinct from other parts of Colombia. Here, Joropo dance and music reigns, with international competitions twice yearly. Another big feature on these plains of vast cattle ranches is the *coleo*, or rodeo. Be sure to catch one if you can. The Llanos also offers premier rafting and rock climbing. Updated: Jul 27, 2011.

Tours

At present, most excursions into the Llanos and Selva are arranged through companies based in Bogotá, mostly for the convenience. But these trips are often much more expensive than arranging them with locally based companies. In Leticia, there are many tour agencies offering trips into the jungle and to lodges. Slowly, as the Llanos region becomes more secure, tour operators are opening shop in Villavicencio, providing whitewater rafting and rock climbing excursions, as well as expeditions to Parque Nacional Natural Sierra de la Macarena. Some activities can be done on your own. Nonetheless, because of environmental and security (war) considerations, it is highly advisable to go with a guide, preferably one from the area who knows the situation more in-depth. Updated: Jul 27, 2011.

Lodging

Lodging in the Llanos and Selva tends to be more expensive than in other Colombian regions, a consideration for budget travelers. In the selva, tent camping is not possible due to snakes. A hammock could come in handy, especially in smaller villages. Cheaper inns have common baths and fans. Rooms at mid- and upper-range hostels have private baths. Most hostels have room temperature showers. Only the most expensive hotels have hot water. Air conditioning is a choice in either modest or luxury inns.

These two regions have accommodation alternatives distinct from other parts of Colombia. In the Llanos, there are *hoteles campestres* (upscale country inns complete with swimming pools and horseback riding) and dude ranches. Near Leticia, down in the jungle, there are several jungle lodges. Updated: Jul 27, 2011.

VILLAVICENCIO

465m   384,000   8

At the end of day, the sun paints a mango sky over the flat lands of the llanos, or eastern plains of Colombia. As dusk falls, the birds and wildlife silhouette against the now-indigo heaven. The water of a pond splashes with the retreat of a babilla. How do you enter this world of the llanos that few travelers ever visit? The gateway is Villavicencio, just on the other side of the Cordillera Oriental, two hours from Bogotá.

The highway from the nation's capital to Villavicencio is quite an exhilarating experience in and of itself. The 86-kilometer (52-mi) superhighway climbs out of Bogotá to an altitude of over 3,100 meters (10,168 ft). It then plunges down over 50 bridges and through five tunnels to Villavicencio at 467 meters (1,532 ft) altitude—a descent of almost 2,600 meters (8,530 ft). Túnel de Boquerón, the second tunnel, is 2.4 kilometers (1.5 mi) long, and the last one, Túnel de Buenavista, is over 4.5 kilometers (2.7 mi) long.

Once arriving in Villavicencio, you have entered what *villavos* (residents of Villavicencio) call the Territorio de Paz, or Territory of Peace. On the banks of the Río Guatiquía, the city is the most important cultural and commercial center of the Colombian llanos. Villavicencio is a town of simple pleasures and complex history. Many of the men wear traditional llanero clothing: a poncho folded over one shoulder, hat and boots. You have come to Colombia's version of the wild west, right down to the rodeos. Updated: Mar 18, 2011.

History

Villavicencio was on one of the principal routes for Spaniards on the El Dorado quest. The city was founded on April 6, 1840, by Antonio Vil

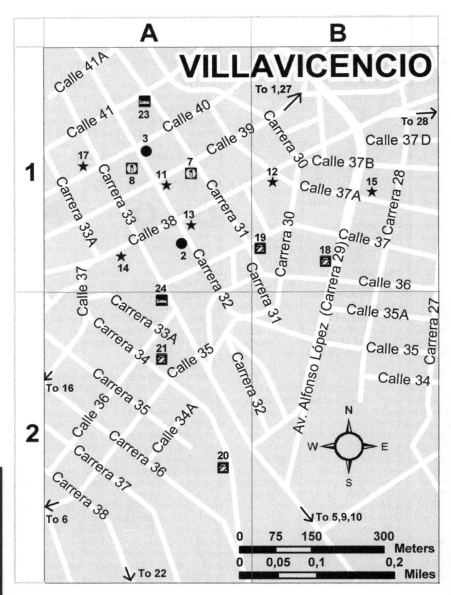

lavicencio y Verastegui. The original settlement was the farmland of Guamalote, which was on a major cattle train route from the plains to Bogotá. It was part of the Estado de Cundinamarca until 1868, when the Territorio de San Martín de los Llanos was established with Villavicencio as the capital. In 1909, the name of the territory was changed to Meta, and in 1959, its status was upgraded to a department. In the latter part of the 20th century and into the new millennium, the town suffered occupations by civil war factions, including paramilitaries. Updated: Jul 04, 2008.

When to Go

You will probably encounter a shower or two anytime you wander to Villavicencio.

● **Activities**

1 Bioparque Los Ocarros A1
2 Banco de la República A1
3 Casa de la Cultura Jorge
  Eliecer Gaitán A1
4 Museo Eduardo Carranza (See 3)
5 Parque de los Fundadores B2

▥ **Eating**

6 Asadero Hato Grande A2
7 El Samán del Parque A1
8 Restaurante Govindas A1

▤ **Nightlife**

9 El Botlón B2
10 El Pentagrama del Llanero B2

★ **Services**

11 Adpostal A1
12 Banco Popular B1
13 BBVA A1
14 Cosmonet A1
15 Hospital Regional de Villavicencio B1
16 Hospital San Antonio A2
17 Instituto de Turismo del Meta A1

▧ **Shopping**

18 Almacén de Discos El Joropo B1
19 Centro Comercial Centauros B1
20 Chinchorroz Saidez A2
21 El Gran Llanerazo A2

▬ **Sleeping**

22 Hotel del Llano A2
23 Hotel Savoy A1
24 Hotel Tabary A2

◆ **Tours**

25 Llanos Travel (See 22)
26 Vergel Aventura Servicios
   Turísticos (See 22)

▦ **Transportation**

27 Aeropuerto Vanguardia A1
28 Jeeps to Restepo B1

The town has 220 days of rain per year, with an annual precipitation of 4,085 millimeters (161 in). The temperature rises as high as 35°C (95°F), and evenings can be as cool as 19°C (66°F). Relative humidity is on average a muggy 78 percent.

Villavicencio is still off the vacation list of most Colombians. Nonetheless, you will still find that some of the country inns charge more during holiday times. Updated: Mar 14, 2011.

HOLIDAYS AND FESTIVALS
Toward the end of March is the annual Concurso Mundial de la Mujer Vaquera, or the International Women's Rodeo (URL: www.mujervaquera.com). Participants come from Colombia, Chile, Brazil, Mexico, Guatemala, Panama, Costa Rica, the U.S. and other countries. A second rodeo event, Encuentro Mundial de Coleo (URL: www.mundialcoleo.com.co), is held October 14-17. The famed Jaropo music festival happens twice a year, from June through July and in December.

Of the religious observances, check out Villavicencio's Easter Week—observed from Palm Sunday to Easter Sunday with processions and a sacred music concert series—or the Novenas de Aguinaldos, from December 16-24. The feast days of the patron saint, Nuestra Señora del Carmen, are held in July. Updated: Mar 18, 2011.

Getting To and Away
Anything from rains to earthquakes can cause landslides on the road from Bogotá to Villavicencio. To check conditions, visit www.coviandes.com. The highway has 103 SOS call boxes and three tollbooths.

BY BUS
The **bus terminal** (Tel: 671-2222, URL: www.terminalvillavicencio.gov.co) is approximately seven kilometers (4 mi) from downtown, on the Anillo Vial, midway between Calle 35 and Carrera 22. It is easily accessible by buseta. It has the usual services, like snack stands and rest rooms, as well as a tourist information booth in front.

LLANOS AND SELVA

Collective pickups and jeeps for Restrepo and other points leave from Calle 37E and Carrera 28.

Buses to Bogotá (2-3 hr, $11) leave with the company **Bolivariano** (Tel: 665-5562/5526) every 15 minutes between 3:25 a.m. and 8:20 p.m., and less frequently before and after these times. The last bus departs at 10:15 p.m.

Transport to Puerto López (1.5 hr, $5) and Puerto Gaitán (3.5 hr, $13) is available 24 hours a day, leaving each hour. Granada (1.5 hr, $5) is serviced by a few different companies, with buses departing every 20 minutes throughout the day and night.

Additionally, there are bus services to Yopal, Arauca, Tame, Puerto Carreño and San José de Guaviare.

BY AIR

Aeropuerto Vanguardia is approximately four kilometers (2.4 mi) from the city, off the road to Restrepo (a right turn at the Monumental de las Harpas). **Villavicencio Aires** (Cra 39, 29c-15, Centro Comercial Llanocentro, 1st floor. Tel: 668-8098, URL: www.aires.aero/aires/Villavicencio.aspx) has daily flights to Bogotá, and **Satena** (Cra. 31, 39-27, 2nd floor. Tel: 662-1260) flies to Bogotá, Puerto Inírida and Puerto Carreño. Updated: Aug 03, 2011.

Getting Around

The **Instituto de Turismo del Meta** (URL: www.turismometa.gov.co) has a list of the official prices for taxis. City busetas also go to points throughout town and many pass near Parque del Hacha or one block down on Carrera 29 ($0.65). Updated: Aug 03, 2011.

Safety

For travelers with their own car or on bike, be aware that the highway from Bogotá has a very steep, downhill grade. Villavicencio is relatively safe during daylight hours. Parque de los Fundadores is OK on weekends, but consider it off-limits during times when no one is around and after dark. Updated: Jul 04, 2010.

Services

TOURISM

Instituto de Turismo del Meta has excellent information on the attractions in Meta Department (Monday-Friday 8-11:30 a.m. and 2-5:30 p.m. Cra. 33, 40-20, Edificio Comité de Ganaderos. Tel: 661-4444, URL: www.

turismometa.gov.co). Better maps of the city and region, however, can be obtained at the Punto de Información Turística in Parque El Hacha (Monday-Friday 7:30 a.m.-6 p.m., Saturday and Sunday 8 a.m.-6 p.m. Cra. 32, between Ca. 35 and 36).

Other offices of importance are: **DAS** (Ca. 37, 42-34. Tel: 672-5188) and **Instituto Geográfico Agustín Codazzi** (Cra. 33a, 37-14, office 401. Tel: 662-6967).

MONEY

Many of Villavicencio's banks are on Calle 38, including: **BBVA** (Ca. 38, 31-74) and **Banco Popular** (Ca. 38, near Cra. 30a), which both have ATMs; and **Bancolombia** (Monday-Friday 8 a.m.-4:30 p.m. Ca. 38, 32-27), which changes American Express traveler's checks in addition to having an ATM.

The city has a quantity of casas de cambio, most located in the **Centro Comercial Centauros** (Cra. 31, 37-32). One is **EuroDivisas** (daily 8 a.m.-1 p.m. and 2-7 p.m. Local 79, 2nd level. Tel: 662-8361). This mall is also where you will find **Western Union/Giros y Finanzas** (Monday-Friday 8 a.m.-noon and 2-5 p.m., Saturday 8:30 a.m.1 p.m. Locals 64-65).

KEEPING IN TOUCH

Villavicencio has a **Telecom** office (Ca. 37, 42-12), but the city has many other local and national call services as well. The post office, **4-72** (Monday-Friday 8 a.m.-noon and 2-6 p.m., Saturday 8 a.m.-noon) is located at Calle 39, 32-02. Internet is somewhat common, with cyber cafés mostly located on Calle 38 past the main plaza; most charge $0.80 per hour. **Cosmonet** (Ca. 38, 33-62) has international calls beginning at $0.30 per minute, as well as broad band Internet. Skype is scarce.

MEDICAL

The principal healthcare provider in Villavicencio is the **Hospital Regional de Villavicencio** (Ca. 37A, 28-53, Tel: 670-5032, E-mail: hospital@hospitalvillavicencio.gov.co). Others serving the needs of villavos are **Hospital San Antonio** (Cra. 42 and Ca. 33) and **Hospital San Luis** (Ca. 35 and Cra. 44D). Pharmacies are especially concentrated on Calle 38, between Carreras 30 and 32.

SHOPPING

El Gran Llanerazo

El Gran Llanerazo has a tremendous selection of crafts from the Meta and Casanare departments. The most predominant items are *cotizas* (sandals) made of cow or pig leather or embroidered jute. For a different fashion statement, try on the ones made of *babilla*, or spectacled caiman (farm-raised, of course, since it is illegal to hunt them in the wild). There is also a wide assortment of leather belts, hats, key chains, sculptures, and products made from wood and horn. Closed on Sunday. Cra. 34, 35-60. Tel: 667-4038. Updated: Jul 04, 2008.

Almacén de Discos El Joropo

The Llanos of Colombia and Venezuela are renowned for their music and dance, both called joropo. Almacén de Discos El Joropo has everything you need to enjoy or perform this musical genre, including recordings, sheet music, instruments and accessories. Even award-winners of the annual Festival de Joropo shop here. The store can put you directly in touch with workshops that make traditional joropo musical instruments, including harps and guitars. Monday-Saturday 9 a.m.-1 p.m. and 2:30-7 p.m., Sunday 9 a.m.-noon. Cra. 29, 36-30. Tel: 671-5134, Cel: 311-475-9413. Updated: Mar 28, 2011.

Chinchorros Saidez

The *chinchorro* is the most comfortable piece of furniture in the Llanos. These broad hammocks are woven as a close-mesh net. Cool on a sultry day and large enough to cocoon yourself in on a chilly night, it is the most perfect hammock you could imagine. Cinchorros Saidez has a fine selection, with a simple single costing $53 and a more elaborately worked one for $125. Doubles (for two people) begin at $140. If you would like to snuggle down with the entire family, family-sized chinchorros are also available. Special orders take one week. Monday-Friday 8 a.m-6 p.m., Saturday 8 a.m.-1 p.m., closed Sunday. ASMEVILL (Asociación de Microempresarios de Villavicencio) market, Ca. 33B, 34-10. Tel: 672-7905, Cel: 312-314-7326/314-392-4807. Updated: Mar 28, 2011.

Things to See and Do

While the greatest attractions lie in the surrouding plains, Villavicencio does have a few things to occupy your time. The Casa de la Cultura Jorge Eliécer Gaitán hosts international film festivals from time to time and the **Banco de la República** (Cra. 32, 37-67) features concerts and exhibits. You can also check out the **Museo Eduardo Carraza** (Cra. 32 and Ca. 40. Tel: 671-4947/662-6327, Cel: 310-286-5945). There are also many parks scattered around the city, as

Festival Nacional de Joropo

The quintessential expression of life on the Llanos is the Joropo, both a musical genre and a dance form. The music is played on a harp, *bandola* (similar to the mandolin) and *cuatro* (a small, four-string guitar), with a continuous beat kept up by maracas. The songs' couplets speak of love, life, loss and adventures. During the dance, women's full skirts swirl as men stomp to the rhythm. The music is a mix of the people who populate the Llanos: indigenous, European and African.

Every year, contestants arrive from all over Colombia and Venezuela for the Festival Nacional de Joropo, which started in 1960. For a week, which spans from the end of June to the beginning of July, Villavicencio's streets fill up with competitions in musical performance, dance and poetry. There are also beauty pageants and horse shows, arts and crafts exhibits, and a gastronomic fair.

well as statues saluting the Llano culture and way of life. An especially spectacular one is Monumento a las Arpas, which has three gigantic harps (10 m/33 ft high by 7 m/23 ft wide), each with 32 strings of water. It is located two kilometers along the Ruta del Piedemonte, at the turnoff for the airport.

Several tourist routes extend out of Villavicencio. Along these routes are quaint villages, hot springs and other glimpses of the Llanos. You can go horseback riding, hiking, birdwatching, whitewater rafting and take wildlife tours along the way. Updated: Jul 04, 2008.

Parque de los Fundadores

(ADMISSION: free) On Saturday and Sunday afternoons, local families hang out at the Parque Los Fundadores, on the south side of Villavicencio. The masterpiece of the park is the Monumento a los Fundadores, which is the last work executed by renowned Colombian sculptor Rodrigo Arenas Betancourt. In the center of the park is a fountain with lights playing off its cascades. Between are several small plazas where you can catch street theater or comedy, enjoy a fresh juice, have your photo taken on a horse or buy artisanal work. If the excitement wears you out, stretch out on the expanses of grass and relax. The park is not considered safe after dark; it is best to

LLANOS AND SELVA

go when villavos go: over the weekend. To get to Parque Los Fundadores, catch a bus that says "Porfía" from the corner of Parque del Hacha of Carrera 32 and Calle 35a, near the fire station. Vía Puerto López, past Unicentro Llano and Carrefour. Updated: Mar 28, 2011.

Bioparque Los Ocarros !

(ADMISSION: $4.40 adults, $3.20 children under 6 years old) Following the zoo trend of creating natural spaces for its resident animals, Bioparque Los Ocarros teaches about the creatures of the Orinoco River Basin. Spread throughout 5.7 hectares (14 ac), it houses 181 species, ranging from land and waterfowl to the majestic jaguar, from inquisitive monkeys to the fearsome caiman and its laid-back cousin, the babilla. Discover the fish of these rivers on Aquarium Island and the many snakes on Serpetarium Isle. All the animals on exhibit have been rescued from traffickers or are donations from people who had them as pets.

Signs give excellent explanations about the ecological importance, status and habitat of each animal (in Spanish), but provide the taxonomic and common English names for the species. You can also hire a guide (Spanish only) for $5.30. Bioparque Los Ocarros also is a research center and clinic. The park is wheelchair accessible. The animals take a siesta come early afternoon, during the hottest part of the day. If you want to see the animals up and about, visit in the morning or late afternoon.

From Calle 37e and Carrera 28, catch a collective jeep heading toward Restrepo and tell the driver to drop you off at Bioparque Los Ocarros ($1.30). The road that goes to the entrance of the park is marked by a sign on the other side of the highway. It is three kilometers (1.8 mi) north of Villavicencio, Ruta del Piedemonte Llanero. Monday-Thursday 9 a.m.-4 p.m., Friday-Sunday 9 a.m.-5 p.m. Tel: 670-9094, Fax: 664-8490, URL: www.corpometa.com/index.php?option=com_content&task=view&id=1&Itemid=2. Updated: Mar 28, 2011.

Tours

At present, only a few tourist agencies operate in Villavicencio. As safety improves, don't be surprised to see even more operators jumping into the field, since the attractions—especially whitewater rafting and rock climbing—will undoubtedly make it one of the hottest places to visit in Colombia. Already you can enjoy some of them, or excursion out into the plains to see its unique wildlife and magnificent sunsets. Updated: Jul 04, 2008.

Vergel Aventura Servicios Turísticos del Llano

Vergel Aventura can take you on whitewater rafting adventures, riding the Class III rapids of Río Ariari in Parque Nacional Natural Sumapaz or on the Río Guatiquía. The trip also involves crossing the river on cable car, a hike through the jungle and swimming in the crystalline pools of two waterfalls ($60-63 per person, including lunch, snacks, guides and transport; $31-57 per person without transport). You can also combine a rafting excursion with canopy, rappelling, paragliding or horseback riding. This company has a three-day/two-night package to Caño Cristales in Parque Nacional Natural La Macarena (2-5 people; $1,130 per person, all inclusive with flight; cheaper with more people). Hotel del Llano, Cra. 30, 49-77. Tel: 682-5353, Cel: 311-281-9328/300-264-3760. E-mail: reservas@vergelaventura.com, URL: www.vergelaventura.com. Updated: Jul 28, 2011.

Llanos Travel

Llanos Travel has a full plate to offer its clients. Hop onto the one-day tours along the tourist Rutas Embrujadas (as far as Granada), Llanera (as far as Puerto López) or Piedemonte (to Restrepo). It costs $55-90, including guide, transportation and lunch. Llanos Travel can also take you to the prime attractions in town, like Parque Las Malocas or Bioparque Los Ocarros. If you can round up 25 people, hire its bus (complete with a music group) to take you around the city. Hotel del Llano, Cra. 30, 49-77. Tel: 671-3278/3245/664-1120, Cel: 325-327-7824. Updated: Mar 28, 2011.

Lodging

The lodging scene in Villavicencio is a bit unusual in comparison to other Colombian cities. It has scores of luxury hotels, but comes up a bit short on mid-range choices. Those hostels that are in the budget category also double as pay-by-the-hour joints. Outside the city, there are many country-club style inns, with bungalows, restaurants and swimming pools. Many of these hotels also have horse stables. Updated: Jul 22, 2010.

Hotel Tabary

(ROOMS: $8-14) Hotel Tabary is probably the best of the cheaper accommodations in Villavicencio. The rooms, for the most

LLANOS AND SELVA

part, are large. The ones in front have plate glass windows overlooking the street. All come with cable TV and private bath—efficiency style, one could call them, with the shower pipe over the stool. The rooms are spic-and-span, due to their daily cleaning and fresh towels. The friendly family is very knowledgeable about what to see and do and how to get around the city. Cra. 33, 36-61. Tel: 672-0529. Updated: Jul 4, 2008.

Hotel Savoy

(ROOMS: $28-46) The Hotel Savoy is a popular place with business travelers looking for a finer hotel at a comfortable price. The large lobby is beyond the reception area, which creates a sense of exclusivity. The clean and modestly decorated guest rooms are medium in size, with cable TV and private bathroom. Hotel Savoy's restaurant serves a vegetarian set lunch ($4, Monday-Saturday noon-2 p.m.), though come early as it often sells out. Ca. 41, 31-02. Tel: 662-2666/2667/5007. Updated: Mar 28, 2011.

Hotel del Llano

(ROOMS: $100-245) Hotel del Llano has for years been considered one of the finest and most respected luxury inns of Villavicencio. Its rooms are spacious, with comfortable beds, private baths, cable TVs and other luxury amenities. The back patio has an Olympic-size swimming pool, as well as a splash area for children. Cra. 30, 49-77. Tel: 671-7000, Cel: 310-773-9130, E-mail: reservas@hoteldelllano.com, URL: www.hoteldelllano.com. Updated: Jul 28, 2011.

Restaurants

Prices tend to be a bit higher in Villavicencio than in other parts of Colombia. The city market is along Calle 37a, between the Ley supermarket and Carrera 26, and sprawls into the side streets. Pick up groceries at the **Ley supermarket** (Monday-Saturday 9 a.m.-8 p.m., Sunday 9 a.m.-6 p.m. Ca. 37b, 29-83).

While in Villavicencio, be sure to try the most typical llanero food—*carne a la vara*, or seasoned meat roasted on an upright spit. Some restaurants are permitted to serve farm-raised capybaras. One recommended place is **Asadero y Restaurante El Cabrestero** (Anillo Vial, across the 7a Brigada military base). Updated: Mar 28, 2011.

El Saman del Parque

For any meal of the day, drop by El Saman del Parque, just a few doors down from Villavicencio's cathedral. This small café is often full with locals stopping by for a coffee prepared with panela. A popular quick snack is the *arepa de choclo con queso* (ground sweet corn and cheese), which is prepared in the beehive oven at the door and served on a banana leaf. Breakfasts are served with eggs as you wish, bread, juice and coffee. For lunch, there's a plate special, and snack foods, beer and *tragos* (coctails) are available in the evenings. Live music entertains the house Monday-Saturday. Daily 7 a.m.-10 p.m., Fridays and Saturdays until 11 p.m. Ca. 39, 32-76. Cel: 312-522-1746. Updated: Mar 28, 2011.

Asadero Hato Grande ♪

(ENTREES: $5.80 and up) Meat-and-potato lovers can get their fill of their favorite dish, Colombian style, at Asadero Hato Grande. This place serves authentic beef from the plains, cooked on an upright spit over a wood fire. The plate overflows with meat, potatoes and yuca ($5.80). For those travelers on a budget, order the plate special, which comes with roasted meat, beans, rice, pasta and salad ($2.65, with soup). The restaurant also cooks up *sancocho de gallina* (a typical chicken stew with plantains, yucca and corn) and has tamales on the weekends. To get there from downtown, Catch the "Ceiba" buseta in front of the fire station near Parque El Hacha. Daily 6 a.m.-10 p.m. Ca. 35, 17-07. Tel: 666-5317. Updated: Jul 04, 2008.

Restaurante Govindas

(LUNCH: $2.50) Like Govindas restaurants all over Colombia, this dining hall offers only vegetarian fare. This one, though, is bare of any plants or other decorations. Only a few posters of Krishna bless the patrons. The set-plate lunch, too, is presented simply. The shop sells whole grain baked goods. Govindas also offers yoga and meditation classes and therapeutic massages. Lunch is Monday-Friday noon-2 p.m. If you'd like something from the bakery, just ring the bell. Cra. 32, 39-42. Tel: 662-2557, Cel: 311-888-3370. Updated: Jul 04, 2008.

Nightlife

Nightlife is hot only on weekends and holidays, and clubs usually open at 6:30 p.m., though the scene doesn't get going until after 9 p.m. To catch some live llanero music, some recommended clubs are **El Botlón** (on the highway toward Puerto López) and **El Pentagrama del Llanero** (in the Unicentro mall on Av. Puerto López). Restaurants on the outskirts of town often have live bands on the weekends. Updated: Mar 18, 2011.

LLANOS AND SELVA

AROUND VILLAVICENCIO

Three scenic routes span out from Villavicencio: Ruta Piedemonte Llanero, Ruta del Almanecer Llanero and Ruta del Embrujo Llanero. You can get to places along these routes independently, with public transport or by booking a tour through an agency in Villavicencio. Security is confirmed to certain points on each of the highways; if you would like to go past these points, be sure to check the current situation locally. On the way, you'll pass a number of rural hotels where you can spend the night, and many of the villages have lodging as well. Updated: Jul 28, 2011.

Ruta Piedemonte Llanero

Ruta Piedemonte Llanero follows the eastern edge of the Cordillera Oriental. On one side, the mountains scrape the sky, and on the other, the endlessly flat land merges with the heavens. The route passes through Bioparque Los Ocarros and Centro-Cultural Etnoturístico El Maguare of the Uitoto indigenous. Restrepo (Km 16) has an interesting church; nearby are the salt flats of Salinas de Upín (3 km/1.8 mi away) and natural pools in the Río Caney. Cumaral (Km 23) has the best rodeo ring in the department. Other attractions include Río Guacavia and Lagos de Samacanda. Some 70 kilometers (42 mi) on are two hot springs spas: Termales Aguas Calientes and Termales de Guaicaramo.

If traveling in your own vehicle, follow Highway 65 northeast out of Villavicencio. For public transportation, hop on a collective pick-up from Calle 37e and Carrera 28 in Villavicencio. Highway 65 continues to Barrancas de Upia, at the border of Casanare department, and Yopal, the capital of that department. From there, other roads connect to towns in Boyacá and other departments. The road is said to be safe as far as Restrepo and possibly as far as Cumaral. Updated: Mar 28, 2011.

Ruta del Amanecer Llanero

Sunsets and sunrises blaze over these eastern plains. The Ruta del Amanecer goes deep into the flatlands, teeming with cattle farms and wildlife. Upon leaving Villavicencio, you will pass the Monument to the Fallen Combatant before passing the military base and oil installations at Apiay. Merecure, Latin America's largest agro-ecological park, is at Kilometer 47, and has lodging, camping, fishing and a zoo. The highway continues to Puerto López, near the geographical center of the nation. All along the way

are agro- or eco-tourist country inn, and there are hotels in Puerto López. Highway 40 continues to Puerto Gaitán on the Río Manacacías, which has white sand beaches where you can practice aquatic sports.

If in your own vehicle, follow Highway 40 east out of Villavicencio. Using public transport, there are buses for Puerto López and other points that leave from the bus terminal. The road is said to be safe as far as Puerto López. Updated: Mar 28, 2011.

Ruta del Embrujo Llanero

The Route of Llanero Enchantment begins its southward journey on Highway 65 from Villavicencio. The first town of note, Acacias (Km 22), is the tourism capital of the Meta Department and has a *malecón* (riverwalk). In mid-October, Acacias celebrates a llanero music festival. Guamal (Km 41) is a vacation spot on the shores of Río Humadea. The road cuts through plains, marshes and African palm plantations, over which herons swoop. At Kilometer 67 is San Martín, the region's oldest city and the heart of the cattle-raising and rodeo district. Mid-November is the International Llano Folklore and Equestrian Ballet Festival in San Martín.

The journey is declared safe as far as Granada, on the Río Ariari. Beyond Granada, you are entering the zone of conflict. Do not travel to towns off the main highway or go walking into the countryside, as there are land mines. Further on are Fuente de Oro, San Juan de Arama (where there is a waterfall and the Termales de Santo Domingo hot springs), Lejanias, Mestas, Vista Hermosa, La Uribe and La Macarena. La Macarena, the village entry point to Parque Nacional Natural Sierra de la Macarena.

If traveling in your own vehicle, follow Highway 65 south out of Villavicencio. Collective pick-ups and jeeps for towns along the route depart from Calle 37e and Carrera 28. Updated: Mar 28, 2011.

PARQUE NACIONAL NATURAL SIERRA DE LA MACARENA!

Those few travelers who ever make it to Parque Nacional Natural Sierra de la Macarena describe crystal-imbedded rock outcroppings from the Cenozoic Era that glitter in the Llano sun. The mountain range is 150 kilometers (90 mi) long and 35 kilometers (21 mi) wide, and gives birth to the Duda,

Further into the Llanos

Further into the Eastern Llanos lie two of Colombia's most unique and hard-to-reach attractions, which are both accessible from Villavicencio: Las Gaviotas and PNN El Tuparro.

Las Gaviotas: Las Gaviotas is a small, self-sufficient ecovillage of 200 people in the Colombian department of Vichara in the Llanos region. Founded by Paolo Lugari in 1971, the community is an award-winning model of environmental sustainability, recognized by the United Nations. Las Gaviotas practices organic farming, uses solar and wind power, and leads a communal lifestyle with shared resources.

About a decade after its establishment, community members started planting Caribbean pine trees in this desolate and otherwise inhospitable environment. Since then, those few trees have expanded into 8,000 hectares (20,000 ac) of forest, altering the the area's climate for the better. The pine's resin, which can be converted to biofuel and made into products for sale, has also become the village's greatest economic venture.

This community of farmers, scientists, engineers and artists has also invented some ecological innovations over the decades, including specialized hand pumps and wine turbines, self-cooling rooftops, and pedal-powered grinders. For more information on Las Gaviotas, visit www.friendsofgaviotas.org/.

Parque Nacional Natural El Tuparro: PNN El Tuparro (Admission: $18 foreigners, $6.25 nationals, $4 children 5-12 years old) is located deep in Colombia's eastern llanos, in the Vichara department, close to the Venezuelan border. This 548,000-hectare (1.4 million-ac) park, which was declared a National Monument and Biosphere Reserve Core Zone in 1982, is made up of green savannah punctuated by rivers, beaches and forests, and surrounded by enormous crystalline rocks. It is home to hundreds of species of birds, as well as monkeys, giant otters, pumas, river dolphins and five primate species.

One of El Tuparro's biggest attractions is the Raudal de Maipures, a six-kilometer (3.7 mi) stretch of unnavigable river current at the confluence of the Tuparro and Orinoco Rivers, where there are waterfalls and rocks covered in venomous coral snakes. El Tuparro's other major draw is its indigenous influence. The park contains an ancient indigenous cemetery of the disappeared Maipures tribe, which is etched with pictographs. Two indigenous Sikuani settlements are located in front of the park's visitor's center, and numerous ruins are scattered throughout the park. Approximately 10,000 members of various native tribes still live on reservations in the area surrounding El Tuparro, and one group, called Guahibos, still reside within the park.

Although it is possible to visit the park independently, it is highly recommended to come with a registered tour operator. One recommended operator is **De Una Colombia** (URL: www.deunacolombia.com), which offers various customizable packages to El Tuparro. Either way, visitors must make a reservation with the National Parks office in Bogotá (Cra. 10, 20-30, 1st floor, Tel: 353-2400, ext 138-139, E-mail: ecoturismo@parquesnacionales.gov.co) prior to arrival. It is possible to spend the night in the park, either in one of the four wooden cabins (capacity for 12 people) or in the small camping area (capacity for 4 tents). Most tour operators arrange accommodation, food and transportation, though.

El Tuparro is not easy to get to, and road access is only possible during the dry season (December-February). The land route from Villavicencio to the park's administrative center takes a brutal 25 hours. Alternatively, you can fly from Bogotá to Puerto Carreño (3 hr, 40 min; 4 flights per week with Satena), then take a boat down the Orinoco River to Puerto Ayacucho, Venezuela. El Tuparro also has two landing strips, and it is possible to fly directly into the park from Puerto Carreño. If you are planning on heading onward to Venezuela, or will take the river route, make sure to get your visa in Bogotá or Puerto Carreño first.

LLANOS AND SELVA

Guayabero, Losada and Güéjar rivers. The only part of the park presently accessible is Caño Cristales, a series of pools and waterfalls. From April to June, its rocks are matted with green algae, then from June to November, those carpets turn a brilliant purple.

The park is still only accessible by air. Although some overland routes do exist, park officials advise against arriving by land because the road passes through the red zone. You can take a plane from Bogotá to Villavicencio (30 min) and then another plane from Villavicencio to La Macarena (1 hr). Additionally, some travel agents in Villavicencio arrange fly-in tours complete with lodging to the one corner of the national park, which is said to be safe.

The Sierra de la Macarena is in the red zone of Colombia's civil war fighting, and the area is largely controlled by the FARC. Trekking and climbing in the park alone is not recommended due to the probability of land mines and other dangers. Go only with an organized tour or guide, who can safely lead you through the park. Guides typically charge $20-25 per day. Most hikes to Caño Cristales last two or three days. Also, check with the national park office in Bogotá about current conditions.

The delicate algae that grows at Caños Cristales is a protected species, so be careful not to disturb it. Do not take any rocks or plants home as a souvenir, and don't leave any trash behind. Stay on the paths and follow your guide's instructions. Updated: Mar 28, 2011.

PUERTO LÓPEZ

 178m   17,000   8

From Villavicencio, traverse the Ruta del Amanecer Llanero due east 78 kilometers (47 mi) and you willarrive at Puerto López. This is Meta Department's principal port on the broad Río Meta. From Alto de Menegua, you can see the plains spreading to all horizons, intertwining with the river. Near the city are Laguna Mozambique and El Ombligo de Colombia (the Bellybutton of Colombia)—the geographical center of the country. One of the most important celebrations here is the Festival de las Colonia, which takes place December 26-30. Various hotels of different classes, including country inns as well as camping, await the tired traveler. Updated: Jul 04, 2008.

Getting To and Away

Buses leave from Villavicencio to Macarena, Arimena and Autollanos hourly from 7 a.m. to 7 p.m. All companies charge $5.30 and take 1.5 hours. One reputable company is Bolivariano.

Puerto López is a principal port on the Río Meta, which flows into the Río Orinoco. With patience, it is possible to catch a boat downstream. Plus, the rivers are said to be heavily patrolled by the Colombian military. Updated: Jul 04, 2008.

FLORENCIA

 266m   151,400   8

Another city where a taste of the jungle may be savored is Florencia, capital of Caquetá Department. Florencia is located on the eastern side of the Cordillera Oriental, just where the mountains tumble down to lush tropical forests. Many Colombians call this city one of the most beautiful in the country. Florencia is a young city, founded only in 1902.

Facing its palm-studded plaza is Catedral Nuestra Señora de Lourdes. Another noteable building is the Roman-villa-styled Palacio de Artes, also called Edificio Curiplaya, where the tourism office is (Tel: 434-7785, E-mail: seculturismo@florencia-caqueta.gov.co, URL: www.florencia-caqueta.gov.co). Also in the center of town is **Museo Caquetá** (Ca. 14, 12-24. Tel: 435-1547, E-mail: wilches_gob@hotmail.com, URL: www.museocaqueta.com), highlighting the region's history and art. Just a kilometer (0.6 mi) from town are the ancient Petroglifos El Encanto rock paintings. Other Florencia attractions include the **Jardín Botánico de la Amazonía** (at the antiguas instalaciones del IDEMA. Tel: 313-376-9441).

Three tourism routes start from Florencia. Within the first 20 kilometers (12 mi) of Florencia, the Ruta a Morelia houses several crystalline-clear swimming holes, like Quebradas El Dedo, La Yuca, La Mochilera and Río Zarabando. Ruta El Caraño, heading north toward Neiva, is also studded with swimming holes and country-style restaurants. There is a jungle hiking path at El Manatial. Misión Nueva Jerusalén, a Gregorian mission, has a museum and a historical trail. Ruta Venecia heads to Puerto Arango, where boat rides may be taken on the Río Orteguaza. Rappelling and birdwatching are other outdoor activities that can be enjoyed.

LLANOS AND SELVA

Florencia has a complete slate of services. There are inexpensive hotels in the center of the city, and several ranches offering lodging are located in the surrounding countryside. Big celebrations in Florencia include the Festival Folklórico de la Amazonía (June) and the Festival Nacional de Música Andina y Campesina (November). Updated: Mar 25, 2011.

Getting To And Away

Florencia is easily accessed by bus from Neiva, Mocoa, Bogotá and other cities. **Satena** (URL: www.satena.gov.co) and **Aires** (URL: www.aires.aero) airlines provide flights to Bogotá, by way of Neiva. Updated: Mar 17, 2011.

MOCOA

 590m   45,600 8

Where the Cordillera Oriental plunges into the Amazon forest is Mocoa. This Putumayo Department capital tucked in an emerald-green landscape is a pleasant stopover for travelers roaming from San Agustín to Pasto, or to take the backdoor crossing into Ecuador. For those who cannot afford to fly down to Leticia, Mocoa also affords a taste of Colombia's jungle. Mass tourism has yet to arrive here.

The focal point of Mocoa is Plaza Santander. Here you'll find Catedral San Miguel with columns gleaming beautiful gold and silver inlays. The city has a multi-ethnic flavor. Over half of the population has migrated from other parts of Colombia, drawn by mining and petroleum exploration. Indigenous nations include the Kafán and Inga.

Many rivers flow through Mocoa, draping the countryside with clear-watered swimming holes and waterfalls. The most spectacular cascade is Fin del Mundo, plunging into the green jungle far below. Hiking into the jungle reveals the region's rich natural beauty and birdlife. Mocoa is also home to many *taitas* (shamans) who can open the door into other worlds. Updated: Mar 03, 2011.

History

San Miguel de Agreda de Mocoa was founded September 29, 1563, by Spanish Captain Gonzalo de Avendaño. Administered by Popayán Province, it was to serve as a base camp for the search for El Dorado. Over the next few centuries, the indigenous Andaquíes nation attacked the settlement several times, burning it to the ground. Mocoa grew into a major commercial center during the latter part of the 19th century. It has been the capital of Putumayo since 1958. During the 1990s and into the 21st century, Mocoa and the Putumayo region was a guerrilla hotbed. In recent years, the Colombian military has waged a concerted effort to clear the region out, making it once more safe to visit Mocoa. Updated: Mar 03, 2011.

When to Go

Mocoa has a humid, tropical climate. Year-round temperatures average 26-28°C (79-82°F). The dry season is September-January, and the rainy season is April-August.

Like other towns in Southern Colombia, Mocoa celebrates Carnaval de Negros y Blancos on January 5 and 6. Carnaval de los Rojos, which highlights indigenous traditions, is celebrated on January 7 in Puerto Limón. The city's birthday party, Fiestas Patronales de Mocoa, is in October. Updated: Mar 03, 2011.

Safety

Mocoa and the roads leading to it are safe; they are heavily patrolled by the Colombian military. Always carry identification, as road patrols are common. Expect extensive baggage searches as well. The civil war's red zone still exists in the Putumayo's deep reaches. Travel toward the Ecuadorian border only during daylight hours. Tap water in Mocoa is not potable; boil or treat it before drinking it. Dengue and other mosquito-borne diseases are present. Mar 03, 2011.

Getting To and Away

BY BUS

Mocoa's bus terminal is two blocks downhill from the main plaza (Ca. 11a, between Cra. 4 and 5). It's an open-air affair, with stands, eateries, bathrooms and baggage keep. Most transport is pick-up trucks, jeeps or minivans.

To Puerto Asís: frequent, during daylight hours; 2 hr, $11.

To San Miguel: 5 hr, $18–TransDorada (hourly), Cootransmayo. If you will be crossing the border, make sure the vehicle is going to the Puente Internacional. Or else go to La Hormiga ($15) and catch another vehicle to the international bridge. TransGuamez goes to **La Hormiga** (9 departures 5 a.m.-11:30 a.m.); the 6:15 a.m. And 11:30 a.m. Services go as far as the Puente Internacional.

To Florencia: 5 hr, $22-24–Cootransmayo (4 departures 8 a.m.-1 p.m.).

To Pitalito: frequent pick-ups; 2.5-3 hr, $8-10. Also, Bogotá-bound buses pass through Pitalito; transfer there for San Agustín.

To Bogotá: most buses leave 3:30 p.m.-8 p.m., 12 hours, $33-35 – Coomotor (2 buses; also 9 a.m., noon), Bolivariano (1 bus), Transipiales (2 buses), Cootranshuila (3 buses; also 1 p.m.), Cootransmayo (4 buses; also 7:30 a.m., 3:30 p.m.). Buses pass through Pitalito and Neiva.

To Pasto: 7 daily, 5 hr–Cootransmayo ($17-20) and Transipilaes ($13).

Coomotor also has services to Ibagué, Honda, Medellín, Armenia and Pereira. Cootransmayo heads to Popayán and Cali. Updated: Mar 03, 2011.

BY AIR
The nearest airport to Mocoa is in Puerto Asís. **Satena** (URL: www.satena.com) has flights to Bogotá, Cali and Puerto Leguizamo.

Border Crossing: San Miguel to Lago Agrio
It is also possible to cross from Colombia into Ecuador through the Putumayo, across the international bridge at San Miguel and on to Lago Agrio, Ecuador. Several foreign travelers report it is now safer and easy to do this route. Take a bus from Mocoa to the Puente Internacional (International Bridge) at San Miguel (5 hr, $18). DAS (Colombian immigration) is just before the bridge. After completing procedures, cross the bridge into Ecuador and catch transport to Lago Agrio to complete Ecuadorian immigration paperwork (45 min, $1).

Begin the trip early in the day, to ensure reaching Mocoa or Lago Agrio in daylight hours. If you need to spend a night on the Colombian side of the border, La Hormiga is said to be better. The situation around San Miguel is still a bit touchy.

Be sure to check into present conditions before starting out on this route, as the Civil War's Red Zone lurks in the not-too-distant jungle. Updated: Feb 11, 2011.

Getting Around
Two city bus routes connect downtown with the market, bus terminal and other points ($0.65). Negotiate taxi fares beforehand; it should cost about $1.70 to points within the city and $2.80 to Vereda Caliyaco. Pick-up trucks to outlying neighborhoods depart from Carrera 6 and Calle 9 ($0.60-1.20). **Ciclomocoa** (Ca. 9, near Cra. 8) has bicycle parts and a repair shop. Updated: Mar 03, 2011.

Services
Most businesses are closed noon-2 p.m. and on Sunday.

TOURISM
Mocoa has no tourism office. Information on community artisans, tour operators and other services may be obtained from **Corpoamazonía** (Corporación para el Desarrollo Sostenible del Sur de la Amazonía) (Monday-Friday 8 a.m.-noon and 2-6 p.m. Cra. 17, 14-85, 2nd floor. Tel: 429-6641, E-mail: carama_de-telecom.com.co, URL: www.corpoamazonia.gov.co). Another good source of information is Felipe of **Hostal Casa del Río** (Vereda Caliyaco, Vía Mocoa-Villagrazón. Tel: 420-4004, Cel: 314-5050, E-mail: casadelriomocoa@gmail.com, URL: www.casadelriomocoa.com). Updated: Mar 10, 2011.

MONEY
Banco Popular (Ca. 8, near Cra. 8) and **BBVA** (Cra. 5, half-block west of Ca. 8) both have ATMs, but no money exchange facilities. No official casas de cambio operate in Mocoa. A few local businesses on Calle 9 change U.S. dollars at poor rates: **Compra Venta Joyería El Dorado** (7-22), **Licores El Ranchito** (7-32) and **Distribuciones Mercacentro** (between Cra. 6 and 7; has best rates). No one exchanges traveler's checks. Updated: Mar 03, 2011.

KEEPING IN TOUCH
The **post office** (Monday-Friday 8 a.m.-noon and 2-5:45 p.m., Saturday 9 a.m.-1 p.m. Ca. 7, 4-25) is the place to send a letter. Half a block away is Telefónica Telecom with national and international phone service, and the cheapest Internet in town. **Llamenet** (Ca. 8, across from the plaza) also has phone and Internet services, and doesn't close at lunch. Updated: Mar 03, 2011.

MEDICAL
Mocoa's public health facility is **Hospital José María Hernández** (Ca. 14, 4 blocks north of Av. Colombia. Tel: 429-6056, Email: hjmh@esehospitalmocoa.gov.co, URL: www.esehospitalmocoa.gov.co). Pharmacies are common throughout downtown. **Farma Sana** (Cra. 6, 8-22. Cel: 311-233-4237) is open 24 hours. Updated: Mar 03, 2011.

The Elixir of the Gods

One of the most sacred medicinal herbs for Amazonian indigenous nations is *yagé*, also called ayahuasca (Banisteriopsis caapi). This hallucinogen opens the doors to other worlds, allowing users to reach deep into themselves and deep into the Spiritual World.

Yagé should only be used for spiritual purposes: to help one find answers and guidance in life. It is not a recreational drug. One's purpose must be clear. The drink is brewed from yagé, chagropanga (Diplopteris cabrerana) and other plants. It needs careful preparation–not only physically, but also spiritually–by a trained *taita* (shaman). Those taking yagé must also prepare themselves. For eight days before the ceremony, they must follow a special diet, eating no fatty meats (preferably only fish); the day before, only fruits and vegetables should be consumed. During this period, they must also refrain from sexual activities. The yagé ceremony is accompanied by sacred music and dance.

On the physical plane, the plant is a strong purgative and toxic. It causes nausea, vomiting, unsteadiness and other symptoms. People with physical conditions, such as urinary tract problems, should probably avoid using yagé. Medications can also cause adverse reactions.

Yagé ceremonies have become a big "tourist attraction." Traditional taitas are concerned about charlatans presenting these "excursions," thus posing physical, psychological and/or spiritual risks to participants. V!VA Travel Guides does not promote such tourism and counsels travelers to exercise caution and respect for this indigenous tradition. Updated: Mar 03, 2011.

SHOPPING

Tive Semamba

At Tive Semamba (Manos Trabajadores), Efigenia Yoge and her *comadres* (close friends) craft jewelry and other items from materials gathered from the surrounding jungles. Seeds, like *frijolillo*, *hsahe* and *achirilla*, are strung together into necklaces and bracelets. Natural fibers *cumare* and *palmiche* are woven into durable bags, skirts and broad "collar" necklaces. *Macana* and *chonta* woods are carved into decorative spears. The women use traditional designs in all their creations. Cel: 310-411-3171, E-mail: tivesemamba@yahoo.com. Updated: Mar 03, 2011.

Things to See and Do

Mocoa offers many opportunities for travelers to savor the Amazon jungle. You can hike around the Centro Experimental Amazónico, in the Serranía de Churmbelo, or to cascades like Hornoyaco and Salto del Indio. The many rivers form cool pools and spectacular waterfalls, including Balneario Caliyaco, just south of town, and Fin del Mundo, from where Mocoa can be seen on the distant horizon. To check out the city from a different vantage point, you can climb La Loma hill. Several hours to the north is Resguardo El Yungillo, an indigenous village. Updated: Mar 03, 2011.

Centro Experimental Amazónico

(ADMISSION: free) Centro Experimental Amazónico (CEA) is a research station with horticulture, fish tanks with *pirarucú* (the Amazon's largest fish) and animal rescue projects (sometimes CEA takes volunteers). Its three trails wend through the jungle. To the main pond's left are Senderos El Yagé and El Trueno, which braid together through the dense green punctuated by flashes of brilliantly colored, calling birds. These paths lead to a meeting house built on an island in a lagoon and the botanical garden. Another path, departing from the right side of the main pond, climbs high up the hill to a lookout post and back down, uniting with the other trails (4 km/2.4 mi, medium-difficult). Allow three to four hours to hike all three paths. From Calle 9 and Carrera 6, catch a Villagarzón-bound pick-up ($1.20) and get off at the large CEA sign. A taxi costs about $5.50. Walking there takes about 1.25 hours. Daily 9 a.m.-3 p.m. Km 8, Vía Mocoa-Villagarzón, Vereda San Carlos. Updated: Mar 11, 2011.

LLANOS AND SELVA

Reserva Natural Fin del Mundo !

(ADMISSION: $1.10 adults, $0.65 children) Some may believe the Fin del Mundo (End of the World) exists at the very tip of South America. But in the north of the continent, in Colombia's Putumayo, is another place where the world seemingly ends. A beautiful waterfall plunges 80 meters (262 ft) into the jungle. An hour's walk through the forest leads to the first pool where you can swim, Pozo de los Dantas, at the foot of a small cascade. The river continues meandering, forming numerous small waterfalls and swimming holes edged by rough sand beaches.

Visitors must leave the falls area before 4 p.m. Nature reserve owners hire horses ($6 one way), do guided hikes ($12) and offer camping ($3.50-5 per person). Take a Villagarzón-bound pick-up ($1.20) from Calle 9 and Carrera 6 and get off at the large Fin del Mundo sign. A taxi costs about $5. Walking there takes about one hour. From the highway, follow the painted rocks to the entry (10 min). The hike uphill to Fin del Mundo takes about 1.5 hours. Daily 7 a.m.-5 p.m. 6 km (3.6 mi) South of Mocoa, Vía Puerto Asís (Villagarzón), Vereda San José del Pepino. Cel: 312-362-3892. E-mail: centroecoturisticofindelmundo@hotmail.com. Updated: Mar 18, 2011.

Tours

Most tour operators in Mocoa are community-based outfits focused on eco-tourism. **Ecoturayah** (Vereda San Carlos, Vía Mocoa-Villagarzón. Cel: 312-561-0631/573-6205, E-mail: ecoturayah@hotmail.com, URL: www.ecoturismoputumayo.com) provides guides for hiking in the surrounding forest and at CEA. This organization also offers canyoning in Reserva Natural Wasiyaco and spelunking in Caverna Refugio Ime as well as cultural and shamanic tours. Ecoturayah has bilingual (Spanish/English) services. **Yapay** (Cel: 320-706-4136, E-mail: ricordiaz@hotmail.com) offers not only hiking with certified guides, but also adventures like rappelling in waterfalls, mountain biking, caving and rafting. This agency also explores the indigenous shamanic worlds. Updated: Mar 03, 2011.

Lodging

Lodging in Mocoa is a fairly simple affair. Few hotels have hot water or air conditioning. A number of basic residencias are near the bus terminal. Several places on the outskirts of town have campsites.

On the road south to Villagarzón are **Fin del Mundo** ($3.50-5 per person. 6 km/3.6 mi south of Mocoa, Vía Puerto Asís/Villagarzón, Vereda San José del Pepino. Cel: 312-362-3892, E-mail: centroecoturisticofindelmundo@hotmail.com) and **Ecoturayah** (10 km/6 mi south, Vereda San Carlos. Cel: 312-573-6205, E-mail: ecoturayah@hotmail.com, URL: www.ecoturismoenputumayo.com). Updated: Mar 17, 2011.

Hotel Central

(ROOMS: $6-16) Hotel Central is a family-oriented, walk-up hostel a half-block from Mocoa's main square. For decades, the owners having been greeting travelers passing through this corner of the Putumayo jungle. They offer simple rooms: some accommodations are small and windowless; others are larger with exterior windows. The best are on the upper story. Be sure to ask to see several rooms before deciding. Cheaper rooms share clean common baths. More expensive ones have private bath and television. Ca. 8, 6-18. Tel: 429-5141. Updated: Mar 17, 2011.

Hostal Casa del Río !

(BEDS:$9, ROOMS: $18-23) Casa del Río, which opened its doors in 2010, is right on the Rumiyaco River at the Caliyaco swimming spot. Caliyaco is one of the most popular swimming areas in Mocoa, so guests have the priviledge of having it at their toes. The hostel has six double rooms and two four-bed dorms; each room has its own bathroom and some have their own TVs. Its hammocks, open-air showers, big garden with a variety of plants and flowers, and main communal area with a self-catering kitchen are all perks. A TV room and free WiFi are the icing on the cake. Vereda Caliyaco, Vía Mocoa-Villagarzón. Tel: 420-4004, E-mail: casadelriomocoa@gmail.com, URL: www.casadelriomocoa.com. Updated: Mar 03, 2011.

Hotel Inga Real

(ROOMS: $28-39) On the corner of Plaza Santander is Hotel Inga Real, one of Mocoa's more upscale hotels. A fantastic mural created with different tropical woods is at the foot of the stairs leading up to the reception. Hotel Inga Real offers clean, good-sized rooms with cable TV. All accommodations have private bath with glass-doored, hot-water showers. Some rooms have exterior windows, and others have interior ones. Guests may dine at the cafetería-bar downstairs (an advantage, as breakfast is not included in the room rates). Ca. 8, 6-50, Edificio La Carreta, 2nd floor. Tel: 429-6616. Updated: Mar 17, 2011.

Restaurants

Like lodging, eating in Mocoa is pretty basic. Most restaurants offer standard Colombian fare, though a few pseudo-international options are served. Local specialties include smoked meats and *cachama*, a type of river fish. *Tacacho mocoano* is green plantain mashed with gravy and pork cracklings. Street vendors sell *chantaduros*, a palm fruit steamed over a wood fire.

Several local grocery stores are along Carrera 6, between Calles 8 and 9. The public market is two blocks downhill from the main square, next to the bus terminal. Updated: Mar 17, 2011.

Restaurante Al Humo 🍴

(ENTREES $4.50-7) Many years ago *abuelita* (grandma) Guillermina wowed the region with her smoked meats. Several generations later, the family is continuing the tradition with Restaurante Al Humo. This small eatery built of bamboo serves up Grandma's recipes for smoked pork ribs, chops, chicken and cachama fish. All dishes are served with tacacho mocoano, yucca and salad. The heaping portions are presented on black-burnished pottery. Sausages and kabobs are also on the menu. Indecisive diners can choose a sampling plate with a variety of meats. Monday-Saturday noon-11 p.m., Sunday 5-10 p.m. Ca. 9, 16-20 (Av. Colombia, Km 00). Cel: 313-871-3093, E-mail: alhumo6900@hotmail.com. Updated: Mar 17, 2011.

Restaurante China Hong Kong Huang

(ENTREES: $6-18) In a small interior patio bedecked with red lanterns, across from Plaza Santander, is Mocoa's local Chinese restaurant. Its menu is composed of chow mein, chop suey and fried rice prepared with beef, chicken or pork. National favorites like *arroz con pollo* (rice with chicken) also make the menu. The ample Chinese dishes may be ordered in full, half or quarter portions. Ca. 8, 7-42. Cel: 320-214-7303. Updated: Mar 17, 2011.

Restaurante Casa Real

(ENTREES: $8-12) In Restaurant Casa Real, the lunchtime atmosphere is bustling. Waitresses swiftly move from table to table, serving plates of the daily special ($3.50) to hungry customers. This diner is often busy from breakfast to dinner. Restaurante Casa Real not only prepares down-home meals, it also presents light snacks like empanadas and *pan de bono* (a small bread made of corn meal, yucca and cheese), and such Colombian classics as bandeja paisa.

Monday-Friday 7 a.m.-8:30 p.m., Saturday 8 a.m.-8:30 p.m. Ca. 7, 6-20. Tel: 429-5610. Updated: Mar 17, 2011.

SIBUNDOY

 2000m   13,540   8

Heading from Pasto eastward, the highway passes through Laguna de la Cocha and then enters the Putumayo and continues to that department's capital, Mocoa, before turning north toward Pitalito, near San Agustín. The road is a virtual rollercoaster through the mountains until it reaches the Valley of Sibundoy, a largely indigenous area with roots deep in the Nudo de los Pastos (the Knot of the Pastos), which unravel into the Cordillera Oriental and Occidental. From here, multitudes of streams flow eastward to join the Putumayo and Amazon Rivers are born.

The village existed long before the Spaniards' first visit in 1534. Inca Huayna Cápac had conquered the local population in 1492 and established a Quechua-speaking settlement here. These settlers were the ancestors of the modern-day Ingas. The population is still largely indigenous and wears long blue and violet ponchos.

Every year in February, the Return of the First People Carnaval (Klestrinyé) is held, which includes traditional music and dance. Sibundoy is renowned for its artisan work, especially mask carving. **Rescate Kamentsa** (Ca. 18, 12-13, Barrio Oriente. Cel: 310-523-4747, E-mail: analuciamuchavisoy@yahoo.es) is one Kamsá artisan cooperative creating masks, musical instruments, and woven and beaded articles. Sibundoy's principal park is full of fallen tree trunks carved with symbols and the mythology of the Inga and Kamsá nations.

Several basic hostels provide lodging. **Villa Beatriz** (Cel: 311-754-0110/460-5903, E-mail: agmajaba@yahoo.com) has two eco-tourism inns and camping. **La Orquídea** (Vereda La Cumbre. Cel: 312-857-2154, E-mail: cmedinasuarez@yahoo.es) offers cabañas and camping, as well as tour guide services.

At the beginning of this millennium, people could only travel as far as Sibundoy, 80 kilometers (48 mi) west of Mocoa. Now the entire Pitalito-Pasto circuit can be done safely. The war zone has been pushed deep into the Putumayo jungle. Updated: Feb 23, 2011.

Getting To and Away

Sibundoy is accessible by public transportation from Pasto (several companies with daily departures; 3 hr, $6) and from Pitalito by way of Mocoa (10 hr, $14). Updated: Feb 23, 2011.

LETICIA

 95m   37,000   8

Welcome to the last outpost of Colombia, on the far southeastern corner of the country. Leticia forms part of the triple frontier, along with Tabatinga, Brazil, and Santa Rosa, Peru. Twenty-five kilometers (15 mi) downstream is Benjamin Constant, a major Brazilian port on the river and an alternative point for taking a boat on the Amazon to Manaus. Leticia is where some travelers first step foot in Colombia. Others say their last goodbye here before taking a boat upstream to Iquitos, Peru, or downstream to Brazil.

Although it is the most developed of the three border cities, Leticia is still a small town. Everything is within walking distance. Parque Santander is the hub of social life. During dawn and dusk, the trees are a riot of *pericos* (small green parrots). In this park, the Victoria Regia Amazonica pool has the largest water lilies in the world. Nearby are two wonderful sculptures: Alegoria Cómica del Amazona by Aida Orrego and another of leaping pink dolphins. Upon arriving in Leticia, you have to pay an entry tax of $9 and show your international yellow fever vaccination certificate. Updated: Aug 03, 2011.

History

The history of Leticia includes many legends. One legend goes back to the Spanish and Portuguese exploration of the Río Amazonas. When Begnino Bustamante established San Antonio in 1867 on orders of the Peruvian government (to prevent Colombia from staking a claim on the river), he called it San Antonio, after a cross inscribed with this name was found at the site where a Portuguese explorer and his expedition had starved to death.

Peru and Colombia had a number of confrontations in the region, intensifying in 1911 until the Salomón-Lozano Treaty of 1922, giving Colombia access to the Amazon River and at which time the town's name was changed to Leticia. Why Leticia? Perhaps not for Santa Leticia, as one would think. Another tale says it was named for the indigenous woman a Colombian soldier had fallen in love with.

In 1933, 300 armed Peruvians invaded Leticia, proclaiming it part of that nation once more. Another bilateral agreement was signed in 1934, creating a demilitarized zone around Leticia, unhindered navigation on the Amazon and Putumayo Rivers, and a pledge of non-aggression on the part of both countries. To ensure Leticia would remain loyal to Colombia, the federal government populated the town with *bogotanos* (people from Bogotá). In the 1960s and '70s, Leticia's economy boomed thanks to the drug trade. Once the drug cartel was brought down, Leticia fell into onto hard times, relying heavily on tourism. Updated: Jul 28, 2011.

When to Go

Leticia has two distinct seasons. The dry season lasts from June to September. The rainy season begins in October with rainfall gradually increasing, being heaviest from January to May. Temperatures are fairly constant throughout the year, with days reaching 31-32°C (87-90°F) and nights falling to 21-22°C (70-72°F). The Amazon flows heaviest in May and lowest in September, with a 15-meter (49-ft) difference between the two stages.

Weekends are fairly busy, with shoppers coming in from Colombian, Peruvian and Brazilian river settlements. You might have a hard time finding a hotel room at this time. Updated: Jul 28, 2011.

HOLIDAYS AND FESTIVALS

The big event on Leticia's calendar is the Festival Internacional de la Confraternidad Amazónica, which is celebrated every year on July 15-20. Participants come from Colombia, Peru and Brazil for this tri-country fair that includes cultural and sporting activities. Other holidays observed in Leticia are: Leticia's founding on April 25; Fiestas de San Pedro in July; Festival Internacional de Música Popular Amazonense El Pirarucú de Oro, a celebration of music and dance from the Amazon region, in November; and the Parade of Año Viejo on December 31. Updated: Jul 29, 2011.

Getting To and Away

Leticia is accessible by river and air. The only road that exists is a dry-weather track to Tarapacá (with public transport only as far as Km 18) and to Tabatinga.

BY BOAT

Leticia's port is at the end of Calle 8. The street is quite muddy in the rainy season. From the three floating docks, catch a launch to villages along the Amazon and its tributaries. Two types of boats work these routes. There's the fast boat with an enclosed passenger compartment and the *peque-peque,* an open canoe with a long-shafted outboard motor. In the past, it was cheaper to take a boat from Puerto Asís to Leticia, but this route now goes right through the war zone, where there is heavy fighting and bombing occasionally reported.

For boats to Santa Rosa, Peru, or Tabatinga, Brazil, go directly to the docks. There are launches that leave every 15 to 20 minutes between 6 a.m. and 8 p.m. Both trips cost $1.30 each way.

Ask around the docks for information about slow-boat peque-peques to the different villages. Peque-peques to Puerto Nariño ($11.50, about 6 hr) leave two times a week.

Several agencies at the end of Calle 8 sell tickets for fast boats to Parque Nacional Natural Amacayacu ($12.50), Mocagua ($13.50) and Puerto Nariño ($14). It is recommended to buy your passage the day before.

For information on international boats to Manaus, Brazil, and Iquitos, Peru, see "Colombia-Brazil-Peru Border Crossings".

BY AIR

Leticia's Aeropuerto Internacional Vásquez Cobo is 1.5 kilometers (1 mi) from downtown. Avenida Vásquez Cobo in front of the airport becomes Carrera 10. **Copa Airlines Colombia** (URL: www.copaair.com), which now owns AeroRepública, flies to Bogotá daily (about $120-175 one way, including taxes). **Aires** (URL: www.aires.aero) and **Satena** (URL: www.satena.com) also have flights to Bogotá ($97-135 each way, including taxes). The Aires flights leave daily at 2 p.m. Flights are cheaper on some days rather than on others. Shop around and check the companies' websites. Updated: Aug 03, 2011.

Getting Around

Busetas leave from Parque Orellana to the villages and the Lagos (5:45 a.m.-6:20 p.m., $0.60-2.25), and to Tabatinga and the Tikuna village Maria Azzu (6 a.m.-6:20 p.m., $1-1.30). Mototaxis, with you riding on back,

charge $0.60 around town and $1.30 to the Policía Federal post in Tabatinga. Taxis cost $2-3.25, depending on the distance.

Renting a motor scooter is a different way to get around. Many shops along Calle 11, Avenida Internacional and Carrera 10 rent motorcycles. The going price is about $3.25 per hour, $18.50 for a half day and $25 for 24 hours. Updated: Aug 03, 2011.

Safety

It is pretty safe within the town of Leticia, though residents advise against walking toward the airport, the river or the border after 10 p.m. It's recommended that visitors stay in the immediate downtown area. In terms of the civil war, people will tell you "it's a whole jungle away."

As in any place in the tropics, mosquito-borne diseases are a concern. Get the yellow fever vaccine at least 10 days before arriving. The tri-border region undergoes a fairly rigorous spraying program to control Aedes and Anopheles denizens. Nonetheless, take proper precautions against mosquito bites, especially if venturing into less-populated areas.

If going swimming, avoid the hours near sunrise and sunset (when piranha and other fish are feeding), the dry season (when water is shallow), or if you have an open or bleeding wound. Updated: May 09, 2009.

Services

TOURISM

Leticia's tourism office, **Secretaría de Medio Ambiente y Desarrolo Productivo** (Monday-Friday 7 a.m.-noon and 2-5 p.m. Ca. 9, 10-86. Tel: 592-5944, URL: www.leticia-amazonas.gov.co), has city maps in English or Spanish as well as information about things to see and do. The **Departamento de Fomento Ecoturístico (D.A.F.E.)** (Monday-Friday 8 a.m.-noon and 2-5 p.m. Ca. 8, 9-75. Tel: 592-7569, E-mail: fondoprom_amazonas@yahoo.es, URL: www.fondodepromocionamazonas.com) has good pamphlets about ecotourism in Leticia and other parts of Colombia. Other important offices include:

Parque Nacional Natural—Buy your Amacayacu ticket here, or apply to volunteer at one of the region's national parks (students, professionals or those with national park experience). Monday-Friday 8 a.m.-noon and 2-5 p.m. Cra. 9, 6-100, 2nd floor. Tel: 592-7124.

Instituto Geográfico Agustín Codazzi— Monday-Friday 7:30-11:30 a.m. and 2-4 p.m. Cra. 11, 9-14.

DAS (Colombian immigration)—The office in town only handles extensions (Monday-Friday 7:30 a.m.-noon and 2-6 p.m. Ca. 9, 9-62. Tel: 592-4877/4878). For entry or exit stamps, go to the office at the airport (Monday-Friday 7:30 a.m.-noon and 2-6 p.m., Saturday-Sunday 8 a.m.-noon and 1-4 p.m.).

Brazilian consulate—Monday-Friday 8 a.m.-noon and 2-4 p.m. Cra. 9a, 13-84. Tel: 592-7384, Fax: 592-8116, E-mail: brvcleticia@yahoo.com.br.

Peruvian consulate—Monday-Friday 8 a.m.-12:30 p.m. Ca. 11, 5-32. Tel: 592-7204, Fax: 592-7755, E-mail: conperu@telecom.com.co.

MONEY

Although there are ATMs and exchange houses in town, it is best to come to Leticia prepared with enough money. Changing traveler's checks is an especially uncertain affair. Banks do not exchange cash; for this, go to a casa de cambio.

Banco de Bogotá (corner of Cra. 10 and Ca. 7) has an ATM that accept Visa, MasterCard, Cirrus, Plus and ATH cards. **BBVA** (Monday-Friday 8-11:30 a.m. and 2-4:30 p.m. Corner of Cra. 10 and Ca. 7) gives cash advances on Visa, and has an ATM.

Money exchange house can change U.S. dollars, euros, Colombian pesos, Brazilian reais or Peruvian soles. Shop for the best rates, which are slightly better than in Bogotá. Two casas de cambio are: **Cambios Alliance 3** (Monday-Friday 8 a.m.-noon and 2-6 p.m., Saturday 8 a.m.-noon. Cra. 11, 7-50) and **Amazonas Cambios** (Monday-Friday 8 a.m.-noon and 2-6 p.m., Saturday 8 a.m.-noon. Ca. 8, 10-95).

There are also a number of exchange (cambios, truco) stands along Calle 8 past Carrera 11, toward the riverfront and on the lefthand side. For money wiring, **Western Union** is in Supermercado León (Monday-Friday 8 a.m.-noon and 2-6 p.m., Saturday 8 a.m.-noon. Ca. 8, 9-60).

KEEPING IN TOUCH

Telecom (Monday-Friday 8 a.m.-noon and 2-5 p.m., Saturday 8:30-11:30 a.m. Cra. 11 and Ca. 9) charges $0.06 per minute for local and $0.12 per minute for national calls. Its rates for international calls are probably the best in town: $0.25 per minute to the U.S. and $0.35 per minute to the U.K.

On average, shops charge $0.12 per minute for local/national calls. To mail postcards, head to the **post office** (Monday-Friday 8 a.m-noon and 2-6 p.m., Saturday 8 a.m.- noon. Ca. 8, 9-65).

There are plenty of places to use the Internet, especially on Carrera 10, between Calles 11 and 13, and on Calle 9. Surprisingly, many are open until late and almost all have Skype. An hour of Internet use costs around $0.50-1.

MEDICAL

Hospital San Rafael de Leticia (Cra. 10, 13-78. Tel: 592-7075, E-mail: hsanrafael1@telecom.com.co) is the region's medical facility. There are several pharmacies on Carrera 10, around Calle 8.

LAUNDRY

Lavandería Aseo Total (Monday-Saturday 6 a.m.-9 p.m., Sunday 8 a.m.-1 p.m. Cra. 10, 9-32. Tel: 592-6051) will do your wash according to your specifications. Depending on the type of service (wash, dry, fold and/or iron), the cost is $0.90-1.05 per pound. If you get your duds in early enough, they'll be ready by the afternoon.

CAMERA

Leticia has several photo shops. However, there are limited options, so stock up prior to your arrival.

Leticolor Digital (Monday-Friday 8 a.m.-12:30 p.m. and 2-7 p.m., Saturday 9 a.m.-12:30 p.m. and 2-7 p.m., holidays 9 a.m.-12:30 p.m., closed Sunday. Ca. 8, 9-42. Tel: 592-4778, Cel: 311-440-1614, E-mail: camiloandrescastillo@yahoo.es.com) has digital and disposable cameras, digital cards, 400ASA UltraMax Kodak film, batteries, camera cases and develops film.

Foto Reina (Monday-Saturday 7 a.m.-7 p.m., Sunday 7 a.m.-noon and 1-7 p.m. Cra. 10, 8-14. Tel: 592-3882) repairs conventional cameras, and has an assortment of digital camera cards, 100 and 400ASA color film and batteries. Updated: Mar 18, 2011.

SHOPPING

Pasaje Orellana

To stock up on supplies, steer over to Pasaje Orellana. The shops have a good selection of hammocks and mosquito nets (try Cacharrería Mohemed). For sloshing through the omnipresent mud, there are plenty of gum boots. Pick up anything else you need here, too, including toothpaste and flashlights. For reading materials, cut across the park to **Cerrajería Asertec** (Monday-Saturday 7 a.m.-8 p.m., Sunday 7 a.m.-noon. Cra. 11, 7-60), which has books in English, Spanish, Portuguese and other languages. Daily 7 a.m.-4 p.m. Backside of Parque Orellana, one block from the river. Updated: Mar 28, 2011.

Tienda Naturalista Artesanal El Manantial
On the front porch, Doña Edilma displays the crafts of Colombian and Peruvian communities from the area. There are many things you can take home as a memento of your trip: bows and arrows, wildlife hand-carved in precious woods, jewelry made of jungle seeds and scales of the piricurú fish, walking canes and paintings. She also has a wide assortment of natural medicines that is said to cure anything from high fever to low sex drive. Daily 7 a.m-8 p.m. Cra. 11, 6-96. Updated: Mar 28, 2011.

Casa Brasil Uirapuru
Casa Brasil has a full assortment of crafts from the indigenous and mestizo settlements along the Amazon River and its tributaries. There's a very fine assortment of bark paintings and hardwood sculptures of local wildlife, like jaguars and pink dolphins. But there's much more that will catch your eye. In the back is Museo Uirapuru, a collection of indigenous crafts and artifacts (no photos allowed). Casa Brasil only accepts MasterCard and Visa, and can ship purchases overseas. Monday-Saturday 8:30 a.m-noon and 2:30-7:30 p.m., Sunday 9 a.m.-noon. Ca. 8, 10-35. Tel: 592-7056, Cel: 321-452-2622. Updated: Mar 28, 2011.

Things to See and Do
Once you begin scratching the surface, you discover there are so many things to do and see while waiting for a boat out of Leticia. Of course, there are tours into the jungle and visits to Parque Nacional Natural Amaracayu and Isla de los Micos. On the Brazilian and Peruvian sides of the rivers, there are jungle lodges where you can hang out for a few days. Go canoeing or drop a fishing line into the tributaries at Lagos Yahuarcacas, where you can see the world's largest water lily. In Leticia, check out the Museo Etnográfico del Hombre Amazónico (The Ethnographic Museum of the Amazon Man) and the free

weekly movies at the university. Other sites on the road to Tarapacá include the Serpentario Armero-Guayabal (snake and reptile house), AmaZOOnas, and the Tikuna and Huitoto "Kilometer" villages. Puerto Nariño and Lago Tarapoto, homes of the pink dolphin, are just a few hours away, too. Updated: Jul 07, 2008.

Museo Etnográfico del Hombre Amazónico !
(ADMISSION: free) Who are the indigenous nations living in the Amazon region? What are their customs? How did the arrival of the white man affect the nations? These and other questions are answered at the Museo Etnográfico del Hombre Amazónico in the Banco de la República's cultural center. This museum also houses many fine examples of tools and crafts made and used by the Yucuna, Huitoto and Tikuna peoples. The collection is the effort of Franciscan Capuchin Mission monks. Banco de la República's cultural center also has a library that has story hour for children and other programs, and hosts free exhibits and special events. Monday-Friday 8 a.m.-noon and 2-6 p.m., Saturday 8 a.m.-noon. Banco de la República Area Cultural, Cra. 11, 9-43, between Ca. 9 and 10. Tel: 592-7729, URL: www.banrepcultural.org/leticia. Updated: Mar 28, 2011.

Reserva Tanimboca
Dosel is the term used for the highest part of the tree canopy, usually about 35-40 meters (115-130 ft) up. Climb to those heights at Reserva Tanimboca and explore an 80-meter (300-ft) trail from tree-to-tree, through a neighborhood inhabited by lizards, birds and monkeys ($40 per person). Other activities include ecological land walks and kayaking on the Río Tacana ($15). Night excursions through the jungle ($20-50, depending on number of participants, including transportation) or in search of caimans are other options. Reserva Tanimboca also has lodging available in treehouses; one house fits three people and the other sleeps five (about $60 per person, depends on number of people). From Parque Orellana, catch a buseta to the Kilometer villages and hop off at Kilometer 8 (5:45 a.m.-6:20 p.m., $0.80). Many tour agencies also offer outings to Reserva Tanimboca. The reserve has an office in Leticia (Cra. 10, 11-69). Kilometer 8, Vía Tarapacá. Tel: 592-7679, Cel: 311-204-3532/310-827-9412/280-8072, URL: www. tanimboca.org. Updated: Mar 28, 2011.

LLANOS AND SELVA

Serpentario Armero-Guayabal

(ADMISSION: $4 adults, $3 children) Slinking through the dense underbrush, coiling around the boughs of trees and slithering through the rivers' roots are creatures whose eyes are watching you explore the Amazon. Some are venomous, others harmless, and still others would love to give you a big hug before swallowing you whole! All of these serpents play a role in keeping the jungle healthy. Serpentario Armero-Guayabal can help you get a close-up view of these snakes safely and will teach you about conservation efforts on their behalf. It is operated by Nativa, a non-profit conservation organization. Another project of Nativa is AmaZOOnas, a reserve of native animals, principally reptiles (including caimans). Catch a buseta from Parque Orellana to the Kilometer villages and hop off at Kilometer 11 (5:45 a.m.-6:20 p.m., $1.05). Daily 8 a.m.-4 p.m. Reserva Tanimboca, Vía Tarapacá. Tel: 592-7679, Cel: 310-791-7470/321-207-9909, URL: www.nativa.org. Updated: Mar 28, 2011.

Tours

Leticia certainly doesn't lack tour agencies eager to take you into the jungle. Also, as soon as you step foot in Leticia, whether stepping out of the airport or onto the dock, you'll be greeted by independent guides offering their services. It's hard to know who has a good track record, so check around with other travelers.

Jugalvis "Juancho" Valenca Pérez (lobby of Hotel Anaconda, Cra. 11, 7-34. Cel: 311-206-6341) is one highly recommended independent guide who does specialized trips. For example, he does a five-day, four-night excursion that focuses purely on medicinal plants ($1,050 for two people, all inclusive). Updated: Jul 07, 2008.

Decameron Explorer

Decameron Explorer offers all types of options for getting to know the Amazon region. Jungle jaunts include boat trips to Lago Tarapoto to observe pink dolphins, hikes on Isla de los Micos, night safaris to search for caimans and special birdwatching excursions. If you feel a bit more energetic, they can also take you kayaking on local lakes or canopying at Reserva Tanimboca. Cultural activities include trips to indigenous villages and sessions with medicine men. Visit the agency to see its complete menu of services. Cra. 11, 6-11. Tel: 592-4196, E-mail: amazonas.receptivosexplorer@decameron.com, URL: www.decameron.com. Updated: Mar 28, 2011.

Lodging

Budget accommodations are quite pricy in Leticia. But then again, they have you over the proverbial barrel here. The usually-reliable standby, camping, is not a viable option due to climatic and fauna-related factors. Leticia hostels run at least $9 per night, and these are probably your cheapest options. Some budget travelers prefer to hop on a boat to Puerto Nariño to spend a few days there instead. Most places will not have hot water, but will provide you with at least a fan. Air conditioning is also available, for a price. The more expensive hotels have swimming pools. Shop around, especially in the low season, when cheaper deals can be struck. Updated: Jul 22, 2010.

BUDGET

Mochileros

(BEDS: $9) Mochileros is a European-style backpacker hostel. It has once-splendid facilities, including common rooms with a book exchange and board games, a communal kitchen, a laundry area and a rooftop terrace. The dorms have sturdy wooden bunks and lockers for securing backpacks. Unfortunately, it's a bit neglected these days. If you want to check it out, call ahead because the front desk isn't staffed all the time. The administrator will meet you and give you a key. Cra. 5, 9-117. Tel: 592-5491, Cel: 314-280-6558, E-mail: javierespiritu@yahoo.es/jamersonx@hotmail.com. Updated: Apr 30, 2009.

Residencias del Centro

(BEDS: $10.50) Although it is officially called Residencias del Centro, everyone still calls it Residencias Colombia. The orange and green sign hanging out front just says "Residencias." It is the most centrally located of the cheaper hotels in Leticia. All rooms are large, with a built-in bed, window and fan. The common baths are basic but clean. The friendly owners are knowledgeable about the region and can assist you in finding an independent guide. Cra. 10, 8-52. Tel: 592-4311. Updated: Jul 08, 2008.

Mahatu

(BEDS: $11.50, ROOMS: $25-30) This hostel is deep in the Amazon jungle, and offers its guests an exotic garden with an Indian maloka hut, a guest kitchen, bicycles, computer access and reliable information about the Amazon. Take a taxi from downtown Leticia ($1.80) to get to the hostel or contact Mahatu for complimentary pickup from the port or

LLANOS AND SELVA

airport. Cra. 7, 9-69. Tel: 592-7384, Cel: 311-539-1265, E-mail: gusrenalvarado@hotmail.com/mahatuhostel@gmail.com, URL: www.mahatu.com. Updated: Mar 28, 2011.

MID-RANGE

Hospedaje Los Delfines !
(ROOMS: $20-35) Hospedaje Los Delfines is a fine place to stay if you can afford to spend a bit more. All the rooms are nicely furnished and include a private bathroom, fan, mini-bar and screened windows. Hammocks abound in the courtyard and there is a TV in the common room. This hotel has something that distinguishes it from the others: It has its own water treatment plant, which is checked regularly by health officials. Cra. 11, 12-85. Tel: 592-7488, Cel: 310-309-9194, E-mail: losdelfinesleticia@hotmail.com/fondoamazonia@hotmail.com. Updated: Jul 28, 2011.

Residencias Amira
(ROOMS: $30-35) This place used to be one of the more economical hotels in Leticia, but it has been upgraded. Now, Residencias Amira offers only rooms with private bathrooms and fridge. All rooms have two to four beds—a mix of singles and doubles. The common balcony is a great place to sit to enjoy the cooler evenings. This place seems a bit overpriced when compared to similar-quality hotels in town. Ca. 9, 9-69. Tel: 592-7767, Cel: 310-585-4114, E-mail: diverleones@hotmail.com. Updated: Mar 28, 2011.

HIGH-END

Hotel Anaconda
(ROOMS: $73.50-134) Not the most expensive hotel in Leticia, the extras Hotel Anaconda piles on makes it excellent value. The 50 rooms all come with balconies, some with a view of the Amazon River. These large suites have good beds, private bathrooms with both cold and hot water, air conditioning, TV and mini-bar. The pool (with a slide) is not only open to guests, but also to the paying public (adults $4,

children $2.50). Hotel Anaconda has its own water and energy plants to guarantee that its guests never go without either. All of this and much more continue to make this well-established hotel a Leticia favorite. Cra. 11, 7-34. Tel: 592-7119, Fax: 592-7005, E-mail: reservas@hotelanaconda.com.co/leticia@hotelanaconda.com.co, URL: www.hotelanaconda.com.co. Updated: Mar 28, 2011.

Decalodge Ticuna
(ROOMS: $105-180) The Ticuna had always been one of Leticia's premier hotels. Since Decameron has taken it over, it has blossomed into a spectacular lodge. Open the door to a bungalow and you enter another world. The anteroom has a hammock, as well as cane chairs. Beyond is the bedroom decorated with regional artesanía and contemporary paintings. Before entering the hot-water bathroom, there is a powder room whose shelves are stacked with snowy-white towels. The grounds include a pool with a fountain and a lookout tower from which you can watch the sun set over the Amazon. Cra. 11, 6-11. Tel: 592-6600/4237, E-mail: contactus@decameron.com, URL: www.decameron.com. Updated: Mar 28, 2011.

Restaurants
Like accommodations, food in the heart of the jungle costs more, though you'll still be able to find a daily plate special for under $2. Not only can you score fresh produce and meats at the **municipal market** (daily 6 a.m.-4 p.m. Ca. 8, half-block from the river), but it also has inexpensive eateries, some with a river view. Be careful about drinks when dining at the market. General stores and supermarkets are all along Calle 8. Bakeries, which seem to occupy every corner, are great places to go to grab a cheap breakfast or snack. At night, check out the tent city of grill stands that sets up on the corner of Avenida Internacional and Calle 7.

Stock up on purified water at **Gaseosas Leticia** (Ca. 8, between Cra. 8 and 9), which has a 24-hour, seven-day dispenser. If you bring your own clean container, five liters costs $0.35 and 20 liters $0.75. It also sells full *garrafones* (jugs); five liters cost $2 and 20 liters go for $11.25.

While in Leticia, be sure to try some of the local delicacies, like *mojojoy* (a worm), or the pirarucú and gamitana fish. Another regional fish you might encounter on your plate is *acarahuasú*, otherwise known to aquarium enthusiasts as the Oscar (Cichlidae astronauts ocellatus). Updated: Aug 03, 2011.

Mimo's

(ICE CREAM: $1.50-5) Mimo's is the place to go for any kind of ice cream treat, from simple soft-serve cones ($1.50-3.25) to gourmet sundaes ($2.25-4.25). There are even special creations for the kids, like the snowman and the Medusa with gummy-worm hair. No sweat for those on a diet, Mimo's has a full line of dietetic ice creams and sauces. You can also take home a liter of one of the 15 flavors of hand-dipped helado to share with your family or fellow travelers. Daily 10 a.m.-9 p.m. Cra. 11, 7-26, across from Parque Orellana. Tel: 592-5129. Updated: Mar 28, 2011.

Restaurante Sancho Panza

(LUNCH: $1.60-2.10) Restaurante Sancho Panza, a favorite eatery for villagers of more modest means, is located on Leticia's main drag. The front veranda has a few tables and inside this faded red wood building is a long counter. Only simple comidas corrientes are on the menu here, with the usual soup, meat-beans-rice-plaintain bandeja and drink. It's enough food to ensure that even Sancho Panza wouldn't go away hungry. Breakfast is also served if you have an early boat to catch.Daily 6 a.m.-9 p.m. Cra. 10, 8-72. Tel: 592-5982. Updated: Jan 24, 2011.

Restaurante Tropical !

(LUNCH: $2.65) The décor of Restaurante Tropical is just as delightful as the food it serves. Jungle kitsch abounds among the plants and aquariums. The jaguar with the safari helmet is a kick. The tables out on the front porch are a delightfully cool place to enjoy breakfast ($2.65-3.20), a blue plate special ($2.65), or a sandwich or burger with fried potatoes ($1.60-2.65). Besides the usual fruit drinks and beer, Restaurante Tropical also mixes up caipirinhas ($1.60). Cra. 10, 8-112, local 3. Tel: 592-7934. Updated: Jul 07, 2008.

Restaurante El Sabor

(LUNCH: $3.50-6.50) Restaurante El Sabor is one of the old standbys for visitors to Leticia, and for locals, too. It offers foods straight off the BBQ grill. Pull up a table on the palm-thatch patio in front or in the large dining room inside and order up a serving of pork, beef or chicken, or fish. All meals come with soup, salad bar, and a pitcher of Amazon fruit drink made with purified water. A vegetarian plate of beans, rice, vegetables and egg salad can also be requested. Monday-Saturday 6 a.m.-11 p.m. Ca. 8, 9-15. Tel: 592-4774. Updated: Jul 29, 2011.

Cozinha da Fazenda

(ENTREES: $2.65-10.50) Cozinha da Fazenda is a truly international restaurant here at the triple border. It has a Portuguese name in Spanish-speaking Leticia and a menu that offers French toast and pancakes for breakfast ($1.60 for one, $3.20 for a stack of three). For other meals, it has pizzas with your choice of toppings (small $5.30, medium $8, large $10.50). Sandwiches are another major feature, with meats, four cheeses or the Romeo y Julieta (cheese and guava paste) ($2.65-3.20). The only liquors poured are the Brazilian classics caipirinha and caipiroska. Cozinha da Fazenda is one of the few vegetarian options in Leticia. Daily 6 a.m.-11 p.m. Cra. 9, 7-48. Updated: Mar 28, 2011.

Tierras Amazónicas

(ENTREES: $5-9) The menu at Tragadero y Beberdero Tierras Amazónicas is a plank of wood, befitting for this old jungle space. Its full bar offers such regional drinks as caipirinha cocktails ($2.65) and chuchuwasa (an aphrodisiac drink made from a bark). Turn over the plank and you'll realize that this establishment is much more than a mere drinking hole. It is a restaurant that offers a full Colombian-Brazilian-Peruvian menu with 16 ways to prepare your fish fresh out of the Amazon, whether pirarucú or piranha ($5-9). Tuesday-Sunday noon-3 p.m. and 6:30-11 p.m. (food until 10:30 p.m.). Ca. 8, 7-50. Tel: 592-4748, Cel: 312-378-8761/313-203-3915 Updated: Aug 04, 2011.

Nightlife

Leticia has a pretty active nightlife scene, though most in-town establishments are closed Tuesday nights. The most grooving nights are Wednesday to Saturday. There are all types of places, from the sit-down bars to cumbia-samba-vallenato-reggaeton discos. Along Avenida Internacional, heading to the border, there are establishments that are open all week and until dawn. However, be advised that these double as strip joints and brothels. Updated: Jul 07, 2008.

Club de Billar y Cafetería Barbacoas

Folks are at Club de Billar y Cafetería Barbacoas before the parrots begin their morning song to way after they return home to roost, talking over coffee or a drink out on the sidewalk café or shooting a game of pool inside. If you're looking for a wake-up brew or a night cap, this is the place to stop. Women who sit alone: be warned that service will be a longer wait for you. Monday-Saturday 5 a.m.-2 a.m., closed Sunday. Cafeteria service only until 10 p.m. Cra. 10, 8-28. Updated: Jul 08, 2008.

Mosshe's Bar

This corner bar is where people meet to have a drink at the end of a long, hot day. There is a sidewalk café outside and inside, a red sofa wraps around sinuous walls. Chic black and chrome fixings are scattered throughout, and the ambience is set by a mix of rap, blues, tropical and contemporary Brazilian music. Most liquors come by shot ($1.85-$4.20), half-bottle or full-bottle ($21-105). Mosshe's even has Bailey's Irish Cream on hand, as well as cocktails such as martinis, screwdrivers, Manhattans, caipirinhas and piña colada ($4.20-6.35). Sunday-Thursday 5 p.m.-2 a.m., Friday and Saturday 5 p.m.-4 a.m., closed Tuesday. Cra. 10, 10-12, across from Parque Santander. Tel: 592-7422. Updated: Jul 08, 2008.

AROUND LETICIA
ISLA DE LOS MICOS

Isla de los Micos (Island of the Monkeys) is a standard stop on tours of the Amazon. Thirty-five kilometers (21 mi) upstream from Leticia, this 450-hectare (1,112 ac) island is home to our distant primate cousins, capuchin monkeys—a not-so-elusive bunch of creatures. Take an interpretive hike through primary tropical forest, observe the flora and fauna, and go fishing and kayaking on Lago Tucuchira. Birdwatching is particularly rewarding. Tours visit Huitoto and Tikuna settlements on this island, too. Contact any of the tour agencies in Leticia about a day tour that includes Isla de los Micos. Updated: Mar 28, 2011.

PARQUE NACIONAL
NATURAL AMACAYACU !

(ADMISSION: $7.50 nationals, $20 foreigners, $4 children under 12) Located 60 kilometers (36 mi) upstream from Leticia, Parque Nacional Natural Amacayacu is one of the most easily (and safely) accessible jungle national parks. Its 293,500 hectares (725,254 ac) on the banks of the Amazon and Amacayacu Rivers is home to more than 150 species of mammals, including pink and gray dolphins, danta, jaguar, manatee, nutria and the tití leoncita (the smallest primate in the world). This place is also a reptile haven full of crocodiles, anacondas and boas. Parque Nacional Natural Amacayacu has one of the most diverse populations of birds, housing almost 500 species, making this

a must-stop for birdwatchers. Amacayacu is one of the most virgin tropical forests, with thousands of species of plants and trees. You can explore the park by canoe up its many waterways or on foot along marked trails, or undertake the six-day hike from one extreme of the park to the other accompanied by a specialist guide.

The concessions (hotels, restaurants, tours) have been privatized; Decameron now administers everything. Lodging has improved, but prices have risen steeply. This is the only lodging option within the park. For shared accommodation, prices are $46-55, and for a maloka cabin, prices range $120-145 for a single and $70-85 for a double. Prices are per person, and include breakfast and dinner, but not boat transportation. A cheaper alternative is to stay in a neighboring *Resguarda Indígena* (indigenous village), like Mocagua. If you choose to do this, request to speak with the *curaca*, or head of the village, upon arriving to ask permission to stay. Lodging in these hamlets costs approximately $6 per person.

Buy your ticket to Amacayacu from the national park office in Leticia. You can contact a tour agency in Leticia or Decameron Explorer at **Hotel Decameron Ticuna** (Cra 11, 6-11, Leticia. Tel: 592-6600) for making plans to go to the park, or take a public launch (see Getting To and Away from Leticia for details).Students and professionals of biological sciences/ecology and individuals with national park experience can apply at the national park office in Leticia to be a volunteer. Updated: Mar 28, 2011.

Fundación Maikuchiga

This foundation works with the indigenous communities of Parque Nacional Natural Amacayacu to reduce the hunting of and trafficking of Amazonian wildlife. Committed to the conservation of the Amazon's rich biodiversity, the organization rescues, cares for and rehabilitates monkeys. It also facilitates educational programs about the environment in schools in the Colombian Amazon. You can visit the Maikuchiga's Monkey Trail to see the various monkeys in rehabilitation at its Animal's House. This guided tour is led by a member of the Mocagua community. Fundación Maikuchiga also takes volunteers; contact it for more information on such opportunities. Cra. 9, 6-100 (201), Leticia. E-mail: fundacionmaikuchiga@gmail.com/casadelosanimales@gmail.com, URL: http://maikuchiga.org / http://maikuchiga.blogspot.com. Updated: Aug 09, 2011.

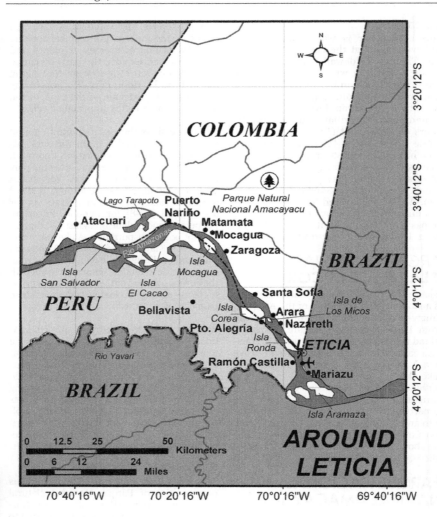

AROUND LETICIA

TABATINGA, BRAZIL

85m   45,300   97

On the other side of the border, just a kilometer (0.6 mi) from downtown Leticia, is its Brazilian cousin, Tabatinga (pronounced ta-ba-CHEEN-ga). If you just want to sample Brazil's cooking and fine Garota chocolates, you don't need to do any formal border procedures. Just walk down doen Leticia's Avenida Internacional. At the border, it becomes Avenida Amizade. Its principal port, Porta da Feira, down by the market, bustles with peque-peques arriving from indigenous villages and the next Manaus-bound boat

loading up. If you're heading down river, stop into the Polícia Federal to get your passport stamped. Although it is the larger city, Tabatinga has fewer services than Leticia, where most travelers prefer to stay. However, there are hotels and restaurants as well as money and communication facilities. Many people here speak Spanish, or at least *portunhol* (a mix of Portuguese and Spanish). Updated: Jul 02, 2010.

Getting To and Away

BY BOAT

Tabatinga has two river ports: the principal one, **Porta da Feira**, at the end of Rua Santo

Dumont in the market area, and the **Porto Fluvial de Tabatinga** (Tel: 097-3412-2219) at the end of Rua Duarte Coelho. Boats for Benjamin Constant and Manaus leave from both ports. Local boats to Leticia (daily 6 a.m.-8 p.m., $1.35) and Santa Rosa (daily 6 a.m.-8 p.m., $3.50) depart from the Porta da Feira.

BY BUS/TAXI

Catch a buseta from Avenida Amizade to Leticia, Tabatinga's airport or the Tikuna village Maria Azzu (6 a.m.-6:20 p.m., $0.95-1.25). Mototaxis ($1.50) and taxis ($2-3.25, depending on distance) also run these routes.

BY AIR

Tabatinga's airport is about four kilometers (2.4 mi) along Avenida Amizade. TRIP Airlines flies to Tefé and Manaus several times a week. See Colombia-Brazil-Peru Border Crossings for more information. Updated: Aug 09, 2011.

Services

TOURISM

Tabatinga has no tourism office. An important institution in town is the **Polícia Federal** (daily 8 a.m.-noon and 2-6 p.m. Av. Amizade 650), where you'll need to have your passport stamped upon arriving from (or leaving for) Manaus. If you need a visa for Colombia, there is a consulate in Tabatinga (Monday-Friday 8 a.m.-1 p.m. Rua General Sanpaio 623).

MONEY

Banco do Brasil (Av. Amizade and Rua Marechal Mallet) has an ATM that accepts Visa, MasterCard and Cirrus. To change dollars, euros or reais, go to **CNM Câmbio e Turismo** (Monday-Friday 8 a.m.-noon and 2-4 p.m. Av. Amizade 2017, in the yellow ochre shopping center. Tel: 97-3412-2600, Fax: 97-3412-3055, E-mail: cbnmtur@ahoo.com.br).

KEEPING IN TOUCH

You can find a few Internet cafés on Avenida Amizade. The **Correios (post office)** (Monday-Friday 8 a.m.-4 p.m.) is on this same boulevard, between Rua Santos Dumont and Rua Coronel Berg. Updated: Jul 09, 2008.

Lodging

Hotel Internacional Bagpackers

(BEDS: $8-16) If your boat from Manaus gets in after dark, this budget backpacker's hostel is three blocks from Tabatinga's Por-

ta da Feira. With a dorm room and several rooms with private bath, this bare-boned inn has a common kitchen and a space to hang out. Rua Pedro Texeira 9, 2nd floor. Cel: 312-585-8855. Updated: Mar 14, 2011.

SANTA ROSA, PERU

 50m   100s 📞 51+65

On an island directly across from Leticia is the smallest of the triple border towns, Santa Rosa. In reality, it is so small it doesn't seem to be worth the census-taker's time to make a call and count. The town isn't much, but it is the jumping-off point for travelers looking for a boat up the Amazon River to Iquitos. A paved way parallels the riverbank. The walk frays into dirt paths disappearing into the dense vegetation. However, this main "street" is as far as you ever need to go in Santa Rosa. Your launch from Leticia or Tabatinga will pull up among the many other canoes shoved against the shore. To the left is where the next boat for Iquitos may be loading up. Also along this stretch are the Peruvian *migración* (immigration) post, about a half-dozen basic hotels, a handful of restaurants and other businesses. From the street vendors, you can pick up a comic book or other last-minute items for your sojourn. Updated: Jun 17, 2009.

Getting To and Away

The only way to get to or from Santa Rosa is by launch, leaving from the main street. Boats depart for Leticia ($1.35) and Tabatinga, Brazil ($3.25), between 6 a.m. and 8 p.m.

Santa Rosa is a more convenient departure point for cargo ships than Islandia is, so most leave from here. Several agencies on the main drag sell tickets for the *rápido* (fast) boat and the weekly flight to Iquitos. See Colombia-Brazil-Peru Border Crossings for more information. Updated: Jul 09, 2011.

Services

The most important office in Santa Rosa is **immigration** (Monday-Saturday 8 a.m.-noon and 2-6 p.m.), about 50 meters (180 ft) to the right of the boat docks, past Hotel Diana. There are no banks in Santa Rosa. Hospedaje El Mirador, about 120 meters (400 ft) from the boat dock, changes money. To stay in touch with the outside world, the main phone office is 30 meters (100 ft) to the right of immigration, in the Snack Bar

Sabor Peruano "mall." There is no Internet in Santa Rosa. Updated: Jul 09, 2008.

COLOMBIA-PERU-BRAZIL BORDER CROSSING

Leticia may be the end of the road for Colombia, but it is also the crossroads of the Amazon jungle. From here, many adventurers set sail for Brazil or Peru, fulfilling a lifelong dream of traveling on one of the world's greatest rivers, the Amazon—or as the locals call it, the Río Amazonas. Get ready to embark for your next destination, whether upstream to Iquitos, Peru, or downstream to Manaus, Brazil.

Immigration

Regulations and procedures frequently change. Check with your ticket agent to see if the boat stops for migración. If not, you may need to take care of these formalities the day before your boat leaves. See the respective cities for addresses and hours.

Colombia—Get your passport stamped at the airport DAS office. If you need a visa to enter, there is a consulate in Tabatinga, Brazil.

Peru—The immigration post is in Santa Rosa, on the other side of the river from Leticia.

Brazil—Immigration formalities are handled by the Polícia Federal in Tabatinga, not on the Colombia-Brazilian border. Brazil has a consulate in Leticia. Citizens of some countries need a visa for this country, including those from the U.S., Canada and Australia. You'll need the form, a 5x7-centimeter photo, your yellow fever vaccination certificate, an ongoing ticket (or credit card or sufficient funds) and the fee ($50 for Aussies, $140 for U.S. citizens). The consul speaks Spanish and English, as well as Portuguese.

If you are only making a day trip into a neighboring town, you will not need to go through immigration. If you are going to a jungle lodge in a neighboring country, check with your tour operator to see if you will need to go through the bureaucracy. This is especially important for nationalities needing a visa for Brazil.

Transportation

The three river towns are all connected to larger cities in their respective countries by air and by river. A few things to keep in mind if you choose to do the age-old way, by boat:
• Speak only with the captain of the boat. Confirm departure date and time, and prices.

• Compare prices with different boats, and inspect the vessel for cleanliness. Pay only the captain or another authorized person, and obtain a receipt. You can also purchase your ticket from an authorized agent.

• Larger boats have cabins (some even with air conditioning). However, these are more expensive than the hammock space on the deck, and tend to be hot and stuffy. If you opt to travel swinging along in your hammock, be sure to choose a spot away from the fumes and noise of the engines, the insect-attracting lights, and the bathrooms. Bring rope not only to hang your hammock, but also to hang cloth for privacy. Board early (often it is possible to do so the night before) to land a choice spot.

• Use a mosquito net and repellent, and don't forget to take your malaria medication.

• Secure your belongings very well. Lock your bags, and always keep the key with you. Be particularly vigilant when the boat pulls into a port village during the trip because this is when most thefts happen.

• Food will be provided, as will drinks (often made with river water). Bring along fresh fruits, comfort foods and purified water. Have your own cup as well, plus some diarrhea medication, just in case.

• It gets remarkably cool at night on the river. Light, warm clothing and a blanket (or cloth hammock) will keep you warm.

TO IQUITOS, PERU:

By Boat

Most cargo ships to Iquitos depart from Santa Rosa rather than from Islandia a bit further down river. Every day one leaves in the evening, usually between 6 and 9 p.m. Take a good look at the ship before you commit yourself. Do all your negotiations with only the authorized ticket seller or at the ship's administration office aboard (3 nights/2 days: hammock $36, cabin $58).

Fast boats ($77, 12 hr) also ply this route, departing from Tabatinga, Leticia. These rápidos leave at 5 a.m. on Wednesday, Friday and Sunday from Tabatinga's Porto da Feira. You can purchase your ticket in advance in Leticia or Iquitos at **Almacén El Repuesto** (Leticia: Ca. 7 10-72. Tel: 592-7156, Cel: 311-

217-6770; Iquitos: Raimundi 390. Tel: 065-241-468). In Tabatinga and in Santa Rosa, buy tickets directly from the boats at the dock a day or two before you intend to depart. Tickets may be paid for in U.S. dollars, Peruvian soles, Colombian pesos or Brazilian reais. Passage includes breakfast, lunch and sodas.

By Air

North American has a charter flight from Santa Rosa to Iquitos on Sunday at 10 a.m. More information can be obtained at the rápidos ticket office in Santa Rosa, just before the immigration post.

TO MANAUS, BRAZIL:

By Boat

Boats to Manaus leave from both of Tabatinga's ports. Some of the ships doing the Manaus route are Voyagers III and IV (URL: www.portaltabatinga.com.br/voyger.htm), Oliveira V, Manuel Monteiro I and Sagrado Coração de Jesus (which is the best). All have the choice of hammocks on deck or cabins. Suites have all the comforts, including TV, mini-fridge and air conditioning. Brazilian boats now purport to prepare drinks with purified water. Buy your ticket directly from the administrator on board. Other slow boats leave from Benjamin Constant, Brazil, 1.5-2 hours downstream from Tabatinga.

Tabatinga-Manaus: Wednesday and Sunday 2 p.m.; 4 nights: hammock $83, shared cabin $152 per person, $303 for two-person cabin.

Manaus-Tabatinga: Wednesday-Saturday 3 p.m.; 6-7 days: hammock $138, shared cabin $207 per person, two-person cabin $414.

Rápidos leave for Manaus from the Porta da Feira.

Tabatinga-Manaus: Friday 8 a.m.; $105, 36 hr.

Manaus-Tabatinga: Wednesday 7 a.m., 40+ hr.

By Air

Planes leave from Tabatinga's airport, about four kilometers (2.4 mi) south on Avenida Amizade. Busetas from Leticia's Parque Orellana go there (5:45 a.m.-6:20 p.m., $1.85), or you can arrive by taxi ($2.65). Flights are to Manaus or to Tefé, from which connections to Manaus can be made. Tickets may be purchased at **CNM Câmbio e Turismo** (Monday-Friday 8 a.m.-noon and 2-4 p.m. Av. Amizade 2017, in the yellow ochre shopping center. Tel: 97-3412-2600, Fax: 97-3412-3055, E-mail: cbnmtur@yahoo.com.br).

TRIP (URL: www.voetrip.com.br) is the only airline that currently services the route between Tabatinga and Manaus (2 hr 40 min, about $270-345 each way). Flights from Tabatinga leave for Manaus daily at 2:45 p.m. The return trip—from Manaus to Tabatinga—leaves at 11:35 a.m. Updated: Aug 09, 2011.

PUERTO NARIÑO

 110m   2,000   8

At the confluence of Río Loretoyacü into the Amazon, 75 kilometers (45 mi) west of Leticia, is Puerto Nariño, the Pesebre del Amaznas (Cradle of the Amazon). This small village surrounded by jungle is a tranquil place to spend a few days. Its biological and ethnic diversity gives ample opportunity for exploration, including walking trails and canoeing on the slow Loretoyacü to Lago Tarapoto in search of pink dolphins. It is part of the Ticoya indigenous reserve of the Tikuna, Cocoma and Yagua peoples, who make up 90 percent of the town's population.

Puerto Nariño is on the itinerary of tours that go to Lago Tarapoto and is increasingly popular among backpackers, since it is quieter and less expensive than Leticia. The town begins with a flat, narrow plain on the waterfront, then the land begins to rise like a multi-tiered cake. No cars venture the streets of Puerto Nariño, because in truth, there are no streets, just a well-laid out, well-signed grid of sidewalks. Puerto Nariño is a national model of an ecological village, with recycling and organic waste management programs, and of the development of eco-ethno-tourism. Updated: May 18, 2009.

History

The first permanent settlement at the mouth of the Loretoyacü River was a product of love. After marrying, Luis Eco Vargas of the Huitoto nation and his Tikuna bride Cándida Cuelto arrived here to set up a homestead. In 1954, Franciscan Capuchin monks opened the Internado Indígena San Francisco, a boarding school teaching sustainable agriculture to children from villages all along the river. Puerto Nariño's official founding date is August 18, 1961, when the town was recogized as a *corregimiento* (settlement). It became a municipio in 1984. The Resguardo Indígena Ticoya

LLANOS AND SELVA

was established as a conservation area in 1990, incorporating 32 indigenous settlements of Tikuna, Cocoma and Yagua, with Puerto Nariño as the principal seat. Updated: Jul 08, 2008.

When to Go

Although the seasons are similar to those of Leticia, it doesn't get as hot in Puerto Nariño. The dry season is from June to September. Rains start in October, with heaviest precipitation falling from January to May. The average temperature in Puerto Nariño is 25°C (77°F), with the heat rising to as high as 32°C (90°F). July is the coldest month, with temperatures averaging only 17°C (63°F). It is also very muggy. Humidity runs 85 percent, and annual rainfall is 3,440 millimeters (136 in). Updated: Jul 09, 2011.

HOLIDAYS AND FESTIVALS

Puerto Nariño has a few impressive events on its calendar. April 1 is the Aniversario del Municipio, the town's birthday party, with special events and parties. May 19-21 brings the Encuentro de Guías de Naturaleza, a conference of nature guides, with field trips. September 7-9 is the Seminario Internacional de Turismo Sostenible, the International Sustainable Tourism seminar, with conferences and field trips. December 29-31 marks the Festival Autóctono de Danza, Murga y Cuento, a gathering of nations to share dances, songs and stories. Updated: Jul 09, 2011.

Getting To and Away

The only place really to go from Puerto Nariño is Leticia. All boats leave from the village's dock. Fast boat to Leticia leave daily at 7:30 a.m., 11 a.m. and 4 p.m. ($11.50, 2 hr). Pequepeques go to Leticia on Monday and Wednesday in the early morning (roughly 6-7 a.m.); the trip takes about four to five hours and costs around $5.30. Updated: Jul 08, 2008.

Safety

Puerto Nariño is a safe town. When out after dark, though, be sure to take a flashlight. Do not wander alone in the jungle or go off the paths; take a guide with you. Beware of Yachingo, Father of the Jungle, the local version of Big Foot! Mosquitoes are common, so take the proper precautions: use mosquito nets and get a yellow fever vaccination. Camping is not advisable due to snakes. Spiders and scorpions are also common, so shake out your clothes before putting them on. As fearsome as it looks, the whip scorpion is not deadly. Take care around the waterfront after dark when caimans are more active. Also, avoid swimming

early mornings and late afternoons when fish—including piranha—are feeding. Do not enter the water if you have an open wound or are bleeding. Keep hands out of the water at these times, also. Updated: Jul 09, 2008.

Services

TOURISM

The tourism office, **Coordinación Turismo y Cultura**, in the Alcaldía, provides good pamphlets on the area's attractions Monday-Friday 7 a.m.-noon and 2-5:45 p.m. Cra. 7 and Ca. 5. Cel: 321-450-0380/311-257-76911, E-mail: coordinacionlocal@gmail.com, URL: www.puertonarino-amazonas.gov.com).

MONEY

Puerto Nariño has no banks or exchange houses. Obtain plenty of Colombian pesos before leaving Leticia.

KEEPING IN TOUCH

You can make local and national calls from **Comcel** (Monday-Saturday 8 a.m.-noon and 2-7 p.m., Saturday 8-10 a.m. Cra. 6 and Ca. 8). **Compartel** (Monday-Saturday 8 a.m.-noon, 2-5 p.m. and 6-9 p.m. Cra. 6 and Ca. 5) provides slow Internet as well as national and international call services.

MEDICAL

Puerto Nariño's hospital is up Calle 5 at Carrera 4. You can purchase medications there or at the general store across from the waterfront Parque Principal. Updated: Mar 18, 2011.

SHOPPING

Associación Artesenal Möwacha

Associación Artesanal Möwacha is a collective of mostly women from the indigenous nations of Puerto Nariño. Inside this modest building are rooms displaying Tikuna, Cocama and Yagua crafts. All the traditional artesanía is here, including bows and arrows, pottery and baskets, depending on the speciality of the nation. Jewelery made from jungle seeds and feathers are also created for you to have a memento of your visit to this village. Off the back patio are workshops where the women pass the day working together. Daily 6 a.m.-5 p.m. Cra. 6, left of Ca. 8, before the bridge. Tel: 311-274-5944. Updated: Mar 18, 2011.

Things to See and Do

For such a small village, Puerto Nariño has an amazing amount of things to see and do.

LLANOS AND SELVA

It is a good base for getting to know the jungle and indigenous villages. One of the most astounding features of Puerto Nariño is the museums. There also are paths for learning about the medicinal and agricultural uses of the jungle, and there are *miradores* (lookout towers) to watch the rivers flow past.

The biggest attraction, however, is Lago Tarapoto, where you can observe pink dolphins and the majestic Victoria regia water lily. Don't forget that just a half-hour down-river is the Parque Nacional Natural Amacayacu. Updated: Jul 08, 2008.

Museums

While in Puerto Nariño, be sure to drop into one or more these interesting museums:

Casa Museo Etnocultural Ya Ipata Ünchi—Ya Ipata Ünchi (Casa of the Monkeys) has exhibits displaying the artesanía and explaining the cultures of the Tikuna, Cocama and Yagua. Admission is free, but tipping guides is appreciated. Monday-Friday 7 a.m.-noon and 2-5:45 p.m. Cra. 7 and Ca. 5. Free, though tip to the guide is appreciated.

Casa Artesanal Tachiwagü—A *maloka* (traditional comunal hut) that teaches the indigenous world vision. Admission is $0.50. Monday-Friday 9 a.m.-noon and 2-5 p.m. Cra. 6, between Ca. 5 and 6.

Fundación Omacha—Taking its name from the Tikuna word for the pink dolphin, this organization works on the conservation of the Amazon's aquatic denizens. It accepts volunteers; visit its website for more information. Village side of the Quebrada Menoe as it enters the Río Loretoyacü. E-mail: info@omacha.org/moralula@yahoo.com. mx, URL: omacha.org.

Centro de Interpretación Natütama—Natütama (Underwater World) is another non-profit working on conservation issues and eco-education that welcomes visitors. The center has over 70 life-size carvings of plant and animal species of the Río Amazonas waterways. Wednesday-Monday 8 a.m.-12:30 p.m. and 2-5 p.m., closed Tuesday. On south bank of Quebrada Menoe as it enters the Río Loretoyacü. Cel: 312-410-1925, E-mail: info@natutama.org/fundacionnatutama@yahoo.com, URL: www.natutama.org. Updated: Mar 28, 2011.

Senderos and Miradores

A network of trails and lookout towers helps visitors appreciate the natural beauty of this region. The journey to any of these attractions begins on Carrera 6, where signs begin to point you in the direction for each. Although a guide is not necessary, one would help you understand and learn about the flora and fauna better.

Mirador Naipata—From Naipata, Casa en el Árbol, just outside Puerto Nariño, you can see the Río Loretoyacü flow into the Amazon.

Mirador Mowa—This tower overlooking the Río Amazonas and jungle is located in the indigenous village 20 de Julio, a 30-minute walk or 10-minute boat ride from Puerto Nariño.

Sendero Ecológico—A path leading through the forest that shows medicinal, fruit, hardwood and ornamental plants.

Sendero Ecológico Mitológico—A project of the students at the Internado de San Francisco. A guided tour of this trail will teach you about the ecology and mythology of the jungle flora.

Sendero Ecológico Nama Aruku—The Path of Knowing is designed and maintained by students of INEAGRO to show the botanical richness of the region and the ancestral uses of plants.

Sendero Interpretativo Puerto Nariño San Martín—This trail through secondary growth rainforest leads to the Tikuna village of San Martín on the edge of Parque Nacional Natural Amacayacu. Updated: Mar 28, 2011.

Lago Tarapoto !

The Río Loretoyacü bulges a bit to one side, creating Lago Tarapoto, a beautiful lake surrounded by jungle and speckled with mangrove islands. Along its shores are isolated indigenous hamlets hidden in the dense vegetation. This is a place of magic, where pink dolphins leap from silver waters. Here, along the shallow, quiet waters of channels branching off the lake, is Victoria regia, the world's largest water lily. Explore this lake by boat, swimming in the cool waters or dropping a line in for piranha.

To see the river and Lago Tarapoto, you can hire a boat with guide. Paddle canoes are the most ecological ($12-15). Peque-peques are the next best ($21 for 4-5 people, with guide). They are slow, but fuel efficient.Try to avoid taking a tour with a speed boat, as it disturbs the pink dolphins and other aquatic

LLANOS AND SELVA

life. You have a better chance of seeing dolphins in early morning and late afternoon. Victoria regia water lilies grow in the backwaters of the lake. Updated: Mar 28, 2011.

Indigenous Villages

Several indigenous villages are accessible by path or by boat from Puero Nariño. Sendero Interpretativo Puerto Nariño San Martín leads to the Tikuna hamlet of San Martín, not too far from Parque Nacional Natural Amacayacu. Unfortunately, it has become affected by tourists, and people are now charging for photos. Mocagua, another Tikuna settlement near the national park, is more traditional (contact Henry do Santos, Cel: 312-354-4717/313-397-5861). Another traditional Tikuna village, 20 de Julio, is known for its artisan work and has a mirador. San Juan del Socó on Río Loretoyacü is another village you can boat to.

San Martín and 20 de Julio can be reached by path from Puerto Nariño. Follow the signs from Carrera 6. For the other two, check with villagers about a canoe to take you there, or go in one of the boats leaving three times daily. Some of these hamlets, like Mocagua, have overnight stays. Speak with the *curaca* (village leader) if you are interested. Updated: Mar 28, 2011.

Tours

Guides are mostly independent in Puerto Nariño. You can ask around or go to the Internado Indígena San Francisco for someone to show you the wonders of the area. To see the river and Lago Tarapoto, you can hire a boat with guide. You can also ask around about renting a canoe to paddle up Río Loretoyacü to Lago Tarapoto. Fray Hector at **Alto del Águila** (Cel: 311-502-8592, E-mail: altodelaguila@hotmail.com) can assist ($8-10 during daylight hours). Updated: Jul 08, 2008.

Student Guides

The Internado de San Francisco de Loretoyacü has a program in ecologically conscious ethnotourism. As part of their training, the youth serve as guides for the Sendero Ecológico-Mitológico on the school's grounds, as well as for other attractions. No tip is encouraged, as this is a curricular activity. If you are interested in acquiring a student guide or in supporting the project, contact Sor Nubia Stella Torres or Sor Edelmira Pinto at the school. Internado de San Francisco de Loretoyacü, 1 km (0.6 mi) west of Puerto Nariño (follow the signs from Cra. 6). Cel: 311-276-8117/8123, Updated: Mar 28, 2011.

Lodging

In terms of lodging, Puerto Nariño has a half-dozen inns offering a peaceful night's rest. Most are simple hostels, but even those vacationers looking for a bit more luxury have a decent selection of places to spend the night. Budget travelers generally head for Puerto Nariño if they want to stay a while in the Leticia area. Here, lodging is cheaper and is closer to many of the prime attractions, including virgin jungle. The town has electricity only until 10 p.m., so be sure to keep a flashlight and candles on hand. Updated: Jul 22, 2010.

Alto del Águila ♪

(BEDS: $8) Fray Hector has created a tranquil retreat overlooking the Río Loretoyacü. Alto del Águila's three cabañas are airy and comfortable. Watch the sunset from the tower, which you'll have to share with two possessive macaws. Evenings are pleasurably spent on the back porch, conversing with Fray Hector. The brother is a most gracious host. If he's full, he can arrange for you to stay at the Hermana Vicentinas' cabañas at the Internado de San Francisco. A curfew of sorts exists, as the sisters let guard dogs loose at night.

From Carrera 6, follow the signs for Internado de San Francisco. Upon reaching the school, cut across the grounds to the grassy trail that leads to Alto del Águila. Also, you can hire a boat from the village to take you to the dock just below the hostel. One kilometer (0.6 mi) from the village, just past Internado de San Francisco school. Cel: 311-502-8592, E-mail: altodelaguila@hotmail.com. Updated: Jul 08, 2008.

> **VIVA ONLINE REVIEW**
> ALTO DEL AGUILA
>
> *"Alto del Águila is a magical place where you can see the biological richness of the Colombian Amazon.*
>
> November 23, 2010

Hospedaje Manguare

(ROOMS: $7-10) Hospedaje Manguare is an inexpensive option in the heart of Puerto Nariño. It is convenient for exploring the trails and miradores of the area. In this small hostel at the back of her home, Doña Isabel offers simple rooms, some with several beds, sharing a clean common bath. After hiking around, you might need to clean your muddy clothes. Conveniently, guests are allowed to wash clothes, which is a plus in this town with no laundromat. Ca. 4, 5-68. Cel: 310-309-0863/311-276-4873, E-mail: cabanaturisticas@hotmail.com. Updated: Mar 28, 2011.

Hotel Casa Selva

(ROOMS: $61-119) Hotel Casa Selva has blossomed into the most expensive and luxurious place in Puerto Nariño. This two-story white beauty has 12 rooms around the interior patio. Shuttered windows and balconies make these quarters bright and airy. All come with private bath and fan. A common room with hammocks is the perfect place to rest after a day of sightseeing. Catch the sunset over the Río Loretoyacü from the mirador on the grounds. Cra. 6, 6-78. Cel: 311-280-7319/521-9297/320-233-7318, E-mail: casaselvahotel@yahoo.es, URL: www.casaselvahotel.com.

Across the way is **Hostal Asaí**, also run by Casa Selva. This hostel is more economical, costing only $30 per person. Cra. 6, 6-65. Tel: 592-6656, Cel: 311-477-8973, E-mail: hostalasai@yahoo.es. Updated: Mar 28, 2011.

Restaurants

You can pretty much count on one hand the number of restaurants in Puerto Nariño. Therefore, you don't have too much choice, especially in the evenings. Most of the restaurants have set hours for serving meals, so you will have to plan accordingly. In general, food is a bit more expensive here. There are several rustic eateries that serve lunch in the back part of the **Perros Fredy** building (Cra. 7, between Ca. 6 and 7). The place to pick up groceries in town is the general store on Carrera 7, between Calles 7 and 8, near the waterfront. A basic market sets up during the day at Carrera 7 and Calle 8. Updated: Jul 08, 2008.

Perros Fredy

(LUNCH: $2.65) Perros Fredy is more than just hot dogs and hamburgers. It also has some simple à la carte dishes, like steak ($2.65-3.70). Additionally, Perros Fredy serves a standard comida corriente with drink that is made with purified water ($2.65). You can choose to sit inside at the short counter and chat with the señora, or at a table out on the porch. This is the only restaurant with continuous hours. Daily 6 a.m.-10 p.m. Cra. 7, between Ca. 6 and 7. Updated: May 18, 2009.

Restaurante Tucunare

(LUNCH: $2.65) This restaurant is nothing fancy—just a large, simple eatery serving nothing but down-to-earth meals. It is also one of the more economical restaurants in Puerto Nariño—its breakfasts cost $2.10 and the luncheon specials are $2.65. Unfortunately, Restaurante Tucunare is not open for dinner. Breakfast 7-9 a.m., lunch noon-2 p.m. Cra. 6, between Ca. 6 and 7. Updated: Jul 09, 2008.

Restaurante Margaritas

(LUNCH: $3.70) From the outside, it looks like just the front gate of a home, but once you enter Restaurante Margaritas, you are struck by the large maloka. This diner is haughtily proud of the fact that many tour groups stop here on trips to Lago Tarapoto. The quality of its service and its prices reflect it. Breakfasts cost $2.65. Lunch is the standard fish, beans, rice, yuca and patacones, accompanied by soup and drink ($3.70). For dinner, you can choose between the à la carte menu ($4.20) or the set meal ($3.70). Daily 7-9 a.m., noon-2 p.m. and 6:30-8 p.m. Ca. 7, between Cra. 6 and 7. Updated: Jul 09, 2008.

!!!!!

LLANOS AND SELVA

Index

INDEX

INDEX

INDEX

Environmental Tips for Travelers

By Nicola Robinson, Nicola Mears and Heather Ducharme, Río Muchacho Organic Farm, Ecuador.

While traveling in a foreign country, it is important to minimize your impact. Here are some tips you should keep in mind while on your trip. Some of this advice may be more difficult to take on board while traveling than it would be to incorporate into your daily lives at home. However, even if you only put into practice three or four of the suggestions, on the road or at home, it will certainly help reduce your impact on the planet.

GARBAGE

- Carry a water bottle and always check if there is somewhere to fill it up at your hotel/restaurant—most hotels and restaurants have purified water in 20-liter bottles called *botellones*. These places usually also sell water in small bottles and might be reluctant to begin with as they think they are losing a sale. Of course you will need to pay for the refill also. If you have to buy bottles, buy the biggest you can and just refill from there, especially if you plan to be in the same place for a while.

- Purify your own water to avoid creating garbage.

- Try to avoid excessive wrapping and plastic bags, which are all too readily dished out for each small purchase. If you can, explain to the shop keeper why you want to give the bag back. If you shop in a local market, take your own bag or have them place everything in one large plastic bag instead of numerous small ones.

- Use a digital camera instead of film. The process of developing film can produce a lot of waste, and unwanted photos are non recyclable and often end up in the trash.

- Use a reusable container for soap so you can use your own instead of the small hotel soaps, which come individually wrapped. If you use hotel soap, use one and take the remainder with you—it will just be thrown out.

- Avoid using excessive cosmetic products such as hairspray, mousse, aftershave and perfume, or try to find effective environmentally friendly alternatives such as biodegradable shampoos and crystal deodorants, which last longer (most containers for these products are non recyclable). Avoid using disposable products such as plastic razors and single-use contact lenses.

- Try to use rechargeable batteries or eliminate use of batteries entirely. For example, use a wind-up or solar torch or radio.

- Use recycled paper for letters home, trip diaries and toilet paper.

- Buy in bulk if you are traveling in a large group to reduce packaging.

- Recycle whatever you can in the country you are traveling. Some products that can not be recycled in the host country can be recycled in your home countries (such as batteries), so please take them home if possible.

INDEX

FOOD AND HEALTH

• Avoid eating foods that you know are from endangered or threatened species (research these before you come to the country). Buy and eat locally grown and locally processed foods wherever possible, rather than food shipped from long distances, which use more energy and packaging.

• Consider using alternative natural medical products for common travelers' illnesses. This may be healthier for you and keeps you from leaving behind pharmaceuticals in the local water and soil (this is becoming a detectable problem in first world countries, thought to affect aquatic organisms like fish and frogs).

NATURE, FLORA AND FAUNA

• Avoid buying souvenirs of local fauna. Many stores sell cases of bright colored butterflies, spiders and insects which are caught by the hundreds in the Amazon. The sales people will tell you that they are not caught but that they raise them—it is not true!

• Avoid buying souvenirs that are made with endangered species or species that have to be killed to be made into a craft. Support crafts made from renewable resources.

• Don't collect insects, flora and fauna without a permit. Leave them for everyone to enjoy.

• When walking, stay on the trails and close gates behind you.

CAMPING AND WATER

• Use toilets where they exist. If there are no toilets, bury human waste in a hole 20 centimeters deep. Human waste should be buried at least 50 meters from water sources.

• Use biodegradable soaps and detergents.

• Don't wash shampoo and detergent off directly in rivers, but rather as far away as you can (4 meters minimum).

• Avoid making fires.

• Use a T-shirt when snorkeling as sunscreen is harmful to marine life.

TRANSPORT

• Use public transport instead of private (e.g. bus instead of rental car) when possible to reduce fossil fuel use. Share rental cars and taxis with others. If possible, walk or use a bicycle. It not only helps the planet, but it keeps you in shape as well!

ELECTRICITY

• Lights, fans, TVs, radios, or computers: If you are not using it, turn it off!

INDEX

TRAVELING WITH CHILDREN AND BABIES

• Try and teach your child about the local environmental issues. Point out good and bad practices.

• Encourage your child to snack on fruit, which has a biodegradable wrapper!

• If traveling with a baby, why not use cotton diapers? Disposable diapers are becoming a major waste issue in developed countries and are becoming a desirable product in the developing world. Using cotton will set a good example to others and reduce the promotion of disposable diapers.

LOCAL ENVIRONMENTAL ISSUES

• Try to learn about the important environmental issues in the country. Good environmental practices (e.g. reduce, reuse, recycle!) are often the same in different countries, but the specific issues are often different (e.g. different recycling options, different endangered habitats and species, different laws and policies, etc.)

• Think about where you are eating and staying, and support the more environmentally friendly businesses. If you stay in an eco-lodge, talk to the owners/managers, ask how they manage their garbage (including human waste), if they recycle and if they use grey water systems to reuse their water. Where do their building materials, food, and power come from? Do they practice or contribute to conservation? Do they support the local community? Be constructive rather than critical if you don't get a good response—some people truly think that it can be called an ecolodge if it is built with natural materials.

• Many countries have interesting volunteer opportunities with environmentally oriented organizations, and volunteering is an option. Research carefully—some volunteer opportunities are not what they say they are. The Web site www.volunteersouthamerica.net has links to several free and low-cost volunteer opportunities around South America.

The following is a list of helpful environmental Web sites for further information:

Advice and links to places you can buy environmentally friendly products: **www.ecomall.com** and **www.greenhome.com**

Ministry of the Environment, Colombia (in Spanish): **www.minambiente.gov.co**

A list of endangered species around the world by the International Union for Conservation of Nature and Natural Resources: **www.iucnredlist.org**

INDEX

Packing lists

(indicates something that might not be available in Colombia)*

GENERAL PACKING LIST:

There are a number of items that every traveler should consider bringing to Colombia:

- ☐ Medicines and prescriptions (Very important. Bringing all relevant medical info and medicines may well save you a lot of grief in Colombia)
- ☐ Photocopies of passport and other relevant ID documents
- ☐ Paperback novels (sometimes you'll be sitting on buses, in airports, or somewhere else for a long time. It is possible to find and/or exchange books in several places in Colombia, but don't count on much selection if you don't read Spanish)
- ☐ Plug converter (many older buildings in Colombia have 2-prong outlets only, although the voltage is the same)
- ☐ A good camera (see photography section)
- ☐ Water bottle (bottled water is readily available in Colombia, but you may want your own bottle)
- ☐ Sunglasses & sun hat
- ☐ Motion sickness medicine
- ☐ Lip balm
- ☐ *Tampons (difficult to find outside the major cities)
- ☐ Condoms and other contraceptives
- ☐ *Foot powder
- ☐ Antacid tablets, such as Rolaids
- ☐ Mild painkillers such as aspirin or ibuprofen
- ☐ *GPS device (especially for hikers)
- ☐ Watch with alarm clock
- ☐ Diarrhea medicine (i.e. Imodium)
- ☐ Warm clothes (The highlands are cooler than you think)

BACKPACKER PACKING LIST:

- ☐ Rain poncho
- ☐ Plastic bags
- ☐ *Swiss army knife/Leatherman
- ☐ Toilet paper
- ☐ *Antibacterial hand gel
- ☐ Small padlock

CARIBBEAN COAST PACKING LIST:

- ☐ Extra film/camera supplies
- ☐ Waterproof disposable camera for snorkeling
- ☐ Sunscreen
- ☐ Good, wide brimmed hat
- ☐ Long pants, lightweight
- ☐ Long-sleeved shirt, lightweight

RAINFOREST PACKING LIST:

- ☐ Rubber boots (most jungle lodges have them, call ahead)
- ☐ *Bug spray (with Deet)
- ☐ Flashlight
- ☐ Waterproof bags
- ☐ Rain poncho
- ☐ First aid kit
- ☐ *Compass
- ☐ Whistle
- ☐ Long-sleeved shirt and pants
- ☐ Malaria/yellow fever medicine
- ☐ Original passport
- ☐ Mosquito net (if your destination does not have one; call ahead)
- ☐ Biodegradable soap

INDEX

ADDITIONAL ITEMS TO PACK:

☐ _____
☐ _____
☐ _____
☐ _____
☐ _____
☐ _____
☐ _____
☐ _____

ANTI-PACKING LIST: THINGS NOT TO BRING TO COLOMBIA:

- x Expensive jewelry. Just leave it home.
- x Nice watch or sunglasses. Bring cheap ones you can afford to lose.
- x Go through your wallet: what won't you need? Leave your drivers' license (unless you're planning on driving), business cards, video-club membership cards, coffee club card, social security card and anything else you won't need at home. The only thing in your wallet you'll want is a student ID, and if you lose your wallet you'll be grateful you left the rest at home.
- x Illegal drugs. You didn't need us to tell you that, did you?
- x Stickers and little toys for kids. Some tourists like to hand them out, which means the children pester every foreigner they see.
- x Really nice clothes or shoes, unless you're planning on going to a special event or dining out a lot.

INDEX

V!VA TRAVEL GUIDES BRINGS YOU A TEAR-OUT LIST OF USEFUL CONTACTS IN COLOMBIA

Feel free to tear out or photocopy this sheet for your use—stick it in your pocket or tuck it in your bag.

EMERGENCY NUMBERS

All emergencies	112 or 123	Immediate attention center	156
Fire	119	Red Cross	132

MEDICAL

Fundación Santa Fe de Bogotá
Calle 119 No. 9-33, Bogotá
Tel: 1-603-0303
URL: www.fsfb.org.co

Medihelp Services, Cartegena
Carrera 6a, 5-101, Bocagrande, Cartagena
Tel: 5-665-2255
URL: www.medihelpservices.com

Dentist (Bogotá): Antonio Flórez—Calle 134 No. 13 - 83, office 806, Edifício El Bosque, Bogotá. Tel: 1-520-0108, Cel: 1-310-878-5179, Fax: 1-626-7868, E-mail antonioefa2004@yahoo.com. Speaks Spanish and English.

ENGLISH-SPEAKING LAWYERS (CRIMINAL)

Chávez-Herrera & Morano
International P.A.
Calle 32, 5-09, oficina 315, Cartagena
Tel: 1-286-8305/288-9466
Fax: 1-288-9466
E-mail: chhm@coldecon.net.co

Rodrigo Martínez-Torres
Calle 37, 15-78, Bogotá
Tel: 575-664-4584/7128
Fax: 1-664-2659
E-mail: rmartinezt@etb.net.co

TRAVELER GUIDANCE

South America Explorers' Club
E-mail: don@saexplorers.org
www.saexplorers.org

Tourist Information Office
Carerra 8, 9-83, Plaza de Bolívar, Bogotá
Tel: 1-327-4916

POST OFFICE (CORREOS)

Bogotá—Carrera 7 and Calle 13, Ed. Murillo Toro
Cartagena—Carrera 7, 8B-20

INT'L COUNTRY CODES

United States and Canada—1
United Kingdom—44
Australia—61

TRANSPORT

Taxis: In Bogotá—Compañía Taxis Verdes, Tel: 355-5550, or Abandera Radio Taxi, Tel: 288-8888. In Cartagena—Comunicamos Tele Taxi, Tel: 660-0000.

COMPLETE THE SECTIONS BELOW FOR YOUR CONVENIENCE:

My Tour Operator:

My Hotel Address:

Taxi Directions to My Hotel:

INDEX

AIRLINES IN BOGOTÁ:

Aerogal (Ecuadorian)
Calle 92, 15-48, local 209
Tel: 1-618-0511, Fax: 1-621-0657
E-Mail: reservasbog@aerogal.com.ec
URL: www.aerogal.com.ec/

American Airlines (US)
Carrera 7, 26-20
Tel: 571-439-7777
URL: www.aa.com

Avianca (Colombian)
Avenida 19, 4-37, local 2
Tel: 1-800-012-3434
www.avianca.com

Continental Airlines (U.S.)
Carrera 7, 71-52, torre A, local 2
Tel: 1-800-944-0219
URL: www.continental.com

COPA (Panamanian)
Carrera 9A, 99-02, local 108
Tel: 1-800-550-7700
URL: www.copaair.com

Iberia (Spanish)
Calle 85, 20-10
Tel: 1-413-9794
URL: www.iberia.com

Lan Chile (Chilean)
Calle 100 8A-49, torre B, 7th floor, office 708
Tel: 1-651-3970, Fax: 1-611-5560
URL: Lan.com

Satena (Colombian)
Avenida El Dorado, entrada 4
Tel: 1-800-091-2034
E-mail: atencionalusuario@satena.com
URL: www.satena.com

Taca (El Salvador)
Calle 114, 9-45
Tel: 637-3900
URL: www.taca.com

Varig (Brazilian)
Carrera 7, 33-24
Tel: 1-350-5749
URL: www.varig.com

EMBASSIES IN BOGOTÁ:

United States
Calle 24 Bis, 48-50
Tel: 1-315-0811, Fax: 1-315-2197
E-mail: ACSBogota@state.gov
URL: bogota.usembassy.gov/

United Kingdom
Cra. 9, 76-49
Tel: 1-326-8300, Fax: 1-326-8302
E-mail: ConsularBogota@fco.gov.uk,
URL: http://ukincolombia.fco.gov.uk/en

Canada
Carrera 7, 114-33, 14th floor
Tel: 1-657-9800, Fax: 1-657-9912
E-mail: bgota@international.gc.ca
URL: www.canadainternational.gc.ca/colombia
-colombie/index.aspx?lang=eng

Australia (Consulate)
Carrera 16, 86A-05
Tel: 1-236-2828, Fax: 1-610-9707

Germany
Carrera 69, 25B-44, 7th floor
Tel: 1-423-2600, Fax: 1-429-3145
URL: www.bogota.diplo.de

France
Carrera 11, 93-12.
Tel: 1-638-1400, Fax: 1-638-1430
URL:www.ambafrance-co.org/spip.
php?rubrique=2

Netherlands
Carrera 13, 93-40, 5th floor
Tel: 1-638-4200, Fax: 1-623-3020
Email: bog@minbuza.nl
URL: www.mfa.nl/bog

Israel
Calle 35, 7-25, 14th floor
Tel: 1-327-7500. Fax: 1-327-7555
E-mail: info@bogota.mfa.gov.il.
URL: http://bogota.mfa.gov.il

Japan
Carrera 7, 71-21, Torre B, 11th floor
Tel: 1-317-5001, Fax: 1-317-4989
E-mail: info@embjp-colombia.com
URL: www.colombia.emb-japan.go.jp/emba-
jada.htm

Switzerland
Carrera 9, 74-08, 11th floor
Tel: 1-349-7230, Fax: 1-349-7195
URL: www.eda.admin.ch/bogota

INDEX

Useful Spanish Phrases

CONVERSATIONAL

Hello	Hola
Good morning	Buenos días
Good afternoon	Buenas tardes
Good evening	Buenas noches
Yes	Sí
No	No
Please	Por favor
Thank you	Gracias
It was nothing	De nada
Excuse me	Permiso
See you later	Hasta luego
Bye	Chao
Cool	Chévere
How are you (formal)	¿Cómo está?
" " (informal)	¿Qué tal?
I don't understand	No entiendo.
Do you speak English?	¿Habla inglés?
I don't speak Spanish.	No hablo español.
I'm from England/U.S.	Soy de Inglaterra/los Estados Unidos

HEALTH/EMERGENCY

Call....	¡Llame a...!
an ambulance	una ambulancia
a doctor	un médico
the police	la policía
It's an emergency.	Es una emergencia.
I'm sick	Estoy enfermo/a
I need a doctor	Necesito un médico.
Where's the hospital?	¿Dónde está el hospital?
I'm allergic to...	Soy alérgico/a a
antibiotics	los antibióticos.
penicillin	penicilina
peanuts	maní
shellfish	los mariscos
milk	leche
eggs	huevos
wheat	trigo

GETTING AROUND

Where is...?	¿Dónde está...?
the bus station	la estación de bus?
a bank	un banco
an ATM	un cajero automático
the bathroom	el baño
Where does the bus leave from?	¿De dónde sale el bus?
Left, right, straight	Izquierda, derecha, directo.
One city block	Un cuadro
Ticket	Boleto

ACCOMMODATION

Where is a hotel?	¿Donde hay un hotel?
I want a room.	Quiero una habitación.
Single/Double/Marriage	Simple/Doble/Matrimonial
How much does it cost per night?	¿Cuanto cuesta por una noche?
Does that include breakfast/taxes?	¿Incluye el desayuno/los impuestos?
Is there 24-hour hot water?	¿Hay agua caliente veinticuatro horas al día?

Notes...

CPSIA information can be obtained at www.ICGtesting.com
Printed in the USA
BVOW11s1331260214

346065BV00010B/390/P